March 7–10, 2016
Sonoma, CA, USA

Association for Computing Machinery

Advancing Computing as a Science & Profession

IUI'16

Proceedings of the 21st International Conference on Intelligent User Interfaces

Sponsored by:

ACM SIGCHI & ACM SIGAI

Supported by:

Microsoft Research, Google, IBM Research, and Tableau Software

Association for
Computing Machinery

Advancing Computing as a Science & Profession

The Association for Computing Machinery
2 Penn Plaza, Suite 701
New York, New York 10121-0701

Notice to Past Authors of ACM-Published Articles
ACM intends to create a complete electronic archive of all articles and/or other material previously published by ACM. If you have written a work that has been previously published by ACM in any journal or conference proceedings prior to 1978, or any SIG Newsletter at any time, and you do NOT want this work to appear in the ACM Digital Library, please inform permissions@acm.org, stating the title of the work, the author(s), and where and when published.

ISBN: 978-1-4503-4137-0 (Digital)

ISBN: 978-1-4503-4469-2 (Print)

Additional copies may be ordered prepaid from:

ACM Order Department
PO Box 30777
New York, NY 10087-0777, USA

Phone: 1-800-342-6626 (USA and Canada)
+1-212-626-0500 (Global)
Fax: +1-212-944-1318
E-mail: acmhelp@acm.org
Hours of Operation: 8:30 am – 4:30 pm ET

Printed in the USA

Welcome

It is with great pleasure that we welcome you to beautiful Sonoma, California and the 21st edition of ACM International Conference on Intelligent User Interfaces – ACM IUI 2016. ACM IUI is "where HCI meets AI," or where the academic research communities of Human-Computer Interaction (HCI) and Artificial Intelligence (AI) intersect. As the premier international forum for reporting outstanding research and development on intelligent user interfaces, the conference welcomes submissions describing work at the cross-section of these two fields and other related fields, such as psychology, behavioral science, cognitive science, computer graphics, design, the arts, and many others. Members of the ACM IUI community are interested in improving the symbiosis between humans and computers, increasing the intelligence of both in the process.

The call for papers attracted 194 long and short paper submissions, 31 poster paper submissions, 11 demo paper submissions, and 17 student consortium submissions. The final program of the conference includes 2 keynotes, 49 long and short papers (25.3% acceptance rate), 15 posters, 6 demos, 2 workshops, 1 tutorial, and 12 student consortium papers. We are particularly excited for the keynotes by two distinguished speakers that will open the first and third days of the conference. The opening keynote will be given by Xavier Amatriain, VP of Engineering at Quora, on the topic of the "Past, Present, and Future of Recommender Systems: An Industry Perspective." The closing keynote will be given by Professor Elisabeth André, from Augsburg University and a long-time member of the ACM IUI community, on the topic of "Socially-Sensitive Interfaces: From Offline Studies to Interactive Experiences."

The conference could not be organized without the help of a large number of individuals who generously volunteered much of their own time. Their names can be found on the following pages. All of the members of the organizing committee have done a fantastic job of coordinating the many moving parts that go into putting on a great conference. We must also particularly thank our 34 senior program committee members for coordinating the papers review process and the 91 members of the program committee for providing high quality reviews. And, most important, we must thank the authors for their diligent work that resulted in so many great submissions. These have allowed us to develop the excellent program that is the enduring heart of the conference.

Another key for any great conference is a collection of strong sponsor organizations and generous corporate supporters. Our sponsors ACM, SIGAI, and SIGCHI are instrumental in making the conference happen year in and year out. This year, SIGCHI and SIGAI were particularly generous in providing financial support for our student travel grants, which have enabled 19 students to attend the conference that might not have otherwise. Our corporate supporters, Microsoft, IBM, Google, and Tableau have been supremely generous and the conference would be weaker without their contributions.

We hope you will find the program engaging and the mix of academic disciplines broadens your perspective on computing. We also hope the conference will provide you with a valuable opportunity to share ideas with other researchers and practitioners from around the world, whether through presenting your own work formally or through informal discussions during the banquet or coffee breaks. With luck, those shared ideas will manifest themselves in exciting papers at next year's conference and ultimately have impact far beyond the conference!

If you have any suggestions for how to improve the conference either this year or in the future, please do not hesitate to let us know.

Jalal Mahmud, Jeffrey Nichols, John O'Donovan
IUI'16 General Chairs

Cristina Conati, Massimo Zancanaro
IUI'16 Program Chairs

Table of Contents

Session: Personalization

Session: IUI for Entertainment and Health

Session: Recommender Systems

Session: Wearable and Mobile IUI 1

Session: Invited Speaker 2

Session: Wearable and Mobile IUI 2

Session: Information Retrieval and Search

Session: IUI for Education and Training

IUI 2016 Conference Organization

General Chairs:	Jeffrey Nichols (Google Inc, USA) Jalal Mahmud (IBM Research, USA) John O'Donovan (UC Santa Barbara, USA)
Program Chairs:	Cristina Conati (University of British Columbia, Canada) Massimo Zancanaro (Bruno Kessler Foundation, Italy)
Poster and Demo Chairs:	Nava Tintarev (University of Aberdeen, U.K.) Bongwon Suh (Seoul National University, South Korea) Matt Dennis (University of Aberdeen, U.K.)
Workshop and Tutorial Chairs:	Ido Guy (Yahoo Labs, Israel) Jill Freyne (CSIRO, Australia)
Student Consortium Chairs:	Tracy Hammond (Texas A&M University, USA) Aaron Adler (BBN Technologies, USA)
Proceedings Chair:	Bart Knijnenburg (Clemson University, USA)
Publicity Chairs:	Chris Trattner (Know-Center, Austria) Denis Parra (PUC, Chile)
Webmasters:	Byungkyu Kang (UC Santa Barbara, USA) Saiph Savage (West Virginia University, USA; and UNAM, Mexico)
Sponsorship Chair:	Jian Wang (LinkedIn, USA)
Treasurer Chair:	Yuheng Hu (University of Illinois at Chicago, USA)
Registration Chair:	Liang Gou (IBM, USA)
Student Volunteer Chairs:	Dan Afergan (Google Inc, USA) Kiley Sobel (University of Washington, USA)
Steering Committee Chair:	Antonio Krüger (DFKI, Germany)
Steering Committee:	Elisabeth Andrè (Augsburg University, Germany) Polo Chau (Georgia Tech, USA) Carlos Duarte (University of Lisboa, Portugal) Lewis Johnson (Alelo, USA) Tsvi Kuflik (University of Haifa, Israel) Mark Maybury (United States Air Force, USA) Jeffrey Nichols (Google Inc, USA) Doug Riecken (Dow Jones, USA) Michelle Zhou (IBM, USA)

Senior Program Committee:

Antonio Krüger (DFKI)
Elisabeth Andrè (Augsburg University)
Liliana Ardissono (University of Torino)
Lora Aroyo (VU University Amsterdam)
Sumit Basu (Microsoft Research)
Shlomo Berkovsky (CSIRO)
Mark Billinghurst (University of Canterbury)
Gautam Biswas (Vanderbilt University)
Peter Brusilovsky (University of Pittsburgh)
Andrea Bunt (University of Manitoba)
Andreas Butz (University of Munich)
Charles Callaway (FBK)
Giuseppe Carenini (University of British Columbia)
Marc Cavazza (University of Tesside)
Joyce Chai (Michigan State University)
Fang Chen (NICTA)
Wai-Tat Fu (University of Illinois at Urbana-Champaign)
Ido Guy (Yahoo Labs)
Tracy Hammond (Texas A&M University)
Eelco Herder (L3S Research Center)
Per Ola Kristensson (University of Cambridge)
Tsvi Kuflik (The University of Haifa)
Henry Lieberman (Massachusetts Institute of Technology)
Pasquale Lops (University of Bari)
Yukiko Nakano (Seikei University)
Jeffrey Nichols (Google)
Nuno Nunes (University of Madeira)
Petteri Nurmi (Helsinki Institute for Information Technology HIIT)
Nuria Oliver (Telefonica R&D)
Fabio Paternò (CNR-ISTI)
Saiph Savage (West Virginia University)
Frank Shipman (Texas A&M University)
Oliviero Stock (FBK-IRST)
Simone Stumpf (City University)
Jean Vanderdonckt (Université Catholique de Louvain)

Program Committee

Daniel Afergan (Tufts University)
Salvatore Andolina (University of Helsinki)
Lisa Anthony (University of Florida)
Joerg Baus (DFKI)
Roman Bednarik (University of Eastern Finland)
Larry Birnbaum (Northwestern University)
Nis Bornoe (Aalborg University)
François Bouchet (Université Pierre et Marie Curie)
Oliver Brdiczka (Darmstadt University of Technology)
Gaelle Calvary (Grenoble Institute of Technology)
Federica Cena (University of Torino)
Duen Horng (Polo) Chau (Georgia Institute of Technology)
Gregorio Convertino (Xerox Research Center Europe)
Florian Daiber (DFKI)
Victor de Boer (VU University Amsterdam)
Nadja De Carolis (University of Bari)
Alexander De Luca (University of Munich)
Matt Dennis (University of Aberdeen)
Eyal Dim (University of Haifa)
Sidney D'Mello (University of Notre Dame)
Casey Dugan (IBM)
Guillaume Durand (National Research Council of Canada)
Serge Egelman (University of California, Berkeley)
Angus Forbes (University of Illinois at Chicago)
Victor Fragoso (West Virginia University)
Cristina Gena (University of Turin)
Werner Geyer (IBM T.J. Watson Research)
Ilya Goldin (Pearson)
David Gotz (IBM Research)
Anna Goy (University of Torino)
Joseph Grafsgaard (North Carolina State University)
Tiago Guerreiro (IST/UTL)
Jason Harley (McGill University)
Chris Harrison (Carnegie Mellon University)
Axel Hoesl (University of Munich)
Enamul Hoque (University of British Columbia)
Sharon Hsiao (ASU)
Yun Huang (Northwestern University)
Sazzad Hussain (CSIRO)
Ali Jahanian (MIT)
Juho Kim (Stanford University)
Sebastien Lalle (University of British Columbia)
Shyong Lam (Google)
Christian Lander (DFKI)
Joel Lanir (University of Haifa)
Q. Vera Liao (University of Illinois at Urbana-Champaign)

Program Committee (continued):

Agnes Lisowska Masson (University of Fribourg)
Markus Löchtefeld (Lancaster University)
Hao Lu (Google)
Maurizio Marchese (University of Trento)
Judith Masthoff (University of Aberdeen)
Kasia Muldner (ASU)
Michael Nebeling (ETH Zurich)
Jason Orlosky (Osaka University)
Luc Paquette (Teachers College)
Alexandros Paramythis (Contexity AG)
Denis Parra (University of Pittsburgh)
Martin Pielot (Telefonica Research)
Katrin Plaumann (Ulm University)
Martina Rau (University of Wisconsin)
Norbert Reithinger (DFKI)
Francesco Ricci (Free University of Bolzano-Bozen)
Michael Rohs (University of Hannover)
Thijs Roumen (Hasso Plattner Institute)
Carmen Santoro (ISTI-CNR)
Olga Santos (UNED)
Gianluca Schiavo (FBK - IRST)
Johannes Schoening (Hasselt University - tUL - iMinds)
Daniel Sonntag (DFKI)
Danny Soroker (IBM Research)
Lucio Davide Spano (University of Cagliari)
Robert St. Amant (North Carolina State University)
Ben Steichen (Santa Clara University)
Carlo Strapparava (FBK-irst)
Luis Sucar (INAOE)
Rajan Vaish (University of California)
Matteo Valoriani (Politecnico di Milano)
Alan Wecker (Haifa University)
Anbang Xu (IBM Research - Almaden)
Sang Ho Yoon (Purdue University)
Hong Yu (Georgia Institute of Technology)
Yong Zheng (DePaul University)

Additional reviewers:

Michael Barz
Annalina Caputo
Qiaozi Gao
Marco de Gemmis
Marco Guerini
Leo Iaquinta
Changsong Liu
Andreas Luxemburger
Diego Magro
Mohammad Mehdi Moniri
Giovanna Petrone
Claudia Picardi
Vo Ngoc Phuoc An
Carlos Torres
Sari Sadiya
Lanbo She
Shaohua Yang

IUI 2016 Sponsors & Supporters

Sponsors: SIGCHI — acm SIGAI

Supporters

Gold Tier: Microsoft Research

Silver Tier: Google — IBM Research

Bronze Tier: tableau SOFTWARE

Past, Present, and Future of Recommender Systems: An Industry Perspective

Xavier Amatriain
VP of Engineering
Quora

Abstract

In 2006, Netflix announced a $1M prize competition to advance recommendation algorithms. The recommendation problem was simplified as the accuracy in predicting a user rating measured by the Root Mean Squared Error. While that formulation helped get the attention of the research community, it put the focus on the wrong approach and metric while leaving many important factors out, in particular the UI.

In this talk I will talk of the Netflix Prize as the past of recommendations. I will then describe the present from an industry perspective based on my personal experience at Netflix first and Quora now . I will describe the different components of modern recommender systems such as: personalized ranking, similarity, explanations, context-awareness, or search as recommendation. I will also review the usage of novel algorithmic approaches such as Factorization Machines, Restricted Boltzmann Machines, SimRank, Deep Neural Networks, or Listwise Learning-to-rank. We will see how those components and algorithmic approaches can be used to recommend not only movies, but also questions, answers, topics, or users.

But, most importantly, I will give many examples of prototypical industrial-scale recommender systems with special focus on the user interface and its interaction with the algorithms. It is clearly in the interface of the UI and the novel algorithms where the future of recommender systems lays.

ACM Classification

H.3.3 [Information Search and Retrieval]: Information Filtering

Author Keywords: Recommender Systems, User Interfaces

Short Bio

Xavier Amatriain is VP of Engineering at Quora, where he leads the team building the best source of knowledge in the Internet.

IUI 2016, March 7–10, 2016, Sonoma, CA, USA.
ACM 978-1-4503-4137-0/16/03.
DOI: http://dx.doi.org/10.1145/2856767.2856798

With over 50 publications in different fields, Xavier is best known for his work on Machine Learning in general, and Recommender Systems in particular. Before Quora, he was Research/Engineering Director at Netflix, where he lead the team building the famous Netflix Recommendation algorithms. Previously, Xavier was Research Scientist at Telefonica Research and Research Director at UCSB. He has also lectured at different universities both in the US and Spain and is frequently invited speaker at conferences, companies, or summer schools. He has served as General Chair for the ACM Recommender Systems conference in 2010, Track Chair for WWW 2016, and PC member for many conferences including most recently KDD 2016.

Predicting Attitude and Actions of Twitter Users

Jalal Mahmud[1], Geli Fei[2*], Anbang Xu[1], Aditya Pal[3*], Michelle Zhou[4*]

[1]IBM Research - Almaden, jumahmud@us.ibm.com, anbangxu@us.ibm.com
[2]University of Illinois at Chicago, gfei2@uic.edu
[3]Facebook Inc, aditya.pal@gmail.com
[4]Juji Inc, mzhou@acm.org

ABSTRACT
In this paper, we present computational models to predict Twitter users' attitude towards a specific brand through their personal and social characteristics. We also predict their likelihood of taking different actions based on their attitudes. In order to operationalize our research on users' attitude and actions, we collected ground-truth data through surveys of Twitter users. We have conducted experiments using two real world datasets to validate the effectiveness of our attitude and action prediction framework. Finally, we show how our models can be integrated with a visual analytics system for customer intervention.

Author Keywords
Attitude; Social Media; Twitter; Brand

ACM Classification Keywords
H.5.2 [Information Interfaces and Presentation]: User Interfaces - Interaction styles.

General Terms
Human Factors; Design; Measurement.

INTRODUCTION
In the last few years, social media such as Twitter has emerged, and different brands have social media presence to attract their potential customers. People express various opinions about such brands in social media. Some people may like a brand (e.g., Delta Airlines, Fitbit), some may show neutral attitude, and others may dislike the brand. Some may have formed an attitude towards a brand very recently, and others may have an attitude for quite a long time. Some people have attitude with higher confidence than others, some may remember their attitude well and some are more likely to change their attitudes. People also take different actions (e.g., buy a product/service corresponding to that brand, recommend others to buy) based on their attitude about a brand. Prior works on sentiment/opinion analysis [3, 4, 6, 7, 10, 11, 12, 14] can be useful to know whether a user may like/dislike a brand. A recent work on attitude modeling [1] also describes inferring attitude towards controversial topics in terms of sentiment, opinion and actions. However, such works do not address whether such attitudes are persistent (e.g., an individual formed an attitude for a long time) or temporary (e.g., an individual formed an attitude recently). They also do not provide the strength of attitude (e.g., whether the individual has attitude with high/low confidence). Furthermore, they do not address how well a user remembers his/her attitude or whether the user is likely to change the attitude. Such fine-grained information of consumer attitude can be useful for social media marketers who would directly engage such consumers on social media platforms [5]. Furthermore, predicting social media actions (e.g., retweeting a tweet) as described in Gao et al. is inadequate for such scenario where marketers would be more interested to know whether a consumer will take actions outside the social media.

Motivated by such a need, we present computational models to predict a Twitter user's attitude in terms of a number of characteristics such as *attitude favorability* (How much a consumer likes or dislikes an attitude object), *attitude persistence* (whether an attitude is persistent), *attitude confidence* (strength of attitude), *attitude accessibility* (How well a consumer remembers attitude about the object) and *attitude resistance* (How likely a consumer keeps the present attitude). Our work is inspired by marketing literature where attitude is described in terms of such characteristics [13].

Since there are no publicly available ground truth data of attitude characteristics, we have collected such data using self-report surveys conducted among Twitter users. Using the ground-truth data, we developed statistical models to predict users' attitude. Our classification based models of attitude characteristics are based on features extracted from users' historical tweets. Such models can classify whether a user has specific characteristics of attitude, and also output the likelihood of those attitude characteristics. We have also developed statistical models to infer likelihood of different action intention (e.g., intention to buy a product) based on one's attitude. Similar to our models for predicting different attitude characteristics, our models for predicting action

* This work was done while the author was with IBM Research.

IUI '16, March 7–10, 2016, Sonoma, CA, USA
Copyright 2016 © ACM 978-1-4503-4137-0/16/03...$15.00.
DOI: http://dx.doi.org/10.1145/2856767.2856800

intentions are also trained from features derived from users' historical tweets.

We performed extensive experiments using two real world datasets to validate the effectiveness of our models. For attitude characteristics, we observed mixed result. While attitude favorability can be predicted within 65-69% AUC, prediction accuracies of other characteristics are low to moderate (52-59% AUC). Action intentions can be predicted within 56-67% AUC. We have also integrated our prediction models with a visual analytics system that recommends Twitter users with specific attitude towards a brand, and thus allows potential intervention. Below we list the summary of contributions of this work:

- A survey study of understanding attitude of Twitter users towards multiple brands.
- Models to predict attitude of Twitter users towards a brand in terms of a set of characteristics.
- Models to predict users' intention to take different actions based on their attitudes.
- Experiments demonstrating the effectiveness of our models.
- A visual analytic system that integrates our models and allows customer intervention.

SURVEY STUDY - METHODOLOGY

We collected two real-world datasets from Twitter. Our first dataset is about "Delta" airlines, and the second dataset is about "Fitbit" exercise equipment.

Survey Questions: We created the surveys using SurveyGizmo (http://www.surveygizmo.com/), a popular survey-building tool. Our survey questions were designed to capture various aspects of attitude [13]. Table 1 and 2 shows questions that were included in the Delta survey. Similarly, Table 3 and 4 shows questions that were included in the Fitbit survey. Response to each question was on 5-point Likert scale. Note that, some attitude variables are measured using multiple questions. Response to such variables is computed as an average of the response of those questions. A high value of favorability means user likes the brand more, and low value means the opposite. A high/low value of persistence means user has more/less persistence attitude. Similarly, a high value of accessibility means user can remember the attitude easily, and low value means the opposite. A high value of resistance means user is more likely to stay with the brand, and low value means the opposite. A low value on the response to each action intention means the user is less likely to perform the action, and high value means the opposite.

Survey Participants:

We identified 7534 Twitter users who tweeted about "Delta" airlines during March 2014 to June 2014. They were identified using the keyword @delta in Twitter's Search API. We sent them requests to participate in our survey. To do so, we constructed 6 Twitter accounts and these accounts were used for sending the surveys. These accounts were constructed in a way to appear as genuine as possible, so that a survey request from them does not appear to be a phishing or marketing campaign to target users and the risk of them getting marked as spam by Twitter is mitigated. We offered $50 Amazon gift card to 1 out of every 100 survey participants. Similarly, we identified 5261 Twitter users who tweeted about "Fitbit" exercise equipment (identified using the keyword @fitbit in Twitter's Search API), and sent request to participate in our survey. Similar to our "Delta" airlines survey, we created 6 Twitter accounts to send survey requests to Twitter users and we offered $50 Amazon gift card to 1 out of every 100 survey participants. We ensured that each participant took the survey only once. We also made sure study participants' privacy was protected. We anonymized our ground truth data so that participants were not identifiable afterwards. Before taking the survey, each participant was told that their survey responses will be anonymized, and they gave us explicit consent (by reading consent statement and indicating in the user interface of the survey) to pull their tweets from Twitter. We did not ask their Twitter id to protect their privacy, instead we asked them to give access to their tweets using oAuth. These tweets were linked to their survey responses but was anonymized, so users ID or personal data was not stored.

Attitude Characteristics	Questions
Favorability	How much have you liked your travel experience with Delta Airlines?
Persistence	How often have you used Delta Airlines for your travel? How long have you used Delta Airlines for your travel?
Confidence	Based on your answers, how certain are you about your answers?
Accessibility	How well do you remember your attitude about Delta Airlines?
Resistance	How likely will you switch to another airlines if Delta reduces efficiency of service? How likely will you switch to another airlines if Delta reduces comfort of service? How likely will you switch to another airlines if Delta increases cost of service?

Table 1. Questions to assess attitude about Delta

Survey Responses:

823 users responded to our Delta survey (10.9% response rate) and 507 users responded to our Fitbit (9.6% response rate) survey. We manually inspected survey responses and removed incomplete and inconsistent responses. Finally, we had 751 survey responses for Delta and 447 survey

responses for Fitbit. For each user who responded, we collected their most recent 3200 tweets (max limit enforced by Twitter) using Twitter's REST API. If they had less than 3200 tweets, then we collected all their tweets. We also checked their tweets and they were all English.

Action Intentions	Questions
Buy	How likely are you going to buy ticket of your next trip from Delta airlines?
Recommend	How likely are you going to recommend others to fly by Delta airlines?
Prohibit	How likely are you going to tell others not to fly by Delta airlines?

Table 2. Questions in Delta survey to assess action intentions

Attitude Characteristics	Questions
Favorability	How much have you liked your experience with Fitbit?
Persistence	How long have you used Fitbit?
Confidence	Based on your answers, how certain are you about your answers?
Accessibility	How well do you remember your attitude about Fitbit?
Resistance	How likely will you switch to another fitness device if Fitbit reduces efficiency (e.g., calorie tracking)? How likely will you switch to another fitness device if Fitbit reduces comfort (e.g., comfort to wear)? How likely will you switch to another fitness device if Fitbit increases cost? How likely will you switch to another fitness device if Fitbit reduces visual attractiveness?

Table 3. Questions to assess attitude about Fitbit

Action Intentions	Questions
Buy	How likely are you going to buy next fitness device from Fitbit?
Recommend	How likely are you going to recommend others to buy fitness device from Fitbit?
Prohibit	How likely are you going to tell others not to use Fitbit?

Table 4. Questions in Fitbit survey to assess action intentions

CLASSIFICATION APPROACHES

We developed statistical models to classify each attitude characteristics and action intention. Such models used a set of features extracted from users' historical tweets. For simplicity, we developed binary classifiers for each attitude characteristics. Thus, we first converted each attitude characteristics into binary values (using mean as threshold).

Feature Extraction.

- *Unigram features:* This feature represents all unigrams extracted from tweets.
- *Sentiment features*: We use a sentiment/opinion dictionary that contains a list of words with their positive/negative sentiment polarity. We count total number of positive/negative words in user's tweets and used that positive and negative counts as features.
- *Context-based Sentiment/Opinion feature*: This is similar to the above sentiment/opinion feature; however, it looks for sentiment words that appear in the surrounding area of the brand name (e.g., textual patterns like "awesome delta"). Thus, we counted how many times positive sentiment words in the dictionary co-occur with the brand name and how many times negative sentiment words in the dictionary co-occur with the brand name and used those counts as feature values.
- *Domain-specific sentiment feature*: This feature is similar to the above *Context-based Sentiment/Opinion feature*, however, it is computed by matching words in users' tweets with a domain-specific sentiment dictionary which we constructed from training users' tweets.
- Length of use feature: This feature captures the attitude-persistence of a user and is obtained by taking the timestamp difference of a user's latest and oldest mention of the brand.
- *Frequency feature*: This feature represents how often the user mentions the brand.

Statistical Models.

Once we computed the above mentioned features, we developed statistical models using WEKA [15]. We tried a number of classifiers such as Naive Bayes, SMO (SVM), Random Forest from WEKA and performed 5-fold cross validation. SMO and Random Forest based classifier achieved comparable performance. In experiment section, we report experimental result for SMO classifier.

EXPERIMENTS

Here we describe experiments we have performed to validate the effectiveness of our approach.

Attitude Classification

Table 5 shows the result of our attitude prediction for Delta and Fitbit datasets in terms of F1 and AUC. We observe mixed result for attitude characteristics prediction. Attitude favorability can be predicted with reasonable accuracy (65%-69% AUC). However for other attitude characteristics, we found moderate to low prediction accuracy. It is more intuitive that textual and sentiment based feature extracted from users' historical tweets contain predictive information to predict attitude favorability (i.e., how much they like/dislike a brand). Attitude accessibility and resistance were more difficult to predict which could be either due to the reason that our survey users did not provide very reliable response for those dimensions or users' historical tweets did not contain enough predictive feature for predicting them.

	F1		ROC Area (AUC)	
	Delta	Fitbit	Delta	Fitbit
Favorability	0.71	0.68	0.69	0.65
Persistence	0.61	0.57	0.59	0.57
Confidence	0.58	0.56	0.56	0.55
Accessibility	0.55	0.53	0.53	0.52
Resistance	0.53	0.53	0.52	0.52

Table 5. Result of Attitude Classification

	F1		ROC Area (AUC)	
	Delta	Fitbit	Delta	Fitbit
Buy	0.68	0.65	0.67	0.63
Recommend	0.65	0.60	0.64	0.58
Prohibit	0.60	0.58	0.58	0.56

Table 6. Result of Action Intention Classification

Action Intention Classification

Table 6 shows the result of action intention prediction for both datasets in terms of F1 and AUC. Overall, action intentions can be predicted within reasonable accuracy (56% to 67% AUC). In each case, buy action achieves best performance, while prohibit action seems harder to predict. We think one of the difficulties of predicting prohibit action comes from the particularly unbalanced training data, as prohibit action is an extreme action that not many users would do.

SYSTEM FOR CUSTOMER INTERVENTION

We integrated our prediction models with a visual analytics system for customer intervention. We iteratively designed such a system. First, the system uses simple keyword filtering to identify a set of Twitter users who have recently discussed the brand in their tweets. Their attitudes and action intentions are computed based on their tweets and presented to agents for intervention. The design is shown in Figure 1 and includes two main components: the *attitude & intention component* and the *detailed view component*. The *attitude & intention component* (right in Figure 1) shows an overview of customer attitudes and action intentions in a number of dimensions including favorability, persistence, confidence, accessibility, resistance, buy, recommend, and prohibit. A bar chart visualizes the distribution of the customers' attitude or action intention values along a dimension. The number in a bar denotes the total number of customers in the corresponding segment (see Figure 1). The system allows agents to create visual filters on any individual bar chart in the *attitude & intention component* by selecting a range on the axis, and customers within the selected range would then be shown in the *detailed view component* (left in Figure 1) to reflect the selection. The filtering feature helps agents identify target customers for intervention.

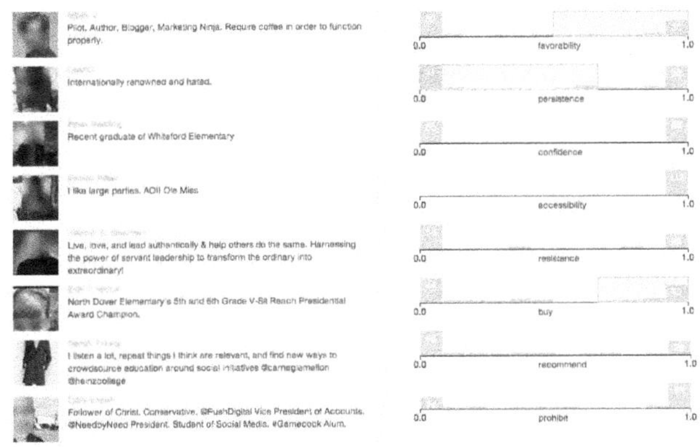

Figure 1. A screenshot of the visual analytics system

LIMITATIONS

Our work has several limitations. We found that accuracy of our prediction models are not high. This can be due to various factors. First, our survey responders might not provide reliable response. We understand that self reported ground truth is not perfect. In our experiments, we did manually check responses of the survey to see if there was any inconsistency in response, and deleted some inconsistence response. In future we will explore other forms of ground truth collection. Second, our models are trained such that features extracted from historical tweets of users are used to predict their attitude and action intention. Such tweets may not contain enough information to predict users' attitude and intentions. In future, we plan to experiment with more features (e.g., features used in [8] to predict re-tweeters) and their relationships to find if prediction accuracy can be improved.

CONCLUSIONS AND FUTURE WORK

This work is a first exploration to predict one's attitude towards a brand in terms of a set of characteristics, and likelihood to take different actions based on attitudes. Our models are trained and tested using two real-world datasets. We have found that most of the attitude characteristics and action intentions can be predicted with moderate accuracy (60-65%). Furthermore, we have integrated our prediction models to a visualization interface to demonstrate usage in customer intervention. In future, we plan to explore how to construct attitude models which are easily scalable across multiple brands and apply our models in real-world scenarios.

REFERENCES

1. Gao, H. Mahmud, J., Chen, J., Nichols, J, Zhou, M.X. Modeling User Attitude Toward Controversial Topics in Online Social Media. In *Proc.* ICWSM 2014.
2. Hoyer, W.D., Maclnnis, D.J. Pieters, R. Consumer Behavior. 5th Edition, 2008.
3. Hu, X.; Tang, J.; Gao, H.; and Liu, H. 2013a. Unsupervised sentiment analysis with emotional signals. In Proc. of the WWW 2013, 607–618.
4. Hu, X.; Tang, L.; Tang, J.; and Liu, H. 2013b. Exploiting social relations for sentiment analysis in microblogging. In Proc. of the WSDM 2013, 537–546.
5. Jansen, B. J., Zhang, M., Sobel, K., et al. 2009. Twitter power: Tweets as electronic word of mouth. Journal of American Society for Information Science & Technology, 60(11), 2169-2188.
6. Jiang, L.; Yu, M.; Zhou, M.; Liu, X.; and Zhao, T. 2011. Target dependent twitter sentiment classification. In Proc. of the HLT '11, 151–160.
7. Kim, J.; Yoo, J.; Lim, H.; Qiu, H.; Kozareva, Z.; and Galstyan, A. 2013. Sentiment prediction using collaborative filtering. In Proc. of the ICWSM 2013.
8. Lee, K.; Mahmud, J.; Chen, J., Zhou, M.X., Nichols, J. 2014. Who Will Retweet This? Automatically Identifying and Engaging Strangers on Twiteer to Spread Information. In Proc. IUI 2014.
9. Li, F.; Huang, M.; and Zhu, X. 2010. Sentiment analysis with global topics and local dependency. In *Proc.* AAAI 2010.
10. Li, D.; Shuai, X.; Sun, G.; Tang, J.; Ding, Y.; and Luo, Z. 2012. Mining topic-level opinion influence in microblog. In *Proc.* CIKM 2012.
11. Lin, C., and He, Y. 2009. Joint sentiment/topic model for sentiment analysis. In *Proc.* CIKM 2009.
12. Pang, B. and Lee, L. 2008. Opinion mining and sentiment analysis. Foundations and Trends in Information Retrieval (2).
13. Schiman, L., and Kanuk, L. 2010. Consumer Behavior, 10th edition. Prentice Hall.
14. Tan, C.; Lee, L.; Tang, J.; Jiang, L.; Zhou, M.; and Li, P. 2011. User-level sentiment analysis incorporating social networks. In Proc. of KDD 2011.
15. Witten, I.H., Frank, E., and Hall, M.A. 2011. Data mining: Practical machine learning tools and techniques, 3rd Edition. Morgan Kaufmann.

Encouraging Diversity- and Representation-Awareness in Geographically Centralized Content

Eduardo Graells-Garrido*
Telefónica I+D
Santiago, Chile

Mounia Lalmas
Yahoo Labs
London, UK

Ricardo Baeza-Yates
Yahoo Labs
Sunnyvale, USA

ABSTRACT
In centralized countries, not only population, media and economic power are concentrated, but people give more attention to central locations. While this is not inherently bad, this behavior extends to micro-blogging platforms: central locations get more attention in terms of information flow. In this paper we study the effects of an information filtering algorithm that decentralizes content in such platforms. Particularly, we found that users from non-central locations were not able to identify the geographical diversity on timelines generated by the algorithm, which were diverse by construction. To make users see the inherent diversity, we define a design rationale to approach this problem, focused on the treemap visualization technique. Then, we deployed an "in the wild" implementation of our proposed system. On one hand, we found that there are effects of centralization in exploratory user behavior. On the other hand, we found that the treemap was able to make users see the inherent geographical diversity of timelines. We measured these effects based on how users engaged with content filtered by the algorithm. With these results in mind, we propose practical actions for micro-blogging platforms to account for the differences and biased behavior induced by centralization.

ACM Classification Keywords
H.3.3 Information Storage and Retrieval: Information Search and Retrieval—*Information Filtering*; H.5.2 User Interfaces: Graphical user interfaces (GUI).

Author Keywords
Centralization; Location Bias; Information Filtering; Information Visualization.

INTRODUCTION
In his book on user experience, Bill Buxton wrote that *"in order to design a tool, we must make our best efforts to understand the larger social and physical context within which it is intended to function"* [8]. In today's global Web, it is not clear if current social platforms consider those different contexts when building their user interfaces or defining their content-based algorithms. This would not be a problem in an uniform, unbiased world, but our world is neither uniform [22] nor unbiased [29]. One of these biases is *centralization* [24], an organizational schema for governments that can be beneficial for the population, for development, and for the economy, because of the concentration of political, economical and media powers. However, at the same time, it can create regional inequalities within a country [25], making national growth biased toward central locations. Given that centralization is part of the social context of users, in this work we evaluate whether this bias affects the informational and exploratory behavior of users on the Web, particularly in micro-blogging platforms. We do so through the following research questions:

> Does centralization affect how people perceive information, and how people behave when browsing informational content in micro-blogging platforms? If so, how can we encourage non-centralized exploration?

To answer our research questions, we analyzed the usage of Twitter by people in Chile interested in politics. This case study is perfect for our analysis for two reasons. On the one hand, Chile is a highly centralized country toward its capital region [4, 17]. Although this region is indeed near the geographical center of continental Chile, the country spans over 4,300 km (2,671 mi) from north to south, with only 175 km (108 mi) in average from east to west, having a geographical configuration that is not particularly fit for centralization. After returning to democracy, various initiatives attempted to decentralize the country, but enormous political and economical resistance allowed for only small progress towards this, if any [14]. On the other hand, Chile is one of the developing countries with the highest Internet penetration rate [10], and Twitter is actively used by politically-involved Chileans [40].

A previous study [20] determined that centralization is reflected in the way users interact in Twitter, creating regional inequalities in information flow with respect to user location. The authors developed an information filtering algorithm that generates geographically diverse timelines. By construction, the algorithm allows all locations to be present in a timeline. In this paper, we evaluate this algorithm through a user study. We find that users from central locations have a different sense of diversity, interestingness, and informativeness than users from peripheral locations.

The results from the user study imply that, even though in theory the algorithm solves the problem, in practice users might not notice it. After analyzing these differences, we hypothesize that centralization generates a *diversity- and representation-awareness* problem, and thus we define a design rationale to

*Corresponding author: `eduardo.graells@telefonica.com`. Work carried out while the first author was a PhD student in the Web Research Group, at Universitat Pompeu Fabra, Barcelona, Spain.

IUI 2016, March 7–10, 2016, Sonoma, CA, USA.

ACM 978-1-4503-4137-0/16/03 ...$15.00.
DOI: http://dx.doi.org/10.1145/2856767.2856775

address these issues. In compliance with our design rationale we then test a visualization of categorical news headlines by Weskamp [41] in our context, *i. e.*, in geographically diverse timelines with micro-posts instead of headlines. We hypothesize that this interface eases the identification in timelines by making geographical diversity salient through the usage of *squarified treemaps* [6], a well-known information visualization technique. We evaluate this design in an exploratory application deployed on the Web. The analysis of interaction data reveals that, even though there are differences in how people behave with respect to their geographical origin, our design facilitates diversity- and representation-awareness from a geographical point of view.

Our results show that centralization affects the perception and behavior of politically-involved users in Chile. They also demonstrate that awareness of social and geographical contexts when designing algorithms and user interfaces improves user perception in the presence of these systemic biases. Finally, considering that many countries are centralized [17, 24, 25], our findings and implications can be used by micro-blogging platforms to make their systems aware of important factors of social contexts.

STATE OF THE ART

This paper deals with *centralization* [24], in particular considering its geographical aspect. Geography is an important attribute to be considered in the study of social networks and Web platforms. In the context of Twitter, even though most of user ties are geographically local [35], more than a third of mentions and links are inter-countries [26]. To understand how a virtual population is distributed, each user's location must be determined, a meta-attribute not always available. When geolocating users in micro-blogging platforms, a simple approach is to query a gazetteer with the user's self-reported location [21], but there are more complex and accurate approaches that involve entity recognition [1] and language models [11]. In our context, location classifiers can become biased when the population is imbalanced [37], and care must be taken when parameterizing such algorithms.

Despite being a virtual platform, Twitter users reflect or are influenced by physical world phenomena. For instance, the number of international flights between countries is the best predictor of non-local ties [39]; tweets can predict gross community happiness by comparing aggregated word usage related to mood in communities [36]; interaction and publishing behavior on Twitter is related with cultural dimensions [19]; and international communication is still dominated by physical distance [18]. Communication and tie formation in Twitter are influenced by geography and culture—two aspects deeply connected with centralization. In Chile, the informational behavior of the population is centralized [20]. Thus, in our work, we evaluate if centralization influences user perception of geographically diverse timelines.

We focus on geographical diversity because under population imbalance and centralization, it is expected that timeline content is also imbalanced, both in volume and in popularity metrics (*e. g.*, number of retweets). Then, we propose to filter timelines using methods that increase geographical diversity of its content. Diversification can be performed by minimizing similarity between items in a recommendation list [42], maximizing entropy of a set of content features [13], as well as context-specific diversification methods [31]. In the case of Twitter, diversified timelines (in its information entropy sense) have been found to be easier to remember and more engaging [13]. In this paper we build upon such work, by evaluating perception of timelines generated by an information filtering algorithm [20], which, in turn, is based on two previous algorithms that aim to generate diverse information sets [13, 31].

We focus on how user location influences those perceptions and how engagement differs in terms of location and user interface. Park *et al.* [33] showed that the presentation of news headlines in clusters generates more clicks on news than non-clustered displays. We extend their design guidelines by using *squarified treemaps* [6] to maintain clustered representations of micro-posts while, at the same time, making diversity visually salient and noticeable. Treemaps have been used before to visualize content from micro-blogging platforms by Archambault *et al.* [3], although their approach is different to ours: they visualize clustered keywords, whereas we visualize entire tweets using a design inspired by *Newsmap.jp* [41], a treemap visualization of news headlines. In the context of political diversity, it has been acknowledged that visualization-based interfaces help people behave differently [15].

It is known that people from different cultures behave in different ways when communicating, not only on micro-blogs [18] but also on other forms of communication, like instant messaging [23]. In our work, we propose that centralization introduces differences in how users behave, and thus, these differences should be accounted for when designing systems.

BACKGROUND

In this section we briefly describe the dataset and methods used by Graells-Garrido *et al.* [20], which provide the background of this work. Although the defined methods are general, we restrict ourselves to Twitter, a micro-blogging platform where users publish status updates called *tweets* with a maximum length of 140 characters. Users can *follow* other users, establishing directed connections between them. When user A *follows* user B, tweets and *re-tweets* made by B will show up in A's timeline. A timeline is a list of tweets in reverse chronological order. Users can annotate tweets using *hashtags*, *i. e.*, keywords that start with the hash character #.

Context: Municipal Elections in Chile. In the first user study on this paper we analyze a dataset of tweets from Chile. Centralization in Chile is characterized through geography at the *regional level*, *i. e.*, the first-level administrative division of the country. Chile has 15 regions, and the capital *Región Metropolitana* (translated as *Metropolitan Region*, and *RM* hereafter) is the most central one [4, 17].

The dataset is composed of tweets crawled on October 28th, 2012, in the context of municipal elections held in Chile that day. The event had a distinctive hashtag (*#municipales2012*), which, among other related hashtags (e.g. *#tudecides*), keywords (e.g. *vote*), location and candidate names, were used as queries for the *Twitter Streaming API*.[1] In total, this dataset contains 157,648 users who published 724,890 tweets. To explore the representativity of the sample, we estimated the Pearson product-moment correlation coefficient r between virtual and physical population, and between account rate and household Internet Access Rate in Chile [30]. Because of population imbalance, we estimated the correlation of the logarithms of population, obtaining $r = 0.95$ ($p < 0.01$). The user and household Internet access rates correlate at $r = 0.68$ ($p < 0.01$). Therefore, we consider the sample spatially representative of the physical population at the regional level.

Because its content is about local elections happening nationwide, this dataset is suitable to study the effects of centralization. The analysis made in [20] consists on the determination of potential centralization patterns in information flow. It was made by aggregating *mentions*, *replies* and *retweets* with respect to origin and destination locations of the involved user accounts. Then, an interaction graph between locations was built, in which the authors estimated *betweenness centrality* using random walks [32]. Betweenness centrality was chosen instead of other centrality metrics because it represents *"the potential of a point for control of information flow in the network"* [16]. The use of a random walk allowed the authors to consider the user distribution instead of binary edges in the graph, as well as to build a baseline graph based on the population distribution of the physical world. Then, by comparing both graphs, it was possible to determine whether informational behavior in Twitter, in terms of to whom people interact with, is centralized. It was found that: *1) RM* is the most central location in Twitter discussion; *2)* that centralities are significantly different between observations (interactions) and expectations (physical world population distribution); and *3)* the observed centrality of *RM* is higher than the expected one, and the centralities of all other locations exhibit the opposite behavior, implying that centralization also affects informational behavior in political discussion of Chileans in Twitter.

Building Geographically Diverse Timelines. The influence of centralization makes content from peripheral locations harder to find. One way to help to reduce this bias is through generation of geographically diverse timelines where all regions are represented regardless of their centrality. This can be achieved through the usage of information filtering techniques.

In this paper, we use an information filtering algorithm previously defined Graells-Garrido *et al.* [20]. This *Proposed Method* (hereafter *PM*) mixes two other known algorithms:

1. The first algorithm [13] is greedy and based on *information entropy*. Entropy is estimated with respect to several content-based features extracted from tweets (presence of links, topical information in hashtags, author connectivity and experience, age of content, and so forth). At each iteration, the algorithm selects a tweet from a candidate pool that maximizes the current entropy of the filtered timeline. In [20] this algorithm was modified to consider popularity (number of retweets) as a feature, by preferring candidate tweets who are more popular than others.
2. The second algorithm is known as *Sidelines* [31]. Because the complexity of the information features considered in [13] can be greater than those of geography (*e. g.*, consider the number of hashtags against the number of locations), the entropy contribution of these dimensions can be higher than the entropy contribution of geography. Thus, geographical diversity is enforced by *sidelining*, *i. e.*, when a tweet is selected for inclusion by the first algorithm, its location is not considered at the following n iterations.

The mixed algorithm applies both base algorithms simultaneously: tweets are selected according to their entropy contributions, but only considering those from locations that have not been sidelined. With this schema a timeline of s tweets can be built, with ensured information and geographical diversity. Whether these timelines are perceived as more diverse, interesting and informative than baseline timelines (including the first base algorithm [13]) is what we evaluate in the next section.

USER PERCEPTION OF DIVERSE TIMELINES

We describe the user study performed to evaluate how users perceive timelines generated with the *PM* algorithm [20] in comparison with those of baseline conditions. Our hypothesis is that centralization influences user perception, given that it is part of the cultural context of users. Users are grouped according to their geographical origin: a centralized location (*RM* group) or a peripheral one (*NOT-RM* group). Then, users are asked to compare three attributes of timelines: *diversity*, *interestingness* and *informativeness*. Note that interestingness and informativeness are related to relevance and coverage, respectively. However, we used user-centered terms as our study targeted end-users who may have been more familiar with the terms we chose.

Conditions and Datasets. In addition to the *Proposed Method* (*PM*), we consider the following baseline conditions: *Popularity Sampling* (*POP* hereafter): we select the s most popular tweets in terms of retweets; and *Diversity Filtering* (*DIV* hereafter): an implementation of the algorithm that maximizes information entropy of each timeline [13]. Because the different conditions require pairwise comparisons, we split the dataset from [20] in three:

1. *morning-noon*: 140,211 tweets published by 52,403 users between 10:00AM and 2:30PM.
2. *afternoon*: 180,824 tweets published by 63,388 users between 2:30PM and 9:00PM.
3. *night*: 401,029 tweets published by 106,942 users between 9:00PM and 2:00AM (next day).

This division of time matches the local culture where lunch happens between 1:00PM and 2:30PM, and dinner around 9:00PM. For each dataset we built filtered timelines with *PM*, *DIV*, and *POP*. We excluded retweets as our focus is on standalone, source tweets.

Participants. Participants were recruited using *snowball sampling* in Twitter using open calls to volunteer in the study, which were retweeted by participants. No compensation was offered. We recruited 125 participants. Of them, 81 were male,

[1] `https://dev.twitter.com/docs/streaming-apis`

41 were female and 3 opted to not say. In terms of age, 1 was 18–19, 59 were 20–29, 54 were 30–39, 4 were 40–49, 1 was 50+ years old and 6 opted not to say. All participants were from Chile (87 in *RM* and 38 in *NOT-RM*). Experience with social networks was asked using a five-point Likert scale: those from *RM* scored 3.73 ($\sigma^2 = 0.59$), and those from *NOT-RM* scored 3.68 ($\sigma^2 = 0.58$).

Experimental Setup. For each sub-dataset we generated three timelines (with $s = 30$ tweets) using *PM*, *DIV*, and *POP*. Timelines were displayed with a format that resembled Twitter user interface.

Procedure. The study had a *within-subjects* design. First, participants were asked to fill a questionnaire about demographic information and other features such as Twitter usage. Then, in at most three steps, users performed a series of comparisons between two timelines rendered side by side, each one generated by a different condition. To avoid sequence effects, the order of pairwise comparisons (*POP/PM*, *POP/DIV*, *DIV/PM*) and the order of sub-datasets (*morning-noon*, *afternoon*, *night*) were randomized in both, the position on the screen (left or right) and the experimental step. Hence, all the participants contributed to all conditions whenever possible, as some participants were expected to not do all comparisons being an on-line, volunteered study. Additionally, not all participants were expected to do a full read of timelines, and thus we discarded comparisons where the total reading time of both timelines was less than one minute.

Task. Participants were instructed to read the two timelines side by side, and then answer the following questions:

1. *Which of the two timelines is more diverse?*
2. *Which of the two timelines is more interesting?*
3. *Which of the two timelines is more informative?*
4. *Optional: Please explain your answers. Add examples if needed.*

Questions 1 to 3 had a seven-point Likert scale from -3 to 3, where -3 (or 3) means that the timeline on the left (or right) was perceived as more *diverse*, *interesting* or *informative* than the other, and a value of 0 means that there was no perceived difference. Question 1 asked for general diversity as we did not want to prime participants into thinking primarily about geographical diversity, although we explained that it should be considered in its widest sense, including geography, by adding the following subtitle to the question: "*Consider diversity in its widest sense (geographical, demographical, topical, temporal, etc).*" Question 4 presented a free-text form element. After answering the four questions, a pause screen was shown for 15 seconds to allow participants to rest.

Statistical Model. The aforementioned questions define three dependent variables: *diversity*, *interestingness* and *informativeness*. For each dependent variable we built the following statistical model (using *R formula syntax*):

$$Y \sim C(\text{comparison}) \times C(\text{location}),$$

where Y is an ordered response variable, $C(\text{comparison})$ is a dummy variable that encodes the specific pairwise comparisons performed in the study, and $C(\text{location})$ is a variable that encodes whether users are from *RM* or not. The operator $\times$ encodes the main effects plus the interaction between factors.[2]

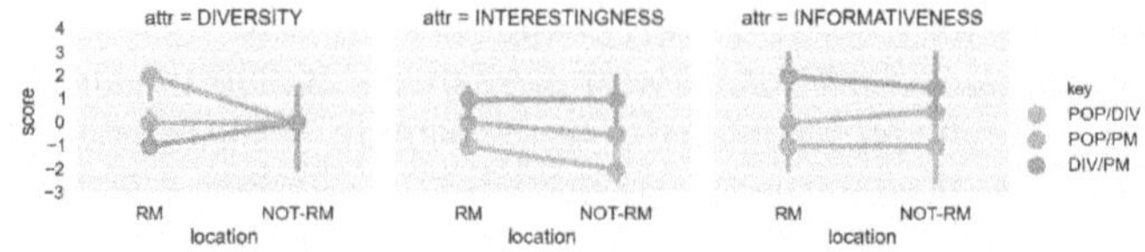

Figure 1: Point plots of median scores given by participants in comparisons of diversity, informativeness and interestingness. For each pairwise comparison, a positive value indicates that the approach on the right of the label was perceived to be more diverse, interesting, and informative than the one on the left, and *vice-versa*.

Over this model we performed a *generalized linear model* regression with a *proportional odds model* [27]. This model is also known as *ordered logistic regression*, and is used when modeling ordinal dependent variables. It extends the logistic regression model by allowing more than two categories, considering the order of the responses, and not assuming equidistant items in the Likert scale. If the statistical interaction was not found to be significant, then we performed another regression without the interaction terms (*i. e.*, using the $+$ operator instead of $\times$).

Results

In total, participants performed 238 comparisons: 84 for conditions *POP/DIV*, 80 for conditions *POP/PM*, and 74 for conditions *DIV/PM*. The following are the interpolated medians of pairwise comparisons given by users:

- *POP/DIV*: diversity (0), interestingness (-1), informativeness (-1). Users perceived both as equally diverse, but POP is found to be more interesting and informative.
- *POP/PM*: diversity (1), interestingness (0), informativeness (0). PM is found by users to be more diverse than POP, and both are perceived as equally interesting and informative.
- *DIV/PM*: diversity (-0.5), interestingness (1), informativeness (2). DIV is found by users to be slightly more diverse than PM, but PM is perceived as more interesting and informative.

Figure 1 showcases the medians of pairwise comparisons between conditions (questions 1, 2 and 3), considering individual differences according to location. It can be observed that statistical interactions could appear in the three attributes under consideration, specially with diversity. To formalize this intuition, we applied the regression defined previously to the user scores of comparisons. The following list describes the fit of those regressions:

- Diversity: the regression with interaction terms (log-likelihood $= -447.21$, AIC $= 910.41$, cond. H $= 1,900$) presented a significant interaction, and is used for analysis.
- Interestingness: the regression with interaction terms did not present significant terms according to the likelihood ratio test. The regression without interaction (log-likelihood

[2] $A \times B = A + B + A * B$.

Result #	Variable	Effect	β	Odds-Ratio	95% C.I.	p
R1	Diversity	Location *RM* and condition *POP/PM*	1.291	3.637	$[0.317, 2.278]$	0.010
R2	Interestingness	Location RM	0.686	1.985	$[0.307, 1.069]$	< 0.001
R3	Interestingness	Comparison *POP/DIV*	-1.404	0.246	$[-1.885, -0.933]$	< 0.001
R4	Interestingness	Comparison *POP/PM*	-0.859	0.423	$[-1.353, -0.373]$	< 0.001
R5	Informativeness	Location *RM*	1.364	3.910	$[0.869, 1.872]$	< 0.001
R6	Informativeness	Comparison *POP/DIV*	-0.926	0.396	$[-1.618, -0.241]$	0.008
R7	Informativeness	Location *RM* and comparison *POP/DIV*	-1.201	0.301	$[-2.148, -0.261]$	0.012
R8	Informativeness	Location *RM* and comparison *POP/PM*	-1.543	0.214	$[-2.577, -0.521]$	0.003

Table 1: Significant effects from the user study, including coefficients, effect sizes (Odds-Ratios) and confidence intervals. We only include effects with significant p-values ($p < 0.015$).

$= -430.84$, AIC $= 873.67$, cond. H $= 460$) is used for analysis.

- Informativeness: the regression with interaction terms (log-likelihood $= -429.35$, AIC $= 874.70$, cond. H $= 200$) presented a significant interaction, and is used for analysis.

The condition numbers of the respective Hessians indicate that the fits are not ill-defined. Table 1 shows the significant factors of each regression. We identify each result as Ri, to reference it later in the discussion. We mention only those that are significant according to their p-value (considering $p < 0.05$).

Discussion of Results

The experimental results support our hypothesis. Moreover, they give us two important insights. First, *popularity is more valued than diversity*. Users give more value to popularity than diversity, considering value as the mixture of informativeness and interestingness. Even *POP*, that is not geographically diverse, is perceived as more interesting than *DIV* (R3) and PM (R4). Likewise, *POP* is perceived as more informative than *DIV* (R6, R7 -*RM* only-) and PM (R8 -*RM* only-). Yet, the Odd-Ratios (OR) of these results are low, and thus, while there is an effect, this effect is subtle. Second, *perception of timeline properties depends on the geographical origin of users*. By design, we expected *PM* to be perceived as more diverse by users than *POP*, and more informative/interesting than *DIV*. However, this happened *only when users come from* RM (R1). Moreover, just being from *RM* indicates that users are more prone to find content interesting/informative, regardless of its diversity (R2, R5). The high odd-ratios of these results indicate that the effect is strong. The interaction between location and comparisons of *POP* and the diversity-driven algorithms *DIV* and *PM* (R7, R8), indicates a slight (given its ORs) accentuation of the effect.

Qualitative Feedback. Users' answers allowed us to validate the motivations and design decisions behind the proposed algorithm [20]:

> "In terms of diversity, *[PM]* is partly more diverse because it is more geographically diverse. I was in doubt to choose *[POP]* as more diverse because it contained some tweets about several topics, but at the end I preferred geography" [*P76, NOT-RM*].

> "I feel `[PM]` has much more information related to many locations, unlike timeline *[DIV]* which is focused on informing only about *[RM]*" [*P50, RM*].

One reason popularity was considered in the algorithm was to avoid potential noise present in *DIV*, because noisy information is likely to increase entropy. This difference, as well as the similarities between both approaches, was noted by some users:

> "It seems to me that both timelines *[DIV,PM]* are similar in the background, although *[PM]* has an informative emphasis, more than merely anecdotal as *[DIV]*. In a way, it could be said that *[DIV]* is slightly more diverse in comparison to *[PM]*, but in my judgement those 'diverse' tweets were not interesting enough, instead they are more likely to be 'noise' in the main topic of both timelines" [*P47, RM*].

> "I find *[POP]* more interesting as it talks about a particular topic, while *[DIV]* is about self-referential stuff that is not always of common interest" [*P86, NOT-RM*].

The above answers also surface the different concepts users have when considering diversity, as some users consider topical and geographical diversity, whereas others explicitly stated *personal opinions* as a source of diversity. However, users agree that a noticeable difference between *PM* and *DIV* relies on the fact that *PM* presents tweets from popular users:

> "In general, timeline *[PM]* is based on known sources or journalists. Timeline *[DIV]* is about people from the community giving their impressions on what is going on, which is interesting but it doesn't have any backup information" [*P38, RM*].

> "It could be said that timeline *[DIV]* has a diversity of users that are not, in contrast with those of timeline *[PM]*, notable personalities of the 'Twitter world', however this is not enough for it to be considered more diverse (...). In terms of informativeness, timeline *[PM]* is ahead, since it is comprised of Twitter users dedicated to inform, it is expected for it to contain more complete tweets in terms of what was going on" [*P47, RM*].

If informativeness and interestingness are linked with user status, then the answers above support the quantitative results where *PM* was more interesting and informative than *DIV*. However, this feedback did not explain the differences reported in diversity by users.

Diversity and Representation. From these insights, we hypothesize that people from central locations find *PM* more diverse, and any approach more informative/interesting, because they are not used to see information from peripheral locations. It is known that the geographical span of ego-networks in Twitter is small [35], and thus, exposing those users to views from other locations expands their vision.

In contrast, people from peripheral locations do not see differences in diversity, nor find the content informative/interesting, because they are used to be exposed to views from *RM*. For peripheral users, before filtering, the timeline content focused prominently on the centralized and most populated locations; after, it contained a wider set of locations, but still not prominently their own. This concept is known as *out-group ho-*

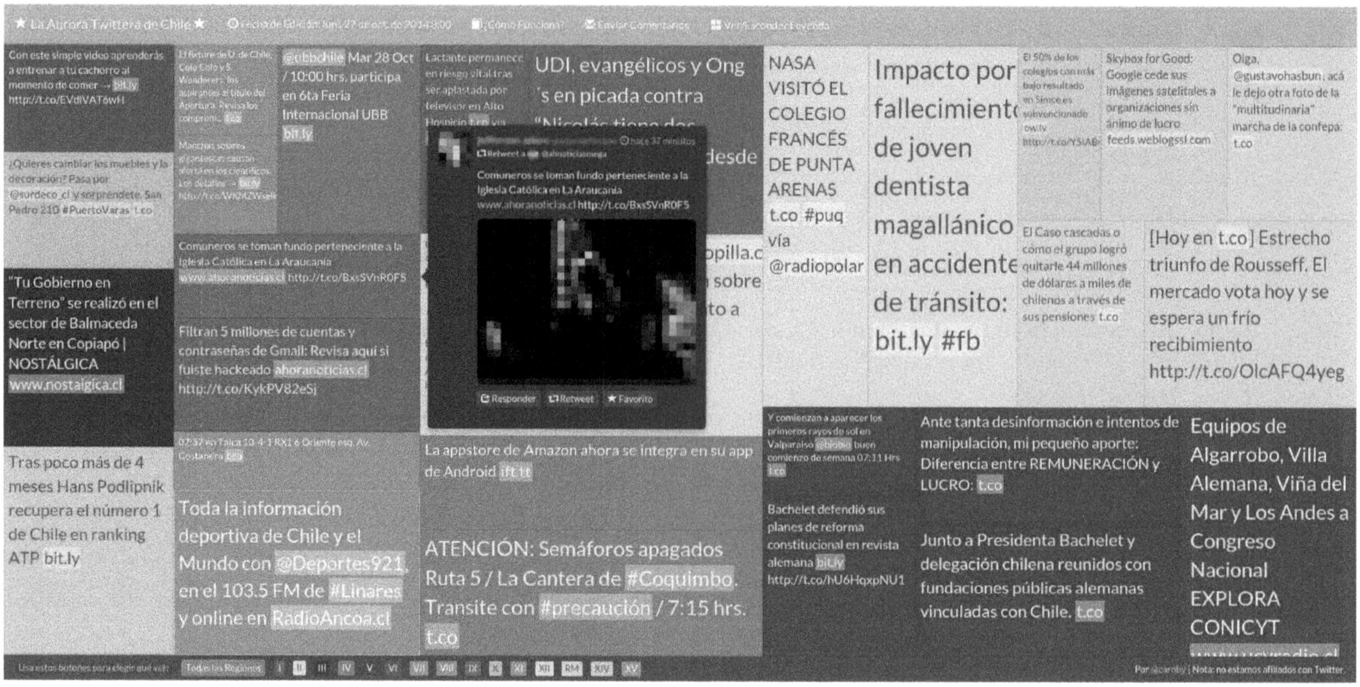

Figure 2: Screenshot from **http://auroratwittera.cl**, the URL of our prototype implementation. The bottom bar contains the location filters. The upper bar contain navigational links to an *About* page and a feedback form.

mogeneity [38], and it can be described through the phrase *"they are alike, we are diverse"* [34]. We recall that the source dataset guarantees the presence of local content, given that it is about nationwide municipal elections happening at the same time. This implies that users did not recognize the presence of their locations in the generated timelines. Hence, in the next section we seek to enhance *representation-awareness* of users, to help users to recognize their presence in the timeline.

A DIVERSITY-AWARE PLATFORM

We propose a platform design that seeks to increase awareness of representation caused by diversity in timelines generated by the *PM* algorithm. The platform is deployed "in the wild" [12], *i. e.*, we target end-users in their everyday use of Twitter.

Design Rationale: Awareness Through Identification

Since *PM* timelines are geographically diverse by definition, perhaps what people from peripheral locations need is to *become aware* of their representation in the information stream. We propose to increase this awareness by facilitating *identification* as defined by Butler [7], *i. e.*, identification relies upon differences with the others. In our context, this means that by emphasizing differences with the others, we can facilitate identification (and thus, representation-awareness). We do so by making diversity salient, allowing users to *see* the geographical diversity present in the timeline.

Making Diversity Salient. Prior work determined that presentation [33] and visualization [15] change the way users behave in the presence of diverse information. In particular, the grouping of news headlines according to agreement with political positions improved user access to diverse information, measured in clicks on those headlines [33]. Then, clustering content in locations would make easier for users to quickly see their own locations represented. However, it must be applied with care because our context is different. In political contexts, information is usually classified into a bipartite separation of groups (*e. g.*, *democrats* and *republicans*, *conservative* and *liberal*, etc.), whereas in our case the number of locations is larger (*i. e.*, 15 Chilean regions), creating the need to scroll on the screen and thus inducing a positional bias, by giving more importance to those clusters already visible without scrolling.

To avoid scrolling and its associated positional bias, we consider a previous visualization of news headlines by Weskamp [41], which uses a 2D space-filling layout algorithm to partition the available screen space: the *squarified treemap layout* [6]. We visually encode locations as *internal nodes* and tweets as *leaves*. Sibling leaves appear together. The *area size* of each leaf depends on the number of retweets of the corresponding tweet, and the number of followers and friends of its author, in inverse proportions to population location. In this way, screen space is shared in a fair way between locations, as shown in Figure 2. Each leaf node is colored according to its location (*hue*) and its recency (*saturation*). Internal nodes are not displayed as they are not needed.

User Interaction. To interact with the visualization, users can *click* a leaf node to display a pop-up with detailed information about the corresponding tweet, with buttons to perform core Twitter interactions (reply, retweet, mark as favorite, follow) and a text format that resembles the typical tweet presentation. To *filter locations*, for each location we display a button that, when clicked, updates the treemap to display only tweets originated from the selected location.

Prototype
We implemented a prototype of the user interface (see Figure 2) using the *d3.js* [5] library. This interface is named *"Aurora Twittera de Chile"* (*AT* hereafter) and is available at `http://auroratwittera.cl`. Every 30 minutes a *"new issue of AT"* was generated by the filtering algorithm (having $s = 30$ as size for each timeline and $n = 5$ for turns in the sideline step in *PM*).

We used the same implementation of the filtering algorithm *PM* from the first user study, with two differences: first, for performance reasons, we did not use a location classifier for all tweets in the dataset. Instead, we considered only tweets from accounts with a known self-reported location, although we did consider non-geolocated tweets retweeted by those accounts. Second, we avoided repeated authors or tweet content in the same timeline, and we discarded tweets where almost all text was in uppercase letters to avoid *shouting*.

Input tweets were downloaded with a crawler using the *Twitter Streaming API*. As query keywords we used location names, political terms, and other terms of interest that appear constantly on the news, as well as mentions to media accounts, both at national and local levels. Each issue had a specific URL in the form `http://auroratwittera.cl/timeline/ID`, which allowed users to access it at a later time, as well as saving a permanent link. In addition, if the URL contained the code of a location (*e. g.*, `http://auroratwittera.cl/#RM`) the interface displayed immediately the tweets related to that location in the same way as if a location filter button had been pressed.

Social Bot @todocl. Since social bots can generate social discussion and behavioral changes based on their activity [2], we created a social bot on Twitter, with username *@todocl*, to publicize *AT* and recruit users. *@todocl* presented itself as a social experiment to establish an informative community about current happenings in Chile using Twitter, and published three types of tweets:

- Whenever a timeline was generated, *@todocl* published two tweets with a link to its corresponding *issue*: one mentioning four users who authored "featured tweets", and one mentioning four users with "featured retweets" (in both cases users were selected randomly from filtered timeline).
- After publishing those tweets, every minute *@todocl* retweeted one tweet featured in the current issue.
- Every hour past 45 minutes, *@todocl* published 15 tweets, one per location, featuring a link to the current issue with each specific location in the URL, as well as an attached image with a *word cloud* of their most representative terms obtained with *Term Frequency/Inverse Document Frequency* (TF-IDF).

This implementation, comprised of filtering algorithm, user interface and social bot, creates a platform where users can access geographically diverse information, in the form of an external application to Twitter, as well as injected into the platform itself. We evaluate this application next.

EVALUATION WITH INTERACTION DATA
In this second study, we evaluate user behavior based on the interaction data obtained from *AT*, in particular at differences with respect to centralization. Our hypothesis is that the presentation using treemaps will help users overcome the awareness problems, due to the reasons specified in our design rationale. Note that *AT* is not a task-based system, *i. e.*, we do not expect users to visit the site to perform a specific task. Instead, the system is designed as an exploratory interface to geographically diverse timelines. By being exploratory, common evaluation metrics such as task accuracy or task performance cannot be applied. Instead, we evaluate user interaction with our system from the point of view of three dimensions: diversity-awareness, representation-awareness, and interestingness. From the analysis of those dimensions, we elaborate plausible explanations of potential differences in behavior as indicated by statistical analysis.

Experimental Setup
In this experiment we analyze interaction data obtained from user interaction with our implementation in *AT*. Each interaction is considered an event. We logged implicit events on the server, such as *session created/restored*, and from the client browser using Javascript, such as *timeline and UI loaded*, and *pings*. As explicit events we logged clicks on every element of the user interface, allowing us to identify whether users filtered locations, clicked on links, asked for a more detailed view of a tweet, as well as clicking on the Twitter native buttons to reply, mark as favorite, or follow a tweet's author.

Using the logged events we analyze user behavior from three dimensions derived from interaction data and related to the problem at hand:

- *Diversity-Awareness*: defined as the number of different locations that generated the content the user interacted with. Every time the user interacted with content, we logged the location of the author that published it. Thus, we define a variable named *distinct locations* that encodes the number of different locations the user has interacted with. Note that we assume that users who clicked elements from a tweet are aware of the content they are clicking.
- *Representation-Awareness*: defined as the likelihood of selecting specific locations for browsing by users. We define a variable named *filter likelihood* that is 0 if the user has not selected specific locations using the location filters from the UI, and 1 otherwise.
- *Interestingness*: defined as the number of interactions with content by the user per day. We define a variable named *content events* that sums the number of clicks in links, the number of tweets seen with more detail, the number of tweets marked as favorite or replied, as well as the number of times other users have been followed. Given that some users visited the site more than once, we normalize this variable according to the number of different days each user has accessed the site.

Participants. We gathered interaction data from October 1st, 2014 until January 20th, 2015. The server logged each user request and was able to identify sessions based on cookies

Figure 3: Design baselines implemented for the study. Left: standalone tweets (each in its own box). Right: clustered tweets by location.

placed on user browsers. IP addresses were used to identify each user's location, using the GeoIP Legacy Database.[3] The User Agent information was used to determine if the user was browsing from a mobile device; those users were served with a minimal version of the site but were not considered in the study because of platform heterogeneity (in terms of interaction capabilities, screen sizes, etc.). From 16,969 valid interaction events, we have 321 users, of which 193 are in *RM* and 128 are in *NOT-RM*. We discarded users who were active in the site for less than 10 seconds or that were in the top 5% of dwell time,[4] as well as those who deactivated Javascript or could not be geolocated using GeoIP.

Conditions. To evaluate the effect on user behavior of both, location and user interface, we developed two alternative baseline conditions to compare with our proposed design: *1) Baseline*, where each tweet is rendered independently of the others, and tweets are sorted by their time of publication. Each tweet is displayed inside a box with a bordered color and a legend at the bottom to indicate its originating location; and *2) Clustered* [33], where tweets are clustered by location. Each location is represented as a box with a bordered color and a legend at the top to indicate the originating location of its tweets. Both baselines are shown in Figure 3. It can be seen that, although they are text-based, they include visual cues that indicate differences in location. Also, both have the same interactive location filters as our condition, *Treemap*.

When a user accessed *AT*, if it was his/her first visit, a random condition was assigned. Because we tracked users using cookies, in following requests users received the same interface according to their initial assignment. The distribution of users is as follows: *baseline* was assigned to 97 users; *clustered* to 98 users; and *treemap* to 126 users.

Setup. We consider a *between-subjects* design, as participants were exposed to one condition only. When users loaded *AT* we gathered the following user information: *IP address*, *HTTP Referrer* and *User Agent*. Then, we logged each interaction with elements of the user interface. If the user requested the page through an URL with a location code, we considered it as an initial click on a location filter, because such links were generated by the social bot, and the user explicitly chose to follow them instead of the main URL. Finally, the user interface sent a ping every ten seconds to the server to track the time spent on the website even in the absence of interactions, to capture the dwell time of passive users.

Statistical Model. For analysis, we evaluate the effect of location and condition in the dependent variables defined earlier: *distinct locations*, *filter likelihood* and *content events*. We consider the two categorical independent variables *location* (*RM* or *NOT-RM*) and *condition* (*baseline*, *clustered*, or *treemap*). Both are included in the following statistical model:

$$Y \sim C(\text{condition}) \times C(\text{location}).$$

As in the previous study, we consider main effects of each factor as well as the interaction between them. The C element in the formula generates *contrasts* as dummy variables.

Over this model we perform *generalized linear model* regressions. The link function used for regressions of *distinct locations* and *content events* is the *Negative Binomial* distribution, which is commonly used to model over-dispersed count data. For *filter likelihood* we use *logistic* (*logit*) regression, because we model a probability. For each variable, if the statistical interaction was not found to be significant, we performed another regression without the interaction term.

Results

Figure 4 shows the distributions of our variables. Additionally, we include the distribution of the number of days each user has visited the site, because it is used to normalize the variable content events, which is not normalized in the figure.[5] The following list describes the regression of each variable:

- Variable distinct_locations (mean $= 0.364$, std $= 1.013$, max $= 10$): the *N.B.* regression (deviance $= 248.44$, $\chi^2 = 453$, log-likelihood $= -240.45$) has intercept $\beta = -1.987$ (95% C.I. $[-2.683, -1.290]$, $p < 0.001$).
- Variable filter_likelihood (mean $= 0.436$, std $= 0.497$, max $= 1$): the *logit* regression (log-likelihood $= -212.41$, $p = 0.002$) has non-significant intercept $\beta = -0.289$ (95% C.I. $[-0.779, 0.201]$, $p = 0.247$).
- Variable content_events (mean $= 1.688$, std $= 3.313$, max $= 33$): the *N.B.* regression (deviance $= 374.79$, $\chi^2 = 564$, log-likelihood $= -518.79$) has non-significant intercept $\beta = 0.105$ (95% C.I. $[-0.328, 0.538]$, $p = 0.635$).

Table 2 shows the significant coefficients of each regression. We show only those with a p-value lesser than 0.05. We identify each result as Ri, to reference it later in discussion. As effect sizes we analyze Odd-Ratios (OR). In contrast with our first study, no interaction terms were significant.

Discussion of Results

Diversity- and Representation-Awareness. With respect to diversity-awareness, we found that people from *RM* are more likely to be diverse-aware (R10, OR $= 2.473$), which is coherent with the results from the first user study, given the main

[3] `http://dev.maxmind.com/geoip/legacy/geolite/`

[4] Those users presumably left their browser windows open.

[5] We applied a N.B. regression to the number of days, but no effect of condition/location was found.

Result #	Variable	Effect	β	O.R.	95% C.I.	p
R9	distinct_locations (N.B.)	Condition *treemap*	0.732	2.080	[0.092, 1.373]	0.025
R10	distinct_locations (N.B.)	Location *RM*	0.950	2.473	[0.348, 1.553]	0.002
R11	filter_likelihood (logit)	Condition *treemap*	0.7541	2.126	[0.207, 1.301]	0.007
R12	filter_likelihood (logit)	Location *RM*	−0.494	0.610	[−0.955, −0.033]	0.036
R13	content_events (N.B.)	Condition *treemap*	0.628	1.873	[0.167, 1.088]	0.008

Table 2: Significant effects from the user study, including coefficients, odds-ratios, and confidence intervals.

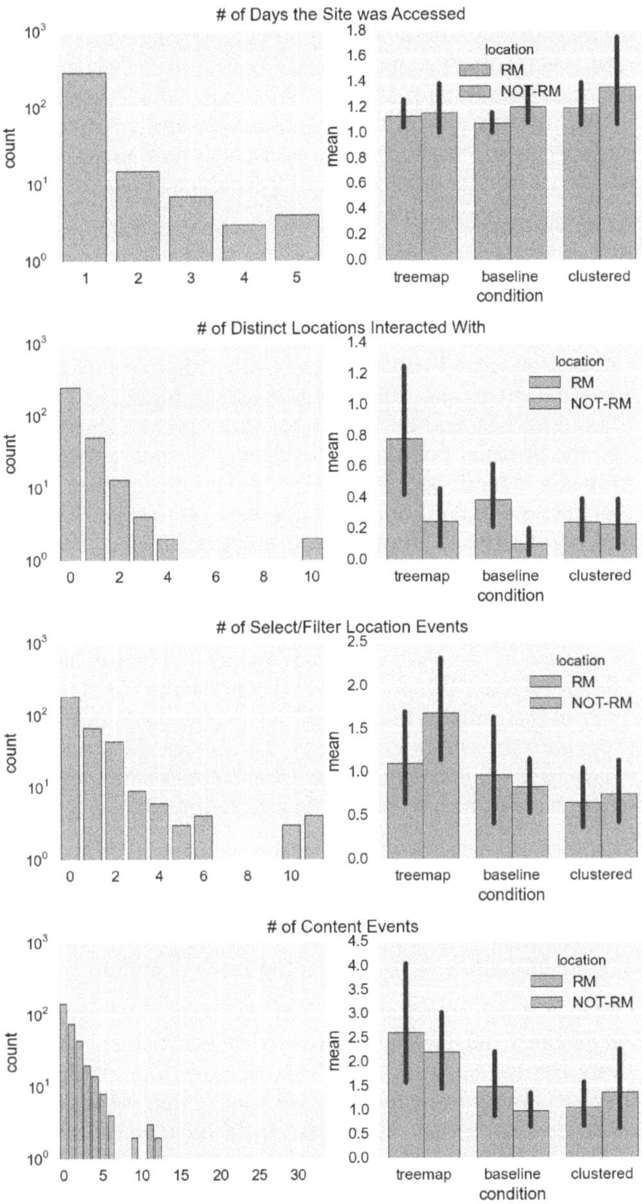

Figure 4: Distribution of each variable analyzed from interaction data. For each variable we include a histogram (left) and a bar plot (right) to compare means between groups.

effect of location with the distinct location variable. Moreover, we found that people exposed to the treemap condition were as likely to be diverse-aware (R9, OR = 2.080), which means that people from *NOT-RM* exposed to the treemap can be as diversity-aware as people from *RM*.

With respect to representation-awareness, we found that people from RM is less likely to select specific locations (R12, OR = 0.60), which means that people from NOT-RM is more likely to do so. Moreover, we found that people exposed to the treemap condition were more likely to select specific locations (R11, OR = 2.126).

Interestingness. We did not find an effect of location on the number of content events, which means that users from all locations were equally engaged with content. However, we found that people exposed to the treemap condition were more likely to interact with content (R13, OR = 1.873). Its OR indicates that using the treemap increases the chances of interaction with content by 87.3%.

Our research question asks: *how can we encourage non-centralized exploration?* As interpreted from our first user study, it should never be just about the algorithm, but also about how users respond to what the algorithm returns to them. This response is influenced not only by the algorithm, but also by the user interface used. At the beginning of this section we stated that the main purpose of *AT*'s design was to make users more diversity- and representation-aware. We believe we succeeded, because, regardless of geographical origin (*i. e.*, no statistical interaction), the treemap design showed good properties on the three dimensions under consideration. These properties, in terms of diversity, representation, and user interest, indicate that a good way to encourage such behavior is by allowing users to explore content using non-traditional user interfaces. In fact, the clustered condition did not have any significant effect, even though it was expected [33]. As outlined in our rationale, the number of clusters can make exploration more difficult for users.

IMPLICATIONS

In the literature, cultural differences [22] have been acknowledged in the study of communication systems [23] by suggesting specific features and interaction mechanisms pertinent to each culture. As we have found in our studies, Chilean information seekers and content explorers in Twitter are affected by centralization. Their perception of content is different, and their interaction with exploratory interfaces is also different.

This implies that location with respect to centralization (*i. e.*, central or peripheral) introduces an individual difference to be accounted for in system design. If this difference is not considered, user exploration can be biased toward central locations. While centralized exploration is not inherently bad (*i. e.*, there could be genuine interest in central location content given contingency or current news), the purpose of decentralization is to make users aware of the geographical diversity of the information space. What we do on-line, influences our off-line lives, and thus, such awareness would help users in today's *"culture of real virtuality"* [9] to reaffirm their identities on the Web by recognizing their local traits and culture on content.

To do so in exploratory settings, we propose the following design changes in micro-blogging platforms:

1. Search results are ranked (presumably) by relevance and popularity. Centralized contexts (such as many Latin American countries) will have biased popularity metrics toward central locations. A diversity-aware algorithm (*e. g.*, *PM*) would help in this case.
2. Currently, Twitter offers two options related to geography in its search page: "Everywhere" (the default) and "Near me". We suggest to change the default value according to the user's context, *i. e.*, use "Near me" when users are from peripheral locations.
3. Since including geographical diversity in timelines is not enough, because users may not be aware of it, techniques to make them *see* this difference can help. We recommend platforms to use visualization techniques such as treemaps to display timelines. The original design by Weskamp [41] has proven to be useful when visualizing news headlines as it *"allows many interesting comparisons and readings of how we differ culturally"* [28]. Our results provide evidence of the good properties of treemaps, in particular in displaying the differences derived from user location and its relation to centralization.

By considering these implications and suggestions, micro-blogging platforms will allow users to *decentralize* part of their exploratory behavior. Or, they could keep a centralized exploration in a *conscious* way. The important outcome is that users will be able to choose *how* and *what* to explore.

CONCLUSIONS

In his essay *"In praise of shadows"*, Junichirõ Tanizaki wonders what if the fountain pen, an *"insignificant little piece of writing equipment"*, would have been invented in Japan, as in spite of its insignificance it *"had a vast, almost boundless, influence on our culture"*. In that line of thinking, we wonder "*what if global web platforms would have emerged in countries with severe systemic biases?*" Perhaps algorithms would have considered those biases and user interfaces would have been adapted to mitigate their effects. To this end, we studied the specific case of Chile, a highly centralized country [17]. With Chilean users, considering their geographical origin from a centralization point of view, we analyzed through carefully designed experiments the differences in users' perception of diversity when exploring geographically diverse timelines.

In a user study with labeling tasks, we found that centralization induces differences in perception of what is interesting, what is informative, and what is diverse. In particular, only users from the centralized location were able to identify the geographical diversity present in the constructed timelines. Inspired by a visual design by Weskamp [41], we used information visualization to make users *aware* of such diversity, addressing what we called the *diversity- and representation-awareness* problem. We deployed this design on the Web to display timelines generated with a diversity-aware algorithm, and spread information about it using the social bot *@todocl*.

By analyzing logged interaction data, we observed that users behave differently according to their geographical origin. We identified different interaction signals in central and peripheral users. Furthermore, we also observed that the proposed design improves exploration and diversity- and representation-awareness, regardless of geographical origin of users. These results were used to define design implications and suggestions for micro-blogging platforms. We believe that consideration of our implications will have noticeable and positive consequences on information access by users in centralized contexts, which are not uncommon in Latin America [17].

As of September 2015, *@todocl* has more than 5,000 followers. We see this is as an indication of the need to provide content aggregators like *AT*, that focus on diversification of specific social-context related aspects [8].

Limitations and Future Work. Critics might rightly say that our experiments suffer from biased user sampling and the lack of counterbalanced designs. Currently, given centralization and the unequal population distribution, finding users from *NOT-RM* is hard, because *RM's* population is greater and has more access to the Internet in comparison to other locations, making it more difficult to find users willing to participate from non-central locations. Our snowball sampling method provided a way to find a large enough population to gain important insights in the first study. In the second study, all users mentioned by *@todocl* were geographically diverse, and those users retweeted *@todocl*'s tweets, improving the representativity of the sample. In terms of design, we could not validate users until the end of each study. Thus, because several users would have been discarded, the ideal counterbalanced designs would have proven to be unbalanced in practice.

The Web is increasingly being more accessed from mobile devices than from desktops. In our case, of 1335 detected mobile users, 68% could be geolocated using the IP address. Considering those users in a new mobile-friendly version of our site will allow us to study differences in a mobile context.

Finally, we will approach further studies from two perspectives. On the one hand, the lack of qualitative feedback in our second study imply that we cannot fully demonstrate a solution to diversity-awareness, although we believe that we have found evidence toward that conclusion. On the other hand, our results apply to one country only. Thus, we will seek to generalize our results by replicating our studies in other Latin American countries.

Source Code. We have published the code needed to replicate this experiment in `https://github.com/carnby/aurora`.

Acknowledgments. We thank Pajarito, Denis Parra, Luz Rello, and Sergio Salgado for their helpful comments. This work was partially funded by Grant TIN2012-38741 (Understanding Social Media: An Integrated Data Mining Approach) of the Ministry of Economy and Competitiveness of Spain.

References

1. Abel, F., Hauff, C., Houben, G.-J., Stronkman, R., and Tao, K. Semantics + filtering + search = Twitcident. Exploring information in social web streams. *Proceedings of the 23rd ACM Conference on Hypertext and Social Media.* 2012, 285–294.
2. Aiello, L. M., Deplano, M., Schifanella, R., and Ruffo, G. People are strange when you're a stranger: impact and influence of bots on social networks. *Links*, 697(483,151), 2012: 1–566.
3. Archambault, D., Greene, D., Cunningham, P., and Hurley, N. ThemeCrowds: multiresolution summaries of Twitter usage. *Proceedings of the 3rd international workshop on Search and mining user-generated contents.* 2011, 77–84.
4. Atienza, M., and Aroca, P. Concentración y crecimiento en Chile: una relación negativa ignorada. *EURE (Santiago)*, 38(114), 2012: 257–277 (In Spanish. Title translation: Concentration and growth in Chile: an ignored negative relation).
5. Bostock, M., Ogievetsky, V., and Heer, J. D^3 data-driven documents. *IEEE Transactions on Visualization and Computer Graphics*, 17(12), 2011: 2301–2309.
6. Bruls, M., Huizing, K., and Van Wijk, J. J. Squarified treemaps. Springer, 2000.
7. Butler, J. Precarious life: the powers of mourning and violence. Verso, 2006.
8. Buxton, B. Sketching user experiences: getting the design right and the right design. Morgan Kaufmann, 2010.
9. Castells, M. The rise of the network society: the information age: economy, society, and culture. John Wiley & Sons, 2011.
10. Center, P. R. Internet seen as positive influence on education but negative on morality in emerging and developing nations. `http://www.pewglobal.org/2015/03/19/internet-seen-as-positive-influence-on-education-but-negative-influence-on-morality-in-emerging-and-developing-nations/`. 2015.
11. Cheng, Z., Caverlee, J., and Lee, K. You are where you tweet: a content-based approach to geo-locating Twitter users. *Proceedings of the 19th ACM International Conference on Information and Knowledge Management.* 2010, 759–768.
12. Crabtree, A., Chamberlain, A., Grinter, R. E., Jones, M., Rodden, T., and Rogers, Y. Introduction to the special issue of "The turn to the wild". *ACM Transactions on Computer-Human Interaction (TOCHI)*, 20(3), 2013: 13.
13. De Choudhury, M., Counts, S., and Czerwinski, M. Identifying relevant social media content: leveraging information diversity and user cognition. *Proceedings of the 22nd ACM Conference on Hypertext and Hypermedia.* 2011, 161–170.
14. Eaton, K. Designing subnational institutions regional and municipal reforms in postauthoritarian Chile. *Comparative Political Studies*, 37(2), 2004: 218–244.
15. Faridani, S., Bitton, E., Ryokai, K., and Goldberg, K. Opinion space: a scalable tool for browsing online comments. *Proceedings of the SIGCHI Conference on Human Factors in Computing Systems.* 2010, 1175–1184.
16. Freeman, L. C. A set of measures of centrality based on betweenness. *Sociometry*, 1977: 35–41.
17. Galiani, S., and Kim, S. Political centralization and urban primacy: evidence from national and provincial capitals in the Americas. In: *Understanding long-run economic growth: geography, institutions, and the knowledge economy.* University of Chicago Press, 2008, 121–153.
18. Garcia-Gavilanes, R., Mejova, Y., and Quercia, D. Twitter ain't without frontiers: economic, social, and cultural boundaries in international communication. *Proceedings of the 17th ACM Conference on Computer Supported Cooperative Work & Social Computing.* 2014, 1511–1522.
19. Garcia-Gavilanes, R., Quercia, D., and Jaimes, A. Cultural dimensions in Twitter: time, individualism and power. *International AAAI Conference on Weblogs and Social Media.* 2013.
20. Graells-Garrido, E., and Lalmas, M. Balancing diversity to counter-measure geographical centralization in microblogging platforms *(short paper). 25th ACM Conference on Hypertext and Social Media.* 2014.
21. Hecht, B., Hong, L., Suh, B., and Chi, E. H. Tweets from Justin Bieber's heart: the dynamics of the location field in user profiles. *Proceedings of the 2011 annual conference on Human Factors in Computing Systems.* 2011, 237–246.
22. Hofstede, G., Hofstede, G. J., and Minkov, M. Cultures and organizations, software of the mind: intercultural cooperation and its importance for survival (3rd edition). McGraw-Hill Professional, 2010.
23. Kayan, S., Fussell, S. R., and Setlock, L. D. Cultural differences in the use of instant messaging in Asia and North America. *Proceedings of the 2006 20th anniversary conference on Computer Supported Cooperative Work.* 2006, 525–528.
24. Kollman, K. Perils of centralization: lessons from church, state, and corporation. Cambridge University Press, 2013.
25. Krugman, P. The role of geography in development. *International regional science review*, 22(2), 1999: 142–161.
26. Kulshrestha, J., Kooti, F., Nikravesh, A., and Gummadi, K. P. Geographic dissection of the Twitter network. *Proceedings of the 6th International AAAI Conference on Weblogs and Social Media.* 2012.

27. McCullagh, P. Regression models for ordinal data. *Journal of the royal statistical society. Series B (Methodological)*, 1980: 109–142.

28. Meirelles, I. Design for information: an introduction to the histories, theories, and best practices behind effective information visualizations. Rockport Publishers, 2013.

29. Merton, R. K., and Sztompka, P. On social structure and science. University of Chicago Press, 1996.

30. Ministerio de Desarrollo Social, G. d. C. CASEN Survey. `http://observatorio.ministeriodesarrollosocial.gob.cl/casen_obj.php`. 2011.

31. Munson, S. A., Zhou, D. X., and Resnick, P. Sidelines: an algorithm for increasing diversity in news and opinion aggregators. *International Conference on Weblogs and Social Media*. 2009.

32. Newman, M. E. A measure of betweenness centrality based on random walks. *Social networks*, 27(1), 2005: 39–54.

33. Park, S., Kang, S., Chung, S., and Song, J. NewsCube: delivering multiple aspects of news to mitigate media bias. *Proceedings of the SIGCHI Conference on Human Factors in Computing Systems*. 2009, 443–452.

34. Quattrone, G. A., and Jones, E. E. The perception of variability within in-groups and out-groups: Implications for the law of small numbers. *Journal of Personality and Social Psychology*, 38(1), 1980: 141.

35. Quercia, D., Capra, L., and Crowcroft, J. The social world of Twitter: topics, geography, and emotions. *The 6th International AAAI Conference on Weblogs and Social Media*. 2012.

36. Quercia, D., Ellis, J., Capra, L., and Crowcroft, J. Tracking gross community happiness from tweets. *Proceedings of the ACM 2012 conference on Computer Supported Cooperative Work*. 2012, 965–968.

37. Rout, D., Bontcheva, K., Preoţiuc-Pietro, D., and Cohn, T. Where's@ wally?: a classification approach to geolocating users based on their social ties. *Proceedings of the 24th ACM Conference on Hypertext and Social Media*. 2013, 11–20.

38. Rubin, M., and Badea, C. They're all the same!... but for several different reasons: a review of the multicausal nature of perceived group variability. *Current Directions in Psychological Science*, 21(6), 2012: 367–372.

39. Takhteyev, Y., Gruzd, A., and Wellman, B. Geography of Twitter networks. *Social Networks*, 34(1), 2012: 73–81.

40. Valenzuela, S., Arriagada, A., and Scherman, A. Facebook, Twitter, and youth engagement: a quasi-experimental study of social media use and protest behavior using propensity score matching. *International Journal of Communication*, 8, 2014: 25.

41. Weskamp, M. newsmap. `http://newsmap.jp`. 2004.

42. Ziegler, C.-N., McNee, S. M., Konstan, J. A., and Lausen, G. Improving recommendation lists through topic diversification. *Proceedings of the 14th International Conference on World Wide Web*. 2005, 22–32.

TagFlip: Active Mobile Music Discovery with Social Tags

Mohsen Kamalzadeh[1], **Christoph Kralj**[2], **Torsten Möller**[2], **Michael Sedlmair**[2]
[1]Simon Fraser University, Burnaby, Canada, mkamalza@sfu.ca
[2]University of Vienna, Vienna, Austria, christoph.kralj@gmail.com,
torsten.moeller@univie.ac.at, michael.sedlmair@univie.ac.at

ABSTRACT
We report on the design and evaluation of TagFlip, a novel interface for active music discovery based on social tags of music. The tool, which was built for phone-sized screens, couples high user control on the recommended music with minimal interaction effort. Contrary to conventional recommenders, which only allow the specification of seed attributes and the subsequent like/dislike of songs, we put the users in the centre of the recommendation process. With a library of 100,000 songs, TagFlip describes each played song to the user through its most popular tags on Last.fm and allows the user to easily specify which of the tags should be considered for the next song, or the next stream of songs. In a lab user study where we compared it to Spotify's mobile application, TagFlip came out on top in both subjective user experience (control, transparency, and trust) and our objective measure of number of interactions per liked song. Our users found TagFlip to be an important complementary experience to that of Spotify, enabling more active and directed discovery sessions as opposed to the mostly passive experience that traditional recommenders offer.

Author Keywords
Music discovery; recommendation; user controlled; fine tuning; folksonomies; social tags; user-centred design; minimal effort; exploration; user interface; transparency

ACM Classification Keywords
H.5.2. Information Interfaces and Presentation (e.g. HCI): User Interfaces — Evaluation/methodology, graphical user interfaces, user-centered design

MOTIVATION
In the past decade, the amount of music we can have immediate access to has increased dramatically as music streaming services that provide access to millions of songs for a small subscription fee have risen in popularity. In the year 2015, most such services house more than 30 million songs. With such a broad range of choices, discovering new music and deciding what to listen to can become a burden. While this well established phenomenon [30] is not new to the age of music streaming, the effects of it have become more pronounced as the hesitation of having to pay for each individual track has diminished.

Recently, there has been a surge in both academic and commercial efforts to build interfaces and algorithms that can integrate these growing online libraries into our daily music consumption routines. Some solutions have focused on minimizing user interaction and relying on advanced recommendation algorithms. In such cases, the user's immediate role has been reduced to choosing a starting point (like a song, or a genre), and liking/disliking songs, with the rest being decided by other factors such as the user's preference profile, the context of listening, or various measures of content and user similarity. While these solutions excel in simplification, they suffer from issues such as lack of transparency[1], lack of user control, and pigeon-holing the users in their preference profiles [17, 37].

On the other end of the spectrum, elaborate interfaces have been developed that give the users control over various aspects of music retrieval, such as the parameters of a recommender algorithm. Although these interfaces have been shown to overcome some of the mentioned issues of recommender systems, they are generally complex and are designed with large screens and prolonged periods of user engagement in mind. This is in discrepancy with the typical situations in which we listen to music, such as when commuting and at work [15]. To fully exploit the potential of massive music libraries, it is crucial for novel methods of music discovery to naturally squeeze into these periods of everyday music listening. Commercial recommendation services like Spotify and Apple Music have identified this need and strive to provide simple interfaces to their vast libraries. This has, however, left them suffering from the usual issues that plague non-interactive recommender systems, as mentioned above.

With TagFlip we attempt to identify the sweet-spot between user control and interaction effort. Our goal is to put the user back in control of the music retrieval process while keeping the required effort minimal. Using a rich dataset of social tags from Last.fm, TagFlip morphs the conventional seed-based recommender that is well equipped for passive listening, into an interface that invites the user to explore and discover new music and musical styles by specifying tags—to perhaps break out of a comfort-zone and take a left-turn. At the same time, it minimizes the friction between listening and active discovery by diminishing both the mental load and physical interaction effort required from the user to initiate the discovery process, choose various styles of music to explore, and express or change his/her preferences.

[1]often referred to as the black-box issue with recommender systems

IUI 2016, March 7–10, 2016, Sonoma, CA, USA.

ACM 978-1-4503-4137-0/16/03 ...$15.00.
http://dx.doi.org/10.1145/2856767.2856780

Identifying the necessity of adapting to the increasing mobility of music listening, TagFlip was designed with small screens (roughly five inches in diagonal) in mind. With minimal required effort, TagFlip can fit well into the periods of idle time that we typically fill by interacting with our phones. Sitting in the bus, exercising, taking a few moments of rest mid work, or sitting on the couch holding our phones and paying a bit of attention to the TV are all examples of these times.

We evaluated TagFlip in comparison to Spotify's mobile application in a lab study with 16 participants. Our users rated TagFlip on par with Spotify in usability and higher in three of our four recommendation constructs (*interface and interaction adequacy*, *control and transparency*, and *attitudes and behavioural intentions*). We also observed that TagFlip required significantly fewer screen touches for discovering a new liked song across all users. In our interviews, half of our users desired to have TagFlip on their own phones and almost all of them pointed out that it filled a crucial empty space in music recommendation, especially for specific and highly controlled discovery.

In summary, the main contributions of our work are twofold:

- Providing insight into the design and evaluation of tag based interactive music discovery tools, along with design considerations and topics for future research.
- Identifying the strengths of such systems and providing evidence that social tags can be effectively employed as direct means for user control in music recommendation.

BACKGROUND AND RELATED WORK

A review of state-of-the-art in music retrieval techniques and interfaces that are designed to exploit massive scale libraries reveals two dominant poles in terms of the level of user engagement. On one end of the spectrum are purely algorithmic approaches that minimize user involvement, while on the other end, we have elaborate and often complex interfaces that strive to put the user at the front and centre. These two extremes cater to the *satisficing* and *maximizing* behaviours that Schwartz et al. [31] explore. In the former case, the user is looking for something that is "good-enough", whereas in the latter, the user tries to maximize the degree to which the selected item adheres to his/her preferences at the moment.

Music consumption literature has confirmed how the listeners' behaviours fit this spectrum and how where the user ends up on it can depend both on the users' general enthusiasm and knowledge about music [11, 14, 16] and the listening context [4, 16]. Most current tools fall on the satisficing or maximizing extremes of the spectrum. Besides recommenders, the emerging notion of curated radio stations and playlists in services like Spotify and Songza is also very close to the satisficing end of the engagement range, with the added human touch in their creation. The role of the user is, of course, not neglected in algorithmic recommender systems. However, it lives as a personalized profile built based on various elicited or inferred preferences over longer periods of time, the inner workings of which are predominantly hidden from the user. Hence, while such systems excel at requiring absolute minimal interaction, when the user leaves the boundaries of pure satisficing, they fall short of providing any apparatus for increased user engagement and control. The popular like/dislike button that accompanies this type of recommendation is far from having any immediately visible feedback or a meaningful effect on the recommender algorithm. The user cannot specify what aspects of the music caused the like/dislike, and does not know what influence the action will have on future recommendations. Often times, prolonged use of these services accompanied with frequent like/dislikes leads to the user being enclosed in a bubble of his/her own computed taste profile with no way of knowing what went wrong or how to break out; an effect which is often called pigeon-holing in the recommendation literature [17]. On the maximizing end, we have the possibility of selecting specific musical entities like songs or albums, which bring about maximum user control on the music content at the expense of large interaction effort. Novel interfaces that fall in between are mostly designed for large screens and complex interaction and do not fit the current rapid shift to mobile music listening and discovery. As such, a rather unexploited space remains where minimal interaction and high user control meet, one that has also been identified by previous work [16].

The importance of transparency, control, and feedback during various stages of recommendation is well known [32], and has given birth to conversational and critiquing recommender systems [7, 8], which are dedicated to increasing user involvement in recommendation algorithms, through user feedback on attributes of recommended items. More recently, interfaces have been designed to explain recommendations to users [28, 41], or allow them to visually manipulate aspects and parameters of recommendation algorithms [5, 23, 40]. Faceted filtering and recommendation [46] is another more manual technique that allows the user to quickly combine various attributes in search. When it comes to music, such systems have for the most part not been designed for efficiency, simplicity, and mobile use and are predominantly based on a limited facet space [9, 45, 47], unlike TagFlip which houses more than 350 tags of various kinds.

An early effort toward increasing user control in recommendation of music was the MusicSun [26], which gave users lists of artists based on one of nine directions (*rays*) of similarity to a seed artist, with each ray representing a web-mined word. Another example is Tasteweights [5], which allowed the user to manipulate factors from his/her own taste profile, along with information from Wikipedia, Facebook friends' preferences, and experts from Twitter, to tune the recommendation list. While these and similar efforts are valuable steps in the right direction, they are first and foremost designed for prolonged sessions of use or come with interfaces that are often too elaborate, fitting larger than mobile screens.

A body of research has focused on visualizing large music libraries to simplify their exploration. This generally involves depicting the musical entities, such as artists or songs, on a 2D or 3D map with the assistance of dimensionality reduction techniques, and allowing the user to traverse or zoom the map. The input to these techniques can be any type of descriptor, like features extracted from the audio itself, or metadata. Some pioneering studies on this front include MARSYAS3D by Tzanetakis and Cook [38], Islands of Music by Pampalk et al. [27], and the artist map by van Gulik et al. [39]. In general, these types of interfaces either do not offer sufficient user control, or suffer from issues similar to that of controllable recommenders discussed above, namely, a need for large displays and more indulgent exploration, rather than efficient and minimal interaction.

Identifying the need for simplicity coupled with higher possibility of user control than what pure satisficing interfaces facilitate, Baur et al. [1] introduced the *Rush* technique, which gave the user a choice between multiple recommended items, each of which could sway the algorithm in a different direction than others. Unlike TagFlip, the interface was built for creating homogeneous playlists from songs already known by the user, rather than discovery and song by song recommendation. A later version of *Rush* [2] added the possibility of controlling the similarity to operate based on artist, genre, tempo, or songs form the same artist. In comparison, TagFlip provides finer grained control over music selection by utilizing social tags, which cover a much broader range of music descriptions. Furthermore, the user can easily combine various tag filters using TagFlip, but *Rush 2* does not allow combining similarity axes.

A number of tools have previously used social tags as basis for interactive recommendation. Vig et al. [42] used tags of movies in a critiquing-based recommender, allowing users to decrease or increase the weight of each tag of a recommended movie to get the next one. While their approach bears similarities to ours in using a rich set of social tags, the interface is not built with music in mind, and does not fit the dynamic and song-to-song nature of music listening. Wang et al. [44] built an interface for querying music with multiple weighted tags. With this tool the user can click and drag on a tag in a tag cloud to increase or decrease its importance in recommendation. The study is, however, mostly algorithm oriented and explores the retrieval techniques rather than user experience. In a similar fashion, the Music Explaura system [12] used interactive tag clouds (*textual auras*) as basis for recommending artists. Users of this system experienced a steep learning curve. Although they expressed interest and surprise at the concept once explained to them, most did not immediately realize the meaning of the tag clouds and the fact that they could manipulate them. Meerkat [25] also used tags as means for personalizing radio stations. Unlike us though, the authors focused only on the functionality, finding that people liked having this level of control on their music. However, they left out design completely and the interface was not tested for usability. Furthermore, none of the above tools were designed for mobile devices.

With TagFlip, we went through an interative user centred design process to identify and address the key design issues involved with bringing tags into interactive discovery and recommendation. In the next section, we explain the various design decisions made through-out this process and provide implications for design of future tag based tools.

TAGFLIP

In this section we first discuss how we selected and processed data for TagFlip. Then, we explain our interaction paradigm and design requirements for the interface and report on what we learned throughout the design process.

Data and platform

Among the myriad types of data that can be utilized as the basis for music recommendation, classification, and retrieval, few are easily understandable for the average non-technical music listener. While recommendations based on collaborative filtering or audio content can be accurate according to algorithmic precision measures, the data underlying such algorithms is not translatable to tangible and easy to interpret attributes of music, as such, it is not directly user controllable.

On the contrary, the massive tag spaces formed in social music tagging platforms such as Last.fm can be rich sources of semantic music attributes that are understandable to the average user. These spaces (often called folksonomies) can play a key role in bridging the semantic gap between the users' description of music and how recommenders work. The terms present in the Last.fm folksonomy range from arguably every music genre and sub-genre imaginable, to moods, activities, and niche musical terms popular in smaller communities. Each song/tag annotation also has a score attached to it, which represents the percentage of taggers of the song who used the term to annotate it [36].

On the down side, with all this information come several issues, a variety of which and possible approaches to addressing them have been discussed by Lamere [18]. These include issues such as the cold-start problem (unpopular music gets very few tags), synonymy (multiple tags having the same meaning), polysemy (tags having multiple different meanings), and noise (spelling errors and terms with no meaning in the music domain). To alleviate some of these, our first step in employing Last.fm tags in our tool was a robust preprocessing phase, in which we utilized the available information on the popularity of songs (listener and play count), the scores of tags, and language processing techniques to remove meaningless or subjective tags, fix spelling errors, identify meaningful compound terms, extract usable information out of unusable tags, and remove subjective or vague terms. This process is explained in detail in supplementary materials. In the end, we had a cleaned set of 358 tags.

TagFlip was built for Android, and our music library contained 100,000 songs and 1.3 million song/tag associations. The music was a subset of the Million Song Dataset [3], which covers a broad range of contemporary music, and the audio was played from Spotify, using its Android SDK [34].

Interaction paradigm

The core user interaction in TagFlip consists of a repeated two phase exchange between the system and the user. The beginning of playback resembles a conventional recommender or search system. The user can either start from a specific song, or describe the desired music using a combination of tags. Once a song is played, TagFlip displays its top tags (Figure

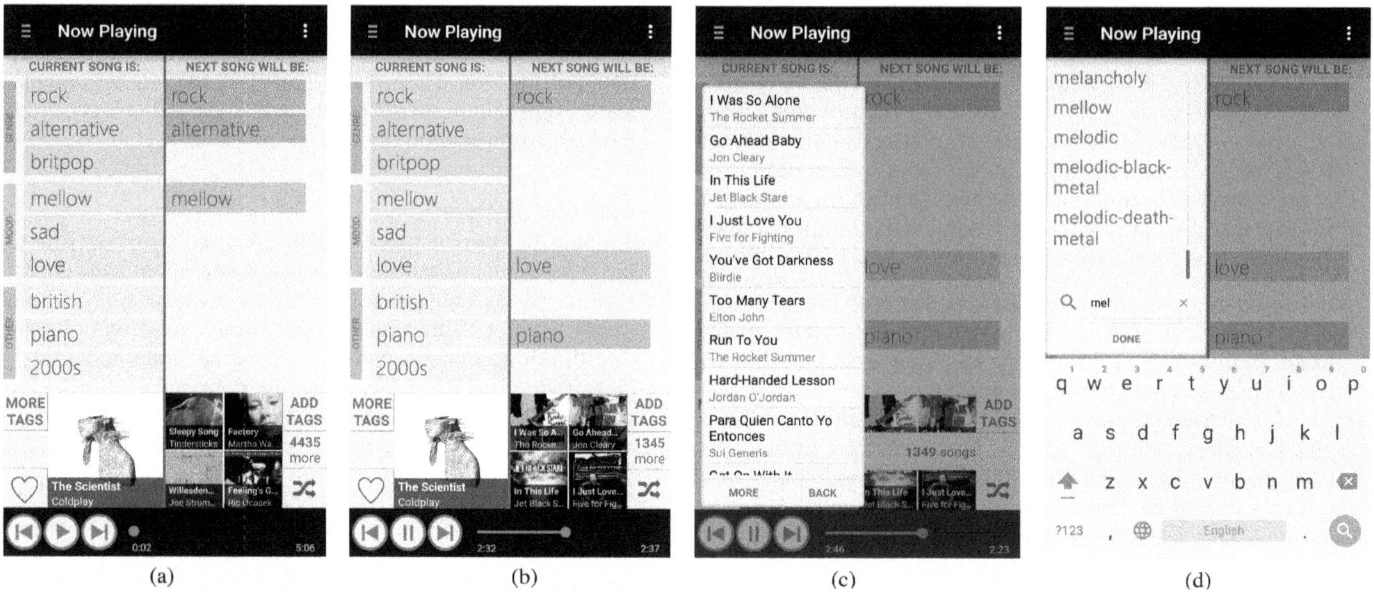

Figure 1. Screenshots of TagFlip. (a) What is displayed when a song is played from library. (b) After the user has modified the tags for the next song. (c) Viewing a list of upcoming songs. (d) Adding tags from a full list.

1(a)), and indicates which ones are being considered for retrieving future songs. The tags are grouped into genre, mood, and "other" categories. By default, three tags are "pinned", two genre tags and one mood tag. These define the future direction of music playback by constraining the library to songs that match all of them. A playlist based on this direction is built and set for the user who does not desire further engagement. This constitutes one phase of the exchange. The album arts of the next four songs are displayed in the bottom right of the screen, the number of songs that match the selected criteria is shown, and the complete list of songs can be accessed by tapping this number (Figure 1(c)). A shuffle button below the number of songs does the task of randomizing the order of upcoming songs.

The second phase involves the user modifying the set of tags used in finding future songs by simply tapping on any of the tags to pin or unpin it (Figure 1(b)). Each tap immediately updates the set of planned songs and this is made visible to the user through updating the number of matching songs and the next four album arts. Once the next song is played, the interface is updated to reflect its tags while keeping the previously pinned tags intact (which are by design also present in the new song), and thus, the exchange continues. In summary, the key factors that differentiate this core interaction paradigm in TagFlip from earlier efforts are:

1. High impact interaction instances: This is crucial for achieving high control coupled with minimal interaction effort. Each pinning or unpinning of a tag can greatly influence the set of future songs. In addition, as most songs have several diverse tags associated with them, one pin/unpin can lead the user to music that is similar to the previous song in some aspects and vastly different in others. This way, the user covers a larger span of the library than what would be possible with a conventional seed-based recommender system, without completely changing seeds or switching playlists.

2. Fine tuning: Another key differentiator between TagFlip and previous tools is how easily it enables fine tuning based on tags of the currently playing song. The lack of such functionality in current music discovery tools and a need for it has been stressed out by Kamalzadeh et al. [16], who call it *adjusting control*. Many of the participants in our final user study were particularly excited about this concept.

3. Low interaction effort: Previous studies have shown that users are interested in meaningfully altering aspects such as the mood of their music listening session with efforts as low as what skipping a song requires [16]. We used this as a guideline to what each tag pin/unpin should need. The only overhead of a pin/unpin compared to a skip is finding the desired tag on the screen. This leads us to the next factor.

4. Low mental load: To minimize the mental effort for selecting which tags to pin/unpin, TagFlip shows a summarized set of each song's tags categorized into "genre," "mood," and "other" terms. This gives the user an overview of the possibilities and obviates the need for extensive thinking. If a user desires, (s)he can view all other tags of a song using the "more tags" button and pin them with the same tapping action.

5. Scalability of control: Following the satisficing/maximizing spectrum and guidelines provided by earlier studies [4, 16], a key design requirement for TagFlip was the possibility to organically scale from coarse to fine-grained user control in conjunction with low or high user engagement. By allowing the users to pin as many tags as they wish, the system supports a range of control on the retrieved songs. With few pinned tags the system resembles a conventional recommender or radio station, but pinning tags can rapidly increase user control. If further control is needed, the user can quickly bring up a list of all tags in the system as a pop-up on the main screen (Figure 1(d)), using the "add tags" button, and quickly search and add tags from it. This addition is directly visible beneath the pop-up dialog.

6. Transparency: This is one of the key pillars of building trust and increasing user satisfaction with recommendation systems [37], the lack of which leads to the black-box issue. The two phase exchange in TagFlip is by nature explanatory and transparent. The user can clearly see the effect of each pin/unpin in the number of matching songs and the next four album arts. Furthermore, the fact that the number keeps decreasing as more tags are pinned informs the user that the songs will match all the pinned tags, rather than just any of them. As was proven in our lab study, this mechanism made it clear to users how the system worked and resulted in high user perceived transparency.

7. Small screen: Staying within the confines of smartphone screens underlined all steps of TagFlip's design. Apart from the necessity to acknowledge the rapid migration of music consumption to mobile devices, adhering to such limits would simplify redesigning the interface for a desktop environment while still conforming to the minimal interaction effort requirements. The small screen size helped us narrow down the absolutely critical user tasks to support and forced us to think in terms of "what should be left out" instead of "what should be added". Several usability tests during various stages of design (from low to high fidelity prototypes, to an actual application) informed these decisions.

Design process and decisions

TagFlip started from the idea of the user being in control of high-level aspects of music. In its path from paper prototype to working application, which took 18 months, several design possibilities were explored and tested. Three stages of formative usability tests with a total of 10 different participants were performed through-out this process. Out of nine initial designs, two made it to the medium fidelity prototyping stage which was done in a desktop Java environment, and one to Android. We now elaborate on a few key findings of this process and the choices that were made according to them.

Individual tag blocks or a left/right flow:

Coming out of paper prototypes, we had two thoroughly different competing designs for TagFlip (available in supplementary materials). In one, each tag was housed in a separate square block, and there was no high level separation between the current and next songs in the interface. Instead, each block displayed the strength of each tag in the currently playing song and provided a slider for choosing the strength for the same tag in the next song. This design was based on the faders of a mixing board. Our usability tests showed this to be a confusing system image and lacking organization, with many users not noticing the current and next separation in each block. This lead us to choosing the current presentation, where a flow from left to right implicates a shift from current to next, resembling how we read and write in English. We also found it was important to clearly separate the two sides of the interface to further amplify the current/next concept. This is what lead to the addition of the vertical line in-between, and every UI element on each side only pertaining to its corresponding time stamp; current or next (except for the play bar in the bottom).

Strength of tags:

One of the earliest ingredients of TagFlip was the ability for the user to specify how strong the association between the retrieved music and the pinned tags should be, as an added level of user control. This is similar to what the interactive tag cloud systems discussed earlier provided [12, 44]. The earliest prototypes explored ways of supporting such a task by the use of sliders, interactive bars, knobs, and text size. However, heuristic evaluations and usability tests with users revealed that such a functionality could lead to a confusion between strength of the tag and how much they cared about it. Also, for some users, the tags had a binary meaning; they either belonged with a song or did not. Our tests showed that most users did not care about having this functionality at all. This fact, plus the added complexity that such a feature would incur on the interface, lead us to removing it from the later versions of TagFlip.

Communicating target set sizes:

To provide full transparency, TagFlip employs a strict retrieval policy, where all the target songs should include all the user requested tags. Therefore, adding too many tags or certain unpopular combinations can lead to an empty set of songs. This could also happen if all the songs in the set have been played without the user changing preferences. In such a scenario, if a song has to be played (through tapping the next button or the current song ending), TagFlip automatically removes the least popular tag to retrieve music. In our design process, we considered adding visual encodings that would either prevent the user from pinning tags that would lead to an empty set, or help the user easily rectify the problem if such a thing were to happen. We used horizontal bars placed on the right end of the screen in front of each tag. The size of each bar reflected the size of the resulting set of songs, if the corresponding tag was to be added. Once a tag was added, the bar changed colour, and its size indicated how much one would expand the target set if the tags was removed. However, our usability tests proved that this encoding was often confused with the above *tag strength* concept. Hence, the encoding was completely removed. In the final version, the interface would just inform the user that no songs were found, and would suggest the removal of the least popular tag.

Categorizing tags into genre, mood, and other:

Previous studies have shown genre and mood to be two of the top attributes of music for users in selecting/looking for music or managing their libraries [15, 35, 43]. Therefore, we found it sensible to categorize tags into these two, as a way of reducing cognitive load. The "other" category was added to house terms that could not be classified as genre or mood. Context of listening has also been reported to play an important role in music selection, but words relating to context were not popular in our dataset, making it pointless to place them in a separate category. We decided that the three top terms from each category could sufficiently describe a song. Categorization was done based on lists of genres and moods which we built by combining and cleaning various lists from the web. In cases were these lists intersected (e.g. "romantic") we prioritized the genre list. It is noteworthy that since user input is never dependant on this categorization, the accuracy of these lists is not of importance; they are used solely to organize the presentation.

Limiting the main screen to nine tags:
Early prototypes of TagFlip presented all tags of the currently playing song in the main screen and made each category scrollable. This created visibility issues with part of the pinned tags being hidden if scrolled out of the screen. To mitigate this, we limited the number of tags shown by default for each song to nine. Where available, these were equally distributed into the three above explained categories. If a category contained less than three tags for a certain song, we filled the screen by including more than three tags from other categories. The user had the possibility to view the rest of a song's tag by clicking the "more tags" button in Figure 1.

EVALUATION

To evaluate TagFlip, we compared it to Spotify's mobile app, which has a library of more than 30 million songs, in a lab study designed around comparing the applications in their music discovery capabilities. The setup was refined through three pilot tests, and 16 participants (8 female, median age = 26) were recruited for the main study. Nine of these had a background in computer science, and nine had a Bachelor's or higher degree. We chose Spotify as a point of comparison as it is one of the most popular music streaming/recommendation services, and most of our participants either used it regularly or had experience with it. We decided against comparing TagFlip to an in-house made conventional recommender (with seed attributes and like/dislikes) because it would end up as just a less powerful version of TagFlip with no tag based navigation, and would presumably give us unrealistically positive results. With this test, we intended to investigate whether there is room for an interface like TagFlip in our user's daily music consumption, and to that end, the sensible route was to compare it to the state-of-the-art in commercial systems. Besides similar music recommendation (radio stations based on songs or genres) and community made playlists, Spotify also houses features such as top charts, artist pages and albums, and similar artists. All of these were open to participants.

We employed a within subjects design with a mixed methods approach [19] which consisted of questionnaires, interviews, videos of each session, and usage logs (with TagFlip only). The participant first filled a questionnaire covering basic music listening habits such as average hours of listening per day and use of streaming/recommendation services, and demographics. Then, the participant used each interface for 10 minutes (balanced order between participants). The task was to find new songs that (s)he liked and had not heard before (or had heard a long time ago and forgotten about), and to save the found songs by tapping the heart button in TagFlip, or adding them to a playlist in Spotify. Before the 10 minute main task, each user was also given five minutes with each interface in order to get familiar with it. During this time, the participant could ask questions about the interface from the experiment conductor. After finishing the 10 minute task with each interface, the participant filled two questionnaires according to his/her experience with it; one for general usability, and one for recommendation aspects. For the former, we used the SUS questionnaire [6], and for the latter, we built a 22 item questionnaire with 5 point Likert scale answers, based on the ResQue framework [29]. After both tasks were performed, a semi-structured interview was conducted, which mainly revolved around how the participants usually discovered new music, and how they would compare the two interfaces. The study was done on an HTC One M7 phone (4.7 inch screen) which was connected to loud speakers. For each participant, the study took roughly one hour, after which the participant was compensated 10 Euros.

Following the ResQue framework [29], we categorized our questions on recommendation aspects into four main constructs: **(1)** Quality of recommendations, **(2)** Interface and interaction adequacy, **(3)** Control and transparency, and **(4)** Attitudes and behavioural intentions. Based on these constructs, number of user interactions, and the liked songs, we formulated 7 hypotheses categorized into three higher level ones and four sub-hypotheses about each construct in our recommendation questionnaire. These seven were designed to question both the subjective and objective user experiences with TagFlip and Spotify:

- ***H1:*** *The overall user rating for recommendation aspects of TagFlip will be higher than Spotify (aggregate score based on all 22 questions)*
- ***H1.1 to H1.4:*** *TagFlip will be rated higher than Spotify in all the four constructs of recommendation.*
  - ***H1.1*** *Quality of recommendations*
  - ***H1.2*** *Interface and interaction adequacy*
  - ***H1.3*** *Control and Transparency*
  - ***H1.4*** *Attitudes and behavioural intentions*
- ***H2:*** *The number of interactions (screen touches) per liked song will be smaller for TagFlip.*
- ***H3:****The number of songs liked will be larger for TagFlip.*

H1 and its four sub-hypotheses gauge the subjective reaction from our participants, As discussed earlier, the key differentiators of TagFlip relate to precise user control and high transparency, coupled with low interaction effort. These factors align with the *control and transparency* and *interface and interaction adequacy* constructs from our questionnaire (H1.2 and H1.3). We predicted that better performance in these two categories would also lead to an overall better experience with TagFlip (H1), and better user rating in the other two constructs (H1.1 and H1.4). H2 was intended for helping us objectively test whether TagFlip actually required small interaction effort for exerting high control and reaching desired music. Finally, H3 was born out of the assumption that a better experience with TagFlip would lead to more liked songs.

Questionnaire results

Eleven participants said they used online streaming services on a regular basis, and the most popular service was Spotify. The medians for size of personal music collection, active listening hours (focused), and passive listening hours (during

Construct	Question Type	Question	TagFlip	Spotify
Quality of recommendations	Positive	The recommended songs matched what I was looking for	3	3
		The recommendations I received better fit my interests than what I may receive from a friend	**2**	1.5
		I enjoyed the recommended songs	3	3
		The recommender system helped me discover new music that I like	3	3
	Negative	A recommendation from my friends better suits my interests than the recommendations from this system	2	2
		The recommended songs were not enjoyable for me	**0.5**	1
		I could not find new music that I liked using the recommender	**0**	1
Interface and interaction adequacy	Positive	The app made it clear why the songs were recommended to me	**3**	1.5
		The app provided an adequate way for me to express my preferences	**3**	2.5
		I easily found the recommended songs in the interface	3	3
		I found it easy to find songs that I liked using the recommender system	3	3
	Negative	It was difficult to tell the app what I was looking for	**0.5**	2
		Looking for a list of recommended songs required too much effort	2	**1**
		It required too much effort to find what I liked using the recommender system	1	1
Control and Transparency	Positive	I felt in control of telling the app what music I wanted to find	3	3
		I understood why the songs where recommended to me	**3**	2
	Negative	It was difficult to understand why some songs were recommended	1	1
		I did not feel in control of specifying and changing my preferences	**0**	1
Attitudes and behavioural intentions	Positive	Overall, I am satisfied with the recommender	3	3
		I think I would like most of the songs that I find with this app if I use it again	3	3
	Negative	The recommender can not be trusted	**0.5**	1
		The recommended songs confused me	**0.5**	1

(a)

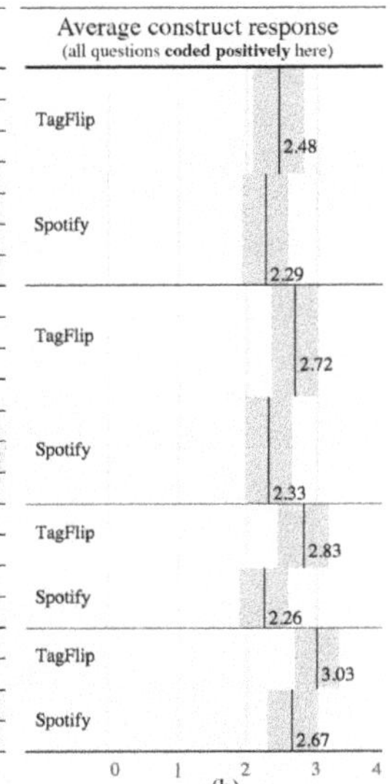

(b)

Figure 2. Part (a) shows median responses for all the questions regarding recommendation aspects, coded from 0 to 4, with 4 being the best response for positive questions and 0 being the best for negative ones. In part (b), average scores for all constructs along with 95% confidence intervals are shown. Here, negative questions were reverse coded to contribute positively.

other activities) were 5895.5 songs, "30 minutes to 1 hour"[2], and "2 - 4 hours"[3] respectively.

On the usability side, both interfaces scored similarly on the SUS questionnaire[4] (TagFlip: $M = 75.63$, $\sigma = 10.97$; Spotify: $M = 72.66$, $\sigma = 18.67$) with no significant difference in a paired sample t-test; $t(15) = 0.54, p = 0.60$. For some participants, the main screen in TagFlip was not immediately clear at first glance. However, they quickly realized the interaction concept and how the songs were retrieved once they started tapping on the tags and observing the next four songs and the size of the target set being updated and decreasing with each added tag, in the bottom right of the screen.

Figure 2 shows the median response to all the questions regarding recommendation aspects for both interfaces, classified into the four above mentioned constructs, and further grouped into positive and negative. Responses were coded into scores from 0 to 4. In positive questions, 4 is the best response, and in negative questions 0. For each question, the better median value is highlighted. As shown in the table, TagFlip tops Spotify in 11 of the 22 questions, while it's beaten in one. Using reverse codes for negative questions, the aggregate score over all 22 questions turned out to be significantly higher for TagFlip (TagFlip: $M = 3.03, \sigma = 0.51$; Spotify: $M = 2.51, \sigma = 0.66$; $t(15) = 3.12, p < 0.01, d = 0.78$). This **confirms H1**. Response histograms for all 22 questions are provided in supplementary materials.

Looking at individual constructs, TagFlip scored significantly higher in three of the four. These were *interface and interaction adequacy* ($t(15) = 2.26, p = 0.04, d = 0.56$), *control and transparency* ($t(15) = 3.86, p < 0.01, d = 0.97$), and *attitudes and behavioural intentions* ($t(15) = 2.54, p = 0.02, d = 0.63$). These numbers **support H1.2, H1.3, and H1.4** as well. In the *quality of recommendations* construct, although TagFlip scored higher, the difference was not found to be significant ($t(15) = 1.88, p = 0.08$), **leaving H1.1 unconfirmed**.

Objective measures

To test H2 and H3 we analysed the videos captured from the participants' interactions with both interfaces. We counted each touch of the screen (including a non-broken scroll) as one interaction. Since the act of adding a song to a playlist in Spotify, which was what the participants were instructed to do if they liked a song, required three taps (compared to one tap in TagFlip) we counted each of these three tap sequences as one interaction in Spotify. Each instance of typing in a search box anywhere in the interfaces was also counted as one interaction.

The number of interactions with TagFlip were smaller for all but one participant, and this was found to be a significant effect; TagFlip: $M = 144.56, \sigma = 37.00$; Spotify: $M = 209.56, \sigma = 54.64$; $t(15) = -5.85, p < 0.01, d = -1.48$. A look at our videos made it clear why such a large difference existed. With Spotify, participants spent a lot of time switching between various charts, playlists, and radio stations; actions that need several taps. In contrast, in TagFlip most of the interaction happened in the main screen with the tags or the list of upcoming songs.

Beyond that, we were specifically interested in how effective the participants' interactions were. While it is generally difficult to objectively measure such a concept between two fundamentally different interfaces, we chose to measure the number of interactions per liked song as a way to approximate effectiveness. This value was found to be significantly smaller for TagFlip ($M = 25.61, \sigma = 15.07$) than Spotify ($M = 34.58, \sigma = 18.47$); $t(15) = -2.05, p = 0.04$. As such,

[2] Asked in ranges: <15m, 15m -30m, 30m - 1h, 1h - 2h, > 2h

[3] Asked in ranges: < 1h, 1h - 2h, 2h - 4h, 4h - 6h, > 6h

[4] SUS gives a score between 0-100

our data supports H2 as well. Looking just at the number of liked songs, we saw very close numbers for the two interfaces for most users (TagFlip: $M = 7.00, \sigma = 3.10$ Spotify: $M = 7.06, \sigma = 3.09$), with no significant difference found in a paired sample t-test ($t(15) = -0.79, p = 0.938$). As such, our **results do not support H3**.

Another measure to look at is the number of tags pinned when recommendations were played. With Spotify, the user has only one point of control, which is realized through selecting a seed song for recommendation or a pre-compiled playlist. With TagFlip, participants had an average of 2.27 tags pinned through-out their 10 minute exploration, which indicates a level of desired control higher than what one tag can achieve. A comparison between recommendations that lead to a like by the user and those that did not, reveals a significant difference between the number of pinned tags in the two cases; Liked: $M = 2.46, \sigma = 0.74$; not liked: $M = 2.24, \sigma = 0.75$; $t(15) = 2.382, p = 0.03, d = 0.60$. This can suggest that either the songs chosen with more specific constraints turned out to be of higher quality for the user, or that participants were more likely to think they liked a song if they applied more control toward retrieving it.

Interview results

We manually coded the interviews to identify prevalent concepts. The most prominent comment about TagFlip (mentioned by all participants) was the level of control it provided to the user. Participants appreciated the fact that it was easy to specify exactly what type of music they liked to hear as opposed to the more unpredictable experience with Spotify. As one user put it in simple terms *"You made tags useful"*. Another said jokingly, *"Sometimes you have your own ideas about what your music should be. It is not always what the powers that be think about it."* Another participant said *"in Spotify, you get a radio, like it or not!"*. Some of the participants who used TagFlip second actually complained about the fact that they could not combine criteria in Spotify, and some even asked whether they had missed the feature in its interface. One participant said that with Spotify, she kept trying to reach a *"pleasant stream"* but was not able to. With TagFlip on the other hand, she could easily reach that state; she could choose a number of tags and then expect to like most of the songs and *"prevent radical changes"*. Seven participants actually mentioned that they did not like Spotify's recommendations or playlists because of too little control. On the other hand, eight participants also liked the fact that Spotify could sometimes require a smaller effort and that playlists were human made. For instance, one user mentioned the fact that you sometimes need some *"up and down"* and a *"good mix"*, which the community made playlists can provide.

Another popular concept among the gathered responses was what we call *fine tuning*. Eleven participants specifically liked how TagFlip let them tune their experience based on the tags of each played song. One of our users called this *"local control"*, complaining that no other tool he had used supported it. *"It helped me narrow down my mood"* was how he summarized this experience. We observed this phenomenon first hand as well. Participants would often see a tag and react to it with amusement or add it to the next song. *"hah, 'sexy', why not?!"* and *"'groovy', exactly!"* were examples of this. A similar comment noted how easily one could get diverse styles of music from TagFlip. As one participant put it *"I could easily go from blues to funk to rock to 70's, so I got a lot more"*. Other salient themes in interview responses related to the size of the next four album arts being too small (6 users), and appreciating the system's transparency (5 users).

Based on how excited the participants were about TagFlip, and whether they explicitly asked to have the app on their own phones (without us mentioning it) we classified them into two groups (ENTH: enthusiastic, REST: rest of the users). Seven participants belonged to ENTH. Out of the nine members of REST, another seven were still open to using TagFlip for active discovery, but were not as excited as ENTH members. Looking at the interview transcripts, we found that all members of ENTH mentioned the *fine tuning* aspect of TagFlip, while only four of the second group did so. Using Fisher's exact test, this was found to be a significant effect ($p = 0.03$). A similar association was seen for people who mentioned that they did not like Spotify's recommendations (5 from ENTH and only 2 from REST), however, this was not found to be significant ($p = 0.13$). We also observed a significant difference between the groups in terms of the differences between the number of liked songs with the two interfaces (ENTH: mean of differences between number of liked songs in TagFlip/Spotify = 1.71, $\sigma = 2.70$; REST: $M = -1.4, \sigma = 2.87$; $t(13.44) = -2.26, p = 0.04, d = -1.23$). This indicates that our enthusiastic group liked more songs in TagFlip than Spotify, compared to the rest of the participants. In addition, the earlier-mentioned significant difference between the number of interactions per liked song was created by ENTH users (ENTH: mean difference in interactions per liked song = $-19.32, \sigma = 14.15$; REST: M = $-1.24, \sigma = 14.95$).

DISCUSSION

Is there room for TagFlip?

While there is plenty of existing commercial and academic work on music discovery, most of it has focused on algorithm perfection rather than actively engaging the user. Hence, with this paper, our main goal was to foray into the less explored space of user-controlled music recommendation on mobile devices, and test the possibility of utilizing social tags to accommodate such control.

Out of our five hypotheses on subjective experience, four were supported in our results. These included the aggregate user feedback for recommendation aspects (H1), interface and interaction adequacy (H1.2), control and transparency (H1.3), and attitudes and behavioural intentions (H1.4). A careful look at individual questions reveals the main driving force behind these to be the way TagFlip provided means for users to easily manipulate and fine-tune their recommendations, and how it exposed its logic of operation to them (H1.2). This lead to a high level of perceived control and transparency (H1.3). Although the improvement in the overall quality of recommendations was not found to be significant (H1.1), the participants' trust toward TagFlip greatly benefited from its transparency and high control, leading to a significant difference in the fourth recommendation construct as well (H1.4). This is an interesting phenomenon, suggesting that the users' trust does not necessarily depend on the quality of the recommended items, but also on how much agency they had in the process. A similar effect was reported by McNee et al. [22], who found that higher control leads to higher loyalty, even despite more user effort and comparable recommendation accuracy.

Analysis of our interviews revealed a strong relation between mentioning the *fine tuning* aspect of TagFlip and being in the enthusiastic group of participants who asked to have TagFlip on their own phones as soon as possible. This concept has been largely absent from music recommenders. With current tools, to achieve similar results, users would have to identify the keywords they are interested in, and then manually type them in a search box and hope for the best. Besides minimizing the effort in both high-level and fine-tuning control, our way of presenting music can also lead to spontaneous explorations when it shows an intriguing tag. Our users often chose tags out of amusement, wonder, or sheer curiosity in looking at the number of conforming songs for various tag combinations. As such, TagFlip also enables the user to easily change course significantly with some tags, while keeping other tags pinned, to simultaneously achieve overall similarity.

Moving on to objective measures, we observed considerably different behaviours in user interaction between the interfaces. As mentioned before, most of our users' interactions with Spotify were directed at navigating the various UI elements, such as scrolling through lists of songs and playlists or switching between them. These actions incurred a large number of screen touches, significantly more than with TagFlip, where most interactions happened in the main screen, pinning/unpinning tags or scrolling the list of upcoming songs. Data from these observations supported our hypothesis on interaction effort (H2), which indicates that TagFlip was successful in keeping interaction effort minimal; one of its core design requirements. That said, the number of liked songs with the two apps was surprisingly close, with similarly close and relatively small standard deviations. This could hint at an unknown factor playing a role here. Perhaps this measure is not appropriate for gauging overall performance with the apps, as it might be rooted in an unconscious tendency to like an equal number of songs with both. Nevertheless, we believe that the above difference in interactions per liked song can still be meaningful and indicate a smaller effort required by TagFlip for finding a comparable number of new songs.

Our results suggest that music discovery based on social tags can be a viable solution to increasing user control in music recommendation. More importantly, our iterative design process gave us valuable insight into the users' expectations, reactions, and mental models regarding tag-based discovery. Our principal challenge in designing TagFlip was figuring out the appropriate way of laying out all the required information for the user within the confines of a mobile device, without causing cognitive overload and requiring intricate interaction. Our ability to design this interface with high usability and user satisfaction compared to one of the most popular commercial tools suggests that there is room for expanding tag-based interfaces out of the academic space and integrating them into consumer-facing services, in order to make user interaction with massive music libraries more efficient, directed, and transparent. We will now discuss some of the key findings of our design process.

Design considerations and remaining questions

TagFlip went through major changes in its prototyping stages. Some of our designs, beginning from paper prototypes and all the way to the current iteration, are included in supplementary material. Earlier, we discussed a few of our design choices in building TagFlip. Some of our key findings in the final evaluation were the following:

Full tag list presentation:
TagFlip uses an alphabetically ordered list of tags with the option to search, if the user desires to start listening by specifying tags rather than from a song. Some users found the mental load associated with this task to be too heavy. An interesting question would be how the list of all tags can be presented in a way that reduces the friction of thinking about what to choose. One solution could be a sorting of the list based on the users' listening histories.

Control on tag strength might improve satisfaction:
We discussed how tag strength was left out of the final interface due to the confusion between it and how much users cared about a tag or how popular it was. In our lab study, non of our participants expressed a need for such a feature. However, perhaps its addition can increase user satisfaction by having higher quality recommendations. TagFlip prioritizes songs that have all the requested tags over those that have some but with higher strength. While our participants were mostly content with the recommended material, in a couple of instances they complained that a tag did not belong with a song. Hence, future work can investigate the importance of such a feature and whether it can enhance user experience.

Communicating target set sizes; probably not required:
The tested design in TagFlip (informing the user that no exact match was found and encouraging the removal of a tag) proved to be sufficient in dealing with empty target sets. In the few times that this happened in our lab study, users quickly reacted to the message by removing the tags they cared least about.

Categorizing tags helps:
A third of our participants liked the categorization into mood/genre/other, one felt it was not needed, and the rest did not have specific opinions about it. As such, we did not find enough evidence to suggest that alternate designs could perform better in giving the user a high level idea of the type of music that is played.

Limiting the main screen vs. full scrolling:
Although showing only nine tags on the main screen appeared to be a reasonable choice in our usability tests, many of our users in the final user study kept trying to scroll the list up and

down instead of navigating to the "more tags" page. An interesting design space to explore in the future would be ways of showing all tags of the playing song in the main screen while still keeping the cognitive load to a minimum.

Excluding certain types of music:
Some of the users that took part in our usability tests and the final lab study expressed a need for telling the system that they did not want to hear a certain type of music, by excluding a certain tag. The positive nature of tags makes this difficult to support. One solution would be to use methods such as Latent Semantic Analysis to transform the folksonomy into a set of topics [20, 33]. Having this information, one could then define topics as being contrary to each other, and thus utilize the available information on each song to exclude it from a recommended set. This was, however, beyond the scope of TagFlip at this stage.

Integration with conventional applications:
Some of our participants tried clicking on the album art of the current song, expecting to be taken to a dedicated page for the album or artist, and some mentioned they were more interested in artist-based exploration than song-based. An interesting avenue to explore is ways of integrating such functionalities into a tag-based navigation interface, or adding the latter to the more conventional music streaming tools.

Limitations and further future work

Our lab study was intended for understanding the capabilities of TagFlip compared to what people use in their daily lives. A natural next step would be a longitudinal field study, having TagFlip be part of the users' daily music consumption routines for weeks, while studying how it is used and how naturally it fits. The design questions discussed earlier could then be tested for and analysed in a more realistic environment [21].

A potential confounding factor, which is inherent to the methodological choice we took, is the *demand characteristic effect* [13, 24]. This effect describes the possible tendency of participants to subjectively rate our tool higher because they realize we built it. Being aware of this potential threat, we tried to alleviate it by carefully avoiding to bias our participants in any way. For instance, we did not tell the participants that used Spotify first about the second app that they were going to compare it to; they were only told that we were comparing two apps. In addition, the fact that TagFlip did not end up being rated significantly better than Spotify in the more general questions about recommendation quality, can suggest that such an effect was not strong. On the other hand, since most participants had previous experience with Spotify's app, a boost to usability ratings for Spotify is also expected.

The library of music used in TagFlip contained "only" 100,000 songs, and this had tangible negative effects on user experience compared to Spotify with more than 30 million songs. For instance, as our study was performed in Austria, some users pointed to our lack of local songs as an issue. As such, having a larger library and one that better reflects the interests of the target audience can improve user satisfaction.

Another limitation of TagFlip relates to its tag data. Although we meticulously cleaned the Last.fm data from half a million tags to 358, we did not perform any synonym modelling. While this may not be necessary for certain tag types (genre, instrument, etc.) having such a model can improve the experience with mood tags. Moreover, as some songs have few tags, auto-tagging algorithms [10] could be used to propagate more tags to such songs, to get a more uniform library.

CONCLUSION

The primary goal in designing TagFlip was to increase user involvement and control in the process of music recommendation, while keeping the user's mental and interactive effort as small as possible, and fitting the design in a small phone screen. With the positive results of our evaluations, we believe TagFlip has succeeded in its mission. The consensus among our 16 participants of the lab study was that our tool fills an important space that is unsupported by conventional recommender services, and seven of them asked to have the app on their own phones as soon as it was possible. Considering the fact that Spotify's library is more than 300 times larger than ours and its mobile interface has been refined for years, we find it encouraging that TagFlip could perform as well in usability, and come out on top in most recommendation aspects.

In a lab study, we had participants compare TagFlip to Spotify's mobile application, in terms of usability and music recommendation capabilities. Out of our seven hypotheses to test TagFlip, five were supported by our results. In subjective user feedback, these related to (1) aggregate rating in recommendation aspects, (2) interface and interaction adequacy, (3) control and transparency, (4) attitudes and behavioural intentions. The fifth confirmed hypothesis concerned the objective measure of number of interactions per liked song, indicating that TagFlip required less effort from users for discovering a comparable number of new liked songs.

Based on our design process and final evaluation, we reported on a number of design considerations and open design questions regarding tag based music listening and discovery interfaces. Among other things, we found that grouping tags into categories such as genres and moods can help give the user a holistic understanding of the played music; that providing a way to exclude certain types of music based on tags might help enhance user experience; that having a very clear separation between tags of the current song and constraints for the next is crucial; and that facilitating control on strength of tags might improve perceived recommendation quality but comes at the expense of added complexity and confusion.

In future work, we plan to expand our understanding of how TagFlip can fit into the music listeners' daily lives through a long term study. This would also serve as a platform for further studying and comparing alternative solutions to some of the design questions posed earlier. In addition, we intend to improve our library and dataset by including more songs and enhancing our tag space through methods such as auto-tagging and synonym modelling.

REFERENCES

1. Baur, D., Boring, S., and Butz, A. Rush: Repeated Recommendations on Mobile Devices. In *Proceedings of the 2010 International Conference on Intelligent User Interfaces (IUI '10)* (2010), 91–100.
2. Baur, D., Hering, B., Boring, S., and Butz, A. Who Needs Interaction Anyway? Exploring Mobile Playlist Creation from Manual to Automatic. In *Proceedings of the 2011 international Conference on Intelligent User Interfaces (IUI '11)* (2011), 291–294.
3. Bertin-Mahieux, T., Ellis, D. P., Whitman, B., and Lamere, P. The Million Song Dataset. In *Proceedings of the 12th International Society for Music Information Retrieval Conference (ISMIR '11)* (2011), 591–596.
4. Boland, D., Mclachlan, R., and Murray-smith, R. Engaging with Mobile Music Retrieval. In *Proceedings of the 2015 International Conference on Human-Computer Interaction with Mobile Devices and Services (MobileHCI '15)* (2015), 484–493.
5. Bostandjiev, S., O'Donovan, J., and Höllerer, T. TasteWeights: A Visual Interactive Hybrid Recommender System. In *Proceedings of the 2012 ACM conference on Recommender systems (RecSys '12)*, ACM Press (2012), 35–42.
6. Brooke, J. SUS: A Quick and Dirty Usability Scale. Tech. rep., 1996.
7. Burke, R., Hammond, K., and Yound, B. The FindMe Approach to Assisted Browsing. *IEEE Expert 12*, 4 (Jul 1997), 32–40.
8. Chen, L., and Pu, P. Critiquing-based recommenders: Survey and emerging trends. *User Modeling and User-Adapted Interaction 22*, 1-2 (2011), 125–150.
9. Dachselt, R., Frisch, M., and Weiland, M. FacetZoom: A Continuous Multi-scale Widget for Navigating Hierarchical Metadata. In *Proceeding of the 2008 SIGCHI Conference on Human Factors in Computing Systems (CHI '08)* (2008), 1353–1356.
10. Eck, D., Lamere, P., Bertin-Mahieux, T., and Green, S. Automatic Generation of Social Tags for Music Recommendation. In *Advances in Neural Information Processing Systems (NIPS '07)* (2007), 385–392.
11. Greasley, A. E., and Lamont, A. Exploring engagement with music in everyday life using experience sampling methodology. *Musicae Scientiae 15*, 1 (2011), 45–71.
12. Green, S., Lamere, P., Alexander, J., and Maillet, F. Generating Transparent, Steerable Recommendations from Textual Descriptions of Items. In *Proceedings of the 2009 ACM Conference on Recommender Systems (RecSys'09)*, ACM Press (2009), 281–284.
13. Intons-Peterson, M. J. Imagery paradigms: How vulnerable are they to experimenters' expectations? *Journal of Experimental Psychology: Human Perception and Performance 9*, 3 (1983), 394.
14. Jennings, D. *Net, Blogs and Rock 'n' Roll: How Digital Discovery Works and What it Means for Consumers.* Nicholas Brealey Publishing, 2007.
15. Kamalzadeh, M., Baur, D., and Möller, T. A Survey on Music Listening and Management Behaviours. In *Proceedings of the 13th International Society for Music Information Retrieval Conference (ISMIR '12)* (2012), 373–378.
16. Kamalzadeh, M., Baur, D., and Möller, T. Listen or Interact? A Large-Scale Survey on Music Listening and Management Behaviours. *Journal of New Music Research* (in press).
17. Konstan, J. A., and Riedl, J. Recommender systems: From algorithms to user experience. *User Modeling and User-Adapted Interaction 22*, 1 (2012), 101–123.
18. Lamere, P. Social tagging and music information retrieval. *Journal of New Music Research 37*, 2 (2008), 101–114.
19. Lazar, J. *Research Methods In Human-Computer Interaction.* Wiley, 2010.
20. Levy, M., and Sandler, M. Learning Latent Semantic Models for Music from Social Tags. *Journal of New Music Research 37*, 2 (June 2008), 137–150.
21. McGrath, J. E. Methodology matters: Doing research in the behavioral and social sciences. In *Readings in Human-Computer Interaction: Towards the Year 2000*, 2nd ed. Morgan Kaufmann, 1995, 152–169.
22. McNee, S., Lam, S., Konstan, J., and Riedl, J. Interfaces for Eliciting New User Preferences in Recommender Systems. In *User Modeling 2003*, P. Brusilovsky, A. Corbett, and F. de Rosis, Eds., vol. 2702 of *Lecture Notes in Computer Science*. Springer Berlin Heidelberg, 2003, 178–187.
23. O'Donovan, J., Smyth, B., Gretarsson, B., Bostandjiev, S., and Höllerer, T. PeerChooser: Visual Interactive Recommendation. In *Proceedings of the 2008 SIGCHI Conference on Human Factors in Computing Systems (CHI '08)* (2008), 1085–1088.
24. Orne, M. T. Demand Characteristics and the Concept of Quasi-controls. *Artifacts in Behavioral Research: Robert Rosenthal and Ralph L. Rosnows Classic Books* (2009), 110.
25. Oudenne, A. M., Kim, Y. E., and Turnbull, D. S. Meerkat: Exploring Semantic Music Discovery Using Personalized Radio. In *Proceedings of the 11th International Conference on Multimedia Information Retrieval (MIR '10)* (2010), 429–432.
26. Pampalk, E., and Goto, M. MusicSun: A New Approach to Artist Recommendation. In *Proceedings of the 8th International Conference on Music Information Retrieval (ISMIR '07)* (2007).

27. Pampalk, E., Rauber, A., and Merkl, D. Content-based Organization and Visualization of Music Archives. In *Proceedings of the 10th ACM International Conference on Multimedia (MULTIMEDIA'02)* (2002), 570–579.

28. Pu, P., and Chen, L. Trust building with explanation interfaces. In *Proceedings of the 15th International Conference on Intelligent User Interfaces (IUI'06)* (2006), 93–100.

29. Pu, P., and Chen, L. A user-centric evaluation framework of recommender systems. In *UCERSTI Workshop of RecSys'10* (2010), 14–21.

30. Schwartz, B. *The Paradox of Choice*. Harper Perennial, 2004.

31. Schwartz, B., Ward, A., Monterosso, J., Lyubomirsky, S., White, K., and Lehman, D. R. Maximizing Versus Satisficing: Happiness Is a Matter of Choice. *Journal of Personality and Social Psychology 83*, 5 (2002), 1178–1197.

32. Sinha, R., and Swearingen, K. The Role of Transparency in Recommender Systems. In *Proceedings of the 2002 SIGCHI Conference on Human Factors in Computing Systems (CHI' 02)* (2002), 830–831.

33. Sordo, M., Gouyon, F., Sarmento, L., Celma, O., and Serra, X. Inferring Semantic Facets of a Music Folksonomy with Wikipedia. *Journal of New Music Research 42*, 4 (2013), 346–363.

34. Spotify Android SDK. `https://developer.spotify.com/technologies/spotify-android-sdk/`.

35. Stumpf, S., and Muscroft, S. When Users Generate Music Playlists: When Words Leave off, Music Begins? In *Proceedings of the 2011 International Conference on Multimedia and Expo (ICME '11)* (2011), 1–6.

36. Sturm, B. L. The State of the Art Ten Years After a State of the Art: Future Research in Music Information Retrieval. *Journal of New Music Research 43*, 2 (2014), 147–172.

37. Tintarev, N., and Masthoff, J. A Survey of Explanations in Recommender Systems. In *Proceedings of the 2007 IEEE International Conference on Data Engineering Workshop* (2007), 801–810.

38. Tzanetakis, G., and Cook, P. MARSYAS3D: A Prototype Audio Browser-editor Using a Large Scale Immersive Visual and Audio Display. In *Proceedings of the 2011 International Conference on Auditory Display* (2001), 250–254.

39. van Gulik, R., Vignoli, F., and van de Wetering, H. Mapping Music in the Palm of Your Hand, Explore and Discover Your Collection. In *Proceedings of the 5th International Society for Music Information Retrieval Conference (ISMIR'04)* (2004).

40. Verbert, K., Parra, D., Brusilovsky, P., and Duval, E. Visualizing Recommendations to Support Exploration, Transparency and Controllability. In *Proceedings of the 2013 International Conference on Intelligent User Interfaces (IUI '13)*, ACM Press (2013), 351–361.

41. Vig, J., Sen, S., and Riedl, J. Tagsplanations: Explaining Recommendations Using Tags. In *Proceedings of the 2009 International Conference on Intelligent User Interfaces (IUI '09)* (2009), 47–56.

42. Vig, J., Sen, S., and Riedl, J. Navigating the Tag Genome. In *Proceedings of the 2011 International Conference on Intelligent User Interfaces (IUI '11)*, ACM Press (2011), 93–102.

43. Vignoli, F. Digital Music Interaction Concepts: A User Study. In *Proceedings of the 5th International Society for Music Information Retrieval Conference (ISMIR '04)* (2004), 415–420.

44. Wang, J.-C., Shih, Y.-C., Wu, M.-S., Wang, H.-M., and Jeng, S.-K. Colorizing Tags in Tag Cloud: A Novel Query-by-Tag Music Search System. In *Proceedings of the 2011 ACM International Conference on Multimedia (MM '11)*, ACM Press (2011), 293–302.

45. Wang, J.-C., Wu, M.-s., Wang, H.-m., and Jeng, S.-k. Query by Multi-tags with Multi-level Preferences for Content-based Music Retrieval. In *Proceedings of the 2011 IEEE International Conference on Multimedia and Expo (ICME '11)* (2011), 1–6.

46. Yee, K.-P., Swearingen, K., Li, K., and Hearst, M. Faceted metadata for image search and browsing. In *Proceedings of the 2003 SIGCHI Conference on Human factors in Computing Systems (CHI '03)* (2003), 401–408.

47. Zhu, S., Cai, J., Zhang, J., Li, Z., Wang, J.-c., and Wang, Y. Bridging the User Intention Gap: An Intelligent and Interactive Multidimensional Music Search Engine Categories and Subject Descriptors. In *Proceedings of the 2014 ACM International Workshop on Internet-Scale Multimedia Management (WISMM '14)* (2014), 59–64.

Expense Control: A Gamified, Semi-Automated, Crowd-Based Approach For Receipt Capturing

Maximilian Altmeyer[1,2], **Pascal Lessel**[2,3], **Antonio Krüger**[2,1]
[1]Saarland University, [2]DFKI GmbH, [3]Saarbrücken Graduate School of Computer Science
Saarbrücken, Germany
{first name}.{last name}@dfki.de

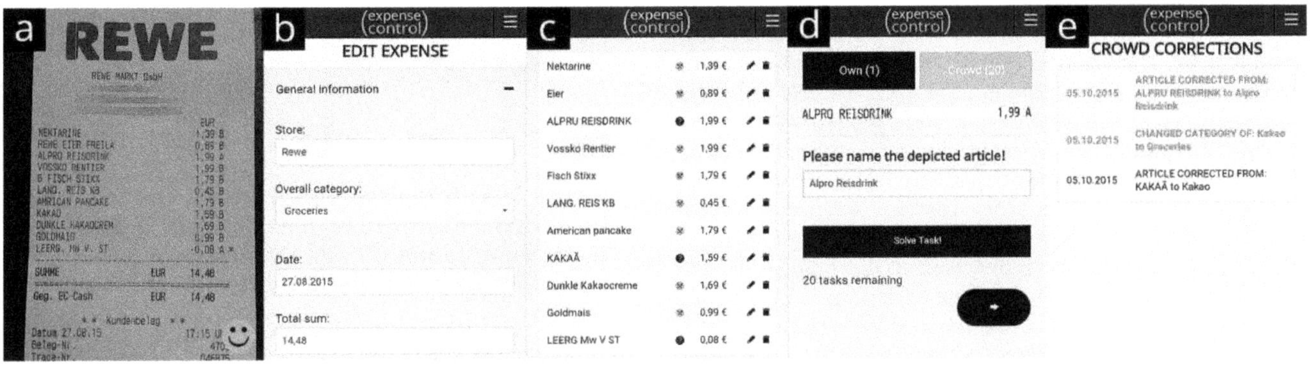

Figure 1: Workflow of our app. a) Photographing the receipt. b) Recognized general information. c) Extracted articles and categories. d) Microtask to be solved by the crowd. e) Corrections performed by the crowd

ABSTRACT

We investigate a crowd-based approach to enhance the outcome of optical character recognition in the domain of receipt capturing to keep track of expenses. In contrast to existing work, our approach is capable of extracting single products and provides categorizations for both articles and expenses, through the use of microtasks which are delegated to an unpaid crowd. To evaluate our approach, we developed a smartphone application based on a receipt analysis and an online questionnaire in which users are able to track expenses by taking photos of receipts, and solve microtasks to enhance the recognition. To provide additional motivation to solve these tasks, we make use of gamification. In a three-week-long user study (N=12), we found that our system is appreciated, that our approach reduces the error rate of captured receipts significantly, and that the gamification provided additional motivation to contribute more and thereby enrich the database.

Author Keywords

Gamification; Crowdsourcing; Wisdom of Crowds; OCR; Digital Household Accounting Book

IUI'16, March 07–10, 2016, Sonoma, CA, USA.

DOI: http://dx.doi.org/10.1145/2856767.2856790

ACM Classification Keywords

H.5.m. Information Interfaces and Presentation (e.g. HCI): Miscellaneous

INTRODUCTION

Optical character recognition (OCR) has improved significantly in recent years [27] and is used in various domains, for example to digitize printed documents (e.g. books) [16], to translate text in real time [35] or to provide assistive technologies for blind and visually impaired users [3]. However, OCR results are still error-prone and heavily depend on the quality of both the picture taken and the printed text [11]: the higher the quality of the picture and text, the better the results, and inversely. This makes it hard to achieve reliable OCR results in domains that are confronted with e.g. text fonts that are hard to recognize, pale ink, or crumpled paper [37,40] and gets even worse when taking pictures with a smartphone camera because of bad lighting and distortion of the picture [11].

One approach to fix spelling errors is using crowdsourcing which relies on the concept of the wisdom of crowds [34]. This concept states that a group of people is able to come to a better decision than an individual [34] and is often used to overcome problems that cannot adequately be solved by computers [7, 18] or to enhance algorithms by combining methods from artificial intelligence and crowdsourcing [4]. In this paper we investigate a crowd-based approach to enhance the outcome of OCR. Our goal is not solely to correct spelling errors, as done in existing work [1, 6, 12, 26] but also semantically enhance OCR results and attach meaningful metadata by the use of designated microtasks solved by an unpaid crowd. We evaluated our approach in the domain of receipt capturing to keep track of expenses with a special focus on extracting single articles, corresponding prices and an appropriate categorization. Existing attempts in this field using rule-based mechanisms [32] or machine learning methods [40] did not provide this information, probably because extracting those entities adds substantial difficulty to the OCR problem space. The increasing interest in self-tracking [24, 39], and the desire to track expenditures, additionally strengthen the need for a solution to this problem.

We developed a budgeting application (cf. Figure 1) for smartphones that allows for tracking expenses by taking pictures of receipts to extract relevant entities such as the total sum, store name, single articles and their corresponding prices, and a categorization of both the receipt and each article. To enhance the recognition algorithm, we used the outcome of different microtasks that were solved by users of our app. Solving these microtasks is not motivated by monetary rewards because it may negatively influence the quality of the generated solutions [25]. Instead, we use gamification - the use of game elements in non-game contexts [8], as it has already been successfully used in the field of crowdsourcing [6, 10, 21, 36]. The presented system is able to run in a self-sustained manner without using any external crowdsouring platforms. In a three-week-long user study, we found that the error rate when extracting entities from receipts can be significantly reduced with the help of crowd-solved microtasks and that the outcomes of these microtasks additionally improve entity extraction in future receipts. Moreover, we were able to confirm positive effects of the gamification elements on the willingness of subjects to participate.

The paper is structured as follows: we first review the challenges in performing OCR in the receipt analysis domain by inspecting German receipts from different stores, and report the results of an online study. We then consider related work and introduce how we integrated the findings into a smartphone prototype. Finally, we report and discuss the results of a user study using our prototype.

DOMAIN-SPECIFIC CHALLENGES AND REQUIREMENTS

To identify technical challenges, we inspected receipts to draw conclusions about their content and structure. We furthermore utilized an online questionnaire and reviewed popular budgeting applications informally to establish requirements for our prototype. More information about the online questionnaire and the receipt analysis can be found in [20].

Receipts Analysis

One major problem when extracting entities from receipts automatically is the absence of a uniform format [32]. We therefore inspected 117 German receipts from 85 different shops to deduce an abstract model for German receipts. We analyzed all receipts using two reviewers, each one inspecting every receipt, and thereby identified three sections (see Figure 2a):

1. **Header**: In 84.7% of all receipts, the store's name was provided as plain text. In addition, this region contains information about the store's address (95.3%), its telephone number (83.5%), the date of purchase (100%), or the website (41%). We found that the name of the store has no consistent format (since it is of arbitrary length and content); nor could be a fixed location identified for the store's name within the header region.

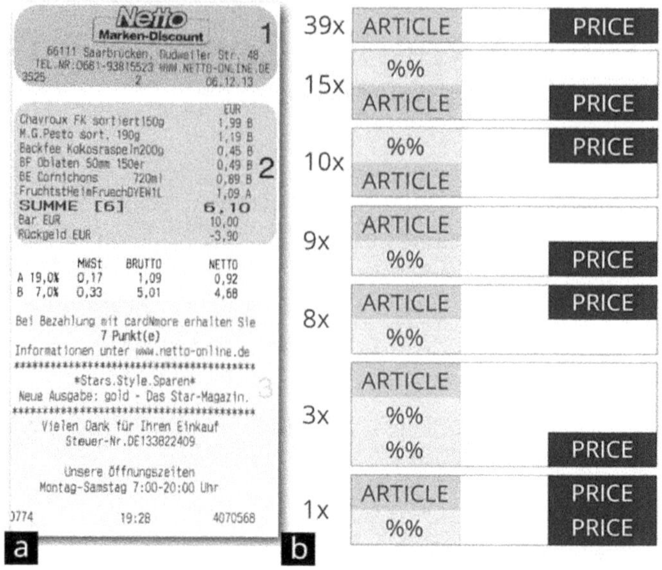

Figure 2: a) A typical receipt from a German supermarket with the identified regions: header (1), body (2), additional information (3). b) Arrangement patterns of articles and prices; % denotes additional information

2. **Body**: The body contains listed articles together with their prices as well as the total sum of the purchase. Since we aim for extracting single articles together with corresponding prices, we further examined how prices, article names and additional information (like article numbers, quantity, etc.) are aligned, and determined seven different patterns within our sample, as depicted in Figure 2b). We also analyzed the chosen wordings for the total sum of a receipt and found that there are 18 different representations used in our sample: most often the German word for "sum" was used (39), followed by "total" (31), and 16 remaining words that were distributed with high variance.

3. **Additional information**: This section contains entries not directly necessary for the capturing process. However, we found that there may be information (e.g. a web address) that could be helpful if the header is not recognized.

Based on these findings, we deduced four challenges when extracting relevant entities from receipts:

C1: *Identification and extraction of the store's name*
The analysis showed that it is hard to identify and extract the store's name because of its arbitrary length, content and format. Matters were complicated further due to the fact that no fixed location could be determined.

C2: *Identification of articles and extraction of their prices*
The layout examination of articles and corresponding prices revealed that it is not possible to simply match prices with

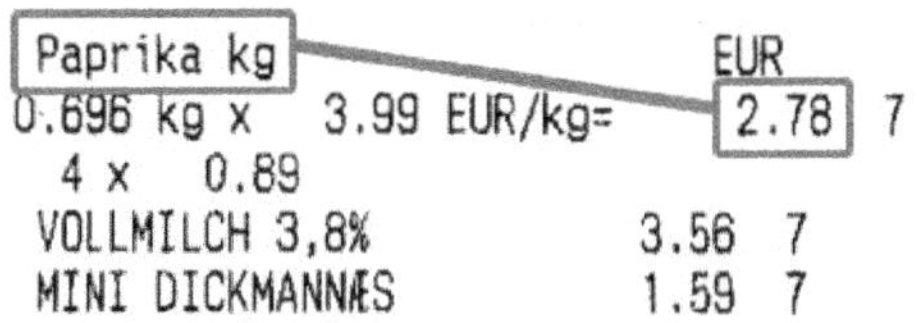

Figure 3: Article name (red rectangle on the left) and corresponding price (red rectangle on the right)

words of the same line to extract the article name because there is no consistent format or structure given (cf. Figure 2b). Moreover, article names are also of arbitrary length, making a purely programmatic approach more or less impossible. Figure 3 illustrates the problem of matching an article name to the corresponding price.

C3: *Categorization of single articles and the whole expense*
We consider deducing categories for single articles and the whole expense hard, since no information allowing inference of a category can be found on the receipt.

C4: *Identification and extraction of the total sum*
As our analysis reveals, although there are a lot of receipts using the same wording, which could be used to identify the total sum in most cases, there is still an incomplete set of further wordings that need to be considered.

Online Questionnaire

We setup an online questionnaire to obtain information about participants shopping behavior, their interest in keeping track of expenses, and their attitude towards automatic receipt capturing to establish requirements for our prototype. The questionnaire was available for six weeks.

Participants
We recruited 238 participants (Female: 101). Concerning age, the data is skewed young (<18: 2.73%, 18-25: 51.26%, 26-30: 13.03%, 31-40: 10.92%, 41-60: 19.33%, >60: 2.73%). This can be explained by the way the questionnaire was promoted (social media and student mailing lists).

Results
Although 82.35% of the participants were not keeping track of their expenses, only 12.18% claimed to be uninterested in doing so. Asked for causes, participants stated that the main reason is the high amount of effort to track expenses manually (stated by 57.98%). We therefore conclude that our prototype needs to ease the process of tracking expenses (**R1**). Participants reported visiting weekly farmer's markets and other specialized markets at least infrequently (5.88%), which makes a manual way to record expenses necessary (**R2**), since there are not always receipts provided. We moreover learned that the majority of people who own a smartphone (83.61%) always have it available (70.85%) while shopping or at least most of the time (21.11%). Additionally, a majority (64.71%) of participants stated that for receipt capturing they would prefer to take a photo with their smartphone. These two findings suggest that an application for mobile devices is the most suitable platform for our system (**R3**). 46.64% of the participants prefer to categorize the whole purchase instead of single items. Still, 16.38% would want every single item categorized, and 27.31% want both (single items and the whole purchase). Therefore, both options should be offered (**R4**). Concerning the evaluation period, 82.35% prefer monthly records of their purchases, which requires statistics and filters to allow for monthly aggregation (**R5**).

Informal Budgeting App Review

After establishing requirements based on the online questionnaire, we informally reviewed 10 budgeting apps, with a special focus on popular apps as reported in [2], to establish a core set of requirements for our prototype. We discovered that all reviewed apps contained statistics allowing aggregation of expenses at least by month and by category. Additionally, the amount of money spent was visualized using different types of charts. We therefore require the prototype to offer the possibility to visualize expenses in a statistical manner (**R6**). We furthermore learned that there should be a way of seeing all expenses together with the possibility to filter for different time intervals (**R7**). Other core functionalities that should be offered are editing and deleting expenses (**R8**). Based on the review, we additionally identified 10 different categories by taking the most provided categories within the applications into account. This information was used to build a basis set of categories (groceries, electronics, personal hygiene, fashion, household, pet needs, gardening, freetime, other) to be used for the categorization of expenses.

RELATED WORK

We inspected related work in the domain of crowdsourcing in general, approaches using crowdsourcing to correct OCR results, and related work in the domain of automatic receipt capturing as these domains are relevant for our work.

Crowdsourcing Picture Classification

There exist many approaches using crowdsourcing to solve problems that cannot be solved by machines in a simple way. For example, Von Ahn and Dabbish [36] developed the ESP Game, in which randomly paired players see images they need to tag. Every time they agree on a word, they receive points and the word is accepted as a valid tag. The approach confirms that a crowd can be used to annotate pictures and generate meaningful metadata, which is what we also do, but in another domain. Another example showing that a crowd not only succeeds in categorizing entities based on images, but outperforms single users in this task, can be seen in Lessel et al. [21]. The authors make use of crowdsourcing to generate classifications of waste that was inserted into an augmented recycling bin. Based on these classifications, feedback was provided to both the crowd as well as people standing in front of the trash bin, thereby educating them towards sustainable recycling behavior. This approach is also interesting for us since the crowd was not paid; instead, users were motivated through game elements, which we also aim for.

Crowdsourcing and OCR

One prominent approach is the reCAPTCHA system [37], displaying pictures of words extracted from scanned texts to people visiting websites. The extracted words are those that are unrecognizable by OCR. By typing the corresponding word, users can confirm they are human and indirectly fix OCR errors. The approach showed that a crowd is able to correct errors even when the crowd size is low (six users are sufficient) and additionally proved that a post-correction of OCR errors by human beings increases the accuracy compared to standard OCR. These findings support our idea of using a crowd to correct errors in extracted entities. Additionally, the fact that the crowd does not need to be large is an important information for the validation process in our prototype. Nevertheless, the reCAPTCHA system is used to correct OCR errors without regarding semantic coherences, as we do in order to identify and match articles and prices.

The Australian Newspapers Digitization Project (ANDP) [16] followed the idea to use OCR corrections to improve their digitized historic newspaper articles. They created a web service that volunteers could use to correct text passages. More than 9,000 users corrected over 12.5 million lines of text, and the number of volunteers participating in this platform is growing further [31]. This approach also shows the success of a crowd correcting erroneous text regions. However, in line with the reCAPTCHA approach, the focus of ANDP is not to provide microtasks to gain semantic coherences or to use collected information to improve an extraction algorithm, as covered by our work.

Turning crowd-based OCR correction into a game was investigated in the Digitalkoot system [6]. The system aimed to improve the digitalization of old newspaper articles from the National Library of Finland. Two games were developed, both based on pictures of words already extracted by an OCR engine. Over 4,768 people were recruited in 51 days, completing more than 2.5 million tasks by using a gamified and crowd-based approach. This supports our idea of using a crowd-based approach and gamification as a motivator.

Automatic receipt capturing

Considering the digitalization of receipts, there are several attempts to be found in literature. One is the work of Zhu et al. [40] which describes an approach for automatic expense reimbursement using OCR to digitize receipts with the help of conditional random fields and regular expressions. The latter were used to extract entities with limited variation, such as phone numbers or the transaction amount. Conditional random fields were used to extract entities having large variation (e.g. store names). The results show that this system is more robust to recognition errors, but still is far from being accurate, which motivates us to investigate a crowd-based approach in this context.

Receipts2Go [19] is another system that also targets the digitalization of single-sided documents, by capturing them with a cell phone, which is in line with our idea. They also used regular expressions to extract entities with low variety. However, there is no evaluation of this concept, and the question of how well this approach performs remains open. The fact that the authors suggest qualifying an image before processing it, post-processing of OCR results and using results from extractions in the past to improve OCR results, supports our concept, in which we provide live feedback when capturing a receipt and use crowd-generated content from past extractions to infer relevant information for upcoming analysis.

Figure 4: a) Main screen and b) statistics view of our app.

In contrast to our work, both approaches considered only certain elements to be extracted: Individual articles together with corresponding prices, and a proper categorization, were not considered. Since both approaches used regular expressions for the extraction of entities with low variety, we adapted this technique in our algorithm.

The work of Shen and Tijerino [32] relies on ontologies to extract entities from receipts and uses an Object-Relationship Model, which provides information about sets of objects and their relationship, as well as constraints over object and relationship sets. As this approach relies on perfect, flawless OCR results, it may not be directly applicable in our setting, in which receipts are captured with a smartphone camera. Therefore, we additionally use crowdsourcing to correct and classify entities and try to combine information gained through the crowd with static methods described in this work.

To our knowledge, our approach is the first investigating crowdsourcing to reduce the error rate when extracting relevant entities for expense tracking. Using gamification to motivate the crowd enables our system to run in a self-sustained manner and furthermore allows to investigate the effects and the perception of gamification in this domain. This is important since there exists work demonstrating that gamification is not always successful [14] and depends on many different factors [38]. To our knowledge, there seems to be no other work considering the identification and extraction of single articles together with respective prices and categories based on a photographed receipt. In contrast to existing approaches making use of crowdsourcing only to correct text errors, we go a step further and use microtasks to obtain semantically relevant information to enhance our recognition algorithm.

SYSTEM DESIGN

To evaluate our approach, we developed a budgeting application that allows for tracking expenses by taking pictures of receipts. The design of this prototype is based on the requirements we have established, and implements solutions to the aforementioned challenges. To enhance the recognition algorithm, we used the outcome of different gamified microtasks that were solved by an unpaid crowd.

Concept

We designed the concept of our prototype based on the results presented in the last sections. To accomplish **R3**, we decided to target mobile devices and implemented our prototype as an Android application. This also seems to be beneficial regarding the ease of tracking expenses (cf. **R1**) since it offers the possibility to add expenses by taking pictures of receipts with the smartphone's camera. During the conceptualization we also performed a usability test as suggested by Nielsen [29] with 5 participants (3 female), aged 33 on average. We asked them to accomplish tasks within the app and used a think-aloud approach [28]. Participants were also asked to solve 25 microtasks including all task types. Impacts of the usability test on our concept are stated in the following sections.

Budgeting Features

On the home screen of our application (cf. Figure 4a) we show the overall amount of money spent in the current month as well as in the last month (cf. **R5**). Clicking on the monthly expenses directly takes the user to a view showing all expenses from the corresponding month, as this functionality was considered important in the usability study. Furthermore, the last expenses were shown together with categories, total sum, and the store name. The prototype furthermore provides a view in which expenses are visualized in a statistical manner (cf. Figure 4b) based on categories of single articles or the category of the overall expense, which can be set by the user (cf. **R4**, **R6**), and custom time intervals (cf. **R7**). Moreover, the app can show all expenses and filter them by year or by month (cf. **R7**, **R5**). Expenses can always be edited or deleted (cf. **R8**) and may also be added manually (cf. **R2**).

Automated Receipt Capturing

The workflow (cf. Figure 1) of adding expenses by taking a picture of the receipt starts before the user actually takes the photo. As suggested in several related works [11, 19], live feedback on the quality of the picture is given (cf. Figure 5c and Figure 5d) in form of a smiley in the camera view to enhance the OCR outcome. As soon as a picture is taken, it gets preprocessed and text is extracted by an OCR engine on the user's smartphone. We decided to outsource the whole extraction to the user's smartphone to keep the traffic as low as possible for the user and reduce the workload on the webserver, to which the result containing recognized text and corresponding line numbers is sent. On the webserver, we extract all relevant information based on the received OCR result using the outcomes of microtasks solved by the crowd.

In the following sections we describe in more detail how we realized the concept.

Receipt Capturing and Image Preprocessing

As the quality of the picture taken greatly affects the quality of the OCR result [11], we decided to implement different approaches to enhance the picture taken by the user. In a first step, we provided live feedback on the quality of the picture in form of a smiley in the camera view. Whether the smiley is green and smiling (cf. Figure 5c) or red and frowning (cf. Figure 5b) depends on lighting and the orientation of the mobile device, since both attributes have been identified as crucial for good OCR results in the literature [11, 15].

Figure 5: a) Identified horizontally aligned regions, b) Unfavorable position of the camera, c) Suitable picture, d) Region Of Interest (ROI)

To measure whether there is too much distortion or the image is skewed, we implemented an algorithm that identifies horizontally aligned regions on the given picture by using edge detection methods together with morphological closing transformations. In a further step, we calculate bounding boxes for these regions, as shown in Figure 5a). If the boxes are higher than they are wide, we can conclude that the smartphone is in an unfavorable position and distortion might be too high, since we considered words to be wider than high. Based on our receipt analysis, we can also conclude that there is too much noise in the image (e.g. because of other text elements in the background) when the x-coordinates of the bounding boxes are too heterogeneous, since we found that articles on receipts are always in alignment. After the picture was taken, we preprocessed the picture, since this further enhances OCR results [12]: In a first step we again used the algorithm described above to identify horizontally aligned regions. Based on these regions, we identified the region of interest (ROI), i.e. where the receipt is located in the picture. This was done by discarding all horizontally aligned regions where the x-coordinate of the corresponding bounding box was either lower than the calculated mean of all x-coordinates, or higher (with a certain threshold). The remaining regions were consolidated to form another bounding box which represents the region where the receipt is located (represented by the red line in Figure 5d). This area was extracted from the picture to obtain better results when thresholding it. Afterwards, we used similar approaches (thresholding, Gaussian blur, deskewing) as reported in related work [15, 19].

Entity Extraction And Consideration Of Posed Challenges

After preprocessing we used tesseract[1] to extract text regions from the picture on the user's smartphone. The extracted text is uploaded to a webserver, where three steps to extract all relevant entities from the receipt are performed:

1: Receipt Segmentation

At first, we divide the receipt into three regions: header, body and additional information (cf. Figure 2a). To identify the header, we search for the first occurrence of a price, using regular expressions. Once a price is found, the line above is considered to represent the end of the head section. Afterwards, we search for words indicating the total sum in our

[1] `https://github.com/tesseract-ocr`, last accessed January 5, 2016

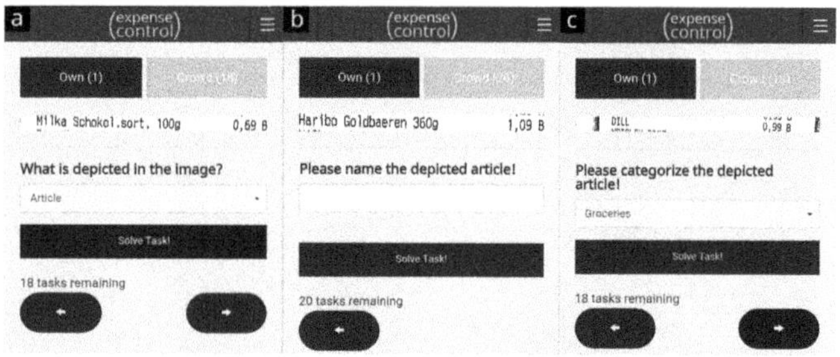

Figure 6: Crowd microtasks: a) Classification, b) Article naming, c) Article categorization.

database, that were collected by solving microtasks, to find the end of the body region. Once we find such a word, we assume the respective line to contain the total price, which can be extracted using regular expressions, targeting **C4**. Moreover the line containing the total sum represents the end of the body region. The remaining part of the receipt is therefore considered to be the additional information region.

2: Extracting the Store's Name
After dividing the receipt in the three parts, we assume to find the store's name in the header region. Moreover, as our analysis revealed, the header may contain entities like the store's address, its URL and the phone number, which serve as store identifiers and can be determined using regular expressions. Once store identifiers are extracted, they can be looked up in the database to find a matching store and thereby overcome **C1**. Every time a user corrects an extracted store in the app, we save the correction in our database and link it to corresponding store identifiers, which allows to deduce the correct merchant in future analysis.

3: Extracting Article Names and Corresponding Prices
As we learned by the receipts analysis, article names and their prices can be found in the body. Therefore, we identify all prices within the body region, using regular expressions. Next, we iterate over all lines in the body and perform a fulltext search as well as use Levenshteins distance [23] to find the content of this line in our database, which contains the outcome of all crowd-solved microtasks. We search in the table containing the corrected versions of entities but also in the table containing the raw, possibly erroneous OCR version of entities to compensate for spelling errors. Once we find a match, a classification (article, additional information) for this line can be made, based on the outcome of the associated classification microtask (cf. Figure 6a). Using these classifications, we can match one of the patterns we found in the receipts analysis (cf. Figure 2b), which allows to infer a match for an article and the corresponding price solving **C2**. Once a line is classified as an article, we can also receive its corrected name by the outcome of the respective article correction microtask (cf. Figure 6b) and its corresponding category through the result of the article categorization microtask (cf. Figure 6c) and thereby also provide a solution for **C3**.

Crowd Microtasks

Whenever a line cannot be classified properly, i.e. the entity cannot be found in our database, a microtask is generated to obtain missing information.

We decided to divide all problems or unknown entities of a receipt into microtasks, instead of creating larger tasks like correcting and classifying a whole receipt at once. This strategy is considered to lead to fewer mistakes, a greater stability in the face of interruption, and provides an easier experience for the user [5]. In the app, each microtask is shown isolated and consist of an image of the unknown receipt line and a short task description, following the suggestions given for crowd user interfaces in [30]. Users can decide to either solve own tasks, which means that these tasks correspond to problems that occurred when analyzing own receipts, or crowd tasks that were generated when analyzing receipts of other users. Every microtask can be skipped by the user, because the contained picture may be of low quality or ambiguous in some cases (e.g. if more than one line was extracted accidentally). If a microtask is skipped by at least six users, we discard the picture, similar to [37], as it cannot be used to infer proper information. However, the owner still can manually update the receipt and thereby provide a solution for the respective microtask. We decided to use three different task types, which we assume to be helpful to match articles and prices, to extract the total sum, and to categorize articles and the overall expense (cf. Figure 6):

Classification Microtasks
Based on the receipt analysis we identified three different types for entities: **article names**, **additional information** (e.g. article numbers or quantity indications) and **total sum**. Given the classification of a line (whether it contains an article, additional information or a total sum), we are able to match articles and prices and furthermore extract an overall sum for the purchase. Therefore, this task is the first task that is generated when an entity cannot be classified. The user is asked to identify the entity to be an article, additional information or total sum, as depicted in Figure 6a). In the usability test, participants had no problems classifying entities as articles or total sums but struggled to classify entities as additional information. As a reason, they stated that the wording seemed too generic for them. We therefore added more specific classification options that are internally mapped to the additional information option.

Article Correction Microtasks
This microtask is created once an unknown entity is identified as an article by the crowd. The user is asked to name a depicted article as shown in Figure 6b). The outcome of this microtask is used to correct OCR errors (spelling errors), identify and distinguish articles and provide a meaningful article name, since the articles are often abbreviated on the receipt. This task also makes it possible to store a relation between the raw text obtained by the OCR engine and the corrected version. This relation is very useful since it can compensate for typical OCR errors (e.g. confusing a zero with the letter "O" or spelling errors) and makes it possible to match abbreviated article names to their corrected versions.

Article Categorization Microtasks
Again, this microtask is generated after an entity was classified as an article, to obtain a meaningful category for it.

Figure 7: Different game elements used in the prototype. a) Points are awarded. b) An achievement is unlocked. c) Personal profile. d) Leaderboard.

The user can decide between ten different categories (cf. Figure 6c) we established in the budgeting apps reviewing process. The categorizations provided by this task are used not only for single articles but also to categorize a whole expense based on the categorizations of each purchased article, as this is required by users (cf. **R7**).

Solving Microtasks

As soon as a minimum amount of users (in our prototype we required at least six participants since [37] indicates that this amount is sufficient) participated in a microtask, a solution is generated for this task. Depending on the type of the task, the method to acquire this solution differs. A classification needs to reach at least least 60% of all votes. Once this is achieved, the raw OCR result gets stored in our database, together with the determined classification. This allows to recognize similar entities in the future, provide input for the entity extraction algorithm, and thus decrease the amount of errors. Once an entity is voted to be an article, both Article Correction and Article Categorization Microtasks are delegated to the crowd. The outcome of these tasks are determined by selecting the option with the most votes. Once an option is chosen, the corresponding article name gets corrected or respectively gets enriched by a category. The owner of the associated receipt gets notified about all changes and corrections that were performed by the crowd (cf. Figure 1e). The textual representations of these changes were significantly shortened after participants considered them as too long in the usability test.

Gamification Elements

To motivate users to solve microtasks and use our app, we integrated different gamification elements and thereby followed the design implications given in [33], stating that a budgeting app should use methods to engage users so that they keep tracking expenses over longer timescales. Gamification has been successfully used in many crowdsourcing systems to motivate and engage users [21, 37]. Furthermore, the use of gamification was able to improve crowd participation and the number of solved tasks in different domains [13]. We decided to integrate points, badges and a leaderboard together with a personal profile to provide attributes to measure fame or reputation, which is considered to motivate and retain users [9]. Points (cf. Figure 7a) can be collected by solving microtasks or receiving badges. A badge is awarded if the user solves an extraordinary amount of microtasks or regularly uses the app (e.g. by scanning receipts; an example is depicted in Figure 7b). However, we did not want to give points without any meaning, but instead decided to grant users advantages based on their score. Since solving microtasks is a service of one user for a whole crowd, we wanted to make sure that microtasks of users working a lot for the crowd are delegated with higher priority than those of users not solving many microtasks to other users. This means that problems that occur when analyzing a receipt of a user who solves many microtasks of the crowd are delegated and potentially solved faster than problems of users solving few microtasks for others. Additionally, we integrated a leaderboard (cf. Figure 7d) since competition is perceived as positive and motivating by many users [25] and is considered a solid retention scheme [9]. To further motivate users, we also showed their current rank and how many points are needed to get to the next rank directly on the home screen of our app. Unlocked badges, the amount of points and the username were summarized in a personal profile (cf. Figure 7c). Users could also see in their profile what they need to do to receive a certain badge and how their points, their rank on the leaderboard and the priorization of their problems are related to each other.

EVALUATION

By the evaluation of our approach, we tried to find evidence for the following hypotheses:

H1 Our prototype subjectively eases keeping track of expenses.

H2 The outcome of designated microtasks solved by a crowd can be used to reduce the error rate of captured receipts.

H3 The outcome of microtasks solved by a crowd can be used to reduce the error rate of new receipts that are unknown to the system.

H4 Gamification motivates users to solve microtasks.

H1 is motivated by findings from our online study suggesting that users are interested in keeping track of expenses but shy away from the huge effort involved. Since our system allows capturing receipts by photographing them, we assume that we ease the capture of expenses. **H2** builds on the assumption that our approach using the outcomes of crowd-solved microtasks lowers the error rate, compared to a baseline without any crowd-based data, when extracting relevant information from captured receipts. **H3** is based on the assumption that solving a certain microtask not only affects a single receipt, but helps to improve other receipts to be captured in the future as well. If we can show that our approach works, i.e. that a crowd solving microtasks indeed leads to a lower error rate when extracting entities from receipts, the question remains open how to motivate a crowd to solve microtasks without using monetary incentives. This leads to **H4** which is motivated by the related work [6, 13, 21, 36] showing that gamification has positive effects in crowdsourcing.

Method

We let participants use our prototype for three weeks and asked them to capture their expenses. At the beginning of the study, the app was locked and automatically generated a password. This password needed to be used to fill out an online questionnaire assessing buying behavior as well as interest in and experiences with tracking expenses. Only after finishing this questionnaire was the app unlocked.

To investigate **H4**, gamification elements were not visible in the first week, so as to acquire a baseline. We decided against a counterbalanced measures design (i.e. reversing the order of half the participants) since deactivating game elements later could have detrimental effects on participants [14]. After the first week, the app was automatically locked again and could be unlocked by finishing the mid-session online questionnaire. In this questionnaire we provided questions about the app usage, how tracking expenses was perceived by the participants, how motivated they were towards solving microtasks, and what could be done to increase their motivation. After this questionnaire was finished, the app was unlocked again and all gamification elements activated. Two weeks later, participants were asked to take part in the post-session questionnaire, which had similar questions as the mid-questionnaire for purposes of comparison. We asked questions about how tracking expenses was perceived and whether participants were motivated to solve microtasks. Furthermore, we investigated whether certain game elements were considered motivational or not, and provided questions related to how far our system eases keeping track of expenses. Both the mid-session as well as the post-session questionnaire, were used to investigate **H1** by posing questions about how the approach was perceived subjectively concerning ease of expense tracking. We used 5-point Likert scales to measure agreement with statements participants were shown to. During the study, we logged all receipts that were added by the participants together with all solved microtasks to investigate **H2** and **H3**. In order to calculate an error rate, we needed to provide a ground truth for comparison with results of our approach. Therefore, we went through all receipts and classified, categorized and corrected all lines of these receipts manually. This was done in two steps: One person provided a ground truth for each line of every receipt that was added by the participants and the other one checked for errors (e.g. spelling mistakes or other interpretation options).

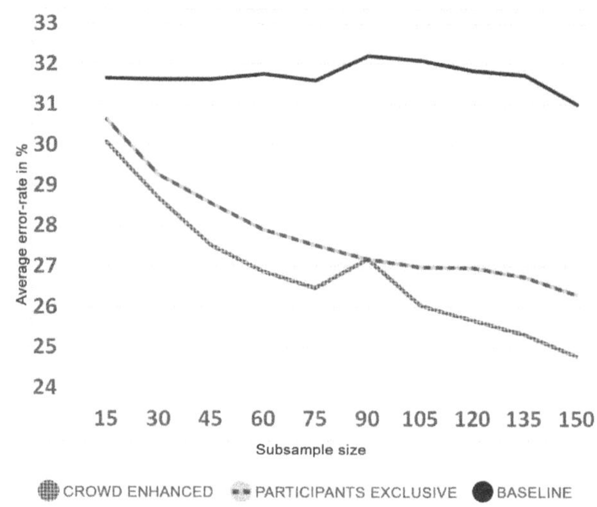

Figure 8: The error rate of new receipts for the CE algorithm (green) and the CEPE algorithm (orange) compared with the baseline algorithm (gray) for different subsample sizes.

Results

In three weeks, 191 receipts were added by 12 participants (5 female, 7 male). The age distribution was skewed young (21-30: 9, 31-40: 1, >40: 2). On average, participants added 15.92 receipts during the study (SD=14.35, Mdn=8). Before the study, only 3 subjects were keeping track of their expenses although 10 participants claimed to be interested in doing so. Three-fourths of the participants go shopping 3-4 times a week, one-eighth go shopping twice a week and one-eighth claimed to go shopping 5-6 times per week. Concerning their buying behavior, participants visit same stores (M=4.42, SD=0.52, Mdn=4) and tend to buy the same products (M=4.33, SD=0.49, Mdn=4).

Perception of the Prototype

Participants stated in the post-session questionnaire that the app eases tracking expenses (M=3.91, SD=1.04, Mdn=4) and that they would rather use our system than manually track their expenses (M=4, SD=1.18, Mdn=4). Moreover, they considered capturing expenses by taking pictures of receipts to be easy (M=4.45, SD=0.68, Mdn=5) and perceived the smiley as helpful for taking a good picture (M=4.27, SD=1.35, Mdn=5). These findings provide evidence supporting **H1**: the prototype eases keeping track of expenses. Moreover, crowd corrections were perceived positively (M=4.38, SD=0.74, Mdn=4.5) and considered meaningful (M=4.5, SD=0.54, Mdn=4.5). Participants also had the feeling that they used the app often (M=3.73, SD=1.35, Mdn=4).

Entity Extraction and Crowd Performance

During the evaluation, 15393 microtask solutions were generated by 12 participants, 1282.75 solutions per participant on average (SD=1053.54, Mdn=1101). To obtain an error ratio for each receipt, we analyzed every captured receipt again, using the outcome of all microtasks (classifications and corrections) solved by the crowd (crowd-enhanced algorithm, CE), and compared the result with an approach that solely relies on assumptions concluded by the receipt analysis without considering the crowd (baseline algorithm). Since it is impossible to deduce categories of articles for the baseline algorithm (that does not utilize any crowd data), we excluded the category in the error rate to obtain comparable results. Thus, the error rate is calculated by the ratio of the amount of wrong entities (wrong classification and/or wrong value of a line) to the overall amount of entities (right classification of a receipt line and correct value).

The baseline algorithm produced an error rate of 31.8% (SD=22.02, Mdn=32%) whereas the CE algorithm reached an error rate of only 10.36% (SD=14.68, Mdn=5). A paired t-test showed a significant effect between these error rates ($t(190)=12.47$, $p<0.01$) supporting evidence for **H2**: the outcome of designated microtasks solved by a crowd can be used to reduce the error rate of captured receipts.

To evaluate whether microtasks of one receipt can be used to enhance newly added receipts, we picked a random subsample with 15 to 150 receipts (10 iterations, increasing the subsample size by 15 each time) and used this as a training sample. We then iterated over all receipts that were not contained in this subsample (the test sample) and applied both the crowd-enhanced algorithm as well as the baseline algorithm. In the CE algorithm, we only considered solutions of microtasks that were related to unknown entities of receipts within the selected training sample to enhance receipts in the test sample. Since participants subjectively claimed to buy the same products, we additionally performed a crowd-enhanced participants exclusive (CEPE) algorithm in which we used receipts of one user for the test set and the receipts of all other users as training sample to avoid having receipts of the same user in the test set and in the training sample. To receive more reliable results, we repeated the subsample selection 50 times for each sample size. Figure 8 shows the error rates for each subsample for all three algorithms. The results support **H3**: the outcome of microtasks solved by a crowd can be used to reduce the error rate of new receipts that are unknown to the system, since both the CE and the CEPE algorithm outperform the baseline algorithm in all sample sizes. We conducted a repeated measurements ANOVA and found a significant effect between the algorithms ($p<0.05$). Pairwise comparisons using the Bonferroni method revealed that the difference between the CE algorithm and the baseline is significant ($p<0.01$), as well as the difference between the CEPE algorithm and the baseline ($p<0.01$). Moreover, the CE algorithm performed significantly better than the CEPE algorithm ($p<0.01$). The fact that the error rate is decreasing with increasing number of receipts further suggests that our approach improves over time (with increasing data retrieved by the outcome of microtasks).

Effects and Perception of Gamification

To obtain insight about how game elements were perceived subjectively by participants, we asked questions concerning fun and engagement in the mid- and post-session questionnaire and compared answers before and after game elements were active in the app. Additionally, all used game elements were specifically addressed in the post-session questionnaire. In the mid-session questionnaire, participants subjectively had the feeling that they solved many of their own (cf. Table 1a) and many crowd microtasks (cf. Table 1b). In the post-session questionnaire the feeling of solving many of their own tasks did not change signifantly. The same was true for the feeling of having solved many crowd tasks. However, participants tended to disagree with the statement that solving their own microtasks was fun or engaging (cf. Table 1c), as well as solving crowd tasks (cf. Table 1d) in the mid-session questionnaire (before gamification was active). In the post-questionnaire for their own tasks, this perception did not change significantly, but improved for crowd tasks significantly (cf. Table 1d), suggesting gamification had an effect. Concerning the game elements used, the highscore was considered most motivating (M=3.75, SD=1.56, Mdn=4.5), followed by points (M=3.67, SD=1.50, Mdn=4) and badges (M=3.42, SD=1.31, Mdn=3.5).

Question	Mid-Session	Post-Session	sig.
a: Solved many own tasks	M=3.58, SD=1.44, Mdn=4	M=3.67, SD=1.56, Mdn=4	p=0.723
b: Solved many crowd tasks	M=4.17, SD=0.93, Mdn=4.5	M=4.17, SD=1.34, Mdn=5	p=1.0
c: Solving own tasks was fun	M=2.58, SD=1.31, Mdn=2.5	M=4.17, SD=1.34, Mdn=5	p=0.131
d: Solving crowd tasks was fun	M=2.58, SD=1.31, Mdn=2.5	M=3.42, SD=1.51, Mdn=3.5	t(11)=2.49, p<0.05

Table 1: Questions and respective answers concerning fun and engagement in the mid- and post-session online questionnaire.

Week 1	Week 2	Week 3	sig.
M=238.25, SD=209.87, Mdn=173.5, Min=27, Max=676	M=569.75, SD=462.05, Mdn=522, Min=0, Max=1258	M=474.75, SD=426.67, Mdn=415.5, Min=0, Max=1169	p<0.05

Table 2: Overview of solved tasks per user/week.

Considering the amount of solved tasks per user in each week, we performed a repeated measurements ANOVA and found a significant effect between the three weeks (cf. Table 2). Pairwise comparisons using the Bonferroni method showed that the difference between weeks 1 and 2 is significant ($p<0.05$) as well as the difference between weeks 1 and 3 ($p<0.05$), whereby week 1 was the baseline phase without any gamification elements. These results show evidence for **H4**: the use of gamification additionally motivates users to solve microtasks. However, the differences between the number of solved microtasks for each participant in every week (cf. Figure 9) and the ordinary perception of gamification, indicate that although gamification overall lead to a higher number of solved microtasks, there seems to be differences in how gamification is perceived and considered motivating. Figure 9 indicates that some participants were not affected by gamification at all. It also shows that the number of solved tasks decreases

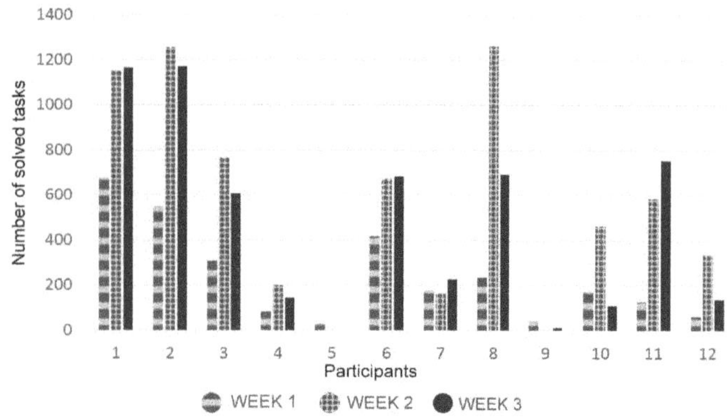

Figure 9: Solved microtasks for each participant/week.

for many participants in the last week again. Although this effect was not significant, it poses the question in how far the used game elements are able to motivate users in the long run.

Discussion

The study showed that participants are interested in keeping track of expenses and appreciate an automated approach to capture receipts. Our prototype was considered to ease the tracking process of expenses, supporting **H1**, and thereby mitigating the main reason for not keeping track of expenses: the high effort involved. The conducted analysis to measure the error ratio of receipts revealed that the crowd-based approach is able to significantly enhance the extraction of relevant information, as it produces roughly only a third as many errors as the baseline approach, showing evidence for **H2**.

The examination of how far the outcome of microtasks solved by the crowd can be used to reduce the error rate of new receipts that are unknown to the system, revealed evidence for **H3** since the error rate of both the CE and the CEPE algorithm performed better than the baseline approach for all training samples. However, the differences to the baseline are not very high, which most probably is explainable by the relatively low size of the crowd (12 participants) and the limited time of our study (3 weeks) leading to a relatively low amount of data. Further investigation is needed to find out in how far the error rate of new, unknown receipts keeps on decreasing with increasing crowd size and duration of the study. An explanation why newly added, system unknown receipts can be enhanced, lies in the increasing amount of collected data which raises the chance of finding receipt entities in the database. The reason why the CE approach performs better than the CEPE approach might be because of the fact that participants tend to buy the same articles and visit same stores (as they have reported), which increases the chance to have same articles in the test and in the training set. This, on the other hand, is beneficial for an approach as done by us, since a user that is solving her own tasks can thereby improve the algorithm to better recognize her products in the future. The number of solved microtasks was significantly influenced by the use of gamification: It increased dramatically in the second week after gamification was introduced and subjectively, solving crowd-tasks appeared to be more fun. However, we also found that the number of solved microtasks got lower in the last week of the investigation, but still was significantly higher than in week one. These results show supporting evidence for **H4**. Nonetheless, as we only investigated the prototype short-term, it is questionable whether this is only a novelty effect. Moreover, the high variance of solved tasks per user suggests that the gamification elements are not motivating for all users. An explanation for this can be found in [17] showing that competition, as was used in our system, can also be demotivating. Figure 9 also shows that two participants were not interested in solving microtasks, independent of whether gamification was active or not, thus necessitating further incentive mechanisms. Again, a long-term study with more participants seems suitable to explore the impacts of gamification on motivation further. A larger amount of participants also allows to have a control group without any game elements throughout the study. We decided against a control group in this work as we wanted to investigate whether the number of solved microtasks increases with gamification for each subject, which demands a within-subject design, especially considering our low participant count.

CONCLUSION

In this paper we investigated a crowd-based approach to enhance the outcome of optical character recognition in the domain of receipt capturing to keep track of expenses. We developed a prototype which made it possible to track expenses by taking photos of receipts and not only recognizes entities, but also enhances them with semantic information. At the same time the presented system does not rely on external crowdsourcing platforms (e.g. Amazon Mechanical Turk) but is able to run in a self-sustained manner without using monetary incentives. We based our approach on an online questionnaire to gain information about participants shopping behavior, their interest in keeping track of expenses and their attitude towards automatic receipt capturing, as well as on a receipt analysis to obtain insights about technical challenges in this field. In a three-week-long user study, we were able to show that our approach was appreciated by the users and eases keeping track of expenses subjectively. This mitigates the main reason for not keeping track of expenses: the high effort involved. We furthermore were able to show that our approach significantly reduces the error rate for captured receipts, and that the outcome of crowd-solved microtasks can be used to enhance recognition for new receipts as well. Moreover, we found evidence that gamification provided additional motivation to users to contribute more, solve a higher amount of microtasks and thereby enrich the database.

In future work we plan to investigate the long-term effects of our approach to test in how far the error-rate further decreases when accumulating more data and whether gamfication can be used to keep users engaged over a longer timespan. Therefore we aim to conduct an in-the-wild study and release the app in the market. Before, we plan to revise our gamification concept in order to motivate a broader range of users and investigate how we can change the design and concept of the microtasks to be more fun and engaging. One promising approach to accomplish this is described in [22], in which users are able to decide about the game elements they want to use, thus leading to a more tailored gamification design.

REFERENCES

1. Hend Al-Rouqi and Hend S. Al-Khalifa. 2014. Making Arabic PDF Books Accessible Using Gamification. *Proceedings of the 11th Web for All Conference. ACM, 2014.* (2014), 1–4. DOI: http://dx.doi.org/10.1145/2596695.2596712
2. Matthias Böhmer, Brent Hecht, Johannes Schöning, Antonio Krüger, and Gernot Bauer. 2011. Falling Asleep with Angry Birds, Facebook and Kindle: A Large Scale Study on Mobile Application Usage. *Proceedings of the 13th International Conference on Human Computer Interaction with Mobile Devices and Services. ACM, 2011.* (2011), 47. DOI: http://dx.doi.org/10.1145/2037373.2037383
3. Erin Brady, Meredith Morris, Yu Zhong, Samuel White, and Jeffrey Bigham. 2013. Visual Challenges in the Everyday Lives of Blind People. *Proceedings of the SIGCHI Conference on Human Factors in Computing Systems. ACM, 2013.* (2013), 2117–2126. DOI: http://dx.doi.org/10.1145/2470654.2481291
4. Justin Cheng and Michael S Bernstein. 2015. Flock : Hybrid Crowd-Machine Learning Classifiers. *CSCW '15 Proceedings of the 18th ACM Conference on Computer Supported Cooperative Work & Social Computing* (2015).
5. Justin Cheng, Jaime Teevan, Shamsi Iqbal, and Michael Bernstein. 2015. Break It Down: A Comparison of Macro- and Microtasks. *Proceedings of the 33rd Annual ACM Conference on Human Factors in Computing Systems. ACM, 2015.* (2015), 4061–4064.
6. Otto Chrons and Sami Sundell. 2011. Digitalkoot: Making Old Archives Accessible Using Crowdsourcing. *Human Computation. 2011.* (2011), 20–25. http://cdn.microtask.com/research/Digitalkoot-HCOMP2011-Chrons-Sundell.pdf
7. Gabriel de la Cruz, Bei Peng, Walter Lasecki, and Matthew Taylor. 2015. Towards Integrating Real-Time Crowd Advice with Reinforcement Learning. *Proceedings of the 20th International Conference on Intelligent User Interfaces Companion. ACM, 2015.* (2015), 17–20. DOI: http://dx.doi.org/10.1145/2732158.2732180
8. Sebastian Deterding and Dan Dixon. 2011. From Game Design Elements to Gamefulness: Defining "Gamification". *Proceedings of the 15th International Academic MindTrek Conference. ACM, 2011.* (2011), 9–15. DOI: http://dx.doi.org/10.1145/2181037.2181040
9. Anhai Doan, Raghu Ramakrishnan, and Alon Halevy. 2011. Crowdsourcing Systems on the World-Wide Web. *Communications of the ACM 54.4 (2011).* 54, 4 (2011), 86–96. DOI: http://dx.doi.org/10.1145/1924421.1924442
10. Carsten Eickhoff, Christopher G. Harris, Arjen P. de Vries, and Padmini Srinivasan. 2012. Quality Through Flow and Immersion: Gamifying Crowdsourced Relevance Assessments. *Proceedings of the 35th International ACM SIGIR Conference on Research and Development in Information Retrieval. ACM, 2012.* (2012), 871. DOI: http://dx.doi.org/10.1145/2348283.2348400
11. Daniel Esser, Klemens Muthmann, and Daniel Schuster. 2013. Information Extraction Efficiency of Business Documents Captured with Smartphones and Tablets. *Proceedings of the 2013 ACM Symposium on Document Engineering. ACM, 2013.* (2013), 111–114. DOI: http://dx.doi.org/10.1145/2494266.2494302
12. Paula Estrella and Pablo Paliza. 2014. OCR Correction of Documents Generated during Argentina's National Reorganization Process. *Proceedings of the First International Conference on Digital Access to Textual Cultural Heritage. ACM, 2014.* (2014), 119–123.
13. Oluwaseyi Feyisetan, Elena Simperl, Max Van Kleek, and Nigel Shadbolt. 2015. Improving Paid Microtasks through Gamification and Adaptive Furtherance Incentives. *Proceedings of the 24th International Conference on World Wide Web. International World Wide Web Conferences Steering Committee, 2015.* (2015), 333–343.
14. Juho Hamari and Harri Sarsa. 2014. Does Gamification Work ? A Literature Review of Empirical Studies on Gamification. *47th Hawaii International Conference on System Sciences. IEEE, 2014* (2014), 3025–3034. DOI: http://dx.doi.org/10.1109/HICSS.2014.377
15. Rose Holley. 2009a. How Good Can It Get? Analysing and Improving OCR Accuracy in Large Scale Historic Newspaper Digitisation Programs. *D-Lib Magazine 15.3/4 (2009)* (2009). DOI: http://dx.doi.org/10.1017/CBO9781107415324.004
16. Rose Holley. 2009b. Many Hands Make Light Work : Public Collaborative OCR Text Correction in Australian Historic Newspapers. *National Library of Australia Staff Papers (2009)* March (2009), 1–28.
17. Chin-Lung Hsu and Hsi-Peng Lu. 2004. Why do People Play On-Line Games? An Extended TAM with Social Influences and Flow Experience. *Information & Management 41.7 (2004).* 41, 7 (2004), 853–868. DOI: http://dx.doi.org/10.1016/j.im.2003.08.014
18. Shih-Wen Huang, Pei-Fen Tu, Wai-Tat Fu, and Mohammad Amanzadeh. 2013. Leveraging the Crowd to Improve Feature-Sentiment Analysis of User Reviews. *Proceedings of the 2013 International Conference on Intelligent User Interfaces. ACM, 2013.* March 1922 (2013), 3–14. DOI: http://dx.doi.org/DOI=10.1145/2449396.2449400
19. Bill Janssen, Eric Saund, Eric Bier, Patricia Wall, and Mary Ann Sprague. 2012. Receipts2Go: The Big World of Small Documents. *Proceedings of the 2012 ACM Symposium on Document Engineering. ACM, 2012.* (2012), 121—-124. http://dl.acm.org/citation.cfm?id=2361381

20. Frederic Kerber, Pascal Lessel, Maximilian Altmeyer, Annika Kaltenhauser, Christian Neurohr, and Antonio Krüger. 2014. Towards a Novel Digital Household Account Book. *CHI'14 Extended Abstracts on Human Factors in Computing Systems. ACM, 2014.* (2014), 1921–1926. DOI: http://dx.doi.org/10.1145/2559206.2581288

21. Pascal Lessel, Maximilian Altmeyer, and Antonio Krüger. 2015. Analysis of Recycling Capabilities of Individuals and Crowds to Encourage and Educate People to Separate Their Garbage Playfully. *Proceedings of the SIGCHI Conference on Human Factors in Computing Systems. ACM, 2015.* (2015), 1095–1104. DOI: http://dx.doi.org/10.1145/2702123.2702309

22. Pascal Lessel, Maximilian Altmeyer, Marc Müller, Christian Wolff, and Antonio Krüger. 2016. Don't Whip Me With Your Games - Investigating Bottom-Up Gamification. *Proceedings of the SIGCHI Conference on Human Factors in Computing Systems. ACM, 2016.* (2016), (to appear). DOI: http://dx.doi.org/10.1145/2858036.2858463

23. Vladimir I. Levenshtein. 1966. *Binary Codes Capable of Correcting Deletions, Insertions, and Reversals*. Vol. 10.

24. Ian Li, Anind Dey, and Jodi Forlizzi. 2010. A Stage-Based Model of Personal Informatics Systems. *Proceedings of the SIGCHI Conference on Human Factors in Computing Systems. ACM, 2010.* (2010), 557. DOI:http://dx.doi.org/10.1145/1753326.1753409

25. Elaine Massung, David Coyle, Kirsten F. Cater, Marc Jay, and Chris Preist. 2013. Using Crowdsourcing to Support Pro-Environmental Community Activism. *Proceedings of the SIGCHI Conference on Human Factors in Computing Systems. ACM, 2013.* (2013), 371–380. DOI: http://dx.doi.org/10.1145/2470654.2470708

26. Günter Mühlberger, Johannes Zelger, and David Sagmeister. 2014. User-Driven Correction of OCR Errors: Combining Crowdsourcing and Information Retrieval Technology. *Proceedings of the First International Conference on Digital Access to Textual Cultural Heritage. ACM, 2014.* 52, 1 (2014), 53–56.

27. M.P. Nevetha and A. Baskar. 2015. Applications of Text Detection and its Challenges : A Review. *Proceedings of the Third International Symposium on Women in Computing and Informatics. ACM, 2015.* (2015), 712–721.

28. Jakob Nielsen. 1992. Evaluating the Thinking-Aloud Technique for Use by Computer Scientists. (1992).

29. Jakob Nielsen. 2000. Why You Only Need to Test with 5 Users. (2000).

30. Bahareh Rahmanian and Joseph G. Davis. 2014. User Interface Design for Crowdsourcing Systems. *Proceedings of the 2014 International Working Conference on Advanced Visual Interfaces - AVI '14* (2014), 405–408. DOI: http://dx.doi.org/10.1145/2598153.2602248

31. Charalampos Saitis, Andrew Hankinson, and Ichiro Fujinaga. 2014. Correcting Large-Scale OMR Data with Crowdsourcing Categories and Subject Descriptors. *Proceedings of the 1st International Workshop on Digital Libraries for Musicology* (2014), 1–3.

32. Zhinian Shen and Yuri Tijerino. 2012. Ontology-Based Automatic Receipt Accounting System. *International Conferences on Web Intelligence and Intelligent Agent Technology (WI-IAT), 2012 IEEE/WIC/ACM. Vol. 3. IEEE, 2012* (2012), 236–239. DOI: http://dx.doi.org/10.1109/WI-IAT.2012.265

33. Stephen Snow and Vyas Dhaval. 2015. Fixing the Alignment: An Exploration of Budgeting Practices in the Home. *Proceedings of the 33rd Annual ACM Conference Extended Abstracts on Human Factors in Computing Systems. ACM, 2015.* (2015), 2271–2276.

34. James Surowiecki. 2005. *The Wisdom of Crowds*. Anchor.

35. Takumi Toyama, Daniel Sonntag, Andreas Dengel, Takahiro Matsuda, Masakazu Iwamura, and Koichi Kise. 2014. A Mixed Reality Head-Mounted Text Translation System Using Eye Gaze Input. *Proceedings of the 19th International Conference on Intelligent User Interfaces. ACM, 2014.* (2014), 329–334. DOI: http://dx.doi.org/10.1145/2557500.2557528

36. Luis von Ahn and Laura Dabbish. 2004. Labeling Images with a Computer Game. *Proceedings of the SIGCHI Conference on Human Factors in Computing Systems. ACM, 2004.* (2004), 319 – 326. DOI: http://dx.doi.org/10.1145/985692.985733

37. Luis Von Ahn, Benjamin Maurer, Colin McMillen, David Abraham, and Manuel Blum. 2008. reCAPTCHA: Human-Based Character Recognition via Web Security Measures. *Science 321.5895* 321, 5895 (2008), 1465–1468. DOI: http://dx.doi.org/10.1126/science.1160379

38. Erika Noll Webb. 2013. Gamification : When It Works, When It Doesnt. *Design, User Experience, and Usability. Health, Learning, Playing, Cultural, and Cross-Cultural User Experience. Springer Berlin Heidelberg, 2013* (2013), 608–614.

39. Mark Whooley, Bernd Ploderer, and Kathleen Gray. 2014. On the Integration of Self-Tracking Data Amongst Quantified Self Members. *Proceedings of the 28th International BCS Human Computer Interaction Conference on HCI 2014-Sand, Sea and Sky-Holiday HCI. BCS, 2014.* February (2014), 151–160. DOI: http://dx.doi.org/10.14236/ewic/hci2014.16

40. Guangyu Zhu, Timothy J. Bethea, and Vikas Krishna. 2007. Extracting Relevant Named Entities for Automated Expense Reimbursement. *Proceedings of the 13th ACM SIGKDD International Conference on Knowledge Discovery and Data Mining. ACM, 2007.* (2007), 1004–1012. DOI: http://dx.doi.org/10.1145/1281192.1281300

Exploring User Attitudes Towards Different Approaches to Command Recommendation in Feature-Rich Software

Michelle Wiebe
University of Manitoba
Winnipeg, Canada
wiebem14@myumanitoba.ca

Denise Y. Geiskkovitch
University of Manitoba
Winnipeg, Canada
denise.geiskkovitch@gmail.com

Andrea Bunt
University of Manitoba
Winnipeg, Canada
bunt@cs.umanitoba.ca

ABSTRACT
Feature-rich software applications offer users hundreds of commands, yet most people use only a very small fraction of the available command set. Command recommenders aim to increase awareness of an application's capabilities by generating personalized recommendations for new commands. A primary distinguishing characteristic of these recommenders concerns the manner in which they determine command relevance. *Social* approaches do so by analyzing community usage logs, whereas, *task-based* approaches mine web documentation for logical command clusters. Through a qualitative study with sixteen participants, in this work we explored user attitudes towards these different approaches and the supplemental information they enable.

Author Keywords
Software learnability; Recommender systems; Explanations

ACM Classification Keywords
H.5.m. Information interfaces and presentation (e.g., HCI): Miscellaneous.

INTRODUCTION
Feature-rich software, such as Photoshop and the GNU Image Manipulation Program (GIMP), can contain hundreds or even thousands of commands. Most users, however, take advantage of very little of an application's power. For example, prior work indicates that people tend to use only a very small percentage (e.g., 5%) of their software's command set (e.g., [9]).

One approach to helping users become more aware of their software's capabilities has been through command recommender systems. These systems monitor the commands that a user is using, and then return new and ideally relevant commands. In determining command relevance, such recommender systems have applied two primary strategies. *Social* command recommender systems apply collaborative filtering techniques on community usage logs (e.g.,[11,12]), whereas *task-based* recommenders mine web documents (describing how to perform particular tasks) for logical command groupings [8].

Prior work indicates that the manner in which an intelligent system communicates and justifies its advice can substantially impact user attitudes towards, and acceptance of the system (e.g., [3,5,7,13]). Prior work also suggests that the nature of such explanations will depend heavily on the system's underlying reasoning techniques [16]. This is particularly true when considering the fundamental differences between social and task-based approaches to command recommendation. For example, in explaining its recommendations, a social recommender could provide statistics on community and "peer" usage, whereas a task-based recommender could list related tasks.

This research seeks to understand how users might respond to social vs. task-based command recommenders from the perspective of the explanations that they facilitate. In particular, we conducted a qualitative laboratory study with sixteen participants to examine how users respond to social vs. task-based command recommendation approaches and how the manner in which the systems justify their recommendations impacts users' attitudes. Our findings point to potential individual differences with respect to preferences and attitudes towards the utility of social vs. task-based recommender systems, and highlight a number of important considerations moving forward.

RELATED WORK
Our coverage of related work focuses on the two areas central to this research: command recommender systems for feature-rich software and intelligent systems that augment their advice with supplementary explanations.

Command Recommenders
Prior work on command recommender systems for feature-rich software has primarily focused on the algorithmic components of providing tailored recommendations. As described above, one primary approach to recommending new commands has been to leverage usage logs collected from an application's community of users [10–12]. An example is CommunityCommands [10,12], which uses collaborative filtering techniques to determine relationships between commands. A second approach to command recommendation has been to use command clusters mined

IUI'16, March 07 - 10, 2016, Sonoma, CA, USA

ACM 978-1-4503-4137-0/16/03$15.00
DOI: http://dx.doi.org/10.1145/2856767.2856814

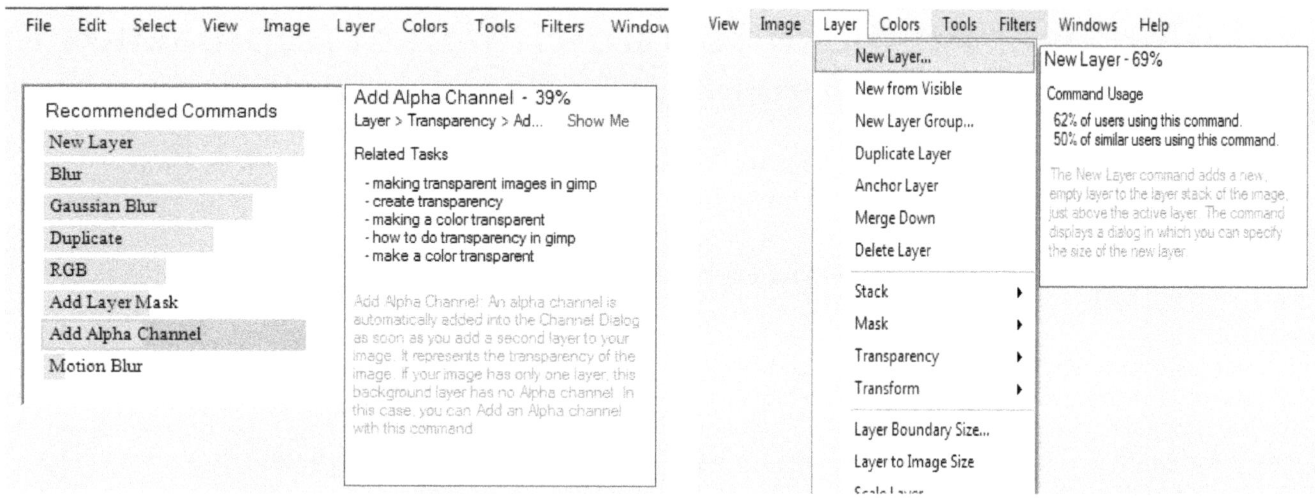

Figure 1: The supplementary information for each recommender system type: Task-Based (Left) and Social (Right). The left shows what the recommendations looked like when displayed in a palette. The right is an example of integrated recommendations.

from web documentation. For example, the QFRecs system [8] leverages Query-Feature Graphs [4] (command-to-task mappings mined from web documentation) as an automatically generated plan library. Using this plan library the system then estimates the user's most likely set of current tasks based on their recent command use. Based on these task estimates, the system recommends additional commands that have been associated with those tasks in online documentation (see [8] for a more detailed description).

In evaluating the above approaches, researchers have focused on assessing the relevance of the system's recommendations to a user's workflow (e.g., [8,12]), as well as the impact of the recommendations on task performance (e.g., [8]) and recommendation uptake (e.g., [10]). Little attention, however, has been provided to the manner in which the systems communicate their recommendations to their users, which is the focus of our work.

Explanations in Intelligent Systems

There is a rich history of exploring why and how intelligent systems should explain their behavior to their users (e.g., [1–3,5,6,13,14]). While a great deal of this work supports the inclusion of such insight [5,13], prior work also suggests that the content of the explanations (or supplemental information) can impact user perceptions of the utility of those explanations and of the system's behavior (e.g., [2,3,6,14]). We extend this work by comparing two types of explanation interfaces for command recommender systems.

THE RECOMMENDER SYSTEMS AND THEIR EXPLANATION INTERFACES

In this section, we describe two explanation interfaces that we implemented and studied as part of this work: one for a social recommender based on the CommunityCommands approach [12], and one for a task-based recommender based on the QFRecs system [8]. In both cases, the systems' explanations provide insight into why the commands have been recommended as opposed to explaining the technical details of the underlying algorithms. We created both recommender systems in a mock GIMP interface.

Guided by previous work on explaining collaborative-filtering based movie recommendations [6], our *social* recommender supplements each command recommendation with the percentage of all users who have used the command, along with the percentage of similar users who have used it (see Fig. 1, Right).

The task-based recommender system, on the other hand, displays a list of tasks associated with each command (see Fig. 1, Left). This list of tasks is taken from the recommender system's underlying Query-Feature Graph, which maps each command in the interface to a set of high-level descriptions of potential tasks involving that command [4].

Both explanation interfaces include the system's confidence in its recommendation (displayed next to the command name) and a tool-tip-like description of the command.

We implemented two presentations techniques for each recommender type, which differ according to *where* the recommendations are located in the interface. With the *integrated* technique, recommendations are presented within the menus (see Fig. 1 Right), whereas with the *palette* technique, recommendations are removed from the menus, found instead in a separate interface component (see Fig. 1 Left). We implemented these two techniques in the event that user response towards the different forms of supplemental information depends on where the recommendations were located in the interface.

STUDY

The goal of our qualitative study was to solicit user attitudes and opinions towards the social and task-based approaches to command recommendation and the two forms of supplemental information that they afford (i.e., information on community usage vs. information on related tasks).

Design

Our primary factor of interest was *system type (social vs. task-based)*, which was a within-subjects factor in our study (i.e., all participants experienced both systems). We also included *recommendation location (integrated vs. palette)* as a between-subjects factor.

Participants

Sixteen participants (7 male, 9 female) took part in the study. Participants were 18-51 years old (mean age 29.5) and were recruited from the university community through the use of public bulletins. Three participants were GIMP novices, 8 reported using the software at least once per year, 4 used it at least once per month and 1 used it at least once per week Participants were provided with a $15 honorarium.

Tasks and Procedure

While our focus was on qualitative data (i.e., attitudes towards the recommender systems and their supplemental information), we wanted participants to be able to experience working with the recommender systems. To do so, we created four isomorphic tasks modeled after online tutorials for the GIMP software. Each task involved a list of steps for the participant to complete. The names of commands were removed from the steps, and only information about what the participant needed to accomplish in that step was included (e.g., "remove all color from image" for the desaturate command).

Using fully implemented versions of the recommender systems as guides, we tailored the actual recommendations generated in the study to ensure that both recommender systems were equally helpful to the tasks at hand. Specifically, we ensured that the needed command was presented in the recommended set of commands for each step. For the social recommender system's, we used GIMP usage data collected through the Ingimp project as the community data source [15]. For the task-based recommender system, we used the Query-Feature Graph as described in [8].

The remainder of the procedure for the study was as follows: Participants completed two tasks, with a maximum of 15 minutes each, with each recommender system (social or task-based). Upon finishing these two tasks, they completed a short system-specific questionnaire. After interacting with both systems, they completed an additional comparative questionnaire, and we conducted a semi-structured exit interview. The order of the recommender systems was counterbalanced, while task order was randomized. The entire study session lasted 60-90 minutes.

Results

Our analysis did not find any interactions between participants' attitudes towards the recommender systems and the location of the recommendations (integrated vs. palette). Thus our description of results considers only recommender system type. We begin by presenting the questionnaire data, and follow this with insight from the interviews as to why participants preferred one system over another.

Questionnaire Item	Task-Based	Social
How satisfied are you with the recommendation application?	5 (1.2)	5.1 (1.3)
This recommendation application would motivate you to learn new commands in the future.	5.19 (0.96)	5 (2.4)
How trustworthy were the recommendations?	4.86 (1.85)	4.81 (1.10)

Table 1: Mean (stdev) responses to questionnaire items administered after each system (1 == low, 7 == high).

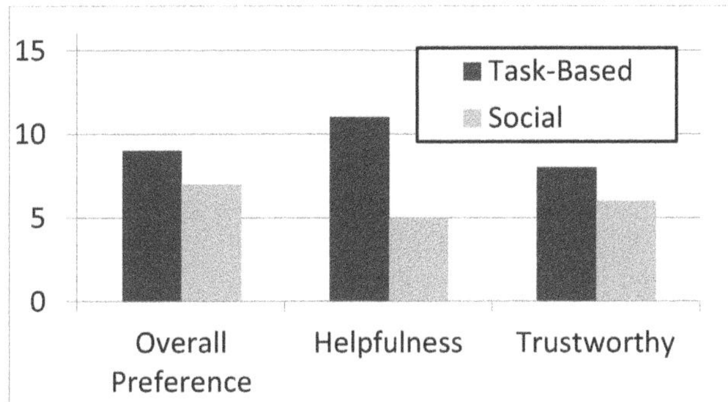

Figure 2: Users' preference overall and in terms of the systems' helpfulness and trustworthiness.

Ratings and Overall Preference Data

The questionnaires administered after each condition revealed limited impact of system type on user attitude toward each system directly after use (see Table 1). As would be expected, an RM ANOVA confirmed that there was no significant impact of system type on participants' mean responses towards their satisfaction with the system, the degree to which they would be motivated to learn new commands, and the trustworthiness of the recommender system ($p >= 0.5$ in all cases). We did, however, see a great deal of variability in participants' responses, which we elaborate on in the next section.

Responses on a comparative questionnaire revealed that users' overall preference between the two systems was almost evenly divided (see Figure 2). There was a larger difference, on the other hand, in terms of which system participants found more helpful (see "Helpfulness" in Fig. 2). Along this dimension, 11 participants favored the task-based system and 5 participants favored the social recommender.

Interviews

In the interviews, we asked participants to explain why they preferred one recommender system over another. Their responses point to a number of key issues for these types of command recommendations and their supplemental information.

Valuing Context of Use: Given the focus on new commands, a number of participants appreciated the additional context that the task-based recommender provides. The following two quotes illustrate this type of feedback:

I found them both helpful, but the list of related tasks gave me more context for what other sorts of things this might do, or might be related to. (P8)

I prefer when the recommendations give me some idea about which task each command can be used rather than what other people use. (P3)

The quotes above suggest that when recommending new commands, an indication of how the command might be relevant to the user's work is appreciated.

Identifying Rare Commands: While not a commonly expressed sentiment, one participant felt that a task-based recommender system had the potential to recommend more nuanced commands that might not be as popular:

The task specific ones were better for lesser known commands that a beginner user may not know about. (P10)

Mixed Views on Command Popularity: As for the social recommender, participants expressed mixed views on the value of "popularity" based recommendations. A couple of participants felt that knowing the popularity of a command could help them decide whether or not it was worth learning:

If a lot of people are using a particular tool, it means that it must be useful, but if it's something that maybe not a lot of people are using, then maybe it's not that useful. (P12)

Whereas many others felt skeptical of the "wisdom on the masses":

I felt that the percentages of users just meant that they might be making the same mistakes that I might be making. So just because everybody jumps off a cliff, doesn't mean it's the right thing to do. (P2)

I want to do it the fastest way. Just because someone recommended it, doesn't mean that it's better. (P5)

It did say the percentage of people use this, but then I think 'what if they could be wrong' (P9)

The above quotes suggest that with social recommender systems, some users are skeptical as to whether others are doing things the "right" or most efficient ways.

Desire for Additional Information: A few participants wanted more insight into where the usage statistics were coming from. Without this information, they lacked confidence that the "similar users" (see Fig.1, Right) had been properly identified:

I trust my coworkers, I know what they're capable of. I don't necessarily trust other people. (P5)

Some other participants felt that sheer usage statistics alone were not sufficient without knowing whether or not the command has been helpful:

Success rate! So if this command was recommended to someone else, and they were successful at their task, that would be interesting to see. Because it's not just recommendation, it's like 'oh yeah they did it, and this is how it turned out.' So it was successful or it wasn't to what extent. (P2)

While doubts concerning data source were most commonly expressed in regards to the social recommender, one participant wanted to be reassured that both data sources had been carefully selected:

I think if I knew exactly where these recommendations came from, for example, the task specific coming straight from a useful website, and the social input coming from experienced users, then I think I'd be more likely to consider it reliable. (P11)

DISCUSSION AND FUTURE WORK

Our results indicate that the type of command recommender system that users' value might to be highly dependent on the individual. Our results also suggest a number of ways that these systems and their supplemental information can potentially be improved in the future. We note, however, that our findings are based on a relatively small sample, which consisted primarily of novice or intermediate GIMP users. Participants in our study also interacted with the recommenders in a task-focused manner, as opposed to, for example, a more exploratory learning context. Future evaluations should explore the generalizability of our findings to larger sample sizes, as well the impact of software expertise and context of use on attitudes and preferences.

Given our participants' split opinions, one interesting avenue for future work would be to explore a hybrid approach for either the recommender itself or for the supplementary information it provides. For example, if both approaches were implemented simultaneously, a user could potentially filter or inspect the recommendations according to the data source that they find most reliable or motivating.

Our results also suggest an opportunity to allow users to tune the systems by letting them refine and restrict the data sources that each algorithm uses. For the social approach, however, this could potentially introduce privacy concerns, as a tightly restricted peer group could also permit detailed monitoring of command usages and workflows.

Finally, in moving beyond qualitative impressions, future field evaluations should examine the impact of the different approaches on recommendation uptake. For example, it could be that the social vs. task-based recommender systems differ in their abilities to ultimately encourage users to experiment with new commands.

CONCLUSIONS

In this paper we explored two different approaches to command recommendation for feature-rich software (social vs. task-based) from the perspective how they explain their recommendations. The results of our qualitative study revealed strong individual differences in users' attitudes towards the systems and their command recommendations. Our results also point to a number of promising avenues for future investigation, including exploring hybrid approaches to command recommendation and creating interfaces that allow users to tailor the systems' data sources.

ACKNOWLEDGMENTS

This work was supported by the National Sciences and Engineering Research Council (NSERC).

REFERENCES

1. Andrea Bunt, Matthew Lount, and Catherine Lauzon. 2012. Are explanations always important? A study of deployed, low-cost intelligent interactive systems. *Proceedings of the ACM Conference on Intelligent User Interfaces*, 169–178. http://doi.org/10.1145/2166966.2166996
2. Andrea Bunt, Joanna Mcgrenere, and Cristina Conati. 2007. Understanding the utility of rationale in a mixed-initiative system for GUI customization. *Proceedings of the International Conference on User Modeling*, 147–156. http://doi.org/10.1007/978-3-540-73078-1_18
3. Kate Ehrlich, Susanna E. Kirk, John Patterson, Jamie C. Rasmussen, Steven I. Ross, and Daniel M. Gruen. 2011. Taking advice from intelligent agents: The double-edged sword of explanations. *Proceedings of the ACM Conference on Intelligent User Interfaces*, 227–134. http://doi.org/10.1145/1943403.1943424
4. Adam Fourney, Richard Mann, and Michael Terry. 2011. Query-feature graphs: Bridging user vocabulary and system functionality. *Proceedings of the ACM Symposium on User Interface Software and Technology*, 207–216. http://doi.org/10.1145/2047196.2047224
5. Shirley Gregor and Izak Benbasat. 1999. Explanations from intelligent systems: theoretical foundations and implications for practice. *MIS Quarterly* 23, 4: 497–530. http://doi.org/10.2307/249487
6. Jonathan L Herlocker, Joseph a Konstan, and John Riedl. 2000. Explaining collaborative filtering recommendations. *Proceedings of the ACM Conference on Computer Supported Cooperative Work*, 241–250. http://doi.org/10.1145/358916.358995
7. Anthony Jameson. 2009. Understanding and dealing with usability side effects of intelligent processing. *AI Magazine* 30, 4: 23–40.
8. Adnan Alam Khan, Volodymyr Dziubak, and Andrea Bunt. 2015. Exploring personalized command recommendations based on information found in Web documentation. *Proceedings of the ACM Conference on Intelligent User Interfaces*, 225–235. http://doi.org/10.1145/2678025.2701387
9. Benjamin Lafreniere, John S Whissell, Charles L. A. Clarke, and Michael Terry. 2010. Characterizing large-scale use of a direct manipulation application in the wild. *Proceedings of Graphics Interface*, 11–18.
10. Wei Li, Justin Matejka, Tovi Grossman, Joseph A. Konstan, and George Fitzmaurice. 2011. Design and evaluation of a command recommendation system for software applications. *ACM Transactions on Computer-Human Interaction* 18, 2: 1–35. http://doi.org/10.1145/1970378.1970380
11. Frank Linton and Hans-Peter Schaefer. 2000. Recommender systems for learning: Building user and expert models through long-term observation of application use. *User Modelling and User-Adaptive Interaction* 10, 2-3: 181–208. http://doi.org/10.1023/A:1026521931194
12. Justin Matejka, Wei Li, Tovi Grossman, and George Fitzmaurice. 2009. CommunityCommands : Command recommendations for software applications. *Proceedings of the ACM Symposium on User Interface Software and Technology*, 193–202. http://doi.org/10.1145/1622176.1622214
13. Pearl Pu and Li Chen. 2006. Trust building with explanation interfaces. *Proceedings of the ACM Conference on Intelligent User Interfaces*, 93–100. http://doi.org/10.1145/1111449.1111475
14. Simone Stumpf, Vidya Rajaram, Lida Li, Margaret Burnett, Tomash Dietterich, Erin Sullivan, Russell Drummond, and Jonathan Herlocker. 2007. Toward harnessing user feedback for machine learning. *Proceedings of the ACM Conference on Intelligent User Interfaces*: 82–91. http://doi.org/10.1145/1216295.1216316
15. Michael Terry, Matthew Kay, Brad Van Vugt, Brandon Slack, and Terry Park. 2008. Ingimp: introducing instrumentation to an end-user open source application. *Proceedings of the ACM Conference on Human Factors in Computing Systems*, 607–616. http://doi.org/10.1145/1357054.1357152
16. Nava Tintarev and Judith Masthoff. 2011. Designing and evaluating explanations for recommender systems. In *Recommender Systems Handbook*. 479–510. http://doi.org/10.1007/978-0-387-85820-3

Task Load Estimation and Mediation Using Psychophysiological Measures

Rahul Rajan
ECE, Carnegie Mellon University
Pittsburgh, PA, USA
rahulraj@cmu.edu

Ted Selker
CITRIS, University of California, Berkeley
Berkeley, CA, USA
ted.selker@gmail.com

Ian Lane
LTI, Carnegie Mellon University
Pittsburgh, PA, USA
lane@cmu.edu

ABSTRACT

Human performance falls off predictably with excessive task difficulty. This paper reports on a search for a task load estimation metric. Of the five physiological signals analyzed from a multitasking study, only pupil dilation measures correlated well with real-time task load. The paper introduces a novel task load estimation model based on pupil dilation measures. We demonstrate its effectiveness in a multitasking driving scenario. Autonomous mediation of notifications using this model significantly improved user task performance compared to no mediation. The model showed promise even when used outside in a car. Results were achieved using low-cost cameras and open-source measurement tools lending to its potential to be used broadly.

ACM Classification Keywords

H.5.m. Information Interfaces and Presentation (e.g. HCI): Miscellaneous

Author Keywords

Cognitive Load; Divided Attention; Psychophysiological Measures; Pupil Dilation; Considerate Systems

INTRODUCTION

People use ubiquitous computing platforms like the mobile phone to access information and interact with others, even when they are socially or physically engaged. People, however, have finite mental resources and can only process a limited amount of information without degradation of task performance. Despite this being the case, there is an increasing trend towards computers being proactive and providing information to the user without being prompted. For cognitively challenging activities like driving, divided attention can have dire consequences. Thus, there is a need for systems to gauge the load on this mental resource in order to predict or preempt degradation in task performance, while interacting with a user.

http://dx.doi.org/10.1145/2856767.2856769

While progress has been made towards gauging this load, we are still a long way off from being able to measure it at a real-time fine-grained level. In the future, such capabilities might avert human mistakes in situations of divided attention. For instance, voice interaction might become the most efficient way for a user to interact with a system, when their manual and visual resources are already occupied. By using a rapid and fine-grained cognitive load measure, dialog or proactive agents would be able to track the ebbs and flows of the load being experienced by the user in real-time. This would allow it to preempt disfluencies and other irregularities in speech, as well as to time its responses and other actions, so as to prevent overloading the user. In the driving scenario, it has been shown that passengers adapt their conversation to the driving situation, which leaves the driver with more resources to perform the driving task when it gets difficult [5, 9]. Interactive agents should aim to emulate such considerate behaviors.

Cognitive load can be gauged by directly modelling the driver via psychophysiological measures, or by modelling driving context and its effect on the driver, or by jointly modelling both [18]. Compared to modelling the external driving context, less progress has been made in modelling the driver's internal state in order to identify when to interrupt them. One advantage of the internal state approach is the potential for these models to generalize to other domains. Modelling external context requires specific sensors and techniques to be considered for each domain separately. Furthermore, a physiological-based approach can be tuned for each user individually, as different users might experience external contexts differently. Recent advances in wearable technologies suggest that monitoring at least a few physiological signals in everyday life might become a feasible option.

In this paper, we evaluate several signals that might be used as part of a psychophysiological approach to gauging cognitive load. We wanted to capture the temporal aspects of divided attention — the transitions in load when addressing and recovering from interruptions, for example. At the same time, we wanted to facilitate data collection that was repeatable, with real-time performance measures that were responsive to task load. To meet these goals, we designed a multitasking scenario with a driving-like primary task, and an intermittent secondary task of attending and responding to notifications. As part of our initial explorations, we present results from two separate user studies. In the first set of results, pupil dilation measures were used to build classification models that can detect which tasks the user is engaged in. We show how the performance of the model varies with changes in the modality and timing of notifications. We do this for each user, as well as across all users. To evaluate the feasibility of using such a model built on pupil dilation measures we conducted a second study. Here the classification model was used to autonomously mediate notifications to users in real-time. We demonstrate its effectiveness by analyzing user task performance with and without mediation. In the following sections, we provide background and discuss related work, before describing the two studies and their results in detail.

RELATED WORK

In cognitive psychology, there is a general consensus that people have limited and measurable cognitive capacities for performing mental tasks [26]. Furthermore, engaging in one mental task interferes with the ability to engage in other tasks, and can result in reduced performance on some or all of the tasks as a consequence [17]. To characterize the demand on these limited resources, psychologists have employed notions like cognitive load and mental workload, which gains definition through the experimental methods that are used to measure it [19].

Measuring Cognitive Load

Cognitive load can be assessed using data gathered from three empirical methods: subjective data using rating scales, performance data using primary and secondary task techniques, and psychophysiological data from sensors [29]. Self-ratings, being post-hoc and subjective in nature, tend to be inaccurate and impractical to use when automated and immediate assessment is required. Secondary task techniques are based on the assumption that performance on a secondary measure reflects the level of cognitive load imposed by a primary task. A secondary task can be as simple as detecting a visual or auditory signal, and can be measured in terms of reaction time, accuracy, and error rate. However, in contexts where the secondary task interferes with the primary task, physiological proxies that can measure gross reaction to task load are needed to assess cognitive load.

Psychophysiological Measures

Psychophysiological techniques are based on the assumption that changes in cognitive functioning cause physiological changes. An increase in cortical activity causes a brief, small autonomic nervous response, which is reflected in signals such as heart rate (HR) and heart rate variability (HRV) [11,27,36], electroencephalogram (EEG) [30, 36], electrocardiogram (ECG) [30], electrodermal activity (EDA) [14, 31], respiration [27], and heat flux [12], eye movements and blink interval [3, 14, 15, 36] and pupillary dilations. Our dataset includes most of these signals as well as additional signals that have been shown to be sensitive to affect like pulse transit time (PTT), facial electromyography (EMG) and skin temperature [22, 28].

In particular, brain activity as measured through event-related potentials using EEG, or as inferred from pupillary responses have received more attention recently because of their high sensitivity and low latency [1, 19, 24]. There has been very little work that correlates these measures with the other physiological measures, or demonstrates how to effectively align them. Furthermore, to the best of our knowledge this is the only work that has focused on tracking cognitive load that is rapidly and randomly changing, since we are interested in teasing out the dynamic nature of instantaneous cognitive load. Lastly, prior work has typically focused on cognitive load arising in single-task scenarios like document editing [15], and traffic control management [31]. In contrast, we employ an increasingly common multitasking scenario, aspects of which we briefly review below.

Multitasking Scenarios

In multitasking scenarios, the distribution of cognitive resources when engaged in two or more tasks is not very well understood. This makes it difficult to assess and predict workload that will be experienced by the user. Theories have been proposed to model how multiple tasks might compete for the same information processing resources [2, 35]. One widely used approach that has been shown to fit data from multitask studies is Wickens' multiple resource theory. This attempts to characterize the potential interference between multiple tasks in terms of dimensions of stages (perceptual and cognitive vs. spatial), sensory modalities (visual vs. auditory), codes (visual vs. spatial), and visual channels (focal vs. ambient) [35]. Performance will deteriorate when demand for one or more tasks along a particular dimension exceeds capacity.

In the case of driving and notification comprehension, both tasks compete for resources along the stages dimension. We would expect performance to deteriorate when there is an increased demand for the shared perceptual resources, i.e. when driving is hard and/or when the notification is difficult to comprehend. If the notification is visual, both tasks might also compete along the modality and visual channel dimensions. We would expect performance deterioration to be greater for visual notifications.

Driving and Language

Listening and responding to another person while driving a car has been widely studied, and has been shown to effect driving performance, particularly with remote conversants [21]. Passengers sitting next to a driver are able to adapt their conversation to the traffic situation, allowing the driver to focus on driving when it becomes difficult [5, 9]. These findings have motivated research towards building dialog systems that are situation-aware and interrupt themselves when required [20]. As mentioned earlier, the focus in most of this work is on monitoring the driving environment, and less on determining the cognitive load of the driver. Recently, there has been an interest in studying the effect that complex linguistic processing can have on driving using physiological measures of pupil dilation and skin conductance [8].

Mediation

Successful dual-task scenarios depend on the availability and requirements of cognitive resources for the secondary task given resource consumption by the primary task [34]. This presents opportunities to increase people's ability to successfully handle interruptions, and prevent expensive errors. McFarlane's seminal work proposed four methods for coordinating interruptions, including immediate, negotiated, mediated and scheduled [25]. Mediation has been widely studied in the desktop computing domain [13, 16], but has not been adequately explored in post-desktop, mobile situations. We believe that ours is also the first study to present results on autonomous mediation using a psychophysiological measure.

STUDY 1: DYNAMIC TASK LOAD ESTIMATION

Our goals in this study were to:

- Collect a dataset[1] consisting of psychophysiological signals from users experiencing fluctuating task loads in a multitasking scenario
- Experiment with building models based on psychophysiological signals that can rapidly track cognitive load in a multitasking scenario
- Study the impact that the timing and modality of an intermittent secondary notification task has on the load experienced by the user

The appeal of testing in real world scenarios is transfer of results. But such experiments suffer from lack of repeatability and reproducibility because of the large number of variables involved. Repeating a route introduces landmarks that become familiar and changes performance. Events of interest happen unpredictably and infrequently. Establishing ground truth is also non-trivial and sometimes requires manual effort like scoring or annotating video recordings, etc. Experiments in the lab can circumvent a lot of these shortcomings by abstracting out the problem. A common practice in psychophysiology, however, is to have a control condition, followed by a test condition, with a rest period in between. As a consequence, the temporal aspects of psychophysiological signals as they fluctuate are lost.

In this study, we wanted the advantage of the lab setting, while still grappling with some of the complexity of real world data. In particular, we wanted to capture the temporal aspects of fluctuating psychophysiological signals while a participant is intermittently multitasking. For the primary task, we chose to use the established ConTRe (Continuous Tracking and Reaction) task [23], which provides a highly controlled yet unpredictable task load for the participant. This allows for consistent and replicable analysis. For the secondary task, the user was intermittently presented with notification prompts that they had to attend and respond to. The timing (mediated vs. non-mediated) and modality (audio vs. visual) of the notifications were treated as independent variables to investigate their impact on the load experienced by the user.

The study was setup so that the driving task would randomly switch between low and high workloads. This was done to simulate a typical driving scenario where drivers episodically experience high workload when they are entering/exiting highways, changing lanes, following navigation instructions, etc.

[1] will be hosted at http://rahulrajan.com/physio_data

Figure 1. Screenshot of the ConTRe Task that displays the yellow reference cylinder with the traffic light on top, and the blue tracking cylinder.

In the mediated condition, the operator would send notifications only during the low driving workload condition, in contrast to their random delivery in the non-mediated condition. With regards to modality, audio notifications were delivered via speakers, and visual notifications through a heads-up display (HUD). The audio notifications were created using Apple's text-to-speech engine on OS X Yosemite (Speaking voice: Alex; Speaking rate: Normal). The HUD used was a Google Glass, which projects the screen at a working distance of 3.5 m, approximately 35° elevated from the primary position of the eye.

Design

The study was designed as a 2 (Audio/Visual *modes*) X 2 (Mediated/Non-mediated *conditions*) repeated-measures within-subjects study. To control for possible effects of order, the study was double counterbalanced for the *mode* and *condition* factors. Additionally, there was a baseline for both the low and high driving workload conditions.

Participants

20 people (10 male, 10 female) participated in our study, recruited through a call sent out to students selected randomly from a graduate school population. The mean age of the participants was 26.4 years, with a standard deviation of 2.7 years. Participants were rewarded with $40 gift cards for completing the study.

Tasks

We elaborate below on the design of the primary ConTRe task and the secondary notification task that make up the multitasking scenario.

Primary Task (T1): ConTRe

The ConTRe task comes as an add-on for OpenDS, an open-source driving simulator [23]. It is an abstracted and simplified task that is comprised of actions required for normal driving, i.e. operating the brake and acceleration pedals, as well as using the steering wheel. This focuses the user's task and simplifies the recording of tracking behavior. Fine-grained measures of performance on the primary task relative to the secondary task requests can be obtained, which is necessary for our investigation.

The vehicle in Figure 1 moves with a constant speed on a unidirectional straight road consisting of two lanes. The simulator shows two cylinders at a constant distance in front of the vehicle: a yellow reference cylinder, and a blue tracking cylinder. The yellow reference cylinder moves autonomously and unpredictably. The lateral position of the blue tracking cylinder is controlled by the user through the use of the steering wheel. The cylinder moves left or right depending on the direction and angular velocity of the steering wheel, i.e the steering wheel controls the cylinder's lateral acceleration. The user's goal is to track the yellow reference cylinder, by overlapping it with the steering wheel-controlled blue cylinder, as closely as possible. Effectively, this corresponds to a task where the user has to follow a curvy road. For the low and high task load conditions, the lateral speed of the reference cylinder was set to values that were empirically determined to create low and high workloads for the user, respectively.

There is a traffic light with two colors placed on top of the yellow reference cylinder. The top light turns on red, whereas the bottom one turns on green. At any time, neither of the lights or only one is turned on. The red light requires that the user respond by depressing the brake pedal, while the green light corresponds to the accelerator pedal. This operates independently of the steering function. As soon as the user reacts to the light by depressing the correct pedal, the light turns off.

Secondary Task (T2): Notifications

The notification task was based on cognitive tests frequently used to measure working memory capacity [6]. Working memory has been purported to be involved in a wide range of complex cognitive behaviors, such as comprehension, reasoning, and problem solving as it is thought to reflect primarily domain-general, executive attention demands of the task [10]. In this work we do not aim to measure working memory per se, but instead want to measure the effect of engaging in a complex cognitive secondary task. Thus, we modify the cognitive tests for our purposes as described below.

In each condition, subjects were presented with a series of twenty items, which included ten equations and ten sentences taken from widely used complex span tasks [6] (see Table 1). The math equations and sentences are representative of the symbolic and verbal types of notifications, respectively, that users typically receive. Using standardized stimuli allows for consistency and replicability. Both types of notifications were randomly interspersed, so as to prevent the driver from getting into a rhythm of expecting either one. After the driver had read or listened to each item, they verbally indicated if the notification was *true* or *false*. Sentences are true when they are make sense, math equations are true when they are valid.

After each item, the subject was presented with an isolated letter, which represents something they had to remember from the notification. After two, three, or four items, the driving task was paused, and they were asked to recall the letters in sequence. This was done to mimic the behavior of drivers who usually attend to notifications while driving and respond to them, or perform other tasks that require more attention when stopped at a light, or while driving down a road with no noticeable gradient or curve at a constant speed [18].

Type	Notification
Math	$2/2+1=1$
Sentence	After yelling at the game, I knew I would have a tall voice

Table 1. Examples of the two types of notifications

Apparatus

The Robot Operating System (ROS Hydro) was used to synchronize signals from the different components of the experimental setup. This includes data from the simulator, physiological sensors, and the audio-visual feeds, all of which were being sampled at different frequencies, on separate machines. Each component publishes messages via ROS Nodes to the server, which synchronizes the data and writes it to disk. A Logitech camera, a mic, and audio mixer were used to capture audio-visual information. Participants controlled the simulator using a Logitech G27 Racing Wheel.

Physiological Sensors

Physiological signals were captured and recorded using the Biopac's BioNomadix monitoring devices for Electrocardiogram (ECG), Photoplethysmograph (PPG), Electromyogram (EMG), respiration, skin temperature, Electrodermal Activity (EDA), and Impedance Cardiography (ICG). Pupil dilation and eye gaze was captured using Pupil Pro hardware[2], which is a head-mounted mobile eye-tracking platform.

Since the hands of the participant were occupied for driving, we placed the PPG and EDA sensors on the participant's left toe & instep, respectively [32]. The facial EMG sensor was placed just above their left eyebrow to measure activation of the corrugator supercilii muscle, which is associated with frowning. Two skin temperature sensors were placed on the tip of the nose and on the left cheek. The ECG, impedance cardiography, and respiration sensors were placed in the default positions, i.e., on the chest and neck.

Methodology

Participants were guided through an informed consent process, followed by an overview of the study. They were aided through the process of having a number of sensors attached to their body for the purposes of recording their physiological responses. The participant was then seated in the simulator and given a demonstration of how visual notifications would be presented on the HUD, and audio notifications delivered over speakers.

The dataset collection was split in two parts: baseline and experimental. The baseline section records physiological measures for low and high driving workload separately. The experimental section records physiological measures for the multitasking scenario described in Section 3.3.

Baseline

Each participant was taken through a series of practice runs to get them comfortable with the primary driving task. When

[2]http://pupil-labs.com/pupil/

Physiological Measures		Performance Measures	
Raw	Derivative	ConTRe Task (T1)	Notification Task (T2)
Electrocardiogram (ECG)	Pulse Transit Time (PTT)	Steering Deviation	Sentence Response Time
Photoplethysmograph (PPG)	Inst. Heart Rate (IHR)	Acceleration Reaction Time	Sentence Accuracy
Impedance Cardiography(ICG)	SKT B − SKT A (SKT)	Acceleration Accuracy	Math Response Time
Respiration		Braking Reaction Time	Math Accuracy
Electrodermal Activity (EDA)		Braking Accuracy	Recall Accuracy
Skin Temp. Nose (SKT A)			
Skin Temp. Cheek (SKT B)			
Electromyography (EMG)			
Pupil Dilation			
Eye Gaze			

Table 2. Collection of measures available in the dataset.

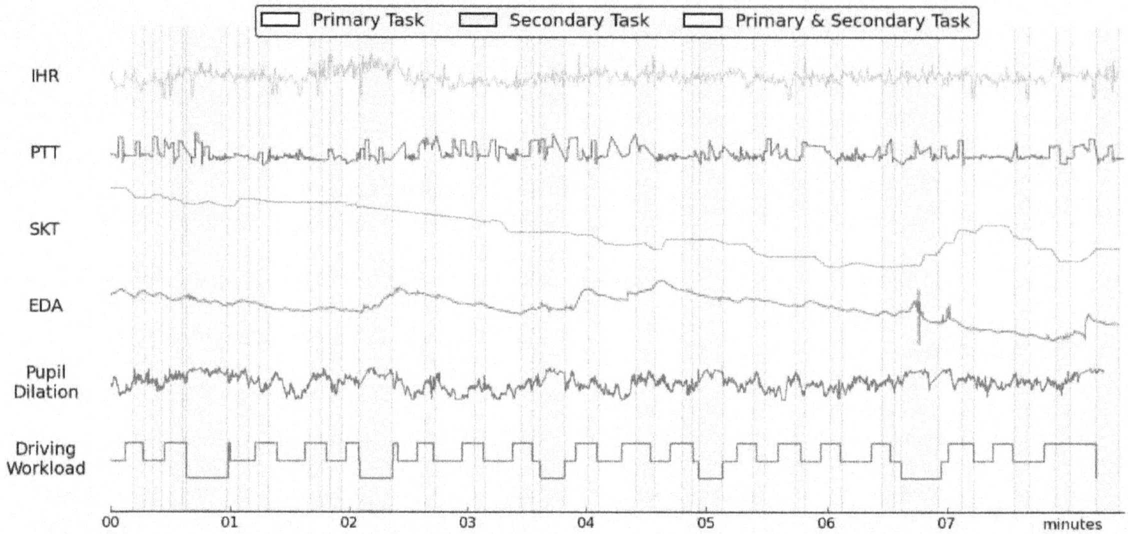

Figure 2. Example physiological measures collected during an audio non-mediated experimental condition. Driving workload is represented as a step function (1: High, 0: Low, -1: Pause). Colored regions delineate when the user was engaged in the primary driving task (T1; white regions), secondary notification task (T2; orange regions), or both (T1 & T2; blue regions).

done with the practice, the low benchmark was recorded using the low workload setting on the simulator. After a minute, they were asked to repeat a series of ten sentences that were read out to them, one-by-one, while they were still performing the primary ConTRe task. The same routine was performed to record the high benchmark using the high workload setting on the simulator.

Experimental

This was followed by another set of practice rounds that combined both the ConTRe task (with the randomly alternating workloads) and the notifications task. The notification task included a set of five items, three of which were equations, with the rest being sentences. This provided the participants with a sense of what to expect during the actual trials. The practice trials could be repeated if necessary. The participants then moved on to the experimental trials. Each participant had a total of four trials, one for each condition. The entire study lasted approximately 2 hours.

Data Processing

The dataset consists of a number of physiological and performance measures which are tabulated in Table 2. We recorded ten psychophysiological signals: EDA, EMG, skin temperatures (nose and cheek), four signals based on cardio-respiratory activity (ECG, PPG, ICG & respiration), and two based on eye activity (gaze and pupil dilation). Apart from the eye-based signals which were sampled at 30 Hz, the rest of the signals were sampled at 2000 Hz.

Three derivative signals were also calculated. Instantaneous heart rate (IHR) was obtained from the ECG signal using the BioSig library[3] which implements Berger's algorithm [4]. Pulse Transit Time (PTT) was obtained by calculating the difference in between the ECG R-wave peak time and the PPG peak time, which is the time it takes for the pulse pressure waveform to propagate through a length of the arterial tree. Difference in skin temperature (SKT) was also calculated by subtracting the temperature of the nose from that of the cheek.

[3]http://biosig.sourceforge.net/

The performance measures encompass both the primary driving task and the secondary notification task. Of interest are the reaction times and accuracies to the red and green light stimuli, and the steering deviation in tracking the reference cylinder. Also recorded are the performance measures for the secondary notification task as shown in Table 2.

Preprocessing & Labelling

In this exploration, 5 of the 13 psychophysiological signals collected were seen to be the easiest and most fruitful to analyze for dynamic task load modelling. They include IHR, PTT, SKT, EDA and pupil dilation (Figure 2). These signals were extracted from the collected data and down-sampled to 40 Hz (except for pupil dilation which remains at its original sampling rate of 30 Hz). Each signal was plotted, and thresholds were determined to filter out unlikely values (from movement artifacts, etc.). Data for each user was standardized (zero mean & unit variance), prior to which outliers that were more than three standard deviations from the average, were filtered out.

Two sets of labels are included in the dataset, a set each for the primary and secondary task. By syncing with the timestamps from both the task logs, we determined the precise primary and secondary task conditions that the participant was under for every physiological sample. The primary task labels denote if the participant is in the low, high, or paused driving workload condition (see Driving Workload in Figure 2). The logs from the secondary task allow us to determine the periods during which a participant was attending to a notification, i.e. blue regions in Figure 2. The orange regions signify the recall part of the secondary task, when the primary driving task was paused.

Feature Extraction

We derived a number of statistical features on the main signal ($x[n]$), the derivative signal ($x[n+1]-x[n]$), and the percentage change ($(x[n+1]-x[n])/x[n]*100$). These features include the mean, median, percentiles (10th, 25th, 75th, 90th), ranges (between min and max, 10th and 90th percentiles, and 25th and 75th percentiles), skewness, and standard deviation.

Features were extracted using a sliding window. To capture temporal properties, windows were overlapped, i.e. their step size was smaller than their length. Different window lengths and step sizes were considered. Specifically, the following pairs of window and step sizes (seconds) were analyzed: (7, 1), (5, 1), (3, 1) and (3, 0.25).

Modelling for Multitasking Scenario

Based on the insights from Wilkin's multiple resource theory described in the Related Work section, the loads that the primary and secondary tasks impose on the user are not mutually exclusive. Both tasks compete for resources along the stages dimension, and along the visual channel dimensions if the notifications are visual. Hence it would be more prudent for the classifier to make predictions on the load the user is under for both tasks separately and simultaneously, instead of attempting to make predictions on some notion of composite or absolute load. Thus, we can view this as a multi-label classification problem. In this formulation, each window is assigned two labels, where each label is drawn from the set of labels that corresponds to the primary and secondary tasks. Given the limited data to train the model on, we reduce our task to a multi-label binary classification problem, and ignore the specific states of the ConTRe (low/high workloads) and notification (attending/recall) tasks. Essentially, at this stage, we are simply trying to predict which tasks (T1 and/or T2) the user is engaged in by analyzing the psychophysiological data.

A sliding window is labelled as T1 if for the duration of a window the participant is only engaged in the primary ConTRe task. If the ConTRe task is paused, and the participant is engaged in recall, the window is labelled as T2. If the participant is attending to a notification while performing the ConTRe task, the window is labelled as both T1 and T2. For simplicity, the transitory unlabelled windows were discarded. The features of the remaining windows, and their corresponding multi-label assignments $\{T1,T2\}$ were fed to a Random Forest classifier, which is an ensemble technique that learns a number of decision tree classifiers and aggregates their results. Models were built across all users, as well as for each user separately to account for individual differences in their psychophysiological response. To evaluate the classifier's performance, we used leave-one-user-out cross-validation for the population models, and 3-fold cross-validation for the individual user models.

The time it takes to comprehend a notification varies by participant. This creates variation in the number of driving and notification task labels generated per participant, which in turn results in a varying baseline accuracy for each user because of the class imbalance problem. Hence, instead of accuracy, we use the Area Under the Receiver Operating Characteristic Curve (ROC AUC) metric to evaluate the classifier, as it is insensitive to class imbalance. ROC curves show the trade-offs between higher sensitivity and higher specificity. Sensitivity refers to the correct detection of a condition or state when it is truly present. Specificity indicates the correct rejection of a state when it is truly not present. The area under the ROC curve is a measure of adequacy on both. Curves corresponding to random or chance classification of 50% would fall close to the diagonal, and result in an ROC AUC score of 0.5 regardless of class imbalance, while the most successful classifications would have an ROC AUC score close to 1.0.

Being a multi-label classification problem, the classifier outputs two probabilities simultaneously: one for the probability of the sample belonging to the primary task (T1), and another for the probability that the sample belongs to the secondary task (T2). We report the macro-averaged ROC AUC scores for the pair of labels, as a measure of how well the classifier is simultaneously able to predict both labels ($T1 \vee T2$). We also report the ROC AUC score for each label, individually, to shed light on how accurately the classifier is able to identify each task.

Results

Of the five physiological signals analyzed, the pupil dilation measures were the only signal to yield results that were much better than random. For this reason, we only list and discuss results using the pupil dilation measures. For the four window and step size combinations considered, mean ROC AUC scores for the population and individual models are shown in Table 3.

Window, Step (s)	Population			Individual		
	T1∨T2	T1	T2	T1∨T2	T1	T2
7, 1	0.85	0.90	0.80	0.84	0.89	0.78
5, 1	0.84	0.89	0.78	0.83	0.88	0.78
3, 1	0.81	0.85	0.76	0.81	0.87	0.75
3, 0.25	0.80	0.86	0.75	0.80	0.86	0.74

Table 3. ROC AUC Scores for population and individual models using different window and step sizes

Condition	T1∨T2	T1	T2
Non-mediated			
Video	0.88	0.90	0.86
Audio	0.90	0.92	0.88
Overall	0.88	0.91	0.86
Mediated			
Video	0.82	0.89	0.76
Audio	0.81	0.88	0.74
Overall	0.81	0.89	0.74

Table 4. Population-based ROC AUC Scores under different timing and modality conditions.

A larger window size tends to provide better results, and this trend holds for both the individual and population models. The population scores are comparable to the average user scores, which tells us that the model based on pupil dilations is generalizable.

Table 3 also shows ROC AUC scores for predicting each label individually. The scores indicate that the models are better at identifying when the user is engaged in the primary driving task (T1) as compared to when the user is engaged in the secondary notification task (T2). This might be because of the differences in load induced by equation and sentence notifications, and also from the differences in the notifications being right or wrong. Our model doesn't account for these yet, but each can potentially be treated as a different class under a label in the multi-label framework.

We also compared how varying the independent variables of timing and modality impacted the ROC AUC scores. The results for these experiments are tabulated in Table 4. Only the analysis on the 7 second long windows are presented here as similar trends were observed for the other combinations. It is clear that mediating when notifications were sent had a larger effect than modality on the model's ability to identify the secondary task. To explain this, we must remember that in the mediated condition, the participant is sent notifications when they are in the low driving-workload state. The multiple resource theory predicts that the cognitive load on the user in this state (low driving-workload + notification) is similar to the cognitive load they experience when they are in the high driving-workload state. Thus, in the mediated condition windows where the user is driving with and without notification, i.e. windows labelled {T1} and {T1,T2}, look similar. In the non-mediated condition, this is not the case, as notifications are also delivered in the high driving-workload states. This allows the classifier to better identify the secondary task (T2) in the non-mediated condition.

STUDY 2: AUTONOMOUS MEDIATION

A classifier was built and tested for its ability to mediate notifications using real-time pupil dilatation measures. The classifier used was a modified version of the the model described above. It was trained on data from the non-mediated condition. During the pilot experiments, models using moving windows that were 5 seconds long with a step size of 1 second gave the most promising results.

The classifier gets standardized input from the pupil dilation data stream, and outputs a {T1,T2} classification every second. Since at this preliminary stage, we are only detecting what tasks the user is engaged in, we make the assumption that if the user is multitasking, i.e {T1,T2} = {1,1}, then the user is experiencing high load. If the user is only engaged in driving it outputs {1,0}.

The experimental setup is similar to the one used in the previous study with some modifications to the design and tasks. These changes are described in detail below.

Design

This study focused on audio notifications only. It was designed as a repeated measures within subject study with only one independent variable, i.e. non-mediated (control) vs. mediated (test) conditions. To control for possible effects of order the study was counterbalanced.

Participants

10 people (all male) participated in our study recruited through a call sent out to students selected randomly from a graduate school population.

Tasks

Since notifications are what the system needs to mediate, they could not be used as the secondary task (T2) that the classifier detects. We therefore increased task load in a different way by using a manual transmission-based gear changing task as the secondary task. The tasks were chosen so as to make it difficult for a user to perform perfectly on the primary and secondary tasks simultaneously.

Primary Task (T1): ConTRe

The primary task remains the same as in the first user study. The participant is engaged in an abstracted driving task, where they track a yellow cylinder with a steering wheel. The participant also has to simultaneously respond to red and green lights on the yellow cylinder by depressing the brake and accelerator pedals, respectively. The ConTRe task was set to alternate between periods of low and high workloads as described in the first study.

Secondary Task (T2): Gear Change

An LCD screen is placed in front of the simulator such that its contents are easily visible below the yellow and blue cylinders presented on the simulator screen. Numbers from 1–6 are presented on the LCD screen, which correspond to the gears on the manual transmission gearbox which is included with the Logitech G27 Racing Wheel. The user was asked to shift to the right gear when the number changed on the screen. To create a high task load for the user, the gear number only changed when the ConTRe task was in its high load setting. The gear number was set to change every 1–3 seconds.

Mediated Task: Notifications
The notification task is a simplified version of the one used in the previous study. To create a continuous task scenario the pause and recall portion of the previous study was eliminated. In this study, notifications only consist of audio math and sentence prompts that the user responds to with a true or false.

Apparatus and Sensors
The apparatus used to conduct, synchronize and record the experiment was the same as before. Only audio notifications were presented to the user. As pupil dilation was the lone physiological measure of interest, the Pupil Pro headset was the only physiological sensor worn by the user.

Methodology
Participants were guided through an informed consent process, followed by an overview of the study. The participant was then seated in the simulator, and was asked to put on the Pupil Pro headset. They were instructed on how to perform the ConTRe task. Once comfortable with the task, the secondary gear changing task was introduced. After this the audio math and sentence notifications were demonstrated to the user. Once the user was familiar with all the tasks, a calibration step was performed to determine the parameters needed to standardize the data before classification. This step simply required the user to perform the ConTRe task in its low workload setting for 10 seconds. This was followed by two experimental trials. These included the test condition in which notifications were autonomously mediated based on task load, and the control condition in which notifications were randomly presented to the user regardless of task load.

Notifications were mediated by delaying them if they hadn't started playing. If they had started playing, and then the system detected that the task load on the user was high, the notification would cut off and repeat itself when the load on the user had reduced. A trigger-happy system that cuts off a notification every time a {1,1} is output by the classifier can be annoying to the user. For better user experience, notifications were mediated only when certain patterns of classification outputs were observed. Based on pilot studies, the protocol was set to delay or cut-off notifications anytime a pattern of either [{1,1}, {1,1}] or [{1,1}, {1,0}, {1,1}] classifications was output by the classifier. The system would then wait for a series of five {1,0} classifications before resuming delivery of notifications.

Measures
Quantitative performance data on primary, secondary, and mediated tasks were collected. From the primary ConTRe task, we collected the following: steering deviation, i.e. the difference in distance between the reference cylinder and the tracking cylinder (sampled at 570 Hz); reaction times to respond to the red and green lights, i.e. the amount of time from when the light went off to when the correct pedal was depressed; and the error rate of depressing the wrong pedal. These measures were automatically recorded by the simulator. An average of 23.8 and 13.7 acceleration stimulus points were presented to each user in the mediated and non-mediated conditions, respectively. Similarly, an average of 21.3 and 11.2 brake stimulus points were presented in the mediated and non-mediated conditions, respectively. Since notifications were being delayed in the mediated condition, these trials were longer that the non-mediated ones. For each user in each condition, the mean steering deviation, reaction times, and reaction errors were calculated.

Performance Measures	M	N	*p*
Primary Contre Task			
Steering Deviation (%)	22.0	23.1	.47
Accel Reaction Time (ms)	980	1014	.67
Brake Reaction Time (ms)	1117	1157	.47
Accel Response Error Rate	0.34	0.23	.07
Brake Response Error Rate	0.25	0.32	**.05**
Secondary Gear Task			
Attempts per stimulus	1.15	1.26	**.015**
Response Error Rate	0.22	0.31	**.05**
Mediated Notification Task			
Math Reaction Time (s)	2.02	2.30	.19
Sent. Reaction Time (s)	2.30	2.53	.32
Math Response Error Rate	0.08	0.08	.82
Sent. Response Error Rate	0.22	0.27	.33

Table 5. Mean performance measures of the primary, secondary and mediated tasks from both the mediated (M) and non-mediated (N) conditions, along with paired t-test two-tailed p-values.

From the secondary gear-changing task, the number of tries the user took to get to the right gear, and the number of times they didn't succeed in reaching the right gear were determined. The mean of these measures for each user in both conditions were then calculated. Per user, an average of 52.2 and 28.3 gear change requests were made in the mediated and non-mediated conditions, respectively.

For performance on the mediated notification task, the response times for the math and sentence prompts were computed. This is the time from when the notification was presented to the driver to when they respond to indicate true or false. The mean response times for notifications are then recorded for each user in every condition. The errors in the responses and the mean per user was also calculated for each condition. An average of 7.5 math and sentence prompts each, were presented to users in both conditions.

The outputs from the classifier, which occur every second, were also recorded for the mediated condition. These will be

System Stimulus	Sensitivity	Specificity	Accuracy
every *H* and *L*	40	72	61
H	90	19	56
HH or *HLH*	83	42	63
HHH	74	68	71
HHHH	58	82	70

Table 6. Evaluation of different types of stimulus to which a system could be designed to respond. The first two rows indicate the overly eager and cautious behaviors, respectively. The next three rows represent different patterns of classifier output.

analyzed to shed light on how the classifier's outputs could inform the system's mediation behavior.

Results

Below we report on results from the experiment. We look at mediation effects on each task by collectively analyzing their corresponding performance measures. Since this presents three sets of comparisons (one for each task), we use the Bonferroni adjusted alpha levels of .017 per test (.05/3) to control for Type I errors. To perform the analysis, we perform a multivariate ANOVA (MANOVA) on the performance measures from each task. As opposed to running multiple univariate F tests on each measure, MANOVA has the advantage of reducing the likelihood of a Type I error, and revealing differences not discovered by ANOVA tests [33]. We also analyze the classifier output with respect to task load, in order to shed light on how a system might mediate notifications more effectively.

Mediation Effects

The analysis of mediation effect on the primary ConTRe task using a repeated measures MANOVA showed no significant effect, $F(5,5)=1.44$, $p=.35$. The means for each of the five primary task measures in both conditions and the paired t-test two-tailed p-values are listed in Table 5.

For the secondary gear-changing task, a repeated measures MANOVA showed a significant effect, $F(2,8)=7.42$, $p=.015$. Further analysis of each of the dependent variables showed a significant difference in the mean number of tries the user took to get to the right gear between the mediated ($M=1.15$, $SD=0.16$) and non-mediated ($M=1.26$, $SD=0.14$) conditions, $t(9)=-3.72$, p=.004. There was also a slightly significant difference in the failure rates between the mediated ($M=0.22$, $SD=0.05$) and non-mediated ($M=0.31$, $SD=0.13$) conditions, $t(9)=-2.26$, p=.05. These are listed in Table 5.

A repeated measures MANOVA for the mediated notification task revealed no significant effect, $F(4,6)=0.98$, $p=.48$. The means for each of the four notification task measures in both conditions and the paired t-test two-tailed p-values are also listed in Table 5.

System Mediation Performance

Since the classifications are done on a sliding window, we can expect a lag from the onset of high task load to when the classifier output indicates so. Another reason for the delay in classifications might be that even though a high load is being imposed on the user, it might take a couple of seconds for them to experience it as such. To find the average delay, the cross-correlation between the alternating load conditions and time-shifted classification outputs was determined for multiple time shifts. Across users the average time-shift at which the cross-correlations were maximum was 4.9 s with a standard deviation of 1.44 s. For further analysis, this number was rounded up, and the classification outputs were time-shifted by 5 s for each user. For simplicity, we represent a {1,0} classifier output as *L* and a a {1,1} classifier output as *H*. The goal of this analysis is to get a sense of how well the classifier was detecting high load situations across users in the study, and how the system's mediation behavior could potentially be improved.

By being overly eager or overly cautious, a system can display two extremes in how it uses the classifier outputs to inform its mediation behavior. The eager system for example reacts immediately to every change in task load *L* and *H* being output by the classifier by playing or pausing a notification. We would expect the system to have high specificity, as it immediately changes its behavior based on classifier output. The cautious system also stops notifications immediately when high task load is sensed *H*, but continues to do so even if an *H* is followed by *Ls* for a specified period of time. Thus it displays low specificity. Under the cautious behavior, a single *H* occurring during a high load section is considered as a true positive (correct classification). Conversely, a single *H* during a low load section is a false positive (incorrect classification). The system's sensitivity, specificity and accuracy are calculated by aggregating the true and false positives over the trials from all users. Results for the overly eager and cautious behaviors are shown in Table 6, along with a few intermediate behaviors which we describe next.

To trade-off between sensitivity and specificity, the system could be designed to mediate notifications only if it sees a particular pattern of classifier outputs. As described above, if a pattern occurs during a high load section it is marked as a true positive, and if it occurs during a low load section it is marked as a false positive. A few example patterns were evaluated, and their results are listed in Table 6. These include patterns such as [*H*,*H*] or [*H*,*L*,*H*] which reduces the sensitivity of the system to the classifier outputs, making it less cautious. This was also the pattern that was actually used by the system in the autonomous mediation study. We can reduce system sensitivity even further by having the system mediate notifications only when it sees [*H*,*H*,*H*] from the classifier. Table 6 also lists evaluation results when [*H*,*H*,*H*,*H*] is the pattern that the system responds to. In this way we get a sense of how the system's mediation behavior would have changed if the protocol was set to respond to different patterns of classifier outputs.

DISCUSSION

This paper presents a dataset of 13 psychophysiological signals to estimate cognitive load. These signals include ECG, PPG, ICG, Respiration, EDA, nose & cheek skin temperatures and the differences between them, EMG, pupil dilation, eye gaze, PTT and IHR (listed in Table 2). These were collected during a dual-task user study that subjected a participant to a series of alternating low and high task loads. The study was designed in this way to mimic the fluctuating loads people experience while driving in the real world. The goal was to capture these fluctuations as reflected in the participants physiological responses.

The dual-task study consisted of a primary driving-like tracking and reaction task, and a secondary notification-based cognitive task. ConTRe was used as the primary task as it focuses on core driving skills and removes learnable contextual cues. This improves data and repeatability of experiment. Similarly, prompts frequently employed in complex span task experiments serve as the notifications presented to a participant. These represent the symbolic and verbal nature of notifications commonly received by people on their smartphones. In the study, the timing and modality of the notifications were treated as independent variables to understand their effects on cognitive load.

The dual-task scenario can be cast as a multi-label learning problem of the primary and secondary tasks. The approach succeeded at building classification models that distinguish whether the user is engaged in the primary task, the secondary task, or both. The model worked for each user and across all the participants. These models were built using statistical features derived from measurements of pupil dilation, which were fed to a random forest classifier. Our evaluations showed that the timing of the notifications has a larger effect on the load experienced by the user than the modality of notification delivery.

We evaluated the impact of this model in a separate real-time notification mediation study. The setup from the first study was altered to include a manual gear changing task instead of the notification itself. Pupil dilation data was streamed to the classifier which output a multi-label classification every second. In the test condition, the system would inhibit notifications if it believed that the user was simultaneously engaged in two tasks. In the control condition, notifications were delivered randomly. The effects of mediation were determined by analyzing the performance measures for each task. Mediation allowed users to reach the right gear (their secondary task) with less errors, and fewer number of attempts per gear change request. Notice that the gear-shifting task uses different perceptual and cognitive skills than the verbal notification task, which is what the model was trained on. Our model transferred and performed well on this mechanical performance stressing activity.

The system's mediation performance was evaluated using cross-correlation measures between the user task loads and time-shifted classifier outputs. We can interpret the results as there being an average lag of 4.9 s between the onset of high task load for the user, and when the system mediated notifications to them. System mediation behavior was also analyzed based on how it responds to different patterns of outputs from the classifier. The trade-off between the system's sensitivity and specificity was demonstrated for these different patterns.

Future work

There are a number of directions future work can take, and we briefly discuss a few here. First, our data analysis did not include moving windows over transitions from low to high workloads and back. We are optimistic that temporal models could be used to detect these transitions, reducing the lag in load detection. Second, improved measures of the load experienced by the users (ground truth) can be obtained by using a composite measure of the different task performance metrics. Reaction times can serve as more reliable proxies for cognitive load than externally imposed task load settings. Third, with more data we can make fine-grained estimations about user load within each task (for example, T1 = 0, 1, 2, 3, etc., based on difficulty of the primary driving task). Fourth, we should explore which physiological signals are more indicative of stress, and which are better suited for estimating cognitive load. Stress is likely to arise when failure at a task is coupled with feelings of lack of control, in situations where participants are evaluated by others [7]. We might hypothesize that stress is an affect. It ebbs and flows at a slower pace than cognitive load, which being reflective of the stages of mental processing, fluctuates more rapidly.

To show that pupil dilation measures can be robust we used an inexpensive off-the-shelf measuring technique. Prior work reports use of expensive eye-trackers with higher sampling rates for pupilometric measurements. Our study succeeded with a consumer webcam (Microsoft LifeCam HD-6000) that has a sampling rate of only 30 Hz. Even when tested outdoors in a car during the day, with no special attempt to control for ambient luminescence (apart from the initial calibration step), the system showed promising results in estimating task load through pupil dilation measures. More work could be done to refine the setup and understand the trade-offs between the fidelity of the equipment, environmental setup, and the robustness of results.

CONCLUSION

We show that technology can know when its appropriate to engage the user. This paper describes a system that can gauge the cognitive load using psychophysiological signals. We created a dataset of 13 physiological measures collected from participants in a multitasking study. They were asked to attend and respond to notifications while performing a primary driving task. We also collected performance measures on these tasks. Of the five most promising physiological measures analyzed, only pupil dilation reliably tracked task load in the near real-time five second range. We demonstrated the effectiveness of using pupil dilation measures for mediating task load in a second multitasking user study. Autonomous mediation of notifications significantly improved participant task performance. Cognitive load assessment is a rich area for exploration, and we hope to inspire other researchers to use our data set to further evaluate models of dynamic task load estimation. By enabling computers to interact appropriately and considerately, we can pave the way for future proactive computing scenarios.

REFERENCES

1. Pavlo Antonenko, Fred Paas, Roland Grabner, and Tamara van Gog. 2010. Using electroencephalography to

measure cognitive load. *Educational Psychology Review* 22, 4 (2010), 425–438.

2. Alan Baddeley. 2003. Working memory: looking back and looking forward. *Nature reviews neuroscience* 4, 10 (2003), 829–839.
3. Jackson Beatty and B Lucero-Wagoner. 2000. The pupillary system. *Handbook of psychophysiology* 2 (2000), 142–162. http://www.nrc-iol.org/cores/mialab/fijc/files/2003/090203_Pupillary_System_.pdf
4. Ronald D Berger, Solange Akselrod, David Gordon, and Richard J Cohen. 1986. An efficient algorithm for spectral analysis of heart rate variability. *Biomedical Engineering, IEEE Transactions on* 9 (1986), 900–904.
5. David Cohen, Akshay Chandrashekaran, Ian Lane, and Antoine Raux. 2014. The hri-cmu corpus of situated in-car interactions. *Proc. IWSDS* (2014), 201–212.
6. Andrew R a Conway, Michael J Kane, Michael F Bunting, D Zach Hambrick, Oliver Wilhelm, and Randall W Engle. 2005. Working memory span tasks: A methodological review and user's guide. *Psychonomic bulletin & review* 12, 5 (Oct. 2005), 769–786. DOI: http://dx.doi.org/10.3758/BF03196772
7. Dan Conway, Ian Dick, Zhidong Li, Yang Wang, and Fang Chen. 2013. The Effect of Stress on Cognitive Load Measurement. In *Human-Computer Interaction–INTERACT 2013*. Springer, 659–666.
8. V Demberg, E Kiagia, and A Sayeed. 2013. Language and cognitive load in a dual task environment. In *Proceedings of the 35th annual meeting of the cognitive science society (cogsci-13)*.
9. Frank A Drews, Monisha Pasupathi, and David L Strayer. 2008. Passenger and cell phone conversations in simulated driving. *Journal of Experimental Psychology: Applied* 14, 4 (2008), 392.
10. Randall W. Engle. 2002. Working memory capacity as executive attention. *Current Directions in Psychological Science* 11, 1 (Feb. 2002), 19–23. DOI: http://dx.doi.org/10.1111/1467-8721.00160
11. Tycho K. Fredericks, Sang D. Choi, Jason Hart, Steven E. Butt, and Anil Mital. 2005. An investigation of myocardial aerobic capacity as a measure of both physical and cognitive workloads. *International Journal of Industrial Ergonomics* 35, 12 (2005), 1097–1107. DOI: http://dx.doi.org/10.1016/j.ergon.2005.06.002
12. Eija Haapalainen, SeungJun Kim, Jodi F Forlizzi, and Anind K Dey. 2010. Psycho-physiological measures for assessing cognitive load. In *Proceedings of the 12th ACM international conference on Ubiquitous computing*. ACM, 301–310.
13. Eric Horvitz, Carl Kadie, Tim Paek, and David Hovel. 2003. Models of attention in computing and communication. *Commun. ACM* 46, 3 (March 2003), 52. DOI: http://dx.doi.org/10.1145/636772.636798
14. C.S. Ikehara and M.E. Crosby. 2005. Assessing Cognitive Load with Physiological Sensors. In *Proceedings of the 38th Annual Hawaii International Conference on System Sciences*. IEEE, 295a—-295a. DOI: http://dx.doi.org/10.1109/HICSS.2005.103
15. Shamsi T Iqbal, Piotr D Adamczyk, Xianjun Sam Zheng, and Brian P Bailey. 2005. Towards an index of opportunity: understanding changes in mental workload during task execution. In *Proceedings of the SIGCHI conference on Human factors in computing systems*. ACM, 311–320.
16. Shamsi T. Iqbal and Brian P. Bailey. 2010. Oasis. *ACM Transactions on Computer-Human Interaction* 17, 4 (Dec. 2010), 1–28. DOI: http://dx.doi.org/10.1145/1879831.1879833
17. Daniel Kahneman. 1973. *Attention and effort*. Citeseer.
18. SeungJun Kim, Jaemin Chun, and Anind K Dey. 2015. Sensors Know When to Interrupt You in the Car: Detecting Driver Interruptibility Through Monitoring of Peripheral Interactions. In *Proceedings of the 33rd Annual ACM Conference on Human Factors in Computing Systems*. ACM, 487–496.
19. Jeffrey Michael Klingner. 2010. *Measuring cognitive load during visual tasks by combining pupillometry and eye tracking*. Ph.D. Dissertation. Stanford University.
20. Spyros Kousidis, Casey Kennington, Timo Baumann, Hendrik Buschmeier, Stefan Kopp, and David Schlangen. 2014. A Multimodal In-Car Dialogue System That Tracks The Driver's Attention. In *Proceedings of the 16th International Conference on Multimodal Interaction*. ACM, 26–33.
21. Tate T Kubose, Kathryn Bock, Gary S Dell, Susan M Garnsey, Arthur F Kramer, and Jeff Mayhugh. 2006. The effects of speech production and speech comprehension on simulated driving performance. *Applied cognitive psychology* 20, 1 (2006), 43–63.
22. Changchun Liu, Karla Conn, Nilanjan Sarkar, and Wendy Stone. 2008. Online affect detection and robot behavior adaptation for intervention of children with autism. *Robotics, IEEE Transactions on* 24, 4 (2008), 883–896.
23. Angela Mahr, Michael Feld, Mohammad Mehdi Moniri, and Rafael Math. 2012. The ConTRe (Continuous Tracking and Reaction) task: A flexible approach for assessing driver cognitive workload with high sensitivity. *Adjunct Proceedings of the 4th AutomotiveUI.* (2012), 88–91.
24. Sandra P Marshall. 2007. Identifying cognitive state from eye metrics. *Aviation, space, and environmental medicine* 78, Supplement 1 (2007), B165—-B175.
25. Daniel McFarlane. 2002. Comparison of Four Primary Methods for Coordinating the Interruption of People in Human-Computer Interaction. *Human-Computer Interaction* 17, 1 (March 2002), 63–139. DOI: http://dx.doi.org/10.1207/S15327051HCI1701_2

26. George A Miller. 1956. The magical number seven, plus or minus two: some limits on our capacity for processing information. *Psychological review* 63, 2 (1956), 81.

27. L J M Mulder. 1992. Measurement and Analysis-Methods of Heart-Rate and Respiration for Use in Applied Environments. *Biological Psychology* 34, 2 (1992), 205–236. <GotoISI>://A1992KA29300007

28. Calvin K L Or and Vincent G Duffy. 2007. Development of a facial skin temperature-based methodology for non-intrusive mental workload measurement. *Occupational Ergonomics* 7, 2 (2007), 83–94.

29. Fred Paas, Juhani E Tuovinen, Huib Tabbers, and Pascal W M Van Gerven. 2003. Cognitive load measurement as a means to advance cognitive load theory. *Educational psychologist* 38, 1 (2003), 63–71.

30. Kilseop Ryu and Rohae Myung. 2005. Evaluation of mental workload with a combined measure based on physiological indices during a dual task of tracking and mental arithmetic. *International Journal of Industrial Ergonomics* 35, 11 (2005), 991–1009. DOI: http://dx.doi.org/10.1016/j.ergon.2005.04.005

31. Yu Shi, Technology Park, Natalie Ruiz, Ronnie Taib, Eric H C Choi, and Fang Chen. 2007. Galvanic Skin Response (GSR) as an Index of Cognitive Load. In *CHI EA '07 CHI '07 Extended Abstracts on Human Factors in Computing Systems*. ACM, 2651–2656. DOI: http://dx.doi.org/10.1145/1240866.1241057

32. Marieke van Dooren, J J G (Gert-Jan) de Vries, and Joris H Janssen. 2012. Emotional sweating across the body: Comparing 16 different skin conductance measurement locations. *Physiology & Behavior* 106, 2 (2012), 298–304. DOI: http://dx.doi.org/10.1016/j.physbeh.2012.01.020

33. Russell T Warne. 2014. A Primer on Multivariate Analysis of Variance (MANOVA) for Behavioral Scientists. *Practical Assessment, Research & Evaluation* 19, 17 (2014), 2.

34. Christopher D. Wickens. 2002. Multiple resources and performance prediction. *Theoretical Issues in Ergonomics Science* 3 (2002), 159–177. DOI: http://dx.doi.org/10.1080/14639220210123806

35. Christopher D Wickens. 2008. Multiple resources and mental workload. *Human Factors: The Journal of the Human Factors and Ergonomics Society* 50, 3 (2008), 449–455.

36. Glenn F. Wilson. 2002. An Analysis of Mental Workload in Pilots During Flight Using Multiple Psychophysiological Measures. *The International Journal of Aviation Psychology* 12, 1 (2002), 3–18. DOI: http://dx.doi.org/10.1207/S15327108IJAP1201_2

What Belongs Together Comes Together. Activity-centric Document Clustering for Information Work.

Alexander Seeliger, Benedikt Schmidt, Immanuel Schweizer, Max Mühlhäuser
Technische Universität Darmstadt
Darmstadt, Germany
{seeliger, schmidt, schweizer, max}@tk.tu-darmstadt.de

ABSTRACT

Multitasking and interruptions in information work make frequent activity switches necessary. Individuals need to recall and restore earlier states of work which generally involves retrieval of information objects. To avoid resulting tooling time an activity-centric organization of information objects has been proposed. For each activity a collection with related information objects (like documents, websites etc.) is created to improve information access and serve as a memory aid.

While the manual maintenance of such information collections is a tedious task and becomes an interruption on its own, the automatic maintenance of such collections using activity mining is promising. Activity mining utilizes interaction histories to extract unique activities based on the stream of interaction with information objects. For activity mining, existing work shows varying success in limited study setups.

In this paper, we present a method for activity mining to generate activity-centric information object collections automatically from interaction histories. The technique is a hybrid approach considering all information types used in previous work – activity stream and accessed content related information. Method performance is evaluated based on interaction histories collected during real work data from eight information workers collected over several weeks. For the dataset our hybrid approach shows on average a performance of 0.53 ARI up to 0.77 ARI, outperforming single metric-based approaches.

Author Keywords

Activity Mining; Document Organization; Information Work

ACM Classification Keywords

H.3.3. Information Search and Retrieval: Clustering

ACM 978-1-4503-4137-0/16/03 ...$15.00.
http://dx.doi.org/10.1145/2856767.2856777

INTRODUCTION

Information work is a challenging work type, characterized by multitasking, frequent interruptions and information overload [20]. During the last decades the execution of information work changed with the advent of a variety of assistive technologies and tools. Notebooks, smart phones and tablets provide access to various networks, and therefore to services enabling advanced means of collaboration and information interaction, anywhere, anytime. Despite this transformation, the characteristics and challenges of information work remained unscathed. In fact, the amount of available information permanently increases [25] and with more devices and more apps there are more sources for interruptions.

The interruption with a task switch is a specific challenge for information work. In this moment, the information worker needs to concentrate on continuing an earlier task and will restore a work environment. Apps need to be opened or closed and information need to be retrieved. Thus, mental and physical *tooling time* (time to get back to the work environment before interruption) emerges. The overall process increases the probability of prospective and retrospective memory failures. Efficiency drops and mistake likelihood increases [1].

To address the challenges of interruptions and activity switches a myriad of personal information management tools have been proposed. One direction is activity-centric information management which organizes information based on activities, the information is used in [26, 2, 7, 12]. Such lists not only improve the access of relevant information but also serve as a memory aid for the prospective and retrospective memory. However, most activity-centric information management approaches require manual work. Individuals create activity objects (sometimes also referred to as tasks) and assign information objects. This is a tedious process which can be an interruption on its own, resulting in a neglected and outdated activity lists.

An alternative is the automatic detection of activities from interaction histories to cluster those information objects which belong to the same activity – a type of activity mining. In this paper, we focus on such activity mining approaches. Systems like CAAD [19], Swish [16] or Transparency [22] track the interaction of a user with information and use the resulting interaction histories to automatically create document clusters which belong to different activities. These systems use interaction history data like access times, access frequencies and access sequences to cluster information belonging to similar activities. This activity mining is a complex problem, because multitasking and interruptions disguise the borders between different activities. A user might search a plane for a business trip while reporting project data with a messenger application. Despite the complexity, existing work shows promising results using (1) activity-based and (2) content-based properties. Unfortunately, there exists no comparison of the usefulness of different property types for activity mining (activity-centric document clustering). Furthermore, all considered approaches use limited study setups, frequently using lab setups. No long term studies which show the performance of such approaches with real data exist at all.

In this paper, we provide two main contributions:

1. An activity mining method for the automatic clustering of activity related information based on interaction histories, using a mixture of activity and content based properties is presented. The method analyzes an interaction history and identifies activities and the information objects used in the activity, even if the activity was interrupted or executed in parallel with other activities. Our method considers activity and content based properties we found in the related work and implements mechanisms to reason about the relevance of the properties for activity-centric document clustering.

2. While related work only contains small studies with data of few hours up to few days [19, 16, 22, 5], we provide an evaluation of our approach with raw data from 8 information workers with 21 up to 47 work day interaction histories, each. Furthermore, we systematize information from the existing body of work on activity-centric document clustering and show the relevance of different activity and content properties. The overall dataset includes 28,045 access events on 7,968 different documents. Our evaluation shows that activity mining as activity-centric document clustering provides useful results to support information workers during their workday.

The paper is structured as follows. First, we introduce related work. Second, we introduce the interaction history properties we use to cluster documents. Third, we specify our activity-centric document clustering method using a hybrid mix of activity and content based properties. Next, we describe our long term study, evaluate our method and discuss the results. Finally, we conclude with a discussion and a short summary.

RELATED WORK

One direction for the support of information work is activity-centric task (or activity) management, using task lists which collect information objects related to the task. These lists require the manual creation and maintenance of the tasks and collections. An early example is Groupbar [26] which provides users with a task-aware window manager. The activity-centered task assistant [2], working spheres [7] and UMEA [12] are just a few examples of such tools with a manual maintenance of task lists with related information objects, utilizing support e.g. from interaction histories or specific visualizations.

Apart from the manual support types, different semi-automatic research prototypes for an activity-centric support of information work exist. Recently, Laevo [11] was introduced as a semi-automatic desktop interface for organizing window configurations of three knowledge work processes (archiving, multitasking, planning). With TaskTracer [24], a semi-automatic approach with automatic detection of task switches was realized. TaskPredictor [24] automatically assigns used documents to tasks. It assumes, that the behavior of users is a mixture of different activities and that each activity is related to a set of information objects. By permanently observing the users actions (document accesses, window focuses, webpage navigation etc.), new assignments can be predicted.

Other work focuses on the automatic creation of activity-centric document clusters from interaction histories. A first example is the Groupbar extension SWISH [16]. SWISH aims at the automation of task-specific window groupings from an interaction history with recorded transitions between windows, considering the window titles. The automatic maintenance of tasks with attached information objects was focused by the Context-Aware Activity Display (CAAD) [19] and the Transparency tool with hierarchical task instance mining [22]. CAAD traces the users behavior and tries to detect behavioral changes. A pattern mining algorithm analyzes the users workflow of used program names and accessed documents to generate context structures which are activity-specific. The hierarchical mining approach uses a simple hierarchical clustering based on semantic similarity of the accessed document content to identify task structures. Brdiczka [5] performs activity mining based on document usage patterns by clustering access events of documents up to a threshold. The evaluations of the automatic approaches are rather limited. Oliver et al. report for SWISH [16] performance values for two data sets. For a data set of one user and five tasks, collected over approximately four hours they report an F-measure of 0.58. The results are improved to a recall of 0.76 by using 1 hour chunks of data and application. The CAAD system by Rattenbury et al. [19] was evaluated by a usefulness study over 1 week usage of 7 persons. Schmidt et al. with hierarchical task instance mining [22] evaluated task execution in a lab simulation with 8 persons working on 7 complex, frequently interrupted tasks. They generated a gold-standard and showed that their algorithm has an F-measure of 0.72 in comparison. Brdiczka [5] evaluates the work data for 3 days of work of 10 persons. His result is an F-measure of 0.32 with a precision of 0.20 for 50 tasks. By limiting the data set to the six most frequent tasks Brdiczka obtains an F-measure of 0.74. All approaches use a different selection of activity and content properties to create activity clusters.

The results show that the automatic detection of activities with related information objects is promising. All approaches we are aware of use activity properties (access sequences, durations, etc.) or content properties (document content, window titles) from interaction histories and use clustering-like techniques. However, none existing work makes use of the combination of content and activity properties. All approaches are evaluated in different setups and show very different results. There exists no comparison of the approaches or the used properties. Furthermore, the evaluations consider only short time spans between few hours up to one week.

ACTIVITY AND CONTENT BASED PROPERTIES FOR DOCUMENT CLUSTERING

In this paper, we develop a method for the automatic clustering of activity related information based on interaction histories. The state of the art has shown that two types of properties are frequently used to create such clusters: (1) activity-based and (2) content-based properties. Activity-based properties have a wider look at how documents are related to each other during activity execution, using environmental and behavioral aspects. Content-based properties just focus on the concrete content of the corresponding document, thus implying that information objects which belong to the same activity also are related on content level.

Defining a Document Relatedness Metric

Before defining concrete document relations, a generic function that expresses relatedness between documents is needed. We define relatedness as a function that consumes both documents A and B and returns a similarity value that is bound between 0 and 1. This function is a *semi-metric* on a document corpus D and is defined as

$$rel : D \times D \rightarrow \mathbb{R} \in [0, 1]$$

and fulfills the following properties:

1. $rel(A, B) \geq 0$ (non-negativity)
2. $rel(A, B) = 0$ if $A = B$
3. $rel(A, B) = rel(B, A)$ (symmetry)

Low values of $rel(A, B)$ indicate that there exist a high relatedness between document A and B. High values indicate that both documents are not related to each other. Most notably, we are interested in activity relatedness which means that two documents are related if they belong to the same activity.

Defining Document Relations via Activity Properties

The first category of document properties tries to extract activity knowledge from interaction histories of documents. By recording the behavior of users working with documents, correlations between documents can be mined.

Before actually defining concrete activity properties, a short introduction to the work execution process of the information worker is given to better understand the difference between activity and task. Each information worker has several goals to achieve but limited capabilities and resources require them to pick a subset of goals based on priorities. To achieve a goal the prospective work is considered as a task which structures and specifies the upcoming activities. The execution of a task is performed by an activity. Activities then transform an object into an outcome which may be interpreted as the achievement of the selected goal. The user decides when a created outcome fulfills the goal [21].

We will focus ourselves on interaction histories of information workers using modern operating systems which follow a WIMP[1]-style interaction paradigm, allowing multiple applications to run at the same time. In the following we present information which can be collected from such a system, using an application which tracks user-system interactions and creates an interaction history. The tracking application we used for our work is presented later in this paper, here we focus on the general information types we have identified from our research and the related work, to be relevant information sources to be used for activity-centric document clustering.

Application Usages

Switching between windows (a change of the active foreground window) indicate an application switch which can – but not necessarily is – an indicator for an activity switch. While the switch can mean a change of focus, a set of applications can also be used together to realize a specific outcome (e.g. a web search and document editing to create a survey). Still, the active window is an important indicator of the awareness.

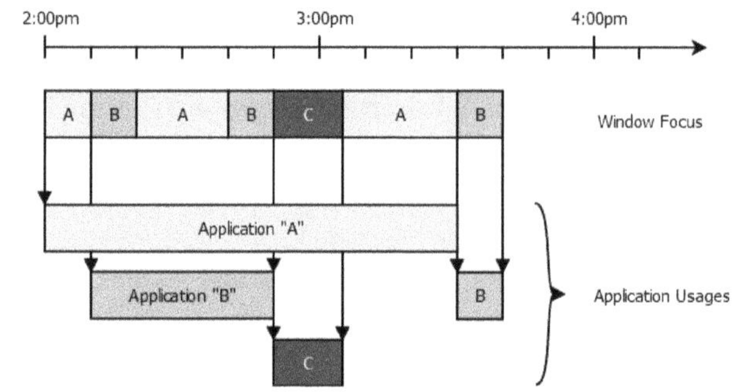

Figure 1. Single window switches will be merged together if the interval between those switches is less than 30 minutes. This merging results in multiple parallel time-lines.

Realization: The use of foreground information helps to determine active application usage times. We assume that a window not necessarily becomes irrelevant once it is hidden. If the resumption time is smaller than 30 minutes, we merge active window times together (see Figure 1). Iqbal and Horvitz [10] have conducted a user study, measuring the probability of task resumption depending on the time spent before the suspension and the resumption time. In this study, the probability for returning to a task within 30 minutes is at least 70%.

A1: Context Applications

Some activities may require the user to use the same subset of applications over and over again. So it is obvious to use all currently used applications as an indicator for the activity relatedness between documents.

Realization: Context applications can be modeled using a vector U containing the current state of each application a_i at a given time t. $U_t = (a_1, a_2, ..., a_A)$. If the application i is used $a_i = 1$ and otherwise $a_i = 0$. When multiple document accesses have been recognized, we can compare all seen application usages for each visit and get a better prediction which applications are really specific for the compared documents.

[1] Abbrv.:Windows, Icons, Menus, Pointers

A2: Time-Related (1): Mostly used together
Often multiple documents are used together, like presentations and notes. We can make use of this and group documents together, when they are used together multiple times.

Realization: Besides collecting the application usage intervals, document accesses are also collected. Documents d_1 and d_2 can then be compared by calculating the proportion of the number of application intervals S_{d_i} in which both documents have been accessed to the number of application intervals in which only d_1 or d_2 was accessed.

$$rel(d_1, d_2) = 1 - \frac{2 \cdot S_{d_1 \cap d_2}}{S_{d_1} + S_{d_2}}$$

This formula returns high relatedness between documents d_1 and d_2, if the number of application usages in which both documents have been accessed is higher than the number of documents in which only one of the documents has been accessed.

A3: Time-Related (2): Parallel Work
Another indicator for activity-relatedness between two documents is parallel work and the according permanent document switching (i.e. keyboard shortcut *Alt-Tab*).

Realization: The calculation of the relatedness for parallel work between d_1 and d_2 with the access times $U_i = (a_{i,1}, a_{i,2}, ..., a_{i,A})$ is defined as the following:

$$rel(d_1, d_2) = 1 - \frac{\sum_{i=1}^{|U_1|} \sum_{j=1}^{|U_2|} \theta(a_{1,i}, a_{2,j})}{|U_1| \cdot |U_2|}$$

with

$$\theta(t_1, t_2) = \begin{cases} 1 & \text{if } abs(t_1 - t_2) < 5 \text{ minutes} \\ 0 & \text{otherwise} \end{cases}$$

We assume parallel work with documents when the time span between their document accesses is less than 5 minutes. Because the metric delivers high relatedness values for a small number of access times, it only delivers values for documents with at least two access times.

Defining Document Relations via Content Properties

Until now we have only highlighted activity-centric properties based on interaction histories as relatedness metrics. In this section we will have focus on the content of documents. Documents may have the same topic and use the same vocabulary. If documents address a similar topic it can be an indicator that the documents are used in the same activity. So comparing the content of documents is the most obvious approach to determine activity relatedness.

C1: TF-IDF
A well-known content similarity measure in information retrieval is TF-IDF [17]. The TF-IDF is the product of term frequency and inverse document frequency. Term frequency $tf(t, d)$ is defined as the number of occurrences of the term t in the document d. Inverse document frequency is defined as the importance of a word to distinguish it from a common word. Then the TF-IDF is defined as

$$\mathsf{tf} - \mathsf{idf}(t, d, D) = \mathsf{tf}(t, d) \cdot \mathsf{idf}(t, D)$$

To compare two documents, the normalized $\mathsf{tf} - \mathsf{idf}$ factor [15] is calculated for each term and each document, resulting in a document-term matrix (TD-matrix). Now the distance between two documents can be computed by comparing its $\mathsf{tf} - \mathsf{idf}$ vectors using the cosine similarity.

C2: Latent Semantic Analysis
Latent Semantic Analysis [14] (LSA) is a statistical method based on the TD-matrix. After building the term-document-matrix a *Singular Value Decomposition* (SVD) [3] is applied. SVD decomposes the matrix into the product of three other matrices, thus we can read the singular values, which characterize the importance of a term in the document corpus. We can then determine which dimensions can be reduced by setting less relevant singular values to zero and recompute the TD-matrix.

In comparison to the TF-IDF metric LSA does not compare the occurrences of words, it compares higher level semantic structures. The reduction of the TD-matrix generalizes conceptual equal terms and removes less important terms. This generalization let LSA solve the problem of synonymy.

C3: Latent Dirichlet Allocation
Blei et al have presented another document classification approach for large collections called *Latent Dirichlet Allocation* [4] (LDA). It is a generative probabilistic three-level hierarchical Bayesian model in which a document is modeled as a random mixture of latent topics. A topic is characterized by a distribution over a fixed vocabulary. In a probabilistic model data is treated as observations that come from a generative probabilistic process including hidden variables.

The goal of LDA is to infer the unknown topic structures from the distribution of words in the documents. The result of LDA is the topic distribution of a document, which can then be compared using a similarity metric over distributions. We use the *JensenShannon* divergence which is based on the *Kullback-Leibler* divergence with some differences. It is symmetric and always delivers a finite value. Furthermore, it is bounded by 1.

DOCUMENT CLUSTERING METHOD USING A HYBRID FEATURE SET

In the following, we present our method for activity-centric document clustering. Until now a couple of relatedness metrics (see table 1) have been presented which can all be used standalone for document clustering. However, using only single metrics could lead to misleading results. Only focusing on activity data will not be able to identify multitasking (e.g. parallel reporting about an activity and programming will be grouped together). Only focusing on document similarity will ignore relatedness which is not on a topic level (e.g. booking a flight and calculating the cost in parallel). To address these issues, our approach focuses on the combination of multiple relatedness properties. A mixture of activity and content related properties will be used at the same time (hybrid feature set). As it turns out, combining multiple document properties to calculate relatedness is not an easy task, especially, when trying to combine different property types, which use different information sources. A first step was already done by

#	Property	Type	Description
A1	Context Applications	*Activity*	The applications which are used indicate which activity is currently performed.
A2	Mostly Used Together	*Activity*	Documents which are used together may have a relationship between each other.
A3	Parallel Work	*Activity*	Documents which are used parallel may have a relationship between each other.
C1	TF-IDF	*Content*	TF-IDF calculates the similarity between documents by comparing word occurrence.
C2	Latent Semantic Analysis (LSA)	*Content*	Similar to TF-IDF but comparing higher semantic structured.
C3	Latent Dirichlet Allocation (LDA)	*Content*	LDA calculates the similarity of documents by comparing topic distributions.

Table 1. Summary of all presented activity and content properties.

defining all relatedness metrics the same way and normalize the outcome. This makes sure that calculating the sum of two metrics does not deliver a value which does not represent the relatedness between documents anymore. This also avoids complicated transformations for the different approaches.

A very easy method to combine multiple document properties is to use the average value of the calculated metrics. However, this approach has two main issues: (1) the quality of the different metrics may vary and (2) the value distribution over the metrics is different. Both challenges need to be addressed.

1. Although it seems quite obvious to give the different relatedness metrics the same amount of influence to the overall combined metric, it can be somehow problematic and counterproductive. Depending on the domain, the amount and the quality of documents, some relatedness metrics may work better than others. To uncover hidden structures of the documents, equal influence for all relatedness metrics is not the best solution. A weighting factor can be used to overcome this issue:

$$rel_{total}(d_j, d_{j'}) = \sum_{i=0}^{n} \rho_i \cdot rel_i(d_j, d_{j'}) \text{ with } \sum_{i=0}^{n} \rho_i = 1$$

   The weighting factor ρ_i controls the influence of each relatedness value rel_i to the overall combined metric. This weighting can be used to give lower quality metrics less influence but high quality metrics a higher influence.

2. When each weight ρ_i is set to the same value ($\rho_i = \frac{1}{n} \forall i$), that does not necessarily give all relatedness metrics equal influence. The influence of the i-th metric of $sim(d_j, d_{j'})$ depends on the relative contribution to the average document relatedness over all pairs [8]. Some metrics may have in average lower or higher values than others. This difference has an impact on the relative proportion of the corresponding metric. To overcome this difference, a normalization factor is calculated from the average contribution:

$$rel_{total}(d_j, d_{j'}) = \sum_{i=0}^{n} rel_i(d_j, d_{j'}) \cdot \frac{\rho_i}{\overline{d_i}}$$

   with

$$\overline{d_i} = \frac{1}{N^2} \sum_{j=0}^{N} \sum_{j'=0}^{N} rel_i(d_{ji}, d_{j'i})$$

   The relative influence of the i-th relatedness metric without the correction is $\rho_i \cdot \overline{d_i}$. Thus it is necessary to correct $rel_i(d_j, d_{j'})$ with the factor $\frac{1}{\overline{d_i}}$. For example, if the influence of all relatedness metrics should be equal, the weighting has to be set to $\rho_i = 1/(n \cdot \overline{d_i})$.

The relevance of both issues is even higher when combining different types of relatedness metrics – activity and content relations. To address these issues optimal weighting parameters depending on the collection of documents must be found and each metric needs to be normalized so that the relative contribution of each metric is adjusted.

Finding the optimal weightings is a complex task because of the independence of each metric and the use of different data sources for calculating relatedness between documents. Fixed parameters for specific domains may not result in good results for every document corpus because in most cases documents have different domains and topics. Even the behavior of each information worker is different and everyone has an own personal bias for organizing documents. It is needed to develop a solution that finds weighting parameters for each document corpus and information worker individually.

Finding Optimal Parameters for Weighting and Clustering

The finding of the optimal weighting parameters can be formulated as an optimization problem which optimizes the generated activity-centric document clusters. Each weighting parameter $\rho_0, \rho_1, ..., \rho_n$ is a variable in the optimization problem which controls the outcome of the clustering. The number of variables depends on the number of metrics that will need to be combined together. The bounds of the variables are the following:

$$\rho_0, \rho_1, ..., \rho_n \in [0, 1] \qquad \text{with} \qquad \sum_{i=0}^{n} \rho_i = 1$$

as the side condition.

We will use an optimization problem solver with continuous variables which tries to find the best solution from all feasible solutions. The optimization function looks like the following:

$$f(\rho_0, \rho_1, ..., \rho_n, D) \to \mathbb{R} \qquad \text{with} \qquad \sum_{i=1}^{n} \rho_i = 1$$

where f is the document clustering function which returns the quality of the activity-centric document groups and D the

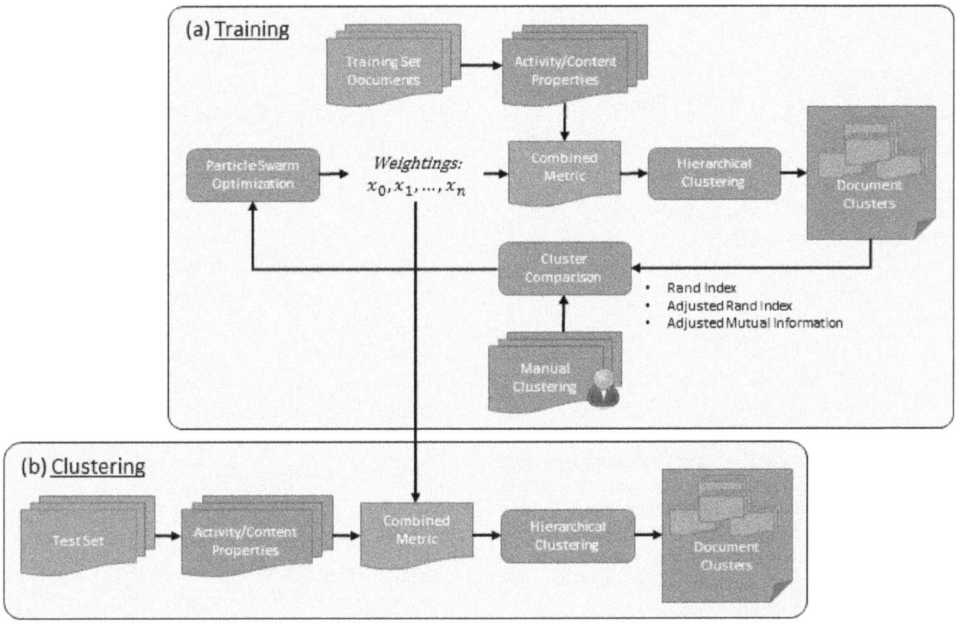

Figure 2. This figure shows the overall process of activity-centric document clustering for information work. The process is twofold: (a) the training phase calculates the weighting parameters for combining the different document properties using a small manual clustered document part and the Particle Swarm Optimization and (b) the actual clustering using the learned parameters from training.

document corpus. The optimization problem optimizes f to its maximum, which means it optimizes the activity-centric document clusters. We define f as the function which returns a value between 0 and 1 and determines if the calculated document clusters have the optimal structure. We let the user manually cluster a small part of the given document corpus and then use this information as a desired result for the clustering of these documents. That means that the system tries to adjust the weighting parameters to exactly match the manual document clusters using the optimization solver. We can then say, that f is a function which returns how much the calculated and the manual assigned clusters differ from each other.

The optimization problem can be solved by an optimization algorithm which will return the best parameter values $\rho_0^*, \rho_1^*, ..., \rho_n^*$.

Particle Swarm Optimization

The Particle Swarm Optimization [13] (PSO) is a computational algorithm which tries to find an optimum by iteratively improving a candidate solution given a quality function. PSO is an evolutionary algorithm trying to improve the quality of the solution stepwise. It is initially inspired by bird flocking, especially, the group dynamics of the birds' social behavior. Reynolds and Heppner argued that the synchrony of flocking requires each bird to maintain an optimum distance between its neighbors. A fundamental hypothesis of PSO is that "social sharing of information among conspeciates offers an evolutionary advantage" [13, 29].

Based on both assumptions PSO works as the following: a population of candidate solutions (particles) moves around in the search-space. The movement is determined by a formula using the particle's position and velocity. It is influenced by the local best known position and better positions found by other particles. This process is repeated over and over again until the maximal number iteration is reached or a given error threshold was passed. In result the swarm is moving towards the best solution but there is no guarantee that a satisfying solution is found.

Creating Activity Related Document Groups

The last step is to create the activity-centric document clusters by performing the actual clustering. For each document pair a feature vector is calculated using the different relation properties presented in this paper. The calculated feature vector is then normalized using the given average contribution value and combined to a single value given the calculated weighting parameters. The result of the combined value for each document pair can be easily represented as a relatedness matrix. The final step is to use the calculated matrix to generate activity-centric document groups.

The *Agglomerative Hierarchical Clustering* algorithm [30] (HAC) is used to cluster documents into activity-centric document groups given a relatedness matrix. It works as follows: at the beginning each document has its own cluster. Document clusters with the highest relatedness values are then merged together until a given threshold has been reached. We have decided to use HAC instead of K-means because we do not know the number of clusters beforehand. Furthermore, HAC has shown significant better results than K-means with varying k in our tests.

EVALUATION

This paper provides a method for the automatic clustering of activity related information based on interaction histories, by combining activity and document properties. In this section a user study will be presented which shows how the presented

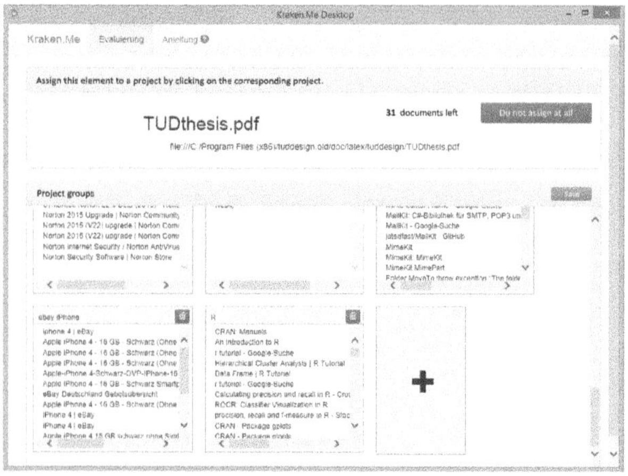

Figure 3. Regularly, the participant of the user study is asked to assign collected documents into activity-centric document groups. The user is shown a document which should be assigned to a group. By clicking on a document group, the shown document is assigned. Furthermore, the user can give each group a short description. If a document is not relevant at all, the document can be marked as irrelevant. Finally, documents can be moved from one group to another.

system (see figure 2) performs on real world data (no predefined scenario nor a restriction was given).

Study Design

Our participants installed a tool to collect interaction histories on their work machines. For this purpose, we used Kraken.me [23]. Kraken.me is a multi-device user tracking suite which offers a variety of different tools for tracking, storing and analyzing all kinds of data on multiple devices. For our purpose Kraken.me was used to generate the interaction histories without any user interruption.

For calculating the performance of the predicted activity-centric document groups, it is needed to have a standard against which the prediction is tested. During the evaluation the user will be asked by the desktop client once a day to assign recorded documents into groups (see figure 3). The user has to manually create new document groups as needed, and give these groups a short description. The user can also decide to remove a document from the list when it is not related to any created group. The manual assignment by the user will then be used as a gold standard to measure the performance of the automatic document clustering algorithm.

Figure 3 shows how the evaluation window looks like and what information is shown to the user. In case of a website, the user sees the title and the URL of the website. In case of a file, the file name and the absolute storage path is shown. When the user wants to create a new group, the user can click on the plus symbol to create one. A title for each activity related document group can be given. The shown document on the top can be assigned by simply clicking on the corresponding document group. Additionally, the user can see the remaining number of documents.

Participants

In the user study eight (8) male persons have participated. All study participants use the computer every day, are technical versed and can be considered as knowledge workers. The following table shows the age structure of the study participants:

Age group	*21 - 30*	*31 - 40*	≥ 60
Participants	6	2	1

Table 2. Age structure of the user study participants.

Timeframe for the Evaluation

Getting enough data for the document clustering algorithm is essential for evaluating the performance with real world data. The collected data must at least reveal multiple activity-centric document groups, so a longer period of usage is needed. Also activity patterns are only getting visible when the user is observed over a longer time. Finally the evaluation was performed from 15. September to 31. October 2014.

Not all participants had time to participate for the full time of the study. From 3 participants (P1, P2, P3) we have data from 47 work days, P4 and P5 have delivered data from 40 work days, P6 delivered data from 26 days and P7 and P8 have participated for 21 work days.

Collected Data

As seen in table 3, we have collected $28,045$ data items in total. From the 8 participants $7,968$ unique documents have been tracked with $15,129$ accesses. Finally $3,902$ software usage intervals were recorded. We did no data cleaning at all, only participants could mark documents as not related.

In this study we have collected a large number of real usage hours. We distinguish between real and parallel usage times. Real usage times describe the active working time on the computer when applications are open. Parallel application usages are the summed usage hours of applications running at the same time, for example when working with Excel and PowerPoint at the same time, the usage times are multiplied by two. Because we monitor each active window change using the foreground process changed event, we can also measure the number of application switches. In total we have monitored $18,336$ application switches over all study participants, so in average each user has switched applications $2,292$-times. It is interesting to see the high average number of application switches of 30.3 times per hour.

Finally, we have calculated the average active duration of a single application window. According to table 3 each application is shown in the foreground for about 7.5 minutes in average. When users are often switching between applications this number is lower than when users are working on one application for a long time.

Performance Measurements

The performance of the presented system can be calculated by comparing the predicted activity related document groups with the gold standard. We calculate the differences between them using cluster comparison measurements. There exist multiple performance measurements for this task:

- **Rand Index** [18] uses a pairwise comparison instead of looking if a single object was classified correctly. Rand

User	Sum	*P1*	*P2*	*P3*	*P4*	*P5*	*P6*	*P7*	*P8*
Documents	*7,968*	2,114	1,197	1,321	588	250	21	322	2,155
Doc. visits	*15,129*	2,985	2,633	1,320	1,251	628	205	496	5,611
Software usages	*3,902*	971	567	1087	261	116	529	134	237
Usage time (real) in hours	*1,758.2*	716.7	79.1	678.8	56.6	15.5	35.2	75.5	100.8
Usage time (parallel) in hours	*2,665.4*	939.7	240.6	888.3	145.7	7.9*	138.4	109.7	195.0
Avg. app usage in minutes	*7.5*	15.5	4.1	13.6	5.2	2.9	3.4	9.8	5.1
Switches	*18,336*	3,634	3,530	3,926	1,684	165	2,455	669	2,273
Switches per h	*30.3*	5.1	44.6	5.8	29.7	10.7	69.7	8.9	22.6

Table 3. Statistics of the collected data set grouped by participants. *: Parallel usage hours for this participant could not be calculated correctly due to an installed application that influenced our observer.

Index has a range from 0 (the predicted classification is not equal to the true classification) to 1 (predicted and true classification are the same). This measure has the disadvantage that the result is highly dependent on the number of clusters and the measure convergence to 1 as the number of clusters increase [28, 6].

- The **Adjusted Rand Index** [9] overcomes the problem of Rand Index. It returns a constant value for two random cluster sets.
- The **Adjusted Mutual Information** uses the entropy and mutual information formula and corrects the effect of a higher rating due to a larger number of document groups. The mutual information is a function which measures the equality of two assignments, ignoring permutations.

  The expected value for the mutual information can be calculated by the formula described by Vinh, Epps, and Bailey (2009) [27].

Study Evaluation

In this section the results of the user study will be presented. First the performance of each relatedness metric at its own is shown. With this knowledge, the best metrics will be selected for a second evaluation. The different metrics will be combined and used to train the weights using the Particle Swarm Optimization. Then the calculated weights will be used on the test set and the performance will be measured.

Evaluation of the Relatedness Metrics at its own

In the first evaluation we look at how the presented relatedness metrics perform standalone. We want to get more details about the quality of each of the relatedness metrics. This result will then be used to select a list of the best metrics for the second evaluation in which we will combine them together.

The evaluation is performed on the complete dataset. For the 8 participants all relatedness metrics were used to predict activity-centric document groups from the collection of documents. In the study we use the Agglomerative Hierarchical Clustering. The threshold θ is varied from 0 to 1 stepwise (0.01) and the best performance values are aggregated. Table 4 shows the aggregated mean (over all best individual values) and best values for each relatedness metric.

Metric	AMI	ARI	RI
C1: TF-IDF	**0.3706** (*0.5387*)	**0.3962**	**0.5606**
C2: LSA	0.3317 (*0.7119*)	0.3475	0.5300
C3: LDA	0.3361 (***0.7519***)	0.3350	0.5226
C4: Document Title	0.2202 (*0.3093*)	0.2004	0.4640
C5: Document Path	0.2891 (*0.5979*)	0.2604	0.4737
A1: Context Apps	0.2314 (*0.3699*)	0.1418	**0.4704**
A2: Time-Related (1)	0.1931 (*0.5029*)	0.1824	0.3562
A3: Time-Related (2)	***0.2950*** (**0.5986**)	**0.1917**	0.3671
R: Random	0.0396 (*0.1546*)	0.0289	0.4194

Table 4. Evaluation of each relatedness metric in average and best values in brackets.

The comparison of all evaluated relatedness metrics (see figure 4) shows a better performance of the content-related relatedness metrics. Only the path metric which uses the document path as the input delivers worse performance. The title metric also does not perform as well as the metrics which use the full content of the document.

In all cases content-related metrics outperform the activity-based approaches. The overall best performance delivered TF-IDF followed by LDA150. Although some paper [4, 14] show better performance of LDA or LSA, in our study the

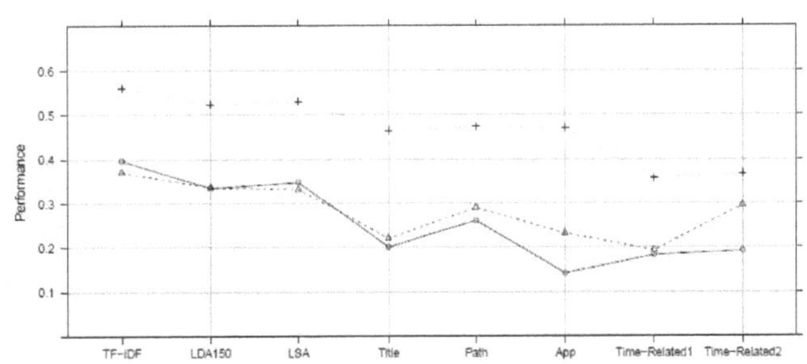

Figure 4. Average single relatedness metric performance comparison

TF-IDF approach was superior. The reason for this may be the smaller set of documents, compared to the used corpora in above mentioned papers. LSA and LDA are designed to work better with a larger number of documents. Overall, this result shows that the content of a document is a very strong indicator to determine activity-centric document groups.

Evaluation of the Combined Hybrid Feature Set

For evaluating the performance of the document clustering using a hybrid feature set it is needed to first learn the combining weightings for a part of the gathered data. Therefore, the collected dataset will be split into two sets (training and test) of equal size. Only the training set will be used to learn weightings using an optimization algorithm. The test set is then used to calculate the quality performance with the learned weightings, so the algorithm only sees the unknown data set. The dataset is separated by time, so that the training set consists of items which were collected in early days of the study and the test set contains items of the second time frame of the study.

From the result presented in the previous section a set of relatedness metrics are selected as candidates for the hybrid feature set approach:

1. **Mix of content and activity metrics**: TF-IDF, Path, App Context, Time-Related (1) and Time-Related (2)
2. **Only activity-based metrics**: App Context, Time-Related (1) and Time-Related (2)
3. **Only content-based metrics**: TF-IDF, Title, Path

The clustering threshold parameter will not be learned during the training, because this parameter works as a personal adjustment setting. The higher the number, the smaller the document groups will become. For the evaluation we will change the parameter stepwise between 0 and 1 by 0.01 steps and calculate the performance. During the training the parameter will be set to a fixed value (here: 0.7). It is not necessary to get the global maximum in the training phase because the threshold value will be varied when calculating the performance of the test set.

Training of Weighting Parameters

In the training phase the best weighting parameters for each study participant are calculated. Therefore, the training set is used as the input for the optimization algorithm which uses the combined relatedness model and adjusts the weighting parameters. The Adjusted Rand Index performance measurement is the function to be optimized. Particle Swarm Optimization is performed with 50 evolutions and 5 particles.

Testing Phase and Results

In the testing phase the real performance of the hybrid feature set document clustering approach is evaluated. The computed weightings which control the influence of each relatedness metric will be used on an unseen set of data. Then the performance of the predicted document groups will be measured.

1. Mix of content and activity metrics

In the first configuration a mixture of content- and activity-based relatedness metrics is used. This configuration is the desired feature set combining both worlds, thus it should deliver the best performance of all configurations.

Metric	*Mean*	*Best*	*Worst*
ARI	0.5287	0.7688	0.1908
AMI	0.5079	0.6942	0.2662
RI	0.6636	0.8711	0.4194

Table 5. Performance results of document clustering approach using a hybrid feature set combining Time-Related (1), Time-Related (2), App Context, TF-IDF, Path.

The document clustering approach with the hybrid feature set outperforms the performance of all single relatedness metrics. The combination of multiple metrics increases the quality of the predicted document groups. In average the Adjusted Rand Index is 0.5287 with a best performance of 0.7688. In comparison to the best single metric (TF-IDF) the combined model is about 0.13 basis points better.

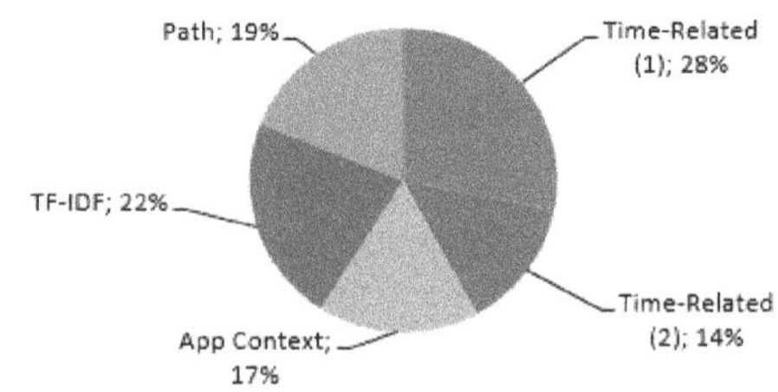

Figure 5. Average weighting parameter values. Configuration: Time-Related (1), Time-Related (2), App Context, TF-IDF, Path.

When looking at the learned weighting parameters the proportion (see figure 5) of the content-based relatedness metrics (41%) are slightly lower than the activity-based approaches (59%). The distribution over all metrics is nearly balanced. Only App Context is rated slightly lower than all other metrics. This result also shows that activity-based approaches help to better understand the structure and relationships between documents.

2. Only activity-based metrics

The second configuration only uses activity-based metrics as a comparison. This allows us to determine the influence of activity approaches in comparison to content-based approaches.

Metric	*Mean*	*Best*	*Worst*
ARI	0.3205	0.6361	0.0256
AMI	0.3522	0.6466	0.1116
RI	0.5582	0.7187	0.4194

Table 6. Performance results of hybrid feature set document clustering approach combining Time-Related (1), Time-Related (2), App Context.

In this configuration the results are getting worse in comparison to the mixed model. The best values from configuration 1 could not be reached without including the documents content.

The proportion of each metrics is almost balanced and can be seen in figure 6. Only the Time-Related (1) metric has a slightly larger influence on the result than Time-Related (2) and App Context.

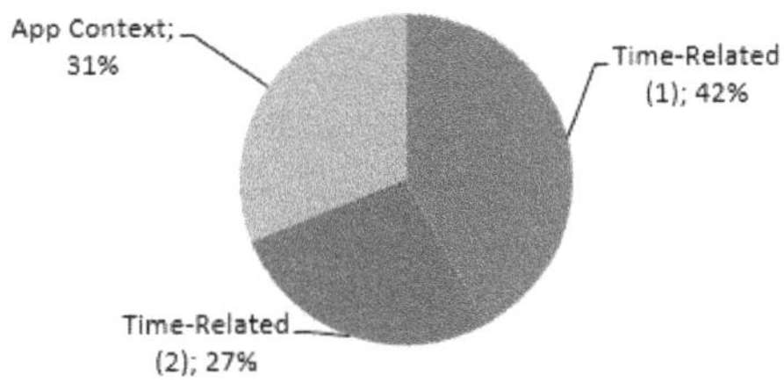

Figure 6. Average weighting parameter values. Configuration: Time-Related (1), Time-Related (2), App Context

3. Only content-based metrics

The last configuration only focuses on content-based metrics. In this configuration the TF-IDF, Path and Title metric is used to determine the relatedness between documents.

Metric	*Mean*	*Best*	*Worst*
ARI	0.3374	0.5263	0.0674
AMI	0.3532	0.5598	0.1533
RI	0.5582	0.6711	0.4194

Table 7. Performance results of the document clustering approach using a hybrid feature set combining TF-IDF, Path, Title.

In table 7 the performance of the combination of content-based relations is presented. This configuration also delivers a lower performance than the mixed model.

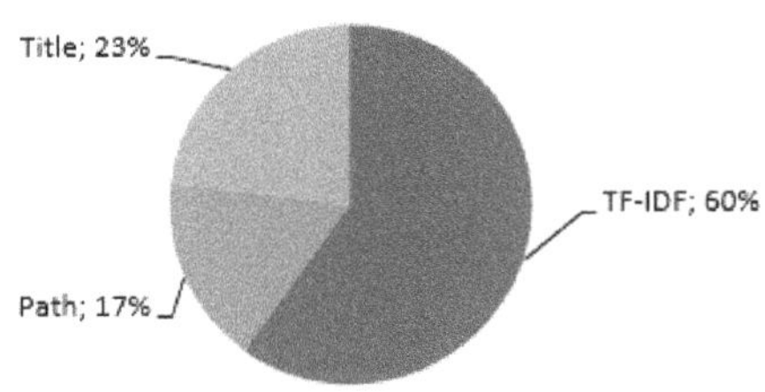

Figure 7. Average weighting parameter values. Configuration: TF-IDF, Path, Title.

The optimization algorithm delivers best results when TF-IDF similarity metric influences 60% of the result. Title and Path metrics equally divide the rest.

Evaluation Summary

The first evaluation has shown that the performance of content-based similarity metrics is better in comparison to activity-based approaches on a real world data set. The best performance was delivered by the TF-IDF method followed by LDA and LSA. The best activity-based metric was Path followed by Title, Time-Related (1), Time-Related (2) and App Context.

In the second part of the evaluation the combined hybrid feature set model was used to predict activity-centric document groups from a collection of documents. Three different configurations were evaluated, the first using activity- and content-based properties, the second using only activity-based approaches and the third using only content-based methods. The mix configuration outperformed all other configurations and has shown a significant performance increase when a mixture of different metrics is used to cluster documents. With an average performance of 0.5287 (ARI) and a best performance of 0.7688 (ARI) the combined model has shown a good performance. The main goal of this paper was to prove if a mixture model of different relatedness metrics can deliver a higher quality of the document groups than using a single approach. The evaluation has exactly shown that this is possible.

DISCUSSION AND CONCLUSION

In this paper we presented two main contributions. On the one hand we introduced an automatic clustering approach of activity related information based on interaction histories, using a mixed model of activity and content properties. Thus, we built on existing work in this domain. However, this paper is the first paper which combines the different methods. On the other hand we provided a long-term user study in an open world scenario, evaluating our and existing approaches on information work of 8 participants. The user study has shown that the hybrid feature set approach outperforms every single approach used in related work. Our approach also adapts to the users preference, and therefore delivers a user-centric view of documents.

Overlapping Clusters

This paper proposes a single cluster assignment of related information. However, information may consist of multiple topics and a single cluster assignment may not be sufficient. One solution is the creation of overlapping clusters by modifying the clustering algorithm and making changes to the cluster comparison metric. Overlapping clusters provide a better structure for multi-topic information but are also more complicated to understand for end-users. Another solution is the use of hierarchical structures which are more familiar to users that know the concept of file systems. Future research in this topic is required that also covers the graphical representation of clusters.

Interactive System

We provided an automatic hybrid clustering approach which has shown promising results in the user study. This opens up the development for an interactive system allowing users to organize their information work that provides far better clustering results than other systems. We could imagine that the weighing parameters can be determined by letting users cluster some information objects manually and/or provide default weightings and let the user correct wrong assignments. Using this knowledge automatic information clustering of the rest of the collection can be achieved. Future research which addresses the user interface (e.g. displaying clusters) and interaction (e.g. manual correction) with the system, may also help to further improve the results.

ACKNOWLEDGEMENTS

This project (HA project no. 479/15-21) is funded in the framework of Hessen ModellProjekte, financed with funds of LOEWE Landes-Offensive zur Entwicklung Wissenschaftlich-ökonomischer Exzellenz, Förderlinie 3: KMU-Verbundvorhaben (State Offensive for the Development of Scientific and Economic Excellence).

REFERENCES

1. Bailey, B. P., and Konstan, J. A. On the need for attention-aware systems : Measuring effects of interruption on task performance , error rate , and affective state. *Computers in Human Behavior 22* (2006), 685–708.
2. Bellotti, V. Managing Activities with TV-ACTA : TaskVista and Activity- Centered Task Assistant. In *Personal Information Management Workshop*, ACM Press (2006), 8–11.
3. Berry, M., Dumais, S., and O'Brien, G. Using linear algebra for intelligent information retrieval. *SIAM review*, December (1995).
4. Blei, D., Ng, A., and Jordan, M. Latent dirichlet allocation. *the Journal of machine Learning research 3* (2003), 993–1022.
5. Brdiczka, O., Su, N., and Begole, J. Temporal task footprinting: identifying routine tasks by their temporal patterns. In *Proceedings of the 15th international conference on Intelligent user interfaces*, ACM Press (2010).
6. Fowlkes, E. B., and Mallows, C. L. A Method for Comparing Two Hierarchical Clusterings. *Journal of the American Statistical Association 78* (1983), 553–569.
7. González, V., and Mark, G. Constant, constant, multi-tasking craziness: managing multiple working spheres. In *Proceedings of the SIGCHI conference on Human factors in computing systems*, vol. 6, ACM Press (2004), 113–120.
8. Hastie, T., Tibshirani, R., and Friedman, J. *The elements of statistical learning*. 2009.
9. Hubert, L., and Arabie, P. Comparing partitions. *Journal of Classification 2*, 1 (1985), 193–218.
10. Iqbal, S. T., and Horvitz, E. Disruption and recovery of computing tasks: Field study, analysis, and directions. In *Proc. CHI 2007*, ACM (2007), 677–686.
11. Jeuris, S., Houben, S., and Bardram, J. Laevo: A temporal desktop interface for integrated knowledge work. In *Proc. UIST 2014*, ACM (2014), 679–688.
12. Kaptelinin, V. UMEA: translating interaction histories into project contexts. In *Proceedings of the SIGCHI conference on Human factors in computing systems*, no. 5, ACM Press (2003), 353–360.
13. Kennedy, J. Particle swarm optimization. *Encyclopedia of Machine Learning 4* (2010), 1942–1948.
14. Landauer, T. K., Foltz, P. W., and Laham, D. An introduction to latent semantic analysis. *Discourse Processes 25*, 2-3 (Jan. 1998), 259–284.
15. Manning, C. D., Raghavan, P., and Schütze, H. *Introduction to Information Retrieval*, vol. 1. 2008.
16. Oliver, N., Smith, G., Thakkar, C., and Surendran, A. C. Swish: Semantic analysis of window titles and switching history. In *Proc. IUI 2006*, ACM (2006), 194–201.
17. Rajaraman, A., and Ullman, J. D. Data mining. In *Mining of Massive Datasets*. Cambridge University Press, 2011, 1–17. Cambridge Books Online.
18. Rand, W. M. Objective Criteria for the Evaluation of Clustering Methods. *Journal of the American Statistical Association 66* (1971), 846–850.
19. Rattenbury, T. *An activity based approach to context-aware computing*. PhD thesis, 2008.
20. Reinhardt, W., Schmidt, B., Sloep, P., and Drachsler, H. Knowledge Worker Roles and Actions - Results of Two Empirical Studies. *Knowledge and Process Management 18*, 3 (2011), 150–174.
21. Schmidt, B. *Information Work Support Based on Activity Data*. PhD thesis, TU Darmstadt, Mai 2013.
22. Schmidt, B., Kastl, J., Stoitsev, T., and Mühlhäuser, M. Hierarchical Task Instance Mining in Interaction Histories. In *Proceedings of the 29th annual international conference on Design of communication (SIGDOC)*, ACM Press (2011).
23. Schweizer, I., and Schmidt, B. Kraken.me: Multi-device user tracking suite. In *Proc. UbiComp 2014*, ACM (2014), 853–862.
24. Shen, J., Li, L., Dietterich, T. G., and Herlocker, J. L. A hybrid learning system for recognizing user tasks from desktop activities and email messages. In *Proc. IUI 2006*, ACM (2006), 86–92.
25. SINTEF. Big data, for better or worse: 90% of world's data generated over last two years. *ScienceDaily* (May 2013).
26. Smith, G., Bausdich, P., Robertson, G., Czerwinski, M., Meyers, B., Robbins, D., and Andrews, D. Groupbar: The taskbar evolved. In *Proc. OZCHI 2003* (January 2003).
27. Vinh, N. X., Epps, J., and Bailey, J. Information theoretic measures for clusterings comparison: Is a correction for chance necessary? In *Proc. ICML 2009*, ACM (2009), 1073–1080.
28. Wagner, S., and Wagner, D. *Comparing clusterings: an overview*. No. 001907. 2007.
29. Wilson, E. O. *Sociobiology: The new synthesis*. Harvard University Press, 2000.
30. Witten, I. H., Frank, E., and Hall, M. A. *Data Mining: Practical Machine Learning Tools and Techniques (Google eBook)*. 2011.

Interactive Intent Modeling from Multiple Feedback Domains

Pedram Daee[1], Joel Pyykkö[2], Dorota Głowacka[2], and Samuel Kaski[1]
Helsinki Institute for Information Technology HIIT
[1]Aalto University, Department of Computer Science
[2]University of Helsinki, Department of Computer Science
firstname.lastname@hiit.fi

ABSTRACT
In exploratory search, the user starts with an uncertain information need and provides relevance feedback to the system's suggestions to direct the search. The search system learns the user intent based on this feedback and employs it to recommend novel results. However, the amount of user feedback is very limited compared to the size of the information space to be explored. To tackle this problem, we take into account user feedback on both the retrieved items (documents) and their features (keywords). In order to combine feedback from multiple domains, we introduce a *coupled multi-armed bandits* algorithm, which employs a probabilistic model of the relationship between the domains. Simulation results show that with multi-domain feedback, the search system can find the relevant items in fewer iterations than with only one domain. A preliminary user study indicates improvement in user satisfaction and quality of retrieved information.

Author Keywords
Exploratory search; intent modeling; multi-armed bandits; relevance feedback; probabilistic user models.

ACM Classification Keywords
H.3.3 Information Search and Retrieval: Relevance feedback; I.2.6 Learning.

INTRODUCTION
The dominant information retrieval paradigm relies on the user's ability to form a precise query, which is difficult at least in the about 50% of search sessions where the user is uncertain about her information need [17]. Furthermore, the information need can shape throughout the search session. For instance, when the user prepares for writing a summary about a particular topic, the search process typically takes several iterations in which the user directs the search by tuning the initial query and the initial search intent, after observing the results. This important type of a search scenario is called *exploratory search* [10, 12, 18].

There is a wide variety of qualitative definitions of exploratory search [19]. Marchionini [12] illustrated exploratory and lookup tasks as an overlapping cloud and suggested that lookup tasks are embedded in exploratory tasks and vice versa. The problem context that motivates the search process is typically characterized in definitions of exploratory search [18]. Imprecise task requirements or open-ended search goals are the two primary attributes often used to define exploratory search with respect to the problem context [11]. The exploratory search process is considered to be cognitively complex with the information seeker being uncertain about the search process [18].

To help the user in exploratory search, her interactions with the system can be employed to infer her search intent. This is challenging for two reasons. First, active interaction is required from the user; however, users are often not willing to invest in actively giving feedback to search systems. Second, even if the interface was appealing enough, the user can only provide a limited amount of feedback, which makes user intent modelling challenging. In this paper we make it easier for the user to give feedback in exploratory search, by allowing feedback on multiple domains, in this case keywords and documents. For this we formulate the user intent modelling task as a new coupled multi-armed bandit problem, instead of using only one multi-armed bandit for one modality as in earlier approaches [14].

The rest of the paper is organized as follows: First we model exploratory search as a learning problem with limited feedback. Next, we propose the *coupled multi-armed bandits* algorithm that employs Thompson sampling with a novel probabilistic user model. We conclude the paper by evaluating the proposed method in a simulation scenario and a user study.

PROPOSED APPROACH

Problem Setting
Let D be a set of documents in a corpus and K be a set of keywords extracted from these documents. For each user, it is assumed that the relevance of each document $d \in D$ is an unknown distribution over [0,1]. This distribution encodes the uncertainty of the user about the relevance of each item, which is a key element of exploratory search. The expected

IUI'16, March 07–10, 2016, Sonoma, CA, USA.

DOI: http://dx.doi.org/10.1145/2856767.2856803

relevance of d for the user is denoted by $E_D[d]$. The document $d \in D$ is more relevant than $d' \in D$, if $E_D[d'] < E_D[d]$. Similarly, it is assumed that the relevance of each keyword $k \in K$ is an unknown distribution over [0,1] with its expected relevance denoted by $E_K[k]$. We call this set of distributions the user intent model. The expected relevances of keywords and documents are connected through a model of the data that defines how keywords belong to documents.

In each session, a user with a fixed but unknown intent model arrives. Each session consists of N iterations. In each iteration, the user provides input based on her intent model as relevance values to keywords and documents, and the algorithm provides a set of new documents and keywords. It is assumed that user feedback consists of samples from the relevance distributions.

The retrieval system should look for the most relevant document $d^* = \arg\max_{d \in D} E_D[d]$ and present it to the user. To solve this maximization the system needs to explore the document space to estimate the expected relevance of documents based on user feedback. At the same time it should exploit the estimates to show relevant documents as early as possible. This kind of a black box optimization problem, where the objective function is unknown and expensive to sample, has been studied in multi-armed bandit [6] and Bayesian optimization [4, 16] literature. A natural performance criterion for these problems is regret, which is the loss due to not presenting the most relevant documents to the user. The cumulative regret after receiving feedback for a set of documents n_D is $cum\_regret = |n_D| E_D[d^*] - \sum_{d \in n_D} E_D[d]$. The goal is to minimize the cumulative regret, which is equivalent to maximizing the sum of expected relevance feedback on documents in n_D. However, since the expected relevance of documents is hidden to the system, this measure cannot be calculated in practice.

In practice, an exploratory search system is successful if it presents to the user items, e.g. documents, that the user finds interesting. How we measure this "interest" is through maximizing the average number of clicks (or other types of positive relevance feedback) on documents in N iterations [15]. Since it is reasonable to assume that the user provides positive feedback mostly on relevant documents, this user behavior model also minimizes the cumulative regret defined from the theory point of view.

By modeling the problem as regret minimization, there is little hope to achieve a reasonable result by only considering the limited feedback on documents. In exploratory search, it is more convenient for the user to express the abstract understanding of her needs in terms of higher-level information, such as a set of keywords. In this paper we take advantage of both feedback on documents and on keywords in order to improve the regret of an exploratory search system. We tackle the problem by modeling it as coupled multi-armed bandits where it is possible to provide feedback both to the arms and the features defining the arms. In our exploratory search problem, the arms are documents and the features are keywords defining the documents.

Connecting Documents and Keywords

We assume there exists a document-keyword matrix M defined as

$$M = \begin{bmatrix} P(k_1|d_1) & \cdots & P(k_{|K|}|d_1) \\ \vdots & \ddots & \vdots \\ P(k_1|d_{|D|}) & \cdots & P(k_{|K|}|d_{|D|}) \end{bmatrix}_{|D|\times|K|}$$

where $P(k_i|d_j)$ specifies the likelihood of document d_j generating keyword k_i. This matrix is generated from the data model that expresses how keywords and the documents are related. An example, which we use, is to consider documents as bags of words and to use normalized *tf-idf* representations of documents. We make the simplifying assumption that the connection between expected relevance of a document and keywords is as follows:

$$E_D[d_j] = \sum_{i=1}^{|K|} E_K[k_i] P(k_i|d_j)$$

With the compact notation $E_D[D] = \left[E_D[d_1], \ldots, E_D[d_{|D|}]\right]^T$, and analogously for keywords, this becomes

$$E_D[D] = M E_K[K] \qquad (1)$$

Note that we made the simplifying assumptions only for the expected relevances; the shapes of the relevance distributions can be different.

Coupled Bayesian Bandits

The user provides relevance feedback to both documents and keywords. The relevance (reward) distributions for document d and keyword k are denoted by $r_d \sim f^D(.|x_d, \theta)$ and $r_k \sim f^K(.|x_k, \theta)$, respectively. The x_d and x_k are the feature (context) vectors associated with d and k. The fixed but unknown parameter θ defines the shared link between these two relevance distributions. After the user has interacted with a set of documents n_D and a set of keywords n_K, we can write the posterior at time $t = |n_D| + |n_K|$ as

$$\pi_t(\theta) \propto \pi_0(\theta) \prod_{d \in n_D} f^D(r_d|x_d, \theta) \prod_{k \in n_K} f^K(r_k|x_k, \theta), \qquad (2)$$

where $\pi_0(\theta)$ is the prior distribution for θ. In order to apply Bayesian bandit methods [1, 9] it is only necessary to be able to perform the following two steps: draw a sample from the posterior at time t, and after that score all the documents and keywords by $E_D[r_d|x_d, \theta^p]$ and $E_K[r_k|x_k, \theta^p]$.

These two steps are the minimum requirements for employing the Thompson sampling algorithm for bandits [1, 7, 9]. In Thompson sampling, the exploration and exploitation are controlled indirectly by the uncertainty in the posterior. We can easily draw a sample from the posterior by using any sampling method, after specifying the shared parameter θ that connects the relevance distributions, and the feature vectors x_d and x_k. These parameters are defined by the user model.

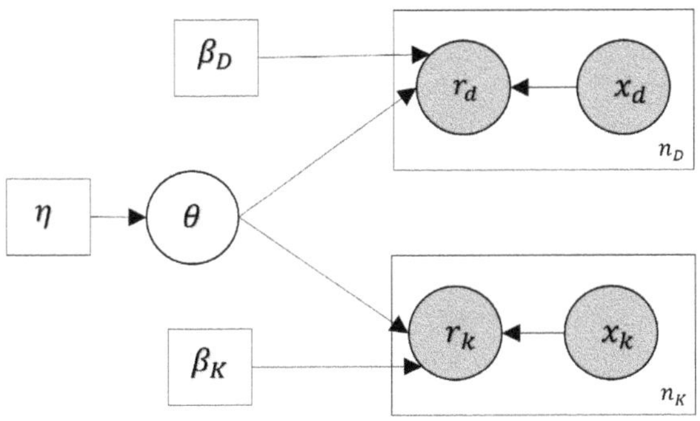

Figure 1. Probabilistic model for user feedback on documents and keywords.

Probabilistic User Model

We propose a simple model for received relevance feedback on documents and keywords. Since the amount of feedback from the user is limited, we need to impose a structure on the expected relevance of items to be able to generalize well. We assume that the expected relevance of keywords is linearly related to their feature vectors by the unknown weight vector θ, i.e. $E_K[K] = M^T\theta$. Based on this linearity assumption and our previous assumption in equation (1), we have $E_D[D] = ME_K[K] = MM^T\theta$. Using this feature transformation, we only need to estimate one set of unknown weights to specify expected relevance of both documents and keywords. Considering Gaussian distributions for relevance, we propose the following model (plate diagram in Figure 1):

$$f^K(r_k|x_k,\theta,\beta_K) = N(r_k; x_k^T\theta, \beta_K^2)$$

$$f^D(r_d|x_d,\theta,\beta_D) = N(r_d; x_d^T\theta, \beta_D^2)$$

$$\pi_0(\theta) = N(\theta; 0, \eta^2 \mathrm{I})$$

Here, x_k is the kth column of M and x_d is the dth column of MM^T; they define feature vectors for keyword k and document d, respectively. Since all the distributions are Gaussian, the posterior is also a Gaussian distribution, with:

$$\pi_t(\theta) = N(\theta; \mu_t, \Sigma_t)$$

$$\Sigma_t^{-1} = \beta_D^{-2}X_{n_D}^T X_{n_D} + \beta_K^{-2}X_{n_K}^T X_{n_K} + \eta^{-2}\mathrm{I} \quad (3)$$

$$\mu_t = \Sigma_t(\beta_D^{-2}X_{n_D}^T R_{n_D} + \beta_K^{-2}X_{n_K}^T R_{n_K})$$

where X_{n_D} is a $|n_D| \times D$ design matrix containing feature vectors for the observed documents in the set n_D, and R_{n_D} is a $|n_D| \times 1$ matrix of the corresponding observed relevance values. With the same logic, X_{n_K} is a $|n_K| \times D$ design matrix containing feature vectors for the observed keywords in the set n_K, and R_{n_K} is a $|n_K| \times 1$ matrix of the corresponding observed relevance values. The computational complexity of (3) comes from the covariance matrix inversion.

The coupled multi-armed bandits algorithm employing Thompson sampling for controlling exploration-exploitation tradeoff is as follows:

ALGORITHM 1: Coupled multi-armed bandits

At time step t

1. draw $\theta^p \sim \pi_t(\theta)$ from (3)
2. for document bandit: select $d^+ = \arg\max_{d\in D} x_d^T\theta^p$
3. for keyword bandit: select $k^+ = \arg\max_{k\in K} x_k^T\theta^p$
4. update the posterior (3) based on user feedback and observed feature vectors

SIMULATION

In each exploratory search session, the simulator considers a small set of documents and keywords as targets, and assumes their expected relevance to be 1. The simulated user employs Latent Semantic Indexing (LSI) and cosine similarity measure to calculate similarities to the targets for all documents and keywords. According to these similarities, an expected relevance value in [0,1] is assigned to each document and keyword, defining $E_D[D]$ and $E_K[K]$.

In each iteration, the algorithm presents five documents and five keywords to the user (by repeating steps 2 and 3 of Algorithm 1). We assume that the simulated user selects document d as relevant with probability equal to relevance value $r_d \sim N(E_D[d], \beta_D^2)$, and provides relevance feedback $r_k \sim N(E_K[k], \beta_K^2)$ for keyword k with probability proportional to $|r_k - 0.5|$. The motivation is that users usually give feedback to keywords that are highly relevant or irrelevant. We used a fixed pool of 750 computer science arXiv articles, with only 50 of them having high expected relevance in the user intent model. The model parameters were set to $\beta_D = \beta_k = 0.3$ and $\eta = 0.5$. We compared our method with variants that only consider feedback on keywords or documents to update the posterior (3).

Based on the simulation result in Figure 2, we can conclude that considering feedback on both documents and keywords will significantly increase the number of relevant items that the user can find with the same number of iterations.

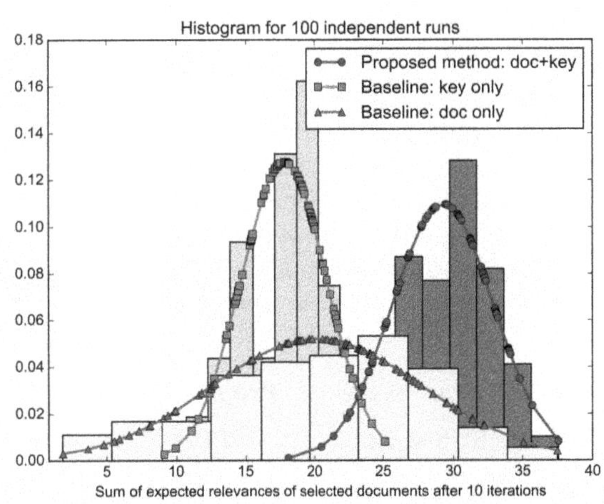

Figure 2. Histogram for 100 independent runs of the methods. The sum of expected relevances of selected documents after 10 iterations is significantly higher when both types of feedback (doc+key) are considered.

USER EXPERIMENTS AND RESULTS

We implemented the proposed method in an existing exploratory search system SciNet [8]. SciNet uses the LinRel algorithm [2] to learn the user intent model based on feedback on keywords visualized on a radar-like interface. In our implementation, we replaced LinRel with Algorithm 1. Furthermore, user interactions with documents, i.e. clicks or bookmarks, are considered as relevance feedback on documents, in addition to feedback on keywords. The computational complexity of both algorithms is the same.

We conducted a preliminary user study on 10 university students and researchers. All the participants were fluent in English and had some background in computer science or a related field. Each participant performed two exploratory tasks in which they had to do a literature survey on a topic and answer three questions in a fixed amount of time. The topics were reinforcement learning and neural networks. The participants reported their knowledge of the topics on 1-5 Likert scale (with 2.2 on average). The user interface and real time performance of the systems were identical, and the participants were naïve about which exploratory search engine was used for each task. In each iteration, five documents were shown to the user and the user could bookmark the relevant ones. All user interactions were logged by the system including the typed query, documents and keywords presented to the user, and documents and keywords that the user interacted with. After each task the participants answered a questionnaire containing SUS [5] and a short version of ResQue [13] using 1-5 Likert scale, where 1 indicates “strongly disagree”. A short interview with each participant was conducted after the tasks.

Answers to all the tasks and the bookmarked documents were rated by experts in a double-blind assessment using a scale from 0 (no answer) to 5 (perfect answer). All the shown documents were assessed on a binary scale based on their relevance to the search topic. The inter-rater agreement between the experts showed that the rankings overlapped more than 80%. One of the users was excluded from the analysis because he did not bookmark any article.

Table 1 summarises different performance measures for the proposed algorithm and the baseline system. The percentage of all the shown articles that were labelled as relevant by the experts was calculated as a measure of the quality of the shown information. For the proposed system this value was 5 percent better compared to the baseline. However, the difference was not statistically significant.

Performance measure	Proposed	Baseline
Average SUS score	**75**	67.2
Average ResQue score	**54.7**	52.3
% of relevant documents	**84.6**	79.1
User task performance	3.45	3.45

Table 1. Performance measures for the proposed and baseline systems. The better value on each row is shown in bold.

The proposed algorithm had better SUS and ResQue scores compared to the baseline. However, due to the small sample size these differences were not statistically significant. It should be noted that most of the questions in SUS and ResQue target areas such as user interface, which was the same in both systems. There are two questions in ResQue that measure the *novelty* and *diversity* of search results [13]: *The recommender system helped me discover new items* and *The items recommended to me are diverse.* In both questions the proposed method scored higher (4.1 and 3.7) against the baseline system (3.5 and 3.3).

User task performance was measured by averaging the expert assessments of the answers for the three questions in each task. The users were hard pressed to gather a report in time, which was also evident in their answers. In these reports both systems achieved the same average performance.

In the interviews, 6 out of 9 users reported higher satisfaction with the proposed system (more diversity and better results), one reported that he could not tell the difference, and two said that the baseline was better.

Overall, the preliminary results indicate that the proposed system gave the users a more satisfying image of the topic they were exploring. Furthermore, the usability of the total system has also improved.

DISCUSSION AND CONCLUSION

In this paper we introduced the *coupled multi-armed bandits* algorithm as the exploratory search method that employs the user feedback on both the retrieved items and their features. Our approach is based on two main ideas. First, we model user behavior as a generative probabilistic model. Second, we couple different sources of feedback in a unified model. Our simulation results and preliminary user study indicate that considering these two sources of feedback can improve the performance and quality of the exploratory search.

From the practical point of view, our algorithm provides the opportunity to exploit several types of relevance feedback that are available for documents, in addition to relevance feedback available for individual keywords. For example in [3] it was shown that it is possible to detect implicit relevance feedback from physiological signals such as electrodermal activity and facial electromyography on documents. We believe that this is an important step for the future of exploratory search applications since an increasing amount of research studies the feasibility of performing information retrieval based on novel types of relevance signals both on keywords and on documents.

ACKNOWLEDGMENTS

This work has been partly supported by the Academy of Finland (Finnish Centre of Excellence in Computational Inference Research COIN), Re:Know funded by TEKES, and MindSee (FP7–ICT; Grant Agreement #611570).

REFERENCES

1. Agrawal, S., and Goyal, N. Thompson Sampling for Contextual Bandits with Linear Payoffs. In *Proc. of ICML,* (2013), 127-135.
2. Auer, P. Using confidence bounds for exploitation-exploration trade-offs. *The Journal of Machine Learning Research*, (2003), 397-422.
3. Barral, O., Eugster, M. J., Ruotsalo, T., Spapé, M. M., Kosunen, I., Ravaja, N., ... and Jacucci, G. Exploring Peripheral Physiology as a Predictor of Perceived Relevance in Information Retrieval. In *Proc. of IUI,* ACM (2015), 389-399.
4. Brochu, E., Cora, V. M., and De Freitas, N. A tutorial on Bayesian optimization of expensive cost functions, with application to active user modeling and hierarchical reinforcement learning. *arXiv preprint arXiv:1012.2599*, 2010.
5. Brooke, J. SUS-A quick and dirty usability scale. *Usability evaluation in industry 189*, (1996), 4-7.
6. Bubeck, S., and Cesa-Bianchi, N. Regret analysis of stochastic and nonstochastic multi-armed bandit problems. *Foundations and Trends in Machine Learning*, (2012), 5(1), 1-122.
7. Chapelle, O., and Li, L. An empirical evaluation of thompson sampling. In *Advances in Neural Information Processing Systems,* (2011), 2249-2257.
8. Glowacka, D., Ruotsalo, T., Konuyshkova, K., Kaski, S., and Jacucci, G. Directing exploratory search: Reinforcement learning from user interactions with keywords. In *Proc. of IUI,* ACM (2013), 117-128.
9. Hoffman, M. D., Shahriari, B., and de Freitas, N. On correlation and budget constraints in model-based bandit optimization with application to automatic machine learning. In *Proc. of AISTATS,* (2014), 365-374.
10. Kammerer, Y., Nairn, R., Pirolli, P. and Chi, E.H. Signpost from the masses: learning effects in an exploratory social tag search browser. In *Proc. of the SIGCHI Conference on Human Factors in Computing Systems*, ACM (2009), 625-634.
11. Kim, J. Describing and predicting information-seeking behavior on the web. *Journal of the American Society for Information Science and Technology*, (2009), 679–693.
12. Marchionini, G. Exploratory search: from finding to understanding. *Communications of the ACM* (2006), 41–46.
13. Pu, P., Chen, L., and Hu, R. A user-centric evaluation framework for recommender systems. In *Proc. of RecSys,* ACM (2011), 157-164.
14. Ruotsalo, T., Jacucci, G., Myllymäki, P. and Kaski, S. Interactive intent modeling: Information discovery beyond search. *Communications of the ACM,* (2014), 58(1), 86-92.
15. Slivkins, A., Radlinski, F., and Gollapudi, S. Ranked bandits in metric spaces: learning diverse rankings over large document collections. *The Journal of Machine Learning Research*, (2013), 14(1), 399-436.
16. Srinivas, N., Krause, A., Kakade, S. M., and Seeger, M. Gaussian process optimization in the bandit setting: No regret and experimental design. In *Proc. of ICML,* (2010).
17. Teevan, J., Alvarado, C., Ackerman, M. S., and Karger, D. R. The perfect search engine is not enough: a study of orienteering behavior in directed search. In *Proc. of CHI,* ACM (2004), 415-422.
18. White, R. W., and Roth, R. A. Exploratory search: Beyond the query-response paradigm. *Synthesis Lectures on Information Concepts, Retrieval, and Services*, (2009), 1-98.
19. Wildemuth, B. M., and Freund, L. Assigning search tasks designed to elicit exploratory search behaviors. In *Proc. of HCIR*. ACM (2012), 1–10

Inferring a Player's Need For Cognition From Hints

Carlos Pereira Santos
Eindhoven University of Technology &
NHTV Breda University of Applied Sciences
Eindhoven, The Netherlands
c.a.pereira.santos@tue.nl

Vassilis-Javed Khan, Panos Markopoulos
Eindhoven University of Technology
Eindhoven, The Netherlands
v.j.khan@tue.nl, p.markopoulos@tue.nl

ABSTRACT
Player behavior during game play can be used to construct player models that help adapt the game and make it more fun for the player involved. Similarly in-game behavior could help model personality traits that describe people's attitudes in a fashion that can be stable over time and over different domains, e.g., to support health coaching, or other behavior change approaches. This paper demonstrates the feasibility of this approach by relating Need for Cognition (NfC) a personality trait that can predict the effectiveness of different persuasion strategies upon users to a commonly used game mechanic – *hints*. An experiment with N=188 participants confirmed our hypothesis that NfC has a negative correlation with the number of hints players follow during the game. Future work should confirm if adherence to hints can be used as a predictor of behavior in different games, and to find other game mechanics than hints, that help predict user traits.

Author Keywords
Player modeling; Player profiling; Games with a purpose; Need for cognition; game design.

ACM Classification Keywords
K.8.0 PERSONAL COMPUTING: General; Games.

INTRODUCTION
Player modeling refers to in-game behavior analysis to represent, explain or predict the player's behavior [9]. Player models are typically applied to adapt or improve gameplay, e.g., the level of challenge, the game characters and the game environment [2]. This approach can be extended to model [3] stable characteristics of users such as personality traits, that can help predict attitudes and behaviors in different contexts, which has also been called player profiling [6]. For example, [6] model personality traits by embedding personality questionnaire items inside a game, thus allowing to profile user personality by logging game play. Such an approach can potentially remove the tedium of using psychometric questionnaires in order to obtain this information from players. [8] go on to embed questionnaire items in social situations enacted in the game. It would be even more beneficial if the game mechanic used to model player traits would be an inherent element of the game tested rather than an in-game administration of a psychometric questionnaire.

IUI'16, March 07-10, 2016, Sonoma, CA, USA
 ISBN 978-1-4503-4137-0/16/03…$15.00
DOI: http://dx.doi.org/10.1145/2856767.2856805

Furthermore, developers can purposely design games with pre-knowledge that specific game mechanics can deduce specific psychometric characteristics of players and use them as a tool to enhance gameplay. This paper demonstrates the feasibility of this approach for the specific case of Need for Cognition (NfC), a personality trait relating to how likely a person is to engage cognitively when confronted with choices rather than apply mental shortcuts and heuristics. This trait has been shown to predict how people might react to hints and persuasive attempts common in the domains of health coaching, choice behavior e.g., see [7], and advertising effectiveness, e.g., see [3]. We report a study that investigates the link between a commonly used game-mechanic – *hints* – with NfC. More specifically, we investigate the players' behavior in following hints and whether that correlates with their need for cognition. To our knowledge no other game has deduced personality traits unobtrusively in a way embedded in a single and specific game mechanic. The importance of our study is applicable not just to gaming but also to a range of other applications such as persuasion and advertisement.

In the remainder of this paper we introduce Need for Cognition and discuss how it can be measured by self-report and by observational measures. We then go on to describe the design of a game, where the game mechanic of providing hints was designed such us to expose the NfC of players. We report an experiment where we tested the correlation of NfC measured through a questionnaire and the number of hints followed in the game.

NEED FOR COGNITION
Need for Cognition (NfC) is associated with the extent to which an individual is inclined to engage in cognitive activities [1]. High NfC defines persons who are more inclined to mental problem solving and assessment of situations with higher degree of elaboration. On the other hand, people with lower NfC are prone to less elaboration and follow more heuristic and empirical strategies.

An individual's NfC can be inferred by applying suitable psychometric tests, as for example [1]. It can also be inferred by observing behavior when offered different choices; for example [5].

NfC is a simple and stable personality trait and it has been applied across multiple contexts including predictions of the effectiveness of social influence strategies for persuasion [5]. To this point it has not been attempted to assess a player's NfC through Player Modeling.

PLAYER MODELLING OF NEED FOR COGNITION

To establish whether player modeling can be used to model NfC, we set out to design a game that would allow differences between people with high NfC and those with low NfC to manifest naturally during game play. This is where game environments excel, offering ample opportunities to exhibit choice behavior within a controlled environment, and where it is straightforward to record player actions.

The approach is to introduce a shortcut mechanism that reduces cognitive load in some choice situations; for example, by introducing a hint system that supports the player's decision process. We designed a two-player turn-based game, where players control the movement of a set of units (Figure 1). Each player has a team and starts with three units. The overall objective is to eliminate the units of the opposing team[1]. In a typical turn the player can only move one out of the three available units. Each unit can only move up to two tiles, and has three main properties: shield, energy (health), and attack power, (displayed in the upper right corner). Small vertical progress bars at the right of each unit represent energy. The key game mechanic is the unit movement; each player per turn has to decide which unit to move and where to move it. The game becomes challenging since on every turn a player can choose from 50 possible moves on average, and for every possible action one needs to consider their opponent's possible moves.

To shortcut considering such a large set of possible moves we introduced a secondary game mechanic that suggests one reasonably good movement - a hint. Hints are displayed directly on the board by lighting tiles, indicating which unit should move and where to. Hints can be requested explicitly by pressing the light-bulb button, or implicitly if a timer times out. The timer is displayed in the game through a progress bar. The time was fixed and was determined based on the average time a player takes to play; during the first testing phase we found that a player took 6 seconds on average, so we set the timer to 4 seconds, to give the opportunity to players to plan their own move.

Hints provide a natural extension to the basic game mechanic as a support for less experienced players.

[1]Play Nanobots at: http://imi.nhtv.nl/nanobots/

Figure 1: *Left* - Nanobots is a game designed to study players' Need for Cognition. The screenshot shows a typical player turn. *Right* - Need for Cognition scale questionnaire embedded into the Nanobots game displayed before a game starts.

At the same time whether the player will rely on the hint could arguably relate to the player's NfC: players with lower NfC should be expected to take more shortcuts during the decision making process by using the hints provided.

The hint mechanic suggests a beneficial movement, but not the optimal one. Note that, if the optimal movement would be offered, playing the game would be contrived, since hint followers would always win.

EXPERIMENTAL STUDY

We conducted an experiment to test the relation between NfC and in game choice behavior.

Measures

Need for cognition was measured with the standard questionnaire of [1]. We logged the number of hints requested, the number of hints followed, the total duration of the game and the score players achieved.

Measures and hypothesis

We hypothesized that player's NfC would correlate negatively with the number of hints explicitly requested in the game (H1). Also, we hypothesized that there is a negative correlation between NfC as measured with the standard questionnaire and the number of hints players would follow in the game (H2).

If found, such negative correlations could be explained by high NfC people taking fewer hints, according to our experiment design, but could also be explained by high NfC taking longer to play the game and thus having more opportunities to follow hints or simply because the game favors people with higher NfC. To address these potential confounds, we tested two more hypotheses: First whether people with high need for cognition play longer than people with low need for cognition (H3); we anticipate that this hypothesis should be rejected. Second, we examine a higher need for cognition correlates with a higher score in the game (H4).

Procedure

We uploaded the game online and on the Google Play-Store as free to play, and also used crowdsourcing to recruit participants. Players were informed of the fact that data was being collected for research purposes, and all logged data was anonymous. The first game is a tutorial that should help players understand the game goal and mechanics. Moreover, to limit the confounding effect of learning the game and especially for different learning speeds across players or for difficulties players have problems adjusting to the game, we considered the first two games as training and did not consider the data of the first and second game. The data is shown below for completeness though. The study only relates the data from the third game onwards.

Participants

A total of 188 participants took part of the study, but, only data from 105 participants was retained, ensuring that all players included in the analysis had played at least 6 games, had answered all the NfC questions.

RESULTS

Explicit requested hints

A Spearman's correlation analysis between the players' (N=105) NfC and the sum of the number of hints explicitly requested by that player between the third and the sixth game, although a clear trend, was not significant ($r = -0.173$, $p = 0.078$); thus H1 could not be accepted.

Hints followed

A Spearman's correlation analysis between the NfC of players (N=105) and the sum of the number of hints followed them between third and the sixth game (inclusive), reveals a significant negative correlation ($r=-0.198$, $p=.043$) in accordance to H2.

Game itself does not bias towards Need for Cognition

The analysis of the average game time depicted in Figure 4, shows a substantial decrease in time spent playing the first game for both high and low NfC players. The duration of games seemed to remain relatively stable in games three to five, confirming that the game was sufficiently understood by that point and excluding sessions 1 and 2 from the analysis avoids confounding learning effects.

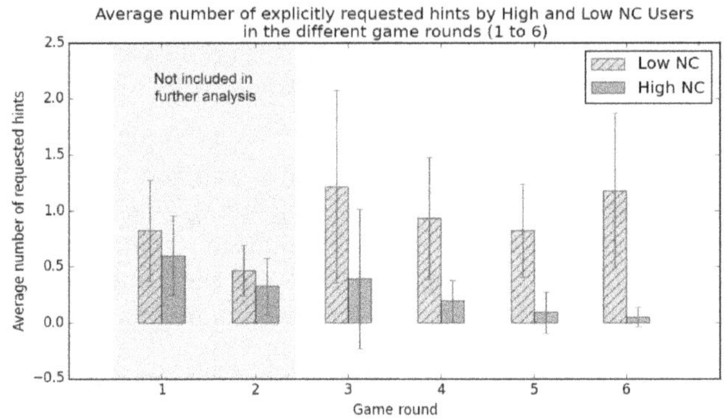

Figure 2: Average explicitly requested hints by high and low NfC players.

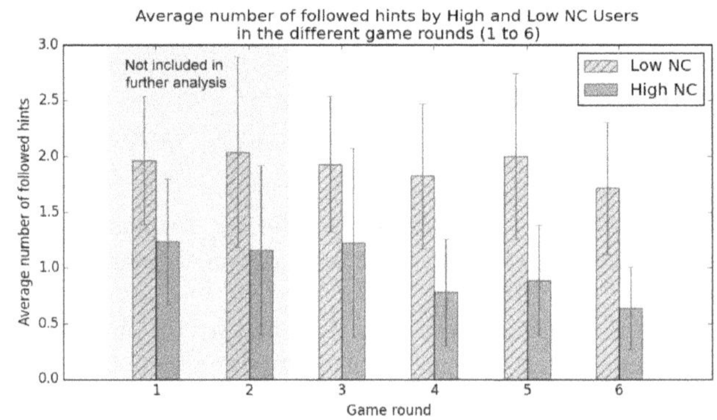

Figure 3: Average hints followed by high and low NfC players.

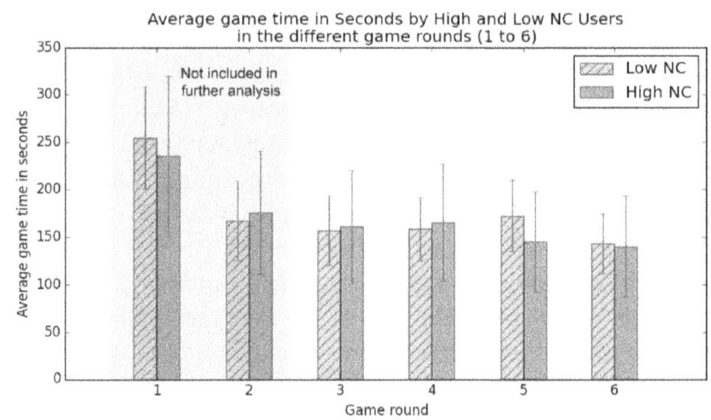

Figure 4: Average game time by high and low NfC players.

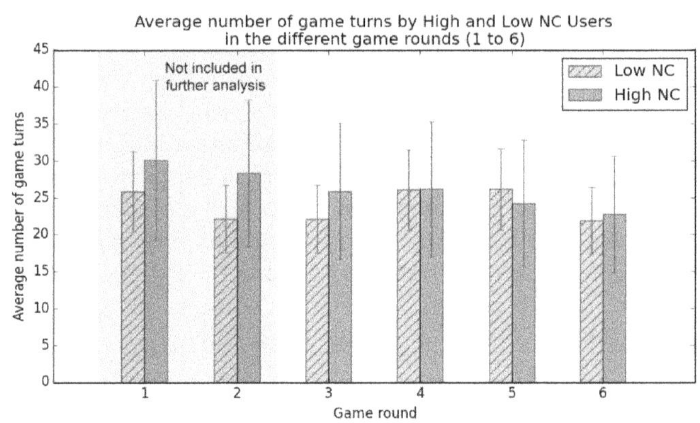

Figure 5: Average number of turns by high and low NfC players.

We also analyzed the average number of turns for both high and low NfC (see Figure 5), and across all games no significant difference was found, therefore invalidating H3. A Spearman's test does not show any correlation between NfC and game score achieved overall ($r=0.002$, $p=0.984$) so H4 could not be retained. In sum, looking at game sessions 3, 4, 5, and 6, we found no significant difference between high and low NfC players. Rejecting both H3 & H4 shows that the game does not favor players with certain NfC.

DISCUSSION

We could not confirm our hypothesis that NfC would influence explicit request of hints. A possible explanation is that the players did not need to explicitly request a hint, because the game automatically provided the hints (the implicit invocation of hints after a certain time period). In hindsight, this complication in the hint mechanic introduces an ambiguity in our results, as we cannot distinguish instances where the player wished to have a hint and got it automatically from situations where the player did not wish to have a hint. Nevertheless, this slight difference taps into different behavioral measures. Explicitly requesting hints addresses the player's need for advise or support, whereas following hints addresses whether the player is actually influenced by the hint. We are planning to investigate this difference in future research.

We could confirm our hypothesis that there is a negative correlation between followed hints and NfC. While we are yet not at the point of reliably testing NfC based on game behavior, this correlation confirms the feasibility of modeling personality traits by player behavior. This finding is an important one because it supports the unobtrusive detection of NfC – a general and salient user trait – with a specific and commonly used game mechanic. Our approach offers several advantages with regards to ensure a pleasurable and unobtrusive profiling of users.

Such profiling can improve players' experiences in several ways. For example, we would recommend in strategy games, like our Nanobots game, high NfC players should get additional (visually and conceptually related) cognitive tasks – e.g. puzzles – to solve before going to a next level while low NfC players will not. In other game types, such as adventure games, high NfC players should get more riddles to solve compared to low NfC players; or in exploration games (e.g. RPGs or puzzle-platforms), low NfC players can get an influential figure (e.g. priest or political leader) to impact their engagement and exploration with the game. Further, other game aspects, such as content purchases high NfC players should get in-depth information and low visual complexity as this would be favorable for them [4]; whereas low NfC players should get more visual complex stimuli. Naturally, future research should seek to evaluate whether the recommendations mentioned above would actually contribute to player experience.

CONCLUSION

We developed Nanobots, a simple strategy game to test whether players' Need for Cognition, a general and stable personality trait correlates with players' behavior regarding hints. As expected, we found a negative correlation between following hints and NfC. This study is the first that provides empirical evidence for such a relation of in-game behavior and a stable personality trait. Game designers, developers and researchers can directly benefit from the unobtrusive detection of NfC, in order to adapt system behavior to the needs of the user. Extending the principle demonstrated in this paper offers a lot of promise. By defining more links between game mechanics and player models, one can provide game designers a set of tools that can help develop better games, but, also to enhance the value and utility of such games.

REFERENCES

1. Cacioppo, J. T., Petty, R. E., & Kao, C. F. 1984. The efficient assessment of need for cognition. Journal of Personality Assessment, 48(3), 306–307.

2. Darryl Charles, A. Kerr, M. McNeill, et al. 2005. Player-centred game design: Player modelling and adaptive digital games. *Proceedings of the Digital Games Research Conference*, 00100.

3. Curtis P. Haugtvedt, Richard E. Petty, and John T. Cacioppo. 1992. Need for cognition and advertising: Understanding the role of personality variables in consumer behavior. *Journal of Consumer Psychology* 1, 3: 239–260.

4. Martin, B. A., Sherrard, M. J., & Wentzel, D. (2005). The role of sensation seeking and need for cognition on web-site evaluations: a resource-matching perspective. *Psychology and Marketing*, *22*(2), 109-126.

5. Maurits Kaptein, Panos Markopoulos, Boris de Ruyter, and Emile Aarts. 2015. Personalizing persuasive technologies: Explicit and implicit personalization using persuasion profiles. *International Journal of Human-Computer Studies* 77: 38–51.

6. Giel van Lankveld, Pieter Spronck, Jaap Van den Herik, and Arnoud Arntz. 2011. Games as personality profiling tools. *Computational Intelligence and Games (CIG), 2011 IEEE Conference on*, IEEE, 197–202.

7. Stephen M. Smith and Irwin P. Levin. 1996. Need for cognition and choice framing effects. *Journal of Behavioral Decision Making* 9, 4: 283–290.

8. Pieter Spronck, Iris Balemans, and Giel Van Lankveld. 2012. Player Profiling with Fallout 3. *AIIDE*. Retrieved 10/10/15 from http://musicweb.ucsd.edu/~sdubnov/mu270d/AIIDE12/01/AIIDE12-038.pdf

9. Georgios N. Yannakakis, Pieter Spronck, Daniele Loiacono, and Elisabeth André. 2013. Player Modeling. *Artificial & Computational Intelligence in Games* 6:45–59.

Driver Classification Based on Driving Behaviors

Cheng Zhang[1], **Mitesh Patel**[2], **Senaka Buthpitiya**[2], **Kent Lyons**[3], **Beverly Harrison**[4]
Gregory D. Abowd[1]
Georgia Institute of Technology[1], Yahoo Labs[2], Technicolor Research[3], Microsoft[4]
chengzhang@gatech.edu, miteshp@yahoo-inc.com, senaka@yahoo-inc.com,
kent.lyons@technicolor.com, 00beverly@gmail.com, abowd@gatech.edu

ABSTRACT
In this paper we develop a model capable of classifying drivers from their driving behaviors sensed by only low level sensors. The sensing platform consists of data available from the diagnostic outlet (OBD) of the car and smartphone sensors. We develop a window based support vector machine model to classify drivers. We test our model with two datasets collected under both controlled and naturalistic conditions. Furthermore, we evaluate the model using each sensor source (car and phone) independently and combining both the sensors. The average classification accuracies attained with data collected from three different cars shared between couples in a naturalistic environment were 75.83%, 85.83% and 86.67% using only phone sensors, only cars sensors and combined car and phone sensors respectively.

Author Keywords
Driver Identification; Driver behavior modeling; Sensor fusion; Smartphones;

ACM Classification Keywords
H.4 Information System Applications : Miscellaneous

INTRODUCTION
Driving is an integral part of everyday life for many people and we are seeing interesting technologies integrated with cars including navigation systems, adaptive cruise control (ACC) and lane-keeping assist systems (LKAS). Many of these systems utilize sensing mechanisms to monitor the car, the environment and the driver. As such, the car is an interesting platform for exploring new ubiquitous computing applications. Unfortunately, these car sensing and computing platforms tend to be proprietary and closed. It is very difficult for developers or researchers to leverage these platforms to build applications.

There are standards for getting some of the car sensing data. Specifically, the On-Board Diagnostic (OBD-II)[1] protocol provides information about the car that is traditionally used to perform car maintenance tasks. Mobile phones offer another platform for rich sensing that can be used to infer information about the car and its driver. As users upgrade their phones, the old phone, which is often a very capable sensing platform, might be put in the car and serve a useful role. Alternatively, these mobile platforms might be integrated into the car as possible open platforms (e.g. Android Auto).

In this project, we explore identifying the driver of the car using the sensing capabilities available on these platforms. There are several applications where such a driver classification could be beneficial. For example, it would be useful for the car and user's mobile phone to streamline the in-car mobile phone experience. Using the visual and touch interface of a phone while driving is dangerous and in many locations illegal. Shifting to a hand-free, eyes-free interface is a possibility but requires extra steps for the user to enter that mode. In contrast, using the traditional phone interface while a passenger in the car poses no problems. Determining who is driving the car (versus a passenger) and communicating that information to the mobile devices in the car could help automatically set the appropriate modes or offer other abilities to personalize the in-car experience. A phone might have a unique identified owner and off-the-shelf techniques can classify if the phone is in a moving vehicle, however, just knowing that a phone (and its owner) is in the car is not sufficient information to adapt a user interface when there are multiple people in the car. The person could be a driver or a passenger.

In this paper, we develop driver identification models using the sensors available on smartphones along with the limited car sensor information available through the OBD-II protocol. We explore using each of these sensing platforms independently and the possibility of fusing the data sources together. We present three experiments from two different data sets. The primary aim of these experiments is to test the capability and the robustness of the classification model. Our first data set involves 14 drivers each driving three different cars and is designed to understand the machine learning challenges in this domain. Our second data set is more naturalistic whereby we collect everyday data from pairs of people that share a car. Our experiments detail the tradeoffs between the number of unique driver classifications we need to make, the impact of different sensor data on classification, and the differences between the more controlled versus naturalistic driving data sets.

[1] http://en.wikipedia.org/wiki/OBD-II_PIDs

IUI'16, March 07-10, 2016, Sonoma, CA, USA.
 ISBN 978-1-4503-4137-0/16/03 $15.00.
DOI: http://dx.doi.org/10.1145/2856767.2856806

RELATED WORK

Researchers have developed a number of solutions for understanding different aspects of user behavior in cars. These systems often use state of the art algorithms in computer vision, low level sensor data and fusion techniques and machine learning algorithms.

For example, in the areas of predicting driver drowsiness, different computer vision based systems have been developed for monitoring driver vigilance by monitoring eye blink rate, head nodding etc [10]. Other research has shown the possibility to detect drunk driving patterns from smartphone sensors [4] and to monitor elders driving pattern through a sensor fusion of accelerometer, camera and GPS [1].

More directly relevant to our research is work that detects various driving events. Research has demonstrated the promise of classifying driving events (e.g. turn events, stop, start) through inertial sensors on a phone [5] [9] and the sensor data from a vechile [7] with different algorithms(e.g. DTW, HMM). Our work is similar in terms of sensing sources, but instead of identifying driving events, we distinguish between different potential drivers of the same car.

Finally, there is some work modeling driving behavior using sensed data but this makes different assumption about data availability. Some research built drivers' profile based on the additional sensors from the car, which is not widely available through OBD-II car ports [6] and others collected the sensors from smartphone to identify the driver vs. passengers [2]. The closest work is [8], which was able to classify different drivers, but it instrumented the brake and gas pedals with customized sensors sampling at high frequencies (1 kHz), which make it less practical to be applied in the real world.

Most of the research above focuses on driving event detection, using customized sensors or having access to proprietary sensors. We instead chose a more practical hardware setting in current real-world scenarios using the ODB interface and a smartphone. The OBD-II interface is available in every car produced after 1996 in the US and phones have been widely used as testbeds for sensor data collection [2] [4] [5] [6]. Thus the challenge we address is using the data from commodity hardware to build a driver classification model.

DATA COLLECTION

To build a driver classification model based on driving behavior, we need data from multiple drivers. We collected data in two different scenarios. In the first data set we collect data from 14 drivers who each drove 3 different cars on a predefined route. With this setup we wanted to understand the ability to classify a many drivers and their associated driving behaviors on a single car with a user-consistent driving task. The second data set was a more naturalistic driving setting where we recruited 3 couples who share a car and collected their everyday driving activities over a 4 day period (Friday to Monday). The data collected under this condition was less controlled, with ad-hoc routes, and hence would allow us to test the robustness of our model.

We equipped cars with an off-the-shelf Bluetooth OBD-II scanner that connects to a Samsung Galaxy S3 Android smartphone placed in the central console with a custom Android data logging application we wrote. In our Android logger application, we used the Torque API[2] which manages Bluetooth connectivity and the sensor data coming from the OBD-II scanner. We log all the sensor streams available through OBD-II scanner as well as the phone sensor data including accelerometer, gyroscope, magnetometer, GPS, temperature and the light sensor. We optimized the application to wake up only when the car is turned on and it would go to sleep after the car is turned off.

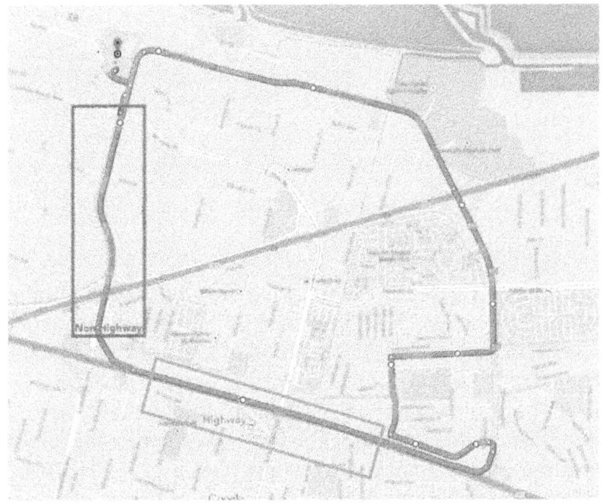

Figure 1: Predefined route followed by users during data collection (image blurred for anonymity purposes).

Procedure

For the first data set, we collected data from 14 (8 male and 6 females) participant drivers who were recruited using convenience sampling from our corporate research lab. All of the participants were asked to drive 3 different cars in a random sequence (2014 Honda Accord, 2013 Honda Accord, 2012 Scion Coup) on a pre-defined route as shown in Figure 1. The predefined car route was 7.2 miles (11.6 km) and included surface streets, freeways, ramps, traffic lights and

[2]https://play.google.com/store/apps/details?id=org.prowl.torque

Sensor & Sensor Location		Dims	Info. Gain
Gyroscope	phone	1	31.9
Torque	car	1	16.43
GPS	phone	1	9.14
Accelerometer	phone	1	8.89
Acc. pedal position D	car	1	0.62
Throttle position manifold	car	1	0.56
Absolute throttle position B	car	1	0.38
Relative throttle position	car	1	0.35
Acc. pedal position E	car	1	0.29
Engine RPM	car	1	0.09

Table 1: Sensors used to classify drivers, the dimensionality of the sensor output, and information gain from each sensor used for driver classification.

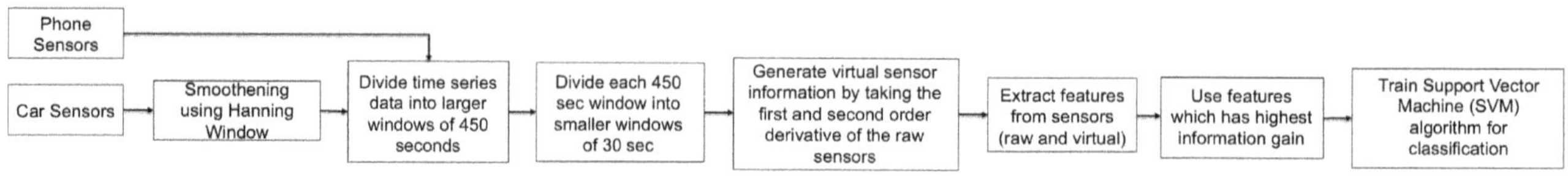

Figure 2: Block diagram used for classification modeling driver classification algorithm

stop signs. Each driver provided driving data for approximately 21.6 miles (34.8 km) in total (7.2 miles per route * 3 cars). The data collection was conducted over 3 days and between 10:30 AM to 4:30 PM. On average, participants took M=20.13 minutes (SD=3.90) to complete the course. Before driving, the participants were given instructions about the route and were asked to report back any deviations. Two participants redid the driving task as they had missed several key points on the route.

For the second dataset, we recruited 3 couples who share a car. The cars owned by the couples were of different makes (Volkswagon Jetta 2013, Honda Element 2004 and Audi A4 2012). As with first dataset, each car was equipped with the OBD-II dongle and a smartphone with our logging application. The smartphones were attached to an external battery so that the phone battery lasted 5-6 days. The couples were asked to keep a log sheet which contained the date, start time, end time and name of the driver so as to get the ground truth of who drove the car with approximate start and stop times so we could label the data collected. The 3 couples drove the car for totals of 203, 279 and 321 minutes with each driver driving the car for more than 1.25 hours.

DATA PROCESSING

Given our focus on driving behavior, we select a subset of sensors from Table 1. For example, the absolute throttle and accelerator provided information about how the gas pedal is pressed by the driver. From the smartphone, we log linear acceleration, gyroscope and acceleration information derived from GPS. The car sensor data from the OBD-II sensor is sampled at approximately 5 Hz whereas the gyroscope, linear acceleration sensor data and GPS data were sampled at 90 Hz, 90 Hz and 1 Hz respectively. We avoided using sensors and features that were related to road or traffic conditions (*e.g.,* instead of speed which is influenced by the traffic/road

Features	Dimensions
Histogram	10 (Car) 30 (Phone)
Entropy of Histogram	1
Power Spectrum	5 (Car) 26 (Phone)
Entropy of Power Spectrum	1
St. Dev. of Power Spectrum	1
Cepstrum	5 (Car) 26 (Phone)
Entropy of Cepstrum	1
St. Dev. of Cepstrum	1
Max, Min, Mean, Median, and Variance per car sensor	1

Table 2: Features extracted from all the sensors (virtual and real)

conditions, acceleration and jerk were used which are more closely related to driving behavior).

We used a Hanning window of size 11 to smooth the OBD-II sensor data. Further, we created virtual sensors by taking the first and the second order derivative of the physical sensor outputs. The time series data is divided into windows of 450s which are further divided into sub-windows of 30s each. The window sizes were optimized to accurately capture small driving changes without significantly compromising classification accuracy, using our first data set.

For each 30s window we extracted a total of 6400 statistical and frequency based features from the physical and the virtual sensors. We iteratively reduced the features based on the ranking of information gain and associated impact on accuracy. Afterwards, we verified the results of the feature pruning using 10-fold cross-validation. Using this process, we reduced the number of features to 1171. Table 2 provides details of the features and the dimensions related to each feature as provided to our model. A classifier was built to classify instances from each 30s sub-window; 15 instances (450s) were aggregated to vote for a driver. If there was a tie for different drivers based on votes/probabilities, we categorized it as a misclassified case. We used a support vector machine (SVM) model with a polynomial kernel with a cost function of one as our driver classification model.

EVALUATION

We performed an off-line evaluation of our approach with leave-one-out cross-validation. We performed three different experiments to test *a*) the model's performance on an artificially large number of drivers, *b*) the impact of driver count on model performance, and *c*) the robustness of the model in natural non-prescribed environments. The first dataset was used for Experiments *a* and *b*; the second naturalistic driving data was used for Experiment *c*.

In Experiment *a*, the SVM model classified the correct driver with an accuracy of 85.00%, 93.22% and 61.42% using only the phone sensors for car 1, 2 and 3 respectively (Table 3) which is far greater than a random chance classification (7.14%). We also tested the accuracy of the SVM model using only car sensor data and a combination of both car and phone sensors. The classification accuracies using only the car sensors were 37.14%, 25.36% and 28.57%, whereas the accuracies were 82.00%, 88.56% and 61.43% when classified using both the car and phone sensors.

In Experiment *b*, we examined the impact of the number of drivers on the classification performance. We used car 1 data from our first dataset and examine the impact on accuracy for between 2 and 14 drivers (Figure 3). The classification ac-

	Pre-defined route - Experiment a (Data set 1)				Naturalistic driving- Experiment c (Data set 2)			
	Car 1 Scion Coup (2012)	Car 2 Honda Accord (2014)	Car 3 Honda Accord (2013)	Mean Car 1,2,3	Car 4 Volkswagon Jetta (2013)	Car 5 Audi A4 (2012)	Car 6 Honda Element (2004)	Mean Car 4,5,6
Phone Sensor	85.00	93.22	61.42	79.88	67.50	75.00	97.50	80.00
Car Sensor	37.14	25.36	28.57	30.36	80.00	87.50	90.00	85.83
Car & Phone Sensor	82.00	88.56	61.43	77.33	62.50	82.50	97.50	80.83

Table 3: Accuracy attained using different datasets and using each sensor source independently and by combining them

curacy for the model using only the car sensor data shows a large drop once the number of drivers is greater than 3. However the classification accuracy was 100% for 2 drivers classification when tested with phone sensors, car sensors and a combination of both car and phone data (Figure 3).

As a final validation of our approach and to test the robustness of our approach in the real-world, we use our second naturalistic dataset, *which was not used in designing our approach*. We again tested the classification accuracy using only phone sensors, only car sensors and the combination of both car and phone sensors (Table 3). The model driver classification accuracy for each car-couple pair was 67.50%, 75% and 97.50% for cars 4, 5 and 6 respectively. Similarly, the classification accuracy using only the car sensors was 80%, 87.50% and 90% and using the combined car and phone sensors was 62.50%, 82.50% and 97.50% for car 4, 5 and 6 respectively.

DISCUSSION

Reflecting on these results, we see that only using the car sensors results in rather poor performance when there were more than 3 drivers. This result is evident in Experiment *a* (Table 3) for car 2 and 3 in particular as well as Experiment *b* (Figure 3). This could be caused by insufficient separation between drivers in the reduced feature space created by just the car sensor data.

The model can classify between a few drivers with higher accuracies using only phone sensors and a combination of car and phone sensors. The classifier gave the best accuracy when tested with fewer drivers. The classification accuracies were 100%, 100% and 100% (2 drivers, Figure 3) using the first dataset when tested with 2 drivers using only phone sensors, only car sensors and combined car and phone sensors.

The results of Experiment *c* shows our model performs well in real-world driving situations. We obtained accuracies of 75.83%, 85.83% and 86.67%. Together our experiments reinforce our model's capability to classify a small set of drivers with data collected in both controlled and naturalistic driving condition.

Lastly, analyzing sensors based on the maximum information gained for both car and phone sensors, we derived that features extracted from Torque sensor (16.43) of the car provided the most information whereas gyroscope sensor of the phone (31.9) provided the highest information (see Table 1). Other sensor information (GPS, accelerometer from phone; acceleration pedal position and throttle position from the car) also provides information necessary to model driving behavior. Reducing the number of features based on information gain not only reduced the overall training features by 82% but provided the same level, if not better, accuracy than using all the 6400 features.

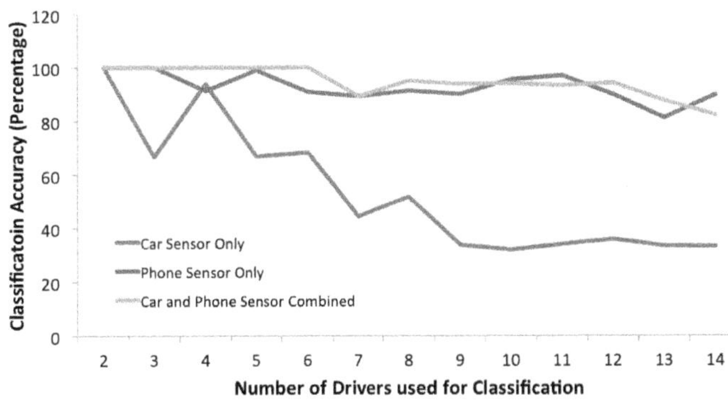

Figure 3: Classification accuracy by incrementally increasing the number of drivers in the model (Experiment b)

FUTURE WORK & CONCLUSIONS

Our aim was to develop and evaluate a driver classification model. We plan to extend this work in three directions. First, we plan to deploy the system to work online in real-time. Second, we plan to use our classification system to develop a variety of advanced mobile applications and/or services (*e.g.*, shift the driver's phone from touch interaction to hands-free mode) for more personalized in-car experiences. Third, we are looking at opportunities to improve our classification accuracies. For example, we are experimenting with a Bayesian network based learning approach (akin to [3]) which learns the importance and dependencies of each sensor.

In this paper, we presented a driver classification model inferred from driving behavior captured by low level sensors. The sensors consisted of car sensors available through the OBD-II scanner and smartphone sensors. The proposed model was tested with each set of sensors independently as well as by using the combined set. Different characteristics of the model such as ability to classify differing number of drivers under different driving conditions from prescribed to naturalistic driving were evaluated. While classifying a large number of drivers is challenging, we found the two driver case to perform well which opens to door for new applications.

ACKNOWLEDGMENTS

The authors would like to thank all the volunteers who took part in the data collection process and all the reviewers for their constructive feedback.

REFERENCES

1. Baldwin, K. C., Duncan, D. D., and West, S. K. The driver monitor system: A means of assessing driver performance. Tech. rep., Johns Hopkins APL Technical Digest, 2004.

2. Bo, C., Jian, X., Li, X.-Y., Mao, X., Wang, Y., and Li, F. You're driving and texting: Detecting drivers using personal smart phones by leveraging inertial sensors. In *Proceedings of the 19th Annual International Conference on Mobile Computing & Networking*, ACM (2013), 199–202.

3. Chickering, D., Heckerman, D., and Meek, C. A bayesian approach to learning bayesian networks with local structure. *CoRR abs/1302.1528* (2013).

4. Dai, J., Teng, J., Bai, X., Shen, Z., and Xuan, D. Mobile phone based drunk driving detection. In *4th International Conference on Pervasive Computing Technologies for Healthcare* (March 2010), 1–8.

5. Johnson, D., and Trivedi, M. Driving style recognition using a smartphone as a sensor platform. In *14th International IEEE Conference on Intelligent Transportation Systems* (2011), 1609–1615.

6. Ly, M. V., Martin, S., and Trivedi, M. Driver classification and driving style recognition using inertial sensors. In *IEEE Intelligent Vehicles Symposium (IV)* (June 2013), 1040–1045.

7. Mitrovic, D. Reliable method for driving events recognition. *IEEE Transactions on Intelligent Transportation Systems 6*, 2 (June 2005), 198–205.

8. Miyajima, C., Nishiwaki, Y., Ozawa, K., Wakita, T., Itou, K., Takeda, K., and Itakura, F. Driver modeling based on driving behavior and its evaluation in driver identification. *Proceedings of the IEEE 95*, 2 (Feb 2007), 427–437.

9. Sathyanarayana, A., Sadjadi, S., and Hansen, J. Leveraging sensor information from portable devices towards automatic driving maneuver recognition. In *15th International IEEE Conference on Intelligent Transportation Systems* (2012), 660–665.

10. Zhang, W., Cheng, B., and Lin, Y. Driver drowsiness recognition based on computer vision technology. *Tsinghua Science and Technology 17*, 3 (June 2012), 354–362.

Adaptive Contextualization: Combating Bias During High-Dimensional Visualization and Data Selection

David Gotz
School of Information and Library Science
University of North Carolina at Chapel Hill
216 Lenior Dr; CB 3360
Chapel Hill, NC 27599 USA
gotz@unc.edu

Shun Sun
School of Information and Library Science
University of North Carolina at Chapel Hill
216 Lenior Dr; CB 3360
Chapel Hill, NC 27599 USA
shunsun@live.unc.edu

Nan Cao
Department of Computer Science and Engineering
NYU Shanghai
1555 Century Ave
Pudong, Shanghai, China
200122
nan.cao@nyu.edu

ABSTRACT
Large and high-dimensional real-world datasets are being gathered across a wide range of application disciplines to enable data-driven decision making. Interactive data visualization can play a critical role in allowing domain experts to select and analyze data from these large collections. However, there is a critical mismatch between the very large number of dimensions in complex real-world datasets and the much smaller number of dimensions that can be concurrently visualized using modern techniques. This gap in dimensionality can result in high levels of selection bias that go unnoticed by users. The bias can in turn threaten the very validity of any subsequent insights. In this paper, we present Adaptive Contextualization (AC), a novel approach to interactive visual data selection that is specifically designed to combat the invisible introduction of selection bias. Our approach (1) monitors and models a users visual data selection activity, (2) computes metrics over that model to quantify the amount of selection bias after each step, (3) visualizes the metric results, and (4) provides interactive tools that help users assess and avoid bias-related problems. We also share results from a user study which demonstrate the effectiveness of our technique.

Author Keywords
Visualization; Visual Analytics; Exploratory Analysis; Intelligent Visual Interfaces

ACM Classification Keywords
H.5.m. Information Interfaces and Presentation (e.g., HCI): Miscellaneous

INTRODUCTION
Large and complex datasets are being gathered across a wide range of application disciplines to support data-driven decision making. From healthcare to advertising to business intelligence, these datasets are often gathered "in the wild" with large numbers of heterogeneous and diverse variables.

Unlike data for traditional *prospective* studies—which is gathered narrowly according to a study design determined a priori with the goal of supporting a specific analytical question—these real-world datasets capture a vast and diverse sample of data from the system under investigation without knowing in advance the types of questions that will be asked. The aim in these settings is to gather data with enough variation and richness that a wide range of ad hoc, targeted analyses can be performed *retrospectively*—after data has been collected— to quickly provide precision data-driven evidence to decision makers or investigators.

As just one example, there is growing interest within the healthcare domain in using "Big Data" to help personalize care and support precision treatment decisions [23]. The so-called Learning Health System [18] concept is receiving heavy investment, with the aim of creating methods and tools that enable a data-driven environment in which evidence that informs medical treatment can be obtained via analysis of large populations of real-world patient data. The subsequent outcomes from those decisions could then be added to the population-based dataset, with new analyses of the updated data producing a powerful learning effect [1, 10, 11].

These sorts of large-scale data-driven analyses, regardless of domain, require analysts to select subsets of data that can be further analyzed to answer a specific question of interest. This *data selection* process is often accomplished using visual analysis technologies [34] which are designed to leverage interactive visualization algorithms to help user quickly and intuitively navigate complex datasets. For example, visual analysis techniques have been applied to problems in the healthcare domain, allowing users to quickly identify and select a cohort of patients for further analysis during population-based studies [37]. This form of visual data selection can be highly effective, supporting an analysis workflow that is both intuitive and high speed.

However, there is a critical limitation that must be overcome when this approach is applied to high-dimensional datasets. More specifically, there is a dramatic mismatch between the relatively small number of dimensions displayed simultaneously even in "multi-dimensional" visualization methods

IUI 2016, March 7–10, 2016, Sonoma, CA, USA.

ACM 978-1-4503-4137-0/16/03 ...$15.00.
http://dx.doi.org/10.1145/2856767.2856779

(e.g., most often less than 20) compared to the very high-dimensional nature of many real-world datasets (e.g., tens of thousands of features in real-world medical data).

This dramatic difference in dimensionality means that users performing visual data selection must apply filters with an exceptionally narrow view of the dataset they are manipulating. Unfortunately, because the variables in many real-world, high-dimensional datasets are highly interdependent, the filters applied during visual data selection can produce large amounts of selection bias which—for the vast majority of variables that are omitted from the visualization—can occur invisibly and go undetected. As a result, the bias that is introduced can be a silent yet critically limiting factor which undermines the quality of all subsequent analyses of the selected data.

In this paper, we present Adaptive Contextualization (AC), a novel approach to interactive visual data selection that is specifically designed to combat the invisible introduction of selection bias. Our approach (1) monitors and models a user's visual data selection activity, (2) computes metrics over the model to quantify the degree of selection bias introduced during the process, (3) visually represents the results for contextual awareness, and (4) provides interactive tools that help users assess bias when it is discovered and revert problematic filters to explore alternative selections. Specifically, our work offers the following contributions:

- **Algorithms for capturing and assessing the introduction of bias during data selection.** We define a context model that captures the sequence of steps performed by a user during the visual data selection process. We then define a multi-dimensional distance metric which quantifies the shift in variable distributions between any pair of steps in our context model. The metric is recomputed automatically as the model changes in response to additional user activity.

- **Visual representations and interaction techniques.** We describe an interactive visual representation for the results produced by the algorithms outlined above. The visualization is updated automatically as users explore a dataset, and provides interactive tools that allow users to investigate the bias metrics and revise their data selection process.

- **An evaluation of AC's effectiveness.** We include results and analysis from a 18-person study evaluating AC as applied to a medical domain problem. The results show that a data selection tool with AC (when compared to a baseline version without AC) improves awareness of variable distribution changes within a dataset during selection and reduces the time required to estimate levels of selection bias.

BACKGROUND AND RELATED WORK

The context-aware visualization methods proposed in this paper are related to several different areas of research including high-dimensional visualization methods, provenance modeling, and previous approaches to intelligent visualization.

High-Dimensional Visualization

The application of interactive data visualization techniques to high-dimensional datasets has been a focus and challenge for the research community for at least twenty years [5]. The challenge is rooted in constraints that derive from the very fundamentals of the data visualization concept. Visualization uses a relatively small number of visual variables (position, shape, size, brightness, color, orientation, texture, and motion) [36] to encode complex information; and relies upon humans' visual perception to interpret the resulting graphics to derive insight.

Using clever graphical arrangements (e.g., parallel coordinates [17] and scatterplot-matrices [7]) as well as multiple coordinated views [35], a single variable can be leveraged to encode more than one variable at the same time. However, even advanced applications of these techniques, as shown in the a recent survey of state-of-the-art parallel coordinates techniques [15] are able to concurrently visualize only a relatively small number of dimensions (most often less than 20).

Given this restriction on the dimensionality of visual representations, research in this area often focuses on data summarization, projection, or ranking. This includes traditional projection methods like principle component analysis (PCA) and multi-dimensional scaling (MDS), visual clustering (e.g., [2, 6, 8, 27]), and a variety of hierarchical summarization methods [9]. Optimization-based techniques can then support algorithmic configuration of these approaches based on specific quality criteria [4]. However, summarization methods result in loss of information due to the reduction in dimensionality. Ranking-based methods, meanwhile, can prioritize dimensions for viewing but do not overcome the limited number of visualized dimensions. As a result, a majority of dimensions can remain invisible.

Provenance Modeling

Visual queries are a key benefit of many interactive visualization systems [28]. User interface controls allow users to change query constraints, while visualization is used to interactively depict the updated dataset. Visual queries can be combined with direct manipulation of the visualization's graphical objects [16] to make exploratory data selection fast and intuitive. Together, these methods can support an exploratory selection process through which users can quickly and interactively focus a visual analysis upon a data subset of interest (e.g., healthcare domain examples [12, 26, 37]).

In recognition of the exploratory and ad hoc nature of these tools, researchers have developed a variety of visual provenance models. These models are designed to capture and record the often complex chain of visual data transformations that users can apply as they explore a dataset [14, 19, 22, 24, 32]. In these most basic form, these models capture trails of user activity to document the origin of a dataset [20] or to allow re-use of a previously saved sequence of analysis operations [3]. This paper adopts a similar approach to monitoring and capturing user activity, but uses this data interactively to actively contextualize a user's ongoing exploratory data selection process.

Intelligent Visualization

The provenance models described above are often captured as evidence documenting how specific visualizations were constructed or how insights were discovered. However, the same models capture detailed information about a user's analytic activity which can support a wide range of intelligent visualization algorithms. For example, algorithms have been designed to compare a user's currently visualized dataset with a representation of his/her visualization history. These have enabled, for example, user interfaces that recommend past visualizations that are most relevant to a user's current activity [30]. A similar approach has allowed for the ranking and recommendation of relevant notes captured by a user in a visualization notebook [31].

Using sequences of steps along a provenance model can also support intelligent visualization applications. For example, behavior-driven visualization recommendation [13] is a technique that analyzes user activity as it is performed to detect patterns that suggest user intent. Alternative visualizations are then recommended with the aim of better supporting a user's analytic needs. In addition, models can be collected and indexed for subsequent searching, supporting collaboration and re-use of visualization-based data selection procedures [22]. At a high level, the AC approach outlined in this paper is perhaps most similar to these intelligent visualization techniques. However, the goal is quite distinct given AC's focus on data quality and bias as introduced during high-dimensional data selection.

MOTIVATING SCENARIO AND BASELINE SYSTEM

As a motivating example for the challenges of high-dimensional data selection, consider the Integrated Cancer Information and Surveillance System (ICISS) managed by the UNC Lineberger Comprehensive Cancer Hospital [21]. Like similar "Big Data" resources in other domains, ICISS gathers large volumes of complex real-world data from multiple sources to build a detailed repository for retrospective analysis. In particular, ICISS integrates the North Carolina Central Cancer Registry (containing a nearly complete sample of all cancer cases in the state) with administrative and claims data for roughly 60% of "general population" patients from across the state. In total, ICISS contains electronic health data for more than six million patients.

ICISS contains a wide variety of data about these patients including demographic data, insurance information, and longitudinal medical data (including diagnoses, lab tests, medications, and procedures). Other variables include census and environmental data, behavioral data, and economic data. All together, this results in a very high dimensional dataset, with the number of distinct variables easily exceeding 100,000.

Researchers hoping to use this data resource to retrospectively study the impact of various cancer treatments or interventions must begin with a critical but challenging first step: they must select—from this complex pool of over six million patients—a representative cohort of patients to study. This is generally accomplished by specifying a series of inclusion/exclusion criteria to whittle the population down to a group that is (1) a manageable size, (2) appropriate for given

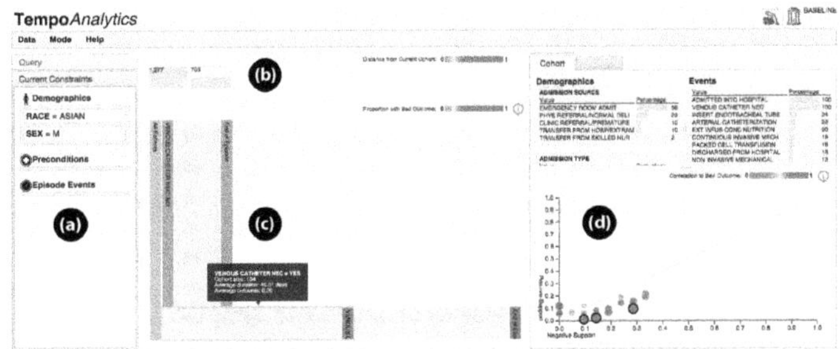

Figure 1. The baseline visualization-based data selection system with four panels: (a) a query/constraint panel; (b) a visual breadcrumb showing steps in the data selection process; (c) an interactive visualization panel allowing user-driven patient subgrouping and inclusion/exclusion constraint definition; and (d) a panel visualizing demographic and clinical event statistics for the selected cohort.

clinical question, (3) representative of the larger population being studied.

For example, to support one recent study at ICISS, researchers studying breast cancer narrowed in on a study cohort by along 12 dimensions, resulting in a study cohort of just 2,640 patients (from the over six million overall). Using traditional methods, this type of iterative selection process can take months of effort, require high levels of technical staff support, and result in a large number of complex custom-built SQL queries and statistical analyses.

Baseline Visual Data Selection System

To support the scenario above, a visualization-based data selection system was developed with a design similar to the recently introduced DecisionFlow system from Gotz and Stavropoulos [12]. Both DecisionFlow and our prototype adopt a design specifically created to allow ad hoc exploration of high-dimensional temporal event data, making it a good match for the electronic health data. Our baseline system, however, provides more capabilities than DecisionFlow. In particular, our baseline system allows users to iteratively apply inclusion/exclusion criteria, more closely matching the workflow outlined in the motivating scenario. We then extend this baseline design by adding the AC methods described in the next section of this paper.

The baseline visualization system, shown in Figure 1, combines (a) a visual query panel for retrieving an initial cohort of patients from a large-scale database; (b) a visual breadcrumb showing the sequence of inclusion/exclusion constraints added during the selection process; (c) an interactive temporal event visualization panel that supports direct manipulation for defining new constraints, and (d) an interactive patient event/demographic panel that visualizes a variety of basic statistics to help users identify interesting variables within the high-dimensional data.

The baseline visualization design allows users to quickly and intuitively select focused cohorts for subsequent analysis. However, the presence of correlations between variables means that selection bias is likely to occur. For example, filtering to include only patients with emergency admissions will skew data toward certain diseases with acute manifestations, while filtering to include patients with certain medications can result in a strong age bias. These changes are often hidden from user's view, however, because—due to the high dimensionality—they are not included in the visualization. In this way, the iterative application of multiple filters, as is typical in the motivating scenario, can produce a final cohort that is dramatically—and invisibly—different than the original.

ADAPTIVE CONTEXTUALIZATION METHODS

This section provides a detailed description of Adaptive Contextualization (AC). This includes a provenance model designed to model user's behavior and the evolving chain of datasets that are defined during interaction. A metric is then defined over this model to quantify differences in variable distributions across the high-dimensional space. Intelligent user interaction capabilities are then adopted automatically update the model, recompute the metrics, and surface the results for visual inspection and manipulation. Together, this AC approach provides users with clear and actionable feedback about the location and degree of bias introduced in response to their interactive data selection activity.

Provenance model

At the core of the AC method is a data structure designed to capture the provenance behind the dataset currently being visualized by the user. This *provenance model* must capture each of the datasets visited by a user over the course of the data selection process with sufficient detail to support the metric defined later in this section.

As shown in Figure 2, the provenance model is represented as a sequential chain of datasets d_i linked by filters f_i. Each filter includes one or more constraints defined by users' interaction with the visualization. The very first dataset visualized by a user, d_0, is the dataset returned by the user's initial query. The final dataset in the chain, noted as d_{active}, corresponds to the user's currently visualized dataset. All other d_i represent datasets created as intermediate steps by the user as part of the interactive data selection process. We note that this structure represents the minimally required provenance model for AC. This representation can be extended as required to support additional provenance-based user interaction capabilities.

Given this basic representation, a visualization system can be instrumented to build and maintain the provenance model in response to user interaction. As new constraints are applied via direct manipulation with the visualization, new datasets are defined and added to the end of the chain. The model supports *reversion*, allowing users to undo one or more filters from the end of the chain. In response to a reversion, the chain of datasets is first pruned back to the selected point while new filters are extended along a new branch within the model. See Figure 2.

Except for small datasets, it can be impractical to store a complete copy of each dataset along the chain. Therefore, AC only requires that two datasets be stored in full: d_0 and d_{active}. Intermediate datasets, if required, can be reproduced by applying the corresponding chain of filters to d_0. AC does require, however, a detailed characterization of the distribution for each variable in each dataset d_i as these are needed by

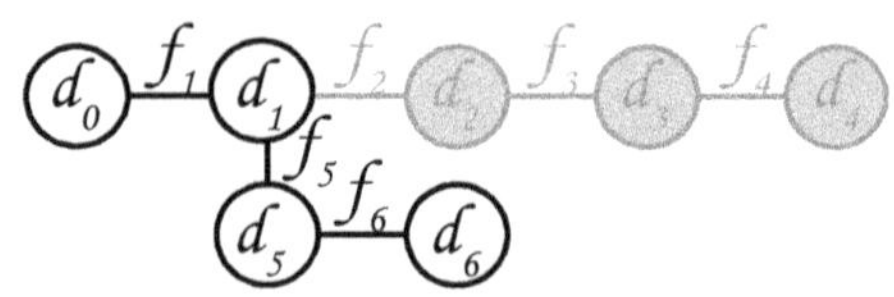

Figure 2. The provenance model captures the sequence of user activity that led to the current dataset. It captures both the datasets at each step (d_i) as well as the filters (f_i) used to arrive at those datasets. When users revert to earlier steps to undo filters, the model pruned (gray circles). A new branch is then created to reflect any subsequent filters. The dataset at the end of the model (in this case, d_6) is the active dataset, d_{active}.

the metric defined in the next section. Therefore, each time d_{active} is updated in response to user interaction, a process runs to compute a detailed high-dimensional *variable distribution vector*, which we note as $\vec{v}_i = \{v_i^1, v_i^2, ..., v_i^n\}$. This vector contains a discrete probability distribution v_i^j for each individual variable j in the n dimensional dataset d_i.

Pairwise Dataset Comparison Metric

The provenance model documents each of the steps in the data selection process by which a user transforms d_0 to d_{active}. To quantify the amount of selection bias introduced, we construct a pairwise dataset comparison metric, $\delta(d_j, d_k)$, which varies from zero (to indicate that two datasets have identical variable distributions) to one (indicting maximally different variable distributions between datasets).

The δ metric builds upon the Hellinger distance [25, 33], a statistical measure designed to quantify the similarity between two probability distributions. For discrete datasets, such as those found in typical visualization applications, a discreet probability version of the Hellinger distance can be computed as follows. For two discrete probability distributions $A = (a_1, ..., a_n)$ and $B = (b_1, ..., b_n)$:

$$H(A, B) = \sqrt{\frac{1}{2}\sum_{i=1}^{n}(\sqrt{a_i} - \sqrt{b_i})^2} \quad (1)$$

where n is the number of discrete values for A and B.

Conceptually, this measure will be used in our algorithm to quantify the difference between the distribution of values observed for the same variable in one dataset versus another dataset (e.g., gender distribution in d_0 versus d_{active}). The uni-variate H evaluates to zero when A and B are identical, and produces a value of one when A and B are maximally different. We choose the Hellinger distance as the basis for our approach because it is both (1) an established measure for comparing distributions, and (2) it can be computed efficiently for discrete probability distributions.

Within our AC algorithm, this discrete form of the Hellinger distance can be applied directly to categorical and ordinal values. Ratio variables, meanwhile, should typically be binned to convert them to ordinal measures before computing the discrete probability distribution. This binning step can prevent n values that are relatively large in comparison to the dataset

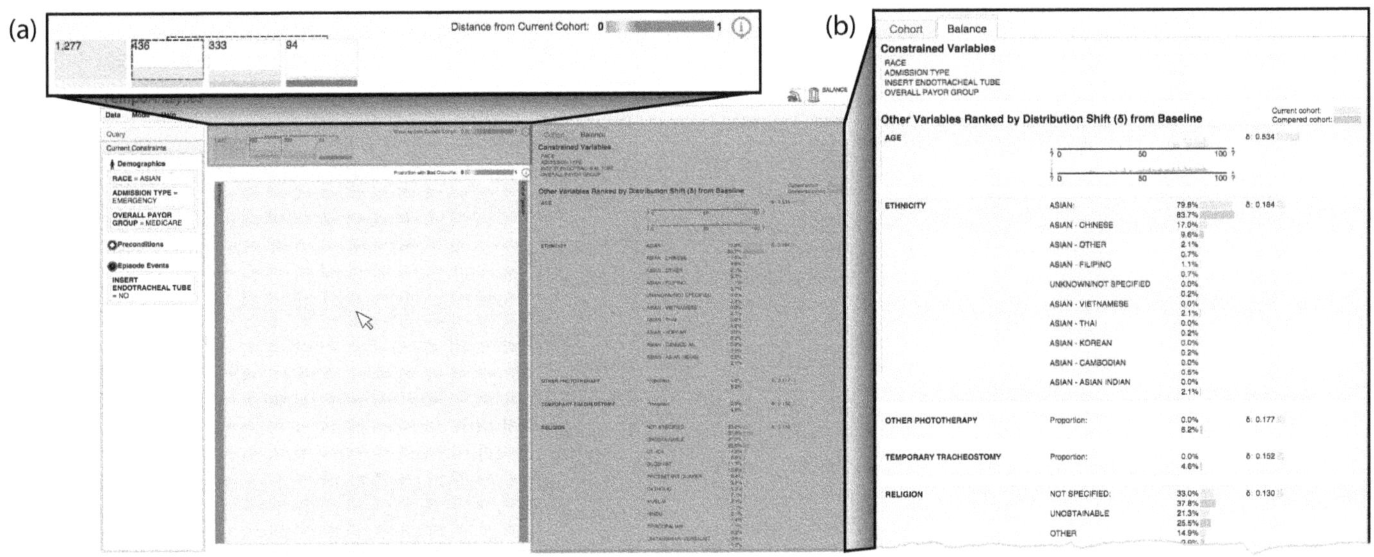

Figure 3. The user interface for our AC-based visualization system extends the baseline interface of Figure 1 in two key ways. First, (a) the breadcrumb panel showing the user's history of datasets includes a visualization of the δ metric and supports new interactions to support dataset comparisons. Second, (b) a new Balance Panel has been added to visualize detailed ranked lists of univariate differences between datasets.

size. As n grows larger, there is risk of over-sensitivity to small changes in variable distributions.

While H provides a uni-variate measure of similarity, the datasets in our work are high-dimensional in nature, often containing tens of thousands of unique dimensions. We therefore define the multi-variate distance measure δ using a weighted average of the uni-variate Hellinger distances across all dimensions m in our dataset:

$$\delta(d_j, d_k) = \frac{\sum_{i=1}^{m} w_i * H(v_j^i, v_k^i)}{\sum_{i=1}^{m} w_i} \qquad (2)$$

where v_j^i and v_k^i are the discrete probability distributions for the ith variable datasets d_j and d_k; and $w_i \in \{0, 1\}$ is the weight for the ith variable. This produces a measure which, like the traditional uni-variate Hellinger distance, ranges from zero (for datasets with identical variable distributions) to one (for datasets whose variable distributions are maximally different).

The weights in this measure are used to ignore distances contributed by dimensions that have been explicitly filtered by the user. More specifically, variables that have been explicitly constrained within of filters f_i found prior to the datasets d_j and d_k within the provenance model are assigned weights of zero. All other variables are assigned weights of one. In this way, the δ measure only considers differences in variable distributions that occur implicitly as a confounding side effect.

For example, consider the motivating medical scenario. If a dataset containing patient medical data was filtered by a user to contain only men, the gender variable would be assigned a weight of zero when comparing the two datasets (all patients vs. men only). This would ensure that the expected differences in gender distribution would not contribute to the result of the distance measure. However, hidden differences in correlated variables (e.g., differences in the prevalence of maternity-related procedures) would be detected.

Metric Visualization and Interaction

As users go about the data selection process using an AC-enabled visualization system, the AC algorithm monitors user interaction and dynamically updates the data provenance model after each filter. As d_{active} changes, new δ values (Equation 2) are computed for each new pair of datasets in the model. The δ values, along with the individual H values computed for each variable (Equation 1) are then made available via the user interface to highlight for users where the largest biases have been introduced.

The δ and H metrics are then used highlight and prioritize areas of emerging selection bias for the user. To present this information, the baseline user interface shown in Figure 1 is expanded to include two new intelligent visualization capabilities. First, highlighted in Figure 3(a), a Contextualized Breadcrumb view provides additional contextual information compared to the baseline breadcrumb design and supports a new set of user interaction capabilities. Second, highlighted in Figure 3(b), a new *Balance Panel* supports detailed univariate comparisons for selected pairs of datasets.

The Contextualized Breadcrumb

The contextualized breadcrumb panel is designed help users understand (1) the filters that have been applied at each step of the data selection process, and (2) how the dataset d_{active} compares to those previously visualized datasets in terms of underlying variable distributions. To achieve this goal, a glyph-based design has been developed as illustrated in Figure 4. In this design, each dataset in the provenance model, starting with d_0 and continuing to d_{active}, is represented by its own glyph. The glyphs are positioned from left to right,

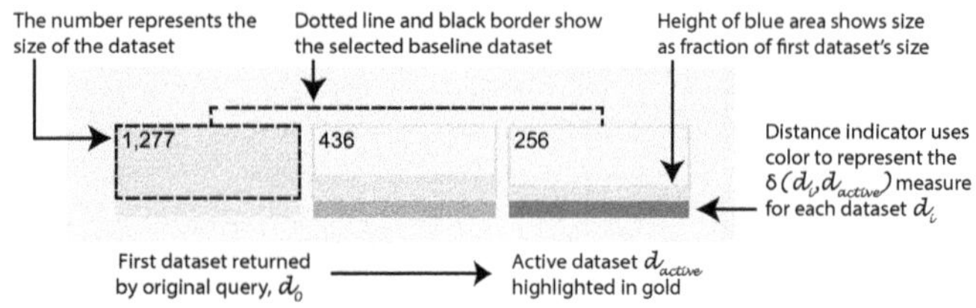

Figure 4. The contextualized breadcrumb view uses color-coded bars at the bottom of each glyph to encode the δ measures. Interaction capabilities revert to prior datasets or select a prior dataset for detailed comparison in the Balance Panel.

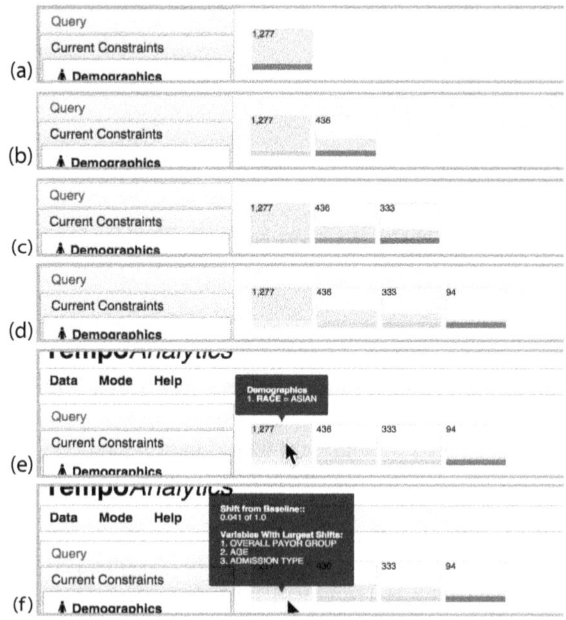

Figure 5. The contextualized breadcrumb view grows the right as users apply new filters. (a-d) The color-coded δ bars are updated in response to these new datasets, providing up-to-date representation of the measured bias. (e) Mousing over the main glyph area shows the filters applied at that step, while (f) hovering over the δ bar.

with d_0 appearing first. As new datasets are visited, the chain of glyphs is extended to the right as shown in Figure 5.

Each glyph shows the size of the dataset with both a number and a blue indicator whose height is proportional to the size of the dataset. This provides a simple bar-chart view of the changing dataset size as filters are applied. In addition, a color-coded rectangle, which we call a *δ bar*, is positioned at the bottom of each dataset's glyph. For each dataset d_i, the color of the bar is determined by the value of $\delta(d_i, d_{active})$. This value is then mapped to a green-to-yellow-to-red color scale. A red δ bar represents a dataset that has major differences in variable distributions compared to the active dataset. A green bar, meanwhile, represents a dataset that is very similar to the active dataset. This explains, for example, why the active dataset (highlighted with the gold border) has a pure green δ: it shows no bias when compared to itself (i.e., $\delta(d_{active}, d_{active}) = 0$).

Users can access additional information via interaction. Mousing over the portion of the glyph containing the blue size indicator shows the specific filter applied to arrive at the corresponding dataset. Meanwhile, mousing over the δ bar provides a high-level summary of the bias detected between the dataset and $d_{actcive}$. In particular, as shown in Figure 5(f), users can see the actual δ score as well as a list of the three variables with the largest difference in distributions as measured by Equation 1.

Finally, users can click on any glyph in the breadcrumb to select the corresponding dataset. If the selected dataset is *not* d_{active}, then the breadcrumb view is updated with a dotted black selection line (see Figure 4) which connects the selected dataset with d_{active}. Coordinated with this selection, the user interface displays the Balance Panel described below to support detailed investigation of the differences between the datasets. Clicking on the active dataset returns the visualization to its normal exploratory data selection model. Right-clicking on a dataset brings up a context menu that allows users to "go back" to an earlier dataset to explore alternative selections.

The Balance Panel

When a dataset d_i (other than d_{active}) is selected in the contextualized breadcrumb view, the Balance Panel (Figure 3b) is presented to the user with the aim of supporting detailed comparisons between the selected dataset and the user's currently active dataset. This panel, in essence, provides users with a prioritized visualization of the individual univariate H scores (Equation 1) that contribute to the overall δ value.

The top of the balance panel provides a list of constrained dimensions. While a detailed list of active constraints are also included in the leftmost sidebar of the user interface (where the query is performed), this section of the panel provides users with a reminder that the listed variables have been explicitly constrained and are therefore omitted from the data that is displayed below it. In particular, these are the dimensions for which w_i is set to zero in Equation 2.

The remainder of the balance panel provides a ranked list univariate visualizations. The visualizations are sorted by H score, placing at the top of the list the variables whose distributions have been changed the most given the filters that created d_{active} from d_i.

The balance panel is critical for users because it allows them to understand *why* a large δ has developed during the data selection process. An example workflow from our motivating scenario is illustrated in Figure 6. First, a user is shown iteratively applying multiple filters (Figure 6(a-c)) before clicking on the contextual breadcrumb to learn which variables have been most biased (Figure 6(d)). The balance view tells the user that the age variable is most biased variable. Using the balance view to look at other datasets in the breadcrumb, the user learns that this bias introduced by a filter to a specific type of hospital admission.

EVALUATION

To evaluate the benefits of AC to users during high-dimensional data selection, we conducted a user study comparing our AC-based visual data selection prototype to a baseline system in which AC features were disabled. The study

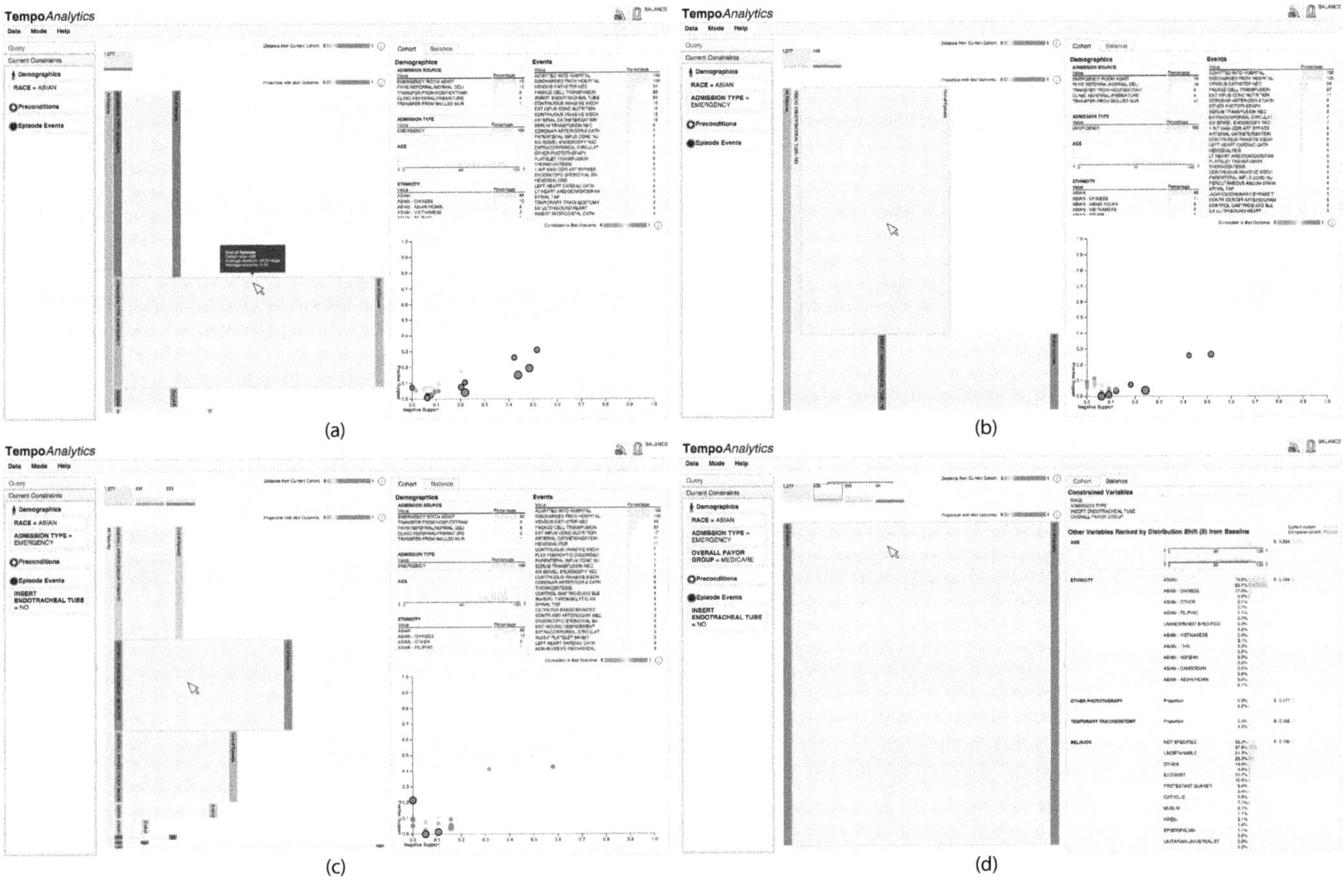

Figure 6. A sample interaction sequence showing a user applying multiple filters to narrow down to a narrow cohort of patients. The breadcrumb at the top shows the growing provenance model as it expands from (a) one step to (d) four steps. In (d), the user has switched to the Balance view to inspect the differences between two datasets as represented by the dotted black line in the breadcrumb view.

required users to perform tasks related to the selection of a patient cohort from a database containing electronic medical record data for approximately 30,000 patients with over 3,000 variables.[1] We note that while the data was medical in nature, the study tasks were designed to require no medical knowledge or background.

Participants and Testing Environment

A total of 18 users (12 female, 6 male) were recruited to participate in the study. All participants were college educated and had ages within the range of 21–50. The participants were randomly assigned into two groups of nine: a *Baseline* group and an *AC* group. None of the participants had any prior experience with any of the software evaluated in the study. The study tasks were performed on a 13.3-inch laptop computer with a display resolution of 1280×800 pixels and a 60 Hz refresh rate.

Procedure

Each user took part in single study session lasting roughly one hour. Each session began with a brief introduction to the data that would be used during the study, followed by a tutorial during which the moderator described the various features of the software that would be used to complete the study tasks. Users in the *AC* group were given access to the advanced AC features described in this paper. Users in the *Baseline* group were given access to a version of the same software but with the AC-related features disabled (see Figure 1). Regardless of group, participants were then instructed to practice with their assigned software tool and asked to perform six specific practice tasks. The moderator provided additional help and instruction when needed during these practice tasks.

Once a user was comfortable using the software assigned to her/his group, the experimental portion of the study began. The participant was asked to perform six formal study tasks that were very similar to the six practice tasks, but focused on different subsets of the study dataset. Both groups of users performed identical tasks with identical data, but with different versions of the software.

While the formal study tasks were performed, the moderator did not provide any assistance or instruction. The moderator recorded both accuracy and time-to-completion for Tasks T1–T4. Tasks T5 and T6 focused on the more subjective tasks of bias assessment and confidence, respectively. Once finished with the study tasks, users completed a post-session questionnaire with nine 5-point Likert scale questions (Q1–Q9) and two free-response questions that asked users to

[1] Variables include demographics, thousands of distinct medical procedures, and other medical events (e.g., admission and discharge).

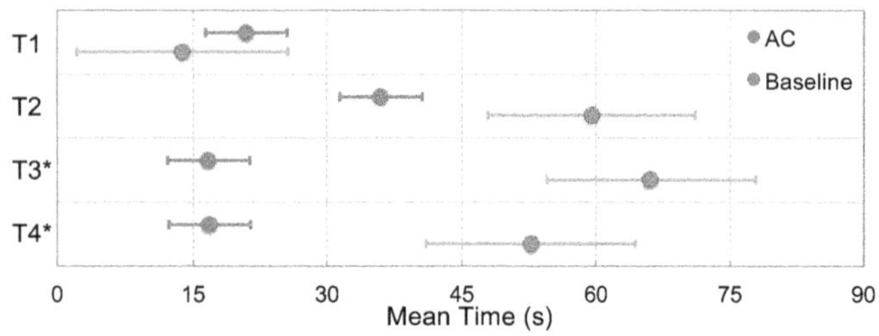

Figure 7. Mean time-to-completion (in seconds) for the four timed tasks in our study (T1–T4). Error bars show the standard error. * Tasks T3 and T4 were performed significant faster by the AC group ($p < 0.01$).

comment regarding the most and least helpful aspects of the software they were given to perform the tasks.

Finally, after the questionnaire, participants in both groups were debriefed by the moderator to gather additional qualitative feedback. Moreover, users in the *Baseline* group were given a demonstration of the full AC prototype and asked to comment regarding the additional features.

Results and Discussion

The results from our study show that AC can help contextualize the visual data selection process, and help users more effectively detect and characterize emerging selection bias. This section presents the results obtained from our study and discusses the implications of those results for AC-based visualization systems.

Study Tasks

Overall, users from both the *AC* and *Baseline* groups completed all tasks (T1–T6) with high accuracy. However, there were statistically significant[2] differences observed in task completion time for two of the four timed tasks as illustrated in Figure 7.

T1: Users were asked to compare the mortality rate for across different patient subgroups within the same dataset. This is a task for which AC was not expected to provide any meaningful benefit, and therefore similar performance was expected across groups. Indeed, both groups answered accurately well with only one incorrect answer. A user in the *AC* group arrived at the wrong answer after confusing the variable "Admission Type" with "Admission Source" and therefore select the wrong variable for comparison. However, the user did perform the task correctly even if the final response did not provide the correct answer.

T2: Users were asked to apply a filter to create a new dataset, then compare the values observed for a single variable across the "before" and "after" datasets. Users in all groups arrived at the correct answer, while *AC* user performed the task more quickly. The difference in timing, however, was not statistically significant given our sample size. We hypothesize that the Balance Panel proved useful for those that completed this task in the least amount of time, but more study is required to reach a stronger conclusion.

[2]Statistical significance for T1–T6 was determined using a standard t-test comparing results between *AC* and *Baseline*.

T3: Users were next asked to compare more broadly the two datasets produced after T2, comparing all variables rather than a single specific dimension. All users were again able to provide accurate answers. However, the *AC* arrived at their answers in significantly less time ($p < 0.01$). This result suggests that the Balance Panel was highly beneficial in helping users characterize differences between datasets.

T4: Users were asked to apply an additional filter, resulting in three datasets in the breadcrumb panel. Users were then asked to identify which of the first two datasets was most similar to the new active dataset that was just created. AC proved most useful in this case. Participants in the *AC* group performed the task significantly faster and provided accurate answers. Meanwhile, participants in the *Baseline* group faced far more difficulty resulting in significantly slower times ($p < 0.01$). Moreover, one user in the *Baseline* group simply abandoned the task claiming it was not possible to answer. The task completion time for this user were therefore omitted from the results shown in Figure 7 and our statistical analysis. The user did remain to complete the study session, but including his results for T4 would have produced an even stronger effect. Moreover, we believe that this user's behavior is emblematic of the much more difficult cognitive work required by participants in the *Baseline* group to complete this task.

T5 and T6: Unlike the previous tasks, T5 and T6 asked participants for subjective assessments. Users asked (T5) to state how representative the final dataset was with respect to the original query result; and (T6) state how confident they were in their assessment. Interestingly, both responded similarly that the final dataset was quite biased (*AC*: mean of 1.89; *Baseline*: mean of 1.69; on a 5 point scale with 1="very biased", 5="highly representative") and had similar levels of confidence in their assessments (*AC*: mean of 3.44; *Baseline*: mean of 3.88; on a 5 point scale with 1="very unsure", 5="highly confident"). The differences were not statistically significant, making it impossible to draw any firm conclusions. However, we do note that the *AC* user were less extreme, reporting in answers for both questions which, on average, were closer to the midpoint of the scale. The subjective feedback reported in the next section provides a more nuanced view of the participants' opinions.

Questionnaire and Moderator Debriefing

Users' feedback gathered via the questionnaire (see Figure 8) suggests that users clearly recognized certain benefits of using an AC-enabled visualization system for data selection[3] Moreover, these benefits appear to come without any penalty in terms of ease-of-use.

Q1–Q4: Q1 asked users how easy or hard it was to "learn how to interpret" the visualization, while Q2 as how easy or hard it was to "learn how to interact with" the visualization tool. Q3 asked users to score how easy the system was to use *after* the initial learning curve. The responses were similar for both the *AC* and *Baseline* groups for all three questions, falling in the middle of the range. This suggests the inclusion

[3]Statistical significance for Q1–Q9 was deterined using a Mann-Whitney U test comparing results between *AC* and *Baseline*.

of AC capabilities does not have any meaningful impact on either the learning-curve of ease-of-use for the system.

From the moderator debriefings, it was observed that users with prior experience with other data visualization tools found the interface very easy and convenient to use, while others took more time to become comfortable. However, even the participants with a steeper learning curve were able to complete the study session within the expected time.

Q5-Q7: The next three questions all suggested that the *AC* group felt more empowered for key selection bias assessment tasks. Q5 asked if it was easy to compare a dataset from one step to a dataset from another step in the selection process. Users in the *AC* group were far more likely to agree, and the difference was statistically significant ($p < 0.05$). Similarly, participants from the *AC* group were in stronger agreement with Q6, which asked users if the system made it easy to detect when a filter produce datasets that exhibited large amounts of selection bias. The difference for Q6, however, was not statistically significant given our relatively small sample size. Finally, the *AC* group was significantly ($p < 0.10$) more likely to agree with Q7, which asked if the visualization made it easy to learn which dimensions were most biased from the original dataset after applying multiple filters.

Q8: Participants responded similarly across groups to Q8, which asked about comparing variable distributions across any arbitrary pair of datasets rather limiting the comparisons to d_{active}. In both the Baseline and AC software prototypes, users would need to revert to a prior dataset using the breadcrumb view, which made this task harder to perform than other comparisons.

Q9: Perhaps surprisingly, users from the *Baseline* group agreed more strongly that the system they used in their study session provided sufficient information to properly assess the validity of the dataset they selected. The differences were not statistically different. However, we believe that the users with AC were provided with a more nuanced view that highlighted areas of bias. This in turn fosters deeper suspicion—and rightly so—within the user population about the quality of their data selection.

These results show that users in the *Baseline* group were equally or more confident in their final data selection. However, this confidence is misplaced as *Baseline* users also found it harder to compare datasets, harder to assess differences in individual dimensions across steps of a data selection process, and performed tasks more slowly and with more cognitive effort. We believe that this highlights the critical benefits AC, without which users may dangerously proceed with an analysis of a dataset both confident of its quality and ignorant of any underlying bias which may threaten then validity of subsequent analysis results.

These conclusions were further supported by the feedback in the open-ended questions at the end of the questionnaire. Users in the *AC* group said the color-mapped indicators for the δ measure of each dataset "useful"/"very helpful" for dataset comparison. Meanwhile, five of the eight users in

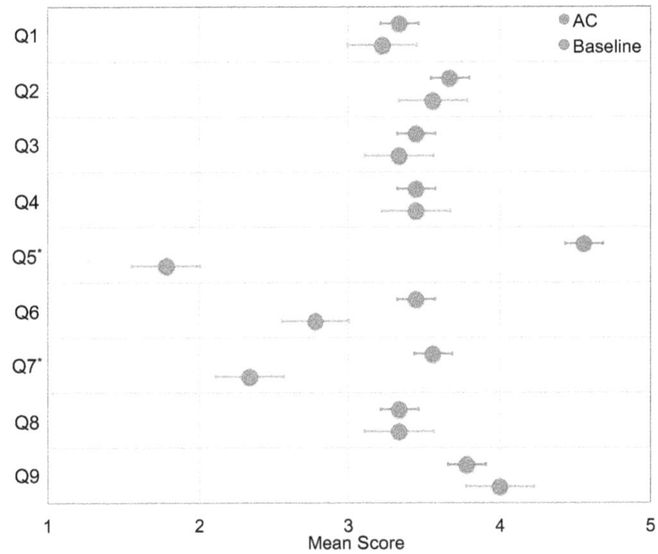

Figure 8. Average responses for each of the nine 5-point Likert scale questions (Q1–Q9). Error bars show the standard error. * Questions Q5 ($p < 0.05$) and Q7 ($p < 0.1$) show statistically significant differences between groups.

the *Baseline* group expressed a wish for more straightforward ways to compare the datasets rather than manually going back and manually comparing variable by variable.

Finally, at the very end of the study session for members of the *Baseline* group, the moderator revealed the AC features that were made available to users in the *AC* group. Every *Baseline* user said the study tasks would have been much easier with these new features. Comments from these users after the reveal included "nice!", "that's cool", and "a significant improvement if you want to compare between cohorts." Meanwhile, users in the *AC* group felt the tasks would have been impossible without the added features, or at least would have been much harder and taken much longer.

Interestingly, one user in the *AC* group brought up in the discussion that he would have had less confidence in his assessments (e.g., T6, Q9) if he had been in the *Baseline* group without access to the AC-based features. However, as already discussed, the study results don't support his assertion. Instead, we believe that users without AC—rather than wishing for features such as those that AC provide—simply proceed with false confidence because the bias being introduced during selection is often hidden within the many variables that have been omitted from the visualization.

CONCLUSION

Large scale datasets are being gathered in many domains with the goal of supporting data-driven decision making. While interactive data visualization can play a critical role in this process, there is a critical mismatch between (1) the very large number of dimensions in many complex real-world datasets, and (2) the much smaller number of dimensions that can be concurrently visualized using modern techniques. This gap in dimensionality can place a user at high risk of hidden selection bias during exploratory data selection tasks. This paper described Adaptive Contextualization (AC), a novel approach to interactive visual data selection that is specifically designed to combat this challenge. The AC approach (1) captures a model of users' visual data selection activity, (2) computes metrics over that model to quantify the amount of selection bias after each step, (3) visualizes the metric results, and (4) provides interactive tools that help users detect and assess the sources of bias as they emerge.

The results from our formal user study provide evidence for the benefits of our approach. However, there remain many avenues for future work. In particular, we plan to examine intelligent ways to help users minimize the impact of bias through the use of intelligent data transformation operations. In addition, we plan to explore other data quality measures which can be computed in similar ways to address challenges beyond selection bias. Finally, we plan to conduct more thorough, longitudinal evaluations of our approach through a series of multi-dimensional long-term case studies [29].

ACKNOWLEDGMENTS

This work was made possible in part by a Data Fellow award from the National Consortium for Data Science (NCDS).

REFERENCES

1. Abernethy, A. P., Etheredge, L. M., Ganz, P. A., Wallace, P., German, R. R., Neti, C., Bach, P. B., and Murphy, S. B. Rapid-Learning System for Cancer Care. *Journal of Clinical Oncology 28*, 27 (Sept. 2010), 4268–4274.
2. Ankerst, M., Berchtold, S., and Keim, D. Similarity clustering of dimensions for an enhanced visualization of multidimensional data (1998). 52–60.
3. Bavoil, L., Callahan, S., Crossno, P., Freire, J., Scheidegger, C., Silva, C., and Vo, H. VisTrails: enabling interactive multiple-view visualizations. In *IEEE Visualization* (Oct. 2005), 135–142.
4. Bertini, E., Tatu, A., and Keim, D. Quality Metrics in High-Dimensional Data Visualization: An Overview and Systematization. *IEEE Transactions on Visualization and Computer Graphics 17*, 12 (Dec. 2011), 2203–2212.
5. Buja, A., Cook, D., and Swayne, D. F. Interactive High-Dimensional Data Visualization. *Journal of Computational and Graphical Statistics 5*, 1 (Mar. 1996), 78–99.
6. Cao, N., Gotz, D., Sun, J., and Qu, H. DICON: Interactive Visual Analysis of Multidimensional Clusters. *IEEE Transactions on Visualization and Computer Graphics 17*, 12 (2011), 2581–2590.
7. Carr, D., Littlefield, R., Nicholson, W., and Littlefield, J. Scatterplot matrix techniques for large N. *Journal of the American Statistical Association 82*, 398 (1987), 424–436.
8. Chen, K., and Liu, L. VISTA: Validating and Refining Clusters Via Visualization. *Information Visualization 3*, 4 (Dec. 2004), 257–270.
9. Elmqvist, N., and Fekete, J. Hierarchical Aggregation for Information Visualization: Overview, Techniques, and Design Guidelines. *IEEE Trans on Visualization and Computer Graphics 16*, 3 (2010), 439–454.
10. Etheredge, L. M. A Rapid-Learning Health System. *Health Affairs 26*, 2 (Mar. 2007), 107–118.
11. Friedman, C. P., Wong, A. K., and Blumenthal, D. Achieving a Nationwide Learning Health System. *Science Translational Medicine 2*, 57 (Nov. 2010).
12. Gotz, D., and Stavropoulos, H. DecisionFlow: Visual Analytics for High-Dimensional Temporal Event Sequence Data. *IEEE Transactions on Visualization and Computer Graphics 20*, 12 (2014), 1783–1792.
13. Gotz, D., and Wen, Z. Behavior-driven visualization recommendation. In *Proceedings of the 14th international conference on Intelligent user interfaces*, ACM (New York, NY, USA, 2009), 315–324.
14. Gotz, D., and Zhou, M. Characterizing users' visual analytic activity for insight provenance. In *IEEE Symposium on Visual Analytics Science and Technology, 2008. VAST '08* (2008), 123–130.
15. Heinrich, J., and Weiskopf, D. State of the Art of Parallel Coordinates. In *Eurographics 2013 - State of the Art Reports*, M. Sbert and L. Szirmay-Kalos, Eds., The Eurographics Association (2012).
16. Hibino, S., and Rundensteiner, E. A. User interface evaluation of a direct manipulation temporal visual query language. In *Proceedings of the fifth ACM international conference on Multimedia*, ACM (New York, NY, USA, 1997), 99–107.
17. Inselberg, A., and Dimsdale, B. Parallel coordinates: a tool for visualizing multi-dimensional geometry. IEEE Computer Society Press (Los Alamitos, CA, USA, 1990), 361–378. ACM ID: 949588.
18. Institute of Medicine. Best Care at Lower Cost: The Path to Continuously Learning Health Care in America. Tech. rep., Sept. 2012.
19. Jankun-Kelly, T. J., Ma, K. L., and Gertz, M. A Model for the Visualization Exploration Process. In *Proceedings of IEEE Visualization* (Washington, DC, USA, 2002), 323–330.
20. Kreuseler, M., Nocke, T., and Schumann, H. A History Mechanism for Visual Data Mining. In *IEEE Symposium on Information Visualization* (2004), 49–56.
21. Lineberger. UNC Lineberger Comprehensive Cancer Center. Integrated Cancer Information and Surveillance System: http://iciss.unc.edu/, 2014.
22. Lu, J., Wen, Z., Pan, S., and Lai, J. Analytic Trails: Supporting Provenance, Collaboration, and Reuse for Visual Data Analysis by Business Users. In *Human-Computer Interaction INTERACT 2011*, P. Campos, N. Graham, J. Jorge, N. Nunes, P. Palanque, and M. Winckler, Eds., no. 6949 in Lecture Notes in Computer Science. Springer Berlin Heidelberg, Jan. 2011, 256–273.

23. Murdoch, T. B., and Detsky, A. S. The inevitable application of big data to health care. *JAMA 309*, 13 (Apr. 2013), 1351–1352.

24. North, C., Chang, R., Endert, A., Dou, W., May, R., Pike, B., and Fink, G. Analytic Provenance: Process+Interaction+Insight. In *CHI '11 Extended Abstracts on Human Factors in Computing Systems*, ACM (New York, NY, USA, 2011), 33–36.

25. Pollard, D. *A User's Guide to Measure Theoretic Probability*. Cambridge University Press, 2002.

26. Rind, A. Interactive Information Visualization to Explore and Query Electronic Health Records. *Foundations and Trends in HumanComputer Interaction 5*, 3 (2013), 207–298.

27. Seo, J., and Shneiderman, B. Interactively exploring hierarchical clustering results. *IEEE Computer 35* (2002), 80–86.

28. Shneiderman, B. Dynamic Queries for Visual Information Seeking. *IEEE Softw. 11*, 6 (Nov. 1994), 70–77.

29. Shneiderman, B., and Plaisant, C. Strategies for Evaluating Information Visualization Tools: Multi-dimensional In-depth Long-term Case Studies. In *Proceedings of the 2006 AVI Workshop on BEyond Time and Errors: Novel Evaluation Methods for Information Visualization*, ACM (New York, NY, USA, 2006), 1–7.

30. Shrinivasan, Y., Gotz, D., and Lu, J. Connecting the dots in visual analysis. In *IEEE Symposium on Visual Analytics Science and Technology, 2009. VAST 2009* (2009), 123–130.

31. Shrinivasan, Y. B., and Gotz, D. Connecting the dots with related notes. In *CHI '09 Extended Abstracts on Human Factors in Computing Systems*, ACM (New York, NY, USA, 2009), 3649–3654.

32. Shrinivasan, Y. B., and van Wijk, J. J. Supporting the Analytical Reasoning Process in Information Visualization. In *Proceedings of the SIGCHI Conference on Human Factors in Computing Systems*, ACM (New York, NY, USA, 2008), 1237–1246.

33. Simpson, D. G. Minimum Hellinger Distance Estimation for the Analysis of Count Data. *Journal of the American Statistical Association 82*, 399 (Sept. 1987), 802–807.

34. Thomas, J., and Cook, K. *Illuminating the Path: The Research and Development Agenda for Visual Analytics*. National Visualization and Analytics Ctr, 2005.

35. Wang Baldonado, M. Q., Woodruff, A., and Kuchinsky, A. Guidelines for Using Multiple Views in Information Visualization. In *Proceedings of the Working Conference on Advanced Visual Interfaces*, ACM (New York, NY, USA, 2000), 110–119.

36. Ward, M., Grinstein, G., and Keim, D. *Interactive Data Visualization: Foundations, Techniques, and Applications*, 1 edition ed. A K Peters/CRC Press, Natick, Mass, June 2010.

37. Zhang, Z., Gotz, D., and Perer, A. Iterative cohort analysis and exploration. *Information Visualization OnlineFirst* (Mar. 2014).

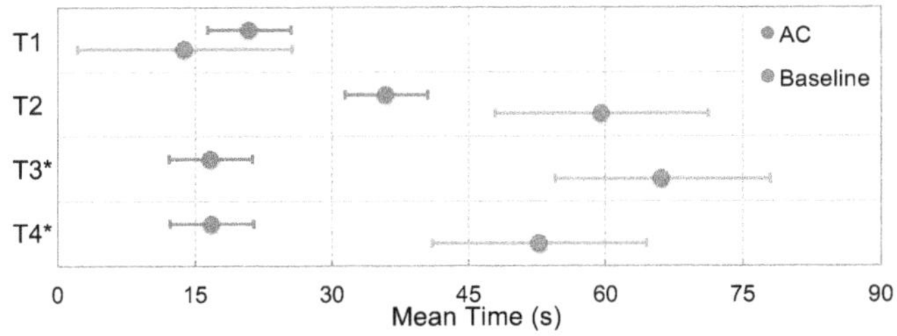

MultiConVis: A Visual Text Analytics System for Exploring a Collection of Online Conversations

Enamul Hoque and Giuseppe Carenini
Department of Computer Science
University of British Columbia, Canada
{enamul, carenini}@cs.ubc.ca

ABSTRACT
Online conversations, such as blogs, provide rich amount of information and opinions about popular queries. Given a query, traditional blog sites return a set of conversations often consisting of thousands of comments with complex thread structure. Since the interfaces of these blog sites do not provide any overview of the data, it becomes very difficult for the user to explore and analyze such a large amount of conversational data. In this paper, we present MultiConVis, a visual text analytics system designed to support the exploration of a collection of online conversations. Our system tightly integrates NLP techniques for topic modeling and sentiment analysis with information visualizations, by considering the unique characteristics of online conversations. The resulting interface supports the user exploration, starting from a possibly large set of conversations, then narrowing down to the subset of conversations, and eventually drilling-down to the set of comments of one conversation. Our evaluations through case studies with domain experts and a formal user study with regular blog readers illustrate the potential benefits of our approach, when compared to a traditional blog reading interface.

Author Keywords
Asynchronous conversations; text visualization; visual text analytics, computer mediated communication;

ACM Classification Keywords
H.5.2 Information Interfaces and Presentation: User Interfaces
I.2.7 Natural Language Processing:Text analysis

INTRODUCTION
With the proliferation of web-based social media, there has been an exponential growth of asynchronous online conversations discussing a large variety of popular issues like 'ObamaCare', 'US immigration reform', and 'Apple iWatch release'. Asynchronous conversations, such as blogs, may start with a news article or editorial opinion, and later generate long thread with hundreds of comments, which readers may become interested in exploring and analyzing to seek variety of information and opinions. However, given a query, traditional blog sites only present the set of relevant blogs as a paginated list ordered by their recency, without providing any high-level summary of the conversations. This navigational support is often inadequate to explore a set of blogs that may be of great interest to readers [19].

For example, consider the issue of 'iPhone bending' that went viral on social media, when the iPhone 6 was launched in September 2014. Soon after the product was released, some people claimed that this new phone can easily bend in the pocket while sitting on it. This incident triggered a huge amount of discussions in Macrumors [28], a blog site that regularly publishes Apple related news and allows participants to make comments. Within a few days, more than a dozen conversations with thousands of comments were generated in Macrumors covering various related issues, such as 'what users reported about the bending issue', 'what Apple says to defend its new product', and 'what are the reactions from the rivals of Apple' etc. In this situation, we could imagine three different users who would like to explore this set of conversations. First, a potential customer, who intended to buy an iPhone may want to explore these conversations to verify whether the bending issue is really serious. Second, a journalist may want to publish a story about what people are saying about the 'bending issue'. Finally, an Apple marketing analyst may want to get a pulse from the online community to make informed decision about how to react to the rumors and possibly redesign the products. In all cases, given the large number of conversations/comments, it would be extremely difficult and time-consuming for a user to explore and analyze all this information with the current blog interfaces, that provide sequential access to conversations/comment and have limited interactive features (such as searching for keywords).

Integrating Natural Language Processing (NLP) and Information Visualization (InfoVis) techniques has been proposed as a promising solution to this and similar textual/information overload problems [11, 40, 41]. In this work, we tightly couple NLP techniques for topic modeling and sentiment analysis with interactive visualizations to support the exploration and analysis of large set of conversations by considering the specific characteristics of the conversational domain. While asynchronous conversations comprise emails, blogs, microblogs (e.g., Twitter), and messaging; in this paper we focus on the blog conversations. In fact, blog conversations exhibit several unique characteristics: unlike microblog or messaging [34], they do not have fixed length comments; furthermore they have finer conversational structure as participants often reply to a post and/or quote a fragment of other comments [21]. In this paper, we consider these unique characteristics in devising

IUI'16, March 07-10, 2016, Sonoma, CA, USA
Copyright 2016 ACM. ISBN 978-1-4503-4137-0/16/03 $15.00
DOI: http://dx.doi.org/10.1145/2856767.2856782

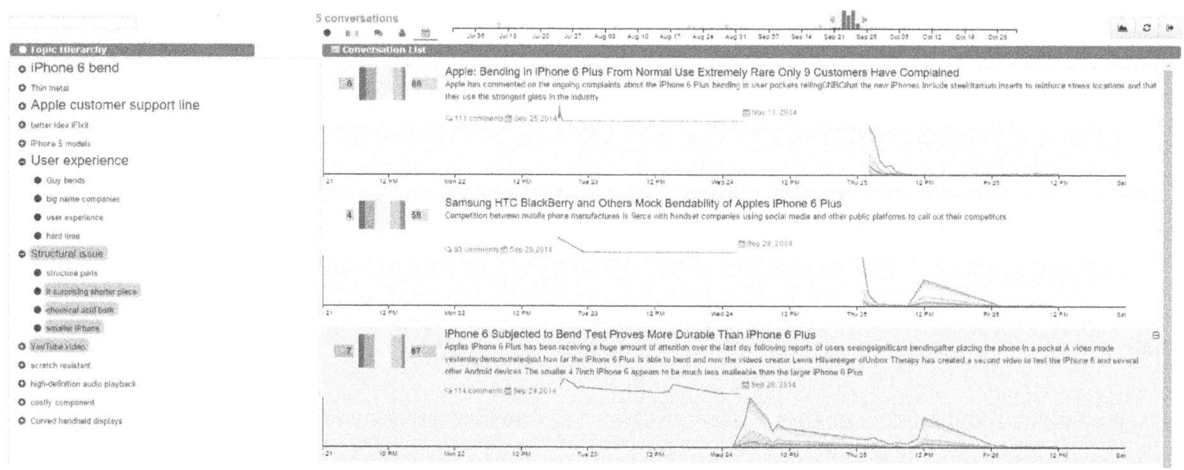

Figure 1. The MultiConVis interface, showing a subset of blog conversations returned by the query 'iPhone bending' from Macrumors in November 2014. Here, the user filtered out some conversations from the list using the Timeline located at the top, and then hovered on a conversation item (highlighted row in the right). As a consequence, the related topics from the Topic Hierarchy were highlighted (left).

both NLP and InfoVis techniques. Our work is closely related to a visual text analytic system named ConVis [17], which was also designed for blog conversations, but focused on supporting the user in exploring a single conversation. As we move from a single conversation to a collection of conversations, critical challenges emerge from the fact that users need to deal with a much larger amount of data, with different levels of granularity. For instance, the number of topics increases drastically for a set of conversations, therefore understanding and exploring these topics can be much more time consuming and cumbersome. Since some of these topics are similar in their semantic meaning, grouping them into a hierarchical topic organization may support the understanding and navigation of topics more effectively.

To address this challenge, we devise a hierarchical topic modeling technique that organizes the topics within a set of conversations into multiple levels, based on their semantic similarity. We then design a visual interface that presents the hierarchical topic structure along with other conversational data as shown in Figure 1. The main contributions of this work are:

1) A **hierarchical topic modeling method** over a collection of conversations. While [17] describes how to effectively extract topics from a single conversation, here we propose a method which creates a topic hierarchy for a whole collection of conversations, by aggregating the topics extracted from each conversation in the collection.

2) The design and implementation of the **MultiConVis** interface, which supports exploration of a collection of blog conversations based on the topic hierarchy and sentiment. In essence, MultiConVis can be seen as an interface built on top of ConVis to allow the user to seemingly switch from exploring a collection of conversations to a single conversation. In particular, MultiConVis initially visualizes all the conversations in the whole collection, next supports the user in filtering out conversations that are irrelevant to her information needs, and then allows her to drill down to a specific conversation, which is visualized with the ConVis interface.

3) The evaluation of MultiConVis through a set of **case studies**, and a **user study** to investigate how the system influences user performance and subjective opinions when compared to a sample, traditional blog reading interface similar to existing interfaces, like Slashdot [37] and Macrumors [28].

RELATED WORK

Research prototypes that aim to support the exploration of a large collection of conversations can be categorized based on the information they extract and visualize: (a) metadata of the conversations (e.g., timestamps, tags, and authors), (b) the results of text analysis such as topic model and opinion.

Metadata visualization

Some earlier works have focused on how to support the exploration of a blog archive using only metadata, for example, by visualizing tags and comments arranged along a time-axis [19], or by providing faceted visualization widgets for visual query formulation according to time, place, and tags [10]. While these works may assist users to find the blogs they are looking for, they are not designed to support users in understanding the actual content (i.e., the text) of these conversations. However, many tasks require the user to get overviews of the actual content of a collection of conversations, such as "Find out what are people feeling about *X* over time." Therefore, our goal is to visualize a combination of various metadata and textual analysis results that are identified as important in our user requirements analysis.

Topic modeling and visualization

In contrast to simply showing the metadata of the conversations, recently there have been some attempts to visualize the topics discussed within a collection of conversations [40, 41, 11]. Recent approaches use probabilistic topic models such as Latent Dirichlet Allocation (LDA), where topics are defined as distributions of words and documents are represented as mixture of topics. Many of these works also consider the temporal aspects of topics by showing the evolution of topics over time. For example, *Themail* visualizes how topics in a collection of email conversations develop over time by arranging keywords selected based on term-frequency inverse document-frequency

(TF-IDF) along a horizontal time axis [40]. *TIARA* [41] represents the temporal evolution of topics from an email collection by applying the ThemeRiver visualization [15], where each layer in the stacked graph represents a topic and the keywords of each topic are distributed over time. From the height of each topic and its content distributed over time, the user can see the topic evolution.

More recent works have tried to move beyond visualizing topics as a flat list, by organizing them into a hierarchy [12, 4, 26]. For example, *HierarchicalTopics* organizes a large number of topics into a tree structure by considering the distance between the probability distributions of topics [12]; and then utilizes a hierarchical ThemeRiver view to explore temporal trends of topics. Using the same algorithm, *TopicPanorama* builds topic hierarchies from multiple corpora (i.e., news, blogs, and microblogs), followed by matching these hierarchies using a graph-matching technique, so that the common and distinctive topics from different corpora can be visualized [26]. It combines a radially stacked tree visualization with a density-based graph visualization to facilitate the examination of the matched topic graph from multiple perspectives. Compared to these approaches that generate static topic hierarchies, *RoseRiver* focused on exploring the evolutionary patterns of hierarchical topics generated at different timeframes by conveying topic merging and splitting relationships over time using Sankey diagrams [4].

Organizing topics into a hierarchy can be very useful to our work as well, because the number of distinct topics in a collection of conversations may be quite high, compared to a single conversation. However, existing hierarchical topic modeling approaches are not designed specifically for conversational data. In contrast, MultiConVis creates a topic hierarchy for a collection of conversations by aggregating the topics of each conversation in the collection. And such topics are generated by taking specific characteristics of asynchronous conversations (e.g., reply-relationship) into account [17].

Opinion visualization

There is a growing interest in visualizing the opinions expressed in conversations, mostly focusing on microblogs [8, 29, 43]. Diakopoulos et al. presented *Vox Civitas* [8] that displayed sentiment and tweets volume over time for events discussed in microblogs to support the tasks of journalistic inquiry. *TwitInfo* [29] was also designed for visualizing microblogs with a focus on providing more accurate aggregation of sentiment information over a collection of tweets. Unlike these works, *OpinionFlow* focused more on visualizing the spreading of opinions about a particular topic (e.g., 'US government shutdown') among participants with a combination of a density map and a Sankey diagram [43]. Often the opinion information is summarized with other important aspects of information spreading such as temporal information, and the connections among conversation threads and authors [44].

A critical issue when abstracting data for sentiment analysis is how to aggregate sentiment information across sentences, comments and conversations. While all the works described above dealt with twitter data, in which tweets are only organized as a list, here we focus on a set of much more structured

Facets \ Levels	Collection of Conversations	One Conversation
Topics	Hierarchy with all topics from all conversations	Conversation-level topics with explicit links to the topic hierarchy and to comments
Time	- Start day/time - Volume of comments over time	Ordinal time representations: comments are ordered chronologically
Sentiment	- Sentiment distribution for each conversation - Sentiment evolution over time for each conversation	Sentiment distribution for each comment
Authors	Number of authors for each conversation	Conversation-level authors with explicit links to comments

Table 1. A summary of how facet elements are abstracted for a collection of conversations vs. one conversation.

blog conversations, where each conversation consists of a set of comments organized in multiple threads with reply-relationships. We exploit this additional structure when we visually represent sentiment over multiple, different levels.

USER REQUIREMENTS ANALYSIS

Why and how people read a collection of blogs has been studied extensively in the fields of computer mediated communication [46, 9, 23], social media [16, 7], human computer interaction [2, 31], and information retrieval [24, 27, 30, 36]. In essence, the primary goals of reading blogs include information seeking, fact checking, and opinion seeking [23, 6], which require the reader to understand what *topics* are discussed in the conversations and what *opinions* are expressed on those topics. Furthermore, users often exhibit a *variety seeking behaviour*, i.e., they tend to switch frequently from a topic to its sub-topics or to a completely different topic [36].

Blog readers also care about temporal aspects of the conversations [16, 7], for instance, the start and end time of a conversation, the chronological position of a comment with respect to the other comments within a conversation [2], and the volume of comments over time when exploring multiple conversations. Information about authors of the comments is also considered to be valuable [16], especially for blogs in which the same users participate frequently.

Table 1 summarizes our design choices for what information our interface should display, in light of current literature on blog readers. The row in the table corresponds to data facets and the columns to whether the facet is for multiple conversations vs a single one. Since the number of topics for a collection of conversations is potentially much larger than for a single conversation, all the *topics* within a collection are organized into a hierarchy, while the topics of each single conversation are organized as a flat list and are explicitly connected to the comments of that conversation. To support the goals related to the *time* facet, the volume of comments over time is computed for each conversation in the collection of conversations, whereas within each conversation the chronological position of the comments is used. For the *sentiment* facet the distribution of sentiments across five polarity intervals (-2 to +2) is computed by counting how many sentences

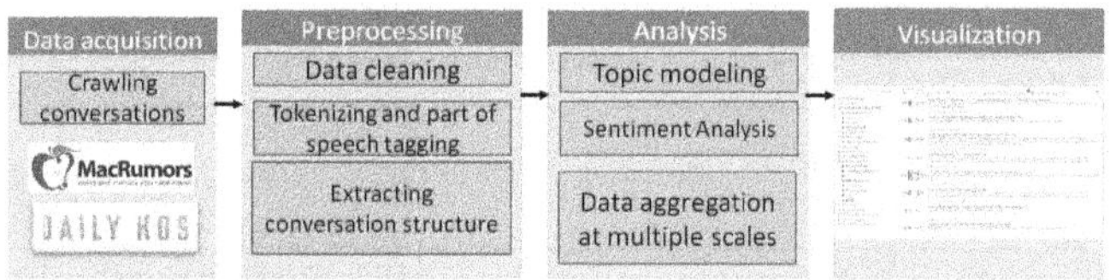

Figure 2. Overview of the MultiConVis system.

fall in each of these intervals. Here, for a collection of conversations, we compute the sentiment distribution for *each conversation*, whereas for one conversation, we compute this distribution at a finer level, i.e., for *each comment*. Finally, for the *authors* facet, while for a set of conversations only counts of authors are computed without providing the detailed list of authors, for one conversation the list of authors for that conversation is shown.

Current literature on blog reading not only inspired our data choices, but also guided the development of MultiConVis interactive visualization techniques. Considering the exploratory nature of blog reading, MultiConVis supports the user in browsing the set of conversations and comments by means of all the key facets (e.g., topics, sentiment and authors). Furthermore, the interface facilitate the exploration through the facets at different levels of granularity: from all conversations, to a subset of conversations, to one conversation. For consistency, elements of the same facet across different levels of granularity have similar visual mapping in terms of color, shape and other visual encoding channels. Finally, to facilitate the exploration and filtering of conversations, important attributes of each conversation (e.g., number of topics/ authors and overall sentiment distribution) are encoded as information scent [42].

SYSTEM OVERVIEW

The MultiConVis system consists of four major components as shown in Figure 2. Given a specified query (e.g., 'iPhone bending'), the *data acquisition module* invokes a blogsite such as Macrumors to crawl the set of conversations obtained from the first page of the search results returned by that site. Next, the *preprocessing module* performs data cleaning to retain only the conversational data in the crawled pages, followed by extracting the conversational structure, i.e., reply-relationships and quotation. We also use a state-of-the-art tagger [33] to tokenize text and annotate the tokens with their part-of-speech tags. After that, the *analysis module* performs topic modeling and sentiment analysis over the whole set of conversations. It then aggregates both metadata and results of text analysis at different granularity levels as described in the user requirements analysis. Finally, the *visualization module* displays the results obtained from the analysis module, and supports the user to interactively explore the conversations.

TEXT ANALYSIS

Topic hierarchy generation

Our topic modeling approach takes a collection of n blog conversations $C = \{c_1, c_2, ..., c_n\}$ that satisfies a user query, and generates a topic hierarchy following a bottom-up approach. In the resulting hierarchy, each node represents the cluster of sentences in the conversations that discuss the topic described by the label of the node. While one could think of a top-down approach to be more suitable for generating the topic hierarchy

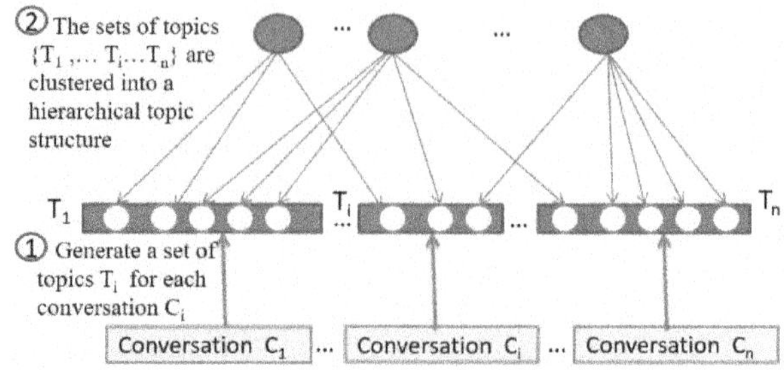

Figure 3. Hierarchical topic model generation.

as it considers the whole set of conversations while generating the initial set of clusters (the roots of the hierarchy); we choose a bottom-up approach because in this way we are able to take into account the conversational structure extracted from each conversation. In other words, we first generate a set of topic clusters for each conversation by taking advantage of its conversational structure, and then we organize these topic clusters from all the conversations into a hierarchy. More specifically, our topic hierarchy generation involves two primary steps as shown in Figure 3: 1) generate a set of topics T_i for each conversation $c_i \in C$; 2) aggregate all the T_i into a hierarchical topic structure for the whole collection.

For **topic Modeling over each conversation**, we adopt the method described in [17]. We briefly summarize it here, because our topic modeling method for a collection of conversations exploits similar data structures and techniques. Topic modeling of a single conversation starts by grouping the sentences of the conversation into a number of topic clusters (*segmentation*). Then, representative key phrases are assigned to each of these clusters (*labeling*).

In essence, topic segmentation applies a Lexical Cohesion-based Segmenter (LCSeg) [13] to each thread in the conversation as shown in Figure 4, where each thread represents a path from the initial message to a leaf message. Notice that after running the LCSeg algorithm, two sentences (e.g., s_1 and s_4) may appear together in the same segment in one thread $(A, C1, C2)$, while falling into different segments in another thread $(A, C1, C4, C5)$. To consolidate all the (possibly conflicting) segmentation decisions made on each thread, we apply an efficient min-cut graph partitioning algorithm [35]. The optimal number of topics for each conversation is automatically determined by maximizing the clustering objective function proposed in [32].

Topic labeling takes the segmented conversation as input, and generates a set of keyphrases to describe each topic cluster in the conversation. This is done by adapting the co-ranking method proposed in [45], in which a list of the top keyphrases is extracted form a graph of words that captures the co-occurrence of each word in the topic cluster with respect to the words in the leading sentence of that cluster, as well as the position of each word with respect to the thread structure of the conversation.

Creating the topic hierarchy over the collection is the key computational contributions of this paper. Once the sets of topics T_i for each conversation c_i are generated, we organize all of them into a single topic hierarchy to create a structured overview of the whole collection of conversations. To achieve

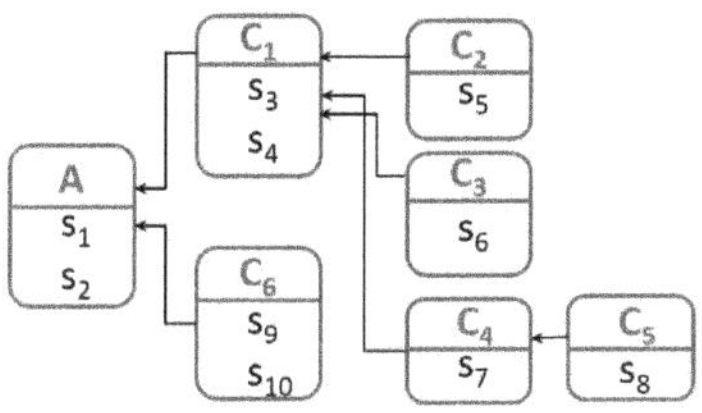

(a)

Thread	Sentences
A,C1,C2	$s_1, s_2, s_3, s_4 \mid s_5$
A,C1,C3	$s_1, s_2, s_3, s_4 \mid s_6$
A,C1,C4,C5	$s_1, s_2 \mid s_3, s_4 \mid, s_7, s_8$
A,C6	s_1, s_2, s_9, s_{10}

(b)

Figure 4. a)Reply-to relationships between the initial post A and the comments $C_1, C_2, ..., C_6$ of a conversation (left). Each post may comprise of one or more sentences as denoted by $s_1, s_2, s_3, ..., s_{10}$. b) the corresponding list of threads along with segmentation results after running the LCSeg algorithm on each of these threads. Here, the segmentation boundary is denoted by '|' (right).

this, we have devised a graph-based method similar to the one that we apply to single conversations. The main difference here is that the nodes of the graph we create are not sentences anymore, but topics.

In particular, we create a weighted undirected graph $G(V_C, E_C)$, where the nodes V_C represent the union of all the topics T_i from the set of conversations $C = \{c_1, c_2, ..., c_n\}$ and an edge weight $w(x;y)$ in E_C, between any two given topic nodes x and y, is generated by computing the average similarity between all pairs of sentences, in which one sentence belongs to topic x and the other one belongs to topic y. More formally, consider S_x is a set of l sentences and S_y is a set of m sentences for topics x and y respectively. Then we compute the edge weight $w(x;y)$ as follows:

$$w(x;y) = \frac{1}{l \times m} \sum_{s_i \in S_x, s_j \in S_y} sim(s_i, s_j) \tag{1}$$

Here, $sim(s_i, s_j)$ is the measure of similarity between a pair of sentences s_i and s_j. This measure is based on cosine similarity between s_i and s_j, if topic x and topic y belong to two different conversations c_x and c_y. Also, the same cosine similarity measure is used when s_i and s_j are from the same conversation, but never appear in the same segment in the segmentation results of the LCSseg algorithm. However, if s_i and s_j are both from the same conversation and they appear together in the same segment at least once, then the similarity is determined by k, where k is the number of times ($k >= 1$) in which s_i and s_j appeared in the same segment. This is based on the intuition that two topics that are from the same conversation and have stronger cohesion in the threads of that conversation should be more likely to be clustered together than those that do not. More formally,

$$sim(s_i, s_j) = \begin{cases} \{CosineSim(s_i, s_j) & \text{if } c_x \neq c_y \\ \begin{cases} k & \text{if } k >= 1 \\ CosineSim(s_i, s_j) & \text{if } k = 0 \end{cases} & \text{else} \end{cases} \tag{2}$$

$$CosineSim(s_i, s_j) = \frac{\sum_{w \in s_i, s_j} tf_{w,s_i} \cdot tf_{w,s_j}}{\sqrt{\sum_{p \in s_i} tf_{p,s_i}^2} \cdot \sqrt{\sum_{q \in s_j} tf_{q,s_j}^2}} \tag{3}$$

$$0 \leq CosineSim(s_i, s_j) \leq 1 \tag{4}$$

Here, $tf_{a,b}$ denotes the term frequency of term a in the sentence b.

Once we have built the graph $G(V_C, E_C)$, we apply the same graph partitioning algorithm used in topic segmentation for single conversation, i.e., approximate solution to n-Cut [35] on $G(V_C, E_C)$. As a result, topic nodes that are mostly similar (i.e., strongly connected in $G(V_C, E_C)$ will form coherent clusters. Each of these clusters can be interpreted as a parent topic (in the topic hierarchy) of all the topic nodes that forms that cluster.

For the final step of topic labeling, we assign a set of keyphrases to each parent topic by taking all the sentences from all the children topic nodes under it, and by then extracting and ranking keyphrases from all those sentences. This process is similar to the topic labeling method described for single conversation, except that given the absence of a thread structure between multiple conversations, we modify the ranking process by creating a graph that only captures word co-occurence relationships.

Sentiment

For sentiment analysis, we apply the Semantic Orientation CALculator (SO-CAL) [39], which has been shown to work well on user-generated content. SO-CAL computes sentiment polarity as numeric values. At first, we generate the polarity for each sentence of the conversation using SO-CAL. We defined five different polarity intervals (-2 to +2), and aggregate the results at various levels. For instance, at the level of a single conversation for each *comment*, we count how many sentences fall in any of these polarity intervals to compute the polarity distribution for that comment. Similarly, when dealing with a set of conversations, for each *conversation* we count how many sentences fall in any of these five polarity intervals to compute the polarity distribution for that conversation.

MULTICONVIS

In order to explore various design choices, we carried out an iterative design process, starting from early mockups and prototypes, to a fully functional system. Throughout this process, we performed formative evaluations [25] to identify potential usability issues and to iteratively refine the prototype. We now present the final design of the MultiConVis interface[1], along with justifications for the key design decisions based on our user requirements analysis and the InfoVis literature.

Visual encoding

Facets: As mentioned earlier, a key design goal of MultiConVis is to facilitate the exploration of a set of conversations at multiple levels of granularity, while maintaining consistent visual mapping across different levels. We maintained consistency in the visual encodings across different levels as follows: 1) Sentiment distributions are represented in the same way (as a stacked bar) for a conversation, for a topic as well as for a comment (see Figure 5(a)). A set of five diverging colors was used in a perceptually meaningful order purple (highly negative) to orange (highly positive) to visualize the distribution of sentiment orientations at all the three different levels of granularity[2]. 2) For all the attributes related to topics/authors facet, the same color coding was used across different levels

[1] See also video demo in supplementary material.

[2] The orange and purple colors were selected instead of the standard green and red to avoid the color blindness effects.

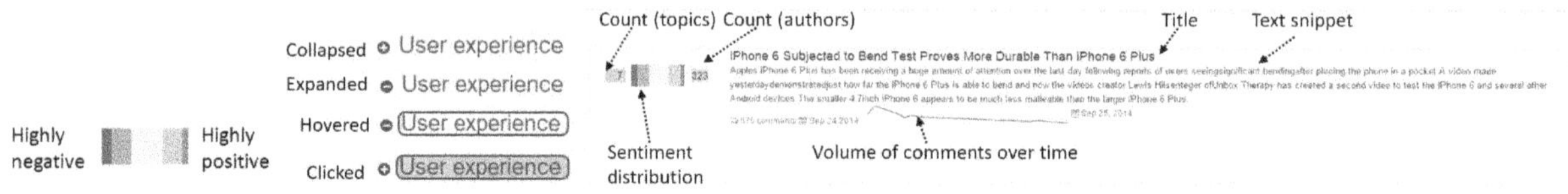

(a) Sentiment distribution (b) Topic in four different states with respect to user interaction (c) Conversation

Figure 5. The main visual encodings in MultiConVis: a) Sentiment distribution is shown as stacked bar; b) Visual encoding of topics changes according to different user interactions; c) Visual encoding of a set of aggregated metadata and text analysis results for a conversation.

Figure 6. A snapshot of MultiConVis for the 'iPhone bending' dataset: the Topic Hierarchy represents the set of topics and their sub-topics as an indented tree (left); the Conversation List shows a set of aggregated metadata and text analysis results for each conversation (row); the Timeline at the top shows the volume of comments over time for all conversations.

to reflect changes with respect to user interactions (see Figure 5(b)).

All conversations: Initially, when the user starts exploring the whole collection of conversations MultiConVis displays three components as shown in Figure 6: 1) a Topic Hierarchy; 2) an overview of the set of conversations (Conversation List); and 3) a Timeline View showing the volume of comments of the whole collection over time. These three components are interactively coordinated, so that any operation in one view is reflected in the other views.

The **Conversation List** shows the current set of conversations, where each item in the list represents a set of aggregated metadata and the results of text analysis for the corresponding conversation (See Figure 5(c)). In particular, we encode the following attributes of each conversation: 1) the overall sentiment distribution using a stacked bar, 2) the number of comments, which is encoded as the height of this stacked bar, 3) the count of topics and authors as horizontal bars, and 4) a sparkline that represents the volume of comments over time in a more space efficient way [14]. In addition, the title and a text snippet of the conversation are shown to the right side of its visual summary. Overall, these attributes summarize the set of conversations, facilitating the discovery of interesting subsets of conversations that are of interest to the user.

The **Topic Hierarchy** visually conveys all the topics in the whole collection of conversations using an indented tree representation. Here, topics are sorted chronologically within each level of the hierarchy. Each topic node is represented by its top keyphrase label returned by the topic modeling method, however, when the user hovers on a topic additional keyphrases are also shown to provide more context about that topic. The font size of a topic node represents how much it has been discussed compared to other topics. We present the Topic Hierarchy as an indented tree, where the parent-child relationship is represented by relative vertical position along with horizontal position. We made this choice because an indented tree representation is much more compact than explicitly showing hierarchical links between topic nodes.

Multi-level exploration

From the whole collection to subsets of conversations: While the user initially gets an overview of all the conversations in the collection, her subsequent goal is to find the subset of conversations that are more interesting or relevant, given her current information needs. We support this goal by providing a set of interactive features: linked highlighting, selection, filtering and reordering. The Timeline View, shown in Figure 6, allows the user to quickly filter out conversations that do not fall within the time range in which the discussions were more active or relevant. In addition to filtering, the user can reorder the set of conversations based on the following

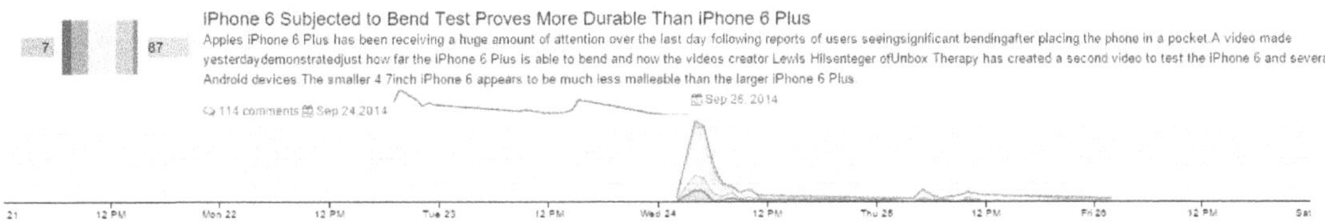

Figure 7. A conversation from the 'iPhone bending' dataset, showing stacked area chart to represent how sentiment distribution evolves over time.

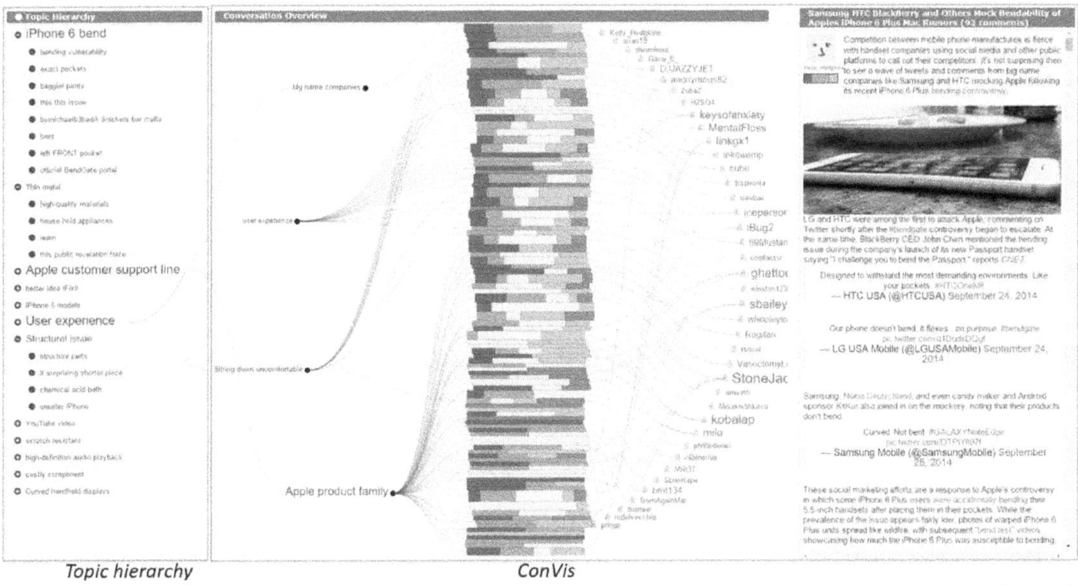

Figure 8. As the user selects a particular conversation, the Conversation List is replaced by the ConVis interface, where the Thread Overview visually represents the whole conversation encoding the thread structure and how the sentiment is expressed for each comment(middle); The Facet Overview presents topics and authors circularly around the Thread Overview; and the Detail View presents the actual conversation in a scrollable list (right). Here, topics are connected to their related comments as well as to their parents in the Topic Hierarchy via curved links.

attributes: number of topics/ authors/ comments, sentiment distribution, and date of the first post of a conversation.

To promote exploration based on the topic facet, we provide coordinated highlighting and selection of conversations by topic. For example, hovering on a topic highlights all the conversations where this topic was discussed, and conversely hovering on a conversation temporarily highlights topics in the Topic Hierarchy. Moreover, when the user selects a topic by clicking on it, a vertical outline is drawn alongside the related conversations, allowing the user to see the conversations in which this topic was discussed, even when she is exploring different conversations/ topics. Throughout the filtering and selection processes, the representation of various attributes from both topics and conversations serve as information scent, thus enhancing the ability of the user to navigate and filter data more effectively [42].

Often, as the user finds a subset of conversations that are relevant to her information needs, she may become interested to know more detailed information about them, for instance to see the temporal evolution of sentiment over time for each conversation. We provide such feature based on user interactions, i.e., as the user clicks on the 'Show timeline' button, the sentiment distribution of comments over time is represented as a stacked area chart, within each conversation item in the list (See Figure 7). This helps the user to understand temporal patterns of sentiment in different conversations, supporting her to fulfill information needs related to the time facet.

Drill down to one conversation: As the user continues her exploration, she may become particularly interested in a specific conversation. In this case, she can drill down into that conversation with the ConVis interface, which was designed to explore a single conversation [17]. Here, an important design question arises: once the exploration has reached a single conversation, should we show ConVis along with both the Conversation List and the Topic Hierarchy, so that the user can simultaneously glance at all of them? Notice that showing all the levels would be extremely challenging because of horizontal space limitations. However, we found this not even to be necessary. Our initial formative evaluations and case studies indicate that users do not need to jump back and forth to the Conversation List while exploring a single conversation. On the contrary, users tend to spend most of the time reading specific comments of the conversation they have decided to focus on before going back to the Conversation List. In light of this, when the user drills down into one conversation the Conversation List is replaced with the ConVis interface, as shown in Figure 8.

Now, we briefly describe the visualization components of the ConVis interface, and how they interact with other views of MultiConVis (a more detailed description of ConVis is provided in [17]). ConVis consists of an overview (Thread Overview) of the conversation along with two primary facets, topics and authors, which are presented circularly around this overview. Once ConVis is displayed within MultiConvis, the

Topic Hierarchy over the whole collection is still shown to provide helpful context to the user in understanding the relationship between the topics of the selected conversation and the topics of the other conversations. As shown in Figure 8, the topics of the selected conversation displayed with ConVis are explicitly linked to the ones in the Topic Hierarchy.

The ConVis Thread Overview visually represents the sentiment distribution of each *comment* of the conversation as a stacked bar, similarly to how the sentiment distribution of a *conversation* was represented in the Conversation List. In addition, three different metadata are encoded within the stacked bar: the comment length (height), ordinal position of the comment in the conversation (vertical position), and depth of the comment (horizontal position). To indicate topic-comment-author relationship, the facet elements are connected to their corresponding comments in the Thread Overview via subtle curved links. These visual links allow the user to perceive the related entities more quickly and with greater subjective satisfaction than plain highlighting [38]. Finally, the Detail View (see Figure 8) displays the actual text of the comments in the discussion as a scrollable list.

The user can start exploring the conversation by hovering the mouse on topics, which highlights the connecting curved links and related comments in the Thread Overview. As such, one can quickly understand how topics may be related to different comments and authors. If the user clicks on a topic, a thick vertical outline is drawn next to the corresponding comments in the Thread Overview. Such outlines are also mirrored in the Conversation View. Besides exploring by the topics/authors, the reader can browse individual comments by hovering and clicking on them in the Thread Overview. In particular, when the user hovers over a comment its topic is highlighted, while when the user clicks on a comment, the actual text for that comment is shown in the Conversation View (by scrolling). In this way, the user can easily locate the comments that belong to a particular topic.

As the user drills down to the conversation, she might become interested to know whether similar topics are discussed in other conversations. At any point, the user can look at the Topic Hierarchy to see what are the other similar topics to her current topic of interest, but not discussed in this conversation. For instance, when the user is exploring the topic 'Thin metal' in the current conversation, she may select a related topic labeled 'Structural issue' in the Topic Hierarchy, which results in abandoning the ConVis interface and switching back to the Conversation List, where the conversations related to 'Structural issue' would be highlighted. Finally, at any time the user can return to the Conversation List by clicking on the 'Back' button.

IMPLEMENTATION

The data acquisition, preprocessing, and analysis components were developed using python and a server-side component (in php) which feeds the data to the visualization pipeline. The visual interface was implemented using a combination of HTML, Javascript (using D3, JQuery, crossfiter, and dc.js libraries), so that the tool can be make available as a web application accessible to a large audience.

EVALUATION

We evaluated the MultiConVis interface in two different ways:1) case studies with different domain experts, 2) a formal user study with regular blog readers. While the case studies provided qualitative evidence for the utility of the MultiConVis system, the user study allowed us to compare the system with a traditional interface. Note that ConVis, the interface for single conversations embedded in MultiConVis, had already been evaluated in a previous user study [18], which showed that ConVis outperformed traditional interfaces along several subjective metrics (e.g., usefulness, enjoyable).

Case Studies

We conducted case studies with three users, whose professions are quite diverse, but who come from populations that could all arguably benefit from MultiConVis:

U1: a regular blog reader who visits the Macrumors blog site several times a week. Therefore, he had a genuine interest in exploring the conversations returned by our 'iPhone bending' query. His primary goal was to verify whether the problem of 'iPhone bending' reported by some customers was really serious or not.

U2: a graduate student in the school of Journalism, who contributes to local newspapers about recent political issues. He had strong interest in our dataset about the recent 'ObamaCare health reform'. His primary goal was to understand and summarize the key opinions expressed by the participants about the ObamaCare health reform.

U3: a business analyst in a social media company, where she often needs to analyze a large amount of conversations to understand how customers react to newly released products. So, her goal in the study was to explore conversations about the 'iWatch release' to identify comments that express negative opinions about the product, which is a task that matches what she performs on a regular basis for her company.

For the purpose of case studies, we have collected three different datasets from two different blog sources: Macrumors [28] (a technology-news related blog site dedicated to the discussion of recent news and opinion relating to the Apple Inc) and Daily Kos [5] (a political analysis blog site) between September to December 2014. To create each dataset, we provide a query to the blog site to retrieve the set of conversations that appear on the first page of the search results.

For each case study, we analyzed the results by triangulating between multiple data collection methods, including observations, notes taken by participants during the analysis session, and semi-structured interviews. In addition, we logged interface actions to better understand the usage patterns.

For lack of space, we can only report the primary results of the case studies. The key findings were that: (a) all three users relied on the topic hierarchy to accomplish their task, (b) each user used the hierarchy differently, (c) all users found the topic hierarchy extremely useful. For instance, while the blog reader started his exploration by quickly scanning through the topics in the hierarchy and then going back and forth between topics and conversations, the journalist explored the topics in the hierarchy more systematically, exploring all the comments about one topic before moving to a new one. Still differently, the business analyst started by skimming through the titles of the conversations. But, as she was skimming through the conversations, she also kept an eye on the topics that were highlighted for each conversation in the topic hierarchy. In this way, she identified controversial topics that were intensely debated in recent conversations.

Overall, the semi-structured interviews revealed that users were very satisfied with the interface. In particular, U1 said *"The comments about that chemical acid bath was buried down in the middle of one conversation, which I don't think I would have noticed with a regular interface. Using MultiConVis, I was able to pick this topic from the hierarchy and then jumped into the related comments without having to read the entire conversations....".* U2 found the topic hierarchy to be very helpful in supporting a systematic exploration of the conversations by organizing the key opinions into meaningful topical groups. More interestingly, he realized the potential utility of MultiConVis system for other exploratory tasks that he would like to perform, *"This tool could be not only useful when I want to write a story, but also to prepare for interviewing a policy maker, or a politician by quickly understanding what topics are triggering the most interesting or controversial discussions in the public spheres."* Finally U3 anticipated that this tool could be very useful to understand what features of their products worked (or didn't work) and then revise the products accordingly, *" The MultiConVis interface would definitely help me to understand the requirements and needs of my customers more effectively. Our current way is just to skim through the comments, often missing the important feedback from customers ...but this interface can help me identify what are the biggest concerns from the customers and get clues about the ways to satisfy their needs."*

User study

We run a formal user study to evaluate the efficacy and usability of the MultiConVis interface compared to an interface that represents the traditional interfaces for blog reading. The aim of the user study is to answer the following two questions: (1) When we compare MultiConVis with the traditional interface for exploring a set of conversations, is there any difference in user performance and subjective reactions? (2) What specific features of the MultiConVis interface are perceived as more/less beneficial by the potential users (e.g., Topic Hierarchy, Timeline etc.)?

Methodology

Since the first research question requires comparisons among two different user interfaces, we conducted a summative evaluation through controlled experiments [25]. The study was designed with two interfaces as conditions: a) the traditional interface for blog reading, and b) *MultiConVis*. Here, the traditional interface shows a set of blog conversations as a linear list, where each item represents a set of metadata of the conversations (e.g., title, number of comments, and posting date). The user can click on any conversation in the list, which results in showing all the comments of that conversation using an indented list representation. In addition, we provided a set of interactions that are common in most blog reading interfaces, i.e., searching for terms and sorting conversations by attributes (e.g., number of comments). A within-subject design was used with interface as the within-subject factor, allowing us to directly compare the measures of each participant with respect to both interfaces. Finally, all study aspects, including instructions and setup, went through several iterations of evaluation and pilot testing.

Task and procedure

At first, a pre-study questionnaire was administered to capture demographic information and prior experience with exploring blog conversations. Then, the participant went through the following steps for each of the two interfaces: 1) In a scripted warm-up session, the interface was introduced to the participant using a sample dataset. 2) The participant was then asked to perform a task based a set of conversations. For each interface, a different set of conversations was provided.

Task: Considering the open-ended nature of blog reading, no specific set of questions was given. Instead, the participant was asked to explore a set of conversations about the given query and then write a single summary of what she thought were the major discussion points and most insightful comments within the conversations. The study lasted approximately 60 minutes and each participant was paid $15 to participate.

We selected two different datasets crawled from the Macrumors site for testing ('iphone bend' and 'ipad release'). The number of conversations in the datasets are kept the same (16 conversations in each dataset) to avoid potential variations due to the amount of conversational data. Also, to counterbalance any potential learning effects due to the order of exposure to specific interfaces and dataset, the order was varied using a 2 x 2 Latin square. During the study, we collected both quantitative data such as task completion time and qualitative data such as observations and questionnaires. Finally, a post-study questionnaire followed by an semi-structured interviews were administered regarding the user's experience with two interfaces.

Participants

We conducted the study with 16 users (aged 18-37, 6 females) who have considerable experience of reading blogs. The participants held a variety of occupations ranging from journalists, engineers, system analysts and students from both graduate and undergraduate levels. They were recruited through emails and social networks (Facebook and reddit posts).

Results analysis

After completing the task with each interface, participants rated six different measures in the form of in-study questionnaires. Since these measures were rated using a standard 5 point Likert scale, standard parametric analysis was not suitable due to the lack of normality [22]. Instead we performed nonparametric analysis i.e., Mann-Whitney's U tests on the responses for each of these measures.

The results of these questionnaires are presented in Figure 9. The pairwise comparisons using Mann-Whitney's U tests indicate that MultiConVis was superior on five different measures out of six: usefulness ($Z = -1.823; p < .05$); enjoyable to use ($Z = -3.697; p < .01$); find insightful comments ($Z = -3.95; p < .01$); find major points ($Z = -2.909; p < .01$); and enable to write more informative summary ($Z = -3.915; p <$

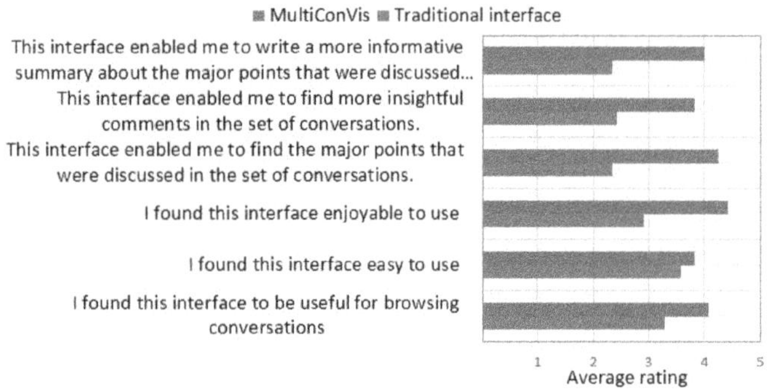

Figure 9. Average rating of interfaces by the participants on six different measures. Longer bars indicate higher rating.

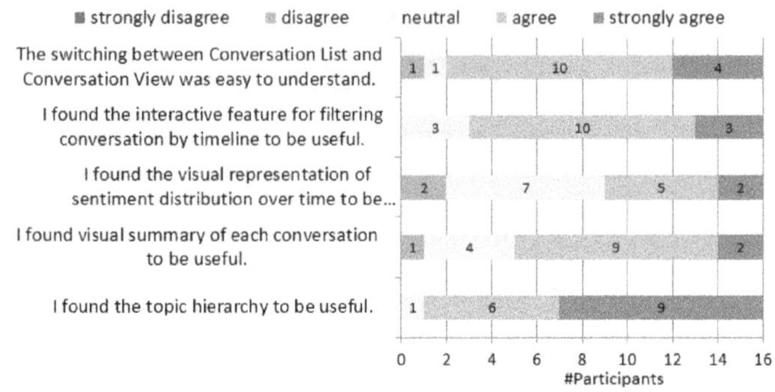

Figure 10. Responses to statements regarding specific features of the MultiConVis interface.

.01). For the other measure i.e., ease of use, MultiConVis was still rated higher over the traditional interface, however the results was not significant. This is interesting, because MultiConVis appears to be as easy to use as the other interface in spite of its complex interface features.

Interface features: Each participant was also asked a set of questions regarding the usefulness of specific features of the MultiConVis interfaces. From Figure 10, we can readily see that the majority of the responses were dominated by positive ratings. Among the interface features, the Topic Hierarchy received the most positive ratings (strongly agree:9, agree:6), followed by the visual summary of each conversation, and interactive filtering by timeline.

Time: The average time required to complete the tasks was not significantly affected by the interfaces, with MultiConVis and the traditional interface requiring 1065 ± 249 and 1029 ± 204 secs respectively.

Overall Preference: In the post-study questionnaire, participants were asked which system they prefer for exploring a collection of conversations. 75 % of the participants indicated a preference for MultiConVis, whereas 25 % preferred the traditional interface. Many of the participants who chose MultiConVis indicated that the utility of Topic Hierarchy was the primary reason for their preference: *"By having a topic hierarchy of the relevant topics, as well as highlighting which conversation refers to which topic, it was very easy to filter out the blogs that were not relevant.'* (P8). They also found the visual summary provided for each conversation was very useful, *"The summary offered by this visualization is quite impressive and throws a lot of instant information."* (P2). Additionally, for the sentiment distribution over time *"...made it very easy to see how opinions changed over time. While investigating bend gate it was clear how the community opinion changed after the event had played out in the media"* (P4).

Those who preferred the traditional interface indicated that they like its familiarity *"I preferred the older style of interface mainly because it's what I'm more familiar with..."* (P1). They also pointed out that sometimes the topic hierarchy was inaccurate (e.g., topic labels did not always make sense to them) *"..maybe with better tagging I'd find it (MultiConVis) more useful..."* (P1), and *"the keywords weren't necessarily the most useful ones or the relevant ones"* (P5).

DISCUSSION

After conducting the evaluation with real users, we reflect upon our visualization design in order to understand to what extent our system can support the kind of tasks the users wanted to perform. Our case studies demonstrate that the system can be useful in a variety of contexts of use, while the formal user study provides evidence that the MultiConVis interface supports the user's tasks more effectively compared to traditional interfaces. In particular, all our participants, both in the case studies and in the user study, appear to greatly benefit from the topic hierarchy and the high-level overview of the conversations. The user study also shows that the MultiConVis interface is significantly more useful than the traditional interface, enabling the user to find insightful comments from thousands of comments, even when they were scattered around multiple conversations, often buried down near the end of the threads. Remarkably, MultiConVis was preferred by the majority of the participants over the traditional interface, suggesting the potential value of our approach for combining NLP and InfoVis.

CONCLUSIONS AND FUTURE WORK

MultiConVis is an interactive visual text analytics system for exploring a collection of blog conversations. Unlike traditional systems, MultiConVis takes the unique characteristics of online conversations into account to tightly integrate NLP and InfoVis techniques. The resulting visual interface aggregates data across different levels, supporting a faceted exploration starting from a whole set of conversations, to a subset of conversations, to one conversation.

We would like to extend our work along the following avenues. First, we would like to explore the possibility of applying higher level argumentation analysis of the conversations [1] by extracting the discourse structure of the posts [20], to better support the user in understanding the opinions expressed about each topic. Second, even though the topic hierarchy was found to be very useful, still in a few cases the extracted topics were either noisy or did not match the user's current information needs. To deal with this problem, we aim to extend the recently proposed interactive topic modeling approach for single conversations [18], to handle a large collection of conversations. Finally, to increase the ecologically validity of our evaluations [3], we would like to perform longitudinal studies to observe how the system is used by real users to satisfy their information needs over an extended period of time.

REFERENCES

1. Kelsey Allen, Giuseppe Carenini, and Raymond T Ng. 2014. Detecting Disagreement in Conversations using Pseudo-Monologic Rhetorical Structure. In *Proceedings of the EMNLP*.
2. Eric Baumer, Mark Sueyoshi, and Bill Tomlinson. 2008. Exploring the role of the reader in the activity of blogging. In *Proc. Conf. CHI*. 1111–1120.
3. Sheelagh Carpendale. 2008. Evaluating information visualizations. In *Information Visualization*. 19–45.
4. Weiwei Cui, Shixia Liu, Zhuofeng Wu, and Hao Wei. 2014. How Hierarchical Topics Evolve in Large Text Corpora. *IEEE Trans. Visualization and Computer Graphics* 20, 12 (2014), 2281–2290.
5. dailykos.com. 2015. Daily Kos. (2015). `http://dailykos.com/`.
6. Kushal Dave, Martin Wattenberg, and Michael Muller. 2004. Flash forums and forumReader: navigating a new kind of large-scale online discussion. In *Proc. ACM Conf. on CSCW*. 232–241.
7. Munmun De Choudhury and Hari Sundaram. 2011. Why do we converse on social media?: an analysis of intrinsic and extrinsic network factors. In *Proceedings of the 3rd ACM SIGMM international workshop on Social media*. ACM, 53–58.
8. Nicholas Diakopoulos, Mor Naaman, and Funda Kivran-Swaine. 2010. Diamonds in the rough: Social media visual analytics for journalistic inquiry. In *IEEE Symposium on Visual Analytics Science and Technology (VAST)*. IEEE, 115–122.
9. Judith Donath, Karrie Karahalios, and Viégas Fernanda. 1999. Visualizing Conversation. *Journal of Computer-Mediated Communication* 4, 4 (1999), 0–0.
10. Marian Dork, Sheelagh Carpendale, Christopher Collins, and Carey Williamson. 2008. Visgets: Coordinated visualizations for web-based information exploration and discovery. *IEEE Trans. Visualization & Comp. Graphics* 14, 6 (2008), 1205–1212.
11. Marian Dork, Daniel Gruen, Carey Williamson, and Sheelagh Carpendale. 2010. A visual backchannel for large-scale events. *IEEE Trans. Visualization and Computer Graphics* 16, 6 (2010).
12. Wenwen Dou, Li Yu, Xiaoyu Wang, Zhiqiang Ma, and William Ribarsky. 2013. HierarchicalTopics: Visually Exploring Large Text Collections Using Topic Hierarchies. *IEEE Trans. Visualization & Comp. Graphics* 19, 12 (2013), 2002–2011.
13. Michel Galley, Kathleen McKeown, Eric Fosler-Lussier, and Hongyan Jing. 2003. Discourse segmentation of multi-party conversation. In *Proc. Annual Meeting on Association for Computational Linguistics*. 562–569.
14. P. Goffin, W. Willett, J.-D. Fekete, and P. Isenberg. 2014. Exploring the Placement and Design of Word-Scale Visualizations. *IEEE Trans. Visualization & Computer Graphics* 20, 12 (Dec 2014), 2291–2300.
15. S. Havre, E. Hetzler, P. Whitney, and L. Nowell. 2002. ThemeRiver: visualizing thematic changes in large document collections. *IEEE Trans. Visualization & Comp. Graphics* 8, 1 (2002), 9–20.
16. Marti A Hearst, Matthew Hurst, and Susan T Dumais. 2008. What should blog search look like?. In *Proc. ACM Workshop on Search in Social Media*. 95–98.
17. E. Hoque and G. Carenini. 2014. ConVis: A Visual Text Analytic System for Exploring Blog Conversations. *Computer Graphics Forum (Proc. EuroVis)* 33, 3 (2014), 221–230.
18. E. Hoque and G. Carenini. 2015. ConVisIT: Interactive Topic Modeling for Exploring Asynchronous Online Conversations. In *Proc. ACM conf. on Intelligent User Interfaces*. 169–180.
19. Indratmo, Julita Vassileva, and Carl Gutwin. 2008. Exploring blog archives with interactive visualization. In *Proc. working Conf. on Advanced visual interfaces*. 39–46.
20. Shafiq Joty, Giuseppe Carenini, Raymond Ng, and Yashar Mehdad. 2013b. Combining intra-and multi-sentential rhetorical parsing for document-level discourse analysis. In *Proc. Annual Meeting on Association for Computational Linguistics*. 486âĂŞ–496.
21. Shafiq Joty, Giuseppe Carenini, and Raymond T Ng. 2013a. Topic Segmentation and Labeling in Asynchronous Conversations. *Journal of Artificial Intelligence Research* 47 (2013), 521–573.
22. Maurits Clemens Kaptein, Clifford Nass, and Panos Markopoulos. 2010. Powerful and Consistent Analysis of Likert-type Ratingscales. In *Proc. Conf. CHI*. 2391–2394.
23. B. K. Kaye. 2005. Web side story: An exploratory study of why weblog users say they use weblogs *(AEJMC Annual Conf.)*.
24. Daekyung Kim and Thomas J. Johnson. 2012. Political blog readers: Predictors of motivations for accessing political blogs. *Telematics and Informatics* 29, 1 (Feb. 2012), 99–109.
25. H. Lam, E. Bertini, P. Isenberg, C. Plaisant, and S. Carpendale. 2012. Empirical Studies in Information Visualization: Seven Scenarios. *IEEE Trans. Visualization & Comp. Graphics* 18, 9 (2012), 1520–1536.
26. Shixia Liu, Xiting Wang, Jianfei Chen, Jun Zhu, and Baining Guo. 2014. Topicpanorama: a full picture of relevant topics. (2014), 183–192.
27. Craig Macdonald, Rodrygo L.T. Santos, Iadh Ounis, and Ian Soboroff. 2010. Blog track research at TREC. *SIGIR Forum* 44, 1 (2010), 58–75.
28. macrumors.com. 2015. Macrumors. (2015). `http://macrumors.com/`.

29. Adam Marcus, Michael S Bernstein, Osama Badar, David R Karger, Samuel Madden, and Robert C Miller. 2011. Twitinfo: aggregating and visualizing microblogs for event exploration. In *Proc. CHI*. ACM, 227–236.

30. Gilad Mishne. 2006. Information access challenges in the blogspace. In *Workshop on Intelligent Information Access (IIIA)*.

31. Sean A Munson and Paul Resnick. 2010. Presenting diverse political opinions: how and how much. In *Proc. Conf. CHI*. 1457–1466.

32. Mark EJ Newman and Michelle Girvan. 2004. Finding and evaluating community structure in networks. *Physical review E* 69, 2 (2004), 026113.

33. nlp.cs.illinois.edu. 2015. Illinois Part of Speech Tagger. (2015). `http://bit.ly/1xtjFHe`.

34. Alan Ritter, Colin Cherry, and Bill Dolan. 2010. Unsupervised modeling of twitter conversations. In *Proc. ACL*. 172–180.

35. Jianbo Shi and Jitendra Malik. 2000. Normalized cuts and image segmentation. *IEEE Trans. on Pattern Analysis and Machine Intelligence* 22, 8 (2000), 888–905.

36. Param Vir Singh, Nachiketa Sahoo, and Tridas Mukhopadhyay. 2010. Seeking variety: A dynamic model of employee blog reading behavior. *Available at SSRN 1617405* (2010).

37. slashdot.com. 2015. Slashdot. (2015). `http://slashdot.com/`.

38. Markus Steinberger, Manuela Waldner, Marc Streit, Alexander Lex, and Dieter Schmalstieg. 2011. Context-preserving visual links. *IEEE Trans. Visualization & Comp. Graphics* 17, 12 (2011), 2249–2258.

39. Maite Taboada, Julian Brooke, Milan Tofiloski, Kimberly Voll, and Manfred Stede. 2011. Lexicon-based methods for sentiment analysis. *Computational linguistics* 37, 2 (2011), 267–307.

40. Fernanda B Viégas, Scott Golder, and Judith Donath. 2006. Visualizing email content: portraying relationships from conversational histories. In *Proc. Conf. CHI*. 979–988.

41. Furu Wei, Shixia Liu, Yangqiu Song, Shimei Pan, Michelle X Zhou, Weihong Qian, Lei Shi, Li Tan, and Qiang Zhang. 2010. Tiara: a visual exploratory text analytic system. In *Proc. ACM Conf. on Knowledge Discovery and Data Mining*. 153–162.

42. Wesley Willett, Jeffrey Heer, and Maneesh Agrawala. 2007. Scented widgets: Improving navigation cues with embedded visualizations. *IEEE Trans. Visualization & Computer Graphics* 13, 6 (2007), 1129–1136.

43. Y. Wu, S. Liu, K. Yan, M. Liu, and F. Wu. 2014. OpinionFlow: Visual Analysis of Opinion Diffusion on Social Media. *IEEE Trans. Visualization and Computer Graphics* 20, 12 (Dec 2014), 1763–1772.

44. J. Zhao, N. Cao, Z. Wen, Y. Song, Y. Lin, and C. Collins. 2014. #FluxFlow: Visual Analysis of Anomalous Information Spreading on Social Media. *IEEE Trans. Visualization & Computer Graphics* 20, 12 (Dec 2014), 1773–1782.

45. Ding Zhou, Sergey A Orshanskiy, Hongyuan Zha, and C Lee Giles. 2007. Co-ranking authors and documents in a heterogeneous network. In *Seventh IEEE International Conf. on Data Mining*. 739–744.

46. Aaron Robert Zinman. 2011. *Me, myself, and my hyperego: understanding people through the aggregation of their digital footprints*. Ph.D. Dissertation. MIT.

Topic Modeling of Document Metadata for Visualizing Collaborations over Time

Francine Chen
FX Palo Alto Laboratory
3174 Porter Drive
Palo Alto, CA 94304 USA
chen@fxpal.com

Patrick Chiu
FX Palo Alto Laboratory
3174 Porter Drive
Palo Alto, CA 94304 USA
chiu@fxpal.com

Seongtaek Lim
School of Information
UC Berkeley
Berkeley, CA 94720 USA
stlim@berkeley.edu

ABSTRACT
We describe methods for analyzing and visualizing document metadata to provide insights about collaborations over time. We investigate the use of Latent Dirichlet Allocation (LDA) based topic modeling to compute areas of interest on which people collaborate. The topics are represented in a node-link force directed graph by persistent fixed nodes laid out with multidimensional scaling (MDS), and the people by transient movable nodes. The topics are also analyzed to detect bursts to highlight "hot" topics during a time interval. As the user manipulates a time interval slider, the people nodes and links are dynamically updated. We evaluate the results of LDA topic modeling for the visualization by comparing topic keywords against the submitted keywords from the InfoVis 2004 Contest, and we found that the additional terms provided by LDA-based keyword sets result in improved similarity between a topic keyword set and the documents in a corpus. We extended the InfoVis dataset from 8 to 20 years and collected publication metadata from our lab over a period of 21 years, and created interactive visualizations for exploring these larger datasets.

Author Keywords
Interactive visualization; small group collaboration; temporal dynamics; topic modeling.

ACM Classification Keywords
H.5.m. Information interfaces and presentation (e.g., HCI): Miscellaneous.

INTRODUCTION
Effective methods for data analysis and visualization of collaborations over time have many useful applications. They can be used for finding people with expertise in some topic area, people with broad interests across disciplines, and people who are recently active or who have had a large amount of experience over time. Other applications include helping management assess the balance of people working on various areas, and to see the impact of their policies on how their team members collaborate over time.

Temporal analysis of group collaborations within an organization can be a difficult task. One reason is that groups dynamically change over time in nonlinear ways [3]. For example, at a research laboratory, people with different skills and interests may collaborate with each other only for a few short-term projects. Thus, a means to analyze the dynamic features of collaboration would be useful.

Document metadata that contains co-author information provides a way to establish the relationships between people in collaborations. Along with who is involved, it is also important to know what they are collaborating on. Sometimes the metadata has information about publication venues (e.g. [17]), which can be used to define areas of interest. However, this is problematic when the dataset is focused on a single venue (e.g. [7]), or when scaling to a dataset with a large number of venues.

Another simple way to define areas of interest is to match the keywords from the document metadata to establish the relationships. The problem with this is that for a given keyword, the number documents (and authors) matching that keyword is relatively small. Hence a large number of keywords would need to be visualized (along with the authors), which is hard to do effectively.

This paper proposes the use of topic modeling to automatically compute areas of interest from document metadata for visualizing collaborations over time. Topic modeling provides more meaningful areas of interest than publication venues. A well-known topic modeling algorithm is Latent Dirichlet Allocation (LDA) [4]. As a dimension reduction technique, it enables better scaling to larger data sets than publication venues or keywords. Unlike simpler venue or keyword metadata, topic modeling provides a vector space of terms which has standard methods, such as cosine similarity, to compute relevance. Moreover, topic modeling enables filtering nodes by

IUI'16, March 07 - 10, 2016, Sonoma, CA, USA

ACM 978-1-4503-4137-0/16/03…$15.00
DOI: http://dx.doi.org/10.1145/2856767.2856787

relevance, which has uses that include focusing on the most relevant nodes and reducing clutter.

Although the topic-model vector space is a reduced space from the high-dimensional vector space of terms, it needs to be further reduced for visualization. For this, the topic-model vector space provides a good way to lay out the topics in the visualization: the similarity scores between topics can be mapped to a 2D plane by multidimensional scaling (MDS).

Another important aspect for people who analyze data is to be able to see sudden surges in activity level. To visualize the changing popularity for the various topics over different time spans, we apply a burst detection algorithm [13] to the activity stream of each topic. The topics change colors to indicate different "heat" levels as different time intervals are selected by the user.

Our visualization interface employs a node-link graph with both fixed and moveable nodes, in conjunction with a time slider. Topics computed from the dataset are represented by persistent fixed nodes, which are placed in the 2D plane to indicate the relative similarity of the set of topics. People who work on different topics at different times are represented by transient moveable nodes, which are placed to indicate the similarity of their publications during a specified time interval to each other and to the fixed topic nodes. As the time slider is manipulated by the user to select a time period, the person nodes may appear, disappear, or move relative to each other and to the fixed topics with animated transitions.

To evaluate the effectiveness of using topic modeling in the visualization, we tested it on a public dataset (InfoVis 2004 Contest [7], extended to 20 years), and a dataset from our lab's publication database (21 years). We compared LDA-based topics to the topics others have automatically or manually defined for the public InfoVis dataset. For both datasets, we examined how well the topics cover the person nodes and the amount of clutter (number of nodes and edges) under different numbers of topics and relevance score thresholds, and the burst activity levels which can be affected by the diversity of topics.

RELATED WORK

In our previous work, Collaboration Map [18] demonstrated a visualization that uses a node-link force directed graph with fixed nodes representing publication venues and moveable nodes representing authors, along with a time interval slider. The use of publication venues is problematic when there are too few venues to be discriminative or too many venues to visualize and therefore does not scale.

In the present work, areas of interest are represented by topics; whereas in [18] the publication venues serve as surrogates for areas of interest. With our approach, the visualization model can be applied to document metadata focused on a single publication venue (e.g. [7]) or scaled to a large number of publication venues by controlling the number of topics. The topics are represented as fixed nodes that are laid out using MDS. Additionally, we perform burst detection on the topic streams to detect highly active topics.

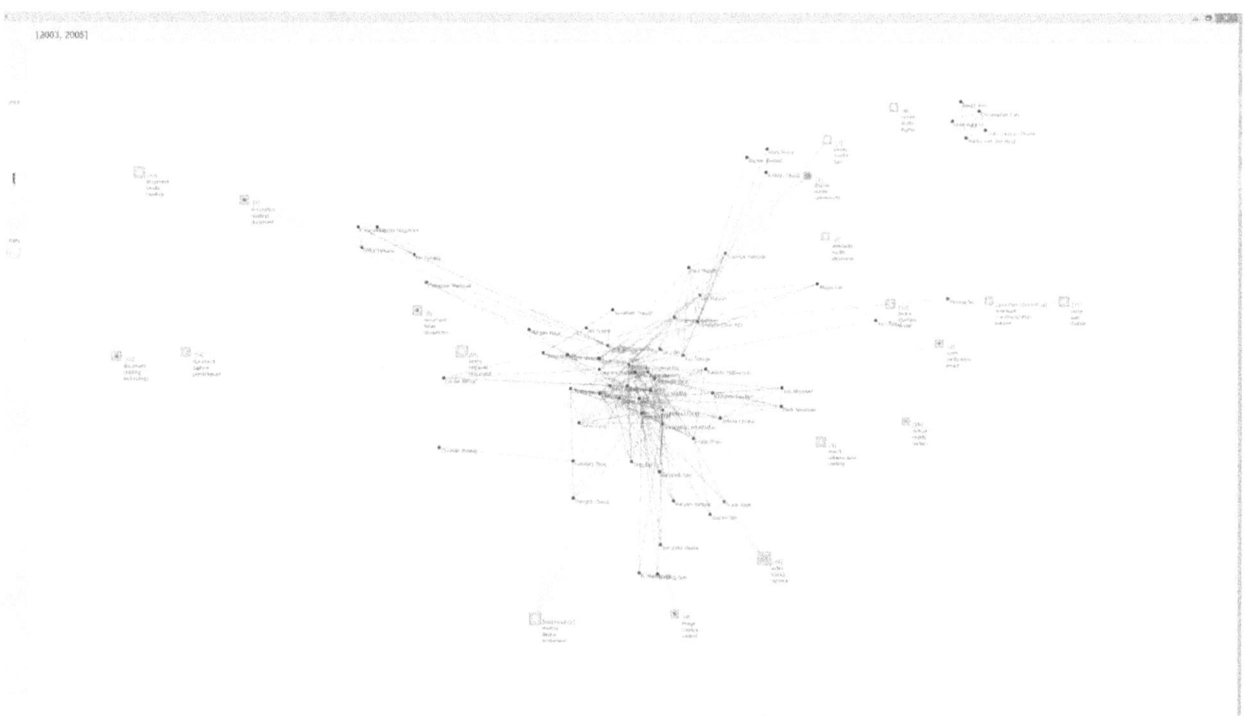

Figure 1. Screenshot of visualization showing topic-based collaborations. The dataset is from our research lab's publication database (Lab21), with 20 topics and relevance score threshold of 0.25. The visualization is rendered on a high-res 4K display.

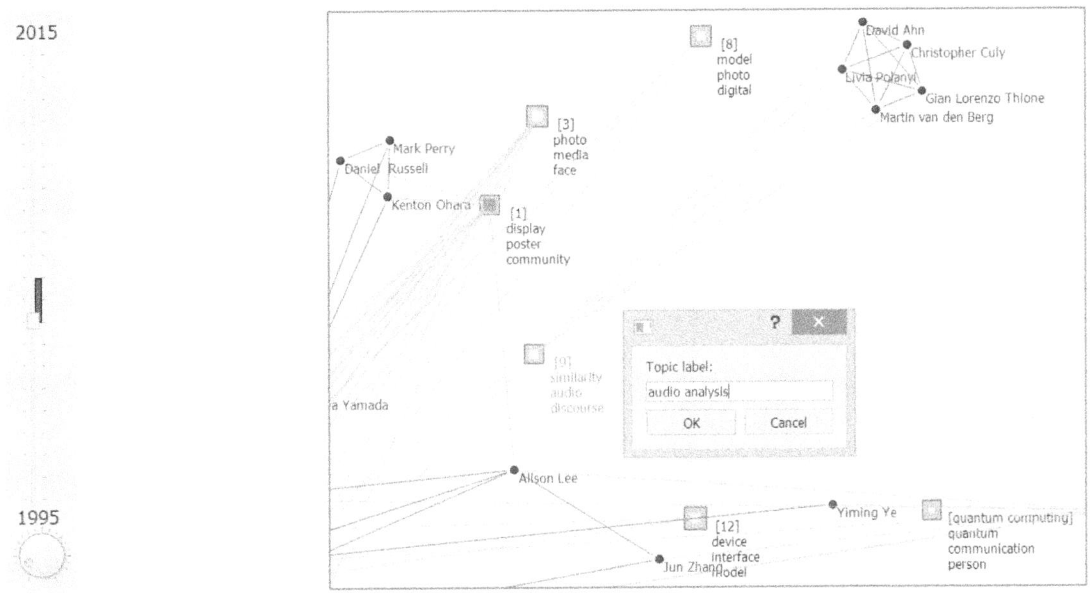

(a) (b)

Figure 2. Close-ups: (a) timeline widget with a slider and a dial to set the interval size, (b) detail showing co-author relations, person-topic relations, topics and burst levels in the selected time period. A pop-up widget for adding a topic label is shown in (b).

Kraker et al. [14] visualize topic evolution using small multiples where at each time step the topics are computed and visualized; this results in the topic locations changing over time. In contrast, the topics are fixed in our visualization and serve as anchors for locating people. Furthermore, active topics are detected and shown in our visualization using different heat levels.

Most of the traditional visualizations for paper publications show a view with nodes representing the papers; examples are the InfoVis 2004 Contest entries [7] and the more recent PivotSlice [25]. In contrast, our visualization focuses on visualizing the collaborations and does not show the papers as nodes.

From the InfoVis 2004 Contest, the entry by Ke et al. [11], which was given a first-place award, has a node-link view of the authors in addition to a view of the papers. The co-author view shows only the authors (without topics or papers) and their relationships in a static view. In contrast, our visualization shows the authors' expertise by displaying links to the topic nodes, and also their co-author relationships for selected time periods in a dynamic interactive view with animations.

Regarding the data analysis aspect of collaboration networks and bibliographic metadata, existing work tends to focus on the theoretical properties of the network graphs (e.g. [16]), which are interesting for studying large scale systems and can help in the design of networking infrastructure, but are less applicable to networks in smaller organizations or teams.

The groups participating in the InfoVis 2004 Contest proposed a number of different methods for identifying keywords characterizing topics, which we refer to as *topic keywords*[1], to use in visualization of the InfoVis dataset. Both Ke et al. [11] and Tyman et al. [23] manually defined topic keywords. Teoh and Ma [22] identified keywords that most frequently occur in the documents in the dataset. Ke et al. [11] took into account temporal information and identified bursts of keyword usage.

Lee et al. [15] used Microsoft proprietary clustering to identify topics for the InfoVis 2004 Contest. Ahmed et al. [1] used a self-organizing-map to cluster documents. Identifying topics using these clustering methods results in a hard clustering of the documents, i.e. assigning each document to one cluster, where documents with similar term distributions are grouped.

We chose instead to use a soft two-sided clustering, Latent Dirichlet Allocation (LDA) [4], a popular method for identifying topics in a document collection. In the LDA model, each document is a mixture of topics, rather than being associated with a single topic, and each word in a document comes from one of the document's topics. Since documents often discuss more than one topic, the LDA model can better reflect the topics in each of the documents in a collection. We examine this in our experiments

[1] Note that a *topic keyword,* which summarizes a topic, should not be confused with keywords in the document metadata.

comparing the InfoVis 2004 topic keywords and LDA-based topic keywords.

The Termite system [5] is a visual analysis tool that provides a table visualization of terms and topics computed using LDA to help users to assess topic model quality. This is useful when a large number of topics is required, since the topic terms are often less coherent and "junk topics" become a problem.

DATA ANALSYSIS AND VISUALIZATION

An overview of the system is shown in Figure 3. We explain these parts in the following sections.

Data Preparation

To prepare a dataset of documents for use in the visualization, the document metadata is preprocessed and analyzed for topics. The results are represented with data structures that can be quickly initialized and run in real time. Typically, the document metadata contains the authors, time information (e.g. year), title, and keywords. Additionally, we require an abstract, because some amount of text is needed for the topic modeling.

Data Preprocessing

The metadata (abstract, keywords, title) is lower-cased and then tokenized into words with punctuation stripped at word boundaries. Stopwords are removed and then a singularizer, which converts plural word forms to singular, is used to normalize the remaining words. These "cleaned" words form the corpus vocabulary and create a vector space of terms V. Each document in the collection, D, is represented as a vector of term counts in V.

Topic Modeling

From the vector representation of documents, topics are identified for use as fixed interest areas in the visualization. As discussed in the Related Work section, there are many approaches to identifying topical keywords, but we use an LDA model, which can better represent the topics. The LDA model is trained on the preprocessed document data.

Given the number of topics desired, k, and the set of documents D represented as term vectors in V, Latent Dirichlet Allocation computes a set of k topics, where each topic is represented by a set of terms and their associated probabilities. We used the Gensim Python software library [8] for this computation. In the visualization, k is predetermined (or alternatively k can be chosen by the user).

For a given dataset, the topics identified by LDA can vary for different runs due to the use of random initialization when learning the model. To reduce the variation in results, we bias the word probabilities for each topic by initializing $\boldsymbol{\beta}$ in Blei et al. [4]. For an LDA model with k topics, $\boldsymbol{\beta}$ is a $k \times V$ matrix where $\beta_{ij} = p(w^j = 1|z^i = 1)$, the probability of word w^j in topic z^i (the notation x^i denotes the ith element of vector x). We first perform hard clustering on the documents in D, with the number of clusters set to the

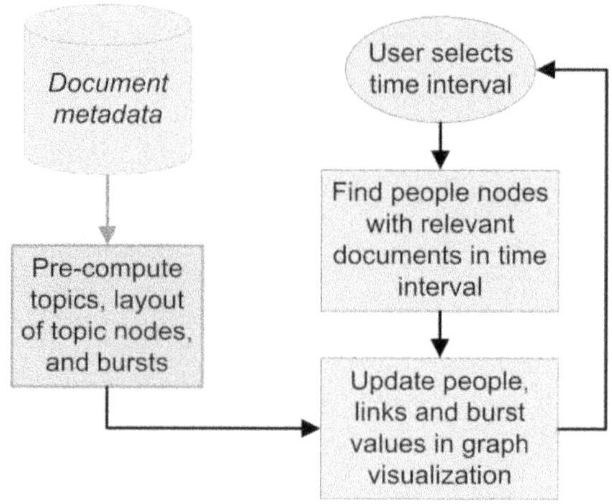

Figure 3. Overview of data analysis and interactive visualization process.

desired number of LDA topics, k. Then we initialize the values of $\beta_{i\cdot}$ for $i \in \{1, \dots, k\}$ with the term distributions from hard clustering. That is, the kth $\beta_{i\cdot}$ is initialized to the vector representing the normalized term distribution of the documents assigned to the kth cluster. We chose to use spectral clustering because the clustering results are less variable.

Dimension Reduction for Scalability

After the topics have been computed using LDA, we further reduce the dimensions for scalability and efficiency. Dimension reduction is performed on V using the LDA topics as follows. Each topic is composed of component terms with associated probabilities of the word conditioned on the topic. The probabilities are sorted and since the values decrease rapidly, we keep only m terms for each topic (we use $m = 10$). The component terms may overlap between the k topics. The union of these component terms creates a subspace V_C of V, with $\dim(V_C) \leq k*m$. By reducing the dimension, we can scale to large datasets. It also makes it more efficient in computation time and memory space. This is important if the data needs to be transmitted to Web browsers for the visualization application.

Layout of Topics

The topics in the visualization are represented by nodes of a graph. These Topic nodes are placed in fixed locations in the layout. To determine the Topic node coordinates for the visualization, we use multidimensional scaling (MDS), based on the normalized cosine similarity between topics in the vector space of terms. We compute the cosine similarity with respect to V_C.

Burst Detection for Topics

Burst detection is computed for the topics. For each topic, the number of relevant documents are found for each time point to generate an activity stream. A burst detection algorithm [13] is applied to the activity stream of each topic. Then for each time point of a topic, a burst level is assigned: {0, 1, 2, 3}, where the highest activity level is labeled 3. These are mapped to different "heat" colors in the visualization: {green, yellow, orange, red}.

Interactive Visualization

The visualization is designed to interactively show the temporal dynamics of the people collaborating over topics. Similar to Collaboration Map [18], we use a node-link force directed graph with two types of nodes (fixed and moveable) and a time interval slider. For scalability, we employ Topic nodes instead of Publication Venue nodes, and the layout of the fixed nodes has been improved by using MDS.

To handle larger numbers of nodes and links, the interactive visualization is implemented in C++ with the Qt application framework [21] and runs on a desktop computer. To better visualize the nodes and their text labels, a high resolution 4K display can be used (Figure 1 and Figure 2b).

Timeline Widget

A timeline widget with a slider and a dial allows the user to select a point in time, set the size of the time interval, and drag it along a timeline (Figure 2a). When the selected time interval is changed, the visualization is updated to reflect the collaborations that occurred in the time interval.

Topic Nodes

The topics in the visualization are represented by square nodes in the graph. The Topic nodes are fixed in the positions obtained from MDS layout computation. Each Topic node is labeled with its top three component terms, i.e. the three terms with largest $p(w^j|z^i)$ along with an ID number.

The user can add a label to a Topic node. The component terms and the user's domain knowledge of the dataset may suggest a word or phrase for labeling a topic. Clicking on a Topic node pops up a widget for entering a topic label. The topic label is visualized in square brackets, replacing the topic ID number used as the default label. Figure 2b shows a topic label being entered in a widget, and the bottom-right of the figure shows a Topic node with a previously entered label "quantum computing".

The Topic nodes are colored based on the maximum burst level of the selected time interval. See Figure 2b. The size of the color patch represents the percent of activity during that time period with respect to the topic's total activity. As the time slider is moved, it is possible to see a topic's popularity level increase and then decrease, simultaneously with the other topics' changing popularity level.

Person Nodes

The Person nodes are transitory and can appear/disappear and move around as the time interval on the timeline widget is manipulated. The movement of the Person nodes is animated.

The selected time interval is used to filter the Person nodes: only the people with documents authored in this period are shown in the visualization. The links between Person nodes with co-author relationships in the selected time period are highlighted (in purple). Links are shown between Person nodes and their relevant Topic nodes (in gray). See Figure 1 and Figure 2b. These links define forces that drive the animation to layout the positions of the Person nodes. The Topic nodes are anchored in the MDS layout locations and do not move.

A Person node can be selected and dragged to see it and its links better. This is useful when there is clutter around the Person node. When the node is let go, it bounces back to its location in the force-directed layout.

A relevance score threshold parameter controls how many Person nodes are filtered and visualized. The nodes with scores above the threshold are retrieved. A Person node's score with respect to a Topic node is based on the cosine similarity of the person's documents to the topic. A document may be relevant to more than one topic. The relevance score can be set to achieve different purposes, such as finding highly relevant Person nodes by using a high value, or to reduce clutter and occlusion by using a moderate value.

Note that the documents are not rendered in the visualization, since the focus of the visualization is collaboration over topics. If desired, a simple feature can be used to get information about the documents; e.g. by showing a list of relevant documents when a Person node or Topic node is clicked.

EVALUATION

We performed evaluation of the computed LDA-based topics and our visualization using these topics to show collaborations among authors over time. The LDA-based topics were compared for similarity to the topics contestants identified as part of the InfoVis 2004 Contest [7]. Then we describe using the visualization to explore larger datasets.

Datasets

Our evaluations were performed using two datasets: (1) a public dataset from InfoVis Contest, (2) publication metadata from our lab.

The InfoVis dataset contains metadata for InfoVis papers spanning 8 years (1995-2002) plus their references, which we refer to as *IV8+R*. The core set of only InfoVis papers we refer to as *IV8*.

We created an extended dataset covering 20 years of InfoVis papers, which we refer to as *IV20*. This dataset is based a cleaned version of IV8+R produced by Ke et al. [11]. From this version we extracted a cleaned version of IV8, and then extended it by adding InfoVis papers from 2003-2014 using the openly accessible metadata in the IEEE digital library [9]. The number of InfoVis papers from IV8 to IV20 increased from 152 to 557, and the number of authors increased from 313 to 1075.

The dataset composed of publication metadata from our lab was extracted from an internal database. It contains metadata from 1995-2015 for 524 publications by 306 authors over a period of 21 years. We refer to this dataset as *Lab21*.

Comparison of Topic Keyword Sets

We first compared the similarity of our LDA-based topics against both the manually and automatically defined topic keywords from the InfoVis 2004 Contest. There were six sets of keywords: two were produced manually and four were computed automatically. These keyword sets are summarized in Table 1.

The keywords were defined on different subsets of the InfoVis 2004 Contest dataset. Lee (ID 3) clustered only the InfoVis papers and not their references. Tyman (ID 5) used topics presented in an Information Visualization class. Keim (ID 2) manually defined topics after manual cleaning that included adding keywords to publications without keywords.

Ahmed (ID 0) removed papers that had no words remaining after preprocessing that included removing infrequent words, removing popular words such as "information" and "visualization", and then created a self-organizing map.

Teoh manually added keywords to documents without keywords and then automatically identified the most frequent keywords. Ke used a burst detection method on the full InfoVis dataset.

Since we performed our evaluation on the IV8 dataset, we identified keywords on IV8 based on Teoh's frequency method and refer to the keywords as "frequent" (ID 6), and on Ke's burst detection method and refer to the keywords as "burst" (ID 7).

Since only a few of the topic keywords overlap across documents, we use the word2vec representation [19] of the keywords when computing similarity. Specifically, we used the word and phrase vectors that were pre-trained on about 100 billion words from part of the Google News dataset [24]. This dataset contains about 3 million words and phrases represented as 300-dimensional vectors.

While a common approach to representing words in a document is to assign each word in the vocabulary an index in a term vector, word2vec learns an embedded representation of words, so that each word or phrase that word2vec was trained on has a reduced dimension, embedded representation. It has been shown that similar words are located in close proximity in the embedded representation [19]; thus, the word2vec representation allows a more fine-grained assessment of the similarity of topic keyword pairs.

To compare the sets of topic keywords from the InfoVis Contest and LDA, the normalized cosine similarity of pairs of topic keyword sets represented using word2vec as $\vec{x}$ and $\vec{y}$ were computed:

ID	*Method*	*# Kwds*	*Manual*	*Dataset*	*Topic Keywords*
0	Ahmed [1]	11	no	IV8+R, filtered	Database Query and Data Mining, System Design, Web Data, Interaction, Graph Drawing, Focus + Context Techniques, Software Visualization, Hierarchy, Multidimensional Data Analysis, Trees, Text and Image Information Retrieval
1	Ke [11]	6	no	IV8+R	data visualization, focus + context, hierarchy, human factors, information visualization, user interface
2	Kiem [12]	5	yes	*N/A*	Information Visualization, HCI, Data Analysis, Computer Graphics, Graph Drawing
3	Lee [15]	5	no	IV8	General, Dynamic Queries, Graph Visualization, Focus + Context Techniques, Tree Visualization
4	Teoh [22]	15	partly	IV8+R, added keywords	text visualization, data mining, database, information analysis, information retrieval, multivariate data, taxonomy, user interfaces, data model, cartography, animation, internet, focus+context visualization, graph drawing, hierarchies
5	Tyman [23]	5	yes	*N/A*	Data, HCI, Implementation, Other, Techniques
6	frequent	15	no	IV8	data visualization, information visualization, world wide web (www), user interface, information retrieval, visualization, internet, focus+context, hierarchy, computer animation, interactive system, spreadsheet, graph drawing, animation, treemap
7	burst	6	no	IV8	information visualization, world wide web (www), user interface, information retrieval, visualization, graph drawing
8	LDA	5	no	IV8	[magnification, nonlinear, …], [document, text, …], [tree, hierarchy, …], [display, analysis, …], [query, database, …]

Table 1. Keyword sets by groups for the InfoVis 2004 Contest dataset. For LDA (ID 8), the two most probable keywords for each topic are shown in square brackets.

$$Sim(\vec{x},\vec{y}) = \frac{\vec{x}\cdot\vec{y}}{|\vec{x}||\vec{y}|}$$

For each similarity computation, one keyword set is considered as the reference, and the other as the test. In part due to the varying number of keywords, the similarities were compared by computing the maximum similarity of each keyword in the reference against all the keywords in the test, and then the average of the keyword similarities in the reference was used as a measure of how well the test keywords align with the reference:

$$\overline{Sim(\vec{x})} = \frac{1}{|R|}\sum_{i\in R}\max_{j\in T} Sim\,(\vec{x_i},\vec{y_j}),$$

where R is the set of reference keywords and T is the set of test keywords.

A heat map indicating the similarity of each reference topic keyword set against each test topic keyword set is shown in Figure 4. Since three of the six InfoVis 2004 keyword sets had five topics, we used the LDA model with five topics for this comparison. We note that the similarity of the topic keyword sets is noticeably lower when the Tyman keywords (5) are the reference set. The Tyman keywords are general words which are not specific to the information visualization domain. We also note that when the LDA keywords are the reference, the similarity with the other keyword sets is also low, except for keyword set 0, Ahmed, which contains 11 keywords and possibly keyword set 3, Lee, who also employed clustering. Keyword set 4, Teoh, which contains the largest number of keywords, 15, also has a relatively high similarity with the other keyword sets. Of the frequency-based keyword sets computed from IV8, we note that both exhibit good similarity with the other InfoVis Contest keyword sets, and that the burst method (ID 6) is a subset of the frequency method (ID 7). In contrast, we observe that LDA, which models documents as a mixture of topics, produces keywords that are less similar on average to the other keyword sets.

We next examine how well each of the different keyword sets match the documents in the IV8 corpus. For this we compute the average normalized cosine similarity of a keyword set against each document. We again use the word2vec term representation. To create the document representation, the word2vec term vector for each of the words in a document is summed, similar to the way that the commonly-used term vectors representing the words in a document are summed to represent the document as a term-frequency vector. That is, the vector representation for a document, $\vec{d}$, is:

$$\vec{d} = \sum_{i\in W}\vec{v}_i,$$

where $\vec{v}_i$ is the word2vec representation for word i and W is the set of words in the document. When a keyword containing more than one term is not in the word2vec vocabulary we used, the word2vec representation of the component words in the phrase are summed and normalized to represent the phrase.

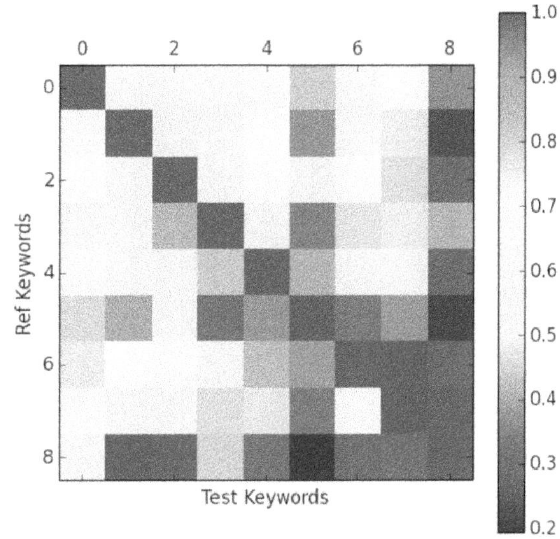

Figure 4. Heatmap showing the similarity of topic keyword sets. The numbers correspond to the ID for the different keyword identification methods shown in Table 1.

We represent LDA topics with one or more of the most probable terms or "topic keywords", i.e. the largest $p(w_i|z_j)$, over the words w_i in topic z_j. When more than one keyword is used to represent an LDA topic, the weighted average of the most probable N keywords is used to represent the topic, with weight $p(w_i|z_j)$ for each keyword w_i. The normalized cosine similarity of the document against each topic (represented as weighted keyword vector) in a keyword set is computed, and the similarity of the best-matching topic, i.e. the maximum document similarity, is selected as the similarity of the document to the keyword set.

The average document similarity for each keyword set is shown in Figure 5. The format of the names in the figure is [*identifier*]-[*info*]-[*#topics*]. For the InfoVis keywords, [*info*] specifies whether the keywords were manually defined or computed. For the LDA models, [*info*] indicates the number of most probable terms used in the similarity computation. We used {2, 3, 10} for comparison. Except for Tyman, the average number of keywords for all the InfoVis keyword sets is 2; the number of keywords shown in our visualization is 3, and 10 weighted keywords were used for similarity computations in our visualization.

From Figure 5 we observe that manually defined keyword sets performed the worse. The LDA keyword sets with two and three keywords per topic generally performed slightly worse than the InfoVis keyword sets in gold. Increasing the number of keywords per LDA topic to 10 improved performance in all cases to better than the InfoVis keyword sets in gold. Based on these results and the observation that the probability of the keywords associated with a topic which rank lower than the first ten is very small, we find

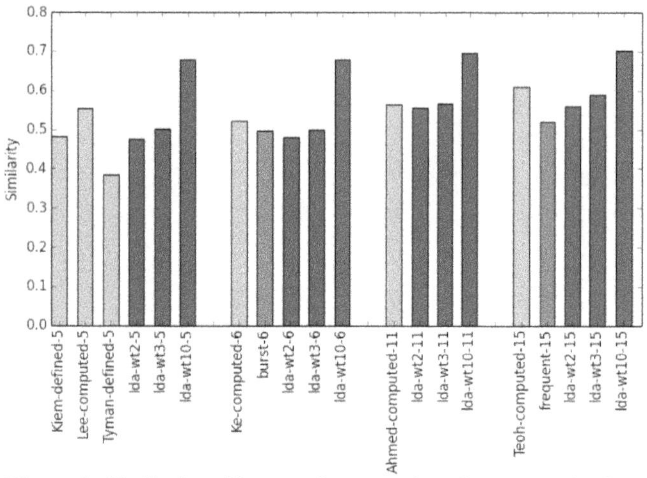

Figure 5. Similarity of keyword sets against documents in the IV8 dataset. The LDA keyword sets are in blue. The InfoVis 2004 Contest keywords are in gold. Frequency-based keywords computed from IV8 are shown in green.

support for using only the top ten keywords in placing the topics and when computing similarity between topics and documents.

Exploring Larger Datasets

We used our interactive visualization to explore the two larger datasets with longer time frames: IV20 and Lab21.

Example on InfoVis 20-year Dataset

As an example, we describe how the visualization shows a person changing his collaborators and topics over time. We ran the visualization on the InfoVis extended dataset IV20, and observed the person Jean-Daniel Fekete. To reduce clutter, the relevance threshold for Person nodes was set to 0.5. We set the time interval size to 3 years, and then we moved the time slider to examine different periods. Close-up regions of some interesting periods are shown in Figure 6. In the period 2002-2004, Fekete collaborated with two people on topic 4 (graph, layout, tree). In 2004-2006, Fekete continued to collaborate with the same two people, and also started collaborating with another person on topic 18 (network, social, structure). Topic 4 and 18 are somewhat similar as shown by their topic words (i.e. "graph" and "network") and their locations in the visualization. Later in 2011-2013, Fekete collaborated with a new group of people on topic 19 (analysis, display, knowledge), which is a different topic located farther in the visualization.

Observations on the Two Datasets

The dimension of the vector spaces V for the IV20 data is 8,252, and for the Lab21 data is 5,626. We use $m = 10$ for the number of highest probability components, so the dimension of subspace V_C subspace is $\leq 10k$, where k is the number of topics. In our tests with $k = 5, 10, 20$, the dimension of V is reduced by a factor of about 30 to 160.

We examine the sizes of the node-link graphs for different number of topics ($k = 5, 10, 20$), and for various relevance scores computed by cosine similarity.

The total number of Person nodes (*p-nodes*) and edges (person-person and person-topic) for different number of topics, *k,* are shown in Figure 7. The number of persons in the IV20 data is 1,075, and in the Lab21 data is 306. By looking at the p-nodes in Table 2, we see that the space of persons (and documents) is well covered. With IV20, for $k = 20$ all 1,075 p-nodes are covered, and for $k = 5$, only 2 p-nodes are missed. With Lab21, for $k = 20$, just 4 of the 302 p-nodes are missed. The missing nodes occur when the person's documents are not in the subspace V_C.

Having good coverage or recall of the p-nodes is important so that parts of the data do not become inaccessible in the visualization, and we see that the coverage is good by the topics and the subspace V_C under the dimension reduction. In contrast, a more simplistic approach such as taking the top k keywords [22] and using keyword matching would provide very poor coverage.

The total number of nodes and edges can be large (see Table 2), which leads to clutter in the visualization. The

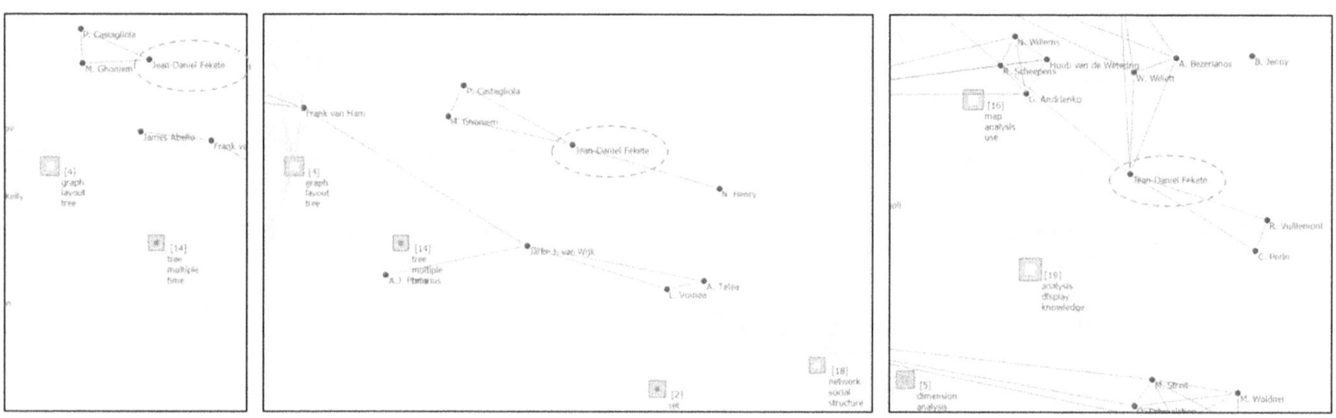

[2002-2004] [2004-2006] [2011-2013]

Figure 6. Time sequence with IV20 data. Close-up of regions in the visualization are shown for three different time periods.

nodes and edges can be filtered by varying the relevance score threshold so that only the more relevant objects are displayed. Figure 7 shows the number of p-nodes and edges retrieved with different relevance thresholds.

Dataset	p-nodes, $k = 5$	edges, $k = 5$	p-nodes, $k = 10$	edges, $k = 10$	p-nodes, $k = 20$	edges, $k = 20$
IV20	1073	3584	1075	3699	1075	3770
Lab21	292	1649	302	1759	302	1850

Table 2. Number of Person nodes (p-nodes) and edges.

The burst results show that there are roughly 5 to 7 bursts per topic over the 20 year periods (for $k = 5, 10, 20$). See Figure 8. For the IV20 data, level 2 bursts occur only at $k = 20$, and for the Lab21 data, level 3 bursts occur only at $k = 20$. One possible explanation is that the topics are more diverse in a research lab database with heterogeneous information than in conference paper metadata focused on a single research area, and that topics also become more diverse when there are more of them at higher k values.

CONCLUSION AND FUTURE WORK

We presented methods for interactive visualization of the temporal dynamics of collaborations over topics. Topic modeling was used to automatically identify topics to serve as landmarks in the visualization, MDS was used for placing the topics in the layout, and burst detection was applied to indicate active topics during a selected time period.

We compared LDA topic modeling against the topic keyword sets from the InfoVis Contest entries. Our results showed that the topic keywords selected by LDA differ more relative to the InfoVis topic keywords than the InfoVis topic keywords differ among each other. We observed that the additional terms provided by LDA-based keyword sets result in improved similarity between a topic keyword set and the documents in a corpus.

We used our topic-based method to visualize two larger datasets with longer time frames, one with only one publication venue, and a second with many venues. Our analysis demonstrated that the use of topic modeling allows for good coverage of the people in the visualization and the potential for scaling to larger datasets.

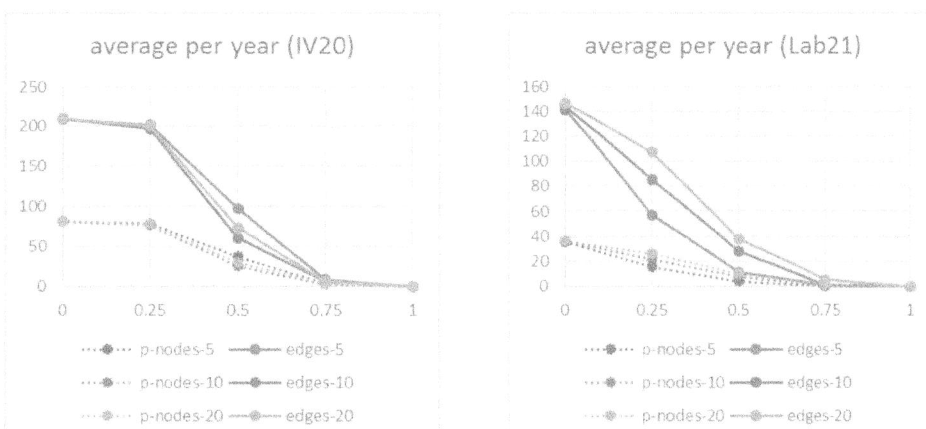

Figure 7. Number of Person nodes (p-nodes) and edges, as the relevance threshold is varied.

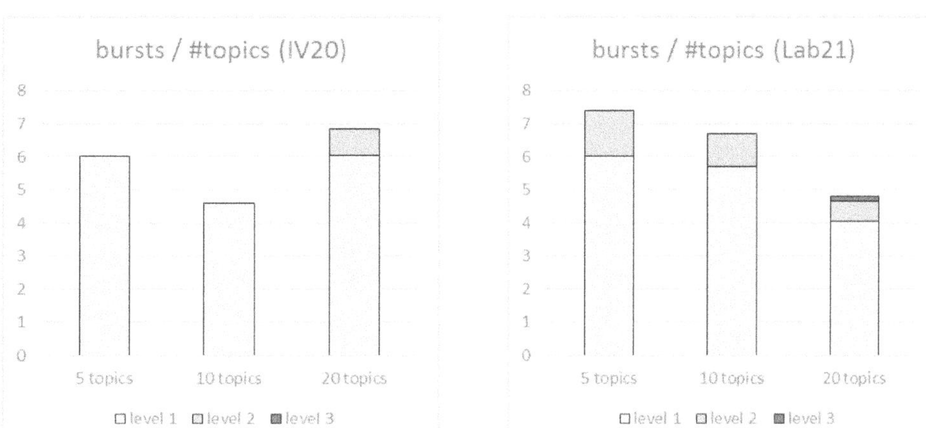

Figure 8. Burst results.

There are several directions in which our work could be improved and extended. These include adapting the visualization to smaller and lower resolution displays such as smartphones. With larger form factors such as wall-sized displays, more topics can be visualized; however, "junk topics" are more likely to occur. A good stop word set eliminates some of the junk topics, but others are due to sparse support [20] and require methods for identifying them (e.g. [2, 5]). Another possible extension is to explore whether alternative representations for the topic nodes may be more informative than the most probable terms that we used; for example, identifying phrases in addition to the single terms provided by LDA.

ACKNOWLEDGMENTS

We thank Bee Liew and Joel Tan for help with collecting the data.

REFERENCES

1. Ahmed, A., Dwyer, T., Murray, C., Song, L., Wu, Y.X. Wilmascope graph visualization. *IEEE InfoVis 2004 Contest Poster Compendium*.
2. AlSumait, L., Barbara, D., Gentle, J., Domeniconi, C. Topic significance ranking of LDA generative models. *Proc. ECML PKDD 2009*, pp. 67-72.
3. Arrow, H., Poole, M.S., Henry, K.B., Wheelan, S., Moreland, R. The temporal perspective on groups. *Small Group Research*, 35, 1 (2004): 73-105.
4. Blei, D.M., Ng, A.Y., Jordan, M.I. Latent Dirichlet allocation. *J. Machine Learning Research*, 3 (2003): pp. 993-1022.
5. Chuang, J., Manning, C. D., Heer, J. Termite: Visualization techniques for assessing textual topic models. *Proc. AVI '12*, pp. 74-77.
6. Faridani, S., Bitton, E., Ryokai, K., Goldberg, K. Opinion space: a scalable tool for browsing online comments. *Proc. CHI '10*, pp. 1175-1184.
7. Fekete, J.-D., Grinstein, G., Plaisant, C. IEEE InfoVis 2004 Contest, the history of InfoVis, www.cs.umd.edu/hcil/iv04contest.
8. Gensim Python software library. http://radimrehurek.com/gensim
9. IEEE Xplore Digital Library. http://ieeexplore.ieee.org/Xplore/home.jsp
10. Jacovi, M., Soroka, V., Gilboa-Freedman, G., Ur, S., Shahar, E., Marmasse, N. The chasms of CSCW: a citation graph analysis of the CSCW conference. *Proc. CSCW 2006*, pp. 91-101.
11. Ke, W., Borner, K., Viswanath, L. Major information visualization authors, papers and topics in the ACM Library. *IEEE InfoVis 2004 Contest Poster Compendium*.
12. Keim, D. A., Barro, H., Panse, C., Schneidewind, J., Sips, M. Exploring and visualizing the history of InfoVis. *IEEE InfoVis 2004 Contest Poster Compendium*.
13. Kleinberg, J. Bursty and hierarchical structure in streams. *Proc. KDD 2006*, pp. 289-298.
14. Kraker, P., Weißensteiner, P., Brusilowsky, P. Altmetrics-based visualizations depicting the evolution of a knowledge domain. *Proc. STI 2014*, pp. 330-333.
15. Lee, B., Czerwinski, M., Robertson, G., Bederson, B.B. Understanding research trends in conferences using PaperLens. *Proc. CHI 2005*, pp. 1969-1972.
16. Leskovec, J., Kleinberg, J., Faloutsos, C. Graphs over time: densification laws, shrinking diameters and possible explanations. *Proc. KDD 2005*, pp. 177-187.
17. Ley, M. Digital bibliography & library project (DBLP). http://www.informatik.uni-trier.de/~ley/db/.
18. Lim, S., Chiu, P. Collaboration Map: Visualizing temporal dynamics of small group collaboration. *CSCW 2015 Companion*, pp. 41-44.
19. Mikolov, T., Sutskever, I., Chen, K., Corrado, G.S., Dean, J. Distributed representations of words and phrases and their compositionality. *Proc. NIPS 2013*, pp. 3111-3119.
20. Mimno, D., Wallach, H.M., Talley, E., Leenders, M., McCallum, A. Optimizing semantic coherence in topic models. *Proc. EMNLP 2011*, pp. 262-272.
21. Qt software application framework. https://www.qt.io/developers.
22. Teoh, S.T., Ma, K.-L. One-For-All: Visualization of the information visualization symposia. *IEEE InfoVis 2004 Contest Poster Compendium*.
23. Tyman, J., Gruetzmacher, G.P., Stasko, J. InfoVisExplorer. *IEEE InfoVis 2004 Contest Poster Compendium*.
24. Word2vec. https://code.google.com/p/word2vec/
25. Zhao J., Collins C., Chevalier F., Balakrishnan R. Interactive exploration of implicit and explicit relations in faceted datasets. *IEEE Trans. on Visualization and Computer Graphics,* 19, 12 (2013): 2080-2089.

Rank As You Go: User-Driven Exploration of Search Results

Cecilia di Sciascio
Know-Center GmbH
Graz, Austria
cdisciascio@know-center.at

Vedran Sabol
Know-Center GmbH
Graz, Austria
vsabol@know-center.at

Eduardo E. Veas
National University of Cuyo
Mendoza, Argentina
eveas@know-center.at

ABSTRACT
Whenever users engage in gathering and organizing new information, searching and browsing activities emerge at the core of the exploration process. As the process unfolds and new knowledge is acquired, interest drifts occur inevitably and need to be accounted for. Despite the advances in retrieval and recommender algorithms, real-world interfaces have remained largely unchanged: results are delivered in a relevance-ranked list. However, it quickly becomes cumbersome to reorganize resources along new interests, as any new search brings new results. We introduce *uRank* and investigate interactive methods for understanding, refining and reorganizing documents on-the-fly as information needs evolve. *uRank* includes views summarizing the contents of a recommendation set and interactive methods conveying the role of users' interests through a recommendation ranking. A formal evaluation showed that gathering items relevant to a particular topic of interest with *uRank* incurs in lower cognitive load compared to a traditional ranked list. A second study consisting in an ecological validation reports on usage patterns and usability of the various interaction techniques within a free, more natural setting.

ACM Classification Keywords
H.5.2. Information Interfaces and Presentation: User Interfaces – Graphical user interfaces (GUI), Interaction styles (e.g., commands, menus, forms, direct manipulation), Evaluation/methodology;; H.3.3. Information Storage and Retrieval: Information Search and Retrieval – Information filtering, Search process; I.2.7. Artificial Intelligence: Natural Language Processing – Text analysis

Author Keywords
search interface; interaction; visual analytics; user study

INTRODUCTION
With the advent of electronic archival, seeking for information occupies a large portion of our daily productive time. Thus, the skill to find and organize the right information has become paramount. Exploratory search is part of a discovery process in which the user often becomes familiar with new terminology in order to filter out irrelevant content and spot potentially interesting items. For example, after inspecting a few documents related to "robots", sub-topics like "human-robot interaction" or "virtual environments" could attract the user's attention. Exploration requires careful inspection of at least a few titles and abstracts, when not full documents, before becoming familiar with the underlying topic.

Advanced search engines and recommender systems (RS) have grown as the preferred solution for contextualized search by narrowing down the number of entries that need to be explored at a time. However, traditional information retrieval (IR) systems strongly depend on precise user-generated queries that should be iteratively reformulated to express evolving information needs. Formulating queries has proven to be more complicated for humans than plainly recognizing information in a visual manner [12]. Hence, the combination of IR with machine learning and HCI techniques has led to a shift towards – mostly Web-based – browsing search strategies that rely on on-the-fly selections, navigation and trial-and-error [23]. As users manipulate data through visual elements, they are able to drill down and find patterns, relations or different levels of detail that would otherwise remain invisible to the bare eye [43]. Moreover, well-designed interactive interfaces can effectively address information overload issues that may arise due to limited attention span and human capacity to absorb information at once.

In turn, RS can be more limited than IR systems if they do not tackle trust factors that hinder user engagement in exploration. As Swearingen et al. [38] pointed out in their seminal work, the RS has to persuade the user to try the recommended items. To fulfill such challenge not only the recommendation algorithm has to fetch items effectively, but also the user interfaces must deliver recommendations in a way that they can be compared and explained [31]. Explanatory interfaces increase confidence in the system (*trust*) by explaining how the system works (*transparency*) [39] and allowing users to tell the system when it is wrong (*scrutability*) [18]. Hence, to warrant increased user involvement the RS has to justify recommendations and let the user customize their generation.

In this work we focus mainly on transparency, controllability and, to some extent, on predictability features that support: (a) exploration of textual document recommendations and (b) refinement of evolving information needs. *uRank* is a visual analytics approach that automatically generates an interactive keyword-based overview of the document collection. It allows users to discover keyword-document relationships – query preview to predict the effect of keyword selection –, as well

IUI 2016, March 7–10, 2016, Sonoma, CA, USA.

http://dx.doi.org/10.1145/2856767.2856797

as keyword-keyword relationships – possible key phrases –. Users refine their interests through a drag-and-drop mechanism that updates a document ranking, representing document relevance scores and query term contribution as stacked bars. We delineate the motivation behind our approach and present the results of two user studies that took place in both, a controlled and an unstructured context.

Our contributions are summarized as: *(i)* a highly controllable and transparent UI for exploratory search of textual documents and *(ii)* two user studies covering the benefits of *uRank* with respect to a traditional list-based UI and usability aspects.

BACKGROUND

Search Result Visualization

Modern search interfaces assist user exploration in a variety of ways. For example, query expansion techniques like *Insyder*'s Visual Query [30] address the query formulation problem by leveraging stored related concepts to help the user extend the initial query. Tile-based visualizations like *TileBars* [13] and *HotMap* [15] make an efficient use of space to convey relative frequency of query terms through – gray or color – shaded squares, and in the case of the former, also their distribution within documents and relative document length. This paradigm aims to foster analytical understanding of Boolean-type queries, hence they do not yield any rank or relevance score. All these approaches rely on the user being able to express precise information needs and do not support browsing-based discovery within the already available results.

Faceted search interfaces allow for organizing or filtering items throughout orthogonal categories, proving their usefulness for inspecting enriched multimedia catalogs [44, 33]. More recently, interfaces supporting rather natural facet-type visual filtering, e.g. geographic or temporal, have also been proposed [29]. However, faceted search relies on structured information, i.e. metadata categories, thus it hardly supports topic-wise exploration of unstructured data.

Rankings conveying document relevance have been discouraged as opaque an under-informative [13]. However, the advantage of ranked lists is that users know where to start their search for potentially relevant documents and that they employ a familiar format of presentation. A study [35] suggests that: *i)* users prefer bars over numbers or the absence of graphical explanations of relevance scores, and *ii)* relevance scores encourage users to explore beyond the first two results. As a drawback, lists imply a sequential search through consecutive items and only a small subset is visible at a given time, thus they are mostly apt for sets no larger than a few tens of documents. Focus+Context and Overview+Detail techniques [28, 15] sometimes help overcome this limitation while alternative layouts like *RankSpiral*'s [36] rolled list can scale up to hundreds and maybe thousands of documents. Other approaches such as *WebSearchViz* [24] and *ProjSnippet* [8] propose complementary visualizations to ordered lists, yet unintuitive context switching is a potential problem when analyzing different aspects of the same document.

Although ranked list are not a novelty, our approach attempts to leverage the advantages provided by lists; i.e. user familiarity, and augment them with stacked-bar charts to convey document relevance and query term contribution in a transparent manner. *Insyder*'s bar graph [30] is an example of augmented ranked lists that displays document and keyword relevance with disjoint horizontal bars aligned to separate baselines. Although layered bar dispositions are appropriate for visualizing distribution of values in each category across items, comparison of overall quantities and the contribution of each category to the totals is better supported by stacked-bar configurations [37]. Additionally, we rely on interaction as the key to provide controllability over the ranking criteria and hence support browsing-based exploratory search.

LineUp [9] has proven the simplicity and usefulness of stacked bars to represent multi-attribute rankings. Despite targeting data of different nature – *uRanks*'s domain is rather unstructured with no measurable attributes –, the visual technique itself served as inspiration for our work.

Recommending Interfaces

In recent years, considerable efforts have been invested into leveraging the power of social RS through visual interfaces [25, 19]. As for textual content, *TalkExplorer* [40] and *SetFusion* [26] are examples of interfaces for exploration of conference talk recommendations. The former is mostly focused on depicting relationships among recommendations, users and tags in a transparent manner, while *SetFusion* emphasizes controllability over a hybrid RS. Rankings are not transparent though, as there is no explanation as to how they were obtained. Kangasraasio et al. [17] highlighted that not only allowing the user to influence the RS is important, but also adding predictability features that produce an effect of causality for user actions.

With *uRank* we intend to enhance predictability through document hint previews, allow the user to control the ranking by choosing keywords as parameters, and support understanding by means of a transparent graphic representation for scores.

Topic Analysis

In addition to methods for visualizing item relevance or distribution of query terms along search results, we consider appropriate to also include in this section another group of methods that support exploration by providing a topical overview of a document set.

Tag clouds have been proposed for browsing document collections [34]. Besides providing a topical overview, such representations are used for keyword-based filtering, but do not provide possibilities to influence a ranking.

Clustering approaches like Scatter/Gather [5] are able to handle very large pools by building hierarchical structures for top-down exploration. IN-SPIRE [20] and InfoSky [1] provide cluster browsing interfaces based on spatial metaphors: a landscape and the outer-space, respectively. Hierarchical cluster exploration is not a trivial task, therefore they are rarely adopted by real-world systems.

Another alternative is topic models, which performs a generative approach, e.g. latent Dirichlet allocation, to capture themes inherent to a document collection [2]. Typical UIs present a topic overview of a collection and allow for further exploration at multiple levels via zooming with keyword search [7] or by navigating a network of interconnected documents, like in *TopicNets* [10]. Topic models owe their flexibility to the fact that they do not correspond to any predefined taxonomy. The model generation process does not infer any semantic information, instead it discovers patterns basing on term co-occurrence. This flexibility could also turn into a weakness, as the topics generated are often not interesting or relevant to users [16]. Moreover, topic models are costly to compute and the exploration and discovery process only works on a pre-existing collection. Although it is possible to interactively change a topic model by joining or splitting topics, these methods aim at improving the model rather than supporting exploratory search [16]. We seek a solution that is not only flexible but also personalizable. Users should be able to construct their own topics as their interests evolve.

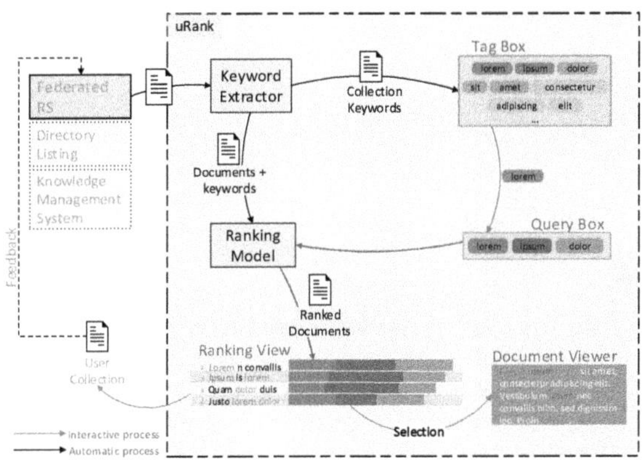

Figure 1. ***uRank*** **visual analytics workflow showing automatic (black arrows) and interactive mechanisms (red arrows)**

URANK VISUAL ANALYTICS

uRank is a visual analytics approach that combines lightweight text analytics and an augmented ranked list to assist in exploratory search of textual documents. Figure 1 depicts the workflow between automatic and interactive mechanisms. Combining these mechanisms enables users to explore a document collection and refine information needs in terms of topic keywords. The workflow is summarized as follows:

1. uRank receives a set of textual document surrogates, i.e. titles and abstracts. The Web-based implementation is currently fed by a RS connected to several sources.
2. The keyword extraction module analyzes all titles and abstracts and returns: (*i*) a list of weighted representative terms for each document, and (*ii*) a set of keywords that describe the whole collection
3. The UI displays a list of documents along with the extracted collection keywords.
4. The user explores the documents and keywords. During this process, the user can discover possible key phrases or relations between documents and keywords at a glance.
5. When the user finds interesting terms, they can interactively select them individually or as group via drag and drop.
6. The document list is re-sorted according to the specified keywords and augmented with colored stacked-bars denoting document scores.
7. The user can select a single document to access more detailed information.
8. Once the user finds a document that suits their search interest, they can add it to their own collection.

User-driven actions (4, 5, 7 and 8) highly depend on the user's search strategy, thus they are rather iterative and interchangeable.

The User Interface

uRank's UI layout is arranged in a multiview fashion that displays different levels of abstraction of a document collection:

Collection overview. The *Tag Box* (Figure 2.A) summarizes the entire collection through augmented keyword tags.

Documents overview. The *Document List* shows titles along with ranking information and the *Ranking View* displays stacked bar charts depicting document relevance scores (Figure 2.C and D, respectively). Together they represent minimal document views. The list and ranking visualization are updated as the user manipulates keyword tags in the *Query Box* (Figure 2.B).

Document detailed view. For a document selected in the list, the *Document Viewer* (see section Details on Demand) displays the title and snippet with color-augmented keywords.

Display space requirements constrain the number of views and their space at a given time. At first, all views appeared juxtaposed, avoiding multiple overlapping views. In the latest version we added the *Bookmark Overview* (Figure 2.E) and removed the *Document Viewer* from the main view and is shown as a modal when the user requires deeper information about a particular document.

Interactions and Visual Design

Our approach relies on a suitable visual encoding and on interactive mechanisms. Visual encoding supports preattentive processing by leveraging the capacity of human vision to absorb great amounts of information at a glance. In turn, interactions enable users to directly or indirectly manipulate the data through the view [42], uncovering pieces of information in the data space that would otherwise pass unnoticed.

Exploring a Document Collection

The *Tag Box* provides a summary of the textual documents as a whole by presenting keywords as tags. Summarizing the collection in a few representative terms allows the user to scan the recommendations and grasp the general topic at a glance, before even reading any of them. This is particularly important in the context of collections brought by RS, where the user is normally not directly generating the queries that feed the search engine.

Figure 2. ***uRank*** **User Interface displaying documents related to** ***recommender systems*****, with ranking updated to match the keywords "collaborative", "item" and "performance". A. The** ***Tag Box*** **presents a keyword-based summary of the document collection, B. the** ***Query Box*** **contains keywords selected by the user, C. the** ***Document List*** **and D. the** ***Ranking View*** **present a list with augmented document titles and stacked bars indicating relevance scores, and E. the** ***Bookmark Overview*** **shows bookmarked documents.**

Tags are organized in descending order to convey document frequency (DF) and visually grouped in five gray-shaded clusters that represent keywords with similar frequencies. Redundant frequency coding is intentional and aims at maximizing distinctiveness among items in the keyword set [43].

At first glance, the *Tag Box* gives an outline of the covered topic in terms of keywords and their relative frequencies. Nevertheless, a bag-of-words representation alone does not supply further details about how a keyword relates to other keywords or documents. To bridge this gap, tags are augmented with two compact visual hints: *i)* the *co-occurence hint* appears as a red circle showing the number of frequently co-occurring keywords across all documents, and *ii)* the *document hint* consists in a pie chart that conveys the proportion of documents in which the keyword is contained. Both hints become visible on mouse over, along with a tooltip on top of the *Tag Box* that provides an accurate explanation of the hints' meaning (Figure 3(a)). Further inspection is possible by clicking on a particular tag, which has a twofold effect:

1. Unrelated documents are dimmed in the *Document List* and *Ranking View*, so that documents containing the keyword remain in focus – even if they are not currently ranked –. This feature allows for predicting the effect of selecting a keyword (Figure 4).

2. Co-occurring terms are brought to focus by dimming unrelated tags in the background (Figure 3(b)), in order to support the user in discovering possible key phrases within the collection.

In the first-generation implementation, the user had to click on the *document-* and *co-occurrence hint* to trigger effects 1 and 2, respectively. A preliminary study showed that clicking on the small hints was unintuitive, therefore we simplified this interaction by triggering both effects together on tag clicks.

The study also revealed that users had difficulties finding a particular keyword, especially when the *Tag Box* was overly populated. For that reason, a text input field and a frequency range slider were added on top of the *Tag Box*. The former provides keyword search functionality, such that when the term is found, the corresponding tag is highlighted and the *Tag Box* scrolls to its position, or an error message pops up otherwise (Figure 5). The frequency slider allows for setting the minimum and maximum document frequency for visible tags. Tags become visible or hidden as soon as the user starts dragging the handles. By default, the minimum value is set to 2 and the maximum value matches the most frequent tag. In Figure 2.A the slider has been set to the range [7, 81], significantly reducing the number of tags in display.

Ranking Documents On The Fly

In theory, recommender and information retrieval systems produce lists where items are already sorted by their relevance with respect to certain criteria. However, it has been argued that user trust and engagement may be hindered if the UI does not provide features for reshaping the search criteria or clear rationale as to what makes and item more relevant than another. Hence, with *uRank* we address controllability and transparency by providing a user-driven method for reorganizing documents as information needs evolve, along with a suitable visual encoding and animated transitions that convey a transparent logic for document relevance.

Document titles are initially listed following the order in which they were supplied. Changes in the document ranking visualization originate from three types of keyword tag manipula-

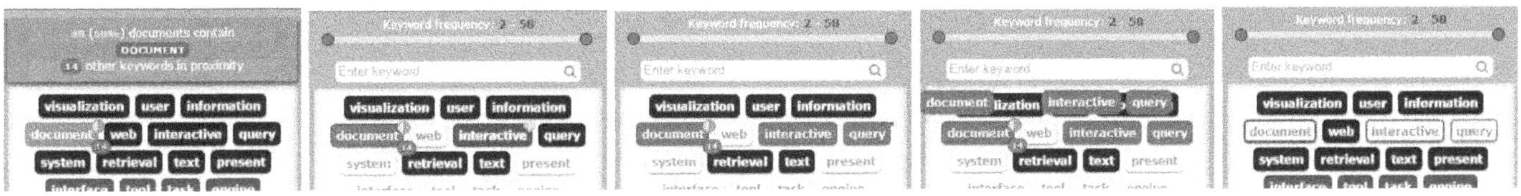

(a) (b) (c) (d) (e)

Figure 3. *Tag Box*. a) Keyword hints and tooltip become visible on hover. b) Clicking on a tag locks the view and frequently co-occurring keywords are highlighted. c) Clicking on additional tags creates a multiple selection. d) A group of tags being dragged with the cursor. e) Dropped tags are cloned in the *Tag Box* and highlighted with the appropriate border stroke

tions in the *Query Box* (Figure 2.B): addition, weight change and deletion.

Tag Addition. Keyword tags in the *Tag Box* can be manually unpinned , dragged with the mouse pointer and dropped into the *Query Box*. Tags can be either dropped one by one (Figure 6) or as a group. After clicking on a tag of interest, the *Tag Box* appears "locked" so that the frequently co-occurring tags remain highlighted. The user then can click on additional tags (Figure 3(c)) and drag them altogether (Figure 3(d)). The *Tag Box* is "unlocked" once the tags are dropped into the *Query Box*. The intention of incorporating multiple drag-and-drop is to assist users in interactively creating their own key phrases. Remembering the sequence of tags that form a potentially interesting key phrase entails higher cognitive effort if the user can only drag tags individually and the sequence vanishes from the bare eye every time the view in the *Tag Box* is unlocked.

Dropped tags are re-rendered by adding a weight slider, a delete button on the right-upper corner – visible on hover – and a specific background color from a categorical palette – Color Brewer's *9-class Set 1* qualitative palette [11] –. Since keyword tags represent category labels, i.e. abstractions of entities into groups, the use of a categorical color scheme allows for clearly distinguishing tags from one another.

In an earlier version, dragged tags were removed from the *Tag Box*, causing position adjustments in subsequent tags to fill the empty gaps. A previous evaluation revealed that this had the undesired effect that previously spotted tags could not be found again in the same place. Therefore, in the current version a clone of a dropped tag remains in its original position in the *Tag Box* and the border is highlighted with the same categorical color assigned in the *Query Box*.

Weight Change. Tag sliders allow the user to adjust the weight of a keyword in document scores. Figure 6 shows tag backgrounds with different levels of intensity after the sliders have been tuned.

Tag Deletion. Tags can be removed from the *Query Box* by clicking on the "delete" icon. The user also has the alternative to clear the *Query Box* and restore the document list to its original state. In any case, animation is used to shift tags to their original positions in the *Tag Box* at a perceivable pace.

Tag manipulations are forwarded to the *Ranking Model* as ranking parameters, which in turn feeds the ranking visualization. This visualization consists of a list of document titles (Figure 2.C) and stacked bar charts (Figure 2.D) depicting relevance scores for documents and keywords within them.

We favor the use of animation to convey ranking-state transitions rather than abrupt static changes. Animated transitions are inherently intuitive and engaging, giving a perception of causality and intentionality [14]. In *uRank*, soft animated transitions for ranking-state changes and document selection help the user intuitively switch contexts. As Baldonado et al. [41] state in their rule of attention management, perceptual techniques lead the user's attention to the right view at the right time.

As the document ranking is updated, the *Document List* is re-sorted in descending order by overall score and list items are translated to their new positions at a perceptible pace. Stacked bars then appear *Ranking View*, growing from left to right and horizontally aligned to each list item. Green or red shading effects are applied on the left side of list items for a few seconds to denote positive and negative shifts.

The total width of stacked bars indicates the overall score of a document and bar fragments represent the individual contribution of keywords to the overall score. Bar colors match the color encoding for selected keywords in the *Query Box*, enabling the user to make an immediate association between keyword tags and bars. Missing colored bars in a stack denote the absence of certain words in the document surrogate. Additionally, each item in the *Document List* contains two types of numeric indicators: position and shift with respect to the

Figure 4. Document hints show which documents contain certain keyword, helping to predict the effect of selecting it

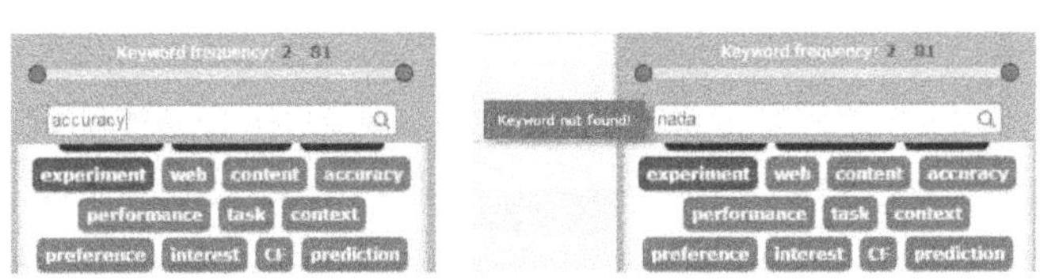

Figure 5. Keyword search in *Tag Box*. (left) Found keyword appears highlighted for a few seconds. (right) Error message pops up otherwise.

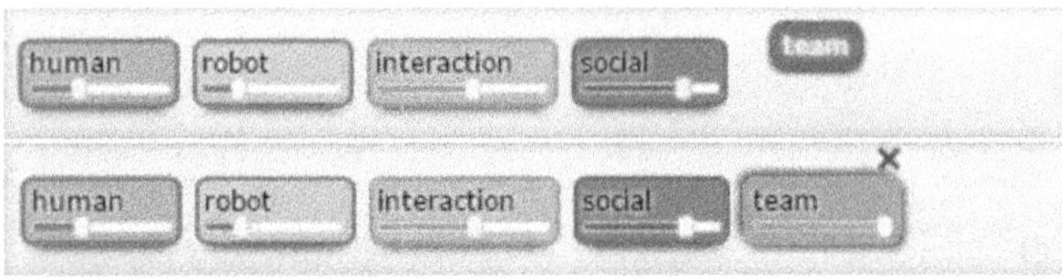

Figure 6. (*top*) Keyword tag before being dropped in *Tag Box*. (*bottom*) Dropped tag extended with weight slider and delete button. Background colors match a categorical scale and weights have been tuned.

immediate previous position. Position is denoted inside a gray circle, whereas shift is indicated as a color-coded number.

This visualization attempts to attract user's attention to likely relevant documents by bringing highly ranked ones to the top and pushing the rest to the bottom. In a previous generation, items with null score were hidden and the list height was shrunk or enlarged to fit only ranked items. Some users argued that such behavior was undesirable or confusing. Therefore, unranked items are currently grouped below the ranked ones, so that they remain accessible even though they are likely irrelevant for the given query.

Optionally, the user can track shifts in particular documents by clicking on the watch – eye-shaped – icon. The watched item remains in focus as it is surrounded with a slightly darker shadow and the title is underlined. Also, watched items remain on top of other elements during list animations.

Details on Demand

Once the user identifies documents that seem worth further inspecting, he/she can drill down one by one to determine whether the initial assumption holds. The *Document Viewer*, as shown in (Figure 7 gives access to textual content – title and snippet – and available metadata for a particular document. Query terms are highlighted in the text following the same color coding for tags in the *Query Box* and stacked bars in the *Ranking View*. These simple visual cues pop out from their surroundings, enabling the user to pre-attentively recognize keywords in the text and perceive their general context prior to conscious reading.

Keyword Extraction

The aforementioned interactive features are supported by a combination of well-known text-mining techniques that extend the recommended documents with document vectors and provide meaningful terms to populate the *Tag Box*.

Document vectors ideally include only content-bearing terms like nouns and frequent adjectives – appearing in at least 25% of the collection –, hence it is not enough to just rely on a list of

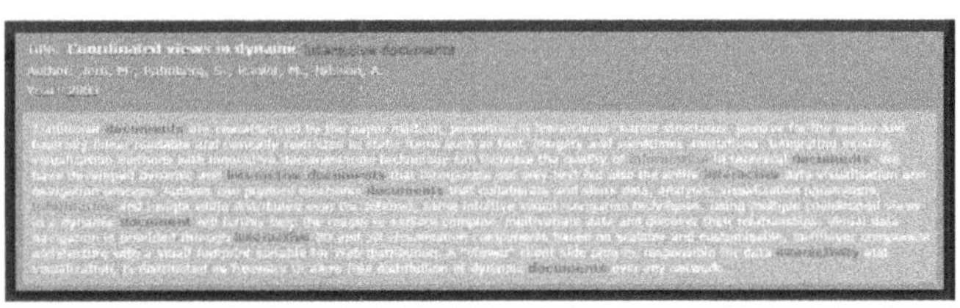

Figure 7. *Document Viewer* shows augmented title and abstract for a selected document. Color-coded terms match the tags in *Query Box*

stop words to remove meaningless terms. Firstly, we perform a part-of-speech tagging (POS tagging) [3] step to identify words that meet our criteria, i.e. common and proper nouns and adjectives. Filtering out non-frequent adjectives requires an extra step. Then, plural nouns are singularized, proper nouns are kept capitalized and terms in upper case, e.g. "IT", remain unchanged. We apply the Porter Stemmer method [27] over the resulting terms, in order to increase the probability of matching for similar words, e.g. "robot", "robots" and "robotics" all match the stem "robot". A document vector is thus conformed by stemmed versions of content-bearing terms.

Next, we generate a weighing scheme by computing TF-IDF (term frequency – inverse document frequency) for each term in a document vector. The score is a statistical measure of how important the term is to a document in a collection. Therefore, the more frequent a term is in a document and the fewer times it appears in the corpora, the higher its score will be. Documents' metadata are extended with these weighted document vectors.

To fill the *Tag Box* with representative keywords for the collection set, all document keywords are collected in a global keyword set. Global keywords are sorted by document frequency (DF), i.e. the number of documents in which they appear, regardless of the frequency within documents. To avoid overpopulating the *Tag Box*, only terms with DF above certain threshold (by default 5) are taken into account. Note that terms used to label keyword tags are actual words and not plain stems. Scanning a summary of stemmed words would turn unintuitive for users. Thus, in order to allow for reverse stemming, we keep a record of all variations matching each stem, and pick the representative word as follows:

1. if there is only one term for a stem, use it to label the tag,
2. if a stem has two variants, one in lower case and the other in upper case or capitalized, use it in lower case,
3. use a term that ends in 'ion', 'ment', 'ism' or 'ty',
4. use a term matching the stem,
5. use the shortest term.

To feed document hints, *uRank* attaches a list of bearing documents to each global keyword. For co-occurrence hints (Figure 2.A), *uRank* tracks by default keyword co-occurrences with a maximum word distance of 2 and at least 10 repetitions.

Document Ranking Computation

Quick content exploration in *uRank* depends on its ability to readily re-sort documents according to changing information needs. As the user manipulates keyword tags and builds queries from a subset of the global keyword collection, *uRank* computes documents scores to arrange them accordingly in a document ranking. We assume that some keywords are more important to the topic model than others and allow the user to assign weights to them.

Document scores are relevance measures for documents with respect to a query. As titles and snippets are the only content available for retrieved document surrogates, these scores are computed with a term-frequency scheme. Term distribution schemes are rather adequate for long or full texts and are hence out of our scope. Boolean models have the disadvantages that they not only consider every term equally important but also produce absolute values that preclude document ranking.

The *Ranking Model* implements a vector space model to compute document-query similarity using the document vectors previously generated during keyword extraction. Nonetheless, a single relevance measure like cosine similarity alone is not enough to convey query-term contribution, given that the best overall matches are not necessarily the ones in which most query terms are found [13, 22]. The contribution that each query term adds to the document score should be clear in the visual representation, in order to give the user a transparent explanation as to why a document ranks in a higher position than another. Therefore, we break down the cosine similarity computation and obtain individual scores for each query term, which are then added up as an overall relevance score.

Given a document collection D and a set of weighted query terms T, such that $\forall t \in T : 0 \leq w_t \leq 1$; the relevance score for term t in document vector $d \in D$ for query terms T is calculated as follows:

$$s(t_d) = \frac{tfidf(t_d) \times w_t}{||d|| \times ||T||},$$

where $tfidf(t_d)$ is the tf-idf score for term t in document d and $||d||$ is the Euclidean norm for vector d. Note that every term t in query T is 1 , such that $1/||T||$ represents a single dot in its unit query vector. Thus the Euclidean norm of T equals the square root of the vector length, i.e. $||T|| = \sqrt{|T|}$.

The overall score of a document $S(d)$ is then computed as the sum of each individual term score $s(t_d)$. Finally, the collection D is sorted in descending order by overall score with the quicksort algorithm and ranking positions are assigned.

Implementation

uRank is a Web-based tool mainly implemented in JavaScript. We made use of libraries like *jQuery*[1] and *d3*[2] for the UI. Keyword extraction is performed entirely on the client side (due to project requirements). For POS-tagging, tokenization, stemming and tf-idf computation we leveraged *jspos*[3] and *NaturalJS* [4]. Other support libraries include *colorbrewer*, for color schemes, and Underscore.js, for diverse functionalities.

STUDY I: URANK VS BASELINE LIST-BASED UI

Exploratory search interfaces have arguably a steep learning curve that often prevents their adoption. The goal motivating this study was to find out how people responded when working with a tool like *uRank* with respect to a traditional list-based UI. The study followed a 2x2 repeated measures design with two independent variables: *tool*: uRank (*U*) and a baseline list-based UI (*L*) – with usual browser tools like Control+F search – and *#items*: *30* and *60*. Thus, every participant worked under the four possible combinations: **U-30**, **U-60**, **L-30** and **L-60**.

[1] https://jquery.com/
[2] http://d3js.org/
[3] https://code.google.com/p/jspos/
[4] https://github.com/amitamb/NaturalJS

Table 1. Cosine similarities between collections gathered during Study I

Task Type	Comparison	WW	Ro	AR	CE	All topics
Q1	U vs L	.55	.79	.58	.74	.66
(focused	U-30 vs U-60	**.71**	**.83**	**.94**	**.67**	**.79**
search)	L-30 vs L-60	.58	**.83**	.56	.56	.63
Q2	U vs L	.70	.86	.84	.86	.81
(focused	U-30 vs U-60	**.84**	**.89**	**.90**	**.93**	**.89**
search)	L-30 vs L-60	.82	.74	.81	.87	.81
Q3	U vs L	.75	.72	.75	.63	.72
(broad	U-30 vs U-60	**.64**	**.88**	**.75**	**.62**	**.72**
search)	L-30 vs U-60	.59	.66	.63	.33	.55

To counterbalance learning effects, we created data sets for 4 different topics and treated *topic* as random variable.

We recruited 24 participants (11 female, 13 male, between 22 and 37 years old), who were mainly graduate and post-graduate students from the computer science the medical domains. None is majoring in the topics selected for the study.

The study simulated an exploration scenario, where the participant receives a list of recommendations while reading a Wikipedia article. There were three tasks per condition: two focused exploration tasks and a broad exploration task. For the former, participants had to find the five most relevant items for a set of two or three given keywords (Q1 and Q2). These tasks reflect the behavior of shifting information interests to a new topic while exploring. The broad exploration task (Q3), which consisted in finding five items relevant to a short text, reflects the need to clarify a textual description, building phrases to describe information needs. All combinations of *tool*, *#items* and *topic* were randomly assigned with balanced Latin Square. For each condition, participants filled a 7-point likert scale NASA TLX questionnaire for subjective workload assessment. In turn, the system recorded selected items and completion time per participant and task.

Workload, Completion Time and Performance.

Figure 8(a) shows that overall workload was significantly lower under the *U* condition, independently from *#items*, $F(1,23) = 35,254, p < .01, r = .2$. It can be observed in Figure 8(c) that this tendency applies to all dimensions. The results also revealed that even though users tended to consume all the time allotted (Figure 8(b)), the lower *subjective* temporal demand (Figure 8(c)) suggests that they felt significantly more relaxed when working with *uRank*.

To analyze performance, we aggregated the collections gathered by all participants and computed cosine similarity across *tool*, *#items*, *topic* and task (Q1, Q2 and Q3). Similarity values in Table 1 between collections produced with and without *uRank* (**U vs L**) denote that overall choices regarding relevant documents matched three out of four times ($M = .73$, $SD = .1$), across all task types and regardless of *#items*.

Collections produced with our tool for the two variations of *#items* (**U-30 vs U-60**) turned quite similar across all topics and task types ($M = .8$, $SD = .12$, with a minimum of .62). In turn, comparisons for the baseline UI with 30 and 60 items (**L-30 vs L-60**) denote greater overall diversity ($M = .67$, $SD = .16$, with a minimum of .33), particularly for broad search task (Q3) respect to focused search (Q1 and Q2). For full results refer to di Sciascio et al.[6].

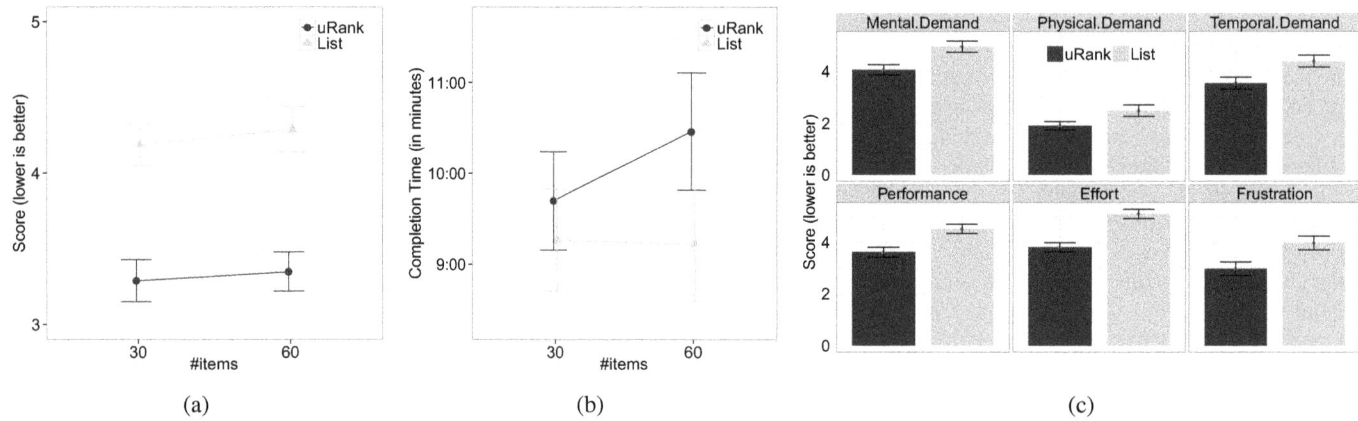

Figure 8. Study I Results. (a) Workload interaction lines show that *uRank* is significantly less demanding. (b) Time completion lines show a regularity towards using all available time. (c) Bar charts reveal lower workload for *uRank* across all dimensions. Error bars represent standard error.

Discussion and Limitations

It is a long-known problem that most users do not go beyond simple keyword search, despite the availability of more advanced UIs. Despite its highly controlled setup, the current study provided evidence that users actually engaged in exploration using *uRank*. Our tool is inherently more complex than a Google-like UI, yet users felt significantly less pressed by time and more confident about their performance. On top of that, participants were first-timers, i.e. they only had a few minutes of training prior to the evaluation tasks.

Nevertheless, the highly controlled and rather unnatural setting poses certain limitations. For example, we balanced the level of knowledgeability by choosing topics in which none of the participants was an expert. Having little or no knowledge about the underlying topic made tasks quite difficult for some of them. Also, exploration was guided towards common “search interests“, which rarely represented the true interests of the users. Taking these limitations into account, we conducted a second user study to observe user behavior during exploratory search in more realistic conditions.

USER STUDY II: ACTION ANALYSIS AND USABILITY

The second study explores the strategies users employ in exploratory search when working with *uRank* in a more natural setting, i.e. without rigid tasks, time-ups or uninteresting topics. Specifically, we were interested in addressing usability aspects and detecting usage patterns.

We sent invitations via e-mail to colleagues in the Computers Science field, which included a link to a Web form with all necessary guidelines. A total of 16 people accepted to take part in the study. A session started with a demonstrative video of the UI features. Thereafter participants had to open the *uRank* Web site in their browsers. They could chose a topic of their preference out of 7 collections, each with approximately 100 documents. The task consisted in freely exploring the collection and bookmarking interesting documents. We suggested between 5 and 10, although not as a strict condition.

The system recorded action logs: tag clicks, single and multiple drag-and-drop interactions, etc. After submitting the session data, users filled a survey consisting of: *(i)* questions addressing usability of specific UI components, and *(ii)* a standard usability questionnaire.

Table 2. User action summary

Type	Action	$M(SE)$	User Count
exploration	tag hover	135.06(21.03)	16
	tag click	2.63(0.50)	16
	keyword search	0.38(0.26)	2
control	ranking update	10.01(2.22)	16
	single tag dropped	4.44(0.68)	15
	multiple tags dropped	0.31(0.12)	5
	tag weight changed	4.13(1.53)	12
	tag deleted	1.13(0.43)	6
	reset	0(0)	0
drill-down	document click	74.81(26.57)	16
	document bookmark	4.63(0.81)	12
	document unbookmark	0.06(0.06)	1
	document watched	1.56(0.64)	9
	document unwatched	0.19(0.10)	3

Action Analysis

In this section we break down action log information according to action-type categories: exploration, control and drill-down. Table 2 presents a summary of recorded user actions.

We contrast action logs against user feedback provided for UI-specific questions. Responses were collected on a 7-point likert scale, where most questions were phrased in a positive tone (1=strongly disagree, 7=strongly agree), e.g. “Looking at the colors in keywords and bars, it was clear how the ranking was computed”. The scale was inverted for negative-tone questions, e.g. “The position indicator in the document list was confusing” (1=strongly agree, 7=strongly disagree), so that all values can be interpreted as “higher is better”.

Exploratory Actions

Action logs show that users extensively hovered on keyword tags (135 times on overage) but in most cases did not click on tags to preview bearing documents and potential key phrases ($M = 2.63$, $SE = 0.5$).

Usage data for the keyword range slider reveal interesting results: only 4 participants interacted with it – with two of them tuning it 117 and 303 times, respectively –, but most

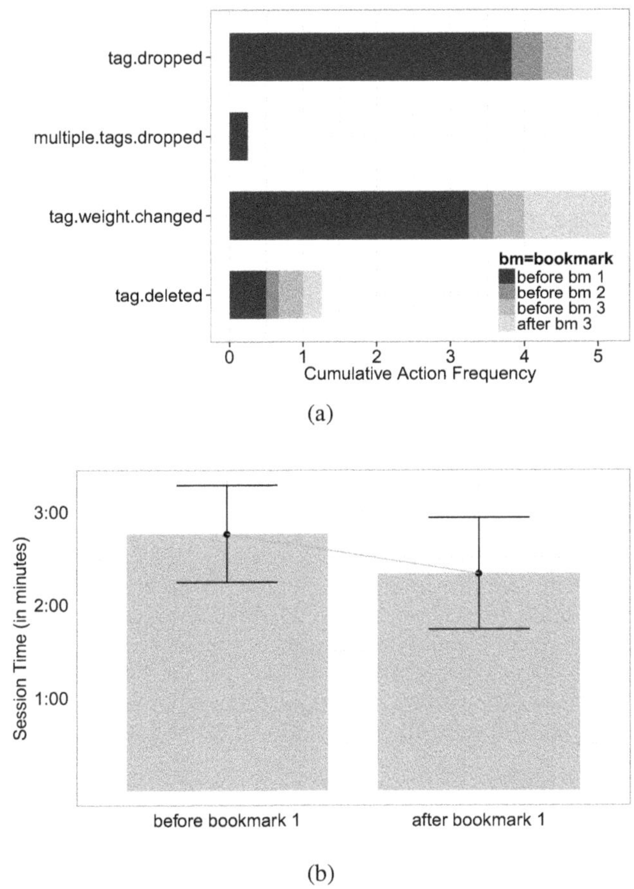

Figure 9. Study II Results. (a) Stacked bars for ranking updates distribution around 1st, 2nd and 3rd bookmark. (b) Bar chart shows average pre- and pos-1st-bookmark session time.

users reported that this feature was useful ($M = 5.09$, $SE = 0.35$). The keyword search feature was also scarcely used: only two participants actively searched for specific terms. This corresponds with previous studies: people preferred browsing the offered keywords to explicitly searching for them [12].

Control Actions

On average, users updated the document ranking 10.01 times. This evidences the role of interactive control features in engaging users in a trial-and-error search process. The rather low usage of tag clicks compared to the number of ranking updates ($2.64 vs. 10.1$) may suggest that users were more interested in immediately discovering the effect of manipulating a tag than in trying to predict it beforehand.

Most control actions corresponded to simple tag additions (4.44 times) and weight changes (4.13). These observations match user responses, as they admitted mostly choosing keywords one by one ($M = 5.82$, $SE = 0.38$) and frequently using the sliders to change keyword weights ($M = 4.77$, $SE = 0.37$).

Multiple drag and drop was only used by roughly a third of the participants (0.31 times), corroborated by the answers to the question "I mostly chose groups of keywords together" ($M = 2.45$, $SE = 0.39$). When asked about how easy it was to use this mechanism, responses were quite neutral ($M = 4.09$, $SD = 0.36$). Perhaps some participants found it too complicated (two of them actively reported so), but the majority just ignored it. We attribute the low usage to its two-step mechanism, evidencing that a one-step increment in the interaction path inherently hinders ease-of-use.

Tag deletions remained in a low rate: two thirds of the participants never performed this action. The rest did it between 2 and 3 times (overall 1.13 times). None reset the ranking.

Drill-down Actions

8 out of 15 participants clicked on a specific document between 15 and 100 times (89 times on average). 4 outliers only inspected document abstracts between 1 and 5 times and 2 more than 300 times. In general, participants admitted that they often read document titles ($M = 6.09$, $SE = 0.2$), and sentences surrounding colored keywords ($M = 4.95$, $SE = 0.34$). The level of agreement to reading full abstracts was moderate ($M = 4.41$, $SE = 0.33$).

Surprisingly, 4 users did not bookmark any document. Excluding them ($N = 12$), users bookmarked 6.1 documents on average, which is not a discouraging number considering that the task did not impose a minimum amount. Participants did not revert their decisions: only one item was unbookmarked by accident and bookmarked again.

The questionnaire revealed that by looking at the colors of tags and bars it was clear for them how the ranking was computed ($M = 5.77$, $SE = 0.26$). Also, they chose their bookmarks mostly by looking at the titles and the ranking ($M = 5.27$, $SE = 0.27$), which denotes that users trusted the recommendations. Summarizing, the evidence suggests that the UI helped participants achieve a high level of self-perceived performance and that they felt confident about their decisions.

Search Strategy Analysis

Control actions represent trial-and-error steps that users perform throughout browser-based exploration. We attempt to discover search patterns thereof by splitting ranking update actions, namely: *tag dropped*, *multiple tag dropped*, *tag weight change* and *tag deleted*, and observing how frequently they occurred: i) before the first bookmark, and i) between subsequent bookmarks. In the current analysis we only considered users that bookmarked at least one document ($N = 12$).

At first glance, Figure 9(a) reveals a strong tendency for tag selections to occur prior to the first bookmark event. All multiple tag drops were performed at this stage, while roughly 75% of all single tag drops fell therein ($M = 3.83$, $SE = 0.75$). As stated before, tag deletions were infrequent (overall, $M = 1.25$, $SE = 0.55$), but appear evenly distributed along all search phases. Weight changes also reach their peak before the first bookmark cut ($M = 3.25$, $SE = 1.24$), then tend to decrease towards the second ($M = 0.33$, $SE = 0.23$) and third bookmarks ($M = 0.42$, $SE = 0.33$), and finally a slight increment appears towards the end ($M = 1.17$, $SE = 0.79$). The distribution of actions depicted in Figure 9(a) suggests that after the first bookmark users were quite certain about the chosen keywords, although they fine-tuned the ranking minimally even after identifying three relevant documents.

This notion is supported by temporal distribution. Considering that an average session lasted approximately 5 minutes, Figure 9(b) reveals that pre- and pos-first-bookmark exploration were balanced (on average 2'45" and 2'20", respectively). Thus, the tipping point in a session was roughly marked by the occurrence of the first bookmark. Control actions in general were executed in the first half of a session. Afterward, users minimally refined query parameters, denoting that they were satisfied with their decisions and dedicated the second half of the session to find other relevant documents.

Finally, the fact that tag drops and weight sliders were extensively used and that tag deletions were scarce may indicate that participants tended to know what they were searching for from the beginning and rarely undid their decisions. This can be validated by looking at the number of keywords per bookmark ($M = 4.32$, $SE = 0.61$), which did not differ significantly from the total number of unique keywords ($M = 5$, $SE = 0.65$).

Usability Analysis

In addition to questions for specific UI features, participants also filled a Software Usability Scale (SUS) questionnaire [4], a standard post-study questionnaire for subjective assessment of usability. Participants were not English native speaker, hence we chose a version with all positive-tone questions [32] for better understanding. To keep consistency with the scoring scale in the *uRank* specific questions, we used a 7-point likert scale instead of a 5-point one. User responses were multiplied by 1.66 instead of 2.5 to obtain overall SUS scores in a range between 0 and 100. Thus, the score s_i for question x_i was computed as $s_i = (x_i - 1) * 1.6$.

Averaging over all questions and participants, the mean raw score amounted to 84 ($SD = 9.4$). *uRank* falls in the 90-95 percentile range in the curved grading scale interpretation of SUS scores [32], thus obtained an **A grade**. These scores are also subdivided into *Usable* (questions 1, 2, 3, 5, 6, 7 and 8) and *Learnable* (4 and 10) subscales [21]. Adjusting multipliers for a 7-point likert scale (2.08 and 8.33, respectively), *uRank* scored an A for *Usable* ($M = 82.8$, $SD = 10.03$) and an A+ for *Learnable* ($M = 90.4$, $SD = 11$).

At the end of the study, users were asked to share their general impressions of the system. Two participants reported some delays in the ranking update after changing tag weights and a few expressed that they would prefer softer colors for tags and bars or even less color diversity. Nonetheless, most positive answers agreed that overall usability and ease of use were good. A few answers even highlighted that animations made it easy to follow the effects of their actions.

Discussion and Limitations

This study revealed which parts of the tool proved most useful and easy to handle. Additionally, it provided some insights on how exploratory search unfolded: for example, control actions occurred mostly before the first bookmark, and then users dedicated to find more interesting documents. This was, to some extent, surprising, as we expected a decreasing, yet less abrupt frequency of ranking updates.

Particularly, this study falls on the opposite side from Study I. The task did not impose any goals or reasons to actually pursue a dedicated search. Therefore, perhaps people were only motivated to try the tool once and see how it works, but did not actually engage in exploring and learning. We expect that conscious exploration would involve several changes of interests and further interactions. The short duration of an average session (5'05") corroborates this assumption.

We believe the only way to produce a realistic situation would be through a longitudinal study, e.g. having an online service where people can obtain an actual profit after interacting with it. Another option could be a more balanced setup, that is less controlled than Study I and less free than Study II. However, defining exactly how an optimal setup should be is out of the scope of this paper.

CONCLUSIONS AND FUTURE WORK

This paper introduced the reasoning line for the visual and interactive design of *uRank*, a visual analytics tool for exploratory search, along with incremental improvements and their rationale. Although originally planned as a recommending interface, it could be extended to generic search interfaces for not only unstructured data like text, but also for structured data. The latter would require that input data previously enriched with semantic information, tags or named entities.

We also presented two complementary user studies that support the design. The first study consisted in a highly-controlled comparative evaluation against a traditional list-based UI. Results revealed that participants found it significantly more *relaxing* to work with *uRank*, despite no important differences in performance or speed. In fact, most of them reported their wish to start actively using *uRank* in their scientific endeavors, e.g. paper writing. The limitations of a strictly controlled study served as starting point for the second study. In this case, we asked users to freely explore documents with *uRank* and bookmark the relevant ones within a topic of interest. This study shed a light on interaction paths and browsing strategies followed during exploratory search. Moreover, the tool received positive critics, as supported by the post-study questionnaires.

In the future we will pursue improvements in the UI, such as a more intuitive mechanism for multiple drag-and drop, and an overview component for navigating large lists. We also plan to extend text-mining methods by enriching keyword with synonyms and semantic relationships. Moreover, we plan to leverage bookmark logs collected during both studies and use them as feedback to improve recommendations with folksonomy-based information, closing the interactive loop with the RS, as shown in Figure 1.

ACKNOWLEDGMENTS

This work is funded by the EC 7th Framework project EEXCESS (grant 600601). The Know-Center is funded within the Austrian COMET Program - Competence Centers for Excellent Technologies - of the Austrian Federal Ministry of Transport, Innovation and Technology, the Austrian Federal Ministry of Economy, Family and Youth and by the State of Styria. COMET is managed by the Austrian Research Promotion Agency (FFG).

REFERENCES

1. Keith Andrews, Wolfgang Kienreich, Vedran Sabol, Jutta Becker, Georg Droschl, Frank Kappe, Michael Granitzer, Peter Auer, and Klaus Tochtermann. 2002. The InfoSky visual explorer: exploiting hierarchical structure and document similarities. *Information Visualization* 1, 3-4 (2002), 166–181. DOI: http://dx.doi.org/10.1057/palgrave.ivs.9500023
2. David M Blei and John D Lafferty. 2009. Topic Models. *Text Mining: Classification, Clustering, and Applications* (2009), 71–89. DOI: http://dx.doi.org/10.1145/1143844.1143859
3. Eric Brill. 1992. A Simple Rule-based Part of Speech Tagger. In *Proceedings of the Workshop on Speech and Natural Language (HLT '91)*. 112–116. DOI: http://dx.doi.org/10.3115/1075527.1075553
4. John Brooke. 1996. SUS - A quick and dirty usability scale. *Usability evaluation in industry* 189, 194 (1996), 4–7. DOI: http://dx.doi.org/10.1002/hbm.20701
5. Douglass R Cutting, David R Karger, Jan O Pedersen, and John W Tukey. 1992. Scatter / Gather : Browsing A Cluster-based Large Document Approach Collections to Scatter / Gather. *Sigir'92* (1992), 318–329. DOI: http://dx.doi.org/10.1145/133160.133214
6. Cecilia di Sciascio, Vedran Sabol, and Eduardo E Veas. 2015. uRank: Exploring Document Recommendations through an Interactive User-Driven Approach. In *Proceedings of the Joint Workshop on Interfaces and Human Decision Making for Recommender Systems, IntRS 2015, co-located with ACM Conference on Recommender Systems (RecSys 2015)*, Vol. 1438. 29–36. http://ceur-ws.org/Vol-1438/paper5.pdf
7. Debasis Ganguly, Johannes Leveling, and Gareth J F Jones. 2013. TopicVis : A GUI for Topic-based Feedback and Navigation. In *Proceedings of the 36th international ACM SIGIR conference on Research and development in information retrieval - SIGIR '13*. 1103–1104. DOI: http://dx.doi.org/10.1145/2484028.2484202
8. Erick Gomez-Nieto, Frizzi San Roman, Paulo Pagliosa, Wallace Casaca, Elias S Helou, Maria Cristina F de Oliveira, and Luis Gustavo Nonato. 2014. Similarity preserving snippet-based visualization of web search results. *IEEE transactions on visualization and computer graphics* 20, 3 (March 2014), 457–70. DOI: http://dx.doi.org/10.1109/TVCG.2013.242
9. Samuel Gratzl, Alexander Lex, Nils Gehlenborg, Hanspeter Pfister, and Marc Streit. 2013. LineUp: visual analysis of multi-attribute rankings. *IEEE transactions on visualization and computer graphics* 19, 12 (Dec. 2013), 2277–86. DOI: http://dx.doi.org/10.1109/TVCG.2013.173
10. Brynjar Gretarsson, John O'Donovan, Svetlin Bostandjiev, Tobias Höllerer, Arthur Asuncion, David Newman, and Padhraic Smyth. 2012. TopicNets: Visual Analysis of Large Text Corpora with Topic Modeling. *ACM Trans. Intell. Syst. Technol.* 3, 2, Article 23 (Feb. 2012), 26 pages. DOI: http://dx.doi.org/10.1145/2089094.2089099
11. Mark Harrower and Cynthia A. Brewer. 2003. ColorBrewer.org: An Online Tool for Selecting Colour Schemes for Maps. *The Cartographic Journal* 40, 1 (June 2003), 27–37. DOI: http://dx.doi.org/10.1179/000870403235002042
12. M Hearst. 2011. User interfaces for search. *Modern Information Retrieval* (2011). http://people.ischool.berkeley.edu/~hearst/papers/mir_revision.pdf
13. Marti A. Hearst. 1995. TileBars: Visualization of Term Distribution Information in Full Text Information Access. In *Proceedings of the SIGCHI conference on Human factors in computing systems - CHI '95*. ACM Press, 59–66.
14. Jeffrey Heer and George Robertson. 2007. Animated transitions in statistical data graphics. *IEEE transactions on visualization and computer graphics* 13, 6 (2007), 1240–7. DOI: http://dx.doi.org/10.1109/TVCG.2007.70539
15. Orland Hoeber and Xue Dong Yang. 2006. The Visual Exploration of Web Search Results Using HotMap. In *10th International Conference on Information Visualisation, IV 2006*. 157–165. DOI: http://dx.doi.org/10.1109/IV.2006.108
16. Yuening Hu, Jordan Boyd-Graber, Brianna Satinoff, and Alison Smith. 2014. Interactive topic modeling. *Machine Learning* 95, 3 (2014), 423–469. DOI: http://dx.doi.org/10.1007/s10994-013-5413-0
17. Antti Kangasrääsiö, Dorota Glowacka, and Samuel Kaski. 2015. Improving Controllability and Predictability of Interactive Recommendation Interfaces for Exploratory Search. In *IUI*. 247–251. DOI: http://dx.doi.org/10.1145/2678025.2701371
18. Judy Kay. 2006. Scrutable adaptation: Because we can and must. In *Lecture Notes in Computer Science (including subseries Lecture Notes in Artificial Intelligence and Lecture Notes in Bioinformatics)*, Vol. 4018 LNCS. 11–19. DOI: http://dx.doi.org/10.1007/11768012_2
19. Bart P. Knijnenburg, Svetlin Bostandjiev, John O'Donovan, and Alfred Kobsa. 2012. Inspectability and control in social recommenders. *Proceedings of the 6th ACM conference on Recommender systems - RecSys '12* (2012), 43. DOI: http://dx.doi.org/10.1145/2365952.2365966
20. M. Krishnan, S. Bohn, W. Cowley, V. Crow, and J. Nieplocha. 2007. Scalable Visual Analytics of Massive Textual Datasets. In *2007 IEEE International Parallel and Distributed Processing Symposium*. IEEE, 1–10. DOI: http://dx.doi.org/10.1109/IPDPS.2007.370232

21. James R. Lewis and Jeff Sauro. 2009. The factor structure of the system usability scale. *Lecture Notes in Computer Science (including subseries Lecture Notes in Artificial Intelligence and Lecture Notes in Bioinformatics)* 5619 LNCS (2009), 94–103. DOI: http://dx.doi.org/10.1007/978-3-642-02806-9_12

22. Christopher D. Manning. 2008. *Introduction to Information Retrieval.* Cambridge University Press.

23. Gary Marchionini. 2006. Exploratory search: from finding to understanding. *Commun. ACM* 49, 4 (2006), 41. DOI: http://dx.doi.org/10.1145/1121949.1121979

24. Tien N Nguyen and Jin Zhang. 2006. A novel visualization model for web search results. *IEEE transactions on visualization and computer graphics* 12, 5 (2006), 981–8. DOI: http://dx.doi.org/10.1109/TVCG.2006.111

25. John O'Donovan, Barry Smyth, Brynjar Gretarsson, Svetlin Bostandjiev, and Tobias Höllerer. 2008. PeerChooser: Visual Interactive Recommendation. *Proceeding of the twenty-sixth annual SIGCHI conference on Human factors in computing systems* (2008), 1085–1088. DOI: http://dx.doi.org/10.1145/1357054.1357222

26. Denis Parra, Peter Brusilovsky, and Christoph Trattner. 2014. See what you want to see: Visual User-Driven Approach for Hybrid Recommendation. *Proceedings of the 19th international conference on Intelligent User Interfaces - IUI '14* (2014), 235–240. DOI: http://dx.doi.org/10.1145/2557500.2557542

27. M.F. Porter. 1980. An algorithm for suffix stripping. *Program: electronic library and information systems* 40, 3 (1980), 211–218. DOI: http://dx.doi.org/10.1108/00330330610681286

28. Ramana Rao and Stuart K Card. 1994. The table lens. In *Proceedings of the SIGCHI conference on Human factors in computing systems celebrating interdependence - CHI '94*. ACM Press, New York, New York, USA, 318–322.

29. Manuela Rauch, Werner Klieber, Ralph Wozelka, Santokh Singh, and Vedran Sabol. 2015. Knowminer Search - a Multi-Visualisation Collaborative Approach to Search Result Analysis. In *Information Visualisation (iV), 2015 19th International Conference on*. 379 – 385. DOI: http://dx.doi.org/10.1109/iV.2015.72

30. Harald Reiterer, Gabriela Tullius, and TM Mann. 2005. Insyder: a content-based visual-information-seeking system for the web. *International Journal on Digital Libraries* (2005), 25–41. http://link.springer.com/article/10.1007/s00799-004-0111-y

31. Francesco Ricci, Lior Rokach, and Bracha Shapira. 2011. Introduction to Recommender Systems Handbook. In *Recommender Systems Handbook*, Francesco Ricci, Lior Rokach, Bracha Shapira, and Paul B. Kantor (Eds.). Springer, 1–35.

32. Jeff Sauro and James R. Lewis. 2012. *Quantifying the User Experience.* Morgan Kaufmann.

33. Christin Seifert, Johannes Jurgovsky, and Michael Granitzer. 2014. FacetScape : A Visualization for Exploring the Search Space. In *Proceedings 18th International Conference on Information Visualzation.* 94–101. DOI: http://dx.doi.org/10.1109/IV.2014.49

34. Christin Seifert, Barbara Kump, Wolfgang Kienreich, Gisela Granitzer, and Michael Granitzer. 2008. On the Beauty and Usability of Tag Clouds. *2008 12th International Conference Information Visualisation* (July 2008), 17–25. DOI: http://dx.doi.org/10.1109/IV.2008.89

35. Guy Shani and N Tractinsky. 2013. Displaying relevance scores for search results. *Proceedings of the 36th international ACM SIGIRâĂŹ13* (2013), 901–904. http://dl.acm.org/citation.cfm?id=2484112

36. Anselm Spoerri. 2004. Coordinated Views and Tight Coupling to Support Meta Searching. In *Proceedings of Second International Conference on Coordinated and Multiple Views in Exploratory Visualization.* 39–48. DOI: http://dx.doi.org/10.1109/CMV.2004.5

37. Marc Streit and Nils Gehlenborg. 2014. Bar charts and box plots. *Nature methods* 11, 2 (Feb. 2014), 117. http://www.ncbi.nlm.nih.gov/pubmed/24645191

38. K. Swearingen and R. Sinha. 2001. Beyond Algorithms Beyond Algorithms: An HCI Perspective on Recommender Systems. *ACM SIGIR 2001 Workshop on Recommender Systems (2001)* (2001), 1–11. DOI: http://dx.doi.org/10.1.1.23.9764

39. Nava Tintarev and Judith Masthoff. 2012. Evaluating the Effectiveness of Explanations for Recommender Systems. *User Modeling and User-Adapted Interaction* 22, 4-5 (Oct. 2012), 399–439. DOI: http://dx.doi.org/10.1007/s11257-011-9117-5

40. Katrien Verbert, Denis Parra, Peter Brusilovsky, and Erik Duval. 2013. Visualizing recommendations to support exploration, transparency and controllability. *Proceedings of the 2013 international conference on Intelligent user interfaces - IUI '13* (2013), 351. DOI: http://dx.doi.org/10.1145/2449396.2449442

41. Michelle Q. Wang Baldonado, Allison Woodruff, and Allan Kuchinsky. 2000. Guidelines for using multiple views in information visualization. *Proceedings of the working conference on Advanced visual interfaces (AVI)* (2000), 110–119.

42. Matthew O Ward, Georges Grinstein, and Daniel A Keim. 2010. *Interactive Data Visualization: Foundations, Techniques, and Application.* A. K. Peters, Ltd.

43. C Ware. 2013. *Information visualization: perception for design* (3rd ed.). Elsevier.

44. Ka-Ping Yee, Kirsten Swearingen, Kevin Li, and Marti Hearst. 2003. Faceted metadata for image search and browsing. *Proceedings of the conference on Human factors in computing systems - CHI '03* (2003), 401–408. DOI: http://dx.doi.org/10.1145/642679.642681

Supporting Multitasking in Video Conferencing using Gaze Tracking and On-Screen Activity Detection

Daniel Avrahami[1], Eveline van Everdingen[2], Jennifer Marlow[1]

[1] FXPAL
Palo Alto, CA 94304 USA
{daniel, marlow}@fxpal.com

[2] Vrije Universiteit Amsterdam
1081 HV Amsterdam, The Netherlands
e.a2.van.everdingen@student.vu.nl

ABSTRACT

The use of videoconferencing in the workplace has been steadily growing. While multitasking during video conferencing is often necessary, it is also viewed as impolite and sometimes unacceptable. One potential contributor to negative attitudes towards such multitasking is the disrupted sense of eye contact that occurs when an individual shifts their gaze away to another screen, for example, in a dual-monitor setup, common in office settings. We present an approach to improve a sense of eye contact over videoconferencing in dual-monitor setups. Our approach uses computer vision and desktop activity detection to dynamically choose the camera with the best view of a user's face. We describe two alternative implementations of our solution (RGB-only, and a combination of RGB and RGB-D cameras). We then describe results from an online experiment that shows the potential of our approach to significantly improve perceptions of a person's politeness and engagement in the meeting.

Author Keywords

Video conferencing; multitasking; gaze tracking; head-pose; intelligent camera switching.

ACM Classification Keywords

H.5.m. Information interfaces and presentation (e.g., HCI): Miscellaneous.

INTRODUCTION

The use of videoconferencing in the workplace has grown significantly over the last decade. This includes the use of dedicated systems, often in dedicated rooms (*c.f.,* [2]) and video conferencing from a personal computer (a desktop or a laptop). Prior work has shown that videoconferencing can be advantageous over audio-only communication ([3, 4]). One challenge for using videoconferencing in the workplace is that participants often need (or want) to engage with other tasks. However, multitasking during videoconferencing is typically regarded as rude or inappropriate. As a result, the need and desire to multitask often leads workers to opt for using an audio-only link, forgoing the benefits of videoconferencing. Since multitasking activities are often related to the meeting itself (for example, looking at a shared document or searching for relevant material), we argue that mitigating the negative perceptions of multitasking in videoconferencing could be beneficial to all parties in the conversation.

In a recent study, Marlow *et al.* [7] found that multitasking during videoconferencing was rated as significantly more polite and acceptable when it took place on the same screen as the videoconferencing than when it took place on a second monitor or on a phone. One explanation for this difference, proposed in [7], is that the ability to see the remote person's eyes, even when they were multitasking, made them appear more engaged. The importance of, and sensitivity to gaze in both face-to-face and video conferencing interaction has been demonstrated many times (*c.f.,* [12]). However, with the price of display technologies dropping, dual-monitor setups are becoming common. Thus, videoconferencing (and multitasking) in such setups needs to be supported.

To improve the communication between participants during videoconferencing, we present a solution that utilizes different cameras for each display. Our solution intelligently switches between the two cameras, based on a combination of head-pose tracking and on-screen events monitoring, in order to provide remote participants with the best head-on view of the user. We describe two implementations: one that relies on two standard RGB cameras, and one that uses one standard RGB camera and one depth camera (RGB-D). Using a controlled online study, we demonstrate the viability of our approach for improving impressions of engagement, politeness, and acceptability of multitasking behavior.

RELATED WORK

Prior work has looked at different methods to infer gaze behavior and adapt information presentation accordingly, both virtually and in collocated settings. Past work has used Kinect-based systems to suggest the best viewpoints from different cameras and angles while continuously displaying a target object on the screen [11] or to identify speakers and camera angles for a group of people having a face-to-face meeting [9, 10].

One impact that multitasking can have on video communication is that it potentially affects gaze. People are

IUI'16, March 07 - 10, 2016, Sonoma, CA, USA

ACM 978-1-4503-4137-0/16/03...$15.00
DOI: http://dx.doi.org/10.1145/2856767.2856801

Figure 1. Looking at the primary monitor (left), looking at secondary monitor without camera switching (center), and looking at the secondary monitor with camera switching (right). While the background behind the user changes, the ability to get a head-on view of the face results in significantly higher ratings of politeness and engagement in the videoconference.

fairly accurate at detecting when eye contact/gaze is being directed at them, and this feeling of direct eye contact can build trust [1]. Prior work pertaining to video conferencing has addressed the role of correcting for gaze direction of a single person. The GAZE-2 system, for example, used multiple webcams on a single screen [12]. Other systems used a single camera and synthetically corrected a remote person's gaze (e.g. [5, 6]). Additional work on inferring engagement in conversation with a conversational agent also incorporated gaze detection mechanisms [8].

However, using video conferencing while interacting with two monitors is also a common scenario in distributed collaboration contexts [7]. In those cases, the range of possible head poses is often too great for synthetic gaze correction. Our emphasis is on following a user's gaze across different monitors and cameras rather than adjusting a single, relatively static eye-gaze view. Additionally, our solution uses information about the user's interaction with the computer. This allows increased reliability when reliance on computer-vision is insufficient.

IMPLEMENTATION

To improve video-conferencing experience in a dual-monitor setting, we implemented a solution that uses head-pose tracking and on-screen activity recognition for automatic camera selection. We make the assumption that each monitor already is, or can be cheaply, fitted with its own webcam. One important aspect of our solution is that while it aims to support multitasking it intentionally does not hide it (the background changes behind the user when the camera view changes, making multitasking clear).

The solution operation is illustrated in Figure 2. The On-Screen Activity Monitor continuously listens for mouse, keyboard and focus-change events. When started, the *Current Camera* is the camera of the primary monitor. On every iteration (typically every frame), the head-pose tracking module determines which monitor the user is looking towards (as illustrated in Figures 1 and 3). Possible return values are: Looking at the same monitor as the current camera (no need to switch), looking at the other monitor (recommend a switch), looking at neither monitors (no need to switch), and uncertain (*low confidence*).

If the result from the head-pose tracking module cannot determine which of the two monitors the user is looking at, the solution examines the location of the latest events recorded by the On-Screen Activity Monitor. Return values can be: the same monitor as the current camera (no need to switch) or the other monitor (recommend a switch).

Based on the return value, the solution will either attempt to switch to the other camera and set it as the Current Camera (see *Transition Smoothing* below), or stay with the same camera. Video from the current camera is then passed for transmission over the network to the remote videoconferencing participant.

Head-Pose Tracking Module

We created two alternative implementation of the head-tracking module that we describe next.

RGB-Only Solution

Our first implementation relies on two RGB cameras, one for each monitor. In this first implementation, face-detection on frames from each camera is performed using a Haar-Cascade classifier. If a face is detected in only one of the cameras, we assume that the user is looking towards that camera's monitor. If no faces are detected by either camera (or if faces of multiple people are detected), the module does not recommend switching. However, if a face is detected in both cameras, we estimate the head-pose in each camera using Haar-Cascade classifiers trained on facial features (specifically, eyes and noses). We use the geometric relationship between detected eyes and nose within the face's bounds to estimate which camera has a view that is closest to a head-on view of the face. If no clear winner is determined, the module marks its result as *low confidence*. The benefit of this solution is that it is cheaper and many existing monitors now come with a webcam built in.

RGB-D + RGB Solution

Our second implementation performs head-pose tracking using a single RGB-D camera, and only uses the second RGB camera to be able to send two views of the user to the videoconferencing application. The benefit of this solution is that it is more accurate and, thanks to using depth information, less susceptible to issues of illumination or problems with recognizing faces with glasses. We implemented this version in C# using the Intel RealSense F200 depth camera.

To use this solution, the system must first be calibrated; calibration allows the system to establish the geometric relationship between head position and orientation and the different monitors. In the calibration stage, the user is asked to look at, and click on circular targets shown at the corners of each monitor. The system records the head-position in 3D space and Eular angles of the head for each target. These are then used at runtime to estimate the user's gaze direction relative to each monitor. For example, for each monitor we compute a horizontal offset based on the head's distance from the camera, horizontal distance from the camera's center, and the yaw value as follows:

$$H_{Monitor} = X_{Head} + Z_{Head} \times \tan(Yaw_{Head})$$

The values are normalized such that a value of 0.0 corresponds to looking at the left edge of a monitor and 1.0 to looking at the right edge of the monitor. A negative value indicates that the user's gaze is to the left of the monitor, a value greater than 1 indicates that the user's gaze is to the right of the monitor. When calculated for both monitors, it is possible that the value for *both monitors* will be within the 0-1 range (or close to it), for example, when the user is looking towards an area close to both screens (see Figure 3c). In those cases, the module marks its result as *low confidence* and the system will rely on the On-Screen Activity Monitor.

Transition Smoothing

One issue that we discovered quickly is that frequent head movements or noise in the vision system can result in the video constantly switching between cameras, leading to poor user experience. We thus introduced a two-stage smoothing mechanism when deciding whether to switch between cameras. First, we only switch to a camera if the user looked towards its monitor for longer than a preset threshold (in our case, 750 milliseconds). Second, we do not switch away from a camera if it was recently switched to; in other words, we remain on a camera for at least a preset threshold (in this case, 1 second). While these thresholds can be adjusted, we found the introduction of this smoothing mechanism to greatly improve the usability of our solution.

One area for exploration in future work is to use knowledge about the application interacted with to predict the duration of the interaction. For example, an instant message window combined with keyboard events might suggest a longer gaze than, say, the appearance of an incoming-email notification.

EVALUATION

To test whether our approach is able to improve perceptions of a videoconference participant's behavior, we conducted a

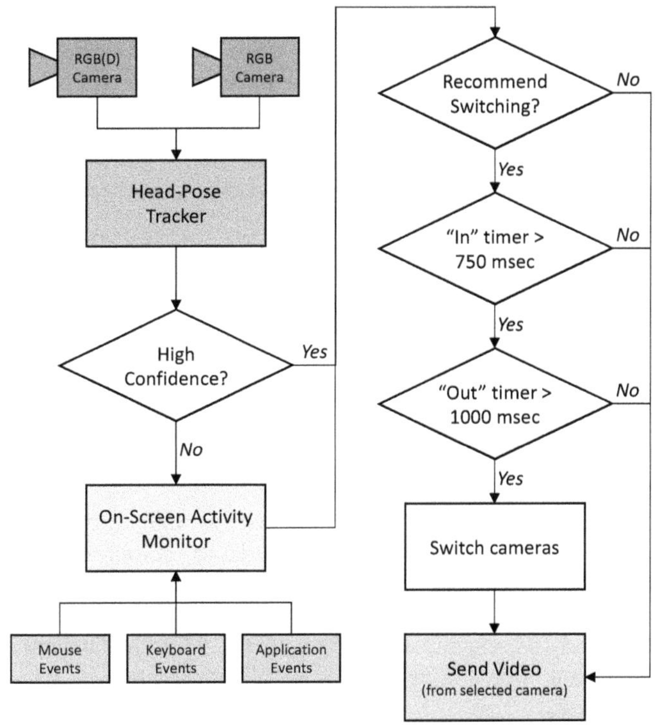

Figure 2. Decision flow of our system. Our system chooses a view of the user to send to remote participants based on head-pose tracking and on-screen activity monitoring.

between-subjects online experiment following the paradigm from Marlow *et al.* [7]. In the study, participants watched one of two 1-minute clips of a videoconference meeting between two people (Person A and Person B) and then answered a series of questions about what they saw and heard. Instructions read, "*On the next page is a clip from a recorded videoconference business meeting between two coworkers, Person A and Person B, where they discussed an advertising campaign. You are asked to watch the video and answer a few questions about what you saw and heard.*"

In the clips, Person A describes three potential locations for an advertising campaign. Person B, who has a dual-monitor setup, listens, occasionally responding with short utterances such as "uh-huh." During the conversation, Person B shifts her gaze between her two monitors (from the primary to the secondary monitor and then back).

The study was a between-subjects design in which participants were randomly assigned to one of two

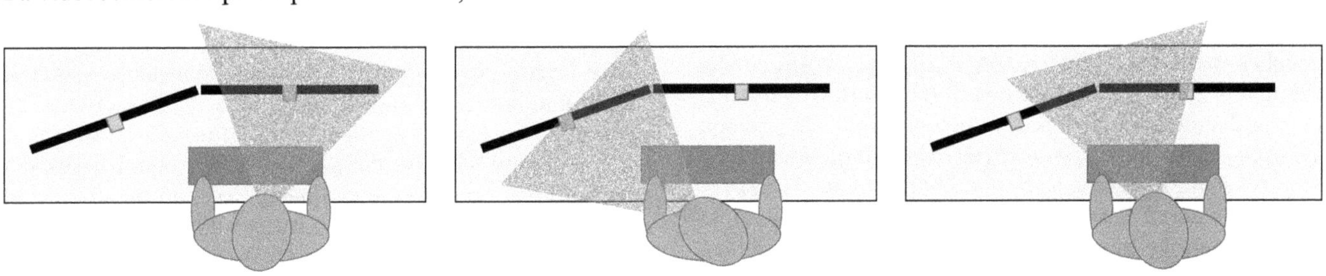

Figure 3. Looking twards monitor 1 (left), towards monitor 2 (middle) and towards the left edge of monitor 1 (right). In the last case, the head-pose tracker has low confidence, and the system relies instead on on-screen activity monitoring.

conditions: the *Dynamic View* condition, in which the view changed between the two cameras when Person B shifted her gaze to the secondary monitor, and the *Static View* condition, in which only the view from a single camera was used.

The study was conducted on the Crowdflower crowdsourcing platform. U.S.-based participants received 40 cents for their participation.

Measures

After watching the video clip, participants were asked to rate a series of statements on a 5-point Likert scale (with 1=completely disagree and 5=completely agree). These statements pertained to the Politeness, Acceptability, and Obviousness of the multitasking by Person B, and rating of Person B's engagement in the meeting.

Participants

138 unique individuals participated in the study. We excluded 32 participants who failed a comprehension question about the video and two participants whose completion time was outside the norm. Our final dataset included 104 respondents (55% women), 53 in the Dynamic View condition and 51 in the Static View condition.

RESULTS

We conducted an ANOVA with Condition (*Dynamic View* vs. *Static View*) as the independent variable and the align-ranked ratings [13] of Politeness, Acceptability of Person B's multitasking, and ratings of Person B's engagement in the meeting. We included Gender and Age as covariates.

The analysis shows that while multitasking was equally obvious to participants in both conditions (M=3.62 for Dynamic vs. M=3.73 for Static, $F(1,102)=.03$, $p=.84$), our camera-switching approach resulted in a significant improvement in ratings of perceived politeness, and acceptability of the multitasking, and higher ratings of engagement in the meeting. As shown in Figure 4, Person B's behavior in the Dynamic View condition was rated as significantly more Polite (M=3.86) than it was in the Static View condition (M=3.25) ($F(1,102)=9.78$, $p<.01$). Person B's behavior was also rated as significantly more Acceptable in the Dynamic View condition (M=3.75) than the Static View condition (M=3.23) ($F(1,102)=6.63$, $p=.01$) and Person B was seen as significantly more Engaged in the Meeting in the Dynamic View condition (M=3.56) than the Static View condition (M=3.07) ($F(1,102)=5.99$, $p<.02$).

We found supporting evidence looking at participants' open-ended responses to the question "Please describe in a few sentences what you saw person B doing." While many participants in the Static View condition described Person B as being distracted, unfocused, or preoccupied (e.g., *Person B was not paying attention to the person talking*), none of the responses in the Dynamic View condition contained negative assessments about Person B's behavior. Additionally, eight participants in the Static View condition referred to Person B's gaze direction, e.g. "*Listening to Person A and then looking off screen*" or "*looking off into another area.*" In

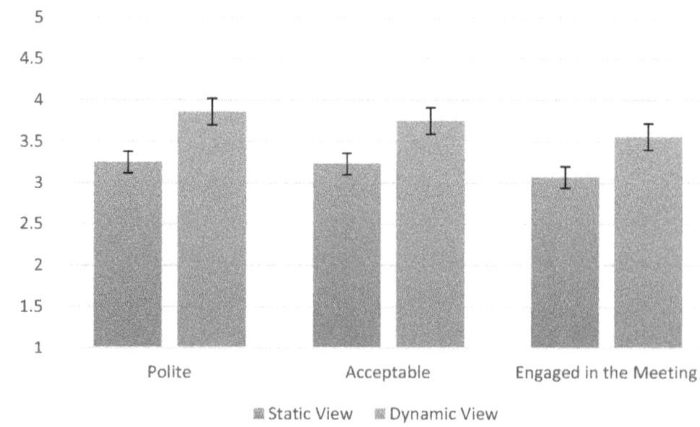

Figure 4. The effect of our system on ratings of Politeness, Acceptability, and Engagement in the Meeting.

contrast, 10 participants in the Dynamic View condition who referred to Person B changing her gaze were focused on the screens and camera angles (e.g., "*switching between two different monitors/screen angles*" and "*Person B was listening, and then looked into a different monitor before switching back*"). This suggests a better comprehension of the multitasking happening on a dual-monitor setup.

DISCUSSION AND FUTURE WORK

In this work, we presented a video-conferencing approach designed for a dual-monitor setup, common in office environments, equipped with dual cameras. Our solution intelligently switches between the two cameras, based on a combination of head-pose tracking and on-screen events monitoring, in order to provide remote participants with the best head-on view of the user.

We evaluated our approach using an online experiment that shows that dynamically switching cameras during multitasking results in significantly higher ratings of perceived politeness, acceptability, and engagement in the meeting. Our solution does not hide the fact that multitasking is taking place – a user is seen turning away for a brief moment before the camera view switches, and the background behind the user changes. Our results thus improve perceptions of behavior, without obscuring it. One limitation of our experiment is that participants were placed in the role of non-participating meeting observer watching two strangers converse. It is important to note that, particularly in multi-person videoconferencing meetings, being a passive observer in a meeting is not uncommon.

In future work, we intend to examine the use of this approach across devices, such as switching between the cameras of a laptop and smartphone. Another area for future exploration is for improving the camera-switching decision process with additional semantic knowledge of the user's activity. For example, the type of application that the user is looking at, or interacting with on the second screen could be used to predict how long the interaction is likely to be, and decide whether to transition to the corresponding camera. Finally, detecting off-screen activities such as writing or sketching on a whiteboard and providing a best view is an interesting area for future work.

REFERENCES

1. Ernst Bekkering and J.P. Shim. 2006. Trust in Videoconferencing. *Communications of the ACM* 49, 7: 103–107.
2. Cisco Project Workplace: http://www.cisco.com/c/dam/assets/sol/tp/project-workplace
3. Owen Daly-Jones, Andrew Monk, and Leon Watts. 1998. Some advantages of video conferencing over high-quality audio conferencing: fluency and awareness of attentional focus. *International Journal of Human-Computer Studies* 49, 1: 21–58.
4. Wei Dong and Wai-Tat Fu. 2012. One piece at a time: why video-based communication is better for negotiation and conflict resolution. *Proceedings of the ACM 2012 conference on Computer Supported Cooperative Work*, ACM, 167–176.
5. Jim Gemmell, Kentaro Toyama, C. Lawrence Zitnick, Thomas Kang, and Steven Seitz. 2000. Gaze awareness for video-conferencing: A software approach. *IEEE Multimedia* 7, 4: 26–35.
6. Dominik Giger, Jean-Charles Bazin, Claudia Kuster, Tiberiu Popa, and Markus Gross. 2014. Gaze correction with a single webcam. *Multimedia and Expo (ICME), 2014 IEEE International Conference on*, IEEE, 1–6.
7. Jennifer Marlow, Eveline van Everdingen, and Daniel Avrahami. Taking Notes or Playing Games? Understanding Multitasking in Video Communication. *Proceedings of CSCW 2016*, ACM, to appear.
8. Yukiko I. Nakano and Ryo Ishii. 2010. Estimating user's engagement from eye-gaze behaviors in human-agent conversations. *Proceedings of the 15th international conference on Intelligent User Interfaces*, ACM, 139–148.
9. Abhishek Ranjan, Rorik Henrikson, Jeremy Birnholtz, Ravin Balakrishnan, and Dana Lee. 2010. Automatic camera control using unobtrusive vision and audio tracking. *Proceedings of Graphics Interface 2010*, Canadian Information Processing Society, 47-54.
10. Gianluca Schiavo, Alessandro Cappelletti, Eleonora Mencarini, Oliviero Stock, and Massimo Zancanaro. 2014. Overt or Subtle? Supporting Group Conversations with Automatically Targeted Directives. *Proceedings of the 19th International Conference on Intelligent User Interfaces,* ACM, 225-234.
11. Fumiharu Tomiyasu and Kenji Mase. 2015. Human-Machine Cooperative Viewing System for Wide-angle Multi-view Videos. *Proceedings of the 20th International Conference on Intelligent User Interfaces Companion,* ACM, 85-88.
12. Roel Vertegaal, Ivo Weevers, Changuk Sohn, and Chris Cheung. 2003. GAZE-2: conveying eye contact in group video conferencing using eye-controlled camera direction. *Proceedings of the SIGCHI conference on Human factors in computing systems*, ACM, 521–528.
13. Jacob O. Wobbrock, Leah Findlater, Darren Gergle, and James J. Higgins. 2011. The aligned rank transform for nonparametric factorial analyses using only anova procedures. *Proceedings of the SIGCHI Conference on Human Factors in Computing Systems*, ACM, 143–146.

Closing the Cognitive Gap between Humans and Interactive Narrative Agents Using Shared Mental Models

Rania Hodhod
Columbus State University
4225 University Avenue, Columbus, GA
hodhod_rania@columbusstate.edu

Brian Magerko
Georgia Institute of Technology
North Ave NW, Atlanta, GA
magerko@gatech.edu

ABSTRACT
This paper proposes a new formal approach for negotiating shared mental models between humans and computational improvisational agents (improv agents) based on our sociocognitive studies of human improvisers. Negotiation of shared mental models serves as a core mechanism for improv agents to co-create stories with each other and with human interactors. The model aims to narrow the gap between human and machine intelligence by providing AI agents that, in the presence of incomplete knowledge about an improv scene, can use procedural representations not only to understand human parties but also to negotiate their mental models with them. The described approach allows flexible modeling of ambiguous, non-Boolean knowledge through the use of fuzzy logic and situation calculus that allows reasoning under uncertainty in a dynamic improvisational setting.

Author Keywords
Computational creativity; cognitive consensus; fuzzy logic; improvisational agents; shared mental models.

ACM Classification Keywords
H.5.2 **[User Interfaces]**: Interaction Style; I.2.11 **[Distributed Artificial Intelligence]**: Intelligent Agents; I.2.3 **[Deduction and Theorem proving]**: Uncertainty, Fuzzy and belief revision.

INTRODUCTION
Interactive narrative research has heavily focused on systems that either provide a) a centralized drama manager agent that mediates a user's narrative experience through the behavior of weakly autonomous agents [1] or b) strongly autonomous systems that represent a story as the interaction of agents pursuing their goals [2–4]. Both of these approaches view interactive narrative systems as an embodiment of authorial intentions; story content is created by an author that is then exposed to the user, depending on the user's interactions/choices with the system. User contributions to the story do not actively create story elements in as much as move the experience in a particular direction within a pre-authored story space. This model puts the computer in a privileged position in the user/machine relationship. Whether story elements are represented as beats [5], plot points [6], [7], planning operators [2], or some other instantial content, contemporary interactive narrative systems privilege the computer over the human interactor as a creative entity in the narrative experience. These systems do not view interactive narrative as a co-creative experience-where each participant has an active role in the creation of story content- which is seen in such real life experiences as improvisational theatre or children playing pretend.

Improvisational theatre is a creative group performance where actors co-construct stories on stage in real time. There is typically no centralized story creator, but rather two or more improvisers who are perpetually negotiating elements of the scene in real time. First, improvisers attempt to define the *platform* of a scene as the introduction (e.g. scene location, characters, the activity they are engaged in, etc.) [8]. Then typically moves towards finding the *tilt* of the scene (i.e. the main conflict or problem to solve in the scene) [9]. Finally, a resolution to the tilt is then attempted, thus ending the scene.

Despite the fact that this general process of defining scene elements is all done as part of the performance on stage, the emergent narrative can still be represented as a plot, like any other play. However, improvisers do not go behind stage and agree on scene elements, nor does the moderator of the scene typically provide explicit scene elements to them[1]. Rather, the elements of a scene are

IUI'16, March 07-10, 2016, Sonoma, CA, USA
© 2016 ACM ISBN 978-1-4503-4137-0/16/03…$15.00
DOI: http://dx.doi.org/10.1145/2856767.2856774

[1] The amount of detail given to performers can vary wildly from troupe to troupe. Some troupes practice giving the entire platform,

perpetually negotiated as part of a performance (what Sawyer calls *collaborative emergence* [12]). Improvisers are continuously adding elements to the scene that have a degree of ambiguity to them (e.g. intending to communicate that one is a pirate by petting a parrot on their shoulder, which could also communicate that one is a zookeeper without any other context provided) or that may be rejected by the other improvisers for a variety of reasons (e.g. it conflicts with their view of the scene, disagrees with it being appropriate material for the audience, etc.). In other words, improvisers continuously negotiate a *shared mental model* (SMM) of what is true in the scene, such as the platform [13]. Our empirical studies of improvisers have shown that this process of building such a model, called *collaborative convergence*, is at the essence of improvised scenes [13] .

Cognitive psychologists provide representations of the mental models that people form when understanding narratives and consequently how humans know, perceive, make decisions, and construct behavior in social situations [14]. A mental model typically contains minimal information (i.e. not every single detail but the main salient points of a phenomenon or experience) described as a set of well-defined, highly organized knowledge [15]. In other words, information is presented with the presumption that minimal processing effort is required [41]. Though, confidence about a particular piece of well-defined knowledge may vary. For example, "cowboys always wear hats" is a simple (Boolean) example of well-defined knowledge. However, people's confidence in this statement might vary from being completely confident (100%) or completely unconfident (0%), which indicates Boolean logic, or perhaps being partially confident in it. For example, being 60% confident about this statement and 40% uncertain is referred to as fuzzy logic. The confidence level in a specific piece of knowledge can act as an indication of the awareness of this knowledge [15].

The concept of mental models is extended to SMMs when it is related to team contexts [16]. SMMs are a hypothetical cognitive construct that incorporates the development of mutual beliefs from the team members' individual mental models until a common mental model is reached by the team members, either explicitly or implicitly. SMMs among team members develop from working and training together on similar tasks [17]. Studies by Yen et al. [17] suggest a close relationship between the existence of a shared mental model and successful team performance; the stronger the shared mental model the better tasks are accomplished. Shared mental models are essential in domains that require co-creation of stories on the fly like improvisation as they enable better communication and mutual understanding between the actors.

The work presented in this paper provides new insights on co-creativity in interactive narrative through supplying the AI agents with the *processes* based in constructing shared mental models that can be used for supporting co-creative interactions with humans, the *knowledge* that those processes operate on, and the application of these processes in the improv theatre domain. Work on computational improvisation has yielded agents that model the cognitive processes central to the human act of theatrical improvisation, but relied on pre-authored narrative structures to construct a story with the user rather than providing the agents with capabilities that allow them to co-create a new story with the user. The paper presents a computational shared mental model that allows improv agents to communicate with each other and with a human actor to reach mutual understanding about the identity of their characters and the nature of their joint activity.

The following section gives an overview of improvisational acting, defining the main cognitive skills involved in this domain and clarifying how human improvisers make use of mind reading [18] and theory of mind [19] to communicate with each other (we are interested in mindreading and theory of mind as they reflect one's ability to understand and interact with others by having some grasp of their mental states and using this understanding to explain and predict their behavior on the basis of these mental states).

IMPROVISATIONAL ACTING

Improvisational acting (improv) is a creative group performance where actors co-construct stories on stage in real time. Performances are constrained by sets of game rules and audience suggestions [13]. Audience suggestions (e.g. "do a scene about plumbers") often provide some semantic priming to help improvisers interpret events, formulate beliefs, and build and repair their mental models.

Improvisers interact through the process of proposing and responding to *offers* (i.e. proposals made by improvisers in a performance to add something to a scene) [13]. Based on an improviser's perception of other improvisers' actions, he builds his hypothesis of his portrayed character, other agents' characters and the activity they are involved in. While making or responding to offers, an improviser is able to model other actors' mental models in the scene, evaluate the outcome of actions, and update goals, which can be referred to as *theory of mind* [19].

Improv actors negotiate their shared mental model solely through presentations to the ongoing scene rather than with explicit communication about the model [20]. Each improviser starts to act and build their individual mental model based on how he or she observes the world that is

as seen in the popular television show, *Whose Line Is It Anyway?* [10], [11].

unfolding on stage. However, improvisers often make presentations that can be perceived or interpreted many different ways [20]. Actors may misinterpret dialogue or misinterpret pantomimed motions. For example, if one actor holds their fists one on top of the other and moves them from side to side, another actor could interpret this as either raking or sweeping, among other possibilities. To handle the ambiguities of these presentations, improv actors' mental models must deal with inexact information.

Improv actors execute motions on stage that are ambiguous. A simple motion like waving a hand can be interpreted multiple ways, including waving to someone, erasing a board, or cleaning a window. These ambiguous presentations and the ease with which improvisers can misinterpret them can cause an individual improviser to develop a mental model that differs from the other improvisers' models. The state where improvisers' mental models differ from each other is called *cognitive divergence*[2]. Through processes of *cognitive convergence*, improvisers repair their divergent mental models to reach a state of *cognitive consensus*, where everyone agrees on the shared mental model [13]. Cognitive consensus can be thought of as the state of "being on the same page."

Improvisers employ different *repair strategies* to deal with divergences as they occur [13]. Repair strategies are either *other-oriented* or *self-oriented*. Other-oriented repair strategies aim to affect someone else's mental model through presenting new concepts (*presentation*) or correcting divergences (*clarification*). Self-oriented repair strategies try to align one improviser's mental model with others' by learning what the other improvisers think is going on. An actor may communicate an idea about what is going on in the scene so that other actors may confirm it (*verification*). Alternatively, the actor may introduce new, vague information to the scene in order to observe how the other improvisers react, hoping that this will reveal some disambiguating information (*blind offer*). Repair strategies help the agents update their mental models and approach cognitive consensus.

RELATED WORK

Virtual improvisational theatre has been the focus of research in digital improv systems. The Computer-Animated Improvisational Theater (CAIT) offered two types of improv agents: Improv Puppets and Improv Actors [21], [22]. Both types of agents could improvise with other agents in real-time under the guidance of human input for how they should act. These agents reason about each other's mental models and can change their own mental model to conform to another's based on observations. However, CAIT cannot allow humans to improvise with these systems as equal co-creators of a narrative because these agents could not create narratives on their own as a result of the absence of the procedural knowledge required for this act. Instead, they worked from pre-authored narrative structures. In the Improv system [23], virtual animated avatars could be scripted to enact a scenario giving the appearance of believable improvisational performances. Neither of these systems, however, applied a deep understanding of how professional actors perform improvisation.

Work on computational improvisational agents has yielded agents that model the cognitive processes central to the human act of theatrical improvisation. One set of agents played the improv game *Party Quirks*, where a human party host tried to discover what characters party guest agents portrayed. The agents needed to develop a shared mental model with the human in order to reach cognitive consensus [20]. However, the agents in *Party Quirks* can only reason about explicit true and false beliefs; they could not reason about information that was partially true [39].

The work described in this paper differs from other work done on joint intentions and shared beliefs, such as STEAM [24], ARITMIS [25], Collagen [26], the STAPLE architecture [27], and work done by Kennedy and Trafton [28]. The common aspect between these architectures is the presence of an explicit representation of team goals, plans and joint commitments, and the use of shared plan theories. Despite the existence of some similarities between STAPLE and our architecture, the main difference appears in the ability of our agents to deal with implicit shared mental models where one agent does not have to explicitly declare its beliefs to other agents. On the other hand, the work done by Kennedy and Trafton on simulation of shared mental models relies on hypothetical declarative knowledge and productions to help the agent to reason about the environment. This can hardly be achieved in a domain like improv because of the absence of pre-authored states that can aid in rule production.

THESPIAN is another system developed by Si et. al [19] that allows the agents to behave based on models of emotions and social normative behaviors in addition to having explicit author-specified plot design goals, but for the agents to decide on an action they are offered bounded look-ahead policy. Since Thespian agents cannot act in the absence of explicit goals and an explicit agreement between the agents and each other, they cannot be used in improvised/co-creative narrative experience.

COMPUTATIONAL SHARED MENTAL MODELS FOR IMPROV AGENTS

The work presented in this paper employs fuzzy logic and situation calculus to provide a mechanism that allows AI agents to reason about uncertain beliefs with degrees of

[2]We currently ignore models built between the actors and the audience, though divergences can exist between them as well.

truth and variable confidence. The fuzzy logic representations we describe here for reasoning, decision making, and shared mental models are integral parts of the **Co**-creative **Co**gnitive **A**rchitecture (CoCoA) (Figure1). The components of CoCoA form the knowledge that improv agents use to understand and contribute to an emergent narrative that they co-create with a human user.

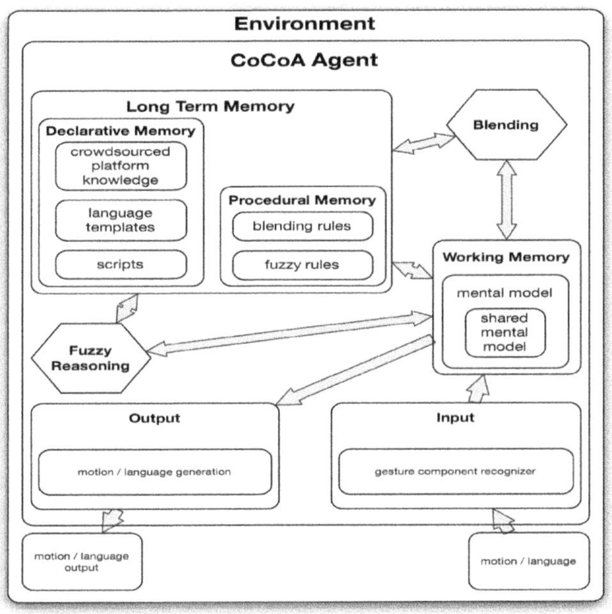

Figure 1. The CoCoA Architecture for Improv Agents

Figure 1 describes the main architecture of this work where the input layer contains a gesture component recognizer (a Microsoft Kinect connected to a specialized gesture code layer), which provides the means to capture a human interactor's posture and gesture. It is worth noting here that the language model has not been completed yet. The Kinect along with the code layer interpret the captured gestures and provides a list of possible actions that can be represented by that posture and gesture. This information is passed to the working memory, which uses fuzzy reasoning (the main focus of this paper) and long term memory knowledge to reason about this information. After the agent decides on his next action based on the knowledge retrieved from the input layer and the fuzzy reasoning module, the decision is passed to the motion/language generation in the output layer, which displays an animated AI agent performing that action as an output.

Human Reasoning and Fuzzy Logic

Human reasoning can be defined as the process of manipulating symbols in order to improve knowledge and make better decisions [22]. One of the strengths of how humans reason about the world is the non-Boolean manner followed when building mental models, which allow them to reason about vague and imprecise knowledge [14]. Mental models not only contain such knowledge but also information about how to use this knowledge. This non-Boolean description of categorical knowledge is informed by contemporary views in cognition and category theory, such as work by Lakoff [30] and Rosch [31]. One way to represent this knowledge is fuzzy logic, which reduces the design complexity of "humanistic" systems, which usually operate in a decision-making environment involving vagueness, imprecision and uncertainty.

In Boolean logic, any concept has only two possible values for its membership in any set: True and False. Fuzzy logic allows the notion of membership in a set to become a matter of degree [32]. In other words, an element x has a degree of membership (DOM) that ranges from 0 to 1 to indicate how much it belongs in a fuzzy set S. A DOM of 0 means x is definitely not a member of S (*false* in Boolean logic). A DOM of 1 means x definitely is a member of S (*true* in Boolean logic). For example, a person of 2 meters high may have a DOM of 0.9 in the set of *tall person* and a DOM of 0.3 in the set of *short person*. Degree of association (DOA) is defined as the degree of membership between two elements in two knowledge categories. In other words, DOAs provide a bidirectional version of degree of membership that indicates how much two elements are associated with each other [23].

Shared Mental Model for Improv Agents

Shared mental models emerge from agents' individual mental models as a perceived shared construct of what everyone knows and thinks. SMMs among team members develop from working and training together on similar tasks [33–35] and from things like team experience and common organizational familiarity.

The aim of our work described in this paper is to design and implement a shared mental model representation for co-creative improvisational agents. The shared mental model is not a shared knowledge construct but rather a socially agreed upon one that resides as two separate models (one in each agent). Yet, cognitive convergence is achieved when the shared mental models coincide as shown in Figure 2.

The main challenge in designing improv agents that can construct shared meaning as part of a performance is to deal with the absence of explicit coordination between agents, either as part of the improvised interactions or behind the scenes. Rather, a shared mental model need be constructed *during* the narrative co-construction/performance.

In an improvised scene, the agents communicate with each other through actions. This form of give-and-take communication helps each agent to understand what the other agents' beliefs might be and consequently allow both mental models to converge to a single model (i.e. shared mental model). Our shared mental model incorporates common individual views of both agents' mental models, see Figure 2. Each individual mental model consists of three components: *beliefs*, *commitments*, and *reasoning and decision-making* modules. The *beliefs component* models the agent's beliefs about itself, other agents and the surrounding world. Those beliefs are associated with confidence factors that show how much the agent thinks his belief is correct. For example, *BEL(agent$_x$, is(agent$_y$, sheriff), medium, 0.513).* This rule states that agent$_x$ has medium confidence in agent$_y$ being a sheriff and this confidence is equal to 0.513.

The *commitments component* encapsulates any obligations (commitments) the agent might have towards other agents. An example of the rules used in this component is COM (agent$_y$, p), which states that agent$_y$ is committed to respond to last action agent$_x$ performed (p). Finally, the *reasoning and decision-making* component provides feedback that notifies the mental model about any inconsistencies that exist (explained later in this paper). For example, the agent might have a certain belief about his partner's character and a new belief about his partner's last action, if the module found that this action cannot be performed by that particular character, an inconsistency flag is raised and the agent has to make a decision on keeping only one of those beliefs based on his confidence in both. Moreover, the reasoning and decision-making component allows the agent to decide on its next move (action) based on his current mental model.

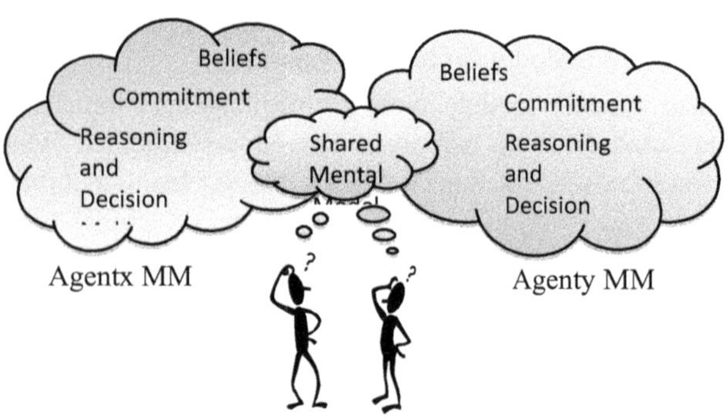

Figure 2. Representation of improv agents' mental models

To formalize the components of a shared mental model computationally, we utilize a hybrid model that incorporates confidence factors, iconicity, probability, and fuzzy logic along with situation calculus. The next sections touch on each of these techniques.

Confidence Factor

In order for an agent to act on a piece of knowledge, the knowledge must exist and the agent must be aware of its existence [36]. AI agents can capture the notion of awareness by unambiguously having an explicit fact that the agent knows specific knowledge. However, these facts will not account for changes in beliefs over time. This can be remedied through the introduction of confidence factors that dynamically change based on changes in the world. Confidence factors are fuzzy values (DOMs on a scale from 0 to 1) that allow an agent to compute the strength of its beliefs in a specific world frame, i.e. at any instant during the scene. For example, in an improvised act, at one instance one improviser can believe his partner is a sheriff with medium confidence and at another instance the same improviser can decrease his confidence in this belief based on their mutual interactions in the scene.

Iconicity Function

A main part of the knowledge that improvisers employ in a scene can be represented by degrees of association between different content and presentation aspects of a scene [37]. Content aspects are part of what improvisers call the *platform*, which includes the scene's location, the characters and their relationship to each other, and the joint activity the characters are participating in [8]. Presentation aspects include the motions improvisers make, the semantic actions these motions represent, and the dialogue improvisers speak. Agents use the DOAs between elements in this knowledge category to interpret presentations from other actors, extrapolate new information about the scene to add to their own mental model, and decide what information to present and how (see Figure 3).

Agents do not always present an element (e.g. a character) in a scene that has the highest DOA to the other elements in its mental model. Rather, an improviser often presents something that is iconic, something that conveys a significant amount of information about the agent's mental model [20]. An element is iconic if it is one of a few elements in a knowledge structure category with its particular DOA to a given element in another category. For example, in the context of an Old West story, only a few characters, like an outlaw, are highly associated with robbing a bank. Therefore, robbing a bank is an iconic activity for an outlaw and, if an actor starts a scene with a bank robbery, they are suggesting very highly that their character is an outlaw. On the other hand, many characters are highly associated with riding horses. Riding a horse is not an iconic activity for an outlaw; it does not provide a lot of information about which character the agent is trying to portray. When an agent makes an iconic presentation, another improviser is less likely to misinterpret the presentation, which reduces cognitive divergences and aids in repairing the shared mental model.

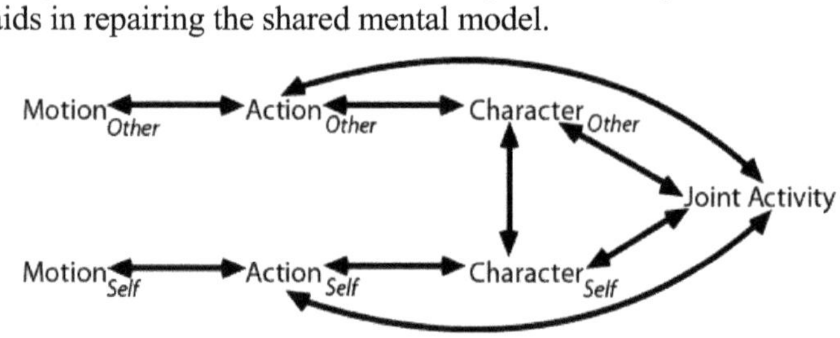

Figure 3. Degree of association (DOA) relationships between knowledge categories

Figure 3 shows the four categories of the knowledge base that exist in the agent's mental model: motions, actions, characters, and joint activities. Those categories are linked via DOAs in a way that allows an agent to infer new knowledge from existing ones. Based on the agent's confidence in his mental model, he decides to either perform an action or extrapolate to new knowledge categories first based on the s DOAs links. For example, if the agent has information about $Action_{other}$ (an action done by the other agent) it can extrapolate to $Character_{other}$ (the other agent's portrayed character) and/or joint activity (the activity the agents are performing together).

Iconicity calculations are similar to those used in [11] for *Party Quirks*. A typical game of *Party Quirks* involves four players: one plays the role of party host, and all others play as party guests. Each party guest is assigned a "quirk" – some special trait for each guest that is public knowledge to everyone except the party host, including the audience. The host player then, within the context of hosting a party, aims to figure out what quirk each guest is portraying through their interactions. A guest typically leaves the scene when the host has successfully guessed their quirk. In *Party Quirks*, iconicity values are computed between two element categories only but these are updated to account for the different element categories of the knowledge structure. To calculate iconicity, we take a pair of elements from two different knowledge structure categories (element $e_1 \in$ category C_1, element $e_2 \in$ category C_2). The iconicity of this pair of elements depends on how far its DOA value is from the average DOA value for pairs of all elements of category C_1 to element e_2 (how easy it is to tell that e_1 is unusual) and how many other elements of C_1 have a similar DOA value (how many possible elements e_1 could be confused with), as shown in Equation 1.

Equation 1: Iconicity of $<e_1 \in C_1, e_2 \in C_2> =$

$1 - [\,(\,1 - |avgDOA(<\forall e \in C_1, e_2 \in C_2>) - DOA<e_1 \in C_1, e_2 \in C_2>|\,)\,] \,/\, (\,(\text{number of } <\forall e \in C_1, e_2 \in C_2> \text{ pairs}) - (\text{number of } <\forall e \in C_1, e_2 \in C_2> \text{ pairs within } 1\,\sigma \text{ of } DOA<e_1 \in C_1, e_2 \in C_2>)\,)$

In other words, the iconicity of a pair of two elements from different categories is [1– (1 – absolute value of (the average of all DOA values for elements of C_1 and element e_2 – DOA between e_1 and e_2)) / (the number of elements in C_1 – the number of elements of C_1 with a DOA to e_2 within one standard deviation of the DOA between e_1 and e_2)]. Iconicity values are all normalized on a scale from 0 to 1.

Probability of Knowledge Selection

An agent can use the iconicity of the elements in its mental model to determine the probability that a given element will be selected from its knowledge category given the current state of its mental model. In other words, despite the fact that it seems reasonable for an agent to present an element with high probabilistic value, this is not always the case because humans do not always do this. Humans can sometime choose to do something that seems reasonable in a specific situational rather than doing another action that seem more probable to be executed in that situational based on the way they perceive the situational (their mental model). On the other side, probabilities for choosing elements in the agent's mental model help it to estimate/measure its confidence that its mental model is correct.

The probability function for mental model elements is given by the following equation:

Equation 2: Probabilistic value of $e_1 \in C_1$ given $e_2 \in C_2$ = (Iconicity of $<e_1 \in C_1, e_2 \in C_2>$ / Σ Iconicity $<\forall\, e_1 \in C_1, e_2 \in C_2>$) That is, the probability that e_1 is the value for C_1 if e_2 is the value for c_2 is (the iconicity of e_1 in $<e_1 \in C_1, e_2 \in C_2>$ / the sum of the iconicities for all elements in C_1 given e_2).

Fuzzy Logic

Fuzzy logic is a valuable tool for dealing with vague knowledge and the approximate nature of human reasoning [30]. It allows reasoning in the presence of linguistic variables that are vague and have no concise definition, such as temperature, probability and confidence using membership functions.

For a linguistic variable X, membership functions on X represent fuzzy subsets of X. The membership function, which represents a fuzzy set A, is usually denoted by μ_A. For an element x of X, the value $\mu_A(x)$ is called the *membership degree* of x in the fuzzy set A. The membership degree $\mu_A(x)$ quantifies the grade of membership of the element x to the fuzzy set A. The value 0 means that x is not a member of the fuzzy set; the value 1 means that x is fully a member of the fuzzy set. The values between 0 and 1 characterize fuzzy members, which belong to the fuzzy set only partially.

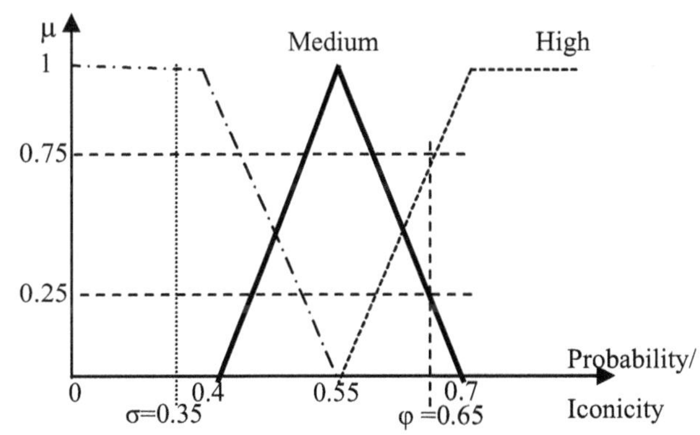

Figure 4. Diagrammatic representation of fuzzy probabilities and iconicity values using trapezoidal and triangular membership functions. The low, medium, and high fuzzy values are used to determine the agent's confidence based on the probability φ and iconicity σ.

For the purpose of this work, we decided to treat iconicity, probability, and confidence factors as fuzzy variables with fuzzy sets low, medium, and high. The aim is to use iconicity and probability input values to compute a confidence value utilizing Triangular and trapezoidal membership functions.

Mapping iconicity (Equation 1) and probabilistic interpretations of likelihood informed by the iconicity function (Equation 2) to a corresponding confidence factor was done through the use of Trapezoidal and Triangular Membership Functions for our fuzzy values (low, medium, and high) (Figure 4). For the membership function of probability, the x-axis represents the inputs of the probabilistic values φ resulted from the iconicity function. The y-axis represents the degree of membership μ of element φ in the fuzzy sets low, medium, and high, where each term x in Probability has a $\mu_{probability}(x)$ characterized by a fuzzy set in a universe of discourse U=[0, 1].

We designed fuzzy rules to evaluate the output confidence factors for iconicity and probability input values. Fuzzy rules can be expressed in "*if... then...*" form. The "*if...*" part is called the *antecedent* and the "*then...*" part is called the *consequent*. Both parts contain linguistic variables defined by fuzzy sets. A linguistic variable can be either a variable whose value is a fuzzy number or values defined in linguistic terms.

Choosing the linguistic values *low*, *medium* and *high* for the iconicity (I), probability (P), and confidence factors (CF) variables, the following fuzzy inference rules were designed:

R_1: IF I is high and P is high THEN CF is high
R_2: IF I is high and P is medium THEN CF is medium
R_3: IF I is high and P is low THEN CF is medium
R_4: IF I is medium and P is high THEN CF is medium
R_5: IF I is medium and P is medium THEN CF is medium
R_6: IF I is medium and P is low THEN CF is low
R_7: IF I is low and P is high THEN CF is medium
R_8: IF I is low and P is medium THEN CF is medium
R_9: IF I is low and P is low THEN CF is low

The designed rules are sufficient to serve the purposes of this work. Consider now an iconicity value of 0.65 and probability of 035. According to the Trapezoidal and Triangular membership function, the iconicity of 0.65 has 0 membership in the low fuzzy set, 0.25 membership in the medium fuzzy set, and 0.75 membership in the high fuzzy set (see Figure 4). The 0.35 probability has 1 membership in the low fuzzy set, 0 membership in the medium fuzzy set, and 0 membership in the high fuzzy set. According to the above noted IF-THEN rules, using fuzzy AND then the fuzzy output can be obtained as follows:

	Membership Grade		
	Low	Medium	High
Rule 1: min(0.75, 0)			0
Rule 2: min(0.75, 0)		0	
Rule 3: min(0.75, 1)		0.75	
Rule 4: min(0.25, 0)		0	
Rule 5: min(0.25, 0)		0	
Rule 6: min(0.25, 1)	0.25		
Rule 7: min(0, 0)		0	
Rule 8: min(0, 0)		0	
Rule 9: min(0, 1)	0		

Table 1. Membership grade of the inference rules

$[A_j(x_o) \wedge B_j(x_o)=m_j$, where m_i is the membership of the output of each rule. Then with w_j denoting the crisp output of rule j as shown in (1), the Centroid Defuzzification Method for the outputs shown in Table 1 applies as follows to produce the crisp output CF: $CF = \Sigma_{i=1}^{n} m_i * w_i / \Sigma_{i=1}^{n} m_i$
In this example, CF= [(0.75*0.55)+(0.25*0.4)] / (0.75+0.25) = 0.513, where 0.4, 0.55 and 0.7 are the centers of gravity of the fuzzy outputs low, medium and high.

The agent can now use this confidence value to represent how confident it is in a specific belief in his mental model as follows: *BEL ($agent_x$, is($agent_y$, sheriff), medium, 0.513).* In plain English, this predicate can be read as: $agent_x$ believes that $agent_y$ is a *sheriff* with medium confidence equal to 0.513. Medium value is chosen here based on the ranges chosen for the data value sets low, medium and high.

Updating Mental Model Beliefs

The previous section illustrates how an agent can compute their confidence about a specific belief. It is worth noting that the agent's beliefs can change as a scene unfolds. Consequently, each agent should be able to update its beliefs and associated confidences based on what it infers from the introduced information. Hence, we designed more fuzzy rules that can help the agent to update his beliefs as the following example:

Fuzzy Rule One: *IF* $agent_x$ has low confidence about $agent_x$'s motion *AND* has medium confidence about $agent_x$ as $character_y$, *THEN* decrease $agent_x$ confidence in $character_y$.

This rule is designed to **decrease** agent B's confidence about agent A's character if agent A did a motion that can be interpreted as related to two different characters X and Y. For example, if one agent holds their fists one on top of the other and moves them from side to side to perform a sweeping motion, an agent could relate this motion to both a waiter character and a janitor character. Other rules were designed to **increase** the agent confidence about his beliefs.

The agents' confidence about the knowledge in their mental models keeps changing based on the actions they take to establish a shared mental model and consequently reach cognitive consensus. Reaching cognitive consensus requires the agents to have the same beliefs as a subset of their individual beliefs. The next section defines how shared mental models make use of various strategies to address cognitive divergence whenever recognized and how this helps the agents to approach cognitive convergence.

SITUATION CALCULUS AND REPAIR STRATEGIES

SMMs are a hypothetical cognitive construct that extends the notion of individual mental models to a team context [17]. Based on an empirical study of the cognition employed by performers in improvisational theatre that focuses on how improvisers create a dramatic or comedic performance in real-time, it has been found that in an improvisational scene, improvisers employ different *repair strategies* to deal with divergences as they occur and that they rely on their shared mental model to decide on the suitable repair strategy to use [13]. Repair strategies are those strategies utilized by improv actors to achieve cognitive consensus when divergences arise. They help the agents update their mental models and approach cognitive consensus. The choice of a repair strategy depends on the status of the agent's mental model in a specific frame of the world. Due to the dynamic nature of the agent's shared mental model, situation calculus is appropriate for the representation of repair strategies because of its ability to capture change based on time along with reasoning about causes and effects of these changes.

Situation calculus is a logic formalism designed for representing and reasoning about dynamic domains [38]. Situation calculus is one way to represent changes in First Order Logic by adding a situational argument to each non-eternal predicate. We used fluents such as BEL ( ) to indicate whether an agent has a specific belief about a relation or a proposition or not and function fluents to describe the state of the world, for example the CONF ( ) function returns how confident agent x is about certain knowledge. Now we have introduced situation calculus, we are going to explain how it is used to represent the repair strategies.

Repair Strategies

Presentation is another-oriented repair strategy (i.e. attempts to change other's model instead of their own). It is the foremost repair technique that demonstrates what an improviser believes to be true and introduces new information that relates to an individual's mental model. Clarification is another other-oriented repair technique used by improvisers to correct any misunderstandings or misinterpretations of information that has already been communicated. It is different from presentation in that it does not introduce any new concepts (unless those new concepts are meant to clarify old ones). For various types of clarification, see [13].

Verification is a self-oriented repair technique. Verification occurs when an improviser has an idea of what another improviser's mental model *might* be, and he often communicates his impression to his scene partner(s) in order to verify it. Verification is not always an exact formulation of what an improviser believes. It can also manifest as a statement that is related to a belief that an improviser wants to test for accuracy (i.e. wants to *verify*). This is one repair strategy that relies on dialogue in improv theatre, however as we do not deal yet with dialogues between agents, situation calculus rules focus only on actions as follows:

A blind offer (related to the canonical improv offer, which is when an improviser presents a new potential contribution to a scene) is the final self-oriented repair technique. Improvisers use this term to describe when they intentionally introduce new, vague, and poorly-defined information. The purpose of this action is for the improviser's scene partner(s) to take the information and expand upon it, using the blind offer as an opportunity to present or clarify their mental model(s). The designed situation calculus rules are as follows:

Each of the above strategies do also have action effects axiom that commits the agent to respond to the interactor's action and successor state axiom that defines how the agent beliefs should change after the execution of the action.

Acknowledgment of Repair Strategies

After an attempted repair, an acceptance state follows that identifies if a repair strategy has failed or succeeded. A repair attempt is said to have failed if the divergence continues or a new one takes its place. The other possibility is that the repair succeeds, which means is met with *acceptance* [13]. Acceptance does not necessarily equate to cognitive consensus, but only defines a state that follows a repair attempt. The ideal form of consensus is true cognitive consensus, which is when an improviser correctly accepts another improviser's mental model. True cognitive consensus can only be identified through explicit confirmation by all the improvisers originally involved in the divergence (a phenomenon we capture in our group interview data [13]). Cognitive consensus, however, can be partial, which means that it is not necessary for *all* mental models to be identical, but at least two mental models that used to be different have become the same (one divergence has been resolved).

EVALUATION

In order to evaluate SMM presented in this paper, we ran two studies. The first study includes a live interaction between a human interactor and our AI agent. The second one includes a series of tests to measure the success of the two AI agents in their attempts to reach consensus in their beliefs.

Study I

In this study, we allowed a human interactor to interact with our improv agent. The agent starts with a mental model that contains only different elements in each of the knowledge categories defined earlier in Figure 3 along with DOAs between one another. Figure 5 shows the portion of the big network in which sheriff and cowboy are elements in the character category. Hold gun and punch are elements in the action category and bar-fight is an element in the joint activity category.

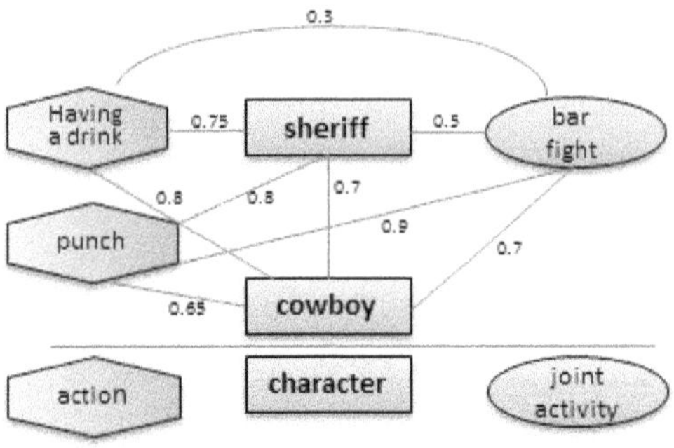

Figure 5. DOMs between, actions, characters, and joint_activities. Sheriff has very strong (0.95) degree of association to hold gun action and medium (0.7) degree of association to the cowboy character. Both sheriff and cowboy have strong and medium DOAs

The player starts to interact with the improv environment using Microsoft Kinect. Now the human interactor is considered as $agent_y$ and the improv agent is $agent_x$. The human interactor starts by holding her hand cupped near her mouth as if she is having a drink. The agent recognizes the motion and extrapolates to action other which is the "having a drink" action. At this point, the agent can extrapolate to either character other or joint activity as shown in Figure3. As seen in Figure 5 'having a drink' action has DOAs with the 'cowboy' and 'sheriff' characters. Since there is no prior information about the scene, the agent just picks the character with the highest association that is cowboy and the following belief is added to the agent's mental model: *BEL ($agent_x$, is($agent_y$, cowboy), medium, 0.513)*. This beleief shows that the the improv agent has a high confidence that the human intercator is a cowboy. On the other hand, another belief is added in the long term memory that the human interactor might be a sheriff with medium confidence equal to 0.75.

Based on the current mental model, the agent chooses to extrapolate to his character (character self) and decides on being an "outlaw". The agent then chooses an action to execute, which was "punch" action. The human interactor "punches" back. Now the agent has to update his confidence about the interactor's character based on the latest action using the rules in Section IV .C. The "punch" action has a medium DOA with the "cowboy" character so the final confidence is updated based on the following fuzzy rule.

Fuzzy Rule: *If* $agent_x$ has <u>medium</u> confidence about $agent_y$'s motion *AND* has <u>high</u> confidence about $agent_y$ character, *Then* <u>decrease</u> $agent_x$ confidence in $agent_y$ character.

Using this knowledge the agent decides to extrabolate to the joint activity which results in adding the following belief

BEL ($agent_x$, joint_activity($agent_y$, bar-fight), medium, 0.513).

The agent chooses to do the "shoot-gun" action. Although the human interactor realized it is a bar-fight, she decided to change the context and chose to make the "sweep a table" move as shown in Figure 6. The agent interprets the move as "sweep table" action but according to his model this action is not likely associated with the cowboy character so he recognizes this as a divergence.

Figure 6. The human interactor is doing the 'sweep a table' action

To address this divergence, the agent decides on the appropriate repair rule to use. Since the agent has credible evidence (medium to high confidence) that he and the human interactor were doing the "bar fight" joint activity, the agent decides to do a clarification repair strategy- that is to amend his partner's mental model. Accordingly, based on the clarification definition, the agent decides to execute an action that is highly associated with his character, so he did the "raise hands up" action by raising his two hands up in a surrender position. It is worth mentioning that in the absence of the repair strategies the agent will keep just responding to the interactor's actions and would not take the initiative to try to change the interactor's mental model.

The human interactor realizes that the agent is still taking the role of an "outlaw" so she acknowledges the repair and chooses to go along with the agent so she decides to be the "sheriff" and moves forward as if she approaches the agent. The agent increases his confidence in the interactor's character and the joint activity; sheriff and bar-fight. The human interactor continues interacting with the agent a couple more times before the agent confidence passes a specified threshold of 90% so the agent announced that he thinks they reach consensus and that he thinks he is an "outlaw", the human interactor is a "sheriff" and they were involved in a "bar-fight".

This study provides some interesting insights about the capability of the shared mental model and how it can serve in producing interesting human computer interactions. Despite the fact that there were some mis-interpretations from both the interactor and the improv agent sides, it was still interesting to see the back-and-forth negotiation between the human interactor and the improv agent. It seems that the fuzzy rules handled the ambiguity and uncertainty embedded in the interactions in a satisfactory way as the human interactor ended up with an enjoyable improv experience.

Study II

In the second study, we ran the two agents without allowing them to reason about the world in any way (choose their actions in a completely random manner). Each agent would guess at his own character, the other agent's character, and their shared joint activity entirely randomly. In these circumstances, the agents would be expected to reach cognitive consensus (complete agreement on both characters and the joint activity in the scene) on a given line only 0.07% of the time, due to the improbability of guessing correctly from our large pool of permutations. After running twenty scenes, each starting with a "blank slate" (no beliefs in either agent's mental model) and each running for one-hundred lines, the agents never once found total consensus. We would only expect total consensus to be found approximately once in over 1500 lines, so this is not a surprising outcome.

In contrast to this control run, we turned the SMMs on and allowed the agents to act out a series of twenty scenes (each continuing for one-hundred lines) in which each agent would attempt to infer the other agent's character, his own character, and their mutual joint-activity based on the actions performed in the scene. Each would then choose actions to perform and present to the other agent based on the actions' DOAs to his current beliefs about his own character and the joint activity. Utilizing this reasoning, the agents found total consensus at some point in 9 out of the 20 runs. Additionally, they reached near consensus (agreement on all but one element in a scene) in seventeen out of twenty runs, and were "one away" from total consensus (or better) in 10.0% of the total lines performed, which is over 4.5 times more often than in the random trials.

These numbers show that, even in the absence of explicit information-sharing between the agents, the reasoning used to populate our shared mental models significantly improved the agents' ability to reach common beliefs about a scene. By inferring the beliefs of other actors based on the visible actions performed, each agent can negotiate and re-assess his beliefs strategically based on its unique set of assumptions about character-action-activity relationships.

CONCLUSION

Mental models underlie everything that happens in a co-created story. Since improv involves the perpetual invention and contribution of new information to a scene, there is a constant potential for errors regarding that information. Therefore, understanding how to create shared mental models and navigate those errors is especially important. The process of cognitive convergence allows improvisers to deal with their mistakes and reach an understanding, using shared mental models as the foundation for their construction of a collaborative scene.

This paper presents a shared mental model for improvisational narrative agents who rely on their beliefs and desires to achieve cognitive consensus in a co-constructed scene through shared mental models, which in turn provides a model for how humans and agents can co-create a scene together through similar implicit means. Fuzzy logic and situation calculus were able to successfully handle the continuous change in the agent's mental model. Turning the SMM on and off proofs the validity of using confidence factors to guide the decision making and provides us with evidence on the validity of the model as it enhances the performance of the agents and allows them to reach cognitive convergence 4.5 times more often than in the random trials when the SMM was turned off.

The model presented in this paper allows the elicitation of implicit objectives that guide the agents to achieve cognitive consensus and recognize when it is achieved. This model provides the flexibility for improv agents to be employed in games environments where they can reason about fuzzy uncertain knowledge and interact with each other and with human users.

Although the generated repair rules were designed for the improvisation domain, they pretty much capture how the negotiation process occurs in other domains too. We always present new things to others (Presentation), ask for clarification when we are confused about something (Verification), or make attempts to clarify things to others (Clarification). Therefore, it seems that these rules are applicable in those domains that share common characteristics with the improvisation domain, such as argumentation (using natural language) or an AI-based dancing game (using gestures).

In its current state, our approach does not capture all of the complexities of a full theory of mind because assessments are only based on DOA. For example, agents with the kind of SMM described here cannot reason about privileged knowledge (e.g. knowledge that only one agent knows because the other agent was not present to hear it), which a full theory of mind can account for. Improv agents would need to reason about all aspects of theory of mind to be able to create all the same kinds of narratives a human can. However, the shared mental models proposed in this paper are enough for improv agents to begin improvising a scene while considering each other's beliefs. Most importantly, we would argue that this model serves as an important step in preserving high user agency and improvisational narrative generation simultaneously, particularly within domains that rely on natural interfaces as a way to introduce ambiguity in the communication between user and computer.

ACKNOWLEDGMENTS

Rania Hodhod and Brian Magerko gratefully acknowledge the grant from NSF (#IIS 0757567).

REFERENCES

1. D. L. Roberts and C. L. Isbell, "A survey and qualitative analysis of recent advances in drama management," *Int. Trans. Systems Science and Applications, Special Issue on Agent Based Systems for Human Learning*, vol. 4, no. 2, 2008.
2. M. Cavazza, F. Charles, and S. J. Mead, "Interacting with virtual characters in interactive storytelling," in *Proc. 1st Int. Joint Conf. Autonomous agents and multiagent systems: part 1*, 2002, pp. 318–325.
3. R. M. Young, M. O. Riedl, M. Branly, A. Jhala, R. J. Martin, and C. J. Saretto, "An architecture for integrating plan-based behavior generation with interactive game environments," *Game Development J.*, vol. 1, no. 1, pp. 51–70, 2004.
4. M. O. Riedl and R. M. Young, "Narrative planning: balancing plot and character," *Artificial Intelligence Research J.*, vol. 39, no. 1, pp. 217–268, 2010.
5. B. Magerko, "Player modeling in the interactive drama architecture," Ph.D Dissertation, Dept. CS and Eng., Michigan Univ., Michigan, USA, 2006.
6. V. Bayon, J. R. Wilson, D. Stanton, and A. Boltman, "Mixed reality storytelling environments," *Virtual Reality J.*, vol. 7, no. 1, pp. 54–63, 2003.
7. R. Aylett, M. Vala, P. Sequeira, and A. Paiva, "Fearnot!–an emergent narrative approach to virtual dramas for anti-bullying education," *in Proc. Int. Conf. Virtual Storytelling. Using Virtual Reality Technologies for Storytelling*, 2007, pp. 202–205.
8. R. K. Sawyer, *Improvised dialogues: Emergence and creativity in conversation*, 1st ed. Westport, CT: Ablex Publishing Corporation, 2003.
9. A. Brisson, B. Magerko, and A. Paiva, "Tilt Riders: Improvisational Agents Who Know What the Scene is About," in *Intelligent Virtual Agents 10th Int. Conf., IVA 2011, Reykjavik, Iceland, September 15-17, 2011. Proceedings*, Reykjavik, Iceland, 2011.
10. R. de Moraes and A. Forrest, "Whose Line - Party Quirks," *Whose Line is it Anyway?*, ABC, Hollywood, CA, 04-Oct-2001.
11. Whose Line Is It Anyway? (UK), *TV.com*. Retrieved September 19, 2012 from http://www.tv.com/shows/whose-line-is-it-anyway-uk/
12. R. K. Sawyer, "Improvisational Cultures: Collaborative Emergence and Creativity in Improvisation," *Mind, Culture, & Activity*, vol. 7, no. 3, pp. 180–185, Aug. 2000.
13. D. Fuller and B. Magerko, "Shared mental models in improvisational performance," in *Proc. the Intelligent Narrative Technologies III Workshop*, Monterey, CA, 2010, pp. 1–6.
14. M. J. Davidson, L. Dove, and J. Weltz. (1999, November). Mental models and usability. Depaul University, Cognative Psychology 404 [Online]. Available: http://www.lauradove.info/reports/mental%20models.htm
15. R. Fagin and J. Y. Halpern, "Belief, awareness, and limited reasoning," *Artificial Intelligence*, vol.34, pp. 39–76, 1988.
16. I. van de Kieft, C. M. Jonker, M. B. van Riemsdijk, "Improving User and Decision Support System Teamwork: An Approach Based on Shared Mental Models," *Workshop Explanation-aware Computing-IJCAI*, Barcelona, Spain, 2011, pp. 61-70.
17. J. Yen, X. Fan, S. Sun, T. Hanratty, and J. Dumer, "Agents with shared mental models for enhancing team decision makings," *Decision Support System J.*, vol. 41, pp. 634-653, 2006.
18. S. SPAULDING, "Embodied cognition and mindreading," *Mind & Language*, vol. 25, no. 1, pp. 119–140, 2010.
19. M. Si, S. C. Marsella, and D. V. Pynadath, "THESPIAN: An Architecture for Interactive Pedagogical Drama," in *Proc. 2005 Conf. Artificial Intelligence in Education: Supporting Learning through Intelligent and Socially Informed Technology*, Amsterdam, The Netherlands, The Netherlands, 2005, pp. 595–602.
20. B. Magerko, P. Dohogne, and D. Fuller, "Shared Mental Models in Improvisational Digital Characters," in *Proc. 2nd Int. Conf. Computational Creativity*, Mexico City, Mexico, 2011, pp. 33–35.
21. B. Hayes-Roth, E. Sincoff, L. Brownston, R. Huard, and B. Lent, "Directed Improvisation," in *Technical Report KSL-94-61*, Palo Alto, CA, 1994.
22. B. Hayes-Roth and R. Van Gent, "Story-Making with Improvisational Puppets and Actors," in *Technical Report KSL-96-09*, Palo Alto, CA, 1996.
23. K. Perlin and A. Goldberg, "Improv: A System for Scripting Interactive Actors in Virtual Worlds," in *Proc. 23rd Annu. Conf. Computer Graphics and Interactive Techniques*, New York, 1996, pp. 205–216.
24. M. Tambe, "Towards flexible teamwork," *in Artificial Intelligence Research J. (JAIR)*, vol. 7, pp. 83–124, 1997.
25. M. D. Sadek, P. Bretier, and F. Panaget, "ARTIMIS: Natural dialogue meets rational agency," in *Int. Joint Conf. Artificial Intelligence*, 1997, vol. 15, pp. 1030–1035.

26. C. Rich and C. L. Sidner, “COLLAGEN: A collaboration manager for software interface agents,” *User Modeling and User-Adapted Interaction*, vol. 8, no. 3, pp. 315–350, 1998.
27. R. A. Subramanian, S. Kumar, and P. Cohen, “Integrating joint intention theory, belief reasoning, and communicative action for generating team-oriented dialogue,” in *Proc. THE NATIONAL Conf. ARTIFICIAL INTELLIGENCE*, 2006, vol. 21, p. 1501.
28. W. G. Kennedy and J. G. Trafton, “Using simulations to model shared mental models,” DTIC Document, 2007.
29. R.A. Subramanian, S. Kumar, and P.R. Cohen, “Confirming Changes in Beliefs and Intentions,” *in Proc. AAAI Spring Symposium: Intentions in Intelligent Systems*, 2007, pp. 46-47.
30. G. Lakoff, *Cognitive models and prototype theory*. In U. Neisser (Ed.), Concepts and Conceptual Development: Ecological and Intellectual Factors in Categorization, Cambridge: Cambridge Univ. Press, 1987, pp. 63–100.
31. E. Rosch, *Principles of Categorization*. In E. Rosch and B. Lloyd (Eds.), Cognition and Categorization, Hillsdale, NJ: Lawrence Erlbaum, 1999.
32. J. Yen and R. Langari, *Fuzzy Logic: Intelligence, Control and Information*. 1st ed., New York: Prentice Hall, 1998.
33. J. R. Rentsch and R. J. Hall, *Members of great teams think alike: A model of team effectiveness and schema similarity among team members*. In M. M. Beyerlein & D. A. Johnson (Eds.), Advances in interdisciplinary studies of work teams: Theories of self-managing work teams, Greenwich, CT: JAI Press, 1994.
34. J. E. Mathieu, T. S. Heffner, G. F. Goodwin, E. Salas, and J. A. Cannon-Bowers, “The influence of shared mental models on team process and performance.,” *Applied Psychology J.*, vol. 85, no. 2, pp. 273–283, 2000.
35. L. L. Levesque, J. M. Wilson, and D. R. Wholey, “Cognitive divergence and shared mental models in software development project teams,” *Organizational Behavior J.*, vol. 22, no. 2, pp. 135–144, 2001.
36. L. O’Brien, *Self-Knowing Agents*. Oxford University Press, 2007.
37. B. O’Neill, A. Piplica, D. Fuller, and B. Magerko, “A Knowledge-Based Framework for the Collaborative Improvisation of Scene Introductions,” *in Proc. 4th Int. Conf. Interactive Digital Storytelling*, Vancouver, Canada, 2011.
38. Situation Calculus - Google Search. Retrieved July 2, 2012 from https://www.google.com/search?q=situational+calculus&ie=utf-8&oe=utf-8&aq=t&rls=org.mozilla:en-US:official&client=firefox-a
39. B. Magerko, C. DeLeon, and P. Dohogne, “Digital improvisational theatre: party quirks,” *in Proc. 10th Int. Conf. Intelligent Virtual Agents*, 2011, pp. 42–47.
40. K. E. Weick and K. H. Roberts, “Collective mind in organizations: Heedful interrelating on flight decks,” *Administrative science quarterly*, pp. 357–381, 1993.
41. S. Nicolle. Mental models theory and relevance theory.*Pragmatics & Cognition 11:2 (2003), 345 – 378.*

No more Autobahn! Scenic Route Generation Using Googles Street View

Nina Runge[1], **Pavel Samsonov**[2], **Donald Degraen**[2], **Johannes Schöning**[2]

[1]University of Bremen, TZI
Digital Media Lab
Bibliotheksstr. 1
28359 Bremen, Germany
nr@tzi.de

[2]Hasselt University – tUL – iMinds
Expertise Centre for Digital Media (EDM)
Wetenschapspark 2
3590 Diepenbeek, Belgium
first.last@uhasselt.be

ABSTRACT

Navigation systems allow drivers to find the shortest or fastest path between two or multiple locations mostly using time or distance as input parameters. Various researchers extended traditional route planning approaches by taking into account the user's preferences, such as enjoying a coastal view or alpine landscapes during a drive. Current approaches mainly rely on volunteered geographic information (VGI), such as point of interest (POI) data from OpenStreetMap, or social media data, such as geotagged photos from Flickr, to generate scenic routes. While these approaches use proximity, distribution or other spatial relationships of the data sets, they do not take into account the actual view on specific route segments. In this paper, we propose *Autobahn*: a system for generating scenic routes using Google Street View images to classify route segments based on their visual characteristics enhancing the driving experience. We show that this vision-based approach can complement other approaches for scenic route planning and introduce a personalized scenic route by aligning the characteristics of the route to the preferences of the user.

ACM Classification Keywords

H.5.m Information interfaces and presentation: Miscellaneous

Author Keywords

Deep Learning; Intelligent User Interfaces, Google Street View; Scenic Routes

INTRODUCTION & RELATED WORK

The rapid development of autonomous vehicles will also radically change the way we perceive the in-car experience [5]. Navigation will no longer be only a tool to navigate from point *A* to point *B* on the shortest or fastest path, but the selection of a route will have an impact on the in-car experience as well. This is already true for travellers and owners of convertibles or motorbikes as the driving itself has an intrinsic motivation for them [1].

There is already a large corpus of related work that explores the generation of scenic or alternatives routes. For example, Hochmair et al. [1, 4] describe an approach to generate scenic routes using different sources of volunteered geographic information (VGI) and data from photo sharing platforms. The *GPSView* system uses a similar approach and adapts an attention-aware technique to community contributed photos and allows travellers to enjoy sightseeing during a trip [13]. As shown by Bolzoni et al. [2], adding category information to points of interest (POIs) makes it easier for tourists to formulate their preferences while planning an itinerary. In order to provide a better navigation experience, Samsonov et al. [10] proposed that navigation systems should also be aware of so-called space usage rules (such as no-swimming signs, no-surfing signs or no-fishing signs) to be able to guide the users to places where they can enjoy certain activities (e.g. swimming or fishing). In the domain of pedestrian navigation multiple applications and research prototypes exist to improve walking experiences. The application *Space Recommender System* [11] merges data from social networks to improve walking experiences in urban spaces, whereas the *Hobbit* application [8] helps people to avoid company in rural areas.

While all these approaches provide interesting alternatives to the shortest or fastest route, the main limitation is that these techniques do not consider the actual view from the road and rely on other data to judge the route's aspects. It has been shown that in order to improve driver experience, it is necessary to take into account a rich set of visual landscape features. For example, Qin et al. [9] showed that the presence of billboards negatively influences scenic qualities and the presence of lakes positively improves the overall driving experience. One could also consider a scenario where a street, that is close to the shoreline, might be directly behind dams, or the view on the ocean is blocked by houses, tunnels or trees (as illustrated in Figure 1). On the other hand, a street further away from the coast might offer a beautiful view over the ocean (e.g. because there is a high plateau). In addition, VGI could also be biased [3] or not uniformly distributed and affect other approaches for scenic route generation. For exam-

IUI'16, March 07 - 10, 2016, Sonoma, CA, USA

ACM 978-1-4503-4137-0/16/03... $15.00
DOI: http://dx.doi.org/10.1145/2856767.2856804

Figure 1. By looking on the map of a route near Copenhagen on the left, a user would expect view from the ocean from all locations, but most of the time it is blocked by trees or wastelands. On the left: The route, and the computed grid. In the middle: the corresponding GSV images. On the right: the outcome of the classification. The categories with the highest probability p are assigned to each grid cell. Image and base map ©Google 2015.

ple, while there will be a high amount of geo-tagged photos taken around a popular sight, it is unlikely that this location will be visible from the road. While these limitations could be overcome by creating a detailed 3D model of the environment and applying scene and visibility analysis [12], such an approach would be computationally very expensive on a global scale. However, it would also not take into account the presence of flora, e.g. trees and bushes, at a location.

To overcome these issues, we propose a pipeline to generate scenic routes based on Google Street View (GSV) data. Our automated system named *Autobahn* crawls GSV images alongside routes and tags and classifies these images using deep learning [7]. In contrast to other photo sharing platforms, building upon GSV has the advantage that these images are taken from a vehicle (in the majority of the cases) on major roads. We provide insights on the technical implementation, as well as a first user study, that compares our approach with the state-of-the-art.

THE AUTOBAHN PIPELINE

Typical automotive navigation between two locations requires a starting point, a destination and routing parameters such as fastest or shortest route. As input, the *Autobahn* system requires the user to additionally select one of the 6 predefined scenic routing parameters in order to align the routing to the user's preferences. An overview on the developed components can be seen in Figure 2. The following sections explain the main components of the pipeline in detail.

Grid Creation

When starting a route generation between two locations, the bounding box of the area is taken as the reference grid for our calculations. The corresponding OpenStreetMap (OSM) data of this area is downloaded through the OSM Overpass API. The area is divided into a grid with cells of one square kilometer size. The cell size corresponds to roughly one-minute driving time, assuming an average speed of 60 km per hour. For each cell, one location is determined by selecting the closest road to the center of the cell. Roads classified as service roads in OSM are excluded as it is highly unlikely that GSV is available on these roads. If a cell does not contain any applicable roads, it will not be processed any further.

Street View Data Collection

In the next step, we generate panoramic images for all sample locations of the grid using GSV. As the GSV API does not allow to retrieve an entire panoramic view as a single image, we reconstruct the panorama by individually downloading image tiles and stitching them together. We iterate through the panorama with a pitch ranging from minus ten to seventy degrees in steps of ten degrees for each 10 degree heading in the 360 degree panoramic image. The resulting 288 images with a resolution of 640×640 pixels are then downscaled to 320×320 pixels. As the positions of all 288 tiles are known, the stitching process is straightforward and a single image of 11520×2560 pixels is generated. As the classification component (described in the next section) is trained on smaller pictures, we scaled panoramic image down by 80%. Figure 1 shows examples of the used 2304×512 pixel panoramas.

Panorama Classification

In order to classify the images, we used the pre-trained neural network created by Zhou et al. [14]. They used crowd workers to assign place tags to different images. This resulted in 205 place categories, such as field, forest, airport terminal or boat deck. The neural network was trained with 2,448,873 images of the ImageNet Database and showed an accuracy 50% on the evaluation dataset and even better results for other datasets, like the easier dataset SUN 205 (66.5% accuracy).

For classifying our panoramic images, we used the Caffe Deep Learning Framework for neural networks [6]. As our use case does simply require a distinction between a few unique place categories, tags related to indoor scenes were discarded.

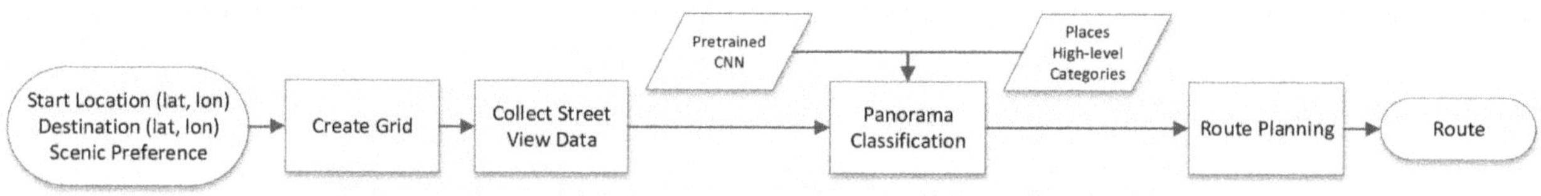

Figure 2. The *Autobahn* pipeline for scenic route generation using GSV images.

In an iterative process, we grouped the 111 trained scenes into 5 high-level scenic categories, namely *sightseeing* (e.g. viaduct, temple, amusement park), *nature and woods* (e.g. valley, alley, garden), *fields* (e.g. wheat field, corn field), *water* (e.g. ocean, harbor, coast) and *mountain* (e.g. butte, snowy mountain, volcano). The sixth category contained all non-scenic tags (e.g. *street*, *industry* and *building*). For each panoramic image, the neural network gives a probability what kind of landscape is most likely visible in the image. We categorized the images based on the category with the highest probability. The most probable tags for three examples on a route in Copenhagen are shown in the Figure 1. We also list all the probabilities for the place classification and the category it belongs to. Three example outputs for a colored grid (with the corresponding categories) based on the panorama classifications can be seen in Figure 4.

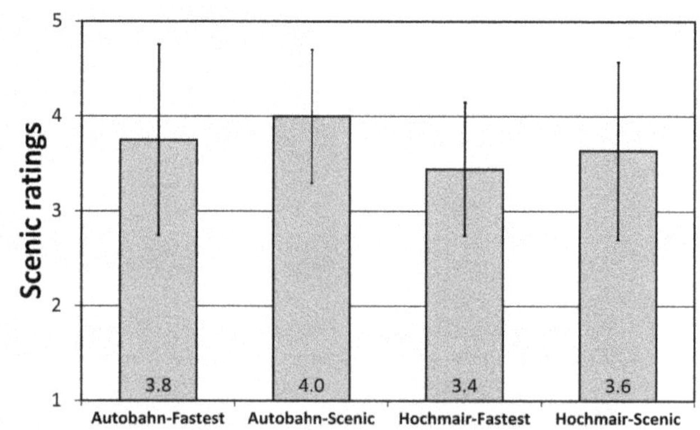

Figure 3. Mean values for a 5-point Likert scale (5=very scenic, 1=not scenic) ratings, error bars indicate standard deviation. Comparing two routes generated by the *Autobahn* system (*Autobahn*-scenic) and the fasted routes from the same start and end points (*Autobahn*-fastest). Same for the routes by Hochmair.

Route Planning

Once a region of interest (ROI) is classified based on the panoramic GSV image, we are able to plan different routes through the ROI. Our algorithm generates a scenic route from a given start point to a finish point through multiple or even all cells containing the scenic qualities constrained to the maximum travel time as selected by a user. For example, a user interested in *mountain views* would start by providing the system with his preference, a start location, a destination, and maximum travel time. The system provides the user with a personalized route in the ROI, maximizing the number of cells classified as *mountain* in the given time.

Since routing is not the main contribution of the paper, we implemented a first approach in two steps. Firstly, a route is created from the given start location to the destination while passing through the scenic cell surrounded by the most other scenic cells. In the second step, we recursively split existing segments by adding the closest scenic point to the route, as long as the overall route length does not exceed the value defined by the user or all points from the grid are added. If adding a point leads to going on a road twice, it is skipped. This routing strategy ensures a high concentration of the scenic preferences, while avoiding there-and-back detours. For routing from *A* to *B* in the algorithm, we used OpenRouteService[1] for the European routes and GraphHopper[2] for the USA routes.

[1]`http://openrouteservice.org`
[2]`http://graphhopper.com`

RESULTS & EVALUATION

We have used our *Autobahn* system to classify GSV images in 10 different ROIs of about 32,000 km^2 around the world. Based on their preferences, users are able to plan various scenic routes throughout these 10 areas. An overview can be seen in Figure 4. The grid view provides an overview of the classified area and provides insight into the generation of scenic routes. In the left image, showing the classification of Malloca, Spain, the following area classifications are visible: cities, fields and areas where a driver could enjoy nice mountain views. We have also classified the main highway system of Belgium, to provide users with an overview on the most scenic parts of the highways system. The interactive website can be accessed at `http://autobahn.edm.uhasselt.be`.

To further evaluate the *Autobahn* system, an online survey was conducted. Three different areas with scenic views were evaluated (Mallorca, Spain; Rhone-Alpes, France; Santa Barbara, USA). For each area, two routes with identical start and finish locations, were created. One route was generated using a default fastest route planning algorithm. The second route took into account the scenic information from our *Autobahn* system. The scenic routes were generated using the *mountain* and *water* tags, this because we expected users to pay more attention to sea and mountain views compared to forests, sightings and fields. In order to compare these results to previous work, we used three routes generated by Hochmair. et al. [1] and their fastest routing alternatives connecting the identical start and finish locations. These routes are located throughout the state of Florida (North Tampa, Odessa and Yankeetown). Each route contains one point every 100 to 500 meters, in average 34 points per route, and variated

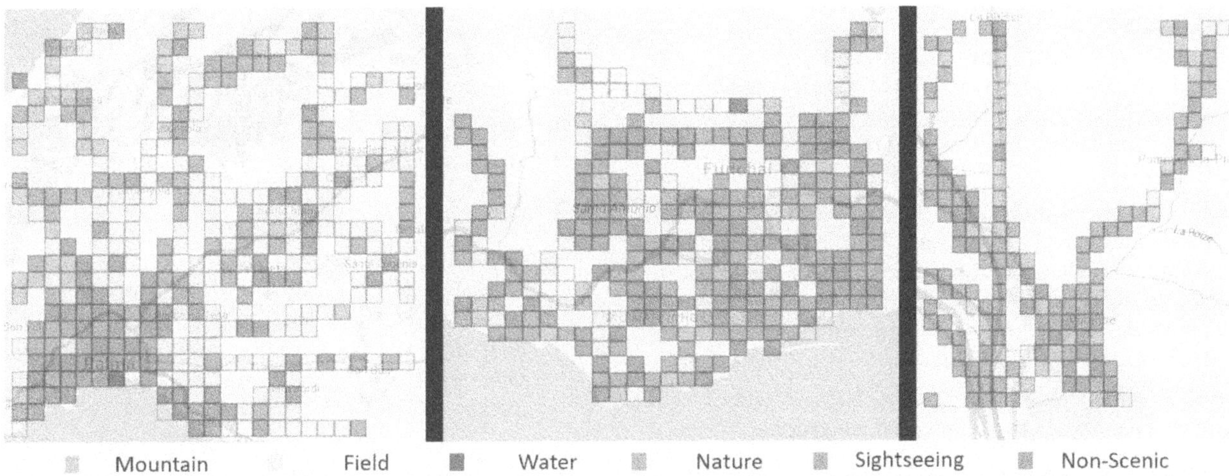

Figure 4. Three example colored grid outputs of *Autobahn*. From the left to the right: Mallorca (Spain), Madeira (Portugal), Rhone-Alpes (France). Base map: ©Google 2015

from 4.8 km to 16.4 km in distance. Both our routes and the routes of Hochmair shared same characteristics in terms of length and ratio between the scenic route and the fastest path. The routes were presented in Latin square order to prevent influences. For each route, the points on that route were sequentially iterated though. For each point, participants were shown the panoramic view on that location for a duration of two seconds. These images are not identical to the ones used for categorizing the grid. After each route, participants were asked to rate that route on a 5-point Likert scale with regard to the scenic qualities. They were also asked if they would like to travel the route in real-life. Participants were able to provide feedback on, why assessed a route scenic or not scenic in a free-text field. The survey took about 30-40 minutes to complete. A total of 24 participants (10 female, 14 male) were unfamiliar with the selected ROI and completed the survey. Participants ranged between 18 and 49 years old ($M = 32.4$, $SD = 9.2$), 18 owned a car and one owned a motorbike. Participants expressed preference to routes generated by the *Autobahn* system, as can be seen in Figure 3 . However a pair-wise comparison of these both results yields no significant differences. The routes generated by Hochmair were also preferred to the fastest routes, again with no significant difference. The free-text field answers revealed similar preferences toward the scenic routes. Participants commented "this is a mountain tour on an island", "nature" and "a lot of greenery" for both the fastest and the scenic routes, but the more subjective answers also expressed a tendency towards the scenic routes, e.g. "nice, cool, beautiful, interesting", compared to "boring and normal" for the fastest path. Participants also expressed overall positive feedback in the general idea behind the *Autobahn* system and were interested in the application for future use.

DISCUSSION & CONCLUSION

In this paper, we presented a novel approach to generate scenic routes based on automatic scene classification using GSV images. We created an automated pipeline that allows the user to define scenic preferences for a routing assignment from a given start location to a destination point. Our pipeline classifies regions using a deep learning into 6 different scenic categories. They are used to align the routing to the preferences of the user. Our results are promising as they visualize the diversity of scenic qualities in a selected region and reveal route qualities that go beyond those currently picked up by comparable systems such as Hochmair et al. [1]. Initial user tests revealed preferences to our routes generated by the *Autobahn* system compared to the fastest path, yet no statistical differences were found. As such ratings are highly subjective and might be influenced by several factors, we believe that the *Autobahn* system provides the first steps into scenic routes generation based on automatic scene classification using GSV images.

One could also imagine various other routing algorithms based on the classified GSV images. Users interested in diversity could be provided with a route through a region which contains a multitude of different scenic qualities. Alternatively, a route could be designed to ensure a highly diverse landscape or, on the contrary, a very monotone drive. Besides scenic routing, we believe the power of classifying GSV data has yet to be fully exploited in a diverse range of applications. As GSV images is constrained to mainly North America and Europe, our system is limited in this regard and lacks coverage in large parts of Asia, Africa and South-America, as well as major cities of Germany and Austria.

As our system can recommend routes with a large variety of different views, we believe that it can complement other approaches for scenic route planning. This will be further explored in the future. The generated grids can be used in regional statistics, such as cross referencing the scenic qualities of regions to health and population related data.

ACKNOWLEDGEMENTS

We thank Hartwig H. Hochmair for providing us with the routes generated by his system. This work was supported in part by the following grants: BOF R-5209, and a Google Faculty Research Award.

REFERENCES

1. Majid Alivand, Hartwig Hochmair, and Sivaramakrishnan Srinivasan. 2015. Analyzing how travelers choose scenic routes using route choice models. *Computers, Environment and Urban Systems* 50 (2015), 41–52.
2. Paolo Bolzoni, Sven Helmer, Kevin Wellenzohn, Johann Gamper, and Periklis Andritsos. 2014. Efficient Itinerary Planning with Category Constraints. In *Proceedings of the 22Nd ACM SIGSPATIAL International Conference on Advances in Geographic Information Systems (SIGSPATIAL '14)*. 203–212.
3. Brent Hecht and Monica Stephens. 2014. A tale of cities: Urban biases in volunteered geographic information. *Proc. of ICWSM* (2014).
4. Hartwig Hochmair. 2010. Spatial Association of Geotagged Photos with Scenic Locations. *Geospatial Crossroads@ GI_Forum* 10 (2010), 91–100.
5. Hillary Page Ive, Wendy Ju, and Kirstin Kohler. 2014. Quantitative Measures of User Experience in Autonomous Driving Simulators. In *Adjunct Proceedings of the 6th International Conference on Automotive User Interfaces and Interactive Vehicular Applications (AutomotiveUI '14)*. 1–3.
6. Yangqing Jia, Evan Shelhamer, Jeff Donahue, Sergey Karayev, Jonathan Long, Ross Girshick, Sergio Guadarrama, and Trevor Darrell. 2014. Caffe: Convolutional Architecture for Fast Feature Embedding. *arXiv preprint arXiv:1408.5093* (2014).
7. Alex Krizhevsky, Ilya Sutskever, and Geoffrey Hinton. 2012. Imagenet classification with deep convolutional neural networks. In *Advances in neural information processing systems*. 1097–1105.
8. Maaret Posti, Johannes Schöning, and Jonna Häkkilä. 2014. Unexpected journeys with the HOBBIT: the design and evaluation of an asocial hiking app. In *Proceedings of the 2014 conference on Designing interactive systems*. ACM, 637–646.
9. Xiaochun Qin, Michael J Meitner, Brent Chamberlain, and Xiaoning Zhang. 2008. Estimating visual quality of scenic highway using GIS and landscape visualizations. In *ESRI Users Conference*.
10. Pavel Andreevich Samsonov, Brent Hecht, and Johannes Schöning. 2015. From Automatic Sign Detection To Space Usage Rules Mining For Autonomous Driving. In *CHI 2015 Workshop on Experiencing Autonomous Vehicles: Crossing the Boundaries between a Drive and a Ride*. ACM.
11. Martin Traunmueller, Ava Fatah gen Schieck, Johannes Schöning, and Duncan Brumby. 2013. The path is the reward: considering social networks to contribute to the pleasure of urban strolling. In *CHI'13 Extended Abstracts on Human Factors in Computing Systems*. ACM, 919–924.
12. Jianwei Zhang, Hiroshi Kawasaki, and Yukiko Kawai. 2008. A Tourist Route Search System Based on Web Information and the Visibility of Scenic Sights. In *Second International Symposium on Universal Communication, 2008 (ISUC '08)*. 154–161.
13. Yan-Tao Zheng, Shuicheng Yan, Zheng-Jun Zha, Yiqun Li, Xiangdong Zhou, Tat-Seng Chua, and Ramesh Jain. 2013. GPSView: A Scenic Driving Route Planner. *ACM Trans. Multimedia Comput. Commun. Appl.* 9, 1, Article 3 (Feb. 2013), 18 pages.
14. Bolei Zhou, Agata Lapedriza, Jianxiong Xiao, Antonio Torralba, and Aude Oliva. 2014. Learning deep features for scene recognition using places database. In *Advances in Neural Information Processing Systems*. 487–495.

An Intelligent Interface for Learning Content: Combining an Open Learner Model and Social Comparison to Support Self-Regulated Learning and Engagement

Julio Guerra
Instituto de Informática, Universidad Austral de Chile, Valdivia, Chile
School of Information Sciences, University of Pittsburgh, Pittsburgh, PA, USA
jdg60@pitt.edu

Roya Hosseini
Intelligent Systems Program, University of Pittsburgh
Pittsburgh, PA, USA
roh38@pitt.edu

Sibel Somyurek
Department of Computer Education and Instructional Technologies, Gazi University
Ankara, Turkey
ssomyurek@gazi.edu.tr

Peter Brusilovsky
School of Information Sciences, University of Pittsburgh
Pittsburgh, PA, USA
peterb@pitt.edu

ABSTRACT
We present the Mastery Grids system, an intelligent interface for online learning content that combines open learner modeling (OLM) and social comparison features. We grounded the design of Mastery Grids in self-regulated learning and learning motivation theories, as well as in our past work in social comparison, OLM, and adaptive navigation support. The force behind the interface is the combination of adaptive navigation functionality with the mastery-oriented aspects of OLM and the performance-oriented aspects of social comparison. We examined different configurations of Mastery Grids in two classroom studies and report the results of analysis of log data and survey responses. The results show how Mastery Grids interacts with different factors, like gender and achievement-goal orientation, and ultimately, its impact on student engagement, performance, and motivation.

Author Keywords
Open Learner Model; Achievement-Goal Orientation; Self-Regulated Learning; Social Comparison

ACM Classification Keywords
H.5.m. Information Interfaces and Presentation (e.g. HCI): Miscellaneous; K.3.1. Computers and Education: Computer Uses in Education

INTRODUCTION
In many courses offered by modern universities, mastery of a subject comes only after considerable practice. Subjects like college-level mathematics, physics, chemistry, or computer science expect students to work with simulations, examine worked-out examples, and practice their skills by solving a large number of problems. Only a limited amount of this practice (typically problems) is usually assigned to students as a part of course requirements; the rest is recommended for students to complete as practice. This division is well-justified, since different students need considerably different amount of practice. Historically, practice examples and problems were provided by textbook authors at the end of every chapter, and teachers recommended them as practice assignments when this chapter is assigned for reading. However, the increased use of computers as learning tools has gradually led to creation of large numbers of computer-based practice systems oriented toward student self-study. For example, in the area of learning programming, we can distinguish several types of practice content that is now supported by many practice-oriented systems: worked-out examples that allow students to examine meaningful problem-solving approaches [6]; program animations that visually demonstrate program behavior [15]; program tracing exercises that engage students in understanding language semantics [5]; and program construction exercises that allow students to practice their composition skills [26].

Years of studies have demonstrated the strong educational benefits of each of the listed kinds of practice content. Moreover, the recent advancement of Web technologies has led to the steady transition of many practice-oriented systems from stand-alone to Web-based, with solid volumes of practice content accessible online. Surprisingly, these shifts have not led to a similar revolution in the use of this practice content. As observed by a recent report [3], overall student exposure to this content is low.

In this work, we present the Mastery Grids system, an intelligent interface for online learning that attempts to resolve this unfortunate situation and considerably increase student work with several types of practice content, from examples to problems. The Mastery Grids interface combines several

IUI'16, March 07 - 10, 2016, Sonoma, CA, USA

ACM 978-1-4503-4137-0/16/03 ...$15.00
DOI: http://dx.doi.org/10.1145/2856767.2856784

design decisions to address several known obstacles to work with practice content: all types of content are accessible from the same integrated interface, avoiding the need to log into different single-content systems; student-changing state of knowledge is visualized in the form of an open learned model (OLM) to support self-regulated learning and guide students to the most appropriate practice topics and content; social comparison in the form of peer and class progress is offered to provide additional motivation and navigation support. We grounded the design of Mastery Grids in self-regulated learning and learning motivation theories, as well as in our past work in social comparison, OLM, and adaptive navigation support. The force behind the interface is the combination of adaptive navigation functionality with the Mastery-oriented aspects of OLM and the Performance-oriented aspects of social comparison. To assess the value of our approach, as well as specific design decisions, we examined different configurations of Mastery Grids in two classroom studies and report the results of analysis of the log data and survey responses. The results show the overall impact of our technology on student engagement, performance, and motivation, as well as insights in the ways in which Mastery Grids interacts with different factors, like gender and achievement-goal orientation.

BACKGROUND

Open Learner Model and Open Social Student Modeling

Open learner models (OLMs), which are also referred to as open student models (OSMs), are an important kind of educational interface that has emerged in the area of personalized learning systems. While in traditional personalized systems, student models that represent the current state of student knowledge are hidden from students and are used solely to personalize the educational process, more recent open student model interfaces introduced the ability to view, explore, and even modify the state of a student's own knowledge [8]. Typically, the state of knowledge is displayed using some form of visualization, such as a set of skillometers [19] or a knowledge map [16]. By visualizing, and sometimes, interacting with her own learning or achievement representation, the learner is given a powerful feedback tool that is known to impact her metacognition and self-regulated learning strategies [9].

Recent projects attempted to enhance the value of OLMs in several ways. The most popular among these efforts is integrating OLM with interfaces to access learning content [18, 25, 22]. In this way, an OLM provides personalized navigation support that helps students to select the most appropriate content for their skill levels. Studies show that this kind of personalized support could increase the efficiency of student work and also increase their motivation to work with learning content [18, 25].

Other researchers have attempted to enhance the engagement power of OLMs by using ideas of social comparison; namely, by allowing students to explore each others' models [7] or to view a cumulative model of the class [13, 4], thus triggering social comparison effects. This approach, which has been referred as Open Social Student Modeling, has demonstrated a considerable positive effect on engagement and efficiency, causes students to complete more practice content, and allows them to move quickly to the next content items [13, 4].

Self-Regulated Learning and Achievement-Goal

Self-regulated learning (SRL) defines the learner as an active participant who monitors and applies strategies to control her own learning process cognitively, metacognitively, and emotionally [29]. A key aspect in SRL is the interdependence between motivation and self-regulating processes [29]. For example, self-efficacy, an element of self-regulation, is viewed as the force behind learning motivation [2] and has a strong influence in goal-setting [23]. Moreover, a self-regulated learner, "who proactively seek[s] out information when needed and take[s] the necessary steps to master it" [28], is closely related to the Mastery-Approach orientation defined by the Achievement-Goal Orientation framework [11]. This framework argues that students' motivation while facing a learning situation translates to different types of goals, and defines a 2x2 classification of goal orientations: *Mastery-Approach* oriented students pursue learning, while *Performance-Approach* oriented students pursue achievement and are usually more sensitive to comparison and scores. *Mastery-Avoidance* students avoid not to learn or learn too little, and *Performance-Avoidance* students avoid to perform worse than others or receive low scores. Relationships between SRL and achievement goals are well studied. For example, students who present high levels of mastery goal orientation and who are intrinsically motivated to learn also present higher levels of SRL elements, including higher self-efficacy and the use of self-regulatory strategies [27].

Researchers have also studied how different goal orientations can be fostered, a finding that suggests that mastery oriented environmental factors (such as learning autonomy) can promote the adoption of mastery goals [10], while performance-oriented elements, like score rankings, can account for the adoption of performance goals, such as competition to score higher than other students [20]. While mastery and performance orientations seem to represent opposite values, they can coexist: a student can present high levels of performance- and mastery-oriented goals at the same time [1]. Our system follows these ideas by integrating mastery orientation provided by OLM, which allows the learner to monitor her own learning progress, and performance orientation is provided by social comparisons features.

MASTERY GRIDS: AN INTELLIGENT INTERFACE FOR PRACTICE-ORIENTED LEARNING CONTENT

The Mastery Grids system is an attempt to design an intelligent interface for accessing learning content that provides support for SRL and allows learners to monitor their course progress. In its core, it follows our earlier work that integrated content navigation with OLM-based knowledge progress visualization [13]. To complement the benefits of OLM, Mastery Grids (MG) also engages the power of the Open Social Student Model by incorporating visualization based on the models of other students. The MG interface presented below adds several features to its first version presented in [17].

The interface of the Mastery Grids system (Figure 1) is composed of several grids showing different aggregations of progress information. In all grids, columns represent topics and rows represent different types of content (such as problems, examples, or animations). The first grid shows an extended OLM that visualizes the learner's own progress over several kinds of practice content. Each cell shows knowledge progress, with one kind of content for one topic using a different density of green color. The third grid (number 2 in Figure 1) represents the average progress of the *reference group* using a varying density of blue color. A combo box in the menu bar allows the student to use the whole class, or just the top students, as a reference group (number 7 in Figure 1). Different colors were used to represent the group average and the learner (blue and green, respectively) in order to implement the differential comparison in the second grid (number 3 in Figure 1). When the group has a higher progress than the learner on a specific kind of content in a specific topic, the corresponding cell in the second grid becomes blue. Otherwise, it becomes green. The intensity of the color represents the intensity of the difference, and a gray color means there is no difference.

In the bottom part (number 4 in Figure 1), a progress grid for each of the students in the group is shown (with the top progressing students shown first). The list does not show the names of the students. To be consistent with the colors used in the first grid, each peer grid is represented in shades of blue and the learner is represented in shades of green, which also facilitates locating the learner in the list. Figure 1 shows the learner in the 3rd position of the list. To speed up the interface loading, the ranked list of peers is only shown when clicking in the button "Load the rest of the learners," which is located below the 3rd grid and does not appear in Figure 1.

By clicking on any topic cell, the user can access the practice content of this topic, shown as activity cells organized in rows by content type (number 5 in Figure 1). By clicking in the activity cells, the content is loaded in an overlaid window. Mastery Grids integrates different types of online "smart" content from different content providers. "Smart" content [3] interactively engages students, provides mechanisms to store and retrieve student activity data, and ultimately, incorporates feedback mechanisms. The captured activity data are processed by MG's back-end services to compute knowledge progress. For example, each programming problem included in the Mastery Grids system shows the correct answer to the student and logs the student response in a User Model server, which can provide summaries of this data back to Mastery Grids. The version presented in this paper includes three types of smart content for a Java programming course: programming problems [14], interactive examples [6], and program animations [24].

To allow for the exploration of a broader design space, different interface components can be loaded in different combinations. A selector widget in the menu bar allows students to select among different progress visualizations for the different content types (number 8 in Figure 1). The user can choose a *full* view in which each grid has separate rows for each content type (as shown in Figure 1), and can also select to display averages by the type of content (for example, showing only progress in examples), or an *overall* view where all the three first grids are collapsed in one grid with one row for the learner progress, one row for the comparison, and one row for the group progress, as shown in Figure 3. The *overall* view mode is set as the default view. In addition, all comparison features can also be completely hidden by clicking the button "Individual" (number 6 in Figure 1), which leaves only the personal part of the interface visible, as shown in Figure 2.

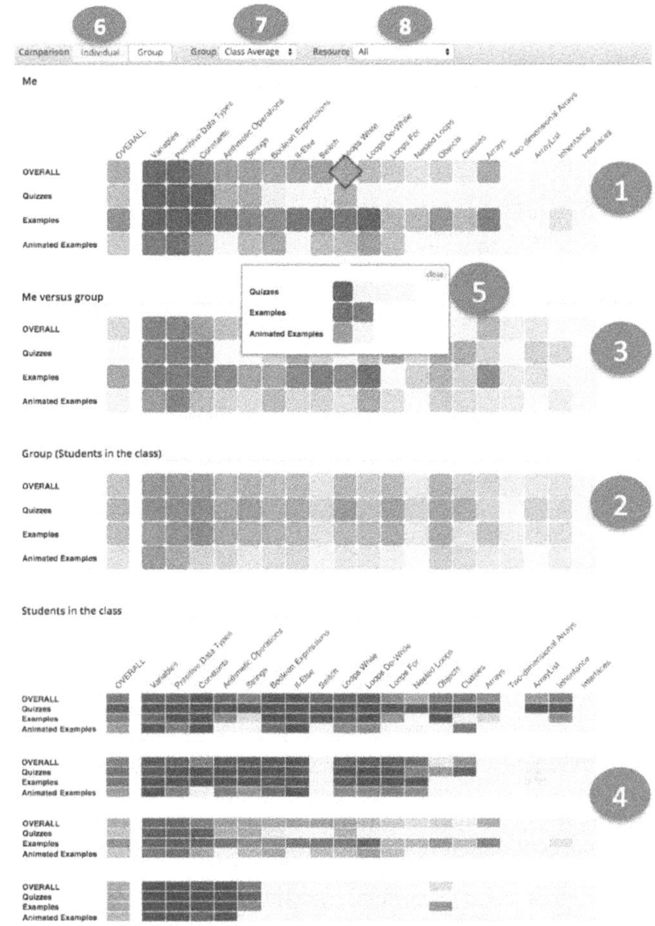

Figure 1. The full Mastery Grids interface. A menu bar contains controls to change the view of the group or the details shown. Circled numbers have been added in the image to support explanations.

The Mastery Grid interface can be configured to hide or show the menu controls (numbers 6, 7, and 8 in Figure 1), as well as to enable or disable the OSSM features for a specific group or for individual users. For example, this allows us to show social comparison features only to some students, or to enable all features for the instructor. Figures 2 and 3 show different configurations of Mastery Grids both with and without social-comparison features, respectively.

CLASSROOM STUDIES

In this work, we reported the analyses and results of two semester-long classroom studies in an introductory Object-Oriented Java programming class during 2014-2015. Classes were taught by the same instructors and had the same setup.

Figure 2. Mastery Grids with minimal features or individual view (all social comparison features have been disabled).

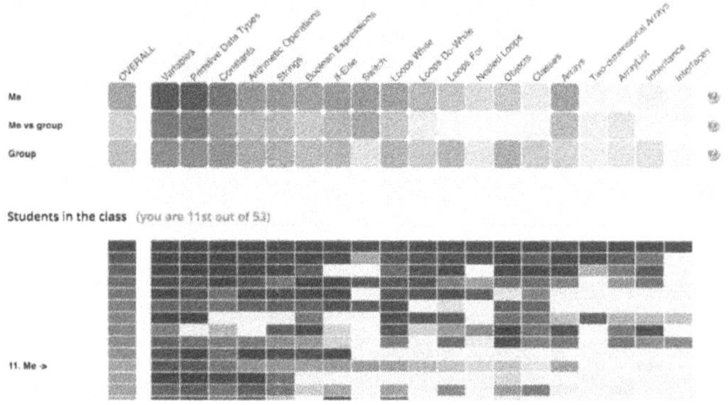

Figure 3. Mastery Grids with social comparison features and collapsed grids, averaging the progress across types of resources.

The studies were designed to explore the engagement effects of the system features, especially the social comparison elements presented in Mastery Grids, and to examine the mediating impact of the learner's motivational characteristics. To support this goal, different features of the system were enabled or disabled to different student groups, which is explained in detail in the next section.

To characterize learners' motivation, we choose the Achievement-Goal Orientation Framework [11] because of its strong relations to Self-Regulated Learning as depicted in the Background section. To measure goal orientation, we use the Achievement-Goal orientation questionnaire [11], which contains 12 questions in a 7-point Likert scale, which corresponds to 3 questions for each of the Achievement-Goal factors: Mastery-Approach ("My goal is to learn as much as possible"), Mastery-Avoidance ("My aim is to avoid learning less than I possibly could"), Performance-Approach ("My goal is to perform better than the other students"), and Performance-Avoidance ("I strive to avoid performing worse than others").

Classroom setup and data collection

Each classroom study was divided into 2 parts. Part 1 started at the beginning of the term, when some details of the study and the Mastery Grids system were introduced to the students with a live demonstration. The Mastery Grids system was initially set up with minimal features, as shown in Figure 2. Instructors offered around 1% of extra credit for participating in the study, including solving at least 10 problems in the system. A pretest was applied in conjunction with an initial measure of the Achievement-Goal questionnaire.

Part 2 started in the fifth week, 3 weeks before the midterm. At this time, students were randomly classified in 4 groups, according to the presence of social features (*social* factor) and/or the presence of the resource selector component (*resource* factor). Pretest scores also balanced the assignment to groups. The four groups are named as follows: *control* or *C* (keep the individual view), *resources-on* or *R* (add the resource selector feature in the menu), *social-on* or *S* (add the social comparison features), *social-resources* or *SR* (add both social comparison features and resource selector). At the beginning of Part 2, an email was sent to all students with a reminder of the study, a reminder of instructions to access the system, and a brief explanation of the new features introduced (for the control group, the email contained only the reminders). A week before the midterm, the Achievement-Goal questionnaire was applied again. At the end of the term and the end of Part 2, a post-test, the achievement-goal questionnaire, and a usability/usefulness survey of the Mastery Grids system were administered. Consent forms were also collected in order to use the data from questionnaires. The three moments wherein the achievement-goal factors were measured are referred to as *initial*, *middle*, and *final* measures.

Table 1. Number of students participating in the studies. Number of female and male students in parentheses.

		Resources		
		Resources On	Resources Off	Total
Social	OSM	23 (12, 10)	20 (8, 12)	43
	OSSM	22 (11, 11)	24 (7, 15)	46
	Total	45	44	89

Activity on the system occurring during Part 1 of the study is referred to as activity *before conditions were introduced* or simply, *Part 1*. Similarly, activity during Part 2 is referred to as activity *after conditions were introduced* or *Part 2*. Recall that during Part 1, all students had access to the same basic features of the system (Figure 2).

The system usage data includes logs of sessions (different log-ins into the system), problems attempted and solved, examples displayed, animations displayed, and other interface interactions, like changes on the resource selector or group selector menu and clicks on the button "load others" (see description of Mastery Grids and Figure 1). Time spent on activities was also recorded. Engagement is measured in absolute scores of system activity and relative scores of activity or time by session in the system.

In total, 89 students who logged into the system at least once (38 female, 48 male; 3 students did not provide gender information) out of 114 students enrolled were used for the analyses in this paper. The number of students in each of the groups can be seen in Table 1. Female and male student counts are shown in parentheses.

In the next sections, we first present analyses on the difference between OSM and OSSM interfaces; i.e. the *OSM* group includes *C* and *R* groups; the *OSSM* group with social features enabled is the combination of groups *S* and *SR*. Then, we briefly analyze the resource selector feature on system usage.

ASSESSING THE OVERALL VALUE OF THE INTERFACE

To explore the value of both the OSM and OSSM, we compared the usage statistics of our classroom studies using the Mastery Grids system to a previous classroom study offered

Table 2. The Mean±SD of system usage statistics: comparison between a portal of course materials and the Mastery Grids system across all groups (MG), the OSM group, and the OSSM group.

Parameters	Portal	MG	p-value	OSM	p-value	OSSM	p-value
Logged-in students	17	89	-	43	-	34	-
Active students	14 (82%)	80 (90%)	-	40 (93%)	-	30 (88%)	-
Sessions	2.71±1.49	7.54±6.05	.000 ***	7.45±5.76	.000 ***	9.37±6.49	.000 ***
Distinct topics	9.21±4.85	9.4±5.6	.97	9.3±5.71	.89	11.47±4.75	.192
Problem attempts	72.36±67.25	78.88±62.18	.556	76.45±54.33	.534	100.83±69.51	.07 .
Distinct problems	32.79±21.67	43.74±28.26	.21	43.6±28.25	.15	53.2±25.86	.01 *
Distinct problems solved	28.43±19.2	41.92±28.13	.126	41.88±28.7	.152	50.77±25.57	.003 **
Success rate	.707±.147	.648±.144	.182	.639±.147	.153	.627±.127	.094 .
Repeats per problem	2.52±1.81	1.8±0.77	.318	1.83±0.84	.402	1.85±0.74	.579
Success per problem	1.8±1.36	1.11±0.35	.1	1.11±0.33	.139	1.12±0.39	.098 .
Failure per problem	0.72±0.61	0.69±0.56	.534	0.72±0.67	.418	0.73±0.45	.338
Examples viewed	13.27±9	32.52±26.23	.019 *	31.02±26.67	.035 *	41.57±24.67	.000 ***

significant level: ***: <.000; **: <.01; *: <.05; .: <.1

in Spring 2008 in which students used a traditional non-adaptive portal to access comparable volumes of the same practice content. The *Portal* presented the content in a simple two-level hierarchy of HTTP links, the first level offered a list of topics and the second level listed links to parameterized problems and interactive examples. Table 2 provides the summary of usage statistics of the *Portal* and the Mastery Grids system across all groups (*MG*), the *OSM* group, and the *OSSM* group. Usage statistics are computed based on the data of *active* users who had at least 5 problem attempts in the portal, whole system (MG), or in a specific condition (OSM or OSSM). Because the OSSM group did not have social features during Part 1, we consider as *logged-in* OSSM users those who logged in during the Part 2 (34 out of 46) and as *active* OSSM users those who have at least 5 problem attempts in Part 2 (i.e, have a reasonable chance to experience "true" OSSM condition). This explains why active users for both the OSM and OSSM groups does not add up to the total active users in the *MG* column: there are 10 students in the OSSM group who had enough activity to be considered as active MG users but did not have enough activity in Part 2 to be considered as *active* OSSM students. In other words, only 30 OSSM students who attempted 5 or more problems during Part 2 are considered as *active* OSSM students. Columns four, six, and eight of the table report the observed significance level (p-values) for the statistical tests that were carried out to compare each usage parameter between the Portal and MG, between the Portal and the OSM group, and between the Portal and the OSSM group, respectively[1].

According to Table 2, the Mastery Grids system performed significantly better than the Portal in engaging students to work with the non-mandatory course materials. The OSM/OSSM interface made the Mastery Grids system arguably more addictive than the basic portal: the average number of sessions and examples viewed were significantly higher in all conditions of the Mastery Grids system (MG, OSM, and OSSM). Progress tracking also allowed students to better distribute their efforts: on average, when using Mastery Grids, students explored and solved more distinct problems.

[1]The One-Way ANOVA or Kruskal-Wallis H test was used, depending on whether the assumptions of the parametric test were met.

This difference becomes significant for the OSSM group, where they accessed about 1.6 times more distinct problems than in the *Portal*. This indicates that the navigation support available in Mastery Grids decreases students tendency of staying with the same content (for example, repeating problems they have already mastered), and as a result, students moved on to new problems more quickly. This data correlates (but not significantly) with a slightly lower *success rate* in the Mastery Grids system. Our data shows that in the absence of mastery indicators and navigation support offering guidance across course topics, students tended to over-stay within topics repeating the same problems even after solving them correctly, which resulted in a larger fraction of successful attempts on the same problems.

These observations indicate that the Mastery Grids system is more beneficial than a traditional portal, in terms of student engagement and effort allocation. In the next sections, we look beyond the engagement level and explore different aspects of the tool, from its impact on student performance to how it affects student navigation patterns, as well as how it interacts with motivational factors.

ASSESSING THE VALUE OF SOCIAL COMPARISON

Effects of OSSM on engagement

To analyze the value of the social comparison component within the overall context of the Mastery Grids system, we compared engagement differences between OSM (C + R) and OSSM (S + SR) groups by examining usage statistics and patterns both before and after conditions were introduced (Part 1 and Part 2). Table 3 shows statistics of usage during Part 1 and Part 2, and within the OSM and OSSM groups. The first row shows the number of students who logged into the system in the corresponding group and part. The other rows show the average usage parameters per student.

There are no significant differences on usage statistics between social and non-social groups before the OSSM conditions were introduced (Part 1 columns in Table 3), which suggests that groups were balanced. Looking at the OSSM (Social) columns in both Part 1 and Part 2, we note a trend of increase of activity and time on the system, while the OSM group tended to decrease the activity from Part 1 to Part 2.

Table 3. Mean and Standard Error (in parentheses) of student usage statistics in Part 1 and 2 of the studies for OSM and OSSM groups.

	Part 1		Part 2	
	OSM	OSSM	OSM	OSSM
Students	43	46	35	34
Sessions	3.26 (.49)	3.5 (.49)	4.77 (.58)	4.5 (.68)
Problem attempts	40.7 (6.2)	34.9 (6.0)	37.3 (5.2)	48.4 (7.6)
Problems solved	22.7 (2.99)	20 (3.2)	20.3 (3.2)	24.1 (3.5)
Success rate	.66 (.03)	.694 (.027)	.57 (.03)	.58 (.03)
Examples viewed	16 (2.6)	16.9 (2.8)	16.6 (2.8)	18.4 (2.8)
Animations viewed	4.84 (.94)	4.3 (.99)	5.14 (1.28)	7.62 (1.41)
Time on the system	4905 (1043)	4803 (1136)	6416 (1016)	5955 (984)
Time on problems	1386 (245)	1606 (568)	2317 (406)	2204 (396)
Time on examples	1342 (356)	1239 (278)	1605 (353)	1162 (231)
Time on animations	568 (234)	375 (108)	452 (117)	595 (146)
Clicks group selector				1.15 (.47)
Clicks load others				1.06 (.30)
Time by session	1633 (331)	1328 (230)	1247 (154)	1501 (244)
Activity by session	21.38 (3.49)	17.05 (2.29)	12.87 (1.75)	23.58 (4.96)

Note also how time measures increase in both groups, and that this increase is smaller in the OSSM group. To see the differences in the increase of activity or time, repeated-measures ANOVA on activity statistics measured in Part 1 and Part 2 was performed among OSM and OSSM groups. In these analyses, we also include a measure of the total activity by session (at the bottom of Table 3) which sums problems attempts, examples, and animated examples displayed by each student, and divides this sum by the number of sessions the student has. Only students who have activity in both Part 1 and Part 2 were considered. Additionally, outliers were found and removed for the statistics *time by session* (1 student presented an extremely long session) and *activity by session* (4 students showed 1 session with an extremely high number of activities in either Part 1 or Part 2).

We found a significant difference on success rate on problems ($p = .007$) between Part 1 and Part 2, which was expected given that Part 2 involves generally more complex problems. A significant interaction between *Time* (Part 1, Part 2) and *Social group* (OSM/OSSM) factors was found on the amount of *activity by session*, $F(1, 55) = 4.972$, $p = 0.03$, $\eta_p^2 = .083$. As it can be seen in Figure 4, students in the OSSM group increased their number of activities per session, while students in the OSM group decreased it. Another significant interaction was found for the factors Time, Gender and Social group on the number of examples displayed, $F(1, 45) = 6.467$, $p = .014$, $\eta_p^2 = 0.126$. Female students in the OSSM group tended to increase the number of examples displayed from Part 1 to Part 2, while male students decreased the number of examples displayed, and both female and male students decreased the number of examples displayed in the OSM group (Figure 5).

We compute the total number of activities by summing problem attempts, distinct examples, and animations displayed. A step-wise regression performed on the total activity in Part 2 showed that total activity in Part 1 ($\beta = 0.515$, $SE = .115$) and *social group* factor ($\beta = 30.431$, $SE = 12.53$) are both significant predictors, $p < .001$ and $p = .019$, respectively. Being in the OSSM group means an increase of about 30 activities, as compared to being in the OSM group. Other factors

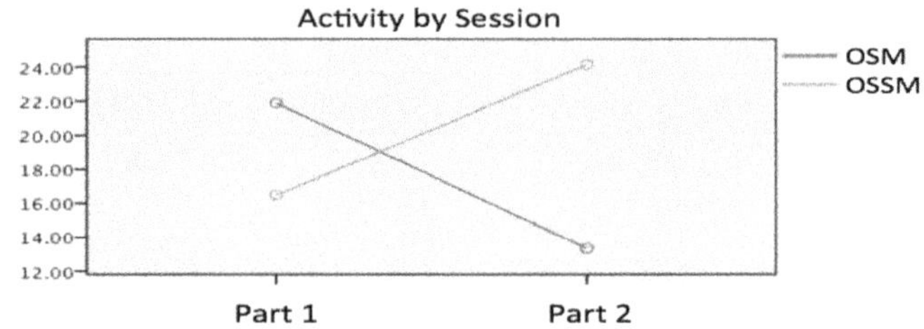

Figure 4. Interaction between Time (Part 1, Part 2) and Social factor (OSM/OSSM).

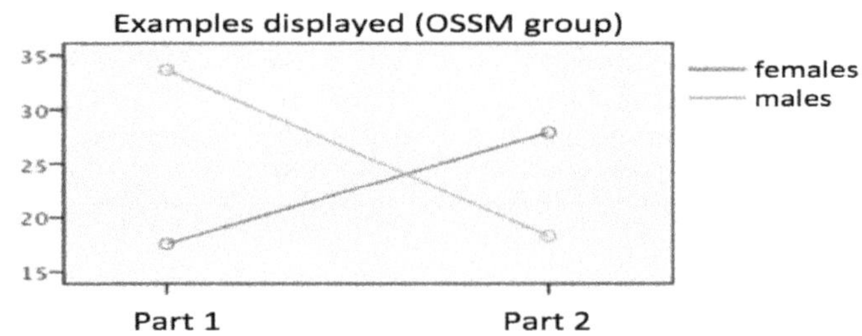

Figure 5. Examples displayed by female and male students in the OSSM during Part 1 and Part 2.

like gender or previous experience did not result in significant predictors and did not enter the step-wise regression model. This confirms the role of social features in engaging students to do more activities.

Effect in performance and instructional effectiveness

We evaluated the effect of the OSM and OSSM on student performance using four measures: (1) *normalized learning gain*, which is defined as the actual gain divided by the possible gain; (2) *course grade*; (3) *success rate*, which is the percentage of correct attempts on problems; and (4) *effectiveness scores*. We conducted several analyses to compare performance differences between the groups (OSM/OSSM). We did not find any differences in the learning gain, success rate, or course grade across the two groups. However, there were some differences in the effectiveness score.

Effectiveness score: To compare instructional effectiveness scores between the OSM and OSSM groups, we looked into instructional effectiveness scores of students, following the approach in [21]. First, we computed $z - scores$ of the performance p_z (correctly answered problems) and time t_z (time spent on problems). Then, the relative effectiveness of a student is computed as the distance between point (p_z,t_z) and the line of zero (0) effectiveness.

For this analysis, we used data from students who attempted at least 5 problems. Although, we did not find a significant difference on the effectiveness scores between the OSM and OSSM groups, differences were found in the change of effectiveness scores among the groups from Part 1 to Part 2. A repeated-measure analysis of variance with both group (OSM/OSSM) and gender as factors showed the main effect of time (Part 1, Part 2) is significant ($F(1, 40) = 27.02$, $p < .001$). The within-subject test indicates that the interaction of time and group is also significant ($F(1, 40) = 4.72$, $p = .036$), in Part 2 the effectiveness scores of the OSSM group ($M = 0.18$, $SE = .426$) were higher than in the OSM group ($M = -2.81$, $SE = .389$). Also, the interaction of gender and group was marginally significant ($F(1, 40) = 3 : 59$, $p = .065$), male students in the OSSM group had higher efficiency scores ($M = 0.12$, $SE = 0.40$) than male students in the OSM group ($M = -0.48$, $SE = 0.37$) during Part 2. In general, we observed a tendency to decrease the effectiveness scores from Part 1 to Part 2, except for male students in the OSSM group.

Effects on navigational patterns

So far, we provided high-level analysis of the intelligent interface in the Mastery Grids system, showed the value of OSSM on engagement, and explored its impact on student performance. In this section, we seek to extend our previous analysis by looking at a micro-level analysis of students' navigation patterns with the goal to understand how the sequence of students' clicks on Mastery Grids cells differs between the OSSM and OSM interface.

We started by classifying students' moves from the current cell to the next cell in the Mastery Grids system into four different groups: (1) *within-topic*, which indicates a move to a cell in the same topic; (2) *next-topic*, which indicates a move from a cell in a topic to the cell in the next topic (according to the sequence of topics in the course), (3) *jump-forward*, which indicates a jump to a cell in a topic that two or more steps further away from the current topic, and (4) *jump-backward*, which indicates a jump to a cell in an earlier topic. A *within-topic* or *next-topic* move represents a sequential navigation, while a *jump-forward* or *jump-backward* move represents a non-sequential navigation pattern. We then computed the ratio of non-sequential navigation for 58 students who had at least one attempt in both Part 1 and Part 2 of the study, and excluded 4 students who had non-sequential navigation scores larger than $2 \times SD$ from the mean. To ensure that these ratios are stable, we considered only 39 (OSM/OSSM : 20/19) students with at least 5 problem attempts in Part 1 and at least 10 problem attempts in Part 2 (the smaller threshold in part 1 is due to the shorter length of the part).

To explore the differences in student patterns between the OSM and OSSM groups, we conducted a repeated measures ANOVA on the non-sequential ratios (Part 1 and Part 2) among OSM/OSSM groups. There was no difference in the non-sequential patterns between the OSM and the OSSM group, $F(1, 37) = 0.50, p > .05$. Similarly, there was no difference in those patterns both before and after social features were enabled in the OSSM; namely, in Part 1 and Part 2 of the study $F(1, 37) = 1.61$, $p > .05$. However, there was a significant interaction between *time* (Part1, Part2) and group (OSM, OSSM), $F(1, 37) = 3.01, p < .10$. More specifically, in the OSM group, the ratio of non-sequential navigation was higher in Part 2 ($M = 0.16$, $SD = 0.08$) than in Part 1 ($M = 0.11, SD = 0.08$).

To investigate further the relationship between the non-sequential patterns on the amount of learning, we performed a step-wise regression to predict the normalized learning gain of students in terms of the following factors: number of total activities on problems and examples, pretest group (low or high by median split), gender, group (OSM/OSSM), and total ratio of non-sequential navigation patterns over the whole semester. The results of the regression showed that only the total ratio of non-sequential navigation made a significant contribution to the learning gain ($\beta = 0.66$, $SE = 0.28$, $p < 0.03$). The non-sequential navigation patterns also explained a significant proportion of variance in the learning gain $R^2 = .20, F(2, 30) = 3.65, p < .04$.

By putting all these results together, the non-sequential patterns increased more in the OSM group than in the OSSM group. This could be due to the social nature of the OSSM that makes students more conservative in their navigation – they tend to sequentially follow their peers rather than browsing the content space by their own, which is often a non-sequential process. More interestingly, there was a positive association between non-sequential navigation patterns and learning gain: those who had a higher proportion of non-sequential patterns gained more knowledge. Although the two groups (OSM and OSSM) were not different in terms of the learning gain, this suggests that students in the social group might gain more knowledge if other adaptive features are added to the social interface, such as individual or personalized guidance. Future studies should be conducted to investigate this hypothesis.

The role of the Achievement-Goal orientation

We now analyze how the motivational profile of the students, as characterized by their Achievement-Goal orientation [11], affects overall engagement in the system and learning effectiveness. For each student, the responses of the Achievement-Goal questionnaire were grouped and averaged by each of the factors. As a result, each student has four scores (Mastery-Approach score, Mastery-Avoidance score, Performance-Approach score, Performance-Avoidance score) for the three moments in the term in which the questionnaires were applied: initial, middle, and final measures.

We first analyze differences in usage between low or high achievement-goal students by classifying students using the median of each of the achievement-goal factors. We used the middle Achievement-Goal measures (measures at the middle of the term) because it is more representative of the state of the goal orientation of the students while using the system. Only 54 students who answered the questionnaire and gave consent are included in these analyses. We found a clear difference on usage only among low and high Mastery-Approach students, while other classifications did not show significant differences. Students in the high Mastery-Approach group have a higher level of activity in all the measures during Part 1. In Part 2, this effect disappeared. A 2x2 ANOVA on usage statistics on Part 2 by the Mastery-Approach factor (low/high) and the group (OSM, OSSM) did not result in any significant main effect or interaction. This suggests that the motivational effect that social features have on the increase of activity observed in the OSSM group might be of another nature than Mastery orientation, and are perhaps related to Performance orientation or a change of Performance orientation during the term.

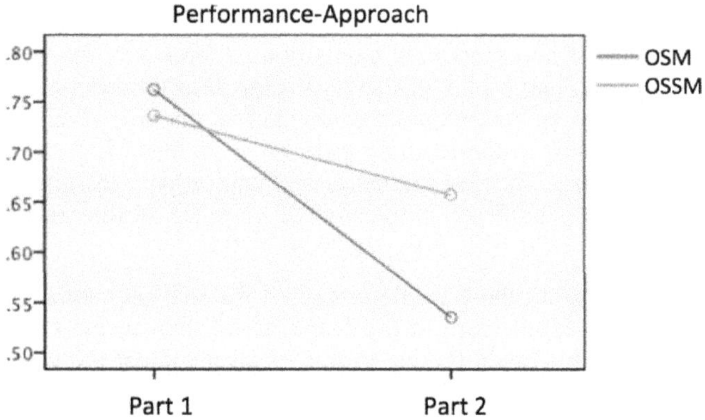

Figure 6. Different decrease of Performance-Approach orientation of students in the OSM and OSSM groups.

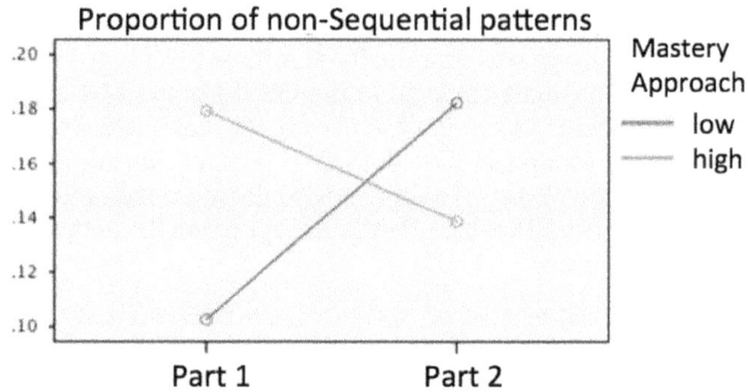

Figure 7. Contrast of the change of the proportion of non-sequential patterns among students in the low and high groups of Mastery-Approach orientation.

We now analyze the change of Achievement-Goal and the interaction with the *Social* factor. Since the literature on Achievement-Goal suggests that Mastery and Performance orientations can be influenced by environmental factors [10], we are interested to see if the use of the system with social comparison features, which are performance-oriented features, has any impact on the change of the goal orientation of the students.

We performed a repeated-measures ANOVA on the initial and final measures of Achievement-Goal orientation between the OSM and OSSM groups. A significant effect on Time (initial, final) exists for all 4 achievement-goal factors, which all consistently decreased during the term. A significant interaction was found for the Performance-Approach orientation and *Social* factor, $F(1,50) = 7.506$, $p = .009$, $\eta_p^2 = .131$. Students in the OSSM group showed lower decrease of the Performance-Approach level than students of the OSM group (Figure 6). These results suggest either that students who did not decrease their Performance-Approach orientation are becoming engaged by the social comparison features, or that social comparison features are influencing students positively in their Performance orientation. Both of these explanations have support in the achievement-goal literature, and further research is needed to establish a causal relationship. It is interesting to highlight that the Social factor presented no interaction effect, nor a main effect on the change of other Achievement-Goal factors like Mastery-Approach orientation. Even when the social comparison features might foster performance orientation, they are not negatively influencing the mastery orientation.

Now, we look at the relations between Achievement-Goal and the proportion of non-sequential navigation patterns (see previous section for details about non-sequential navigation measures). We consider the Achievement-Goal orientation measures taken in the middle of the term. Only students who answer the questionnaire, gave consent, and present at least 5 attempts to problems in Part 1 and at least 10 attempts to problems in Part 2 are considered, resulting in 29 students, 15 in OSM group and 14 in OSSM group. A significant negative correlation between the proportion of non-sequential patterns and the Mastery-Approach orientation score was found, $\rho = -.378$, $p = .043$, $N = 29$. This suggests that highly motivated students are more sequential in their patterns of navigation. A significant negative correlation was also found in the difference of the proportion of the non-sequential patterns (Part 2 - Part 1) and Mastery-Approach level, $\rho = -.429$, $p = .02$, $N = 29$. When looking at the OSM and OSSM groups separately, the negative correlation between the difference of non-sequentiality and the Mastery-Approach orientation is stronger in the OSSM group $\rho = -.62$, $p = .018$, $N = 14$, and is not significant in the OSM group. These results suggest that more motivated students become more sequential in their patterns of navigation after being exposed to social features. Step-wise regression analyses showed that other factors, including goal orientation, gender, and *social* factors were not significant predictors of the non-sequentiality proportion in Part 2. However, a repeated measures ANOVA on the proportion of non-sequentiality patterns at Part 1 and Part 2 found a significant interaction of Time and Mastery-Approach group (low/high), $F(1,27) = 8.135$, $p = .008$, $eta_p^2 = .232$. Figure 7 shows different patterns of the change of the proportion of non-sequential navigation patterns among low and high Mastery-Approach students.

Effectiveness scores (see Section *Effect in performance and instructional effectiveness*) measured in Part 1 and Part 2 did not show any significant correlations with the Achievement-Goal measures (middle). Repeated-measures ANOVA on the effectiveness scores did not show any significant effect of interaction with any Achievement-Goal group (low/high). Regression analyses on effectiveness scores also did not find any significant factor.

The value of peer-level comparisons

The Mastery Grids interface has a number of optional social features that were enabled for the students in the OSSM group: changing the comparison mode through the group selector menu (number 7 in Figure 1), and loading the progress of other students in the class (number 4 in Figure 1) by clicking on the 'load the rest of learner' button in the interface. We analyzed Mastery Grids logs to see how much students clicked on these features. Overall, out of the 34 logged-in OSSM students who logged in the system in Part 2, 18 students clicked at least once on the *group* menu or the *load learners* button, with a median of 2.5 clicks ($Mean =$

$4, Max = 20$). Although students used the social features comparatively few times, there was a statistically significant positive correlation between the number of clicks on these features and overall engagement, ($\rho = 0.41, p < .02$). Those who clicked on these features more had also more activities on problems and examples. Of course, this correlation does not imply causation. The results of the regression analysis also showed that number of clicks on social features had a significant positive impact on the number of activities ($\beta = 5.87$, $SE = 2.25$, $p < 0.02$), which can explain about 18% of the variance ($R^2 = 0.18$, $F(1, 32) = 6.84$, $p < .02$).

THE IMPACT OF INTERFACE COMPLEXITY

To see the value of the resource selector component in the Mastery Grids system, we looked into logs of 45 students who were in the *resources-on* (R) and *social-resources* (SR) groups. In both groups, students were able to switch from the default *overall* view that showed the average progress of content in one row, to the *full* view that showed progress of different content types in separate rows. For example, in the *social-resources* (SR) group, the *full* and *overall* view were similar to those shown in Figure 1 and 3, respectively.

In general, only 11 (24%) students clicked on the resource selector menu, but they did not used it extensively. The average number of clicks on this menu was 1.54 ($SD = 5.33$, $Max = 33$). However, number of clicks on the resource menu was positively correlated with the number of activities that students viewed, $\rho = 0.29$, $p < .06$. Those who clicked more on the resource menu had more problem attempts or example views. This suggests that the presence of a feature alone does not increase students tendency in using it, and that there is a clear trade-off between having a complex interface with different views (the *full* vs *overall* view) and the amount of engagement. Some students might become reluctant to continue working with a complex interface. On the other hand, those who start using such an interface might find it helpful and become even more engaged.

SURVEY ANALYSIS

A usability and usefulness questionnaire was designed to survey student opinion about the system and was applied at the end of the term in both classroom studies. The questionnaire has 2 main sections. Section 1 has 11 questions that refer to the overall usability and usefulness of the OSM features of the system. All surveyed students answered this part. Part 2 contains 14 questions about the usefulness and usability of the OSSM features, which was answered only by the OSSM group. All questions are in a 5-point Likert scale (Strongly Disagree to Strongly Agree). For Section 1, the middle point of the scale (3) is labeled as "No Opinion". In section 2, the middle point of the scale is labeled as "Did not notice". The questions, with their Mean and Standard Error in parentheses, can be seen in Table 4.

Figure 8 shows the distribution of answers. For the analysis and in the figure, questions are grouped by usefulness, usability, and motivation questions. In Section 1, questions 1, 4, 5, 6, 8, 9, and 10 are about the usefulness of the OSM system. Questions 2, 7, and 11 are about usability, and question 3 is about motivation. In Section 2, questions 1, 6, 7, and 8 are general questions about the importance that students give to be able to compare or see others. Questions 2, 3 and 5 are about the usefulness of OSSM features. Questions 4 and 9 are about usability, and questions 10, 12, and 14 are about motivation on OSSM features. Questions 12 and 14 have reversed scales, but are not shown reversed in the figure 8. Finally, questions 11 and 13 ask students about the idea of showing peer names. Some of the question refer to figures showing the features that were included in the questionnaire and are not reproduced here.

Among surveyed students, 63 answered Section 1 and between 20 to 26 students answered Section 2 (only within the OSSM group). In general, the evaluation of the OSM interface, Section 1, is positive in terms of both usability and usefulness. Students also agreed that Mastery Grids motivated them to work in problems and examples. The lower score was given to question 6 ("The interface helped me to plan my class work"), which might has been interpreted as the overall class work plan. We may need to re-phrase the question to stress the idea of planning the work within the system. We further average usefulness questions, usability questions, and motivation questions and test their differences among low and high Achievement-Goal orientation (using the middle measure of the achievement-goal survey). A Krustal-Wallis non-parametric test found a significant difference of usefulness responses among low and high Mastery-Approach students, $\chi^2 = 5.699$, $p = .017$. Other scores (such as usability and motivation) and other achievement-goal measures did not result in significant differences. High Mastery-Approach students were more positive towards the usefulness of the system. A similar analysis was performed for Section 2 within the OSSM group. Questions were classified and 4 scores computed: value (questions 1, 6, 7, and 8), usefulness (2, 3, and 5), usability (questions 4 and 9), and motivation (questions 10, 12 reversed, and 14 reversed). A Krustal-Wallis non-parametric test found significant differences on the value score $\chi^2 = 4.071$, $p = .044$ among Mastery-Approach groups. High Mastery-Approach students value the interface more. A marginally significant difference ($p = .071$) was also found for usability scores, with the same trend: high Mastery-Approach students think the system is more usable.

CONCLUSIONS

This paper presented the Mastery Grids system, an intelligent interface for accessing several kinds of practice content for an introductory programming course. To address several known obstacles to the broader use of valuable practice content, we combined an open learner model, adaptive navigation support, and social comparison technologies. Based on the analysis of literature on learning motivation and self-regulated learning, we expected OSM and social comparison features to provide different motivational dimensions to the tool.

The analyses of data from several classroom studies confirmed the overall engagement impact of our interface and provided important insights about specific interface components such as social comparison and content-level progress

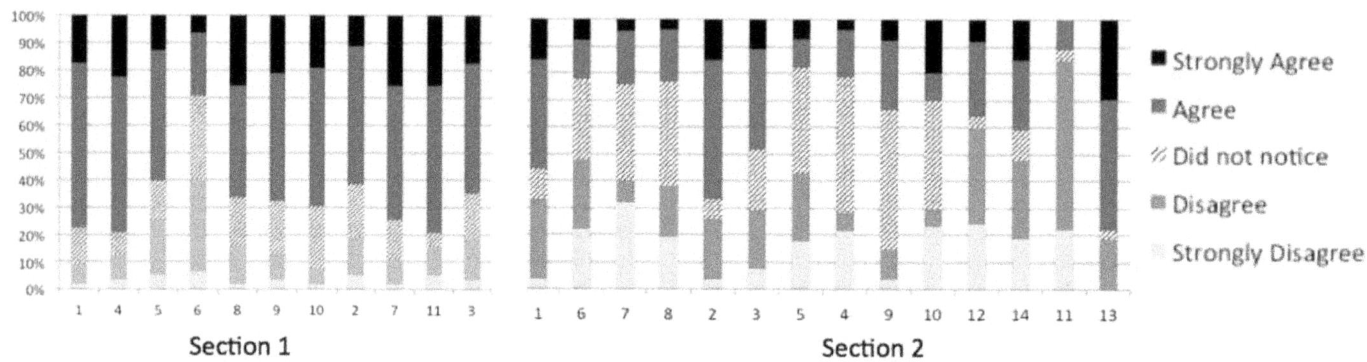

Figure 8. Distribution of responses of Sections 1 and 2 of the Mastery Grids Survey.

Table 4. Questions included in the Mastery Grids Survey. Some of the questions refer to images contained in the survey that are not reproduced here.

	Section 1 questions	M (SE)
1	In general, it was useful to see my progress in Mastery Grids	3.84 (0.11)
2	In general, I liked the interface of Mastery Grids	3.49 (0.13)
3	Seeing my progress in the tool motivated me to work on quizzes and examples	3.60 (0.13)
4	The interface helped me to understand how the class content is organized	3.86 (0.12)
5	The interface helped me to identify my weak points	3.43 (0.14)
6	The interface helped me to plan my class work	2.89 (0.13)
7	It was clear how to access problems and examples	3.87 (0.12)
8	It was useful to see my knowledge progress for each topic (figure 1, A)	3.75 (0.13)
9	It was useful to see how I am doing with individual quizzes and examples (figure 1, B)	3.73 (0.13)
10	The timeline (figure 1, C) was useful	3.79 (0.11)
11	Using green colors in different intensity to show my progress was easy to understand	3.84 (0.14)

	Section 2 questions	M (SE)
1	It is important for me to see the progress of the rest of the class	3.44 (0.19)
2	It was useful to see the progress of the whole class as it is represented in the Group row in Mastery Grids (A)	3.50 (0.18)
3	It was useful to see the progress of the top students as it is represented in the Group row in Mastery Grids (A)	3.30 (0.19)
4	The comparison between the group and myself (B) is easy to understand	3.61 (0.18)
5	It was useful to see the comparison between the selected group and myself (B)	3.33 (0.18)
6	It is important for me to see the progress of individual classmates (C)	3.30 (0.20)
7	In general, it is useful for me to be able to compare my progress with the progress of others	3.44 (0.22)
8	It is important for me to see my position in the class (D)	3.53 (0.20)
9	Visualizing the progress of others using blue colors of different intensities was easy to understand	3.94 (0.17)
10	Viewing my classmates' progress motivated me to work more in quizzes and examples	3.34 (0.22)
11	I think it would be useful for me to know the names of individual classmates in (C)	2.18 (0.17)
12	Viewing that others were more advance than me made me want to quit using Mastery Grids	2.71 (0.24)
13	If names are shown, I will not like to show my name in the list to others	3.91 (0.18)
14	Sometimes I just checked quizzes and examples to catch up with the progress of others rather than to learn more	2.79 (0.24)

visualization. Most importantly, the study demonstrated a significant positive impact of navigation-oriented social comparison interface on student engagement, efficiency, and effectiveness. A more detailed analysis also revealed interesting interactions of social comparison interface with motivational factors. While all achievement-goal orientations tend to decrease during the term, students exposed (and engaged by) social features in the system do not decrease their performance orientation. Student feedback indicated that students find the OSM and OSSM features useful and usable, and that highly motivated students have more positive opinions of these features. These results provide sufficient ground to recommend further exploration and practical use of social comparison technology as a component of interfaces for accessing practice content.

On the other hand, the study has provided some evidence that social comparison could negatively affect the diversity of student navigation, causing students to behave more alike one another. To decrease the unifying effect of social comparison while retaining its engagement value, it might be advisable to combine social comparison and personalized recommendation technologies. Our pilot study of this combination brought positive results [12]. In future work, we plan to further explore the value of OSM and OSSM in the context of practice content access examining different kinds of OLM, different approaches to present social comparison, and different combinations with other navigation support technologies.

ACKNOWLEDGMENTS

This work is supported by the Advanced Distributed Learning (ADL) Initiative (contract W911QY-13-C-0032). The views and conclusions contained in this document are those of the authors and should not be interpreted as representing the official policies, either expressed or implied, of the Department of Defense.

REFERENCES

1. Ames, C. Classrooms: Goals, structures, and student motivation. *Journal of educational psychology 84*, 3 (1992), 261.

2. Bandura, A. *Social foundations of thought and action: A social cognitive theory.* Prentice-Hall, Inc, 1986.

3. Brusilovsky, P., Edwards, S., Kumar, A., Malmi, L., Benotti, L., Buck, D., Ihantola, P., Prince, R., Sirki, T., Sosnovsky, S., Urquiza, J., Vihavainen, A., and Wollowski, M. Increasing adoption of smart learning content for computer science education. In *Proceedings of the Working Group Reports of the 2014 on Innovation & Technology in Computer Science Education Conference*, ACM (2014), 31–57.

4. Brusilovsky, P., Somyürek, S., Guerra, J., Hosseini, R., and Zadorozhny, V. The value of social: Comparing open student modeling and open social student modeling. In *User Modeling, Adaptation and Personalization*. Springer, 2015, 44–55.

5. Brusilovsky, P., and Sosnovsky, S. Individualized exercises for self-assessment of programming knowledge: An evaluation of quizpack. *ACM Journal on Educational Resources in Computing 5*, 3 (2005), Article No. 6.

6. Brusilovsky, P., and Yudelson, M. From webex to navex: Interactive access to annotated program examples. *Proceedings of the IEEE 96*, 6 (2008), 990–999.

7. Bull, S., and Kay, J. Student models that invite the learner in: The smili:() open learner modelling framework. *International Journal of Artificial Intelligence in Education 17*, 2 (2007), 89–120.

8. Bull, S., and Kay, J. Open learner models. In *Advances in intelligent tutoring systems*. Springer, 2010, 301–322.

9. Bull, S., and Kay, J. Open learner models as drivers for metacognitive processes. In *International Handbook of Metacognition and Learning Technologies*. Springer, 2013, 349–365.

10. Ciani, K. D., Middleton, M. J., Summers, J. J., and Sheldon, K. M. Buffering against performance classroom goal structures: The importance of autonomy support and classroom community. *Contemporary Educational Psychology 35*, 1 (2010), 88–99.

11. Elliot, A. J., and Murayama, K. On the measurement of achievement goals: Critique, illustration, and application. *Journal of Educational Psychology 100*, 3 (2008), 613.

12. Hosseini, R., Hsiao, I.-H., Guerra, J., and Brusilovsky, P. What should i do next? adaptive sequencing in the context of open social student modeling. In *Design for Teaching and Learning in a Networked World*. Springer, 2015, 155–168.

13. Hsiao, I.-H., Bakalov, F., Brusilovsky, P., and König-Ries, B. Progressor: social navigation support through open social student modeling. *New Review of Hypermedia and Multimedia 19*, 2 (2013), 112–131.

14. Hsiao, I.-H., Sosnovsky, S., and Brusilovsky, P. Guiding students to the right questions: adaptive navigation support in an e-learning system for java programming. *Journal of Computer Assisted Learning 26*, 4 (2010), 270–283.

15. Levy, R. B.-B., Ben-Ari, M., and Uronen, P. A. The jeliot 2000 program animation system. *Computers and Education 40*, 1 (2003), 1–15.

16. Lindstaedt, S. N., Beham, G., Kump, B., and Ley, T. Getting to know your user unobtrusive user model maintenance within work-integrated learning environments. In *4th European Conference on Technology Enhanced Learning (ECTEL 2009)*, U. Cress, V. Dimitrova, and M. Specht, Eds., vol. 5794 of *Lecture Notes in Computer Science*, Springer-Verlag (2009), 73–87.

17. Loboda, T. D., Guerra, J., Hosseini, R., and Brusilovsky, P. Mastery grids: An open source social educational progress visualization. In *Open Learning and Teaching in Educational Communities*. Springer, 2014, 235–248.

18. Long, Y., and Aleven, V. Active learners: Redesigning an intelligent tutoring system to support self-regulated learning. In *8th European Conference on Technology Enhanced Learning (EC-TEL 2013)*, D. Hernandez-Leo, T. Ley, R. Klamma, and A. Harrer, Eds., vol. 8095 of *Lecture Notes in Computer Science* (2013), 490495.

19. Mitrovic, A., and Martin, B. Evaluating the effect of open student models on self-assessment. *International Journal of Artificial Intelligence in Education 17*, 2 (2007), 121–144.

20. O'Keefe, P. A., Ben-Eliyahu, A., and Linnenbrink-Garcia, L. Shaping achievement goal orientations in a mastery-structured environment and concomitant changes in related contingencies of self-worth. *Motivation and Emotion 37*, 1 (2013), 50–64.

21. Paas, F. G., and Van Merriënboer, J. J. The efficiency of instructional conditions: An approach to combine mental effort and performance measures. *Human Factors: The Journal of the Human Factors and Ergonomics Society 35*, 4 (1993), 737–743.

22. Papanikolaou, K. A., Grigoriadou, M., Kornilakis, H., and Magoulas, G. D. Personalising the interaction in a web-based educational hypermedia system: the case of inspire. *User Modeling and User Adapted Interaction 13*, 3 (2003), 213–267. Questions: interaction between goals. Sequencing? Self-choice? Al-la chapter?

23. Schunk, D. H. Goal setting and self-efficacy during self-regulated learning. *Educational psychologist 25*, 1 (1990), 71–86.

24. Sirkiä, T., and Sorva, J. How do students use program visualizations within an interactive ebook? In *Proceedings of the Eleventh Annual International Conference on International Computing Education Research*, ICER '15, ACM (New York, NY, USA, 2015), 179–188.

25. Sosnovsky, S., and Brusilovsky, P. Evaluation of topic-based adaptation and student modeling in quizguide. *User Modeling and User-Adapted Interaction 25*, 4 (2015), 371–424.

26. Spacco, J., Hovemeyer, D., Pugh, W., Emad, F., Hollingsworth, J. K., and Padua-Perez, N. Experiences with marmoset: Designing and using an advanced submission and testing system for programming courses. In *11th Annual Conference on Innovation and Technology in Computer Science Education, ITiCSE'2006*, M. Goldweber and P. Salomoni, Eds., ACM Press (2006), 13–17.

27. Wolters, C. A., Shirley, L. Y., and Pintrich, P. R. The relation between goal orientation and students' motivational beliefs and self-regulated learning. *Learning and individual differences 8*, 3 (1996), 211–238.

28. Zimmerman, B. J. Self-regulated learning and academic achievement: An overview. *Educational psychologist 25*, 1 (1990), 3–17.

29. Zimmerman, B. J. Self-regulating academic learning and achievement: The emergence of a social cognitive perspective. *Educational psychology review 2*, 2 (1990), 173–201.

User Trust in Intelligent Systems: A Journey Over Time

Daniel Holliday
Centre for HCI Design
City University London
London, United Kingdom
daniel.holliday.1@city.ac.uk

Stephanie Wilson
Centre for HCI Design
City University London
London, United Kingdom
s.m.wilson@city.ac.uk

Simone Stumpf
Centre for HCI Design
City University London
London, United Kingdom
simone.stumpf.1@city.ac.uk

ABSTRACT
Trust is a significant factor in user adoption of new systems. However, although trust is a dynamic attitude of the user towards the system and changes over time, trust in intelligent systems is typically captured as a single quantitative measure at the conclusion of a task. This paper challenges this approach. We report a case study that employed a combination of repeated quantitative and qualitative measures to examine how trust in an intelligent system evolved over time and whether this varied depending on whether the system offered explanations. We discovered different patterns in participants' trust journeys. When provided with explanations, participants' trust levels initially increased, before returning to their original level. Without explanations, participants' trust reduced over time. The qualitative data showed that perceived system ability was more important in determining trust amongst with-explanation participants and perceived transparency was a greater influence on the trust of participants who did not receive explanations. The findings provide a deeper understanding of the development of user trust in intelligent systems and indicate the value of the approach adopted.

Author Keywords
Trust; Intelligent Systems; Qualitative Evaluations; Quantitative Evaluations; Case Study

ACM Classification Keywords
H.1.2 User/Machine Systems: Human Factors

INTRODUCTION

The Need for Trust in Intelligent Systems
While intelligent systems are designed to aid users, they are not without their problems. Intelligent systems are dynamic and, through the use of machine learning algorithms, seek to adapt to the needs and preferences of individual users. In doing so, they typically violate certain fundamental usability principles [6]: 1) control – an intelligent system may modify its behavior without explicit authorization from the user; 2) predictability – an intelligent system may produce a different output, when given the same input, at different points in time; 3) transparency – an intelligent system may not provide any understanding of its inner workings and so its behavior is not comprehensible to the user.

Glass et al. [4] claim that research has placed too great an emphasis on the components and machine learning algorithms of intelligent systems, with insufficient consideration for how users trust their actions. However, trust is a significant factor in determining the adoption of systems that perform tasks on behalf of the user [11]. System ability, control, predictability and transparency have been identified as some of the key factors that influence users' trust in intelligent systems [2, 5, 12, 14]. Therefore, failure to adequately consider and address these factors in the design of an intelligent system is likely to result in a system that is not adopted by users.

What is Trust?
A vast number of definitions of trust exist. It has been studied from various perspectives across a range of disciplines and there is little consensus as to what trust means [10]. Trust is a "highly complex and multi-dimensional phenomenon," in which it is insufficient simply to ask an individual whether they trust or distrust another agent, as they may trust them in some regards but not in others [9]. Trust needs to be considered holistically and examined in its constituent parts rather than simply as a whole [3]. While an individual's initial judgments regarding the trustworthiness of another are founded in their general disposition to trust, their trust changes in response to the degree to which subsequent interactions either confirm or discredit those judgments [7]. Trust beliefs may grow or change over time with repeated interactions [13].

Existing Measures of Trust in Intelligent Systems
While existing research examines the multifaceted nature of user trust in intelligent systems, it does not consider the effect of repeated interactions on trust. In the context of intelligent systems, trust, and its associated factors, is measured solely in post-task questionnaires and interviews [2, 12, 14]. This approach captures users' trust in intelligent systems at a specific point in time but gives no

IUI'16, March 07-10, 2016, Sonoma, CA, USA
© 2016 ACM. ISBN 978-1-4503-4137-0/16/03...$15.00
DOI: http://dx.doi.org/10.1145/2856767.2856811

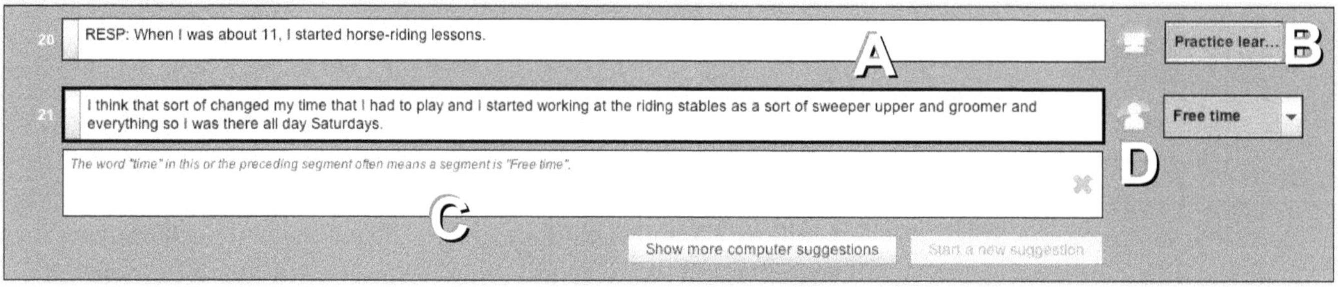

Figure 1. The AutoCoder user interface showing (A) a series of segments, (B) their corresponding codes, (C) a system-generated explanation, (D) an indication of whether the code has been assigned to a segment by the user or by the system.

representation of how trust develops and changes over time. While users' trust journeys have received some consideration in other domains [15], intelligent systems differ from other technologies in a crucial way. The behavior of intelligent systems may change over time as the learning agent receives more training data, which, in turn, will affect user trust.

This paper reports a case study in which a combined quantitative and qualitative approach was used to measure user trust over time in intelligent systems. Existing research has found that explanations increase user trust in intelligent systems [1, 12, 16]. It follows to use an intelligent system with explanations, a mechanism with which to potentially influence trust, to investigate how user trust evolves over time.

METHOD

We set out to investigate users' trust journeys both in cases where the intelligent system offered explanations and in cases where it did not do so. A case study was devised and carried out in which participants were exposed to an intelligent system. Fifteen participants (7 male, 8 female), consisting of full-time postgraduate students and academic university staff across a range of different university departments, were assigned to one of two groups: 1) with-explanations; 2) without-explanations. From hereon, participants in the with-explanation and without-explanation groups will be referred to with participant codes beginning with 1 and 2 respectively.

The Intelligent System Used in the Case Study

The intelligent system used in the case study was the AutoCoder [8]. The AutoCoder is an intelligent assistant designed to aid users in the task of coding qualitative data, i.e. the process of marking segments of a transcript with codes (descriptive words or category names) for analysis in qualitative research. Figure 1 shows the graphical user interface of the AutoCoder and highlights its key features. The AutoCoder automatically codes the segments of the transcript. If the user disagrees with the code allocated by the system, they may correct it to the code that they judge appropriate. The AutoCoder produces system-generated explanations to explain the reasoning behind automatically coded segments. These explanations are based on words, combinations of words and punctuation. Participants in the with-explanation group used the AutoCoder as described above. Participants assigned to the without-explanation group used a modified version of the system in which they did not receive explanations.

Procedure

Participants were asked to code an interview transcript using the AutoCoder. They took between approximately 60 – 90 minutes to complete the task. Quantitative and qualitative measures of user trust were obtained throughout the duration of the task. After participants had manually coded three segments of the transcript, the AutoCoder displayed an alert instructing them to complete a trust assessment (TA). Participants were asked to indicate the extent to which they agreed with the statement, "I trust the AutoCoder to assist me in coding the remaining segments of the transcript." Participants expressed their agreement on a 7-point Likert scale, ranging from 1 (strongly disagree) to 7 (strongly agree). After they had completed the TA and dismissed the alert, the AutoCoder automatically coded the remaining transcript segments. Participants then worked their way through the rest of the transcript, correcting or agreeing with the intelligent system's decisions. The TA was triggered at regular intervals during the remainder of the coding task; capturing participants' trust levels at these times. Following the coding task, participants completed a post-task questionnaire (PTQ), where again, their trust levels were recorded.

Participants' attitudes towards overall trust and the identified factors of trust (perceived system ability, perceived control, perceived predictability and perceived transparency) were gathered by asking them to think aloud during the coding task. Prior to the task, participants were instructed to describe what they were doing, why they were doing it, what they thought the system was doing, why they thought the system was doing what it was doing and any other thoughts that occurred to them. During the session, participants received no prompts beyond efforts to encourage them to continue thinking aloud, such as, "okay," and, "please continue".

In the following section, we describe a subset of our data that examines the trust journeys of participants from the with-explanation and without-explanation groups.

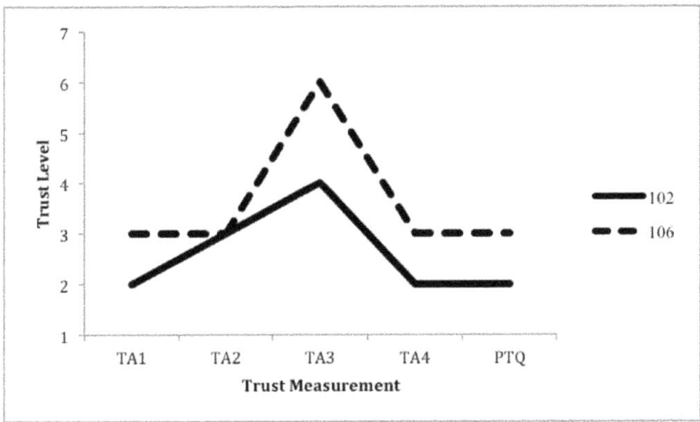

Figure 2. Graph showing the trust journeys of participants 102 and 106 of the with-explanation group.

RESULTS AND DISCUSSION

The repeated measurement of trust at intervals throughout the duration of the coding task brought to light the different patterns in participants' trust journeys that were exclusive to each of the groups. Participant attitudes gleaned from the think aloud help us to understand the reasons for these variations. We now consider the development of trust throughout the duration of the task. Two participants have been chosen from each group and their trust journeys discussed in detail, illuminated by the qualitative data. These participants' trust journeys were representative of each group. Participants 102 and 106 from the with-explanation group and participants 204 and 206 from the without-explanation group were selected as their think aloud qualitative data was the most illuminating, giving useful insight into their trust journeys. We are not able to discuss the trust journeys of all participants in detail and without negating the value of the rich qualitative data in the scope of this paper. In examining the responses and attitudes of these participants in detail, we identify the factors of trust that most greatly influence their overall trust.

With-Explanation Group Pattern – "Hump"

Figure 2 shows the similar trust journeys followed by participants 102 and 106 in the with-explanation group. These participants' initial trust in the AutoCoder was low, before increasing to reach a peak in the middle of the task. Their trust then decreased, returning to its initial level.

At TA1, the AutoCoder had not automatically coded any segments of the transcript. This indicates participants' disposition to trust in the intelligent system. Participant 102 was skeptical of its abilities without evidence to the contrary: *"I wouldn't trust it until I see results. Instinctively, I wouldn't trust it."* Participant 106 was somewhat less hesitant to trust the system, stating he had, *"no reason to trust it but I'm quite confident for some reason. I wouldn't have a reason to distrust it, as such, either."*

While participant 106 perceived the system's ability to have improved by TA2, his trust did not yet increase, as he believed more time was needed for the AutoCoder to learn from more training data: *"[...] it is a learning system and it has learned better how to better answer [...] I think it needs a bit more time to learn."* Participant 102 expressed similar sentiments regarding perceived system ability, although this was sufficient for her trust to increase: *"It is getting better but [...] I think it's got to learn a little bit more."*

At TA3, the trust levels of both participants 102 and 106 reached their highest point. Participant 102 believed that the system had learned to produce a more accurate output based on her own input: *"[...] it seems like it's learned better,"* and participant 106 deemed that the system's ability had improved considerably and that it was, *"really, really getting there."*

However, both participants' trust decreased at TA4. Participant 106 believed that his trust had been misplaced and asserted the AutoCoder's ability had deteriorated: *"I think I got a bit optimistic for the AutoCoder [...] it all started to go a little bit wrong [...] so that's knocked my confidence in it."* Similarly, participant 102's trust was influenced by their perceived ability of the system: *"I wouldn't trust it because [...] I'm looking at how it's answered."*

The trust levels of both participants 102 and 106 remained unchanged in the PTQ. While participant 102's trust level was low, she did feel that the intelligent system's output had been sufficiently correct so as to be beneficial rather than detrimental in completing the task: *"I'm not saying it's a perfect system [...] There are quite a few answers or codes that it put correctly, so it did help."* At the PTQ, participant 106 summarizes his trust journey with the AutoCoder. He describes his increase, then decrease in perceived system ability: *"I got quite confident with it at one point 'cause it seemed to be learning [...] and then we hit a patch where it [...] didn't work so well."*

Without-Explanation Group Pattern – "Downward"

Figure 3 shows the trust journeys followed by participants 204 and 206 of the without-explanation group. The participants' initial trust in the intelligent system is again low but this is, in fact, their highest level of trust in the entire task. This decreases, with both following a similar decline in trust until the task's conclusion.

The participants' disposition to trust in the AutoCoder was captured at TA1, before the system had automatically coded the transcript segments. Participant 204's initial trust level was influenced by the belief that the perceived system ability would be low: *"it will not have had the opportunity yet for enough learning."* Participant 206 was concerned that without having seen the AutoCoder in action, he would be unable to determine how it made its coding decisions: *"I don't know how it works [...] I'm not sure what's going on in the background."*

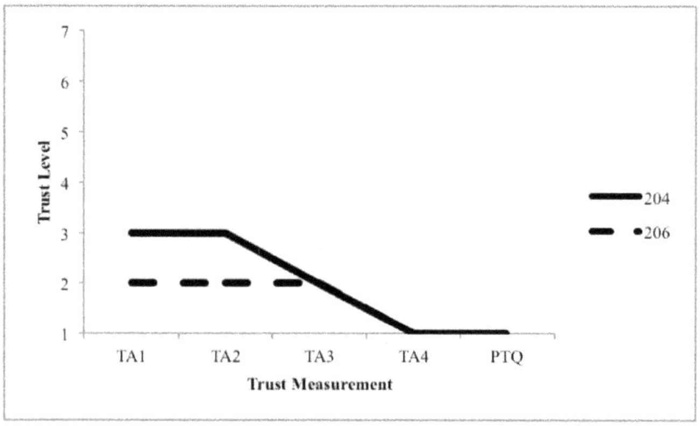

Figure 3. Graph showing the trust journeys of participants 204 and 206 of the without-explanation group.

At TA2, both participants expressed frustration with their inability to understand the AutoCoder's workings due to the poor perceived transparency of the system, with participant 206 stating, *"I just don't understand why it's making the decisions it's making [...] I think that's my biggest problem with it."* Participant 204 declared, *"I don't know at the moment how it's making its decisions."*

The participants' frustration at poor perceived transparency in the intelligent system continued at TA3. Participant 206's trust remained constant, although he was unable to determine the workings of the AutoCoder: *"I don't know how it's doing it. Unless there's something else I'm not seeing, something deeper."* Participant 204's trust reduced when he, also, was still unable to determine how the system was making its decisions: *"I think there is a pattern, probably, but I haven't properly picked it up."*

The trust levels of both participants followed the same downward direction at TA4. Participant 204 attributed this to continued poor perceived transparency of the AutoCoder: *"I feel as though I ought to have picked up on more of a pattern [...] about what I put in and what the machine does [...] I really don't know."* Participant 206, also, was unable to determine the reasoning of the intelligent system, *"'cause recently it seems to have thrown a few random ones in there."*

In the PTQ, both participant 204 and 206's trust in the AutoCoder stayed at the lowest level as a result of continued low perceived transparency. Without an understanding of its workings, participant 204 was unable to ascribe intelligence to the system, even when its output was correct: *"There were times when you thought that might display a glimmer of intelligence [...] But it was probably nothing more than random."* Following the task, participant 206 again emphasizes the importance of perceived transparency in his lack of trust in the intelligent system, *"I don't understand what it's doing. If I have to trust something, I need to understand it myself."*

The repeated measurement of participants' trust levels over time revealed different trust journeys that were exclusive to each of the groups. Through examination of the think aloud, the decrease in trust amongst participants in the with-explanation group can be explained by a reduction in perceived system ability, that is, the perception that the AutoCoder's output was inaccurate. Meanwhile, the reduction in trust of participants in the without-explanation group is founded in poor perceived transparency, that is, that the rationale behind the decisions made by the AutoCoder could not be understood. We can observe differences in the factors of trust and their influence on overall trust. Indeed, emphasizing the contextual importance of perceived transparency over perceived system ability, participant 206 asserted, *"I know it's not going to be perfect and get everything right all the time but I don't know how it's doing it."*

CONCLUSION

The trust levels of participants in the with-explanation group were influenced strongly by the perceived ability of the AutoCoder. The presence of explanations assisted participants in the conception of an accurate mental model, increasing perceived transparency and the high-level understanding that the AutoCoder is a *"learning system."* Participants' trust in the AutoCoder in the without-explanation group was affected by the perceived transparency of the system. Without the presence of explanations, participants found it more difficult to conceive a mental model as to how the AutoCoder worked and, as a result, their level of trust did not increase.

The findings of this case study exemplify the deeper, richer understanding of the development of users' trust over time in intelligent systems that can be obtained by collecting data about the entire user trust journey. The approach employed in this paper reveals how and why users' trust evolves over time, rather than simply what their level of trust is at a single point in time. Furthermore, the reasons for variations in participants' trust, and variations in the factors of trust, could not have been understood without capturing their attitudes through the use of the think aloud protocol.

The think aloud data allow us to understand the 'why's' rather than just the 'what's' of individual users with regards to their trust in an intelligent system. This approach also allows for a greater understanding of the individual factors of trust and the consideration, in the context of intelligent systems, that users may trust the system in terms of one factor (e.g. perceived transparency) but not another factor (e.g. perceived system ability).

There is great value in developing and expanding this approach to measure user trust across multiple tasks carried out over a longer period of time, not limited to a single session. A greater comprehension of not only what engenders trust, but why users trust and how their trust evolves over time - their trust journeys - can lead to the design of more trustworthy intelligent systems.

REFERENCES

1. Bunt, A., Lount, M., and Lauzon, C. Are explanations always important?: A study of deployed, low-cost intelligent interactive systems. In *Proc. IUI 2012*, ACM Press (2012), 169-178.
2. Cramer, H., Evers, V., Ramlal, S., van Someron, M., Rutledge, L, Stash, N., Aroyo, L., and Wielinga, B. The effects of transparency on trust in and acceptance of a content-based art recommender. *User Modeling and User-Adapted Interaction 18*, 5 (2008), 455-496.
3. Gambetta, D. Can We Trust? In D. Gambetta (Ed.) *Trust: Making and Breaking Cooperative Relations*, Blackwell (1988), 213-237.
4. Glass, A., McGuinness, D.L., and Wolverton, M. Toward establishing user trust in adaptive agents. In *Proc. IUI'08*, ACM Press (2008), 227-236.
5. Hoffmann, A., Söllner, M., Hoffmann, H., and Leimeister, J.M. Towards Trust-Based Software Requirement Patterns. In *Requirements Patterns (RePa), 2012 IEEE Second International Workshop on*, IEEE (2012), 7-11.
6. Höök, K. Steps to take before intelligent systems become real. *Interacting with Computers 12*, 4 (2000), 409-426.
7. Kramer, R.M. Trust and distrust in organizations: Emerging perspectives, enduring questions. *Annual Review of Psychology*, *50*, 1 (1999), 569-598.
8. Kulesza, T., Stumpf, S., Burnett, M., Wong, W., Riche, Y., Moore, T., Oberst, I., Shinsel, A., and McIntosh, K. Explanatory Debugging: Supporting End-User Debugging of Machine-Learned Programs. In *Proc. VL/HCC 2010*, IEEE (2010), 41-48.
9. Lewis, J.D., and Weigert, A.J. Trust as a social reality. *Social Forces*, *63*, 4 (1985), 967-985.
10. McKnight, D.H., and Chervany, N.L. Trust and distrust definitions: One bite at a time. In *Proc. Workshop on Deception, Fraud, and Trust in Agent Societies* (2001), 27-54.
11. Muir, B.M. Trust in automation: Part I. Theoretical issues in the study of trust and human intervention in automated systems. *Ergonomics*, *37*, 11 (1994), 1905-1922.
12. Pu, P. and Chen, L. Trust building with explanation interfaces. In *Proc. IUI'06*, ACM Press (2006), 93-100.
13. Rempel, R.E., Holmes, J.G., and Zanna, M.P. Trust in close relationships. *Journal of Personality and Social Psychology*, *49*, 1 (1985), 95-112.
14. Söllner, M., Hoffmann, A., Hoffmann, H., and Leimeister, J.H. How to Use Behavioral Research Insights on Trust for HCI System Design. *Ext. Abstracts CHI 2012*, ACM Press (2012), 1703-1708.
15. Tang, J., Gao, H., Liu, H., and Das Sarma, A. eTrust: Understanding trust evolution in an online world. In *Proc. SIGKDD 2012*, ACM (2012), 253-261.
16. Tintarev, N., and Masthoff, J. Evaluating the effectiveness of explanations for recommender systems. *User Modeling and User-Adapted Interaction*, *22*, 4-5 (2012), 399-439.

An Intelligent Assistant for High-Level Task Understanding

Ming Sun **Yun-Nung Chen** **Alexander I. Rudnicky**
School of Computer Science, Carnegie Mellon University
5000 Forbes Ave., Pittsburgh, PA 15213, USA
{mings, yvchen, air}@cs.cmu.edu

ABSTRACT
People are able to interact with domain-specific intelligent assistants (IAs) and get help with tasks. But sometimes user goals are complex and may require interactions with multiple applications. However current IAs are limited to specific applications and users have to directly manage execution spanning multiple applications in order to engage in more complex activities. An ideal personal agent would be able to learn, over time, about tasks that span different resources. This paper addresses the problem of cross-domain task assistance in the context of spoken dialogue systems. We propose approaches to discover users' high-level intentions and using this information to assist users in their task. We collected real-life smartphone usage data from 14 participants and investigated how to extract high-level intents from users' descriptions of their activities. Our experiments show that understanding high-level tasks allows the agent to actively suggest apps relevant to pursuing particular user goals and reduce the cost of users' self-management.

Author Keywords
Multi-domain; User intention; Spoken dialog system (SDS); Language understanding.

ACM Classification Keywords
I.2.1 Applications and Expert Systems: Natural language interfaces; I.2.7 Natural Language Processing: Language Parsing and Understanding; I.2.11 Distributed Artificial Intelligence: Intelligent agents

INTRODUCTION
Smart devices, such as phones or TVs, now host applications (apps) from different domains. Each app is designed to handle a limited number of domains (usually one). It may be configured by developers to support transition between known apps, but such functionality is not scalable and loses potentially desirable adaptive configuration. On the other hand, users can mentally arrange apps and seamlessly coordinate the information among them. However, this manual process of launching apps one by one may be time-consuming and difficult, especially for elder users and users with (visual) disabilities, although vocabularies of a touch-screen or gestures have been enriched significantly over the past decade [10]. We would want our personal IAs to help organize apps/domains automatically given user requests expressed at the level of intentions. For example, upon receiving "can you help me plan an evening out with my friends?", we would like our agent to find a restaurant with good reviews (YELP), reserve a table (OPENTABLE) and contact friends (MESSENGER).

Conventional multi-domain dialog systems passively select one domain from multiple domains according to a user input, ignoring relationships between domains and the ultimate user intention behind cross-domain behaviors [3, 4, 5, 6, 17, 22, 14, 21, 23, 13]. This paper describes a layer above individual applications, which links them to a specific intention underlying user activities [26, 27]. By doing so (and in combination with other techniques), an agent would be able to manage interactions at the level of intentions, mapping intents into multiple existing applications/functionality. In the example above, the agent may respond "Okay, to *plan a dinner event*, I need to know *where*, *when* and *who*". Here, "*plan a dinner event*" indicates a (in-)correct interpretation of the user intention. (The user would have opportunity to correct the agent when misunderstanding presents.) *Where*, *when* and *who* collectively construct a shared context across app boundaries. Thus, a unified interaction could be provided, instead of concatenating individual domains managed by the user. This paper focuses on an IA which is capable of 1) discovering meaningful intentions from user's past interactions; 2) leveraging surface intentions with groups of apps; 3) talking about intentions via natural language. In the rest of the paper, a real-life multi-domain dataset is briefly described, followed by our framework (HELPR). At the end, we discuss user studies that evaluate our model.

DATA COLLECTION
We logged real-life interactions at app-level from users' smart phones. We then requested two types of user annotation: 1) what apps were used for a particualr goal; and 2) what the goal was (i.e., task description). Meta information such as date, time, location was shown to the user to aid recall. Users were also asked to re-enact the smart phone interaction by talking with a Wizard-of-Oz system. An example of annotation and Wizard-of-Oz dialog is shown in Figure 1.

We had 14 participants and collected 533 sessions; mean age for the 4 male participants was 23.0 and 34.6 for the 10 females. In the group were 12 native English speakers. Details of the collection are provided in [27].

HELPR FRAMEWORK
The agent (see Figure 2) maintains an inventory of past interactions, such as "plan a trip to California", each associated

ACM 978-1-4503-4137-0/16/03$15.00.
DOI: http://dx.doi.org/10.1145/2856767.2856818

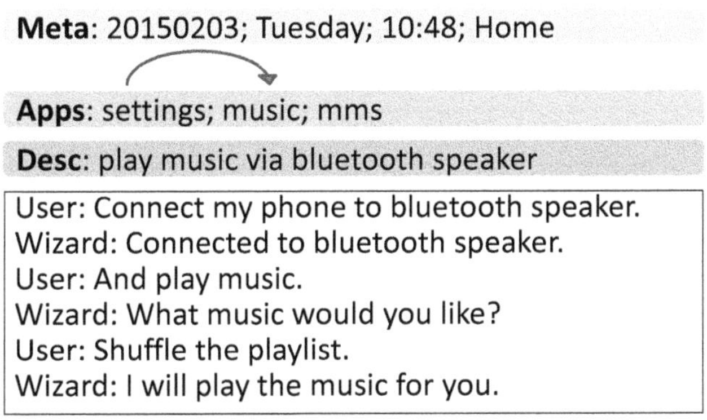

Figure 1. User connected SETTINGS and MUSIC and noted that these two apps were used to *play music via bluetooth speaker*. Wizard-of-Oz dialog was collected and manually transcribed.

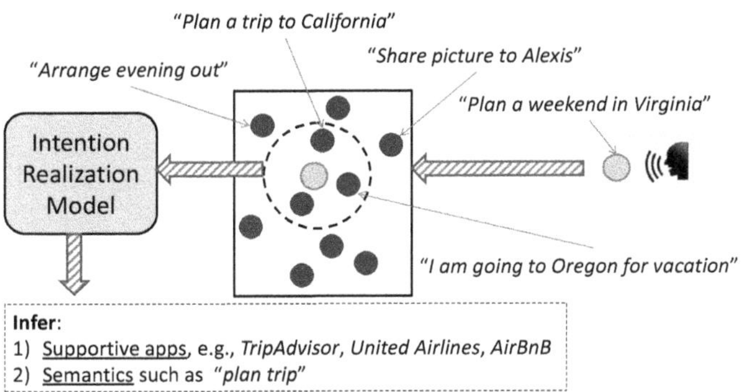

Figure 2. Intention understanding and realization example. Solid nodes denote past interactions (blue) and current input (yellow).

with information such as the sequence of apps used and the utterances spoken by user during the interaction. Given a new input (yellow node), the agent first identifies similar past experience (denoted as the ones within the dashed circle). This is the intention understanding process. Next, an intention realization model is built from those similar interactions to generate 1) supportive apps and 2) natural language reference. Thus, the intelligent agent transparently conveys its understanding of the input intention in these two modalities.

Intention Understanding

We define a complex intention collectively by the set of previous interactions of similar nature. We used two approaches to find such similar past experience. A cluster-based method first groups training examples into K_C clusters (i.e., segmenting the semantic space). The input language is used to identify the closest of these clusters; the members of this cluster define the nature of the intention. We also investigated a K-Nearest Neighbors approach that finds the K_N most similar past interactions given the input.

We anticipate some major differences between cluster-based and neighbor-based intentions. (i) The cluster-based method should provide insight into the basic intentions of a user. This may become useful when the agent is actively learning tasks, i.e., asking user to label the current activity while suggesting one of the list of basic intentions. (ii) Cluster-based method can utilize richer contextual information (such as the apps used or utterances spoken by the user) when segmenting the semantic space of past interactions. Ideally, this yields better clustering performance. Such post-initiate information is not available in the neighbor-based approach, since it does not have a training process. (iii) The cluster-based approach has hard boundaries between intentions. Instances close to the boundaries may not be characterized well by their cluster members, compared with neighbor-based method. However, regardless of the differences between these two approaches, we believe that by referring to shared (past) experience, the agent can (i) better indicate (mis-)understanding of user's intention; and (ii) build rapport with the user [30].

Intention Realization in Two Modes

Supportive Applications

As an intelligent user interface, the agent needs to assist human user in pursuing complex intentions that span multiple domains. We propose two strategies to generate sets of supportive apps. In the first one, we combine the individual app sequences in a set into a single app sequence to cover the activity (denoted as REPSEQ). For example, $\{a_1a_2a_3, a_1a_2a_4, a_1a_3a_4\}$ will yield $a_1a_2a_4$ by majority voting at each position. An alternate strategy would be to have a classifier assign multiple labels (apps ids) to the input (MULTLAB). The advantage of REPSEQ is that it can preserve common ordering among apps. However, from the example above, once the members are selected, the input language has no further influence on the selection of apps. Arguably, during this process we can weight each set member by its closeness to the input; we did not investigate this possibility. In this work, we focus on the quality of the proposed set of apps. At present we do not consider app order.

In the user interface, the agent could a) present the clickable icons of these apps to reduce the navigation through installed apps; b) warm up these apps to speed up the activation; c) build unified conversation based the set of apps.

Language Reference

The human-agent communication channel needs to be transparent in both directions. The agent must be able to verbally convey its understanding of user intention, allowing the user to track the agent's understanding. For example, it can use explicit or implicit confirmation [2], e.g., "do you want to *share a picture*?" Practically this can simply be a template ("do you want to ___?") and the reference to the intention ("share a picture"). Compared with echoing content extracted from the user's most recent input, our approach better communicates the agent's (mis-)understanding, allowing timely detection and recovery of errors.

To enable this we want our agent to automatically infer the semantics from related past experience. Text summarization can be used to generate a high-level description of the intention cluster [9, 15]. Keyphrase extraction provides an alternative [29, 18, 1]. In our case, we mainly need a short content ("share a picture") so the keyphrase approach is more suitable. Even if the automatic generation of semantic summarization is not precise, in context it may still be sufficiently meaningful to the human.

USER STUDIES

Study 1: End-to-End Evaluation

We investigated the differences within: 1) cluster-based vs. neighbor-based intention models; 2) personalized vs. generic setups; 3) REPSEQ vs. MULTLAB realization strategies. For each user, the chronologically first 70% of collected data was to train a personalized mode (in principle mirroring actual data accumulation). The remaining 13 users' first 70% data was combined and used to train a generic model. The number of intentions K_C for the cluster-based intention model and the number of nearest neighbor K_N for the neighbor-based model were tuned. K_C was automatically optimized (from 1 to 10) via gap statistics [28]. K_N was set to the square root of the number of training examples [7]. For REPSEQ we used ROVER [8] to collapse multiple app sequences into one. For MULTLAB, we used support vector machine (SVM) with linear kernel.

There are intra-user and inter-user inconsistencies in the use of language/apps, creating the problem of *vocabulary-mismatch* [16, 24], where interactions related to the same intention may have non-overlapping 1) spoken terms ("take picture" vs. "shoot photo"), sometimes caused by minor differences such as wrong word choice or morphology ("take" vs. "taking"); 2) app choice, e.g., people may use different apps with essentially similar purpose (MESSENGER vs. EMAIL). To address these issues, we applied query enrichment (QryEnr) and app similarity (AppSim). We describe them in detail.

Query Enrichment

QryEnr will expand the query by incorporating words semantically close to it [25], for example $\{shoot, photo\} \rightarrow \{shoot, take, photo, picture, selfie\}$. The chance of observing sparse input feature vectors caused by out-of-vocabulary (OOV) is thereby reduced. In this work, we used `word2vec` with the gensim toolkit[1] on the model[2] pre-trained on GoogleNews [20]. Each word w_t in the pre-processed (lemmatization on verbs and nouns) query $Q = \{w_1, w_2, ..., w_T\}$ yields mass increases for N semantically close words in the feature vector f [27].

App Similarity

In the generic model, a recommended app, e.g., BROWSER may not match the only (or preferred) app on a specific user's phone, e.g., CHROME. Therefore, similarity metrics among apps are also needed to convert all apps in the generic model training data into the ones that are in this user's phone (as a pre-process). The other is to convert the recommendation results to fit this user's installed apps (a post-process). In the real world, pre-process may not be feasible since there are many individual users and adapting the (huge) generic training data for each of the users is expensive. Therefore, in this work we adopted post-processing.

We can construct a similarity matrix among all 132 apps in our collection by three means: (i) rule-based: the app package names can be useful, e.g., com.lge.music is close to com.sec.android.app.music since both contain the string "music"; (ii) knowledge-based: the Google Play store provides a finite ranked list of "similar apps" for each entry; (iii) data-based: app descriptions from the store can be projected into a high-dimensional semantic space to compute similarity. In the rule-based method, we used edit distance with 50 hand-crafted fillers (e.g., "com", "android") removed from package names. For the knowledge-based approach, we used reversed rank ($1/r$) as the similarity. For the data-based approach, we used the `doc2vec` toolkit to train the space for over 1 million apps then used cosine similarity [12]. Knowledge-based and data-based matrices are sparse since some (vendor) apps were not found in our snapshot of the Google database; 15.5% of the cells are non-zero for data-based and only 1.0% for knowledge-based.

[1] `https://radimrehurek.com/gensim/`
[2] `https://code.google.com/p/word2vec/`

	REQSEQ		MULTLAB	
	Personal	Generic	Personal	Generic
Cluster (baseline)	42.8	10.5	55.1	24.0
+QryEnr	44.0	11.0	56.1	27.4
+AppSim	42.8	14.8	55.1	29.2
+QryEnr+AppSim	**44.0**	**15.4**	**56.1**	**38.2**
Neighbor (baseline)	50.8	23.8	51.3	19.1
+QryEnr	54.9	26.2	57.0	22.9
+AppSim	50.8	30.7	51.3	24.7
+QryEnr+AppSim	**54.9**	**32.7**	**57.0**	**30.3**

Table 1. Weighted average F_1 score (%) on test set across 14 participants, using bag-of-word features. Average number of clusters, K_C, in the cluster-based approach is 7.0 ± 1.0 for generic models, and 7.1 ± 1.6 for personalized models. The reported numbers are average performance of 20 K-means clustering results. K_N in the neighbor-based condition is 18.5 ± 0.4 for generic models and 4.9 ± 1.4 for personalized models. AppSim is rule-based.

Results

We compare the apps suggested by our model with the ones actually launched by users (Table 1). This prediction task is difficult; in our corpus, on average each user has 19 unique apps and 25 different sequences of apps. The upper part of the Table corresponds to the cluster-based intention model, the lower part to the neighbor-based intention model. Within each approach, intention realization strategies (QryEnr, AppSim) and their combination are shown.

Bringing more post-initiate information (i.e. set composition) into the clustering process improves performance [27]. But we did not observe better performance for the cluster-based model relative to the neighbor-based model. When the REPSEQ realization strategy is adopted, neighbor-based intention yields a better F_1 score. It is possible that REPSEQ is sensitive to the selection of similar interactions. Arguably, an input may fall close to the intention boundary in the cluster-based setting, which indeed is closer to some interactions on the other side of the boundary as opposed to the ones within the same intention cluster. On the other hand, the MULTLAB approach shows relatively consistent performance in both cluster- and neighbor-based settings, indicating ro-

	REQSEQ			MULTLAB		
	Prec.	Rec.	F_1	Prec.	Rec.	F_1
Baseline	33.3	18.9	23.8	45.8	12.3	19.1
Rule	43.3	24.3	30.7	59.4	15.9	24.7
Knowledge	41.8	22.3	28.7	53.0	14.6	22.6
Data	38.1	21.2	27.0	54.6	13.9	21.7
Combine	**44.7**	**25.0**	**31.7**	**61.0**	**16.4**	**25.5**

Table 2. Comparison of different AppSim approaches on neighbor-based intention in a generic model. Precision, recall and F_1 score are reported. For the data-driven method, the vector dimension $D = 500$.

bustness and self-adaptability with respect to the choice of interactions for similar intentions.

In Table 1, the fact that QryEnr improves F_1 in all conditions indicates that semantic similarity among words can effectively address the *language-mismatch* problem. In addition, although AppSim has no effect on personalized models, it addresses the *app-mismatch* issue in generic model in an intuitive way. Combining QryEnr and AppSim methods together (denoted as "+QryEnr+AppSim") consistently achieves the best performance on F_1. Further inspection shows that QryEnr improves recall while AppSim improves both precision and recall. As we expected, the generic intention model is inferior to the personalized model for our data. We anticipate that with a larger user community (and perhaps grouping of similar users instead of a single generic model) we will observe better performance. Note that, IAs will face a cold-start problem before sufficient data has been accumulated for specific users. Thus, generic models will always be required to ensure reasonable communication.

Table 2 compares the differences across AppSim methods. Applying AppSim improves the baseline in the generic model. The rule-based approach outperforms other two methods, although it requires filters. This is probably due to the sparseness of similarity matrices in the knowledge- and data-based approaches. Nevertheless, combining three similarity scores yields the best performance, showing the effectiveness of leveraging inter-app similarity for this task.

Study 2: Intention Representation in Natural Language

We used Rapid Automatic Keyword Extraction (RAKE[3]) algorithm [1], an unsupervised, language- and domain-independent extraction method, reported to outperform other unsupervised method such as TextRank [19, 11] in both precision and F score. In RAKE, we required that 1) each word have 3 or more characters; 2) each phrase have at most 3 words; and that 3) each key word appear in the text at least once. We did not tune these parameters. We used 3 individual resources and 2 combinations, reflecting constraints on the availability of different contexts in real-life. The three individual resources are manual transcription of user utterances from their dialogs (MANUAL), ASR transcriptions (ASR) thereof and high-level task descriptions (DESC). The number of key phrases that could be generated by each resource or their combination depends on resource size (Table 3).

[3] `https://www.airpair.com/nlp/keyword-extraction-tutorial`

MANUAL	ASR	DESC	DESC + ASR	DESC + MANUAL
20.0	20.3	11.3	29.6	29.1

Table 3. Mean number of phrases generated using different resources

We asked 6 users to first review and refine their own clusters, by showing them all cluster members. Toaid rercall we displayed, 1) context e.g., location, time; 2) task descriptions (e.g., "planning a dinner"), 3) dialogs produced and 4) apps involved. Users could decide whether to split each cluster into subgroups. Then, based on the refined clusters, we generate ranked lists of key phrases using the different resources. Users were asked to provide binary judgment for each phrase in the list (randomized) indicating whether it correctly summarized all the activities in the current (refined) cluster.

To focus on a practical goal, we used Mean Reciprocal Rank (MRR)—"how deep the user has to go down a ranked list to find one descriptive phrase?" Average MRR was 0.64 across different resources and their combinations, meaning that on average the user can find an acceptable phrase in the top 2 items shown; although MRR is lower when individual resource was used, an ANOVA did not show significant differences between resources (and their combinations). Other metrics such as Precision at position K or Mean Average Precision at position K shows DESC+ASR and DESC+MANUAL do best, especially when K is larger. Results indicate that having a task description is useful.

To conclude, if the IA can observe a user's speech commands or elicit descriptions from user (ideally both), it can generate understandable activity references and could communicate more effectively than using alternatives (e.g. lists).

CONCLUSION AND FUTURE WORK

We present a framework, HELPR, that implicitly learns from past interactions to map high-level expressions of goals (e.g., "go out with friends") to specific functionality (apps) available on a smart device. The proposed agent uses language produced by user to identify interactions similar to the current input. A set of domains/apps can be proposed from past experience and used to support current activities. This framework is also capable of generating natural language references to a past experience cluster. As a result, the communication channel would have greater transparency, supporting timely recovery from possible misunderstandings.

Our long-term goal is to create agents that observe recurring human activities, figure out the underlying intentions and then provide active support through language-based interaction (in addition to allowing the user to explicitly teach the agent about complex tasks). The value of such an agent is that it can learn to manage activities on a level more abstract than provided by app-specific interfaces and would allow users to build their own (virtual) applications that combine the functionality of existing apps.

REFERENCES

1. Berry, M. W., and Kogan., J. Text mining: applications and theory (2010).
2. Bohus, D., and Rudnicky, A. I. Constructing accurate beliefs in spoken dialog systems. In *Proceedings of IEEE Workshop on Automatic Speech Recognition and Understanding* (2005).
3. Chen, Y.-N., and Rudnicky, A. I. Dynamically supporting unexplored domains in conversational interactions by enriching semantics with neural word embeddings. In *Proceedings of 2014 IEEE Spoken Language Technology Workshop (SLT)*, IEEE (2014), 590–595.
4. Chen, Y.-N., Sun, M., and Rudnicky, A. I. Leveraging behavioral patterns of mobile applications for personalized spoken language understanding. In *Proceedings of 2015 International Conference on Multimodal Interaction (ICMI)* (2015).
5. Chen, Y.-N., Sun, M., and Rudnicky, A. I. Matrix factorization with domain knowledge and behavioral patterns for intent modeling. In *NIPS Workshop on Machine Learning for SLU and Interaction* (2015).
6. Chen, Y.-N., Sun, M., Rudnicky, A. I., and Gershman, A. Unsupervised user intent modeling by feature-enriched matrix factorization. In *Proceedings of The 41th IEEE International Conference on Acoustics, Speech, and Signal Processing (ICASSP)* (2016).
7. Duda, R., Hart, P., and Stork, D. *Pattern Classification*. John Wiley and Sons, 2012.
8. Fiscus, J. G. A post-processing system to yield reduced word error rates: Recognizer output voting error reduction (rover). In *Proceedings of Automatic Speech Recognition and Understanding Workshop (ASRU)* (1997), 347–352.
9. Ganesan, K., Zhai, C., and Han, J. Opinosis: a graph-based approach to abstractive summarization of highly redundant opinions. In *Proceedings of the 23rd international conference on computational linguistics (COLING)*, ACL (2010), 340–348.
10. Harrison, C., Xiao, R., Schwarz, J., and Hudson, S. E. Touchtools: leveraging familiarity and skill with physical tools to augment touch interaction. In *Proceedings of the SIGCHI Conference on Human Factors in Computing Systems* (2014), 2913–2916.
11. Hulth, A. Improved automatic keyword extraction given more linguistic knowledge. In *Proceedings of the 2003 conference on Empirical methods in natural language processing (EMNLP)*, ACL (2003), 216–223.
12. Le, Q. V., and Mikolov, T. Distributed representations of sentences and documents. In *ICML* (2014).
13. Li, Q., Tur, G., Hakkani-Tur, D., Li, X., Paek, T., Gunawardana, A., and Quirk, C. Distributed open-domain conversational understanding framework with domain independent extractors. In *Spoken Language Technology Workshop (SLT), 2014 IEEE*, IEEE (2014), 566–571.
14. Lin, B.-s., Wang, H.-m., and Lee, L.-s. A distributed architecture for cooperative spoken dialogue agents with coherent dialogue state and history. In *Proceedings of 1999 IEEE Workshop on Automatic Speech Recognition and Understanding Workshop (ASRU)*, vol. 99 (1999), 4.
15. Liu, F., Flanigan, J., Thomson, S., Sadeh, N., and Smith, N. A. Toward abstractive summarization using semantic representations. In *Proceedings of the 2015 Conference of the North American Chapter of the Association for Computational Linguistics (NAACL)* (2015).
16. Lucchese, C., Orlando, S., Perego, R., Silvestri, F., and Tolomei., G. Identifying task-based sessions in search engine query logs. In *Proceedings of the fourth ACM international conference on Web search and data mining*, ACM (2011), 277–286.
17. Lunati, J.-M., and Rudnicky, A. I. Spoken language interfaces: The OM system. *CHI91 Human Factors on Computing Systems* (1991).
18. Medelyan, O. Human-competitive automatic topic indexing. In *Thesis Dissertation, University of Waikato* (2009).
19. Mihalcea, R., and Tarau, P. Textrank: Bringing order into texts. In *ACL* (2004).
20. Mikolov, T., Chen, K., Corrado, G., and Dean, J. Efficient estimation of word representations in vector space. In *Proceedings of Workshop at International Conference on Learning Representations (ICLR)* (2013).
21. Nakano, M., Sato, S., Komatani, K., Matsuyama, K., Funakoshi, K., and Okuno, H. G. A two-stage domain selection framework for extensible multi-domain spoken dialogue systems. In *SIGdial Workshop on Discourse and Dialogue (SIGDIAL)*, Association for Computational Linguistics (2011), 18–29.
22. Rudnicky, A. I., Lunati, J.-M., and Franz, A. M. Spoken language recognition in an office management domain. In *Proceedings of International Conference on Acoustics, Speech, and Signal Processing (ICASSP)*, IEEE (1991), 829–832.
23. Ryu, S., Song, J., Koo, S., Kwon, S., and Lee, G. G. Detecting multiple domains from users utterance in spoken dialog system. In *Proceedings of the International Workshop on Spoken Dialogue Systems (IWSDS)* (2015).
24. Shen, X., Tan, B., and Zhai., C. Implicit user modeling for personalized search. In *Proceedings of the 14th ACM international conference on Information and knowledge management*, ACM (2005), 824–831.
25. Sun, M., Chen, Y.-N., and Rudnicky., A. I. Learning OOV through semantic relatedness in spoken dialog systems. In *16th Annual Conference of the International Speech Communication Association (Interspeech)* (2015).

26. Sun, M., Chen, Y.-N., and Rudnicky, A. I. Understanding user's cross-domain intentions in spoken dialog systems. In *NIPS Workshop on Machine Learning for SLU and Interaction* (2015).

27. Sun, M., Chen, Y.-N., and Rudnicky, A. I. HELPR: A framework to break the barrier across domains in spoken dialog systems. In *International Workshop on Spoken Dialog Systems* (2016).

28. Tibshirani, R., Walther, G., and Hastie., T. Estimating the number of clusters in a data set via the gap statistic. In *Journal of the Royal Statistical Society: Series B (Statistical Methodology)* (2001), 411–423.

29. Witten, I. H., Paynter, G. W., Frank, E., Gutwin, C., and Nevill-Manning, C. G. Kea: Practical automatic keyphrase extraction. In *Proceedings of the fourth ACM conference on Digital libraries* (1999), 254–255.

30. Zhao, R., Papangelis, A., and Cassell, J. Towards a dyadic computational model of rapport management for human-virtual agent interaction. In *Intelligent Virtual Agents*. 2014, 514–527.

SleeveAR: Augmented Reality for Rehabilitation using Realtime Feedback

Maurício Sousa
INESC-ID Lisboa / Técnico Lisboa / University of Lisbon
Lisboa, Portugal
antonio.sousa@ist.utl.pt

João Vieira
Técnico Lisboa / University of Lisbon
Lisboa, Portugal
felixvieira@tecnico.ulisboa.pt

Daniel Medeiros
INESC-ID Lisboa / Técnico Lisboa / University of Lisbon
Lisboa, Portugal
daniel.medeiros@tecnico.ulisboa.pt

Artur Arsénio
Universidade da Beira Interior
Covilhã, Portugal
arturarsenio@di.ubi.pt

Joaquim Jorge
INESC-ID Lisboa / Técnico Lisboa / University of Lisbon
Lisboa, Portugal
jorgej@acm.org

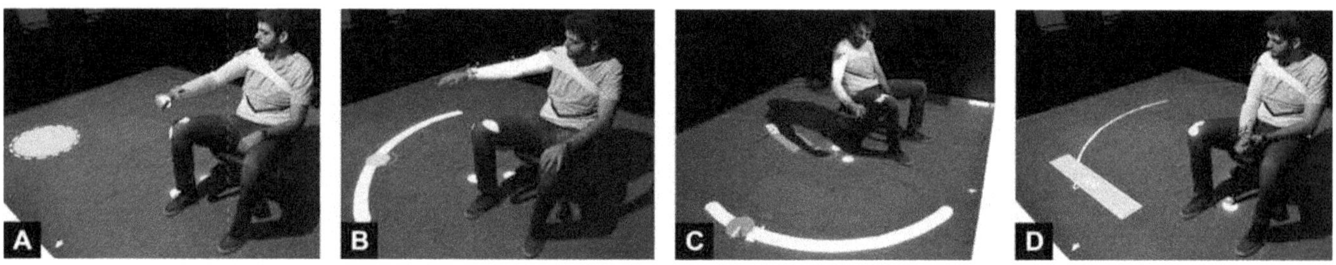

Figure 1. SleeveAR addresses new active projection-based strategies for providing user feedback during rehabilitation exercises. a) Initial position. b) Mid-performance. c) Sleeve Feedback. d) Progress report.

ABSTRACT
We present an intelligent user interface that allows people to perform rehabilitation exercises by themselves under the offline supervision of a therapist. Every year, many people suffer injuries that require rehabilitation. This entails considerable time overheads since it requires people to perform specified exercises under the direct supervision of a therapist. Therefore it is desirable that patients continue performing exercises outside the clinic (for instance at home, thus without direct supervision), to complement in-clinic physical therapy. However, to perform rehabilitation tasks accurately, patients need appropriate feedback, as otherwise provided by a physical therapist, to ensure that these unsupervised exercises are correctly executed. Different approaches address this problem, providing feedback mechanisms to aid rehabilitation. Unfortunately, test subjects frequently report having trouble to completely understand the feedback thus provided, which makes it hard to correctly execute the prescribed movements. Worse, injuries may occur due to incorrect performance of the prescribed exercises, which severely hinders recovery. SleeveAR is a novel approach to provide real-time, active feedback, using multiple projection surfaces to provide effective visualizations. Empirical evaluation shows the effectiveness of our approach as compared to traditional video-based feedback. Our experimental results show that our intelligent UI can successfully guide subjects through an exercise prescribed (and demonstrated) by a physical therapist, with performance improvements between consecutive executions, a desirable goal to successful rehabilitation.

ACM Classification Keywords
H.5.2 Information Interfaces And Presentation: User Interfaces

Author Keywords
Rehabilitation; Augmented Reality; Projection-based Systems

ACM 978-1-4503-4137-0/16/03 ...$15.00.
http://dx.doi.org/10.1145/2856767.2856773

INTRODUCTION
While supervised physical therapy is of utmost importance for the rehabilitation process, individual patient effort also plays a very significant role in their recovery. If we are to support a home rehabilitation process without the presence of a therapist, we must provide feedback to guide patients and correct them

throughout their tasks. Hence, patients must be willing to learn about their condition and perform the prescribed therapeutic exercises without professional supervision. However, it is very hard to correctly perform prescribed movements without help. In the absence of proper guidance, patients may end up injuring themselves. Feedback that normally is given by a professional, by visual forms (the therapist demonstrating what to do), auditory (the therapist giving directions) or physical (the therapist applying physical force). In the absence of a therapist, it would be necessary to provide similar feedback from other sources, to support performing tasks towards desired targets.

To this end, Augmented Reality (AR) is a possible means to provide alternate feedback sources and shows a significant potential in the rehabilitation field. Additionally, tools are already available to help in developing augmented reality applications that interact with the patient's body [7]. When combined with carefully designed and customized feedback mechanisms AR can be of high value to the rehabilitation process [15]. The key idea is to provide more information to patients so that they can easily and safely execute prescribed tasks. This feedback is usually given by a therapist while undergoing physical therapy. In unsupervised settings, a different approach must be followed making sure the therapy goals are achieved and the patient correctly performs the assigned exercises. A possible approach is to take advantage of different senses by using augmented reality stimuli to help patients monitor execution of exercises. Indeed, studies have already shown that augmented reality feedback enhances the motor learning of individuals [15].

In this work, we describe SleeveAR, a novel approach that enhances patient awareness to guide them during rehabilitation exercises. SleeveAR aims at providing the means for patients to precisely replicate these exercises, especially prescribed for them by a knowledgeable health professional. Since the rehabilitation process relies on repetition of exercises during the physiotherapy sessions, our approach contributes to the correct performance of the therapeutic exercises while offering reports on the patient's progress. Furthermore, without rendering the role of the therapist obsolete, our approach builds on the notion that with proper guidance, patients can autonomously execute rehabilitation exercises. In what follows we review related work, detail the SleeveAR approach and discuss its design, informed by health professionals' feedback. We also discuss technical aspects of the implementation and present the results of its evaluation.

RELATED WORK

Our work builds on related research involving computer-assisted rehabilitation approaches and AR feedback using projection techniques. In this section we also discuss video and AR mirror approaches common in movement guidance systems.

Rehabilitation Systems

Nowadays, there are many different rehabilitation systems to help improve the recovery of patients. Many of them have different therapeutic goals and focus on specific injuries, e.g., stroke [4, 8], or limb rehabilitation [13, 6, 9]. Using these systems can greatly influence a patient's rehabilitation outside the clinic. Not only do they allow for a certain quality in performing prescribed exercises, they also enable patients to exercise in the comfortable environment of their homes. This makes it easier to stimulate and motivate them throughout the whole process [4]. Patients' effective rehabilitation is supported on three main concepts: repetition, feedback and motivation [14]. Hence, developing a rehabilitation system should be informed by these three principles and how to approach them. The repetitive nature of rehabilitation exercises can quickly become boring for a patient [12, 6, 5]. Therefore, there is a need to turn these exercises into something less tedious. When dealing with repetitive exercises, the main goal should be divided into several sub-goals. This way patients can achieve incremental success through each repetition. Furthermore, as compared to techniques where success is only achieved after completing the whole task [14], patients also report an increased motivation to improve performance. Nicolau et al. [11] used optical tracking to accurately track patient movements during rehabilitation for therapist control. Gama et al. [7] developed a rehabilitation system in which the user's position was tracked using a Microsoft Kinect. In this system, users could see themselves on the screen with overlaying targets that represented the target position. When an incorrect posture was detected (for instance, shoulders not aligned or arm not fully stretched), users were notified in real-time through visual messages. White arrows on the screen were used as visual cues to guide patients' limbs to the target. For each repetition, points were added to a score, depending on how well users performed. Klein et al.[9] focused on rehabilitating stroke victims which normally end up with one of the arms extremely debilitated. Their research focused on motivating patients to move an injured arm. Even with a small range of motion, it is important for the patient to move it to improve the recovery. The patient would see a virtual arm overlaying the injured arm, which would simulate a normal arm movement. The virtual arm position was calculated based on a few control points around the patients' shoulder and face. The results showed an enhancement of the shoulder range of motion for all test subjects. Also targeting stroke victims, Sadihov et al. [13] proposed a system to aid rehabilitation exercises via an immersive virtual environment. Tang et al. [17, 18] developed Physio@Home, a guidance system to help patients execute movements by following guidelines. The patient would see her/himself on a mirror. On top of the reflection, visual cues indicated the direction to which the arm should move. The exercises were pre-recorded by another person and then replicated by the patient.

Augmented Reality Mirrors

Mirrors allow a person to have visual feedback of his/her body. They enhance the spatial awareness which is useful to learning motor activities. AR mirrors do not necessarily require actual physical mirrors to be implemented. However, Anderson et al. [2] introduce such an approach using an actual mirror with a partially reflective layer facing the user and a diffuse layer in the back. The reflective layer provides a natural reflection while a light-projector overlays images onto the diffuse layer. The result was a mixture of the user's reflection with virtual images. Virtual mirrors can be considered an easier alternative to implement, by allowing any screen to turn into a mirror by means of a color camera. Thus we can generate virtual images on top of the reflection (for instance, for guiding purposes). Already several applications make use of augmented mirrors to guide users, be it for rehabilitation [17, 19, 9] or to support interactions outside rehabilitation [1, 3].

Projection-based Augmented Reality

Using light-projectors for AR has enabled the creation of very interesting applications. Through techniques of projection mapping, it became possible to turn any irregular surface into a projection screen. We can observe this technique applied to different objects. It is regularly used for live shows using buildings as the screen. One example is the promotion of the movie "The Tourist" where projection mapping was applied to an entire building. But it can also be applied to the human body to obtain interesting effects. Using projection mapping we can alter the perception of an object and create optical illusions. This kind of technique can bring great benefits to applications that require guiding feedback by being able to focus projection on a body part for example, just as it is necessary in rehabilitation systems. But for it to be useful, projection mapping should be interactive and applied in run-time instead of being pre-recorded like the examples above.

LightGuide [16], explored projection mapping in a innovative way. The projection was made onto users, using their body as a projection screen. Indeed, real-time visual cues were projected onto the user's hand in order to guide them through the desired movement. By projecting this information in the body part being moved, the user could keep a high level of concentration without being distracted by external factors. Different types of visual cues were developed, having in mind movements that demanded degrees of freedom over three dimensions. For each dimension a different design was planned so that the user could understand clearly in what direction should the hand move. To apply real-time projection mapping onto a moving body part, its position must be known at all time to make sure the light projector is illuminating the correct position. For this, motion tracking devices are used which enable to record the movement of, in this case, a person.

Information Feedback

Our senses are constantly at work to provide us information about our surroundings. We can think about our senses as input devices, each designed for a specific type of information. When patients are engaged on physical therapy, the therapist is constantly interacting with them. This is important in order for patients to steadily improve their performance through rehabilitation. Not only does the therapist tell them what to do but also demonstrates them movement and whenever necessary, physically corrects them. What we observe here is providing three different types of feedback to patients - audio, visual and haptic, each being interpreted by hearing, sight and touch respectively. For an automated rehabilitation system to succeed, these interactions must be simulated by other sources of feedback, in a way that the patient understands what he or she must do in the absence of the therapist. Notably, visual feedback information is often used in rehabilitation systems to communicate with users [8]. As one example of visual feedback from an AR perspective, we have the overlaying of information on an interactive mirror for the user to analyze his performance in real-time [2, 17, 19, 9, 1, 3]. Since there are multiple ways to give feedback, we can see examples where more than one are used at the same time. Combining forms of feedback can convey a better understanding of the tasks by minimizing the amount of information given visually and rely on other senses. However, if not designed with caution, a system can end up overloading the user with too much simultaneous information.

Feedback Applications

Sigrist et al. [15] suggest that different feedback types can complement each other to enhance the user comprehension. Alhamid et al. [1] introduced an interface between a user and biofeedback sensors (sensors that are able to measure physiological functions). Even though this is not aimed at rehabilitation, their approach to user interaction can be analyzed in this vein. Through this interface, users were able to access data about their bodies and health thanks to measurements conveyed by the biofeedback sensors. This system was prepared to interact with the user using multiple response interfaces, each tailored to a specific purpose. The visual interface relied on a projector that showed important messages and results from the biofeedback measurements. On the other hand, the audio interface played different kinds of music depending on the user's current state. For example, if high levels of stress were detected, relaxing music would be played to help the user relax.

One of the most common approaches to visual feedback is the augmented mirror approach already discussed. Its chief advantage is that even without overlaying virtual images, it provides users with a spatial awareness of their bodies. But we could observe other examples of augmented feedback being applied to the mirror, since a simple reflection is not enough to provide guidance. Tang et al. [17] explored two different designs for visual guidance on a mirror aimed at upper-limbs movement. Their first iteration consisted of virtual arrows that pointed at the targeted position for the user's hand. The second provided a trace of tubes placed along a path which represented the complete movement to be performed by the user's arm. However each instanced exhibited some difficulty in depth perception. This kind of visual cues has proven not to be suitable for exercises where users had to move their arms towards or away from the camera.

Anderson et al. [2] tried to provide a more detailed visual feedback by using a full virtual skeleton placed over the user reflection. In this case the goal was to mimic the skeleton's pose and hold it for a specific time. To diminish the lack of depth perception, a second tracker was placed on the user's side. Every time the system detected a large error on the z-axis, a window would appear with a side-view of both the virtual and user's skeleton. Unlike the previous approach, LightGuide [16] does not rely on interactive mirrors or screens to apply its visual feedback. By using a depth-sensor camera and a light projector, they were able to project information on the user's hand. This approach was able to guide the hand through a defined movement by projecting visual cues. All the information projected on the hand was being updated in real-time influenced by the current position given by the tracking device. The visual cues varied according to the desired direction of the movement. If the current movement only required back and forward motion, only one dimension was used. Therefore, the visual cue would only inform the user where to move his hand in the z axis through a little arrow pointing to the correct position. Two dimensional movements would combine the first visual cue by virtually painting the remaining of the hand with a color pattern. The portion of the hand closer to the desired position, would be painted with a different color than the remaining portion. They concluded that by using LightGuide, most of the users could better execute a certain movement than if they were following video instructions.

Our approach follows the work of Sodhi et al. [16] (LightGuide) and Tang et al. [17] (Physio@Home), both of them address movement guidance. But both lack performance review tools, a feature much needed during the rehabilitation process. They also assume that users always execute almost perfect movements, since the error feedback relies only in pointing to the direction of the pre-recorded exercise. Furthermore, the Physio@Home mirror metaphor provides for poor depth perception. We shall see how our interface provides for more intelligent behavior through incremental performance review and more accurate feedback.

INTERACTION DESIGN

SleeveAR deals with the specific scenario of the physical recovery of an injured arm. Our approach steps away from the mirror metaphor by augmenting, with virtual guidance information, several surfaces available to the patient, full arm and floor.

For the purpose of this research, we address basic physiotherapy exercises for upper arm and forearm, also depicted in Figure 2:

Abduction-Adduction. Horizontal movements of the arm away from or towards the center of the body.

Elevation-Depression. All arm movements above or below a vertical plane.

Flexion-Extension. Variations of the angle between the upper arm and the forearm.

Since it is required for patients to precisely perform the prescribed exercises, our approach takes extends physiotherapy sessions with exercises at home completed without direct professional supervision. However, to minimise the risk of further

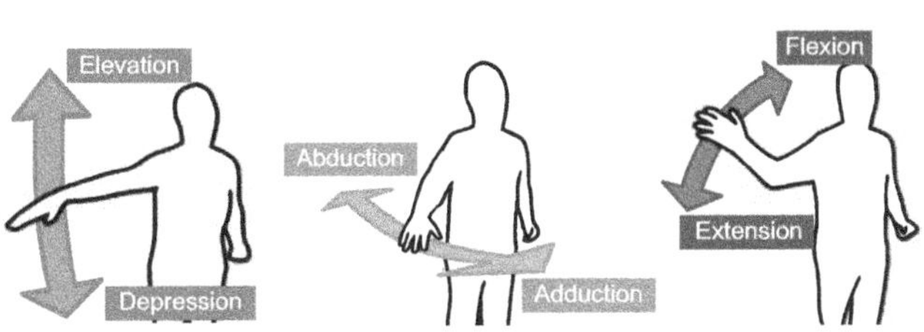

Figure 2. Physiotherapy exercises.

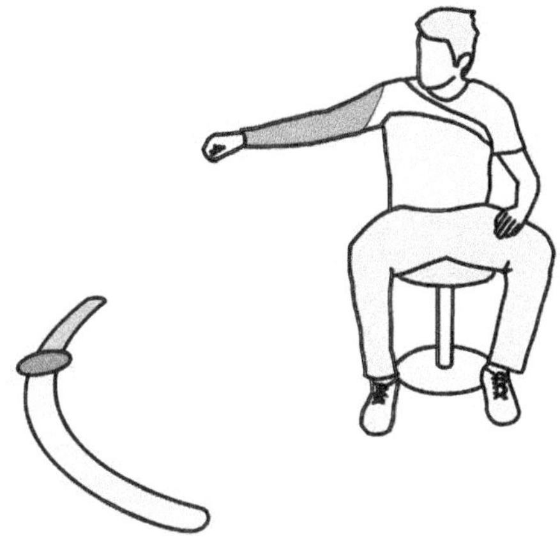

Figure 3. SleeveAR: augmented reality projections on an arm sleeve and onto the floor surface provides both movement guidance and performance feedback.

injuries and promote progress towards recovery, SleeveAR blends movement guidance with incremental performance reports to provide an overall awareness of the recovery process.

Unlike LightGuide [16], our approach takes advantage of the full arm's surface and the floor. By increasing the projection area throughout the whole arm and user's surrounding environment areas, we can successfully improve an user's awareness while a movement is being executed, as depicted in Figure 3.

In addition, the movement to be performed, is recorded by a real health professional, so that the patient can achieve a much more realistic and useful rehabilitation process. Therefore, SleeveAR main objective is to preserve the degree of similarity between the performed exercise and the one prescribed by the therapist.

SleeveAR Workflow

Our approach consists of two main concepts. First, the precise recording of the exercise being demonstrated by a personal therapist. And secondly, the ability to properly guide another person, the rehabilitation subject, during the execution of the pre-recorded exercise. Not only does this provide a vast range of possible exercises, but also it leverages on the therapist's know-how to assign adequate exercises based on a patient's condition and needs. At the same time, our method provides awareness of the rehabilitation progress to ensure the correctness of the patient's movements. In this way, a therapist can demonstrate the prescribed exercises and make sure the patient performs those correctly without requiring close supervision.

Therefore, the SleeveAR process can be divided into three main stages, as depicted in Figure 4. First, the *Recording Stage*, involves the demonstration of the exercise being recorded by the therapist. Next, the *Movement Guidance Stage*, focuses on guiding the patient to recreate the prescribed exercise as

Figure 4. SleeveAR Interaction Workflow

previously recorded. Finally, the *Performance Review Stage* provides the patient with an overview of their performance, by comparing with the original prescribed exercise.

Recording

The prescribed exercises were specifically designed for the current patient's health condition. With this in mind, we wanted to maintain this relation between a therapist and a patient, by giving therapists the power to demonstrate the prescribed exercises to the patient. Based on this demonstration, SleeveAR captures the therapist movements and stores them for a later usage. By giving the therapist the responsibility of demonstrating the exercise, we do not need to worry about the physical limitations of the patient that will use our system to recreate it. We are assuming the recorded exercise is already customized for the patient in question. Given these assumptions, SleeveAR is able to guide a patient through those exercises as best as it can.

Movement Guidance

Our approach divides the task of guiding a patient through an exercise into two stages, reaching the first *initial position* of the exercise (see Figure 1A) and *exercise performance* (Figure 1B). These two stages constitute a simple and clear process for organizing the desired activities to be performed by the patient. To successfully recreate an exercise, the user must first reach the exercise initial position, i.e., the first arm position from the recorded demonstration. To accomplish this first task, a patient must follow SleeveAR's feedback to achieve the correct arm position. After the initial position has been reached, as determined by SleeveAR, the system starts guiding the user through the recorded movement. However, it would be a very difficult task for a patient to exactly recreate the original demonstration of the exercise. To this end, SleeveAR relies on thresholds to allow some leeway in performing recorded motions. In doing so, if it were required of a patient to achieve, for example, a 90 degree arm flexion, they would not need to actually attain the exact angle. Indeed it is enough for them to achieve a flexion within the specified tolerance, which is consistent with the incremental improvement characteristic of therapy. Furthermore, SleeveAR takes into account that no two people are equal. Thus the system does not rely on absolute coordinates to guide user movements. Indeed, by normalizing the joint angles and relying on relative positions, our approach is able to accommodate people with different sized limbs, eg a 1,60m tall therapist can guide a 1,80m patient through recorded movements (or vice-versa). During the guidance task, the two different time sequences (the user's and the therapist's) are compared using the *Dynamic Time Warping* algorithm (DTW) [10], which is appropriate to map the degree of similarity between two temporal sequences that can vary both in timing and speed. Consequently, this approach overcomes the challenge of spotting movement deviations and then provide the correct feedback by dynamically discerning the differences between the two time series. Finally at the end of each exercise, SleeveAR provides an overview of the patient's performance superimposed on the original. This helps a patient in understanding what they might have done wrong and which parts of the exercise can be improved. To successfully guide a patient through their exercises while informing on their performance, we need to plan how SleeveAR interacts with its users. In the next section we describe our techniques to provide real-time and interactive feedback to the user.

Performance Review

Whenever an exercise is completed, SleeveAR provides users with a review of their performance, as shown in Figure 1D. By reviewing their exercise, a patient is able to understand how close they were to the original exercise.

Patients are informed about their performance by two different means. First, and most important, the recorded trajectory is drawn on the floor, followed by the user's most recently executed attempt. These trajectories help visualize what portions of the exercise need to be improved. Second, an overall score is calculated using the DTW algorithm and then translated to a user-friendly percentage value. With this intelligent "gamification" feature, users feel motivated to improve their score and, consequently, improve their performed exercises.

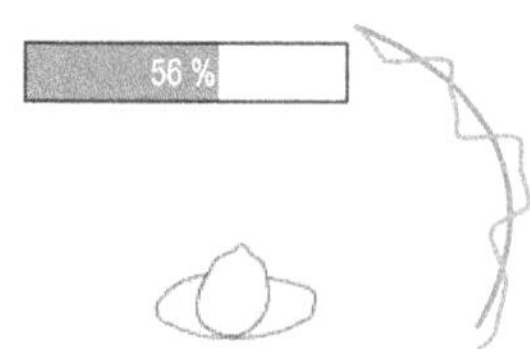

Figure 5. Example top view of the projected performance report.

In Figure 5, we depict the feedback provided after the user's movement is completed. The orange and green line represent the original trajectory and the user's attempt respectively. These are drawn on the floor. The score is depicted using a horizontal bar, which shows the degree of similarity between the performed and the recorded movements.

Real-time Feedback

Our approach provides visual feedback projected both on the user's arm and onto the floor area inside their field-of-view. It also provides audio notifications to inform the user about the end of their movement and important transitions. The motivation behind our technique is to provide users with detailed movement guidance information on the floor, while taking advantage of their peripheral vision and hearing for important notifications regarding body stance errors and cues to start/stop the exercise.

Visual Feedback

Providing useful and minimalist design was our goal when designing our visual feedback. There were some key points we wanted to address when designing it. First, the visual information had to provide the user with a representation of their *current* position, while also showing the target position. Through these representations, users must grasp easily what they need to do in order to achieve the same target position. To provide suitable feedback regarding the full arm we first applied different methods for each arm region.

Forearm. Before creating the forearm visual feedback it is important to understand what type of movement could be executed with this arm region. The forearm is connected to the upper arm by the elbow joint and its range of motion could be summarized in extension and flexing of the arm. When extending or flexing the arm, people change the elbow angle, given by the angle between the upper and forearm. To represent the

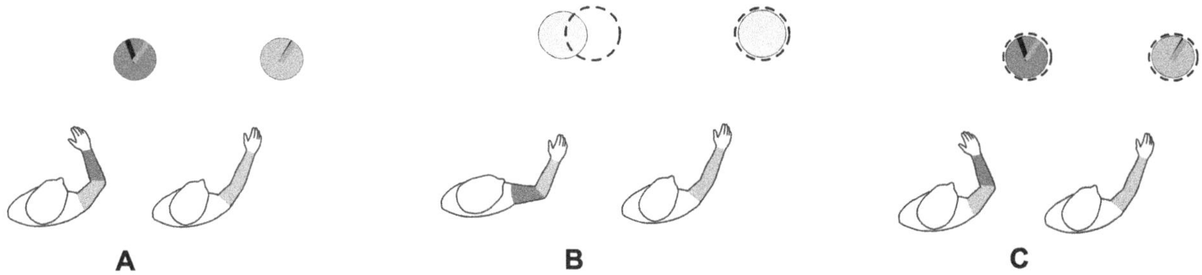

Figure 6. SleeveAR projected visual feedback. a) Forearm flexion feedback. b) Full arm positioning feedback c) Combined Full arm positioning and forearm flexion feedback.

current state, we use a black bar, as depicted in Figure 6A. Whenever the user moves their forearm, this bar moves accordingly. On the other hand, the desired forearm state is represented by the green bar. For the user to achieve this state, they must move their fore arm in order for the black bar to reach the green bar. To improve user awareness we added two additional features. Depending on the distance between the two bars, the circle color would continuously change from red (too far) to green (close enough). Also, whenever the black bar gets too far from its desired position, rotating arrows appear to warn the user that their arm is not correctly positioned.

Upper Arm. As for the upper arm, the type of movement allowed can be represented by the user's pointing direction, which is defined by the vector connecting the shoulder and the elbow joints. Once again, it is necessary to present both the current and the desired state, as shown in Figure 6B . To represent the upper arm current direction, we chose a dotted circumference. By moving the upper arm vertically or horizontally, the dotted circumference should move, away or towards the user respectively, on the floor plane.

Full Arm. Each of the two approaches above are designed to guide each arm region independently. In order to guide the user to a full arm position, we combine both, as depicted in Figure 6C. By replacing the grey circle, used to guide the upper arm, with the elbow angle circle from the forearm design, we are able to combine both simultaneously. All these techniques are used to guide the user to a specific static pose.

Additionally to the floor-projected feedback, SleeveAR projects information on the user's arm. This gives feedback to the user by representing the correctness of the current state of their arm by colors (red==incorrect / green== correct), as shown in Figure 6.

Augmented Floor. During an arm movement, we can not assume that both the upper and forearm remain in a static relation. There are situations were the arm remains fully extended throughout the movement or where the forearm relative position varies during the movement. In this case there is an elbow angle variation which means the forearm desired state is continuously changing. To this end, the feedback must then change during the movement. As for the upper arm, to help the user know where they must move it, a path is drawn showing the direction to where that section must go. The forearm changes the circle proper, while the upper arm controls the dotted circumference that must coincide with the circle. To that effect, if we move the circle throughout the movement path, we are able to continuously inform the user about the desired direction while also updating what specific elbow angle they should observe. Figure 7 illustrates an example where the user is already midway through the exercise.

Audio Feedback

Audio feedback plays an important role in timing and user notification contexts. We recognize the importance of audio to notify users about specific events. In the Recording phase, SleeveAR provides an audible notification when it actually starts recording. In this case, a countdown audio clip is used to prepare the therapist to position themselves at the initial position, before the actual recording starts. Another notification sound is played when the recording stops. As for the Movement Guidance phase, SleeveAR notifies the user whenever an exercise attempt starts. From here on, the main feedback is provided in visual form.

IMPLEMENTATION

We built a prototype in order to assess our assumptions that realtime feedback using projection-based augmented reality can yield better results than mirror-like video approaches in a realistic physical therapy scenario. The developed environment is comprised of input devices to track peoples' arm movements, while providing visual and audio cues to perform complex rehabilitation exercises, including progress report. We chose the Optitrack tracking system to implement our approach. This system relies on body markers to capture movement, but provides better accuracy than depth cameras (future higher-resolution, less noisy depth cameras may render these a viable option for use in domestic settings).

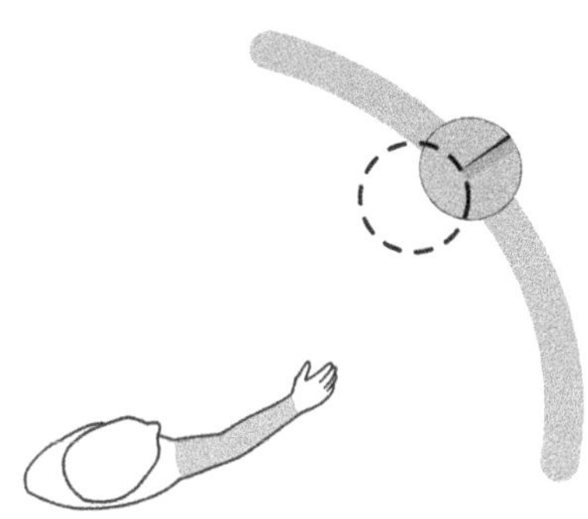

Figure 7. Movement guidance feedback

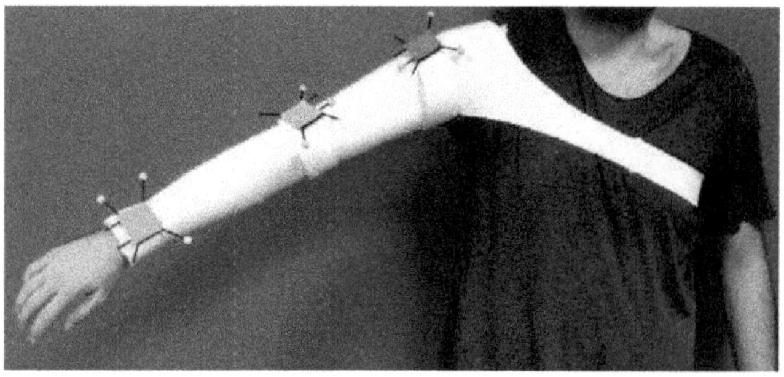

Figure 8. The Sleeve

The Sleeve

We designed a custom sleeve, as shown in Figure 8, made of wool. We employed a white colored cloth to better render light projections. To solve positioning problems, we maintain the sleeve in place using a "belt" strapped around the user's torso which greatly increased its stability. Each of the rigid bodies were still attached to a bracelet and the bracelets were stitched to the sleeve. This significantly improves the rigid bodies relative position stability, while also enabling us to tighten them more or less depending on the user's arm thickness. Another advantage of using our custom sleeve is providing a better surface to project information, due to it being white. This enable us to have a smoother and more neutral surface to project color for example. For our work, we required three different rigid bodies. Each is to be attached to a different arm location, in this case, shoulder, elbow and wrist. Having an easy way to attach and hard-to-displace method of holding our rigid bodies was vital for our work. Rigid bodies moving out of place during a movement could result in unwanted and unexpected results. Therefore, we created a better attachment method, by using a custom designed sleeve.

Given the real-time tracking information, the SleeveAR prototype then generates user feedback according to the specific exercise the user is attempting to execute. Such feedback is provided by controlling speakers to deliver audio notifications and, most importantly, by making usage of a light projector to project information both on the user's arm and floor.

Setup

Aiming for an environment favourable for the performance of rehabilitation exercises, we build our main setup in laboratory space providing the optimal area for tracking and to render projections. The SleeveAR setup is depicted in Figure 9. Multiple infrared motion cameras were installed in the ceiling for position input. Also in the ceiling, we use a commodity short-throw projector, facing downwards, to cover the maximum area surrounding the interaction space. Additionally, two audio speakers were installed as depicted in Figure 9. Our prototype handles essentially two main components:

Tracker Server. The tracker module provides position data from the user's arm captured from ten infrared motion cameras. Also, the tracker server transmits a UPD data stream of data over a local network.

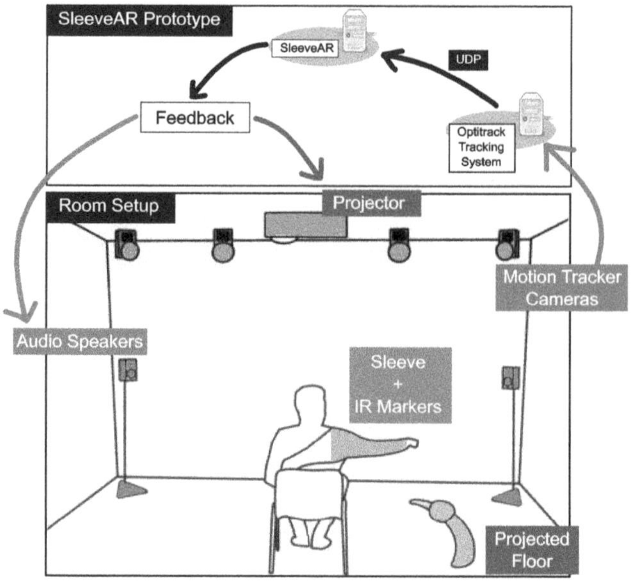

Figure 9. SleeveAR prototype's architecture and room apparatus.

SleeveAR Module. This module deals with the position input data from the tracker server, while processing it to determine the correct response, visual or audio feedback. In addition, the SeeveAR module utilizes the positional vector between the projector and the sleeve's position to determine where to project the arm's feedback techniques. Since, by calculating where the arm's shadow is cast, our prototype is able so superimpose projections on top of the sleeve surface.

EVALUATION

To evaluate SleeveAR, we intended to observe how well subjects can recreate simple arm movements just by following the feedback at their disposal. Five different exercises were defined based on such movements. Each exercise was simultaneously captured using both video and the SleeveAR's Learning component (thus the same movement is recorded both in video and in our system).

This section presents a detailed description of the user tests. We address the experimental methodology employed to test our prototype with test subjects, the category of performed tests, what metrics we used, and features of the collected sensor information. We then present the experimental results together with a critical analysis and discussion in order to achieve a better understanding about our prototype functionality and performance. Finally, as a qualitative assessment, we report the most relevant comments produced by a professional physical therapist after using our system.

Methodology

The test was divided into three stages: 1) *Introduction* 2) *Execution* and 3) *Questionnaire*. The average time spent on the test was approximately 30 minutes, of which two minutes were spent on the *Introduction*, fifteen on the *Test Execution* and the last three on the *Questionnaire*.

Exercises				
1	Abduction	Adduction		
2	Abduction	Elevation	Adduction	
3	Flexion	Abduction	Adduction	Extension
4	Elevation	Depression		
5	Abduction	Depression	Flexion	

Table 1. Arm movements and sequences during the exercises.

At the start of each session, participants received a brief explanation concerning the main goal of our prototype and were given instructions by a team member on the experiment proper. After this brief explanation, each participant performed the test. Each test session consisted of two different stages, the guidance with video and with the SleeveAR. These were shuffled at random in order to avoid experimental bias. In order to gather data for further analysis, we logged all the necessary information about the participant's movements for each exercise.

Finally, we asked participants to fill a brief questionnaire. This included questions concerning the performed tasks both with video and SleeveAR, while also providing some information about the user's profile.

The questionnaire was comprised of a list of statements scored on a 6-point Likert Scale where 1 means that users did not agree at all with a statement and 6 meant they fully agreed with it, as summarized in Tables 2 and 3.

Participants

Our subject group included 18 people, of which 14 were male and 4 were female, one of them being a physical therapist. Participants were on average 26 years old. All participants reported no physical impairment at the time of taking the tests.

Test Execution

On the task execution stage, each of the participants was asked to replicate five different rehabilitation exercises in two distinct sub-stages: *Video*, where the participant watches a video intended exercise at least two times and then, while following the video playing, the participant executes the same movement based on the video observation; and *SleeveAR*, the exactly same previously recorded exercises, now with real-time feedback. To avoid biasing the experiment, half of the participants started with *Video* while other half used *SleeveAR* first. Each exercise consisted of different movement combinations as described on Table 1.

When preparing the experiments, each exercise was simultaneously recorded with a video camera and with motion tracking devices. Under these circumstances, we made sure that the video recorded content and the data recorded by SleeveAR were the same.

In the SleeveAR phase, users would first be presented with a small tutorial which introduced each feedback component (forearm and upper arm) individually and then in combination. After the tutorial, both the SleeveAR and Video phases

It was easy to...	Video	SleeveAR
...perform the first exercise?	6 (0)	6 (0.75)
...perform the second exercise?	6 (0.75)	5.5 (1)
...perform the third exercise?	5.5 (1)	5 (2)
...perform the fourth exercise?	5.5 (1)	5 (2)
...perform the fifth exercise?	5 (1.75)	4 (1)
...follow the guidance information?	5 (1)	5 (0.75)
...see if the arm was in the right position?	5 (1.75)	5.5 (1)
...see if the arm was in the wrong position? *	6 (1.75)	6 (0.75)
...see when the exercise ended?	6 (1)	5 (1)

Table 2. User preferences: Median (Interquartile Range) for both OST and VST approaches. * indicates statistical significance. The values include Median and Inter-Quartile Range (IQR) in parentheses.

followed the same script. Each subject was allowed three attempts for each exercise, the first two served for practice and the last for measurement.

Results and Discussion

The data gathered consists of user preferences and task performance. The main objective was to address the correctness of the executed exercises. Experiments with test subjects were performed for a baseline scenario, consisting of exercise execution through video observation and a patient assisted scenario consisting of real-time feedback supported by the proposed prototype. Furthermore, this evaluation provides a formal study of our feedback techniques. Therefore, the analysis of the results is divided into a *User Preferences Overview* and *Task Performance Overview*.

User Preferences Overview

Since the values obtained from the tasks are two related-samples and come from the same population in a 6-value Likert-scale, we applied the Wilcoxon Signed Ranks test. This test was used to highlight statistically significant differences between the SleeveAR and video observation conditions.

Results from the questionnaire, as shown in Table 2, suggest that there is only one statistically relevant difference between the two tested approaches. Evidencing that, regarding user preferences, test subjects were convinced that they were capable of successfully executing all five exercises under either condition. We identified a significant statistical difference in the question - *It was easy to see if the arm was in the wrong position* - where users preferred SleeveAR to video observation (**p-value = 0.011**). This suggests that users found it easier to detect wrong movements using SleeveAR due to being constantly informed about their movement and corrected in real-time. Additionally, we observed that users seemed more interested in using SleeveAR because of its novelty and interactive feedback. Furthermore, due to the gamification provided during the performance review, the majority of users

It was easy to understand the...	Median (IQR)
...forearm feedback?	6 (0.75)
...upper arm feedback?	5.5 (1)
...full arm feedback?	5 (2)
...movement guidance feedback?	6 (1)
...arm color projection?	5 (1.5)

Table 3. Results from Widget Questionnaire

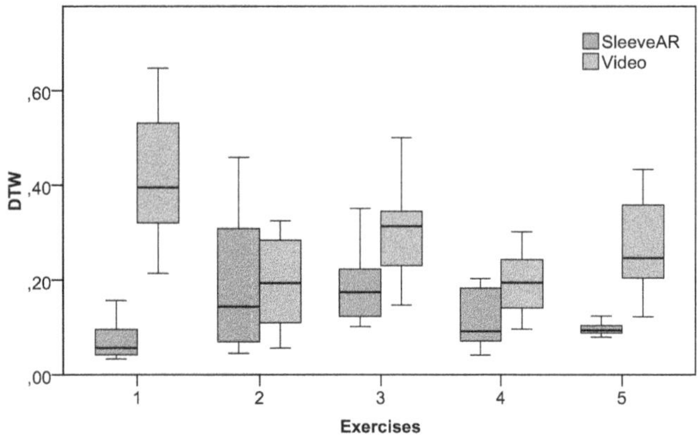

Figure 10. Average results of the Dynamic Time Warping algorithm of each exercise for both approaches (Lower values are better).

were challenging themselves to improve their score on each attempt.

Regarding visual feedback, as listed in Table 3, no statistical differences between the two approaches were observed. As for the floor feedback, some participants complained about their arms occluding visual feedback when looking down at the projections. This can be solved by positioning the floor feedback further away from the user, whenever this condition is detected. Regarding feedback on both arm and floor, some participants stated some difficulty following them simultaneously, even though these were placed in the same field of view.

Task Performance Overview

The user task performance was measured by the degree of similarity between the participants' arm paths and the original path demonstrated by the therapist. To this end we adopted again the *Dynamic Time Warping* algorithm (DTW) [10].

With the application of DTW in mind, the recorded movements can be represented as a temporal sequence of positions. One can then compare the performance values for both the proposed solution and the baseline scenario.

Due to an arm movement being divided by the upper and forearm sections, the DTW was applied to each individually, thus providing us with a more detailed set of values. This separation enables to observe if there were significant performance differences between each arm region.

The final DTW values of each exercise are the result of adding both arm regions' values. It is important to highlight that with the following results, DTW values closer to zero directly represent movements more similar to those of the original demonstration. These results show evidence that SleeveAR provided a higher similarity compared to the original exercise.

For the first exercise, one can observe in Figure 10 the test results (computed from all participants), both using the SleeveAR and just by observing the respective video. In terms of statistic values, participants achieved with SleeveAR an average DTW value of 0.114 and a Standard Deviation of 0.09, versus 0.439 and 0.165, respectively, for video observation. These results clearly suggest that SleeveAR improved participant's performance in the first exercise, i.e., they were able to re-create the original exercise better then by video observation. Based on evidence from the experimental results, similar conclusions can be drawn for the remaining four exercises.

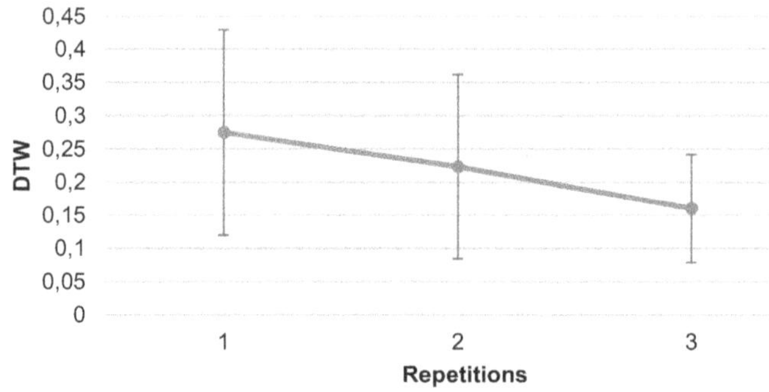

Figure 11. DTW value variation with each repetition using SleeveAR.

We applied a paired T-Student Test to data collected from each exercise on both conditions to assess the performance of our proposed solution on the user's last attempt, under a null hypothesis which stated that SleeveAR and Video observation average DTW were similar. Indeed, for all exercises the computed p-values are lower than 0.05 (0.00002, 0.00001, 0.039, 0.001 and 0.04 for the first five exercises respectively), which invalidates the null hypothesis and showing that, DTW is lower on average for SleeveAR than the video observation.

Focusing on SleeveAR results, Figure 11 presents the average DTW for each of the three trials executed by participants for each exercise. These results clearly show an improvement on a patient's performance in just a small number of repetitions. Not only the average DTW values become smaller, i.e. closer to the original, with successive repetitions, but also the standard deviation appears to diminish. Seemingly, with each repetition, participants are able to see where they performed worse in the previous attempt. These improvements on successive repetitions are statistically meaningful. Indeed, a T-student Test on the slope of the regression line, shown in Figure 11, invalidates the null hypothesis of a zero slope (i.e., performance would not increase with repetitions), with a two tailed p-value of 0.0367, lower than the significance level of 0.05.

Interview with a Physical Therapist

In addition, a professional physical therapist also tested the SleeveAR prototype, conducting the same evaluation exercises performed by the test subjects. We gathered this expert feedback in an interview as a qualitative evaluation of our technique. To recap, our main objective was to improve the guidance of subjects through pre-recorded exercises in order for them to be as close as possible to the original exercise. With this goal in mind, we wanted to investigate in which scenarios this tool might be useful in a regular physical therapy work environment. We also wanted to understand what could be missing in order to improve SleeveAR and make it a complete tool more useful in rehabilitation.

The most significant feedback is now presented, stressing both the positive and negative aspects of the proposed solution.

Missing feedback from one of the three axes. For SleeveAR feedback to be fully complete, it would need to take into account the missing axis of movement when providing real-time feedback. Since this prototype focused on guiding the arm through relatively simple movements, we did not detect this problem. But, subsequently, in the evaluation tests, we realized that it might have helped to take this into account. In the absence of checking the upper arm's rotation, SleeveAR considers some different arm poses to be the same.

Arm obstructs visibility. Occasionally, the right arm might obstruct the user's vision, making it difficult to observe the feedback being projected onto the floor. This issue could be solved by projecting the visual feedback further away from the subject, when such a situation is detected.

Increase number of tracking points in shoulder area. In physical therapy, various arm movements also focus on the shoulder area. So, it would be necessary for our sleeve to include more tracking points around the shoulder instead of only having a tracking point for the shoulder, elbow and wrist.

Potentially useful tool for patient reports. Some physical therapists follow a group of standard arm movements to initially evaluate a patient's condition. They could receive full reports with necessary data that otherwise they would have to measure physically. It could be possible to extend SleeveAR to return additional information about a patient's range of movement after executing a group of exercises. This would allow for an immediate access to information and possibly, a more precise assessment of their condition. In addition, with the possibility of recording movements and later replaying them, SleeveAR could offer a great mechanism for demonstrating to the patient, in a visual form, how much they had improved over the course of their rehabilitation, by displaying recordings of their movements.

A great tool to help a physical therapist when multitasking. While working in a physical therapy gymnasium, therapists often have to look after several patients at the same time. SleeveAR could help the therapist by reducing the number of instances they have to correct a patient and therefore, allowing them focus other patients that might need more help.

Provides a great motivation with the feedback received. The Knowledge of Performance and Results demonstrated in SleeveAR is very satisfactory and could really help in motivating patient while showing their evolution.Being able to show the patients performance by drawing their trajectories over the original exercises helps understanding which parts need improvement. Also, the real-time feedback does a great job at instantaneously showing the patient what to correct on their exercises.

CONCLUSION AND FUTURE WORK

Augmented Reality with visual feedback for rehabilitation is expected to provide a patient with improved sources of information and guidance when executing exercises outside of the controlled environment of the clinic. This is a much desirable scenario than the alternative of exercising with no feedback (and hence there is no possibility to correct a wrong execution). While the state of the art presents several solutions to provide guidance during movement execution, there is still room for improvement, and much research is needed to determine the best combination of different feedback sources. Projecting light on members to guide an individual through a movement showed promising results, but it is still difficult for patients to replicate exactly the prescribed rehabilitation exercise using this information alone.

We have described SleeveAR an intelligent user interface, which combines AR feedback and movement guidance to help rehabilitation exercises. It is intended not only to precisely guide people in performing exercises, but also to provide simple and clear awareness of the correctness or the incorrectness of the required actions, using visual and audio cues.

With SleeveAR, patients are able to formally assess feedback combinations suitable for movement guidance while solving some of the perception problems. SleeveAR also applies different feedback techniques in addition to the ones observed in the state of the art, both on the patient's body (arm and forearm) and on his surrounding floor. The ground projection shows the movements in all axes and allows the sleeve projection to continue in the patient's peripheral field of view. Furthermore, results from user tests suggest that people can replicate previously recorded movements by following multimodal feedback. Future work will address the guidance of real patients during the execution of more complex rehabilitation exercises.

We expect that full body awareness in exercises can be achieved through the usage of multiple projected surfaces (walls, furniture, and even the ceiling).This is particularly interesting to enable a larger range of exercises. Moreover, the perpendicular nature of walls can bring various one-dimensional representations of the exercises, each providing a single detailed point of view in real time. We plan as future work to determine the impact of such approaches on exercise performance.

Yet the setup and apparatus is still a bit complex, far from low cost and easy installation, to be deployed in home settings. Next efforts will focus on using commodity depth cameras to provide a more cost-effective approach. However, the current technique can be efficient, and even cost-effective, for rehabilitation gyms with multiple and concurrent therapeutic sessions.

ACKNOWLEDGMENTS

This work was partially supported by the Portuguese Foundation for Science and Technology (FCT) through the projects TECTON-3D (PTDC/EEI-SII/3154/2012), CEDAR (PTDC/EIA-EIA/116070/2009), and by national funds through FCT with reference UID/CEC/50021/2013. Daniel Medeiros would like to thank CAPES Foundation, Ministry of Education of Brazil for the scholarship grant (reference 9040/13-7). Artur Arsenio's work was partially funded by the Carnegie Mellon University (CMU) – Portuguese program through FCT, project AHA-Augmented Human Assistance, CMUP-ERI/HCI/0046/2013.

REFERENCES

1. Mohammed F. Alhamid, Mohamad Eid, and Abdulmotaleb El Saddik. 2012. A multi-modal intelligent system for biofeedback interactions. *2012 IEEE International Symposium on Medical Measurements and Applications Proceedings* (May 2012), 1–5. DOI: http://dx.doi.org/10.1109/MeMeA.2012.6226653

2. Fraser Anderson, Tovi Grossman, Justin Matejka, and George Fitzmaurice. 2013. YouMove: Enhancing Movement Training with an Augmented Reality Mirror. *Proceedings of the 26th Annual ACM Symposium on User Interface Software and Technology* (2013), 311—-320. http://doi.acm.org/10.1145/2501988.2502045

3. T. Blum and V. Kleeberger. 2012. mirracle: An augmented reality magic mirror system for anatomy education. *Virtual Reality Short ...* (2012), 115–116. http://ieeexplore.ieee.org/xpls/abs_all.jsp?arnumber=6180909

4. N. Alberto Borghese, Renato Mainetti, Michele Pirovano, and Pier Luca Lanzi. 2013. An intelligent game engine for the at-home rehabilitation of stroke patients. *2013 IEEE 2nd International Conference on Serious Games and Applications for Health (SeGAH)* (May 2013), 1–8. DOI:http://dx.doi.org/10.1109/SeGAH.2013.6665318

5. Grigore Burdea. 2002. Virtual Rehabilitation- Benefits and Challenges. (2002).

6. James William Burke, Michael McNeill, Darryl Charles, Philip Morrow, Jacqui Crosbie, and Suzanne McDonough. 2009. Serious Games for Upper Limb Rehabilitation Following Stroke. *2009 Conference in Games and Virtual Worlds for Serious Applications* (March 2009), 103–110. DOI: http://dx.doi.org/10.1109/VS-GAMES.2009.17

7. Alana Da Gama, Thiago Chaves, Lucas Figueiredo, and Veronica Teichrieb. 2012. Guidance and Movement Correction Based on Therapeutics Movements for Motor Rehabilitation Support Systems. *2012 14th Symposium on Virtual and Augmented Reality* (May 2012), 191–200. DOI:http://dx.doi.org/10.1109/SVR.2012.15

8. He Huang, T Ingalls, L Olson, K Ganley, Thanassis Rikakis, and Jiping He. 2005. Interactive multimodal biofeedback for task-oriented neural rehabilitation. *Engineering in Medicine and Biology Society, 2005. 27th Annual International Conference of the* (2005), 2547–2550. http://ieeexplore.ieee.org/xpls/abs_all.jsp?arnumber=1616988

9. Alexandre Klein and Gilda Aparecida De Assis. 2013. A Markeless Augmented Reality Tracking for Enhancing the User Interaction during Virtual Rehabilitation. *2013 XV Symposium on Virtual and Augmented Reality* (May 2013), 117–124. DOI: http://dx.doi.org/10.1109/SVR.2013.43

10. Joseph B Kruskal and Mark Liberman. 1983. The symmetric time-warping problem: from continuous to discrete. *Time Warps, String Edits and Macromolecules: The Theory and Practice of Sequence Comparison* (1983), 125–161.

11. Hugo Nicolau, Tiago Guerreiro, Rita Pereira, Daniel Gonçalves, and Joaquim Jorge. 2013. Computer-assisted rehabilitation: towards effective evaluation. *International Journal of Cognitive Performance Support* 1, 1 (2013), 11–26.

12. Paula Rego, PM Moreira, and LP Reis. 2010. Serious games for rehabilitation: A survey and a classification towards a taxonomy. *Information Systems and Technologies (CISTI), 2010 5th Iberian Conference on* (2010). http://ieeexplore.ieee.org/xpls/abs_all.jsp?arnumber=5556674

13. D. Sadihov, B. Migge, and R. Gassert. 2013. Prototype of a VR upper-limb rehabilitation system enhanced with motion-based tactile feedback. *2013 World Haptics Conference (WHC)* (April 2013), 449–454. DOI: http://dx.doi.org/10.1109/WHC.2013.6548450

14. Christian Schönauer and Thomas Pintaric. 2011. Full Body Interaction for Serious Games in Motor Rehabilitation. *Proceedings of the 2Nd Augmented Human International Conference* ACM Press (2011), 1–8. http://dl.acm.org/citation.cfm?id=1959830

15. Roland Sigrist, Georg Rauter, Robert Riener, and Peter Wolf. 2013. Augmented visual, auditory, haptic, and multimodal feedback in motor learning: A review. *Psychonomic bulletin & review* 20, 1 (Feb. 2013), 21–53. DOI:http://dx.doi.org/10.3758/s13423-012-0333-8

16. Rajinder Sodhi, H Benko, and A Wilson. 2012. LightGuide: projected visualizations for hand movement guidance. *Proceedings of the SIGCHI Conference on Human Factors in Computing Systems* (2012). http://dl.acm.org/citation.cfm?id=2207702

17. R Tang, H Alizadeh, A Tang, Scott Bateman, and Joaquim Jorge. 2014. Physio@ Home: design explorations to support movement guidance. *CHI '14 Extended Abstracts on Human Factors in Computing Systems* (2014). http://dl.acm.org/citation.cfm?id=2581197

18. Richard Tang, Anthony Tang, Xing-dong Yang Scott, and Joaquim Jorge. 2015. Physio @ Home : Exploring visual guidance and feedback techniques for physiotherapy exercises. *Proceedings of the SIGCHI Conference on Human Factors in Computing Systems* (2015).

19. Eduardo Velloso, A Bulling, and Hans Gellersen. 2013. MotionMA: Motion modelling and analysis by demonstration. *Proceedings of the SIGCHI Conference on Human Factors in Computing Systems* (2013), 1309–1318. http://dl.acm.org/citation.cfm?id=2466171

PlaylistPlayer: An Interface Using Multiple Criteria to Change the Playback Order of a Music Playlist

Tomoyasu Nakano **Jun Kato** **Masahiro Hamasaki** **Masataka Goto**
National Institute of Advanced Industrial Science and Technology (AIST), Japan
{t.nakano, jun.kato, masahiro.hamasaki, m.goto}@aist.go.jp

ABSTRACT
We propose a novel interface that allows the user to interactively change the playback order of multiple songs by choosing one or more criteria. The criteria include not only the song's title and artist name but also its content automatically estimated by music/singing signal processing and artist-level social analysis. The artist-level social information is discovered from Wikipedia and DBpedia. With regard to manipulating playback order, existing interfaces typically allow the user to change it manually or automatically by choosing one of a few types of criteria. The proposed interface, on the other hand, deals with nine properties and multiple integrations of them (*e.g.*, vocal gender and beats per minute). To realize the ordering by multiple criteria, a distance matrix is computed from the criteria vectors and is then used to estimate paths for ascending, descending, and random orders by applying principle component analysis or to estimate a path for a smooth order by solving the travelling salesman problem.

ACM Classification Keywords
H.5.5. Information Interfaces and Presentation (*e.g.*, HCI): Sound and Music Computing – Signal analysis, synthesis, and processing; H.5.2. Information Interfaces and Presentation (*e.g.*, HCI): User Interfaces – GUI.

Author Keywords
Music playlist; playback order; visualization; vocal gender; musical commonness; social commonness.

INTRODUCTION
Playlists, lists of songs played back automatically, are a popular way of listening to music. The playback order can be determined using metadata such as artist names and song titles, and the "freshness" of a playlist listened to repeatedly can be increased by randomly shuffling the playback order.

We propose a playlist playback interface, *PlaylistPlayer*, that enriches the listener's experience by allowing interactively changing the playback order based on various properties of the songs and their artists. These properties, derived from content and from web, are visualized in the extended playlist interface (Figure 1). The following three kinds of properties can be visualized and used to change the playback order:

IUI'16, March 07–10, 2016, Sonoma, CA, USA

ACM 978-1-4503-4137-0/16/03...$15.00.
DOI: http://dx.doi.org/10.1145/2856767.2856809

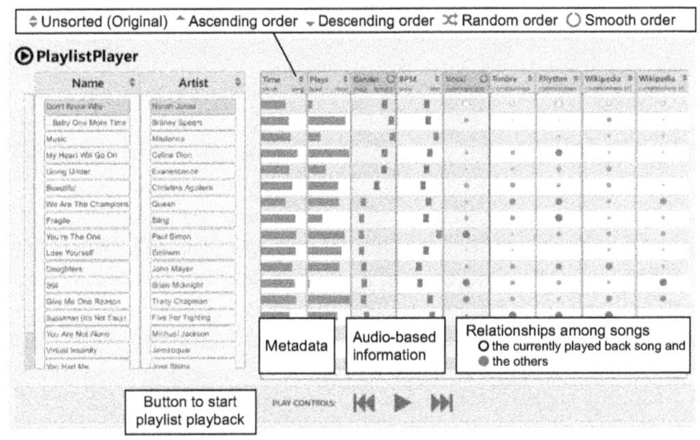

Figure 1. An example PlaylistPlayer screen.

(type 1: absolute values) meta-data:
intrinsic information (song length) and information given by a listener's behavior (the number of views),

(type 2: absolute values) audio-based information:
vocal information (vocal gender) and musical information (beats per minute: BPM),

(type 3: relative values) relationships among songs:
musical commonness [14] (a song's similarity to a set of songs) of vocal timbre, musical timbre, and rhythm; and social commonness (artist-level social relationships between a song and a set of songs) of artist background information on the web.

Any of those properties can be used as a re-ordering criterion, and two or more properties (*e.g.*, vocal gender, BPM and musical commonness) can be used as re-ordering criteria. Integrating multiple properties enables designing a variety of playback orders that match the user's needs.

RELATED WORK
Previous work on playlist generation is related to our interface's changing playback order, and previous work on playlist visualization in order to discover a song is related to our interface's visualization.

Playlist Generation
Common approaches to creating playlists on existing music players such as *iTunes* are to manually select songs, using some conditions to create complex playlists (*Smart Playlist*), or to select songs automatically (*Genius*).

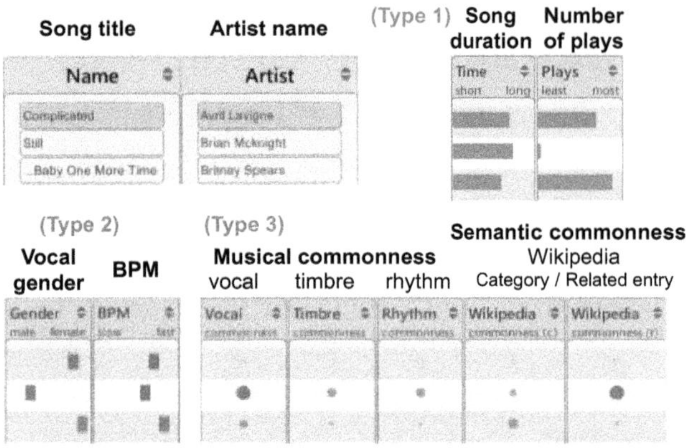

Figure 2. The tabular visualization of all properties.

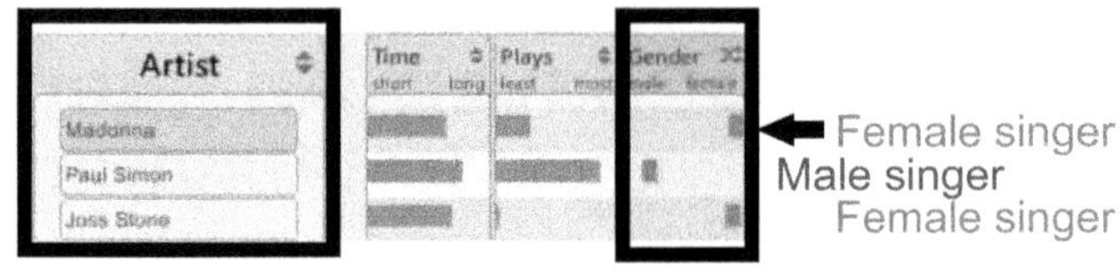

Figure 3. The random order of the vocal gender.

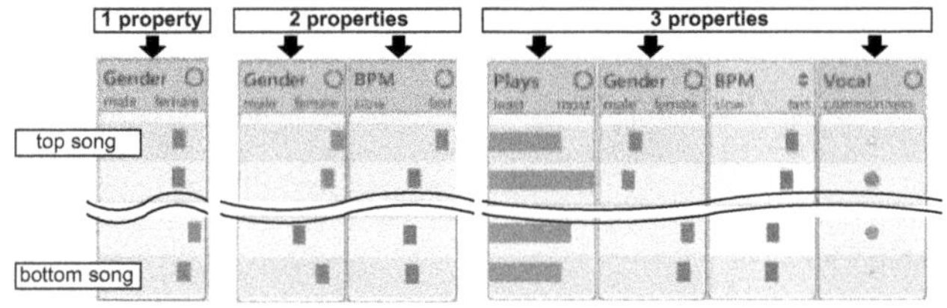

Figure 4. Re-ordering by the smooth order using multiple properties.

On the other hand, much research has also been focused on playlist generation [2, 18]. Research on generating playlists based on smooth transition between one song and the previous and next songs (acoustically similar pieces) [4, 17] is related to our system in terms of playback order. And research considering human behavior during playback (*e.g.*, skipping a song) and generating a playlist by dynamically adapting to the user's preferences [11, 15] is related to our system in terms of using human behavior (*i.e.*, the number of views).

PlaylistPlayer, however, uses metadata, audio data, and behavioral data not for 'generating a new playlist but for changing the order in which an existing playlist is played back'. Moreover, multiple criteria can be used by integrating the individual criteria.

Playlist Visualization

There has been much work in which visualization of relationships among songs was used to browse, to explore, and to discover a song [12]. Some research focusing on combining visualization with playlist generation is related to our system, such as interactive playlist generation [20], generating a thumbnail image that represents audio features of a playlist [19], and printing out album covers for use as tangible interfaces of playlists [8].

There has also been work on visualizing artist relationships based on musical background (*e.g.*, female solo-singer), moods, tempo, genres, active years and decades [7, 20], and associated activities (*i.e.*, members of a band) [9].

PlaylistPlayer, in contrast, uses tabular type visualization as an extension of the standard playlist. Our system visualizes not only *static* values (*i.e.*, metadata and acoustic characteristics) but also *dynamically* changing values (*i.e.*, relationships among songs). In addition, artist relationship includes artists' personal information on the web.

PLAYLISTPLAYER: AN EXTENDED PLAYLIST

PlaylistPlayer is a playlist interface which is an extended classical list-view style playlist. To realize PlaylistPlayer, first the musical characteristics of the audio data for all the songs in the playlist are estimated automatically. The characteristics used in the current implementation are BPM, vocal gender, commonness of vocal timbre, musical timbre, and musical rhythm. Second, we crawl the web for artist-level social relationships among all songs in the playlist.

Finally, we implement an interface for interactions during changing playback order and visualization. In this section we describe the interface and the interactions. The re-ordering, signal processing and web mining methods are described in detail in the next section.

Change Playback Order and Visualization

PlaylistPlayer can change playback order according to the three types of properties listed in the INTRODUCTION. Figure 2 shows all three types with some tabular visualization methods by reference to [16]. Type-1 properties are represented by blue rectangles in horizontal bar graphs. Type-2 properties are represented by colored rectangles (blue or red). For example, if a male probability of vocal gender is high, the rectangle is colored blue and placed at the left side. And type-3 properties are represented by green circles whose sizes depend on relationships (musical or social commonness). The reason for using the commonness instead of the similarity between two songs is to fit to the tabular type visualization.

To change the order, sort/unsorted marks, a smooth mark, and a random mark are placed on top of each property column (Fig. 1). A single triangular shape means ascending or descending order, the circle shape means all song transition are smooth (including a transition between top and bottom songs), and the curved arrow means random order. Random order means that all the songs in the playlist are ordered alternately with regard to the selected properties. For example, if the random mark of the "Gender" property is checked (Fig. 3), a song sung by a male singer is played after a song sung by a female singer. When there are two triangular shapes on one property, that property is not considered when determining the order (i.e., the order is the original predefined order).

The listener can change the order by clicking the marks of one or more properties each time. If two or more properties are selected, these marks are coordinated (Fig. 4).

IMPLEMENTATION

To test the interface, we used 19 songs as listed in Figure 5. They were chosen among 415 English songs performed by various types of artists (solo singers, male/female singers,

song ID	Artist name / Song title
1	Avril Lavigne / Complicated
2	Brian Mcknight / Still
3	Britney Spears / ...Baby One More Time
4	Celine Dion / My Heart Will Go On
5	Christina Aguilera / Beautiful
6	Eminem / Lose Yourself
7	Erykah Badu / On & On
8	Evanescence / Going Under
9	Five for Fighting / Superman (It's Not Easy)
10	Jamiroquai / Virtual Insanity
11	John Mayer / Daughters
12	Joss Stone / You Had Me
13	Madonna / Music
14	Michael Jackson / You Are Not Alone
15	Norah Jones / Don't Know Why
16	Paul Simon / You're The One
17	Queen / We Are The Champions
18	Sting / Fragile
19	Tracy Chapman / Give Me One Reason

Figure 5. Songs used in the evaluation.

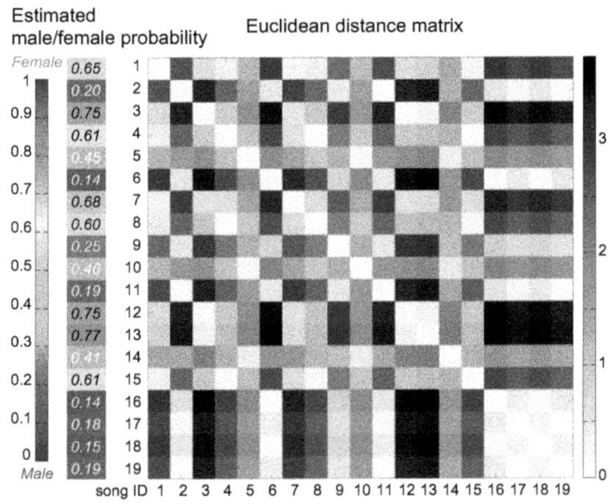

Figure 6. A Euclidean distance matrix calculated from estimated male/female probabilities in the 19 songs.

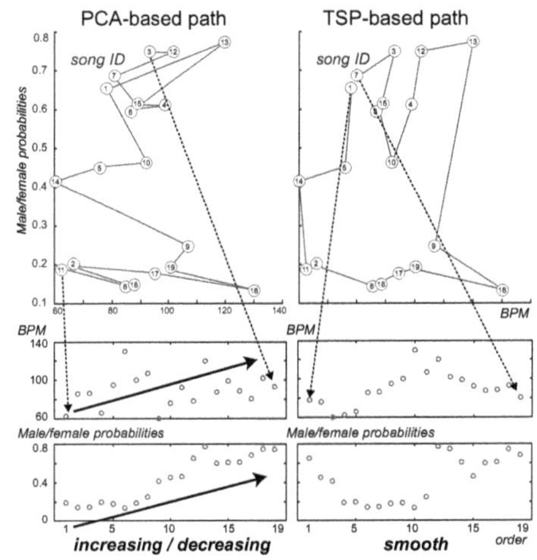

Figure 7. Two types of paths are estimated.

bands, or groups). They were taken from commercial music CDs (*Billboard Top Rock'n'Roll Hits* 1968-1972, *Billboard Top Hits* 1975-1989 and *GRAMMY NOMINEES* 1996-2005).

Re-Ordering using multiple criteria

All properties among songs can be represented as an $N \times N$ Euclidean distance matrix (N is the number of songs of the playlist). If the listener selects two properties as criteria for re-ordering, such as vocal gender and BPM, a distance between two songs is calculated from the 2-dimensional vector. Before calculating the distance, each vector is normalized by subtracting the mean and dividing by the standard deviation. The Euclidean distance matrix A is defined as

$$A = (a_{ij})_{\substack{1 \leq i \leq N,\\ 1 \leq j \leq N}} \quad a_{ij} = \sqrt{\sum_{d=1}^{D} (x_i(d)^2 - x_j(d)^2)}, \qquad (1)$$

where $\vec{x_i}$ and $\vec{x_j}$ are the D-dimensional normalized vectors of two songs (see Figure 6 for concrete examples).

For changing playback order according to those properties, we compute a one-dimensional vector from the matrix to realize the ascending/descending/random order. The one-dimensional vector is computed by applying principle component analysis (PCA) for reduction of dimensions of the distance matrix. Then the one-dimensional vector is sorted.

The path for smooth transition is estimated by solving the travelling salesman problem (TSP). Although the TSP was used for getting acoustically-smoothed transition in previous works [4, 17], the originality of the PlaylistPlayer is that the TSP used to integrate multiple criteria (Fig. 4).

The PCA-based and TSP-based methods can scale up to at least hundreds of songs (completed in a second on a personal computer). Moreover, their computational efficiencies can be increased by using the EM algorithm for PCA [1] and some approximate algorithms for TSP [17]. For the PCA, the most computationally demanding steps of the EM algorithm are $O(NDM)$, where M denotes the number of principle components [1]. For the TSP, the *Minimum Spanning Tree* is $O(m \log m)$ with m being the number of edges [17].

Figure 7 shows that path-estimation results obtained by taking into account two properties (vocal gender and BPM).

Music/singing signal processing

BPM (type 2) of each song is estimated by using the median value of the time intervals between individual beats during one song. To estimate beats, we use modules of Songle [6].

Since we focus on vocal timbre, musical timbre, and rhythm, we extract acoustic features representing them from the musical audio signals [14]. These features are used to estimate the vocal gender (type 2), and the musical commonnesses (type 3) of songs.

Vocal Gender Estimation (type 2)

Our system also uses a vocal gender estimation method [10]. Male/female probabilities of each *reliable frame* (see [10]) are estimated using a probabilistic Support Vector Machine (SVM) [3] and are reduced to a single value by taking the median across the SVM output.

Fifteen songs (13 Japanese and 2 English) sung by fifteen male singers and thirteen songs (11 Japanese and 2 English) sung by thirteen female singers are used as the training set of each model. These songs are solo vocal performances and are from the RWC Music Database (RWC-MDB-P-2001) [5].

Musical Commonness Estimation (type 3)

We use a musical commonness estimation method [14] based on latent Dirichlet allocation (LDA). A song-set (playlist) model can be obtained by summing the hyperparameters of the topic distributions of song models [14].

To train the LDA-based topic model, we used the 415 songs.

Web mining

To provide different type of relations among songs, we focus on artist properties. The artist information is obtained from Wikipedia (http://www.wikipedia.org/) and DBpedia [13]. DBpedia has structured information extracted from Wikipedia. From each artist entry (page) are extracted phrases in the Categories section (*e.g.*, Grammy Award-winning artists) and related entries' names that have a link

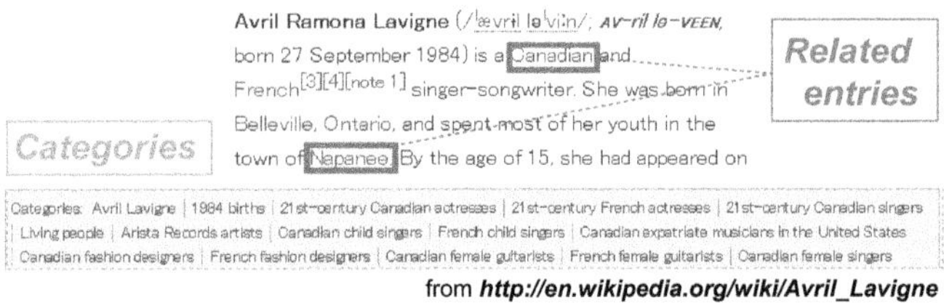

Figure 8. A Wikipedia artist entry (page) and the kinds of information.

with another entry on Wikipedia. An example of the extracted information is shown in detail in Figure 8.

We investigated social information among 335 artists of the 415 songs. The total numbers of social information are 2,154 categories and 15,658 related entries. There was music-related information (*e.g.*, Musical quartets, American pop singers, and genre), personal information (*e.g.*, 1942 births), and information about awards.

Social Commonness (type 3)
We estimate social commonness by using the categories and the related entries as social annotations. The estimation procedure is similar to the musical commonness estimation procedure based on the LDA. An artist-set (playlist) model can also be obtained by integrating artist models.

Evaluation

Accuracies of the proposed estimation methods are calculated for the 19 songs. To evaluate the vocal gender estimation, estimated male/female probabilities are shown in Figure 6 and they are binarized ("male" if the probabilities are equal to or lower than 0.5, "'female" if the probabilities are greater than 0.5). The classification rate was 94.7% (18/19 songs).

Estimated BPMs are comparable to annotated BPMs by a musician. To evaluate the estimation method, we computed five BPMs for each song based on five beat structure candidates estimated by Songle [6]. Then, we chose the BPM that is the closest to the annotated BPM. A root-mean-square value of the difference between the chosen (estimated) BPMs of 19 songs and the annotated BPMs was 0.78.

Estimated musical commonness and social commonness are evaluated based on the Pearson product-moment correlation coefficients between estimated commonness of each song and the number of songs having high similarity with the song [14]. If the correlation coefficients are high, the estimated commonness is appropriate. This means a song having higher (lower) commonness and it is very similar (is not similar) to songs of a song set. The correlation coefficients of the three musical elements (vocal timbre, musical timbre and rhythm) were 0.87, 0.91 and 0.80, and of the two social information (category and related entry) are 0.81 and 0.85.

USER FEEDBACK

To investigate the capabilities, limitations, and potential of our interaction design, we asked seven users to use the system for 20 minutes and collected preliminary user feedback. We chose the users (six males and one female) so that they have different levels of musical experience/knowledge. Six users had experience with musical instruments, and three users had experience with arrangement/composition. The playlist consisted of the 19 songs (Figure 5). All users knew more than 1 song, and four users knew more than 10 songs. After the trial usage, we asked the users to write comments about the two primary functions of the system: 1) song information visualization and 2) changing the playback order.

Positive comments about the capabilities and potential of the interface are listed below.

Visualization of multiple properties This is helpful when exploring the playback order that meets my expectation.

Automatic re-ordering based on content-based criteria 1) Easy to use and much appreciated. 2) Helpful for finding new songs similar to songs of favorite artists. 3) The smooth order creates smooth transitions between songs which are suitable for background music. 4) The random order gives fresh listening experience for a worn-out set of songs.

Both functions 1) Both were useful for listening songs in a new perspective. 2) Both are likely to be helpful for generating a new playlist. 3) The properties for social commonness were useful because they matched the impression of the songs/artists.

There were also negative comments pointing out the limitations of the current implementation.

Visualization of multiple properties 1) The visualization of the social commonness properties was not comprehensive enough. 2) There are sometimes mismatches between visualization results and auditory impression. 3) The type 3 visualization was sometimes confusing.

Automatic re-ordering based on content-based criteria 1) Since there are a lot of properties (nine), the re-ordering operation by integrating them is a bit more complex. 2) The commonness order is hard to comprehend.

Both functions / Other perspective 1) There is too much information for casual listening. 2) Some properties require prior knowledge of music to comprehend the ordering rules. 3) Functions to compare results of sorting and to filter the results based on multiple criteria are desired. 4) Released date of songs can be added as a new property for sorting.

These comments suggest that the interface is effective, but some visualizations/functions should be improved.

CONCLUSION

This paper presents PlaylistPlayer, a playlist playback interface that can be used to change the playback ordering of existing playlists by using multiple criteria interactively. Although this paper did not discuss the "repeat" function, which is an standard function to use for playlist playback, the proposed criteria (or combinations of them) can be used to change after finishing playback of all songs to create various kinds of repeats. In addition, we intend in future work to further improve the interaction in ways inferred from user feedback.

ACKNOWLEDGMENT

This paper utilized the RWC Music Database (Popular Music). This work was supported in part by CREST, JST.

REFERENCES

1. Bishop, C. M. *Pattern Recognition and Machine Learning*. Springer-Verlag New York, Inc., 2006.
2. Bonnin, G., and Jannach, D. Automated generation of music playlists: Survey and experiments. *Journal of ACM Computing Surveys (CSUR) 47*, 2 (2015), 1–35.
3. Chang, C.-C., and Lin, C.-J. Libsvm: A library for support vector machines. *ACM TIST 2* (2011), 1–39.
4. Flexer, A., Schnitzer, D., Gasser, M., and Widmer, G. Playlist generation using start and end songs. In *Proc. ISMIR 2008* (2008), 173–178.
5. Goto, M., Hashiguchi, H., Nishimura, T., and Oka, R. RWC music database: Popular, classical, and jazz music databases. In *Proc. of ISMIR 2002* (2002), 287–288.
6. Goto, M., Yoshii, K., Fujihara, H., Mauch, M., and Nakano, T. Songle: A web service for active music listening improved by user contributions. In *Proc. ISMIR 2011* (2011), 311–316.
7. Gouyon, F., Cruz, N., and Sarmento, L. A Last.fm and YouTube mash-up for music browsing and playlist edition. In *Proc. ISMIR 2011* (2011), 1–2.
8. Graham, J., and Hull, J. J. iCandy: a tangible user interface for iTunes. In *Proc. CHI2008* (2008), 2343–2348.
9. Hamanaka, M., and Yoshiya, M. BandNavi: Band-member backtracker based on member history information. *Journal of Communication and Computer 9*, 2 (2012), 114–121.
10. Hamasaki, M., Goto, M., and Nakano, T. Songrium: A music browsing assistance service with interactive visualization and exploration of a web of music. In *Proc. WWW 2014* (2014), 523–528.
11. Hu, Y., and Ogihara, M. NextOne Player: A music recommendation system based on user behavior. In *Proc. ISMIR 2011* (2011), 103–108.
12. Langer, T. Music information retrieval & visualization. In *Trends in Information Visualization* (2010), 15–22.
13. Lehmann, J., Isele, R., Jakob, M., Jentzsch, A., Kontokostas, D., Mendes, P. N., Hellmann, S., Morsey, M., van Kleef, P., Auer, S., and Bizer, C. DBpedia - a large-scale, multilingual knowledge base extracted from Wikipedia. *Semantic Web Journal* (2012), 1–5.
14. Nakano, T., Yoshii, K., and Goto, M. Musical similarity and commonness estimation based on probabilistic generative models. In *Proc. ISM 2015* (2015), 197–204.
15. Pampalk, E., Pohle, T., and Widmer, G. Dynamic playlist generation based on skipping behavior. In *Proc. ISMIR 2005* (2005), 634–637.
16. Perin, C., Dragicevic, P., and Fekete, J.-D. Revisiting bertin matrices: New interactions for crafting tabular visualizations. *IEEE Trans. Visualization and Computer Graphics 20*, 12 (2014), 2082–2091.
17. Pohle, T., Pampalk, E., and Widmer, G. Generating similarity-based playlists using traveling salesman algorithms. In *Proc DAFx' 05* (2005), 1–6.
18. Song, Y., Dixon, S., and Pearce, M. A survey of music recommendation systems and future perspectives. In *Proc. CMMR 2012* (2012), 395–410.
19. Uota, T., and Itoh, T. GRAPE: A gradation based portable visual playlist. In *Proc. IV 2014* (2014), 361–364.
20. van Gulik, R., and Vignoli, F. Visual playlist generation on the artist map. In *Proc. of ISMIR 2005* (2005), 520–523.

Remind Me: An Adaptive Recommendation-Based Simulation of Biographic Associations

Dominik Gall, Jean-Luc Lugrin, Dennis Wiebusch, Marc Erich Latoschik
{dominik.gall, jean-luc.lugrin, dennis.wiebusch, marc.latoschik}@uni-wuerzburg.de
Human-Computer Interaction
University of Würzburg
Würzburg, 97074, Germany

ABSTRACT
Classical reminiscence therapy has been shown to effectively enhance the stability of memory and identity in people with dementia. Typically, reminiscence therapy uses biography artifacts like photos and personal items and objects. Today, many of these artifacts are from the digital realm providing new options to adapt or even improve the purely analog therapy. In this work we propose a method to enhance reminiscence therapy by computer simulated biographic associations. Our approach provides assistance for associative reasoning on affective stimuli and thus enables access to biographic content so that no deliberate search is required. We develop a recommender model for mapping mental states to biographic content based on similarity. The system dynamically adapts its state and the depicted digital artifacts to the responses of the user. It is a first step towards an immersive reminiscence therapy which will incorporate associated stimuli on multiple channels to increase effectiveness. A preliminary study showed encouraging results concerning the usability of the system.

Author Keywords
Elderly people; dementia; reminiscence therapy; computer-mediated health promotion; immersion;

ACM Classification Keywords
H.5.m Information Interfaces and Presentation (e.g. HCI): Miscellaneous

INTRODUCTION
In 2030, the number of people living with dementia is estimated to be 65.7 million worldwide, doubling every 20 years [17]. Thus, the improvement of the effectiveness of interventions that meet the needs for people with dementia is considered a major issue [14]. A major symptom of dementia is the development of multiple cognitive deficits that manifest by the impairment of memory and disturbance of executive functioning, like abstracting and sequencing [2]. Reminiscence therapy is one of the most popular interventions in dementia care for tackling these symptoms. It is highly rated by caregivers and participants [20]. Also, it has been shown to be a promising intervention for improving the sense of integrity and ameliorate depression in people with dementia [9, 7, 20]. In reminiscence therapy, participants are encouraged to reflect on past experiences with the aid of familiar stimuli from the past, like photographs. In the future items with a dominant visual or auditive aspect will be represented mainly in the digital realm and the number of these items will increase to a great extent. Yet, to our knowledge, technical support for improving the effectiveness of reminiscence therapy is very limited.

To address the challenge of increasing the effectiveness of reminiscence therapy, we present a system that aims to increase immersion on biographic relevant stimuli by simulating associative reasoning on a huge set of personal stimuli. This approach contrasts to traditional methods, where associative reasoning is only supported externally by the caregiver and the directly tangible stimuli. A major aspect of reminiscence therapy is the personal interaction of the caregiver with the participant. Thus, we set high priority on not changing this setting, in order to maintain the effective treatment factors of reminiscence therapy. Our system is designed to facilitate personal interaction during the intervention, not to replace it. Furthermore, the requirement of technical expertise for setup or operation is a major obstacle for the use of information technology devices by caregivers [11]. To that effect we use mobile touch devices that allow low threshold usage in face-to-face or group settings.

The two contributions of this work are as follows: we provide a system, (1) for increasing immersion in reminiscence therapy by simulating association and (2) for enabling automated accessibility of biographic stimuli where no deliberate semantic reasoning is required.

RELATED WORK
Technical approaches that aim to support reminiscence focus on displaying stimuli that are linked by a fixed definition and have to be selected manually. In the CIRCA project [1, 3] a system is developed that allows structured browsing through multimedia archive designed to support communication and

IUI'16, March 07 - 10, 2016, Sonoma, CA, USA

ACM 978-1-4503-4137-0/16/03...$15.00
DOI: http://dx.doi.org/10.1145/2856767.2856816

reminiscence. Hereby the focus is not on adapting content to implicit user behavior. In this context it was found that the use of touch screen interfaces seems to encourage users with dementia to use the system and provides a supportive interaction environment [4].

In [5] and [19] multimedia presentation tools for a set of historic stimuli that also allow the storage of personal data are presented. A framework for interaction with 3D reconstructions of familiar environments is introduced in [6]. Several systems have been proposed that aim to compensate for memory deficits during reminiscence therapy by providing material that has recently been recorded [10, 12, 21]. In [16] a system to support reminiscence in everyday live is presented. A review of information technology aided reminiscence therapy outlines its potential but also a lack of knowledge about the type and content that is beneficial to people at different stages of dementia [11]. To date, assisted selection of stimuli to enhance reminiscene has not been well addressed.

There are two elements that distinguish our work from previous approaches for information technology aided reminiscence therapy. First, our implementation aims to simulate, and thereby stimulate impaired association processes. Second, our implementation gives automated access to stimuli without requiring manual preselection.

OUR PROPOSAL

Our conceptual goal is to facilitate association processes by the simulation of semantic association. Therefore, we propose a system that iteratively aims to activate mental entities that are specified by two conditions: first, the history of previously activated mental entities and second the currently predominant pattern of change between these entity sets. Here the set of currently activated mental entities models the content a user is conscious of. While the pattern of change models the predominant emotional mindset of the user. We propose to simulate this association model by applying an adaptive semantic recommender system to emotion triggering stimuli. Hereby the user navigates through a directed, weighted, complete graph of emotional relevant stimuli. The weights of this graph model the association strength by which two stimuli are linked to each other. They are simultaneously adapted during the navigation through this graph in the following way: first, a set of semantic similarity measures is evaluated. Second the set of these similarity measures is weighted according to their currently estimated relevance.

SYSTEM PROCESS

Our system aims to recommend biographic stimuli that are similar to previously selected content in terms of the currently predominant mental state of the user. This recommendation task presents two technical challenges: first, a model for mapping mental states to similarity of biographic content has to be defined and second, this model has to adapt to the response of the user to the recommended content. Usability for dementia patients was of high priority in the design of our system. Therefore, user interaction is restricted to a simple affectively motivated selection task, where no explicit reasoning is required. The implementation we propose could run on a tablet or smartphone device for a low threshold usage in clinical and care settings. The process of the system, outlined in Figure 1, is structured as follows: initially a set of static distance measures is evaluated on semantic annotated stimuli. An iterative selection task is presented to the user, where several stimuli that are similar to previous selections are recommended. This similarity term is defined by a weighted sum of the static distance measures. Hereby the weights are updated according to the selection behavior of the user.

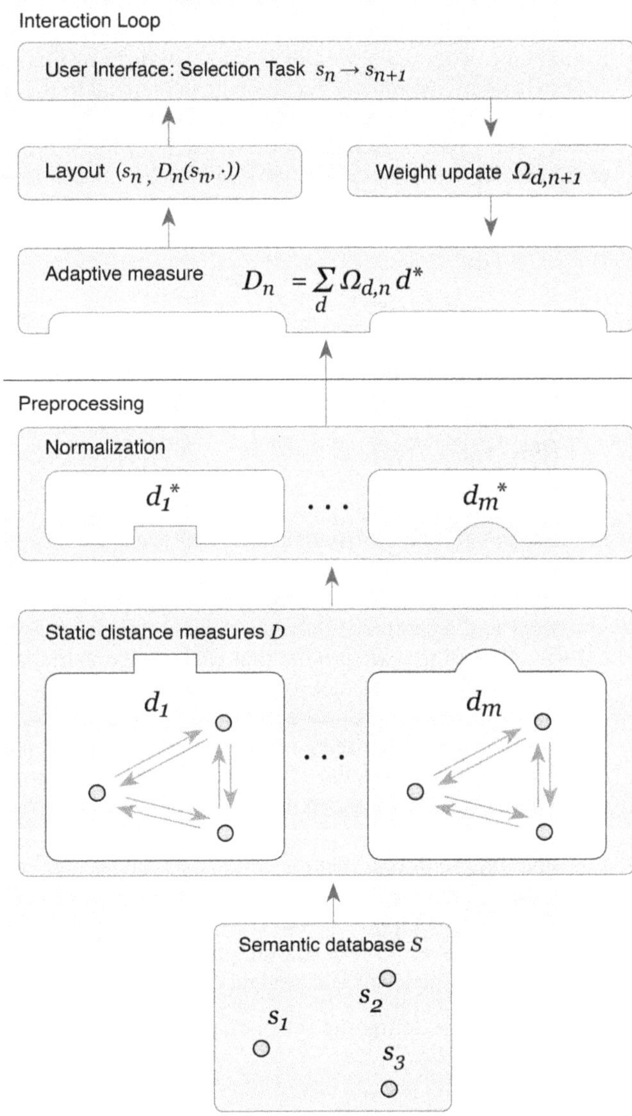

Figure 1. Illustration of the system process. First normalized semantic distance measures are initialized and second an adaptive distance measure is iteratively updated by evaluating user behavior.

Semantic Database

We denote S as the set of stimuli represented in the system. For our demonstration we restricted stimuli to images. These images can either be added and semantically annotated at runtime or be loaded from a database.

Static Distance Measures

A set of semantically motivated distance measures D on the stimuli set S has to be selected. Each of these distance measures models a semantic aspect of non-similarity of two stimuli. These aspects, and hence the measures in D remain static throughout the procedure. For a valid distance measure, we only require non-negativity and coincidence.

For our implementation we chose three distance measures that aim to encode different types of memory cues.

1. For modeling interpersonal memory cues we define a distance measure that relates to the persons that are contained in an image. Therefore, we call P the set of persons that appear at least in one image. Each image is mapped to the set of persons appearing in it by the mapping $p : S \to \mathcal{P}(P)$, where $\mathcal{P}(P)$ indicates the power set of P. First a binary distance measure $d_p : S^2 \to [0, 1]$, indicating the amount of overlap of appearing and not appearing persons. For two images $s_1, s_2 \in S$ the person distance is defined as

$$d_p(s_1, s_2) := 1 - \frac{|R(s_1, s_2)|}{|P|}$$

whereas R denotes the set of persons that either appear on both images s_1 and s_2 or on none of them:

$$R(s_1, s_2) := \{\varphi \in P : (\varphi \in p(s_1) \wedge \varphi \in p(s_2)) \vee (\varphi \notin p(s_1) \wedge \varphi \notin p(s_2))\}$$

For a survey of binary distance measures see [8].

2. For modeling situational memory cues we define a geographical and a temporal distance measure in the canonical way. Therefore, we assume that each image is mapped to the geographical location of its content, i.e. to its latitude and longitude values by the mapping $g : S \to \mathbb{R}^2$. For approximating the geographical distance measure $d_g : S^2 \to \mathbb{R}_0^+$ we use the Haversine formula for great-circle distances between two points [18].

3. For modeling temporal memory cues we assume that each image is mapped to the date and time of its content $t : S \to \mathbb{R}$, presupposing the existence of a reasonable date mapping over $\mathbb{R}$. For the temporal distance measure $d_t : S^2 \to \mathbb{R}_0^+$ the Euclidean distance is used.

For our system we define the set of static distance measures as $D := \{d_p, d_g, d_t\}$.

Normalization

The value range and spread of the above defined distance measures may vary to a great extent. In order to combine the different distance measures, they are normalized in two steps. First a z-score transformation is applied to allow the relative comparison of the selected measures. Therefore, for each distance measure $d \in D$ and each stimulus $s \in S$ the distance to a neighbor $\xi \in S$ is considered as a random variable $d(s, \cdot) : S \to \mathbb{R}$. The z-score transformation is applied on each random variable $d(s, \cdot)$, aligning the standard deviation and center. The resulting standardized random variable is denoted by $z_{d,s}$. Second, in order to increase the significance of further distance measures for small and large outliers a quasi homogeneous transformation is applied. For an overview on homogeneous coordinates see, for example, [13]. This transformation is defined as the first coordinate of the intersection of the line between the origin and the point $z_{d,s}(\eta)$ and the unit circle. Thus, in total for a given neighbor $\xi \in S$ of the stimulus s and a distance measure $d \in D$ the normalized distance function $d^* : S^2 \to [-1, 1]$ is defined as $d^*(s, \xi) := z_{d,s}(\xi)(z_{d,s}(\xi)^2 + 1)^{-\frac{1}{2}}$. Figure 2 informally illustrates the described normalization process.

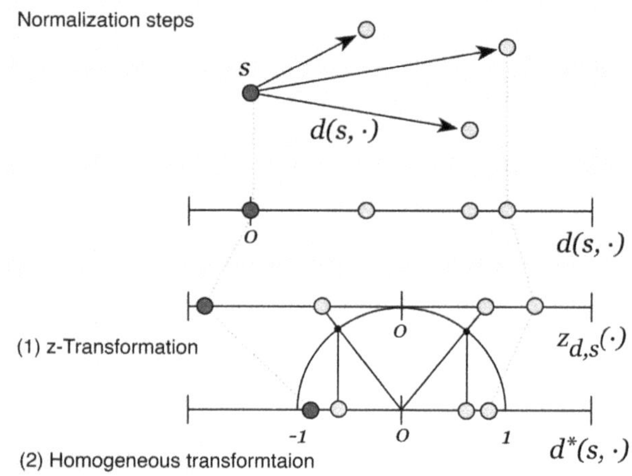

Figure 2. Informal illustration of the normalization process. For the neighbor distances of each stimulus first a z-transformation and second a quasi homogeneous transformation is applied.

Adaptive Measure

To traverse through the image graph the system recommends images in the order of the their distance to the current node within the graph, where this distance adapts to the recent choices of the user. For a given iteration step $n \in \mathbb{N}$ we define this adaptive distance measure $D_n : S^2 \to \mathbb{R}$ as a weighted sum of the static distance measures, as $D_n(s_1, s_2) := \sum_{d \in D} \Omega_{d,n}\, d^*(s_1, s_2)$, where $\Omega_{d,n}$ denotes the weights that are adapted to the traversal behavior. During the traversal of the graph, indicated by the sequence of stimuli $(s_0, \ldots, s_n) \in S^n$ the weights $\Omega_{d,n}$ are defined as the arithmetic mean of $N \in \mathbb{N}$ weight components $\omega_{d,\eta} \in [0, 1]$, so that $\Omega_{d,n} = \frac{1}{N} \sum_{\eta=\max(0,n-N)}^{n} \omega_{d,\eta}$. For an iteration step $\eta \in \{1, \ldots, n\}$ the weight components $\omega_{d,\eta} \in [0, 1]$ model the prediction value of the distance measure d in contrast to the other competing distance measures. That prediction value shall be high if the chosen stimuli is close to the previous stimulus in terms of the distance measure d.

Weight Update

The weight components are defined as the relative difference between the differently measured distances of two subsequent stimuli as follows: for each distance measure $d \in D$ and each iteration step $\eta \in \{0, \ldots, n\}$ we define the distance between the currently and the previously selected stimulus as $\Delta_d(\eta) := d(\eta - 1, \eta)$. The unnormalized weight components $\widetilde{\omega}_{d,\eta}$ are now defined with inverted fraction of these values $\widetilde{\omega}_{d,\eta} := \frac{\sum_{\tilde{d}\in D} \Delta_{\tilde{d}}(\eta)}{\Delta_d(\eta)}$. Here the weight components themselves are defined as the normalization of their counterparts $\omega_{d,\eta} := \frac{\widetilde{\omega}_{d,\eta}}{\sum_{\tilde{d}\in D} \widetilde{\omega}_{\tilde{d},\eta}}$. Thereby it is assured that $\sum_{d\in D} \Omega_{d,\eta} = \sum_{d\in D} \omega_{d,\eta} = 1$. For practical reasons we initially chose an even distribution for the start configuration $\eta \leq N$. For computing one iteration of the interaction loop only the weights have to be updated. This is done in constant time, since only a direct comparison of two stimuli has to be evaluated. Thus, no interference during the interaction with the system is expected.

User-Interface

For the touch user-interface the currently selected stimulus is displayed together with the closest neighbors in terms of the measure D_n. The selected image is prominently displayed on the left and the recommended images are placed in two rows on its right hand side. Hereby the proximity and opacity of the unselected images decreases by their adaptive distance to the selected image. The layout is smoothly updated when one of the recommended images is selected. The selected image takes the position of the focused image, and its closest neighbors in terms of D_{n+1} get recommended, as illustrated in figure 3. Emphasis was put on a low threshold for the usage within the therapeutic setting for people with dementia and caregivers. Touch devices with a low interaction complexity seem to be suitable for that purpose [4].

PRESTUDY

To pre-evaluate the usability of our system we conducted a user study with 15 participants (13 males and 2 females) between the ages of 20 and 60. Participants included students and academic staff. For practicability, only the the person and location measures were used and for the calculation of the weights, N was set to 3. The stimulus set for the study contained 18 images. These images where composed of 18 backgrounds showing 3 different cities and portraits of 9 persons in the foreground. Each image shows one to three persons.

Procedure

First the participants where given an introduction to the system. Then they were given the task to interact with the system for 5 minutes and to switch between a person and a location based selection every 1 to 5 selections. Afterwards the participants completed a questionnaire measuring the intuitive usability of the system. The questionnaire consisted of the QUESI [15] and two questions to evaluated in what extent the recommended images matched their expectations in terms of person or location cues. A five point Likert scale from very negative (1) to very positive (5) was used.

Results

The results of the prestudy are encouraging: the QUESI overall score of intuitive use was 4.19 with standard deviation 1.05. The matching of the recommendations to expectations for person cues was rated on average by 3.67 with standard

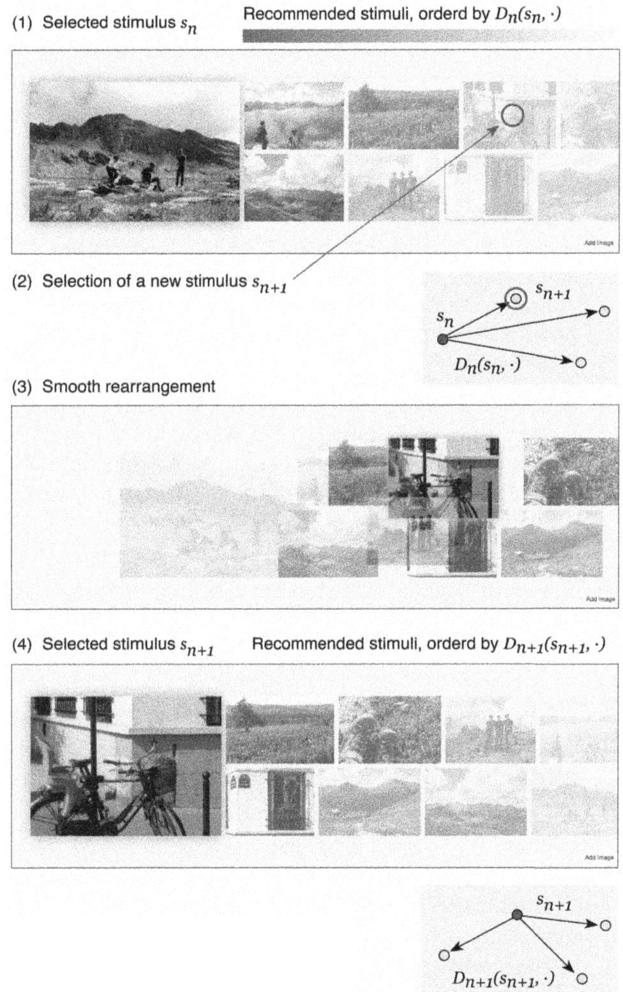

Figure 3. Illustration of the layout for one interaction iteration. The selected image is displayed large, whereas the recommended images are displayed on its right-hand side, ordered and blurred ascending by their adaptive distance to the selected image (1). When a new image is selected (2) the layout is smoothly updated (3) and the adaptive distance measure is updated (4).

deviation 1.11. Whereas for location cues the matching was rated on average by 4.33 with standard deviation 0.90.

CONCLUSION

In this work we proposed a new approach for increasing the effect of reminiscence therapy, by computing semantic similarities to automatically suggest related biographic stimuli (images). A first preliminary study shows encouraging results concerning the system effectiveness. One important part of our future work is to conduct a similar evaluation with patients at different stages of dementia and practitioners. Our second prototype will include additional modalities (audio, video) and further semantic similarity measures, such as inferring user's preferences from viewing duration.

ACKNOWLEDGMENTS

This work was supported by the German Federal Ministry of Education and Research (project InterMem, 16SV7322).

REFERENCES

1. Alm, N., Astell, A., Ellis, M., Dye, R., Gowans, G., and Campbell, J. A cognitive prosthesis and communication support for people with dementia. *Neuropsychological rehabilitation 14*, 1-2 (2004), 117–134.
2. Association, A. P., et al. *Diagnostic and Statistical Manual of Mental Disorders: DSM-5*. ManMag, 2003.
3. Astell, A. J., Ellis, M., Alm, N., Dye, R., Gowans, G., and Campbell, J. Using hypermedia to support communication in Alzheimer's disease: The CIRCA project. *Foundations of augmented cognition* (2005), 758–767.
4. Astell, A. J., Ellis, M. P., Bernardi, L., Alm, N., Dye, R., Gowans, G., and Campbell, J. Using a touch screen computer to support relationships between people with dementia and caregivers. *Interacting with Computers 22*, 4 (2010), 267–275.
5. Caprani, N., Dwyer, N., Harrison, K., and O'Brien, K. Remember when: Development of an interactive reminiscence device. In *CHI'05 Extended Abstracts on Human Factors in Computing Systems*, ACM (2005), 2070–2073.
6. Chapoulie, E., Guerchouche, R., Petit, P.-D., Chaurasia, G., Robert, P., and Drettakis, G. Reminiscence therapy using image-based rendering in VR. In *Virtual Reality (VR), 2014 iEEE*, IEEE (2014), 45–50.
7. Chiang, K.-J., Chu, H., Chang, H.-J., Chung, M.-H., Chen, C.-H., Chiou, H.-Y., and Chou, K.-R. The effects of reminiscence therapy on psychological well-being, depression, and loneliness among the institutionalized aged. *International Journal of geriatric psychiatry 25*, 4 (2010), 380.
8. Choi, S.-S., Cha, S.-H., and Tappert, C. C. A survey of binary similarity and distance measures. *Journal of Systemics, Cybernetics and Informatics 8*, 1 (2010), 43–48.
9. Cotelli, M., Manenti, R., and Zanetti, O. Reminiscence therapy in dementia: A review. *Maturitas 72*, 3 (2012), 203–205.
10. Kikhia, B., Bengtsson, J. E., Synnes, K., Hallberg, J., et al. Creating digital life stories through activity recognition with image filtering. In *Aging Friendly Technology for Health and Independence*. Springer, 2010, 203–210.
11. Lazar, A., Thompson, H., and Demiris, G. A systematic review of the use of technology for reminiscence therapy. *Health education & behavior 41*, 1 suppl (2014), 51S–61S.
12. Lee, M. L., and Dey, A. K. Using lifelogging to support recollection for people with episodic memory impairment and their caregivers. In *Proceedings of the 2nd International Workshop on Systems and Networking Support for Health Care and Assisted Living Environments*, ACM (2008), 14.
13. Li, H., Hestenes, D., and Rockwood, A. Generalized homogeneous coordinates for computational geometry. In *Geometric Computing with Clifford Algebras*. Springer, 2001, 27–59.
14. Livingston, G., Johnston, K., Katona, C., Paton, J., Lyketsos, C. G., of the World Federation of Biological Psychiatry, O. A. T. F., et al. Systematic review of psychological approaches to the management of neuropsychiatric symptoms of dementia. *American Journal of Psychiatry* (2014).
15. Naumann, A., and Hurtienne, J. Benchmarks for intuitive interaction with mobile devices. In *Proceedings of the 12th international conference on Human computer interaction with mobile devices and services*, ACM (2010), 401–402.
16. Peesapati, S. T., Schwanda, V., Schultz, J., Lepage, M., Jeong, S.-y., and Cosley, D. Pensieve: supporting everyday reminiscence. In *Proceedings of the SIGCHI Conference on Human Factors in Computing Systems*, ACM (2010), 2027–2036.
17. Prince, M., Bryce, R., Albanese, E., Wimo, A., Ribeiro, W., and Ferri, C. P. The global prevalence of dementia: a systematic review and metaanalysis. *Alzheimer's & Dementia 9*, 1 (2013), 63–75.
18. Robusto, C. The cosine-haversine formula. *American Mathematical Monthly* (1957), 38–40.
19. Sarne-Fleischmann, V., Tractinsky, N., Dwolatzky, T., and Rief, I. Personalized reminiscence therapy for patients with alzheimer's disease using a computerized system. In *Proceedings of the 4th International Conference on PErvasive Technologies Related to Assistive Environments*, ACM (2011), 48.
20. Woods, B., Spector, A., Jones, C., Orrell, M., and Davies, S. Reminiscence therapy for dementia. *Cochrane Database Syst Rev 2* (2005).
21. Yamagami, T., Oosawa, M., Ito, S., and Yamaguchi, H. Effect of activity reminiscence therapy as brain-activating rehabilitation for elderly people with and without dementia. *Psychogeriatrics 7*, 2 (2007), 69–75.

Empirically Studying Participatory Sense-Making in Abstract Drawing with a Co-Creative Cognitive Agent

Nicholas Davis, Chih-Pin Hsiao, Kunwar Yashraj Singh, Lisa Li, Brian Magerko
Georgia Institute of Technology
School of Interactive Computing
{ndaivs35, chsiao9, kysingh, lisa_li, magerko}@gatech.edu

ABSTRACT
This paper reports on the design and evaluation of a co-creative drawing partner called the Drawing Apprentice, which was designed to improvise and collaborate on abstract sketches with users in real time. The system qualifies as a new genre of creative technologies termed "casual creators" that are meant to creatively engage users and provide enjoyable creative experiences rather than necessarily helping users make a higher quality creative product. We introduce the conceptual framework of participatory sense-making and describe how it can help model and understand open-ended collaboration. We report the results of a user study comparing human-human collaboration to human-computer collaboration using the Drawing Apprentice system. Based on insights from the user study, we present a set of design recommendations for co-creative agents.

Author Keywords
Creativity Support Tools; Computational Creativity; Collaboration

ACM Classification Keywords
H.5.m. Information interfaces and presentation (e.g., HCI): Miscellaneous

INTRODUCTION
Collaboration is a powerful way to help both novices and experts push their creative boundaries and inspire their creative process. As collaborators make complimentary and unexpected contributions, their shared product grows in an emergent manner that would be more creative than what each partner could achieve individually [30]. Developing agents to facilitate collaboration can provide insight into the nature of collaboration as well as means of supporting collaborative creativity. To investigate improvisational collaboration, we developed a co-creative drawing partner called the Drawing Apprentice, shown in Figure 1. This system collaborates with users in real time using turn taking to gradually build a drawing through time [10].

IUI'16, March 07-10, 2016, Sonoma, CA, USA

DOI: http://dx.doi.org/10.1145/2856767.2856795

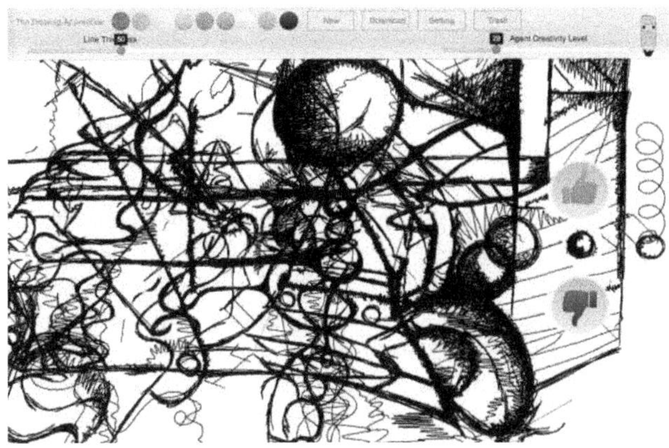

Figure 1: Drawing Apprentice UI and collaborative drawing made with the system.

We employ the cognitive science theory of enaction [34] and its conceptual framework called *participatory sense-making* [15] to model and understand creative collaboration. This framework describes critically important cognitive mechanisms and processes that we have seen evidence of in other collaboration tasks, such as joint activity and cooperation [7,13]. Participatory sense-making has been utilized to characterize collaboration and narrative development in pretend play [7], which is a similarly improvisational and open-ended domain. We used participatory sense-making to inform our system design and analyze improvisational collaboration in the domain of abstract drawing.

Cognitive agents, from the perspective of enaction, interact to gradually determine patterns of regularity and meaning using dynamic feedback loops [15]. Therefore, each collaborator is influenced both by the content of actions (i.e. lines of a drawing) as well as the dynamics of interaction that have emerged during in-the-moment interaction, such as the rhythm of turn taking, area of focus, and manner of motion. This dual feedback system has the potential to lead collaborators into new realms of creative expression with dynamic, multi-layered, and sometimes competing mental models for evaluating what creative contributions 'make sense' in the current situation.

Given the novelty and complexity of open-ended creativity and collaboration as a research topic, our prototype serves primarily as a technical probe to identify the circumstances under which contributions from co-creative agents appear to make-sense. In particular, we investigate three dimensions of participatory sense-making in collaborative drawing:

- To what degree was participatory sense-making present during the collaboration?
- What metrics and features did users employ to determine whether contributions 'made sense'?
- How did users try to define shared meaning structures with the agent, i.e. how did they attempt to teach the system?

We report on a Wizard of Oz-style user study comparing human-human collaboration to human-computer collaboration with the Drawing Apprentice system. We hypothesize that a system that mimics and builds on the contributions of users using real-time feedback can impact the sense-making process of art making with similar benefits as participatory sense-making exhibited in open-ended creative collaboration between two people. Our findings show that the Drawing Apprentice was able to engage users in participatory sense-making that resulted in discovering novel visual ideas and emergent meaning in the drawing. We also present several metrics users employ when evaluating whether contributions from the agent 'made sense.' These findings are then summarized in a set of design recommendations for supporting participatory sense-making with co-creative agents more generally.

RELATED WORK

The work reported here is an interdisciplinary effort nestled between the fields of computational creativity and creativity support tools. Computational creativity is a field of artificial intelligence focused on developing agents that generate creative products autonomously [3,5,38,39]. Creativity support tools, on the other hand, are technologies designed to enhance and augment the user's creativity, typically aiming to improve the quality of the final product [12,32,33,35]. Computers can support human users in their creative process in a variety of ways, including acting as a nanny, coach, pen-pal, and colleague [26]. The Drawing Apprentice can be considered a computer colleague since it collaborates with users on their creative task.

There are some computational creativity projects in other creative domains that explore human-computer co-creativity, such as Weinberg's work in interactive improvisational percussion robots [21]. Weinberg's robot, Shimon, listens to a performer and mimics or adds to the performance of the human collaborator. The system analyzes the music of performers and generates melodic improvisations that are in sync with human collaborators. In practice, the human and robot develop a call and response interaction where each party modifies and builds on the previous contribution. GenJam is another improvisational jazz system that uses a form of genetic algorithms to generate jazz improvisations [2]. The system has acoustic sensors that recognize musical input. A number of jazz improvisation schemes are stored in the program. An accompaniment is selected by the computer and played on a MIDI style system. Biles has performed with GenJam in jazz clubs successfully for several years. He advocates evaluating such systems based on the degree to which the system is useful and meaningful to the artist.

Viewpoints AI (VAI) is a co-creative dance partner that improvises with users in real time as they dance in front of a virtual character projected on a large display screen [22]. Using a Kinect, VAI analyzes the dance gestures of users and selects a complimentary dance move for the virtual character to perform. The system was initially trained by analyzing professional dancers to seed its knowledge base with expert dance moves [23]. Its knowledge base grows as it observes novel moves performed by users. VAI has a similar goal as the Drawing Apprentice to coordinate with users during open-ended creative improvisation. However, drawing results in a creative product that remains visually present and grows over time versus the ephemeral activity of dancing.

Another example of human-computer co-creativity is Magerko et al.'s Digital Improv project [27–29]. In this project, users engage in multiple theatrical improvisation games focused on narrative construction with AI improvisers. In the Digital Improv project, a computationally creative system attempts to recognize actors' actions, interpret them to be relevant to kinds of characters, and respond to these actions in a virtual world. The computer develops a shared meaning with the actors and generates actions according to features of the negotiated narrative context [17–20].

In the domain of artistic creativity, there are a variety of CSTs focused on supporting artistic creativity in the capacity of a coach to train the user's technical skill. For example, ShadowDraw [25] attempts to recognize the object users are drawing and provide them with guidelines in real-time to help draw more accurate representations. iCanDraw [11] helps users draw portraits by providing feedback on how well the user's lines align with the target portrait to enhance the accuracy of drawing their portraits. Projector Guided Painting helps users reproduce classic artworks by using a projector to depict the next color that should be applied to a particular region of the canvas [14].

These CSTs focus on increasing artistic skill and helping users create high quality products, but individuals interested in learning to engage in creative expression for its own intrinsic rewards have unique needs that often fall outside of existing CSTs. These users are not necessarily focused on achieving the best product, but derive enjoyment from the creative process itself, i.e. *autotelic creativity*, rather than task-oriented creativity [6]. A new category of tools was recently recognized that are primarily designed to creatively engage these casual users called *casual creators*, defined as:

> "...an interactive system that encourages the fast, confident, and pleasurable exploration of a possibility space, resulting in the creation or discovery of surprising new artifacts that bring feelings of pride, ownership, and creativity to the users that make them." [5]

Casual creators are systems designed specifically to support the process and experience of creativity. In this context, the fun and enjoyable dimensions of the actual creative experience interacting with the tool are emphasized over the aesthetic quality of the final product.

Potential use cases for the Drawing Apprentice include engaging children with the tool to facilitate creative 'out of the box' thinking by encouraging them to integrate and adapt to novel artistic contributions, thereby increasing their visual lexicon and ability to integrate unexpected contributions. In particular, children on the autistic spectrum may derive unique benefit from the tool by encouraging joint activity and adaptation, which are cognitive skills with which this population traditionally struggles [4,31].

PARTICIPATORY SENSE-MAKING

There are five core ideas to the cognitive science theory of enaction that are helpful in considering the design of a co-creative improvisational agent. First is the notion of *autonomy*, which describes how cognitive agents operate independently, based on their own intrinsic laws, to sustain themselves and continually generate their identity through interaction with the environment according to those laws. A system is defined as 'autonomous' when it can change the laws that govern its interaction with the world by casting a web of significance on the elements in its environment. As autonomous agents interact with their environment, they gradually detect patterns of regularities from dynamic feedback loops, which help them make sense of the environment in a process referred to as *sense-making*. Enaction describes the *emergence* of meaning structures through coordination and coupling between a cognitive agent and some system in the environment. It also adheres to the *embodiment* paradigm in asserting that agents must act with their body to make sense of the environment, which inherently constrains and affords certain types of interaction. Finally, the subjective *experience* of the agent is shaped by the meaning it has imbued into its environment and this influences how future actions are generated and evaluated.

A cognitive agent can be said to exhibit a degree of *structural coupling* with a system in the environment when it has understood the parameters and mechanisms of that system to the extent that it can predict how different actions will affect the system. When additional agents are introduced into the fold, the dynamics of sense-making become more complex because each agent is independently engaging in a process of sense-making with the environment as well as each other. This mutually influencing process is termed *participatory sense-making*, and it is formally defined as:

> A co-regulated coupling between at least two autonomous agents, where: (i) the co-regulation and the coupling mutually affect each other, constituting an autonomous self-sustaining organization in the domain of relational dynamics and (ii) the autonomy of the agents involved is not destroyed (although its scope can be augmented or reduced). [24]

This quote outlines the layered process of meaning making in participatory sense-making where the method for interacting together exists as an additional dimension, here described as relational dynamics, i.e. the rhythm of turn taking, ways of providing feedback, and manner of actions (independent from the content of actions).

For true co-regulation to occur in participatory sense-making, agents must make sense of both these relational or interaction dynamics as well as the content of actions in a dual sense-making process that is unique to participatory sense-making. We expect to find clear examples of such co-regulation in human collaboration, and through our experimentation, we hope to define the types of parameters and mechanisms that would enable a co-creative agent to exhibit the degree of autonomy and sense-making that would give rise to a similar co-regulated participatory sense-making as seen in human collaboration. This type of interaction is defined as the ideal for creative collaboration due to its ability to facilitate emergent meaning in an open-ended interaction that goes beyond what the individual user could have accomplished alone.

Enactivist researchers define cooperation as follows: "cooperation means that each of the subjects is taking account of the other's interests and objectives in some relation to the extrapersonal context, and is acting to complement the other's response [13]." We argue this definition is applicable to improvisational creative collaboration, and the means by which it can be achieved is through a process of co-regulated participatory sense-making. During this dialogical process, the dynamics of the interaction itself become autonomous and have the potential to propel the interaction forward. Interaction dynamics, in the case of digital drawing collaboration, include elements such as the length of a turn, the rhythm of actions within that turn, and the flow or trajectory of the experience, i.e. staying in one region versus moving to another.

We aim to explore with this work how a co-creative agent may be able to facilitate some degree of participatory sense-making without high-level representations of aesthetics and art theory. The quality of sense-making between a human collaboration and computer collaboration can then be compared to identify critical elements that were present in human collaboration, but absent when collaborating with the agent. We can then apply those insights to update the prototype and conduct further experimentation to evaluate whether users were able to achieve cooperation and collaboration in a more meaningful manner.

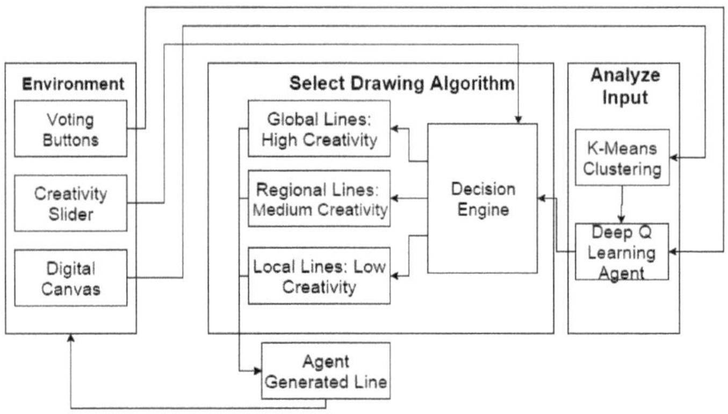

Figure 2: Drawing Apprentice System Architecture Diagram

DRAWING APPRENTICE SYSTEM

In this section, we describe the important technical components of the Drawing Apprentice system architecture and explain how they relate to the user experience. The system is implemented as a web application[1] with a client-server architecture that enables multiple people to collaborate with each other as well as the agent from the Drawing Apprentice system. It was designed for use with stylus- or touch-based interactions, but mouse can also be used.

At the highest level, the system is a co-creative agent that takes user input lines, transforms those lines based on pre-encoded line transformation techniques, and outputs new lines onto the same canvas (see Figure 2). Unique and defining features of input lines set are determined by clustering the data points in the input lines and sending that cluster data into the neural network (see Analyze Input box in Figure 2). This allows the neural network to derive its own classifications scheme based on the data it has been given.

The system was seeded with 12 experimental line transformational algorithms, including simple functions, such as translation, scaling, rotation, as well as more complex techniques that change the individual features of the input lines to create new lines that retain a similarity to the input lines. These more complex transformations are achieved by determining a set of equations to describe the input line and then tweaking individual coefficients in the equations to produce a similar line (see Figures 4 & 5).

Figure 3: The drawing results from the algorithm 1- 3 for low-creativity level (black lines: human, blue lines: agent)

Inspired by the theory of enaction, the system is designed to engage in participatory sense-making by coordinating its actions through real-time feedback. In practice, this means training the system's machine learning algorithms dynamically using real-time feedback from the voting buttons and creativity slider.

The creativity slider in the interface of the Drawing Apprentice constrains which algorithms the system will choose from when reacting to the user's lines. The creativity level roughly corresponds to the general definition of the term 'creativity' in the creativity literature as: novelty, value, and surprise. At low levels of creativity (slider is between 0-33), the system will produce lines that slightly alter the user's input lines without much change. For example, in Figure 3-Algo-2, the system introduces some noise or perturbation to the input line and then redraws it. This type of contribution is almost identical to the user's input line and therefore is not very 'novel' or 'surprising.' Other algorithms at the low level of creativity mimic the user's line, but slightly translate or offset it, e.g. Algo-3 in Figure 3.

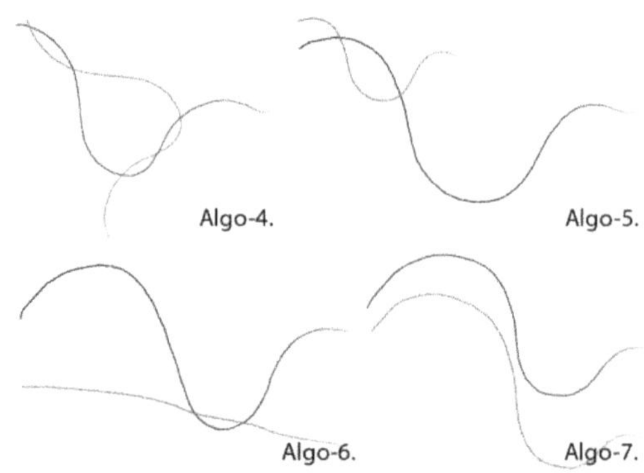

Figure 4: The drawing results from the algorithm 4-7 for mid-creativity level (black lines: human, blue lines: agent)

When the system is set to medium creativity (slider is situated between 33-66), the agent mimics and imitates the user's input with transformations, such as rotation (Algo-4 in Figure 4) and scaling (Algo-5 in Figure 4). The agent also mimics the user's input line with variations, such as slightly modifying the coefficients of equations that describe the user's input line. For example, the height of a curve might change, or the angle at which a corner is made might change.

At high levels of creativity (slider is set to 66-100), the

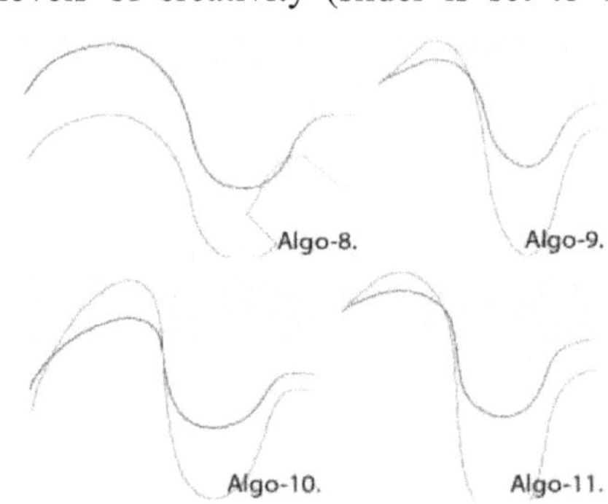

Figure 5: The drawing results from the algorithm 8-11 for high-creativity level (black lines: human, blue lines: agent)

[1] https://adam.cc.gatech.edu/DrawingApprentice/

system increases the novelty of the lines it produces using a few different techniques. For example, the system employs a line mutation algorithms that takes the input line and splices a portion of that line with a portion of another line on the canvas to introduce new content into the line (algo-8 of Figure 5). Another algorithm fits a polynomial function to part of the line that can be approximated using a polynomial (i.e. it passes the vertical line test), and then tweaks some coefficients similar to the medium creativity algorithm, but to a more drastic extent, thereby reducing the visual similarity to the input line. Yet another algorithm segments the input line into many different equations (such that it need not pass the vertical line test), and then tweaks the coefficients on some of those line segments while still maintaining the overall shape. For example, if the user drew a square, the system could produce a rectangle.

As shown in Figure 1, the user is provided with up/down voting buttons to give feedback to the system. This feedback informs the system about which algorithms in particular (within each category of creativity, i.e. low, medium, and high) the user prefers. The voting buttons are designed to train the neural network to learn the circumstances under which each type of transformation algorithm should be used. The decision about how to respond to the user's input line is a mix of the neural net analysis that compares the current input to previous responses, the creativity value, and the feedback the user has provided on each of the algorithms previously.

DRAWING APPRENTICE USER EXPERIENCE

Instead of hard-coding knowledge into the agent to make it creative, the Drawing Apprentice is designed to extract critical information from a user that is already exhibiting intelligence and creativity given the target domain in an open-ended creative task. Therefore, the most general design principle is *whenever possible, offload any higher-level cognitive tasks to the user*, i.e. enable the user to manually specify the boundaries within which the agent should operate throughout the interaction. The agent does not need to know why those parameters exist if those values help facilitate effective collaboration. Known as the *Eliza effect*, researchers have demonstrated that users attribute intentionality to virtual agents if they appear to understand the context of the situation, even when the system may not 'understand' the actions it performs [36,37]. Through interaction and user experience design, defining constraints and parameters can be smoothly integrated into their creative flow or removed altogether as the machine learning algorithms grow in complexity and sophistication.

Turn Taking

Turn taking was designed to facilitate emergent interaction dynamics, meaning the number and length of the agent's lines are dependent upon the user's recent contributions. As soon as the user ends their current line, a timer begins. If this timer passes the arbitrary value of 2 seconds before the user begins their next line, their turn ends, and the system starts to draw. The system's turn will be approximately the same number of lines as the user's turn to mirror the interaction. However, the user may begin drawing at any point, which can lead to synchronous collaboration.

User Feedback

While humans are able to leverage extremely subtle and implicit cues during joint activity and coordination, enabling basic feedback mechanisms, such as voting, begins to approximate a similar process of coordination as human collaboration. From the perspective of optimizing the machine learning algorithms, the human should be required to provide feedback on every contribution made by the system. To maintain the flow of the creative experience, though, the human is never required to provide feedback, but rather users are given the choice to vote whenever it occurs to them, which can be highly variable between users. This presents an interesting opportunity where improving the user experience design might potentially improve the performance of the machine learning algorithms (since more feedback helps train the system).

Character Design

To simulate the dynamism and embodied nature of real-time human collaboration, the Drawing Apprentice character draws lines dynamically, meaning lines do not appear at once in full, but are gradually animated through until their completion. Dynamic line drawing is meant to provide a sense that the system is going through the embodied act of creating a line.

Pilot studies revealed the importance of having a character represent the Drawing Apprentice on the canvas, which is a sentiment echoed in the literature on embodied virtual agents [1,16]. In an early version of the prototype, the character only appeared while the system was drawing. In the pilot studies and during demos watching and talking about the character seemed to excite the participants. Multiple users requested a permanent presence, or 'home' for the character while it was not drawing. We improved the character design and created a home base for the agent to return to after it has completed its drawing. In our context, character design may be able to improve the perceived performance of the agent. With the right animations and visual design, the system might appear more creative and intelligent without any change to the algorithms.

USER STUDY

We hypothesize that a system that mimics and builds on the contributions of users in a real-time drawing collaboration can impact the sense-making process of art creation with similar benefits as participatory sense-making exhibited in open-ended creative collaboration between two people. This user study was designed to help understand participatory sense-making in the domain of collaborative drawing and delineate critical mechanisms that foster it. We investigate to what extent users can effectively work with the Drawing Apprentice in a way that enables the user to

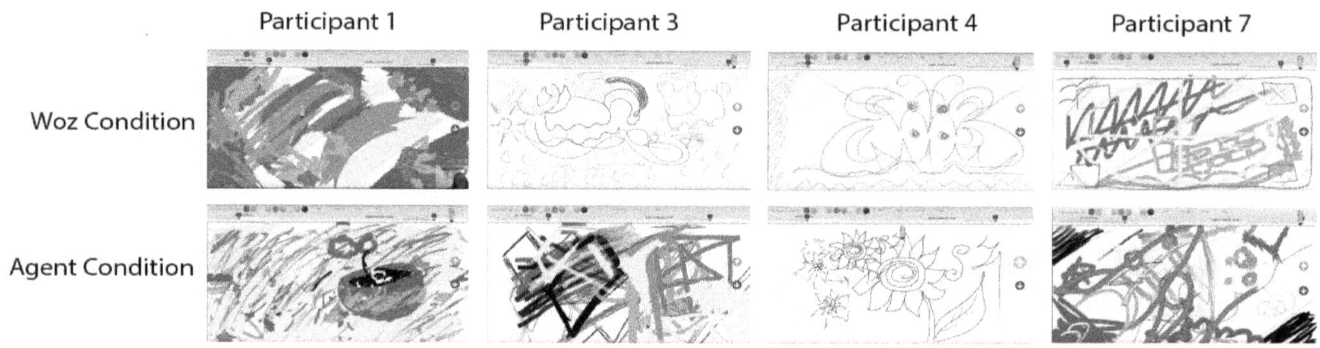

Figure 6: Representative sample of drawings from the user study. Top row: WoZ Condition; Bottom Row: Agent Condition

interactively and co-creatively build artistic meaning as the artwork develops.

Study Design

For this study, we had 7 participants, 4 female, and 3 male with an average age of 25 (ranging from 20-45) recruited from the student population at Georgia Tech. The artistic experience of the group was generally categorized as novice, with an average of 2.15 on a 5 point scale ranging from no artistic experience to 5 years of professional practice in the field. The data generated from the study included video recordings (see Figure 6), the transcribed audio data from the retrospective protocol analysis, the log data from the system, and the survey data.

The experiment was divided into two phases that each included a 12-minute collaborative drawing task, a retrospective protocol analysis, and a survey about the participant's experience interacting with the system. A non-collaborative drawing task was not included because drawing independently lacks any social coordination and participatory sense-making, which were the focus of the current study. Each experimental session lasted approximately one hour. The experiments were conducted using a Microsoft Surface tablet and a capacitive pen as input to the device. The Drawing Apprentice system was running as a web application and expanded to full screen (see Figure 1).

Participants were first oriented with the basic drawing features of the interface (line thickness, color selection, input method), as well as the unique features of the Drawing Apprentice system, such as the voting buttons and creativity slider. The experimenter described how each vote helped the system understand what the user liked, and the creativity slider controlled how 'creative' the agent was, with 0 being less creative and 100 being the most creative.

Participants were then given an open-ended prompt to 'collaborate with the system for 12 minutes to create a drawing.' One drawing task was collaborating with the Drawing Apprentice system (referred to as the agent condition), while the other task was collaborating with a Wizard of Oz agent being controlled by an expert human artist (referred to as the WoZ condition). The interface was the same in both conditions, and participants were not aware of which condition they were experiencing. They also were unaware that an expert human was controlling the system in the WoZ condition. The experimental conditions were randomly ordered to account for learning effects.

In the WoZ condition, an expert human artist controlled the system's drawing contributions from another room. The expert artist was one of the researchers from the team that has been collaborating with novices and experts in the domain of abstract drawing for over ten years. The expert used approximately the same interaction dynamics as the system, waiting 2 seconds after the user was finished drawing to begin the turn, as well as drawing approximately the same amount of lines as the user's last turn. The expert's responses were calibrated using the creativity slider, with low creativity turns closely following the participant's lines, while high creativity resulted in more novel contributions.

During the retrospective protocol analysis, the experimenter prompted the user to explain their thought process throughout the video walkthrough. The survey focused on evaluating the quality of the collaboration and how influential their collaboration was in defining artistic goals.

FindingsThis section presents the preliminary results from the retrospective protocol analysis. We performed a qualitative data analysis on the transcribed interview data using thematic analysis targeting language relating to key themes about participatory sense-making. These findings will help us develop a formal coding scheme that can be used to code the video recordings according to the elements that are identified below as important for participatory sense-making in the domain of drawing collaboration.

A key factor in this analysis is determining why contributions seem to 'make sense' to the user or 'not make sense' to the user. We expect contributions that appear completely erratic to be too far outside the meaning structures developed by the user to be integrated, while contributions that are on the fringe of the user's current meaning have the potential to expand visual ideas and guide interactions in-the-moment. Further, the manner in which interaction occurs can impact whether the agent appears to coordinate with the user, i.e. the rhythm of turn taking, the speed of lines drawn, the size of lines, etc.

Supporting evidence for participatory sense-making comes from participants reporting that the agent was able to contribute to the drawing in the following meaningful ways: (1) build on the contributions of the user, (2) demonstrate a certain degree of coordination and mutual sense-making with the user. In particular, we are interested in whether the agent can help shape these meaning structures such that *creatively engaging*, *unexpected*, and *surprising* meaning emerges through interactions over time.

Wizard of Oz Condition

The first step in the analysis was to delineate how participants described participatory sense-making in the case of human collaboration (WoZ experimental condition). In this circumstance, the thematic analysis focused on concepts related to a structural coupling between the collaborators, during which there was a mutual co-regulation of the activity, meaning both the human and the system defined basic units of meaning that were extended and added on by each participant in a way that would not have occurred without the collaboration.

Making Sense of the Agent

P2 described how the agent influenced the creative process, reporting

> *"I'm definitely taking into account what the agent is doing and some combination of trying to figure out how to sort of control the agent, and also work with it, because it did things that I wouldn't necessarily expect, which is cool."*

P5 describes how echoing and mirroring actions helped anticipate and make sense of the agent, stating

> *"The system tended to echo what I did, and mirror the patterns I made, sometimes in different locations on the screen, but I was able to pretty quickly anticipate the kind of move, not exactly what it would do, but to the point where I was pleased with some of them, or displeased...."*

P5 elaborated this sentiment by describing he was able to find a 'comfort zone' in which the agent would make predictable contributions, "*At that point, I liked what I expected it to do. That didn't really surprise me there, but in a comforting kind of way.*" While unexpected contributions may have inspired the user, achieving basic structural couplings enabled a 'comfort zone' to emerge that provided some stability and predictability in the collaboration that helped contribute to the feeling of a 'dialog' with the system.

Interaction Dynamics

P3 described the experience of WoZ collaboration in distinct categories that help shed light on how the interaction was conceptualized:

> *"There was like me teaching it, or it copies me, or he comes up with something cool, and I copy it, or we were like collaborating on something we both know what's going on. I guess there is just another thing that is random, like I don't know what to draw, and I'll do something random, or he doesn't know what to follow and he does something random."*

As P3 worked to make sense of the agent's behavior, they noted distinct modes of interaction that included both the agent and user copying, working on a joint activity, as well as injecting novel or 'random' contributions to help move the collaboration forward while the user or system were unsure how to contribute. Examples of joint activities include coloring (i.e. filling a shape with one color) as well as one of the collaborators (agent or user) completing each other's thoughts. Achieving joint activity relied heavily on mutual spatial awareness, which is detailed later in the Sense-Making Evaluation section.

The notion of participants copying the agent was introduced again with a strongly positive association from P4. There was a sentiment that when the participant chooses to copy the agent, it signified the agent's contribution were accepted and integrated into the user's current artistic intention, i.e. structural coupling. P4 described this sentiment,

> *"It was really cool. It is taking the accent points from the lines and making them more accented. So I was like OK, I'm going to copy you....I think throughout this interaction, there are times when the system lead me instead of the other way around... I felt a little like the system. I was like: am I just copying it?"*

The system and user were taking turns leading the interaction and suggesting new content and activities in which to engage, demonstrating a mutual co-regulation in the participatory sense-making process. Once users made sense of how the system interacts, the users engaged in a playful process of exploring the boundaries and challenging the system with increasingly 'difficult' inputs. For example, P4 'challenged' the agent, stating "*So, I was like OH! It looks like a butterfly, and I was like haha system! What are you going to do now? So I draw in moons, and I was like OK, what are you going to do?*" Instead of worrying about the outcome of the artwork, P4 was creatively engaged by the dialog that emerged with the system. This interaction inspires the participant to generate lines that test the limits of the system.

Emergent Meaning

P1 described the process of discovering emergent meaning as a result of working with the agent, saying

> *"I drew that, and it started out as random stuff, and it reminded me of a flower or a star, and then the agent drew that, and it reminded me of a halbird....so I extended it, and then the agent extended it further..."*

In this instance, the collaborators formed a brief structural coupling during which the user and agent were both contributing ideas and building onto a core idea that emerged through interaction. P6 also reports meaning emerging through a process of co-regulated structural coupling when he describes redefining his goals about the agent's contributions,

> *"I wanted to make a wagon, a cart thing. But then it made something like this, then I made it a bed instead. Then, it did this really nice hatching on the pillow, which I liked."*

Here, P6 originally intended to draw a cart. However, based on the system's contribution, he redefined that goal as a bed, which was further elaborated by the system.

Agent Collaboration Condition

Next, we describe some illustrative examples during which participants reported participatory sense-making during collaboration with the co-creative agent. Then, we will list some of the most critical evaluation metrics users reported for determining whether or not the agent's contributions 'make sense.'

Making Sense of the Agent

P4 described how she developed a strategy for anticipating the agent's response through experimentation,

> *"I decided to make a spiral, and see if the AI would continue my spiral, but then it made it elsewhere, so I was like that's cool...so I drew a different spiral, to see what it would do, and they did the same thing....so I was like maybe I can use that and replicate smaller things, so I would make a flower, so I anticipated what it did."*

This quote shows evidence that P4 began to make sense of the agent's reactions. P5 also discovered types of actions that elicited good responses, saying "*I did a lot of these Bezier curves because I liked the way it tried to answer me with those....*" This type of predictability was critical for the sense-making process in artistic collaboration.

Interaction Dynamics

Users were able to couple their behavior with the system, but as P5 describes, this required them to submit to how the system worked in a one-sided manner,

> *"This is when I sort of discovered how to work with it on that pattern over there... I'm sort of doing what it's doing, and we're feeding off of each other....I quit fighting it and started collaborating...I'm playing more by its rules. I'm sort of anticipating what I thought it would do."*

This quote demonstrates participatory sense-making, but the process is being regulated mostly by the agent because the participant has to work from the agent's contribution in order to achieve 'collaboration.' This is contrasted to the mutually co-regulated process during which each partner takes turns leading and defining new goals, as seen in human collaboration. P5 surrendered a certain degree of autonomy when he decided to '*play by the agent's rules.*' Some participants were comfortable surrendering this autonomy. However, in some cases, such as P7, dealing with the agent was frustrating, since there was "*a lot of prodding him into doing things. It was more about prodding him, and being concerned about him rather than me doing something creative.*" This type of interaction dynamic could be characterized as trying to lead or control the agent as opposed to engaging in a mutual co-regulation where each party exhibits autonomy. While prodding the agent may reduce the artistic autonomy of users, the dialogical interaction still had the capacity to propel the interaction forward, as P5 describes:

> *"I think if you had just given me a blank canvas and told me to draw anything, as a non-artist, I would have quickly given up, because I didn't know what I was doing. The fact that there was a back and forth, and new things were emerging on the screen, made me want to try to answer it, or to try to prod it to coming up with another addition to the drawing. I was probably more engaged than I would be if I was just drawing on a blank canvas by myself."*

Emergent Meaning

P1 summarized the effect that collaboration with the co-creative agent had on their creative process, saying "*It made it less structured. I did more doodling to see how I could incorporate what the pencil was doing and see how I could interact with it.*" The 'doodling' that P1 described leads to emergent and unpredictable visual elements in the drawing. This type of interaction dynamic helped users discover novel visual ideas. P6 describes how working with the co-creative agent challenged them to move beyond their 'standard' drawing,

> *"It felt nice when I had to change my standard drawing, because that's something I always draw. This was more of a challenge for me to say: let's see what I can come up with to draw."*

Adapting to and incorporating the agent's contributions helped participants draw in ways they would not have done without the collaboration. The challenge for the Drawing Apprentice is determining how to make better unexpected choices that encourage users to incorporate the agent's contributions rather than ignore them. Utilizing user feedback is one method to help facilitate this type of coordination.

Voting Buttons and Creativity Slider

Participants reported being able to make sense of the agent and collaborate with it in both conditions, but the voting buttons and creativity slider were not fully leveraged by

	Making Sense of Agent	Interaction Dynamics	Emergent Meaning
WoZ Collaboration	User anticipated and predicted agent responses	Co-regulated coupling where leader varies between agent and user	Visual ideas emerge from both user and agent and transform over time
Agent Collaboration	User anticipated and predicted agent responses	User leads and controls agent	User incorporates and adapts to agent responses

Table 1: Comparing participatory sense-making between the two collaboration conditions

most participants. The down vote mechanism was used to discourage the system from behaving in a particular manner, such as the style of its lines. For example, P2 reports:

> "*I definitely up voted a lot in the first time, and I down voted a lot more this time. I wanted to try to get rid of the fast lines I couldn't see, which kind of happened....I tried to discourage when it did really really shaky stuff. It kind of helped.*"

Other participants reported being uncertain about how voting affected the system. For example, when directly asked how voting affected the agent, P1 states, "*I don't know. I don't know if they really affected it.*" Other participants experimented to a further degree, but still described uncertainty when voting on the agent's contributions, with P4 reporting "*I'm not sure if the voting buttons did anything, because I down voted it, but it continued to do what it did.*" In general, participants expected immediate feedback from a down vote, such as the system immediately stopping its current drawing task. P2 elaborated one reason why voting was confusing, stating:

> "*It definitely takes several iterations of a down vote for it to figure out exactly what you are trying to discourage, like the line placement, or what type of thing you are trying to discourage, because there probably several things it considers when trying to place a line.*"

This comment highlights the fact that each vote could relate to several parameters of the line, such as its placement, the style (shaky, smooth, curvy, etc.), and the shape. Participants were uncertain how their vote would affect the system due to this ambiguity. For example, P3 stated that each system input "*has a lot of attributes, I don't know if it discards or has a decreased value of all of those, or I just don't like this particular thing.*" Providing users with explicit visual feedback about how their vote affected the algorithms would help address this shortcoming of the system.

Some participants described voting as distracting, or similarly described how they forgot about voting when they were deeply immersed in a drawing task. For example, P5 described his experience with voting, saying "*I tried to use those [voting buttons] this time to reinforce things I liked, but... I found those more distracting.*" When users were deeply engaged in collaboration, they reported thinking less about the voting and creativity mechanisms. For example, P4 stated "*I totally forgot about the creativity slider, and the voting buttons for a while because I was so intrigued by what the system was doing on its own at that level of creativity.*" These mixed sentiments about the feedback mechanisms provide insights for updating the implementation of voting and feedback that will be outlined in the Design Recommendations section.

Sense-Making Evaluation Metrics

Achieving human-level collaboration is the ultimate goal for the type of co-creative system we designed. To do so, it is critical to understand the nature of participatory sense-making in the domain of artistic collaboration and the metrics users employ to evaluate their partner. Next, we describe key concepts that emerged in the thematic analysis when we focused on contributions that appeared random or erratic in a way that was not beneficial and did not lead to emergent meaning. This dimension of the analysis will help inform the continued development of our system as well as other co-creative agents in the artistic domain. The concepts of *spatial awareness*, *visual similarity*, and *perceptual logic* emerged as particularly important when participants described how they evaluated whether contributions from the system made sense.

Spatial Awareness

One of the most common metrics users employed to evaluate whether the system's contributions made sense related to whether the agent exhibited *spatial awareness* of things that were previously drawn. According to participants, the agent should maintain an awareness of visual elements that have been created previously to not 'mess up' what the users have drawn. Participants became frustrated when they perceived the agent as 'messing up' their contribution rather than building off of it. For example, P1 states: "*Usually if I draw actual things, they keep within lines, and you know, you organize the space, and when you have other things encroaching on it, it's hard.*" P4 reported a similar occurrence while collaborating with the agent, stating: "*The system would draw on top of other things we drew, when I specifically avoided those things...so that was annoying.*" It was obvious that the system did not understand what the user's intention was when it drew on top of the participant's lines.

Visual Similarity

The agent's contribution should retain some visual similarity of the user's contribution so that the user can help understand the relationship between their contribution and the system's. When the user was able to see the visual similarity between the agent's and their behaviors, they were able to reason through why it made a contribution, which can reduce their frustration if it 'messes up' something they drew. For example, P2 states: "*This is cool. I like this pattern here. I did that, and he did a more acute angle.*" The agent's contributions that were on top of the user's lines were more acceptable if the user could justify why the agent had created those lines. Typically, visual similarity and close spatial proximity to the user's input lines helped provide clues to participants about why the agent drew a particular object. For example, P3 states "*I was trying to draw two birds, but he just tries to copy...I didn't really like it, because it's not really a bird anymore, but I get why he did that.*" It is important to understand the context in which a contribution is accepted even though the participants report not 'liking' it. This acceptance can lead to emergent meaning as users work to continue to transform the content rather than completely abandoning or ignoring the contribution, as is sometimes the case when the user perceives contributions to be too erratic.

Perceptual Logic

The agent's lines are evaluated as 'messing up' the participants drawing when the agent drew over top of a previous structure without taking into account any of the features of that structure. When the agent did make contributions within or on top of a previously defined shape, it must adhere to what could be termed the prevailing 'perceptual logic' of that region [8,9]. Perceptual logic is a concept that describes how each region or idea in a drawing has its internal set of rules and mechanism that serve to constrain what type of visual contributions seem relevant and logical for the target region. It could be conceptualized as the local style of a particular region.

In some cases, perceptual logic appeared to be based purely on visual relationships, like the repetition of similar patterns (as noted in the previous section on visual similarity), while in other cases, it was based on a semantic definition of the object, such as a house that has different components that are 'right' or 'wrong.' P3 described a perceptual logic of 'orderly geometric shapes', reporting:

> "*I didn't like too much what was going on there because I was trying to actually do like geometric shapes and stuff, so I was thinking something more orderly, so I just moved back and started drawing regular shapes.*"

Contributions that did not adhere to the perceptual logic of 'orderly geometric shapes' did not make sense to the participant. Another example of perceptual logic is when P5 reported:

> "*I didn't like the way it looked. It messed up my swirl, and it wasn't symmetric....if it was going to do it, it should be centered in the spiral, then I might have thought it would have been ok...it seemed arbitrary.*"

The negative sentiment this participant had for that particular violation shows that sometimes perceptual logic is tied up with an emotional response, evidenced when P5 reiterates his sentiments on the spiral, saying "*I really hated that thing inside the spiral, that's what I hated the most.*"

DESIGN RECOMMENDATIONS

Given its prominence in evaluating the agent's behavior, spatial awareness seems to be a foundational skill for a co-creative drawing partner. One method for achieving spatial awareness is by constraining the agent's learning mechanisms to particular regions of the artwork, i.e. executing certain types of drawing behaviors in certain regions based on user feedback. Since drawings develop over time, the perceptual logic in each region is also subject to change as regions grow, transform, and potentially connect with other regions. Given this dynamism, the system's learning algorithms should be temporally sensitive as well. For example, when users re-visit previously established regions, they may be trying to accomplish much different tasks, which could drastically change the perceptual logic that is appropriate. Considering both space and time in the learning algorithms should therefore improve the agent's ability to coordinate with users and engage in participatory sense-making.

In both conditions, participants used repetition to try to train and reinforce behaviors in the agent, but this type of implicit feedback was not registered by the co-creative agent. By analyzing the relationship of the user's input lines for a given turn, it might be possible to classify what type of contribution the user is making, i.e. defining a pattern through repetition, drawing a complete shape, or beginning a joint activity, such as coloring. All these modes of teaching emerged during the study, but the agent's machine learning architecture was not specifically designed to learn in that manner. Additionally, other implicit cues observed during interaction could serve as feedback for the system, such as when the user copied the agent's contribution. Co-creative agents should take this type of mimicry as positive feedback indicating the early stages of a structural coupling that can facilitate participatory sense-making.

Our findings indicated that users did not fully understand how using voting and the creativity slider affected the behavior of the system. This could be mitigated by providing more explicit feedback about how their vote affected the agent's knowledge and drawing behaviors. In addition to describing how votes affect the creativity of the system, our findings indicated that users would benefit by reducing the ambiguity of binary feedback. Disambiguating user feedback could include providing a more continuous evaluation scale (versus the current binary like/dislike), as well as categories of feedback, such as providing independent feedback on the location, style, and content of the agent's drawing contribution.

CONCLUSIONS

This paper described a co-creative drawing partner called the Drawing Apprentice. The system was designed to improvise and collaborate with users in real time on an abstract drawing. We presented the conceptual framework of participatory sense-making from the cognitive science theory of enaction to help understand and categorize the interaction dynamics involved in collaboration. That conceptual framework was then used to compare human-human collaboration and human-computer collaboration during a user study with the Drawing Apprentice system. Our analysis identified how meaning emerged through participatory sense-making in both conditions. We identified critical metrics users employ to evaluate whether the system's contributions 'made sense' and describe how participants worked to train and provide feedback to the system to help coordinate their interactions. We leveraged these findings to propose design recommendations for co-creative agents.

ACKNOWLEDGEMENTS

This work is supported in part by NSF IIS grant #1320520.

REFERENCES

1. Baylor, A. L. Promoting motivation with virtual agents and avatars: role of visual presence and appearance. *Philosophical Transactions of the Royal Society of London B: Biological Sciences* 364, (2009) 1535: 3559–3565.
2. Biles, A. J. GenJam: A genetic algorithm for generating jazz solos. *Proceedings of the International Computer Music Conference*, Citeseer, (1994), 131–131.
3. Boden, M. A. *The Creative Mind: Myths and Mechanisms*. Weidenfeld & Nicolson, London. 1990.
4. Charman, T., Swettenham, J., Baron-Cohen, S., Cox, A., Baird, G. and Drew, A. Infants with autism: an investigation of empathy, pretend play, joint attention, and imitation. *Developmental psychology* 33, 5 (1997), 781.
5. Colton, S., Wiggins, G. A. Computational creativity: The final frontier? *ECAI*, (2012) 21–26.
6. Compton, K. and Mateas, M. Casual Creators. *Proceedings of the Sixth International Conference on Computational Creativity June*, 228. 2015.
7. Davis, N., Comerford, M., Jacob, M. Hsiao, C.-P. and Magerko, B. An Enactive Characterization of Pretend Play. *Proceedings of the 2015 ACM SIGCHI Conference on Creativity and Cognition*, (2015), 275–284.
8. Davis, N., Do, E. Y.-L. Gupta, P. and Gupta, S. Computing harmony with PerLogicArt: perceptual logic inspired collaborative art. *Proceedings of the 8th ACM conference on Creativity and cognition*, (2011) 185–194.
9. Davis, N., Hsiao, C.-P., Popova, Y. and Magerko, B. An Enactive Model of Creativity for Computational Collaboration and Co-creation. In *Creativity in the Digital Age*. Springer, (2015), 109–133.
10. Davis, N., Hsiao, C.-P., Singh, K. Y., Li, L, Moningi, S. and Magerko, B. Drawing Apprentice: An Enactive Co-Creative Agent for Artistic Collaboration. *Proceedings of the 2015 ACM SIGCHI Conference on Creativity and Cognition*, (2015), 185–186.
11. Dixon, D., Prasad, M. and Hammond, T. iCanDraw: using sketch recognition and corrective feedback to assist a user in drawing human faces. *Proceedings of the 28th international conference on Human factors in computing systems*, (2010), 897–906.
12. Edmonds, E. and Candy, L. Computer support for creativity. *International Journal of Human-Computer Studies* 63, (2005), 4-5:
13. Fantasia, V., De Jaegher, H. and Fasulo, A. We can work it out: an enactive look at cooperation. *Frontiers in psychology* 5. 2014.
14. Flagg, M. and Rehg, J. M. Projector-guided painting. *Proceedings of the 19th annual ACM symposium on User interface software and technology*, ACM Press, (2006), 235–244.
15. Fuchs, T. and De Jaegher, H. Enactive intersubjectivity: Participatory sense-making and mutual incorporation. *Phenomenology and the Cognitive Sciences* 8, 4 (2009), 465–486.
16. Gulz, A. and Haake, M. Design of animated pedagogical agents—A look at their look. *International Journal of Human-Computer Studies* 64, 4 (2006), 322–339.
17. Hodhod, R., Piplica, A. and Magerko, B. A formal model of shared mental models for computational improvisational agents. *Proceedings of the 12th Annual Conference on Intelligent Virtual Agents*. 2012.
18. Hodhod, R., Magerko, B. and Gawish, M. Pharaoh: Context-Based Structural Retrieval of Cognitive Scripts. *International Journal of Information Retrieval Research (IJIRR)*, 2, 3 (2012), 58–71.
19. Hodhod, R. and Magerko, B. Pharaoh: Conceptual Blending of Cognitive Scripts for Computationally Creative Agents. *The Twenty-Seventh International Flairs Conference*. 2014.
20. Hodhod, R. and Magerko, B. Closing the Cognitive Gap between Humans and Interactive Narrative Agents Using Shared Mental Models. *21st Annual Intelligent User Interfaces Conference*. 2016.
21. Hoffman, G. and Weinberg, G. Shimon: an interactive improvisational robotic marimba player. *CHI'10 Extended Abstracts on Human Factors in Computing Systems*, (2010), 3097–3102.
22. Jacob, M., Coisne, G., Gupta, A, Sysoev, I., Gav Verma, G., and Magerko, B. Viewpoints AI. *AIIDE*. 2013.
23. Jacob, M., Zook, A. and Magerko, B. Viewpoints AI: Procedurally Representing and Reasoning about Gestures. *Proceedings of DiGRA*. 2013.
24. De Jaegher, H. and Di Paolo, E. Participatory sense-making. *Phenomenology and the cognitive sciences*, 6, 4 (2007), 485–507.
25. Lee, Y. J., Zitnick, C. L. and Cohen, M. F. ShadowDraw: real-time user guidance for freehand drawing. *ACM Transactions on Graphics (TOG)*, 27. 2011.
26. Lubart, T. How can computers be partners in the creative process: Classification and commentary on the Special Issue. *International Journal of Human-Computer Studies* 63, 4-5 (2005), 365–369.
27. Magerko, B., Dohogne, P and DeLeon, C. Employing Fuzzy Concept for Digital Improvisational Theatre. *AIIDE*. 2011.
28. O'Neill, B., Piplica, A., Fuller, D. and Magerko, B. A Knowledge-Based Framework for the Collaborative Improvisation of Scene Introductions. In *Interactive Storytelling SE - 10*, Mei Si, David Thue, Elisabeth

André, JamesC. Lester, Joshua Tanenbaum and Veronica Zammitto (eds.). Springer Berlin Heidelberg, (2011), 85–96.

29. Piplica, A., DeLeon, C. and Magerko, B. Full-body gesture interaction with improvisational narrative agents. *Intelligent Virtual Agents*, (2012), 514–516.
30. Sawyer, R. K. and DeZutter, S. Distributed creativity: How collective creations emerge from collaboration. *Psychology of Aesthetics, Creativity, and the Arts* 3, 2 (2009), 81.
31. Schertz, H. H. and Odom, S. L. Promoting joint attention in toddlers with autism: A parent-mediated developmental model. *Journal of autism and developmental disorders* 37, 8 (2007), 1562–1575.
32. Schneiderman, B. Accelerating Discovery and Innovation. *Communications of the ACM* 50, 12. 2007.
33. Shneiderman, B., Fischer, G., Czerwinski, M. et al. Creativity Support Tools: Report From a U.S. National Science Foundation Sponsored Workshop. *International Journal of Human-Computer Interaction*, 20, 2 (2006), 61–77.
34. Stewart, J. R., Gapenne, O. and Di Paolo, E. *Enaction: Toward a new paradigm for cognitive science.* MIT Press. 2010.
35. Voigt, M., Niehaves, B. and Becker, J. Towards a Unified Design Theory for Creativity Support Systems. GroupSystems (2011), 152–173.
36. Wardrip-Fruin, N. *Expressive Processing: Digital fictions, computer games, and software studies.* MIT press. 2009.
37. Weizenbaum, J. ELIZA---a computer program for the study of natural language communication between man and machine. *Communications of the ACM* 9, (1966), 36–45.
38. Wiggins, G. A. Searching for computational creativity. *New Generation Computing* 24, 3, (2006), 209–222.
39. Wiggins, G. A. A preliminary framework for description, analysis and comparison of creative systems. *Knowledge-Based Systems* 19, 7 (2006), 449–458.

RelaWorld: Neuroadaptive and Immersive Virtual Reality Meditation System

Ilkka Kosunen[1], Mikko Salminen[4], Simo Järvelä[4], Antti Ruonala[2], Niklas Ravaja[2,3], Giulio Jacucci[1,2]
[1]Helsinki Institute for Information Technology HIIT, Department of Computer Science, University of Helsinki
[2]Helsinki Institute for Information Technology HIIT, Aalto University
[3]Department of Social Research, University of Helsinki
[4]Department of Information and Service Economy, Aalto University

ABSTRACT
Meditation in general and mindfulness in particular have been shown to be useful techniques in the treatment of a plethora of ailments, yet they can be challenging for novices. We present RelaWorld: a neuroadaptive virtual reality meditation system that combines virtual reality with neurofeedback to provide a tool that is easy for novices to use yet provides added value even for experienced meditators. Using a head-mounted display, users can levitate in a virtual world by doing meditation exercises. The system measures users' brain activity in real time via EEG and calculates estimates for the level of concentration and relaxation. These values are then mapped into the virtual reality. In a user study of 43 subjects, we were able to show that the RelaWorld system elicits deeper relaxation, feeling of presence and a deeper level of meditation when compared to a similar setup without head-mounted display or neurofeedback.

Author Keywords
Neurofeedback, Virtual Reality, Meditation, Mindfulness

ACM Classification Keywords
H.5.1. Multimedia Information Systems: Artificial, augmented, and virtual realities

INTRODUCTION
In recent years, meditation in its various forms has gained a lot of research attention, specifically mindfulness meditation. While the brain-level effects of meditation are numerous and complex (see e.g. [2]) and clearly in need of considerably more in-depth studying, the wide range of well-being benefits, such as stress reduction, are more well-known (for various meta-analyses, see e.g. [19] [8] [41] [17] [10]). It is suggested that naive meditators would benefit from a system / application, which would help in focusing their attention to the meditation task at hand and closing out all other visual and auditory distractors, especially in a noisy office environment.

Physiological computing [12] applied to develop symbiotic interaction between humans and computers [23], is still an open research area [44]. This includes identifying and recognising psychophysiological states through multidisciplinary investigations coupling machine learning, psychophysiology and human-computer interaction, as well as research on how to integrate such findings in useful applications [22]. Recent work, for example, includes identifying workload for safety in supervisory tasks or driving [5] [43], detecting relevance for implicit feedback in information retrieval[11] [4] [39], research and adaptation in computer games [28] [45] [46], interactive storytelling [16], training cognitive performance [32], and usability testing [20].

Neurofeedback has been proven to be a useful tool in the treatment of various disorders including ADHD [30], epilepsy [48], learning disabilities [13] and autism spectrum disorders [26], to name just a few. However, little research has been done on how neurofeedback could be used to enhance meditation, including mindfulness-based therapies.

Virtual reality technologies have been successfully used in many therapies, especially those that rely on mental imagery: patients with phobias who traditionally have attempted to desensitize themselves within their imagination can face their fears in a controllable virtual environment [36]. Similarly, patients with eating disorders who suffer from distorted body image can work on their self-image through a virtual body [14].

While all these technologies and techniques have been separately proven to be highly effective, and many have been used to treat the same disorders such as depression and stress, combining them all into a single system is still undone.

Our main contribution is a design for a system that combines neurofeedback and virtual reality into a computer-assisted meditation system. We also contribute a user study of 43 subjects that demonstrates that our system is able to generate a deeper level of meditation, greater relaxation and a higher level of felt presence.

DOI: http://dx.doi.org/10.1145/2856767.2856796

In the following we describe the related work before we introduce the design considerations and implementation of the RelaWorld system. Next, we present the user study, and conclude with a discussion.

RELATED WORK

Meditation and Mindfulness

Lutz and colleagues [31] define meditation as a set of complex emotional and attentional regulatory strategies developed for various ends, including the cultivation of well-being and emotional balance. Meditation as a concept covers a broad range of various practices, traditions and even religious belief-systems; it is thus important to always specify the exact meditation technique in question. Different meditation techniques have varying goals, ranging from relaxation to heightened sense of well-being [31]. Many of the currently practiced approaches to meditation, including the currently popular mindfulness-based stress reduction, draw from Buddhist tradition [31]. Lutz, Slagter, Dunne and Davidson [31] divided meditation exercises into two broad categories: focused attention and open monitoring. Later Travis and Shear [51] suggested a third category of automatic self-transcending.

Different meditation techniques and approaches have differing effects not only on self-reported experiences but also at the neural level. Focused attention has been characterized by EEG beta (13-30Hz) and gamma (30-50Hz) band activities, open monitoring by theta (4-8Hz) activation, and automatic self-transcending by alpha-1 (8-10Hz) band activity (for a review, see [51]).

Traditionally, meditation has been considered as something that needs to be exercised almost daily and for long periods. However, recently there has been a growing interest in short-duration meditation or mindfulness programs, which could give results quickly. Previous research has documented promising results of short-duration meditation interventions. Twenty-minute exercises during five consecutive days led to positive improvements in self-reported depression and anger in a sample of students [49]. A study by Zeidan and colleagues [52] hints that a brief mindfulness meditation intervention of only three sessions could also improve cardiovascular variables (heart rate), whereas Steffen and Larson [47] present evidence of reduced cardiovascular reactivity to a stressor during a single mindfulness meditation session.

While there is a multitude of different meditation traditions, practices and exercises, there are only a few prior studies on how well suited they are for VR implementation.

Computer-Assisted Meditation Systems

Various kinds of computer-assisted meditation systems have been proposed in the past. In a study by Baños et al. [3] a virtual environment was successfully used to induce positive moods in elderly people. The system simulated a walk in a park where the participants could stop to listen to relaxing melodies, nature sounds and guided meditation exercises. The participants reported both an increase in positive emotion and a decrease in negative emotions. The system was perceived to be easy to use. The system used a 21" touchscreen with integrated audio speakers.

Chittaro and Vianello [9] proposed a mobile application to help naive meditators practice mindfulness. In their application, called AEON, the users would enter their thoughts on a mobile device that would visualize them as ink on a parchment placed under water. The users can then use the touchscreen to produce waves on the water that progressively dissolve the written thoughts. In a user study with 22 participants that compared the AEON system to two traditional mindfulness exercises, they found the system to be more pleasant and easier than traditional meditation, yet still able to produce a higher level of decentering, an index of mindfulness.

Carissoli et al. [7] examined the effectiveness of a mobile app using a three-week mindfulness-inspired protocol for stress reduction. In a study with 56 participants, they compared a group using the mobile app with a group that listened to relaxing music and a control group. However, while the data showed a trend towards decreased stress levels for both meditation and music listener groups, the results failed to reach statistical significance.

Our work extends these types of meditation systems by adding the immersivity of virtual reality and the possibilities of neurofeedback.

Virtual Reality-Based Therapies

Virtual reality-based systems have been used in the treatment of a wide range of mental disorders, ranging from eating disorders [14], to erectile dysfunction [34]. Virtual reality systems have been especially successful in the treatment of various anxiety disorders including fear of flying, social phobia, PTSD, fear of spiders and fear of heights (for a review, see [36]). In fact, the meta-review concludes that these so,called virtual reality exposure therapies (VRET) are "slightly but significantly more effective than exposure in vivo, the gold standard in the field."

Shaw et al. [42] introduced the Meditation Chamber, an immersive virtual environment for meditation training. The system used skin conductance as the biofeedback mechanism in three guided meditation and relaxation exercises that used head-mounted display for stereoscopic imagery and sound. The system was installed in an exhibition where 411 users tested the system. The majority of the users reported an increase in relaxation, especially those who had little prior experience in meditation. While conceptually similar to our system, it used skin conductance, a measure of peripheral physiology for the biofeedback, while our system utilizes EEG to record brain activity directly.

Gromala et al.[18] combined virtual reality and biofeedback into a system that helps chronic pain patients to manage their pain with guided mindfulness meditation. Their system, the Virtual Meditative Walk, simulated a walking meditation through a forest with a biofeedback adaptation that modified the weather in the virtual world based on the user's skin conductance: as the user relaxed the weather would clear, while anxiety would cause the user to be engulfed in a fog. In a user study of 13 participants, they were able to show that the virtual reality system was significantly more effective in reducing reported pain levels when compared to a control group that simply listened to a guided mindfulness audio track. This system differs from ours in that it used a mounted stereoscopic viewer instead of a head-mounted display for the VR, and skin conductance instead of EEG for the biofeedback.

Neurofeedback Therapies

Neurofeedback is a form of biofeedback where the brain activity, usually measured through EEG, is used for the feedback. Neurofeedback has been successfully used in the treatment of various disorders including ADHD [30], epilepsy [48], learning disabilities [13] and autism spectrum disorders [26].

Hinterberger [50] introduced the Sensorium, a neurofeedback environment that allowed the users to experience their physiological signals, brain waves and heart rate, as sounds and light effects. In a user study of 20 participants, almost all of the participants reported an increase in contentment, relaxation, happiness and inner harmony. Our work extends their idea by replacing the rather simple light effects with a virtual reality environment.

Sas and Chopra[40] described a system called MeditAid that used a special kind of aural neurofeedback to help meditators in a mindfulness practice. They recorded the users' brain activity with EEG and provided real-time audio feedback via binaural beats, a type of entrainment technique where two audio tones are played through headphones at a slightly different pitch. In a user study of 16 participants, all users were able to achieve a deeper level of meditation when using the system. While similar to our work, MeditAid was built around a special kind of audio feedback, while our system is designed to utilize the possibilities of full virtual reality immersion.

Presence

In the field of virtual reality research, the concept of presence has gained significant interest. In their book chapter titled "Presence-Inducing Media for Mental Health Applications" Riva et al. argue that "In general, what distinguishes VR from other media or communication systems is the sense of presence. [...] Specifically, we argue that the higher sense of presence induced by a VR may be used to elicit optimal experiences that will support the process of change." [38]

In a study by Freeman et al. [15] the effect of a virtual environment on the sense of presence was studied in the context of a relaxation exercise, and it was shown that the virtual environment, combined with a guided relaxation audio narrative produced a higher sense of presence than the narrative alone.

While the ability of virtual reality environments to generate the sense of presence is proven, to the best of our knowledge there is little research on how neurofeedback could enhance the sense of presence. Our experiment studies the added benefit of neurofeedback when combined with a virtual reality system.

SYSTEM OVERVIEW

The underlying motivation and design principle of the RelaWorld system was to combine the proven methods of neurofeedback and virtual reality into one package that would allow novice meditators to reap the full benefit of the meditative experience even in the middle of busy every day life. We aim to accomplish this by *immersing* the user into an alternative reality.

Immersion

What defines virtual reality as technology is its ability to *immerse* us into an alternative reality. Janet Horowitz Murray famously described immersion as

> "The experience of being transported to an elaborately simulated place is pleasurable in itself, regardless of the fantasy content. We refer to this experience as immersion. Immersion is a metaphorical term derived from the physical experience of being submerged in water. We seek the same feeling from a psychologically immersive experience that we do from a plunge in the ocean or swimming pool: the sensation of being surrounded by a completely other reality, as different as water is from air, that takes over all of our attention, our whole perceptual apparatus... in a participatory medium, immersion implies learning to swim, to do the things that the new environment makes possible... the enjoyment of immersion as a participatory activity."[33]

Taking cue from the above description, our system surrounds the user in a tropical island paradise. We harness the neurofeedback to generate a completely new type of participatory medium where users, instead of learning to swim, are able to fly utilizing parts of their psychophysiological whole hitherto unavailable for direct control. Instead of being submerged in water, the user is surrounded by an energy bubble that gets more opaque as the user relaxes.

Hardware

RelaWorld is a 3D-virtual reality environment designed for meditation practices. It utilizes the Oculus Rift DK2 head-mounted display, and it has been developed with the Unity3D game engine. See Figure 1.

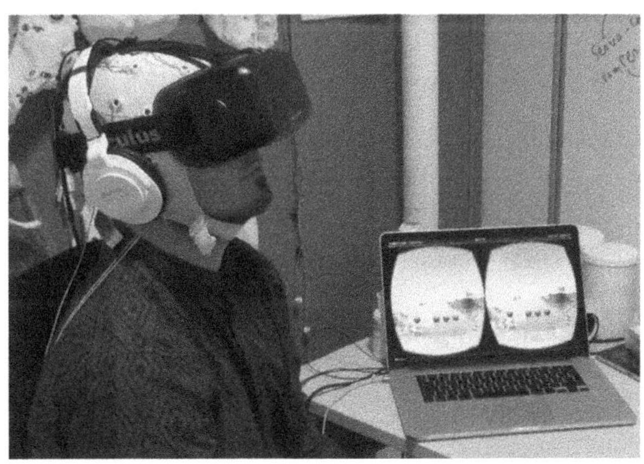

Figure 1. The RelaWorld setup

Virtual world scenarios

In the virtual world, the user is placed sitting on a stone platform, oriented toward seaside scenery. The application has two modes of meditation practices: body scan and focused attention. Both modes use a graphical interface to guide the meditation. In body scan, an HUD-type UI is used to guide the focus (see Figure 2). Focused attention utilizes five focus objects shown floating in front of the user, one object always being highlighted (see Figure 3). As the practise progresses, the meditative performance is reflected with vertical movement of the user, and by varying the opacity of an energy bubble around the user.

Figure 2. Body scan practice

Figure 3. Focused attention practice

Scene design process

Beginning premise

As richness of detail, variety and motion of the visual signal might generate unwanted EEG artifacts, we decided that instead of aiming towards realism, to go for a minimalistic visual language in the scenery. A seaside scene was chosen, being a typical relaxation and meditation setting. A purposefully androgynous figure in the body scan guidance was chosen to take into account all genders.

Directing with details

A practice of level design in games is to guide the players' attention and direction by placing details and movement wherever the designer wants the player to focus. This combined with the design principles of visual hierarchy formed a guideline, by which we placed additional details to most relevant objects. The platform underneath had a detailed texture with a carpet pattern to both create a sense of comfort and to orient the user to the spot. To guide their attention to the meditation task at hand, focus object had a moving glow and highlighted color, body scan UI is visually detailed and bound to view to keep the players' attention at the guidance. The details of background objects are purposefully lesser. The ground is a low-poly with a simple striped texture, the trees have no trunk texture and instead of leaves, the foliage is presented with simple planes. Sky has no cloud coverage, and sun is positioned higher up from the immediate view. Only the waves of the sea have a rich detailing without an orienting purpose. Leaving it rich in detail was based on having a simple but strong immersive effect on the scene. The movement of pollen towards the sea serves a function of drawing the user towards the depth of the scenery; to look into the view, instead of the screen.

Preventing vertigo

As nausea is a common experience in VR, we saw it as important to design against from the get-go. While slow movement in one dimension was already on the safe side of VR-design, we took it a step further. Instead of levitating purely in the air, the user has a sturdy, heavy platform placed underneath the user's feet (see figure 4). That platform moves alongside the user to prevent possible experience of fear of heights and related vertigo. This was successful, as none of the testers reported nausea.

Figure 4. Platform without reference objects

Correcting the height perception

During early tests where the user was sitting on a plain beach just by the sea (see Figure 4), we noticed it was hard to estimate changes in vertical position without looking down. And even then it was hard, since the platform was blocking large part of the view underneath. To solve this, we moved the starting position more inwards from the shore, and added objects of known size around the meditation position and at varying distance: islands, a pathway of stepping stones, and most importantly, trees just next to the user. With their presence, perception of vertical movement increased significantly (see Figure 5).

Figure 5. Vertical starting position with reference objects

Bringing the scene alive
With bare assets present, the scenery appeared lifeless and static. To make it more feel lively, we added subtle animations: gentle waves in the sea, a simulated wind that moves the trees gently pushing floating pollen towards the horizon. To the small pollen objects moving in depth, we applied the Oculus Rift chromatic aberration shader plugin, which added a sense of depth. An audio track of pink noise waves gushing to the shore added immersion, and served as a neutral noise based insulator from sounds of the outside world.

Adjusting the reactivity
When testing different parameters for live data, we found that too direct and immediate reactivity to the changes in the physiology made the experience nervous and jumpy. If the movement reacted fast to even the slightest changes, it was hard for the user to perceive connection between his state of mind and the changes in the adaptation of the environment. Also, the jagged and fast movement distracted concentration and relaxation. This was fixed by adjusting the thresholds and degree of change, so that the experience seemed to reflect a few seconds of change in state of mind, moving the direction smoothly and gently, feeling floaty.

Unpleasantness of single focus
In an early version, focused attention followed strictly the along the lines of traditional meditation practice, and had a single point of focus. Only one of the balls was highlighted per session, and it stayed the same for the whole 10 minutes. This was found to be very straining and boring. Users reported starting to look at the grid of the LED screen, and finding the whiteness of the glow at a single point heavy on the eyes. As a solution, we decided to randomly change the location of the focus object between the balls every 30 seconds and lessened the glow. This made the experience enjoyable and provided the same pace of change in the guidance as in the body scan meditation.

Neurofeedback and Adaptations
We could have used several biofeedback options for the adaption, such as the skin conductance used in the Meditation Chamber [42]. However, we thought observing the brain directly via technology like electroencephalograph (EEG) would make more sense than recording some index of peripheral physiology, such as heart rate or skin conductance, as meditation is inherently cognitive.

Several earlier studies have shown the connection between so-called "brain waves" and cognitive processes, such as alertness. Klimesch et al. [25] showed that the lower alpha band (6.4Hz-8.4Hz) desynchronizes, that is the power decreases, when the subject is alert and expectant. Klimesch [24] also showed that the lower alpha power (6Hz-10Hz) decreases on all sides of the head. Conversely, the theta band power (defined as 4-6Hz, or sometimes as 6-7Hz) has been shown to increase with working memory requirements [21].

The brain activity has been measured during various meditation and relaxation exercises in several previous studies. The theta band (4-6Hz) power has been shown to increase during concentration (including meditative concentration) [1] [27]. Cahn and Polich [6] they concluded that the alpha band (8-12Hz), especially the lower alpha (8-10Hz), decreases during concentration and vigilance. Conversely, the alpha is increased during relaxation, including meditation. The theta band (4-6Hz), especially in the mid-frontal region, seems to increase during concentration and with tasks that employ working memory, but also during meditation.

Based on these findings we decided to design the neurofeedback of the RelaWorld system around the alpha-band and theta-band powers of the EEG. Increase in the power of the theta band (concentration) will produce floating; increase in the alpha band (relaxation) will increase the opacity of the energy bubble surrounding the user.

Adaptations and algorithms
The adaptation is based on theta-band and alpha-band activity of brain. The average of theta and alpha band activity from the six electrodes(F3, F4, C3, C4, P3, P4) generates a stream of two real numbers: one for the theta activity, and another for the alpha activity.

There are two visual adaptations representing the user's performance. Vertical platform movement shows user concentration, while relaxation appears as an energy bubble that becomes more visible the more the user relaxes. At near maximum relaxation level, a particle effect is shown to highlight exceptional performance and to stimulate the opaqueness of the view (see Figure 6).

Figure 6. Bubble at maximum opacity, with star particles

EVALUATION

To evaluate the RelaWorld system, we designed a user study with two types of meditation exercises interspersed with mental tasks.

In this study we had a set of criteria for choosing the exercises for the experiment; they had to be 1) from the same category of meditation exercises, 2) previously studied (at least to a certain degree), 3) easy to learn and instruct to novices, 4) clearly theoretically distinct, 5) predictable in their main effect (even in short term practice with novices), 6) hypothetically more and less suited for VR. Based on these criteria, we chose Point Focus (PF) meditation and Body Scan (BS) meditation as forms of focused attention (FA) meditation for our study. In FA meditation, the task is to focus your attention to a certain single point and keep there, and when your attention starts to drift, bring it back gently (Lutz et al., 2008 [31]). FA may seem easy, but it is actually rather demanding, especially for novices. Its benefits have been associated with development of various attentional and emotional processes (see Lutz et al., 2008 [31]). In BS, the task is to focus on different parts of your own body, letting them relax, and then switching to the next until you have covered your whole body. In PF the task is to focus on a single point in front of you and not be distracted by anything else (this type of exercise is often also called focused attention meditation, but we want to reserve that term for the category of exercises to avoid confusion).

While seemingly different in many ways, these two meditation exercises share the same basic logic of actively controlling your attentional focus on a specific target. The main difference between them is what that focus is: in PF, it is external; in BS, it is internal. In VR, this turns into a difference whether the meditators attention is focused on something inside the virtual environment or outside it. One exploratory research question of our study was to see whether VR would support one type of attentional process better than the other, and consequently whether it would work better with certain types of meditation.

We used two set of questionnaires to evaluate the performance of the system:

(i) The ITC-Sense of Presence Inventory [29]

(ii)The meditation depth questionnaire (MEDEQ) [35]

From the ITC-Sense of Presence Inventory we chose a subset of questions from the full questionnaire so as to keep the experiment duration reasonable. The used the full version of the MEDEQ questionnaire.

Participants

The participants were 43 university students with various major subjects, aged between 20 and 48 years (M=28.7). There were 26 female participants. The participants were paid 40 euros as compensation.

Apparatus

A QuickAmp (BrainProducts GmbH., Germany) amplifier was used to record the EEG, which then went to the OpenVibe [37] framework for real-time analysis. Two frequency bands, the Theta (4-6Hz) and Alpha (8-12) were extracted using fourth order Butterworth bandpass filters. Then we calculated average band power for 100 ms epochs. The resulting values were then send to Unity3D via a TCP connection.

EEG was recorded with 6 electrodes (F3, F4, C3, C4, P3, P4) and the ground electrode was placed at FCz, selected so that the straps of the Oculus headset wouldn't interfere with them. A common reference montage was used during the recordings.

Procedure

When arriving to the lab, the participant at in a comfortable chair. After filling out written consent, the participant was attached to the electrodes. A 5-minute baseline recording took place before the actual experimental tasks, not only for the statistical analyses for controlling the differences in individual levels of the psychophysiological activity, but also to familiarize the participant with the recording apparatus. In the experiment there were 6 meditation exercises, each lasting 10 minutes. Following each exercise was a 3-minute 2-back working memory task for evoking stress and erasing the effects of the last meditation session. After the experiment, we removed the electrodes, thanked the participant and provided a short briefing about the purpose of the experiment. The whole experimental session took between 2 and 2.5 hours.

Design

The experiment employed a 2 (meditation type) X 2 (adaptation) X 2 (medium) design. The two meditation types were focused attention and body scanning, the EEG-based bio-adaptation was either on or off, and the medium was either the Oculus Rift VR-glasses or a computer screen. However, there were only 6 conditions in the experiment. There was no bio-adaptation combined with a computer screen. These two conditions were omitted to keep the total length of the experiment under 3 hours.

RESULTS

In the next sections we compared meditation and presence in the following three conditions with planned contrasts: (a) a control condition (CC) where the participants followed the meditation exercise on a computer screen without a head-mounted display or neurofeedback (NF), (b) a head-mounted display without neurofeedback, and (c) both a head-mounted display and neurofeedback.

We did the statistical analyses with the Linear Mixed Models (LMM) procedure with restricted maximum-likelihood estimation in SPSS (version 21). One at a time, we specified each outcome measure as the dependent variable and the model included the fixed effect for the condition (six different).

Perhaps surprisingly, no statistically significant difference emerged between the two exercises (FA and BS) in any of the outcome measures, except for the part of the meditation depth questionnaire that measures negative feelings, such as boredom. Respondents found FA more boring than BS, but only when they did not use the head-mounted display or neurofeedback. Therefore, the effect of meditation type will not

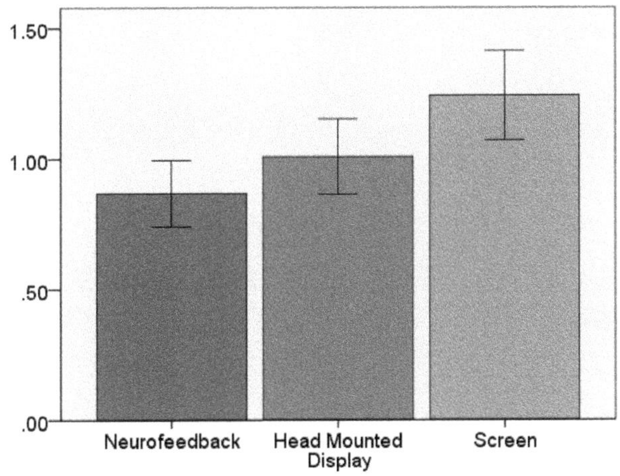

Figure 7. MEDEQ Hindrances: negative feelings during the meditation.

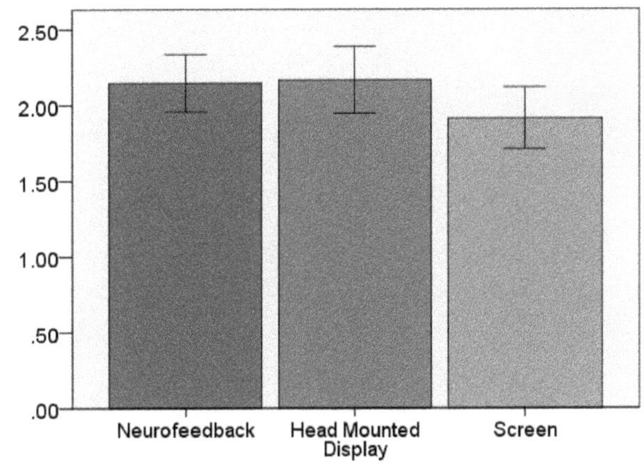

Figure 8. MEDEQ Relaxation: feeling of relaxation during the meditation.

be explored further in the analyses (the data were collapsed across the meditation types when presenting the results).

Meditation Depth Questionnaire

The meditation depth questionnaire showed a general trend: the combination of head-mounted display with neurofeedback was perceived to be the best, while the head-mounted display condition without neurofeedback was rated higher than the control. However, the difference between control condition and head-mounted display was greater, and always statistically significant, than the difference between head-mounted display and neurofeedback, which did not reach statistical significance.

Hindrances

The meditation depth questionnaire measures the meditation experience by dividing it into five stages or factors of increasing depth. The first factor, labeled "Hindrances", deals with the negative feelings associated with the meditation experience, such as boredom and anxiety, and is measured with questions such as "I found it difficult to relax" and "I felt bored." The results can be seen in figure 7. The CC elicited significantly more negative feelings than the head-mounted display condition ($p < 0.01$); while the HMD condition seemed to elicit higher negativity than the NF condition, the difference did not reach statistical significance ($p = 0.091$).

Relaxation

The second factor of the meditation depth questionnaire deals with relaxation and is measured with questions such as "I felt well" and "I became more and more calm and patient". See Figure 8. The CC was the least relaxing and rated significantly lower than the HMD ($p < 0.05$) The head-mounted display and neurofeedback condition elicited almost the same amount of relaxation.

Personal Self

The third factor is labeled "personal self" and deals with aspect of self-reflection elicited by the meditation practice. See Figure 9. It was measured with questions such as "I became aware of a center inside myself" and "I got intuitive insights or understand about my life." Again, the CC received significantly lower score than the HMD ($P < 0.01$) while there was no significant difference between neurofeedback and HMD.

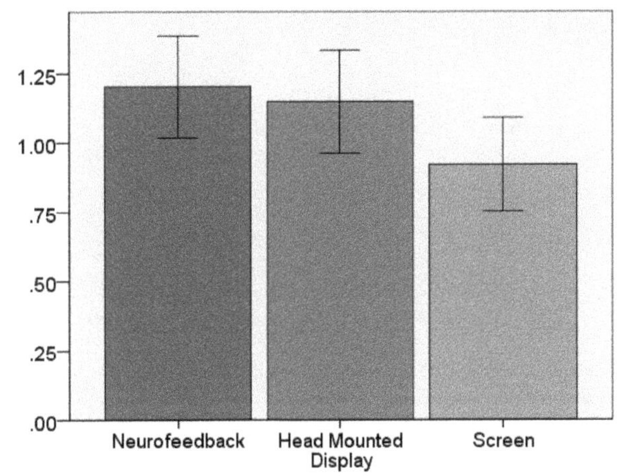

Figure 9. MEDEQ Personal Self: concentration and centeredness

Transpersonal Qualities

The fourth factor, labeled "transpersonal qualities" deals with essential qualities such as joy and love that may arise during meditation. See figure 10. The questions associated with this factor included "I felt love, surrender, connection" and "I experienced boundless joy". The CC was rated significantly lower than the HMD condition ($p< 0.01$) and no significant difference appeared between the neurofeedback and HMD condition.

Transpersonal Self

The final factor of the questionnaire dealt with the deepest levels of meditative experience: feeling of non-duality and infinity of consciousness. See Figure 11. It was measured with questions such as "there was no subject or object anymore" and "I felt myself at one with everything." The control condition again scored significantly lower than the HMD condition ($p< 0.05$) while no significant difference appeared between the NF and HMD conditions.

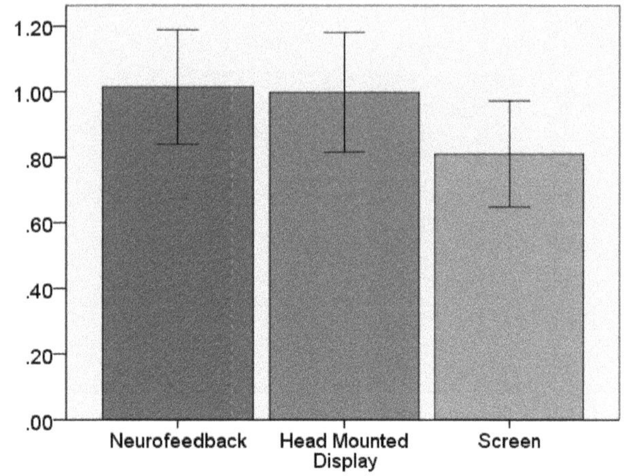

Figure 10. MEDEQ Transpersonal Qualities: experience of essential qualities such as joy and love.

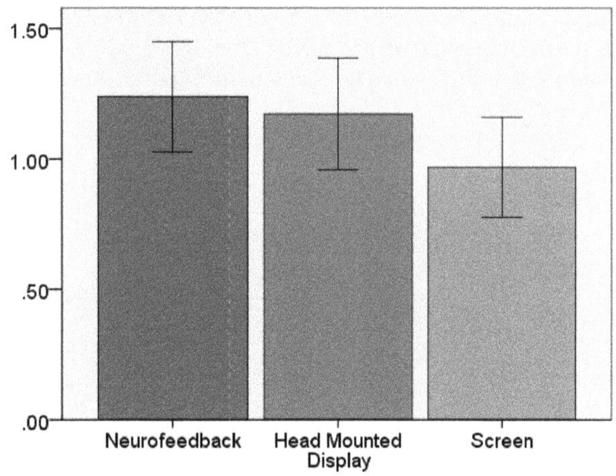

Figure 11. MEDEQ Transpersonal Self: Deepest meditative states of non-duality and infinity of consciousness

Presence

We measured the perceived level of presence using the The ITC-Sense of Presence Inventory [29]. The results show that the combination of neurofeedback and head-mounted display produced the highest level of presence, followed by the head-mounted display without neurofeedback. The screen condition elicited lowest level of presence. See figure 12. These results follow the same trend as those of the meditation depth questionnaire.

DISCUSSION AND CONCLUSIONS

It is well known that VR technology can elicit higher presence than a monitor screen; however, the fact that neurofeedback can increase the feeling of presence even further is something not previously shown (to the best of our knowledge). The results of the meditation depth questionnaire indicate that the system is able to provide added value on all levels of the meditative experience: from the mundane feeling of boredom to the more esoteric states of non-duality, the system was rated better than the control condition. It is also interesting to note that while neurofeedback induced a higher level of presence, it did not directly reflect in the meditation depth questionnaire

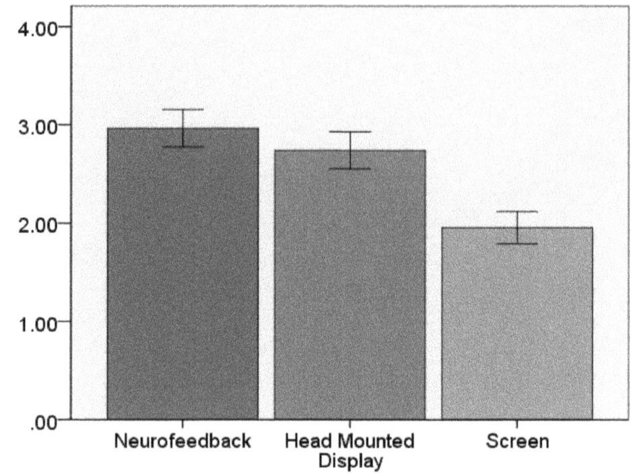

Figure 12. Presence

results. As there was a clear trend of higher ratings for the neurofeedback, this might just be due to the limited sample size.

In this paper we have presented a neurofeedback virtual reality meditation system. The system measures user's brain waves in real time and maps them into levitation and visual effects inside a virtual environment, displayed using a head-mounted device. Our user study shows that the head-mounted display generates higher meditative states when compared to the same system displayed on a normal screen. Neurofeedback further enhances the experience, providing higher levels of presence as reported by the users.

In the next version of the system, we intend to implement individually defined alpha and theta frequency bands (see, for example, [1]) that adapt automatically to each user. In addition to fully using the possibilities of modern VR technology, we plan to implement a walking meditation scenario.

ACKNOWLEDGEMENTS

This work has been partly supported by Academy of Finland (Academy project number 268999) and by the European Commission FP7 framework through the MindSee project (FP7 - ICT; Grant Agreement # 611570).

REFERENCES

1. Aftanas, L., and Glocheikine, S. Human anterior and frontal midline theta and lower alpha reflect emotionally positive state and internalized attention: high-resolution eeg investigation of meditation. *Neuroscience Letters 310*, 1 (September 2001), 57–60.

2. Austin, J. *Zen and the brain: Toward an understanding of meditation and consciousness.* 1998.

3. Baños, R. M., Etchemendy, E., Castilla, D., García-Palacios, A., Quero, S., and Botella, C. Positive mood induction procedures for virtual environments designed for elderly people. *Interact. Comput. 24*, 3 (May 2012), 131–138.

4. Barral, O., Eugster, M. J., Ruotsalo, T., Spapé, M. M., Kosunen, I., Ravaja, N., Kaski, S., and Jacucci, G.

Exploring peripheral physiology as a predictor of perceived relevance in information retrieval. In *Proceedings of the 20th International Conference on Intelligent User Interfaces*, ACM (2015), 389–399.

5. Boyer, M., Cummings, M. L., Spence, L. B., and Solovey, E. T. Investigating mental workload changes in a long duration supervisory control task. *Interacting with Computers* (2015), iwv012.
6. Cahn, B., and Polich, J. Meditation states and traits: Eeg, erp, and neuroimaging studies. *Psychological Bulletin 132*, 2, 180–211.
7. Carissoli, C., Villani, D., and Riva, G. Does a meditation protocol supported by a mobile application help people reduce stress? Suggestions from a controlled pragmatic trial. *Cyberpsychology, Behavior, and Social Networking* (2015).
8. Chiesa, A., and Serretti, A. Mindfulness-based stress reduction for stress management in healthy people: a review and meta-analysis. *The journal of alternative and complementary medicine 15*, 5 (2009), 593–600.
9. Chittaro, L., and Vianello, A. Computer-supported mindfulness: Evaluation of a mobile thought distancing application on naive meditators. *International Journal of Human-Computer Studies 72*, 3 (2014), 337 – 348.
10. Eberth, J., and Sedlmeier, P. The effects of mindfulness meditation: a meta-analysis. *Mindfulness 3*, 3 (2012), 174–189.
11. Eugster, M. J., Ruotsalo, T., Spapé, M. M., Kosunen, I., Barral, O., Ravaja, N., Jacucci, G., and Kaski, S. Predicting term-relevance from brain signals. In *Proceedings of the 37th international ACM SIGIR conference on Research & development in information retrieval*, ACM (2014), 425–434.
12. Fairclough, S. H. Fundamentals of physiological computing. *Interacting with computers 21*, 1 (2009), 133–145.
13. Fernández, T., Herrera, W., Harmony, T., Díaz-Comas, L., Santiago, E., Sánchez, L., Bosch, J., Fernández-Bouzas, A., Otero, G., Ricardo-Garcell, J., Barraza, C., Aubert, E., Galán, L., and Valdés, P. Eeg and behavioral changes following neurofeedback treatment in learning disabled children. *Clinical EEG and Neuroscience 34*, 3 (2003), 145–152.
14. Ferrer-Garcia, M., Gutirrez-Maldonado, J., and Riva, G. Virtual reality based treatments in eating disorders and obesity: A review. *Journal of Contemporary Psychotherapy 43*, 4 (2013), 207–221.
15. Freeman, J., Lessiter, J., Keogh, E., and F.W. Bond, K. C. Relaxation island: virtual, and really relaxing. *Proceedings of the 7th international workshop on presence* (2004).
16. Gilroy, S. W., Porteous, J., Charles, F., Cavazza, M., Soreq, E., Raz, G., Ikar, L., Or-Borichov, A., Ben-Arie, U., Klovatch, I., et al. A brain-computer interface to a plan-based narrative. In *Proceedings of the Twenty-Third international joint conference on Artificial Intelligence*, AAAI Press (2013), 1997–2005.
17. Goyal, M., Singh, S., Sibinga, E., Gould, N. F., Rowland-Seymour, A., Sharma, R., Berger, Z., Sleicher, D., Maron, D. D., Shihab, H., Ranasinghe, P. D., Linn, S., Saha, S., Bass, E., and Haythornthwaite, J. Meditation programs for psychological stress and well-being: a systematic review and meta-analysis. *JAMA internal medicine 174*, 3 (2014), 357–368.
18. Gromala, D., Tong, X., Choo, A., Karamnejad, M., and Shaw, C. D. The virtual meditative walk: Virtual reality therapy for chronic pain management. In *Proceedings of the 33rd Annual ACM Conference on Human Factors in Computing Systems*, CHI '15, ACM (New York, NY, USA, 2015), 521–524.
19. Grossman, P., Niemann, L., Schmidt, S., and Walach, H. Mindfulness-based stress reduction and health benefits: A meta-analysis. *Journal of Psychosomatic Research 57*, 1 (2004), 35 – 43.
20. Hirshfield, L. M., Solovey, E. T., Girouard, A., Kebinger, J., Jacob, R. J., Sassaroli, A., and Fantini, S. Brain measurement for usability testing and adaptive interfaces: an example of uncovering syntactic workload with functional near infrared spectroscopy. In *Proceedings of the SIGCHI Conference on Human Factors in Computing Systems*, ACM (2009), 2185–2194.
21. Inanaga, K. Frontal midline theta rhythm and mental activity. *Psychiatry and Clinical Neurosciences 52*, 6 (1998).
22. Jacucci, G., Fairclough, S., and Solovey, E. T. Physiological computing. *Computer 48*, 10 (Oct 2015), 12–16.
23. Jacucci, G., Spagnolli, A., Freeman, J., and Gamberini, L. Symbiotic interaction: A critical definition and comparison to other human-computer paradigms. In *Symbiotic Interaction*, vol. 8820 of *Lecture Notes in Computer Science*. Springer, 2014, 3–20.
24. Klimesch, W. EEG alpha and theta oscillations reflect cognitive and memory performance: a review and analysis. *Brain Research Reviews 29* (1999), 169 – 195.
25. Klimesch, W., Doppelmayr, M., Russegger, H., Pachinger, T., and Schwaiger, J. Induced alpha band power changes in the human EEG and attention. *Neuroscience Letters 244*, 2 (1998), 73 – 76.
26. Kouijzer, M. E., de Moor, J. M., Gerrits, B. J., Buitelaar, J. K., and van Schie, H. T. Long-term effects of neurofeedback treatment in autism. *Research in Autism Spectrum Disorders 3*, 2 (2009), 496 – 501.
27. Kubota, Y., Sato, W., Toichi, M., Murai, T., Okada, T., Hayashi, A., and Sengoku, A. Frontal midline theta rhythm is correlated with cardiac autonomic activities during the performance of an attention demanding meditation procedure. *Cognitive Brain Research 11*, 2 (2001), 281 – 287.

28. Kuikkaniemi, K., Laitinen, T., Turpeinen, M., Saari, T., Kosunen, I., and Ravaja, N. The influence of implicit and explicit biofeedback in first-person shooter games. In *Proceedings of the SIGCHI Conference on Human Factors in Computing Systems*, ACM (2010), 859–868.
29. Lessiter, J., Freeman, J., Keogh, E., and Davidoff, J. A cross-media presence questionnaire: The ITC-sense of presence inventory. *Presence: Teleoper. Virtual Environ. 10*, 3 (June 2001), 282–297.
30. Lubar, J., Swartwood, M., Swartwood, J., and O'Donnell, P. Evaluation of the effectiveness of EEG neurofeedback training for ADHD in a clinical setting as measured by changes in T.O.V.A. scores, behavioral ratings, and WISC-R performance. *Biofeedback and Self-regulation 20*, 1 (1995), 83–99.
31. Lutz, A., Slagter, H. A., Dunne, J. D., and Davidson, R. J. Attention regulation and monitoring in meditation. *Trends in Cognitive Science 12*, 4 (April 2008), 163–169.
32. Mishra, J., and Gazzaley, A. Closed-loop cognition: the next frontier arrives. *Trends in cognitive sciences 19*, 5 (2015), 242–243.
33. Murray, J. H. *Hamlet on the Holodeck: The Future of Narrative in Cyberspace*. The Free Press, New York, NY, USA, 1997.
34. Optale, G., Munari, A., Nasta, A., Pianon, C., Baldaro, V., and Viggiano, G. Multimedia and virtual reality techniques in the treatment of male erectile disorders. *International Journal of Impotence Research* (1997).
35. Piron, H. The meditation depth index (MEDI) and the meditation depth questionnaire (MEDEQ). *Journal for Meditation and Meditation Research 1*, 1 (2001), 69–92.
36. Powers, M. B., and Emmelkamp, P. M. Virtual reality exposure therapy for anxiety disorders: A meta-analysis. *Journal of Anxiety Disorders 22*, 3 (2008), 561 – 569.
37. Renard, Y., Lotte, F., Gibert, G., Congedo, M., Maby, E., Delannoy, V., Bertrand, O., and Lécuyer, A. Openvibe: An open-source software platform to design, test and use brain-computer interfaces in real and virtual environments. *Presence: teleoperators and virtual environments 19*, 1 (2010).
38. Riva, G., Botella, C., Baños, R., Mantovani, F., García-palacios, A., Quero, S., Serino, S., Triberti, S., Repetto, C., Dakanalis, A., Villani, D., and Gaggioli, A. Presence-inducing media for mental health applications. *Immersed in Media* (2015), 283–332.
39. Ruotsalo, T., Jacucci, G., Myllymäki, P., and Kaski, S. Interactive intent modeling: Information discovery beyond search. *Communications of the ACM 58*, 1 (2014), 86–92.
40. Sas, C., and Chopra, R. Meditaid: a wearable adaptive neurofeedback-based system for training mindfulness state. *Personal and Ubiquitous Computing 19*, 7 (2015), 1169–1182.
41. Sedlmeier, P., Eberth, J., Schwarz, M., Zimmermann, D., Haarig, F., Jaeger, S., and Kunze, S. The psychological effects of meditation: A meta-analysis. *Psychological Bulletin 138*, 6 (November 2012), 1139–1171.
42. Shaw, C., Gromala, D., and Song, M. The meditation chamber: Towards self-modulation. *Metaplasticity in Virtual Worlds: Aesthetics and Semantics Concepts* (2010), 121–133.
43. Solovey, E. T., Zec, M., Garcia Perez, E. A., Reimer, B., and Mehler, B. Classifying driver workload using physiological and driving performance data: Two field studies. In *Proceedings of the SIGCHI Conference on Human Factors in Computing Systems*, ACM (2014), 4057–4066.
44. Spapé, M. M., Filetti, M., Eugster, M. J., Jacucci, G., and Ravaja, N. Human computer interaction meets psychophysiology: A critical perspective. In *Symbiotic Interaction*, vol. 9359 of *Lecture Notes in Computer Science*. Springer, 2015, 145–158.
45. Spapé, M. M., Hoggan, E. E., Jacucci, G., and Ravaja, N. The meaning of the virtual midas touch: An erp study in economic decision making. *Psychophysiology 52*, 3 (2015), 378–387.
46. Spapé, M. M., Kivikangas, J. M., Järvelä, S., Kosunen, I., Jacucci, G., and Ravaja, N. Keep your opponents close: Social context affects eeg and femg linkage in a turn-based computer game. *PLoS ONE 8*, 11 (November 2013).
47. Steffen, P. R., and Larson, M. J. A brief mindfulness exercise reduces cardiovascular reactivity during a laboratory stressor paradigm. *Mindfulness 6*, 4 (2015), 803–811.
48. Sterman, M., and Egner, T. Foundation and practice of neurofeedback for the treatment of epilepsy. *Applied Psychophysiology and Biofeedback 31*, 1 (2006), 21–35.
49. Tang, Y. Y., Ma, Y., Wang, J., Fan, Y., Feng, S., Lu, Q., Yu, Q., Sui, D., Rothbart, M. K., Fan, M., and Posner, M. I. Short-term meditation training improves attention and self-regulation. *Proceedings of the National Academy of Sciences 104* (2007).
50. Thilo, H. The sensorium: A multimodal neurofeedback environment. *Advances in Human-Computer Interaction* (2011).
51. Travis, F., and Shear, J. Focused attention, open monitoring and automatic self-transcending: Categories to organize meditations from vedic, buddhist and chinese traditions. *Consciousness and cognition 19*, 4 (December 2010), 11101118.
52. Zeidan, F., Johnson, S. K., Gordon, N. S., and Goolkasian, P. Effects of brief and sham mindfulness meditation on mood and cardiovascular variables. *The Journal of Alternative and Complementary Medicine 16* (2010), 867–873.

The Effect of Privacy Concerns on Privacy Recommenders

Yuchen Zhao
University of St Andrews, UK
yz39@st-andrews.ac.uk

Juan Ye
University of St Andrews, UK
jy31@st-andrews.ac.uk

Tristan Henderson
University of St Andrews, UK
tnhh@st-andrews.ac.uk

ABSTRACT

Location-sharing services such as Facebook and Foursquare/Swarm have become increasingly popular, due to the ease at which users can share their locations, and participate in services, games and other applications that leverage these locations. But it is important for people who use these services to configure appropriate location-privacy preferences so that they can control to whom they want to share their location information. Manually configuring these preferences may be burdensome and confusing, and so location-privacy preference recommenders based on crowdsourcing preferences from other users have been proposed. Whether people will accept the recommended preferences acquired from other users, who they may not know or trust, has not, however, been investigated.

In this paper, we present a user experiment (n=99) to explore what factors influence people's acceptance of location-privacy preference recommenders. We find that 44% of our participants have privacy concerns about such recommenders. These concerns are shown to have a negative effect ($p < 0.001$) on their acceptance of the recommendations and their satisfaction about their choices. Furthermore, users' acceptance of recommenders varies according to both context and recommendations being made. Our findings are potentially useful to designers of location-sharing services and privacy recommenders.

ACM Classification Keywords

K.4.1 Computers and Society: Public Policy Issues—*Privacy*

Author Keywords

location-based services; location-sharing services; privacy preferences; recommender systems; user acceptance

INTRODUCTION

With the help of social networking sites, location-based services, and smartphones, location-sharing services (LSSs), such as Foursquare/Swarm and Facebook's location check-in mechanism, have been evolving rapidly in recent years. People can now easily share their whereabouts with others, including their families, friends, and even the public, intentionally or unexpectedly. On the one hand, LSSs provide us with convenient features such as personal tracking and discovery of new friends [19]. On the other hand, location-privacy preferences are highly context-aware [1]; sharing information depends on *where* they are and *when* they are in a certain place. Such context-awareness makes the self-configuration of privacy preferences a complex task [9], which may lead to a failure to protect location privacy [20]. Since people treat their location as the most valuable type of personal information [26], the lack of usable location-privacy protection mechanisms may affect the adoption of LSSs. To address these usability and information overload issues, recommenders have been designed to configure location-privacy preferences (semi-)automatically, for instance by recommending preferences based on crowdsourced results (e.g. from people with similar preferences). But people's acceptance of these recommenders and the factors that influence their acceptance have not been investigated sufficiently.

Existing research has mainly focussed on the measurement of metrics, such as the recommendation accuracy, by conducting offline recommender evaluation (i.e. using previously collected user data to construct and test a recommender). But location-privacy preferences are a relatively sensitive domain, compared with other fields where recommenders are used, such as music and movie recommendations, and so poor recommendations could have more serious consequences. Thus simply measuring accuracy may be insufficient. We also need to consider whether people accept these recommenders, or indeed the recommendations made by them. Such acceptance might be affected by subjective factors such as a person's concerns about sharing their preference data with a recommender, and as well as objective factors such as how the recommendations are made, or the type of recommendation being made. Therefore, it is necessary to investigate the influence of both people's subjective factors and these objective factors concerned with the recommender. Understanding this will help us decide which factors we should take into account when designing our recommenders.

In this paper we investigate the following research questions:

- **Q1.** Which subjective factors (e.g. trust in technology, privacy concerns, and perceived quality) will influence a person's acceptance of location-privacy preference recommendations?
- **Q2.** Which objective factors of recommendations (e.g. context and openness) will influence people's acceptance of location-privacy preference recommendations?

The contributions of our work are as follows:

- Using an online user study (n=99), we find that people do indeed have concerns about using recommenders for

IUI 2016, March 7–10, 2016, Sonoma, CA, USA.

DOI: http://dx.doi.org/10.1145/2856767.2856771

privacy-preference prediction. These concerns have a negative influence on their perceived recommendation quality, satisfaction about their choices, and acceptance of the recommendations.

- The openness of a recommendation (with whom the recommender is proposing to share location) has a significant influence on people's acceptance. Recommendations with the highest and lowest openness are both less likely to be accepted.
- Context (specifically time and location) has an effect on people's acceptance of location-privacy preference recommendations.

We believe that our findings are of use to system designers who wish to use recommenders for configuring preferences about sensitive data.

RELATED WORK

To address usability issues in privacy protection, various machine learning classifiers have been used to predict privacy preferences in online social networks [8, 22, 7] and in LSSs [25, 2], thereby helping people to configure their privacy rules (semi-)automatically. These methods learn from individual users' previous privacy decisions and make predictions based on the models that they build. Experimental results demonstrate that these methods can achieve high prediction accuracy.

An alternative approach is to use crowdsourcing knowledge to make recommendations for privacy preferences, such as security configurations on mobile devices [12, 15] and location-sharing preferences [28, 29]. Compared with learning from individual histories, crowdsourcing recommenders learn from the "Wisdom of Crowds". For example, Toch's Super-Ego framework makes predictions based on semantic analysis of locations and the crowdsourcing results in the same semantic categories [27]. In addition, context-aware recommenders [3] based on collaborative filtering (CF) are also used, in which the location and time are treated as contexts and the recommendations are location-sharing preferences. For instance, Xie et al. combine both user-based and item-based CF in a recommender to make location-sharing preference recommendations [28]. They show that crowdsourcing methods can perform as well as machine learning classifiers. Furthermore, such CF recommenders can be used to bootstrap new systems, as they perform particularly well when there are insufficient training data [29].

Research has shown that people's security and privacy behaviours can be affected by social influence [6]. People often trust inaccurate recommendations more than they should [11]. Given that privacy-preference is a sensitive domain, it is important to investigate what factors would influence people's perception on the recommendations and their interactions with the recommenders. Knijnenburg and Jin [17] show that privacy recommendations for location sharing services have a strong persuasive effect on people. We extend their work by exploring what kind of factors from both the recommendations (e.g. source of crowdsourcing and level of openness of recommendations) and the users (e.g. their concerns and perceived recommendation quality) can influence the users' acceptance of the recommendations.

Models and frameworks have been proposed to investigate the effects from other factors beyond recommendation accuracy (e.g. personal characteristics, perceived quality, transparency) in what is referred to as HRI (Human-Recommender Interaction) [21]. For example, Zins and Bauernfeind investigate which factors influence users' satisfaction with recommenders [30]. Their user study mainly focuses on effects from personal characteristics including Internet expertise, product involvement, and Internet purchase attitudes. By applying their model they find that these personal characteristics can influence people's experience when using online recommenders. Pu et al. propose a framework to evaluate recommenders from users' perspectives. They consider a variety of criteria including perceived system qualities, beliefs and attitudes, but do not take into account the influence from the recommender itself [23]. Compared with other existing frameworks, the user-centric evaluation framework proposed by Knijnenburg et al. [18] provides a structured model that covers all the factors in which we are interested, including both the objective factors of the recommender, as well as people's perception, experience and interaction, and personal and situational characteristics. We choose to use this framework, as described in the next section.

METHODOLOGY

Our goal is to investigate the effects of different factors on people's acceptance of location-privacy preference recommendations. To do this, we have designed an experiment based on the framework [18], which allows us to explore the relationships between various objective and subjective factors and the participants' acceptance.

User-centric evaluation of recommenders

In HRI, the evaluation of recommenders not only takes into account the objective factors (e.g. recommendation accuracy) but also the evaluation from the users' point of view (e.g. how good do the users think the recommender is). To study this, a valid framework is needed to precisely describe the factors of the evaluation by the users and build the relationships between these two parts. Knijnenburg et al. [18] have proposed a framework for such user-centric evaluation. The framework provides a way to measure the influences of the objective factors on the users' behaviours in HRI and these influences are considered to be moderated by users' subjective factors.

In this framework, a recommender is defined as a set of Objective System Aspects (OSA) that relate to the underlying recommendation algorithms and graphical user interfaces. OSAs influence the users' perception (e.g. perceived quality of the recommendations) of the recommender. To describe the users' subjective factors in the framework, their perception is defined through a set of Subjective System Aspects (SSA), which have influence on their Experience (EXP) (e.g. their satisfaction about their choices) and Interaction (INT) (e.g. purchasing the recommended products). The SSA is used as the moderators for the OSA's influence on EXP and

INT, which means the influence from OSA to EXP and INT is through SSA. The effects from the Situational Characteristics (SC) such as users' privacy concerns and from their Personal Characteristics (PC) such as demographics and domain knowledge to EXP and INT are also considered in this framework.

To apply this framework to location-privacy preference recommendations, we measure the following factors that might have an effect on acceptance of recommendations:

- *trust*: participants' general trust in technology.
- *quality*: participants' perceived quality of the recommended location-privacy preferences.
- *satisfaction*: participants' satisfaction about their chosen recommendations in the second part of experiment.
- *concern*: participants' privacy concern about using location-privacy preference recommenders.

Specifically we consider *trust* as PC, *quality* as SSA, *satisfaction* as EXP, and *concern* as SC. We use the different sources of crowdsourcing recommendations as conditions, i.e. OSA in the framework. We also introduce the participants' acceptance of the location-privacy preference recommendations into our model as an INT:

- *acceptance*: the percentage of the accepted location-privacy preference recommendations of a participant.

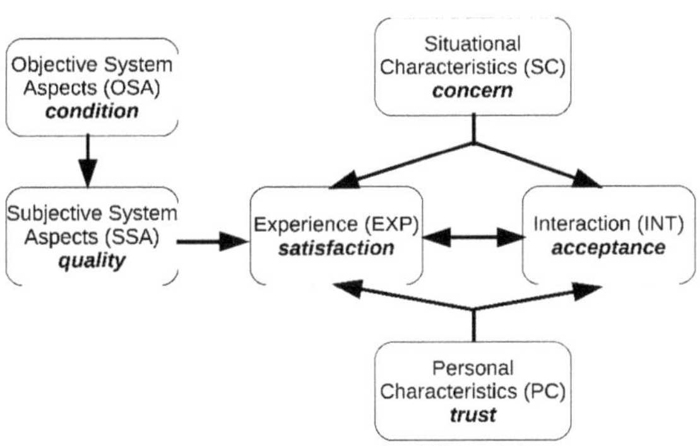

Figure 1. Diagram of the framework for the user-centric evaluation of recommenders as used in our experiment.

Figure 1 shows a diagram of how we apply this framework to privacy-preference recommenders.

Questionnaires

To evaluate the subjective factors in our experiment, we draw on the questionnaires provided by the framework [18]. To measure the above listed factors, we use the following questionnaires: *General trust in technology*, *Perceived recommendation quality*, *Choice satisfaction*, and *System-specific privacy concern* respectively. Each of these questionnaires contain several questions, each of which refers to a *question item*, measured on a five-point Likert scale from *Strongly disagree* to *Strongly agree*.

EXPERIMENTAL DESIGN

We hypothesise that people's acceptance of location-privacy preference recommendations change with different crowdsourcing sources, recommendations with different level of openness, and different contexts (i.e. location category and time). To test this, we conducted an experiment where people used three different location-privacy preference recommenders, and then studied which factors had an influence on their acceptance of the recommended location-privacy preferences.

Participants were invited to login with their Facebook accounts to our experimental system, so that our recommenders could use their real-world Facebook logins to generate recommendations. They were then provided with a prebriefing explaining the various recommenders, and how these recommenders could help with configuring privacy preferences. Next, they were presented with a series of recommendations about locations that existed in their Facebook location check-in histories (as shown in Figure 2). Each recommendation was presented as if it had been made using a particular source of data. For instance, in Figure 2 we see a recommendation that was generated using information from a participant's Facebook friends (in actual fact all recomendations were made randomly, so as to maintain objective accuracy without having it influence *quality*, *satisfaction*, or *acceptance*). Finally, participants were asked to complete a series of questionnaires about their perceived quality of the recommendations, their satisfaction, and system-specific concerns (as shown in Figure 3).

To recruit participants, we advertised our experiment through university mail lists and Facebook groups (to avoid biasing the samples, we used "location-sharing preference" instead of "location-privacy preference" in our experiment and advertisements). 164 participants tried to access our experiment and 99 of them had at least 10 distinct location check-in histories on their Facebook and completed the experiment. Each participant who completed the experiment received a £5 Amazon voucher for their participation. The study design was scrutinised and approved by our institutional ethics committee.

Prebriefing

Our prebriefing explained the various recommenders, which were:

- *same-location* recommender: using the preferences of people who have been to the same location;
- *similar-people* recommender: using the preferences of people who have similar previous location-sharing preferences;
- *Facebook-friends* recommender: using the preferences of people's Facebook friends.

Participants were provided with three examples to familiarise themselves with the recommenders, and a quiz was used to ensure that they understood the concepts. After successfully completing the quiz, participants were asked to login with their Facebook accounts using the PRISONER platform that has been designed for privacy-sensitive social media experiments [14]. This ensured that we would only collect the minimum amount of data required for our purposes. To make our proposed recommenders look realistic, we asked for additional permissions such as a Facebook friends list, even though this was not needed.

To guarantee that we had enough data to generate recommendations, only participants with more than ten distinct location check-ins could proceed to the next part of the experiment.

Exploring recommendations

The purpose of the second part of our experiment was to measure the participants' acceptance of the recommended location-privacy preferences. Firstly, participants were asked about their demographic information including age and gender. Then we used a questionnaire to measure *trust*, one of the subjective factors in our experiment. The other questionnaires about *quality*, *satisfaction*, and *concern* were shown after the participants went through all the recommendations because we want to know whether these factors would be influenced after the participants using different recommenders.

Conditions were altered on a within-subjects basis. Each participant was presented with 30 location-privacy preference recommendations (10 for each recommender). For each recommender, we randomly selected 10 location check-ins from the participant's Facebook data as the contexts of the recommendations. For each recommendation (Figure 2), the participant was provided with the context of their previous check-in, a map of the location of this check-in, and the recommended preference from one of our recommenders. The context contained the name of the location and the time slot (i.e. morning, noon, afternoon, evening, or night) of the check-in. The recommended preference (i.e. with whom the check-in was shared) is randomly selected among *Only Me*, *Friends*, *Friends of friends*, and *Public*. For each recommendation, we asked the participants if they would like to use the recommended preference in the future visit to the place at the certain time. To collect more realistic decisions about the recommendations, we have used real check-in data to make recommendations rather than using locations they have never visited.

Final questionnaires

In the third part of the experiment, we collected data on the participants' subjective factors when using our recommenders; specifically we collected data on *quality*, *satisfaction*, and *concern*. Participants were presented with seven questionnaires. The first six evaluated the *quality* and *satisfaction* of the various recommenders. When answering the questionnaires for a particular recommender, participants were shown with their choices to the recommendations from this recommender made in the second part of the experiment, to remind them with their decisions (Figure 3). One final questionnaire measured overall *concern* with the recommenders.

After answering all the questionnaires, in the last step, participants were given opportunities to provide free-text comments of their opinions and suggestions about our recommenders.

RESULTS

99 participants completed our experiment. Table 2 shows their demographic information.

Table 1. Demographic Information

Category	Options	Participants(%)	Facebook(%)
Gender	Female	63	51
	Male	37	49
Age	18-24	74	21
	25-34	24	27
	35-44	2	20
	45-54	0	16
	55+	0	16

Table 2. The demographics of our experiment (Participants) compared with the overall UK Facebook over-18 user population (Facebook). The Facebook data were taken from the Facebook Adverts Manager in October 2015.

Overall, we find a negative effect of *concern* on *acceptance*. For the objective factors of recommendations, the level of openness of the recommended location-privacy preferences and the contexts of the recommendation both influence people's acceptance. The source of crowdsourcing does not influence their acceptance significantly.

Analytical approaches

In our study, we consider *trust*, *quality*, *satisfaction*, and *concern* as the subjective factors. Each of these factors is evaluated using various question items in the questionnaires. Before we evaluate their effects on *acceptance*, we need to first establish their validity. We do this using Confirmatory Factor Analysis (CFA), which can establish both convergent and discriminant validity. Convergent validity ensures that the question items in the same questionnaire measure the same factor, while discriminant validity ensures that two different questionnaires measure two different factors. To maintain convergent validity, question items with low loadings (i.e. the R^2 value) may be removed until the average variance extracted (AVE[1]) from each factor is larger than 0.5. To maintain discriminant validity, if two factors are highly correlated, one of them will be removed. By applying CFA we can refine the answers to our questionnaires and increase the validity of the factors in our experiment.

To find out whether there are effects between different factors, we need to propose several hypotheses about these effects and test them to discover significant effects. Structural Equation Modeling (SEM) is an integrative modeling technique that tests all proposed hypotheses simultaneously. By applying SEM, we can combine and analyse the detected effects in an integrative structure that allows us to link all the detected effects together. In our experiment, we use Lavaan [24] to implement both the CFA and SEM analyses.

Privacy concerns lower acceptance of recommendations

We are interested in the effects of *concern*, *trust*, and conditions on *quality*, *satisfaction*, and *acceptance*.

[1]The AVE for a given factor is the average of the R^2 values of the factor's question items.

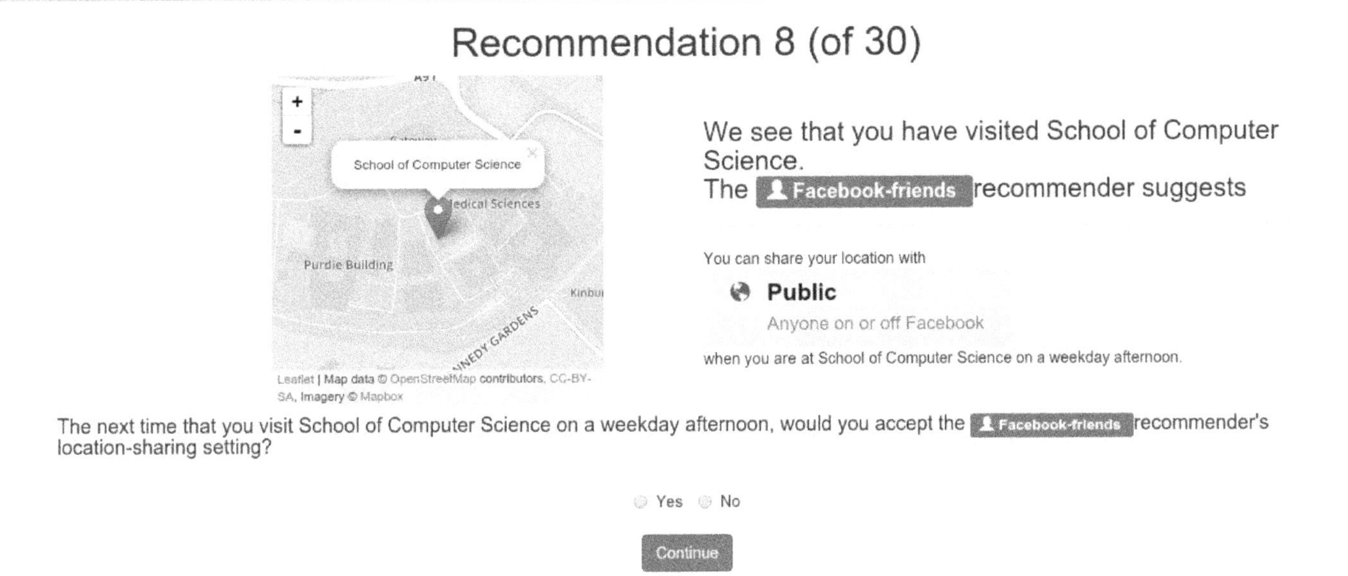

Figure 2. Each participant in our experiment was presented with 30 recommendations made by our 3 recommenders (10 recommendations from each recommender), and asked if they would accept the recommendation.

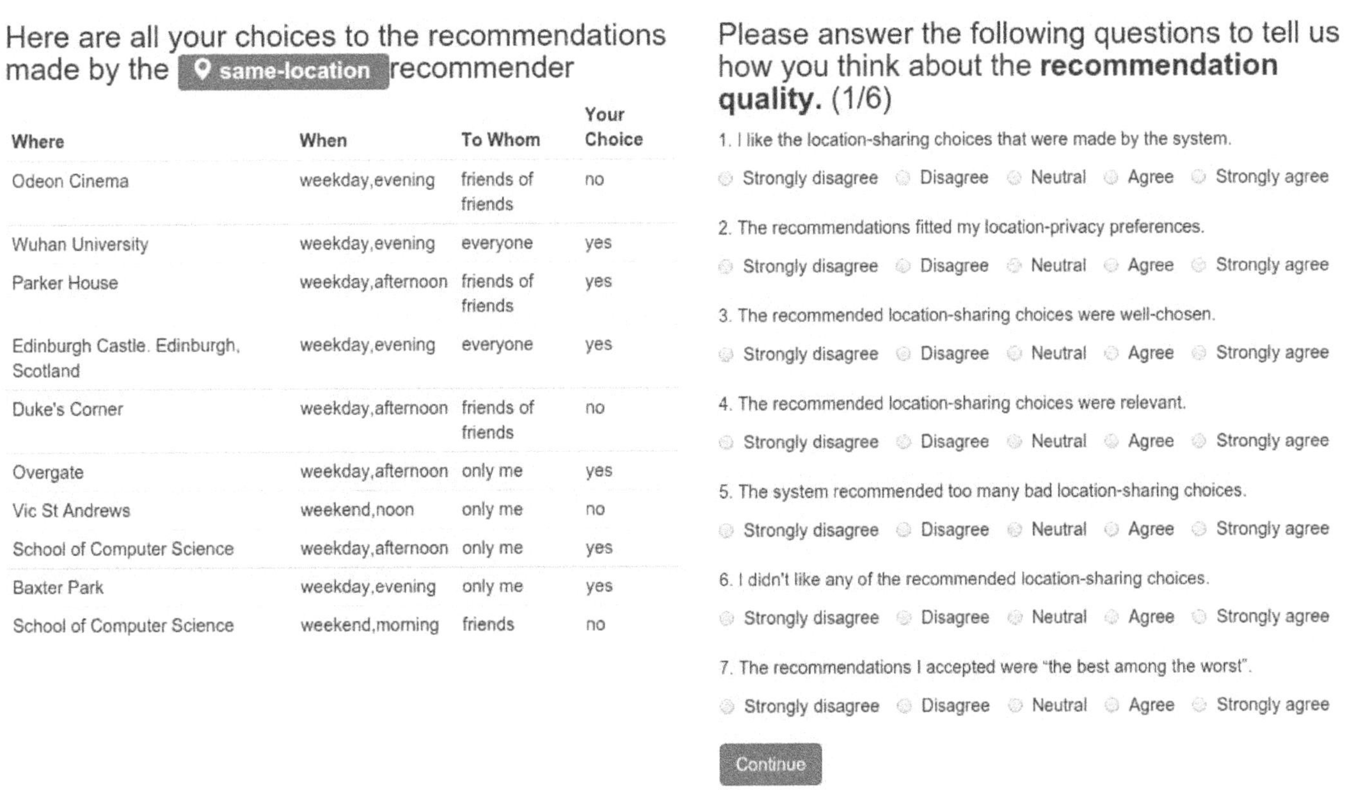

Where	When	To Whom	Your Choice
Odeon Cinema	weekday,evening	friends of friends	no
Wuhan University	weekday,evening	everyone	yes
Parker House	weekday,afternoon	friends of friends	yes
Edinburgh Castle, Edinburgh, Scotland	weekday,evening	everyone	yes
Duke's Corner	weekday,afternoon	friends of friends	no
Overgate	weekday,afternoon	only me	yes
Vic St Andrews	weekend,noon	only me	no
School of Computer Science	weekday,afternoon	only me	yes
Baxter Park	weekday,evening	only me	yes
School of Computer Science	weekend,morning	friends	no

Figure 3. Questionnaires were used to collect data on perceived recommendation quality (*quality*), satisfaction of choices (*satisfaction*), and concerns about our system (*concern*). Participants were also presented with their choices as a reminder.

Construct	Question items	R^2	AVE
Quality	I like the location-sharing choices that were made by the system.	0.858	
	The recommendations fitted my location-privacy preferences.	0.789	
	The recommended location-sharing choices were well-chosen.	0.822	
	The recommended location-sharing choices were relevant.	0.440	
	The system recommended too many bad location-sharing choices.	0.469	
	I didn't like any of the recommended location-sharing choices.	0.328	
	The recommendations I accepted were "the best among the worst".	0.321	**0.575**
Satisfaction	I like the recommendations that I've accepted.	0.510	
	Some of my chosen location-sharing choices could become part of my default location-privacy settings.	0.506	
	I would recommend some of the chosen location-sharing choices to others/friends.	0.544	**0.520**
Concern	I'm afraid that the system discloses private information about me.	0.470	
	The system invades my privacy.	0.861	
	I feel confident that the system respects my privacy.	0.586	
	I'm uncomfortable providing private data to the system.	0.524	
	I think the system respects the confidentiality of my data.	0.571	**0.602**

Table 3. Results of Confirmatory Factor Analysis (CFA). Question items with low R^2 values are removed in the refined results. The general trust to technology (*trust*) is removed because it only has two question items to keep its AVE greater than 0.5. Both the convergent validity and the discriminant validity of our model hold.

Table 3 shows the refined results of CFA after eliminating low-loading question items. *Trust* only has two question items to make its AVE larger than 0.5 and so it is eliminated from our later SEM analysis, as each factor needs at least 3 question items. Our model's convergent validity holds because the AVEs are greater than 0.5 and its discriminant validity holds too because all the correlations between two different factors are lower than the square roots of the AVEs of both the factors.

After refining the factors, we apply SEM to our refined factors by adding relationships between them. All answers to the question items are modeled as ordinal variables. We use the *same-location* recommender as the baseline condition and introduce two dummy variables *friends* and *similar* to represent the conditions of the *Facebook-friends* recommender and the *similar-people* recommender.

To avoid missing any significant relationships in the SEM model we analyse every possible relationship between factors: for *quality*, we study $quality \sim concern + similar + friends$; for *satisfaction*, we study $satisfaction \sim concern + similar + friends + quality$; and for *acceptance*, we study $acceptance \sim concern + quality + similar + friends + satisfaction$.[2] The fit[3] of our SEM model is adequate: $\chi^2_{125} = 483.67, p < 0.001$; $root\ mean\ squared\ error\ of\ approximation\ (RMSEA) = 0.098$; $Comparative\ Fit\ Index\ (CFI) = 0.977$; $Turker-Lewis\ Index\ (TLI) = 0.972$.

Figure 4 shows four significant ($p < 0.001$) effects in our SEM analysis. *Concern* (SC) has a negative effect on both the *quality* (SSA) and the *satisfaction* (EXP), which means that people with higher privacy concerns about our recommenders perceive lower quality of our recommendations and are less satisfied about their choices. *Quality* acts as a mediator between *concern* and *acceptance* (INT), influencing *acceptance* positively. Another positive effect is from *quality* to *satisfaction*.

Our experimental results indicate that people's **privacy concerns** about location-privacy preference recommendations play an important role when they use such recommenders. We regress all of the "Neutral" answers in our *concern* questionnaire into a baseline *concern* and regress all of the participants' answers to their *concern* factors. We find that 44% of these participants have higher *concern* than the baseline. Their privacy concerns about using our recommenders have a negative influence on their acceptance (mediated by their perceived quality) and their satisfactions about their choices (both directly related and mediated by their perceived quality). Location-privacy preferences are inherently sensitive because they contain both location information and people's privacy settings (i.e. whether they share, and if so, to whom they share the locations). Hence it is not surprising that *concern* influences both *acceptance* and *satisfaction*.

We do not find significant effects from *friends* (OSA) or *similar* (OSA) on *quality*, *satisfaction*, nor *acceptance*. In other words, our participants do not perceive the qualities of the recommended location-privacy preferences to be different even when we claimed that they were made from different crowdsourcing sources.

Openness and context affect acceptance

In addition to the conditions (i.e. the source of crowdsourcing) that were controlled in our experiment, we consider other factors that may influence participants' acceptance of recommendations. These include the level of openness of the recommended location-privacy preferences, and the contexts of the recommendations.

[2] *Trust* was eliminated at the CFA stage.

[3] The cut-off values of good fit proposed by Hu and Bentler [13] are: $CFI > 0.96, TLI > 0.95, RMSEA < 0.05$. However, Kenny et al. [16] recommend not computing the RMSEA for models with small degree of freedom and small sample sizes.

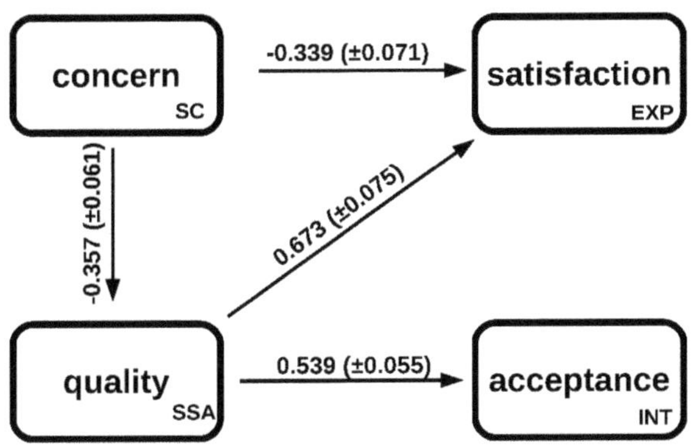

Figure 4. The structured equation modeling (SEM) results. $p < 0.001$ for all coefficients. Numbers above arrows mean the $\beta - weight(\pm standard\ error)$ of the effect. *Standard deviation* = 1. **The *concern* has negative effects on *acceptance* (moderated by *quality*) and *satisfaction* (directly and moderated by *quality*).**

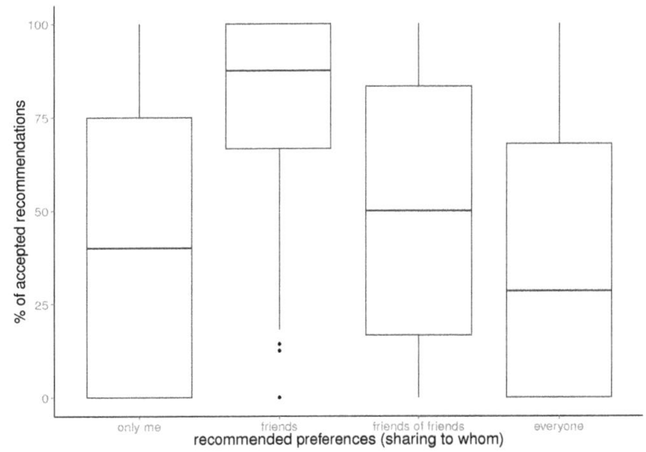

Figure 5. Distribution of all participants' acceptance (the percentage of accepted recommendations) of different recommended location-privacy preferences (sharing to whom). The least open preference (*only me*) and the most open preference (*everyone*) are least accepted. For the sharing-preferences (i.e. *friends*, *friends of friends*, and *everyone*), the less open preference is more accepted. (ANOVA: $F = 33.45, df = 3, p < 0.001$)

We evaluate the different acceptance of the recommended preferences for different levels of openness (i.e. with whom the recommender suggests a location is shared). Figure 5 shows the distribution of decisions for levels of openness from very low (sharing with only myself) to high (sharing with the public). The preference with the highest openness has the lowest acceptance, which means people are less likely to accept highly open location-privacy preference recommendations. Nevertheless, the preference with the lowest openness (sharing to only me) also has low acceptance. This means that people not only consider privacy issues, but also care about the benefits (e.g. social needs) from sharing their locations. For example, one of our participants' feedback includes:

- "... if i (*sic*) would only share something to 'only me', then why would i (*sic*) share at all?"

When the benefits are guaranteed (i.e. sharing to someone), the recommendations of low openness location-privacy preferences get higher acceptance.

To study context, we manually analyse the categories given by Facebook of all the locations in our recommendations and merge similar categories with each other. By this means, we have four categories: *Entertainment*, *Residential*, *School/University/Library*, and *Transport*. For the time dimension, we use the five time slots from our previous work [29]: *morning* (07:00–11:59), *noon* (12:00–13:59), *afternoon* (14:00–16:59), *evening* (17:00–20:59), and *night* (21:00–06:59).

Figure 6 shows that for different contexts, our participants have different acceptance of the recommended location-privacy preferences (two-way ANOVA to examine the interaction effect of time and location: $F = 2.039, df = 12, p < 0.05$). In all of the time slots, recommendations for *School/University/Library* locations are most accepted. Since we advertised our experiment through university mail lists and university Facebook groups, we believe that the majority of our participants are university students. This implies that our participants accept our recommendations mostly in the contexts where they conduct regular daily lives. The *Transport* category experiences the lowest acceptance of recommendations in the three time slots including *morning*, *noon*, and *afternoon*. Comments made by participants may explain this:

- "... for example, I was at the airport. This informs all Facebook users that I will be away for potentially a longer period of time than usual and could put myself at greater risk of property theft etc. ..."
- "... I think a better recommender could consider sharing a place by how regularly you go there or how far from where you normally are it is ie how exotic it is."

It appears that the **regularity** of contexts and the **potential risks** caused by the false positive location-privacy preference recommendations (i.e. sharing the locations which people do not want to share) in different contexts have influences on people's acceptance. We plan to study these questions in future research.

DISCUSSION

We find several effects from both objective and subjective factors on people's acceptance of location-privacy preference recommendations in our user study. We combine these effects together in Figure 7.

As shown in Figure 7, our aim is to design a system where people have both high acceptance of the recommended location-privacy preference and high satisfaction of their choices. These are listed in the left box that represents users' subjective factors. Since we cannot directly manipulate these subjective factors, a system designer must measure the influential objective factors (the right box) and adjust recommendation strategies to making recommendations that people are more likely to accept. Our experimental results indi-

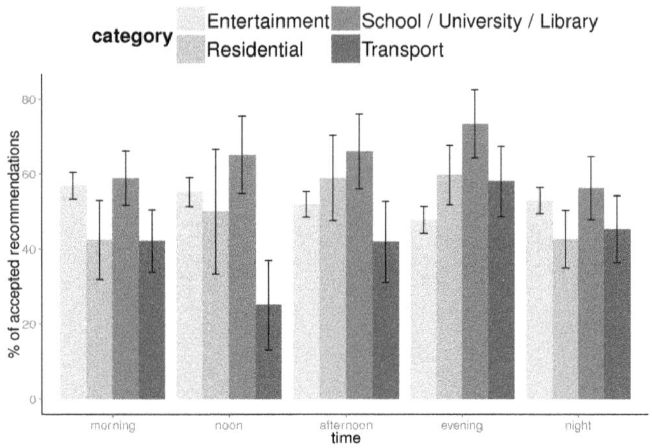

Figure 6. Participants' acceptance of the recommendations made for different location categories. For each time slot, our participants have the highest acceptance of recommended location-privacy preferences in the *School/University/Library* category, which is the most regular context for them (two-way ANOVA: $F = 2.039, df = 12, p < 0.05$).

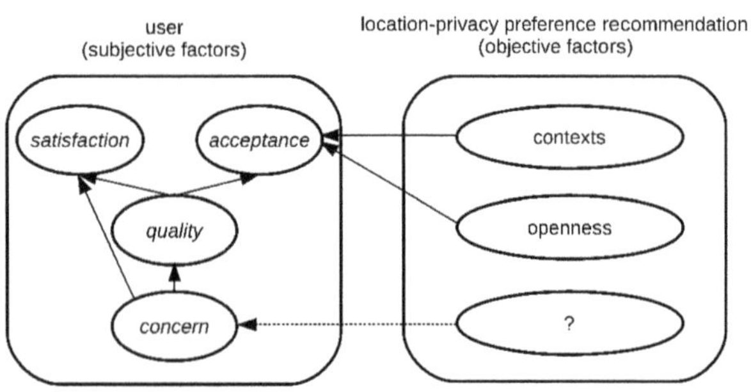

Figure 7. The effects of the subjective factors (left side) of users and the objective factors (right side) of location-privacy preference recommendations. The arrows in solid line mean the detected effects in our experimental results. The dash line means a potential effect from an unknown objective factor (marked as ?) to *concern*. Recommender system designers can only control the objective factors on the right side to influence the subjective factors on the left side.

cate that the contexts of the recommendations and the level of openness of the recommendations, which can be measured by recommender designers, will influence the *acceptance*. We therefore suggest that these two factors should be taken into account in the implementation of location-privacy preference recommenders. In addition, we found the effect from the *concern* on the left side, but we do not know the factors (marked as ? in Figure 7) on the right side that can influence the *concern*, which is our future work. We now discuss our recommendations in further detail.

Be cautious about the level of openness

The first effect we find is the openness of the recommended location privacy preferences. To our surprise, the lowest-openness recommendations do not receive the highest acceptance. In fact, the acceptance of the lowest-openness recommendation is the second lowest and the highest-openness recommendation has the lowest acceptance. This means that people are not likely to give up the benefits of sharing their locations for complete location-privacy, nor vice versa. This suggests that location-privacy recommenders should be careful with such extreme recommendations. When extreme recommendations are made, additional information, such as explanations or request for consent, might be necessary to increase people's acceptance. Meanwhile, overexposing recommendations would decrease people's acceptance. To avoid this happening, enabling people to control the maximum openness that they allow the recommender to make is also a possible solution. This is supported by our participants' feedback:

- "If the system had a 'never share publicly' option that would work best for my preferences. ..."
- "There should be a 'maximum exposure' option ..."

In addition, customised recommendations that can provide finer-grained openness might also be beneficial:

- "..., however I would like some more customization. ..."
- "The recommenders should take into account the preferences I've set in the past."
- "Would need to learn a bit more about my own preferences as well as aggregating those from other sources to be useful for me."

An outstanding research challenge for customisation is how to make recommendations by using different types of customised preferences because people may have different ways to categorise and name the recipients of their location.

Recommendations should be context-aware

The second effect we find is from the contexts for the recommendations. We observed that our participants have higher acceptance of recommended location-privacy preferences in their most regular context than others. Combined with our post-experiment feedback, we postulate that the **regularity** of and the **potential risks** (e.g. being away from home for a long time) of overexposure in different contexts may also influence people's acceptance. In future work, we plan to investigate these factors in more detail. But our current results imply that system designers may wish to let users choose in which contexts they want to use the recommender, or tune recommendations to context. We also suggest that recommenders in other domain such as mobile application recommendations may be context-aware [3], since there are evidences from existing research [4] indicate that people's mobile application usage is highly dynamic with contexts

Recommenders must consider privacy and security

Our experimental results demonstrate that 44% of our participants have privacy concerns when using our recommenders and this concern has a negative effect on their acceptance of the recommended location-privacy preferences and their satisfactions about their choices. People may decide that providing their privacy preferences to a recommender is risky due to its higher sensitivity than other preferences. This type of concern is the *concern* in our experiment. Thus it is necessary to implement location-privacy preference recommenders in a privacy-aware fashion [29].

In addition to privacy, users may also be concerned about security. Recommenders are vulnerable to a series of attacks due to their open structure. One example is the shilling attack [10], which means the malicious users might be able to inject fake profiles and preferences to influence the outcome. Attacks may also be passive, such as the inference attack [5], which means the attackers might be able to infer the location-privacy preferences of certain target users by passively observing the change of the recommendations with the help of some auxiliary information. Additional work is needed to investigate whether these vulnerabilities would contribute to people's concerns and decrease their likelihood of contributing their data to the system. Accordingly, it is important to find solutions to detect and alleviate these attacks.

LIMITATIONS

In our experiment, we find the effects from both the subjective and objective factors on people's acceptance of location-privacy preference recommendations. That said, we note some limitations in our experiment that we hope to overcome in our future work.

First, to ensure the participants were familiar with the contexts of the recommendations, for each participant, we only used their own location check-in history as the contexts for making recommendations. Compared with asking them to consider the recommendations hypothetically in some places they have never been, the answers through our method are more likely to reflect their true decisions. This means, however, that we failed to evaluate their acceptance of the recommended location-privacy settings when they actually enter new places. In future work, we hope to deploy our recommender in real world environments and evaluate people's acceptance of recommended location-privacy preferences *in situ*.

A second limitation is that we used a random recommendation generator rather than real recommenders. This was done to keep the objective quality of the recommendations the same for all participants, since the performance of real recommendations for a specific user could be influenced by the quality of their own preference. By using the same random recommender for all participants, we could ensure that all the changes we observed were due to the changes that we controlled. As a consequence, the overall performance of the recommendations was impacted inevitably. Since the source of crowdsourcing was shown to not have an influence on people's acceptance when the recommenders have the same performance, it would be useful to investigate which crowdsourcing source has the best objective performance when deploying a system in the real world.

CONCLUSIONS

In this paper, we conduct an online user experiment to investigate which objective and subjective factors influence people's acceptance of location-privacy preference recommendations. Our results show that the openness of the recommended location-privacy preferences and the contexts of the recommendations both have effects. Meanwhile, people's privacy concerns about using our recommenders have a negative influence on their acceptance of the recommended location-privacy preferences and the satisfaction about their choices. Compared with existing research focusing on the objective performance (i.e. recommendation accuracy), our work sheds light on the parameters that system designers might want to control and the issues which need to solved when designing location-privacy preference recommenders in order to make them more acceptable to users.

Our future plans are to investigate solutions, both technical and social, for alleviating the security and privacy issues that affect users' concerns about privacy preference recommenders. We believe that this will result in systems that are both technically better, and better accepted by users.

REFERENCES

1. D. Anthony, T. Henderson, and D. Kotz. Privacy in Location-Aware Computing Environments. *IEEE Pervasive Computing*, 6(4):64–72, Oct. 2007. doi:10.1109/MPRV.2007.83.

2. G. Bigwood, F. Ben Abdesslem, and T. Henderson. Predicting Location-Sharing Privacy Preferences in Social Network Applications. In *Proceedings of the First Workshop on recent advances in behavior prediction and proactive pervasive computing (AwareCast)*, 2012.

3. M. Böhmer, G. Bauer, and A. Krüger. Exploring the design space of context-aware recommender systems that suggest mobile applications. In *2nd Workshop on Context-Aware Recommender Systems (CARS)*, 2010.

4. M. Böhmer, B. Hecht, J. Schöning, A. Krüger, and G. Bauer. Falling asleep with Angry Birds, Facebook and Kindle: A Large Scale Study on Mobile Application Usage. In *Proceedings of MobileHCI 2011*, pages 47–56, 2011. doi:10.1145/2037373.2037383.

5. J. a. Calandrino, A. Kilzer, A. Narayanan, E. W. Felten, and V. Shmatikov. "You might also like:" Privacy risks of collaborative filtering. *Proceedings of the IEEE Symposium on Security and Privacy*, pages 231–246, 2011. doi:10.1109/SP.2011.40.

6. S. Das, T. H.-J. Kim, L. A. Dabbish, and J. I. Hong. The Effect of Social Influence on Security Sensitivity. In *Proceedings of SOUPS'14*, July 2014.

7. C. Dong, H. Jin, and B. P. Knijnenburg. Predicting Privacy Behavior on Online Social Networks. In *Proceedings of ICWSM*, pages 91–100, 2015.

8. L. Fang and K. LeFevre. Privacy wizards for social networking sites. In *Proceedings of the WWW conference*, page 351, 2010. doi:10.1145/1772690.1772727.

9. S. Furnell. Managing privacy settings: lots of options, but beyond control? *Computer Fraud & Security*, 2015(4):8–13, Apr. 2015. doi:10.1016/S1361-3723(15)30027-0.

10. I. Gunes, C. Kaleli, A. Bilge, and H. Polat. Shilling attacks against recommender systems: a comprehensive survey. *Artificial Intelligence Review*, 42(4):767–799, Dec. 2014. doi:10.1007/s10462-012-9364-9.

11. J. L. Harman, J. O'Donovan, T. Abdelzaher, and C. Gonzalez. Dynamics of human trust in recommender systems. In *Proceedings of RecSys 2014*, pages 305–308, 2014. doi:10.1145/2645710.2645761.

12. B. Henne, C. Kater, and M. Smith. On Usable Location Privacy for Android with Crowd-Recommendations. In *Proceedings of TRUST 2014*, pages 74–82, 2014. doi:10.1007/978-3-319-08593-7_5.

13. L. Hu and P. M. Bentler. Cutoff criteria for fit indexes in covariance structure analysis: Conventional criteria versus new alternatives. *Structural Equation Modeling: A Multidisciplinary Journal*, 6(1):1–55, Jan. 1999. doi:10.1080/10705519909540118.

14. L. Hutton and T. Henderson. An architecture for ethical and privacy-sensitive social network experiments. *ACM SIGMETRICS Performance Evaluation Review*, 40(4):90–95, Apr. 2013. doi:10.1145/2479942.2479954.

15. Q. Ismail, T. Ahmed, A. Kapadia, and M. K. Reiter. Crowdsourced Exploration of Security Configurations. In *Proceedings of CHI 2015*, pages 467–476, 2015. doi:10.1145/2702123.2702370.

16. D. A. Kenny, B. Kaniskan, and D. B. McCoach. The Performance of RMSEA in Models With Small Degrees of Freedom. *Sociological Methods & Research*, 44(3):486–507, Aug. 2015. doi:10.1177/0049124114543236.

17. B. P. Knijnenburg and H. Jin. The persuasive effect of privacy recommendations for location sharing services. In *SIGHCI 2013 Proceedings*, 2013. doi:10.2139/ssrn.2399725.

18. B. P. Knijnenburg, M. C. Willemsen, Z. Gantner, H. Soncu, and C. Newell. Explaining the user experience of recommender systems. *User Modeling and User-Adapted Interaction*, 22(4-5):441–504, Oct. 2012. doi:10.1007/s11257-011-9118-4.

19. J. Lindqvist, J. Cranshaw, J. Wiese, J. Hong, and J. Zimmerman. I'm the mayor of my house: Examining Why People Use foursquare - a Social-Driven Location Sharing Application. In *Proceedings of CHI 2011*, pages 2409–2418, 2011. doi:10.1145/1978942.1979295.

20. M. Madejski, M. Johnson, and S. M. Bellovin. A study of privacy settings errors in an online social network. In *2012 IEEE International Conference on Pervasive Computing and Communications Workshops*, pages 340–345, Mar. 2012. doi:10.1109/PerComW.2012.6197507.

21. S. M. McNee, J. Riedl, and J. A. Konstan. Making recommendations better: an analytic model for human-recommender interaction. In *Proceedings of the CHI 2006 extended abstracts*, pages 1103–1108, 2006. doi:10.1145/1125451.1125660.

22. K. D. Naini, I. S. Altingovde, R. Kawase, E. Herder, and C. Niederée. Analyzing and Predicting Privacy Settings in the Social Web. In *Proceedings of UMAP 2015*, pages 104–117, 2015. doi:10.1007/978-3-319-20267-9_9.

23. P. Pu, L. Chen, and R. Hu. A user-centric evaluation framework for recommender systems. In *Proceedings of RecSys 2011*, pages 157–164, 2011. doi:10.1145/2043932.2043962.

24. Y. Rosseel. lavaan: An R Package for Structural Equation Modeling. *Journal of Statistical Software*, 48(2), 2012. doi:10.18637/jss.v048.i02.

25. N. Sadeh, J. Hong, L. Cranor, I. Fette, P. Kelley, M. Prabaker, and J. Rao. Understanding and capturing people's privacy policies in a mobile social networking application. *Personal and Ubiquitous Computing*, 13(6):401–412, Aug. 2009. doi:10.1007/s00779-008-0214-3.

26. J. Staiano, N. Oliver, B. Lepri, R. de Oliveira, M. Caraviello, and N. Sebe. MoneyWalks: A Human-Centric Study on the Economics of Personal Mobile Data. In *Proceedings of UbiComp 2014*, pages 583–594, 2014. doi:10.1145/2632048.2632074.

27. E. Toch. Crowdsourcing privacy preferences in context-aware applications. *Personal and Ubiquitous Computing*, 18(1):129–141, Dec. 2012. doi:10.1007/s00779-012-0632-0.

28. J. Xie, B. P. Knijnenburg, and H. Jin. Location sharing privacy preference: analysis and personalized recommendation. In *Proceedings of IUI 2014*, pages 189–198, 2014. doi:10.1145/2557500.2557504.

29. Y. Zhao, J. Ye, and T. Henderson. Privacy-aware Location Privacy Preference Recommendations. In *Proceedings of Mobiquitous 2014*, pages 120–129, 2014. doi:10.4108/icst.mobiquitous.2014.258017.

30. A. H. Zins and U. Bauernfeind. Explaining Online Purchase Planning Experiences with Recommender Websites. In *Information and Communication Technologies in Tourism 2005*, pages 137–148, 2005. doi:10.1007/3-211-27283-6_13.

Data Portraits and Intermediary Topics: Encouraging Exploration of Politically Diverse Profiles

Eduardo Graells-Garrido*
Telefónica I+D
Santiago, Chile

Mounia Lalmas
Yahoo Labs
London, UK

Ricardo Baeza-Yates
Yahoo Labs
Sunnyvale, USA

ABSTRACT

In micro-blogging platforms, people connect and interact with others. However, due to cognitive biases, they tend to interact with like-minded people and read agreeable information only. Many efforts to make people connect with those who think differently have not worked well. In this paper, we hypothesize, first, that previous approaches have not worked because they have been direct – they have tried to explicitly connect people with those having opposing views on sensitive issues. Second, that neither recommendation or presentation of information by themselves are enough to encourage behavioral change. We propose a platform that mixes a recommender algorithm and a visualization-based user interface to explore recommendations. It recommends politically diverse profiles in terms of distance of latent topics, and displays those recommendations in a visual representation of each user's personal content. We performed an "in the wild" evaluation of this platform, and found that people explored more recommendations when using a biased algorithm instead of ours. In line with our hypothesis, we also found that the mixture of our recommender algorithm and our user interface, allowed politically interested users to exhibit an unbiased exploration of the recommended profiles. Finally, our results contribute insights in two aspects: first, which individual differences are important when designing platforms aimed at behavioral change; and second, which algorithms and user interfaces should be mixed to help users avoid cognitive mechanisms that lead to biased behavior.

ACM Classification Keywords

H.4.3 Information Storage and Retrieval: Information Search and Retrieval—*Information Filtering*; H.5.2 Information Interfaces and Presentation: User Interfaces—*Graphical user interfaces (GUI)*

Author Keywords

Homophily; Selective Exposure; Recommender Systems; Information Visualization.

*Corresponding author: **eduardo.graells@telefonica.com**. Work primarily carried out while the first author was a PhD student in the Web Research Group, at Universitat Pompeu Fabra, Barcelona, Spain.

IUI 2016, March 7–10, 2016, Sonoma, CA, USA.

ACM 978-1-4503-4137-0/16/03 ...$15.00.
DOI: http://dx.doi.org/10.1145/2856767.2856776

INTRODUCTION

Research from social sciences has shown that, while everyone seems to have a voice on the Web, people tend to listen and connect to those with similar beliefs in political and ideological issues. Such behavior can be explained in terms of homophily [44], a cognitive bias. Homophily is present in many situations and can be beneficial, as communication with culturally alike people is easier to handle. However, with respect to ideological issues it can have serious consequences, both off- and on-line. On one hand, groups of like-minded users tend to disconnect from other groups, polarizing group views [58]. On the other hand, Web platforms recommend and adapt content based on interaction and network data of users, *i. e.*, who is connected to them and what they have liked before. Because one of their main goals is to maximize user engagement, recommendation algorithms often push content that reinforces homophily in behavior by displaying mostly agreeable information. Such biased reinforcement, in turn, makes further recommendations consisting of even more polarized content, confining users to *filter bubbles* [48].

Until now, most approaches have focused on how to motivate users to read challenging information or how to motivate a change in behavior through recommender systems and display of potentially challenging information. This direct approach has not been effective as users often do not value diversity or do not feel satisfied with it [46]. Motivated by this scenario, our work aims at understanding how to encourage exposure to diverse people from an ideological point of view on micro-blogging platforms. Our research questions are:

Is it possible to encourage exploration and acceptance of user profiles recommended on the basis of political diversity? If so, which factors influence this behavior?

We propose an indirect approach using an advanced user interface, because we believe that neither a recommender system nor a user interface alone are enough to encourage unbiased behavior. Our hypothesis is that an indirect, mixed approach helps users to overcome the cognitive dissonance produced by exposure to potentially challenging information.

To achieve this mixed approach, our work combines the output of a recommender algorithm with a visual depiction. The recommender algorithm is aimed at recommending people who may think differently based on a proxy latent space modeling of topics, named *intermediary topics* [31]. Intermediary topics are latent topics that users, with distant views on some sensitive issues, have in common (*e. g.*, a music genre, a cuisine type). These topics are our means to introduce users to each other, knowing that first impressions matter [4], thus giving connection a chance to happen.

The visual depiction is aimed, first, at providing a pleasing and joyful view of the user's own interests, and then to provide a visual display of recommended profiles. Particularly, our proposal is a visualization of user profiles called *data portrait* [20], with the purpose of making users aware of their own interests and the image they project on a social platform. The visualization of recommendations – of people to "follow" – is based on a hierarchical visualization technique displaying how *recommendees* can be grouped. Both concepts allow users to receive recommendations in the context of their data portrait.

Our system was deployed "in the wild" to evaluate its effects on users, using a proof-of-concept implementation of a recommender system based on the intermediary topics paradigm. We focused on Chile, a Latin-American country with one of the highest Internet penetration rates among developing countries [13], and whose population actively discuss politics on Twitter [60]. As found in a previous study, such discussion is homophilic [28], making it a good candidate for analysis. We analyzed how Chilean users interact with their portraits and explore the recommendations within the realm of *Casual Information Visualization* [52]. We did not frame our evaluation using specific tasks to be performed by users, as these would not reflect scenarios for our system. Instead, we analyzed user behavior employing user engagement metrics [41], as these are more appropriate for studying non-goal oriented user behaviors. The main results of our experiment are:

- The usage of visualization to depict recommendations alongside a data portrait allowed users to explore more recommended profiles, regardless of the recommender algorithm used to generate them.
- Behavioral differences in terms of political involvement influenced how users interacted and engaged with our system.
- On a standalone basis, neither recommender system or visualization help users to exhibit a conscious (unbiased) exploration. However, their combination is effective when users have political content in their profiles.

These results have implications on the design of systems aimed at exploring user generated content: a one-size-fits-all approach misses the opportunity of giving users tools to get the best out of their exploring experience. We discuss design implications in terms of who can be targeted with systems like ours and when to consider presenting diverse recommendations. Our main conclusion is that indirect approaches like these data portraits can help users to make conscious decisions in these biased scenarios.

RELATED WORK

Homophily and Content Recommendation

Homophily is the tendency to form ties with similar others, where similarity can be bound to factors ranging from socio-demographic to behavioral and intra-personal ones [44]. In micro-blogging platforms, the presence of homophily in how individuals interact has been shown to be reflected in the structure of their ego-network, which has allowed to predict user attributes [1, 56], including political leaning [7]. Likewise, its presence has been used to recommend people to interact with [14, 35].

In this paper, we focus on recommendations on micro-blogging platforms based on user similarity. Similarity can be defined in different ways. For instance, two users might be similar if they use the same *hashtags* [12], follow the same accounts [26], mention the same entities [45], or have similar *latent topics* [53] as estimated using Latent Dirichlet Allocation (LDA hereafter) [9]. However, similarity is not the only feature to consider when recommending information or people to follow. Other features include content quality and popularity [15], network relevance (*friend of a friend*) [14], explainability [40], and centrality measures [34].

In our work, we propose *intermediary topics* [31] as a feature to consider when recommending users to follow. The intuition behind intermediary topics is that they focus on homophily on the basis of specific shared latent topics computed using LDA [9]. LDA has been found to be reliable for user classification [51], and in our context, it has successfully identified latent topics that could act as intermediary between people with diverse political profiles [28].

Using topics and relationships between them, represented through the so-called *topic graphs*, for recommendation purposes is not new. For instance, Gretarsson *et al.* [33] visualize topic graphs to ease knowledge discovery. Our context is different. We do not attempt to visualize them; instead, we use the intermediary topics as input features for generating the recommendations. We nonetheless experiment with visual depiction of recommendations, through the paradigm of data portraits, because the visualization of social recommendations has been shown to boost user satisfaction [32].

Encouraging Exposure to Diverse Content

Exposure to exclusively agreeable information or like-minded people reinforces and polarizes individual and group stances on ideological issues [47, 59]. Various works have looked into ways to improve the exposure to challenging information, by employing algorithms for content selection, as well as changing the depiction of this type of information. The degrees of success vary, but results have not been as good as expected in terms of behavioral change.

Opinion Space [23] is a self-organizing interactive visualization of an information space. In it, individual opinions of participants in debate were visualized according to their *opinion profiles*, built automatically for each participant after answering questions about key political issues. Although the visual approach did not reduce selective exposure, it generated more engagement than baseline text-based interfaces and users were more respectful with those having opposite opinions. In *NewsCube* [49], several automatically determined aspects of news stories in political contexts are presented to allow users to access diverse points of view of news events in political contexts. Each aspect is displayed in its own cluster, allowing users to see the diversity of available points of view. This clustered presentation augments the number of interactions with news, but not the number of interactions with different, opposing, clusters [16]. Munson *et al.* [46] tested different ways of altering a user interface without changing its core interaction mechanisms, by changing the sorting order of information and highlighting items pertaining to opposite points of view with respect to the user. It was found that only a minority of users, called *diversity-aware*, values diversity. In discussion forums, Liao *et al.* [42] added *position indicators* of stance polarization to participants, improving agreement of users with those of opposing views when their positions were not consistently moderate, or when the information seekers were looking for highly accurate information.

One possible reason of why direct approaches have not worked is the *selective exposure* [37] mechanism. Selective exposure makes users discard potentially challenging information, either by not reading it, not accepting the recommendation, or preferring an agreeable alternative, regardless of the factual value of the agreeable information item. Through selective exposure, users avoid *cognitive dissonance* [24], a state of discomfort that affects persons confronted with conflicting ideas, beliefs, values or emotional reactions. Thus, if users were to receive recommendations of users who think differently, the selective exposure mechanism would likely prevent them for even browsing the recommendations.

In our work, we apply an indirect approach, where we use intermediary topics [31] to recommend people with potentially distant opinions (as captured by LDA), and yet with specific interests in common. In contrast to the approaches above mentioned, the recommendations are not based on their (non)-alignment on politics or sensitive issues. Instead, we build a data portrait of users of micro-blogging platforms, and show recommendations in that context, emphasizing the similarity of users in terms of their alignment on intermediary topics.

Information Visualization

Our work is related to the field known as *Casual Information Visualization*, defined by Pousman *et al.* [52] as *"the use of computer mediated tools to depict personally meaningful information in visual ways that support everyday users in both everyday work and non-work situations."* The focus on everyday situations means that there does not need to be a concrete task to be completed, nor a specific analytic insight to be expected.

Yi *et al.* [67] identify four cognitive processes that lead to insights gained through visualization: *provide overview*, *adjust*, *detect pattern*, and *match mental model*. Those relevant to our context are *provide overview* and *match mental model*. To provide an overview of profiles and match mental models of portrayed users, we use *word clouds* as the primary element of our proposed visualization. Word clouds have a long history in information visualization [63]. Although not appropriate for analytical tasks, word clouds are expressive, familiar, and popular with users, as they help them expressing themselves [64]. We use word clouds both to provide an overview of a profile and as a navigational tool to explore it, in a coordinated view with other visual elements of the portrait.

Other visualization techniques such as *WordTrees* [65] and *PhraseNets* [61] have been employed to depict structure in text. Although we model data portraits as bipartite graphs between user interests (keywords) and user generated content (micro-posts), we do not focus on relations between words nor the text structure, and thus, we use *word clouds* instead of any of the above mentioned techniques.

Visualization of micro-blog data covers a wide range of applications, including event monitoring [21, 43], visual analysis [19], group content analysis [3], and ego-networks [39]. We use *data portraits* [20] to visually represent user profiles. Data portraits are *"abstract representations of users' interaction history"* [66], and have been built for personal informatics systems [5], Twitter profiles [22] and discussion forums [66], among others. Particularly, we borrow heavily from the work of Viégas *et al.* [62] in visualizing e-mail archives. E-mail archives are "known datasets", and users have expectations of what they will find on such portraits. If those expectations are fulfilled, the enjoyment of the application is greater. In addition, by reflecting on their past, users discover unknown patterns about themselves and their relationships. We rely on this potential enjoyment and discovery to provide a positive experience for users, as a way to mitigate the cognitive dissonance that could be caused by our recommendations.

Graphical techniques used in recommendation contexts include controllable Venn-diagrams [50], network graphs [32, 33], *dust and magnet* [2], and compound graphs [27]. These are targeted at either expert users who know how to control such visualizations, or task-based systems. Instead, similarly to the *Hax* application [57], we propose *circle packing*, a hierarchical visualization technique [17], to create a casual and user friendly depiction of our generated recommendations, as it does not rely on user-controllability nor user expertise. However, differently from *Hax*, which builds a user interface to find audiences to broadcast information, our user interface allows users to find people to interact with.

METHODS AND DESIGN RATIONALE

For our work, we consider the micro-blogging platform Twitter, where users publish micro-posts known as *tweets*, each having a maximum length of 140 characters. Each user can *follow* other users, making their tweets available in his/her own *timeline*. Because of homophily [44], people tend to connect with like-minded individuals and do not think of the possible benefits of connecting with people of different (including opposing) opinions in sensitive issues. We design an intelligent system that recommends people to a target user, to study: (1) what factors affect the exploration and acceptance of recommendations built having politically diverse profiles into consideration, and (2) how to encourage unbiased behavior.

We introduce a data portrait design used in conjunction with a recommendation algorithm to recommend politically diverse profiles who share intermediary topics [28, 31]. Although the data portrait is about each user's own data, we use it as a context to visually present the generated recommendations.

Portraying People's Data

Data portraits [20] can be used to create a self-image to present the target user. Based on the enjoyment and self-reflection experimented in "known data" scenarios [62], our rationale is that we reinforce the non-conflicting interests of users when browsing their own profiles, while allowing to contextualize recommendations according to these interests.

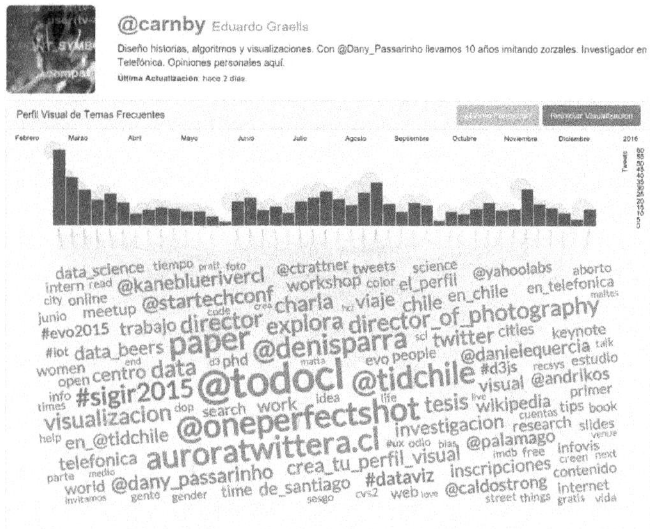

Figure 1: Our data portrait design. In the image, the portrait of the Twitter account *@carnby* (of Eduardo Graells-Garrido).

Our proposed design is displayed in Figure 1. User interests are estimated by counting the frequencies of the n-grams (with $n \leq 3$) of the words appearing in their timeline. The word cloud layout is based on *Wordle* [64], allowing for a tighter yet flexible representation of words.[1] Note that common word clouds follow two patterns of rotation: random angle or 90°. The first pattern makes reading the elements of the word cloud hard, whereas the second provides some sense of structure usually not present in the data. To promote a playful appearance, we decided to use rotated text. We used a fixed rotation for all words of -7°. This value was chosen arbitrarily after manual experimentation. As a way to compensate for the slight text rotation, to maintain readability we used a sans-serif font [55].

The color coding of word cloud elements is based on the type of keyword. We consider three categories: *hashtags (#7570b3)*, *mentions (#d95f02)* and *regular words (#1b9e77)*. This palette is based on the color-blind friendly *Set2* palette by Harrower *et al.* [36], although we darkened the colors to provide a better contrast. Each word has an invisible box that serves as clickable area, and as indicator when a particular word is highlighted when the box is visible.

To provide temporal information, we include a histogram of tweeting activity. This histogram encodes the number of tweets published or retweeted during a given time window. The number of bins is computed using Sturge's formula ($k = \lceil \log_2 n + 1 \rceil$) by the *d3.js* library [10]. Each bin is accompanied with a circle positioned on its upper-left corner, which is a turn-on/off switch for a tweet to be displayed in an overlay window. Although all circles are similar in size, their ratios vary slightly according to the popularity of the most popular tweet in the bin. Circles allow the user to select a bin regardless of its size, a feature particularly useful for time windows with low activity.

[1] We use the implementation by Jason Davies available at `http://www.jasondavies.com/wordcloud/`.

Finally, although users may want to change the background image of the data portrait, just like they can change the background on Twitter, we did not consider background customization to keep full control of aesthetics. Instead, we added their avatars and self-reported descriptions.

Interactions and Component Linkage. We link user interests and time (bins) using *Bézier* curves. The links are always visible, to make the structure behind the data portrait explicit to the user. Those links are displayed in a non-highlighted state. To highlight links and change the state of the portrait, the following interactions are available:

- When users click on a specific word, the corresponding bins are highlighted and connected through *Bézier* curves (see Figure 2, right).
- A click on a specific bin has two consequences:
  - A tweet overlay is displayed with the most popular tweet in it (see Figure 2, left). This tweet is context-dependent: if no word was selected before, it displays the overall most popular tweet; otherwise, it displays the most popular tweet relevant to the corresponding user interest. When a tweet is overlaid, the circle assigned to the current bin is highlighted.
  - The words related to all tweets in the bin are highlighted (see Figure 2, center).
- When displaying a tweet overlay, if the user clicks its corresponding highlighted circle, the circle is desaturated (*i. e.*, colored in gray), and the tweet overlay is hidden (see Figure 2, center).

The visualization can be reset by clicking on the *"Reset Portrait"* button (*"Reiniciar Visualización"*). Additionally, we display a *"How it Works?"* button (*"¿Cómo Funciona?"*), which then displays a pop-up window with instructions.

Influence and Pilot Study. Our proposed design is built upon the results of a pilot study [30] and the design of *Themail* [62], a data portrait of e-mail conversations. In the pilot study, a data portrait was built following an organic design to depict user profiles with recommendations injected inside it. The design was positively received by users, because displaying their interests allowed them to discover new things about themselves. It had, however, no impact on user behavior in terms of recommendations. In addition, several issues with the interface were raised, which were addressed in the new design (as shown in Figure 1), namely: consideration of time, a meaningful color palette for words, personalization of the data portrait, and better readability.

Recommending People Using Intermediary Topics

Our proposed approach aims at recommending people that, while having a potentially distant position in political issues, have shared interests with the target user. We do so by defining a proof-of-concept recommender algorithm. In this algorithm, the scoring of each recommendation is calculated by weighting two scores: 1) a content-based distance using LDA; and 2) an user similarity score based on *intermediary topics* [31], which we use as a proxy of shared interests. By weighting factors, this allows selecting a candidate that has intermediary topics with the target user, but is distant in terms of profile-wide

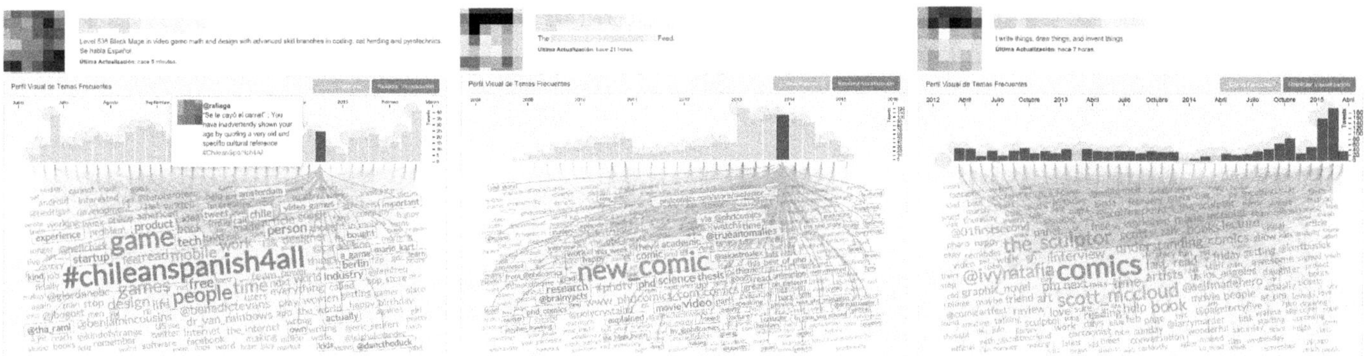

Figure 2: State of the data portrait after several interactions. Left: a click on the histogram will display a tweet overlay, with links to all related keywords to the corresponding bin. Center: a click on the bin circle will deactivate the tweet overlay to ease exploration. Right: a click on a keyword will link related histogram bins. The source profile identities have been blurred to maintain anonymity.

topics as captured by LDA if the target user is politically vocal. On the other hand, users that are similar in political content but with no intermediary topics would not be recommended to each other, as recommendations are based on shared interests characterized through intermediary topics.

These topics are obtained by running LDA over a corpus of user documents or *microblogs* [53], and then creating a topic graph where nodes are topics. Two topics are connected through a weighted edge if both topics contribute content to at least one user. Edge weights are based on the fraction of users that contribute to each edge. Then, weighted closeness centrality is estimated in the graph, as a measure of how topics can make people closer. Intermediary topics are defined as those in the top 50% central topics, and have been found to be shared among a politically diverse set of people [28].

Notations. We represent a user u as a vector:

$$\vec{u} = [p_0(u), p_1(u), \ldots, p_k(u)],$$

where k is the number of latent topics, and $p_i(u)$ is $P(t_i \mid u)$ as defined by the LDA model for a topic t_i. Next, given two users, u_1 and u_2, we define their topical distance as the normalized *Kullback-Leibler Symmetric Distance* [8]:

$$KLD(u_1 \parallel u_2) = \sum_{i=0}^{k} \{\vec{u}_1[i] - \vec{u}_2[i]\} \log\left(\frac{\vec{u}_1[i]}{\vec{u}_2[i]}\right).$$

To normalize a distance into the range $[0, 1]$, given a set of distances, we divide each one by the maximum distance found.

Similarity Considering Intermediary Topics. We estimate *similarity with respect to intermediary topics* and not with respect to all topics, as we want to recommend users who might not be close in distance terms (*e. g.*, they could have ideological differences), but share intermediary topics. The set of intermediary topics for user u is defined as:

$$IT(u) = \{i : \vec{u}[i] \geq \varepsilon,\ t_i \text{ is an intermediary topic}\},$$

where ε is a threshold for topical significance, which depends on the context. For instance, the default value used in the *gensim* library is 0.01 [54].

We define similarity with respect to intermediary topics as the *Jaccard Similarity* between two users:

$$JIT(u_1, u_2) = \frac{|IT(u_1) \cup IT(u_2)|}{|IT(u_1) \cap IT(u_2)|}.$$

Using this formula, when two users share all intermediary topics, $J(u_1, u_2) = 1$, and when users do not share any intermediary topic, $J(u_1, u_2) = 0$.

Algorithm Formalization. Each candidate for recommendation is scored using a *F-Score* [6] of *latent topical distance* and *similarity with respect to intermediary topics*:

$$\text{score} = (1 + \gamma^2) \times \frac{\mathrm{S}(u_1, u_2) \times (1 - \mathrm{D}(u_1, u_2))}{\gamma^2 \times (1 - \mathrm{D}(u_1, u_2)) + \mathrm{S}(u_1, u_2)}.$$

where S is similarity, D is distance, and the balance factor γ indicates the importance given to the distance in comparison to the importance given to similarity. For instance, $\gamma = 1$ gives equal importance to both factors, $\gamma = 0.5$ gives more importance to distance, and $\gamma = 2.0$ gives more importance to similarity.

Having estimated a measure of how close two users are, as well as how similar their sets of intermediary topics are, we can formalize our algorithm to recommend people with intermediary topics as follows. Given a target user u, a candidate set of recommendations C, a balancing factor γ, and the number of desired recommendations n, we estimate the score for all candidates and return the top-n scored candidates.

Displaying Recommendations with Circle Packing

The set of recommendations is displayed below the main data portrait as a separate unit, although both are clearly part of the same system.

Our algorithm generates a list of recommended accounts to follow. Each recommended account contains an avatar, a username, a biography, and a link to the full profile on Twitter. For each of those accounts we know the set of latents topics according to the LDA model. To prepare recommendations for visualization, we cluster accounts based on their common latent topics. We implemented a simple scheme, where two

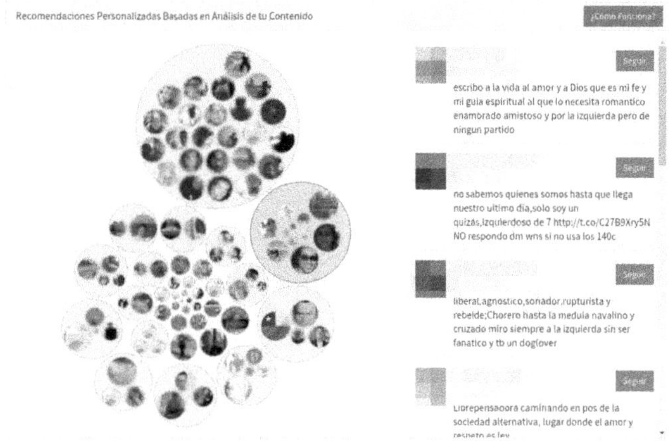

Figure 3: Display of recommendations using Circle Packing. The recommended profile identities have been blurred to maintain anonymity.

users are in the same cluster if their most contributing latent topic is the same. More complex clustering methods could be explored, but this is not the focus of this paper.

Visual depictions have the potential to change how users perceive recommendations. First, visualization of social recommendations has been shown to increase user satisfaction [32]. Second, explaining recommendations is important, as explanations increase user involvement and acceptance [40]. Using visualization techniques to display recommendations allows us to depict the underlying structure behind them, hence providing an *implicit* explanation. Conversely, when using text only, recommendations have to be explained in natural language, since something like *"Topic 5"* is meaningless. Hence, visualization is a natural way to overcome this.

We employ an *enclosure diagram* built using *Circle Packing* [17] to display clustered recommendations. Circle Packing (*CP* hereafter) is a hierarchical visualization technique, where each node of the hierarchy is represented as a circle, with nesting according to the hierarchy. Even though this kind of diagram does not use effectively all the space available (for instance, unlike treemaps [11]), CP *"effectively reveals the hierarchy"* [38], and has an attractive organic appearance. Additionally, circles maintain aspect ratio (unlike cells in a treemap), which is useful to display avatars of different sizes, as seen on previous applications in social query systems [57]. An example visualization is shown in Figure 3.

Interactivity. Our design shows the CP visualization of the hierarchical structure of recommendations, but no actual detailed recommendation is shown at first. A message indicating that users can interact with the visualization is displayed instead. Then, when users click on a cluster, the cluster is highlighted and a list on the right of the visualization displays a detailed list of the corresponding recommendations. In the detailed list, each recommendation profile contains the account name, the full name of the recommended user, and the self-reported biography. The account name is linked to his/her profile on Twitter, and a "Follow" (*"Seguir"*) button allows the user to directly follow the recommended account.

DEPLOYMENT "IN THE WILD"

We detail how we tested our platform, by deploying a proof-of-concept implementation in an uncontrolled setting [18]. This implementation is available at `https://github.com/carnby/aurora`.

Aurora Twittera: A Chilean News Aggregator Platform

We implemented the visual designs using the *d3.js* library [10], and the recommendation algorithms using the LDA implementation from the *gensim* library [54]. We incorporated both, the data portrait design and the recommender system, in a Web platform named *Aurora Twittera* [29] (available at `http://auroratwittera.cl`), *AT* hereafter. *AT* is targeted at Chilean users (hence the `.cl` domain). It is a news aggregator that constantly crawls tweets about Chilean news, specially with respect to political events, but also news on other topics (*e. g.*, sports, cultural events).

Building Portraits

In *AT*, users could create their "Visual Profiles" (*"Perfiles Visuales"*) by connecting their Twitter accounts with the site. Since users had to log-in to the site to browse their portraits, we could gather rich interaction data, which we then analyzed.

After pressing the *"Create Your Profile"* button, users were redirected to the Twitter website, which asked for login credentials and permission to modify their accounts. We asked for these permissions to have a *"Follow"* button next to each recommendation. A scheduler service processed queued portraits, both, those newly created and those queued for update. Tweets were downloaded using the Twitter API using the user credentials. Then, we estimated the user interests according to the methodology described in the previous section and identified the intermediary topics using LDA. We considered the top-300 user interests according to frequency, a number chosen based on the width and height of the data portraits, which is suitable for a 1024x768 screen resolution.

From the up-to-date dataset of users in *AT* we generated, every day, a list of candidate people who tweeted in the previous 48 hours, and for whom we estimate their latent topics using the entire corpus of users who published tweets in those 48 hours. This regularly updated list of candidates allowed us to present fresh recommendations to users.

Promoting the System

AT has a social bot in Twitter, with username *@todocl*. The social bot *@todocl* published tweets mentioning users when their portraits were ready (usually within less than one minute after sign-up), and every three days when their portraits were updated. Although portrait updates were daily, notification was limited to every three days to avoid spamming. Additionally, to promote our system we performed a number of actions:

- Created several *demo portraits* for people to browse, and publicized them on *@todocl*'s timeline. The demo portraits were of popular user accounts. Sometimes the portrayed users, when being mentioned to notify them about the availability of their portraits, retweeted our announcements.
- Created a campaign on `http://ads.twitter.com` aimed at Chilean desktop users in Twitter who were active for at

least one month. As result, 42,190 promoted tweets were displayed, with an engagement rate (as reported by Twitter) of 0.51%.

- Added a "Share my Profile" button to the data portrait. When clicked, the system published a tweet from the portrayed user's account, inviting her/his followers to visit the data portrait.

The system was open to everyone. However, the user interface was available in Spanish only, and recommendations considered only Chilean users.

EVALUATION WITH INTERACTION DATA

Our hypothesis is that an indirect approach, through the mixture of data portraits and recommendations using intermediary topics, allows users to overcome the cognitive dissonance produced by exposure to potentially challenging information. To test this hypothesis our evaluation followed a *between-groups* design. For each user who signed up on the system, a random pair of conditions $\langle UI, RecSys \rangle$ was assigned. In both cases, user interface and recommender system, we considered a baseline condition in addition to our proposed one.

The *User Interface* conditions were:

- *Baseline*: The baseline recommendation UI (see Figure 4), which displays recommendations in a similar way to current mainstream user interfaces.
- *Circle Pack*: The visualization of recommendations using circle packing (see Figure 3 Top).

The *Recommender System* conditions were:

- *KLD*: recommendations generated using Kullback-Leibler Symmetric Distance only, *i. e.*, considering the most similar users according to all LDA topics.
- *IT*: recommendations generated using our proposed method based on intermediary topics (with balancing factor $\gamma = 1$).

In this way, we can compare whether using visualization influences how users explore recommendations, and whether including intermediary topics in the recommendation makes users behave in a less biased way.

For each user, we had the following independent variables:

- *Political Content*: Its value is 1 if the list of the top-50 user interests has a non-empty intersection with a list of political keywords (including hashtags); the value is 0 if the intersection is empty. We considered this variable as binary, *e. g.*, a user could use few political keywords, but if used very often, then it is arguably a user interested in politics.
- *Hub Ratio*: Number of followed accounts divided by the number of followers, which measures the tendency of users to follow others based on their own popularity.
- *Mention Fraction*: Fraction of tweets that mention someone else (excluding retweets).
- *RT Fraction*: Fraction of tweets that are retweets.
- *Tweet Ratio*: Number of tweets per day, defined as total number of tweets published divided by the account age.
- *URL Fraction*: Fraction of tweets that contain a URL (excluding retweets).

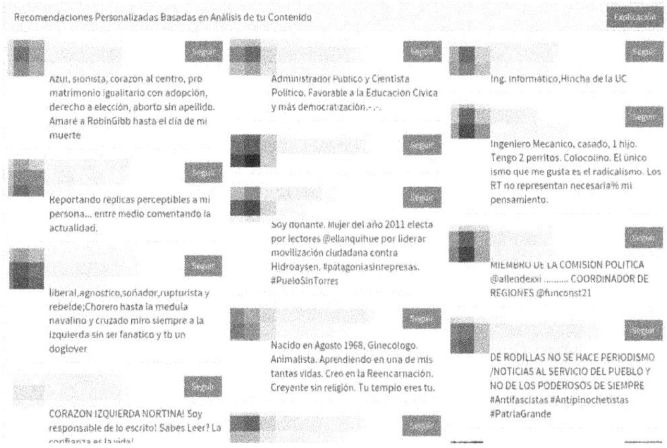

Figure 4: Baseline design of recommendations. The recommended profile identities have been blurred to maintain anonymity.

The interaction data we considered are explicit actions performed on the user interface:

- *Recommendation Exploration*: Number of clicks on elements in the user interface related to recommendations (*e. g.*, click on a profile link or circle pack nodes).
- *Recommendation Acceptance*: Whether the user accepted at least one recommendation.

Since *AT* is a *Casual InfoVis System* [52], users were not expected to perform specific tasks, nor instructed to do so. Although we compare interaction data between conditions to evaluate the differences in behavior, we still require a feedback mechanism to understand how users perceive the system. We analyze user engagement using *implicit feedback* [41], where positive user engagement is used as our proxy of a positive perception of the system through the following variables:

- *Number of Days*: Number of days the user visited his/her data portrait.
- *Dwell Time*: Time (in seconds) spent interacting with or browsing the data portrait with embedded recommendations.

For our analysis, we consider the following factorial model:[2]

$$
\begin{aligned}
Y = {} & C(\text{ui}) \times C(\text{recommendation}) \times C(\text{pol\_content}) \\
& + \text{tweet\_ratio} + \text{hub\_ratio} + \text{RT\_fraction} \\
& + \text{URL\_fraction} + \text{mention\_fraction},
\end{aligned}
$$

where $C(X)$ creates dummy variables for the corresponding categories of the independent variable X, and $\times$ represents the independent factors and the interactions between them.[3] We use this model for two types of regression: Negative Binomial (NB) generalized linear models, and logistic (logit) regression. NB is used for over-dispersed count data, and logit is used to model dichotomous outcomes in terms of probabilities. In both models, if the statistical interactions between factors were found to be not significant, we analyzed the same model without interaction terms.

[2] Specified in R's formula syntax.

[3] $A \times B = A + B + A * B$.

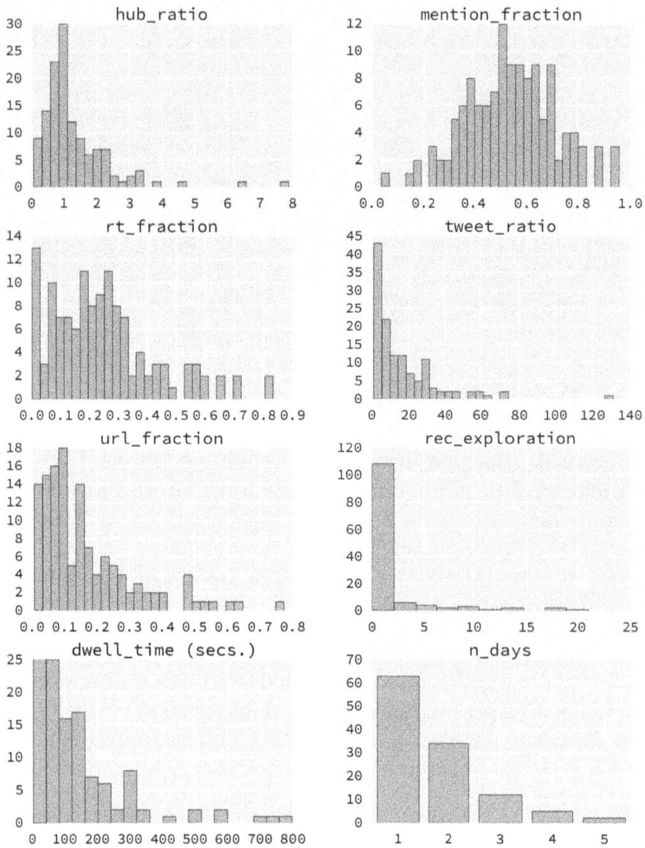

Figure 5: The first five plots display the distribution of characteristics (independent variables) of portrayed users. The last three plots display the distributions of interaction data variables under study.

Participants

As our study focuses on Chilean users and Chilean politics, we discarded users whose self-reported Twitter location was not Chile, or whose IP address was not detected as Chilean by the GeoIP database. We also discarded users whose interaction data was not reliable, *e. g.*, having Javascript-blocking extensions in their browser. Lastly, we discarded users who spent less than 5 seconds on the site, and those whose tweet ratio was less than one.

As result, we have 129 valid portraits, created between 18 February and 17 March 2015. For the recommendation conditions, 59 users were assigned to *KLD*, and 70 to *IT*. With respect to the user interface, 59 users were assigned to the *Baseline*, and 70 to the *Circle Pack* condition. Finally, 69 users had political content in their portraits, and 60 did not. The means of independent variables are: *hub ratio*, 1.30; *mention fraction*, 0.54; *RT fraction*, 0.25; *tweet ratio*, 16.54; and *URL fraction*, 0.17. Figure 5 shows the distributions of these independent variables.

Regression Results

The 129 portrayed users generated 1,707 interaction events. The following are the mean and max values found for each variable, as well as the results of the statistical analysis:

- *Recommendation Exploration* events (mean = 1.53, max = 21): the first NB regression did not contain significant interactions. The NB model without interactions is (log-likelihood = -169.59; deviance = 168.51; $\chi^2 = 221$).
- *Recommendation Acceptance*: 5.42% of participants accepted at least one recommendation. The first logit regression did not contain significant interactions. The logit model without interactions is (log-likelihood = -14.67, $p = 0.002$).
- *Number of Days* (mean = 1.81, max = 8): none of the performed NB regressions reported significant terms.
- *Dwell Time*: We discarded the top decile from the analysis because some users left the browser window open (the maximum dwell time observed was 9 hours), leading to $N = 116$, with mean = 147.66, and max = 798 seconds. The NB model with interactions contained significant terms (log-likelihood = -688.68, deviance = 95.89, $\chi^2 = 80.5$).

Figure 5 shows the distributions of the independent variables. Table 1 displays the regression coefficients with a p-value smaller than 0.05, and the corresponding 95% confidence intervals and p-value. We refer to each result as Ri. We discuss our results focusing first on recommendations, and then user engagement. As effect size for the logit regression coefficients, we consider the Odds-Ratio (OR) of each result. The OR is a measure of how associated a factor is to the outcome under analysis. If the OR is greater than 1, then the presence of the factor is considered to be associated with the outcome. If the OR is lesser than 1, then the opposite association holds. An OR of 1 indicates no association. The OR of each coefficient is defined as OR $= exp(\beta)$. In the case of the NB regression, the effect size of each coefficient is defined as ES $= exp(|\beta|) * \text{sign}(\beta)$. This ES means how much would the outcome increase (or decrease) with a one unit increase of the dependent variable.

Recommendation Exploration

We discuss the extent to which users explored the recommendations, and whether they accepted them (users followed the recommended users).

We found two positive effects that increase the tendency to explore recommendations. The strongest effect is the RT Fraction (R5, ES = 41.721). This can be interpreted as users who tend to retweet more, are more likely to explore recommendations because they are looking for sources to retweet. The second positive effect is the usage of Circle Pack (R2, ES = 11.750). This ES indicates that exploration recommendations increase when users are exposed to CP, if all the other factors are held constant. This effect validates our design choice of using CP.

The negative effects are the usage of Intermediary Topics (IT) and Tweet Ratio. In the case of IT, users exposed to its generated recommendations decrease exploration (R3, ES = -3.157). This effect indicates that users tend to behave homophilically, probably because the recommendees' profile information can make their political leaning explicit (*i. e.*, by using a politically-explicit avatar or self-reported description). However, its effect size is small in comparison to the positive effects found. Likewise, a one unit increase in Tweet Ratio

R#	DV	IV	β	Effect Size	95% C.I.	p-value
R1	Rec. Exploration	Intercept	-2.104	–	$[-3.961, -0.247]$	0.026
R2	Rec. Exploration	UI(CP)	2.464	11.750	$[1.510, 3.417]$	< 0.001
R3	Rec. Exploration	REC(IT)	-1.150	-3.157	$[-1.937, -0.362]$	0.004
R4	Rec. Exploration	Tweet Ratio	-0.030	-1.031	$[-0.053, -0.007]$	0.012
R5	Rec. Exploration	RT Fraction	3.731	41.721	$[1.468, 5.994]$	0.001
R6	P(Rec. Acceptance)	REC(IT)	-4.383	0.012	$[-8.547, -0.219]$	0.039
R7	P(Rec. Acceptance)	Pol. Content(True)	3.354	28.617	$[0.061, 6.647]$	0.046
R8	P(Rec. Acceptance)	Mention Fraction	-12.079	5.68×10^6	$[-21.958, -2.200]$	0.017
R9	P(Rec. Acceptance)	RT Fraction	9.872	19,380.060	$[1.026, 18.717]$	0.029
R10	Dwell Time	Intercept	4.825	–	$[3.971, 5.680]$	< 0.001
R11	Dwell Time	UI(CP), Pol. Content(True) and REC(IT)	2.187	8.908	$[0.785, 3.590]$	0.002

Table 1: Regression Coefficients for the dependent variables under study. Only significant terms are shown for each regression.

decreases exploration (R4, ES $= -1.031$). This may indicate that users who tend to publish more tweets are less likely to explore recommendations because they are generating content–instead of looking for sources; they *are* the sources.

Recommendation Acceptance

There are two significant positive effects. The strongest one is RT Fraction (R9, OR $=$ 19380.06). We interpret this in concordance with previous interpretations, where users were looking for sources of information to retweet from. The second positive effect is the presence of political content on a user portrait (R7, OR $= 28.617$). Hence, if the other variables are held constant, the odds of accepting a recommendation increase more than 28 times if the user is interested in politics. This aligns with results obtained in our first pilot study [30].

The negative effects are Intermediary Topics and Mention Fraction. In the case of IT (R6, OR $= 0.012$), this effect size confirms the homophilic behavior of the user population as already hinted by the previous result in recommendation exploration. The other negative effect is Mention Fraction (R8, OR $= 5.68 \times 10^6$), which suggests that users with high fraction of mentions have almost negligible odds of accepting a recommendation. This suggests that users who already have a network of connections to interact with, do not need (or feel the need) to add new people in their networks.

User Engagement

We defined two variables related to user engagement: number of days that each user visited the site, and dwell time. Both variables allow to measure positive engagement with the site: someone who returns to the site in a different day may do so because s/he finds it useful, and someone who spends more time on the site, in a single session, may do so because s/he finds it interesting.

We observed that 45% of participants returned to the site at least a second time on a different day. However, what causes this return cannot be explained by our regression model, implying that in terms of visits per day, all users were engaged equally. With respect to dwell time, none of the standalone variables or main effects were found to be significant, nor the pairwise interactions. The only factor found significant is the triple interaction between Intermediary Topics, Circle Pack and Political Content (R11, ES $= 8.91$). In the NB model, this can be interpreted as follows: dwell time increases by 8.91 seconds when these three conditions are present, and all other factors are held constant. Note that, if all possible interactions and main effects related to user interface, recommender system, and political content would be significant, there would still be an increase in dwell time by 2.06 seconds when those three conditions are present. As post-hoc testing we separated users into I_Y ($N = 23$), those who comply with the interaction (*i. e.*, are exposed to conditions IT and CP, and have political content in their profiles), and I_N ($N = 93$), those who do not. We compared the distribution of recommendation acceptance in both groups using a non-parametric Mann-Whitney U test, and found that the groups are not significantly different. This means that both groups have the same acceptance rate, but different dwell times, something that has been linked with increased satisfaction with exploratory systems [25].

Overview of Results

Some results, positive and negative, support the motivation behind this work. On one hand, visualization of recommendations increased exploration. On the other hand, our proposed algorithm was not interesting for users, and was out-performed by a fully-homophilic baseline. Our results are not enough to fully support our hypothesis, although we found partial evidence in its favor: there is an effect of our mixed approach, but not for all users.

It is well known that a majority of users are *challenge-averse* [46], so it could be expected that politically-engaged users exposed to our conditions would have had a negative (*e. g.*, less engaging) experience. This was not the case – users who were exposed to our proposed conditions and are politically-involved present a comparable (and even slightly more positive) experience when using the site. In the next section we discuss why this positive experience can be linked with conscious (unbiased) behavior.

DISCUSSION

Recommendation and Individual Differences. To analyze individual differences, we focused on behavioral signals that could be extracted from user profiles, and applied a statistical model to find which ones influence user behavior with our system. Some variables were not significant: *hub ratio* (connectivity) and *URL fraction* (type of content that is shared). The significant variables were *tweet ratio* (publishing behavior), *mention fraction* (interaction with others), and *RT Fraction* (information diffusion). Knowing that some users have the tendency to explore (or not) recommendations allows identifying the users who are more likely to benefit from them, and use simpler algorithms for those users who are not.

Furthermore, the user related variable that influenced recommendation acceptance was the presence of political content. In line with our motivation, arguably only politically-involved people are affected by selective exposure, in the sense that they look for political content, whereas non-politically involved people discard political content because of lack of interest instead of selective exposure. Not all users are interested in politics, therefore, not all users are interested in, nor need, political diversity on their timelines.

Our visualization proposal was effective: when visualizing recommendations instead of using the baseline text interface, users' exploration of recommendation was equivalent, or even greater, than when recommendations were non-diverse. We used an aesthetically attractive design based on circle packing [17], which had the property of displaying part of the underlying structure in recommendations. In that aspect, we did not find a main effect of visualization in reducing homophilic behavior of recommendation acceptance. In fact, homophilic behavior was confirmed: the non-diverse recommendation algorithm increased the likelihood of acceptance. However, due to the statistical interaction found, there is a potential usage of visualization when mixed with algorithms that recommend more diverse information.

"Indirect" Approaches and Unbiased Behavior. As an indirect approach to exposing users to people of opposing views, we proposed a data portrait [20] context for users to explore their own content. These data portraits serve to display recommendations, where users could explicitly see how the system modeled their generated content, and implicitly understand the structure of the recommendations made to them. Thus, when addressing the biased behavior of users, micro-blogging platforms may want to include other profile UIs, specially those based around data portraits [20] and *Casual InfoVis* systems [52].

Previous attempts at directly exposing users to opposing information had detrimental effects, given that a majority of users are *challenge-averse* [46]. For instance, in *Opinion Space* [23], although users did behave differently when using a visualization-based UI, their dwell times were not significantly different, and their political behavior was not less biased. Our own results showed that politically-involved users under our proposed conditions did not behave in a less biased way, although they had slightly longer sessions. This is the key difference – their extra-time browsing recommendations (from 2 to 8 seconds, with an average of 1.53 explored profiles) indicates that, whether they accepted or discarded recommendations, they took their time to explore/decide. We hypothesize that this is a *conscious* decision-making process when exploring recommendations. Note that such consciousness cannot be achieved by direct approaches because they activate cognitive dissonance [24].

Limitations and Future Work. In this work we used a proof-of-concept recommendation algorithm, based on the concept of intermediary topics. Although these topics have been shown to contain politically diverse profiles in the population under study [28], there is a need to quantify in formal terms its differences with fully homophilic algorithms. For instance, we focused on the political diversity of users provided by intermediary topics, but not on whether they actually had opposing views in sensitive issues or not. Moreover, critics might rightly say that sentiment analysis could be used as proxy for opposed opinions instead of latent topics. However, these techniques are not language-agnostic and culture-independent, something relevant in our context (a population with Spanish as primary language), and thus this should be analyzed and tested as well. Finally, our results indicate that our algorithm has lesser acceptance than baseline algorithms. Perhaps by considering more features expected by users, like network features [14], results could be improved.

CONCLUSIONS

Behavioral and content differences influence how users perceive a *Casual InfoVis* system [52]. In our research, while trying to understand how to encourage connecting with others who think differently, we found that being politically open, and the informational and interaction behavior of users, are important features that influence interaction. This is important to be aware for the following reason. When designing systems for specific tasks, user characteristics can be assumed by visualization designers. However, in open systems like ours we cannot predict who will use the system nor their expertise level. In addition, in biased scenarios there does not seem to be a one-size-fits-all solution. Because we presented an exploratory system, our evaluation was not a task-based one focused on algorithm/visualization efficiency. Instead, we performed an "in the wild" evaluation [18], where we focused on individual differences and user interaction with the interface, as well as user engagement metrics [41]. This allowed us to obtain deep insights on user behavior and exploratory styles.

To conclude, our results show that systems that aim at unbiasing user behavior should consider an indirect approach, which can be evaluated with engagement metrics in addition to context-specific metrics (*e. g.*, recommendation acceptance). Furthermore, our work also shows that an unbiased behavior is not one that performs more actions (*e. g.*, accepting more recommendations of people who thinks differently). On the contrary, it is one that allows users to avoid the cognitive heuristics that bias the activity, enabling them to make conscious choices.

Acknowledgments. We are grateful to Daniele Quercia for inspiration and discussion. We thank Shiri Dori-Hacohen and the anonymous reviewers for valuable feedback, and Andrés Lucero for help with the user studies. This work was partially funded by Grant TIN2012-38741 (Understanding Social Media: An Integrated Data Mining Approach) of the Ministry of Economy and Competitiveness of Spain.

References

1. Al Zamal, F., Liu, W., and Ruths, D. Homophily and Latent Attribute Inference: Inferring Latent Attributes of Twitter Users from Neighbors. *International Conference on Weblogs and Social Media*, 270, 2012:
2. An, J., Quercia, D., Cha, M., Gummadi, K., and Crowcroft, J. Sharing political news: the balancing act of intimacy and socialization in selective exposure. *EPJ Data Science*, 3(1), 2014: 1–21.
3. Archambault, D., Greene, D., Cunningham, P., and Hurley, N. ThemeCrowds: multiresolution summaries of Twitter usage. *Proceedings of the 3rd international workshop on Search and mining user-generated contents*. 2011, 77–84.
4. Asch, S. E. Forming impressions of personality. *The Journal of Abnormal and Social Psychology*, 41(3), 1946: 258.
5. Assogba, Y., and Donath, J. Mycrocosm: visual microblogging. *42nd Hawaii International Conference on System Sciences*. 2009, 1–10.
6. Baeza-Yates, R., and Ribeiro-Neto, B. Modern Information retrieval: the concepts and technology behind search, 2nd. Edition. Addison-Wesley, Pearson, 2011.
7. Barberá, P. Birds of the same feather tweet together: Bayesian ideal point estimation using Twitter data. *Political Analysis*, 23(1), 2015: 76–91.
8. Bigi, B. Using Kullback-Leibler distance for text categorization. In: *Advances in Information Retrieval*. Springer, 2003, 305–319.
9. Blei, D. M., Ng, A. Y., and Jordan, M. I. Latent Dirichlet allocation. *The Journal of Machine Learning Research*, 3, 2003: 993–1022.
10. Bostock, M., Ogievetsky, V., and Heer, J. D^3 data-driven documents. *IEEE Transactions on Visualization and Computer Graphics*, 17(12), 2011: 2301–2309.
11. Bruls, M., Huizing, K., and Van Wijk, J. J. Squarified treemaps. Springer, 2000.
12. Brzozowski, M. J., and Romero, D. M. Who should I follow? Recommending people in directed social networks. *International Conference on Weblogs and Social Media*. 2011.
13. Center, P. R. Internet seen as positive influence on education but negative on morality in emerging and developing nations. `http://www.pewglobal.org/2015/03/19/internet-seen-as-positive-influence-on-education-but-negative-influence-on-morality-in-emerging-and-developing-nations/`. 2015.
14. Chen, J., Geyer, W., Dugan, C., Muller, M., and Guy, I. Make new friends, but keep the old: recommending people on social networking sites. *Proceedings of the SIGCHI Conference on Human Factors in Computing Systems*. 2009, 201–210.
15. Chen, K., Chen, T., Zheng, G., Jin, O., Yao, E., and Yu, Y. Collaborative personalized tweet recommendation. *Proceedings of the 35th international ACM SIGIR conference on Research and Development in Information Retrieval*. 2012, 661–670.
16. Chhabra, S., and Resnick, P. Does clustered presentation lead readers to diverse selections? *CHI'13 Extended Abstracts on Human Factors in Computing Systems*. 2013, 1689–1694.
17. Collins, C. R., and Stephenson, K. A circle packing algorithm. *Computational Geometry*, 25(3), 2003: 233–256.
18. Crabtree, A., Chamberlain, A., Grinter, R. E., Jones, M., Rodden, T., and Rogers, Y. Introduction to the special issue of "The Turn to The Wild". *ACM Transactions on Computer-Human Interaction (TOCHI)*, 20(3), 2013: 13.
19. Diakopoulos, N., Naaman, M., and Kivran-Swaine, F. Diamonds in the rough: social media visual analytics for journalistic inquiry. *IEEE Symposium on Visual Analytics Science and Technology (VAST)*. 2010, 115–122.
20. Donath, J., Dragulescu, A., Zinman, A., Viégas, F., and Xiong, R. Data portraits. *ACM SIGGRAPH 2010 Art Gallery*. 2010, 375–383.
21. Dörk, M., Gruen, D., Williamson, C., and Carpendale, S. A visual backchannel for large-scale events. *Transactions on Visualization and Computer Graphics*, 2010: 1129–1138.
22. Dragulescu, A. Lexigraphs: Twitter data portrait: jakedfw. `http://vimeo.com/2404119`. 2009.
23. Faridani, S., Bitton, E., Ryokai, K., and Goldberg, K. Opinion space: a scalable tool for browsing online comments. *Proceedings of the SIGCHI Conference on Human Factors in Computing Systems*. 2010, 1175–1184.
24. Festinger, L. A theory of Cognitive Dissonance. Stanford University Press, 1962.
25. Fox, S., Karnawat, K., Mydland, M., Dumais, S., and White, T. Evaluating implicit measures to improve web search. *ACM Transactions on Information Systems (TOIS)*, 23(2), 2005: 147–168.
26. Goel, A., Sharma, A., Wang, D., and Yin, Z. Discovering similar users on Twitter. *11th Workshop on Mining and Learning with Graphs*. 2013.
27. Gou, L., You, F., Guo, J., Wu, L., and Zhang, X. L. Sfviz: interest-based friends exploration and recommendation in social networks. *Proceedings of the 2011 Visual Information Communication-International Symposium*. 2011, 15.
28. Graells-Garrido, E., Lalmas, M., and Baeza-Yates, R. Finding intermediary topics between people of opposing views: a case study. *International Workshop on Social Personalisation & Search co-located with the 38th Annual ACM SIGIR Conference*. 2015.

29. Graells-Garrido, E., Lalmas, M., and Baeza-Yates, R. Encouraging diversity- and representation-awareness in geographically centralized content. *Proceedings of the 21st International Conference on Intelligent User Interfaces (to appear)*. 2016.
30. Graells-Garrido, E., Lalmas, M., and Quercia, D. Data portraits: connecting people of opposing views. arXiv: 1311.4658 [cs.HC].
31. Graells-Garrido, E., Lalmas, M., and Quercia, D. People of opposing views can share common interests. *Proceedings of the companion publication of the 23rd international conference on World Wide Web (poster)*. 2014, 281–282.
32. Gretarsson, B., O'Donovan, J., Bostandjiev, S., Hall, C., and Höllerer, T. Smallworlds: visualizing social recommendations. *Computer Graphics Forum*. 2010, 833–842.
33. Gretarsson, B., O'donovan, J., Bostandjiev, S., Höllerer, T., Asuncion, A., Newman, D., and Smyth, P. Topicnets: visual analysis of large text corpora with topic modeling. *ACM Transactions on Intelligent Systems and Technology (TIST)*, 3(2), 2012: 23.
34. Gupta, P., Goel, A., Lin, J., Sharma, A., Wang, D., and Zadeh, R. WTF: the who to follow service at Twitter. *Proceedings of the 22nd international conference on World Wide Web*. 2013, 505–514.
35. Hannon, J., Bennett, M., and Smyth, B. Recommending Twitter users to follow using content and collaborative filtering approaches. *Proceedings of the fourth ACM Conference on Recommender Systems*. 2010, 199–206.
36. Harrower, M., and Brewer, C. A. ColorBrewer. org: an online tool for selecting colour schemes for maps. *The Cartographic Journal*, 40(1), 2003: 27–37.
37. Hart, W., Albarracín, D., Eagly, A. H., Brechan, I., Lindberg, M. J., and Merrill, L. Feeling validated versus being correct: a meta-analysis of selective exposure to information. *Psychological bulletin*, 135(4), 2009: 555.
38. Heer, J., Bostock, M., and Ogievetsky, V. A tour through the visualization zoo. *Commun. Acm*, 53(6), 2010: 59–67.
39. Heer, J., and boyd, danah. Vizster: visualizing online social networks. *IEEE Information Visualization (InfoVis)*. 2005, 32–39.
40. Herlocker, J. L., Konstan, J. A., and Riedl, J. Explaining collaborative filtering recommendations. *Proceedings of the 2000 ACM conference on Computer supported cooperative work*. 2000, 241–250.
41. Lalmas, M., O'Brien, H., and Yom-Tov, E. Measuring user engagement. Morgan & Claypool Publishers, 2014.
42. Liao, Q. V., and Fu, W.-T. Can you hear me now? Mitigating the echo chamber effect by source position indicators. *Proceedings of the 17th ACM conference on Computer supported cooperative work & social computing*. 2014, 184–196.
43. Marcus, A., Bernstein, M. S., Badar, O., Karger, D. R., Madden, S., and Miller, R. C. Twitinfo: aggregating and visualizing microblogs for event exploration. *Proceedings of the SIGCHI Conference on Human Factors in Computing Systems*. 2011, 227–236.
44. McPherson, M., Smith-Lovin, L., and Cook, J. M. Birds of a feather: homophily in social networks. *Annual review of sociology*, 2001: 415–444.
45. Michelson, M., and Macskassy, S. A. Discovering users' topics of interest on Twitter: a first look. *Proceedings of the fourth workshop on Analytics for noisy unstructured text data*. 2010, 73–80.
46. Munson, S. A., and Resnick, P. Presenting diverse political opinions: how and how much. *Proceedings of the SIGCHI Conference on Human Factors in Computing Systems*. 2010, 1457–1466.
47. Myers, D. G., and Lamm, H. The polarizing effect of group discussion: the discovery that discussion tends to enhance the average prediscussion tendency has stimulated new insights about the nature of group influence. *American Scientist*, 1975: 297–303.
48. Pariser, E. The filter bubble: what the Internet is hiding from you. Penguin UK, 2011.
49. Park, S., Kang, S., Chung, S., and Song, J. NewsCube: delivering multiple aspects of news to mitigate media bias. *Proceedings of the SIGCHI Conference on Human Factors in Computing Systems*. 2009, 443–452.
50. Parra, D., and Brusilovsky, P. User-controllable personalization: a case study with SetFusion. *International Journal of Human-Computer Studies*, 2015:
51. Pennacchiotti, M., and Popescu, A.-M. Democrats, republicans and Starbucks afficionados: user classification in Twitter. *Proceedings of the 17th ACM SIGKDD international conference on Knowledge Discovery and Data Mining*. 2011, 430–438.
52. Pousman, Z., Stasko, J. T., and Mateas, M. Casual information visualization: Depictions of data in everyday life. *IEEE Transactions on Visualization and Computer Graphics*, 13(6), 2007: 1145–1152.
53. Ramage, D., Dumais, S., and Liebling, D. Characterizing microblogs with topic models. *International Conference on Weblogs and Social Media*. 2010, 130–137.
54. Řehůřek, R., and Sojka, P. Software framework for topic modelling with large corpora. *Proceedings of the LREC 2010 Workshop on New Challenges for NLP Frameworks*. May 22, 2010, 45–50.
55. Rello, L., and Baeza-Yates, R. Good fonts for dyslexia. *Proceedings of the 15th International ACM SIGACCESS Conference on Computers and Accessibility*. 2013, 14.

56. Rout, D., Bontcheva, K., Preoţiuc-Pietro, D., and Cohn, T. Where's @Wally?: a classification approach to geolocating users based on their social ties. *Proceedings of the 24th ACM Conference on Hypertext and Social Media*. 2013, 11–20.

57. Savage, S., Forbes, A., Toxtli, C., McKenzie, G., Desai, S., and Höllerer, T. Visualizing targeted audiences. *COOP 2014-Proceedings of the 11th International Conference on the Design of Cooperative Systems, 27-30 May 2014, Nice (France)*. 2014, 17–34.

58. Sunstein, C. R. The law of group polarization. *Journal of Political Philosophy*, 10(2), 2002: 175–195.

59. Sunstein, C. R. Going to extremes: how like minds unite and divide. Oxford University Press, 2009.

60. Valenzuela, S., Arriagada, A., and Scherman, A. Facebook, Twitter, and youth engagement: A Quasi-experimental study of social media use and protest behavior using propensity score matching. *International Journal of Communication*, 8, 2014: 25.

61. Van Ham, F., Wattenberg, M., and Viégas, F. B. Mapping text with phrase nets. *IEEE Transactions on Visualization and Computer Graphics*, 15(6), 2009: 1169–1176.

62. Viégas, F. B., Golder, S., and Donath, J. Visualizing email content: portraying relationships from conversational histories. *Proceedings of the SIGCHI conference on Human Factors in computing systems*. 2006, 979–988.

63. Viégas, F. B., and Wattenberg, M. Tag clouds and the case for vernacular visualization. *Interactions*, 15(4), 2008: 49–52.

64. Viegas, F. B., Wattenberg, M., and Feinberg, J. Participatory visualization with Wordle. *IEEE Transactions on Visualization and Computer Graphics*, 15(6), 2009: 1137–1144.

65. Wattenberg, M., and Viégas, F. B. The word tree, an interactive visual concordance. *IEEE Transactions on Visualization and Computer Graphics*, 14(6), 2008: 1221–1228.

66. Xiong, R., and Donath, J. PeopleGarden: creating data portraits for users. *Proceedings of the 12th annual ACM symposium on User interface software and technology*. 1999, 37–44.

67. Yi, J. S., Kang, Y.-a., Stasko, J. T., and Jacko, J. A. Understanding and characterizing insights: how do people gain insights using information visualization? *Proceedings of the 2008 Workshop on BEyond time and errors: novel evaLuation methods for Information Visualization*. 2008, 4.

ChordRipple: Recommending Chords to Help Novice Composers Go Beyond the Ordinary

Cheng-Zhi Anna Huang
Harvard University
czhuang@fas.harvard.edu

David Duvenaud
Harvard University
dduvenaud@seas.harvard.edu

Krzysztof Z. Gajos
Harvard University
kgajos@seas.harvard.edu

ABSTRACT

Novice composers often find it difficult to go beyond common chord progressions. To make it easier for composers to experiment with radical chord choices, we built a creativity support tool, CHORDRIPPLE, which makes chord recommendations that aim to be both diverse and appropriate to the current context. Composers can use it to help select the next chord, or to replace sequences of chords in an internally consistent manner.

To make such recommendations, we adapt a neural network model from natural language processing known as WORD2VEC to the music domain. This model learns chord embeddings from a corpus of chord sequences, placing chords nearby when they are used in similar contexts. The learned embeddings support creative substitutions between chords, and also exhibit topological properties that correspond to musical structure. For example, the major and minor chords are both arranged in the latent space in shapes corresponding to the circle-of-fifths.

Our structured observations with 14 music students show that the tool helped them explore a wider palette of chords, and to make "big jumps in just a few chords". It gave them "new ideas of ways to move forward in the piece", not just on a chord-to-chord level but also between phrases. Our controlled studies with 9 more music students show that more adventurous chords are adopted when composing with CHORDRIPPLE.

Author Keywords

Music; Songwriting; Chords; Harmony; Embeddings; Creativity Support Tools, Recommender Systems, Neural Language Models

ACM Classification Keywords

H.5.5 [Sound and Music Computing]: Modeling, Systems

INTRODUCTION

Novice composers often find themselves consciously or unconsciously falling back to familiar sets of chords, because these chords are what they are "used to hearing" and where their fingers are used to falling on their instrument. In the corpus of 200 rock songs curated from the *Rolling Stone Top 500 Hits* [14], we see a long-tail phenomenon where a few chord progressions are used in many songs while most other chord progressions are rarely used, akin to the Zipf distribution of words in natural languages. In fact, a recent article showed that the evolution of our harmonic language, among other musical facets in contemporary western popular music, has stagnated for more than fifty years [11].

However, the challenge is often not only to find something that is novel, but to use these chords in a way that serves a personal musical impetus. In practice, novice composers often find it difficult to use more elaborate chords because they are less certain about their effects and how to integrate them into their own music in a way that feels both original and connected.

To address this challenge, we are developing CHORDRIPPLE (shown in Figure 1 and short-handed as CR)—a system that helps composers be more adventurous by recommending chords that are similar to the chords that they are using thus preserving the composer's original musical intent, but that are a little more unusual. By proposing such chords as possible alternatives to the composer's current chord choice, the system helps the composer see less familiar chords in the light of their own musical discourse, allowing them to easily experiment with the alternatives by substituting them into the current musical context.

We introduce a novel intervention called RIPPLE, which are chord recommendations that not only suggests alternative chords to the current chord but also recommends a reworking of its content. The name RIPPLE is an conceptual analogy to rippling effects, which in this case is the changing of one chord causing the change of its surrounding chords.

Chord recommendations are enabled by a machine learning model that captures chord similarity based on how likely different chords are to be used in similar musical contexts. We trained this model on a corpus of 200 rock songs curated from the *Rolling Stone Top 500 Hits* [14]. This model allows the system to recommend chords that are novel for a particular musical context but still similar to the chords used by the composer.

To evaluate how CR impacts composers' creative process, we recruited 14 undergraduate music students, and asked them to use CR to further develop chord progressions for a piece they were working on. We observed both positive and negative impacts of the tool on the creative process. Positive impacts include the tool helping composers explore a wider palette of chords, to create chord progressions that were "fresh and different throughout". It gave them "new ideas of ways to move forward in the piece", not just on a chord-to-chord level but between several phrases. It encouraged them to make "big jumps

IUI 2016, March 7–10, 2016, Sonoma, CA, USA.

http://dx.doi.org/10.1145/2856767.2856792

Figure 1. A walkthrough, starting with two chords (step 1), of how CHORDRIPPLE is used to help inspire the next chord (steps 2, 4) and for exploring substitutions (step 3, where the bottom four choices are substitutions of the second chord, which are from the RIPPLE effect of choosing the third chord. As shown, chord recommendations here include both single substitutions and also chords that change the context (what is around a chord change), namely RIPPLES.

in just a few chords". They sometimes altered their intentions of extending or closing a phrase based on the recommendations they saw. Instead of following the path of least resistance, the recommendations often made them think and work harder. However, some composers found the choices to be too many and that not all chord recommendations were always relevant to what they were trying to achieve. We propose that future systems of this kind should focus recommendations to what is most relevant under the composer's current intentions. For example, the intention of "make it longer" versus "I'm trying to end here" would entail very different chord recommendations.

As the first study was more exploratory and open-ended, we conducted a second study that was more controlled where students performed transformations on given chord sequences with three design variations of CHORDRIPPLE. We found that the presence of adventurous chord recommendations resulted in students composing more novel chord progressions. Yet we did not observe that recommending more difficult to use chords with RIPPLESallowed students to adopt more of them when compared to just recommending the chords themselves.

The contributions of this paper are threefold. First, we built CR, a creativity support tool that helps composers try more adventurous options; CR supports both adding new material to an existing chord sequence and re-editing existing material (thanks to RIPPLES). Second, we adapted a machine-learning model to learn chord similarity based on actual chord usage. Third, we conducted evaluations that yielded insights into how tools like CR can be integrated into composers' creative practice.

PRIOR RESEARCH

There have been a number of creativity support tools that assist novice composers in composing chord progressions. Most systems are designed to address the musical problem of harmonizing a given a melody [1, 8, 9, 13].

While these systems all use a data-driven approach, each system strives for a different goal and objective in recommending chords. For instance, [8, 13] allows users to adjust the overall "mood" quality of the accompaniment through knobs such as "happy" which adjusts the weight between the transition matrices of a hidden Markov model for the major and minor key. Users can also modify chords individually, but the recommended chords are restricted to only the most typical chords given the local musical context. [9] provided users with a novel interface with control axes that corresponded to principal components of variances of differential transition dynamics in western popular music, allowing users to more effectively explore a wide range of variations on accompaniment sequences.

[1] takes a hybrid approach of also using music-theory to guide the choice of chords for accompaniment. [4] works with chord sequences by themselves and by performing non-negative matrix factorization on a windowed transition matrix, the system allows users to interpolate between different chord progressions to create their own mix.

CR instead presents a composer with sets of diverse chords that are appropriate but more rarely used in a particular musical context. The support for exploring novel and diverse inspirational examples is critical because they help users to generate more novel and diverse artifacts [6, 10, 12].

CHORDRIPPLE

CR provides two mechanisms to help composers adopt novel chord choices in their compositions. First, CR recommends chord substitutions ranging from typical to adventurous (yet still musically appropriate). Second, because the change of one chord in the middle of a phrase may cause the need to change its context, (a concept we name the RIPPLE effect), the system also includes chord recommendations of varying lengths that change a chord's surrounding chords. We designed the first mechanism to help composers create raw adventurous material, while the second mechanism to make it easier to for composers to make adventurous revisions to existing material.

Modeling chords for recommendation

To build a system capable of recommending chords, we first need a model of chord transitions and similarities. To represent chords, we use chord symbols that abstract chords into attributes, such as its root, chord type (such as major, minor, diminished), inversion and bass, extensions and alterations, which can amount to many possible unique chords.

Like words in natural language, the distribution of chords follows a Zipf-like distribution. For example, Figure 2 shows chord frequency in the Bach chorale corpus (BACH) in *music21*. A handful of chords are used very frequently, while many chords are rarely used.

Modelling rarely-used chords and chord transitions is difficult. For some applications it is common to reduce the number of chords to 24, treating all chords as either major or minor rooted in one of the 12 pitch classes. However, this comes with the compromise of conflating chords that bear very different transition dynamics. For example, even though `I64` is an inversion of `I`, it serves a very different function in a cadence. Moreover, as our goal is to make adventurous chord recommendations, we need to be able to model how rare inversions and extensions are used. Hence, we keep all the chord attributes as annotated, which for example results in 92 unique chord symbols in the BACH corpus.

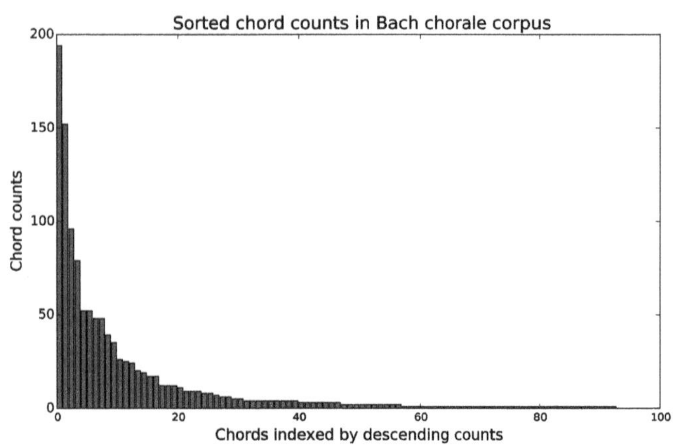

Figure 2. The occurrence count distribution of chords in roman numerals used in Bach chorales as annotated by Tymoczko [15] in the *music21* Bach-chorale corpus [2].

CHORD2VEC

To model chord transitions and similarities, we adapt a neural-network model from natural language processing known as WORD2VEC [7] to the music domain as CHORD2VEC. This model learns chord embeddings from a corpus of chord sequences, placing chords that are used in similar contexts nearby in a vector space. The learned embeddings support substitutions between semantically similar chords. This allows chords that are rarely or never seen in a particular musical context to be recommended if they are nearby in the embedding to other chords that are commonly used in that musical context.

As shown in Figure 3, this model is a skip-gram neural network. Hyperparameter m specifies the dimensionality of the continuous latent embedding, and w specifies the size of the considered context. Latent embeddings of each chord are defined by matrices U, indexed by the input chord, and V, which is indexed by $t+l$, where $-w \leq l \leq w$ indicates output chord c_{t+l}'s relative time position in a sequence with respect to the input chord c_t.

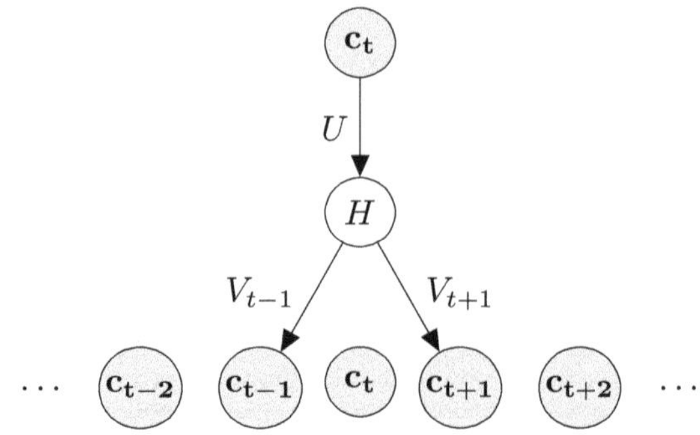

Figure 3. Skipgram neural network with window size $w = 1$.

We use u_i to denote the vector representation of chord i. We use c_t to refer to the chord used at time t, and u_{c_t} and v_{c_t} to refer to the input embedding (U) and output embedding (V) of the chord c_t. Following [7], we define $p(c_{t+l}|c_t)$ as the softmax of the dot product between a chord and its context, as in Eqn. (1), where $-w \leq l \leq w$. The training objective of the model is to maximize the log-likelihood of all chord sequences independently, as in Eqn. (2). Maximizing this objective has the side-effect of puttings chords used in similar contexts close to each other in the input embedding U.

$$P(c_{t+l}|c_t) = \frac{\exp\left(v_{c_{t+l}}^T u_{c_t}\right)}{\sum_{i=1}^{|W|} \exp\left(v_{c_i}^T u_{c_t}\right)} \tag{1}$$

$$L(c_0 \ldots c_{T-1}) = \sum_{t=1}^{T} \sum_{-w \leq l < w,\ l \neq 0} \log P(c_{t+l}|c_t) \tag{2}$$

Trained embedding for recommendation

To support CHORDRIPPLE, we trained CHORD2VEC on a corpus of 200 Rock songs (all transposed to `C`) from the *Rolling Stone Top 500 Hits* [14] containing 98 distinct chords, using latent dimension $m = 10$ and window size $w = 1$.

Data and exploratory experiments

In our experiments, we use the two aforementioned annotated corpora, *Bach Chorales* from *music21* [2] annotated by Tymoczko [15] and *The Rolling Stone: Top 200* corpus transcribed and annotated by Temperley and Clercq [14]. To model the rich palette of chord alterations, we retain all chord attributes from the original chord annotations. We experiment with both transposing chords to the key of `C` versus preserving the chords in their original keys. By transposing we assume that key does not have a major influence on how chords are used. By keeping songs in their original key one can also model key-specific trends at the expense of having less counts on each chord.

Visualizing the axes of the latent embedding

To gain more intuition on how the latent embeddings capture musical semantics, we trained a toy bigram version of CHORD2VEC with hidden layer size $m = 1$ for ease of interpretation. We reduced the number of chord symbols by requiring that they have at least 5 occurrences, which left 30 chords. We can see that these 1-D embeddings approximately capture functional harmony. In Figure 4, we see that chords close in U share similar target chords, for example, `V` and `viio` chords and its inversions and seventh chords are closely related, as they are often followed by some form of tonic chords. In Figure 5, chords close in V serve as similar target chords, for example as a phrase moves into a cadence, chords that transition to a `I64` are likely to choose `ii7` as an alternative or directly move to a `V` chord.

Visualizing embedding when trained in original keys

When training CHORD2VEC on the ROCK corpus with songs kept in their original keys, the learned embedding exhibits topological properties that correspond to musical relationships. The model had a hidden layer size of $m = 10$ and window size of $w = 1$. The x and y axes in Figure 6 correspond respectively to the first two principal components of the projection layer U. It shows that the major and minor chords are both arranged in the latent space in shapes corresponding to the circle-of-fifths. One interpretation of this result is that the tonic and dominant tension relationships are relatively strong in songs of all keys, causing them to push each other apart, some stronger than others causing the angles of the polygon to be different.

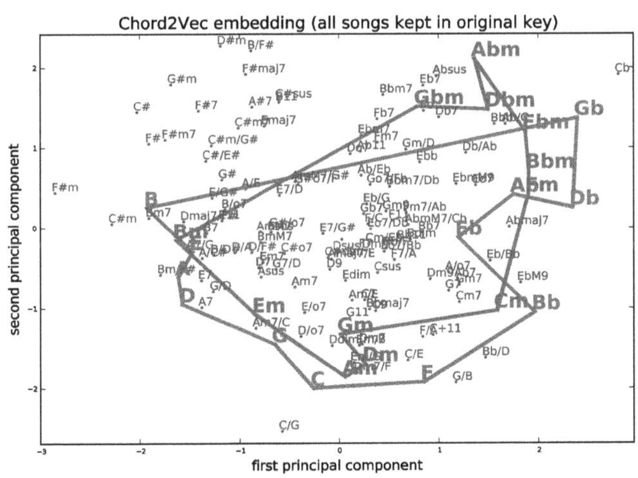

Figure 6. The CHORD2VEC projection layer U with hidden layer size $m = 10$ projected onto its first two principal components. The model was trained on the ROCK corpus with songs kept in original key, and then. Major and minor chords are both arranged in the latent space in shapes corresponding to the circle-of-fifths.

System Design

CR recommends a mix of adventurous and commonly-used chords based on the current context. To recommend more adventurous chords, we use the latent embedding learned from CHORD2VEC to query chords that are the most similar to a composer's current chord choice.

Following [7], we define the similarity between chords through the cosine distance of their embeddings vectors, as in Eqn. (3). Hence, given a chord c_i, we can query the embedding for the k closest chords to c_i to recommend to users as substitutions, by starting with Eqn. (4).

$$\text{similarity}(c_i, c_j) = \frac{u_{c_j}^T u_{c_i}}{||u_{c_j}||\,||u_{c_i}||} \quad (3)$$

$$\text{mostSimilar}(c_i) = \arg\max_{c_j} \text{similarity}(c_i, c_j) \quad (4)$$

These queried chords are not necessarily the most typical in the current musical context as preference has been put on being similar to a composer's current chord choice. To recommend what is typical given a musical context, we learn a distribution $P(c_t|c_{t-1})$ using a simple bigram model. WORD2VEC also learns a similar probabilistic model, but conditioned on both c_{t-1} and c_{t+1}. For simplicity in the current implementation we adopt a bigram model for these queries.

RIPPLES

We call recommendations that affect more than one chord RIPPLES. A RIPPLE can help smooth out transitions between chords, making it potentially easier for users to swap in more adventurous chords. It can also give new ideas of how to move forward or backward from a chord. The basic RIPPLE recommends both a substitution for the current chord (c_t) and also a reworking of its context. There are two steps involved in generating such RIPPLES. First, the substitution (c_t^s) is generated either by querying the CHORD2VEC embedding or by inward conditioning on the current context, in this case (c_{t-1}, c_{t+1}). Next, the immediate current context (c_{t-1}, c_{t+1}) can be reworked by conditioning on its larger outer context and the newly substituted chord, (c_{t-2}, c_t^s, c_{t+2}).

We can derive different kinds of ripples through a cascade of inward and outward conditionals. For example, one can imagine regenerating the larger context $\{c_{t-2}, c_{t+2}\}$ by conditioning outward from the newly substituted context (c_{t-1}^s, c_{t+1}^s). For each of the conditioning and substitution steps, we can also imagine sampling them to generate more variations.

We initially ranked the chord recommendations by the transition likelihood (Eqn. (2)) of the new sequence, using dynamic programming under the bigram model. Table 1 gives an example of chord recommendations from CR when given the most basic chord progression, `C F G C`. We clearly see that the recommendations from a purely NGRAM model are much more conservative, consisting of mostly `C` and `F` chords, while WORD2VEC is much more adventurous, recommending chords that can help composers break out of commonly used chords.

However, if we only consider how well the ripple recommendations flow in and out of the substitution chord, we will be neglecting the original structure of the sequence. For example, in Table 2, when regenerating the context for the chord F in the sequence C F Dm G C, the smoothest path to transition into its substitutions F or F/A is to precede and follow it with the chord C. The result is not very exciting and by returning to C it breaks down the phrase into two sub-phrases.

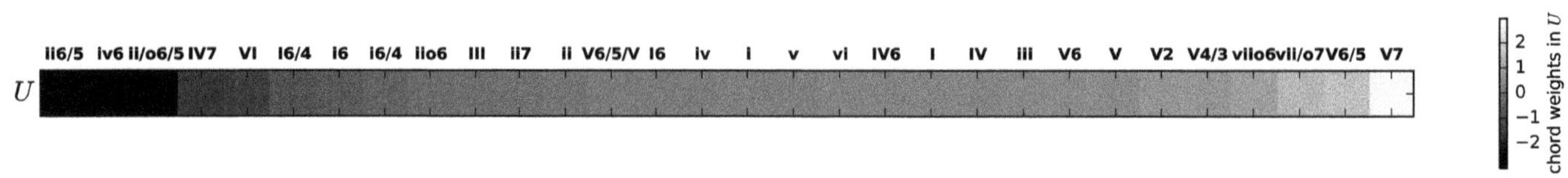

Figure 4. The inputs weights U of the bigram CHORD2VEC on the Bach chorales, with latent embedding size $m = 1$. Some predominant and subdominant chords cluster on the left while all the dominant chords cluster on the right.

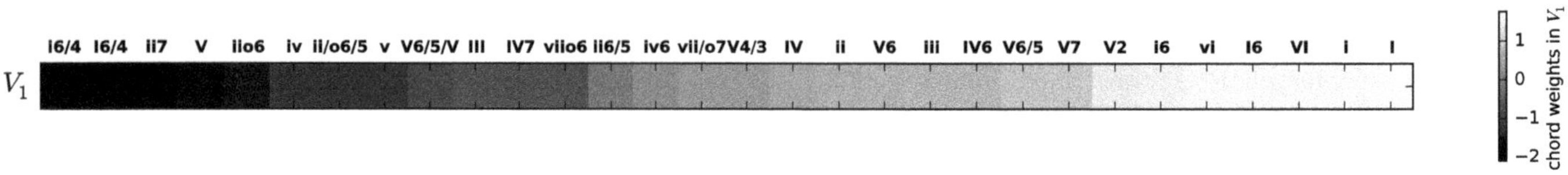

Figure 5. The output weights V of the bigram CHORD2VEC on the Bach chorales, with latent embedding size $m = 1$. Tonic-like chords cluster on the left end while mostly predominant and subdominant chords on the right

C F **G** C	single sub, *above*	triplet subs, *above*	outward subs, *below*
N-GRAM	**C, F**	**C** F **C** F, C **C** F **C**	C **C** G **F**, C **Am** G **Am**
WORD2VEC	**Ab7, Dm7**	C **F Ab7 Cm**, C **C Dm G**	C **F7** G **B**, C **F/A** G **C7**

Table 1. Comparison between chord recommendations from N-GRAM and WORD2VEC the G chord, third in the chord sequence C F G C. The chords in bold function as substitutions (sub) for the original sequence. The labels *above* and *below* indicate where these recommendations would appear relative to the input textbox in CR.

To preserve the original structure or add meaning variation to that structure, we need to also consider the similarity of the chords in the regenerated context to that of the original. This can be achieved by maximizing both the transitional likelihood between the substitution chord, it's regenerated immediate context and the larger original context and also the distance between the immediate context to the substitution chord in the regenerated sequence and the original sequence, as shown in Eqn. (5). We denote the new sequence with substitutions as $\mathbf{C^s}$ and the original sequence as $\mathbf{C}$, and use k_1 and k_2 to denote the start and end index offsets for the sequence of substitution. λ controls the balance between smooth transition and similarity to original sequence. The is the RIPPLE recommendation implemented in the second version of CHORDRIPPLE where we used $\lambda = 1$.

$$\text{cost}(\mathbf{C^s}, \mathbf{C}) = -L(\mathbf{C^s}) + \lambda \cdot \text{sim}(\mathbf{C^s}, \mathbf{C}) \quad (5)$$

$$\text{sim}(\mathbf{C^s}, \mathbf{C}) = \sum_{-k_1 < l < k_2} \log \text{similarity}(c^s_{t+l}, c_{t+l}) \quad (6)$$

The example in Table 2 shows the advantages of this additional constraint. Not only does it regenerate the context with chords that respect more the original function of the chord, it also regenerates the context in a way that is stylistically consistent with the substitution chord (using a seventh chord C7 to lead into F7).

User interface

To make it easier for composers to experiment with these recommendations, we designed a user interface that allows composers to see alternatives in relation to their own choices, akin to autocompletions. As users type their chord sequences

Ripple method	Generated sequence
Transition likelihood only	**C F/A C** G C **C F7 C** G C
Similarity to context	**Cm F/A Ab** G C **C7 F7 D** G C
Original sequence	C F Dm G C

Table 2. Comparison between ripple recommendations that only take transition likelihood into consideration when regenerating the context, versus recommendations that also consider the similarity of the regenerated context to the original

into the input text box shown in Figure 1, suggested chord sequences appear in parallel both above and below, with chord changes highlighted in bold. Users can listen to how their chord sequence might sound if they had chosen a particular suggested sequence. More typical chord recommendations are near the text box, while more adventurous ones are at the fringes. Composers can use the recommendations to help select the next chord, or they can go back to earlier chords and see the bolded changes ripple backwards.

As shown in Figure 1, chord sequences below the text box are recommendations for what can be changed around the current chord. For example, the first five rows below show the top five typical continuations. The bottom two rows show how the chord before the most recent chord be approached differently, which in step 2 of Figure 1 is the second chord in the sequence. Cropped from above the text box are pairs of recommendations that include a single substitution for the current chord and triple substitutions for the chord and its contexts. The top half are the adventurous ones and the bottom half the typical. By clicking on the USE button, users can easily replace their own chord sequence with one of the recommended. A walk through of Figure 1 is given in the next section.

EVALUATION

We conducted two user studies in order to understand how CR impacts the compositional process, each with different degrees of emphasis on external and internal validity. First, we wanted to understand how music students would relate to the the tool, and in what ways the tool can assist them in composing chord progressions. We also wanted to observe if the tool can help students go beyond their usual palette of chords. In this exploratory study, we asked students to use the tool to help them create variations of chord progressions in their own music. They were hence more intrinsically motivated. For the second study, we conducted a controlled experiment to specifically study the effects of adventurous and RIPPLE recommendations respectively on the novelty of students' chord progressions and their satisfaction. Each student was asked to perform transformations on given chord sequences with three design variations of CR.

EXPERIMENT 1: STRUCTURED OBSERVATIONS

We want to understand how CR impacts the compositional process. What kind of goals and expectations do composers have when working with the tool? How does the tool support or alter their intentions? How do they choose between different chord recommendations? To answer these questions, we took a structured-observation approach [5] to our studies. We recruited 15 participants to use CR to further develop the chord progressions they were working on for a piece. We logged their edit traces. We interviewed the participants both before and after the composing task. For the last ten participants, we audio-recorded and transcribed their interviews, and screen captured their interactions with CR.

Participants

We recruited 14 undergraduate music students and a graduate student in the applied sciences with an interest in music. The total of 15 participants included five females and ten males. We paid them $10 each for a 55-minute study session. Fourteen participants were undergraduate music students from three local universities. All the music students had some composing experience, ranging from composing for harmonization assignments in music theory classes to writing their own symphonic pieces. Most students played either the guitar or the piano, and used the instrument as a means to composing chord sequences. Most students composed roughly in the genres of pop, rock and jazz, or with traditional classical harmonies.

The composition tasks

We asked each participant to bring in a piece that they were currently working on that involved chord progressions. We suggested three possible tasks for using our tool: (1) to create variations of their existing chord sequences, (2) to use a few chords from their chord sequences as a seed to growing a new sequence, (3) to compose a new chord sequence from scratch. These tasks were structured enough to provides us with some degree of uniformity for comparison and generalization across participants, but still open enough to support individual expression.

Procedure

Each participant was asked to bring their scores and sketches of a current piece they were working on, with the chord progressions they used in guitar-tablature-like notation. Each session began with a short semi-structured interview on their background in music, how they compose, the role of chords in their music. They were then asked to walk-through how they composed the piece that they brought in. After the initial questions, participants were introduced to CR. To familiarize them with the chord notation used by the interface, participants were asked to type in the chords sequences that they brought in. We then suggested to them three possible short compositional tasks to perform with CR, which we will further outline below. Depending on how much time a participant took to complete the first task, each participant typically completed one to two of the tasks. During the task, participants were asked to adopt a think-aloud protocol. To further understand why and how participants were making decisions at particular moments, we interjected with probing questions. After each task, we conducted a short semi-structured interview for retrospective verbal accounts of how they felt the tool had impacted their creative process.

Two detailed walkthrough of CR usage

We start by walking through a long and short example to illustrate how composers use the tool, how they make decisions, and the impact of the tool on their creative process and the creative outcome.

Composing a second phrase as a variation

Participant 7 (P7) came in with the following chord progression for a minimalistic piece, where this sequence would be looped: C Am Dm F C+. He wanted to explore what else he could do with it. Before he started, he decided he wanted to keep the sound of the augmented chord C+ at the end to preserve the identity of the phrase, but "break out of the really diatonic stuff in the middle". When seeking substitutions for the second chord, he manually replaced Am with Em, which are both possible tonic substitutions that can function as tonic prolongations of C. In this case the composer explored closely related chords, while the tool suggested a more unusual alternative Bb.

> C **Bb** Dm F C+: "This one is not diatonic, [it makes] an aggressive shift, which I like. I feel like that's something that could be used as a climatic sudden moment not so much as a thing that can be repeated".

Even though he liked the effect of Bb, it was not appropriate for the current context as the chord sequence at stake was supposed to be looped, but the suggested chord was meant to be a one-time "sudden surprise change". He then reverted back to the second chord being Am. Figure 7 shows the alternatives recommended by the tool. The chord recommendations Fmaj7/C and Fmaj7 on the top two row are the chords that are most similar to Am according to the WORD2VEC model. In this case, these chords are also mutually similar, being inversions of each other. The bottom two chords, Em and F, are the most likely chords given the current surrounding context being C and Dm. In roman numerals, they would be `I iii ii` and `I IV ii`, the latter being more common than the former. The composer eventually chose Fmaj7/C, which holds the bass note of the previous chord C. He liked that the chord was an inversion and that it was a major 7 chord, saying "It's a good sound. It's different from what I am using".

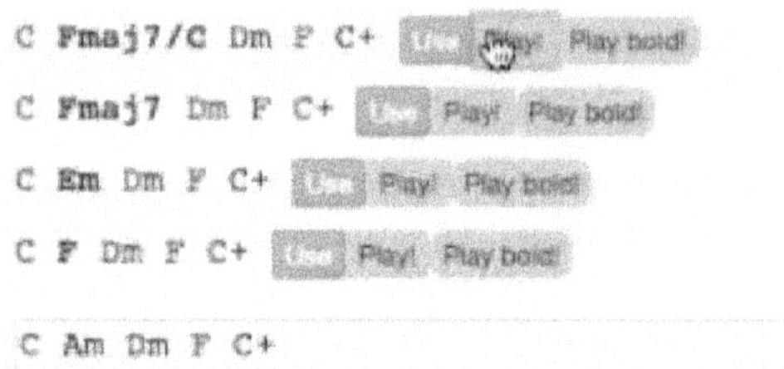

Figure 7. Chord recommendations for Am, the second chord in the sequence C Am Dm F C+. The top two rows are SIM **type recommendations, while the bottom two rows are** IN-RIPPLES.

At the end, the composer came up with two new phrases for his piece, C Fmaj7/C Gm7 F C+ and C Fmaj7/C Bb C Cm G. For the second to the last chord, he chose Cm because he realized it links to two phrases with an interesting internal logic, that is, C "opened" up to go to C+ in the first phrase, while in the second phrase C went in the opposite direction and "contracted" to Cm. The tool gave him "ideas of ways to move forward in the piece, previously I just had this as a repeating progression". He felt the chord sequences were consistent with his style in a way that they bore "grains of progression" that [he] uses a lot, but at the same time the tool helped him go beyond the ordinary. The tool helped him to explore the in-between space:

> "If I am trying to come up with something tonal but [with] variation ... I have difficulty. It's either really tonal or its not and I am not good at the in between, sort of like tonal but breaks free, so that's I think what I accomplished here a little bit".

Using RIPPLES *to change what was fixed*

Participant 8 (P8) came in with a 12-chord long sequence. He had come up with the first two chords, `CM7 Em7`, on the guitar and he "felt like [he] could go somewhere with it" and that he could "really make that build". But when he went to the piano, it took "a different direction".

For the study, we decided to start with the same two chords, `CM7 Em7`, and see what other directions the tool would take it to. The composer initially worked forward, exploring continuations (Figure 1 STEP 2), and then chose `Dm7` as the third chord. In Figure 1 STEP 3, he continued to work forward, and marked the most untypical continuation as the MOST CREATIVE . But upon seeing that there were also recommendations for how to change the existing chords (bottom four rows), he chose `CM7 Bm7 Dm7`, which replaced the original second chord `Em7` with `Bm7` (result shown in Figure 1 STEP 4). This recommendation was based on its surrounding chords `CM7` and `Dm7`. Note that `Dm7` was a chord inspired by the tool earlier.

Even though the composer originally thought of the first two chords as fixed, he was flexible and open to changing them when he saw a substitution he liked. This example also illustrates how the tool could inspire a cascade of changes.

Overall expectations and attitudes towards CR

Participants' reactions to CR were mixed. We give a few brief examples of how participants reacted to CR for the different tasks. For the task of seeking variation to an existing chord sequence, we saw two contrasting intentions from composers. For example, P14 was open to new ideas of how the sequence could be varied: "I was more open to changing up the direction of it or the feeling of it". Meanwhile, for P7, it was the opposite. He had a more specific idea about what the desired variations would sound like and how they would relate back to the original sequence: "[I am] more picky about how I am changing it. [It] took longer [than composing from scratch] to go through [the chord recommendations] and find the right chord".

For the task of starting from scratch, we also saw two contrasting experiences. For example, P7 felt that composing with CR was much faster than improvising on a piano: "I like it when I'm composing from scratch. I have less an idea of what I want, hearing what's next, makes the process quicker". In contrast, P15 found it difficult to generate a chord sequence from scratch, partly because this way of working was foreign to him. He usually writes songs by collaborating with his friend who would first compose a melody and pass it on to him, and he then would come up with chords to accompany it.

Choosing between chord recommendations in CR

There are often several different levels of decisions at play when a composer is trying to decide which chord to choose. For example, [3] outlined four decision levels in a compositional process, which consists of the objective, the musical idea, grammaticality and technical aspects. Moreover, a composer's decision-making criteria are dependent on the stage she is in in the compositional process and also where she is structurally in the piece. Furthermore, a composer might be trying specifically to find the chords she is hearing in her mind [P9] or be open to new ideas [P14].

The different decision levels are often interconnected. A composer may have an overall objective of "breaking out of diatonic harmony" [P7]. Similarly, P14 says "I'm looking more for less conventional chords". These aesthetic aspirations can impact what composers consider as grammatically plausible. On the other hand, a certain chord may work well grammatically but "changes feel" [P14], changes what the phrase is expressing. This elevates the level of decision to that of the musical idea.

When choosing between recommendations in CR, composers often anticipate what subsequent changes or continuations may be needed. For example, choosing one chord may lead to the need to change the next two chords [P14] because it does not flow well into those two chords which are themselves a unit. P1 struggled between a chord she liked more but would require more work to complete the phrase, versus a chord that would conclude the phrase immediately.

Impact of CR on the composition process

Upon first encountering the tool, many participants felt compelled to listen to all of the recommendations. P14 commented "I want to listen to all of them, even if it might not make sense just looking at it, because why not, maybe it will spark something". P15 felt the options were too many and that it was hard to choose between them. It was "like too many ice-cream flavours when you only want three". In contrast, P9 said "I use this like an inspiration and so seeing, having it suggest a ton of stuff to me, I was just like getting more information faster".

Participants had different interpretations on the nature of the recommendations and their effects. P9 described the tool as "yelling at you with things you won't think about", and when he "sees something crazy, try it, get more crazy". This sentiment was echoed in P6. Upon seeing a chord recommendation that increased tension, she was inspired to want even "more intensity, so [she] added a 7th'. P12 said the tool helped him "see where it can go from here". P9 likened the tool to a co-pilot that gives him validation when he sees the chords he wants to try out among the suggested chords. Many composers were delighted to explore a wider palette of out-of-key, extended, altered and inverted chords. P7 said the tool helped him stay "out of straightforward diatonic space", and that it suggested "new places to go". While others found some of the out-of-key chords to be irrelevant: "It doesn't go together. I just feel like it's random" [P14].

Let us zoom into out-of-key chords for a moment. Composers find it harder to workout out-of-key chords manually: "It is hard to generate these chords without hearing how they sound first" [P8]. CR helped composers imagine and hear how to transition to and from and between out-of-key chords, making them more accessible.

> "That's a big jump for me to make in just a few chords, something I'm not able to do on my own, play around and land there" [P7].

P7 pointed out that CR helped him infer which key he was in by suggesting continuations that showed him "this is where you are going" [P7]. He said he would otherwise have forced the sequence to end in the wrong key and destroyed it: "it saved me from myself", said P7.

P8 described the experience of working with CR as faster than working things out in his head, while P6 felt it was a much faster process then improvising on a piano:

> "It is just faster, instead of doing that in my head, these are all the options that make sense, just try them and see if one of these are what you are thinking about" [P8].

The tool at times altered the workflow of the composer by inspiring new directions. For example, P7 originally planned to fix the beginning and the end of the phrase and just work on the middle. But upon seeing the chord recommendations for the middle chords, he chose chords that suggested new directions which required the changing of the ending chords.

EXPERIMENT 2: CONTROLLED EXPERIMENT

In contrast to the first study, we designed a controlled experiment to measure how the level of adventurousness of chord recommendations and how RIPPLES respectively impact the novelty of students' chord progressions and their level of satisfaction.

Task, procedure, participants

The task was to transform a given 8-chord long progression to reflect the character and mood of an image, such as Van Gogh's Starry night. The participants were told that they would not be evaluated on how well the chord progression reflects the image, but that they can see the image as a source of inspiration.

The independent variable of this experiment was the recommendation type. We designed three variations of CHORDRIPPLE: for the current active chord, recommends

- SINGLETON-TYPICAL: only single-chord substitutions that are the most typical given the context
- SINGLETON-ADVENTUROUS: only single-chord substitutions that are similar to current active chord but less typical in the given context
- RIPPLE: single-chord substitutions as in SINGLETON-ADVENTUROUS and also RIPPLE substitutions that include them as the middle chord.

Each participant was first asked to complete a tutorial that involved trying out all the functionality of CHORDRIPPLE. After completing the tutorial, each participant was asked to complete all three conditions. The order of the conditions was randomized. Each condition was paired with a different initial chord progression and image.

Similar to the first set of studies, we recruited 11 music student from local universities. One student had to leave early for class and did not complete the study. The system crashed for another student in the middle of a condition. At the end, we collected 9 complete logs.

Hypotheses

We test two hypotheses regarding how recommendation type might have an impact on the novelty of chord sequences composed and students' satisfaction.

- H1: SINGLETON-ATYPICAL will result in more novel sequences (and higher satisfaction) than SINGLETON-TYPICAL
- H2: RIPPLE will result in more novel sequences (and higher satisfaction) than SINGLETON-ATYPICAL.

Design and analysis

We used a within-subjects design with one factor (recommendation type) with three levels (SINGLETON-TYPICAL, SINGLETON-ATYPICAL, and RIPPLE). We measured two variables: the user's satisfaction with the chord progressions they composed on a 5-point Likert scale, and also the novelty of their top-rated chord progression. We define NOVELTY of a chord progression $c_{0..T-1}$ as the average of the inverse counts (as measured in the ROCK corpus) of the constituent chords, as shown in Eqn. (7).

$$\text{novelty}(c_{0..T-1}) = \sum_{i=0}^{T-1} \frac{1}{N_{c_i}} \quad (7)$$

We used the nonparametric Friedman test to first check if there are differences among the different levels. If the test is significant, we then perform the planned pairwise comparisons following the hypotheses and use the nonparametric Wilcoxon signed-rank test to see if they are statistically significant.

Main effects and discussion

There was no effect of the recommendation type on the satisfaction of the student's ratings on their best chord progression. The means and standard deviations of the ratings in each of the conditions are shown in Table 3. Note that the statistical tests computed are within-subjects and the table is just for giving an overview on the distributions of students' ratings.

We did, however observe a main effect in recommendation type on the novelty of students' best-rated chord progressions. The means and standard deviations of the NOVELTY scores in each of the conditions are shown in Table 3, again just to show the overall differences across conditions. The Friedman's test shows that there are differences in novelty among the three conditions within subjects, and that the effect is significant ($\chi^2(2, N = 9) = 12.67$, $p = 0.0018$). We found that when composing with the SINGLETON-ATYPICAL design variation of CR, students generated chord progressions more novel than when using the SINGLETON-TYPICAL design. The Wilcoxon signed-rank test shows that this effect was statistically significant ($p = 0.0039$), as shown in Table 4. Hence, this supports the novelty aspect of H1.

We did not observe a statistically significant effect for the pair RIPPLE between SINGLETON-ATYPICAL ($p = 0.0977$). Hence, H2 is not supported. We also performed a post-hoc pairwise comparison and found that the RIPPLE condition resulted in progressions that were more novel than the SINGLETON-TYPICAL and the effect was statistically significant ($p = 0.0273$).

These results show that recommending more adventurous chords can help students compose more novel chord progressions. In particular, our chord embedding model was able to make chord recommendations that help students go beyond the ordinary. We did not observe that RIPPLES made it easier for students to incorporate more adventurous chords. We speculate that it is because RIPPLES tend to smooth things out and use less atypical chords in a row. Moreover, novelty itself does not always lead to satisfying progressions. For example, a chord progression may contain many novel chords but incoherent.

Furthermore, there are also many reasons why a RIPPLE might be chosen, beyond smoothing out the transitions between the original context and recommended novel chord. For example, a RIPPLE may be used because it is an interesting variation of the original context, or because the RIPPLE changes more chords at once and allows users to more quickly explore different ideas.

BROADER DISCUSSION AND DESIGN IMPLICATIONS

We have observed that CR had many positive effects on composers' compositional process, although the particular outcomes depended on the person and the details of the task they were working on. Therefore, while this approach is overall helpful, a one-size-fits-all solution is not optimal.

There are several factors that affect how adventurous the composer may want the chord recommendations to be. First, a composer's musical and stylistic aspirations would influence their receptiveness to less frequently heard chords. For example, P3 described his goal as writing a "poppy" song that would be easy to relate to, and wanted to use chords that the general audience would find familiar. P5 was seeking chords that carried the sound typical of a genre. Many other students had the goal of "breaking out", and wanted to use chords that would be less likely encountered if they were improvising on their instruments.

Also, adventurousness is contextual. P8 considered using a triad among a chord sequence of mostly seventh chords as a bold move, as the triad really "stands out". At other times, the intention of the composer may be to find "something simple" so that it does not take away from the other more "iconic moments" of the phrase [P8].

We specifically designed CR to provide suggestions ranging from very typical to very adventurous, so that it could accommodate the diverse needs of composers. However, CR currently takes a fixed approach, splitting its recommendations to be half typical and half adventurous, but composers at times wanted more of one kind. Composers sometimes found some of the recommendations to be too similar to each other.

We propose that designers could include a mechanism that explicitly allows composers to adjust how typical to adventurous they want the recommendations to be. Systems should also allow composers to control the scope of diversity for recommendations, so that they could adjust between widely exploring the chord palette versus zooming into the variations of a particular sound. Furthermore, composers have different goals for different parts of a piece. For example, the intention of "making it longer" versus "I'm trying to end here" would entail very different chord recommendations. The former may include chords that open up new directions while the latter would focus on chords that provide a resolution. We propose that there could be a "knob" that allows users to control the amount of "tension" desired in the chord recommendations. It may also be possible to automatically infer a composer's intention for "conclusiveness" based on the musical context and the chords she has explored so far. The advantage of a knob is that it affords the user with more fine-grained control and the potential to explore a wider range of possibilities iteratively. The advantage of inferred intentions is that they can be used to automatically adapt the chord recommendations, allowing composers to see only what is relevant and thus making the process of composing faster.

ACKNOWLEDGEMENT

I had countless discussions with Ken Arnold throughout the duration of this work. Hubert Ho helped me tirelessly in all aspects of logistics. I want to thank MuseAmi for their feedback and support during summer 2015, especially Eric Humphrey and Leigh Smith at MuseAmi Labs.

Measure	SingletonTypical	SingletonAtypical	Ripple
Self-rated satisfaction	4.5 (0.707)	4.06 (0.682)	4.222 (0.939)
Novelty	0.021 (0.035)	0.147 (0.091)	0.063 (0.085)

Table 3. The mean (standard deviation) of the two measures, self-rated satisfaction and NOVELTY, of student's best chord sequence in the three conditions.

SingletonTypical – SingletonAtypical	SingletonTypical – Ripple	SingleAtypical – Ripple
$S = -22.50, p = 0.0039$	$S = -18.50, p = 0.0273$	$S = 14.50, p = 0.0977$

Table 4. Comparisons on the novelty of student's best chord sequence between all the pairs of conditions, reporting the test statistic S and two-tailed significance p from the the Wilcoxon signed-rank test.

REFERENCES

1. Chuan, C.-H., and Chew, E. A hybrid system for automatic generation of style-specific accompaniment. *Proceedings International Joint Workshop on Computational Creativity.* (2007).
2. Cuthbert, M. S., and Ariza, C. music21: A toolkit for computer-aided musicology and symbolic music data.
3. Delalande, F. Towards an Analysis of Compositional Strategies. *Circuit: Musiques contemporaines 17*, 1 (2007).
4. Fukayama, S., Yoshii, K., and Goto, M. Chord-sequence-factory: A chord arrangement system modifying factorized chord sequence probabilities. *International Society for Music Information Retrieval Conference ISMIR* (2013).
5. Garcia, J., Tsandilas, T., Agon, C., and Mackay, W. E. Structured observation with polyphony: a multifaceted tool for studying music composition. In *DIS '14: Conference on Designing Interactive Systems*, DIS '14, ACM (2014), 199–208.
6. Marsh, R., Landau, J., and Hicks, J. How examples may (and may not) constrain creativity. *Memory and Cognition 24*, 5 (1996), 669–680.
7. Mikolov, T., Sutskever, I., and Chen, K. Distributed representations of words and phrases and their compositionality. *Advances in Neural Information Processing Systems.* (2013), 1–9.
8. Morris, D., Simon, I., and Basu, S. Exposing parameters of a trained dynamic model for interactive music creation. *Proc AAAI 2008* (2008), 784–791.
9. Nichols, E., Morris, D., and Basu, S. Data-driven exploration of musical chord sequences. *Proceedings of the 13th international conference on Intelligent user interfaces IUI 09* (2009), 227.
10. Nijstad, B. A., Stroebe, W., and Lodewijkx, H. F. Cognitive stimulation and interference in groups: Exposure effects in an idea generation task. *Journal of Experimental Social Psychology 38*, 6 (2002), 535 – 544.
11. Serrà, J., Corral, Á., Boguñá, M., Haro, M., and Arcos, J. L. Measuring the evolution of contemporary western popular music. *Scientific reports 2* (2012).
12. Siangliulue, P., Arnold, K. C., Gajos, K. Z., and Dow, S. P. Toward collaborative ideation at scale: Leveraging ideas from others to generate more creative and diverse ideas. In *Proceedings of the 18th ACM Conference on Computer Supported Cooperative Work and Social Computing*, CSCW '15, ACM (New York, NY, USA, 2015), 937–945.
13. Simon, I., Morris, D., and Basu, S. MySong: automatic accompaniment generation for vocal melodies. In *Proceedings of ACM CHI 2008 Conference on Human Factors in Computing Systems*, vol. 1 (2008), 725–734.
14. Temperley, D., and Clercq, T. D. Statistical Analysis of Harmony and Melody in Rock Music. *Journal of New Music Research 42*, 3 (Sept. 2013), 187–204.
15. Tymoczko, D. Local Harmonic Grammar in Western Classical Music. Available at `http://www.dmitri.mycpanel.princeton.edu/mozart.pdf`.

Learning Item Temporal Dynamics for Predicting Buying Sessions

Veronika Bogina
Information Systems Dept.
The University of Haifa,
Haifa 31905, Israel
sveron@gmail.com

Tsvi Kuflik
Information Systems Dept.
The University of Haifa
Haifa 31905, Israel
tsvikak@is.haifa.ac.il

Osnat Mokryn
Information and Knowledge Management Dept.
The University of Haifa
Haifa 31905, Israel
omokryn@univ.haifa.ac.il

ABSTRACT

Identifying whether an e-commerce session will end up in a buy is an ongoing research topic. A session predicted as a non-buying one may trigger recommender systems, thus increasing the probability of a buy. Alternatively, a session predicted as a buying session may enable recommender systems to predict additional items.

In this work, we suggest a prediction model leveraging the temporal characteristics of both the session and the items clicked in that session. Our method introduces a buying probability per session as a function of the clicked-items recent purchase history, and the session temporal characteristics.

Empirical results on imbalanced e-commerce dataset with more than nine million sessions demonstrate that we achieve high Precision, Recall and ROC in predicting whether a session ends up with a purchase. In a wider perspective, our findings shed light on the importance of considering items temporal dynamics in e-commerce sites recommendations.

Author Keywords

Electronic commerce; Recommender Systems; Temporal Dynamics; Machine Learning; Imbalanced Data Set

ACM Classification Keywords

I.2.6 [Artificial Intelligence]: Learning; I.2.1 [Artificial Intelligence]: Applications and Expert Systems.

INTRODUCTION

E-commerce companies use recommender systems to both help customers overcome the information overload, caused by the large number of products that are available on their sites, and increase sales. Products can be recommended based on previous purchases history, top-seller statistics, customer's demographics, context, and more [22].

IUI'16, March 07-10, 2016, Sonoma, CA, USA

DOI: http://dx.doi.org/10.1145/2856767.2856781

Moe [17] observed that when potential buyers click through different items on an e-commerce website they have different objectives and defined a topology map for storing websites visits. These maps categorize sets of clickstreams as buying, browsing, searching, or visit-based knowledge building. These clickstreams can be referred to as sessions.

Temporal Dynamics, e.g., item popularity and user ratings over time, were studied by Koren [13], who found that they can affect user preferences and thereby the interaction between users and items. Tang [23], revealed that the trending of products changes with time, week by week, or even day by day, due to user interest change, demand shifts ignited by some external events or simply because a product is out of inventory.

Temporal trends were studied not only in recommender systems [5,7,13,14,15,23] but also in general Web search. Google Trends is Google's feature that uses the time series index of the volume of queries users enter into Google search. For example, the volume of queries on a particular brand of a watch during the second week of May might be helpful in predicting the June sales report for that brand, when it is released in June. In [6] the authors claim that by using Google Trends they can predict the present, in other words: Google queries help predict economic activity.

Following the above, our goal is to address the following research question: *How can a session's temporal dynamics, as well as the in-session clicked item's recent purchase trend, be used in predicting buying sessions*?

The rest of the paper is organized as follows. First we present related work from two aspects: session-based recommendations and temporal dynamics. Then we present the trends modeling approach. From then on the details of our experiment are described. Thereafter we present the evaluation of our method. Finally, conclusions and suggestions for future work are presented.

RELATED WORK

So far, most of the research in recommender systems was geared towards using temporal dynamics in collaborative filtering (CF). As far as we know little attention was paid to e-commerce sessions and predicting whether they end up with a purchase.

Session-based Recommendations

Session-based recommenders have been researched lately in the music domain. Park et al. [15] coined the term "Session-Based CF," They presented a modified User-based CF that uses session information to capture sequence and repetitiveness in the listening process. Zheleva et al. [9] developed a session-based hierarchical graphical model using Latent Dirichlet Allocation, and showed that their model could facilitate playlist completion based on previous listening sessions or songs that the user has just listened to.

Dias & Fonseca [6] took one step further by using temporal context and session diversity in music recommendation for recommending the next song. For session presentation they used five features: time of day (users tend to listen to different songs at different periods of time), weekday (users song preferences are different in weekday and weekend), day of month (users tend to listen more happy music in the beginning of the month and sad – towards the end), month (users preferences are not the same during different seasons) and song diversity. They showed that the inclusion of temporal information, either explicitly or implicitly, increases significantly the accuracy of the recommendation, when compared with traditional session-based CF.

Poggi et al. [20] focused on session based admission control systems and suggested a method for learning to prioritize Web sessions according to their generated revenue. Their goal was to prevent websites overloading. Using traditional machine learning techniques and Markov-chain models, they were able to estimate the probability of the user's purchasing intentions based upon early navigation clicks. In their model, they rely on the following features: date and time of transaction (discretized to a few categories), tag (identifying the type of transaction performed by the page), whether the user is logged in at this moment, whether s/he is a returning customer, whether s/he bought in the past, and the length of the current session (in number of transactions). They defined buying probability $\Pr(buy|p)$ given that the last k tags in the session are those described by path p. No temporal dynamics of the items were taken into account.

Temporal Dynamics

Koren [13] examined two major temporal effects. The first addresses the fact that an item's popularity may change over time. For example, movies can go in and out of popularity as triggered by external events such as the appearance of an actor in a new movie. The second major temporal effect allows users to change their baseline ratings over time. For example, if user tends to rate an average movie as "4 stars", either his rating scale or the identity of the rater within a household can change over time. Hence, the average rate may change to "3 stars".

Additional work on temporal dynamics was done by [1] on Twitter, where they discovered that temporal features can be successfully exploited for improving the accuracy of personalization. They showed that interests of individual users in a topic evolve differently over time.

TEMPORAL FEATURES AND DYNAMICS

Given the contribution of temporal considerations presented above, we suggest to leverage the use of temporal dynamics of both the items and the sessions for a session-based prediction of a purchase.

Along with the session temporal characteristics, we suggest the use of the trendiness of items, to determine the *session's trendiness*. A session is as trendy as the trendiest item clicked in it recently.

Dataset

We used the Yoochoose RecSys challenge dataset [21] that contains two log files: click events log and buy events log. The click events log contains clicks entries for sessions and items, where each entry has session id, a timestamp (the time when the click occurred), an item id and the category of the item. The buy events log contains buy events for sessions that already appear in the click-events log and ended with a buy. Each entry contains a session id, a timestamp (the time when buy occurred), an item id, a price and a quantity. Table 1 provides the dataset statistics.

#clicks	#buying sessions	#non-buying sessions	#items
33003944	509696	8740032	52739

Table 1. Data Statistics

Items Trends Modeling

To model the trends we performed the following process: The data set was randomly split into two subsets: 80% of the sessions were used for a learning phase (*Temporal Model Building Data*) and the remaining 20% were used for experimentation (*Experimental Data*). The proportion of buy and not buy (5% vs 95%) was kept in these datasets.

Trends Model Building and Session's Trendiness

For each item in the Model Building Data subset two entries in two lookup tables were created: buy and not buy.

For every item, in every day, an entry in the *Buy Lookup Table*, containing the number of buying sessions it appeared in was calculated. Similarly, in the *Not Buy Lookup Table*, the number of not buying sessions per each day it appeared in was calculated. For example, at day 91 (that relates to our start day in the data – April, 1) item1 appeared in the six buying sessions and eight not buying sessions (see Table 2).

To model the trending behavior of each item we examine its recent purchase history over a short time window. Heuristically, we chose a time window of three days. If the number of buying sessions, it was clicked in, was not decreasing, that means, increasing or remaining the same (essential product), then such item is included in the session generation phase. If not, it is ignored. We also require that it was clicked in sessions in at least two days before the current day, ignoring new items that appeared one day ago and for which we could not examine tendency by only one appearance. For example, according to Table 2 – if session's date is day 94 and item1, item2 and item3 appear in this session. Item3 will not be included in further analysis, since we can see decreasing tendency over the three last days. For item 1 – it is increasing and for item2 it is not decreasing, it is constant.

Item/Day	91	92	93
Item1	6	8	9
Item2	5	5	5
Item3	7	5	4

Table 2. Lookup table for buy

Session Temporal Features

The following features are used in building the session representation feature vector:

- *Session Trendiness* – we take a naïve approach. Since in our Model Building Phase we've created two lookup tables – one for "buy" events and another one for "not buy" events, we calculate the trendiness of each item as its buying probability over the last n days as follows:

  $$\Pr(buy_i = 1) = \frac{\#buy\ sessions\ for\ the\ last\ n\ days\ i\ appears\ in\ , i \in s}{\#sessions\ for\ the\ last\ n\ days\ i\ appears\ in, i \in s}$$

  The trendiness of the session is then determined according to the trendiest item in this session:

  $$\Pr(buy_s = 1) = \max \Pr(buy_{i \in s} = 1)$$

- *Number of clicks in the session*. This is not the same as the number of items that appear in the session, since the same item could be clicked several times.

- *Session dwell time* - represents session length, it sums up all dwell times that were spent on examining all item in the session. Here we followed the same idea as Yi et al. [23] that used dwell time as a proxy to quantify how likely a content item is relevant to a particular user.

- *Session start hour* – captures the fact that people tend to buy differently, depending on the hour of the day. For example, in the data set we had people purchased more at 9am and 7pm than any other hour during the day, probably before their work day starts and after it is over.

- *Month* – the data included purchase sessions from April till September, the most "buying" month was August. *Week of the year* – correlates with the month.

- *Day of the week* – we've seen that on Sundays and Mondays people tend to purchase more than on other week days.

- *Day of the year* – mapping of each day to a number between 1 and 365. For example, day 91 relates to our start day in the data – April, 1. This feature is used in the proposed model at the Learning phase.

Feature Selection

After applying WEKA's feature selection process, the selected features (by WEKA) were: trendiness of the session, number of clicks in the session, session dwell time and session start hour. Hence, we created a vector that represents each session and contains the selected features mentioned above.

EXPERIMENT

To evaluate our method, we use the RecSys challenge data set and compare different classifiers, as well as the effect of different features.

Handling Imbalanced Data

The remaining 20% of sessions (that were not used for trends modeling, described above) were still an imbalanced dataset, where classification categories are not equal in size. In such cases, according to [10], classifiers will have a good accuracy classifying items belonging to the main category, but poor performance on the other one. Recent literature suggests a variety of approaches to deal with data imbalance [15,19].

We have used SMOTE [5] to balance the 20% data set. It is the combination of oversampling and undersampling techniques. It combines Informed Oversampling of the minority class with the Random Undersampling of the majority class. Moreover, since our data is a low-dimensional, SMOTE is beneficial in this case, as it operates on the feature space rather than data space.

Classification

In recommender systems, one common practice is to use ensembles of classifiers [11]. Any hybrid technique that combines the results of several classifiers could be seen as an ensemble method. Netflix winners [2] used combination of many different methods in their study. The two most common ensemble techniques are Bagging and Boosting [11]. Bagging ("Bootstrap Aggregation") was initially proposed by Breiman [3] and it combines outputs from several machine learning techniques for improving the performance and stability of prediction or classification. This technique is a special form of the averaging method.

In our experiment we've used two classifiers and decided to present those that performed well on our features: Bagging classifier and NBTree. WEKA [16] allows to choose for Bagging different base-learn classifiers. 1R is a classifier that uses the minimum-error attribute for prediction, discretizing numeric attributes. RepTree is a decision tree algorithm. NBTree is a hybrid of decision trees with Naive Bayes classifiers learned from the instances that reach the leaves. It appears to be a viable approach to inducing classifiers, where many attributes are relevant for classification, yet conditionally independent given the label [12]. The above classifiers were selected for presentation here because they performed well on our dataset (other classifiers that were used include Logistic Regression and Random Forest, but due to the limited space their results are not presented and discussed).

We conducted 10-fold cross validation experiments using WEKA on the *Experimental Data*, in two scenarios: One included all selected features and another without the session trendiness feature. The trendiness of items is evaluated over a time window of three days.

RESULTS

Our experimental results show that using temporal and dynamic characteristics indeed enables a good prediction for whether a session will end up in a purchase.

Table 3 details the set of measures evaluating the results of our method while applying Bagging with 1R, RepTree as base-learner and NBTree. All previously explained and selected features were used. Specifically, we can see from the results in Table 3 that Bagging with 1R classifier performs best, followed by NBTree and Bagging with RepTree. It is easy to see that Bagging with 1R outperforms all classifiers in all measures but the ROC where NBTree (that in general came up second) performed best.

	Bagging 1R	Bagging RepTree	NBTree
Precision	**0.937**	0.852	0.926
Recall	**0.930**	0.848	0.918
F-measure	**0.929**	0.848	0.918
ROC	0.939	0.926	**0.948**

Table 3. Three days history with all selected features

In order to evaluate the effect of the trendiness feature, we ran the classifiers again, this time without using this feature.

Table 4 shows the results for the same set of classifiers (but without the session trendiness). We can see that the results without using the session trendiness feature are clearly less distinctive using all three classifiers. It is interesting to note that while in general the performance of all classifiers is worse, this time the Bagging with RepTree outperforms all other classifiers, and suffers least.

	Bagging 1R	Bagging RepTree	NBTree
Precision	0.649	0.824	**0.840**
Recall	0.643	**0.808**	0.766
F-measure	0.641	**0.806**	0.755
ROC	0.682	**0.889**	0.811

Table 4. Three days history without trendiness feature

DISCUSSION, CONCLUSION AND FUTURE WORK

In this paper we introduced a novel method that used temporal dynamics of the items together with the temporal features of the session to perform a session-based buying prediction – whether the session ends up with a "buy" or not. We further showed that using the recent temporal dynamics of the item, i.e., its current trendiness, improves the prediction accuracy.

In retrospective, however, the real challenge is to predict, *during* the session, whether it is going to end with a purchase. This work could be a first step in creating a novel real-time recommender system that integrates temporal dynamics into the reasoning process of an online prediction mechanism. This mechanism may guide an online recommender for improving the shopping experience to the benefit of both the buyer and the seller. As we envision the process, first we predict if a session is going to end up with a purchase or not. In this way we can identify sessions that are candidate for recommendation – that are not buying sessions and recommend them items that might change it to be buying session.

This work was done using a specific data set; hence it is limited to the characteristics of the data set and the information that is available here. Before drawing any general conclusions, there is a need to repeat this experiment in different datasets, and in different domains.

In the future we plan to check temporal dynamic on additional datasets. We further intend to improve our prediction by using hidden Markov chains.

REFERENCES

1. Abel, F., Gao, Q., Houben, G. J., & Tao, K. (2011, June). Analyzing temporal dynamics in twitter profiles for personalized recommendations in the social web. In Proceedings of the 3rd International Web Science Conference (p. 2). ACM.
2. Bell, R. M., Koren, Y., & Volinsky, C. (2007). The BellKor solution to the Netflix prize.
3. Breiman, L. (1996). Bagging predictors. Machine learning, 24(2), 123-140.
4. Breiman, L. (2001). Random forests. Machine learning, 45(1), 5-32.
5. Chawla, N. V., Bowyer, K. W., Hall, L. O., & Kegelmeyer, W. P. (2002). SMOTE: synthetic minority over-sampling technique. Journal of artificial intelligence research, 321-357.
6. Choi, H., & Varian, H. (2012). Predicting the present with google trends.Economic Record, 88(s1), 2-9.
7. Dias, R., & Fonseca, M. J. (2013, November). Improving music recommendation in session-based collaborative filtering by using temporal context. In Tools with Artificial Intelligence (ICTAI), 2013 IEEE 25th International Conference on (pp. 783-788). IEEE.

8. Ding, Y., & Li, X. (2005, October). Time weight collaborative filtering. InProceedings of the 14th ACM international conference on Information and knowledge management (pp. 485-492). ACM.
9. E. Zheleva, J. Guiver, E. Mendes Rodrigues, and N. Milic-Frayling, ´ "Statistical models of music-listening sessions in social media," Proc. of World Wide Web, 2010.
10. Ganganwar, V. (2012). An overview of classification algorithms for imbalanced datasets. International Journal of Emerging Technology and Advanced Engineering, 2(4), 42-47.
11. Kantor, P. B., Rokach, L., Ricci, F., & Shapira, B. (2011). Recommender systems handbook. Springer.
12. Kohavi, R. (1996, August). Scaling Up the Accuracy of Naive-Bayes Classifiers: A Decision-Tree Hybrid. In KDD (pp. 202-207).
13. Koren, Y. (2010). Collaborative filtering with temporal dynamics.Communications of the ACM, 53(4), 89-97.
14. Lathia, N., Hailes, S., Capra, L., & Amatriain, X. (2010, July). Temporal diversity in recommender systems. In Proceedings of the 33rd international ACM SIGIR conference on Research and development in information retrieval(pp. 210-217). ACM.
15. Lewis, D. D., & Catlett, J. (1994). Heterogeneous uncertainty sampling for supervised learning. In Proceedings of the eleventh international conference on machine learning (pp. 148-156).
16. Mark Hall, Eibe Frank, Geoffrey Holmes, Bernhard Pfahringer, Peter Reutemann, Ian H. Witten (2009); The WEKA Data Mining Software: An Update; SIGKDD Explorations, Volume 11, Issue 1.
17. Moe, W. W. (2003). Buying, searching, or browsing: Differentiating between online shoppers using in-store navigational clickstream. Journal of consumer psychology, 13(1), 29-39.
18. Park, S. E., Lee, S., & Lee, S. G. (2011, May). Session-based collaborative filtering for predicting the next song. In Computers, Networks, Systems and Industrial Engineering (CNSI), 2011 First ACIS/JNU International Conference on(pp. 353-358). IEEE.
19. Pazzani, M., Merz, C., Murphy, P., Ali, K., Hume, T., & Brunk, C. (1994). Reducing misclassification costs. In Proceedings of the Eleventh International Conference on Machine Learning (pp. 217-225).
20. Poggi, N., Moreno, T., Berral, J. L., Gavalda, R., & Torres, J. (2007). Web customer modeling for automated session prioritization on high traffic sites. InUser Modeling 2007 (pp. 450-454). Springer Berlin Heidelberg.
21. RecSys Challenge: http://2015.recsyschallenge.com/challenge.html
22. Schafer, J. B., Konstan, J., & Riedl, J. (1999, November). Recommender systems in e-commerce. In Proceedings of the 1st ACM conference on Electronic commerce (pp. 158-166). ACM.
23. Tang, L. (2015). Top-k Recommendation with Temporal Dynamics. arXiv preprint arXiv:1506.02190.
24. Yi, X., Hong, L., Zhong, E., Liu, N. N., & Rajan, S. (2014, October). Beyond clicks: dwell time for personalization. In Proceedings of the 8th ACM Conference on Recommender systems (pp. 113-120). ACM

A Live-User Study of Opinionated Explanations for Recommender Systems

Khalil Muhammad
Insight Centre for Data Analytics
University College Dublin
khalil.muhammad@insight-centre.org

Aonghus Lawlor
Insight Centre for Data Analytics
University College Dublin
aonghus.lawlor@insight-centre.org

Barry Smyth
Insight Centre for Data Analytics
University College Dublin
barry.smyth@insight-centre.org

ABSTRACT

This paper describes an approach for generating rich and compelling explanations in recommender systems, based on opinions mined from user-generated reviews. The explanations highlight the features of a recommended item that matter most to the user and also relate them to other recommendation alternatives and the user's past activities to provide a context.

ACM Classification Keywords

H.3.3 Information Search and Retrieval: Information filtering; H.5.2 User Interfaces: Evaluation/methodology

Author Keywords

Recommender Systems; Explanations; Opinion Mining

INTRODUCTION

Recommender systems attempt to learn about a user's preferences in order to make targeted suggestions about the items they may be interested in. Recently researchers have turned their attention to explaining recommendations to make it easier for users to make informed decisions, with a view to increasing conversion rates and leading to more satisfied users [1–5]. Early work explored the utility of explanations in collaborative filtering systems with [1] reviewing different models and techniques for explanation based on MovieLens data. They considered a variety of explanation interfaces leveraging different combinations of data (ratings, meta-data, neighbours, confidence scores etc.) and presentation styles (histograms, confidence intervals, text etc.) concluding that most users recognised the value of explanations.

Bilgic and Mooney [6] used keywords to justify items rather than disclosing the behaviour of similar users. They argued that the goal of an explanation should not be to "sell" the user on the item but rather to help the user to make an informed judgment. Elsewhere, keyword approaches were further developed by [2] in a content-based, collaborative hybrid capable of justifying recommendations as: *"Item A is suggested because it contains feature X and Y that are also included in items B, C, and D, which you have also liked."*; see also the work of [7] for related ideas based on user-generated tags instead of keywords. Explanations can also relate one item to others. For example, Pu and Chen [3] build explanations that emphasise the tradeoffs between items, such as *"Here are laptops that are cheaper and lighter but with a slower processor"*. In this paper we describe the results of a user study designed to evaluate the relative merits of different styles of recommendation explanations. The recommendation setting, and the explanations produced are novel in the sense that item descriptions and user profiles are mined directly from user-generated reviews.

OPINION MINING FOR RECOMMENDATION

This paper builds on recent work [8–11] by the community about mining opinions from user reviews to generate user profiles and item descriptions for recommender systems. The work of [10, 11] is especially relevant and describes how shallow opinion mining techniques can be used to extract rich feature-based item descriptions (item *cases*) based on the features that users refer to in their reviews and the polarity of their opinions. An in-depth description of this approach is beyond the scope of this paper and the interested reader is referred to [10, 11] for further details. However, in the interest of what follows we will briefly summarise the type of opinion data that can be produced for the purpose of recommendation and this forms the basis for our explanations. Without loss of generality, we will do this using a reference dataset of TripAdvisor hotel reviews that is available privately for academic use only. The dataset comprises of information about 2,370 hotels, 150,961 users and 227,125 reviews from June to August 2013.

Generating Item Descriptions

Each item/hotel h_i is associated with a set of reviews $R(h_i) = \{r_1, \ldots, r_n\}$, the opinion mining process extracts a set of features, $f_1, \ldots, f_m$, from these reviews, as described in [10, 11]. Each feature, f_j is associated with an *importance* score and a *sentiment* score as per Equations 1 and 2. The importance score, $imp(f_j, h_i)$, is the relative number of times that f_j is mentioned in $R(h_i)$. The sentiment score, $s(f_j, h_i)$, is the degree to which f_j is mentioned positively or negatively in $R(h_i)$.

$$imp(f_j, h_i) = \frac{count(f_j, h_i)}{\sum_{\forall f' \in R(h_i)} count(f', h_i)} \quad (1)$$

DOI: http://dx.doi.org/10.1145/2856767.2856813

$$s(f_j,h_i) = \frac{pos(f_j,h_i)}{pos(f_j,h_i)+neg(f_j,h_i)} \quad (2)$$

$$item(h_i) = \{(f_j, s(f_j,h_i), imp(f_j,h_i)) : f_j \in R(h_i)\} \quad (3)$$

An item/hotel case description is a representation of these features and scores as per Equation 3. Note, $pos(f_j,h_i)$ and $neg(f_j,h_i)$ denote the number of mentions of f_j labeled as positive and negative during the sentiment analysis phase. So $s(f_j,h_i)$ values close to *1* mean that positive opinions dominate whereas a score close to *0* means that negative opinions dominate.

Generating User Profiles

Similarly, we can generate a profile of a user u_T based on the reviews that they have written by extracting features and importance information from these reviews as in Equation 4.

$$user(u_T) = \{(f_j, imp(f_j,u_T)) : f_j \in R(u_T)\} \quad (4)$$

We give more meaning to the frequency with which the user reviews a particular feature, rather than the average sentiment of the user's opinions, since the frequency of mentions is a better indication of which features matter most to a user. For users that have not written any reviews, we can build their profiles by mining opinions from reviews that they have found helpful in the past, or by mining those features that tend to dominate in the hotels that they have stayed in.

FROM OPINIONS TO EXPLANATIONS

Our aim is to describe an approach for generating explanations for each item in a set of recommendations $H = \{h_i ... h_k\}$ generated for some user u_T. The novelty of our approach stems from how we leverage opinion information in two ways: (1) to highlight those important features (*pros* and *cons*) of an item that likely matter to u_T; (2) to emphasise those features that distinguish the recommendation relative to other items, such as alternative recommendations or past bookings.

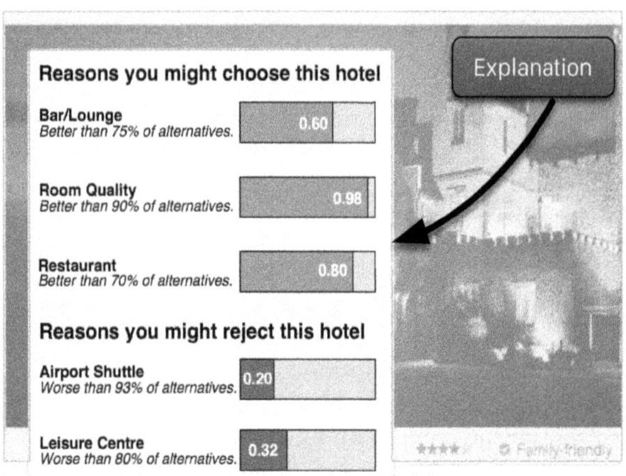

Figure 1. An example explanation showing *pros* and *cons* that matter to the target user along with sentiment indicators (horizontal bars) and information about how this item fares with respect to alternatives.

Core Explanation Components

To begin with, we present in Figure 1 an example explanation for one particular hotel. There are a number of components

	Feature	Importance	Sentiment	better/worse
PROS	Bar/Lounge *	0.25	0.71	75%
	Free Breakfast	0.22	0.79	10%
	Room Quality *	0.18	0.98	90%
	Restaurant *	0.15	0.80	80%
	Shuttle Bus	0.06	0.75	10%
CONS	Airport Shuttle *	0.21	0.20	90%
	Leisure Centre *	0.11	0.32	80%
	Swimming Pool	0.10	0.45	33%
	Room Service	0.5	0.46	20%
	⋮	⋮	⋮	⋮

Figure 2. An example of an explanation structure showing *pros* and *cons* that matter to the user along with associated importance, sentiment, and better/worse than scores.

worth highlighting. First, the explanation is made up of a number of features that have been extracted from the reviews of this hotel and that are known to matter to the user; these are features that the user has mentioned in their own past reviews. Second, these features are divided into *pros* and *cons*, the former with positive sentiment scores $s(f_j,h_i) > 0.7$ and the latter with more negative sentiment scores $s(f_j,h_i) < 0.7$. The *pros* might be reasons to choose the hotel whereas *cons* might be reasons to avoid it. In the case of our data, there are significantly more positive sentiments than negatives, thus a sentiment threshold of 0.7 provides a reasonable split between pros and cons. Third, each feature is associated with a *sentiment bar* that shows the actual sentiment score for that feature. And finally, each feature is associated with an additional piece of explanatory text that highlights how the hotel compares to other relevant items called a *reference set* H' — such as alternative recommendations as in this example — in terms of this feature; the aim here is to provide the user with some additional explanatory context by relating the feature to other hotels that may be relevant to their decision.

Generating a Basic Explanation Structure

To generate an explanation like the one shown in the previous section, we start with a *basic explanation structure* that is made up of the features of the item in question (h_i) which are also present in the user's profile u_T. These features are divided into *pros* and *cons* based on their sentiment score $s(f_j,h_i)$ and ranked in order of importance $imp(f_j,u_T)$.

We also compute so-called *betterThan* (BT) and *worseThan* (WT) scores as in Equations 5 and 6 with respect to some suitable reference set H'. These scores calculate the percentage of items in the reference set for which f_j has a better sentiment score (for *pros*) or worse sentiment score (for *cons*) in h_i. Suitable reference sets include the set of alternative recommendations and the users own past bookings; in this section we assume the former.

$$BT(f'_j,h_i,H') = \frac{\sum_{h_c \in H'} 1[s(f'_j,h_i) > s(f'_j,h_c)]}{|H'|} \quad (5)$$

$$WT(f'_j,h_i,H') = \frac{\sum_{h_c \in H'} 1[s(f'_j,h_i) < s(f'_j,h_c)]}{|H'|} \quad (6)$$

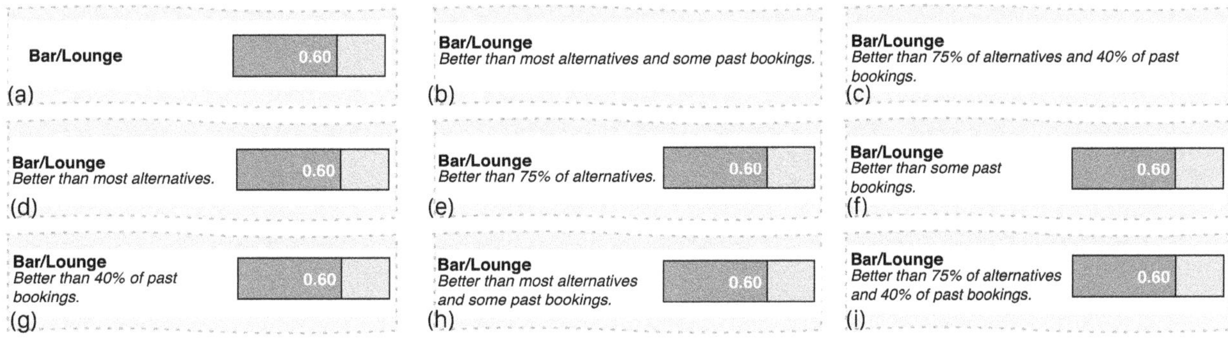

Figure 3. Fragments of explanation interfaces showing all 9 variations (a)-(i); examples of complete interfaces are shown in Figure 4.

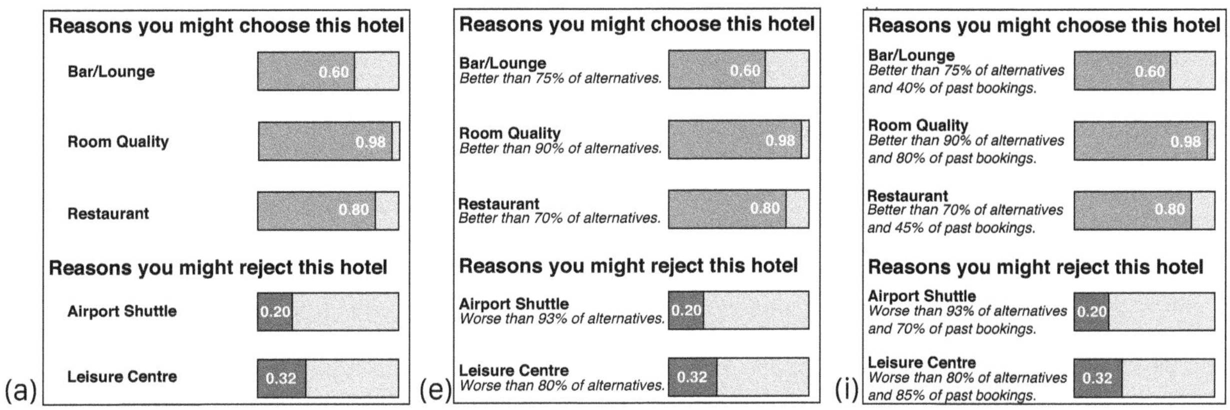

Figure 4. Full sample explanations for the variations (a), (e) and (i).

Figure 2 shows an example basic explanation structure with set of 5 *pros* and 4 *cons*. For each we can see its importance to the user, its sentiment score from the hotel's reviews, and the corresponding better/worse scores. In this case the reference set is the alternative recommendations suggested alongside this hotel (which are not shown here). For example, we see that the *Bar/Lounge* feature, with a sentiment score of 0.6, is better than 75% of the alternative recommendations.

From Basic to Compelling Explanations

Not every feature in the previous example makes for a compelling reason to choose or reject the hotel in question. For example, the *Free Breakfast*, while positively reviewed, is only better than 10% of the alternative recommendations. If this feature is important to the user then there are better alternatives to chose from. In contrast, this hotel's *Room Quality* beats 90% of the alternatives and so may offer a strong reason to prefer this hotel. To simplify the explanations that are presented to users, and make them more compelling, we filter out features than have lower better/worse scores ($< 50\%$) so that only those features that are better/worse than a majority of alternatives remain; these features are indicated with an asterix in Figure 2. They are all features that matter to the user and they distinguish the hotel as either better or worse than a majority of comparable items, e.g. alternative recommendations.

In summary then, to produce an explanation for some recommended item h_i for user u_T given some reference set of related items H' we first identify those features of h_i that matter to u_T, based on their profile. Next we separate these features into *pros* and *cons*. And then we eliminate those *pros* that are not better than a majority of the reference set and those *cons* that are not worse than a majority of the reference set. Finally, we rank-order these remaining (compelling) features by importance to u_T for inclusion in the final explanation.

EVALUATION

We have described an approach to generating novel recommendation explanations based on opinions mined from user-generated reviews. These explanations can be generated to help justify a recommended item to the user by highlighting features that matter to them. We argue that the user can make a more informed decision when the features of the item being explained are separated into *pros* and *cons*, and then augmented with sentiment and contextual information.

Setup

We prepared a range of different explanation styles/interfaces as the initial part of a user study. All of the interfaces separated features into *pros* and *cons*, but each variation was different in terms of whether sentiment bars were used, which reference sets were chosen (alternative recommendations vs. past bookings), and whether the better/worse scores were presented as precise percentages or not. For reasons of space we cannot show the complete set of all 9 interfaces. Instead, in Figure 3 we present the relevant (single-feature) fragments from each of the 9 interfaces and the reader is also referred to Figure 4

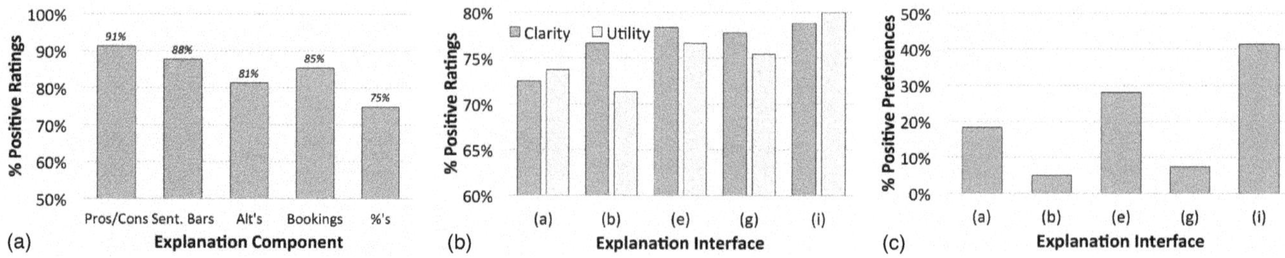

Figure 5. Results of ratings and preferences obtained from live-user study to assess the utility and clarity of different explanation interfaces

for three examples of the complete explanation interfaces. For instance, the fragment in Figure 3(e) indicates that this interface type includes sentiment bars, a reference set made up of alternative recommendations, and that percentage better/worse scores are used. An example of a complete explanation corresponding to this style is shown in Figure 4(e).

We recruited 181 participants, the majority as post-graduate researchers in a number of local universities. In each case, after some evaluation preliminaries where we explained the purpose of the study, we asked them to review the 9 different explanation interfaces and evaluate their overall clarity and utility (on a scale of 1 to 10); the presentation order was shuffled to avoid ordering effects. Based on these ratings we selected the top-5 explanation styles overall and asked the users to select one as their preferred style. After they reviewed all 9 interfaces we asked them to rate the usefulness of the different explanation components (*pros/cons*, sentiment bars, relationship to alternative recommendations or past bookings, and the use of percentages in better/worse scores). Next, we will describe a subset of the results obtained.

Results

To begin, Figure 5(a) shows the percentage of positive ratings (ratings of 5 or higher) received for each of the different types of explanation components. In general the ratings were very high, particularly for the use of *pros/cons* and sentiment bars (both with an average rating of higher that 7). Users expressed a slight preference for reference sets made up of past bookings compare to alternative recommendations, perhaps indicating that they found it easier to relate recommendations to hotels they had stayed in formerly rather than other recommendations that they had little or no knowledge about. In any event these ratings suggest that, in isolation, users found each of the various explanation components to be useful.

For reasons of space we cannot show the individual ratings scores for each of the 9 interfaces here. However, based on the ratings provided (as referred to above) we selected the top-5 most highly rated styles — variations (a), (b), (e), (g), and (i) — as shown in Figure 3. The clarity and utility scores for these top-5 versions are presented in Figure 5(b). In fact, for convenience we show the percentage of *positive ratings* (ratings of 5 or higher) in terms of clarity and utility. Note too that the explanation interface labels refer to the corresponding labels in Figure 3. We can see a preference for those styles that include richer forms of explanation data — styles (e), (g), and (i) — with clarity and utility scores in excess of 75% in each case. Explanation styles that included only the sentiment bars or the reference information – (a) and (b) — while highly rated overall did not score quite as well, especially with respect to utility. This makes sense. The participants found the various types of explanation components to be useful in their own right but even more so in combination. And in particular, the combination of sentiment bars, reference set comparisons, and percentage better/worse scores (interface (i)) achieved the highest number of positive ratings in terms of utility (80%) without any significant compromises in terms of clarity (78%).

The participants, after reviewing and rating individual interface styles, were asked to select a single favourite from the top-5 most highly rated variants. The results presented in Figure 5(c) shows the percentage of preferences that each of the top-5 most highly rated interfaces received. Again we see a strong preference for explanation style (i) which echoes its strong clarity and utility ratings above. Here, variation (i) was selected as the preferred interface by 42% of the respondents with the next best scoring variant (e) securing less than 30% of the preferences. Variant (e) was also high scoring in terms of its clarity and utility scores, but it did not rate as highly when it came to a user's single preference. Interestingly, variant (g) which scored as well as (e) and close to (i) in terms of clarity and utility ratings, did not feature prominently in the respondents final preferences; it secured less than 10% of their votes. This agrees with the preference users seem to hold for past bookings as a reference set versus alternative recommendations (see Figure 5 above); variation (g) used past bookings whilst (e) used alternative recommendations. And in the end, the combination of both reference sets in variation (i) clearly appealed to a majority of respondents.

CONCLUSIONS

We have described a novel approach to generating rich and compelling recommendation explanations mined from user-generated reviews. The results of a live-user study suggest that users found this approach to explanation to be useful, and expressed a preference for interfaces that combined a number of different explanation components. This evaluation is preliminary and limited as its focus has been solely on the explanation interface and we have not fully explored the role of these explanations in a live recommendation setting — this is a matter for future work.

ACKNOWLEDGMENTS

This work is supported by the Insight Centre for Data Analytics under grant number SFI/12/RC/2289.

REFERENCES

1. J. L. Herlocker, J. A. Konstan, and J. Riedl, "Explaining Collaborative Filtering Recommendations," in *Proceedings of The 2000 ACM Conference on Computer Supported Cooperative Work*, CSCW '00, (Philadelphia, USA), pp. 241–250, ACM, Dec. 2000.
2. P. Symeonidis, A. Nanopoulos, and Y. Manolopoulos, "Providing Justifications in Recommender Systems," *IEEE Transactions on Systems, Man, and Cybernetics - Part A: Systems and Humans*, vol. 38, pp. 1262–1272, Nov. 2008.
3. P. Pu and L. Chen, "Trust-Inspiring Explanation Interfaces for Recommender Systems," *Knowledge-Based Systems*, vol. 20, pp. 542–556, Aug. 2007.
4. M. Coyle and B. Smyth, "Explaining Search Results," in *Proceedings of The 19th International Joint Conference on Artificial Intelligence*, (Edinburgh, UK), pp. 1553–1555, Morgan Kaufmann Publishers Inc., July 2005.
5. G. Friedrich and M. Zanker, "A Taxonomy for Generating Explanations in Recommender Systems," *AI Magazine*, vol. 32, pp. 90–98, June 2011.
6. M. Bilgic and R. J. Mooney, "Explaining Recommendations: Satisfaction vs. Promotion," in *Proceedings of Beyond Personalization Workshop at the 2005 International Conference on Intelligent User Interfaces*, (San Diego, USA), pp. 13–18, Jan. 2005.
7. J. Vig, S. Sen, and J. Riedl, "Tagsplanations: Explaining Recommendations using Tags," in *Proceedings of The 13th International Conference on Intelligent User Interfaces*, (Florida, USA), pp. 47–56, ACM Press, Feb. 2008.
8. K. Yatani, M. Novati, A. Trusty, and K. N. Truong, "Review spotlight: a user interface for summarizing user-generated reviews using adjective-noun word pairs," in *Proceedings of the SIGCHI Conference on Human Factors in Computing Systems*, (New York, NY, USA), pp. 1541–1550, ACM, 2011.
9. J. Huang, O. Etzioni, L. Zettlemoyer, K. Clark, and C. Lee, "Revminer: An extractive interface for navigating reviews on a smartphone," in *Proceedings of the 25th annual ACM symposium on User interface software and technology*, (New York, NY, USA), pp. 3–12, ACM, 2012.
10. R. Dong, M. Schaal, M. P. O'Mahony, and B. Smyth, "Topic Extraction from Online Reviews for Classification and Recommendation," in *Proceedings of the 23rd International Joint Conference on Artificial Intelligence*, IJCAI '13, pp. 1310–1316, AAAI Press, 2013.
11. R. Dong, M. P. O'Mahony, and B. Smyth, "Further Experiments in Opinionated Product Recommendation," in *Proceedings of The 22nd International Conference on Case-Based Reasoning*, (Cork, Ireland), pp. 110–124, Sept. 2014.

PanoSwarm: Collaborative and Synchronized Multi-Device Panoramic Photography

Yan Wang
Columbia University
2960 Broadway, New York, NY, USA
yanwang@ee.columbia.edu

Sunghyun Cho
Samsung Electronics
95, Samsung 2-ro, Giheung-gu, Yongin-si, Gyeonggi-do, Korea, 446-811
sodomau@postech.ac.kr

Jue Wang
Adobe Systems
801 N 34th Street, Seattle, WA, USA
juewang@adobe.com

Shih-Fu Chang
Columbia University
2960 Broadway, New York, NY, USA
sfchang@ee.columbia.edu

ABSTRACT

Taking a picture has been traditionally a one-person task. In this paper we present a novel system that allows multiple mobile devices to work collaboratively in a synchronized fashion to capture a panorama of a highly dynamic scene, creating an entirely new photography experience that encourages social interactions and teamwork. Our system contains two components: a client app that runs on all participating devices, and a server program that monitors and communicates with each device. In a capturing session, the server collects in realtime the viewfinder images of all devices and stitches them on-the-fly to create a panorama preview, which is then streamed to all devices as visual guidance. The system also allows one camera to be the host and send direct visual instructions to others to guide camera adjustment. When ready, all devices take pictures at the same time for panorama stitching. Our preliminary study suggests that the proposed system can help users capture high quality panoramas with an enjoyable teamwork experience.

Author Keywords

photography; multi-device; collaborative; synchronized; panorama

ACM Classification Keywords

H.5.3 Group and Organization Interfaces: Collaborative computing

DOI: http://dx.doi.org/10.1145/2856767.2856778

Figure 1. Severe ghosting artifacts observed in the conventional panorama stitching approaches.

INTRODUCTION

Photography has been largely a one-person's task since the invention of the camera in the 18th century. While setting up the scene may require group effort, the camera has always been designed for a single photographer who controls all the key factors in the capturing process, from scene composition and camera setting to the shutter release time. Thus, despite the rapid advances on camera hardware in recent years, the basic workflow of taking a picture, i.e. a single camera controlled by one photographer, largely remains unchanged.

Unfortunately, a single camera cannot satisfy all the creative needs that consumers may have. As a representative example, taking multiple shots and stitching them into a panorama has become a standard feature in most modern image capturing apps on mobile devices. However, it does not work well for highly dynamic scenes that contain fast moving objects such as pedestrians or cars, which can easily lead to severe ghosting artifacts due to their fast motion in the capturing process (see Figure 1). To avoid such artifacts, it is desirable to have all photos covering different parts of the scene to be taken at exactly the same time, which is beyond the current capability of a single consumer camera.

In this paper, we propose a novel system that allows multiple regular mobile devices to dynamically form a team, and work collaboratively in a synchronized fashion to capture a high quality panorama of a dynamic scene. Our system includes a networked server that continuously collects low-resolution viewfinder images from all participating devices during a capturing session, analyzes their content to discover the relative camera positions, and stitches them into a preview panorama. On the client side, each camera continuously streams all the information from the server and presents it on a unique capturing interface. On the interface each user can see not only how his/her own image contributes to the final result, but also a direct visualization of the scene coverage of other cameras. Guided by the visualization, the user's task is to move the camera relative to others to increase the scene coverage of the panorama while avoiding gaps and holes in-between cameras. Our system also allows one user to become the "host", who can send visual guidance to other users on how to move their cameras. When all the cameras are ready, the host sends a signal through the server to capture all the final images at approximately the same time, and renders a high quality panorama from them as the final output. With the simultaneous photo capturing design, the notorious ghost effects in conventional single camera settings can now be alleviated.

By also allowing a group of users to work as a team to capture a single photo, our system introduces an entirely new social photo capturing experience. The recent development of mobile device cameras enables consumers to take high quality pictures anywhere at anytime, and further allows them to be shared on social networks right after being captured, transforming photography into an essential component in our daily social lives. The creative community also started to explore new ways to allow a group of users to collaboratively develop a photo story using photos from different users [1, 12]. However, all these social interactions happen *after* the photos have been taken. In contrast, our system enables teamwork and user interactions *before* a photo is taken, when the users are at the same physical location together.

The main design goal of the system is twofold: (1) on the technical side, we aim to provide a mechanism for consumers to capture high quality panoramas using regular mobile devices, which cannot be achieved otherwise with existing software; and (2) on the user experience side, we aim to provide an enjoyable social photography experience for consumers with different levels of photography skills. To evaluate whether our system achieves the above goals, we conducted a preliminary user study by recruiting user groups to use the system to capture panoramas of real scenes. The result suggests that our system is capable of capturing high quality panoramas, and the process is enjoyable. It also provides us insights on how to further improve the user experience, and guidance for designing future larger scale studies.

RELATED WORK

Panorama Stitching

Panorama stitching has been extensively studied in computer vision and graphics in the last decade [5], and the underlying technologies have significantly advanced to allow efficient implementations on mobile phones [20], sometimes with realtime preview [3]. There are many mature software products for creating panoramas as post-processing, such as Realviz Stitcher and Canon PhotoStitch. It also became a standard feature in the photo capturing modules of mobile platforms, such as Apple iOS 7 and Windows Phone 8. All these solutions require the user to take a series of images that cover the scene, while maintaining some amount of partial overlap among the images for the purpose of alignment [13].

A well-known difficulty for panorama stitching is moving objects [15], which often cause ghosting artifacts as they appear in different positions in different images. Although various computational solutions have been proposed to reduce the artifacts [8], their effectiveness and application range are limited, and some of them require additional user input that is tedious to provide [2]. Another solution to this problem is to develop special hardware systems that hook up multiple cameras to take all shots at the same time, such as the Mrotator One-Shot Photographic head produced by Agno's. However, these devices are expensive and bulky, designed for high-end professional tasks rather than consumer applications.

Various applications and interfaces have also been developed for panorama stitching, especially on mobile devices. Looking At You [9] is an interface using mobile sensors such as gyroscopes and face tracking to help users view large imagery on mobile devices. Videos can also be integrated within panoramic contexts, providing a browsing experience across both the temporal and spatial dimensions [14]. However, none of the works address collaborative capturing or the ghosting artifacts in the panoramas.

Multi-Camera Arrays

Building multi-camera array systems using inexpensive sensors has been extensively explored. These systems can be used for high performance imaging, such as capturing high speed, high resolution and high dynamic range videos [18, 19], or the light field [17]. These systems however are not designed for multi-user collaboration. Some of them contain large-scale, fixed support structures that cannot be easily moved around, and they all require special controlling hardware for sensor synchronization. Our approach, in contrast, uses existing hardware and software infrastructure (e.g. wireless communication) for camera synchronization, thus can be easily deployed to consumers. More importantly, user interaction plays a central role in our capturing process, but not in traditional camera arrays.

Collaborative Multi-User Interface

Multi-user interface design is also a rising topic, especially in the HCI community. The "It's Mine, Don't Touch" project [11] builds a large multi-touch display in the city center of Helsinki, Finland for the users to do massively parallel interaction, teamwork, and games. Exploration has also been done about how to enable multiple users to do painting and puzzle games on multiple mobile devices [4].

In addition to trials on different applications, researchers in Computer Support Cooperative Work (CSCW) provide insights about collaborative interface as well. Kittur. et al. suggested that for complicated tasks having high interdependency on each sub-task, it requires more organization and coordination rather than merely involving more workers for an efficient collaboration [10]. More specifically, a host may help reduce the comminication overhead and thus improve the efficiency [7].

The above research inspires us that it is possible to naturally introduce social interactions from the users' conflicts in using the interfaces. Our work benefits from this observation, but it also differs from these interfaces in that we make panorama stitching as the primary goal, providing users a means to obtain motion-artifact-free panoramas, which has its unique technical challenges and cannot be done with the interfaces mentioned above.

Collaborations in Photography

Collaboration has deep roots in the history of photography, as shown in a recent art project that reconsiders the story of photography from the perspective of collaboration [6]. This study created a gallery of roughly one hundred photography projects in history and showed how "photographers co-labor with each other and with those they photograph."

Recent advances on Internet and mobile technologies allow photographers that are remote to each other in space and/or time to collaboratively work on the same photo journalism or visual art creation project. For example, the 4am project [1] gathers a collection of photos from around the world at the time of 4am, which has more than 7000 images from over 50 countries so far. The "Someone Once Told Me" story [12] collects images in which people hold a card with a message that someone once told them. In addition, shared photo album is an increasingly popular feature among photo sharing sites (e.g. Facebook) and mobile apps (e.g. Adobe GroupPix), which allows people participated in the same event to contribute to a shared album. All these collaborative applications focus on the sharing and storytelling part of the photography experience, but not the on-the-spot capturing experience.

PhotoCity is a game for reconstructing large scenes in 3D out of photos collected from a large number of users [16]. It augments the capturing experience by showing the user the existing 3D models constructed from previous photos, as a visualization to guide the user to select the best viewpoint for taking a photo. In this way, photos of different users can be combined together to form a 3D model. However, this system is designed for *asynchronized* collaboration, meaning that photos are taken at different times. In contrast, our system focuses on *synchronized* collaboration for applications that require all images to be taken at the same time.

DESIGN GUIDELINES

Recall that the motivation of our system is twofold. On the one hand, we wish to provide a new photography functionality that enables capturing panoramas of highly dynamic scenes using regular mobile devices. On the other hand, we want to make this tool intuitive and fun to use, and to encourage interactions among people who are at the same location at the same time regardless of their current social relationship. To realize these two goals, we design our system with the following guidelines:

Encourage social interactions among users with a collaborative interface. As mentioned above, we propose to encourage more social interactions in the photography process by developing a collaborative capturing system, where every user contributes to only a portion of the final image.

Provide a clear, easy-to-follow workflow. Panorama stitching is a fairly complicated process even for a single user. Having multiple users to work collaboratively in a realtime capturing session requires a clear workflow where each step is intuitive and easy to follow. The types of actions and interactions in each step should be limited so users can quickly learn them on the spot, with limited training and practicing.

Provide clear roles and tasks for different users. Given each user equal responsibility and capability in a single session may introduce conflict and confusion. It is desirable to have a single host user that plays the role of coordinating all other users and making sure each step is done correctly. Other users then play a supporting role and follow instructions given by the host. The two types of roles need to be provided with separate sets of user controls.

Provide live preview and keep users in the loop. When capturing panoramas using traditional tools, the users generally have little idea on how the final image will look like until the capturing is completed. It would be especially frustrating if the system fails to generate a good result after intensive teamwork. Thus, the system needs to constantly keep users in the loop, giving them immediate visual feedback after any camera movement, as well as a live preview of the final result.

Limit the duration of a capturing session. The longer a capturing session takes, the more likely that users may feel frustrated or tired and give up in the middle. Thus, the system should be able to converge quickly, e.g. within 1 minute.

USER EXPERIENCE

Following the design guidelines listed above, we created PanoSwarm, a collaborative panorama capturing application that lets users work together in a synchronized fashion for capturing and stitching a panorama. Let us follow a group of users: Alice, Bob and Carol as they use PanoSwarm to capture a panorama of an interesting and dynamic scene.

Team Formation

Alice, Bob and Carol all have PanoSwarm app installed on their iPhones. Carol first opens the app on her iPhone, and selects the option of starting a new capturing session, which automatically makes her the *host user* of the session. A unique QR code then appears on her screen, allowing Alice and Bob

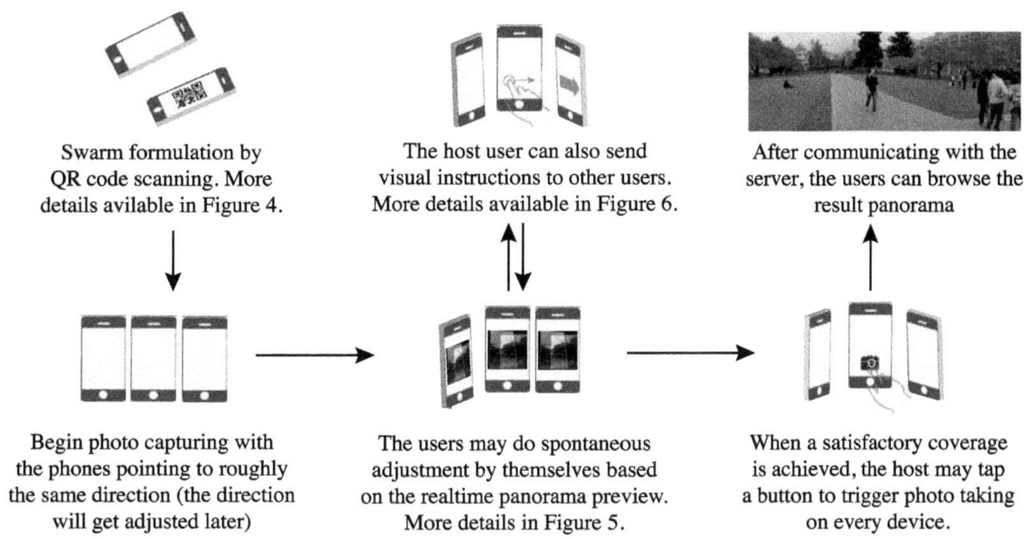

Figure 2. Flow chart of our PanoSwarm system. For clarity, only the critical components for each procedure are rendered on the phone screens in the figure.

to scan using their devices and join the session. Alice scans the code first, and the same QR code automatically appears on her screen, so she can pass it to Bob.

Guided View Finding

After all three users join the session, they make a selection on the UI to enter the capturing mode. Initially, they point their cameras to roughly the same direction, so the system can determine their relative camera positions based on the overlapped portions of the images, and then they begin to adjust the camera directions with the help of the interface. On each user's screen, a preview panorama automatically appears, with colored bounding boxes showing the contribution from each camera. Being the host, Carol then guides Alice and Bob to adjust their cameras to increase the scene coverage of the panorama. She selects Alice's camera on her screen and swipes to the left. On Alice's screen, she immediately sees a red arrow pointing to the left, indicating that she is instructed to turn her camera that way. She then gradually moves her camera towards the left, and sees that the panorama is updated in realtime according to her camera motion. The red arrow only exists for a short period of time and then disappears. Carol monitors Alice's camera motion on her own screen, and she feels the movement is not enough. So she keeps sending the swipe gesture to Alice to instruct her to keep moving, until her camera is turned into the desired direction.

Similarly, Carol selects Bob's camera and uses the swipe gesture to instruct him to turn his camera to the right, which Bob follows. However, Bob moves his camera too far and his image can no longer be stitched with other ones. This is reflected on the panorama preview, and Bob notices it and moves his camera back. Finally, Carol directly talks to Alice and Bob to move their cameras up a little bit, to capture more on the building and less on the ground.

Capturing

When Carol feels the current preview panorama is good to capture, she clicks the button to trigger the capture event. Alice and Bob simultaneously see a countdown on their own screens, and they keep their cameras still before the countdown reaches zero. When it happens, all cameras take pictures at the same time. After a short delay, they then stream the high quality panorama from the server for browsing.

The overall user experience chart is also provided in Figure 2 for better illustration.

Design Guidelines Revisited

The design guidelines and user workflow are not as illustrated at the first place. We refined the user workflow and design guidelines iteratively, the insights from which are discussed here. In our initial attempt, PanoSwarm was built as an entirely decentralized system. However we found in this setup the capturing process is hard to converge, as every user has a different idea on how to improve the panorama, and they usually adjust their cameras simultaneously, making their efforts to be contradictory most times. We found that having a host can greatly improve the capturing efficiency, and often lead to much better results, given that camera adjustments are made sequentially and accordingly.

Adding the host role certainly has some drawbacks. From a system design perspective, it introduces a weak point and makes the system less robust. If the hosts device is malfunctioning then the entire system is broken. From social interaction point of view, it introduces rigid authority that limits the ways that users can potentially collaborate.

SYSTEM DESCRIPTION

The PanoSwarm system consists of two components: (1) an Internet or local server that communicates with each participating devices; and (2) a mobile app (currently implemented on the iOS platform) that runs on each device. The server

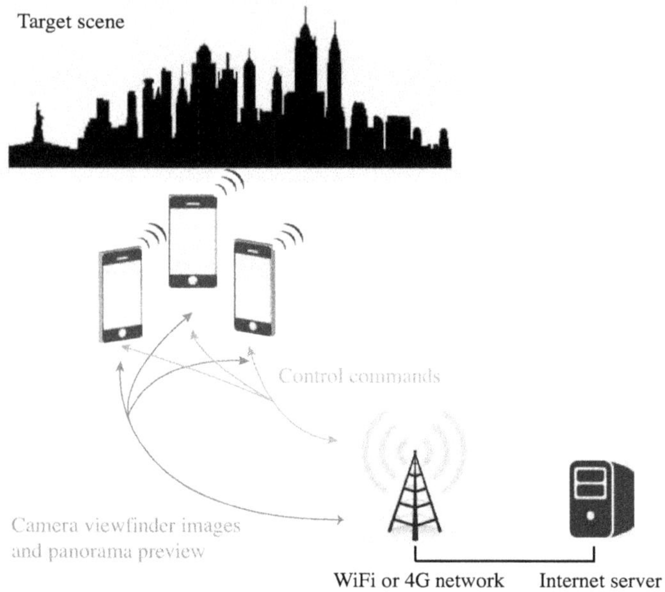

Figure 3. Technical framework of the proposed system.

and the app communicate using standard HTTP protocols. Given the amount of data being transmitted in realtime, the system requires WiFi or 4G network to be available to function smoothly, which is usually not a problem in urban areas. the system framework is shown in Figure 3.

Dynamic Team Formulation

Our system allows users that are physically at the same location to dynamically and temporally form a team for a capturing task. This flexible setup allows users who even do not know each other before to work together as a team. Specifically, when the app launches, it registers itself with the server and obtains a group ID, which is encoded in a QR code and being displayed on the main interface, as shown in Figure 4. Note that every user forms a minimal group consisting of only one user when the app is launched.

A user A can then scan another user B's QR code to join the group that B is currently in. After scanning, device A is assigned with the same group ID as B, and A's QR code on the main interface is replaced by the QR code of B. After A and B are in the group, they can both add news users into the session. In this way a large group can be quickly formed.

On the server side, the server program keeps track of which devices (represented as a unique combination of IP address and port) are associated with the same group ID, and among them which one is the host. When the host taps the "OK" button on the UI to end team formation and enter the actual capturing process, a unique section ID is assigned to this group.

Live Panorama Preview

During the capturing process, each participating device sends a downsized version (maximum dimension is 300 pixels in our implementation) of the current viewfinder image to the sever at the rate of 3 frames/second. The server collects images from all devices and generates a coarse preview

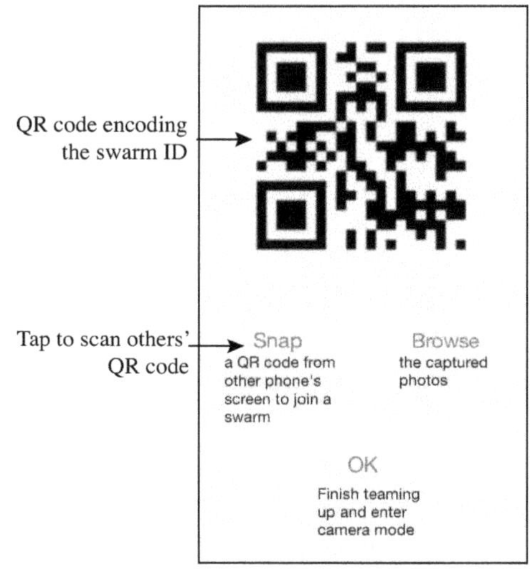

Figure 4. The main interface for easy team formulation. User can join other people's team by simply tapping the "Snap" button and scan others' QR code.

panorama in realtime on the fly, which is then streamed back to each device. We use low resolution images in realtime communication in order to prevent network congestion and server processing burden, so as to maintain a smooth user experience.

The preview panorama serves for two main purposes. First, it gives each user a direct visualization of how his/her own image contributes to the final panorama, and in which direction he/she should move the camera to increase the scene coverage. Without such a preview, it would be really hard for users to mentally reconstruct the relative camera positions, even they could see the viewfinder images of other devices.

The online preview also turns panorama capturing into a WYSIWYG experience. In the traditional panorama capturing workflow, the user is required to finish capturing all the images at first, then invoke an algorithm to stitch the panorama offline. However, given panorama stitching is not a trivial task and involves using advanced computer vision techniques, it may fail at times, and the user either has to give up or re-capture the whole series of images. The lack of instant feedback makes this task to be unpredictable. With the live preview provided by our system, the user can instantly see how his/her camera motion affects the final result, and has the opportunity to adjust the camera to avoid/correct any errors or artifacts in the final result, before capturing the actual images. It thus significantly increases the success rate of the system. This is particularly important for collaborative teamwork, as it takes a significant amount of effort for all participating users to accomplish a collaborative session, thus a bad result is particularly discouraging.

Computing panorama in realtime is technically challenging, even for downsized images. To maintain computational efficiency, we implemented a simplified version of the panorama stitching algorithm on the server, which only uses SIFT feature matching to estimate affine transforms for alignment. Other advanced operations, such as exposure correction, lens distortion correction, and seamless blending are not per-

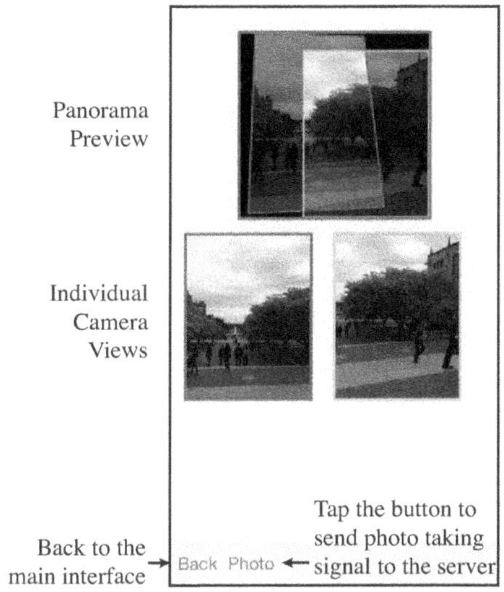

Figure 5. The user interface for the spontaneous adjustment.

formed in the preview stage, but only in the final rendering stage. Such stitching is performed whenever a new viewfinder image is received by the server. We implemented this method using C++ on a server machine with a Core i7 3.2GHz CPU, which achieves 20 fps panorama updating for one PanoSwarm session with four clients.

Guided Camera Adjustment

As mentioned earlier, the users start a capturing session by pointing their cameras to roughly the same object. Then, based on the guidance of the live panorama preview, the users adjust each individual cameras to increase the scene coverage. The adjustments can be made either spontaneously by individual users, or under the guidance of the host user, as we will discuss in this section.

Spontaneous Adjustment. In addition to the live panorama preview, our system also provides additional visualization to help users make spontaneous camera adjustment. As shown in Figure 5, overlaid on the live panorama preview in the upper half of the interface, each user's camera is visualized within a colored bounding box. At the lower half of the interface, each user's viewfinder image is displayed in boxes in corresponding colors. Each user is assigned with a unique color, and a user can quickly identify his/her own color by looking at the border of the panorama preview in the upper half, thus to find the corresponding scene coverage in the panorama. It is also easy for the host user to find out the scene coverage of any devices by reading the colors of the bounding boxes.

Once a specific user identifies his/her color, he/she can then move the camera gradually away from the common initial position to increase the scene coverage. Since the preview is updated in realtime, the user instantly sees the impact of the movement to the final result, as well as the relative camera positions of all the devices. The goal of each user is to maximize the coverage of the panorama preview, while maintaining a reasonable amount of scene overlap (typically 1/5 of the size of the image) with adjacent cameras, which is required by the stitching algorithm.

(a) The host user swipes up-left on the camera view of the other user, suggesting her to turn the camera up-left.

(b) A red arrow is rendered on the user's screen to prompt the host user's suggestion.

Figure 6. The interface showing the host led adjustment process.

Instruction-based Adjustment. One problem for spontaneous adjustment is that different users may start conflicting or duplicating adjustments at the same time. For instance, after initialization, two users may start moving their cameras towards the same direction. After they realize that someone else is doing the same adjustment, they may turn their cameras back at the same time again. Thus, the lack of coordination may make the process hard to converge.

To avoid this problem, our system allows the host user to directly give instructions to other users to guide the overall camera adjustment process. Specifically, when the host user finds a user A is contributing too little to the panorama (e.g. because of too much overlap), he/she can easily identify user A's camera in the second row in the interface, based on the color of the bounding box. By simply touching A's camera view and swiping along the direction that the host wishes A to move, a command containing the target user (i.e. A) and the swiping direction will be sent to the server, and then forwarded to A's device. Once the instruction is received on A's device, a red arrow will be rendered on A's screen, prompting the user to turn the camera to the suggested direction. The red arrow has a relatively short lifespan and will disappear shortly. If the host user wishes a large movement of A's camera, he/she can swipe multiple times to encourage A to continue the movement until desired camera orientation is reached. This process is illustrated in Figure 6, with 6(a) indicating the host's view, and 6(b) showing user A's screen.

Photo Capturing

Once all the cameras have reached their desired scene coverage, the host user can trigger the photo capturing event by tapping a button on the user interface. As discussed earlier,

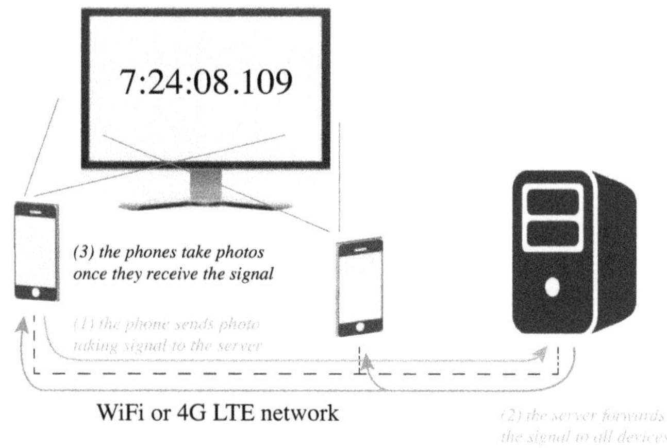

Figure 7. The experiment to verify the effectiveness of the proposed approach of simultaneous photo capturing.

allowing all devices to capture simultaneously is essential for taking motion-artifact-free panoramas in highly dynamic scenes. Our approach for achieving this is to send a signal to the server, and the server will forward this signal to all the devices in the same session. Once a device receives the signal, the app automatically triggers the camera to take a picture, and then upload it to the server for final panorama stitching.

To verify whether this approach can produce accurate synchronization, We first test its feasibility in a controlled environment. As shown in Figure 7, we display a millisecond level clock on a computer screen, and set up two smartphones that both point to the clock. We implement the signal forwarding system mentioned above, and let one of the phones send out the photo taking signal to the server. Both phones will immediately take a photo of the clock once they receive the signal form the server, including the phone that sent out the signal initially. Using this design, variance of the signal arrival delay between the server and the clients can be directly measured, by comparing the difference of the time shown in the photos taken by individual cameras.

We conducted this experiment using WiFi connection as well as 4G LTE networks, and observed time differences on different devices to be well below 100ms. In WiFi networks, the difference is generally smaller than 40ms. This small difference is usually negligible in real panorama capturing tasks, and would not introduce noticeable artifacts.

PRELIMINARY EVALUATION

We implement the proposed system as an iPhone app, and provide a video to demonstrate the system in action, available at `https://www.youtube.com/watch?v=PwQ6k_ZEQSs`. We designed our evaluation to answer three questions: can PanoSwarm help user capture good panoramas of challenging scenes? Is the proposed interface intuitive to learn and use? Furthermore, can PanoSwarm effectively encourage social interactions among people?

Methodology

We compared two interfaces: the built-in panorama capturing procedure in iOS, and the proposed PanoSwarm system.

Participants. We conducted two user study sessions. For the first session, we recruited four users (A1-A4, all male, user group A) from an open e-mail list at a private university. For the second one, we recruited another three users (B1-B3, one female, user group B) at a large public university. All participants self-reported that they extensively used their mobile devices for their photography needs, but had diverse experiences with panorama capturing. Three users were enthusiasts that took panoramas at least once a week (A1, A2 and B1). Three users were casual users that tried a couple of times a year (A3, A4 and B2). User B3 had never tried capturing a panorama before. In addition, the age of the participants ranged from 21 to 32.

Training. At the beginning of each user study session, we trained our participants on how to use our system by going through all the steps once in a capturing session. One of the authors played the role of the host user and explained every step verbally and answered questions, until the subjects had no more questions and can take proper actions in each step. We also explained to user B3 the basic knowledge of panorama stitching, given that he had never done it before.

Tasks. Immediately following the training session, we asked participants to complete at least three capturing sessions of different scenes. When arrived at each scene, before using our system, we asked for one volunteer to take a panorama using the built-in panorama stitching tool in iOS. For each capturing session, we tried to intervene as little as possible, mostly just helped fix some occasional technical issues such as network and device failure. We let the users themselves to decide who should be the host user and which part of the scene to photograph. We also did not give the users specific goals to achieve.

Debrief. We debriefed the participants after they completed their tasks. We asked them for their overall impressions, how PanoSwarm compares to iOS panorama stitching tool, and their overall feedback. In addition, we also asked the participants to complete a short questionnaire.

Results and Findings

In our study user group A finished three capturing sessions and generated three panoramas, and user group B produced six panoramas in six sessions. Every capturing session resulted in a reasonable panorama without dramatic failure such as failed alignment or producing large holes in the panorama, indicating the direct and live panorama preview in the capturing process can effectively help users prevent disasters.

In Figure 8 we show a few panoramas captured by the subjects and compare them with the ones captured by the built-in iOS tool. It suggests that our system can faithfully capture all dynamic objects in the scene, thanks to the simultaneous shutter release on all the devices. In contrast, the iOS tool had difficulties to deal with moving objects and produced obvious ghosting artifacts. It also shows that the differences in exposure time among the devices are small enough to produce high quality results.

Table 1 shows the duration of each capturing session. Some interesting observations can be made from this data:

Figure 8. Comparisons of the panoramas produced by iPhone (top) and our proposed system (bottom) on dynamic scenes. From top to the bottom, each row shows iPhone's result in scene A, our result in scene A, iPhone' result in scene B, and our result in scene B. Note the ghosting artifacts (highlighted in red) in iPhone's results, and the fast-moving, artifact-free objects (highlighted in green) in our results, which are also highlighted in the right column.

Table 1. The duration of each capturing sessions of the two user groups.

	# of users	Time (in seconds)
Group A	4	67, 54, 57
Group B	3	38, 24, 26, 23, 24, 28

1. For both user groups, the first session took noticeably more time than the following sessions, possibly indicating that the users need more time to get familiar with the interface and workflow when using the app for the first time.

2. After the first session, the duration of the capturing sessions quickly came down and became relatively stable, suggesting that the users can learn how to use the app fairly quickly.

3. The average session duration for group A is almost twice as long as that of group B. While the two groups consist of different users, we hypothesize that this is largely due to the different sizes of the groups. Group A has one more

user, thus it may have significantly increased the required user effort for collaboration.

In terms of system scalability, we have tested our system on up to eight devices, and found no issues in the network latency in a WiFi environment. However the server, which is a laptop, did reach 100% CPU occupation. We think it is feasible to accommodate more than eight devices by using a more powerful server (note the complexity of the matching algorithm is linear to the device number because we have the gyroscope and compass readings).

Ease of Use

We also asked about the subjects' opinions about the ease of use of the interface, as well as how they like it compared to iPhone's panorama, in the questionnaire. All users agreed that the system is easy to learn, with better capability than iPhone's default tool, except B3, who had not used any panorama tool before. User B2 commented that "*iPhone does a great job for static scene panoramas. however, it is not very good in two things: 1. Lack of ability for dynamic scene, e.g. ghost shadow. 2. You need to hold steady while moving the phone. PanoSwarm does a good job in both of these.*" User A4 commented that "*from the early prototype I have seen, I think this app fills a totally different need than the native iphone panorama. When messing with the native app you notice that people in frames sometimes get cut off because they are moving- we didn't see anything like that with this app. There is of course the overhead that you need more people with PanoSwarm, but like I mentioned earlier I think this is a cool feature*".

Since our interface provides multiple dynamic views, such as the panorama preview and the live viewfinder images from all devices, we asked the subjects which view is the most important and intuitive to them. The users' answers were highly consistent: they all agreed that **the live panorama preview is almost the only view that they looked at during the capturing sessions**, and the live viewfinder images at the bottom of the interface were not particularly useful. This suggests that for future improvement, we could potentially remove all viewfinder images and focus on improving the live panorama view.

Social Interactions

In the evaluation, we noticed that although we did not explicitly require the users to make interactions when using our app, this process naturally generates social activities. **We observe that people naturally started to talk to each other in the process as the primary communication channel, while the host user also used the app to send out visual instructions**. People talked primarily in the early stage of a capturing session, to figure out which area is his or her responsibility. After that the users mainly used the panorama preview to adjust their directions, with occasional instructions from the host.

When asked whether they would like to use the app in the future with their friends, all users commented positively. User B3 never had any panorama capturing experience, but he commented that "*maybe not on daily basis. It looks time-consuming for me to take photos like that. But in some situations I'd like to use it to keep memories, e.g., in an event with a lot of friends.*".

We also found that while the users prefer using the mobile UI to send the movement instructions, they used verbal instructions for stepping forward/backward. This is because our interface does not support these instructions, but we also found that they did this with no difficulty. This may be because stepping forward/backward is one-dimensional movement, which is easy to verbally instruct, while adjusting the camera orientation to the left/right or up/down can be more difficult to be done verbally. We could potentially add functionalities for giving instructions for stepping forward/backward into the user interface, but it may discourage organic natural user interactions. It would be interesting to explore what is the right balance here.

DISCUSSION

While we are glad that the preliminary study shows that users found PanoSwarm effective and useful, there are many ways we can improve it in future work. There are also many interesting questions left unanswered that we would like to address in future studies.

The Size and the Skill Level of the Team

Our preliminary study only involved teams of 3 and 4 users. We observed that in general the 3-user team had shorter capturing sessions than the 4-user team (27 seconds v.s. 59 seconds in average), given that there was one less camera to adjust. Increasing the number of users will increase the computational load of the server, which may make the server less responsive. However, more users in a session may make the task more challenging and potentially generate more rewarding panoramas with larger scene coverage. The questions that is interesting to us is, ignoring the computational issues, is there a sweet spot for the number of users in a single session to maximize the overall experience? Our hypothesis is that the answer to this question highly depends on the skill levels of individual users in the session. If all users are experts, then perhaps a larger team is preferred. On the contrary, if all users are novices, then having smaller teams would reduce the chance of failure. It is however unclear what happens if the users have mixed skill levels. We plan to conduct more studies in the future to explore along this direction.

Can Strangers Work Together?

The two user study teams in our preliminary study were formed by people that already know each other before. Thus, there is less a barrier among them to work together to accomplish a task. However, it is unclear whether total strangers are willing to team up, and furthermore, accomplish the task effectively. We included the question "do you wish to use PanoSwarm with strangers in the future" in our questionnaires, and the turned-around opinions are mixed. Some of the users show interests, for example, user A4 commented that "*of course, I think this is an amazing experience to share with someone I do not know. Great way to break the ice/ meet people who share similar interests (b/c you guys are taking pics of the same stuff)*". But more users are inclined to only use it with friends. An especially interesting view from user B3, who never used panorama stitching before, is that he prefers to not using the app with strangers, but is willing to show off to other people as a conversation starter by using it with his friends. As one of the main motivation of the project is to encourage social interactions among people who otherwise would not interact with each other, we plan to conduct future studies to evaluate its effectiveness on doing so.

Other Collaboration Modes

Our current app has a fixed setup where one host user controls the overall capturing process. When asked what can be further improved, one subject commented that "*I'm not too keen on the idea of a single host controlling where others should move. I think there should be a way to make it more fun for all the users.*" This inspires us to develop an alternative collaboration mode, where each user has equal responsibilities and power in the capturing process. For example, instead of sending instructions to other users for camera adjustment, each user can send all other users a signal indicating where he/she plans to move the camera, and make sure it does not conflict with other users' intentions that have already been broadcasted. This setup does require more calibrated collaboration, but may be more fun to advanced use and can provide a stronger sense of accomplishment. We plan to implement this mode and further study it.

CONCLUSION

We presented PanoSwarm, the first collaborative photography tool that helps multiple users work together to capture high quality panoramas of highly dynamic scenes, which cannot be done with traditional single camera panorama capturing workflow. Our system employs a client-server framework. The server collects all viewfinder images and stitch them on-the-fly for live panorama preview. The client interface shows the preview to the user and allows the host user to send visual instructions with gestures to other users for coordinated camera adjustment. Our preliminary user study suggests that the proposed system can provide a unique, enjoyable experience for users in addition to capturing high quality panoramas.

REFERENCES

1. 4am project. `http://4amproject.org/`.
2. Agarwala, A., Dontcheva, M., Agrawala, M., Drucker, S., Colburn, A., Curless, B., Salesin, D., and Cohen, M. Interactive digital photomontage. *ACM Trans. Graph. 23*, 3 (Aug. 2004), 294–302.
3. Baudisch, P., Tan, D., Steedly, D., Rudolph, E., Uyttendaele, M., Pal, C., and Szeliski, R. Panoramic viewfinder: Shooting panoramic pictures with the help of a real-time preview. In *Proc. UIST* (2005).
4. Boring, S., Gehring, S., Wiethoff, A., Blöckner, A. M., Schöning, J., and Butz, A. Multi-user interaction on media facades through live video on mobile devices. In *Proc. SIGCHI* (2011).
5. Brown, M., and Lowe, D. G. Automatic panoramic image stitching using invariant features. *IJCV 74*, 1 (Aug. 2007), 59–73.
6. Collaboration: Revisiting the history of photography. `http://www.aperture.org/event/collaboration-revisiting-history-photography/`.
7. Dabbish, L., and Kraut, R. E. Controlling interruptions: Awareness displays and social motivation for coordination. In *Proceedings of the 2004 ACM Conference on Computer Supported Cooperative Work* (New York, NY, USA, 2004), 182–191.
8. Davis, J. Mosaics of scenes with moving objects. In *Proc. CVPR* (1998).
9. Joshi, N., Kar, A., and Cohen, M. Looking at you: Fused gyro and face tracking for viewing large imagery on mobile devices. In *Proc. SIGCHI* (2012).
10. Kittur, A., Lee, B., and Kraut, R. E. Coordination in collective intelligence: The role of team structure and task interdependence. In *Proceedings of the SIGCHI Conference on Human Factors in Computing Systems* (2009), 1495–1504.
11. Peltonen, P., Kurvinen, E., Salovaara, A., Jacucci, G., Ilmonen, T., Evans, J., Oulasvirta, A., and Saarikko, P. It's Mine, Don't Touch!: Interactions at a large multi-touch display in a city centre. In *Proc. SIGCHI* (2008).
12. "Someone Once Told Me" project. `http://www.someoneoncetoldme.com/`.
13. Szeliski, R. Image alignment and stitching: A tutorial. *Found. Trends. Comput. Graph. Vis. 2*, 1 (Jan. 2006), 1–104.
14. Tompkin, J., Pece, F., Shah, R., Izadi, S., Kautz, J., and Theobalt, C. Video collections in panoramic contexts. In *Proc. UIST* (2013).
15. Top panorama problem #3: Ghosting. `http://www.theperfectpanorama.com/articles/problem-3-ghosting.html`.
16. Tuite, K., Snavely, N., Hsiao, D.-y., Tabing, N., and Popovic, Z. Photocity: Training experts at large-scale image acquisition through a competitive game. In *Proc. SIGCHI* (2011).
17. Venkataraman, K., Lelescu, D., Duparré, J., McMahon, A., Molina, G., Chatterjee, P., Mullis, R., and Nayar, S. Picam: An ultra-thin high performance monolithic camera array. *ACM ToG 32*, 6 (Nov. 2013).
18. Wilburn, B., Joshi, N., Vaish, V., Levoy, M., and Horowitz, M. High-speed videography using a dense camera array. In *Proc. CVPR* (2004).
19. Wilburn, B., Joshi, N., Vaish, V., Talvala, E.-V., Antunez, E., Barth, A., Adams, A., Horowitz, M., and Levoy, M. High performance imaging using large camera arrays. *ACM ToG 24*, 3 (July 2005), 765–776.
20. Xiong, Y., and Pulli, K. Fast panorama stitching for high-quality panoramic images on mobile phones. *IEEE Trans. on Consum. Electron. 56*, 2 (May 2010), 298–306.

Recognizing Human Actions in the Motion Trajectories of Shapes

Melissa Roemmele*
roemmele@ict.usc.edu

Andrew S. Gordon*
gordon@ict.usc.edu

Soja-Marie Morgens†
smorgens@soe.ucsc.edu

Louis-Philippe Morency‡
morency@cs.cmu.edu

ABSTRACT
People naturally anthropomorphize the movement of nonliving objects, as social psychologists Fritz Heider and Marianne Simmel demonstrated in their influential 1944 research study. When they asked participants to narrate an animated film of two triangles and a circle moving in and around a box, participants described the shapes' movement in terms of human actions. Using a framework for authoring and annotating animations in the style of Heider and Simmel, we established new crowdsourced datasets where the motion trajectories of animated shapes are labeled according to the actions they depict. We applied two machine learning approaches, a spatial-temporal bag-of-words model and a recurrent neural network, to the task of automatically recognizing actions in these datasets. Our best results outperformed a majority baseline and showed similarity to human performance, which encourages further use of these datasets for modeling perception from motion trajectories. Future progress on simulating human-like motion perception will require models that integrate motion information with top-down contextual knowledge.

Author Keywords
Touch/Haptic/Pointing/Gesture; Animation; Crowdsourcing; Machine Learning

ACM Classification Keywords
H.5.m. Information Interfaces and Presentation (e.g. HCI): Miscellaneous

INTRODUCTION
A skilled animator can create the illusion of life in nonliving objects by moving them in a humanlike manner, producing motion pictures with engaging narratives of anthropomorphic characters [32]. The perception of humanlike actions in object trajectories has been a longstanding interest in psychology, where its study bridges perceptual psychology and social psychology [3, 6, 7, 33]. In an influential early study, Fritz Heider and Marianne Simmel crafted a short film depicting the movements of two triangles and a circle in and around a box with a door, and asked subjects to describe what they saw [11]. These subjects instinctively anthropomorphized the two triangles and circle as humanlike characters, producing rich narratives about the social relationships, emotional states, and intentions of these objects. These studies led Heider to later propose an influential theory of how people attribute mental states to others in social interaction [10].

This relevance to social interaction has motivated several computer scientists to take an interest in Heider and Simmel's early film, with attempts to build automated systems that could perceive the film in much the same manner as Heider and Simmel's experimental subjects. Thibadeau [31] takes a symbolic approach to the perception of actions in the Heider-Simmel film. Beginning with the 2D coordinates of every line and arc in every other frame of the 1690-frame film, the system analytically generates symbolic descriptions of each frame that are matched to defined action schemas, such as opening the door or going outside the box. Pautler et al. [25] follows a related approach, beginning with object trajectory information from an animated recreation of the Heider-Simmel film. An incremental chart parsing algorithm with a hand-authored action grammar is then applied to recognize character actions as well as their intentions. These two rule-based approaches allow for the recognition of gross motor actions (moving to a location, hitting another character), but may not be appropriate for defining other motion trajectories like limping, shivering, tickling, and dancing. Current paradigms for AI recognition problems assume people only "know it when they see it," emphasizing the importance of systematically analyzing human data for these tasks, in contrast to the previous approaches. Accordingly, the problem of automatically interpreting motion trajectories may best be tackled using data-driven techniques applied to a wide array of crowdsourced examples.

In this paper, we describe our efforts to use machine learning to recognize human actions in the motion trajectories of shapes. To perform this task, we created novel animation data using a framework by which people can author animations in the style of Heider and Simmel. The resulting contribution, which we make available to the community, are two labeled datasets that enable a more systematic study of how people

*Institute for Creative Technologies, University of Southern California, Los Angeles, CA, USA
†University of California Santa Cruz, Santa Cruz, CA, USA
‡Language Technologies Institute, Carnegie Mellon University, Pittsburgh, PA, USA

IUI'16, March 07–10, 2016, Sonoma, CA, USA
© 2016 ACM. ISBN 978-1-4503-4137-0/16/03...$15.00
DOI: http://dx.doi.org/10.1145/2856767.2856793

perceive anthropomorphized actions in motion trajectories. We present initial results on two different supervised machine learning approaches for automatically recognizing actions in these datasets. In the first approach, we selected motion features to encode animations as sets of "spatial-temporal words" that were learned by a simple classifier. In our second approach, we replaced this feature selection process with a Recurrent Neural Network that automatically learned a feature representation of animations according to their action labels. The best results of these systems show significant improvement over a majority voting baseline and approximate a human measure of performance on this task, demonstrating the potential for future systems to exhibit human-like motion perception.

RELATED WORK

Because of its practical application to fields like robotics, human-computer interaction, and surveillance, there is a great deal of research devoted to recognizing human actions in video data. Increasingly utilized for this task are techniques for extracting the high-level 2D motion trajectories like those used in our work. For instance, Rao et al. [27] isolated changes in motion characteristics at particular spatial points in order to compute 2D motion trajectories for actions in videos (e.g. opening a door). Messing et al. [21] used a similar approach, where the velocities of particular key points on a person's body were tracked across videos of that person engaging household activities like eating or answering a phone. Such activities could then be recognized according to these "velocity histories" of the tracked keypoints. Vrigkas et al. [35] computed motion curves from videos using optical flow measurements. They identified the action associated with these motion curves by determining the longest common subsequences between these curves and those of known actions.

Some research on action recognition has successfully borrowed methods from text classification research. One such approach that we explore in this paper is to analyze discrete video segments as visual "words" that define the action portrayed in the video, in the same way textual words define the meaning of a document. Niebles et al. [23] used this technique with latent topical modeling algorithms, with the result that videos displaying similar actions (the "topics") were grouped together. Just as certain words are more important than others for determining the topic of a document, certain visual words may be particularly good cues for recognizing an action. Accordingly, Hoai et al. [13] automatically discovered the most discriminative temporal video segments that maximized recognition of mouse behaviors like sleeping and grooming. Like actions, gestures have also been recognized using visual word approaches [12, 36]. This work is particularly relevant to the current effort given that the animations in our dataset are generated by trajectories of underlying hand gestures.

Recent improvements on video-based action recognition are largely based on the new deep learning paradigm in computer vision. These models stack layers of neural networks to establish a "deep" hierarchical representation of the input data that maps directly to classification labels without the need for additional feature encoding. Baccouche et al. [2] and Karpathy et al. [14] observed significant performance gains over previous models using deep learning on existing action recognition datasets. We examine in this paper whether the benefits of deep learning on video classification also apply to the more abstract task of perceiving actions in animations of shapes.

Our work fits alongside other research exploring the connection between action perception and language. There is a growing body of work on automatically generating natural language descriptions of events shown in video [26, 29, 34]. Some effort has been given to the specific task of describing motion trajectories with verbs, as is the goal of our work. In particular, Koller et al. [17] designed finite state automata for labeling the motion trajectories of cars with German motion verbs. The automata encoded the attributes of a car's trajectory that have to be detected in order for the car to be described with a particular verb. Kojima et al. [16] employed a similar rule-based approach for doing this, using the trajectories of people's heads instead of cars. Action verbs were applied by evaluating predicates defining changes in motion for the people and objects in the video. Mathe et al. [20] automatically learned a semantic representation of motion verbs by discovering intervals with similar motion features across several videos depicting the same verb. Finally, Morrison et al. [22] used animations to categorize verb semantics by manipulating the motion features of animations and clustering the verbs people used to describe animations with similar motion features. Among these efforts, our work is the first to examine the verb labeling task as a machine learning classification problem where action labels are automatically acquired from a comprehensive dataset of motion trajectories.

DATA COLLECTION

Other researchers have created animations that resemble Heider and Simmel's film for use in their own studies. For instance, the Frith-Happe animations used in autism research [1] show two interacting triangles intended to elicit mental state attributions from observers. In Barrett et al. [3], research participants created similar animations by playing a game in which they acted out intentional actions with digital arrowheads, i.e. one player moved their arrowhead to "chase" or "fight" another player's arrowhead. However, the animations in these studies were not designed explicitly for automated action recognition across a large vocabulary of actions. To serve this goal, we created two new datasets of animated shapes whose motion trajectories are encoded transparently as time series data. In particular, each animation is represented as a series of frames sampled every 20 milliseconds, with each frame containing the position and rotation values of each shape in the animation at the time point for that frame. The position values are defined as (x,y) coordinates, and the rotation values are angles in degrees. In the first dataset of "Charades" animations (Figure 1), an animation depicts exactly one action and is annotated with a single label. In the second dataset of "Theatrical" animations (Figure 2), an animation is annotated with a sequence of actions whose depiction conveys a story, just like Heider and Simmel's film.

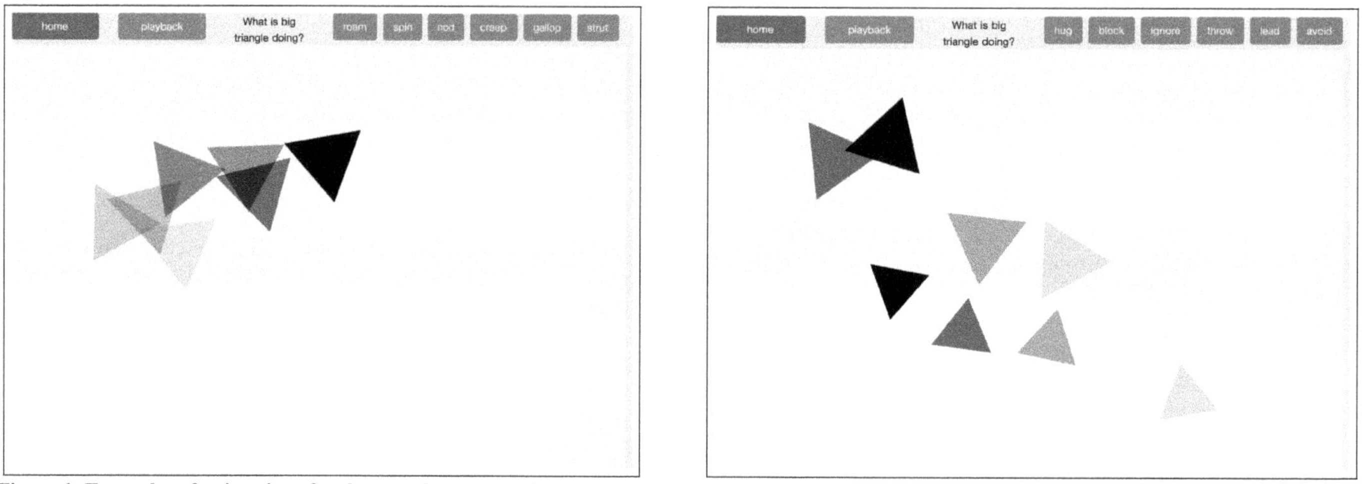

Figure 1. Examples of animations for the one-character action "roam" (left) and two-character action "ignore" (right) in the Charades game interface

Charades Animations

The Charades dataset was generated through a web-based game called *Triangle Charades* [28]. This game utilizes the same concept as the classic party game Charades, in which players convey concepts or entities using non-verbal language only. Here, players illustrate actions through a software interface by animating 2-D triangles resembling those in Heider and Simmel's film. Triangle Charades has two modes of play: "authoring" mode and "guessing" mode. In authoring mode, players are shown an English-language verb with a valency of either one (a one-character action like *spin* or *bolt*) or two (a two-character action like *hit* or *chase*). For one-character actions, players animate a single triangle as the agent of the action. For two-character actions, players are shown two triangles of distinct sizes, and instructed to animate the larger triangle as the agent of the action and the smaller triangle as the target of the action (e.g. "make the big triangle fight the little triangle"). Players animate the triangles by simply dragging them on a multitouch-enabled computer like an iPad. Animations cannot exceed 60 seconds in length. In guessing mode, shown in Figure 1, a player views an animation authored by another player, and then guesses from a set of six action labels which action the animation is depicting. A match between the guesser's selected action and the author's intended action is considered a correct selection. If the guess is incorrect, the guessed verb is eliminated and the player selects another verb until the correct one is selected, completing the guessing round.

The vocabulary of action labels for Charades animations was defined through guided intuition. The linguistic resource *English Verb Classes and Alternations* [19], which catalogs English verbs according to their syntactic behavior and semantics, was used to identify 200 verbs whose semantics involve whole-body motion. Since many verbs were synonymous, they were then manually clustered based on perceived similarity. The most canonical verb in each cluster was then selected to represent that action. For instance, the verb *hit* was picked to reference the action conveyed by the cluster of verbs *hit*, *collide with*, *jab*, *punch*, and *box*. The final vocabulary consisted of 31 one-character actions and 31 two-character actions, which are listed in Table 1. This dataset distinguishes between far more labels than any other known work on abstract action recognition, where typically only five or six labels were considered.

We used the crowdsourcing platform Crowdflower[1] to recruit people to play Triangle Charades. Additional players came through self-signup, yielding a total of 214 authors and 660 guessers for one-character animations, and 95 authors and 483 guessers for two-character animations. These players authored a total of 3041 one-character animations guessed a total of 9862 rounds (mean of 3.24 guessing rounds per animation), and 1762 two-character animations guessed 8655 rounds (mean of 4.91 rounds per animation). We used players' guessing data to validate that animations were perceived in accordance with the actions they intended to illustrate. To do this, we computed the number of guessing attempts it took guessers to correctly identify the action intended by the author of an animation, with 1 being the minimum number of guesses per animation and the maximum being 6. Only animations guessed by at least two players and guessed correctly in fewer than 3.5 average guesses (better than random chance) were included in the final validated dataset. Our final dataset contained 2060 one-character animations and 1158 two-character animations[2]. The mean length of these animations was 5.65 seconds for the one-character dataset and 6.45 seconds for the two-character dataset.

Theatrical Animations

In addition to determining which animations to include in the dataset, the guessing data also provides a measure of human performance on this action recognition task. In particular, recognition accuracy can be quantified as the mean number of guesses taken to select the correct action across all animations, where 1 is perfect accuracy on the task and 3.5 indicates no systematic recognition beyond random chance. This measure can also be used to examine recognition accuracy specifically on animations of the same action label. In the results

[1] http://www.crowdflower.com
[2] Available at https://github.com/asgordon/TriangleCOPA

1-character	*accelerate, bolt, bow, creep, dance, decelerate, drift, flinch, fly, gallop, glide, hop, jump, limp, march, meander, nod, roam, roll, run, scurry, shake, spin, stroll, strut, stumble, swim, trudge, turn, waddle, wave*
2-character	*accompany, approach, argue with, avoid, bother, capture, chase, creep up on, encircle, escape, examine, fight, flirt with, follow, herd, hit, huddle with, hug, ignore, kiss, lead, leave, mimic, play with, poke, pull, push, scratch, talk to, throw, tickle*

Table 1. List of action labels

Figure 2. A Theatrical animation portraying the action sequence "creep up on" followed by "flinch"

section below, we use this analysis to directly compare automated recognition performance to human performance both overall and by action label.

Our second dataset of animations, which we term "Theatrical" animations, directly resemble Heider and Simmel's film (Figure 2). In addition to a "big" triangle and a "little" triangle, these animations feature a circle and a box with a hinged opening (the "door"). Each Theatrical animation is intended to convey a story by depicting a sequence of actions with different characters participating in each action. This dataset is less constrained than the Charades dataset, where only one action is depicted across an entire animation and the action type (one or two character) as well as character roles (big triangle as agent, little triangle as target) are pre-specified. To create the Theatrical dataset, we employed another web application called the *Heider-Simmel Interactive Theater* [8]. Here users apply the same touch-and-drag method as in Triangle Charades to author a movie (max 90 seconds) featuring the shapes and the door, without any instructions about what actions to depict. An animator on our team used the Heider-Simmel Interactive Theater to create 100 animations portraying sequences of both one-character and two-character actions. The mean length of these animations was 9.39 seconds. The same animator then annotated these actions using the Charades labels, establishing a gold standard test set for recognizing sequences of actions[3]. There were additional action labels in this gold standard that are not in Table 1, such as interactions between a particular character and the door and/or box (e.g. *knock*, *enter*, *exit*). After removing these labels, the mean length of the gold standard sequences for the current work was 2.24 action labels per animation.

[3]Available at https://github.com/asgordon/TriangleCOPA

EXPERIMENTS

The Charades dataset and Theatrical dataset offer two different opportunities for automated action recognition. In the Charades dataset, the goal is to predict a single action label for an entire animation. Conversely, the Theatrical animations contain more than one action per animation, so the task is to distinguish boundaries between sequential actions and label each action in the sequence. As we will discuss, the latter task is significantly more challenging, largely because recognizing transitions between actions is known to be as difficult as recognizing actions alone [37]. In this paper, we focus on the task of recognizing individual actions in Charades animations. We then demonstrate an initial application of the Charades-based models to the Theatrical animations in order to establish a starting point for future work on recognizing sequences of actions in motion trajectories.

We explored two alternative approaches to recognizing actions in Charades animations. In the first approach, we modeled animations as bags of spatial-temporal visual words, which were then used as features by a classifier to predict action labels. Our second approach applied the deep learning paradigm for classification, through which a recurrent neural network (RNN) was trained to predict labels from layered representations of motion trajectories. These approaches differ both in how they model the features as well as temporal structure of their data. First, the spatial-temporal words model relies on hand-selected features to encode animations, whereas the RNN automatically constructs features directly from the trajectory data. Second, the bag-of-words approach only considers temporal structure within a given interval of an animation rather than temporal relations between intervals. In contrast, the RNN models long-range temporal dependencies across an entire animation. The details of each model and their specific application to the current task are described below.

Spatial-Temporal Words Model

A spatial-temporal word is a categorical representation of an object's motion at a particular duration of the animation. Motion sequences can be encoded as sets of spatial-temporal words, an approach that has worked successfully for similar tasks such as video-based activity classification and gesture recognition [12, 23, 36]. To apply this approach, we split each animation into uniform-length intervals and computed the motion features of the shapes at each interval independently. The features we selected were those that have worked well for analyzing other types of motion trajectory data such

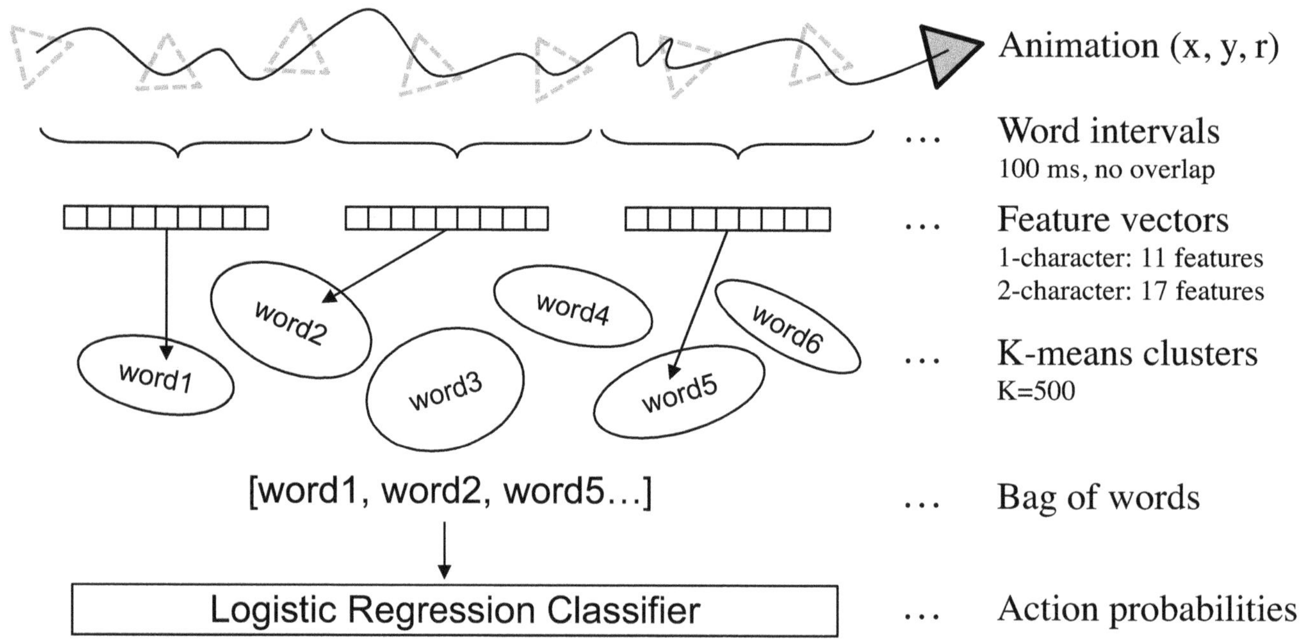

Figure 3. Spatial-temporal words model

as hand gestures [30] and pen sketches [9]. These features are all position-invariant, meaning that they are not affected by the absolute positions of the shapes in an animation but rather their change in position across frames.

Table 2 lists the motion features used by this model. The first 11 features constituted the feature set for one-character action recognition. For each interval in an animation, we calculated these features for the motion trajectory of the agent character performing the depicted action. The presence of two characters, one the agent and the other the target of an action, required additional features to be used for the two-character animations. For each interval in the two-character animations, we calculated the one-character features for the agent of the action. We then also calculated the mean of the six two-character features shown in Table 2 for the relative motion between the agent and target characters. With the addition of these features, the feature set for recognizing two-character actions contained 17 features total.

After computing its features, each interval was transformed into a word by categorizing it according to its feature-based similarity to other intervals. Intervals were assigned to clusters using the k-means algorithm with the Euclidian distance metric, and each interval was subsequently represented as the index of the cluster center closest to that interval. The set of cluster indices can be thought of as the "dictionary" of spatial-temporal words. Each animation was then encoded as a word vector composed of the number of times each word in the dictionary occurred in that animation. Because they have different feature sets, we generated separate dictionaries for the one-character and two-character datasets. We used each dictionary to transform the corresponding animations of that action type into bag-of-words vectors, which could then be used as input to a classification algorithm to predict action labels.

Figure 3 illustrates the full pipeline of the spatial-temporal words model. Interval length, offset length between intervals, and number of words (clusters) in the dictionary are all hyperparameters in this model. Once the animations are encoded as bag-of-words vectors, any classifier can be trained to assign labels from this feature representation. We chose Logistic Regression because it provides straightforward probability estimates describing the likelihood of each label being predicted for a given animation. This probability estimation enabled us to evaluate the model's performance relative to human recognition, as we explain in the next section. We also chose to use Naive Bayes since it is commonly employed for text-based bag-of-words classification tasks and could possibly apply just as well to classifying spatial-temporal words.

Recurrent Neural Network Model

Encoding animations as spatial-temporal words enables them to be efficiently learned by a simple linear classifier, but this approach relies on assumptions that are difficult to verify. In particular, the trajectory features used in above approach (e.g. distance, rotation, velocity) were selected based on previous research and intuition, but it is possible that a different set of motion features would be more useful for the current recognition task. Moreover, even when the dictionary size is fixed, it is unclear if the k-means clustering will result in meaningful differences between words. If random changes in the initialization of the clusters yield a different assignment of intervals to words, it becomes difficult to determine what information is captured by the words. Morever, the hyperparameters of interval length, offset length between intervals, and dictionary size must be manually defined in this model. These decisions create extra overhead for the spatial-temporal word

	Name	Description
1-character features	Distance	agent's change in position between adjacent frames
	Rotation	agent's change in rotation between adjacent frames
	Angle	arctangent of Distance
	Angle Offset	difference between Angle and Rotation
	Velocity	derivative of Distance
	Rotational Velocity	derivative of Rotation
	Acceleration	derivative of Velocity
	Rotational Acceleration	derivative of Rotational Velocity
	Jerk	derivative of Acceleration
	Curvature	curvature of the agent's change in position between adjacent frames
	Angle Change	derivative of Angle
2-character features	Relative Distance	distance between agent and target at each frame
	Relative Angle	arctangent of Relative Distance
	Relative Velocity	derivative of Relative Distance
	Relative Acceleration	derivative of Relative Velocity
	Relative Jerk	derivative of Relative Acceleration
	Relative Angle Change	derivative of Relative Angle

Table 2. List of motion features used in spatial-temporal bag-of-words model

model since they can only be made by inefficiently trying all possibilities.

Recurrent Neural Networks (RNNs) avoid this overhead because they directly learn from input sequences without requiring any manual feature engineering. RNNs have become a state of the art technique for processing sequence data, and have recently demonstrated success specifically on action recognition tasks [2, 14]. We aimed to determine whether an RNN with no explicit knowledge of spatial-temporal words could recognize actions in Charades animations with comparable performance. To do this, we applied an RNN derived from the Elman network [5], whose general architecture consists of an input layer, one or more recurrent hidden layers, and an output layer all connected adjacently by weights. For our task, the input layer encodes the shapes' motion trajectories in the animation, while the hidden layers represent the continuous underlying state of the animation so far. The output layer is equivalent to a Logistic Regression classifier, using the values in the hidden layer to predict action label probabilities for the animation. Figure 4 illustrates this architecture with two hidden layers. The size (number of units) in each hidden layer is a hyperparameter. The weight matrices connecting the layers are the parameters that ultimately determine the probability estimates used to predict actions. The values of these parameters are updated through backpropogation during training (see [18]). For each animation, the model iterates through each frame of the animation and uses both the position and rotation data in the current frame and the hidden values at the previous frame to compute the hidden values at the current frame. The same recurrence is applied when there are multiple hidden layers: for each hidden layer, the state at the current frame is computed from the previous layer combined with the state of the current layer at the previous frame. Once the entire animation is processed, the values of the outermost hidden layer across the entire animation are averaged, and the average values are passed to the output layer. The Logistic Regression classifier (typically referred to as a softmax classifier) in the output layer uses these values to compute the probabilities of predicting each possible action label for that animation. When used to classify an animation, the RNN ultimately selects the action with the highest probability as the recognized action. As implied by the term "deep", RNNs are known to learn better representations of the input data as the number of hidden layers increases. We evaluated this claim for our task by training both an RNN with a single hidden layer and an RNN with two hidden layers. In both cases, the hidden layer interfacing with the output layer encodes a feature representation of the animations that can be used to predict action probabilities. The hidden layer representation can thus be viewed an alternative to the bag-of-words representation used in the spatial-temporal words model. We compared these two alternative feature encodings for the same animations by using Logistic Regression to classify them. We identified that if both models performed similarly, then we could conclude that the RNN feature representation was equivalent to the word-based representation for the action recognition task. Such a result would favor the use of RNNs for this task because they avoid the cost of manual feature engineering as well as the uncertain assumptions required by the spatial-temporal words model. We sought to evaluate this possibility in our experiments.

Methodology

For the experiments presented here, we randomly split each dataset into training, validation, and test sets, allocating 20% of the data to the validation set, another 20% to the test set, and using the remaining 60% for training. For each dataset, we trained the four models described above: the spatial-temporal words model with Logistic Regression (Words + LR), the spatial-temporal words model with Naive Bayes (Words + NB), the 1-layer RNN, and the 2-layer RNN. Additionally, we computed a baseline majority voting model that always predicted the most frequent action label in the test set. We used the validation data to set the interval length, offset length, and dictionary size hyperparameters for the spatial-

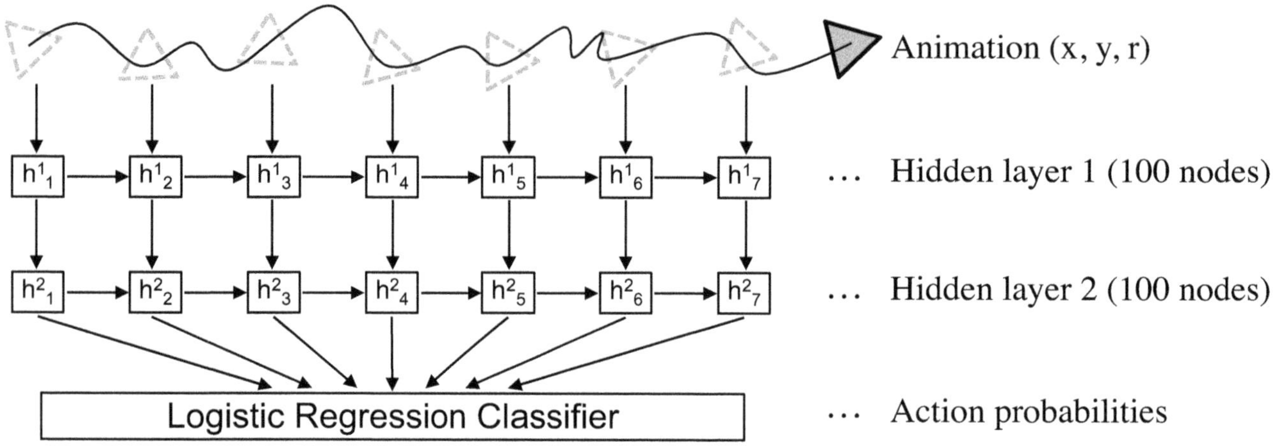

Figure 4. Recurrent neural network model

temporal words models. For both interval length and offset length between intervals, values of 5 frames, 10 frames, 15 frames, and 20 frames were evaluated as well as dictionary sizes of 100, 200, 300, 400, and 500. Similarly, we used the validation set to select the optimal hidden layer sizes for the RNN models, evaluating performance with 100, 300, and 500 hidden layer nodes. In training both the word-based Logistic Regression and RNN models, we performed a max of 1000 iterations of parameter updates, with early stopping if the training error had not improved in 50 iterations. For the RNN models, the RMSProp algorithm [4] was utilized to iteratively update the parameter weights of each model. After selecting the best performing configurations of all four models on the validation sets, we applied these models to the test sets, the results of which we discuss in the next section.

RESULTS AND DISCUSSION

The recognition accuracy of all models on the testing data appears in Table 3, with the best result from each dataset indicated in bold. Regarding the hyperparameters selected through validation, both spatial-temporal words models used an interval length of 100ms, an offset length of 0ms, and a dictionary size of 500 words. For the RNN models, the hidden layer size was 100 nodes (for both layers in the 2-layer RNN). We used the compute-intensive randomized test with stratified shuffling [24] to evaluate the statistical significance of differences in accuracy between models.

The accuracy of the majority baseline was 5.3% for the one-character dataset (predicting the action “hop” for all animations) and 5.6% for the two-character dataset (predicting “fight” for all animations). While all models exceeded this baseline, the difference was statistically significant only for certain models. Different patterns emerged from one-character and two-character experiments. The one-character recognition accuracy was lower across all models. The Words + LR model, with an accuracy of 12.6%, was the single model to significantly outperform the baseline. This model also significantly outperformed both of the RNN models. The results of the two-character models were more dramatic. Here all models showed significant improvement over the baseline. The Words + LR model demonstrated similar accuracy (12.5%) to the corresponding one-character model. The Words + NB model and 2-layer RNN performed significantly better than the Words + LR model with accuracies of 22.0%, and 25.0%, respectively. The 2-layer RNN for two-character animations obtained the best performance of all models, though its 25% accuracy did not significantly differ from the corresponding Words + NB model. While these results show that the spatial-temporal words representation is meaningful for this task, it’s interesting that this representation was much better utilized by Naive Bayes than by Logistic Regression. Naive Bayes assumes that each word is generated entirely independently from others, and while this seems incorrect for this task, it’s possible that it made recognition easier. The improvement of the 2-layer RNN over the 1-layer model, while not significant, suggests that it would be useful to explore even deeper RNNs for this task as additional layers may further improve performance. The two-character results show that the RNN models automatically built a feature representation as useful as the spatial-temporal words representation for the two-character data. Given that the spatial-temporal words representation demands more manual effort and makes more assumptions that may or may not be correct, RNNs may be a more straightforward approach to this problem. Moreover, while the current results leave it unclear, intuition suggests that the ability of RNNs to model long-range temporal structure would be informative for recognizing actions perceived in long motion trajectories.

One explanation for the weaker one-character results is that these actions are inherently harder to recognize than two-character actions when animated with shapes. However, as revealed in the next section, this performance disparity doesn’t appear in humans. This suggests the relative motion between the agent and target of an action was particularly informative to these models, whereas they were less sensitive to the structure contained in the motion trajectory of a single shape. Further work is needed to identify what features humans perceive in these trajectories that the current models fail to account for.

	Baseline	Words + LR	Words + NB	1-layer RNN	2-layer RNN
1-character	0.053	**0.126*†**	0.085	0.080	0.073
2-character	0.056	0.125*	0.220*‡	0.185*	**0.250*‡**

*Significantly better than baseline ($p < 0.05$)
†Significantly better than 1-layer RNN and 2-layer RNN ($p < 0.05$)
‡Significantly better than Words + LR ($p < 0.05$)

Table 3. Classification accuracy on Charades animations

	Baseline	Human	Words + LR	1-layer RNN	2-layer RNN
1-character	3.499	2.139	**2.623*†**	2.817*	2.806*
2-character	3.574	2.114	2.419*	2.261*‡	**2.147*‡**

*Significantly better than baseline ($p < 0.05$)
†Significantly better than 1-layer RNN and 2-layer RNN ($p < 0.05$)
‡Significantly better than Words + LR ($p < 0.05$)

Table 4. Classifiers' mean number of guesses until correct on 6-choice Charades task, compared to humans

Guessing Task

The accuracies in Table 3 are all fairly low, leading one to conclude that machine learning approaches perform poorly on this task. However, comparing the models' performance to human recognition suggests a different interpretation of the results. To make this comparison, test set accuracy can be evaluated according to the Charades guessing task, which measures the mean number of guesses until correct when the choice is constrained to only six labels. For every guessing round completed by a human player, the classifiers also performed this guessing task by predicting an action label for the animation from the same set of six actions shown to the player. Of these six labels, the model selected the one it assigned the highest probability, and this selection continued until the correct label was predicted. Table 4 shows the results of this task alongside human performance as well as a baseline approach. Here, the baseline selected actions simply in the order that they were presented to the player in the guessing round. We omitted the Naive Bayes model from this guessing task because its probability estimates are known to be poorly calibrated [38]. We again used stratified shuffling to evaluate the statistical significance of our results. The relative performance between models shows a similar pattern to Table 3, but new findings emerge from the comparison to human and baseline performance. Here, all models significantly outperform the baseline, signifying that they have all captured factors influencing action recognition to some degree. In accordance with the previous results, the Words + LR model was the best one-character guesser of all models at 2.623 mean guesses until correct. It made significantly better guesses than both the 1-layer and 2-layer RNN. For the two-character data, both the 1-layer RNN (2.261 mean guesses) and the 2-layer RNN (2.147 guesses) had significantly better guessing performance than the Words + LR model. Looking at human performance, players were generally better at guessing than any of the models, with players taking 2.139 mean guesses to select the correct one-character action in the test set, and 2.114 mean guesses for two-character animations. However, guesses made by the 2-layer RNN on the two-character animations did not differ significantly from the corresponding human guesses. Based on this we can conclude that the 2-layer RNN approximated human performance on recognizing two-character actions in motion trajectories.

The guessing task also enables us to examine recognition accuracy for each action label separately. Figure 5 visualizes the results in Table 4 to show the mean number of guesses for test animations corresponding to the same action label. For each action label in the one-character and two-character datasets, the guessing performance of the best model on the corresponding dataset is compared to human guessing for that action label. This analysis reveals interesting distinctions between the human and model recognition. In particular, while human performance was consistent across different actions, the models showed more variance in their ability to recognize specific actions. For instance, looking at the two-character actions recognized in fewer than 1.5 average guesses, only "play with" was recognizable to this degree for humans, compared to nine actions ("lead", "avoid", "push", "examine", "chase", "follow", "pull", "hug", and "encircle") for the 2-layer RNN. However, the model's strong guessing performance on these actions was countered by particularly weak performance on other actions. The actions "huddle with", "accompany", and "fight" all took more than 3 average guesses to identify, whereas even the least recognizable action for humans was identified in under 3 average guesses (2.750 guesses for "herd").

While an ideal comparison with human performance would measure human accuracy choosing from the full set of action labels, this six-choice guessing task is a more practical estimation of human performance. Choosing from over 30 labels for annotating a given animation is more cognitively demanding and time-consuming, and could deter a crowdsourcing approach to data collection. Moreover, this guessing task is useful in that evaluates the accuracy of probability estimates rather than just the accuracy of the best prediction. That RNNs are good at guessing suggests they are good at explicitly modeling the probability distribution over action labels.

Theatrical Recognition

Our second experiment was to move beyond single-action recognition in order to recognize sequences of actions in the Theatrical animations. We assessed the challenges of this

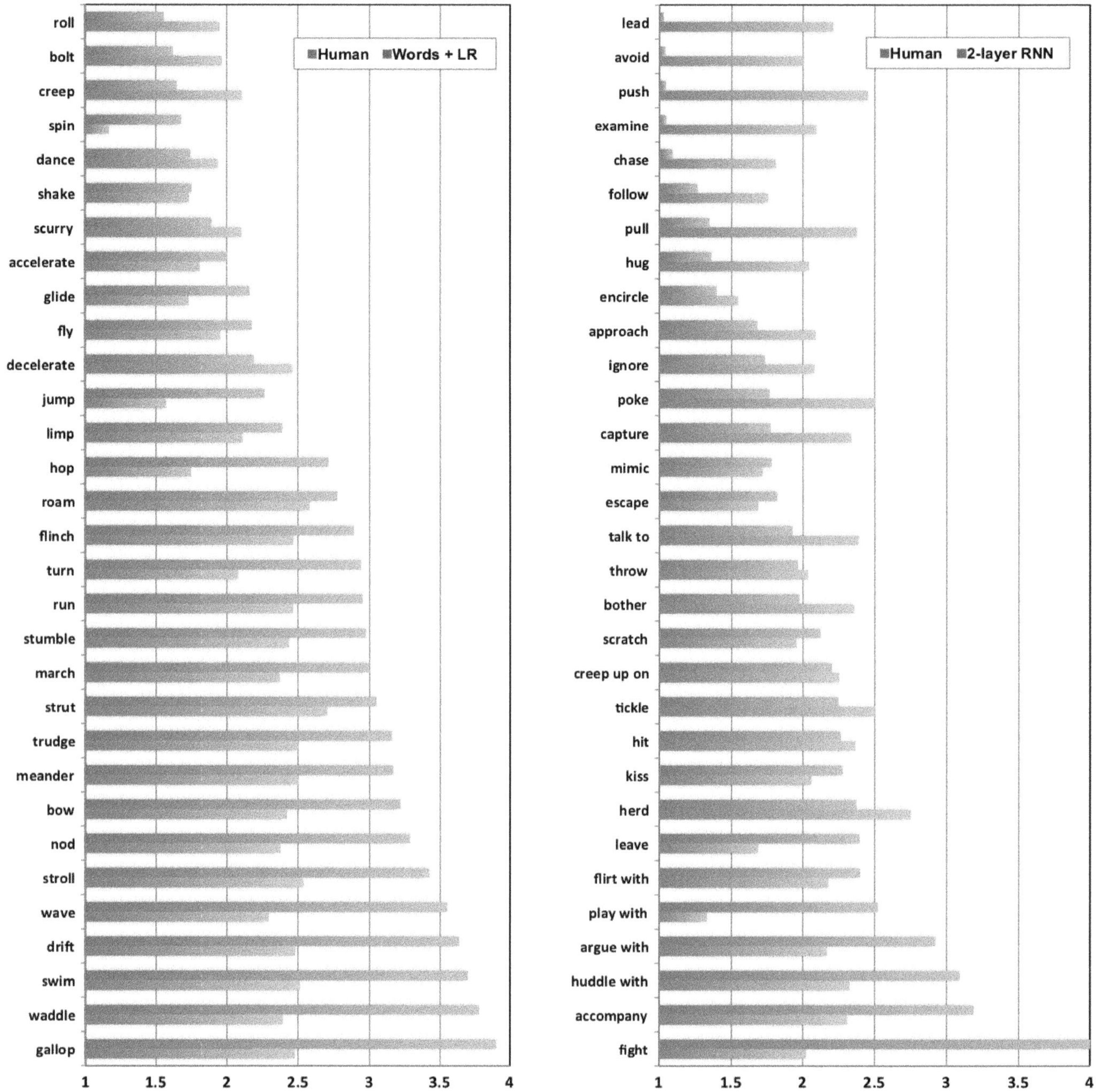

Figure 5. Comparison between humans and best model on mean number of guesses until correct for each verb in test set

task by using the 2-layer RNNs trained on the Charades animations to naively generate action sequences in which each action is predicted independently of other actions in the sequence. RNNs are well suited to this sequence labeling task because they explicitly model temporal relations across all frames of an animation. To establish a baseline approach to the Theatrical recognition task, we divided each Theatrical animation into segments of 150 frames (3 seconds) and applied both the one-character and two-character RNNs to recognize the action in each segment. In particular, for each character in the animation, the one-character classifier was given that character's motion trajectory in order to calculate the probabilities of the one-character labels for the action performed by the character. Additionally, for each ordered pair of characters in the animation, the two-character classifier was given those two characters' motion trajectories in order to determine the probabilities of the two-character actions where the first character in the pair is the agent of the action and the second character is the target. Thus, for the Theatrical animations with three characters (the big triangle, little triangle, and circle), we ran the one-character RNN three times (on each of the three characters), and the two-character RNN six times (on each of the six ordered pairs of characters). The probability estimates resulting from each on the nine RNN instances were pooled, and the action with the highest probability across all distributions was the action predicted for that animation segment. This procedure was repeated for each segment in the animation in order to yield a sequence of action labels.

Because the length of the predicted action sequence could differ from the number of gold standard actions for a particular animation, we evaluated the output in terms of precision and recall (without regard to the order of actions in the sequences) as opposed to accuracy. Precision was 1.4% and recall was 2.3%, with a resulting F-score of 1.8%, revealing that this recognition problem has a non-trivial solution. The poor performance can be attributed to the low accuracy on the previous Charades task, but also to the difficulty of automatically inferring what was predetermined in the Charades animations: the number of actions as well as the boundaries between them, and the roles of the characters participating in an action. This suggests that need for integrating motion trajectory information with top-down knowledge about the narrative context of an animation.

CONCLUSION AND FUTURE WORK

How and why people anthropomorphize abstract objects is a topic that has fascinated researchers across many disciplines. In this work, we showed how the high-level perception of human actions in motion trajectories can be modeled using machine learning, specifically by both a spatial-temporal bag-of-words model and a recurrent neural network. This is unique from previous work that attempted to analytically define trajectory features for actions based on a limited set of examples. We provide two new datasets that facilitate further analysis of this perceptual process. Our initial action recognition results on these datasets show the promise of further machine learning work on behavior classification from motion cues.

Our results suggest that accurate action recognition may require more than just detecting local motion cues, however. While using more sophisticated motion features might yield better recognition performance on the Charades dataset, the Theatrical animations, just like Heider and Simmel's film, are interpreted within a narrative context. Knowledge of this context is missing in the Charades animations even for humans, a likely reason why their own recognition is low. Contextual information such as the characters' actions in previous segments of the animation would likely provide a better model for recognition. New research has demonstrated how the recurrent neural network model used to recognize single-action animations in this work can be extended to model contextual dependencies between sequences of actions [2]. In order to successfully apply such an approach, it would be necessary to author and annotate additional Theatrical animations well beyond the current set of one hundred presented in this work.

We have focused on action perception as a bottom-up process, whereby motion reveals an action which in turn yields an explanation. But perception research suggests this is just as much a top-down process [15], as previous explanations for a shape's behavior influence how its motion is subsequently recognized. In particular, the beliefs, emotions, goals, social relationships, and personality traits attributed to the shapes in these animations lead to behavior interpretations which in turn generate further inferences about the internal states of these shapes. Simulating this process in machines requires deep commonsense reasoning that goes far beyond the task of action recognition and lies outside the scope of current machine perception research, but it is certainly a long-term vision for this work.

ACKNOWLEDGEMENTS

This research was supported by the Office of Naval Research, grant N00014-13-1-0286.

REFERENCES

1. Abell, F., Happe, F., and Frith, U. Do triangles play tricks? Attribution of mental states to animated shapes in normal and abnormal development. *Cognitive Development 15*, 1 (2000), 1–16.
2. Baccouche, M., Mamalet, F., and Wolf, C. Sequential deep learning for human action recognition. *Human Behavior Understanding* (2011), 29–39.
3. Barrett, H. C., Todd, P. M., Miller, G. F., and Blythe, P. W. Accurate judgments of intention from motion cues alone: A cross-cultural study. *Evolution and Human Behavior 26*, 4 (2005), 313–331.
4. Dauphin, Y. N., de Vries, H., and Bengio, Y. Equilibrated adaptive learning rates for non-convex optimization. In *Deep Learning Workshop, International Conference on Machine Learning* (2015).
5. Elman, J. L. Finding structure in time. *Cognitive science 14*, 2 (1990), 179–211.
6. Gao, T., McCarthy, G., and Scholl, B. J. The wolfpack effect perception of animacy irresistibly influences interactive behavior. *Psychological science 21*, 12 (2010), 1845–1853.
7. Gao, T., Newman, G. E., and Scholl, B. J. The psychophysics of chasing: A case study in the perception of animacy. *Cognitive psychology 59*, 2 (2009), 154–179.
8. Gordon, A. S., and Roemmele, M. An authoring tool for movies in the style of Heider and Simmel. In *Interactive Storytelling*. Springer, 2014, 49–60.
9. Hammond, T., and Paulson, B. Recognizing sketched multistroke primitives. *ACM Transactions on Interactive Intelligent Systems (TiiS) 1*, 1 (2011), 4.
10. Heider, F. *The Psychology of Interpersonal Relations*. Psychology Press, 1958.
11. Heider, F., and Simmel, M. An experimental study of apparent behavior. *The American Journal of Psychology* (1944), 243–259.
12. Hernández-Vela, A., Bautista, M. A., Perez-Sala, X., Ponce, V., Baró, X., Pujol, O., Angulo, C., and Escalera, S. Bovdw: Bag-of-visual-and-depth-words for gesture

recognition. In *21st International Conference on Pattern Recognition (ICPR)*, IEEE (2012), 449–452.

13. Hoai, M., Torresani, L., De la Torre, F., and Rother, C. Learning discriminative localization from weakly labeled data. *Pattern Recognition 47*, 3 (2014), 1523–1534.

14. Karpathy, A., Toderici, G., Shetty, S., Leung, T., Sukthankar, R., and Fei-Fei, L. Large-Scale Video Classification with Convolutional Neural Networks. *2014 IEEE Conference on Computer Vision and Pattern Recognition* (2014), 1725–1732.

15. Kinchla, R., and Wolfe, J. The order of visual processing: top-down,bottom-up, or middle-out. *Perception & psychophysics 25*, 3 (1979), 225–231.

16. Kojima, A., Izumi, M., Tamura, T., and Fukunaga, K. Generating natural language description of human behavior from video images. In *15th International Conference on Pattern Recognition*, vol. 4, IEEE (2000), 728–731.

17. Koller, D., Heinze, N., and Nagel, H. Algorithmic characterization of vehicle trajectories from image sequences by motion verbs. In *IEEE Computer Society Conference on Computer Vision and Pattern Recognition*, IEEE (1991), 90–95.

18. LeCun, Y., Bengio, Y., and Hinton, G. Deep learning. *Nature 521*, 7553 (2015), 436–444.

19. Levin, B. *English verb classes and alternations: A preliminary investigation*. University of Chicago Press, 1993.

20. Mathe, S., Fazly, A., Dickinson, S., and Stevenson, S. Learning the abstract motion semantics of verbs from captioned videos. In *IEEE Computer Society Conference on Computer Vision and Pattern Recognition Workshops*, IEEE (2008), 1–8.

21. Messing, R., Pal, C., and Kautz, H. Activity recognition using the velocity histories of tracked keypoints. In *IEEE 12th International Conference on Computer Vision*, IEEE (2009), 104–111.

22. Morrison, C. T., Cannon, E. N., and Cohen, P. R. When push comes to shove: A study of the relation between interaction dynamics and verb use. In *Working Notes of the AAAI Spring Symposium Workshop: Language Learning, an Interdisciplinary Perspective* (2004).

23. Niebles, J. C., Wang, H., and Fei-Fei, L. Unsupervised learning of human action categories using spatial-temporal words. *International journal of computer vision 79*, 3 (2008), 299–318.

24. Noreen, E. W. Computer intensive methods for hypothesis testing: An introduction, 1989.

25. Pautler, D., Koenig, B. L., Quek, B.-K., and Ortony, A. Using modified incremental chart parsing to ascribe intentions to animated geometric figures. *Behavior research methods 43*, 3 (2011), 643–665.

26. Ramanathan, V., Liang, P., and Fei-Fei, L. Video Event Understanding Using Natural Language Descriptions. *2013 IEEE International Conference on Computer Vision* (2013), 905–912.

27. Rao, C., Yilmaz, A., and Shah, M. View-invariant representation and recognition of actions. *International Journal of Computer Vision 50*, 2 (2002), 203–226.

28. Roemmele, M., Archer-McClellan, H., and Gordon, A. S. Triangle charades: a data-collection game for recognizing actions in motion trajectories. In *IUI* (2014), 209–214.

29. Rohrbach, M., Qiu, W., Titov, I., Thater, S., Pinkal, M., and Schiele, B. Translating Video Content to Natural Language Descriptions. *2013 IEEE International Conference on Computer Vision* (2013), 433–440.

30. Sadeghipour, A., Morency, L.-P., and Kopp, S. Gesture-based object recognition using histograms of guiding strokes. In *Proceedings of the British Machine Vision Conference* (2012).

31. Thibadeau, R. Artificial perception of actions. *Cognitive Science 10*, 2 (1986), 117–149.

32. Thomas, F. The illusion of life: Disney animation, 1995.

33. Tremoulet, P. D., and Feldman, J. Perception of animacy from the motion of a single object. *Perception 29*, 8 (2000), 943–952.

34. Venugopalan, S., Xu, H., Donahue, J., Rohrbach, M., Mooney, R. J., and Saenko, K. Translating Videos to Natural Language Using Deep Recurrent Neural Networks. In *Human Language Technologies: The 2015 Conference of the North American Chapter of the ACL*, Association for Computational Linguistics (2015), 1494–1504.

35. Vrigkas, M., Karavasilis, V., Nikou, C., and Kakadiaris, I. A. Action recognition by matching clustered trajectories of motion vectors. In *VISAPP (1)* (2013), 112–117.

36. Wang, T.-S., Shum, H.-Y., Xu, Y.-Q., and Zheng, N.-N. Unsupervised analysis of human gestures. In *Advances in Multimedia Information Processing*. Springer, 2001, 174–181.

37. Weinland, D., Ronfard, R., and Boyer, E. A survey of vision-based methods for action representation, segmentation and recognition. *Computer Vision and Image Understanding 115*, 2 (2011), 224–241.

38. Zhang, H., and Su, J. Naive bayesian classifiers for ranking. In *Machine Learning: ECML 2004*. Springer, 2004, 501–512.

SCEPTRE: a Pervasive, Non-Invasive, and Programmable Gesture Recognition Technology

Prajwal Paudyal, Ayan Banerjee, and Sandeep K.S. Gupta
IMPACT Lab, `http://impact.asu.edu`
Arizona State University, Tempe, Arizona
{Prajwal.Paudyal, abanerj3, sandeep.gupta}@asu.edu

ABSTRACT
Communication and collaboration between deaf people and hearing people is hindered by lack of a common language. Although there has been a lot of research in this domain, there is room for work towards a system that is ubiquitous, non-invasive, works in real-time and can be trained interactively by the user. Such a system will be powerful enough to translate gestures performed in real-time, while also being flexible enough to be fully personalized to be used as a platform for gesture based HCI. We propose SCEPTRE which utilizes two non-invasive wrist-worn devices to decipher gesture-based communication. The system uses a multi-tiered template based comparison system for classification on input data from accelerometer, gyroscope and electromyography (EMG) sensors. This work demonstrates that the system is very easily trained using just one to three training instances each for twenty randomly chosen signs from the American Sign Language(ASL) dictionary and also for user-generated custom gestures. The system is able to achieve an accuracy of 97.72 % for ASL gestures.

Author Keywords
Sign language processing; gesture-based interfaces; assistive technology; wearable and pervasive computing.

ACM Classification Keywords
K.4.2 Social Issues: Assistive technologies for persons with disabilities; H.5.2 User Interfaces: User-centered design

INTRODUCTION
Non-verbal communication is a big part of day-to-day interactions. Body movements can be a powerful medium for non-verbal communication, which is done most effectively through gestures [6]. However the human computer interfaces today are dominated by text based inputs and are increasingly moving towards voice based control [9]. Although speech is a very natural way to communicate with other people and computers, it can be inappropriate in certain circumstances that require silence, or impossible in the case of deaf people [26]. Expressibility is also lost because a lot more could be communicated if machines were trained to recognize gestures on top of the traditional User Interface(UI) elements like text input and speech. These factors have inevitably nudged us towards gesture based communication.

There are several challenges that need to be addressed and solved before we can fully implement such methods. The first one is the lack of a common protocol for gesture based communication, and the second one is the lack of a framework that can successfully translate such communication gestures to meaningful information in real-time. Another important aspect of designing gesture based communication methods is that they need to be pervasive and non-invasive. A survey of ASL users that was taken as part of this research to better assess such requirements, which is summarized in Table 2. The participants of this survey were university students between ages of 19-38, who had completed or were working towards an ASL course at ASU. Everybody in the survey was comfortable conveying simple ideas using ASL.

The system that is proposed as part of this work, SCEPTRE, fulfills these requirements. The entire system is comprised of an Android smartphone or a Bluetooth enabled computer and one to two commercial grade Myo devices that are worn on the wrist to monitor accelerometer, electromyogram(EMG) and orientation. Data is aggregated and preprocessed in the smartphones and is either processed locally or sent to a server. This flexible approach makes it very pervasive as the users can walk around anywhere with the ready-to-use system [4],[2]. Furthermore the devices can be worn underneath a shirt inconspicuously. In the future smart-watches equipped with EMG sensors can be used instead. The main challenge of this research was to develop a method to store, retrieve and most importantly match gestures effectively, conclusively and in real-time.

There are various known methods for gesture recognition and time-series analysis, such as Support Vector Machines, Linear Correlation, Hidden Markov Models, and Dynamic Time Warping [24], [14], [7], [10]. Two classes of methods are usually used for time-series analysis and data-matching: One is the learning based, in which models are developed and stored and the other one is the template based, in which the new time-series data is compared to a saved template. Although learning based models were tried, the template based models were preferred to allow user-driven training with the least number of repetitions and to make sure the system is usable

IUI 2016, March 7–10, 2016, Sonoma, CA, USA.

http://dx.doi.org/10.1145/2856767.2856794

in real-time. A very compelling advantage of utilizing a user-trained approach is that the gesture space can start small and can gradually grow as it is being used. This will also give the users an ability to discover a pattern of expression, train their own system and use that to communicate seamlessly even with users of other systems or languages. Due to the flexibility of the system, a user who is well versed in a particular gesture based system such as ASL, can choose to train the system according to the specifications of that language. She can then add custom gestures or shortcuts to add to that system if desired.

To demonstrate this, the system was first trained by randomly selecting ten control-oriented signs that are intuitive to use such as drawing a square or a letter in the English alphabet in the air with one or both hands. Other more intuitive gestures such as 'twisting one hand' or 'waving right' etc. were also used. The recognition rate on these 'custom' gestures can be kept very high since the system is designed in such a way that while using non-language based signs, the system is able to guide a user to select only those signs that are sufficiently 'different' from the signs that the system is already trained in; this is achieved in a similar way as if a test gesture was being recognized. The system accepts a new gesture only if recognizing the gesture causes no loss in overall accuracy. This is called the 'guided' mode in the system.

To demonstrate the extendibility of the system, it was then trained for 20 ASL signs by turning the 'guided mode' off. Experiments were done both when the system was trained in these signs by the user, and when the system was used with training data only from the other 'pool' of users. Due to the vast difference in EMG signals between users, the latter experiments did not yield very favorable results. However, recognition rates of 97.72% was achieved when all three of EMG, accelerometer and orientation sensors were used and the database consisted of three instances of the gesture trained by the same user. Using any two of the three sensors, the highest recognition accuracy of 95.45% was achieved when using EMG sensors paired with orientation sensors. With only one of the sensors the highest accuracy that was achieved was 93% for orientation sensor. Data was collected from 10 healthy adults between the ages of 22 and 35, each of whom performed a total of 20 ASL gestures.

Usage

The system is envisioned to be used in two primary use cases:
1. User-to-user communication where at least one user uses a sign language: In this scenario, the user wishes to communicate with a person using a gesture based communication medium, but the other person cannot understand that mode of communication. The first user, then begins the translation mode and performs a gesture. The hub receives the data, processes it and sends the recognized output to the user via a text message or audio message as seen in Figure 2 or converted to animated models as facilitated by systems like that described by Marshall et al. [31].

2. User-to-computer Interactions: In this scenario, the user of system uses ASL or some form of custom gestures to communicate with a computer system. The gestures transmitted can be converted to a regular language for communication purposes just as one would use an audio input to form sentences, or they can be used to trigger specific actions according to pre-configured preferences. For example a user may use a certain gesture to signal she wants to control a certain device. The smartphone hub can then trigger a connection to that device, say a garage door, and the user can give a specific gesture command to open the door, and then another one to disconnect as seen in Figure 1.

RELATED WORK

Most existing work on sign language recognition utilize image/video based recognition techniques while some other utilize data gloves [21], [19], [12], [17], [29]. Although a high accuracy is achieved in the aforementioned data-glove based approaches, one major drawback is that the system is wired and invasive as it interferes with day-to-day activities of the user. According to Fang et al. [12], commercially existing data-gloves are also too expensive for large scale deployment. The system that we propose, utilizes Bluetooth enabled sensors that appear in wearables such as smart-watches, and are thus pervasive and non-invasive. They can also be easily worn underneath a shirt to make them less conspicuous.

The image and video based recognition systems [33, 23, 16, 18, 5] use either annotated fingers, color bands etc, or just plain raw images and video from users to translate gesture based communication. Some studies also utilized multiple cameras [37] to enhance the accuracy by some margin. However, image and video based systems are dependent on presence of cameras in the right positions and are affected by background colors. Another drawback to these systems is that image and video processing is computationally expensive which makes the recognition system's response time slower. Also, heavy dependence on Hidden Markov Model (HMM) based methods makes training the system cumbersome and data intensive. Unlike these approaches, using portable wristwatch like sensors to detect gestures is far less invasive and a template based recognition approach does not require many training data-sets. The computational complexity also decreases as there is no need to deal with data-intensive images and videos, this allows the system to be real-time as well as environment independent.

Li et al. [20] has done a study on combining accelerometer and EMG sensors to recognize sub-word level gestures for Chinese Sign Language and Chen et al. [8, 39] show that combination of multiple sensors helps to increase the recognition accuracy. Following this path, we add the EMG measurements from eight built-in pods in the Myo device to get information that can be leveraged to detect subtle finger movements and configurations which are essential for detecting certain signs and distinguishing them from others. The orientation sensors help to distinguish between signs that have a similar movement and muscle patterns but different rotational primitives. Accelerometer sensors detect movement and position of the hands. The combination of all these sensors into one commercial grade, wireless sensor has given the ability to deploy gesture and sign-language recognition abilities in a far more practical and user-friendly way. Bluetooth technol-

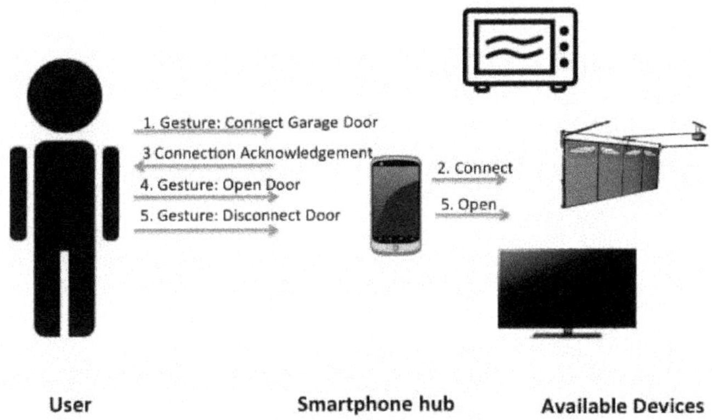

Figure 1. Usage for HCI/ Control system.

Figure 2. Usage for Person-to-Person Communication.

Table 1. Summary of existing Gesture Recognition tools.

Existing Gesture Recognition Algorithms	Mobile	User Extendable	Requires Video	Real Time	User Independent	Invasive	Language Independent
[21]	×	×	×	✓	×	✓	×
[19]	NA	×	×	×	✓	✓	×
[12]	×	✓	×	NA	✓	✓	×
[33]	×	×	✓	✓	×	✓	×
[8]	×	×	×	✓	×	✓	×
Sceptre(Proposed)	✓	✓	×	✓	×	×	✓

ogy for transfer of data makes the system wireless and easy to use. The overall accuracy is also increases due to the use of all three types of signals.

Thus by coupling pervasive technologies with simple algorithms we achieve high accuracy rates and great mobility. Starner et al. propose a solution that might be user and language independent as possibilities, however an implementation is not provided [33]. Moving this system towards complete user-independence is part of future work. The visual nature of sign language communication is however not limited to just hand gestures; expressions and body gait also play important parts in the overall communication. However analyzing facial expressions and body gaits will be part of future work.

PRELIMINARIES

American Sign Language Specifics

Signs in ASL are composed of a number of components: the shape the hands assumes, the orientation of the hands, the movement they perform and their location relative to other parts of the body. One or both hands may be used to perform a sign, and facial expressions and body tilts also contribute to the meaning. Changing any one of these may change the meaning of a sign [15], [3], [35], [11]. This is what gives sign-language the immense power of expressibility, however this also means that multi-modal information has to be processed for sign-language recognition.

Orientation is the degree of rotation of a hand when signing. This can appear in a sign with or without movement. The gyroscope sensors provide rotation data in three axes, which is utilized in recognizing orientation. Data from EMG sensors is utilized in detecting muscle tensions to distinguish hand-shapes, which is another very important feature of the signs.

Location, or *tab*, refers to specific places that the hands occupy as they are used to form words. ASL is known to use 12 locations excluding the hands [36]. They are concentrated around different parts of the body. The use of a passive hand and different shapes of the passive hand is also considered valid locations. Movement or sig, refers to some form of hand action to form words. ASL is known to use about twenty movements, which include lateral, twist, flex, opening or closing [34]. A combination of accelerometer and gyroscope data is instrumental in distinguishing signs based on movement and signing space.

Sign language is a very visual medium of communication, the system that this paper proposes however tries to capture this visual information, in a non-visual manner to ensure pervasiveness. Thus, multi-modal signals are considered to get as close of an estimate as possible.

Problem Description

The primary task of the system is to match gestures. Since multi-modal signals are being considered, they are compared individually to the signals stored in the database and the results are combined. The form of the input data is described in detail Section Methodology, but in short it consists of an array of time-series data. The gesture database has pre-processed iterations of the same gesture along with other gesture data. The problem that the system is solving is comparing this test gesture data to each of the existing sample data using DTW

Algorithm 1 Problem Description.

```
procedure MATCH GESTURES(test)
    for (i in 1 to database_size) do
        template ← next_template
        for (j in 1 to number_of_sensors) do
            distance[j] ← dist(test[j], template[j])
        end for
        Overall_dist = combine(distance)
    end for
    Output = min(Overall_dist)
end procedure
```

Figure 3. Myo Devices and Android Smartphone with the Sceptre App showing.

and Energy based techniques as appropriate and then combining the results at the end to give a distance score. Then, at the very end, the task is to recognize the gesture based on the least distance. Algorithm 1 provides a high level overview of this approach.

REQUIREMENTS

The need/demand for sign language recognition software for accessibility has been previously established, but accessing if there is a need or demand for systems that can utilize an established natural language as a human computer interface has not been studied (to our knowledge). As part of this research a survey was taken where 13 users of ASL expressed their opinions on these topics that included their willingness to use a gesture based system, the perceived practicality of using ASL for HCI, the acceptable time constraints for user to user and user to computer communications etc. The results of the survey are summarized in Table 2.

Extendability

With more and more systems with voice command interfaces, it only seems plausible that a system that understands sign language will be desirable. To the question 2 in the survey, more than 75% of the ASL users agreed that they were very likely to use ASL for HCI, and the rest would be somewhat likely to use such a system. More than 75% people also responded that it was very important that the system be easily trainable, and another 15% thought it was somewhat important. This follows from the knowledge [15] that ASL (and sign language in general) varies a lot over geographical, racial and cultural bounds. Thus, the ability to add unrecognized signs or new signs easily is very important. When ASL users were asked if they were likely to use the system if it could be trained using 3 training instances, more than 76% said very likely and the rest responded they were somewhat likely to spend the time training. This requirement puts the constraint on the system that it has to be relatively easy to train. This system can be trained using only three instances of training per sign. The relationship between training instances and accuracy is summarized in SectionResults and Evaluation.

Time Constraints

Communication is a real-time activity and the need for fast response times in both person-to-person communication as well as HCI is well established. A timing delay of 0.1 s is considered 'instantaneous' while a delay of 0.2 s to 1 s is noticeable to the user, but generally acceptable. If a system takes more than 1 s, then some indication needs to be given to user about the 'processing' aspect [22]. The survey question regarding timing backs this up: while more than 76% of ASL users said they were very likely and an additional 15% said they were somewhat likely to use the system if the response time was under 3 s, this number falls to 53% and 0% very likely responses when the response times were 3-7 s, and more than 7 s respectively. This establishes a strict constraint for recognition time for the system. To meet these standards the system has to be light-weight and should not rely on computationally expensive methods. Also, if the processing is delayed due to unpredictable issues like client network sluggishness, a proper indication has to be given to the user of the wait.

Non-Invasiveness

Historically there has been a certain stigma associated with signing. It was only in 2013 that the White House published a statement in support of using sign language as an official medium of instruction for children, although it has been known to be a developmentally important for deaf children for years [1]. Given this stigma, and due to other more obvious reasons like usability, an interpretation system should be as non-invasive as possible. The survey results confirm this, as more than 90% thought that it is important or very important for the system to be non-invasive.

Pervasiveness

The other disadvantage of using more invasive technology like data-gloves or multiple-cameras is that it makes the system either tethered to a certain lab based environment settings or it requires bulky equipment that discourages its use in an everyday setting [21, 19, 12]. This makes the use of smartwatch like wireless equipment that can work on the streets as well as it works in a lab more desirable.

To make sure that the proposed system meets these requirements some performance metrics are decided upon which are discussed in detail in Subsection Performance Metrics and subsequently the system is tested w.r.t to these metrics as discussed in Subsection Design of experiments.

SYSTEM ARCHITECTURE

The system consists of two Myo Devices connected via Bluetooth to an Android device which acts as a hub as shown in Figures 3 and 4. For the EMG part a Bluetooth enabled computer is used to obtain the data since the Myo framework

Table 2. Summary of ASL users' survey on a continuum from very unlikely (0) to very likely (5).

Question	1	2	3	4	5
Interest in trying solutions for gesture based HCI	0	0	1	3	9
Interest in using ASL for gesture based HCI	0	0	3	4	6
Likeliness to use a system that requires 3 trainings instances	0	0	3	1	9
Importance of non-invasivenss	0	1	3	2	7
Likeliness to use if wait time 0-3 s	0	1	2	4	6
Likeliness to use if wait time 3-7 s	1	1	4	5	2
Likeliness to use if wait time 7-10 s	4	4	5	0	0
Likeliness to try a prototype	0	1	3	4	5
Likeliness of the use of this system by a native speaker for communication	0	1	1	5	6

Figure 4. Deployment: A user with a wrist-band devices on each hand performing a gesture.

does not yet facilitate streaming EMG data to smart phones. For tests that do not use EMG data, Android device collects and does some pre-processing on the data of the gesture performed and stores this as time-series data. All this is sent to the server for processing. Three to four instances for each gesture data are collected, processed and stored. A high level overview of the pre-processing that is done to the data before it is stored in the database is summarized in Figure 5.

At test time when a gesture is performed, the system processes the gesture-data in a similar way as described above. In the Architecture Figure 6, this is encapsulated in the 'Preprocessing' block. After this is done, the system compares this data with the other gesture data stored in the database using a specialized comparison method. The comparison method comprises of testing accelerometer data, orientation data and EMG data by different methods and later combining the results before calculating a 'nearness' score for each pair. After this step a ranking algorithm is employed in the server to compute a list of stored gestures that are closest to the test gesture and best one is returned. Details on these techniques is given in Section Methodology. The system using the same methods of comparison is able to help the user be selective in the signs that the system is trained on, this is called the 'guided mode' as explained in Subsection Training. A smart ranking architecture is used when the size of the database grows to ensure that the results come back in acceptable time to be a real-time application. This is discussed in more details in Subsection Ranking and Optimization. The system also periodically uploads all recognized gesture data and other meta-data like user specific accuracy, new signs trained etc. to the server. This information can be used to make future predictive methods more efficient which is not part of this work.

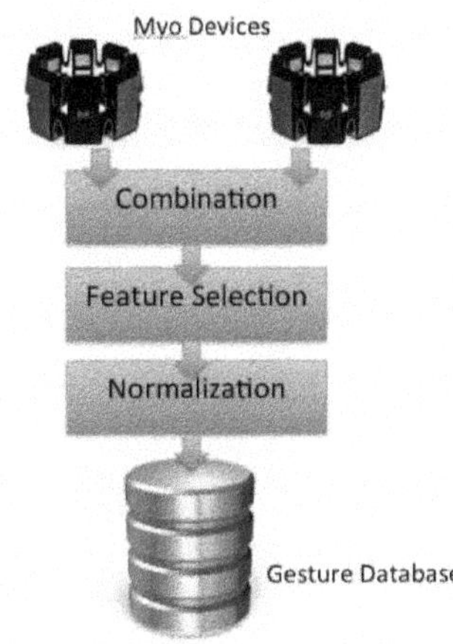

Figure 5. Pre-processing: Data is collected from the Myo devices, processed and then stored in Database.

Training

Training the system requires two Myo devices, a hub for data collection, and server for processing. The hub and the server may be one and the same. A typical training sessions consists of the following steps: 1. The user selects either the 'guided mode' or 'ASL' mode. (in the smartphone interface) 2. She selects a sign from a dropdown list, or creates a new sign. 3. She performs the sign. 4. The system annotates the input data with the name of the sign and stores the data. 5. If guided mode was selected, the system performs a scan of the sign database specific to the user and determines if there are any clashes. If not, the user is asked to repeat the sign two more times after which the sign is ready to use. If however there was a clash, then the user is suggested to choose another sign instead. 6. If the 'ASL' mode was selected, the system does not give such feedback, and simply asks the user to train the system two more times. 7. The gesture is ready to use.

METHODOLOGY

The overall methodology of gesture recognition consists of the following steps as shown in Figure 6.

Pre-processing

Data is collected from two Myo devices while the gesture is being performed (Figure 5). As soon as the end is detected or

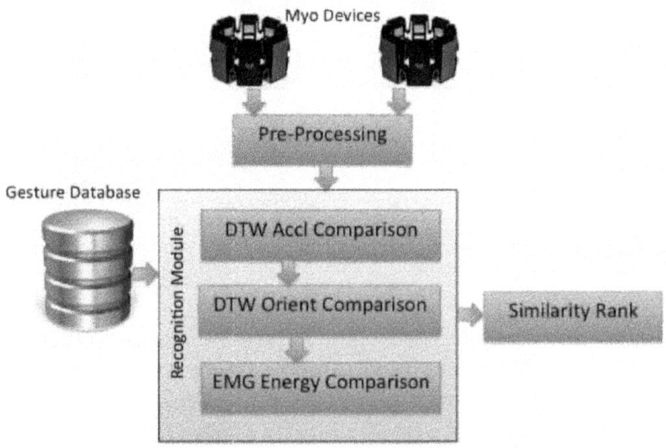

Figure 6. Gesture Comparison and Ranking: New data is collected, processed and compared with existing gesture data to get a ranked-list of similarities.

signaled, the pre-processing begins. The data collected from two hands is aggregated into one data-table then stored into a file as an array of time-series data. At 50 Hz. of sampling rate a 5 s. gesture data will consist of: 6 accelerometer Vectors of length 250 each, 6 gyroscope Vectors of Length 250 each, 6 orientation Vectors of Length 250 each, 16 EMG Vectors, Length 250 each. We combine all this for simplicity into a 34×250 matrix. Each time-series is transformed to make sure the initial value is 0, by subtracting this value from all values in the time-series. This will help prevent errors when the user performs the sign in a different starting positions. Normalization is then done by representing all values as floats between 0 and 1 by min-max method.

Orientation values are received in the form of three time-series in terms of unit quaternions. The pitch, yaw and roll values are obtained from the quaternion values w, x, y and z by using the following equations:

$$roll = tan^{-1}(\frac{2(wx+yz)}{-x^2y^2}) \quad (1)$$
$$pitch = sin^{-1}(max(-1, min(1, 2(wy - zx))))$$
$$yaw = tan^{-1}(\frac{2(wz+xy)}{-y^2z^2}).$$

EMG Energy

After correctly identifying the location of each of the individual pods of the two Myo devices, data is stored and shuffled in such a way that the final stored data is aligned from EMG pod-1 to EMG pod-8. This gives flexibility to the end-user as she no longer has to remember 'how' to put on the devices, and can thus randomly put either Myo device on either hand and expect good results. This is a great leap towards the pervasiveness and ease of use of this technology.

While we found that the DTW based testing worked very good for accelerometer and orientation comparisons, the EMG comparison numbers were not satisfactory. This is because, EMG activations seem to be much more stochastic and a 'shape' based comparison did not yield good results. The

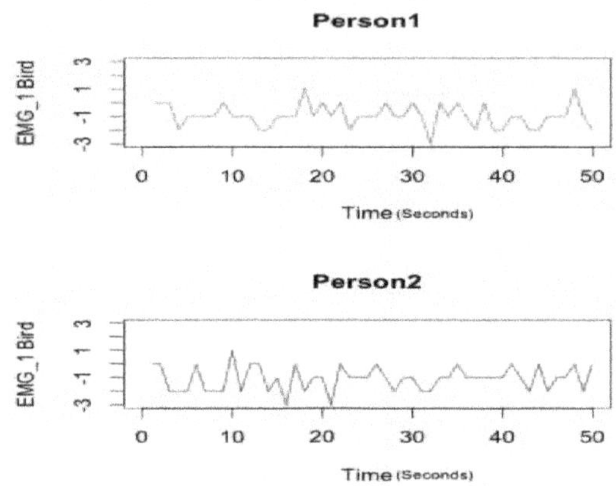

Figure 7. Variation in EMG signals between two users.

shapes formed by performing the same gesture for two different people are drastically different as seen in Figure 7, but they also differ in shape significantly enough between two repetitions by the same person to not give a small DTW distance. However, it was found by experimentation that gestures tend to activate the same EMG pods when repeated. Thus an energy based comparison was tried:

EMG energy 'E' on each pod is calculated as the sum of squares of x[n] , the value of the time-series at point 'n' .

$$E = sum(x[n]^2). \quad (2)$$

Dynamic Time Warping

We used four different approaches for comparing accelerometer and orientation data: a. Euclidian distance b. Regression c. Principal Component Analysis (PCA) and d. DTW. Euclidian distance simply compares the two time-series using mean-squared error. Regression analysis fits a model to the time-series and uses this model to compare best fit for the test gesture. Given a set of features from the time-series for a gesture, PCA derives the optimal set of features for comparison. According to [25], DTW is a well-known technique to find an optimal alignment between two given (time-dependent) sequences under certain restrictions. It was found that DTW based methods gave best results. DTW based approached proved ideal in our use-case since it could gracefully handle the situations when the sign was performed slower or faster than the stored training data, or performed with a small lag. Traditionally, DTW has been used extensively for speech recognition, and it is finding increasing use in the fields of gesture recognition as well [30], specially when combined with Hidden Markov Models [38]. SCEPTRE takes a simpler approach by randomly re-sampling the training and test datasets based on the least number of points in either one, then doing a DTW based distance analysis on them. First a DTW analysis of Accelerometer Data is run and a ranked list of 'probable' signs is passed on for DTW based analysis of orientation Data which in turn creates an even shorter ranked list to be processed by the final EMG algorithm.

On another approach, the normalized distances from each of the outputs is taken and the sum of squares of the final out-

Algorithm 2 Overall Gesture recognition method.

procedure GESTURERECOGNITION
  $t \leftarrow$ elapsed time from start of the experiment
  $test\_gesture \leftarrow$ get gesture data from the user
  $S_G \leftarrow$ query list of recognized gestures from database
  $normalized\_accl \leftarrow accel\_values - first\_accl\_value$
  $normalized\_orient \leftarrow orientation - first\_orientation$
  $normalized\_emg \leftarrow emg\_values - first\_emg\_value$
  for each trained gesture $T_G \in S_G$ **do**
    $dtw\_accl \leftarrow dtw(training\_accl, normalized\_accl)$
    $dtw\_orient \leftarrow dtw(training\_orient, normalized\_orient)$
    $T_G^E \leftarrow$ calculated energy of each pod for the training gesture
    $emg\_energy\_diff \leftarrow T_G^E$ - test_emg_energy
    $scal\_lim \leftarrow \{0, 1\}$
    $scaled\_emg\_diff \leftarrow$ scale(emg_energy_diff,scal_lim)
    $scaled\_accl\_dist \leftarrow$ scale(dtw_accl, scal_lim)
    $scaled\_orient\_dist \leftarrow$ scale(dtw_orient, scal_lim)
    $combined\_nearness \leftarrow$ compute nearness from Eq. 3
  end for
  Sort T_G with respect to combined nearness.
  $recognized\_gesture \leftarrow$ top T_G in the sorted list
end procedure

put is taken as an indication of 'closeness' of a test sign to a training sign. This is the approach that was chosen due to its computational simplicity and speed.

Combination

The overall 'nearness' of two signs is computed to be the total distance between those signs which is obtained by adding up the scaled distances for accelerometer, orientation and EMG as discussed above. An extra step of scaling the distance values between (0,1) is performed so as to give equal weight to each of the features. Also, since we have 8 EMG pods and only 3 each of accelerometer and orientation sensors, we use the following formula for the combination. The formula is for combining accelerometer sum of distances and EMG sum of distances. Similar techniques were applied for the other combinations. An algorithmic summary can be found in Equation 3.

$$dist = (8cs(sc\_accl\_comb) + 3cs(sc\_emg\_comb))/24. \quad (3)$$

where $cs()$ is a function that returns the sum of columns, sc_accl_comb is a data frame that holds the combined accelerometer DTW distances for both hands for all trained signs, and sc_emg_comb is a data frame that holds the combined EMG energy distances for both hands for all trained signs. The overall algorithm that is employed for recognition is summarized in Algorithm 2.

Ranking and Optimization

Timing constraints due to the real-time nature of the application requires us to optimize the recognition algorithm to be efficient, specially as the gesture space increases. As the number of gestures in the database increases to beyond 60, as we can see in Figure 8, the recognition time for identifying one gesture goes beyond the .5 s mark, which we have chosen to represent a real-time timing constraint. Thus, to deal with this situation, we modify our comparison algorithm to first compare to one stored instance of each gesture, then choose the top 'n' number of gestures which when compared to 'k' of each, still allowing the time-constraint to be fulfilled. We then, proceed with the normal gesture comparison routine on only these gesture instances and thus keep the recognition time within our constraints. All the variables for this method viz. the 'n', 'k' are calculated dynamically by what is allowed by the timing constraint 'tc', thus making this approach fluid and adaptable to more vigorous time constraints if required. The overall optimization algorithm is summarized in Algorithm 3.

Algorithm 3 Optimization to meet time constraints.

$databasesize \leftarrow sizeofgesturedatabaseforuser$
$time\_to\_compute \leftarrow estimatedtimefrompreviousiterations$
if $time\_to\_compute < time\_contraint$ **then**
  Compute Similarity Score with one template per gesture
  $top\_gestures \leftarrow list(top\_gestures, time\_to\_compute, time\_constrant)$
  Utilize Algorithm 2
  END
end if

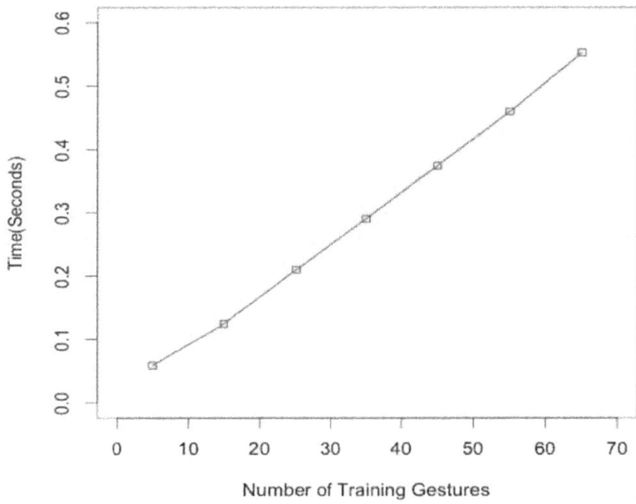

Figure 8. Database Size vs. Recognition Time.

RESULTS AND EVALUATION

Design of experiments

Experiments were designed to test the application with scalability in mind. The system begins on an "empty slate" and the gestures are trained interactively. Since a template based comparison is being utilized, we store the entire data set plus some features. After all the data is collected, the system is ready to be trained for another gesture. A sample application screen can be found in Figure 3. It is advised to provide 3-4 training instances of the same gesture to improve accuracy of recognition but that is not required. We test the system with 1, 2, 3, and 4 instances of each gesture to determine the correlation between number of instances saved and the recognition accuracy rate. That is all that is needed at the training phase. During testing phase we evaluate our system based on time it takes for recognition and on combination of features that produce the best results. Then we evaluate how recognition time increases with the increase in the number of gestures.

The way gestures are performed by the same person are generally similar but they have a tendency to vary slightly over time. Although, considering signals generated by a portable device that the user can put on and off by herself, provides the system a lot of portability and pervasiveness, it comes with a drawback that the signals we receive might not always be the same. To account for this experiments were performed that allowed users to put on the devices themselves, they were allowed to face any direction, and perform the gesture as long as they stayed in the Bluetooth range of the hub. Also, samples were collected over multiple sessions to account for variability in signing over time. The test subjects were 10 University students between the ages of 20 and 32 who performed the gestures in multiple sessions while also varying direction they were facing and if they were standing up/sitting down. The subjects viewed a video recording of the gestures being performed by ASL instructors before performing them with the system.

Prototyping and Choice of Gestures

20 ASL signs were chosen to prototype the system. They were carefully chosen such that a. A good mix of the various ASL components as discussed in Section Preliminaries and b. To include signs that are very close in some components but different in others. The choice of signs and the break-down of components for 10 of the 20 chosen signs is summarized in Table 3. The other 10 signs that were chosen are hurt, horse, pizza, large, happy, home, home, mom, goodnight, wash. Detailed analysis of system performance is give in Section Results and Evaluation.

Performance Metrics

The system is evaluated on each of the requirements discussed in Section Requirements. Pervasiveness of the system is justified since it is wireless and can work in Bluetooth range of the hub device which can either do the processing itself or offload it to a cloud server. Invasiveness is a harder metric to evaluate, as this seems to be more subjective. However, with wearable devices like smartwatches, wristbands such as FitBit, Myo becoming increasingly compact, wireless and even stylish [13], the proposed system is much less invasive then any of the alternatives. (see Related Work). Accuracy is undoubtedly one of the fundamental performance metrics for any recognition system. This basic function of the system is to facilitate real-life conversations, thus the system has to be able to function in real-time. Another aspect of the system is that it is extendable, thus the ease in scalability to a larger number of signs is very important. With the increase in the gesture space, the recognition time will also increase, the system should be able to scale up with a reasonable recognition time. Although there is a slight dip in recognition rate, the potential for scalability showcases the system's flexibility. Thus the experiments focus on these three metrics to evaluate the system:

1. Recognition time
2. Extensibility
3. Recognition rate (Accuracy)

Device Requirements

The device requirements for the experiments are:

Sensors: a. EMG, accelerometer and orientation (or Gyroscope) sensors that go between the wrist and elbow of a user on both hands. The desired frequency of each channel is 50 Hz. b. Wireless interface to transmit raw data from each of these sensors. c. A smartphone that acts as a hub to receive, pre-process, communicate the data to server, and later to display the results. d. A server that stores previous data in an individualized database per user, compares gestures, finds a match, and sends information back to the smartphone.

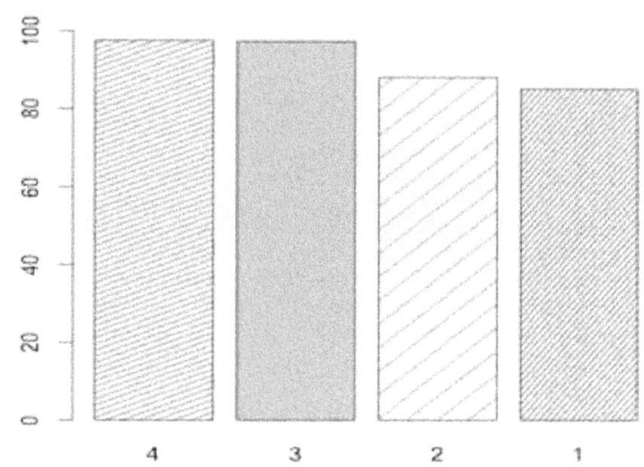

Figure 9. Training Data vs. Accuracy.

All experiments were performed with the setup described in Section System Architecture with devices with the following configurations:

Two Myo Sensors: Medical Grade Stainless Steel EMG sensors, Highly sensitive nine-axis IMU containing three-axis gyroscope, three-axis accelerometer, three-axis magnetometer. Expandable between 7.5 - 13 inches, wieghing 93 grams with a thickness of 0.45 inches. Communication channel: Bluetooth. Processor:ARM Cortex M4 Processor Hub Specifications(Android): OS: Android OS, v5.0 Chipset: Qualcomm MSM8974 Snapdragon 800 CPU: Quad-core 2.3 GHz Krait 400 Memory: 2 GB RAM Mac Specifications(Server) Processor:3.06GHz Intel Core i3 processor with 4MB level 3 cache; supports Hyper-Threading Momory: 8 GB DDR

Results

It was determined through experiments that three is a good choice for the number of training instances for each gesture. This formed a good compromise between usability and results as shown in Figure 9. Thus, each gesture was performed three times at varying times in the day. Then all data was aggregated, and annotated according to the gesture performed. The testing comprised of taking one dataset and comparing it with all other data sets and then estimating the correct gesture. With the 'guided mode' turned on, a recognition rate of 100% was achieved as expected. Then 20 randomly selected ASL Signs were used. The best accuracy was obtained by a tiered-combination method of all three features. The relative accuracy of other methods can be seen in Figure 11. This helps confirm that the combination of all three features produces the highest results.

Figure 8 shows how the recognition time increases with the increase in the number of gestures that are stored in the system. With 65 gestures in the database, a recognition time of

Table 3. Component breakdown of 10 of the chosen signs.

Number	Name of Sign	Location(Tab)	Movement	Orientation	Number of Hands
1	Blue	Around the Face	Wrist-Twist	Away from signer	1
2	Cat	Around the face	Outward and closing	Towards center	2
3	Cost	Trunk	Wrist-Flex	One towards signer one towards center	2
4	Dollar	Trunk	Two Wrist-Flexes	One towards signer one towards center	2
5	Gold	Side of the head	Away from center, change hand-shape twist	Towards the signer	1
6	Orange	Mouth	Open and close twice	Towards user	1
7	Bird	Mouth	Pinch with Two fingers	Away from signer	1
8	Shirt	Shoulder	Twice Wrist Flex	Facing down	2
9	Large	Trunk	Both Hands Away from Center	Facing away from signer	2
10	Please	Trunk/Chest	Form a circle	Both facing towards signer	1

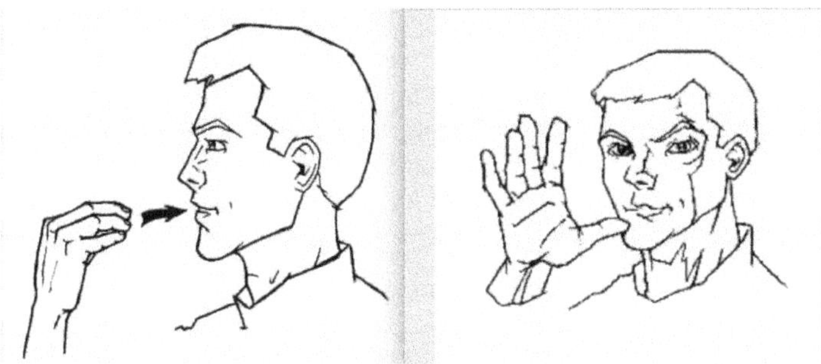

Figure 10. Gesture for 'Mom' Vs. 'Eat'.

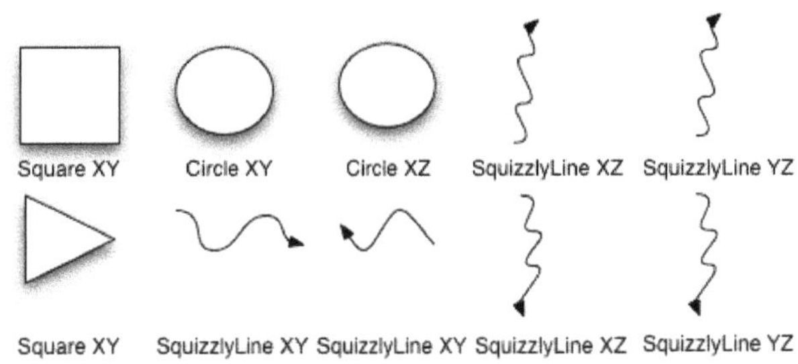

Figure 12. User Trained Gestures.

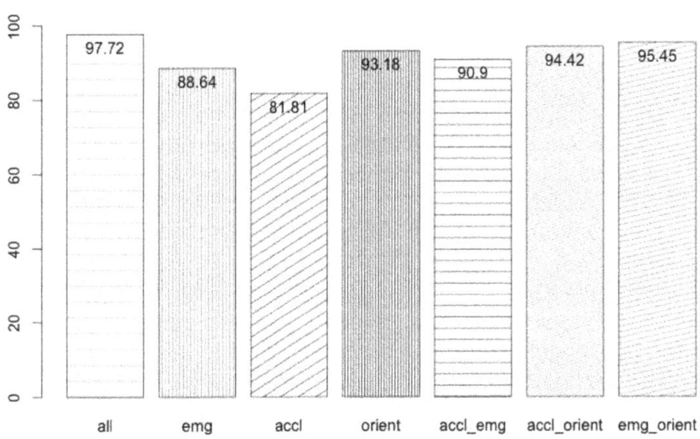

Figure 11. Features vs. Accuracy.

0.552 s was achieved. (processed on a 3.06 GHz Intel Core i3 8 GB RAM Mac). This fast response time means that the system qualifies for use for real-time communications. This time can be further improved upon by utilizing a more powerful server and optimizing the data queries, which will be part of future work.

Figure 13 shows the performance of the system based on recognition results for a combination of the features. The gestures tested were 'day', 'enjoy', 'eat', 'happy', 'home', 'hot', 'large', 'mom', 'pizza', 'shirt', 'still', 'wash' and 'wave'. The different sub-figures show that although comparing solely based on accelerometer performs good for some gestures like 'happy', it is ineffective in distinguishing between others like 'day'. This can be explained because the nature of performing this gesture is very similar to other gestures in overall hand movements, but are different when it comes to finger configurations. Thus the performance gets better as shown in Figure 13c when EMG sensors are brought into the equation. Like we discussed earlier, the least number of recognition errors overall occur when all three of the sensor data are fused as seen in Figure 13d. This gives an insight on where the system is error-prone and thus can be optimized. Server level Optimization based on such input will be part of future work. We envision a server that continuously monitors success-failure data and becomes better by implementing machine learning algorithms to give weights to the different features.

These results can be understood better in context with the breakdown information given for each gesture in Table 3. For instance, Figure 10 shows screenshots of a person performing the gesture 'mom' and another one performing 'eat'. These two gestures are very similar in 'Location' and 'Movement' but are distinctive when it comes to 'HandShape' and 'Orientation of Hand'. Thus, while the system isn't able to distinguish between these two gestures based on Accelerometer information only as seen in Figure 13a, the system does well when EMG information is included as seen in Figure 13c.

The guided mode as discussed in Usage was trained using 3 iterations each of 10 custom signs shown in Figure 12. An

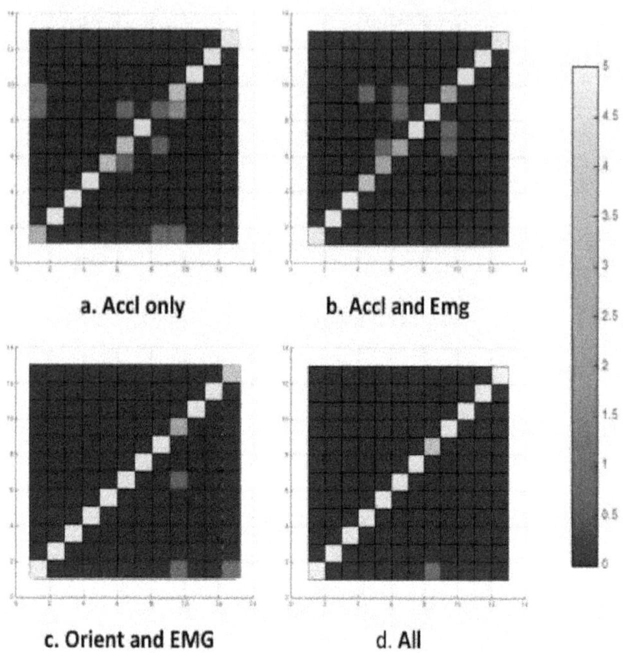

Figure 13. Gesture Recognition vs. Features used.

accuracy of 100% is achieved for this mode as expected, because clashes are detected at training time and avoided.

The results in Figure 11 show an accuracy of 97.72% for 20 ASL signs when all accelerometer, orientation and EMG are used. The database consisted of signs from 10 different people, and each person performed each sign 3 times. This table also lists the accuracy of other variations in the combination of these three input signals. The accuracy varied when individual databases were separated, however it stayed in the (97-100)% bracket when all signals were used on a dataset consisting of template gestures from the test user.

DISCUSSION

Continuous Processing: The gestures that were recognized in this test were isolated in nature. A start and stop button, or a timer was utilized to gather data. This was done to test the algorithms in isolation first. However, when the system is actually deployed to the public, a continuous monitoring algorithm has to be utilized. This can be done by using windowing methods and optimizing based on best results. However, we expect that the system will require a lot more training.

Dictionary Size: Another thing that can be improved upon is the dictionary size and the support for Signed Alphabet. Signed alphabet give an ASL user the ability to use English Language Alphabet to visually spell out a word. This is an important aspect of sign language communication since not all english words or ideas have sign language counterparts. The dictionary size used is currently 20 ASL words and 10 user invented gestures. The video based sign language dictionary website signasl.org currently has over 30,000 videos for sign languages in use, so there is a lot of room to grow into.

Framework Limitations: Currently due to limitations of the Myo framework for Android, final tests involving EMG data signals had to be done using laptop computers. Two Mac computers were used to gather the data simultaneously via Bluetooth channels and then combine them and store them to a cloud based data storage system. A separate script was triggered to process the stored data at test time. With the anticipated release of new framework for Myo Devices, this computation can be done at the mobile phone level and data can be sent to the server only at designated intervals.

User Independence: EMG data fluctuates a lot between people. This is apparent from Figure 7. More research can be done on data gathering and feature selection of the EMG data pods to come up with a 'unifying' framework that works for everyone. This will be a definitive direction in attaining user-independence while using EMG signals.

Search Algorithm: The search algorithm that is implemented can be improved upon to decrease the recognition time. Hierarchal searching can be done, in which training gestures are clustered according to the energies in each time-series data, and only those gestures are compared which have comparable energies.

SCEPTRE in collaboration with other HCI techniques such as brain-driven control [27, 28, 32] can revolutionize the way people interact with computers. In addition to the uses of HCI or Sign Language Communication, this technology can also be extended to uses in the domains of activity recognition, food intake estimation or even physiotherapy.

CONCLUSIONS

DTW and energy based comparison methods are fast and highly effective. Template based comparison techniques have a great advantage of lossless information storing. Comparing accelerometer and orientation data between gestures is best done by using Dynamic Time Warping methods which muscle movement (EMG) data is best compared by comparing total energies in each pods. The structure present in Sign Languages like ASL can be divided into components which explain the success of certain signals in recognizing them. The overall accuracy of the system is increased by a smart combination of these signals without compromising on speed, recognition rate, or usability. The sensors that are used are non-invasive and versatile thus allowing people to effectively utilize them in day-to-day situations without drawing much attention. The future direction of this research is in incorporating continuous sign processing, user independence in the system and increasing the dictionary size.

ACKNOWLEDGEMENTS

This project was partly funded by NIH NIBIB (Grant #EB019202) and NSF IIS (Grant #1116385). We thank Julie Stylinski, Lecturer at ASU for her invaluable ASL domain knowledge and for facilitating the survey. We thank all the survey participants as well as volunteers that helped to train/test the system. We thank Subhasish Das of IMPACT lab, ASU for his technical contribution to get the project going.

REFERENCES

1. Daphne Bavelier Aaron J. Newman. A critical period for right hemisphere recruitment in american sign language processing. In *Multimodal Signals: Cognitive and Algorithmic Issues*, pages 76–80, 2002.
2. Frank Adelstein, Sandeep KS Gupta, Golden Richard, and Loren Schwiebert. *Fundamentals of mobile and pervasive computing*, volume 1. McGraw-Hill New York, 2005.
3. B.J. Bahan. *Non-manual Realization of Agreement in American Sign Language*. UMI Dissertation Services. UMI, 1996.
4. Ayan Banerjee and Sandeep KS Gupta. Analysis of smart mobile applications for healthcare under dynamic context changes. *Mobile Computing, IEEE Transactions on*, 14(5):904–919, 2015.
5. Sara Bilal, Rini Akmeliawati, Amir A Shafie, and Momoh Jimoh E Salami. Hidden markov model for human to computer interaction: a study on human hand gesture recognition. *Artificial Intelligence Review*, 40(4):495–516, 2013.
6. Baptiste Caramiaux, Marco Donnarumma, and Atau Tanaka. Understanding gesture expressivity through muscle sensing. *ACM Transactions on Computer-Human Interaction (TOCHI)*, 21(6):31, 2015.
7. Feng-Sheng Chen, Chih-Ming Fu, and Chung-Lin Huang. Hand gesture recognition using a real-time tracking method and hidden markov models. *Image and vision computing*, 21(8):745–758, 2003.
8. Xiang Chen, Xu Zhang, Zhang-Yan Zhao, Ji-Hai Yang, Vuokko Lantz, and Kong-Qiao Wang. Hand gesture recognition research based on surface emg sensors and 2d-accelerometers. In *Wearable Computers, 2007 11th IEEE International Symposium on*, pages 11–14. IEEE, 2007.
9. Philip R Cohen and Sharon L Oviatt. The role of voice input for human-machine communication. *proceedings of the National Academy of Sciences*, 92(22):9921–9927, 1995.
10. Andrea Corradini. Dynamic time warping for off-line recognition of a small gesture vocabulary. In *Recognition, Analysis, and Tracking of Faces and Gestures in Real-Time Systems, 2001. Proceedings. IEEE ICCV Workshop on*, pages 82–89. IEEE, 2001.
11. E. Costello. *Random House Webster's American Sign Language Dictionary*. Random House Reference, 2008.
12. Gaolin Fang, Wen Gao, and Debin Zhao. Large vocabulary sign language recognition based on fuzzy decision trees. *Systems, Man and Cybernetics, Part A: Systems and Humans, IEEE Transactions on*, 34(3):305–314, 2004.
13. Sandeep KS Gupta, Tridib Mukherjee, and Krishna Kumar Venkatasubramanian. *Body area networks: Safety, security, and sustainability*. Cambridge University Press, 2013.
14. Deng-Yuan Huang, Wu-Chih Hu, and Sung-Hsiang Chang. Vision-based hand gesture recognition using pca+ gabor filters and svm. In *Intelligent Information Hiding and Multimedia Signal Processing, 2009. IIH-MSP'09. Fifth International Conference on*, pages 1–4. IEEE, 2009.
15. T. Johnston and A. Schembri. *Australian Sign Language (Auslan): An introduction to sign language linguistics*. Cambridge University Press, 2007.
16. Daniel Kelly, Jane Reilly Delannoy, John Mc Donald, and Charles Markham. A framework for continuous multimodal sign language recognition. In *Proceedings of the 2009 international conference on Multimodal interfaces*, pages 351–358. ACM, 2009.
17. Kyung-Won Kim, Mi-So Lee, Bo-Ram Soon, Mun-Ho Ryu, and Je-Nam Kim. Recognition of sign language with an inertial sensor-based data glove. *Technology and Health Care*, 24(s1):S223–S230, 2015.
18. Oscar Koller, Jens Forster, and Hermann Ney. Continuous sign language recognition: Towards large vocabulary statistical recognition systems handling multiple signers. *Computer Vision and Image Understanding*, 141:108–125, 2015.
19. T Kuroda, Y Tabata, A Goto, H Ikuta, M Murakami, et al. Consumer price data-glove for sign language recognition. In *Proc. of 5th Intl Conf. Disability, Virtual Reality Assoc. Tech., Oxford, UK*, pages 253–258, 2004.
20. Yun Li, Xiang Chen, Jianxun Tian, Xu Zhang, Kongqiao Wang, and Jihai Yang. Automatic recognition of sign language subwords based on portable accelerometer and emg sensors. In *International Conference on Multimodal Interfaces and the Workshop on Machine Learning for Multimodal Interaction*, ICMI-MLMI '10, pages 17:1–17:7, New York, NY, USA, 2010. ACM.
21. Rung-Huei Liang and Ming Ouhyoung. A real-time continuous gesture recognition system for sign language. In *Automatic Face and Gesture Recognition, 1998. Proceedings. Third IEEE International Conference on*, pages 558–567. IEEE, 1998.
22. Robert B Miller. Response time in man-computer conversational transactions. In *Proceedings of the December 9-11, 1968, fall joint computer conference, part I*, pages 267–277. ACM, 1968.
23. Sushmita Mitra and Tinku Acharya. Gesture recognition: A survey. *Systems, Man, and Cybernetics, Part C: Applications and Reviews, IEEE Transactions on*, 37(3):311–324, 2007.
24. Louis-Philippe Morency, Ariadna Quattoni, and Trevor Darrell. Latent-dynamic discriminative models for continuous gesture recognition. In *Computer Vision and Pattern Recognition, 2007. CVPR'07. IEEE Conference on*, pages 1–8. IEEE, 2007.

25. Meinard Müller. Dynamic time warping. *Information retrieval for music and motion*, pages 69–84, 2007.
26. Yuji Nagashima. Present stage and issues of sign linguistic engineering. *HCI, 2001*, 2001.
27. Koosha Sadeghi Oskooyee, Ayan Banerjee, and Sandeep KS Gupta. Neuro movie theatre: A real-time internet-of-people based mobile application. 2015.
28. Madhurima Pore, Koosha Sadeghi, Vinaya Chakati, Ayan Banerjee, and Sandeep KS Gupta. Enabling real-time collaborative brain-mobile interactive applications on volunteer mobile devices. In *Proceedings of the 2nd International Workshop on Hot Topics in Wireless*, pages 46–50. ACM, 2015.
29. Nikhita Praveen, Naveen Karanth, and MS Megha. Sign language interpreter using a smart glove. In *Advances in Electronics, Computers and Communications (ICAECC), 2014 International Conference on*, pages 1–5. IEEE, 2014.
30. Lawrence R Rabiner. A tutorial on hidden markov models and selected applications in speech recognition. *Proceedings of the IEEE*, 77(2):257–286, 1989.
31. Éva Sáfár and Ian Marshall. The architecture of an english-text-to-sign-languages translation system. In *Recent Advances in Natural Language Processing (RANLP)*, pages 223–228. Tzigov Chark Bulgaria, 2001.
32. Javad Sohankar, Koosha Sadeghi, Ayan Banerjee, and Sandeep KS Gupta. E-bias: A pervasive eeg-based identification and authentication system. In *Proceedings of the 11th ACM Symposium on QoS and Security for Wireless and Mobile Networks*, pages 165–172. ACM, 2015.
33. Thad Starner, Joshua Weaver, and Alex Pentland. Real-time american sign language recognition using desk and wearable computer based video. *Pattern Analysis and Machine Intelligence, IEEE Transactions on*, 20(12):1371–1375, 1998.
34. W.C. Stokoe, D.C. Casterline, and C.G. Croneberg. *A Dictionary of American Sign Language on Linguistic Principles*. Linstok Press, 1976.
35. W.C. Stokoe, ERIC Clearinghouse for Linguistics, and Center for Applied Linguistics. *The Study of Sign Language*. ERIC Clearinghouse for Linguistics, Center for Applied Linguistics, 1970.
36. R.A. Tennant and M.G. Brown. *The American Sign Language Handshape Dictionary*. Clerc Books, 1998.
37. Christian Vogler and Dimitris Metaxas. Asl recognition based on a coupling between hmms and 3d motion analysis. In *Computer Vision, 1998. Sixth International Conference on*, pages 363–369. IEEE, 1998.
38. Andrew D Wilson and Aaron F Bobick. Parametric hidden markov models for gesture recognition. *Pattern Analysis and Machine Intelligence, IEEE Transactions on*, 21(9):884–900, 1999.
39. Xu Zhang, Xiang Chen, Yun Li, Vuokko Lantz, Kongqiao Wang, and Jihai Yang. A framework for hand gesture recognition based on accelerometer and emg sensors. *Systems, Man and Cybernetics, Part A: Systems and Humans, IEEE Transactions on*, 41(6):1064–1076, 2011.

Look at Me: Augmented Reality Pedestrian Warning System Using an In-vehicle Volumetric Head Up Display

Hyungil Kim*
Department of Industrial and Systems Engineering, Virginia Tech
Blacksburg, USA
hci.kim@vt.edu

Alexandre Miranda Anon, Teruhisa Misu, Nanxiang Li, Ashish Tawari, Kikuo Fujimura
Honda Research Institute USA
Mountain View, USA
amiranda, tmisu, nli, atawari, kfujimura@hra.com

ABSTRACT
Current pedestrian collision warning systems use either auditory alarms or visual symbols to inform drivers. These traditional approaches cannot tell the driver where the detected pedestrians are located, which is critical for the driver to respond appropriately. To address this problem, we introduce a new driver interface taking advantage of a volumetric head-up display (HUD). In our experimental user study, sixteen participants drove a test vehicle in a parking lot while braking for crossing pedestrians using different interface designs on the HUD. Our results showed that spatial information provided by conformal graphics on the HUD resulted in not only better driver performance but also smoother braking behavior as compared to the baseline.

Author Keywords
Augmented reality (AR); pedestrian collision warning; head up display; depth perception; driver vehicle interface.

ACM Classification Keywords
H.1.2 User/Machine Systems: Human factors; H.5.1 Multimedia Information Systems: Artificial, augmented, and virtual realities; H.5.2 User Interfaces: Evaluation/methodology.

INTRODUCTION
Recent advances in sensor technology and pedestrian detection algorithms [2, 9] allow automakers to introduce pedestrian collision warning as an advanced driver assistant system (ADAS). Once pedestrians are detected in the vehicle's path, the warning is given to the driver typically through auditory alarms or simple visual symbols [17]. Since such warnings often lack spatial information, drivers need to further localize (i.e., recognize direction and distance of) approaching pedestrians for appropriate decision and reaction. This is a perfect opportunity to use AR in the vehicle; AR HUDs can overlay conformal graphics on top of the vehicle's path to notify the driver of the specific location of pedestrians.

Taking advantages of AR HUDs, we aim not only to guide drivers' attention for faster detection, but also to help them localize the threats earlier. Thus drivers can have more time to prepare for the appropriate reaction. In this paper, we introduce a novel interface design for pedestrian collision warning using a volumetric head up display and evaluate usability of the new interface.

RELATED WORK
AR HUDs can support diverse use-cases by guiding drivers' attention to relevant environmental elements. Many researchers have shown the benefit of AR HUDs as promising driver vehicle interfaces that leverage currently available ADAS such as navigation aids, forward collision warning, blind spot warning, lane departure warning and left turn aid [1, 19, 12, 5, 22]. Regarding pedestrian collision warning, Pomarjanschi et al. showed that highlighting pedestrians with gaze-contingent cues helps reduce the number of collisions [18]. Lim et al. compared driver performance in pedestrian detection using two different types of video see-thru night vision displays [15]. However, most user studies have been conducted in driving simulators with either videotaped or virtual reality driving scenes, where ecologically valid color and depth perception are virtually impossible.

To support better localization, AR HUDs can further guide driver's attention in the third dimension of depth. Some user studies have quantified depth perception provided by different display technologies for AR HUDs: monoscopic, stereoscopic, multi-view and volumetric displays [11, 4, 21, 1]. Our previous work demonstrated that a volumetric display with dynamically adjustable focal plane outperformed a traditional monoscopic display [1]. However, the effects of depth perception on driving performance are yet to be fully understood.

Driver performance in pedestrian collision avoidance can be evaluated by detection performance (e.g., detection distance, reaction time), braking behavior (e.g., pedal

IUI'16, March 07-10, 2016, Sonoma, CA, USA
© 2016 ACM. ISBN 978-1-4503-4137-0/16/03...$15.00 DOI: http://dx.doi.org/10.1145/2856767.2856815

* This work was done when the first author was a research intern at Honda Research Institute USA.

(a) Test vehicle with a volumetric HUD (b) Traditional warning (c) Virtual shadow

Figure 1: Two interface designs implemented in the in-vehicle volumetric HUD prototype

response, maximum deceleration) and final outcome of vehicle measures (e.g., stopping distance, time to stop) [7, 14]. Braking behavior can be further modeled and characterized into normal or hard braking by analyzing deceleration profiles (changes in headway, speed and acceleration during braking maneuver) [6, 16].

EXPERIMENTAL USER STUDY

The main objective of this study is to answer two questions regarding pedestrian collision warning; (1) Can visual warnings on HUDs improve driver performance? (2) Can spatial information provided by AR HUDs change braking behavior? To answer those questions, we ran an experimental user study. Sixteen experienced drivers were asked to drive a test vehicle in a parking lot and brake for crossing pedestrians while using different interface designs for pedestrian collision warning. We designed a two factor repeated measures experiment, such that participants completed the driving tasks under each of six conditions: 3 interface designs (no warning, traditional warning - brake sign, and new warning - virtual shadow), and 2 levels of distance to the target pedestrians (near vs far). First we asked participants to drive without any warning signs for both distance conditions, which served as baseline. Then participants completed the rest of four experimental conditions. The order of interface design experienced was counterbalanced to minimize learning effects. We also randomized the location of road events and randomly added no event trials to minimize drivers' anticipation of pedestrian presence. During each driving trials, we time stamped location, velocity, and acceleration of the test vehicle for further analysis.

Apparatus

Volumetric Display and Depth Perception

We implemented design ideas on our in-vehicle volumetric HUD that can show computer graphics at variable depths from 8m to optical infinity with about 17° field of view (Figure 1.a). Volumetric displays form a visual representation of an object in a 3D space using multiple focal planes, as opposed to stereoscopic displays that simulate depth by presenting offset images to the left and right eye at a fixed focal plane [3]. Our volumetric display with time-multiplexed multi-focal planes can fast switch virtual images between far and near distance, creating a flicker-free appearance of the virtual objects rendered sequentially at different depths. This provides depth cues such as not only binocular disparity but also accurate accommodation, convergence and motion parallax without head or eye tracking. Since it projects computer graphics at the same focus distance of the target objects, drivers do not need to shift focus between virtual objects on the display and real objects in the scene. Therefore, it helps reduce perceptual (e.g., dual images and defocus blur) and safety issues caused by focal depth mismatch [8, 13, 20, 23, 24]. We believe 8m focus depth is reasonable for collision warning because we need to warn the driver in advance to avoid collision. For example, when we consider the generally accepted 2 second rule, the driver needs to be warned 13m ahead of the threat at 15mph. For any hazard occurring within 8m, a complementary auditory alarm could be more effective.

Pedestrian Localization

In this study, we used a wizard of Oz method to simulate pedestrian localization technology by experimental manipulation. We assumed our capability of detecting and localizing pedestrians (e.g., via V2P communication [10]). To simulate this, we pre-defined locations of pedestrians and a trigger point for pedestrians to emerge. When the test vehicle passed the pre-defined trigger point, a global positioning system (GPS) triggered the visual warning to appear. This was accomplished by an excellent quality real time kinematic GPS: OxTS RT4003 with less than 20 cm localization error. This event also transmitted to the (acted) actual pedestrian by a walkie-talkie. We sent the signal to the pedestrian about a half second in advance, considering the time delay of his reaction based on our pilot test and practice.

Interface Design

In the ***traditional warning***, a "BRAKE" sign is shown to notify drivers of presence of pedestrians in the vehicle's path (Figure 1.b). It was based on head up warnings currently available in some luxury cars. Regardless of distance to the target, the sign remains the same at the center of the display until the car stops.

In the new warning, a ***"virtual shadow"*** is shown to notify drivers of direction and distance of an approaching pedestrian (Figure 1.c). Inspired by actual shadows, the shadow is attached to the target pedestrian, appears larger as the car approaches and finally disappears when the car passes. The size of a virtual shadow is proportional to the typical size of pedestrians and the direction of tether tells from which direction the pedestrian is approaching.

Distance to the Target Pedestrians

We introduced two different levels of distances to the target pedestrians that might affect the driver's perceptual risk and yield different braking behaviors. The near targets appeared when the time to collision (TTC) was 2.5 sec. The 2.5 sec TTC was set to be short enough to induce last second hard braking and selected from referencing previous braking study literature [15]. We doubled the distance for the far targets to encourage timed-normal braking.

Driving Tasks

In our user study, we gave participants a realistic parking lot scenario where they are asked to drive with constant speed of 15 mph until they arrived at the pre-defined parking area designated for them. While driving they were asked to brake for any crossing pedestrians. The road events prompting drivers' reaction were always actual pedestrians. In visual warning conditions, drivers additionally saw computer graphics on the HUD.

Dependent Variables

To characterize driver braking behavior and performance, we analyzed deceleration profiles during each braking maneuver and defined dependent variables (Figure 2) such as car reaction time (T_{react}), braking time (T_{brake}), time to stop (T_{stop}), maximum deceleration (G_{max}) and stopping distance (D_{stop}). We defined car reaction time as the elapsed time between the onset of a stimulus (when the car passes pre-defined trigger line) and the beginning of the car's deceleration. Braking time was defined as time spent for decelerating. Reaction and braking time add up to equal time to stop. Braking behavior was characterized by the process measures including reaction time, braking time, and maximum deceleration. Faster reaction followed by longer braking time along with smaller maximum deceleration was considered smoother timed braking behavior. Driver performance in pedestrian collision avoidance was evaluated by the final outcome of vehicle measure, stopping distance or gap from the target when the car stopped.

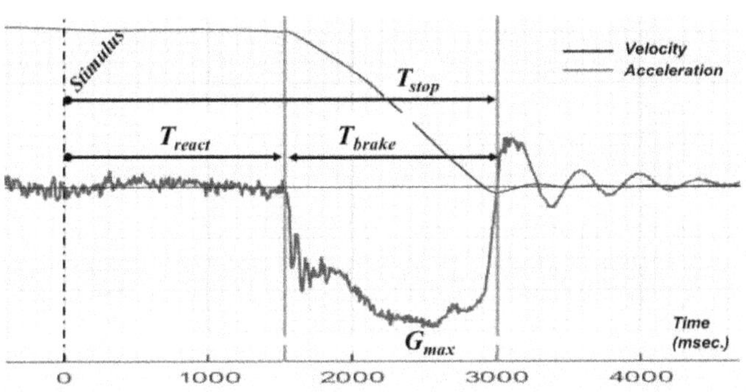

Figure 2. Dependent variables derived from deceleration profile

Results

We eliminated data from two participants who completely ignored the visual cues. Post-test interview revealed that they did not want to rely on technology, but rather believed in their own driving skill and experience. Therefore, we analyzed data from 14 participants using two-way repeated measure Analysis of Variance (ANOVA) to examine the effect of interface design and target distance. We found significant main and interaction effects on all five dependent variables, and performed post-hoc contrast tests for the planned comparisons. The results are summarized by mean and interaction plots (Figure 3).

Reaction, Braking Time and Time to Stop

Post-hoc tests (Figure 3. a and c) revealed that the virtual shadow reduced reaction time while increased braking time which resulted in the same level of time to stop compared to the baseline for both near and far targets. The traditional

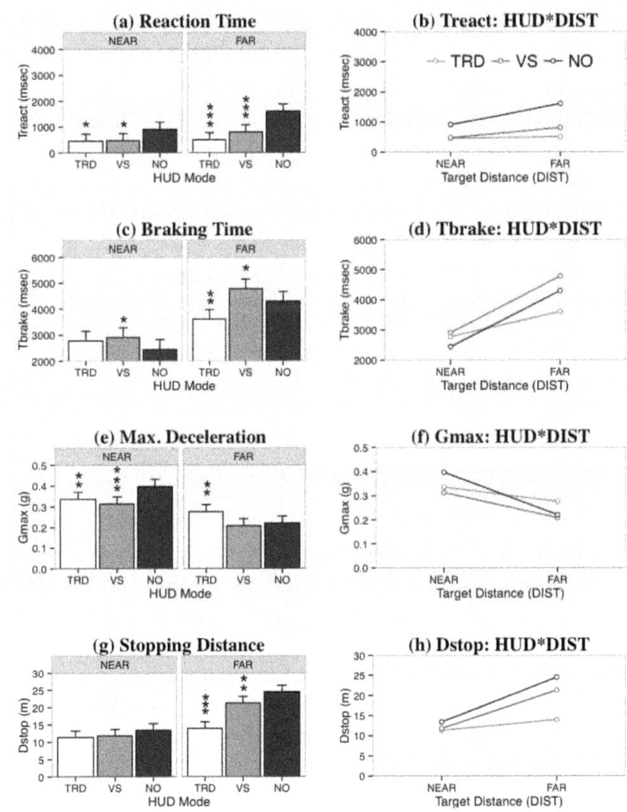

Figure 3. Driver Braking Behavior and Performance. Mean and interaction plots of data from 14 participants. Mean values are reported with 95% confidence intervals. Group differences are reported with *p-values* from the contrast tests compared to the baseline *('***' $p < 0.001$, '**' $p < 0.01$, '*' $p < 0.05$.)* TRD = Traditional warning, VS = Virtual Shadow, NO = No warning.

warning reduced both reaction time and braking time, which resulted in reduced time to stop. More interestingly, as shown in the interaction plot (Figure 3b), target distance did not affect reaction time when drivers used traditional warning.

Maximum Deceleration

Figure 3 (e) and (f) summarizes the post-hoc test results. For the near targets, both interface design reduced maximum deceleration. For the far targets, the traditional warning showed even higher maximum deceleration than the baseline.

Stopping Distance and Gap

For the far targets, both interface designs reduced stopping distance, which resulted in larger gaps leading up to the pedestrians. The interaction plot indicates drivers had similar stopping distances (i.e., traveled distances) regardless of target distance when their using the traditional warning.

DISCUSSION

In this study, we investigated the effect of visual warning presentation methods on drivers' performance and braking behavior in pedestrian collision avoidance. Before presenting any visual warning, we evaluated drivers' baseline performance when they did not have any warnings. In general, partial counterbalancing within the treatment conditions would limit internal validity of the study. However, we intended to run a pretest-posttest design where our main interest was behavioral changes while using warning systems compared to drivers' usual (intact) behavior. Therefore, we did post-hoc contrast tests for the planned comparisons focusing on mean differences in both performance and behavior compared to the baseline.

In terms of driver performance, both the traditional warning sign and the virtual shadow reduced stopping distances (or increased gaps from the pedestrian) for the far targets. This result suggests that visual warnings, whether they provide spatial information or not, improved driver's performance. For the near target we did not find any improvement.

In terms of braking behavior, both interface designs reduced reaction time implying that visual cues help with driver's faster detection. Interestingly traditional warnings caused even harder braking for the far target, which is not necessarily required to avoid collision. Actually drivers showed similar braking behavior regardless of target distance in response to the warning signs. This is probably because the sign lacks spatial information about approaching pedestrians. On the contrary, the virtual shadow resulted in smoother braking for both near and far targets. This result suggests that spatial information presented by conformal graphics resulted in smoother braking behavior. The trend is more obvious when we compare behavioral changes caused by target distance among three interface designs. For example, the interaction plots in Figure 3 (b) and (d) show the same differential effect of target distance between virtual shadow and no warning conditions where only stimuli for the driver were actual pedestrians. This implies that virtual shadows may provide the same level of depth cues as actual pedestrians.

CONCLUSION

In summary, this study suggests that pedestrian collision warning improves driver performance as compared to the baseline, regardless of cue presentation method. However, only conformal presentation of warning cues further results in smoother braking behavior by helping drivers' localization of pedestrians.

In this study, we introduced a novel interface design for pedestrian collision warning that casts virtual shadows of approaching objects that are immersed in the real world, taking advantage of our volumetric HUD. We also developed realistic driving scenarios and a test protocol for usability evaluation of pedestrian collision warning systems. This is one of the first usability evaluations of in-vehicle head up displays with 3D presentation capability. The proposed design and findings can be extended to other use-cases such as cross traffic alerts to avoid collision with vehicles backing up in parking lots, given that high performance object detection and localization technology is available.

REFERENCES

1. Karlin Bark, Cuong Tran, Kikuo Fujimura, and Victor Ng-Thow-Hing. 2014. Personal Navi: Benefits of an Augmented Reality Navigational Aid Using a See-Thru 3D Volumetric HUD. In Proceedings of the 6th International Conference on Automotive User Interfaces and Interactive Vehicular Applications, pp. 1-8. ACM. DOI=http://dx.doi.org/10.1145/2667317.2667329
2. Rodrigo Benenson, Mohamed Omran, Jan Hosang, and Bernt Schiele. 2014. Ten years of pedestrian detection, what have we learned?. In Computer Vision-ECCV 2014 Workshops, pp. 613-627. Springer International Publishing.
3. Barry G. Blundell. 2012. Volumetric 3D Displays. In Handbook of Visual Display Technology, pp. 1917-1931. Springer Berlin Heidelberg.
4. Nora Broy, Simone Höckh, Annette Frederiksen, Michael Gilowski, Julian Eichhorn, Felix Naser, Horst Jung et al. 2014. Exploring Design Parameters for a 3D Head-Up Display. In Proceedings of The International Symposium on Pervasive Displays, p. 38. ACM. DOI=http://dx.doi.org/10.1145/2611009.2611011
5. Chris Dijksterhuis, Arjan Stuiver, Ben Mulder, Karel A. Brookhuis, and Dick de Waard. 2014. An Adaptive Driver Support System User Experiences and Driving Performance in a Simulator. Human Factors: The Journal of the Human Factors and Ergonomics Society 54, no. 5 (2012): 772-785.

6. Daniel Fambro, Rodger Koppa, Dale Picha, and Kay Fitzpatrick. 2000. Driver braking performance in stopping sight distance situations. Transportation Research Record: Journal of the Transportation Research Board 1701: 9-16.
7. Gregory M. Fitch, Myra Blanco, Justin F. Morgan, Jeanne C. Rice, Amy Wharton, Walter W. Wierwille, and Richard J. Hanowski. 2010. Human Performance Evaluation of Light Vehicle Brake Assist Systems: Final Report. No. HS-811 251.
8. Joseph L. Gabbard, Gregory M. Fitch, and Hyungil Kim. 2014. Behind the glass: Driver challenges and opportunities for AR automotive applications. Proceedings of the IEEE 102, no. 2: 124-136.
9. Alexander Gepperth, Egor Sattarov, Bernd Heisele, and Sergio Alberto Rodriguez Flores. 2014. Robust visual pedestrian detection by tight coupling to tracking. In Intelligent Transportation Systems (ITSC), 2014 IEEE 17th International Conference on, pp. 1935-1940. IEEE.
10. Honda, Vehicle to pedestrian communication. Retrieved December 15, 2015 from http://world.honda.com/news/2014/4140904New-Connected-Car-Automated-Driving-Technologies-ITS/print.html
11. Aira Hotta, Takashi Sasaki, and Haruhiko Okumura. 2011. Depth perception effect of dynamic perspective method for monocular head-up display realizing augmented reality. Proc. IDW ‘11: 521-524.
12. Hyungil Kim, Xuefang Wu, Joseph L. Gabbard, and Nicholas F. Polys. 2013. Exploring head-up augmented reality interfaces for crash warning systems. In Proceedings of the 5th International Conference on Automotive User Interfaces and Interactive Vehicular Applications, pp. 224-227. ACM. DOI=http://dx.doi.org/10.1145/2516540.2516566
13. Ernst Kruijff, J. Edward Swan II, and Steven Feiner. 2010. Perceptual issues in augmented reality revisited. In ISMAR, vol. 9, pp. 3-12.
14. Martin Langham, and Nicholas Moberly. 2003. Pedestrian conspicuity research: a review. Ergonomics 46, no. 4: 345-363.
15. Ji Hyoun Lim, Omer Tsimhoni, and Yili Liu. 2010. Investigation of driver performance with night vision and pedestrian detection systems—Part I: Empirical study on visual clutter and glance behavior. Intelligent Transportation Systems, IEEE Transactions on 11, no. 3: 670-677.
16. Gustav Markkula, Ola Benderius, Krister Wolff, and Mattias Wahde. 2012. A review of near-collision driver behavior models. Human Factors: The Journal of the Human Factors and Ergonomics Society 54, no. 6: 1117-1143.
17. Mobileye, Pedestrian Detection. Retrieved December 15, 2015 from http://www.mobileye.com/technology/applications/pedestrian-detection/
18. Laura Pomarjanschi, Michael Dorr, and Erhardt Barth. 2012. Gaze guidance reduces the number of collisions with pedestrians in a driving simulator. ACM Transactions on Interactive Intelligent Systems (TiiS) 1, no. 2: 8.
19. Mehdi Saffarian, Joost CF De Winter, and Riender Happee. 2013. Enhancing driver car-following performance with a distance and acceleration display. Human-Machine Systems, IEEE Transactions on 43, no. 1: 8-16.
20. Missie Smith, Nadejda Doutcheva, Joseph L. Gabbard, and Gary Burnett. 2015. Optical see-through head up displays' effect on depth judgments of real world objects. In Virtual Reality (VR), 2015 IEEE, pp. 401-405. IEEE.
21. Yasuhiro Takaki, Yohei Urano, Shinji Kashiwada, Hiroshi Ando, and Koji Nakamura. 2011. Super multi-view windshield display for long-distance image information presentation. Optics express 19, no. 2: 704-716.
22. Cuong Tran, Karlin Bark, and Victor Ng-Thow-Hing. 2013. A left-turn driving aid using projected oncoming vehicle paths with augmented reality. In Proceedings of the 5th International Conference on Automotive User Interfaces and Interactive Vehicular Applications, pp. 300-307. ACM. DOI=http://dx.doi.org/10.1145/2516540.2516581
23. Daniel R. Tufano. 1997. Automotive HUDs: The overlooked safety issues. Human Factors: The Journal of the Human Factors and Ergonomics Society 39, no. 2: 303-311.
24. Daniel J. Weintraub. 1992. Human factors issues in head-up display design: The book of HUD. No. SOAR-92-2. DAYTON UNIV OH RESEARCH INST.

Context Matters?: How Adding the Obfuscation Option Affects End Users' Data Disclosure Decisions

Jing Wang
Samsung Research America
Mountain View, CA, USA
jingwang84@gmail.com

Na Wang
Samsung Research America
Mountain View, CA, USA
na.wang1@samsung.com

Hongxia Jin
Samsung Research America
Mountain View, CA, USA
hongxia.jin@samsung.com

ABSTRACT
Recent advancement of smart devices and wearable technologies greatly enlarges the variety of personal data people can track. Applications and services can leverage such data to provide better life support, but also impose privacy and security threats. Obfuscation schemes, consequently, have been developed to retain data access while mitigate risks. Compared to offering choices of releasing raw data and not releasing at all, we examine the effect of adding a data obfuscation option on users' disclosure decisions when configuring applications' access, and how that effect varies with data types and application contexts. Our online user experiment shows that users are less likely to block data access when the obfuscation option is available except for locations. This effect significantly differs between applications for domain-specific dynamic tracking data, but not for generic personal traits. We further unpack the role of context and discuss the design opportunities.

Author Keywords
Data obfuscation; privacy; tracking; user behavior; mobile.

ACM Classification Keywords
H.5.m. Information interfaces and presentation (e.g., HCI): Miscellaneous.

INTRODUCTION AND BACKGROUND
Smart devices and wearable technologies empower end-users to track an unprecedentedly wide range of personal data. The *Quantified Self* can bring many benefits, such as promoting health behaviors, improving energy saving, and enabling personalized recommendations [1,10,20,26]. However, the digitalized personal information also eases privacy and security attacks.

Data obfuscation techniques, among other data protection mechanisms, have accordingly been developed to enhance end users' control. While other protection mechanisms control when users' personal data can be disclosed with whom at what level of details for what purposes [14], well-known obfuscation schemes are focused on anonymization, noise addition, and data points removal [12].

IUI'16, March 07-10, 2016, Sonoma, CA, USA
© 2016 ACM. ISBN 978-1-4503-4137-0/16/03...$15.00
DOI: http://dx.doi.org/10.1145/2856767.2856817

A huge incentive to have fine-level protection for service providers, developers, and end users is to not completely lose data access. However, providing every possible control option is not just technically infeasible, but would also make decisions too complex and tedious for end users, especially on mobile platforms, causing them reluctant to adopt such designs [3,6,25]. Thus, understanding the effects of adding control options is critical.

Prior work studied providing options that allow sharing at different levels of details [11] and sharing with subsets of social connections [8]. Our study, in contrast, is to examine options that can obfuscate heterogeneous data. It strives to answer 1) how does adding an obfuscation option affect users' overall disclosing likelihood? 2) How does the application context affect that effect, as people's disclosure decisions are personal and context-dependent [19]? 3) For different data types, does that effect follow similar patterns? If not, how does it vary?

We conducted an online user experiment with 143 participants to address the research questions. Our analysis shows that adding an obfuscation option increases the likelihood that users would allow mobile apps to access their personal data except for locations. Moreover, this effect depends on the application context for domain-specific dynamic tracking data, but not so for generic and static personal traits. We further characterize the differences between contexts and discuss design opportunities to make obfuscations context-aware for selective data types.

METHOD
We studied the effects of adding a data obfuscation option using an online user experiment with manipulations on the obfuscation option's presence and the application context.

Study Design and Measurements
To manipulate the application context, we selected two fictitious health-related mobile apps for the experiment, a fitness app and a medical app, to encompass different data tracking purposes that might influence users' decisions. The fitness app provided workout tracking, while the medical

app estimated heart disease risks through biometric tracking. Their purposes (directive vs. diagnostic) are typical types that apply to personal tracking technologies in all domains [21]. We chose the health domain deliberately, in which personal data tracking is prevalent and thereby its research bear high impacts [15].

12 data types were sampled for participants to decide how apps can access. Such a sample was primarily intended to cover a spectrum of sensitivity, including information usually considered highly sensitive (i.e., fine and coarse locations, medications/treatments taken) as well as information that is moderately or not very sensitive (i.e., physical activities, heart rate, blood pressure, cholesterol, weight, height, age, gender, and race) [15]. They were also expected to have varying degrees of relevance to the two apps' functionalities, which may also affect user decisions.

The other manipulation, the availability of the obfuscation option, was to either remove or add this option to two other options—releasing raw data as they were originally captured and not releasing data at all. We specified obfuscation as anonymization, considering end users found it easiest to comprehend and most comfortable to use [2]. In user interfaces, we referred to it as *Protected Release (PR)*, the releasing raw data option as *Fully Release (FR)*, and the not releasing option as *No Release (NR)* for simplicity.

The PR option's availability and the app context constituted the independent variables of our study, together with their interaction. The dependent variable of our interest was users' tendency to release their data. We measured it as the ratio FR + PR : NR, in which choices of FR and PR were modeled as 1 and NR as 0. Here we counted PR as a form of releasing because people who would choose PR were still revealing their data rather than completely keeping private. We also measured several other variables to control individual differences using established scales, such as users' general and mobile privacy concerns, technical competence, and demographics [16,17,18,22].

Participants

We recruited participants through Amazon Mechanical Turk, a popular recruiting source for online user experiments [9]. We restricted participation to Turk workers with good reputation and located in the US. After filtering out responses that did not pass our comprehension-testing questions, we ultimately refined to 143 valid responses. These responses consisted of 70 males and 73 females, and their age ranged from 19 to 72 with a median of 33.5.

Procedure and User Interfaces

Participants were randomly assigned to one of the 2 (PR unavailable vs. available) x 2 (fitness app vs. medical app) experimental conditions. They were first given brief descriptions of their assigned app's key features and explanations of the two/three options they could select, depending

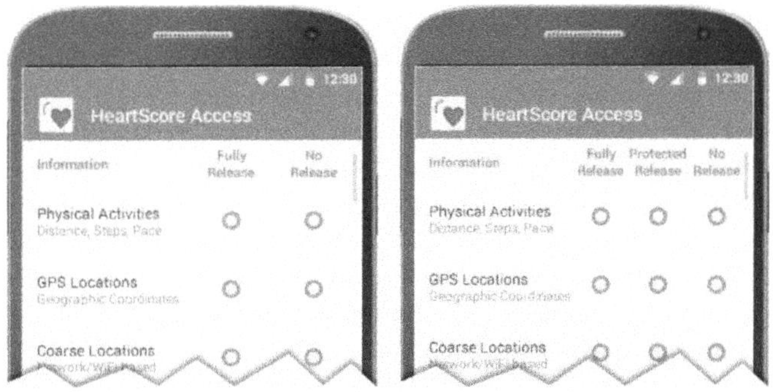

Figure 1. The mockup interfaces for access configurations in the medical app condition (*left: PR unavailable; right: PR available*).

on the condition of PR's availability. Explaining the options did not involve excessive overhead but only used one short sentence for each. Then they were asked to configure the app's access as they would at a newly installed app's first launch using the interfaces partially shown in Figure 1. No default setting was applied in the interfaces. In the end, participants rated the scales on control variables.

RESULTS

We estimated participants' data release likelihood through building generalized linear models for each data type, with a random intercept and a logit link function. Additionally, participants' ratings confirmed our assumption that the 12 data types are associated with varying sensitivity levels.

The Effect of Adding the Obfuscation Option

Our generalized linear models suggest that adding the data obfuscation option significantly increases participants' data release likelihood for most data types. Three decision patterns emerged, associated with different types of data. For fine and coarse locations, the disclosure likelihood remains about the same regardless of the obfuscation option's presence. Though the likelihood significantly grows for all the other data types when the obfuscation option is available, its variance does not differ between apps for readily observable personal traits, mostly demographic information, while depends on the app contexts for health tracking data.

Insignificant Effects on Location Release Likelihood

Adding the obfuscation option does not effect any significant changes on the ratio FR + PR : NR regarding disclosing fine and coarse locations ($p_{fine} = .481$, $p_{coarse} = .543$). A closer look at the decision distribution reveals that the obfuscation option serves as a replacement of releasing raw data, which applies to both apps (Figure 2).

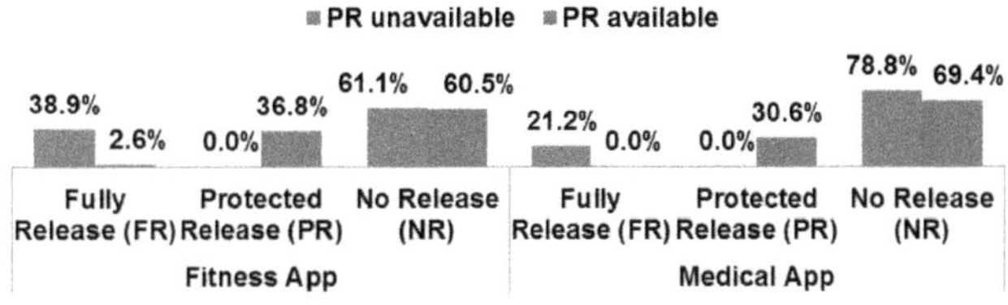

Figure 2. User decisions on disclosing fine locations to the fitness app (left; n = 74) and the medical app (right; n = 69).

Figure 2 illustrates that participants were generally conservative about allowing apps to access their locations, although they were more open towards the fitness app, which offers real-time GPS tracking of workout activities. When PR was present, participants who would otherwise choose FR almost all shifted to PR (i.e., the proportion of selecting FR dropped to nearly 0%). This suggests that FR was not an appealing option even for users who wanted to benefit from location disclosure. They had to sacrifice their privacy when no intermediate options are available.

Context-independent Effects on Personal Trait Release Likelihood

The ratio FR + PR : NR significantly increases when the data obfuscation option becomes available for configuring access to readily observable personal traits, while the effect of adding the obfuscation option does not depend on the app contexts. In statistical terms, the application contexts do not have significant interaction effects with the availability of the obfuscation option. This pattern applies to data types including age, gender, race, and height, most of which are demographic information and relatively static.

PR did not just attract participants who would otherwise choose FR, but also attracted the ones who would otherwise prefer NR. For the fitness app, FR + PR : NR regarding age, gender, race, and height were 1.68, 1.50, 3.69, and 0.61 times higher with PR available than unavailable, respectively. Those ratios for the medical app were increased by 1.56, 6.78, 0.67, and 3.58 times respectively when PR was added. Although the percentage of increases seemed distinct among the four data types, the availability of PR did not reverse the relative releasing propensity between the two apps: if FR + PR : NR for the fitness app was lower (or higher) than for the medical app when PR was absent, then it remained lower (or higher) even when PR became present. Figure 3 shows participants' choice distribution on disclosing personal traits using age as an example.

Context-dependent Effects on Health Tracking Data Release Likelihood

Similar to personal traits, the ratio FR + PR : NR also increases significantly for controlling access to health tracking data when the obfuscation option is introduced. However, this effect of adding the obfuscation option depends upon application contexts, namely the interaction between the application contexts and the availability of the obfuscation option is significant. Data types following this pattern are specific to the health domain, including physical activities,

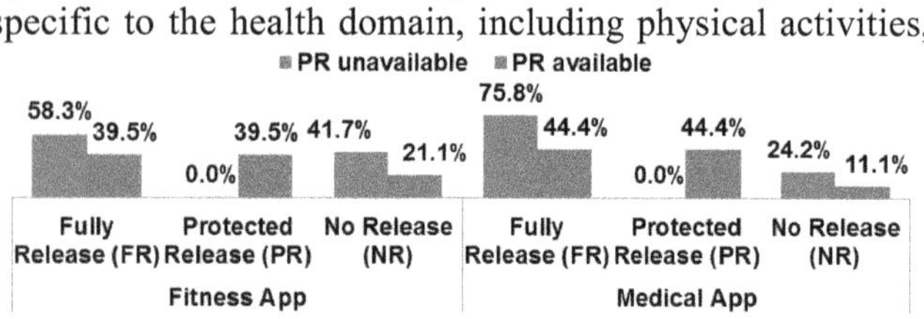

Figure 3. User decisions on disclosing age to the fitness app (left; n = 74) and the medical app (right; n = 69).

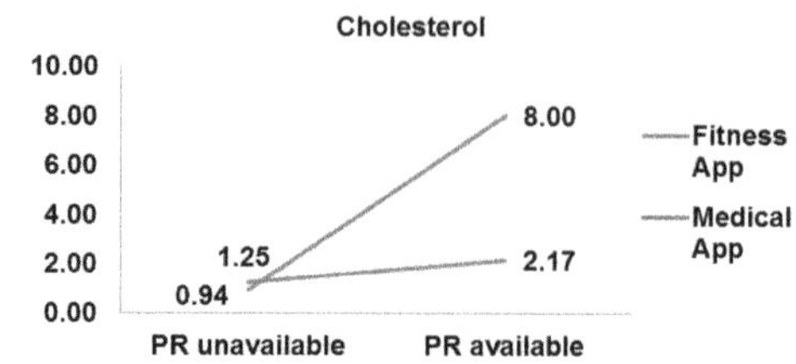

Figure 4. The ratio of FR + PR : NR regarding cholesterol data.

weight, heart rates, blood pressure, cholesterol, and medications/treatments taken, most of which can constitute rich and dynamic data traces. Given the space limit, we only plot the distribution of participants' decisions on releasing cholesterol to illustrate the interaction effects in Figure 4.

As Figure 4 demonstrates, participants were relatively more conservative about releasing their health tracking data to the medical app than to the fitness app when they had to choose either FR or NR. Once they had the additional option of releasing with some protection (i.e., PR), the ratios FR + PR : NR for the medical app remarkably jumped, surpassing those ratios for the fitness app except for the one regarding weight, which in the medical app was already slightly larger than the fitness app when PR was not available (1.75 vs. 1.40). Test results regarding physical activity data were different from the other five types of health tracking data: Neither the main effect of PR's availability nor that of the application context was significant, despite the significance of their interaction effect.

Participants' responses to our open-ended questions partially confirmed our interpretation of their decisions. Locations were repeatedly mentioned as sensitive data they would not allow most parties to fully access. Age, gender, height, and race were often cited as not quite "*an issue*" to share, especially if they were related to app functionalities.

The Role of Application Contexts

The interaction effects between obfuscation availability and application contexts outline the overarching role of application contexts in users' decision-making on disclosing personal traceable data, separating these data types from the general static personal attributes. To further understand the underlying differences of the application contexts, we characterize contexts by decomposing each option along two attributes—user *perceived data's relevance to app functionalities* and *privacy concern level* with allowing the app to access the data. These two attributes are apparently specific to the app context, and they correspond to perceived *benefit* and *risk*, which are commonly considered to jointly shape people's decisions (e.g., [5,11,13]).

We map the average of perceived *benefit* and *risk* associated with each option onto 2-dimentional panels. Both attributes were rated on a 7-point Likert scale (1: not relevant/concerned at all; 7: extremely relevant/concerned). Figure 5 illustrates the mapping for cholesterol data, while the other five data types (i.e., physical activities, weight, heart rate, blood pressure, medications/treatments taken) follow similar patterns and are left out for the interest of space. The bubbles are colored to represent different disclosing options, and their sizes reflect the percentage the option was selected. The Euclidian distance between bubbles indicates the relative distance participants perceived between options (see [7,24] for more details on the part-worth utility mapping approach).

Two key observations from Figure 5 can help explain the context dependency of the obfuscation availability's effect. When PR was not available, FR and NR options were perceived much closer regarding the medical app (Euclidian distance 1.20 points) than the fitness app (Euclidian distance 3.03 points). When PR became available, the NR option drifted away from the other options (Euclidian distance to FR increased to 3.32 points) in the medical app, while the distance between NR and FR in the fitness app remained similar (Euclidian distance 2.71 points).

This pattern occurred in the medical app largely aligns with Simonson's compromise effect [22]: the presence of the obfuscation option made *not releasing* an extremely distinct option from both the *releasing raw data* and the *obfuscation* options; participants had to compromise to choose *not releasing* data at all when they did not have the obfuscation option. In contrast, the options of *not releasing* and *releasing raw data* were already perceived distinct in the fitness app. When the obfuscation option was added, participants more or less maintained their preferences, especially the ones who chose *not releasing at all*.

DISCUSSION AND CONCLUDING REMARKS

In this paper we analyzed the effect of introducing an obfuscation option on end users' disclosure decisions on a variety of personal data. Our results indicate that users are more likely to release their data, either in the original or anonymized form, when the obfuscation is available. Location data is an exception of this effect, for which the obfuscation option almost substitutes the releasing raw data option. Furthermore, this effect for personal tracking data, including physical activities, heart rate, blood pressure, cholesterol, medications/treatments taken, and weight, depends on what application requests to access them. These findings extend previous studies [2,4,11], which were primarily focused on location sharing, to other types of personal data. The effect on location sharing in our study also does not align with compensatory theories as [11] suggests, which may be due to the potentially less perceived benefits from location sharing in the two health apps we studied than in the location sharing application [11] examined.

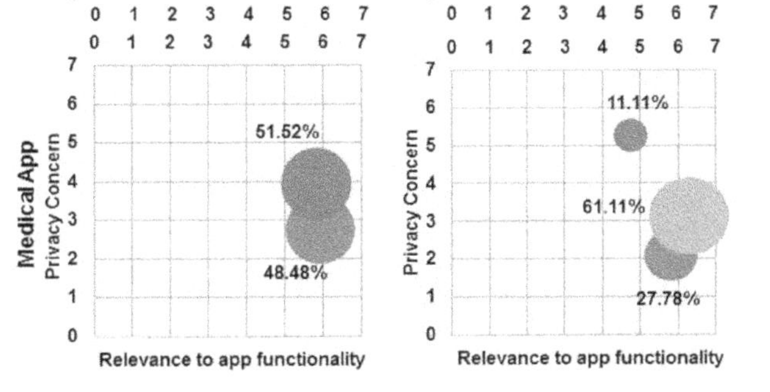

Figure 5. Subjective position and selection percentage of each option for disclosing cholesterol to fitness and medical apps.

Our subsequent analysis on the context's role shows that in contexts where the two options (i.e., releasing raw data and not releasing data at all) are perceived to have similar utilities when obfuscation is absent, adding the obfuscation option can substantially distinguish them and turns the not releasing option a compromise choice if the obfuscation is unavailable. Anonymization improves the distinctiveness between the two extreme options, indicating that the risk of being identified may be users' major concern with releasing data to the medical app and the obfuscation option to anonymize data substantially relieves this concern. Additionally, most types of the tracking data are evidently more relevant to the medical app's functionalities than the fitness app's, but users are less open to share. This suggests that users' decisions may depend on factors beyond utilities, such as the types of inferences apps claim to generate, which deserves further investigation.

Our findings present opportunities to combine intelligent control with data obfuscation techniques. For locations, system default settings may be simplified to unselect the fully release option, while customize the choice between protected release and no release basing on users' concerns with sharing locations. For tracking data, modeling the subjective distance between extremely opposite options may help predict users' choices when obfuscation options are added.

Our study is a first step towards a better understanding of managing heterogeneous personal tracking data from smart devices. Our immediate plan is to expand the investigation to other domains and data types, and incorporate additional attributes (e.g., time, location) to deconstruct end-users' decision contexts in the longer term. We invite scholars leveraging our findings to advance the research on user behavior and decision on data obfuscation.

ACKNOWLEDGMENTS

We thank the anonymous reviewers for their valuable feedback on earlier drafts of the paper.

REFERENCES

1. Ernesto Arroyo, Leonardo Bonanni, and Ted Selker. 2005. Waterbot: exploring feedback and persuasive techniques at the sink. In *Proceedings of the SIGCHI Conference on Human Factors in Computing Systems* (CHI '05), 631-639. http://dx.doi.org/10.1145/1054972.1055059
2. A.J. Bernheim Brush, John Krumm, and James Scott. 2010. Exploring end user preferences for location obfuscation, location-based services, and the value of location. In *Proceedings of the 12th ACM international conference on Ubiquitous computing* (UbiComp '10), 95-104. http://dx.doi.org/10.1145/1864349.1864381
3. Luke Church, Jonathan Anderson, Joesph Bonneau, and Frank Stajano. 2009. Privacy stories: confidence in privacy behaviors through end user programming. In *Proceedings of the 5th Symposium on Usable Privacy and Security* (SOUPS '09), Article 20. http://dx.doi.org/10.1145/1572532.1572559
4. Sunny Consolvo, Ian E. Smith, Tara Matthews, Anthony LaMarca, Jason Tabert, and Pauline Powledge. 2005. Location disclosure to social relations: why, when, & what people want to share. In *Proceedings of the SIGCHI Conference on Human Factors in Computing Systems* (CHI '05), 81-90. http://dx.doi.org/10.1145/1054972.1054985
5. Mary J. Culnan and Pamela K. Armstrong. 1999. Information Privacy Concerns, Procedural Fairness, and Impersonal Trust: An Empirical Investigation. *Organization Science* 10, 1 (January 1999), 104-115. http://dx.doi.org/10.1287/orsc.10.1.104
6. Lujun Fang and Kristen LeFevre. 2010. Privacy wizards for social networking sites. In *Proceedings of the 19th International Conference on World Wide Web* (WWW '10), 351-360. http://dx.doi.org/10.1145/1772690.1772727
7. George P. Huber. 1974. Multi-attribute utility models: A review of field and field-like studies. *Management Science* 20, 10: 1393-1402.
8. Simon Jones and Eamonn O'Neill. 2011. Contextual dynamics of group-based sharing decisions. In *Proceedings of the SIGCHI Conference on Human Factors in Computing Systems* (CHI '11), 1777-1786. http://dx.doi.org/10.1145/1978942.1979200
9. Aniket Kittur, Ed H. Chi, and Bongwon Suh. 2008. Crowdsourcing user studies with Mechanical Turk. In *Proceedings of the SIGCHI Conference on Human Factors in Computing Systems* (CHI '08), 453-456. http://dx.doi.org/10.1145/1357054.1357127
10. Predrag Klasnja and Wanda Pratt. 2012. Healthcare in the pocket: mapping the space of mobile-phone health interventions. *Journal of Biomedical Informatics* 45, 1: 184-198.
11. Bart P. Knijnenburg, Alfred Kobsa, and Hongxia Jin. 2013. Preference-based location sharing: are more privacy options really better?. In *Proceedings of the SIGCHI Conference on Human Factors in Computing Systems* (CHI '13), 2667-2676. http://dx.doi.org/10.1145/2470654.2481369
12. John Krumm. 2009. A survey of computational location privacy. *Personal Ubiquitous Comput.* 13, 6 (August 2009), 391-399. http://dx.doi.org/10.1007/s00779-008-0212-5
13. Robert S. Laufer and Maxine Wolfe. 1977. Privacy as a concept and a social issue: A multidimensional developmental theory. *Journal of Social Issues* 33, 3: 22-42.
14. Scott Lederer, Jennifer Mankoff, and Anind K. Dey. 2003. Who wants to know what when? privacy preference determinants in ubiquitous computing. In *CHI '03 Extended Abstracts on Human Factors in Computing Systems* (CHI EA '03), 724-725. http://dx.doi.org/10.1145/765891.765952
15. Mary Madden and Lee Rainie. Americans' Attitudes about privacy, security and surveillance. Retrieved December 17, 2015 from http://www.pewinternet.org/2015/05/20/americans-attitudes-about-privacy-security-and-surveillance/
16. Naresh K. Malhotra, Sung S. Kim, and James Agarwal. 2004. Internet Users' Information Privacy Concerns (IUIPC): The Construct, the Scale, and a Causal Model. *Info. Sys. Research* 15, 4 (December 2004), 336-355. http://dx.doi.org/10.1287/isre.1040.0032
17. Sampada S. Marathe, S. Shyam Sundar, Marije Nije Bijvank, Henriette van Vugt, and Jolanda Veldhuis Vrije. 2007. Who are these power users anyway? Building a psychological profile. Paper presented at *the 57th Annual Conference of the International Communication Association* (ICA '07).
18. D. Harrison McKnight, Vivek Choudhury, and Charles Kacmar. 2002. Developing and Validating Trust Measures for e-Commerce: An Integrative Typology. *Info. Sys. Research* 13, 3 (September 2002), 334-359. http://dx.doi.org/10.1287/isre.13.3.334.81
19. Helen Nissenbaum. 2010. *Privacy in context: Technology, policy, and the integrity of social life*. Stanford Law Books.
20. Moon-Hee Park, Jin-Hyuk Hong, and Sung-Bae Cho. 2007. Location-based recommendation system using Bayesian user's preference model in mobile devices. In *Proceedings of the 4th International Conference on Ubiquitous Intelligence and Computing* (UIC'07), 1130-1139.
21. John Rooksby, Mattias Rost, Alistair Morrison, and Matthew Chalmers Chalmers. 2014. Personal tracking as lived informatics. In *Proceedings of the 32nd annual ACM Conference on Human Factors in Computing Sys-*

tems (CHI '14), 1163-1172. http://doi.acm.org/10.1145/2556288.2557039

22. Itamar Simonson. 1989. Choice based on reasons: The case of attraction and compromise effects. *Journal of Consumer Research* 16, 2: 158-174.
23. Smith, H. Jeff, Sandra J. Milberg, and Sandra J. Burke. 1996. Information privacy: measuring individuals' concerns about organizational practices. *MIS Quarterly* 20, 2: 167-196.
24. Venkat Srinivasan. 1988. A Conjunctive-Compensatory Approach to the Self-Explication of Multi-attributed Preferences. *Decision Sciences* 19, 2: 295–305.
25. Katherine Strater and Heather Richter Lipford. 2008. Strategies and struggles with privacy in an online social networking community. In *Proceedings of the 22nd British HCI Group Annual Conference on People and Computers: Culture, Creativity, Interaction - Volume 1* (BCS-HCI '08), 111-119.
26. Jing Wang, Patrick C. Shih, and John M. Carroll. 2015. Life after weight loss: design implications for community-based long-term weight management. *Computer Supported Cooperative Work* 24, 4: 353-384.

Socially-Sensitive Interfaces: From Offline Studies to Interactive Experiences

Elisabeth André
Human-Centered Multimedia, Augsburg University
Universitätsstr. 6a, D-86159 Augsburg, Germany
andre@informatik.uni-augsburg.de

ABSTRACT
Recent years have initiated a paradigm shift from pure task-based human-machine interfaces towards socially-sensitive interaction. In addition to what users explicitly say or gesture at, socially-sensitive interfaces are able to sense more subtle human cues, such as head postures and movements, to infer psychological user states, such as attention and affect, and also to enrich system responses with social signals. However, most approaches focus on offline analysis of previously recorded data limiting the investigation to prototypical behaviors in laboratory-like settings. In my presentation, I will focus on challenges that arise when integrating social signal processing techniques into interactive systems designed for real-world applications. From a technical perspective, this requires effective tools able to synchronize, process, and analyze relevant signals in online mode. From a user perspective, appropriate strategies need to be defined to respond to social signals at the right moment in time without disturbing the flow of interaction.

I will discuss two interaction styles for socially-sensitive interfaces. In the area of information retrieval, the concept of *empathic stimulation* has been used to optimize the selection and presentation of data. The basic idea is to exploit sensory data on the users' emotional state to provide them with cues that inspire their curiosity during the data exploration task. In the domain of social coaching, the concept of *social augmentation* has been employed to give people ambient feedback on their behavior while being engaged in a social interaction. The presentation will be illustrated by examples from various national and international projects following these two interaction styles

Author Keywords
Social signal processing; affective computing

ACM Classification Keywords
H.5.2. User Interfaces: Interaction styles

IUI 2016, March 7–10, 2016, Sonoma, CA, USA.
ACM 978-1-4503-4137-0/16/03.
http://dx.doi.org/10.1145/2856767.2856799

Biography
Professor Elisabeth André is a Full Professor of Computer Science at Augsburg University, Germany, and Chair of the Research Unit Human-Centered Multimedia. She received her Diploma and Doctoral Degrees in Computer Science from Saarland University. Before joining Augsburg University, she has been working as a principal researcher at the German Research Center for Artificial Intelligence (DFKI) in Saarbrücken. In addition, she has held various visiting appointments, most recently an invited professorship at Université Paris-Sud, France. Elisabeth André has a long track record in multimodal human-machine interaction, embodied conversational agents, affective computing and social signal processing.

Elisabeth André is on the editorial board of various renowned international journals, such as ACM Transactions on Intelligent Interactive Systems (TIIS), IEEE Transactions on Affective Computing (TAC), Journal of Autonomous Agents and Multi-Agent Systems (JAAMAS), and AI Communications. In 2013 and 2015, she was acting as Panel Chair for Systems and Communication Engineering in the Starting Grant evaluations of the European Research Council (ERC). Currently, she is serving as a General Co-Chair of the 18th ACM International Conference on Multimodal Interaction (ICMI).

In 2007, Elisabeth André was nominated Fellow of the Alcatel-Lucent Foundation for Communications Research. In 2010, she was elected a member of the Academy of Europe, the German Academy of Sciences Leopoldina, and AcademiaNet. She is also an ECCAI Fellow (European Coordinating Committee for Articial Intelligence).

Enhancing Audience Engagement in Performing Arts Through an Adaptive Virtual Environment with a Brain-Computer Interface

Shuo Yan[1], Gangyi Ding[1], Hongsong Li[1], Ningxiao Sun[2], Yufeng Wu[1], Zheng Guan[1], Longfei Zhang[1], Tianyu Huang[1]
Key Laboratory of Digital Performance and Simulation Technology[1], Digital System Laboratory[2]
Beijing Institute of Technology, Beijing, 100081, China
{shuoyan, dgy, lihongsong, ningxiao, wuyufeng, guanzheng, longfeizhang, huangtianyu}@bit.edu.cn

ABSTRACT
Audience engagement is an important indicator of the quality of the performing arts but hard to measure. Psychophysiological measurements are promising research methods for perceiving and understanding audience's responses in real-time. Currently, such research are conducted by collecting biometric data from audience when they are watching a performance. In this paper, we draw on techniques from brain-computer interfaces (BCI) and knowledge from quality of performing arts to develop a system that monitor audience engagement in real time using electroencephalography (EEG) measurement and seek to improve it by triggering the adaptive performing cues when the engagement level decreased. We simulated the immersive theatre performances to provide audience a high-fidelity visual-audio experience. An experimental evaluation is conducted with 48 participants during two different performance studies. The results showed that our system could successfully detect the decreases in audience engagement and the performing cues had positive effects on regain audience engagement. Our research offers the guidelines for designing theatre performances from the audience's perception.

Author Keywords
Audience engagement; brain-computer interface (BCI); electroencephalography (EEG); adaptive user interface

ACM Classification Keywords
H.5.2. Information interfaces and presentation: User Interfaces: Input devices and strategies, Evaluation/methodology, User-centered design; J.5. Computer Applications: Arts and Humanities: Performing arts

IUI'16, March 07-10, 2016, Sonoma, CA, USA.
© 2016 ACM. ISBN 978-1-4503-4137-0/16/03...$15.00
DOI: http://dx.doi.org/10.1145/2856767.2856768

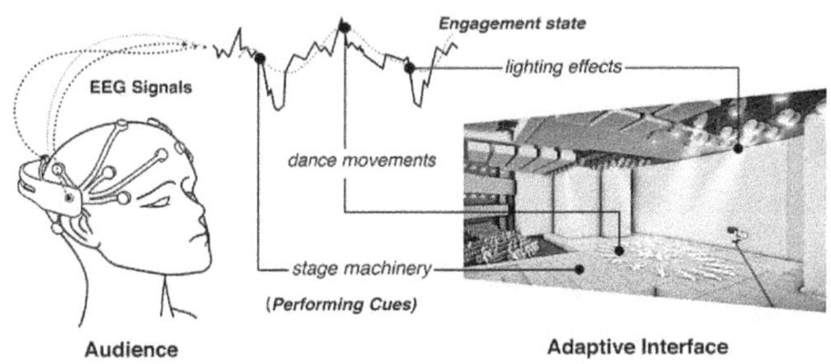

Figure 1. The audiences interact with an adaptive virtual environment of theatre performance that monitors their reactions through the measured EEG signals and adaptively creates real-time performing cues to improve audience engagement.

INTRODUCTION
Audience engagement refers to the effect that a show arouses audience emotions, stimulates their physical reaction, and triggers their cognitive development [28]. It is generally difficult for the audiences to stay focused on the theatre performing arts (such as opera, dance, etc.) with less audience participation, compared with the stand-up comedies and the live music shows [29]. The importance of audience feedback has been detailed in an extensive literature review and the gauging of audience engagement has proved to be a key measure of quality in the performing arts [27]. However, during the design stage of theatre performance arts, it is a challenge for stage directors to predict the audience engagement.

To address this issue, we need to answer the following questions: First, how to measure audience engagement in theatre performing arts? Second, how could we design and generate adaptive performing cues as immediate stimulus to engage the audience and response to their emotional feedback without disrupting the performance? Finally, how to integrate both the measurement system and the adaptive performing cues in one system, which enables the stage directors to improve the design of theatre performances.

Recent development in the BCI techniques has enabled us to measure the audience engagement with off-the-shelf devices with reasonable accuracy. In addition, more and more stage designers have adopted digital performance technique to improve their design. The digital performance technique provides the stage designer a virtual environment in which they can create, manipulate, and test the performance elements in a totally interactive way.

Based on this two development, we seek to improve audience engagement by proposing an interactive design tool that measures the audience engagement and adaptively creates immersive theatre performance experience in a virtual environment in real-time. To do that, we propose a novel approach that combines neuroscience and theatre performing arts. We measure the audience engagement in real-time using neural signals obtained from an off-the-shelf wireless EEG headset. The immersive theatre performance experience is generated by a game engine and can be adjusted interactively. The concept of the proposed system is illustrated in Figure 1.

RELATED WORK

Digital Performance

Theatre and performance in digital culture has been developed from simulation to embeddedness since the emerging of advanced technologies, including 3D modeling of theatre architecture, animated scenery, performance simulation using motion capture, along with simulations of audience interactions and hypermedia content [19].

Digital performance applies digital technology to reconstruct and archive performing arts events. The technique helps performance director and actor to establish a virtual environment to generate the performance scenes, to rehearse the theatre performance, and adjust the narrative structures [10]. However, current digital performance techniques only concentrate on the design of the performance itself without combining the audience emotional states. It has not acknowledged that the audience response could also contribute to the performance.

Brain-Computer Interface

BCIs are rapidly growing technology that draws on brain signals as user input. A BCI is a system that provides computer application with access to real-time information about user cognitive state, on the basis of measured brain activity [31]. In HCI viewpoint, the BCI systems can be categorized into three types: the active BCI, the reactive BCI, and the passive BCI. The active BCIs allow users directly communicate with a technical system by consciously control mental activity. However, these systems usually require extensive tuning and training on both the system and the user, and are rarely generalizable across multiple users [2, 25]. The reactive BCIs derive outputs from the brain activities arising in response to the external stimulations, and the modulated activity is mapped to an artificial control signal. Thus, the attention of the user focus in visual, auditory, or tactile perception is modulated for the purpose of communication, and thereby occupied.

Current research has shown a paradigm shift towards passive BCI systems, which implicitly monitor user conscious and unconscious brain activity [35]. The brain activity is assimilated to an input and can be used to adapt the application to the user's mental state [12]. The system has already been used for user and machine errors detection and adapt user cognitive load [12, 13, 31]. Adaptive interfaces based on passive BCIs, generating a loop that iterates between measurement, evaluation and redesign to create interfaces that automatically adapt depending on the cognitive state of the user [31]. In order to provide pleasant and optimal user experience, user current cognition state and the context-sensitivity become the key information of the interactive system.

Sensing Audience in Performing Arts

Current audience engagement measurement divides into two categories: the explicit and the implicit. Explicit measurement includes post-performance surveys, focus groups, audience interviews and real-time response devices. Physiological measures could be used to measure implicit engagement biometrically [18]. The implicit measurement technique includes the Galvanic Skin Response (GSR), electroencephalograph (EEG), electromyography (EMG), and functional magnetic resonance imaging (fMRI), etc.

The seminal work of Celine Latulipe provides an extensive overview of research in audience engagement [18]. Based on the empirical and theoretical work of Peter Lang [19], she explored how GSR can be used to provide real-time audience feedback to performers while watching different performance videos. The GSR measures the conductivity of user's skin, which response to autonomic nervous system arousal [5]. The similar measurement could also be found in recent work from Chen Wang [34], which extended the experimental paradigm by simultaneously measuring a group of participants in a live performance. However, even though these studies have proved that GSR measurement is a valid representation of audience engagement, neither of their systems has content-related performing cues that automatically adapt depending on the cognitive state of the audience.

There are few studies using physiological measurements for creating adaptive scenes in performing arts. For example, Many Worlds, a research of developing adaptive interface that watches audience members as they watch it, allowing them to influence the sequence of scenes as the film unfolds [14]. The researchers required four volunteers from the audience to be attached to sensors, which monitor and track their heart rate, EEG brain waves, perspiration, and muscle tension respectively. An off-the-peg software tools utilized real-time analysis to change the direction or the scenes in a movie.

There are also possibilities in measuring facial expressions or using EMG to measure facial muscle activations. These data are more linked to audience's emotions, but have poor form factors for detecting in a theatre setting. Because the facial expressions during a performance may not be particularly illuminating, and it is difficult to recognize massive parallel facial expression of an audience. It's also possible to measure neural signal. Calvo-Merino and her colleagues presented their neuroscientific study of aesthetic perception in the context of the performing arts [7]. They use fMRI to investigate the brain areas whose activity during passive watching of dance stimuli was related to independent aesthetic evaluation of the same stimuli. The study shows that there are visual and sensorimotor brain areas in the occipital cortices and right premotor cortex, which have an automatic aesthetic response to dance. The result provides us insight into how visual stimulus mechanism could improve the evaluation of performing arts. However fMRI, much like fNIRS, is mostly be used to build functional maps of brain activity [31].

Measuring Audience Engagement with EEG

Electroencephalography (EEG) is a well-studied method of non-invasive BCIs to measure the brain's electrical activity [3, 23, 33]. The greatest advantage of EEG is high temporal resolution, complex patterns of neural activity can be recorded occurring within fractions of a second after a stimuli has been applied. But, it provides low spatial resolution compared to fMRI, which makes it difficult to determine where the signals originated from in the brain. Further, eye movements, muscle noise, heart signals, and line noise often produce distracting artifacts in EEG recording. To overcome these issues, we could remove artifacts by filtering the noise signal while preserving the essential EEG signals.

EEG frequencies (see Figure 2) have been extensively studied and can provide insight into user mood and emotions such as excitement, meditation, pleasure and frustration [9, 12, 21]. EEG measures are also sensitive to cognitive states including engagement and attention, working modality and perception of user machine errors [9, 11, 32]. The following formula is widely used to estimate participant task engagement based on the amplitudes of α, β, and θ waves, the EEG measured engagement is a ratio value without a unit [26].

$$EEG \quad engagement = \frac{\beta}{\alpha + \theta}$$

Now, commercially available, low-cost wireless EEG headsets have made this approach even more feasible [24]. The headset can be used in general public setting, offers no risk to the user, and do not require specific knowledge or training before use it. Also, EEG has been used make accurate classifications of various cognitive tasks [20, 31]. FOCUS [15] and LET'S LEARN [1] designed EEG-augmented reading system using content-related videos to improve user's reading engagement. However, the systems are not been formally studied. PAY ATTENTION [30] is relevant to our research, it designs an embodied story-telling agent, using adaptive spoken volume and gestures to attract user's attention when detect their engagement level decrease. Although the system could successfully detect the significant drops and regain user attention, it has not specified that whether various changes of behavioral cues affect audience differently. Our research based on the non-invasive, passive BCI system to monitor audience engagement and enhance the user-system performance by creating an interface that response to user's cognitive state controlled by EEG data.

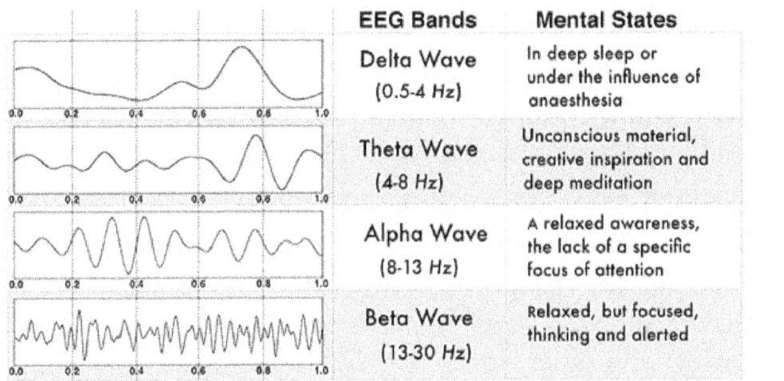

Figure 2. EEG bands and their frequencies, specifications.

In summary, no BCI technique has been used to improve the design quality of the performance art from the audience perspective. In addition, there are few virtual environment performances available that enable the stage designer to adjust the performing cues and evaluate the overall effect in an interactive way. We design an immersive theatre performance virtual environment to create adaptive content-related performing cues to improve audience engagement in various conditions based on the user's unconscious engagement level measured in real-time.

SYSTEM DESIGN

In this section, we present the design and implementation detail of the proposed system.

System Overview

The proposed system includes three levels: the interface level, the logic level, and the engine level. The interface level includes the input interface, which is an Emotiv™ EEG headset, and the output interface, which is a 3D projection system. The logic level consists of parsing the EEG data and determining when to initiate the performing cues. It also includes the software module that simulates and renders the virtual scenes of a show under the design process. The engine level includes the main functions developed based on CryEngine™, a game engine.

The user of the system wears an Emotiv™ EEG headset, which captures the EEG signal during the experiments. The obtained EEG signal then was analyzed to determine the levels of audience engagement. Our algorithm determines the decreases of audience engagement and triggers the performing cues to regain the values. A virtual environment, including the main performance contents and the performing cues, is implemented via CryEngine™. The final results of the virtual performance contents is rendered and projected on an immersive 3D circular-screen.

Measuring EEG-based Engagement

In our study, we integrated EEG into the proposed system to determine the right moment to employ performing cues. The Emotiv™ headset consists of 14 electrode sensors and 2 bipolar reference electrodes spatially organized using the International 10-20 System [16]. It connects wirelessly via Bluetooth and a USB dongle to a computer. It does not require any special training and is comfortable and usable enough for audience to use in a simulated theatre environment. Once the system detected the loss of engagement, the content-related performing cues should be evoked and regained audience engagement in a certain time.

The Emotiv™ hardware filter the signal via the common mode rejection, the digital notch filters at 50Hz and 60Hz, as well as the proprietary algorithms to remove EMG artifacts (such as eye movements, eye blinks, muscle activities) and other noise. The device samples at a rate of 128Hz and is sensitive to frequencies in the range of 0.2-45Hz, which broken into Delta, Theta, Alpha, and Beta waves using Fast Fourier Transforms. For the purpose of our research, when estimating audience engagement with Emotiv™, we used two pairs of electrodes (O1- O2, T7-T8), for those are highly relevant to the visual attention and the positive arousals respectively [6, 17]. The EEG levels for Alpha, Beta, and Theta frequencies were read in from the headset. We estimated the engagement values $E(i)$ by averaging obtained data from the four electrodes based on the above EEG engagement formula. We smoothed the engagement values $E(i)$ by using the moving average filter:

$$E_s(n) = \frac{1}{N} \sum_{i=n-N+1}^{n} E(i)$$

Where $E_s(n)$ corresponds to the smoothed engagement value at n frame, $E(i)$ is the engagement value at i frame, and N is a 10-second timeframe, which is chosen after pre-testing to identity minimum times that ensure sufficient data to accurately make predictions.

Detecting Decreases and Re-engagement

EEG signal measured by Emotiv™ is user-dependent, which makes it difficult to determine the state of engagement for various audiences. We set two thresholds as follows, for the individual audience to separate three distinctive status of audience engagement $S(n)$: positive arousals (1); stable engagement (0), and less interests (-1) from an audience engagement curve $E_s(n)$.

Detecting decreasing thresholds

$$S(n) = -1, when \quad E_s(n) - E_s(n-1) < 0 \quad and \quad E_s < \bar{E}$$

Where $S(n)$ = -1 represents the status of less interests, n is the current frame number, $\bar{E}$ is the average engagement value of all $E(i)$ from the beginning of EEG recording to the current frame. This creates a constantly updating "average" engagement level (gray curve in Figure 3) for each individual audience. When $S(n)$ output -1, a drop point was marked (see Figure 3) and a performing cue should be triggered and displayed at the same time.

The success of re-engaging audience

Similarly, another threshold (or the re-engaging threshold) is set to determine whether the performing cues re-engaged audience successfully and how the performing cues would affect the engagement values differently.

$$S(n) = 1, when \quad E_s(n) - E_s(n-1) > 0 \quad and \quad E_s > \bar{E}$$

If $S(n)$ output is 1, the performing cue was determined to successfully re-engage the audience. We set up a 15-second interval (based on pre-test results) as response time due to a 5-second delay from the smoothed engagement value.

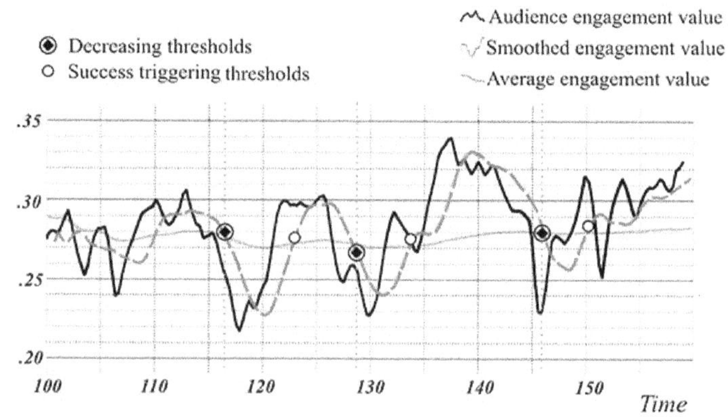

Figure 3. A preliminary test by using our algorithm, when detecting the drops, the adaptive cues will be triggered to regain audience engagement.

Theatre Performing Cues

We design the performing cues based on the classic theatre performing theory. A theatre performance is a synthetic process, which comprises of the performers' acting and the dynamic stage machinery. The stage machinery is designed for the production of theatrical effects, such as the scenic design, the lighting, the sound effects, and the special effects (illusions of the supernatural or magical, see Figure 4) [8].

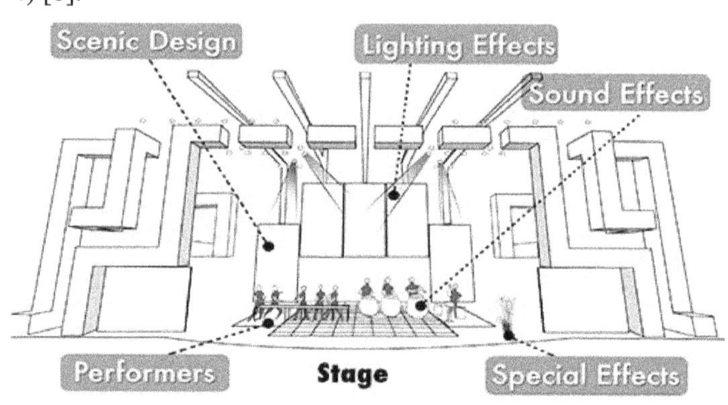

Figure 4. A basic structure of theatre performance.

The basic theatre performing cues is listed in Table 1. The scenic design (partnered with lighting design) helps the audience see and identify the location of the play [22]. In our study, we adjusted the stage set by dynamically moving the display blocks, which can be assembled into various shapes with textures controlled by the video players. The stage special effects, such as smoke or fog, invoke a specific sense of mood or atmosphere that has been reported to enrich performing scenarios and attract the audience immediately. The lighting effects helps the audience focus only on certain areas, performers, props, and or a set piece, which may be the main focus or the emphasis in that scene. The sound effects are the artificial reproduction of sounds that intend to intensify actions and supply realism in the theatre [8].

Theatre Performing Cues		Objects	Dynamic Changes
Stage Machinery	Scenic Design	Background screen; flying system; stage floor	*Horizontal, vertical movement; multi-angled rotating; dynamic matching*
	Special effects	Particle system; theatre property	*Sunlight, smoke, firework, random glowing trail...*
	Lighting effects	Light installations	*Color, size, intensity, shape, direction changing; focusing, spotlighting, composing...*
	Sound effects	Program music; actor voice; instrument	*Volume, rhythm, emotion, scene effects changing*
Performers	Motion	Main actor; figurant	*Complex movement, creative interaction*
	Costume	Apparel; accessories	*Color, shape, texture changing*

Table 1. The specification of theatre performing cues.

For instance, we could simulate sounds like shouts, horse's hooves or any other effect, which either too vast in scope or too complex to be present on stage. For the performers, research in the field of neuroaesthetics attempts to identify the brain processes underlying aesthetic experience for actors' motion, the work shows that the audience are most engaged by the large, complex dance movements [7].

The crucial question is that the theatre performance generally has a narrative structure, with a setup, a build, a climax and a denouement crossing all different types [18]. The process of building up the audience emotion is very important to give a clear performance structure. Therefore, in our study, we worked with stage directors to create content-related performing cues for two performances: an opera and a modern dance. Moreover, we noticed that the theatre performing cues often coordinated with multiple effects. For example, if we want to enhance the change of actor's status, we could employ obvious movement, a follow spot or sounds of footsteps to generate multiple cues, which create more impressive scenarios compared with the single cues. Thus, we divided each performance into several phases according to the performance content. In each phase we designed pairs of content-related single and multiple cues as performing stimulus when detect drops in audience engagement. We attempt to prove the hypotheses that by triggering our performing cues, the audience EEG-monitored engagement level will increase. And we are also trying to analyze how the single and multiple cues could have different influence to the engagement levels.

In our work, CryEngine™ is used to design and implement two theatre performances. We created these single and multiple cues in Flow Graph, which is a visual scripting system that is embedded in CryEngine™ Sandbox Editor. Scene, lighting, sound and special effects as stage machinery entities, could be built and set up vividly. We developed a real-time control subsystem to analyze the decreasing thresholds and establish commands to directly control the single and multiple performing cues in the Flow Graph Editor via TCP/IP networks. The system established separate threads for signal receiving and analyzing, which guaranteed the synchronization error of triggered commands and performing cues in 0.1 seconds. We also used motion capture devices (VICON™ Vantage) to record and obtain performers' original skeleton information. More implementation details of the performing cues in each performance will be described in the experiment session.

EXPERIMENT DESIGN

We designed and conducted a set of experiments including two types of theatre performance. Below we describe our experimental setup, procedure, and measurements.

Experimental Setup

We conducted a 3×1 between participants experiment, which consists two studies (two types of theatre performances). Each study includes three levels: (1) no performing cues, (2) single performing cues triggered by decreasing thresholds in EEG-measured audience engagement levels, (3) Multiple performing cues triggered by decreasing thresholds. 48 participants (24 males and 24 females) were took part in our experiment. Each condition had an equal number of participants (8 males and 8 females). The participants from different culture background and recruited from the same university. The average age was 24.4 (SD = 5.18) with a range of 19-49. All the participants had no prior experience in BCI system and their familiarity with the two theatre performances was low (M = 1.96, SD = 1.24) in the scale of one to seven. In order to create an immersive theatre performance experience, we set up the experiment in a 30 square meters testing place of our laboratory, we used a 135 degrees circular-screen projection system to present the simulated theatre performances in 3D mode. We placed the audience seat right in front of the circular-screen. Figure 5 shows the scenario of our experiment.

Experimental Procedure

The experiment consists of four main phases for each performance:

1) Introduction: Before start, the participants were asked to fill out a form for their basic information and being given a description of the experiment procedure. Then they were brought into the testing room. The researchers aided them putting on Emotiv™ to ensure good connectivity. Once the headset connection was established, the researchers helped participants put on 3D glasses and left the room. The participants started watching the simulated theatre performance on the circular-screen.

(2) Calibration: There is a 20-second calibration phase, which attempted to help audience to adapt with the device and get baseline to establish the decreasing thresholds later. In the calibration phase, the system did not employ any performing cues.

(3) Test: During this phase, the single and multiple cues were triggered according to the experimental conditions. The opera "Siegfried" and the modern dance "The Tramps of Horses" were implemented in the virtual environment for the audiences across various cultures. In the single cues condition, the single performing cues would be triggered when identified drops by monitoring the audience real-time engagement data. In the multiple cues condition, the system triggered multiple performing cues when detected drops in engagement levels. The system would continue triggered next cues right after a 15-second interval for response to the last cue without success. Due to the narrative of theatre performance, audience engagement level could be re-engaged by the performance itself. However, the difference between the performing cues and performance was that the performing cues, as theatre assistive tools, had distinct visual or auditory changes without disturbing the performance content. In no performing cues condition, the system would only detect significant drops when the decreases across the means of smoothed engagement level. In the last phase, the participants were asked to retell the content of the performance in detail as a recall task.

(4) Evaluation: At the end of the experiment, the researchers had the participants remove the headset and fill out a post-experiment questionnaire to receive subjective feedback of our system.

Objective and Subjective Measurement

The objective measurements included 10 key points with the help of stage director that measured the participants' ability to recall the details of each performance. The experimenter counted the key points that the participants mentioned, and rated a score from 0-5.

The post-experiment questionnaire included twelve questions, as a subjective measurement, it was taken by the means of a seven point rating scale (7 point is the highest score) used to measure participants' responses. It included checks on the effective of our performing cues and questions from the audience's perception of the adaptive theatre performance and whether these performing cues help to attract attention and enrich the performance content.

We utilized these measurements to confirm our algorithm could successfully identify significant drops in no performing cues condition. And we verified that the theatre performing cues enhanced the positive arousals on audience engagement in both single and multiple cues conditions.

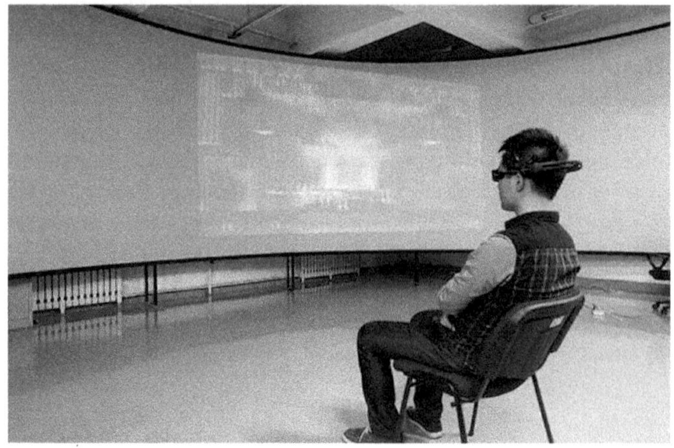

Figure 5. An audience watches the adaptive theatre performance in 3D mode.

EXPERIMENT

"Siegfried"

We chose the classical opera "*Siegfried*" as one of the experimental performance, which is the third of the four operas that constitute "*The Ring of the Nibelung*" by Richard Wagner. We chose a five minutes scene, in which Siegfried waited for Fafner who obtained the ring and transformed himself as a dragon, to appear and fight with him. The scene consisted of three main phases: (1) the actor of Siegfried was playing a tune on his horn and trying to summon the dragon, (2) the dragon out of its cave and appeared in the dark forest at the back of the stage, (3) Siegfried fight with the dragon and stabbed in its heart.

We created pairs of single and multiple cues in each phase. One cue last 15 seconds and was obviously different from the performance content, but extracting emotional features and mapped to the scene design, lighting, sound, special effects, etc. Figure 6 shows the simulated performance compared with live performance and examples of single and multiple performing cues.

Performing Cues Design

Single Performing Cues: (1) We created sound effect to mimic a wood-bird song; Illumination of the moving brick wall. (2) The leaves blew heavily in the wind as the dragon appeared; White spotlight tracked the actor of Siegfried when he was singing. (3) A lightning streaked from sky across the dark forest; Actor interacted with the dragon in a dynamic "backward-forward" fighting move.

Multiple Performing Cues: (1) A wood-bird flew past the stage with the sound of drumming; Brick walls, rocks around the actor of Siegfried were illuminated sequentially in large-scale. (2) When the dragon was out of the cave, the ground was flaking and piles of leaves on the tree were slipping off; High-frequency color lights focused only on the actor and dragon by using white and red spotlight respectively. (3) Actor came close to the dragon amid thunder and lightning, while the back brick walls moved away from the center of the stage; when the actor fight with dragon in "backward-forward" move, red flames would be lighted on the sword and small fires were reflected on the ground.

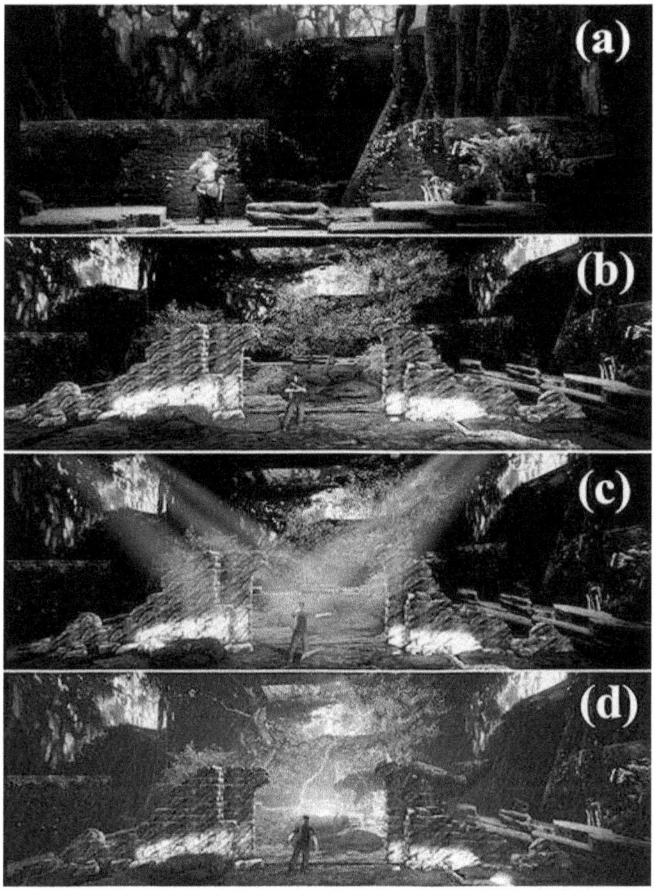

Figure 6. (a) Live performance of "Siegfried" (b) The simulated performance (c) Single cues of color lights (d) Multiple cues of actor's complex fight moves with lightning, thunder and red flames effects.

Object Results

We utilized one-way analysis of variance (ANOVA) to analyze our data from objective and subjective measurements.

To verify our system working effectively, we processed the engagement data from participants in three conditions using our algorithm to identify the times when triggered single and multiple performing cues. We analyzed the average engagement values in a 20-second timeframe before and after each performing cue. In no cues condition, the results showed that the average engagement levels 20 seconds before the triggering time were significantly higher than the average engagement levels 20 seconds after that, $F(1, 58) = 10.261$, $p = 0.002$, proving that our algorithm could correctly detecting significant decreases in audience engagement. Furthermore, we analyzed the data in single cues $F(1, 58) = 0.427$, $p = 0.515$, multiple cues $F(1, 58) = 0.326$, $p = 0.569$, conditions also in a 20-second interval before and after the triggering time, the results showed that there were no significant difference. Figure 7 showed the analysis in three levels. The results also be supported by comparing the time of status in "$S(n) = 1$" in single cues and multiple cues condition $F(1, 30) = 4.598$, $p = 0.040$, which showed that the participants obtained more positive arousals by triggering multiple performing cues than single performing cues (see Figure 9).

The recall task also supported our hypothesis that the score (in the scale of one to five) of correct answer out of 10 key points were on average 1.91 ($SD = 0.95$), 2.28 ($SD = 0.84$), and 3.37 ($SD = 0.94$) in no performing cues, single cues, and multiple cues conditions, respectively.

The result showed that the participants in multiple cues condition had better recall of the performance than in single cues condition, and participants in both of the two conditions were better than in no performing cues condition.

Subjective Results

We applied Likert scale method to the data from the questionnaire. This prediction was supported by the results that participants felt significantly clear narrative of the performance, the (no cues/single cues/multiple cues) results were on average 2.06 ($SD = 0.68$), 3.68 ($SD = 0.87$), 5.31 ($SD = 0.79$), respectively. Also, participants in single and multiple performing cues conditions reported that the performance was seamlessly embedded with the adaptive cues without distractions compared with no cues condition, the results were on average 5.25 ($SD = 0.93$), 4.93 ($SD = 0.77$), 4.87 ($SD = 0.61$). The results showed that the performing cues we designed were enabled to re-engage audience engagement, and the multiple cues had obviously better recall of performing content than in the single cues condition.

"The Tramps of Horses"

We chose modern dance *"The Tramps of Horses"* as another experimental performance, which typically represents a creative choreography with strong rhythm. We divided into four phases: (1) the dancers lined in two rows moved together with the strength and speed of their motions, (2) dancers from the back were disappeared, while seven performers were dancing creatively together with three others who playing Chinese drums, (3) the seven performers and three instrument players made the synchronous action rhythmically with a life growth background scene, (4) all the performers appeared on the stage, their complex movements built the tension as it went toward the climax at the end.

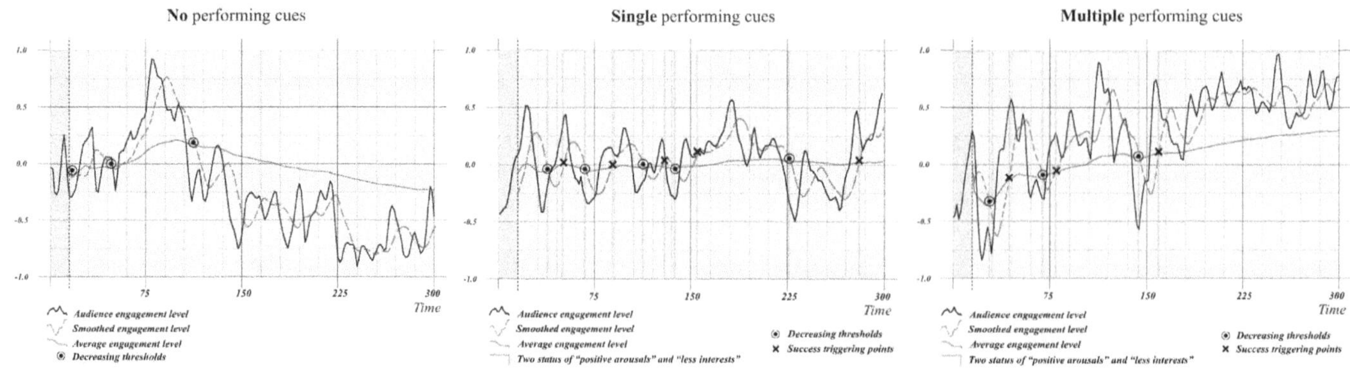

Figure 7. The analysis of three conditions in "Siegfried". Our algorithm correctly detected the decreasing thresholds in audience engagement, and regained the engagement level in a certain time. Multiple performing cues had a better effect on increasing positive arousals than single performing cues.

Performing Cues Design

Single Performing Cues: (1) A slight white spotlight with defined routine tracked performers' movements in rows. (2) A red spotlights followed the leader of dancers augmented his complex movements. (3) Sound effect of plants growing. (4) Water curtain effect; Fireworks effect around the edge of the stage.

Multiple Performing Cues: (1) A strong white spotlight traced the performers horizontally with the undulating movement of front illuminated bulks. (2) Three more performers turned somersaults across the stage with the track of individual red spotlight and then disappeared. (3) Colored lights with high frequencies in the sound of plants growing. (4) Red scattering light with water curtain fluid from top of the stage; Sparking with fireworks effect around the stage with the rotating of LED screen (See Figure 8).

Object Results

First, in no performing cues condition, the results showed that the average engagement levels 20 seconds before the decreasing thresholds were significantly higher than the average engagement levels 20 seconds after that, $F(1, 58) = 9.848$, $p = 0.002$, proving that our algorithm correctly detected decreases in audience engagement. Moreover, to confirm that the performing cues would successfully attract audience attention, we analyzed the data in single cues $F(1, 58) = 0.292$, $p = 0.590$, multiple cues $F(1, 58) = 0.567$, $p = 0.457$, conditions also in a 20-second interval before and after the triggering time. The evidence showed that there were no significant differences in both the single and multiple cues conditions. This also be supported by comparing the time of status in "$S(n) = 1$" in single cues and multiple cues condition $F(1, 30) = 1.477$, $p = 0.234$, which showed that the triggered positive arousals in both conditions were almost the same. The results had also been supported by our recall task: the score of correct answer were on average 1.96 ($SD = 0.92$), 3.09 ($SD= 0.84$), and 3.56 ($SD = 0.85$) in the no performing cues, single cues, and multiple cues conditions, respectively.

Figure 8. (a) Live performance of "The Tramps of Horses" (b) The simulated performance (c) Single cues of fireworks effect (d) Multiple cues of water curtain and red scattering light.

These results showed that in both single and multiple cues conditions, the participants had better recall of the performance content than no performing cues condition.

Subject Results

We also investigated that whether the participants involved in the multiple cues condition felt more attracted than in the single cues condition. The results showed that there were no obvious difference between the two conditions, the results were on average 4.37 (*SD* = 0.80), 4.81 (*SD* = 0.91). It showed that the performing cues we designed were enabled to re-engage audience engagement, however there were no big distinctions of effects between the single cues and multiple cues conditions.

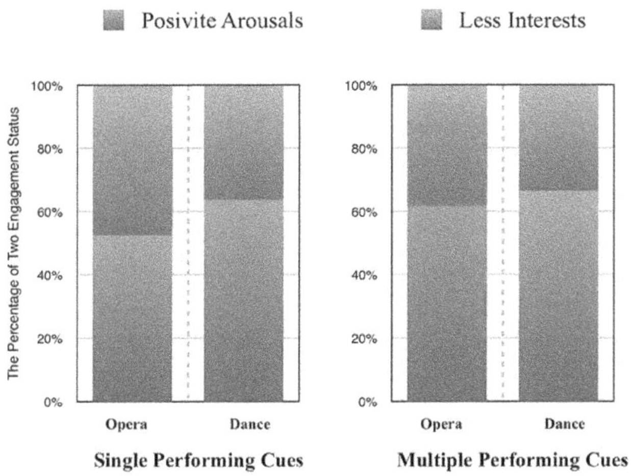

Figure 9. The percentage of two engagement status for averaging all participants in the single and multiple cues conditions of two types of theatre performance.

DISSCUSSION

The experiment showed that we could successfully detected significant decreasing thresholds by using our algorithm, and proved our hypothesis that the use of adaptive theatre performing cues could regain audience engagement in real-time across different types of theatre performances. Our results supported the hypothesis that by using performing cues the participants had better recall of the performance content.

Despite the positive results from our research, we investigated whether the participants would positively rate in multiple cues condition than in single cues condition, the data showed that in opera experiment the audience felt more attracted by triggering multiple performing cues than single performing cues, however there were no significant differences between the two conditions in the experiment of modern dance. This was because that modern dance usually has a fast-paced narrative rhythms, the detection of decreasing thresholds in audience engagement would only happened in certain moments. This evidence showed that the performing cues might have different impacts on attracting audience attention according to various performance types.

We also found that most of the participants did not felt been interrupted during the virtual theatre performance with the embedded performing cues. Our results had proved that the content-related performing cues would re-engage audience engagement unconsciously based on EEG-measured data while keeping the performance rhythm smooth. However, we have not found any significant difference between the male and female participants, but a few females mentioned that they were more impressed by the dynamic changes of lighting and special sound effects. These results lend credence to the idea that performing cues could improve audience engagement, which could be a positive factor in the future of theatre performance design from the audience perception.

Due to the limitation of simulated an immersive theatre environment in our laboratory, some complex features, for example performers' facial expressions, might need high-accuracy motion capture device to create more vivid scenes. While our system achieved its predicted goal of increasing audience attention by monitoring their engagement data in real-time and triggering performing cues when detected drops in audience engagement levels. Our engagement values were based on EEG signals, which were easily to be affected by other signals such as muscle artifacts due to the limitation of the EEG technology. Although we employed filters to remove noise signals, we still need to validate the presented engagement values were excluded irrelevant signals.

CONCLUSION AND FUTURE WORK

To successfully adjust performing content from audience perception into theatre performance in real-time, the system should be able to correctly measure and response to audience engagement state. In our research, we created an adaptive system, which enhances the theatre performance experience by real-time monitoring audience engagement levels from EEG data and employs performing cues that stage designers could use to regain audience attention when detecting significant decreases. We found that the adaptive theatre performance with embedded performing cues could improve the audience recall ability across various types of performances unconsciously. We hope our research serves as a springboard for further investigation into the field of performing arts to employ digital techniques, which could aid the design of theatre performance to create more fluid interactions with audience.

In future work, we should think about the following questions: How could our system be improved to integrate EEG monitoring with other biometric measures such as heart rate, blood pressure to improve the adaptability? Generally, the theatre performances were presented for the crowds, how could we assess the effects of social interaction during an adaptive performance to verify the effectiveness? Our future work will seek to answer these questions and towards understanding of various performing cues affect audience response across types of performances to improving our system.

ACKNOWLEDGMENTS

We would like to thank China National Opera House and the Secondary School of Beijing Dance Academy for their supports and help. The research leading to these results has received funding from National Natural Science Foundation of China under Grants No.61202243, and No.60975013, Key Technologies Research and Development Program Foundation of China under Grants No.2012BAH38F05. This publication only reflects the author's views.

REFERENCES

1. Andujar, M., and Gilbert, J. E. Let's learn! Enhancing User's Engagement Levels Through Passive Brain-Computer Interfaces. *Ext. Abstracts CHI 2013*, ACM Press (2013), 703-708.
2. Ayaz, H., Shewokis, P., Bunce, S., Schultheis, M., and Onaral, B. Assessment of cognitive neural correlates for a functional near infrared-based brain computer interface system. In *Augmented Cognition, HCII 2009, vol. 5638 of Lecture Notes in Computer Science.* Springer Berlin / Heidelberg, 2009, 699-708.
3. Berka, C., Levendowski, D.J., Lumicao, M.N., Yau, A., Davis, G., Zivkovic, V.T, Olmstead, R. E., Tremoulet, P. L. EEG correlates of task engagement and mental workload in vigilance, learning, and memory tasks. *Aviation, Space, and Environment Medicine 78*, Supplement 1(5), B231-B244.
4. Blankertz, B., Dornhege, G., Krauledat, M., Muller, K. and Curio, G. The non-invasive Berlin Brain-Computer Interface: Fast acquisition of effective performance in untrained subjects. *NeuroImage.* 37, 2:539-550.
5. Bouscein, W. 1992. *Electrodermal Activity*. Plenum Press, New York, USA.
6. Brefczynski, J. A., and DeYoe, E. A. A physiological correlate of the 'spotlight' of visual attention. *Nature Neuroscience*, Volume 2, 1999, 370-374.
7. Calvo-Merino, B., Jola, C., Glaser, D.E., Haggard, P. 2008. Towards a sensorimotor aesthetics of performing art. *Consciousness and Cognition.* 17, 3: 911-922.
8. Cruse, W. 2014. Stagecraft theatre. *ENCYCLOPAEDIA BRITANNICA.*

   http://global.britannica.com/art/stagecraft#toc40210
9. Cutrell, E., Tan, D. BCI for passive input in HCI. In *Proc CHI'07*, 2007.
10. Dixon, S. 2015. Digital Performance: A History of New Media in Theater, Dance, Performance Art, and Installation. The MIT Press, 2015.
11. Ferrez, P. W., and Millan. You are wrong! Automatic detection of interaction errors from brain waves. In *Proc IJCAI'05* (2005).
12. George, L., and Lecuyer, A. An overview of research on "passive" brain-computer interfaces for implicit human-computer interaction. *International Conference on Applied Bionics and Biomechanics ICABB 2010, workshop "Brain-Computer Interfacing and Virtual Reality",* Oct 2010.
13. Girouard, A., Solovey, E. T., and Jacob, R. J. K. Designing a passive brain computer interface using real time classification of functional near-infrared spectroscopy. *International Journal of Autonomous and Adaptive Communications Systems* (2010).
14. Grant, C. 2013. Many Worlds: The movie that watches its audience. *BBC News* http://www.bbc.co.uk/news/technology-21429437
15. Huang, J., Yu, C., Wang, Y. T., Zhao, Y. H., Liu, S-Q., Mo, C., Liu, J., Zhang, L., and Shi, Y. C. 2014. FOCUS: enhancing children's engagement in reading by using contextual BCI training sessions. In *Proc CHI'14*, 1905-1908.
16. Jasper, H. H. 1958. The ten-twenty electrode system of the International Federation. *Electroencephalography and Clinical Neurophysiology*, 371-375.
17. Jatupaiboon, N., Pan-ngum, S., and Israsena, P. 2013. Real-Time EEG-Based Happiness Detection System. *The Scientific World Journal*, Volume 2013, 618649.
18. Latulipe, C., Carroll, Erin A., and Lottridge, D. 2011. Love, hate, arousal and engagement: exploring audience responses to performing arts. In *Proceedings of the SIGCHI Conference on Human Factors in Computing Systems* (CHI '11), 1845-1854.
19. Lang, P. 1995. The emotion probe: Studies of motivation and attention. *American Psychologist.* 50(5): 372-385.
20. Lee, J. C., and Tan, D. S. 2006. Using a low-cost electroencephalograph for task classification in HCI research. In *Proc* UIST*'06*, 81-90.
21. Molina, G., Tsoneva, T., and Nijholt, A. Emotional brain-computer interfaces. In *Proc ACII'09*, IEEE (2009), 1-9.
22. Napoli, R., Gloman, C. 2006. Scenic Design and Lighting Techniques: A Basic Guide for Theatre. Focal Press, 2006.
23. Niedermeyer, E., and F. H. Lopes Da Silva. 1993. Electroencephalography: Basic principles, clinical applications and related fields, 3rd edition, Lippincott, Williams & Wilkins, Philadelphia.
24. Nijholt, A., Bos, D. P.-O., Reuderink, B. Turning shortcomings into challenges: Brain-computer interfaces for games. Entertainment Computing 1, 2 (2009), 85-94.
25. Pfurtscheller, G., Neuper, C., Guger, C., Harkam, W., Ramoser, H., Schlogl, A., Obermaier, B., and Pregenzer, M. Current trends in Graz Brain-Computer (BCI) research. *IEEE Transactions on Rehabilitation Engineering* 8, 2 (2000), 216-219.

26. Pope, A.T., Bogart, E.H., Bartolome, D.S. 1995. Biocybernetic system evaluates indices of operator engagement in automated task. Biological Psychology. 40(1995), 187-195.
27. Radbourne, J., Johanson, K., Glow, H., and White, T. 2009. The audience experience: measuring quality in the performing arts. *International journal of Arts Management* 11, 3:16-29.
28. Radbourne, J., Glow, H. and Johanson, K. 2010. Hidden stories: listening to the audience at the live performance. *Double dialogues*, no.13, summer, 1-14.
29. Santoro, C., and G. Troilo. 2007. The Drivers of Hedonic Consumption Experience: A semiotic analysis of rock concerts. In *Consuming Experience.* Abingdon, UK, and New York: Routledge.
30. Szafir, D. and Mutlu, B. 2012. Pay attention! Designing adaptive agents that monitor and improve user engagement. In *Proceedings of the SIGCHI Conference on Human Factors in Computing Systems (CHI '12)*, 11-20.
31. Tan, D., Nijholt, A. 2010. Brain-computer interface: Applying our minds to human-computer interaction. Springer, 2010.
32. Tan, D. Brain-computer interfaces: applying our minds to human-computer interaction. In *Proc CHI Workshop: "What is the Next Generation of Human-Computer Interaction?"*, 2006.
33. Teplan, M. Fundamentals of EEG Measurement. *Measurement Science Review*, vol 2, section 2, 2002, 1-11.
34. Wang, C., Geelhoed, Erik N., Stenton, Phil, P., and Cesar, P. 2014. Sensing a live audience. In *Proceedings of the SIGCHI Conference on Human Factors in Computing Systems* (CHI '14), 1909-1912.
35. Zander, T., and Kothe, C. Towards passive brain-computer interfaces: applying brain-computer interface technology to human-machine systems in general. *Journal of Neural Engineer* 8, 2(2011), 025005.

Facial Expression Recognition in Daily Life by Embedded Photo Reflective Sensors on Smart Eyewear

Katsutoshi Masai
Keio University
Yokohama, Japan
masai@imlab.ics.keio.ac.jp

Yuta Sugiura
Advanced Institute of Science and Technology (AIST)
Koto, Tokyo, Japan
yuta.sugiura@aist.go.jp

Masa Ogata
Keio University
Yokohama, Japan
ogata@ayu.ics.keio.ac.jp

Kai Kunze
Keio University
Yokohama, Japan
kai@kmd.keio.ac.jp

Masahiko Inami
The University of Tokyo
Bunkyo, Tokyo, Japan
inami@inami.info

Maki Sugimoto
Keio University
Yokohama, Japan
sugimoto@ics.keio.ac.jp

ABSTRACT
This paper presents a novel smart eyewear that uses embedded photo reflective sensors and machine learning to recognize a wearer's facial expressions in daily life. We leverage the skin deformation when wearers change their facial expressions. With small photo reflective sensors, we measure the proximity between the skin surface on a face and the eyewear frame where 17 sensors are integrated. A Support Vector Machine (SVM) algorithm was applied for the sensor information. The sensors can cover various facial muscle movements and can be integrated into everyday glasses.
The main contributions of our work are as follows. (1) The eyewear recognizes eight facial expressions (92.8% accuracy for one time use and 78.1% for use on 3 different days). (2) It is designed and implemented considering social acceptability. The device looks like normal eyewear, so users can wear it anytime, anywhere. (3) Initial field trials in daily life were undertaken.
Our work is one of the first attempts to recognize and evaluate a variety of facial expressions in the form of an unobtrusive wearable device.

Author Keywords
Wearable; Smart Eye Glasses; Eyewear Computing; Facial Expression Recognition

ACM Classification Keywords
H.5.m. Information Interfaces and Presentation (e.g. HCI): Miscellaneous

DOI: http://dx.doi.org/10.1145/2856767.2856770

Figure 1. User Wears Our Smart Eyewear

INTRODUCTION
The concept of Affective Computing has been around recently [17] and a number of researchers are gaining more and more insights into affect detection using various approaches [1]. One of the approaches is recognizing facial expressions from video sequences. However, this approach is only reliable in an experimental setting.

Our goal is to recognize people's facial expressions in daily life. Keltner et al. described that our facial expressions provide information about our emotional states [8]. Facial expressions can let us intuit affective states including state of mind, wellbeing, social interaction, etc. because they change spontaneously over the course of a day depending on our mental and physical condition and when we interact with the environment. Although we can tell our own facial expressions, we are not usually aware of our facial expressions or their flow in daily life as it requires cognitive effort. Therefore, we believe quantifying the state of facial expressions in daily life will help us better understand our affective states and lifestyle.

For recognizing people's facial expressions in daily life, we have developed a wearable device that can recognize facial expressions, specifically a smart eyewear. We believe that "wearability" is important for tracking users over the long term. Moreover, as discussed by Picard et al., a wearable can provide a good opportunity to learn about user's affective patterns in daily scenarios [16]. In this approach, we leverage the skin deformation caused by the movement of facial muscles. We use 17 photo reflective sensors that are integrated into the front frame of glasses to detect the skin deformation around the eyes. The sensors we used for our prototype are small and are potentially integrated into everyday glasses. Thus, the usability in daily life is higher than that of the camera-based system in terms of tracking and suitability in social contexts. Our method can consider various facial movements robustly by applying SVM to data acquired from 17 photo reflective sensors that are distributed into the front frame of the glasses.

In this paper, we focus on recognizing eight facial expressions (Figure 2): Neutral, the universal six facial expressions (Happiness, Disgust, Anger, Surprise, Fear, and Sadness) defined by Ekman [3], and contempt, which is sometimes considered as a universal facial expression [12]. We only consider facial expressions since our system only detects skin deformation caused by facial expression changes. We discuss the insights into our affective states acquired from our system. We do not consider complex facial expressions such as a fake smile though they are an interesting area to understand our minds and lifestyle more deeply.

The aims of our work are as follows. (1) Enabling the recognition of eight of a wearer's expressions that are defined as universal (neutral, happiness, disgust, anger, surprise, fear, sadness, and contempt) with a wearable device. We used 17 photo reflective sensors that cover most movements of facial muscles and applied SVM to make the system robust. (2) Social acceptance. We designed and implemented our system as a form of eyewear (fully packaged) because eyewear fits the context of daily usage (Figure 1). Hence, users can wear it anytime, anywhere. To achieve this, we use small photo reflective sensors to capture facial expressions. Those sensors can be integrated into everyday glasses. (3) The observation and analysis of the distribution of facial expressions with long-term use of our system.

RELATED WORK

Facial Expression Recognition

There are a number of notable works related to facial expression recognition in computer vision. According to Tien et al., the general approach to automatic facial expression analysis (AFEA) consists of three steps: Face acquisition, facial data extraction and representation, and facial expression recognition [19]. One AFEA approach achieved the high accuracy of 91.5% for recognizing basic expressions [11] using the Cohn-Kanade Database [7]. However, there are three major problems with camera-based systems in terms of usability in daily life. First, one of the biggest problems is a limited field of view tracking. Most works use a single fixed camera installed in the environment. The camera has difficulty tracking users continuously over a wide area for a long time. Also, users

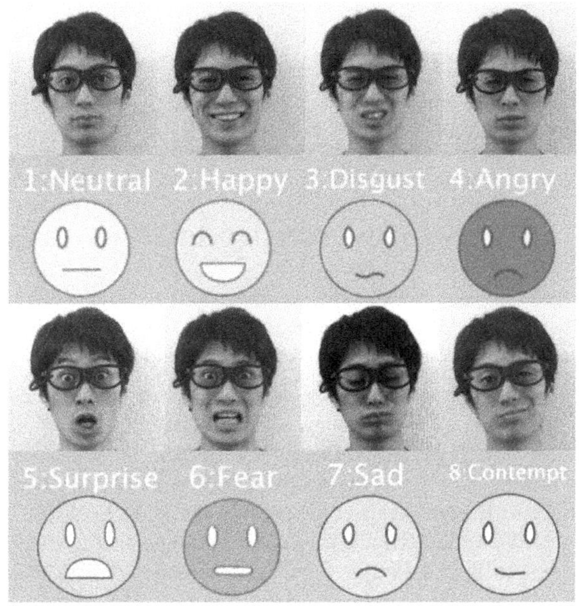

Figure 2. Variation of Recognizable Facial Expressions

are difficult to track when they move constantly or there is an obstacle between them and the camera. Second, the AFEA camera systems mostly work best with a clear image of a face from a frontal view. However, in real environments, a frontal-view of a face is not always available. A facial image acquired from a non-frontal view reduces accuracy of facial expression recognition. Finally, a camera-based system does not fit social contexts: Even if we solve the problems above with a wearable camera, people still have mental resistance to being captured on camera in their daily lives due to privacy issues. In addition, the camera needs a certain distance from users to capture their facial expressions and so designing the device acceptable to society is difficult. Thus, Kimura et al. proposed a eyeglass-based hands-free videophone [9]. It can yield a frontal face image with fish-eye cameras and capture facial expressions. However, the system is wired to laptop computers, and its size and weight were not comfortable for practical use.

Facial Expression Recognition With Wearable Devices

The one of the first approaches that tried to detect facial expressions with a wearable device was Expression Glasses [18], which can recognize specific expressions (confusion/interest) by measuring facial muscle movement using piezoelectric sensors. Gruebler and Suzuki designed a wearable device that can read positive facial expressions using facial EMG signals [6]. It has to be attached to the side of a face, but it can record the user's affective state for more than four hours with high accuracy. It can be used during therapeutic interventions and to support medical professionals. Li et al. used a depth camera and strain gauge to capture displacement of strain signals from upper facial expressions inside a head-mounted display [10]. They also mapped the input signals to a 3D face model. All of them use contact-base sensors. These prior works showed good performances under experimental conditions. However, the measurement processes are

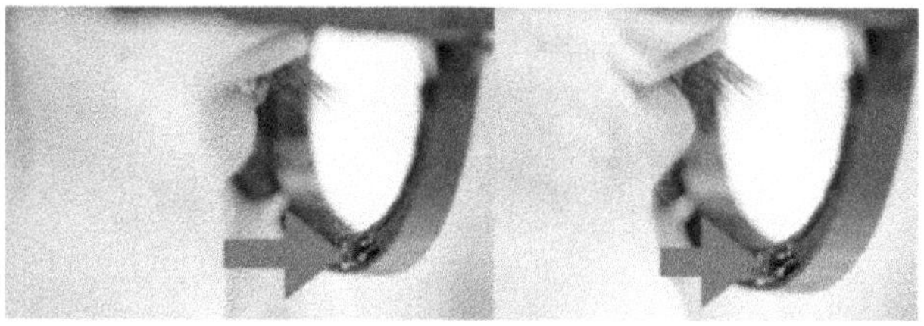

Figure 3. Skin Deformation due to Facial Expression Change

sensitive to losing physical contact with displacement sensors or electrodes. Also, the comfort of wearing the device can be an issue.

Sensing with Photo Reflective Sensors

Fukumoto et al. used photo reflective sensors to capture skin deformation at the corners of eyes and cheeks [5]. The two photo reflective sensors were attached to the outside of glasses to detect happy facial expressions (smiles/laughter) with a practical threshold determination. This method does not scale well for multiple users because of the diversity of the appropriate threshold. In addition, due to the limited number of sensors, it can miscategorize other facial expressions as the target ones. Nakamura et al. proposed a device with one photo reflective sensor, which intuitively and seamlessly controls augmented reality information using the natural movement of eyebrows when users try to focus and stare at something [13].

Other than detecting facial expressions, photo reflective sensors are used for capturing skin deformation on various parts of the human body. For example, Ogata et al. leverage skin deformation of forearms to use skin as an interface (SenSkin) [14]. This work uses two arrays of six photo reflective sensors to detect gestures (pinch, touch, pull-up, pull-down, pull-right, and pull-left) on the skin surface. Their previous work (iRing) also leverages skin deformation of the finger to capture finger gestures and external input [15].

FACIAL EXPRESSION RECOGNITION WITH EMBEDDED PHOTO REFLECTIVE SENSORS ON SMART EYEWEAR

One of the enabling technologies for affect recognition in real life is eyewear computing. The emerging field of eyewear computing is perfect for affect recognition, as the head (the location of most of our senses as well as the brain) is a natural position for sensing due to human physiology. The remaining problem is social acceptance, yet with smaller and smaller Printed Circuit Boards(PCB), sensors, and actuators, we can now build smart glasses that are not much different in appearance from normal eyewear, making them acceptable from fashion and comfort perspectives to the general public.

In this study, we use a large number of photo reflective sensors and apply a machine learning method in consideration of skin deformation caused by facial expressions. This approach has three advantages on facial expression recognition. (1) An adaptive and robust recognition on variety of users and their facial expressions due to the rich sensor information and

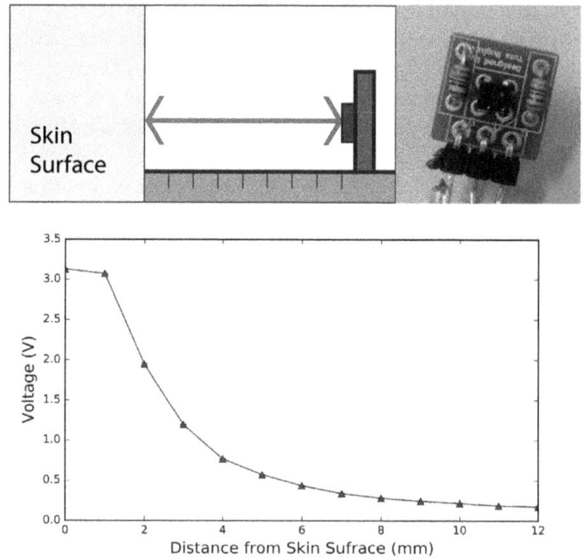

Figure 4. Characteristics of Photo Reflective Sensor to Skin Surface

learning framework. (2) Non-contact measurement: The sensors are noninvasive and they don't need physical contact that is difficult to keep reproducibility and worsen wearing comfort. (3) Smart appearance: The sensors can be integrated into everyday glasses because of the small form factor (e.g SG-105: 3.2 x 2.7 x 1.4 mm). Thus, the users are able to wear the device in various daily scenes.

To capture facial expressions, we leverage skin deformation caused by the movement of facial muscles. When users move their facial muscles, three-dimensional skin deformation occurs. Each facial expression includes different movements of facial muscles. The movements of eyelids, eyebrows, nose, and cheeks cause the 3 three-dimensional skin deformation around eyes. The movement of a mouth also causes the skin deformation under eyes because the muscle movement around the mouth influences cheek shape. According to [4], those movements are the greater part of action units with that the Facial Action Coding System codes human facial expressions. Therefore, placing sensors to capture skin deformation around eyes makes it possible to detect most facial movements related to facial expressions that should be recognized [20]. Skin deformation is captured by measuring the distances between various spots of the eyewear and skin surface on a face. These distances change with different facial expressions. 17 photo reflective sensors integrated into the eyewear frame measure these distances.

In addition, there are two more advantages of our approach. First, it is simple: The processing needed to interpret the readings is minimal, so no elaborate feature extraction needs to be done. Thus, we can keep the processing cost and energy consumption small, which is important for real-time recognition. Second, it is low cost in price: We just use photo reflective sensors with a micro processing unit.

Photo Reflective Sensor

As discussed in Related Work, photo reflective sensors are sometimes used in HCI field to measure human skin movement [5, 13, 14, 15]. We use IR reflective sensors. The sensor is composed of an IR LED and IR photo transistor.

Figure 4 shows a basic characteristics of skin surface reflection captured by an IR photo reflective sensor. We measured the voltage from the sensor that changes in accordance with the distance between the sensor and the skin surface. 30 samples were collected at each position. The figure indicates the average and standard deviation at each distance. The standard deviation is quite low (at most 0.014 V).

The correspondence is not linear, but we can obtain proximity. In the closer distance, the photo reflective sensor shows a higher resolution.

Usage Scenarios

We can assume various scenarios using our device. First usage scenario is "Happiness Map". Given we can achieve facial expression recognition in daily life, one simple way to apply it is to combine facial expressions with location and demography. People can search for the "happiest" place to live or work by looking at others' facial expressions. They can also obtain an overview of how events and policies change the affect state of a region or country.

The second is a "Care System for Older Adults". Facial expressions can provide insights into how people live their lives. Our system can be used as a care system for older adults. They can get an overview of their situation (and potential deterioration of the mood). Since more and more elderly people live away from their children, they tend to feel lonely more easily than before. Our system can help them and their children to take appropriate and productive care of both (e.g., our system notifies the children of the appropriate times to give their parents a call and talk to them when the system detects they are feeling sad and smiling less).

The third is "Collaborative Media Tagging". Facial expressions or emotions can be used to enhance contents. If a lot of people read a book or watch a video with their facial expressions recorded, the content can be indexed and made searchable.Also, content creators could obtain a better grasp on their techniques, making their storytelling more effective (e.g. what surprises a reader/watcher and what does not).

Finally, our device can be used for mental management. Emotional impact is a very delicate problem, as people should feel empowered by technology not influenced or even oppressed. Still given the rise of depression and other mental illnesses related to emotional imbalances, we believe people can benefit from devices that can help them understand and motivate to alter their emotional state. However, these influences should be aligned with the user's long-term goals (not influencing them in "unwanted ways"). Tsujita and Rekimoto outlined a basic example: We can increase people's happiness by making them smile more [21]. Yoshida et al. proposed an emotion evoking system [22]. This mirror system changes facial expressions artificially and revealed that the artificial facial expression can change the user's emotion. Their work shows the interrelation between the cognition of facial expression and emotion. Along those lines, we wonder what would happen if we applied technologies to change some of the symptoms of mental disease. For example, a depressed person usually talks little with others and stays in bed longer (i.e., is less physically active). If a system successfully encourages this person to be more social and active with the assistance of caring people who got his/her information, our work might help deal with his/her mental illnesses. Of course, the proposed solution may not work in every case (e.g. when personalization is needed) and depend on the severeness. However, it may be a promising first step.

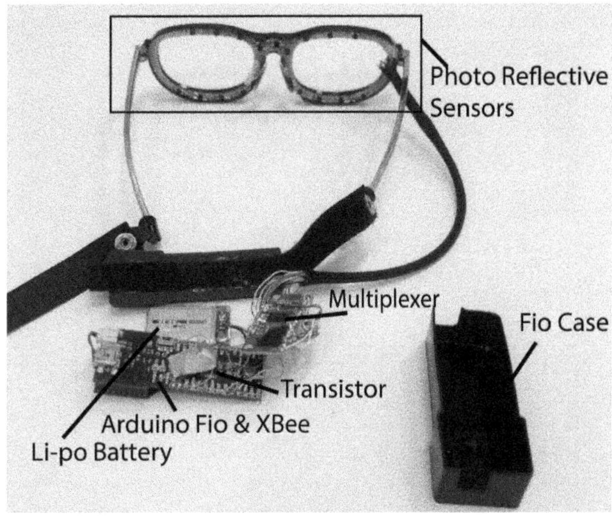

Figure 5. System Components

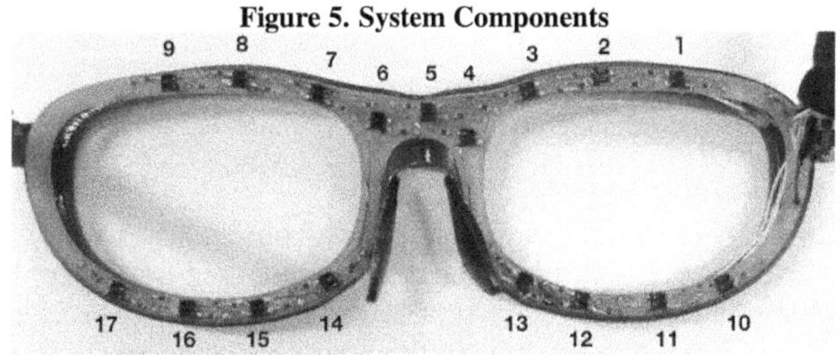

Figure 6. The Placement of Photo Reflective Sensors

IMPLEMENTATION

Hardware

Our prototype includes 17 photo reflective sensors (SG-105), a 16-channel multiplexer (CD74HC4067), a transistor (IRLU3410PBF), Arduino Fio, Xbee, and li-po battery. The weight of the prototype is around 60g. The front frame is 3D printed, and the temple is taken from commercial eyewear. We applied an eyewear band to stabilize the position of the eyewear. The transistor is used to modulate LED of the photo reflective sensors because the sensors are easily influenced by ambient light such as fluorescent light. We measure the difference between the values with LED on and off by switching it on and off frequently at around 80 Hz. With this method, it is possible to reduce the influence of ambient light. Xbee enables serial communication via zigbee at 57600 bits per second.

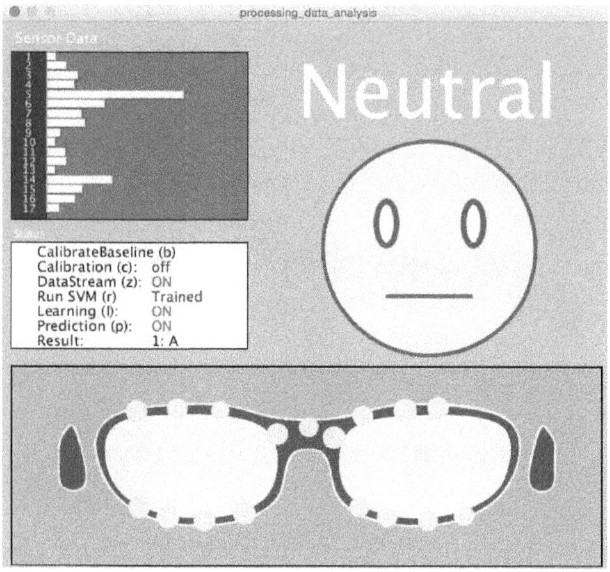

Figure 7. User Interface

Software

In an Arduino environment, input from each sensor is converted into 10-bit data. The data is smoothed out by applying five pieces of data in a row to the moving average in order to reduce the noise and is then sent to Java/Processing. In Processing environment, we normalize sensor data and apply an SVM algorithm with rbf kernel (C = 10, gamma = 1.0) to classify facial expressions in real-time. Figure 7 shows the visualization of our system. The emoticon shows the result of classification. The bar graph represents the raw data. The yellow circles correspond to the positions of each sensor, and their sizes correlate to the normalized values of each sensor. We use only one piece of frame data because we aim at classifying facial expression states.

Machine Learning

1. When a user wears our eyewear device and makes a neutral expression, we set the baseline of each data(BLV) as 0.5.

2. The range of each sensor value ($Range$) is determined during the calibration process. In this stage, a user dynamically moves his/her facial muscles, and the maximum (Max) and minimum (Min) values of each data are determined. With these values, the normalized sensor value (NSV) is calculated as follows. The raw data collected from each time frame is defined as $SensorInput$. $Tolerance$ is chosen as 40 experimentally.

$$Range = (Max - Min) + Tolerance \tag{1}$$

$$\begin{cases} NSV = 0.5 + (SensorInput - BLV)/Range \\ if\, NSV > 1,\, then\, NSV = 1 \\ if\, NSV < 0,\, then\, NSV = 0 \end{cases} \tag{2}$$

$Range$ includes $Tolerance$ since there is a tradeoff with relying only on the acquired data.

- Advantage: Normalization can set the appropriate range of each sensor by measuring the range of sensor data that is different among them according to the geometry of each user's face and the position in which each sensor located. The normalization can improve the robustness because it can accommodate the distance changes between the sensors and the skin surface.
- Disadvantage: The position of the device during calibration phase is not always stable. If a user moves his/her facial muscles too dynamically, this movement changes the position of the eyewear. It changes Max and Min values in an unwanted way. Also if the facial movement during calibration is not enough, it can reduce the information. Therefore, we cannot always normalize the sensor values in the right way.

3. During the learning phase, normalized data is stored with a facial expression label where users choose a desired output for the normalized input. For each label, input from one frame is used.

4. For real-time classification, the normalized value is applied to SVM that is trained with the dataset collected at the previous step.

Algorithm

In addition to the trained data that includes the output label and normalized input, the calculated value (CV) from two different sensor is also used for SVM. The calculation formula for $(S_i, S_j \mid 1 \leqq i, j \leqq 17)$ is shown below

$$\begin{cases} CV = (S_i - S_j)/2 + 0.5 \\ if\, CV > 1,\, then\, CV = 1 \\ if\, CV < 0,\, then\, CV = 0 \end{cases} \tag{3}$$

Sensor placement is shown in Figure 6. We considered the calculated value from adjacent sensors integrated into the lower part of the front frame and sensors that have a vertical relationship. The adjacent sensors of the lower part are important because the surface is smooth and skin is considered as an elastic model, thus they correlate with each other as discussed by Ogata et al. [14]. The data from the sensors that have a vertical relationship also helps because the relationship between the position of the eyewear and the face can be partly considered. All told, we used 33 dimension (normalized input: 17 + adjacent data: 7 [(10,11), (11,12), (12,13), (13,14), (14,15), (15,16), (16,17)] + vertical data: 9 [(1,10), (2,11), (3,12), (4,13), (5,14), (6,15), (7,16), (8,17), (9,17)]).

SYSTEM EVALUATION

For the evaluation, we conducted three experiments. In the first experiment, we obtained a dataset to evaluate the accuracy immediately after user-dependent training with a confusion matrix to prove user dependency. Also, the trade-off between the number of sensors and accuracy was evaluated in this dataset. In the second experiment, we had a trial for multiple day use to check a possibility of long term use. In the third experiment, we proved the robustness while walking. We also described the observations from a demonstration at SIGGRAPH Emerging Technologies 2015.

Evaluation 1 in Basic Setup

We asked eight users (six males and two females / four Japanese, one French, one Chinese, one Taiwanese, and one Sri Lankan / average age: 27.3) to participate in our evaluation. They were asked to sit in a chair and mimic the pictures of an American male making facial expressions described by Ekman [3]. Each time a user looks straight and makes a neutral facial expression, we set the baseline for each sensor. We collected data of eight facial expressions in different poses: Look straight (three times), look up (three times), look down (three times), look left (two times), look right (two times), and take off and put on again (two times). In one recording of each facial expression, 10 pieces of data were collected at regular 50-millisecond intervals. Overall, 1200 pieces of data (8 facial expressions * 10 datasets * 15 times) were collected from all users. All recordings were performed indoors (Figure 8).

Accuracy with User-Dependent Training

First, we tested the accuracy of each user's performance with user dependent training. For each dataset, one recording (10 data) of each facial expression are divided, with the former half as training set (5*8*15 = 600 data) and the latter half as test set (600 data). The training set was applied to SVM with rbf kernel (C = 10, gamma = 1.0). We achieved 92.8% accuracy on average (Facial-Expression-based result was 84.3% - 97.8%. User-based result : 84.8% - 99.2%.). By learning the data of each face direction, our device can classify correctly regardless of the facial expression. Table 1 shows the confusion matrix of the results. As seen in the matrix, disgust can be similar to anger or fear. In addition, surprise and fear are close facial expressions with a 4.7% error to each other.

Table 1. Confusion Matrix (with User-Dependent Training)

	Classified Results								
		N	H	D	A	Su	F	Sa	C
Actual Value	Neutral(N)	96.8%	0.7%	0.2%	0%	1.2%	1.0%	0.2%	0%
	Happiness(H)	0.3%	98.3%	0.5%	0%	0%	0%	0%	0.8%
	Disgust(D)	1.7%	0.2%	84.3%	3.2%	0%	5.5%	3.7%	1.5%
	Anger(A)	0.3%	0%	0.7%	96.5%	0.8%	0.3%	1.3%	0%
	Surprise(Su)	2.0%	0%	1.2%	0.2%	91.2%	4.7%	0.8%	0%
	Fear(F)	1.5%	0%	4.2%	0.8%	4.7%	87.5%	0%	1.3%
	Sadness (Sa)	4.5%	0%	2.5%	1.8%	0.8%	4.7%	85.7%	0%
	contempt(C)	1.5%	0.3%	0%	0%	0%	0.3%	0%	97.8%

User Dependency

Second, we evaluated the user dependency. We trained with each user's training data and tested with all users' test data. The results can be seen in Table 2. The scores are quite low: Accuracy is 48.0% at most (using training data from User A and test data from User G). This result suggests that, with the current system, a user requires individual training for classification.

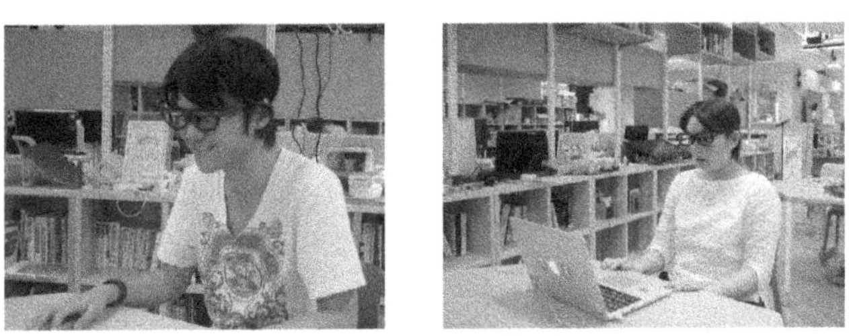

Figure 8. Experimental Setting

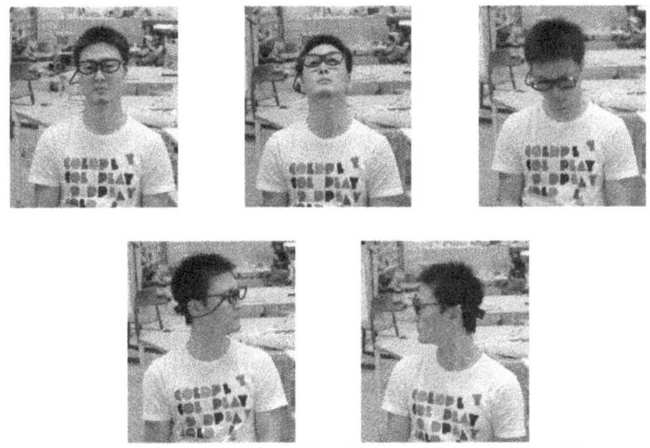

Figure 9. Evaluation with Different Face Directions

Table 2. User Dependency Matrix

	Test Data								
		A	B	C	D	E	F	G	H
Training Data	A	99.2%	36.8%	31.8%	34.5%	28.8%	40.5%	48.0%	28.3%
	B	39.2%	98.7%	23.3%	13.5%	30.0%	33.8%	32.8%	26.7%
	C	42.5%	22.3%	84.8%	37.7%	21.0%	37.3%	40.7%	22.2%
	D	19.8%	29.8%	33.5%	85.0%	32.0%	25.3%	30.5%	18.0%
	E	23.3%	27.3%	18.7%	20.8%	89.3%	17.3%	39.8%	39.5%
	F	44.3%	34.2%	28.2%	27.8%	27.7%	97.3%	35.0%	34.2%
	G	43.8%	31.0%	24.7%	20.0%	27.7%	28.8%	88.7%	28.5%
	H	12.5%	25.2%	15.7%	14.8%	26.2%	17.8%	29.8%	95.2%

Table 3 shows the confusion matrix of all the results. Though there is user dependency, happy expressions can be recognized with relatively high accuracy (71.9%). The other facial expressions did not show good performances (e.g. sadness: 17.2%, contempt: 22.7%).

Table 3. Confusion Matrix(User-Dependency)

	Classified Results								
		N	H	D	A	Su	F	Sa	C
Actual Value	Neutral(N)	74.9%	1.1%	6.3%	1.3%	5.2%	3.2%	2.6%	5.3%
	Happy(H)	5.3%	71.9%	2.6%	5.1%	0.4%	7.7%	2.8%	4.2%
	Disgust(D)	15.8%	7.5%	23.5%	12.2%	14.0%	17.5%	4.1%	5.2%
	Angry(A)	14.9%	7.8%	13.4%	26.6%	13.8%	15.5%	4.9%	3.1%
	Surprise(Su)	27.1%	3.2%	10.1%	4.1%	30.9%	11.7%	8.9%	4.2%
	Fear(F)	14.5%	6.5%	11.4%	8.8%	17.3%	27.7%	5.5%	8.2%
	Sad (Sa)	27.8%	8.6%	7.4%	6.4%	15.9%	13.6%	17.2%	3.1%
	contempt(C)	29.5%	7.8%	8.6%	5.0%	11.7%	11.2%	3.7%	22.7%

Figure10 shows the distribution of sensor value on each facial expression from User A. The sensor number was associated with Figure 6.

Number of Sensors

Next, we evaluated the trade-off between accuracy and the number of sensors. We used all data from eight users. We separated data into training set (4800 data) and test set (4800 data) and applied SVM in the same way as in Basic Setup Analysis. For the selection of sensors, first we chose one sensor with which the result of SVM showed the best accuracy. Next, we added to SVM one more sensor different from the sensors we had already used to obtain the best accuracy. We repeated the process until all sensors were used. For this analysis, we only applied the normalized 17 dimensional data to SVM.

As Figure 11 depicts, the experimental result shows 84.1% accuracy with 17 sensors. The accuracy improves with more sensors. With 13 sensors, our system achieves more than 80% (81.0%) accuracy. Sensors 1, 9, 12, and 15 are left out. The sensor numbers correspond to those in Figure 6. Sensors 1 and 9 and also 12 and 15 are located at symmetric positions

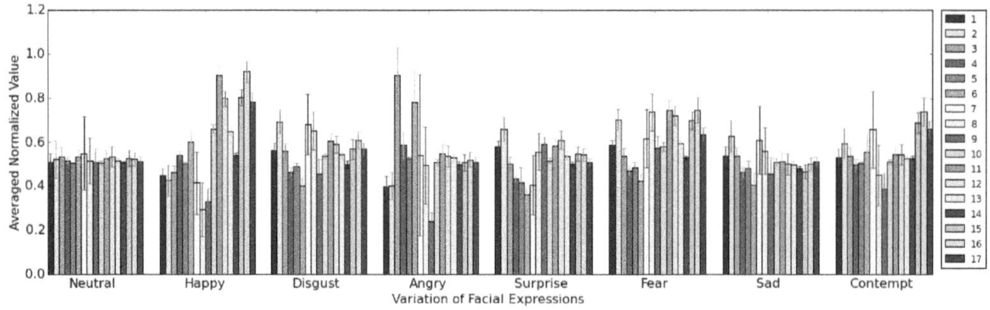

Figure 10. Distribution of Sensor Value on Each Facial Expression

at the opposite ends of the frame. The further the sensor from the center of the face, the longer the distance between eyewear frame and skin surface on face. We think it makes the sensors have less information because they can be influenced more by ambient light and photo reflective sensors works well with closer distance than 10.00 mm.

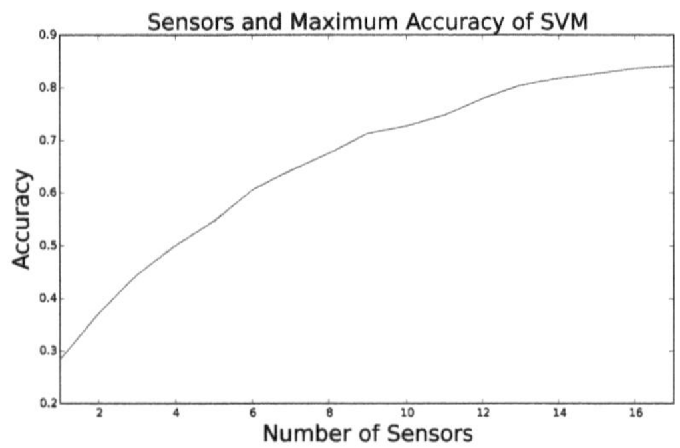

Figure 11. Trade-off of Number of Sensors

Evaluation 2: Robustness for Multiple Use

We also collected data from three of the participants on different days with the same procedure (only when they look straight). For each day, we collected data about eight facial expressions three times (8*10*3 = 240 data). We used data collected from three different days. We used data from two days as training data and the data from the other day as test data. The results are shown in Table 4. On the whole, the averaged accuracy for three users was 78.1%. It suggests the possibility of long-term use. In the confusion matrix, the most dominant error was classifying 33.3% of the anger cases and 23.3% of fear cases as disgust.

Table 4. Accuracy on a different day

	Day1	Day2	Day3	Average
A	83.8%	91.7%	90.4%	88.6%
E	72.9%	70.8%	69.2%	71.0%
F	86.3%	69.6%	68.8%	74.9%

Evaluation3: Usage during Walking

For this experiment, we collected 480 pieces of data from each user. Four users participated (two males and two females / two Japanese, one Chinese, and one German / Age: 25-59). Users were asked to sit in a chair and wear the device. After the calibration, we collected 10 pieces of data of eight facial expressions when they looked straight. We repeated the process three times (Data set A: 240 data). After that, users were asked to walk in a corridor at natural speed. We collected 10 pieces of data of eight facial expressions three times while they were walking. (Data set B: 240 data) We used Data set A as training set and Data set B as test set. The result was an average of 73.2%, which is slight worse than in Evaluation 2. We assume this is because walking caused to change the eyewear position.

Demonstration at SIGGRAPH Emerging Technologies 2015

We have demonstrated our eyewear device at SIGGRAPH Emerging Technologies 2015. During the demonstration, we had more than 200 users from international background. We found that the size and shape of eyewear needs to be adjusted to each user for accurate recognition. There are three major issues we had. 1) The eyewear device sometimes slipped out of place when some user changed facial expressions. It changed the accuracy of the recognition because the device based on the proximity sensing between front frame of the eyewear and skin surface on face. 2) Specific sensors located between users' eyebrows saturated and did not work well for users who have well - defined features despite they did not show any facial expression. 3) The sensors placed on the top measures the distance to eyelid or eyebrows depending on the shape of users' face or the position of the eyewear. Therefore, the meaning of sensor data can be different with each user, requiring individual training and calibration. Due to these 3 reasons, the eyewear should be customized to each user. We observed that the eyewear seems to work better for Caucasian compared to Asian people as they tend to have more expressive faces.

FIELD TRIALS

As initial field trials in daily life, we recorded facial expressions of a user in a daily living/home scenario: A 90 minutes time series consists of playing Go game with a computer (a board game involving two players originated in China, 32 minutes), playing with a dog (16 minutes), watching a sitcom (an episode of "Friends", 22 minutes), and programming on a desk (20 minutes). Also, playing a shooting game with friends(won and lost: 10 minutes) and watching an episode of

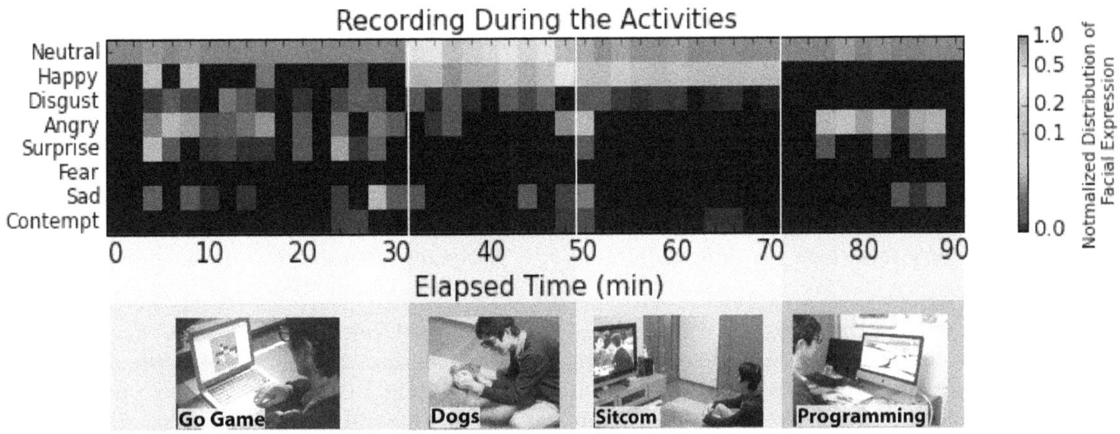

Figure 12. Recording of Facial Expressions for long time

crime drama "Crime Scene Investigation(CSI)" (45 minutes) were recorded on the other day so that we can compare 1) the activities include social interaction (human-human, human-animal: "game", "playing with dog") and the activities include several activities performed alone by the user and 2) the same activity in different contexts (e.g. gaming win-lose, tv comedy-drama). Figure 12 shows the frequency distribution of recognized facial expressions during the recording period. The figure presents a normalized distribution in each 2min with a logarithm contrast enhancement.

The distribution of facial expressions varied on the activities. For instance, many happy expressions were observed during interacting with the dog. The sitcom also caused happy expressions at intervals of neutral ones. While playing Go Game, negative expression was sometimes shown, but at the end, happy expression was dominant probably because he must have won finally.

When the user did the activities by himself, the user tended to show fewer facial expressions. For example, the programming activities induced the angry expression; yet, the dominant expression is neutral. On the other hand, the user shows other more diverse facial expressions (not neutral) while interacting with the dog. The user also showed diverse facial expressions while playing the shooting game with the user's friend. The result is shown in Figure 13. During the game, the user presented more facial expressions such as happy and angry expressions while playing with another person comparing to the time when the user played alone with the computer (the go game). Social interaction seems to cause more facial expressions. In other words, facial expressions can be an indication for communication between people.

However, the distribution of facial expressions also varies according to the results of the interactions (in our case the game)(Figure 14). When the user won a game, the user showed more happy expression, especially in the latter half. During the lost game, the user showed negative expressions and the dominant expression is anger. However, we can still recognize that the user enjoyed the lost game, because the user frequently showed a happy expression.

When watching the one episode of the sitcom "Friends", the user sometimes showed happy expression. On the other day, the user watched the episode of the drama "CSI" that includes the scene such as murder, dissecting the human body and bleeding. The user showed the disgust expression and surprise expression. The user showed the different expressions that correspond to the contents of TV. The distribution of facial expressions can be a good feedback for the contents creators.

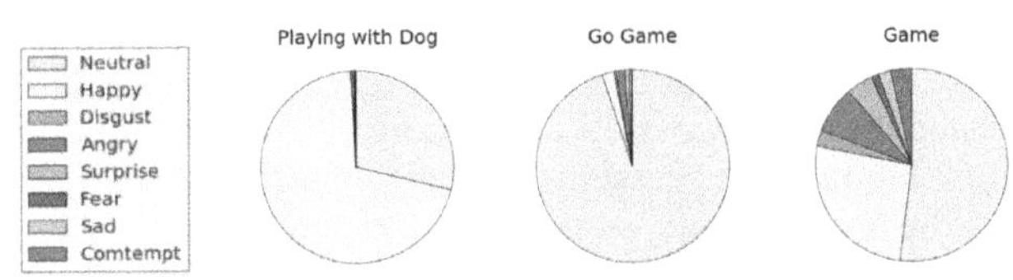

Figure 13. Facial Expression Ratio during Activities

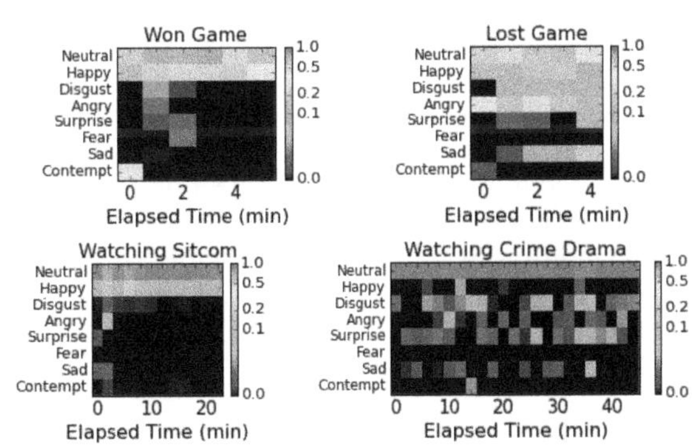

Figure 14. Comparison between Activities

DISCUSSION

We achieved high accuracy 92.8% in the basic setup. It shows a potential of our proposed approach even though many users mentioned that they did not identify the clear difference between surprise and fear, fear and disgust, and disgust and anger when they looked at the pictures for the instruction. If a user makes a very similar facial expression for anger and disgust, most disgust cases may be miscategorized as anger or vice versa.

The user dependency matrix shows the need for user dependent training. In the current conditions, it is necessary to have a personalized training. We do not think this is a big problem as discussed by Scheirer et al. [18], eyewear is a personalized item. Thus, we can design personalized eyewear, and it can be used for a long time by one user. However, we believe external datasets help to reduce the cost of the learning phase and improve the accuracy of recognition. We might try to classify a group of people that share the same culture on facial expressions.

In the long term use and walking situations, the accuracy was reduced. It can be changed due to the physical condition of the device such as the position of the device, artifacts from ambient light. Another factor to reduce accuracy was the difficulty of reproducing the same facial expressions in different conditions and trials. For example, it is difficult for users to make exactly the same specific facial expression many times. They make slightly different facial expressions with different intensities. It makes similar facial expressions difficult to classify. This is controversial because our facial expressions in daily life have the same characteristics. However, it can be solved by increasing the number of training dataset with many trials.

In field trials, "angry" facial expressions were recognized during computer programming or Go game. However, it can be related to mental effort, confusion or frustration instead of "angry" emotion as facial expressions contain the information more than basic emotions. For example, Shichuan et al. suggested the existence of 21 expressions [2]. The information of complex facial expressions is useful in terms of understanding the user in depth, we may consider other sensory inputs to predict them. We regard our work as a first step to recognize complex facial expressions.

LIMITATIONS

We assume only facial expression changes cause skin deformation. However, physiological behavior such as yawning, rubbing one's eyes, and resting one's cheek in one's hand can also cause skin deformation. These can be artifacts of facial expression recognition. Moreover, reflection to skin or sensor value from photo reflective sensors changes in accordance with the condition of a user's face. Factors such as tanned skin, sweat, makeup, and a swollen face in the morning may require users to do external calibration and training.

The eyewear only collects data from the sensors around eyes. Although movement of the mouth is partly detectable, there are several mouth movements our system cannot detect because mouth movement and cheek deformation do not have one-to-one correspondence. For instance, the movement of opening a mouth lowers cheeks slightly, which makes the distance between the eyewear frame and the skin surface longer. Therefore, our system cannot recognize which movement of mouth or cheek makes the distance longer.

CONCLUSION AND FUTURE WORK

We presented a novel smart eyewear that recognizes a wearer's facial expressions. With the eyewear device, we conducted an experiment to recognize eight universal facial expressions. The experimental result shows recognition rates: 92.8% for one-time use and 78.1 % for continuous use in a different day after a training process. Also, we designed our prototype looks like everyday eyewear by using small photo reflective sensors so as to be socially acceptable. This enables facial expression recognition by our smart eyewear in daily life. Our system still has room for improvement in terms of calibration and accuracy, yet we believe it is an important step for quantifying the flow of facial expressions toward assessing affect in daily life.

We regard following three issues as our future work.
First, during the experiments, the participants made intentional facial expressions, although the goal of our work is to capture natural facial expressions. Of course, these are similar, but it is true there is certain gap between intentional and natural expressions. To capture unintentional facial expressions, we need to design a natural learning process.

Second, we use photo reflective sensors that function on the basis of IR reflection. Because sunlight contains enormous amounts of IR light, sensor data saturates when the sensors are exposed to direct sunlight. With the current system, the sensors are not covered by anything and are easily influenced by strong ambient light though we apply light modulation to LED of a photo reflective sensor. Therefore, we will design an optical filter to reduce the influence of ambient light.

Finally, we used a classification algorithm, thus the intensity of facial expressions is not measured. This means the current system cannot measure complicated facial expressions such as one that contains a smile and surprise. Since our facial expressions are not always simple in daily life, and the subtle differences may have different meanings in our affect, we need to consider those complicated or subtle facial expressions to detect affect deeply as a future work.

ACKNOWLEDGMENTS

This research was supported by CREST, JST

REFERENCES

1. R.A. Calvo and S. D'Mello. 2010. Affect Detection: An Interdisciplinary Review of Models, Methods, and Their Applications. *Affective Computing, IEEE Transactions on* 1, 1 (Jan 2010), 18–37. DOI: http://dx.doi.org/10.1109/T-AFFC.2010.1

2. Shichuan Du, Yong Tao, and Aleix M. Martinez. 2014. Compound facial expressions of emotion. *Proceedings of the National Academy of Sciences* 111, 15 (2014), E1454–E1462. DOI: http://dx.doi.org/10.1073/pnas.1322355111

3. Paul Ekman. 1989. The argument and evidence about universals in facial expres-sions. *Handbook of social psychophysiology* (1989), 143–164.

4. Paul Ekman and Wallace V Friesen. 1977. Facial action coding system. (1977).

5. Kurara Fukumoto, Tsutomu Terada, and Masahiko Tsukamoto. 2013. A Smile/Laughter Recognition Mechanism for Smile-based Life Logging. In *AH*. ACM,

New York, NY, USA, 8. DOI: http://dx.doi.org/10.1145/2459236.2459273

6. A. Gruebler and K. Suzuki. 2014. Design of a Wearable Device for Reading Positive Expressions from Facial EMG Signals. *Affective Computing, IEEE Transactions on* 5, 3 (July 2014), 227–237. DOI: http://dx.doi.org/10.1109/TAFFC.2014.2313557
7. T. Kanade, J.F. Cohn, and YingLi Tian. 2000. Comprehensive database for facial expression analysis. In *Automatic Face and Gesture Recognition, 2000. Proceedings. Fourth IEEE International Conference on.* 46–53. DOI: http://dx.doi.org/10.1109/AFGR.2000.840611
8. Dacher et al. Keltner. 2003. Facial expression of emotion. In *Handbook of affective sciences.* Oxford University, New York, NY, USA, 415–432.
9. Shinji Kimura, Masaaki Fukuomoto, and Tsutomu Horikoshi. 2013. Eyeglass-based Hands-free Videophone. In *Proceedings of the 2013 International Symposium on Wearable Computers (ISWC '13).* ACM, New York, NY, USA, 117–124. DOI: http://dx.doi.org/10.1145/2493988.2494330
10. Hao Li, Laura Trutoiu, Kyle Olszewski, Lingyu Wei, Tristan Trutna, Pei-Lun Hsieh, Aaron Nicholls, and Chongyang Ma. 2015. Facial Performance Sensing Head-mounted Display. *ACM Trans. Graph.* 34, 4, Article 47 (July 2015), 9 pages. DOI: http://dx.doi.org/10.1145/2766939
11. Gwen Littlewort, Ian Fasel, M Stewart Bartlett, and Javier R Movellan. 2002. Fully automatic coding of basic expressions from video. *University of California, San Diego, San Diego, CA* 92093 (2002).
12. David Matsumoto. 1992. More evidence for the universality of a contempt expression. *Motivation and Emotion* 16, 4 (1992), 363–368. DOI: http://dx.doi.org/10.1007/BF00992972
13. Hiromi Nakamura and Homei Miyashita. 2010. Control of Augmented Reality Information Volume by Glabellar Fader. In *Proceedings of the 1st Augmented Human International Conference (AH '10).* ACM, New York, NY, USA, Article 20, 3 pages. DOI: http://dx.doi.org/10.1145/1785455.1785475
14. Masa Ogata, Yuta Sugiura, Yasutoshi Makino, Masahiko Inami, and Michita Imai. 2013. SenSkin: Adapting Skin As a Soft Interface. In *Proceedings of the 26th Annual ACM Symposium on User Interface Software and Technology (UIST '13).* ACM, New York, NY, USA, 539–544. DOI: http://dx.doi.org/10.1145/2501988.2502039
15. Masa Ogata, Yuta Sugiura, Hirotaka Osawa, and Michita Imai. 2012. iRing: Intelligent Ring Using Infrared Reflection. In *Proceedings of the 25th Annual ACM Symposium on User Interface Software and Technology (UIST '12).* ACM, New York, NY, USA, 131–136. DOI: http://dx.doi.org/10.1145/2380116.2380135
16. R.W. Picard and J. Healey. 1997. Affective wearables. *Personal Technologies* 1, 4 (1997), 231–240. DOI: http://dx.doi.org/10.1007/BF01682026
17. Rosalind W Picard. 1995. Affective computing. (1995).
18. Jocelyn Scheirer, Raul Fernandez, and Rosalind W. Picard. 1999. Expression Glasses: A Wearable Device for Facial Expression Recognition. In *CHI '99 Extended Abstracts on Human Factors in Computing Systems (CHI EA '99).* ACM, New York, NY, USA, 262–263. DOI:http://dx.doi.org/10.1145/632716.632878
19. Yingli Tian, Takeo Kanade, and JeffreyF. Cohn. 2011. Facial Expression Recognition. In *Handbook of Face Recognition*, Stan Z. Li and Anil K. Jain (Eds.). Springer London, 487–519. DOI: http://dx.doi.org/10.1007/978-0-85729-932-1_19
20. Ying-li Tian, Takeo Kanade, and Jeffrey F. Cohn. 2001. Recognizing Action Units for Facial Expression Analysis. *IEEE Trans. Pattern Anal. Mach. Intell.* 23, 2 (Feb. 2001), 97–115. DOI: http://dx.doi.org/10.1109/34.908962
21. Hitomi Tsujita and Jun Rekimoto. 2011. Smiling Makes Us Happier: Enhancing Positive Mood and Communication with Smile-encouraging Digital Appliances. In *Proceedings of the 13th International Conference on Ubiquitous Computing (UbiComp '11).* ACM, New York, NY, USA, 1–10. DOI: http://dx.doi.org/10.1145/2030112.2030114
22. Shigeo Yoshida, Tomohiro Tanikawa, Sho Sakurai, Michitaka Hirose, and Takuji Narumi. 2013. Manipulation of an Emotional Experience by Real-time Deformed Facial Feedback. In *Proceedings of the 4th Augmented Human International Conference (AH '13).* ACM, New York, NY, USA, 35–42. DOI: http://dx.doi.org/10.1145/2459236.2459243

Towards Using Mobile, Head-Worn Displays in Cultural Heritage: User Requirements and a Research Agenda

Natalia Vainstein
The University of Haifa
Haifa, Israel
tsvikak@is.haifa.ac.il

Tsvi Kuflik
The University of Haifa
Haifa, Israel
ylanir@is.haifa.ac.il

Joel Lanir
The University of Haifa
Haifa, Israel
nataliashtepa@gmail.com

ABSTRACT

Augmented reality (AR) technology has the potential to enrich our daily lives in many aspects. One of them is the museum visit experience. Nowadays, state of the art mobile museum visitor guides provide us with rich personalized, context aware information. However, these systems have one major drawback – they force the visitor to hold the guide and to look at its screen. The utilization of smart-glasses technology allows providing a wearable AR display without the necessity to hold the guide and to look at it and without distracting the user from the real object. This paper describes initial steps towards the implementation of a head-worn display (HWD) museum visitor guide – the results of users' requirements elicitation process, the implementation of a first research prototype and initial insights gathered during the process.

Author Keywords

Augmented reality; Head-worn display; Museum visitors' guide.

ACM Classification Keywords

H.1.2 [User/Machine Systems]: Human factors,
H.5.1 [Multimedia Information Systems] Artificial, augmented, and virtual realities, H.5.2 [User Interfaces] User centered design

INTRODUCTION

Wearable technologies have the potential to enrich our daily lives in many aspects. One of them is the museum visit experience. Nowadays, state of the art mobile museum visitor guides enable museums and other cultural heritage (CH) sites to move away from short textual labels allowing minimal information near exhibits and providing visitors with rich, personalized, context-aware multimedia presentations [1,8]. However, these systems have one major drawback – they force the visitor to hold the guide and to focus on its display (or they provide only audio). The utilization of HWD technologies allows providing a wearable AR display without the necessity to hold the guide and to look at it and without distracting the user from the real object. In recent years, large numbers of relatively low-cost, see-through smart glasses are appearing. Mirza and Sarayeddine [13] reviewed state of the art see-through technologies and the key challenges these technologies face in order to develop a platform that will enable affordable HWDs for the consumer market. Their focus is on see-through technologies for wearable AR displays. Form factor, cost, ease of use, and display performance are reported as major challenges for consumer adoption of AR HWDs. A comparison of the various technologies and how they relate to these aspects found out that "Of the various waveguide technologies discussed, the reflective type seems to be the most promising for large scale consumer deployment. The main advantages are the lower cost, plastic substrate, and lack of color issues. Optical technologies are finally emerging that will enable consumer oriented wearable AR display products to become a reality in the near future".

This study focus on exploring the potential of HWD to enhance the museum visit experience. HWD are not new in the area of CH and museum guides [17]. Still, to date, few prototype implementations in museums have been demonstrated ([3] and [15] are two examples), and even fewer actual HWD guides exist in actual museums. We follow a user centered design in the development of a HWD museum guide. Thus, we first aim to fully understand user requirements for such a guide. We present the opinions of potential users about the needs and usefulness of a HWD museum guide, trying to understand also the reasoning and general guidelines that stem from these requirements. These requirements drive the development of a smart glasses museum visitors' guide prototype which later will be evaluated in a museum setting, with the ultimate goal of improving the overall museum visit experience.

The rest of this paper is organized as follows: first we introduce some related work; next we present the requirements elicitation and analysis study, followed by a description of an initial prototype that was developed and lessons learned in the process. Finally, we describe the future evaluation of the system, planned to take place in a realistic setting.

IUI'16, March 07-10, 2016, Sonoma, CA, USA
© 2016 ACM. ISBN 978-1-4503-4137-0/16/03…$15.00
DOI: http://dx.doi.org/10.1145/2856767.2856802

BACKGROUND AND RELATED WORK

The museum is a unique area for experimentation with novel, mobile technology, as described in [1]. AR and VR were already experimented in museums more than twenty years ago [16], however, only in recent years, with the appearance of commercial small, light-weight wearable devices, the potential of HWDs in museums has started to materialize. Past studies were carried out to evaluate the potential contribution of HWDs and AR to the field of CH. Damala et al. [7] experimented with an AR-based museum guide, using a portable computer, (without a HWD) and found out that "AR assisted interfaces can indeed successfully facilitate visitors intuitively switch their focus and attention from the physical to the digital space and vice versa, even in the complex context of the museum space." Schiele et al. [14] describes a wearable VR device, which includes image recognition capability. By looking at real objects, the users received a VR presentation of animations and sound. Most of the users gave a positive feedback to the system. Mase et al. [12] presented the Meta Museum concept and the VisTa system which uses a VR HMD system that visualizes the evolution of an ancient village in Japan. The authors noted that they plan also to produce a see-through (AR) system, but no further details were provided. An application of a HWD as a museum guide was developed and demonstrated by Sparacino et al. [15] at the museum wearable project, where smart glasses were part of a mobile, personalized and context aware museum visitors guide system. The system was made by a lightweight CPU hosted inside a small shoulder pack and a small, lightweight HWD which was called then private-eye display. The display was a commercial monocular, VGA-resolution, color, clip-on screen attached to a pair of sturdy headphones. The system provided personalized information by using position and time information for inferring users' interests and assigning the user to one of three different types (that determines the information provided to the visitor). The exhibit objects were augmented with video, images and text, displayed around the object of the interest. Vlahakis et al. [17] presented three implementations of a visitor guide for an archeological site, two of them were handheld devices and one was a Laptop with an HMD and earphone devices that had also an AR display. The system included descriptions, navigation information, and personalization of a visitor's tour in the archeological site. Visitors of the Olympia site in Greece tested the guide. They praised the guide for realism, but indicated that during walking they felt uncomfortable to wear it. Recently, Chang et al. [6], described a mobile guide system (not HMD based) that integrates art appreciation instruction with AR that was designed as an auxiliary tool for painting appreciation. The learning performance of three groups of visiting participants was explored: AR-guided, audio-guided, and nonguided. The results showed that compared to the audio- and nonguided participants, the AR guide effectively enhanced visitors' learning effectiveness, promoted their flow experience, and extended the amount of time the visitors spent focusing on the paintings. Banowosari et al. [3] briefly presented a design concept of an AR application using smart-glasses for the Indonesia Wayang Museum, suggesting some guidelines for presentation preparation and interaction.

On a different aspect, Alce et al. [2] explored the applicability of the Wizard of Oz method for eliciting users' feedback about the use of simulated smart glasses with AR capability in the scenario of a city tour and found it to be a useful tool for that purpose. However, they focused mainly on the classical usability aspects of their simulated system. As we can see, most HWD studies in CH focused on exploring and demonstrating the potential of AR and HWDs to enrich and enhance the museum visit experience. However, only few of them went beyond demonstration and collection of users' feedback to the specific application or tried to study and address users' needs. In this study, somewhat similar to [2, 3] we focus on users and understanding their requirements from smart-glasses based museum visitors' guide.

USER REQUIREMENTS FOR GLASSES-BASED GUIDE

Given our focus on understanding visitors' needs first, a qualitative study was carried out to understand the requirements of potential users for a smart-glasses museum guide. The study involved 17 participants (ages 19-57), who have visited a museum at least once. Data was collected by semi-structured interviews, where for each question the participant was asked to explain the reason for the answer. Before the interviews, participants wore and experimented with a Vuzix M100 smart glasses device to understand the potential for such a device at the museum. Users' requirements were elicited from the transcripts of the interviews. During the interviews, 94% (16 out of 17) of the participants answered that they think that a HWD museum guide will be useful and they will be glad to use it.

During the interview the participants indicated requirements with features that they would prefer to have in the guide and features that they would prefer not to have in the guide. After a qualitative analysis of the interview results, we assembled together several topics for requirements. These topics are discussed next (Given the fact that users provided several requirements in different categories, the numbers do not add up to 17).

System proactiveness

An important feature of a HWD mobile guide is its ability to provide continuous information related to its surrounding. However, in a context-aware system, the question is whether the system should keep the user in control, only responding to user requests, or should the system take initiative and propose information and services. Most participants (11 out of 17) preferred to keep the user in control, where the user decides when to receive information. Five participants preferred a proactive system in which the system anticipates what the user is doing and provides information accordingly. Three of them asked for a location (gaze) aware system. Three participants asked to be able to set up the mode of operation (proactive/passive). This preference for control over proactiveness is in sync with user preferences with a handheld mobile guide [11].

Interaction with the device

There are many options for how to interact with information when using a HWD. Users' interaction preferences for a HWD mobile guide varied greatly. There were 12 requests to control the glasses with an accompanied mobile device, 8 requests for using physical touch on the side of the glasses (through buttons or slide gestures), 5 requests for voice commands and 6 requests for mid-air hand gestures. It is interesting to note that 8 participants objected to voice commands, mostly because of the quiet environment of the museum, and the request for privacy.

Device characteristics

A large group of requirements related to the device's characteristics. The users wanted a light weight device (17), and the ability to adjust/remove the display (11). Some users preferred a display for both eyes located at the center of the glasses (7) while others preferred a one eye, top display similar to Google glass or the Vusix M100 (6). It is interesting to note that even aesthetics of the device was commented as important by one user.

Information delivery

When asked about what type of information they would like to receive, visitors expressed a wide variety of preferences towards different types of media. This included text (6), Audio (14), video (11), and images (11). This demonstrates the need for a variety of media options. Having information registered to the real-world position of the museum objects (i.e., see-through AR), was also important (13). It is interesting to note that a large number of users objected to text (10) as they said it is not easy to read with the glasses. Some objected to video (4) as it distracts the visitor from the museum and some (4) objected to audio.

Personalization and privacy

Most users want to be able to choose from multiple content items (13), yet they still expect personalization (10), and acknowledge that the system should monitor them for that (12). Some also agree that the system would collect information about them from external sources (4). Others asked to be in control of data collection (2). The users expected the system to implicitly recognize their interest (like when standing a long time in front of an exhibit) and accordingly extend its explanations (3), or provide users with the ability to explicitly do that (6). However, some users objected to the need to choose content (4), and some objected to any need for filling up any form for personalization (6). There was some objection to monitoring (4) and data collection from external sources (6), and one participant mentioned that data should not be saved after the visit.

Additional features

Users seem to be aware of classical functions and limitations of mobile devices at the museum. They asked for indoor navigation support (8), recommendations (6), group interaction (1), addressing different audiences, e.g. children (1) translation capabilities (1) and presenting battery status (1). In addition, some users expressed the need for multilingual guide (2) and the need for operating instructions in the users' language (1).

User preference about content presentation

Two users found the ability to control the size of the virtual image using the glasses an important option (2). Other requests were that text size should be readable (3), audio volume should be adjustable (1), the user should be able to select the type of media presented (2), fast forward it (2), stop it (2), and that the guide should proactively stop presentation when the user moves away (3).

Training

One participant explicitly asked that "At the beginning of the visit the user should receive training". According to the participant, no matter which type of interaction this device uses, thorough training should take place.

PROTOTYPE DEVELOPMENT

We developed the first prototype of a HWD image-recognition guide. It enables the user to easily receive information about exhibits of interest. For this prototype, four artworks at the Hecht museum[1] were used for initial experimentation.

Architecture and system

The system includes two parts (see Figure 1): a client and a server. The client is an Android application, which is installed on a Vuzix M100 smart glasses. The server includes server implementation and an image recognition function. The image recognition is implemented using Speeded-Up Robust Features (SURF) algorithm [4]. C++ Open CV libraries were used for development. In addition we added a decision rule for images similarity, based on the similarity found between the image taken by the user and a set of exhibits images taken from different angles.

For receiving information about a specific exhibit, the user should press a button on the smart glasses. At this point, the Android application takes a picture from the user's viewpoint and transfers it to the server that performs image recognition. Once the object of interest is identified, the server sends appropriate complementary information to the Android application for presentation (Figure 1 illustrates the process).

[1] http://mushecht.haifa.ac.il/

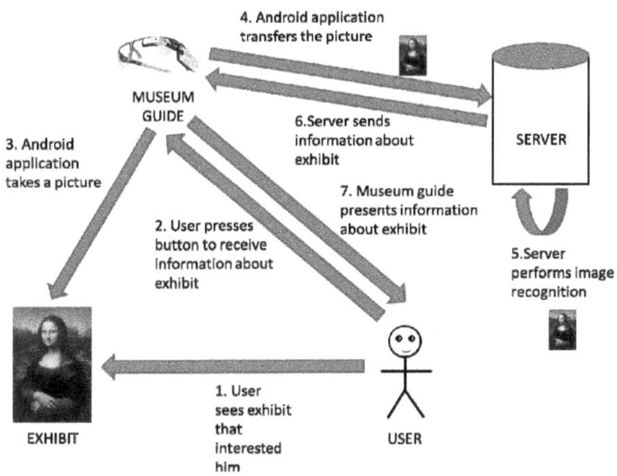

Figure 1: System architecture

Lessons learned

Lessons learned from the HWD museum guide prototype implementation include:

1. The reference images should be with minimum background and frames of the pictures. The backgrounds and frames of the pictures can be similar for different exhibits. This similarity inserts noise to the image recognition process.
2. For better image recognition, it is important to use reference images with similar quality to the pictures that the user takes in real time. It is important to note that image processing utilities, can change the image quality.
3. Taking pictures with a particular device and a particular application causes all pictures to be of the same image dimensions. For exhibits with nonstandard dimensions, this fact makes it difficult to capture this exhibit in order to store it in the database.
4. Taking pictures with extreme angles can worsen the results of the image recognition.

DISCUSSION

Considering the requirements, it is clear that users are well aware of the potential of mobile technologies and use their current experience when considering a smart glasses based museum visitors guide. They are looking for a product with rich functionality – that will provide both information and navigational support (which are two main types of support needed by visitors to CH sites). Most users prefer to remain in control, deciding when and where information should be presented, although proactiveness is preferred by a minority. In addition, users want personalization and are aware that it requires monitoring their behavior, and to some extent, giving up their privacy. Moreover, usability in general seems highly important and with this respect, the need to cater to a wider variety of users, with different preferences with respect to types of media and ways of interaction is brought up. It is clear that users will be looking for a high quality product, as they are used nowadays to high quality smartphones, which make the task of developing a research prototype highly demanding (as it is with more traditional mobile guides). It is worth noting that in general, research prototypes intended to be evaluated in realistic setting, need to be of high quality and sometimes become systems used by visitors on a daily basis, which is a major benefit, as can be seen in [9,10,11].

It is important to note that in this study, we refer to requirements that are relevant nowadays. Today people do not use smart-glasses as they use smart-phones. This fact can influence the proposed requirements, as in the future, some of the results may change in accordance with the progress of the technology.

This work describes the first steps of our research. For better understanding of the usefulness of the new technology, we will compare a handheld museum guide with a HWD guide. The different modalities of presenting and interacting with information can influence the ease of use and general experience of the visitor. Potential users might be accustomed to handheld devices, and there might be issues with acceptability of a new technology. On the other hand, the HWD affords handless interaction and promises a less mediated, and possibly more engaging experience.

CONCLUSIONS AND FUTURE WORK

We presented potential user requirements for a HWD museum-guide. The requirements seem to be challenging. As they are diverse and sometime contradicting. Hence, addressing them all requires developing a very flexible and configurable system. Following the requirements definitions, an initial research prototype was developed. There are works, which compare different algorithms, including SURF, for recognition of museum objects [5]. In the next step, we are going to extend the prototype implementation to object recognition for supplying users' requirements. Then, the prototype will be evaluated and improved in an iterative manner, following a user centered design process until a satisfactory system will be available. The next step will be comparing the use of HWD with a more conventional museum visitor's guide at a real museum. Two versions of a museum visitors guide system will be used. One is an existing handheld, personalized, context aware museum visitors' guide system that has been developed and deployed in the museum, while the second will be the same system, adapted to enable users' interaction through the mobile glasses. In the user studies, with regular museum visitors, the following aspects will be evaluated: usability, the overall visit experience and the impact of the systems on group interaction when the visitor comes with a group of friends – a common scenario. Data will be collected in two complementary ways: by system logs that will enable to analyze visitors' movements through the museum, time spent at POIs and information viewed, and by questionnaires and interviews.

REFERENCES

1. Ardissono, L., Kuflik, T., & Petrelli, D. (2012). Personalization in cultural heritage: the road travelled and the one ahead. *User modeling and user-adapted interaction*, 22(1-2), 73-99.
2. Alce G., Wallergård M. and Hermodsson K. (2015) WozARd: A Wizard of Oz Method for Wearable Augmented. *Advances in Human-Computer Interaction*, vol. 2015, p. 10.
3. Banowosari L. Y., Rahmah M., Rizky G. A. and Fuady M. A. R. (2013). Design Concept of Augmented Reality Application with Glasses for Indonesia Wayang Museum. *International Journal of Advances in Engineering & Technology*, vol. 6, no. 4, pp. 1564-1570.
4. Bay H., Ess A., Tuytelaars T. and Gool L.V. (2008). Speeded-Up Robust Features (SURF), Computer Vision and Image Understanding, vol. 110, no. 3, pp. 346–359.
5. Bay H., Fasel B. and Gool L. V. (2006). Interactive museum guide: Fast and robust recognition of museum objects. *Proceedings of the first international workshop on mobile vision.*
6. Chang, K. E., Chang, C. T., Hou, H. T., Sung, Y. T., Chao, H. L., & Lee, C. M. (2014). Development and behavioral pattern analysis of a mobile guide system with augmented reality for painting appreciation instruction in an art museum. *Computers & Education*, 71, 185-197.
7. Damala A., Cubaud P., Bationo A., Houlier P., Marchal I. (2008). Bridging the gap between the digital and the physical: design and evaluation of a mobile augmented reality guide for the museum visit. *in DIMEA '08 Proceedings of the 3rd international conference on Digital Interactive Media in Entertainment and Arts*, New York.
8. Kraemer, H., & Kanter, N. (2014). Use and re-use of data how Collection Management Systems, Transmedia and Augmented Reality impact the future of museum. *In Virtual Systems & Multimedia (VSMM), 2014 International Conference on (pp. 214-216). IEEE.*
9. Kuflik, T., Stock, O., Zancanaro, M., Gorfinkel, A., Jbara, S., Kats, S. & Kashtan, N. (2011). A visitor's guide in an active museum: Presentations, communications, and reflection. *Journal on Computing and Cultural Heritage (JOCCH)*, 3(3), 11.
10. Lanir J., Kuflik T. ,Dim E. ,Wecker A. J. , Stock O. (2013). The Influence of a Location-Aware Mobile Guide on Museum Visitors' Behavior. *Interacting with Computers*, vol. 25, no. 6, p. 443–460.
11. Lanir J., Kuflik T., Wecker A. J., Stock O., Zancanaro M. (2011). Examining proactiveness and choice in a location-aware mobile museum guide,. *Interacting with Computers*, vol. 23, no. 5, p. 513–524.
12. Mase K., Kadobayashi R., Nakatsu R. (1996). Meta-Museum: A Supportive Augmented-Reality Environment for Knowledge Sharing," *in In ATR Workshop on Social Agents: Humans and Machines*, Kyoto, Japan.
13. Mirza K. and Sarayeddine K. (2012). Key challenges to affordable see through wearable displays: The missing link for mobile AR mass deployment. *Optivent* S.A, Rennes, France.
14. Schiele B., Jebara T. and Oliver N. (2001). Sensory-Augmented Computing: Wearing the Museum's Guide. *IEEE Micro*, vol. 21, no. 3, pp. 44 - 52.
15. Sparacino F. (2002). The Museum Wearable: real-time sensor-driven understanding of visitors' interests for personalized visually-augmented museum experiences. in *Museums and the Web* , Boston.
16. Styliani, S., Fotis, L., Kostas, K., & Petros, P. (2009). Virtual museums, a survey and some issues for consideration. *Journal of cultural Heritage*, 10(4), 520-528.
17. Vlahakis V., Ioannidis N., Karigiannis J., Tsotros M., Gounaris M., Stricker D., Gleue T., Daehne P. and Almeida, L. (2002). Archeoguide: An Augmented Reality Guide for Archaeological Sites. *IEEE Computer Graphics and Applications*, vol. 22, no. 5, pp. 52-60.

SweepSense: Ad Hoc Configuration Sensing Using Reflected Swept-Frequency Ultrasonics

Gierad Laput Xiang 'Anthony' Chen Chris Harrison
Human-Computer Interaction Institute
Carnegie Mellon University
5000 Forbes Avenue, Pittsburgh, PA 15217
{gierad.laput, xiangche, chris.harrison}@cs.cmu.edu

ABSTRACT
Devices can be made more intelligent if they have the ability to sense their surroundings and physical configuration. However, adding extra, special purpose sensors increases size, price and build complexity. Instead, we use speakers and microphones already present in a wide variety of devices to open new sensing opportunities. Our technique sweeps through a range of inaudible frequencies and measures the intensity of reflected sound to deduce information about the immediate environment, chiefly the materials and geometry of proximate surfaces. We offer several example uses, two of which we implemented as self-contained demos, and conclude with an evaluation that quantifies their performance and demonstrates high accuracy.

Author Keywords: Acoustic sensing; mobile devices; interaction techniques; novel input.

ACM Classification: H.5.2 [Information interfaces and presentation]: User Interfaces - Input devices and strategies.

INTRODUCTION
Today, almost all general-purpose computing devices contain a speaker and microphone. We propose utilizing these ubiquitous sensors to bring novel sensing abilities to devices without extra or special hardware (e.g., [8,11]). Specifically, we emit inaudible frequency sweeps using the built in speaker, and capture the reflected waveforms using the built in microphone. These sounds are then analyzed and classified to infer some aspect of the environment.

Our work was originally inspired by the field of soundscape ecology [18]. We learned that different environs (natural or otherwise) have significantly different acoustic properties—the composition and spatial configuration of flora and geological features act as acoustic filters, passing some sounds while attenuating others. This can introduce selective pressure, leading to e.g., animals communicating using frequencies that carry farthest in their habitats (see e.g., [5,12]).

IUI'16, March 07-10, 2016, Sonoma, CA, USA
© 2016 ACM. ISBN 978-1-4503-4137-0/16/03···$15.00
DOI: http://dx.doi.org/10.1145/2856767.2856812

This inspired us to run experiments in our lab, sweeping through a range of frequencies emitted from a laptop, and looking at attenuation due to the environment. We noticed that changes in physical configuration could alter the signal, for example, a door being opened or the lid of our laptop being repositioned; it can even capture subtle relationships between wearable devices and the human body, such as knowing when headphone buds are removed from the ears.

Such actions appear to expose different facets and/or materials, with different acoustic reflectance characteristics. Additionally, in enclosed "chambers", such as the ear canal, cars, rooms and similar, certain frequencies may become standing waves [6], with amplifying effects. Finally, a sound wave reflected off multiple surfaces will return to the microphone at different phases, producing characteristic interference effects. These effects all interact to produce a "sound signature", which can be used for classification.

RELATED WORK
Modal analysis [2] and swept frequency acoustic interferometry (SFAI) are well known in fields such as material identification [21], structural analysis [7] and petrogeology [4]. In the HCI domain, acoustic-based input sensing can be categorized into three general approaches. First are time difference of arrival (TDoA) and time of flight (ToF) localization techniques, most commonly in the form of "sonar," which has seen extensive use (see e.g., [19,23]). Additionally, sensing acoustic Doppler shifts [1] has also proven to be useful (see also [24] for an overview).

More similar to our approach are acoustic fingerprint-based techniques, which use an uncontrolled, but characteristic signal to distinguish between possible states. Approaches can be active—as in the case of Mujibiya et al. [15] and Takemura et al. [22]–or passive, such as Skinput [10]. Conceptually related to our approach is Touch & Activate [16], which enabled ad-hoc touch sensing on objects using swept frequency vibrations. In contrast to our technique, the latter used a piezo contact microphone and a piezo buzzer physically attached to an object and relied chiefly on physical resonance (as opposed to reflectance). The authors cite Touché [20] as inspiration, which used swept frequency *electrical* signals for ad hoc capacitive sensing. As discussed in both papers, applications can often suffice without a full sweep. However, this requires *a priori* knowledge of discriminative frequency bands in different contexts, which precludes general and immediate use.

SWEEPSENSE

Our approach, which we call *SweepSense,* can open new interactive opportunities in contexts where there are speakers and microphones present. Using a device's built-in speaker, we emit a repeating 20ms ultrasound linear frequency sweep. Acoustic sweeps can be generated programmatically (e.g., using various audio APIs such as minim, and BASS audio I/O) or pre-cached using synthesis software (e.g., Audition, Audacity). Further, we use low-level audio API calls (e.g., using callbacks whenever audio samples are captured) to more closely monitor incoming data from the microphone. Most audio APIs expose these types of callbacks, such as the `sample(float[])` function call in minim, or the `setRenderCallback()` in iOS CoreAudio. Meanwhile, captured audio samples are stored in a circular buffer (~100ms or less), where frequency analysis and machine learning are eventually performed.

Next, the captured signals are transformed into frequency space using a Fast Fourier Transform (FFT) and only the inaudible spectrum components of interest are saved (e.g., 20-40kHz for a device capable of sampling at 96kHz). In addition to the raw FFT values, we also compute a series of standard features (derived from [17]): RMS, average power, spectral center of mass, max/min index and values, standard deviation, and spectral band ratios. These features are passed to a Sequential Minimal Optimization-based Support Vector Machine (SMO-SVM), provided by the Weka Toolkit [9]. Note that this model must be trained with data before it can provide real-time classification.

EXAMPLE IMPLEMENTATIONS

We implemented two illustrative applications as self-contained demos. These represent different scales of use, and serve as examples of discrete and continuous sensing.

Discrete Sensing: Smart Ear Buds

SweepSense may be useful in small-scale applications, such as ear buds (Figure 1). For example, when both ear buds are in, music plays as usual. However, if both ear buds are removed, the music can be automatically paused. Also, a phone call could be answered by removing a single bud.

Implementation. For our ear bud application, we used a pair of generic, Samsung in-ear headphones. To avoid crosstalk, we emit a 20 to 22kHz sweep through the left ear bud and a 23 to 25kHz sweep through the right bud. These headphones contain an integrated microphone approximately 20cm down the cord, which we use to capture sound. Using this setup, we can detect four possible states: 1) both buds in, 2) left bud out, 3) right bud out, and 4) both buds out (Figure 1 and Video Figure). We used a SVM model trained using Weka's Quad SMO [9] with default parameters.

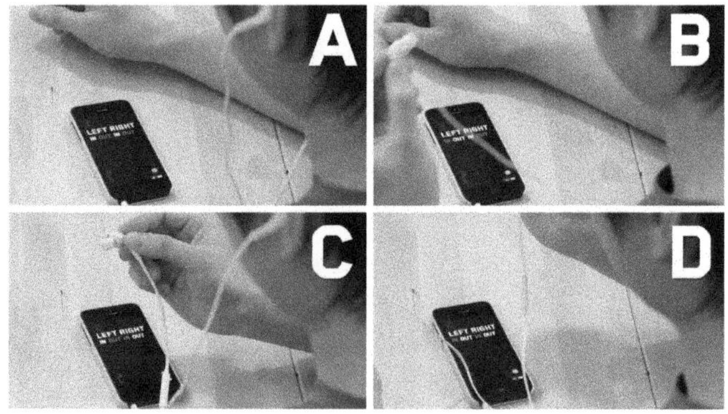

Figure 1. SweepSense can detect whether (A) both ear buds are in, (B) left is out, (C) right is out, or (D) both are out.

Other researchers have achieved similar functionality, but only through additional hardware. For example, small capacitive sensors can be added to ear buds to detect skin contact, as demonstrated in Buil et al. [3]. Metzger et al. used infrared proximity sensors [14] to detect gestures performed around the ear. Most recently, Manabe and Fukumoto [13] showed that a low cost supplementary circuit could be used to detect physical taps on headphones, which physically actuate the speaker diaphragm. SweepSense achieves equivalent functionality and could be integrated to existing devices with just a simple software update.

Continuous Sensing: Laptop Lid Configuration

Contemporary laptops use a special purpose sensor to detect lid configuration, but this is presently limited to detecting open or closed states (i.e., binary). SweepSense could be used to infer *continuous* angular position of the lid without any hardware modification (Figure 2). This could be used, for example, to lock the screen when the lid is lowered, or to sense lid-based gestures e.g., leaning backward to trigger full-screen, or wiggling to minimize windows.

Implementation. For our laptop lid angle application, we emit a continuous 20-40kHz sweep from a 2013 MacBook Air's 2013 built-in speakers (located where the display

Figure 2. SweepSense can infer continuous laptop lid angle. Here the lid is positioned at 100, 70, 50 and 30° (A-D); Sweepsense reports 97, 70, 51 and 30° respectively. Far right (E), a 1Hz "wiggle" gesture is performed and visible in the raw signal.

meets the main chassis). The microphone is located on the left side bezel of the base. Our machine learning setup uses an SVM regression model with a radial basis function kernel (γ=0.01), trained using Weka's SMOReg implementation [9] using default optimization parameters. Our regression model was trained to infer angular positions between 30° and 110°, allowing our system to behave like a virtual lid angle sensor (see Fig. 2 and Video).

We note that although lid sensing can be achieved using accelerometers, it is rare for laptop lids to have accelerometers solely for this purpose. Meanwhile, most laptops have a speaker and microphone. Thus, SweepSense brings new capabilities through software, and more critically, without any additional hardware.

USER STUDY

We sought to evaluate the feasibility of our approach through multiple user studies. In response, we recruited two separate groups of participants, (32 total, 11 female, mean age=24, STDEV=5.5), and each experiment took about 30 minutes. All participants were paid $10 for their time. This section describes the studies in detail.

Ear Bud Experiment

To evaluate ear bud configuration sensing, we had 24 participants (9 female, mean age=24) use our off-the-shelf, Samsung-branded in-ear headphones in two different locations: a large, open social area in an academic building and a medium-sized office (12 participants for each location). Although we created an iOS version of our SweepSense recognizer (Figure 1 and Video Figure), we used a laptop to run the experiment. To better emulate real-world use, music was played in the ear buds throughout the experiment.

Following a brief explanation, participants were asked to replicate a series of ear bud configurations (depicted in Figure 1), which were shown as photographs on the laptop screen. Each configuration was requested five times in a random order (during which time ten classifications were made over a ten second period). Of note, the system performed live classification with no per user training or calibration. In total, we collected 1200 classification attempts for each configuration. Overall accuracy was 94.8% (SD=1.3%); Table 1 provides a confusion matrix.

Laptop Lid Angle Experiment

For the ear bud experiment, it was important to capture test data from a variety of users, as everyone's ears are different. However, since the laptop was constant in this experiment, we recruited a smaller pool of eight participants (2 female, mean age=25). Further, we wanted to test whether SweepSense could generalize across a *range* of environments. For this experiment, we used a classifier trained specifically for our MacBook Air 2013. Meanwhile, we visited participants in a location of their choosing, which included a variety of commonplace settings such as a cafe, study hall, food court, conference room, and shared lab space (mean ambient noise 55.6dB, SD=5.72dB). Overall, we found no significant effect based on location.

	Both-in	Left-out	Right-out	Both-out	Accuracy
Both-in	1150	15	28	7	*95.8%*
Left-out	70	1112	1	22	*92.7%*
Right-out	5	0	1142	53	*95.2%*
Both-out	1	0	51	1148	*95.7%*

Table 1. Confusion matrix for earbud placement classification.

In this experiment, a small *protractor* was placed along the right side of the laptop, near the hinge, allowing participants to accurately orient the lid to any requested angle. A randomized list of angles from 30° to 110° in 10 degree increments was requested verbally (e.g., "please set the lid to 60 degrees"). Each angle appeared twice, for a total of 18 trials. Once the participant was satisfied with their lid positioning, 20 angular estimates (captured over a period of approximately three seconds) were made using the pre-trained classifier and averaged to produce a final estimate.

Results show that the mean angular error was ±4.1° (SD=1.7°) for angles between 30°-100°, summarized in Figure 4. Note that error increases substantially beyond 100°, which we hypothesize is due to the screen no longer strongly participating in reflecting sound downwards towards the microphone (i.e., sound mostly emanates away from the laptop). Finally, our regression model achieved a correlation coefficient (R^2) of 0.988, evaluated using 10% of the dataset we withheld for testing.

DISCUSSION

There are several drawbacks of note. One is our dependence on low frequency ultrasound, which may be audible to children, some adults and pets. However, the technique is not reliant on any single frequency, and our machine learning approach makes it easy to increase the lower bound frequency assuming the hardware supports it. In practice, this audibility issue does not appear to be a critical problem given that ultrasonic sensors have enjoyed commercial success for decades (e.g., automatic door openers) without issue.

Secondly, we found that many devices do not support high sampling rate audio output (we utilized 96kHz for our laptop example, but found that 44.1kHz is a more common upper bound). This reduces audio output fidelity, especially in the ultrasonic range. However, systems today are not engineered for this purpose, and so with purposeful integration, higher ultrasound frequencies might be better supported for applications like we suggest in the future.

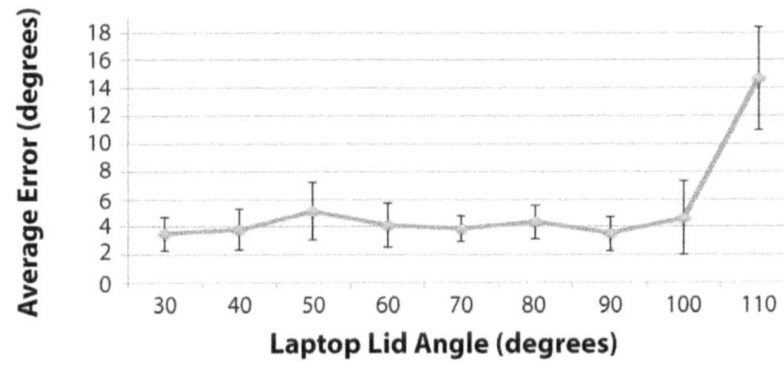

Figure 4. Our regression model can predict laptop lid angle. Below 100°, the mean angular error is ±4.1°.

Finally, acoustic leakage is another issue. For example, if ear buds are partially inserted, our classifiers will struggle to make accurate predictions. More training data would help, but as with other classification systems, this may be a significant challenge. Finally, classifiers may need to be device and model specific—for example, our MacBook lid angle demo is not immediately portable to a Dell laptop.

In general, SweepSense introduces interactive opportunities in environments where speakers and microphones are present. One possibility for future work is in living rooms, which often contain speakers for entertainment and where microphones are increasingly common (e.g., Microsoft Kinect, Smart TVs). This could allow, for example, occupant sensing and detecting whether people are sitting or standing, which could be used to e.g., intelligently pause media. Meanwhile, vehicles generally contain speaker systems, and increasingly feature microphones for Bluetooth-connected telephony and voice navigation functions. SweepSense could allow for occupancy sensing in all seats, enabling e.g., richer safety applications. Few cars today track the status of their windows, and typically only know if doors are opened or closed. With SweepSense, cars could infer the *analog* state of both windows and doors (albeit susceptible to noise in certain cases).

CONCLUSION

Uniquely, and in contrast to prior work, SweepSense uses in-air, reflected, swept-frequency ultrasound. This approach adds to a growing body of work that can take advantage of devices' existing speakers and microphones, allowing such techniques to be deployed with a simple software update. In the future, we hope to explore larger contexts that have speakers and microphones, such as public address (PA) systems in subway stations and supermarkets, and sound systems at concert venues and stadiums.

REFERENCES

1. Aumi, M., Gupta, S., Goel, M., Larson, E. and Patel, S. DopLink: using the doppler effect for multi-device interaction. In *Proc. UbiComp '13*. 583-586.
2. Brandt, A. (2011). "Noise and Vibration Analysis." John Wiley & Sons, Ltd., UK.
3. Buil, V., Hollemans, G., and Wijdeven, S. van de. Headphones with touch control. *Proc. MobileHCI '05*. 377-378.
4. Chevron Corporation. "Chevron, GE Form Technology Alliance." Retrieved April 11, 2014 from: http://investor.chevron.com/phoenix.zhtml?c=130102&p=irol-newsArticle_Print&ID=1895989
5. Cocroft, R and Rodríguez, R. The Behavioral Ecology of Insect Vibrational Comm. *BioSci*.,55. '05. 323-334.
6. Cox, T., D'Antonio, P. and Avis, M. Room sizing and optimization at low frequencies. *Journal of the Audio Engineering Society*, 52(6), 2004, pp. 640-651.
7. Gloth, G. and Sinapius, M. Analysis of swept-sine runs during modal identification. *Mechanical Systems and Signal Processing*, 18(6), Nov. 2004, pp. 1421-1441
8. Gupta, S., Morris, D., Patel, S. and Tan, D. SoundWave: using the doppler effect to sense gestures. In *Proc. CHI '12*. 1911-1914.
9. Hall, M., Frank, E., Holmes, G., Pfahringer, B., Reutemann, P. and Witten, I. The WEKA Data Mining Software: An Update; *SIGKDD Explorations*, 11(1), 2009.
10. Harrison, C., Tan, D. and Morris, D. Skinput: appropriating the body as an input surface. In *Proc. CHI '10*. 453-462.
11. Hwang, S., Bianchi, A. and Wohn, K. VibPress: estimating pressure input using vibration absorption on mobile devices. In *Proc. MobileHCI '13*. 31-34.
12. Kime, N., Turner, W. and Ryan, M. The transmission of advertisement calls in Central American frogs. *Behavioral Ecology*, 11(1), 2000, pp. 71–83.
13. Manabe H. and Fukumoto, M. Headphone taps: a simple technique to add input function to regular headphones. In *Proc. MobileHCI '12*. 177-180.
14. Metzger, C., Anderson, M., Starner, T. FreeDigiter: A Contact-free Device for Gesture Control. *Proc. ISWC '04*. 18-21.
15. Mujibiya, A., Cao, X., Tan, D., Morris, D., Patel, S. and Rekimoto, J. The sound of touch: on-body touch and gesture sensing based on transdermal ultrasound propagation. In *Proc. ITS '13*. 189-198.
16. Ono, M., Shizuki, B. and Tanaka, J. Touch & activate: adding interactivity to existing objects using active acoustic sensing. *In Proc. UIST '13*. 31-40.
17. Peeters, G. A large set of audio features for sound description similarity and classification in the CUIDADO project. Tech. report, ICRAM, 2004.
18. Pijanowski, C., Villanueva-Rivera, J., Dumyahn, L., Farina, A., Krause, L., Napoletano, M., Gage, H. and Pieretti, N. Soundscape Ecology: The Science of Sound in the Landscape. *BioScience*, 61(3), 2001, pp. 203.
19. Priyantha, N. B., Chakraborty, A., and Balakrishnan, H. The Cricket Location-Support system. In *Proc. MobiCom '00*. 32-43.
20. Sato, M., Poupyrev, I. and Harrison, C., Touché: enhancing touch interaction on humans, screens, liquids, and everyday objects. In *Proc. CHI '12*. 483-492.
21. Sinha, D., Springer, K., Han, W., Lizon, D., and Houlton, R. Swept-frequency acoustic interferometry technique for noninvasive chemical diagnostics. In *Proc. 3rd International Conference On-Site Analysis*, 1995.
22. Takemura, K., Ito, A., Takamatsu, J. and Ogasawara, T. Active bone-conducted sound sensing for wearable interfaces. In *Proc. UIST '11 Adjunct*. 53-54.
23. Tarzia, S., Dick, R., Dinda, P. and Memik, G. Sonar-based measurement of user presence and attention. In *Proc. Ubicomp '09*. 89-92.
24. Watanabe, H., Terada, T. and Tsukamoto, M. Ultrasound-based movement sensing, gesture-, and context-recognition. In *Proc. ISWC '13*. 57-64.

Chalkboarding: A New Spatiotemporal Query Paradigm for Sports Play Retrieval

Long Sha*
QUT/Disney Research
long.sha@hdr.qut.edu.au

Patrick Lucey*
STATS LLC/Disney Research
plucey@stats.com

Yisong Yue
Caltech
yyue@caltech.edu

Peter Carr
Disney Research
peter.carr@disneyresearch.com

Charlie Rohlf
STATS LLC
crohlf@stats.com

Iain Matthews
Disney Research
iainm@disneyresearch.com

ABSTRACT

The recent explosion of sports tracking data has dramatically increased the interest in effective data processing and access of sports plays (i.e., short trajectory sequences of players and the ball). And while there exist systems that offer improved categorizations of sports plays (e.g., into relatively coarse clusters), to the best of our knowledge there does not exist any retrieval system that can effectively search for the most relevant plays given a specific input query. One significant design challenge is how best to phrase queries for multi-agent spatiotemporal trajectories such as sports plays.We have developed a novel query paradigm and retrieval system, which we call Chalkboarding, that allows the user to issue queries by drawing a play of interest (similar to how coaches draw up plays). Our system utilizes effective alignment, templating, and hashing techniques tailored to multi-agent trajectories, and achieves accurate play retrieval at interactive speeds. We showcase the efficacy of our approach in a user study, where we demonstrate orders-of-magnitude improvements in search quality compared to baseline systems.

Author Keywords

Spatiotemporal Retrieval; User Interfaces; Sports Analytics

ACM Classification Keywords

H.3.3 Information Search and Retrieval: Query Representation; H.5.2 User interfaces: Graphical User Interfaces (GUI)

INTRODUCTION

Like many data-rich domains, sports analytics is currently experiencing an explosive growth in both the quantity and granularity of data sources [35]. For instance, STATS SportVU generates location data for every player, ball, and referee at 25 Hz along with detailed logs for events such as passes, shots, fouls, etc. Given the overwhelming amount of data now being collected, the interest in effective information management and access for sports data has correspondingly grown as well.

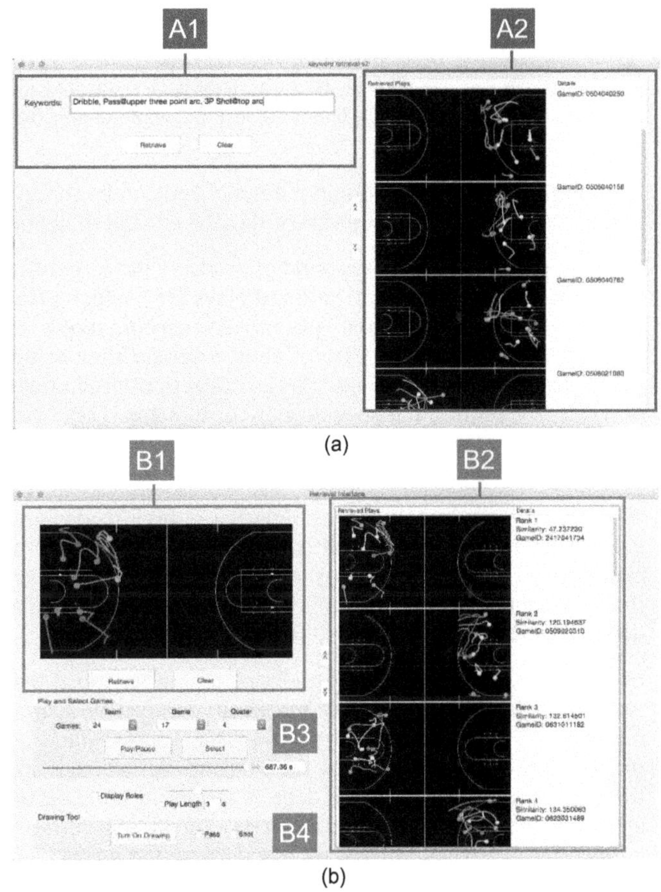

Figure 1. (a) Conventional methods for sports play access are based on "keywords" (A1), which lack specificity and requires the user to browse through a large collection before finding the specific plays of interest (A2). (b) To improve retrieval effectiveness, we instead use a "chalkboard" (B1), which is an intuitive and powerful query format that allows the user to specify plays similar to how a coach draws up plays, and can capture the rich semantics required for effective sports play retrieval (B2). The user can use the "selection tool" (B3) to select specific trajectories, or use the "drawing tool" (B4) to draw a query.

In many sports domains, an important unit of information is a "play" or a short sequence of plays. Roughly speaking, a play comprises the deliberate behavior of one or more players that

*Part of this work was done while Sha and Lucey were at Disney Research

IUI 2016, March 7–10, 2016, Sonoma, CA, USA.

ACM 978-1-4503-4137-0/16/03 ...$15.00.
DOI: http://dx.doi.org/10.1145/2856767.2856772

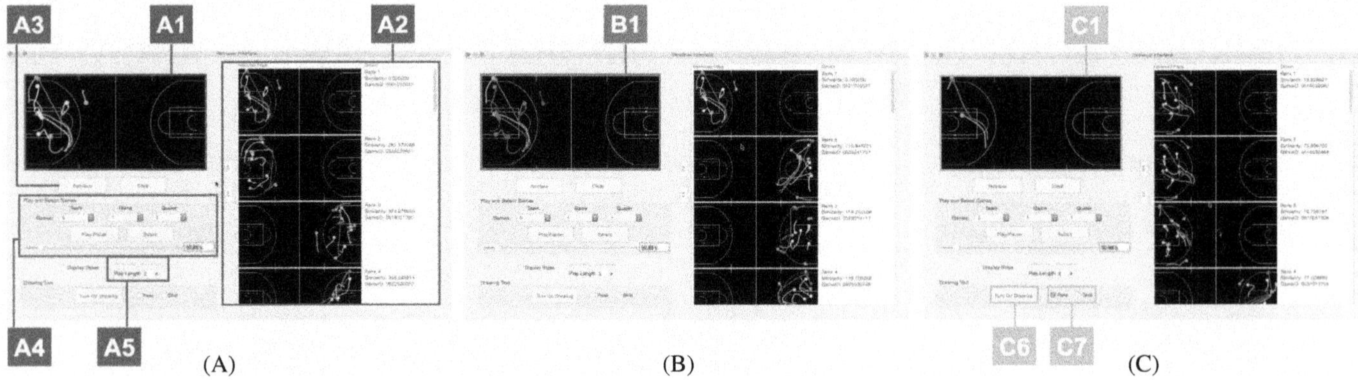

Figure 2. Our Chalkboarding query language can take three different input types. (A) Exemplar-based where a user can play an existing game in the database and choose a short segment play as query – features include: (A1) Visualization window of play containing player and ball trajectories (red=ball, green=offensive-players, yellow=defensive-players, dots=end-of-trajectory), (A2) Retrieval window which displays the most relevant plays in terms of rank, (A3) Retrieval button, (A4) Game-selection and scroll-bar to scrub through game of interest, (A5) Specify length of trajectories in seconds. (B) Manipulating exemplars where a user can select just a subset of trajectories which they deem relevant – it is the same interface except for (B1) the visualization window where the user can right-click to select the trajectories of interest. (C) Drawing plays where the user draws the play of interest like a coach would on a chalkboard – additional features include (C1) visualization window where the user draws the play of interest, (C6) draw tool selection button, (C7) toggle buttons to include actions in play (note, the user must also select the length of the play).

is designed to achieve a certain outcome, and can be thought of as short annotated trajectories of the players and the ball.

Conventional approaches to sports play access has largely focused on improving categorization of plays [38], which offers limited utility when the goal is to *retrieve specific plays*. Indeed, the lack of specificity from categorizations often results in the user to browse through a large collection of candidate plays before finding the specific play of interest. For example, in Figure 1(a), a user may search for all three point shots resulting from a pass from the right (A1).

A key challenge in sports play retrieval is how to design a query format that is both intuitive to use and rich enough to enable precise specification of an information need. Given the spatiotemporal nature of plays, it is clear that one must depart from conventional text-based query formats.

In this paper, we present a new query paradigm for sports play retrieval, which we call ***Chalkboarding***. Instead of searching plays using "keywords", we use a visual representation of player trajectories - inspired by the "x's and o's" a coach uses to draw up plays. Figure 1(b) depicts our basic setup: given an example play as the input query (B1), the system retrieves a ranked list of plays ordered by relevance to the query (B2). With a chalkboard, a user can use the "selection tool" (B3) to select trajectories for a particular example or use the "drawing tool" (B4) to draw a query. As such, Chalkboarding is an intuitive yet powerful query format that allows the user to specify plays similar to how a coach draws up plays, and can thus capture the rich semantics required for effective sports play retrieval.

We view Chalkboarding as complementary to existing categorization methods. Much like how the early work on information access for the World Wide Web was largely dichotomized into directory/taxonomy versus query/retrieval paradigms [45], we view our approach as the first instance of the query/retrieval paradigm for sports plays to complement the existing approaches for the directory/taxonomy paradigm.

Note that the two types of approaches can be integrated together for improved performance (e.g., one can retrieve for only certain types of plays).

An immediate technical question that arises from our Chalkboarding query format is how to measure relevance between the query and a candidate play, i.e., how to interpret the query. For instance, sports plays are multi-agent trajectories, and so relevance estimation requires solving a potentially combinatorial alignment problem between the agents in the query and in the candidate play.

In this paper, we also present a retrieval system tailored towards retrieval of multi-agent trajectories. Our system utilizes a role representation technique based on [36, 4] that can be used to quickly and accurately find the best agent-to-agent alignments between the query and a candidate play (or between two plays) for a variety of spatiotemporal distance and similarity measures. We then leverage this representation to develop efficient templating and hashing techniques for fast indexing of a large repository of plays. Our full-stack system can thus achieve accurate retrieval at interactive speeds.

We validate our system using a variety of empirical evaluations, ranging from analyzing the accuracy/efficiency tradeoff of the various system components, to conducting a user study on the end-to-end task of sports play retrieval. Our retrieval user study demonstrates that our Chalkboarding system can achieve orders-of-magnitude improvements in search quality compared to systems based only on categorization, which showcases the efficacy of our approach.

CHALKBOARDING QUERY LANGUAGE

Our Chalkboarding query language is based on a spatiotemporal trajectories,and uses the x,y (and z if available) positions of players and the ball as the primary input. Trajectories can either be drawn by hand or extracted/selected from recorded trajectories from real games (or a mix of both). Fig-

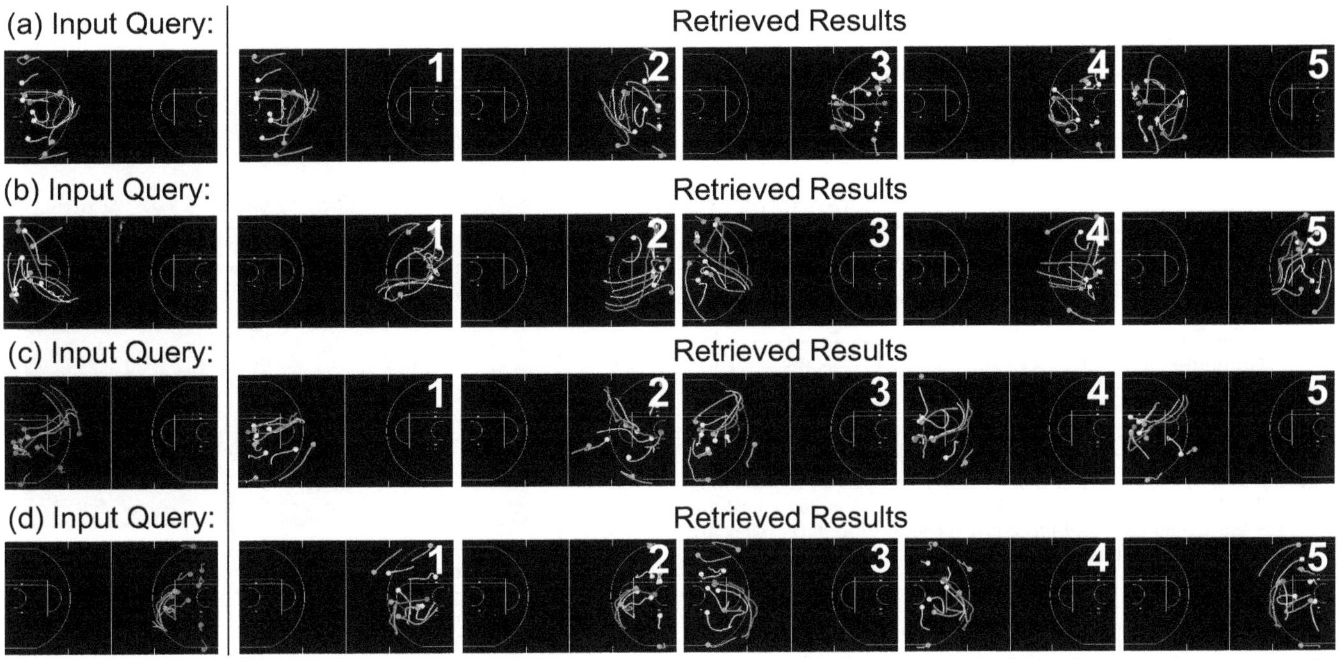

Figure 3. Different input queries using the whole game-exemplars (Query (a) and (b))and select only the trajectories of interest (Query (c) and (d)).

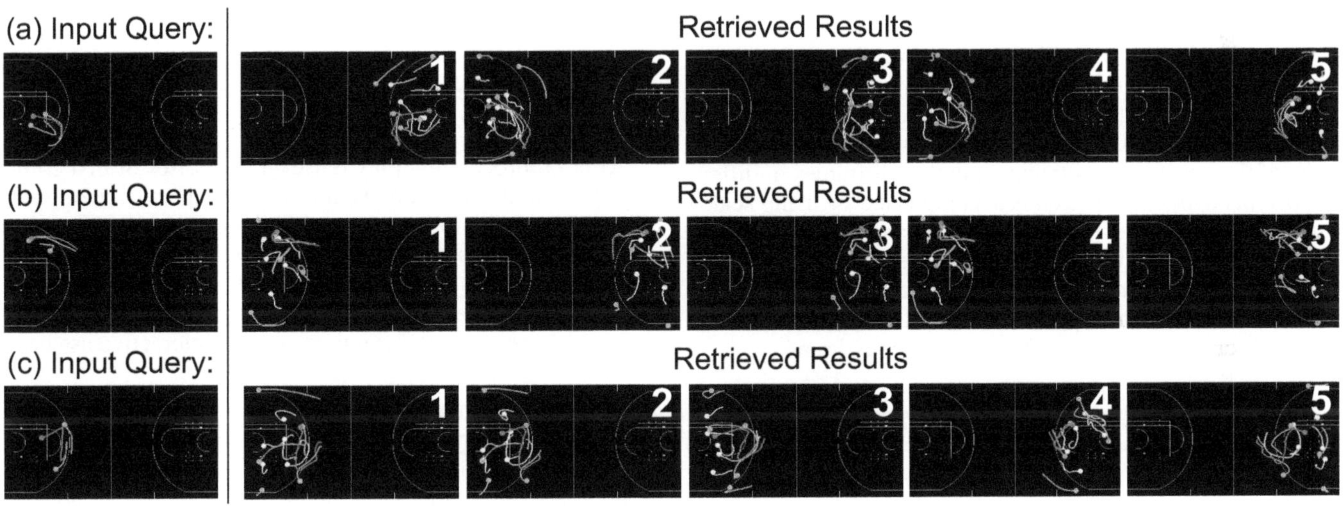

Figure 4. Different input queries using user drawn plays.

ure 2 illustrates the subtle differences between the various input queries.

Exemplar-based query: A user can use a short play sequence from an existing game as the query (Figure 2(a)). The features include: (A1) a visualization window of play containing player and ball trajectories, (A2) a retrieval window which displays the most relevant plays, (A3) a retrieval button, (A4) a game-selection and scroll-bar to scrub through game of interest until the portion of game is found, and (A5) a time-window selection. The last feature is quite important as the current system requires the user to define a time-window to the nearest second (1-5 seconds), and all searches will be constrained to look for trajectories fitting that time duration.

Manipulating exemplar-based queries: A user can also manipulate an existing play sequence before using it the query (Figure 2)(b)). The primary manipulation we consider in this paper is erasing irrelevant players (B1). More generally, one could also consider adjusting the trajectories of an existing play as well.

Drawing-based query: A user can draw a play of interest on the chalkboard. Again, the interface is similar to the other two with the only difference being that the visualization window is now a canvas in which the user draws their input play (C1). To select the drawing feature, a "draw-tool" selection button needs to be enabled (C6) and to include semantics such as "pass" or "shot" onto the trajectories, we have a toggle button for those actions included (C7).

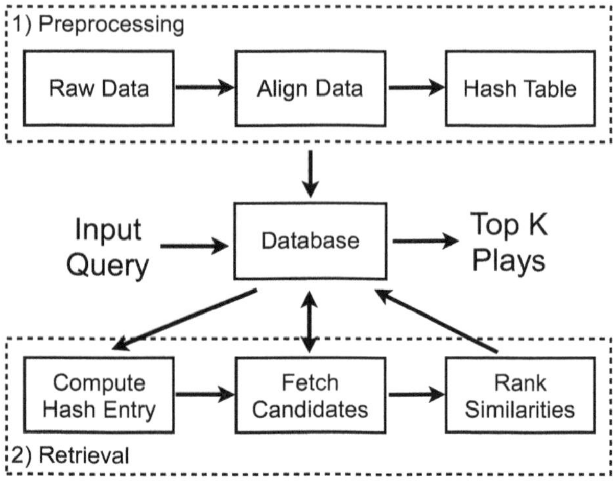

Figure 5. Our retrieval system is divided into two parts, preprocessing and retrieval. The first part aligns the raw data and builds a hash table while the second part contains a fast retrieval procedure. They are explained separately in this section.

Drawing-based query on broadcast feed: Additionally, the user can also draw on a broadcast feed of a game. To draw the play on the broadcast view is a more intuitive way of interaction. This requires an additional process of court calibration. To calibrate the court from the broadcast view with the standard overhead view, we utilize a two-step calibration method based on [12, 47] and [8]. The first step is template-based matching similar to [12, 47]. In order to do landmark matching on the court, we synthesize a relatively clean overhead view of the court by annotating a number of frames in different perspectives. Calibration is accomplished by using scale-invariant feature transform (SIFT) [34] and random sample consensus (RANSAC) [18] to match every frame to one of the templates and find the correspondence. To deal with ill-posed initial conditions, pointless calibration [8] is applied by using the calibration matrix from the previous frame.

The query types are all expressed in the format of multi-agent trajectories, and can be viewed as differing ways of constructing such trajectories. In particular, the exemplar-based and drawing-based input types represent subtractive versus additive query construction procedures: the exemplar-based queries take a full-set of multi-agent trajectories and subtract irrelevant players, whereas the drawing-based queries directly construct the trajectories of the relevant players. Note also that exemplar-based queries strictly require the user to have already identified a play of interested (e.g., from browsing existing plays), whereas drawing-based queries can be constructed without any other information.

Examples of exemplar-based and drawing-based queries are depicted in Figures 3 & 4, respectively. Note that the top-ranked retrieval plays are much more specific to the input query than those that could be retrieved from a text-based (i.e., categorization) query.

CHALKBOARDING RETRIEVAL SYSTEM

Figure 5 shows an overview of our retrieval system. To enable quick and accurate retrieval, "intelligent preprocessing" of the raw trajectory data is required. This preprocessing takes the form of using a role-based representation to enable fast alignment of trajectories, using a simple similarity measure to estimate relevance, followed by learning a hash-table to find the most relevant plays quickly.

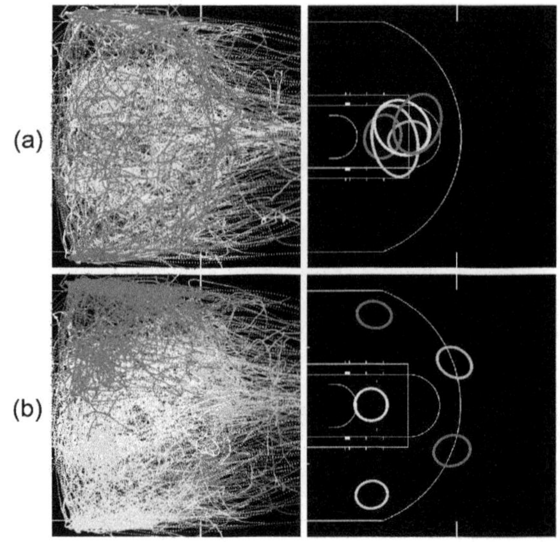

Figure 6. (a) Shows the raw trajectories (left) and the covariance (right) of each player during a quarter of play, which shows that players can be located in any part of the court. (b) However, if we align the player positions to a formation template at each frame, we show that players are spaced into a formation.

After preprocessing, play retrieval comprises of first computing the hash entry from the query to find the most likely candidates, and then followed by local search to rank the candidate plays. Descriptions of these modules are given in the following subsections. Our full-stack system can retrieve relevant results from a repository of hundreds of thousands of plays in less than second, and can thus support interactive use cases.

Role Representation for Fast Alignment

To measure play similarity, we employ an agent-to-agent trajectory comparison method. The advantages of using such an approach are: i) the representation is lossless (i.e., no quantization is required), ii) only a limited number of additional features are required to be stored (and not an overcomplete set of hand-crafted features which maybe hard to store in memory), iii) the representation is visual and interpretable, and iv) it allows for full interactivity with the data (i.e., users can select the precise time-window and agents of interest).

A drawback however, is the problem of permutations. An example of this problem is shown in Figure 6(a) where we show the raw trajectories and the covariances of each player across a quarter of a match. Here we can see players tend to move all around the court and not in one distinct area. In terms of matching trajectories, this means we would have to check all permutations, which in the case of basketball is $5! = 120$ (if we compare the trajectories of both teams it is 120^2).

Although exhaustively comparing all trajectories would yield the optimal agent-to-agent alignment, recent research in

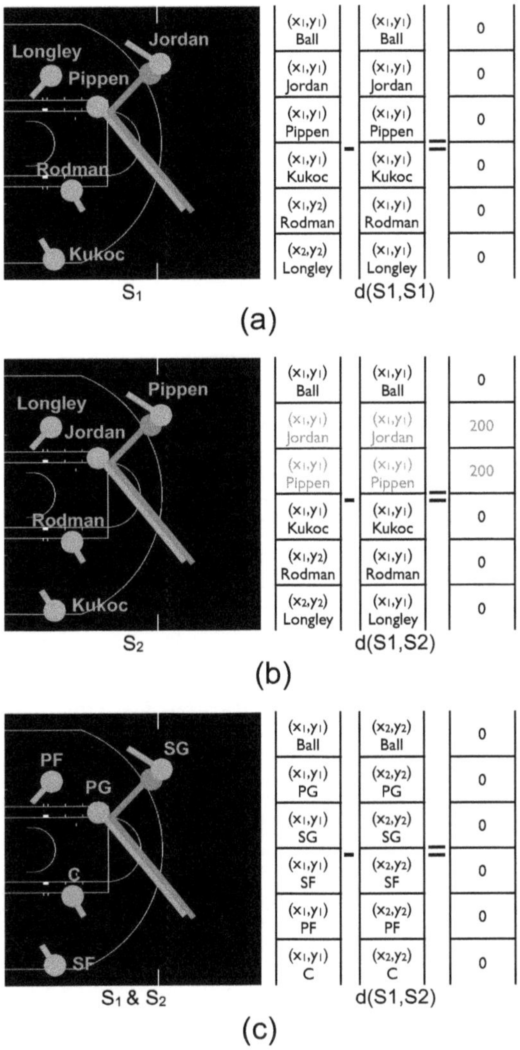

Figure 7. A toy example of the data alignment problem. (a) $\mathbf{S}_1$ is the play of interest, if we find an exactly identical play, the distance between them $d(\mathbf{S}_1, \mathbf{S}_1)$ should be zero. (b) However, if there is another same play S_2, but player Jordan and changed their roles, the distance $d(\mathbf{S}_1, \mathbf{S}_2)$ will no longer be zero due to the misalignment of these two players.

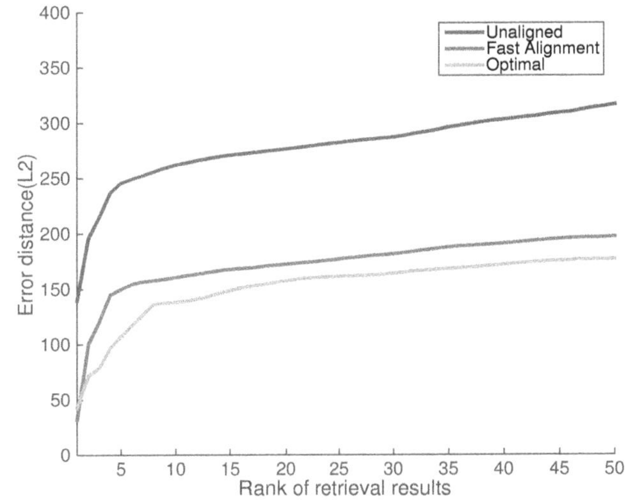

Figure 8. The plot of distance against retrieved-result ranks. Red curve is the optimal result and our role-based representation (yellow) is much closer to the red curve than identity-based representation (blue). And it is also much faster than exhaustively permuting the data.

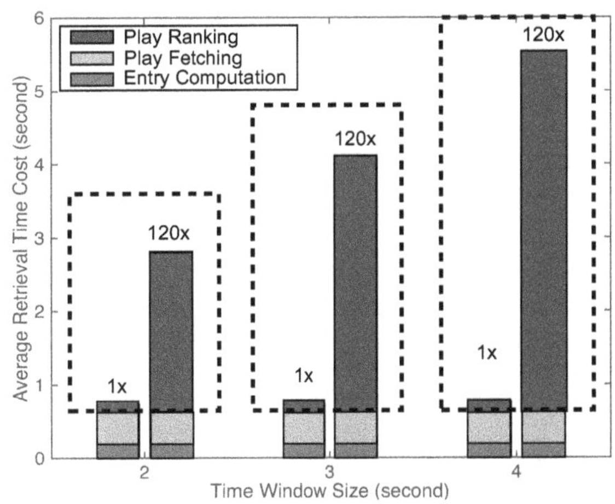

Figure 9. The time cost of our role-based representation (left bar of each pair) and exhaustive permutation (right bar of each pair). The test uses an 100,000-sample database and only the attacking team is considered.

multi-agent systems have shown that matching the trajectories to a predefined formation template can yield near-optimal agent-to-agent alignments [36, 4] in a single pass. We discuss the choice of distance metric in the next section on relevance estimation.

Figure 7 depicts a toy example that illustrates the intuition behind the formation-based approach [36, 4]. We can represent the play in Figure 7(a) as $\mathbf{S}_1 = [\mathbf{s}_{\text{ball}}, \mathbf{S}_{\text{offTeam}}]$, where each individual trajectory can be described as the vector $\mathbf{s} = [x_1, y_1, \ldots, x_F, y_F]^T$, and F is the number of frames in a play. Team behavior can then be described as the trajectories of the five players: $\mathbf{S}_{\text{offTeam}} = [\mathbf{s}_{\text{Jordan}}, \mathbf{s}_{\text{Pippen}}, \mathbf{s}_{\text{Kukoc}}, \mathbf{s}_{\text{Longley}}, \mathbf{s}_{\text{Rodman}}]$. If the team runs exactly the same play at some other point in time, then those two plays will already be pre-aligned (i.e., each player runs the exact same trajectories in both plays), and the distance between them will be zero (for any distance metric).

If we instead compare $\mathbf{S}_1$ with $\mathbf{S}_2$ from Figure 7(b) using the same representation as $\mathbf{S}_1$, then the distance will not be zero as Jordan and Pippen have switched positions. However, if we discard the identity of the player and use their role information at that frame – $\mathbf{S}_{\text{offTeam}} = [\mathbf{s}_{\text{PG}}, \mathbf{s}_{\text{SG}}, \mathbf{s}_{\text{SF}}, \mathbf{s}_{\text{PF}}, \mathbf{s}_{\text{C}}]$, the distance between $\mathbf{S}_1$ and $\mathbf{S}_2$ both plays are seen as the same as the distance is zero (Figure 7(c)). In addition to normalizing for permutation, the role-representation is also robust to substitutions, and agnostic to team identity.

In terms of preprocessing, we first calculate the formation template directly from data in way similar to [4]. At each frame, we then assign each player for each team to one of five roles (PG=point-guard, SG=shooting-guard, SF=small-forward, PF=power-forward and center=C). We do this by first calculating the cost matrix between the template and the current frame snapshot. We then use the Hungarian algorithm [29] to make the assignment, which results in a single

	l_2	l_∞	DTW	Frechet	LCSS	Edit
ACC	0.773	0.755	0.787	0.741	0.430	0.412

Table 1. The average accuracy of each metric in 5-fold cross validation experiment.

role feature being added to the raw position data, which is basically just an extra column in the database.

We also run a sliding window (i.e., 1-5 seconds) and do a majority vote to determine which role that player was in for different time-windows (i.e., 1-5 seconds), which results in an additional 5 columns in the database of features, and is still very lightweight. In order to make all the plays comparable, we rotate all the plays that are conducted on the right side of court by 180 degrees so that the coordinates of all the plays are aligned.

To show that our fast alignment method approximates the optimal alignment, we randomly selected 10 queries and chose the top 50 retrieved results. Figure 8 shows the plot of the average distance against the curve of three different alignment methods (see next subsection for metric distance used). The best performing alignment method was that of the exhaustive method. The next best was our fast-alignment using the role-representation which was a close approximation to the optimal alignment. The worse performing alignment algorithm was that of identity, where the initial representation was fixed for the entire play.

Figure 9 shows the timing comparison, where we see that the role-representation alignment method is substantially faster than exhaustive alignment. This experiment was conducted on a 3.2GHz, 8GB RAM computer. It should be noted that only the attacking team is considered in this test. Had both teams (offense and defense) been involved in the retrieval task, the time cost difference would be even more significant by another order of magnitude.

Relevance Estimation

Relevance estimation is the problem of determining which plays in the data repository is most relevant to an input query, and is typically addressed by producing a ranking of decreasing similarity to the input query [42, 37]. Given that our approach compares agent-to-agent trajectories, we need a suitable similarity metric to capture the differences between plays.

We use a supervised classification experiment to evaluate which distance measure is most suitable for measuring play similarity. We asked a domain expert to annotate 1666 three-second plays into 38 classes based solely on the ball trajectory. We conducted the experiment via 5-fold cross validation and we compared six different metrics on the aligned trajectories: l_2 distance, l_∞ distance, Frechet distance, dynamic time warping (DTW), longest common subsequence (LCSS) and edit distance (Edit). For LCSS and edit distance, we use the SAX [30] to transform the time series into symbol series representation, which eliminates the effect of absolute position and focuses on the shape of trajectories. We used nearest neighbor as our classifier.

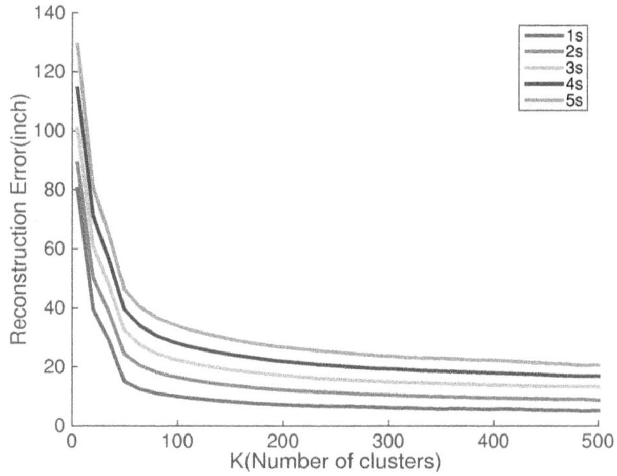

Figure 10. The reconstruction error against the number of clusters for time window sizes from 1 to 5 seconds.

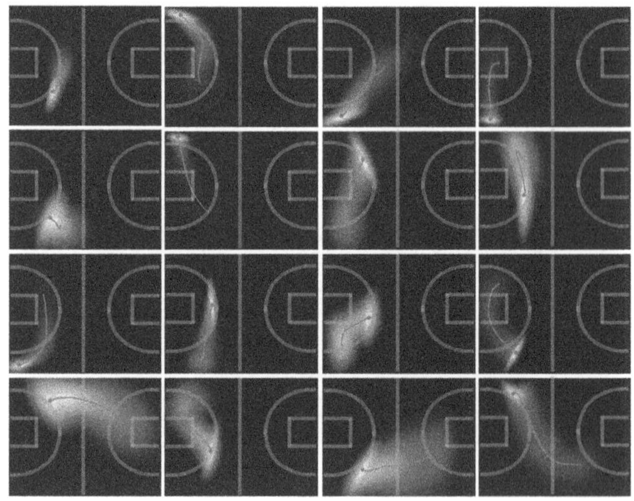

Figure 11. Some examples of the ball trajectories distribution in each cluster with 3-second time window. Red curve is the mean trajectory and the small red circles are the end points.

Table 1 shows the classification accuracy. We can that the first four metrics all worked reasonably well. To test if there were any significant differences between these four metrics we used the Mann-Whitney U significance test, which we chose as the number of examples per class were imbalanced. After running our significance tests, we found that there was no significant difference between these four. As such, we used the l_2 distance as our similarity measure as it is the easiest to deploy.

Hashing for Fast Indexing

In our dataset, we had over 600 hours worth of tracking data ($\sim$30GB), making similarity comparisons between a query and the entire database an expensive task. For example, if we were to break the database into a series of three second plays, this would equate to 4 million different examples. If each comparison took 30ms, searching the entire dataset would take 120secs – far too long to be usable as an interactive retrieval system.

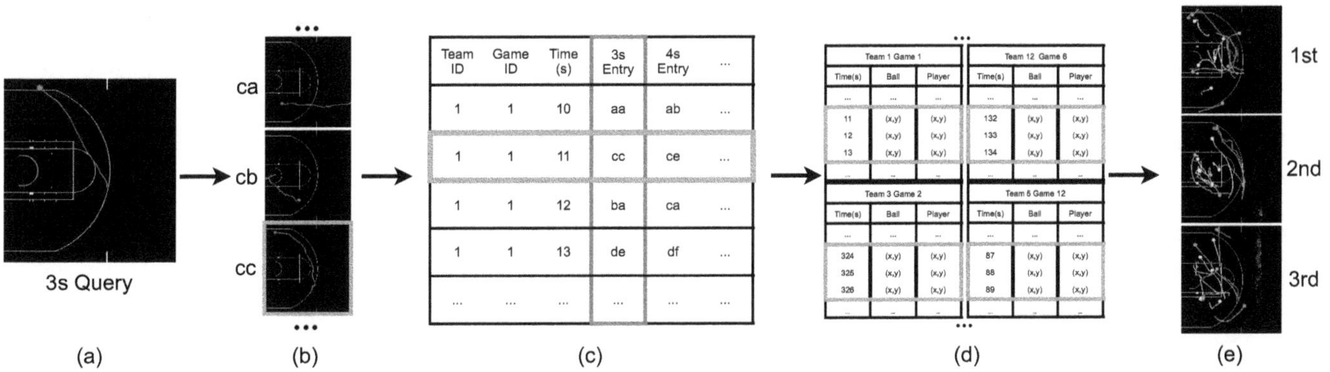

Figure 12. An example of our retrieval process: (a) 3-second query with only ball trajectory, (b) Compare to the centroid of each cluster, (c) Acquire the plays with entry cc (cluster index) from hash table, only look at 3s entry (red column) in this case, (d) According to the game index, fetch the corresponding plays from raw tracking data, (e) Find the top K nearest neighbor.

The standard approach to improve retrieval speed is to use a hash-table or some other kind of indexing [37]. Based on domain experts' opinions as well as our own observations while building the initial version of the system, we used the ball trajectory as our index feature. To learn the dictionary of indexes, we applied K-means clustering using the l_2 distance on all ball trajectories for time-windows of 1, 2, 3, 4 and 5 seconds. To choose K, we inspected the reconstruction error plots (Figure 10), which we chose to be around 60 clusters. Examples of some of the clusters for the 3 second trajectories are shown in Figure 11.

In addition to using the spatial location, ball-actions (e.g., pass, dribble, shots) were incorporated by further splitting the clusters into semantic clusters. To ensure that each cluster contained less than 1000 plays, we further divided clusters which had more than 1000 plays into sub-clusters by applying another round of K-means on the specific cluster until this was achieved (K was chosen according to the size of plays within the current cluster – e.g., if a cluster had 2000 plays, we used K=3).

In terms of preprocessing, we use each frame as the starting point of the ball trajectory and obtain the ball trajectory for various time-windows (1-5 seconds). For each time-window, we then compare that trajectory to the centroid trajectory within the hash-table for the various time-windows. We then assign the index value of the closest centroid trajectory to that frame for each time-window.

Summary of Retrieval Process

Figure 12 depicts the end-to-end process of computing similarity measures of plays in our repository against an input query. Given an input query (Figure 12(a)), we first compare its ball trajectory against the centroids of every cluster (Figure 12(b)). In this case, cluster 'cc' has the best match, and acquire the 3-second plays from that cluster using a hash table lookup (Figure 12(c) and Figure 12(d)). Finally, we perform alignment and similarity matching between the query and the plays in the cluster, and return a ranking of the most similar plays. Note that our approach can continuously run in the background and produce increasingly better rankings of retrieved plays over time, e.g., by checking the next best cluster from Figure 12(b) (although the top retrieved plays tend to be from the best cluster and so does not change).

USER STUDY EXPERIMENTS

Since Chalkboarding is designed to help users to quickly find similar plays in a huge database, we validated our system via an user study on the end-to-end task of play retrieval. The goal of the user study was to compare the search quality of rankings generated by Chalkboarding versus conventional keyword-based queries.

Baseline

The baseline system that we compare against is a keyword-based retrieval system. A basketball expert provided the keywords (action + coarse location) for each retrieval task, so that users with little prior knowledge do not need to select the keyword themselves.

Experiment Design

We selected eight retrieval tasks for our user study that are representative of basketball plays which are shown in Figure 13. For the Chalkboarding system, the first four plays are provided as exemplar-based queries which the users can use. For the remaining four queries, we only showed them the exemplar figures with selected trajectories and asked the users to draw the queries on the chalkboard as a drawing-based query.

We evaluated the retrieval quality via an interleaved evaluation, where the top thirty results from the Chalkboarding and baseline systems combined via the Team-Draft Interleaving method [9] into a single ranking (see Figure 14). The combined ranking is then embedded in the retrieval window of the Chalkboarding retrieval interface (pane B2 in Figure 1(b)), after which the user will scan the results top-down and select the relevant plays.

This setup offers two benefits: i) it is a blind paired test that can control for user- and task-specific variability, which is often more reliable and sensitive than two-sample or A/B

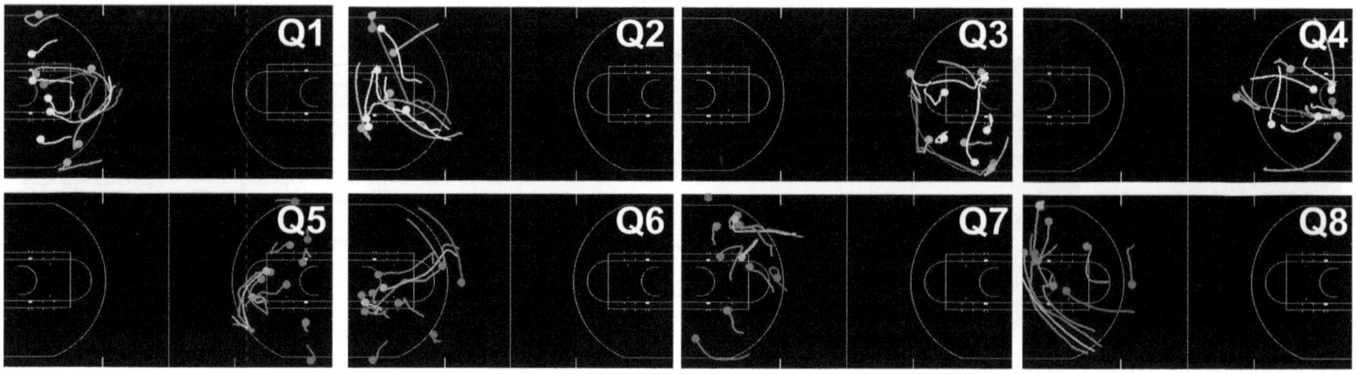

Figure 13. Depicting the eight test queries for our user study. These queries cover a wide range of plays in competitive basketball.

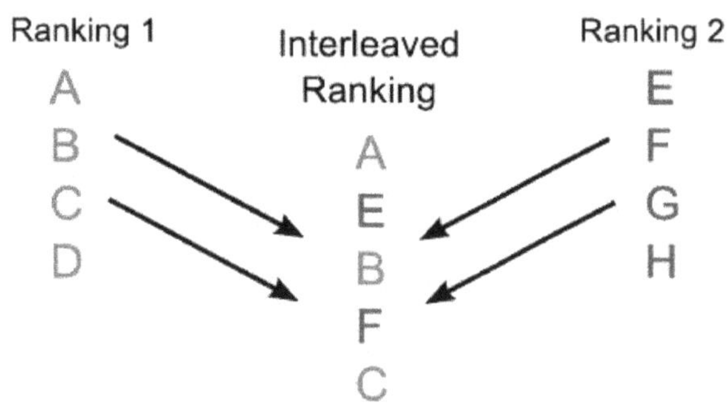

Figure 14. Depicting an interleaving of two rankings.

tests [9]; and ii) by only presenting a single ranking, interleaving allows for evaluation to be conducted in a natural usage context.

Procedure

We recruited ten volunteers with a wide range of basketball knowledge to participate in our user study. We first provided every volunteer with a ten minute introduction to ensure they understood basic basketball concepts. In particular, we used a ninth retrieval task as a demonstration for how to recognize relevant plays.

Every participant was allocated half an hour to perform all eight retrieval tasks. After the initial demonstration, all felt comfortable issuing Chalkboarding queries.

Participants used our Chalkboarding interface to retrieve each query and the result panel showed interleaved results from both systems. They were asked to scan the results top-down and highlight retrieved plays that they think are relevant to the input query. For most users, it took about ten minutes to acclimatize to the interface. After this time however, the average time it took to determine play relevance was around fifteen seconds.

Benchmark Results

Using the relevance judgments of the participants, we performed a benchmark comparison using two standard retrieval evaluation metrics: average precision [42, 37, 49] and expected reciprocal rank of the first result [10]. Let r_j denote the rank of the j-th relevant document, then the average precision of a ranking can be defined as:

$$\texttt{AvgPrec} = \frac{1}{\#rel} \sum_j Prec@r_j,$$

where $Prec@r_j$ is the precision of the top r_j items in the ranking (i.e., fraction of relevant results in the top r_j). The expected reciprocal rank is defined as:

$$\texttt{ERR} = \frac{1}{r_1},$$

which is simply the inverse of the rank of the first relevant result. Average precision is more recall-focused (i.e., places more emphasis on the rank location of all relevant results), whereas expected reciprocal rank is more sensitive to initial search time to finding the first result. For our setting, we computed both of the evaluation measures on the two virtual ranking functions embedded in the interleaved ranking, and over the pooling of both top-30 results (i.e., pooling based retrieval evaluation [37]).

	Q1	Q2	Q3	Q4	Overall
Chalkboarding	0.78	0.88	0.73	0.91	0.83
Keyword	0.06	0.17	0.24	0.09	0.14
Win / Lose	10 / 0	10 / 0	10 / 0	10 / 0	40 / 0

	Q5	Q6	Q7	Q8	Overall
Chalkboarding	0.90	0.71	0.83	0.85	0.82
Keyword	0.06	0.13	0.03	0.18	0.10
Win / Lose	10 / 0	10 / 0	10 / 0	10 / 0	40 / 0

Table 2. Comparing the mean average precision aggregated across all users for each query. Query 1-4 used exemplar-based queries in our system and 5-8 used drawing-based query. The "Win / Lose" rows show the number of users for whom Chalkboarding achieved a higher average precision. We see that Chalkboarding achieves orders-of-magnitude better retrieval quality.

Table 2 shows the results for average precision. The top two rows of the tables show the mean average precision aggregated across all ten users for each system. Recall that the first four retrieval tasks performed were using exemplar-based queries and the second four were using drawing-based

	Q1	Q2	Q3	Q4	Overall
Chalkboarding	0.83	0.85	0.63	1	0.8262
Keyword	0.03	0.06	0.14	0.04	0.07
Win / Lose	10 / 0	10 / 0	10 / 0	10 / 0	40 / 0

	Q5	Q6	Q7	Q8	Overall
Chalkboarding	0.95	0.82	0.95	0.9	0.90
Keyword	0.03	0.11	0.02	0.14	0.08
Win / Lose	10 / 0	10 / 0	10 / 0	10 / 0	40 / 0

Table 3. Comparing the expected reciprocal rank of the first relevant result across all users for each query. Comparing the mean average precision aggregated across all users for each query. Query 1-4 used exemplar-based queries in our system and 5-8 used drawing-based query. The "Win / Lose" rows show the number of users for whom Chalkboarding found a relevant result earlier in the ranking. We see that Chalkboarding achieves orders-of-magnitude better retrieval quality.

	Q1	Q2	Q3	Q4	Q5	Q6	Q7	Q8
Chalkboarding	10	9	7	10	10	9	10	8
Keyword	0	1	3	0	0	1	0	2

Table 4. Showing users' reported interface preference for each query. We see that users overwhelmingly preferred Chalkboarding over the baseline system.

queries. In both settings, our Chalkboarding system substantially outperformed the baseline system. It should be noted that the difference in retrieval quality is very large for all queries.

The "Win / Lose" rows in Table 2 show the breakdown of how many individual users experienced higher average precision using Chalkboarding compared to the baseline system. We see that our Chalkboarding system wins for every user on every retrieval task.

Table 3 shows the results for expected reciprocal rank, and is structurally analogous to Table 2. We again see that our Chalkboarding system achieves significantly better performance compared to the baseline approach.

Subjective Evaluation

We also conducted two subjective evaluations. In the first evaluation, we showed participants both the keyword-based interface (i.e., Figure 1(a)) and the Chalkboard interface and asked them which interface they prefer to use for each retrieval task. All participants had previous experience with keyword-based search interfaces and naturally understood how to use our keyword-based interface. Table 4 shows the results. For most retrieval tasks, the participants unanimously preferred Chalkboarding over the baseline system. Only for queries 2, 3, 6 and 8, some users still like to use the search bar because those plays were easy to describe.

We finally asked the participants to answer a short survey regarding their user experience, and the results are shown in in Figure 15. All participants agreed that our system was more enjoyable to use because it had more functions as well as being more intuitive. In terms of effectiveness, two users with rich basketball knowledge thought the two systems were similar because they didn't think using terminology to describe

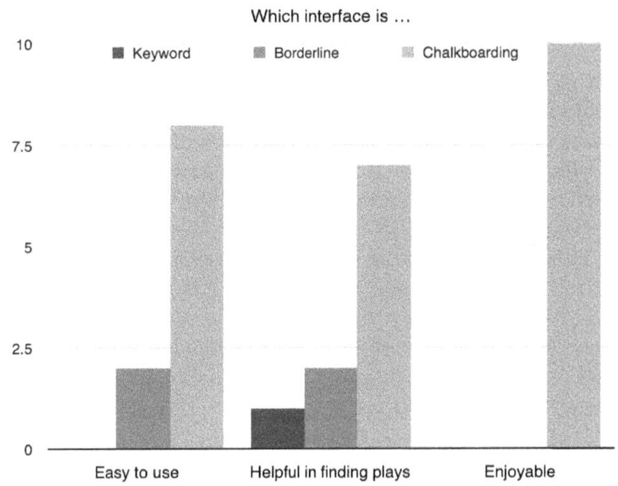

Figure 15. Showing results of our subjective survey. We see that users largely preferred the Chalkboarding system and found it easy and enjoyable to use.

a play is more complex than drawing. But for other users, instead of using domain knowledge to describe a play, drawing a play was definitely easier to find what they want. Seven participants thought Chalkboarding was more helpful for play retrieval, while the remaining three were neutral.

In our open-ended discussions about the system after the user study, the main criticism raised by the three participants who did not find Chalkboarding more helpful is that it is sometimes also important to acquire all the plays of one category. One suggestion was to have a hybrid system, where the user could use both the key-word and Chalkboard for their input query. Another criticism was that the user had to assign a role to each player, which some felt was unnecessarily complicated. We agree with this comment as this step can be automated. In future iterations, we intend to include this automated role assignment feature which will make the interface simpler.

RELATED WORK

The study of information retrieval enjoys a long and rich history in the information science and computer science communities [42, 37]. The overwhelming majority of previous work has been based on text-based or other types of tokenized query formats, which are unsuitable for sports play retrieval due to the inherent spatiotemporal nature of plays.

The most commonly studied type of retrieval and recommender systems that incorporate spatial or temporal data are those that are "location-aware", i.e., make use of information regarding the user's location to retrieve or recommend more relevant information [1, 48]. However, such approaches generally do not study new query formats.

Indeed, the use of free-form or "ad-hoc" queries in (mostly) unstructured corpora has proven to be significantly more user-friendly than more structured query types (e.g., SQL) [42, 37], and have come to dominate the commercial search industry. In a sense, our Chalkboarding approach can be viewed as a new variant of ad-hoc retrieval designed for spatiotemporal trajectory domains.

The primary complement to the query/retrieval paradigm within the broader field of information management and access is the directory/taxonomy paradigm [45]. Previous work on information access in the sports domain have largely focused on the directory/taxonomy paradigm via improving categorization of plays [38, 13, 3], which offers largely orthogonal benefits compared to the query/retrieval paradigm. However, similar to how one can construct a taxonomy of queries in web search [6], we have shown that integrating the two types of approaches can offer further benefit. Other work in sports analytics have largely focused on developing advanced metrics to evaluate player performance [19], analyzing video [32], or analyzing basic spatial patterns [39, 50].

Our approach bears affinity to other work on redesigning the interface between the human user and the data repository for various information retrieval and gathering tasks [5, 11, 16, 43]. Oftentimes, tuning system components such as the relevance estimation method results in relatively modest improvements in performance (cf. [49]), whereas designing a new interface to either accept richer inputs or produce richer outputs can lead to orders-or-magnitude improvements in overall system quality.

From the technical perspective, the primary challenge that we study is how to compare the similarity between two multi-agent trajectories. There have been ample previous work studying how to measure similarity between trajectories and time series [14, 44, 15, 21, 52], but they are largely focused on single trajectories rather than multi-agent ones. We build upon recent work that leverage a "role-based" representation [36, 46] that can compactly and efficiently characterize group behavior and formation in the sports domains.

The role representation is used primarily for alignment purposes and leaves open the question of what similarity measure to use for comparing individual pairs of aligned trajectories. One popular line of research focused on elastic measure that address warping and shifting effects in space and/or time [14, 2, 27, 28, 41, 31], while another line of research focused on finding the most simlar or dissimilar points in two trajectories in order to ensure some notion of robustness (e.g., via the Hausdorff distance) [33, 25]. As the latter is designed to measure distance between polygons and does not take the direction of trajectories into consideration [52], in this paper, we test some representative algorithms from the former category to find an ideal one for our task.

All modern retrieval systems require fast indexing in order to quickly search through a large repository, and one popular approach (which we also adopt) is to use a hash table [23, 51]. In different domains, the hash function is designed differently for specific applications. In general, the goal of hashing is to minimize time cost. Our approach is built on the concept of locality sensitive hashing (LSH) [24, 20], which is designed to place similar samples into a same address. Such an approach has also been applied in other settings where a similarity measure or ranking is required [26, 40].

DISCUSSION OF LIMITATIONS & FUTURE WORK

In a sense, our approach can be thought of as the simplest approach that can support effective sports play retrieval, and motivates many directions for future work. For instance, we can incorporate more sophisticated categorization techniques in order to further refine our query language (i.e., further combine the query/retrieval and directory/taxonomy paradigms). From an interface design standpoint, one obvious area for improvement is spatial manipulation of existing or pre-drawn trajectories (i.e., slightly translating or rotating an existing trajectory).

There are other important information access tasks beyond retrieval, most notably including summarization and personalized curation [11, 43]. A typical interface for the summarization setting is to construct clusters of results and describe the relationships between clusters. Chalkboarding can also be used to improve categorization systems by creating exemplars for clustering purposes.

From a system design standpoint, it would be highly beneficial to further improve retrieval speeds. For instance, many applications designed on top of web search require issuing multiple search queries, which is impractical given our current system. It is possible that using a hierarchical hashing/indexing technique and/or coresets [22, 17] can substantially improve retrieval speed.

From a relevance estimation standpoint, our choice of distance measures can be improved. For instance, one of the early breakthroughs in conventional information retrieval is the concept of "inverse document frequency" [42], which essentially states that tokens that appear in many documents in the corpuse (e.g., stopwords such as "the") are not as indicative of relevance more rare words. It would be interesting to incorporate this concept into our our trajectory distance measures. More generally, one can consider applying machine learning to develop even more accurate measures given appropriate training data [49, 7].

Another interesting direction is to incorporate more spatial regularities into the query processing. For example, understanding spatial equivalence classes [39, 50] can enable the retrieval system to understand that the left corner three point shot is (almost) equivalent to the right corner three point shot, which can further improve the accuracy of the system.

Beyond sports domains, query formats such as Chalkboarding could be applied to a wide range of spatiotemporal retrieval settings. Perhaps the most natural data domain is other types of behavioral tracking data, such as animal behavior.

CONCLUSION

We have presented Chalkboarding, which is a new query format that can naturally capture complex semantics of multi-agent trajectories for sports play retrieval. We have also presented a retrieval system tailor towards efficient and accurate sports play retrieval. Our full-stack system can achieve accurate retrieval at interactive speeds, and we demonstrate its effectiveness in a retrieval user study where our approach achieves orders-of-magnitude improvement in retrieval effectiveness over baseline methods.

REFERENCES

1. Bennett, P. N., Radlinski, F., White, R. W., and Yilmaz, E. Inferring and using location metadata to personalize web search. In *Proceedings of the 34th international ACM SIGIR conference on Research and development in Information Retrieval*, ACM (2011), 135–144.
2. Berndt, D. J., and Clifford, J. Using dynamic time warping to find patterns in time series. In *KDD workshop*, Seattle, WA (1994), 359–370.
3. Bialkowski, A., Lucey, P., Carr, P., Yue, Y., and Matthews, I. "win at home and draw away": Automatic formation analysis highlighting the differences in home and away team behaviors. In *MIT Sloan Sports Analytics Conference (SSAC)* (2014).
4. Bialkowski, A., Lucey, P., Carr, P., Yue, Y., Sridharan, S., and Matthews, I. Large-scale analysis of soccer matches using spatiotemporal tracking data. In *ICDM* (2014).
5. Brandt, C., Joachims, T., Yue, Y., and Bank, J. Dynamic ranked retrieval. In *ACM International Conference on Web Search and Data Mining (WSDM)*, ACM (2011), 247–256.
6. Broder, A. A taxonomy of web search. *ACM Sigir forum 36*, 2 (2002), 3–10.
7. Burges, C. J. From ranknet to lambdarank to lambdamart: An overview. Tech. Rep. MSR-TR-2010-82, Microsoft Research, 2010.
8. Carr, P., Sheikh, Y., and Matthews, I. Point-less calibration: Camera parameters from gradient-based alignment to edge images. In *IEEE Workshop on Applications of Computer Vision (WACV)*, IEEE (2012), 377–384.
9. Chapelle, O., Joachims, T., Radlinski, F., and Yue, Y. Large-scale validation and analysis of interleaved search evaluation. *ACM Transactions on Information Systems (TOIS) 30*, 1 (2012), 6:1–6:41.
10. Chapelle, O., Metlzer, D., Zhang, Y., and Grinspan, P. Expected reciprocal rank for graded relevance. In *ACM Conference on Information and Knowledge Management (CIKM)*, ACM (2009), 621–630.
11. Chau, D. H., Kittur, A., Hong, J. I., and Faloutsos, C. Apolo: making sense of large network data by combining rich user interaction and machine learning. In *Proceedings of the SIGCHI Conference on Human Factors in Computing Systems*, ACM (2011), 167–176.
12. Chen, J., and Carr, P. Mimicking human camera operators. In *Applications of Computer Vision (WACV), 2015 IEEE Winter Conference on*, IEEE (2015), 215–222.
13. Chen, S., Feng, Z., Lu, Q., Mahasseni, B., Fiez, T., Fern, A., and Todorovic, S. Play type recognition in real-world football video. In *IEEE Winter Conference on Applications of Computer Vision (WACV)* (2014).
14. Chen, Y., Nascimento, M., Ooi, B. C., and Tung, A. Spade: On shape-based pattern detection in streaming time series. In *Data Engineering, 2007. ICDE 2007. IEEE 23rd International Conference on* (April 2007), 786–795.
15. Eichmann, P., and Zgraggen, E. Evaluating subjective accuracy in time series pattern-matching using human-annotated rankings. In *Proceedings of the 20th International Conference on Intelligent User Interfaces*, ACM (2015), 28–37.
16. El-Arini, K., and Guestrin, C. Beyond keyword search: discovering relevant scientific literature. In *ACM SIGKDD International Conference on Knowledge Discovery and Data Mining (KDD)*, ACM (2011), 439–447.
17. Feldman, D., Faulkner, M., and Krause, A. Scalable training of mixture models via coresets. In *Neural Information Processing Systems (NIPS)* (2011), 2142–2150.
18. Fischler, M. A., and Bolles, R. C. Random sample consensus: a paradigm for model fitting with applications to image analysis and automated cartography. *Communications of the ACM 24*, 6 (1981), 381–395.
19. Franks, A., Miller, A., Bornn, L., and Goldsberry, K. Counterpoints: Advanced defensive metrics for nba basketball. In *MIT Sloan Sports Analytics Conference (SSAC)* (2015).
20. Gionis, A., Indyk, P., and Motwani, R. Similarity search in high dimensions via hashing. In *Conference on Very Large Databases (VLDB)*, vol. 99 (1999), 518–529.
21. Gudmundsson, J., Laube, P., and Wolle, T. Computational movement analysis. In *Springer handbook of geographic information*. Springer, 2012, 423–438.
22. Har-Peled, S., and Mazumdar, S. On coresets for k-means and k-median clustering. In *ACM Symposium on Theory of Computing (STOC)*, ACM (2004), 291–300.
23. Huston, S., Culpepper, J. S., and Croft, W. B. Indexing word sequences for ranked retrieval. *ACM Transactions on Information Systems (TOIS) 32*, 1 (2014), 3.
24. Indyk, P., and Motwani, R. Approximate nearest neighbors: towards removing the curse of dimensionality. In *ACM Symposium on Theory of Computing (STOC)*, ACM (1998), 604–613.
25. Junejo, I. N., Javed, O., and Shah, M. Multi feature path modeling for video surveillance. In *IEEE International Conference on Computer Vision and Pattern Recognition (CVPR)*, vol. 2, IEEE (2004), 716–719.
26. Kafai, M., Eshghi, K., and Bhanu, B. Discrete cosine transform locality-sensitive hashes for face retrieval. *Multimedia, IEEE Transactions on 16*, 4 (2014), 1090–1103.

27. Keogh, E., and Ratanamahatana, C. A. Exact indexing of dynamic time warping. *Knowledge and information systems 7*, 3 (2005), 358–386.

28. Keogh, E. J., and Pazzani, M. J. Scaling up dynamic time warping for datamining applications. In *Proceedings of the sixth ACM SIGKDD international conference on Knowledge discovery and data mining*, ACM (2000), 285–289.

29. Kuhn, H. W. The hungarian method for the assignment problem. *Naval Research Logistics Quarterly 2*, 1-2 (1955).

30. Lin, J., Keogh, E., Lonardi, S., and Chiu, B. A symbolic representation of time series, with implications for streaming algorithms. In *Proceedings of the 8th ACM SIGMOD workshop on Research issues in data mining and knowledge discovery*, ACM (2003), 2–11.

31. Listgarten, J., Neal, R. M., Roweis, S. T., and Emili, A. Multiple alignment of continuous time series. In *Neural Information Processing Systems (NIPS)* (2004), 817–824.

32. Liu, T.-Y., Ma, W.-Y., and Zhang, H.-J. Effective feature extraction for play detection in american football video. In *IEEE Multimedia Modelling Conference (MMM)*, IEEE (2005), 164–171.

33. Lou, J., Liu, Q., Tan, T., and Hu, W. Semantic interpretation of object activities in a surveillance system. In *Pattern Recognition, 2002. Proceedings. 16th International Conference on*, vol. 3, IEEE (2002), 777–780.

34. Lowe, D. G. Object recognition from local scale-invariant features. In *IEEE Conference on Computer Vision and Pattern Recognition*, vol. 2, Ieee (1999), 1150–1157.

35. Lowe, Z. Lights, cameras, revolution. Grantland, March 2013.

36. Lucey, P., Bialkowski, A., Carr, P., Morgan, S., Matthews, I., and Sheikh, Y. Representing and discovering adversarial team behaviors using player roles. In *IEEE Conference on Computer Vision and Pattern Recognition (CVPR)* (2013).

37. Manning, C. D., Raghavan, P., Schütze, H., et al. *Introduction to information retrieval*, vol. 1. Cambridge university press Cambridge, 2008.

38. McQueen, A., Wiens, J., and Guttag, J. Automatically recognizing on-ball screens. In *MIT Sloan Sports Analytics Conference (SSAC)* (2014).

39. Miller, A., Bornn, L., Adams, R., and Goldsberry, K. Factorized point process intensities: A spatial analysis of professional basketball. In *International Conference on Machine Learning (ICML)* (2014).

40. Qin, J., Liu, L., Yu, M., Wang, Y., and Shao, L. Fast action retrieval from videos via feature disaggregation. In *BMVC*, BMVC (2015).

41. Sakurai, Y., Yoshikawa, M., and Faloutsos, C. Ftw: fast similarity search under the time warping distance. In *Proceedings of the twenty-fourth ACM SIGMOD-SIGACT-SIGART symposium on Principles of database systems*, ACM (2005), 326–337.

42. Salton, G., and McGill, M. J. *Introduction to modern information retrieval*. McGraw-Hill, Inc., 1986.

43. Shahaf, D., Guestrin, C., and Horvitz, E. Metro maps of science. In *ACM SIGKDD International Conference on Knowledge Discovery and Data Mining (KDD)*, ACM (2012), 1122–1130.

44. Toohey, K., and Duckham, M. Trajectory similarity measures. *SIGSPATIAL Special 7*, 1 (2015), 43–50.

45. Wall, A. History of search engines: From 1945 to google today.

46. Wei, X., Sha, L., Lucey, P., Morgan, S., and Sridharan, S. Large-scale analysis of formations in soccer. In *Digital Image Computing: Techniques and Applications (DICTA), 2013 International Conference on*, IEEE (2013), 1–8.

47. Wen, P., Cheng, W., Wang, Y., Chu, H., Tang, N., and Liao, H. Court reconstruction for camera calibration in broadcast basketball videos. *Visualization and Computer Graphics, IEEE Transactions on PP*, 99 (2015), 1–1.

48. Yahi, A., Chassang, A., Raynaud, L., Duthil, H., and Chau, D. H. P. Aurigo: an interactive tour planner for personalized itineraries. In *Proceedings of the 20th International Conference on Intelligent User Interfaces*, ACM (2015), 275–285.

49. Yue, Y., Finley, T., Radlinski, F., and Joachims, T. A support vector method for optimizing average precision. In *ACM Conference on Information Retrieval (SIGIR)*, ACM (2007), 271–278.

50. Yue, Y., Lucey, P., Carr, P., Bialkowski, A., and Matthews, I. Learning fine grained spatial models for dynamic sports play prediction. In *IEEE International Conference on Data Mining (ICDM)* (2014).

51. Zhang, S., Yang, M., Cour, T., Yu, K., and Metaxas, D. N. Query specific rank fusion for image retrieval. *Pattern Analysis and Machine Intelligence, IEEE Transactions on 37*, 4 (2015), 803–815.

52. Zhang, Z., Huang, K., and Tan, T. Comparison of similarity measures for trajectory clustering in outdoor surveillance scenes. In *Pattern Recognition, 2006. ICPR 2006. 18th International Conference on*, vol. 3, IEEE (2006), 1135–1138.

AppGrouper: Knowledge-graph-based Interactive Clustering Tool for Mobile App Search Results

Shuo Chang*[1], Peng Dai[2], Lichan Hong[2], Cheng Sheng[2], Tianjiao Zhang[2], Ed H. Chi[2]

[1]GroupLens Research
University of Minnesota
schang@cs.umn.edu

[2]Google Research
Google Inc.
daipeng, lichan, csheng, cathyzhang, edchi@google.com

ABSTRACT

A relatively new feature in Google Play Store presents mobile app search results grouped by topic, helping users to quickly navigate and explore. The underlying Search Results Clustering (SRC) system faces several challenges, including grouping search results in topical coherent clusters as well as finding the appropriate level of granularity for clustering. We present *AppGrouper*, an alternative approach to algorithmic-only solutions, incorporating human input in a knowledge-graph-based clustering process. AppGrouper provides an interactive interface that lets domain experts steer the clustering process in early, mid, and late stages. We deployed and evaluated AppGrouper with internal experts. We found that AppGroup improved quality of algorithm-generated app clusters on 56 out of 82 search queries. We also found that the internal experts made more changes in early and mid stages for lower-quality algorithmic results, focusing more on narrow queries. Our result suggests, in some contexts, machine learning systems can greatly benefit from steering from human experts, creating a symbiotic working relationship.

Author Keywords

Interactive machine learning; Clustering; Search Result Clustering

ACM Classification Keywords

H.1.2. User/Machine Systems

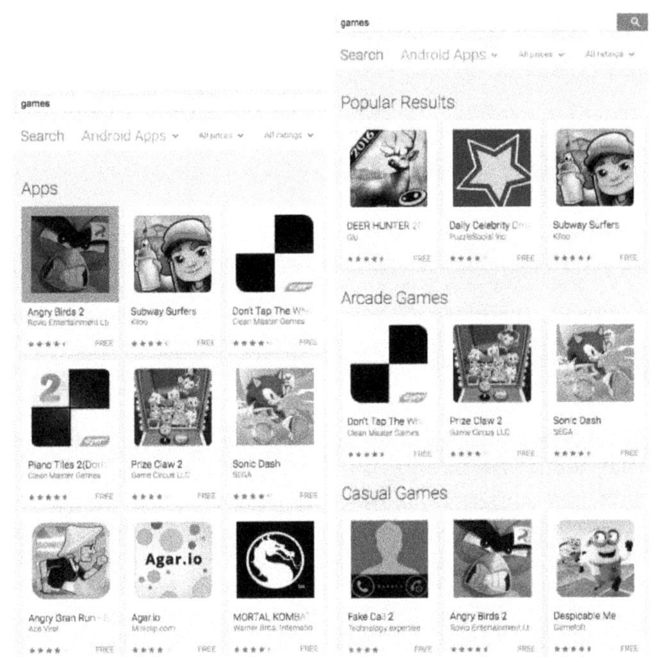

(a) List (b) Grouped by topic

Figure 1. Example of search results for the query "games" in Google Play Store: (a) Left side shows search results in grid; (b) right side shows search results grouped by topic.

INTRODUCTION

Presenting search results grouped by topic (Figure 1b) is a popular alternative to displaying results in plain ranked lists (Figure 1a), enabling users to explore and navigate topic space of search results. This technique is now used in many well-known websites, such as Google Play Store, Pinterest, Google News, etc., and has attracted attention from the research community, where the technique is referred to as Search Results Clustering (SRC for short).

Despite past efforts [6, 12, 17], purely algorithmic SRC techniques do not generally create production-quality document clusters due to the complexity of the unsupervised clustering problem. Search results change all the time due to new documents, changes in user interests, and discovery of new ranking signals. Therefore, the dynamic nature of search results requires an efficient on-the-fly clustering process. Furthermore, many properties of the clusters affect the final user experience, for example, whether there are descriptive labels for clusters; whether documents in clusters are semantically coherent; whether clusters cover all relevant topics under a search query.

*Work was done during internship at Google.

IUI 2016, March 7–10, 2016, Sonoma, CA, USA.
Copyright © 2016 ACM 978-1-4503-4137-0/16/03 ...$15.00.
http://dx.doi.org/10.1145/2856767.2856783

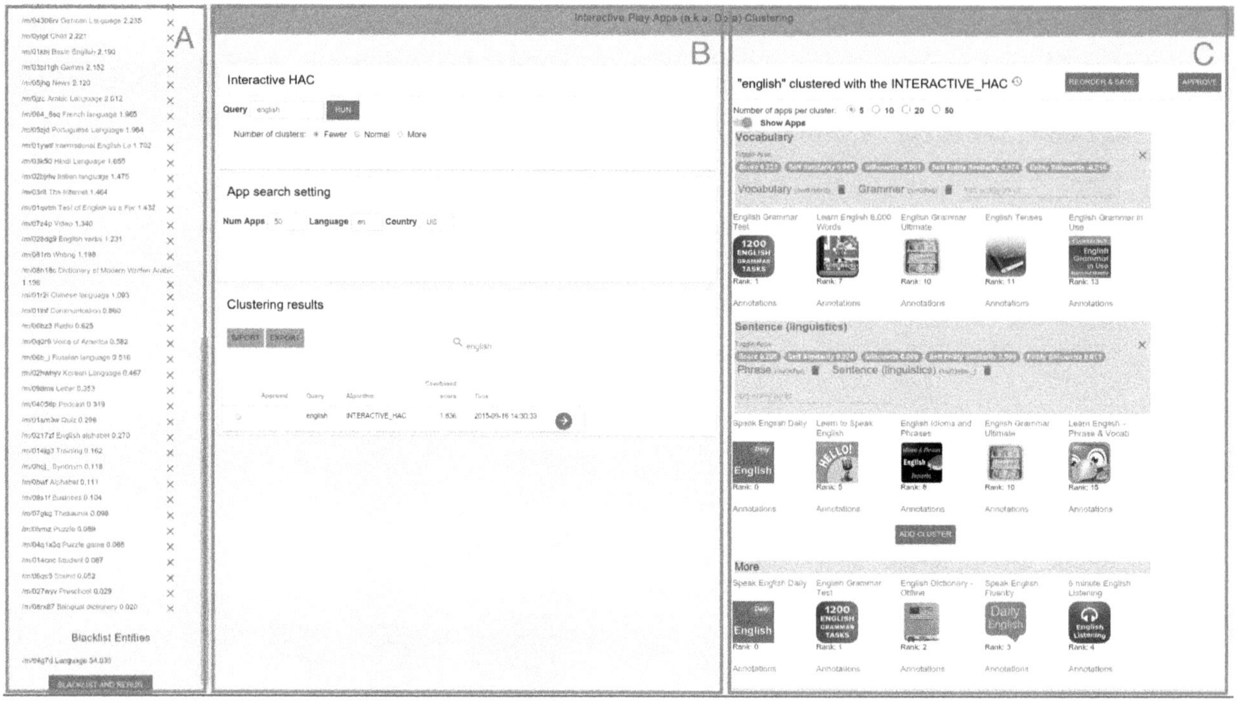

Figure 2. Interface of AppGrouper — an interactive app clustering tool for Google Play Store — consists of three parts: A) side bar with a list of topic labels used in clustering, B) control panels for loading and running clustering, and C) editable app clusters.

We propose an interactive machine learning approach that combines human intelligence with machine intelligence for app search clustering in Google Play Store. Inspired by prior work [17], we design a knowledge-graph-based clustering process for a query and its associated ranked apps: extract topic labels from apps, cluster topic labels, and assign apps to topic label clusters. This process not only provides topic labels that describe the app clusters, but also opens up opportunities for expert input. For example, once major topic clusters are associated with a query, experts can create or edit the name for a cluster based on its content. For instance, even though the search results for "games" change over time, its topical clusters such as "action games", "arcade games", etc., remain relatively stable, and we can create cluster names for these clusters.

We hypothesize that expert input into clustering process can substantially improve app clusters from Search Results Clustering algorithms. Apart from incremental improvements such as picking appropriate names for clusters, experts can provide useful feedback in the process of generating topic clusters.

We built AppGrouper, an interactive clustering system (Figure 2) that generates app clusters while incorporating expert decisions in the process. AppGrouper provides an interface that depicts algorithm-generated, topic-label clusters and accepts expert input in multiple stages of clustering process: (1) *Early stage*: refining input to clustering algorithm; (2) *Mid stage*: steering the algorithm to generate more or less fine-grained clusters; and (3) *Late stage*: editing topic label clusters and topic labels.

This paper offers the following contributions: (1) We presented a novel interactive machine learning approach, including a knowledge-graph-based clustering process and a visual interface, to solve SRC problems. (2) We designed and implemented AppGrouper, an end-to-end system that injects human judgements into the clustering process during its various stages. (3) Through evaluation with experts, we showed signficant quality improvements of the clustering results generated through AppGrouper, and offer some implications for designing interactive machine learning systems in general.

This paper is structured as follows. We first survey related work and situate our research. Next, we introduce the problem of search results clustering in app search. Then, we describe the interactive clustering system, elaborating on the knowledge-graph-based clustering algorithm and how we incorporate expert decisions. We follow this by presenting an evaluation of AppGrouper. Finally, we conclude with a discussion of the findings and design implications.

RELATED WORK

AppGrouper is an interactive clustering system that enables human intervention in Search Results Clustering process. Our work is broadly related to the general domain of interactive machine learning. For the closely related area of Search Results Clustering, most research attention has gone into algorithm solutions.

Interactive Machine Learning

Interactive machine learning combines human judgments with machine learning. Prior work has experimented with interactive machine learning in various applications, including image segmentation [11], document clustering [5, 10], image search [13] and specialized tasks such as grouping social network contacts [1].

Expert input to machine learning system comes in different forms depending on the underlying machine learning algorithms and application domains. Regardless of the types of input, machine learning systems need to be transparent in depicting its results to enable efficient human input [14]. For image segmentation, Fails et al. [11] asked users to provide training samples to machine learning algorithm. Vig et al. [18] enabled end users to critique the results of recommender algorithm and tuned hyper-parameters of the underlying algorithm accordingly.

A subtle and important difference in our work is that we ask for expert input on an internal intermediate model of the clustering process. In previous works [3, 4], users gave feedback of documents that should or should not be together (must-link and cannot-link constraints), guiding algorithm to generate clusters that satisfy these constraints. However, we must design a system that clusters a changing set of apps, because the search results are updated all the time. To be precise, if expert-provided constraints are simply on what apps do or do not belong to a cluster, these constraints may become irrelevant over time, because search results are dynamic. Instead, AppGrouper asks for expert input on an internal model — topic clusters, which specify what topics belong together. Dynamic search results are then assigned to these topic clusters during serving.

Search Results Clustering

Much research attention has been drawn into improving algorithms for clustering search results, as surveyed by Carpineto et al. [6]. Early works focus on approaches that derive features from texts of search result documents and cluster documents based on these features on the fly. One early clustering system called "Scatter/Gather" [16] interactively clusters text document using a bag-of-words model. Later, Ferragina et al. [12] proposed clustering on extracted phrases from search results. Osinski et al. [15] projected text documents into a latent topic space and then performed clustering. More recently, Carpineto et al. [7] presented a meta clustering system that combines outputs from several clustering systems and showed improvements.

Apart from topically-coherent search result clusters, descriptive labels for clusters are critical for good user experience [6]. Practitioners have realized this and spent considerable effort into description-centric clustering algorithms, as evident by commercial search result clustering systems such as *Lingo3G* and *CarrotSearch*. Scaiella et al. [17] contributed to description-centric approach by presenting a topical clustering system. The system annotates text documents with topic entities from Wikipedia and clusters these topic entities together with documents. AppGrouper uses similar knowledge-graph-based approach to cluster apps. However, algorithm-generated clustering results are not perfect, resulting in sub-optimal user experiences when browsing these clusters. We are interested in augmenting the algorithmic solutions and build an interface that enables human interactions with algorithm to fix these problems.

BACKGROUND: APP SEARCH RESULTS CLUSTERING

Why Clustering Search Results

Grouping search results by topic helps users to better discover new areas for exploration. Generally speaking, for navigational search queries, presenting search results in lists seems reasonably effective, which directs users to the particular apps they want to install, e.g., "angry bird". The same approach offers sub-optimal user experience for broad categorical search queries, e.g., "games". Clustering search results for categorical search queries assists users to better achieve the following goals:

- *Explore the topic space related to search queries.* For example, users are interested in discovering what games are available when they search for "games". Users can easily see all genres of games through app clusters shown in figure 1b.
- *Navigate to interesting subtopics.* If users are interested in certain subtopic, they can quickly navigate to the groups of search results related to that subtopic. For example, if a user is interested in "casual game" apps, she can easily navigate to these apps as shown in figure 1b.
- *Discover less popular results.* Search engines typically rank less popular (e.g., less clicked) results toward the bottom of result lists, attracting less attention from users. Grouping results by topics makes less popular results from a diverse set of topics more visible to users: assuming the first 4-5 listed results for query "games" are all action game apps, clustered search results might make arcade game apps and casual game apps more prominent than organic ranked results.

Challenges of Clustering

Search Results Clustering, unlike the popular usage of clustering as a data exploration method, generates clusters that are shown to end users of search engine. This user-facing application creates the following requirements for clustering:

- **P1: Semantically meaningful topic labels for clusters.** Descriptive labels are important for users to understand *what are included in clusters.* Furthermore, topic labels should be sub-concepts under a search query, so that users understand *why clusters are presented.* For example, topic label "tool" would be inappropriate for the query [weather app], because "tool" is a parent concept encompassing all "weather

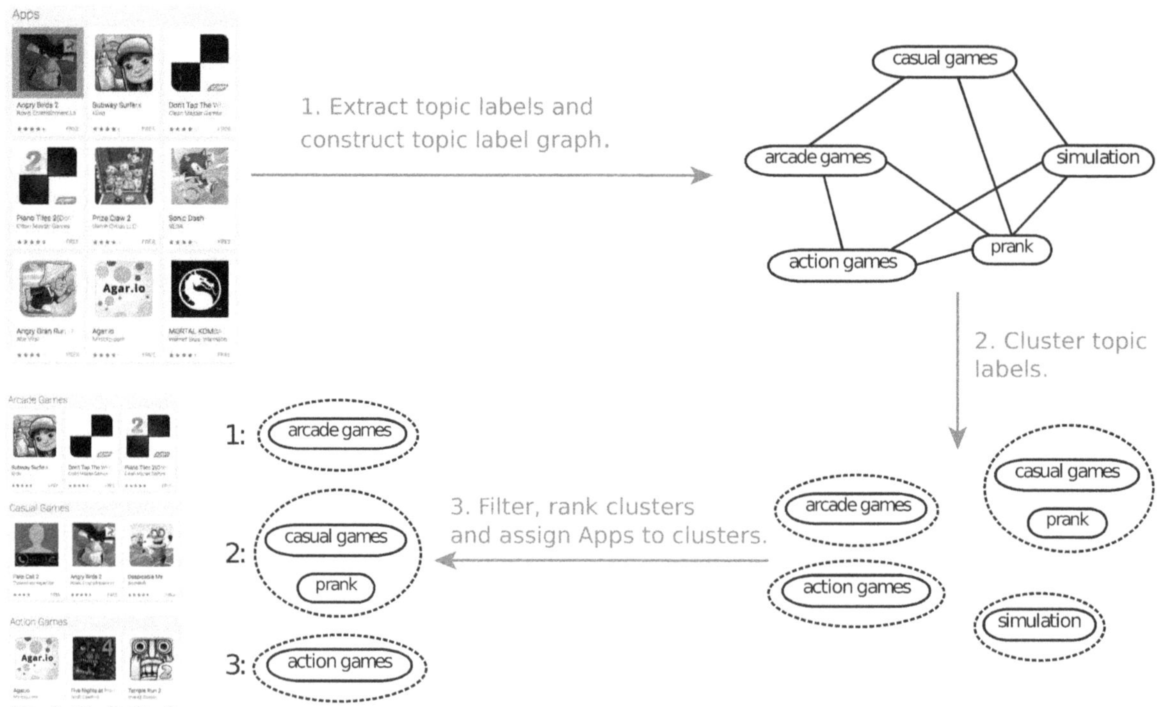

Figure 3. The knowledge-graph-based clustering process, which has three major steps, to generate app clusters for search query [games].

apps". This is a great challenge for topic-model-based clustering algorithms, which typically do not capture hierarchical semantic relationships perfectly.

- **P2: Topical coherence within clusters and separation between clusters.** This is a common objective but also a long standing challenge for all document clustering algorithms. For example, query [game] should not cluster "blackjack" and "angry bird" together when there are other arcade games and card games available.

- **P3: Appropriate granularity of clusters.** High granularity results in small number of cluster, and low granularity results in large number of clusters. Granularity of clustering is query dependent, therefore number of clusters is also query dependent. For example, a "Blackjack" cluster is suitable for search query [card games] but might not be for search query [games], because it is too fine-grained. In recent work, Scaiella et al. asked Amazon Mechanical Turkers to evaluate topicality of search result clusters from their proposed system and two commercial systems, and found that around 20% of clusters should be merged [17].

- **P4: Balanced cluster sizes.** The sizes of clusters, i.e., number of apps in clusters, should be balanced. If one or two clusters contain most search results while the other ones contain only few results, the interface essentially degenerates to plain lists of search results.

- **P5: Clusters should cover most search results.** It is a common practice to include an "other" cluster that contains results not belonging to any cluster. However, when clusters do not cover many results, users have to find targeted result in a very big "other" cluster, defeating the goal of presenting clusters.

Generating clusters with these properties (especially *P1, P2 and P3*) poses a great challenge for the algorithm, but where artificial intelligence struggles human intelligence may excel. For example, experts can judge whether a label describes apps in a cluster, understand concept hierarchy between cluster labels and search query (e.g., "tool" is an inappropriate cluster for search query "weather app"), and evaluate whether apps in one cluster are topically coherent, while algorithms face challenges for many of these tasks.

THE APPGROUPER SYSTEM

We build an interactive clustering system, AppGrouper, that incorporates expert decisions into multiple stages of a knowledge-graph-based clustering algorithm. In this section, we describe several key aspects of AppGrouper, including the clustering algorithm, the user interface, and ways of eliciting and using expert input.

Knowledge-Graph-based Clustering Algorithm

Instead of directly clustering apps, the algorithm extracts topic labels (mapped to concepts in knowledge bases such as DBpedia [1]) from search results, runs clus-

[1] http://wiki.dbpedia.org/

tering on a semantic graph of topic labels, and assigns search results to topic clusters. Knowledge-graph-based clustering algorithm have been somewhat explored in prior work [17].

This approach is made possible with increasingly accurate topic annotation systems, capable of extracting topics from text [8], image [19] and even video [2]. In our system, the topic extraction algorithm is a state-of-the-art entity recognition algorithm that runs over the app meta-data, including its title, descriptions, reviews, etc. The result of the entity recognizer is then fed into a regression-based ensemble learner that generates the most likely topic labels.

In describing the clustering algorithm, we introduce the following notations:

$A = \{a_1, ..., a_n\}$ denotes the set of apps returned by search engine for a query;

$T = \{t_1, ..., t_m\}$ denotes the set of topic labels extracted from A using a topic annotator system for apps;

$C_t = \{T_1, ..., T_k\}$ denotes k clusters of topic labels; $C_a = \{A_1, ..., A_k\}$ denotes k app clusters.

The clustering algorithm optimizes for generating app clusters with previously introduced properties, which we formally define as follows:

- **P2**: Apps within the same cluster are coherent and apps in different clusters are distinct:

$$coherence(C_a) = \sum_{A_x \in C_a} \sum_{a_i, a_j \in A_x} sim(a_i, a_j) \quad (1)$$

$$separation(C_a) = \sum_{a_i \in A_x, a_j \in A_y} [1 - sim(a_i, a_j)], \quad A_x, A_y \in C_a \quad (2)$$

- **P3**: Granularity of clusters is query-dependent, and choosing the right numbers of clusters for different queries is difficult. We penalize clustering results that have too many or too few clusters with the following equation (σ_{lower} and σ_{upper} are lower bound and upper bounds).

$$num\_clusters(C_a) = \begin{cases} \sigma_{lower} - |C_a|, & |C_a| < \sigma_{lower} \\ |C_a| - \sigma_{upper}, & |C_a| > \sigma_{upper} \\ 0, & otherwise \end{cases} \quad (3)$$

- **P4**: App clusters have balanced sizes:

$$balance(C_a) = max_{A_x \in C_a} |A_x| - min_{A_y \in C_a} |A_y| \quad (4)$$

- **P5:** App clusters cover most search results:

$$coverage(C_a) = \sum_{A_x \in C_a} |A_x| \quad (5)$$

Since we want to generate a clustering result that simultaneously optimizes all the objectives above, we formulate the problem as a multiple objectives optimization, defining the objective function as weighted sum of the above properties:

$$\begin{aligned} \alpha_1 \cdot coherence(C_a) + \alpha_2 \cdot separation(C_a) + \\ \alpha_3 \cdot num\_clusters(C_a) + \alpha_4 \cdot balance(C_a) + \\ \alpha_5 \cdot coverage(C_a) \end{aligned} \quad (6)$$

We set the weights $\alpha_1 ... \alpha_5$ and the range of number of clusters $[\sigma_{lower}, \sigma_{upper}]$ through human evaluations, aligning the objective function with expert-judged quality of clustering results.

To generate app clusters optimized for the objective function (6) defined above, we design a multi-stage clustering process, which we will describe with an example shown in figure 3:

1. In Step 1, we obtain topic labels for the search result apps by using a topic annotation system. The topic semantic relation graph is used to construct the topic label graph (as shown in the figure for the search query [games]). The weights of edges in the graph reflect the topical relevance between nodes, computed as the similarity between sets of apps covered by two topic labels.
2. In Step 2, after obtaining the topic label graph, we run a standard clustering algorithm, Hierarchical Agglomerate Clustering (HAC for short), on the graph. Like most other clustering algorithms, HAC requires a hyper-parameter, which is the minimum similarity threshold that two nodes can be merged into same cluster in the process of building a hierarchical tree. We exhaustively search for the optimal value for this parameter that maximizes the objective function (6) by running HAC with varying values of the threshold. In the example, this optimal result has four clusters.
3. In Step 3, to obtain balanced clusters, we filter out clusters that cover too few apps (the "simulation" cluster) and then we rank order the topic clusters. We rank the topic clusters by assigning apps to those clusters and computing the quality of the clusters based on the app assignments. The rank order of the topic clusters affects numbers of apps assigned to clusters, because we assign apps to the ranked clusters in a greedy way. In ranked order, apps are assigned to the first cluster that matched its topic label. For example, in the figure, we assign all apps that are associated with "arcade games" to the first cluster, then remaining apps that are associated with either "casual games" or "prank" to the second cluster and finally remaining apps that are associated with "action games". To obtain the ordering that maximizes balance, we exhaustively search all orderings. Finally, we make a "more" cluster that includes all apps not included in app clusters.

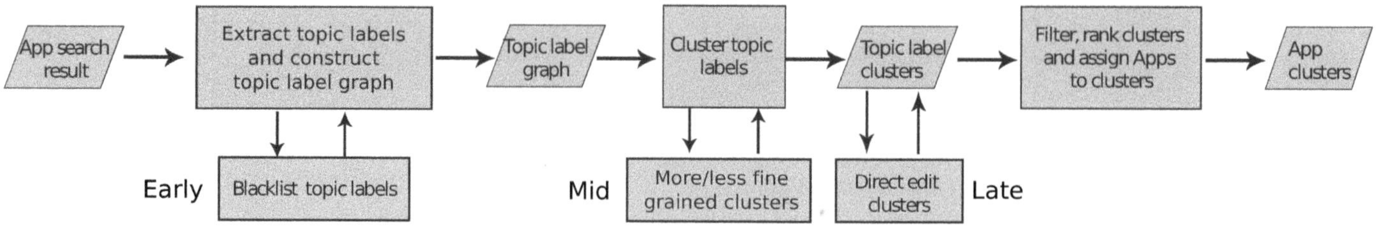

Figure 4. A flow chart with expert decisions in the clustering process. Parallelograms represent data, while rectangles represent process. The three orange boxes on the bottom show expert input in the clustering process in early, mid and late stages.

This clustering process has a couple of advantages over past search result clustering search results approaches. First, the process generates topic labels that describe app clusters; human can easily understand and give critique on clusters of topic labels. Second, knowledge-graph-based clustering is computationally more efficient than computing the clustering on the fly, because clustering systems can store the relative stable topic clusters and assign dynamic search results on the fly to these clusters. For example, users would expect to see the subtopics "action games" and "arcade games" for the query [games], even if the pool of search result changes over time. If humans make edits on topic label cluster, these edits have a long lasting effect.

User Interface

AppGrouper, shown in Figure 2, has a visual interface that lets users load pre-computed clusters and interactively generates new clusters using the algorithm previously described. The interface has three main components: a sidebar on the left (A in figure 2), panels in the middle (B in figure 2) and clusters on the right (C in figure 2).

The panels (B in figure 2) in the middle affect the clusters shown on the right. From top to bottom, the first panel lets users run clustering on a user-specified search query and indicate a preference on the number of clusters; the second panel lets users configure the language of apps shown in clusters; the third panel presents users all clustering results previously computed and lets users search for and select clusters to show.

The right side (C in figure 2) of the interface shows clusters with topic labels for a search query (either newly computed or loaded from previously computed results). Figure 2 shows the clustering result for the query [English]. There are two topic label clusters - one having topic labels "Vocabulary" and "Grammar" and another having topic labels "Phrase" and "Sentence". Each topic cluster has an algorithmically-chosen cluster label (e.g., "Vocabulary") — the topic label that covers most apps in each cluster. The green round boxes contain measurements of clusters' various properties, e.g., coverage of apps and coherence of apps. There is an app cluster with label "More" on the bottom, containing all apps returned from search engine. By clicking on the radio buttons beneath the title of clustering result, users can change the number of apps to show in each cluster. We will describe how users can modify clustering results with other buttons on this panel in the following section.

The left sidebar (A in figure 2) shows all the topic labels in the topic label graph, excluding labels already included in clusters. We will elaborate in the following section how users use this list of topic labels.

Expert Decisions in the Clustering Process

Using AppGrouper, users can inject their judgments at various stages of the clustering process, as shown in Figure 4. As previously discussed, the algorithm is optimized for a set of weighted clustering properties. Expert decisions can help to ensure that *topic labels are semantically meaningful for app clusters*, *app clusters are topically coherent* and *the granularity of clusters is appropriate*, while making the tradeoff decisions between these requirements. We describe the way which we integrate expert judgments in the clustering process below.

Early stage. When the algorithm builds a topic label graph, users can "blacklist" semantically inappropriate topic labels (**P1**), which contribute to low-quality clustering results. For example, if the topic label "game" is included in topic label graph for the query [games for girls], a "game" cluster will most likely be generated. This is bad because "game" is a broader concept than the original query and this "game" cluster will likely include all search results.

Figure 5 shows the left sidebar, zoomed in, depicting a list of topic labels, which are sorted by the percentages of apps covered by that topic, shown to the right of labels. Users can click on topic labels to check their definitions, click on the cross buttons to add labels to blacklist and click on "blacklist and rerun" to re-execute the clustering process.

Mid stage. When the clustering algorithm generates clusters from the topic label graph, users can indicate preferences on a larger or smaller number of clusters, resulting in more or less fine-grained clusters (**P3**). The predetermined range for the number of clusters ([8, 12]) does not work for queries that have a very narrow or a very broad concept. For example, we find that three clusters ("weather service", "temperature" and "digital data") cover most apps related to the query [weather app] and have appropriate granularity. In other cases, we

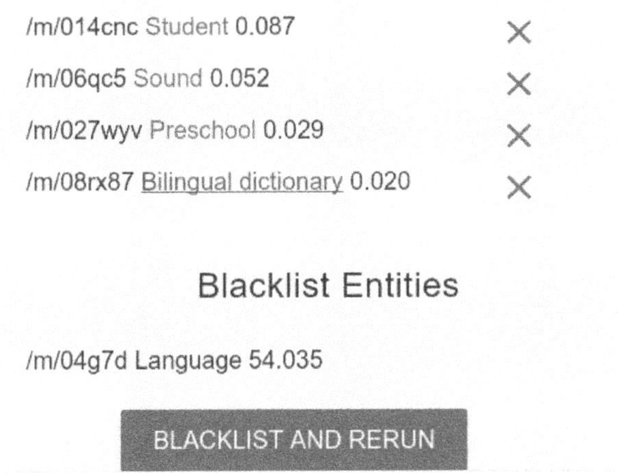

Figure 5. The interface to blacklist topic labels.

see algorithm generated "mega clusters" (large clusters that include many incoherent topic labels), and we break them by increasing the number of clusters. By giving users control over the granularity of clusters, they can make case-by-case adjustments.

Figure 9 shows the panel for adjusting the number of clusters. Users can choose "Fewer" or "More" clusters and click on "run" to get a clustering result with coarser or finer granularity. Under the hood, when users make these selections, we change the range $[\sigma_{lower}, \sigma_{upper}]$ ($[4, 8]$ for "Fewer" and $[12, 16]$ for "More") in equation 3.

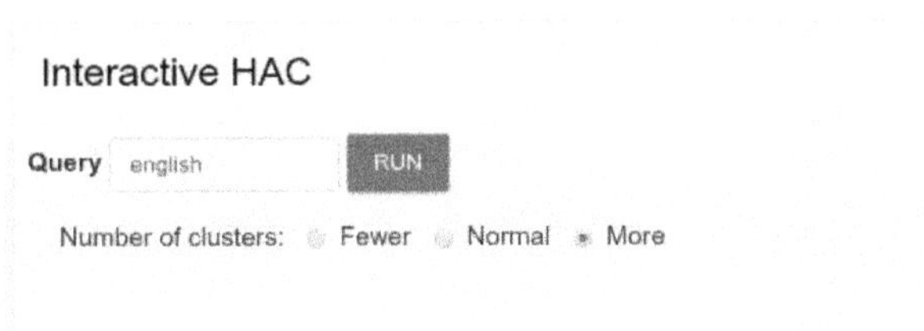

Figure 6. The interface to adjust the granularity of clusters.

Late stage. After the clustering algorithm runs, we present the topic label clusters together with the resulting app clusters and let users make direct edits, including adding/removing clusters, adding/removing topic labels of the clusters, and editing the user-facing names for the clusters. In contrast to early and mid stages' human input, which trigger rerunning clustering algorithm on topic label graph, directly editing topic clusters results in instant and deterministic changes. Experts use this functionality to make minor adjustments to the clusters. After manual edits on the clustering, we pass the edited clusters to another algorithmic step to rank-order the clusters, which is a step that is too tedious for experts.

Figure 7 shows the zoomed-in app cluster panel in figure 2. Users can make edits as follows: (1) delete a topic label from a cluster or even an entire cluster by clicking on the deletion buttons highlighted in two smallest red boxes; (2) add a cluster by clicking on "add cluster" button and add topic labels to a cluster by entering the ids of labels, which are listed in the sidebar (figure 5); (3) rewrite names for clusters by double-clicking on the box highlighted at the top. Whenever users add/remove a cluster or topic label, the system re-assigns the apps in all affected clusters instantly, keeping users informed of the effect of their actions.

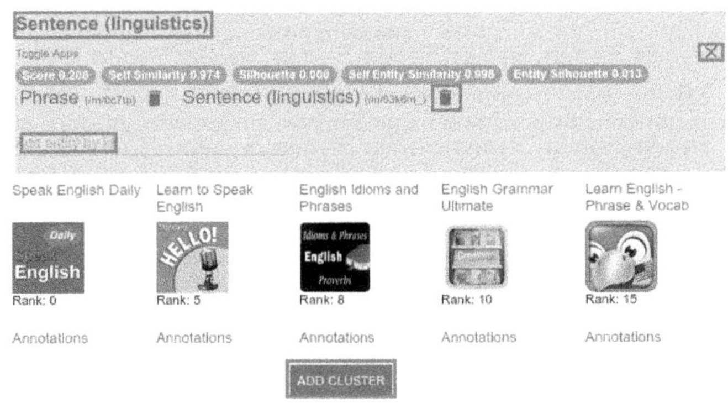

Figure 7. The interface to make direct edits on topical cluster.

EVALUATION

We evaluated AppGrouper with domain experts. Apart from testing our hypothesis that expert input improves clustering quality, we are curious about how experts use AppGrouper and whether they show different patterns of usage for different queries. For example, perhaps broadness of the query might affect how the system is used to guide the clustering algorithm. We have the following research questions to guide our evaluation.

- **RQ1**: Does AppGrouper help a domain expert to improve algorithm generated clustering results?
- **RQ2**: How does the expert use AppGrouper?
- **RQ3**: Does the expert interact with the clustering process in the same way for all queries? Does the broadness of queries matter?

Setup

The participants in our evaluation are domain experts, the targeted users of AppGrouper. These domain experts are engineers who are tasked with making app clusters for search queries in Play Store. In their previous practice, internal experts generated app clusters with algorithm, filtered in only high quality results, made minor changes on cluster titles and shipped the clusters to production.

During the week of September 14, 2015, we deployed AppGrouper with our domain expert who used the system to generate clustering for a wide range of search queries. We randomly sampled 82 search queries, 41 broad queries and 41 narrow queries, from top 1000 search queries in Play Store. We define broad and narrow queries as follows: we sort queries based on number of topic labels associated and categorize the top 25% queries as broad and the bottom 25% as narrow.

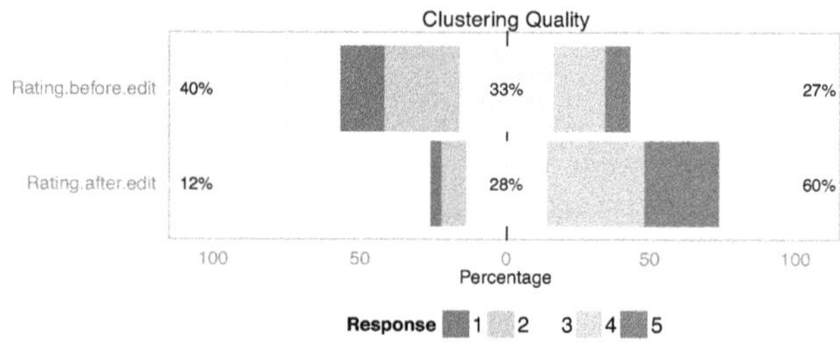

Figure 8. Comparison of ratings on algorithmically-generated app clusters and ratings on expert-guided app clusters using AppGrouper. Clusters generated with expert guidance received higher rating than those without. The colored areas in boxes indicate the percentage of clustering results with certain rating.

The expert's task was to use AppGrouper to make topic clusters for these 82 queries, each of which is expected to take 3 minutes on average. At the end of the task, we had a 30 minute interview with the domain expert. The interview was recorded for later analysis. Note that the expert was not allowed to rewrite the names for clusters, which would make the clustering easily recognizable as human-manipulated.

Another domain expert (referred to as "judge") compared the quality of these 82 clusters with the quality of clusters generated from the clustering algorithm alone. For each search query, we asked the judge to blindly rate the quality of two randomly ordered clusters on a five-point Likert scale (1–5, where 5 means high quality).

Findings

Through analysis of quality evaluations on app clusters and usage log of AppGrouper, we summarize the findings as follows.

AppGrouper helped improve quality of clustering results.

Figure 8 shows that the second expert rated expert-guided app clusters more highly than algorithm-generated app clusters. A Wilcoxon Signed-Ranks Test indicates that the median ratings on app clusters using AppGrouper, $median = 4$, are significantly higher than the median ratings on algorithm generated initial app clusters, $median = 3$ ($Z = 403.5, n_1 = n_2 = 82, p < 1e-6$). [2]

Another result reinforces the finding from a different perspective: 68.3% of the results are evaluated to be better; 14.5% of the results are evaluated to be unchanged; only 17.1% of the results are evaluated to be worse after edits made through AppGrouper. In a related manuscript under preparation, we show that having two experts reaching agreement on which two clustering results is better is actually quite difficult, with Cohen's Kappa as low as 0.33. In other words, when the expert made an improvement to algorithmically-generated clusters, the improvement appears to be significant.

The expert mainly guided in the late stage of clustering process.

Our analysis of the server log of AppGrouper reveals how the expert used AppGrouper to interactively make clusters. Table 1 shows that the expert made changes in the late stage, i.e., added/removed cluster or topic labels in clusters, for 98.8% of the queries, while only gave input to clustering process in early and mid stages for less than 20% of the queries.

A plausible explanation is that guidance operations are more costly in early and mid stages. Indeed, as shown in Table 1, both blacklisting topic labels in early stage and tuning the granularity of clusters in the mid stage have significantly higher system response time than directly editing topic label clusters in late stage, because these actions caused rerunning of the clustering algorithm.

Stage	Early	Mid	Late
Median response time (s)	12	9	0
% queries w/ human input	13.4%	19.5%	98.8%

Table 1. Response times of user actions and percentage of queries receiving human guidance in early, mid and late stages of clustering process. User actions in early and mid stage have significantly higher delay than that in late stage. The expert more frequently gave input in late stage than early and mid stages.

The expert used AppGrouper differently for broad and narrow queries.

As we expected, the algorithm generates more clusters for queries with broad concepts than for queries with narrow concepts (shown in figure 9). This difference is statistically significant using MannWhitney test ($U = 319$, $n_1 = n_2 = 41$, $p < 1e-6$, one-sided). When judged by humans, the quality of app clusters for narrow queries, $median = 2$, is significantly lower than the quality of app clusters for broad queries, $median = 3$, (MannWhitney $U = 576.5$, $n_1 = n_2 = 41$, $p < 0.01$, one-sided), as shown in figure 10.

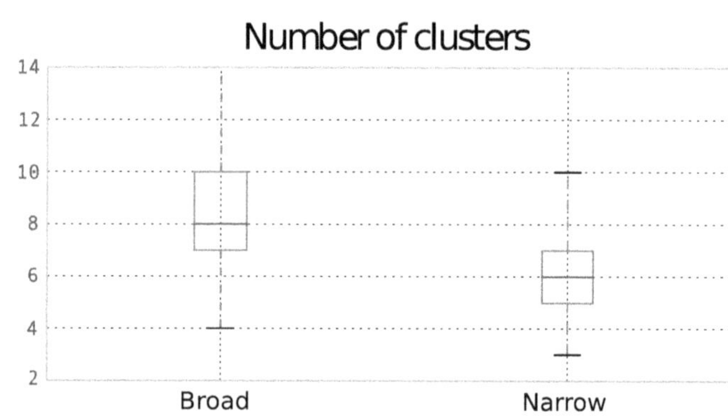

Figure 9. Comparison of number of clusters generated by algorithm for broad and narrow queries. Broad queries on average have more clusters than narrow queries.

[2]Because ratings on five-point Likert scale is ordinal, Wilcoxon Signed-Ranks Test is more appropriate than a t-test.

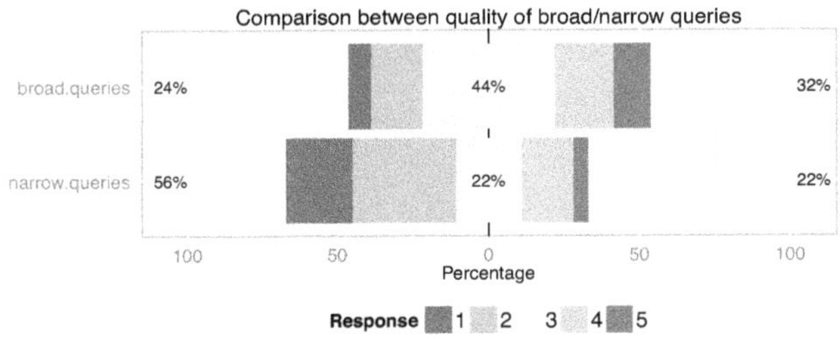

Figure 10. Comparison of quality ratings on algorithmically-generated app clusters for broad and narrow queries.

These different properties result in different user behavior in modifying clusters. Though the expert spent slightly more time on broad queries (figure 11a), the expert made more edits on narrow queries (shown in figure 11b). This difference is marginally significant (MannWhitney U = 691, $n_1 = n_2 = 41$, $p = 0.08$, one-sided).

Our hypothesis is that the number of clusters and the quality of results both contribute to this behavior. On the one hand, broad queries on average have more clusters, requiring more cognitive effort and time to evaluate the clustering results. On the other hand, lower-quality narrow queries took more time to edit. When comparing the type of actions, we find that the expert is much more likely to blacklist topic labels and adjust the number of clusters on narrow queries than on broad queries (table 2): 70% cases when the expert gave input in early and mid stages were on narrow queries.

	Early stage	Mid stage	Late stage
broad	18.2%	25%	50%
narrow	81.8%	75%	50%

Table 2. Breakdown of actions in different stages on broad and narrow queries. The engineer more frequently interacted with clustering process in early and mid stages on narrow queries.

DISCUSSION

AppGrouper improves quality of app clusters.

The interview corroborates our quantitative finding that interactive clustering using AppGrouper improves quality of clusters generated from algorithm. We asked the expert what difficulties he had working with algorithm generated clusters and whether AppGrouper was helpful. The expert responded *"the major pain point was that I had to throw away a lot of [algorithm generated] results. I find it [AppGrouper] super helpful, it helps me to achieve what was not possible."*. Using AppGrouper, these engineers can edit topic label clusters and *"look at the app clusters being updated in real time"*, allowing them to *"be experimental"* and *"higher chance to save a result"*.

Most results only require minor changes.

Why did the expert edit 98% of the queries in the late stage of the clustering process? In our log analysis, we find that the expert mainly edited clustering result by adding or deleting clusters or topic labels. We suspect that the long response time of making changes in the early and mid stages contributes to this behavior, so we asked the expert about his strategy of choosing what features to use. The expert gave a somewhat surprising response — *"Time is not a issue. Quality is more of a concern. I do not choose features [to use] based on time. At least half of the queries are good, only requiring remove a topic label or a cluster."*.

The expert also appreciated the feature that filters and reorders user-modified clusters when saving clusters: *"The clusters are ordered; ranking is important. I trust the algorithm (on filtering and reordering)."*

The expert gave input in the early and mid stages of the clustering process for hard queries.

Why was the expert 3 times more likely to blacklist topic labels and adjust the granularity of clusters when editing lower quality narrow queries than editing broad queries? The expert explained the situations to use these two features: *"[clustering results for] queries that can not reach quality standard by my manual edit. These are usually hard queries."*. Narrow queries on average have worse initial quality ("hard queries"), therefore the expert was more likely to resort to changing clustering results in the early and mid stages. For blacklisting topic labels, *"I blacklist topic labels that are synonyms of [the original] query, topic labels that have larger concept than query, and dominating topic label, say, topic label that cover over 60% apps."* For adjusting granularity of clusters, *"I change number of clusters when I see mega cluster [cluster that has many incoherent topic labels] or too few clusters on a broad query."*

The expert optimizes his effort in improving the quality of app clusters.

Operations in the early and mid stages have uncertain outcome, while operations in the late stages have deterministic outcome. The expert commented *"It sometimes does not work the way I want it, sometimes generates surprisingly good result."*. The setup of our evaluation experiment, using AppGrouper to edit app clusters in limited time, mimics real tasks the internal experts face in their work. The expert naturally tried to reduce his effort on each clustering result while improving quality. In this circumstance, we observed that the expert preferred edits that have a deterministic outcome, and was only willing to take actions that have an uncertain outcome for difficult cases.

DESIGN IMPLICATION

AppGrouper is a system that enables human guidance during an otherwise-automatic clustering process, leveraging human wisdom to tackle challenges inadequately addressed by the clustering algorithm. AppGrouper is designed to the specific application of making clusters for search results in Play Store, but can be extended for other Search Results Clustering problems and other

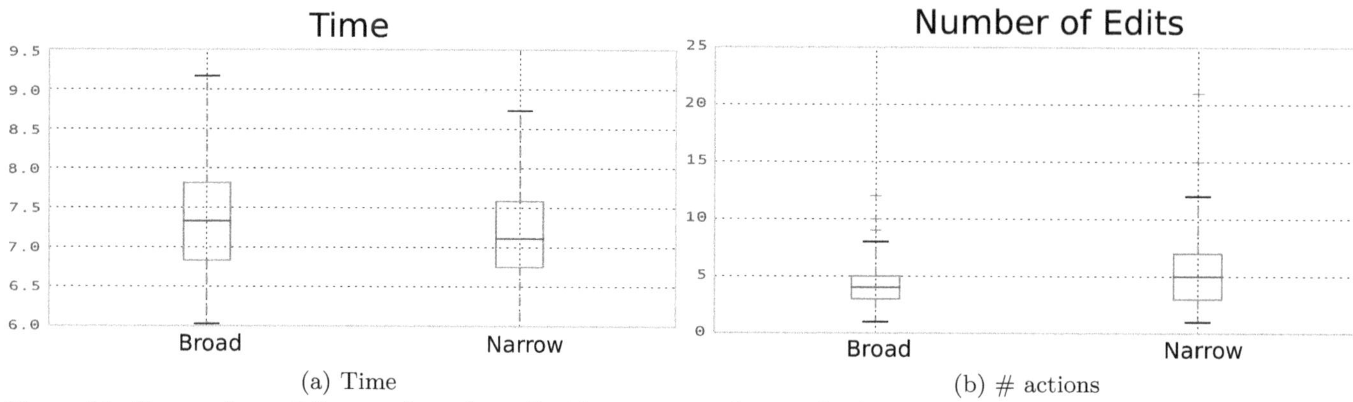

Figure 11. Comparison of time and number of actions on app clusters for broad and narrow queries. The expert spent more time (on log scale) on broad queries, but made more edits to narrow queries.

closely-related applications, such as topic modeling and knowledge extraction [9].

How to design systems that efficiently incorporate human judgment into machine learning is an open research area. By building AppGrouper and observing how it is used by domain experts, we summarize our key lessons as:

- **Make the machine learning process transparent.** Appropriate abstraction and visualization of the underlying machine learning process helps users understand both the strengths and the weaknesses of the process; helping users to give the relevant feedback. In our case, knowledge-graph-based clustering enables users to operate on clusters of topic labels, which are easier to understand and edit than clusters of discrete apps. Providing feedback at several stages while trusting the algorithm performing most tedious tasks on clustering, ranking, and filtering lets users focus on areas the machine learning process needs the most help.

- **Expose appropriate level of complexity.** Admittedly, not all machine learning processes can be easily abstracted and understood by average users. Thus, the system should be designed according to the expertise of users. In our case, we designed interactions at various stages of the algorithm, which enables users to engage at the appropriate control level with the clustering process.

- **Give users control.** This is perhaps the greatest challenge in designing an interactive machine learning system. Giving users control of and clear feedback about their actions are desirable features of good UI, but interactive machine learning system sometimes can not offer these, due to the computation delay and uncertainty of the underlying machine learning algorithm. We observed that an expert preferred making edits that have deterministic outcome over using features that might result in surprisingly good outcomes. We also observed that the expert tended to interact in earlier stages when clustering tasks are hard.

CONCLUSION AND FUTURE WORK

This work makes three major contributions:

- We designed AppGrouper, an interactive system for guiding the topic clustering of app search results in Google Play Store.

- We identified key challenges in making high-quality clusters that can be served in a real production system. We proposed a knowledge-graph-based clustering process that groups topic labels from search results into topic clusters, and then assigns the apps to these topic label clusters. We designed features that enable human guidance at various stages of the clustering.

- We deployed AppGrouper and evaluated it with domain experts, finding that clustering results generated from the interactive clustering process are significantly higher quality than those from a pure algorithmic process. Our observations on the pattern of usage of AppGrouper offers several lessons learned for designing interactive machine learning systems.

In the future, we plan to explore ways to improve machine learning based on human guidance. We believe that the role of human experts in a mixed-initiative system can go far beyond correcting mistakes made by machines. Instead, together in a symbiotic working relationship, the sum is greater than its parts.

ACKNOWLEDGEMENT

I thank Google for providing me the internship opportunity. I appreciate help from Jilin Chen, Zhiyuan Cheng, Sagar Jain in this project and their support during my internship. I also want to thank Max Harper, Daniel Kluver and Vikas Kumar from Grouplens research at University of Minnesota for their feedback on this manuscript.

REFERENCES

1. Saleema Amershi, Bongshin Lee, Ashish Kapoor, Ratul Mahajan, and Blaine Christian. 2011. CueT: Human-guided Fast and Accurate Network Alarm Triage. In *CHI*.

2. Hrishikesh Aradhye, George Toderici, and Jay Yagnik. 2009. Video2Text: Learning to Annotate Video Content. In *IEEE International Conference on Data Mining Workshops*.

3. Pranjal Awasthi, Maria-Florina Balcan, and Konstantin Voevodski. 2014. Local algorithms for interactive clustering. In *ICML*.

4. Sugato Basu, Arindam Banerjee, and Raymond J. Mooney. 2004. Active Semi-Supervision for Pairwise Constrained Clustering. In *Proceedings of the 2004 SIAM International Conference on Data Mining (SDM-04)*.

5. Sumit Basu, Danyel Fisher, Steven M. Drucker, and Hao Lu. 2010. Assisting Users with Clustering Tasks by Combining Metric Learning and Classification.. In *AAAI*. AAAI Press.

6. Claudio Carpineto, Stanislaw Osiski, Giovanni Romano, and Dawid Weiss. 2009. A survey of Web clustering engines. *Comput. Surveys* 41 (2009).

7. Claudio Carpineto and Giovanni Romano. 2010. Optimal Meta Search Results Clustering. In *SIGIR*.

8. Shuo Chang, Peng Dai, Jilin Chen, and Ed H. Chi. 2015. Got Many Labels?: Deriving Topic Labels from Multiple Sources for Social Media Posts using Crowdsourcing and Ensemble Learning. (2015).

9. Jason Chuang, Sonal Gupta, Christopher D. Manning, and Jeffrey Heer. 2013. Topic Model Diagnostics: Assessing Domain Relevance via Topical Alignment. In *International Conference on Machine Learning (ICML)*.

10. Marie desJardins, James MacGlashan, and Julia Ferraioli. 2007. Interactive Visual Clustering. In *IUI*.

11. Jerry Alan Fails and Dan R. Olsen, Jr. Interactive Machine Learning. In *IUI*.

12. Paolo Ferragina and Antonio Gulli. 2005. A Personalized Search Engine Based on Web-snippet Hierarchical Clustering. In *Special Interest Tracks and Posters of the 14th International Conference on World Wide Web*.

13. James Fogarty, Desney Tan, Ashish Kapoor, and Simon Winder. 2008. CueFlik: Interactive Concept Learning in Image Search. In *CHI*.

14. Todd Kulesza, Margaret Burnett, Weng-Keen Wong, and Simone Stumpf. 2015. Principles of Explanatory Debugging to Personalize Interactive Machine Learning. In *IUI*.

15. Stanislaw Osinski and Dawid Weiss. 2005. A Concept-Driven Algorithm for Clustering Search Results. *IEEE Intelligent Systems* 20, 3 (May 2005), 48–54.

16. Peter Pirolli, Patricia Schank, Marti Hearst, and Christine Diehl. 1996. Scatter/Gather Browsing Communicates the Topic Structure of a Very Large Text Collection. In *CHI*.

17. Ugo Scaiella, Paolo Ferragina, Andrea Marino, and Massimiliano Ciaramita. 2012. Topical clustering of search results. In *WSDM*. ACM Press, New York, New York, USA.

18. Jesse Vig, Shilad Sen, and John Riedl. 2011. Navigating the Tag Genome. In *IUI*.

19. Jason Weston, Samy Bengio, and Nicolas Usunier. 2011. WSABIE: scaling up to large vocabulary image annotation. (2011).

Beyond Relevance: Adapting Exploration/Exploitation in Information Retrieval

Kumaripaba Athukorala[○] **Alan Medlar**[⋆] **Antti Oulasvirta**[◇] **Giulio Jacucci**[○] **Dorota Głowacka**[○]

[○] Department of Computer Science, University of Helsinki

[⋆] Institute of Biotechnology, University of Helsinki

[◇] Department of Communications and Networking, Aalto University

[○] first.last@cs.helsinki.fi, [⋆] alan.j.medlar@helsinki.fi, [◇] antti.oulasvirta@aalto.fi

ABSTRACT

We present a novel adaptation technique for search engines to better support information-seeking activities that include both lookup and exploratory tasks. Building on previous findings, we describe (1) a classifier that recognizes task type (lookup vs. exploratory) as a user is searching and (2) a reinforcement learning based search engine that adapts accordingly the balance of exploration/exploitation in ranking the documents. This allows supporting both task types surreptitiously without changing the familiar list-based interface. Search results include more diverse results when users are exploring and more precise results for lookup tasks. Users found more useful results in exploratory tasks when compared to a baseline system, which is specifically tuned for lookup tasks.

Author Keywords

Exploratory search; models of search behavior; reinforcement learning; lookup search; adaptive systems.

ACM Classification Keywords

H.5.m. Information Interfaces and Presentation (e.g. HCI): Miscellaneous

INTRODUCTION

We present a new technique to support two common categories of search tasks: (1) exploratory search, where the goals are ill-defined and may change as search progresses, and (2) lookup search, where the user has a specific target in mind [33, 40]. A lookup search begins with the user expressing their information need as precisely as possible to reach the correct area of the information space, followed by quickly browsing through relevant results, until finally settling on the most appropriate item. By contrast, user behavior in exploratory search is highly dynamic. Users begin exploration with no clear search goals in mind and issue search queries that are imprecise at first. They browse through the search results and iteratively reformulate their queries using new keywords they discover. In contrast to lookup tasks, exploratory search tasks may last from a couple of hours to even years [33].

IUI 2016, March 7–10, 2016, Sonoma, CA, USA.

DOI: http://dx.doi.org/10.1145/2856767.2856786

Our work addresses the observation that most information retrieval (IR) systems target only lookup search, even though exploratory search is almost as common [8]. Most IR systems present a ranked list of documents in descending order of their relevance to the issued search query, aiming to optimise the precision and recall of the search results. However, in exploratory tasks users are uncertain how to formulate search queries [14]. Retrieving the best matching results for the search query might trap the user in their initial query context and this may contribute to user perceptions that exploratory search is challenging.

While most prior work focuses on creating specialized interfaces for exploratory search [17], we present an approach that can support both lookup and exploratory search tasks with no changes to the familiar list-based search interface. Although specialized interfaces might be useful for exploratory tasks, they may not be ideal for lookup tasks. Research shows that, in general, users prefer the simple interfaces used to support lookup tasks [24]. We study an approach that can simultaneously support exploratory and lookup searches.

Our approach identifies the user's search task and adapts the search results accordingly. It only requires adaptations to the retrieval algorithm, which is reflected in the diversity of the returned results. Recent work demonstrates that setting the search engine's parameters so that the search results better match the level of user's knowledge of a specific area improves user satisfaction and performance in exploratory search [4]. Reinforcement learning techniques provide a way to parametrize the search system to trade off between exploration – presenting the user with diverse topics, and exploitation – moving towards more specific topics. While [4] determines an optimal parameter setting for exploratory search for a specific type of user, it does not differentiate between exploratory and lookup search. However, in order to support the diverse needs of users of search engines, it is vital for an adaptive search system to distinguish between exploratory and lookup search, and adjust its parameters and search results accordingly. Empirical studies show that lookup and exploratory search can be distinguished by behavioral characteristics, such as query length, reading time, and task completion time [2]. We show how these behavioral characteristics can be utilized by a search engine to automatically detect what type of search the user is conducting and thus allow the search engine to provide tailored support for this specific task type. Unlike previous studies, our approach does not require any changes to the system's interface and does not require the user to specify beforehand what type of search they are planning to do.

To subject our proposed approach to empirical evaluation, we developed a prototype system that embodies this concept. Our prototype focuses on information-seeking tasks in the context of scientific literature search – but note that this approach is suited for other search domains as well. We selected scientific literature search because exploratory search is one of the most common purposes of search among researchers [3]. We used the arXiv data set as our document corpus because it is freely available and commonly used by researchers.

To evaluate the system, we designed an experiment that captures the key elements of exploratory and lookup tasks. In the experiment, researchers from the computer science field performed both exploratory and lookup tasks using our system and a baseline system. Our hypothesis is that by adapting the search system to set a higher exploration rate for exploratory tasks and a zero exploration rate for lookup tasks, we would improve user performance. As the baseline system, we use a traditional search system which sets the exploration rate to zero to maximize performance in lookup tasks. Results of our user study show that the adaptability of a search engine to both exploratory and lookup search behaviors improves user satisfaction and performance in search.

BACKGROUND

In this section we briefly review contributions of various research communities to the study of exploratory search. We revisit the existing approaches to shed light on some of the open problems in exploratory search. This review also guides us in formulating our approach to exploratory search.

Relevance Feedback

The first key approach developed by the IR community was relevance feedback: users mark documents as relevant or non-relevant and the query model is updated accordingly. Initial experimental studies showed that interactive IR systems benefited from term relevance feedback [30], though evidence from later studies showed these features to be rarely used and, therefore, do not improve retrieval results. The reasons are two-fold [30]: (1) relevance feedback often leads to context traps, and (2) the cognitive load of selecting relevant documents is high compared to typing a new query. Improved modeling of information-seeking behavior would allow an IR system to suggest more relevant results and avoid getting stuck in context traps.

Faceted Search

Faceted search aims to avoid the context trap by using global features instead of contextual ones [42]. It organizes information according to a faceted classification system, allowing users to explore collections of documents by applying multiple filters. Such systems classify information elements along explicit global dimensions, enabling the classifications to be accessed and ordered in multiple ways. As the number of global features is often very large, the process, however, can quickly become overly demanding as users have to go through a large number of options [42]. Improved modeling of user behavior and needs would allow a reduction in the number of facets and thus enhance user experience.

Reinforcement Learning

In exploratory search, the information-needs of a user are constantly evolving, and hence modeling is crucial for acquiring information on search intent as well as query reformulation [39]. Recently, reinforcement learning techniques have been applied to modeling exploratory search [20, 29, 37]. Reinforcement learning allows a system to balance exploitation (moving toward more specific topics) and exploration (presenting the user with alternative topics). The main disadvantage is the "cold start" problem: these systems need a number of sessions to adjust to a users information needs. A recent study showed that systems employing reinforcement learning techniques can optimally balance exploitation and exploration for a given set of users [4]. The study compared different levels of exploration in the retrieval algorithm and identified the right balance that improves user performance, satisfaction and interactions with results in exploratory search. This study provided useful cues for designing our adaptive search system.

Adaptive Systems

Text classification has been a popular topic in machine learning for decades. However, applications related to the problem of online adaptive learning only appeared relatively recently [19]. Most examples of text stream applications include e-mail classification [12], e-mail spam detection [32] and sentiment classification [9]. Various adaptive learning strategies have been used in this domain, including individual methods like case-based reasoning [11], and ensembles, either evolving or with an explicit detection of changes by means of change detectors [1, 10, 21]. All these methods adapt to the gradual change in either user interests or data distribution. Our proposed approach allows the system to adjust to the information needs of the user and the type of search they are conducting.

Exploratory Search Interfaces

The lack of success of relevance feedback techniques is often attributed to user interface design failing to conveniently provide feedback at suitable levels of granularity. In response, a variety of systems were designed to support user feedback, including intelligent user interfaces that assist the user in comprehending an information space [7, 13], visualizations that summarize results for faster relevance judgement [27, 31, 34], as well as interactive visualizations that allow the user to indicate the direction of exploration [20]. These systems are very useful but designed only for exploratory tasks. For lookup tasks, users find such visualizations to be a distraction and, in general, users prefer simple interfaces [24]. This brings us to an important question: is it possible to keep the interface simple and yet provide extra support for exploratory information seekers? To this end, we need a system that could predict the task type in the course of a search session and dynamically adapt the search engine according to the task type.

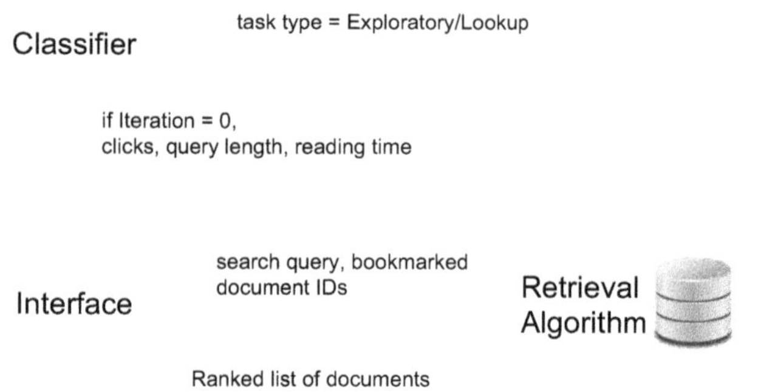

Figure 1. System Overview: the user types in a query and investigates the first page of the search results. Based on the user interaction with the search results displayed on the first page, the search is classified as either lookup or exploratory. The result of the classifier is passed on to the search engine, where the exploration rate of the retrieval algorithm is set according to the search task. Once set, the exploration rate is kept constant for the remainder of the search session.

Models of Exploratory Search

Models of user behavior in information search help us to provide personalized support. Information Foraging Theory is a promising model of exploration that predicts the information seeker's decision from the expectation of information gain [35]. There are also models that assist the search systems in predicting user perception of the results from implicit interactions, including search satisfaction [22], frustration [18], and disambiguating exploration and struggling scenarios [23], as well as predicting the domain knowledge of the user [16]. A recent study reports how to distinguish between exploratory and lookup tasks from implicit measures of search behavior [2]. This study has important implications for designing adaptive search systems. We integrate a similar model in our search system to predict the task type in the course of a search session.

Summary and Contribution

In this section, we briefly summarized some of the existing approaches to exploratory search ranging from IR methods, such as relevance feedback and faceted search, through machine learning methods, most notably reinforcement learning, to adaptive search systems and visualizations for exploratory search. Although all of these methods and systems can clearly improve support for exploratory search tasks, they often need a long training period to spot the gradual change in user behavior or require the users to explicitly state that they are planning to conduct an exploratory search. Additionally, most existing systems use specific visualization techniques that can only support exploratory search, which means that the user cannot rely on the same system to conduct both lookup and exploratory searches. Contrary to previous studies, our approach uses simple behavior characteristics, such as clicks and reading time, to automatically classify the search type and automatically adjust the search engine parameters without the need for additional user feedback or visualization techniques.

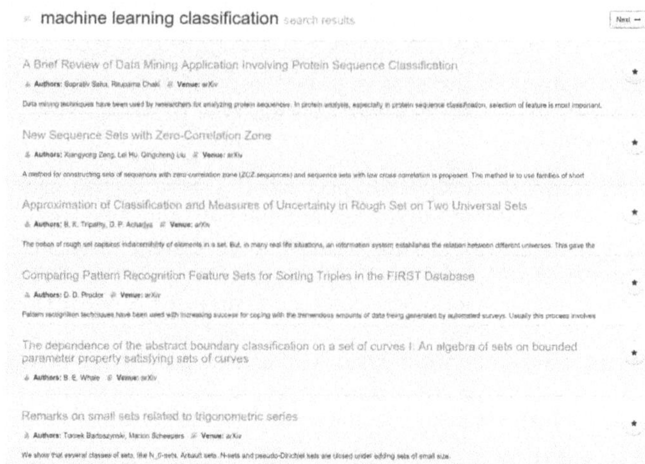

Figure 2. Interface: the user types in a query at the top of the page and a set of search results is displayed. When the title of a document is clicked, the document's abstract is displayed below. The user can bookmark the documents that they like by clicking on the circle next to the title. By clicking the "next" button at the top of the page, the user is taken to the next search iteration.

APPROACH

Our system can be broadly divided into three parts: the user interface, the task type classifier and the search engine containing the document ranking algorithm. The current version of the system operates on $\sim$1 million documents obtained from the arXiv repository.

System Overview

The overview of the system is presented in Figure 1. After typing in the search query, the user is presented with 20 documents, where seven documents are visible without scrolling. Figure 2 shows the interface of the system. We display more documents than in traditional IR systems because in exploratory tasks users examine more results [41]. The initial set of documents is ranked based on the Okapi BM25 algorithm [38]. Next, to see more documents the user can indicate which documents interest him by clicking on the circle next to a given document and thus provide a relevance score of 1 to that document – we refer to this action as *bookmarking*. The user can bookmark as many or as few documents as he wishes. After clicking the "next" button in the top right corner of the page, a new set of documents is displayed based on the feedback provided by the user so far. Documents that do not receive an explicit relevance feedback are assumed to receive a relevance score of 0. While the user is interacting with the first Search Engine Results Page (SERP), the user interface logs three actions performed with the first SERP: the length of the query, total number of clicks (cumulative clicks), and the total time spent reading the clicked documents. These logged interactions are passed on to the classifier to categorise a given search session as either lookup or exploratory, which, in turn, allows the system to set the exploration rate at an appropriate level for the proceeding iterations. Note that the bookmark actions are not used by the classifier, rather they are used by the reinforcement learning algorithm to determine the relevance feedback given to the documents.

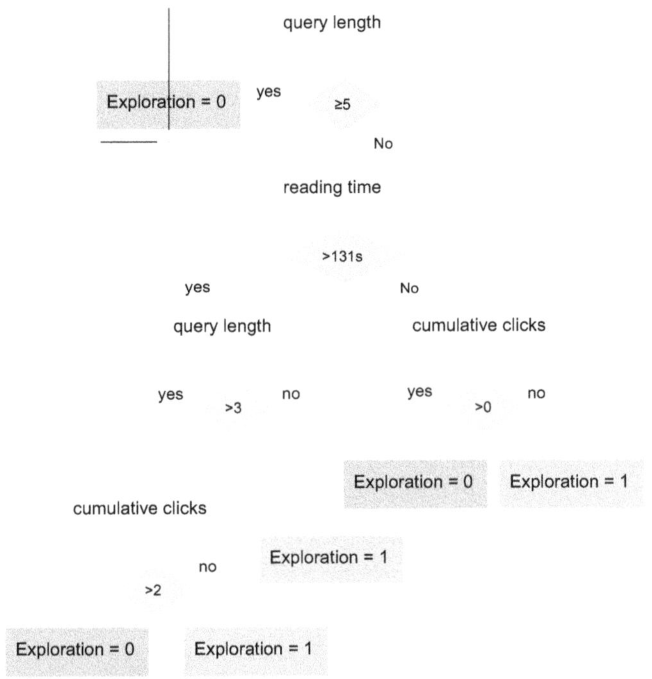

Figure 3. C4.5 decision tree trained using 10-fold cross-validation. When the user clicks the next button after exploring the first search engine results page, the interface sends query length, reading time, and cumulative clicks to the classifier. The classifier uses this decision tree to predict whether the search task type is exploratory or lookup.

Classifying Search Type

To build the classifier, we followed a previous study which identifies implicit search behaviors to distinguish exploratory search from lookup [2]. In that study, exploratory and lookup tasks were operationalized according to the preciseness of the search goal and the complexity of the search task. According to that operationalization, there are core exploratory/lookup tasks with dominant exploratory (high complexity and open-ended goals) or dominant lookup (low complexity and precise goals) characteristics. There are also borderline tasks with mix-characteristics. They designed an interface similar to Google scholar for the arXiv data. The interface included 40 results in first SERP and seven items were visible without the need to scroll. In all other aspects this interface is similar to our interface in Figure 2. The only difference is that our interface has the bookmark feature which is not a problem because the classifier does not use the bookmark interaction as a feature. They conducted a controlled study with six search tasks (two core exploratory and lookup tasks, and one borderline task from each category) and demonstrated how a classifier separates the two task categories from six observable search behaviors: query length, query duration, maximum scroll depth, cumulative clicks, proportion of browsing, and reading time. According to their data, query length, scroll depth, reading time, task completion time, and cumulative clicks are the most discriminative features. We used the data set reported in the same study and trained three different classifiers using 10-fold cross-validation to distinguish known item search and knowledge acquisition tasks [36]: C4.5 decision tree, bagging classifier, and random forest classifier. C4.5 decision tree performed the classification task with 80% accuracy, while bagging and random forest classifiers performed with 79% and 81% accuracy, respectively. We chose the C4.5 decision tree because its transparency allows us to simply understand the exact cause of classification failures, and its performance is comparable to the other classifiers tested.

We selected known item search and knowledge acquisition tasks because known item search is the most common lookup task and knowledge acquisition is one of the main purposes of exploratory search [33]. The classifier identified three features that could best distinguish the two tasks with 80% accuracy: (1) query length – total number of terms in the first query. A term is defined as "a string of characters separated by some delimiter, such as a space, a colon, or a period" [25]; (2) reading time – the time users spent investigating clicked documents; and (3) cumulative clicks – the total number of links in the results page clicked by the user. A schematic of the decision tree is given in Figure 3. We integrated the classifier into our system. As indicated in Figure 1, the classifier receives the user interaction data from the search interface when the user selects the next button to progress to the second iteration. Then, the classifier predicts whether the task is exploratory or lookup and passes this information on to the document ranking component, which sets the exploration rate according to the task type. The interface sends which articles were bookmarked to the retrieval algorithm.

Ranking Documents

In order to help the user to explore the document space, we use LinRel [6], which is used from the second iteration onwards. Suppose we have a matrix D, where each row d_i is a tf-idf feature vector representation of documents presented so far. Let $r = (r_1, r_2 ... r_t)^\top$ be the column vector of relevance scores received from the user up to time t. We estimate the expected relevance r_i of a document d_i as $\mathbb{E}[r_i] = d_i \cdot w$, where the vector w is estimated from user feedback. LinRel estimates $\hat{w}$ by solving $r = D \cdot w$ and estimates relevance score for each d_i as $\hat{r_i} = d_i \cdot \hat{w}$

In order to deal with the exploration/exploitation trade-off, we present documents not with the highest score $\hat{r_i}$, but with the largest upper confidence bound for the relevance score. Thus, if σ_i is an upper bound on standard deviation of relevance estimate $\hat{r_i}$, the upper confidence bound of document d_i is calculated as $r_i + \gamma\sigma_i$, where $\gamma \geq 0$ is a constant used to adjust the confidence level of the upper confidence bound. In each iteration, LinRel calculates

$$s_i = d_i \cdot (D^\top \cdot D + \lambda I)^{-1} D^\top, \quad (1)$$

where λ is the regularization parameter which is set to 1 if each of the feature vectors sums up to 1 (following [6]) and the documents that maximize $s_i \cdot r + \frac{\gamma}{2}\|s_i\|$ are selected for presentation. The first term $s_i \cdot r$ effectively ranks all documents based on their similarity to the documents the user has selected so far and thus it narrows the area of the search space (exploitation). The second term $\frac{\gamma}{2}\|s_i\|$ is an exploration term which ensures that the user is presented with a more diverse set of results. The value of γ can range from 0 to infinity.

The higher the value of γ, the more diverse, or exploratory, the results are. Based on the results of the classifier described above, i.e. whether a given search is classified exploratory or lookup, the value of γ is set to either 0 or 1. If $\gamma = 0$, then the system only exploits – this setting is used in searches classified as lookup. If a given search is classified as exploratory, then the value of γ is set to 1. According to [4], with $\gamma = 1$ the system provides optimal support for exploratory search, maximizing user satisfaction and the number of selected documents by the user.

USER STUDY

The purpose of this study is to empirically evaluate our hypothesis that an adaptive search system, which dynamically adjusts the exploration rate according to the task type, improves user performance compared to traditional search systems that are designed to support only lookup tasks. Our system uses a classifier that takes the user interaction data – cumulative clicks, query length, reading time – as input and predicts whether the user is performing an exploratory or lookup search task. We refer to this system as the *full system*. The *baseline system* that we use treats all the tasks as lookup tasks with the exploration rate fixed at 0. We particularly selected this setting for the baseline system because most of the existing search systems are similarly tuned to exploit the search query with no adaptation to task type [33].

Participants

We recruited 18 researchers from a Computer Science (CS) department because researchers have more experience in exploratory search tasks [3]. Eight of the participants were PhD students and 10 were masters thesis writers. All the participants are researchers in the machine learning domain. We selected the machine learning domain because our data set well covers this domain and also in our department it is easy to get help from experts in this domain to assess the task performance. Four participants were female, which reflects the 20% gender distribution in the CS department. According to the background questionnaire, all the participants often explore unfamiliar topics for research purposes (mean = 3 in 5 point Likert Scale where 1 = never, and 5 = daily). Google scholar is the primary literature search tool for 16 participants, while others use a combination of tools including Google Scholar, ACM digital library and arXiv.

Design

We designed a within subject study, where every participant performed two search tasks – one exploratory and one lookup – in each system (full system and baseline system) resulting in 4 tasks in total per participant. We needed both exploratory and lookup tasks to validate the performance of the classifier. To avoid order effects, we counter-balanced the sequence of performing the tasks and the search system using the Latin square design.

Tasks

Lookup tasks were designed according to a typical known item search scenario, where the participants look for an article that they have come across before. An expert researcher from the machine learning domain selected six articles for the known item search task, where three of them were from the topic image annotation, and the others are from the topic face recognition. We selected these topics because none of the participants were directly involved in research on these topics before, which creates a homogeneous set of participants to avoid biasing the results. Additionally, an expert tested the retrievability and availability of these articles in our data set. We randomly picked one article from each topic and asked the participants to skim through them two hours prior to the study. We described the lookup tasks using the following template:

> *"Do you remember the article that you read two hours ago about the topic X. Imagine that you are conducting a literature review on topic X and decided to refer to this particular article. Try to find this article using the given search system."*

In exploratory search tasks, users typically search for the purpose of learning [40]. To situate the participants in a natural exploratory search setting, prior to the study we asked them to provide a list of topics that they would like to learn about but have limited knowledge of. Then, we selected two unique topics from the given list and assigned one topic per system. In this way, we ensured that there was a genuine motivation to learn for the participants. Table 1 shows the search topics each participant selected for exploratory search tasks.

Measurements

We logged all the details related to the performed search tasks: task type (exploratory or lookup), system used (full system or baseline), search topic for exploratory tasks, search query, and target article for lookup tasks. The system logged the classifier predicted task type for all the tasks performed in both systems as well as all the user interaction data – clicks, duration of result page browsing, depth of scrolling, and time spent reading clicked articles, bookmarked articles, and user feedback on interacted articles. We also collected qualitative feedback on the search system through interviews. An external expert reviewer from the machine learning domain rated, on a binary scale, the relevance of all the articles returned by both systems for the exploratory tasks. The reviewer was unaware of which system was used by the participants.

Procedure

Prior to the study, we provided a background questionnaire to capture the knowledge and research experience of the participants. In this questionnaire, we also asked the participants to give a list of search topics that they would like to learn about for the exploratory search tasks. We only selected those participants who listed at least two machine learning topics that have sufficient articles in our data set.

To situate the participants in the known item search scenario, before the study we invited them to our lab and provided them with two articles to skim through. We asked the participants to imagine that they came across these two articles while searching for literature and instructed them to follow their natural skimming behavior in such a scenario. To prevent them from memorizing the content, we did not tell them

Participant	System	Search topic
1	Full	clustering
	Baseline	dimensionality reduction
2	Full	heart rate classification
	Baseline	unbalanced training set
3	Full	crowd sourcing
	Baseline	collaborative media
4	Full	semi-supervised learning
	Baseline	chaotic theory
5	Full	semantic analysis
	Baseline	lens correction algorithms
6	Full	abstract argumentation
	Baseline	read error correction
7	Full	probabilistic models
	Baseline	data mining
8	Full	dimensionality reduction
	Baseline	artificial neural network
9	Full	deep learning
	Baseline	topic models
10	Full	neural networks
	Baseline	random forests
11	Full	support vector machines
	Baseline	string kernels
12	Full	Bayesian nonparametric
	Baseline	computer vision
13	Full	brain signals
	Baseline	clustering
14	Full	topic segmentation
	Baseline	speech tagging
15	Full	graph matching
	Baseline	time series analysis
16	Full	bootstrapping
	Baseline	compressed sensing
17	Full	social network analysis
	Baseline	deep neural networks
18	Full	reinforcement learning
	Baseline	speech recognition

Table 1. List of search topics each participant selected for the exploratory tasks. We randomly assigned the selected topics for the full system (Full) and the baseline system.

about the upcoming lookup task where they had to re-find the same articles. We informed them that the purpose of this part of the study is to observe their skimming behavior. We did not restrict the time allowed for skimming and the participants spent on average 13 minutes skimming both articles. Then, we allowed them to return to their usual work and come back to the study after 2 hours. This way, we ensured that the participant has some memory of the article that they skimmed through but forgot the exact details, such as the title and author information [28].

All the studies were conducted in a controlled laboratory room, on a laptop computer with an external 27-inch display. Before the study began, we demonstrated how the search system works and the participants performed a training task to become familiarized with the system. Every participant performed one exploratory task and one lookup task with each system, resulting in four tasks in total. The participants were not aware of the two different systems as both the baseline and the full system have the same interface. For exploratory tasks, we allocated 25 minutes and instructed the participants to spend the entire time searching. For the lookup tasks, we allowed 15 minutes maximum and they could end the task as soon as they found the article. The system automatically terminated the search session at the end of the allocated time. Then, the system loaded the list of articles that the participant either clicked or bookmarked to provide an explicit feedback on the relevance of each article on the scale from 1 to 5 (where 1 = not relevant, 5 = highly relevant). After every task, we conducted a semi-structured interview about their experience with the search system. Each study lasted approximately 90 minutes and we compensated each participant with a movie ticket.

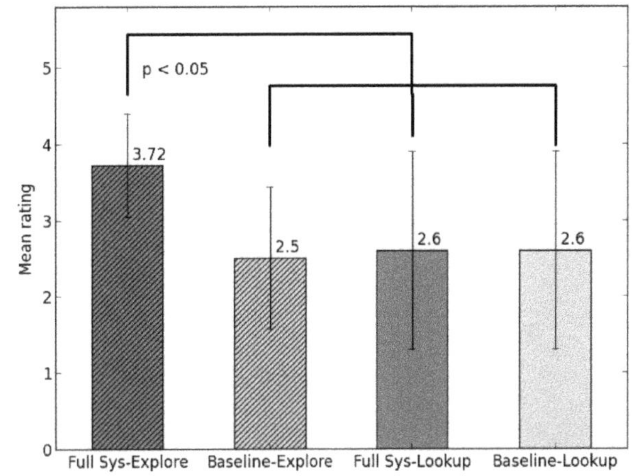

Figure 4. Mean rating given by the participants to the articles that they bookmarked in the full system (Full Sys) and the baseline system for exploratory (Explore) and lookup tasks.

RESULTS

The 18 participants performed 72 search tasks in total (18 exploratory tasks $\times$ 2 systems + 18 lookup tasks $\times$ 2 systems = 72). No data points were excluded. We analyzed both the quantitative and qualitative feedback from the participants as well as the interaction data and expert ratings.

User Perception

To understand whether there is a noticeable difference in the user perception of the two systems, we analyze the explicit scores users gave to the bookmarked items (Best score = 5, worst score = 1). We also analyze the qualitative feedback each participant gave during the interview to corroborate the scores given to the bookmarked items.

User rating: We found that users gave higher ratings for documents retrieved during exploratory tasks using the full system compared to the baseline system. Figure 4 shows the mean rating users gave to both systems for lookup and exploratory tasks (ratings are given on a 5 point Likert scale). Repeated measures ANOVA showed that the system has a statistically significant effect on the user given rating ($F(1,71)$ =

Actual task	Classifier outcome: Exploratory	Classifier outcome: Lookup
Exploratory	92%	8%
Lookup	31%	69%

Table 2. Accuracy of the classifier according to the user study data.

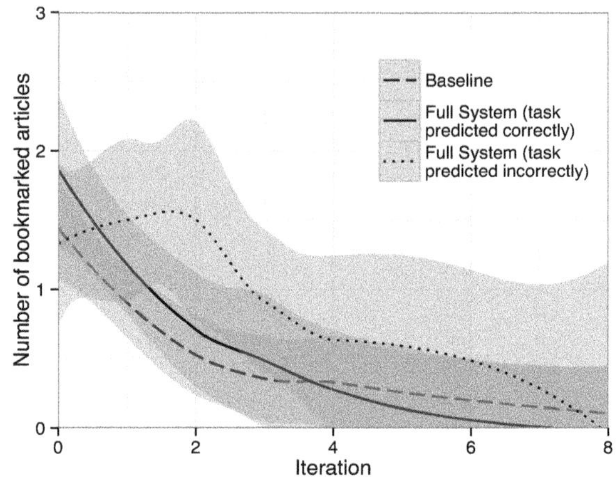

Figure 5. User behavior is influenced by incorrect classification of lookup tasks. When lookup tasks are incorrectly treated as exploratory tasks with a higher exploration rate, users tend to select more items.

4.7, $p < 0.05$). According to post hoc Tukey's test with bonferroni correction, in the exploratory tasks, participants gave a significantly higher rating for the results in the full system (mean = 3.72, s.d. = 0.6, $p < 0.05$) than the results in the baseline system (mean = 2.54, s.d. = 0.92). These results provide quantitative evidence that in exploratory tasks users perceived the results retrieved by the adaptive search system to be more useful.

However, users gave lower ratings for lookup tasks performed in both systems. The mean rating given for lookup tasks in both the full system and the baseline coincide and there is no statistically significant difference ($p > 0.05$, Tukey's test). This result suggests that even though users bookmark documents in lookup tasks, they do not find them to be relevant enough to give them a high score.

Qualitative feedback: Interviews further confirmed that users perceive the full system to be better for exploratory search tasks. Eight participants stated that the full system gave them different directions to explore: "I found new areas that I didn't know before" [Participant 15], "It gave me a range of options beyond what I directly typed. In other search engines I only see things related to my query" [P11]. Four participants mentioned that when they conduct exploratory searches in general, they spend a lot of time reading a single review article to learn about other related areas, but with the full system they found these areas right away: "normally I spend a couple of hours reading a book or a review to find the other topics, then in here I noticed a lot of articles not directly related to my query. When I checked them I realized, this is actually another interesting topic" [P2]. In the baseline system during exploratory tasks three participants stated that they got stuck in one topic: "Over iterations the topic got narrower and I did not know how to find other topics in here" [P8].

For lookup tasks, users gave, on average, lower ratings for articles retrieved in both systems. This is because in lookup tasks, the users' goal is to find a known item and their ratings are bimodal – rating the target item with score 5, and all the other items with the lowest scores, even if they are closely related to the target. For example, when rating a document that was very similar to the target, a participant gave it a score of 2, saying "This article is relevant, but not the one I want. So I give it 2" [P5].

According to the interviews with the participants whose lookup tasks were misclassified as exploratory, we found that most of them had forgotten the paper they were looking for: "I am sorry, I totally forgot [the details of] what I was looking for" [P16], "All I remember is one of the authors is from Facebook. I didn't find anything [relevant]" [P3].

Classifier Accuracy

We calculated the overall accuracy of the classifier by considering the entire 72 search tasks regardless of the system and calculated the percentage of the tasks that were correctly classified as exploratory/lookup. Among the 72 tasks, the classifier accurately classified 58, leading to an overall accuracy of 81%. Further analysis of how well the classifier distinguished exploratory and lookup tasks showed that it accurately classified 92% of exploratory tasks and 69% of lookup tasks (Table 2). The overall accuracy of the classifier in the full system was 78% (89% exploratory, 67% lookup), beating a random classification (50%) by a clear margin.

Further analysis of the incorrectly classified lookup tasks showed that these users issued very short search queries with two keywords, such as "deep learning", "image captioning" or "face recognition", and reading time was longer than 131 seconds. According to the classifier (Figure 3), when search queries are shorter than 3 words and reading time is longer than 131 seconds, they are classified as exploratory. This behavior is concordant with statements made by these users during their interviews that they had forgotten the details of the target article, which would have forced them to employ an exploratory strategy.

As further evidence that the users of misclassified lookup tasks behaved differently compared to those classified correctly, Figure 5 shows LOESS [15] regression lines for how the number of bookmarked articles varies as a function of the iteration number for different systems. LOESS is a

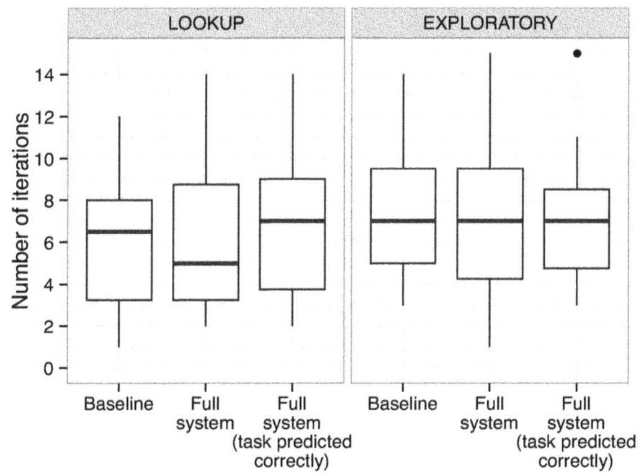

Figure 6. Boxplots of the number of iterations users spent performing lookup and exploratory tasks using the baseline, full system (all data) and full system when the classifier correctly predicted the task type.

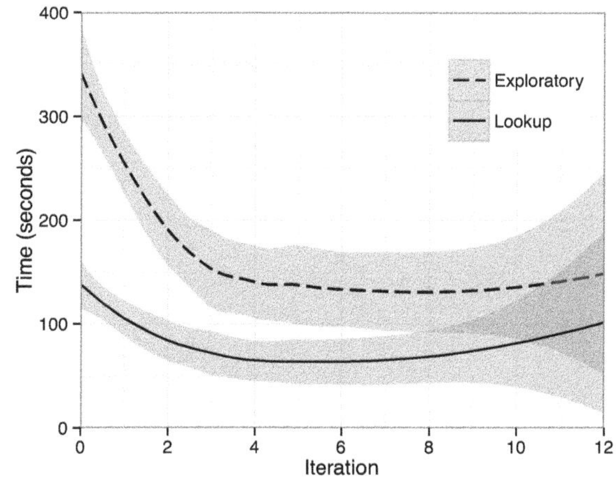

Figure 7. LOESS curves of the iteration duration for lookup and exploratory tasks. Plot only includes experiments from the full systems where the classifier correctly identified the task type. The shaded region indicates the 95% confidence interval.

method for local regression that produces a smooth curve using weighted least squares over a sliding window. Being nonparametric, LOESS does not require the data fit a single global function, but can instead highlight localised trends. Users with misclassified lookup tasks tended to bookmark more articles during the early iterations of the search session compared to both the baseline and the correctly classified full system. If these users are actually employing an exploratory search strategy, then it is indicative of a lack of user motivation in those lookup tasks, and we may, therefore, be underestimating the efficacy of the classifier.

User Behavior

We analyzed user search behavior in terms of: (1) the number of search results users clicked or bookmarked – referred to as *interactions*, (2) the number of times the user requests a new set of results by clicking the next button – referred to as *iterations*, (3) the number of bookmarked articles over iterations. Furthermore, to understand if there is a difference between the user perceived relevance and the actual relevance (according to an expert) in exploratory tasks, we compare the bookmarked articles with expert judgement.

Interactions: In exploratory search tasks, there is a higher number of interactions in the full system (mean = 15.7 interactions/participant) than in the baseline system (mean = 11.5 interactions/participant). In lookup tasks, there are fewer interactions than in exploratory tasks (lookup tasks in full system: mean = 5.2 interactions/participant, lookup tasks in baseline system: mean = 5.3 interactions/participant). According to the repeated measures ANOVA test, the task type has a significant effect on the number of interactions ($F(1,71) = 15.5$, $p = 0.0002$), however the effect of the system on the number of interactions was not significant ($F(1,71) = 0.71$, $p = 0.41$). We conclude that regardless of the system, users interact with more results in exploratory tasks than in lookup tasks.

Iterations: There were no significant differences between the number of iterations users spent with either system when performing either lookup or exploratory tasks ($p > 0.05$, paired t-tests). Figure 6 shows boxplots of the number of iterations users spent with each system performing lookup and exploratory tasks. During lookup tasks, users spent on average 6.11 (s.d. 3.20) and 6.06 (s.d. 3.57) iterations using the baseline and full systems, respectively. The average number of iterations was longer for exploratory tasks: 7.33 (s.d. 3.43) iterations with the baseline and 7.05 (s.d. 3.47) iterations with the full system. Discarding results where the classifier in the full system incorrectly predicted the task type did not lead to a statistically significant difference in the number of iterations spent in either system ($p > 0.05$, Welch's t-test).

There is a consistent difference, however, between the time taken for each iteration depending on the task type. In Figure 7 we consider only those experiments where the classifier correctly identified the task type. Users spent, on average, less time on each iteration during lookup tasks than exploratory tasks. For example, during the first iteration (between the search query and the classifier running) users spent on average 138 seconds performing lookup tasks, but 341 seconds for exploratory tasks.

User Bookmarks Vs. Expert Assessment: While expert assessment showed no difference between either system with respect to the number of relevant articles, users of the full system bookmarked more articles in the initial iterations compared to the baseline. Figure 8 shows how the number of bookmarked articles varies as a function of the iteration number for both baseline and full systems performing exploratory tasks. For a given search query, both baseline and full systems initially show the user the same articles, which is reflected in users bookmarking the same number of articles in the first iteration (iteration 0 in the graph). From the next iteration, the two systems diverge in terms of the number of articles that users bookmark. By the third iteration (iteration 2 in the graph), the users of the baseline system bookmarked less than 1 article per iteration on average. In the full system, however, the number of bookmarked articles declined gradually until

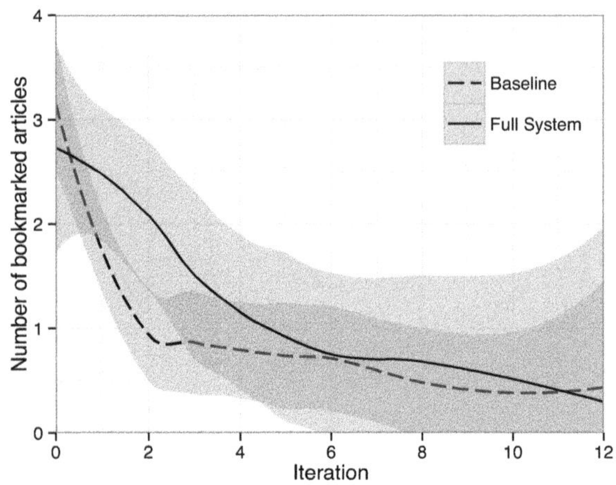

Figure 8. LOESS curves of the number of articles bookmarked at each iteration during exploratory tasks using the baseline and full system. The shaded region indicates the 95% confidence interval.

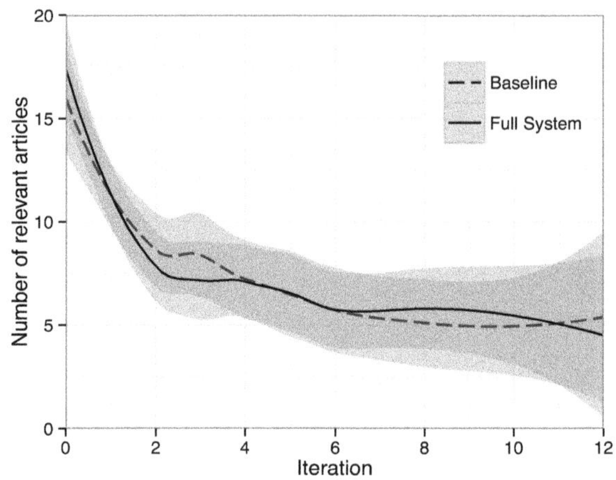

Figure 9. LOESS curves of the number of articles marked as relevant by an expert at each iteration during exploratory tasks using the baseline and full system. The shaded region indicates the 95% confidence interval.

converging with the baseline at around iteration 6. This trend suggests that while users of the full system are exposed to more relevant documents initially, the user feedback eventually overrides the exploratory terms in the ranking equation, leading to convergence with the baseline system.

We contrast these results with the expert assessment of article relevance at each iteration (Figure 9), which suggests that there is no difference between the performance of the full system compared to the baseline. This demonstrates the subjective nature of exploratory search and the need to support individual users' information needs.

DISCUSSION AND CONCLUSIONS

We contribute an approach for designing an information search system capable of supporting both exploratory and lookup search tasks. Exploratory search is gaining importance as more information is available through the web [33], yet it is considered to be one of the most challenging search tasks [3]. Perhaps this is due to the fact that most of the existing search systems are designed to support either lookup or exploratory searches but not both [13, 20]. Users are reluctant to switch between search systems for different search goals or deviate from familiar list based search interfaces to other visualizations introduced in exploratory search systems [24]. We demonstrate a new approach which aims to predict the search task type from implicit measurements of search behavior and dynamically set the parameters of the underlying retrieval algorithm.

Our approach involves using a classifier to predict whether the search goal is exploratory or lookup using three features – clicks, query length and reading time. In line with previous work [2], our results show that exploratory tasks can be distinguished from lookup tasks using search behaviors measured only from the interactions within the first SERP. The overall accuracy of our classifier is 81%, which is comparable with the 85% accuracy reported in [2]. This is an important finding given that the exploratory search tasks in our study are truly motivated by the participants. However, the accuracy of the classifier was lower in the lookup tasks (69%). According to the interviews with the participants of the misclassified lookup tasks, it is clear that they had forgotten the details of their target item and their behavior is very similar to the struggling behavior in lookup tasks reported in literature [23]. One possible reason is that the lookup tasks in our study setting were not as natural as exploratory tasks and the users did not have a true motivation to find the target or pay enough attention when skimming the articles. We see more opportunities in the future to further investigate other possible approaches to improve the classifier accuracy for lookup tasks by incorporating models that disambiguate struggling vs. exploration [23]. Overall, we showed empirically that it is possible to automatically separate search intentions early on in the course of the search session [8].

According to the mean scores users gave to the selected documents, it is evident that users noticed an improvement in the search results retrieved through our approach. A recent study which motivated the trade-off we made between exploration and exploitation in exploratory tasks also reported similar user feedback [4]. Even though the search interface and the visible features are identical in the two systems, users still favored the full system for exploratory tasks.

This finding shows that users are sensitive to the changes in the exploration parameter and a higher exploration rate is necessary for exploratory search tasks. Users' ratings also show how their expectations change according to the task type. In typical known item search tasks, as in our study, users are only interested in finding the target item [26] and they are less interested in other relevant items. For this reason, the overall mean rating for lookup tasks is lower. Another interesting finding is that users gave a similar rating for the baseline system regardless of the task type. This is unexpected because the baseline system does not adapt to the task type.

User behavior analysis sheds light on how the proposed approach influences search strategies – number of interactions, iterations and bookmarked articles. In exploratory tasks, users interacted with more results than in lookup tasks and went through more iterations [23, 33, 40]. Our approach had no significant influence on the number of interactions or iterations. These findings are interesting because they show that users were not overwhelmed by the diverse areas covered by the higher exploration rate in exploratory tasks. At the same time, we can conclude that even in the studies where the classifier incorrectly predicted the task type (22%), users followed the same strategy. This suggests that maybe the classifier incorrectly predicted the task type because the user is indeed following an exploratory strategy in lookup tasks and vice versa. However, further investigation with more studies in an uncontrolled setting would be required to make conclusive remarks.

We observed an interesting difference between the number of results that the users bookmarked as relevant and the expert rated as relevant. Even though the results from both the full system and the baseline system appear equally relevant to an expert, this is not the case for the user. Users tend to bookmark more documents as relevant in initial iterations in the full system compared to the baseline system. The expert reviewer only knew the initial search topic of the user but not the changes in user interests over time. This shows that the relevance of search results is highly subjective and can change throughout the search session [40]. As suggested in the literature, in exploratory search as users gain more knowledge on a given topic, their search interests might deviate from the original topic [5]. This is further justified by the interview findings, where users stated that they found more interesting topics different from their search topic in the full system. This finding further confirms that our approach is appropriate because in exploratory tasks it is not sufficient to retrieve results only relevant to the search query.

Our results show that in cases where lookup tasks are misclassified as exploratory, the user had to bookmark more items than in correctly classified cases (Figure 5). This suggests that users have to examine more items to find the target item. In known item search tasks the goal is to reach the target item as fast as possible [33], and having to bookmark several items indicates that it slows down the lookup process and would lead to frustration [18]. This behavior is similar to struggling behavior in lookup searches [18]. This finding points to the importance of accurately setting the exploration rate. While too few exploratory tasks were misclassified for a similar comparison, we note that tasks performed in the baseline are equivalent to misclassified exploratory tasks in the full system. In the baseline system users bookmarked fewer items than in the full system (Figure 8), which, combined with the interviews, suggests that users saw fewer articles of interest. In the current version of our system, the classifier is only run after the first iteration, however, these findings suggest a possible means to correct misclassified tasks from the second iteration onwards by monitoring user activity as the search progresses. We note that for correctly classified tasks, iteration time trivially distinguishes lookup from exploratory tasks during the initial iterations (Figure 7). The next version of the system could combine our current classifier with subsequent user bookmarking and timing information across iterations, taking a more holistic approach to task classification.

We see several future opportunities to further improve the proposed approach. An important open challenge is how to make the exploration/exploitation trade-off transparent to the user. This step needs more careful investigation of how to show the system predicted task type to the user and allow the user to correct the system's prediction. However, it is also important to avoid overloading the user with too much information as it would become a distraction [24]. It is also important to validate the classifier in a realistic setting by collecting longitudinal data. To this end, we intend to deploy our prototype system to the public. However, this brings additional challenges, such as how to identify the ground truth of the actual search task. We are investigating approaches how to unobtrusively obtain this data from the user.

ACKNOWLEDGEMENTS

This work was partly supported by The Finnish Funding Agency for Innovation (under projects Re:Know and D2I) and by the Academy of Finland (under the Finnish Centre of Excellence in Computational Inference).

REFERENCES

1. Adä, I., and Berthold, M. R. Eve: a framework for event detection. *Evolving systems 4*, 1 (2013), 61–70.
2. Athukorala, K., Głowacka, D., Oulasvirta, A., Vreeken, J., and Jacucci, G. Is exploratory search different? a comparison of information search behavior for exploratory and lookup tasks. *JASIST* (2015).
3. Athukorala, K., Hoggan, E., Lehtiö, A., Ruotsalo, T., and Jacucci, G. Information-seeking behaviors of computer scientists: Challenges for electronic literature search tools. In *ASIST* (2012).
4. Athukorala, K., Medlar, A., Ilves, K., and Głowacka, D. Balancing exploration and exploitation: Empirical parameterization of exploratory search systems. In *CIKM* (2015).
5. Athukorala, K., Oulasvirta, A., Głowacka, D., Vreeken, J., and Jacucci, G. Narrow or broad?: Estimating subjective specificity in exploratory search. In *CIKM*, ACM (2014), 819–828.
6. Auer, P. Using confidence bounds for exploitation – exploration trade-offs. *JMLR 3* (2002), 397 – 422.
7. Baldonado, M. Q. W., and Winograd, T. Sensemaker: an information-exploration interface supporting the contextual evolution of a user's interests. In *CHI*, ACM (1997), 11–18.
8. Belkin, N. J. Some (what) grand challenges for information retrieval. In *ACM SIGIR Forum*, vol. 42, ACM (2008), 47–54.
9. Bifet, A., and Frank, E. Sentiment knowledge discovery in twitter streaming data. In *Discovery Science* (2010).

10. Bifet, A., and Gavalda, R. Learning from time-changing data with adaptive windowing. In *Proc. of SDM* (2007).
11. Bouchachia, A. Incremental learning with multi-level adaptation. *Neurocomputing 74*, 11 (2011), 1785–1799.
12. Carmona-Cejudo, J. M., Baena-García, M., del Campo-Ávila, J., Morales-Bueno, R., and Bifet, A. Gnusmail: Open framework for on-line email classification. In *Proc. of ECAI* (2011).
13. Chau, D. H., Kittur, A., Hong, J. I., and Faloutsos, C. Apolo: making sense of large network data by combining rich user interaction and machine learning. In *CHI* (2011), 167–176.
14. Chowdhury, S., Gibb, F., and Landoni, M. Uncertainty in information seeking and retrieval: A study in an academic environment. *Information Processing & Management 47*, 2 (2011), 157–175.
15. Cleveland, W. S. Robust locally weighted regression and smoothing scatterplots. *Journal of the American statistical association 74*, 368 (1979), 829–836.
16. Cole, M. J., Gwizdka, J., Liu, C., Belkin, N. J., and Zhang, X. Inferring user knowledge level from eye movement patterns. *Inf. Proc. Manag.* (2012).
17. Diriye, A. M. *Search interfaces for known-item and exploratory search tasks*. PhD thesis, UCL (University College London), 2012.
18. Feild, H. A., Allan, J., and Jones, R. Predicting searcher frustration. In *SIGIR* (2010).
19. Gama, J. a., Žliobaitė, I., Bifet, A., Pechenizkiy, M., and Bouchachia, A. A survey on concept drift adaptation. *ACM Comput. Surv. 46*, 4 (2014), 44:1–44:37.
20. Głowacka, D., Ruotsalo, T., Konyushkova, K., Athukorala, K., Kaski, S., and Jacucci, G. Directing exploratory search: Reinforcement learning from user interactions with keywords. In *IUI* (2013).
21. Gomes, J. B., Menasalvas, E., and Sousa, P. A. Learning recurring concepts from data streams with a context-aware ensemble. In *Symposium on applied computing* (2011).
22. Hassan, A., and White, R. W. Personalized models of search satisfaction. In *CIKM* (2013), 2009–2018.
23. Hassan, A., White, R. W., Dumais, S. T., and Wang, Y. Struggling or exploring?: disambiguating long search sessions. In *WSDM* (2014), 53–62.
24. Hearst, M. *Search user interfaces*. Cambridge University Press, 2009.
25. Jansen, B. J., and Pooch, U. A review of web searching studies and a framework for future research. *JASIST 52*, 3 (2001), 235–246.
26. Jenkins, C., Corritore, C. L., and Wiedenbeck, S. Patterns of information seeking on the web: A qualitative study of domain expertise and web expertise. *IT & society 1*, 3 (2003), 64–89.
27. Käki, M. Findex: search result categories help users when document ranking fails. In *CHI*, ACM (2005), 131–140.
28. Kane, M. J., and Engle, R. W. Working-memory capacity, proactive interference, and divided attention: limits on long-term memory retrieval. *Journal of Experimental Psychology: Learning, Memory, and Cognition 26*, 2 (2000), 336.
29. Karimzadehgan, M., and Zhai, C. Exploration exploitation tradeoff in interactive relevance feedback. In *CIKM* (2010), 1397–1400.
30. Kelly, D., and Fu, X. Elicitation of term relevance feedback: an investigation of term source and context. In *SIGIR* (2006), 453–460.
31. Kules, B., Wilson, M., Schraefel, M. C., Shneiderman, B., et al, and et al. From keyword search to exploration: How result visualization aids discovery on the web. Tech. Rep. HCIL-2008-06, University of Maryland, 2008.
32. Lindstrom, P., Delany, S. J., and Mac Namee, B. Handling concept drift in text data stream constrained by high labelling cost. In *Int. Florida Art. Intell. Research Society Conf.* (2010).
33. Marchionini, G. Exploratory search: from finding to understanding. *Com. ACM 49*, 4 (2006), 41–46.
34. Matejka, J., Grossman, T., and Fitzmaurice, G. Citeology: visualizing paper genealogy. In *CHI Extended Abstracts*, ACM (2012), 181–190.
35. Pirolli, P., and Card, S. Information foraging. *Psych. rev. 106*, 4 (1999), 643.
36. Quinlan, J. *C4.5: Programs for Machine Learning*. Morgan-Kaufmann, Los Altos, California, 1993.
37. Radlinski, F., Kleinberg, R., and Joachims, T. Learning diverse rankings with multi-armed bandits. In *ICML* (2008), 784–791.
38. Sparck Jones, K., Walker, S., and Robertson, S. E. A probabilistic model of information retrieval: Development and comparative experiments. *Info. Proc. & Manag. 36*, 6 (2000), 779–840.
39. White, R. W., Bennett, P. N., and Dumais, S. T. Predicting short-term interests using activity-based search context. In *CIKM* (2010).
40. White, R. W., Kules, B., and Drucker, S. M. Supporting exploratory search. *Comm. ACM 49*, 4 (2006), 36–39.
41. White, R. W., and Roth, R. A. Exploratory search: Beyond the query-response paradigm. *Synth. Lec. on Inf. Conc., Retr., and Serv. 1*, 1 (2009), 1–98.
42. Yee, K.-P., Swearingen, K., Li, K., and Hearst, M. Faceted metadata for image search and browsing. In *CHI* (2003).

A $-Family Friendly Approach to Prototype Selection

Corey Pittman
University of Central Florida
4000 Central Florida Blvd
Orlando, FL 32816, USA
cpittman@knights.ucf.edu

Eugene M. Taranta II
University of Central Florida
4000 Central Florida Blvd
Orlando, FL 32816, USA
etaranta@gmail.com

Joseph J. LaViola Jr.
University of Central Florida
4000 Central Florida Blvd
Orlando, FL 32816, USA
jjl@cs.ucf.edu

ABSTRACT
We explore the benefits of intelligent prototype selection for $-family recognizers. Currently, the state of the art is to randomly select a subset of prototypes from a dataset without any processing. This results in reduced computation time for the recognizer, but also increases error rates. We propose applying optimization algorithms, specifically random mutation hill climb and a genetic algorithm, to search for reduced sets of prototypes that minimize recognition error. After an evaluation, we found that error rates could be reduced compared to random selection and rapidly approached the baseline accuracies for a number of different $-family recognizers.

Author Keywords
Classifier; Gesture recognition; Rapid prototyping; User interfaces; $-family; Prototype selection

ACM Classification Keywords
H.5.2 Information interfaces and presentation: User interfaces, input devices and strategies; I.5.5 Pattern recognition: Implementation, interactive systems

INTRODUCTION
$-family recognizers, such as $1 [17], $N [2], 1¢ [6], and $P [15], are 2D gesture recognizers designed to be accessible to all developers. They are suitable for rapid prototyping, have low coding overhead, rely only on simple geometry and nearest neighbor prototype matching, utilize intuitive internal representations of gestures, are easy to debug, and achieve high accuracy with as little as one prototype per gesture [15, 17]. By possessing these characteristics, it is not surprising that $-family recognizers have gained significant popularity. However, developers who employ these recognizers may also be interested in $-family like methods that address related topics in gesture recognition such as rejection criteria for malformed gestures, synthetic data generation, and prototype selection. In this paper, we begin to tackle the latter.

IUI'16, March 7–March 10, 2016, Sonoma, CA, USA.
© 2016 ACM. ISBN 978-1-4503-4137-0/16/03...$15.00.
DOI: http://dx.doi.org/10.1145/2856767.2856808

It is easy to acquire a large dataset. One can collect numerous gesture samples from friends, family, coworkers, and volunteers; record samples online and return them to a local repository; select gestures from publicly available datasets such as [3, 9, 16, 17]; or generate countless synthetic samples from an online service [7]. However, with $-family recognizers that are 1-nearest neighbors template matching algorithms, each new training sample incurs an additional penalty in recognition time and storage space, both of which are often restricted or must be minimized as much as possible. It is therefore necessary to winnow the dataset down to a small subset of samples that exhibit high discriminatory power—that best separate the gesture classes. This prototype (or instance) selection problem is well studied [4], but most solutions are complex (requiring expert knowledge), are slow, or have high coding overhead, and are consequently juxtaposed to $-family ideology in one way or another. Alternative recognizers, like Rubine's linear classifier [12], have also been used for 2D gesture recognition but feature more complex mathematical structures and are therefore less approachable.

In a $-family friendly context, a promising set of solutions for prototype selection are stochastic methods such as genetic algorithms and hill climbing [10, 11, 13]. These methods have been shown to achieve high accuracy, but involve only random template selection and recognizer evaluation. As a result, there is little bookkeeping and little coding overhead, and therefore can be added to any project with only minimum effort.

PROTOTYPE SELECTION
In this work, we propose two potential selection methods to be applied to $-family recognizers: Genetic Algorithms and Random Mutation Hill Climb. Both stochastically search for optimal solutions using online repeated cross-validation of the candidate solutions.

Genetic Algorithm
Genetic algorithms test the fitness of a population consisting of multiple candidate solutions for a number of generations. At the end of each generation, children are created from the higher fitness candidates (parents) from the population. Genetic algorithms leverage mutation and crossover operators to facilitate the exploration of new areas within the search space.

In the context of prototype selection, each candidate solution is a subset of the complete dataset. During initialization, a random collection of prototypes is selected to populate each of the candidate solutions and a recognizer is generated from those prototypes. To evaluate the fitness of a candidate, a random selection of prototypes is recognized, and the resultant accuracy is the fitness of the candidate. This operation is carried out for each of the candidates in the population. Next, the highest fitness candidates are selected to be carried over into the next generation, while the remaining candidates are replaced with children generated by mutating (changing one of the selected prototypes of a candidate) and crossing over (randomly selecting prototypes from two different candidates) candidates from the current generation. This new generation then repeats the processes of the previous generations until either the maximum number of generations pass or a solution that can correctly recognize all the prototypes during fitness evaluation is found. In our implementation, we used single point mutation and uniform crossover as our genetic operators. We also used elitism to carry over the top 50% of each generation. For the fitness evaluation, each candidate solution was evaluated by attempting to recognize $32k$ prototypes from the dataset, where k is the total number of prototypes in each candidate solution. The fitness is the accuracy of this result.

Random Mutation Hill Climb

Of all the methods we considered, Skalak's [13] approach to prototype selection using *random mutation hill climb* (RMHC) is perhaps the most appropriate technique with respect to coding overhead, complexity, understandability, speed, and accuracy. In his initial formulation, prototypes are represented as integers that index samples in a training set, and the selection is encoded into a single bit string. The bit string is randomly mutated one bit at a time. On each iteration, the fitness of the encoded prototype bit string is evaluated utilizing a 1-nearest neighbor classifier. If the fitness of the mutated string is greater than all previously identified solutions, the mutated string becomes the new best (fittest) solution. This process terminates after a predetermined, but low, number of iterations. Our approach is identical except that we store an array of integers that index samples in a training set, and we randomly mutate whole integers rather than individual bits in order to reduce coding complexity. However, there are also a number of optimizations that we employ to speedup the process.

There is no sense in considering a solution in which not every class is represented. When the target prototype count is low, for example, this situation is easy to encounter, and significantly many more mutations are required to achieve high accuracy as compared to the following alternative. Instead, we ensure that there is at least one prototype per gesture when performing a mutation. For each class we keep a counter of selected prototypes that represent the class. When a prototype is to be mutated, if its associated class count is one, we randomly select another prototype from within the same class. Otherwise, there is no restriction. Finally, if the fittest solution wins its second mutation round and has classified a sufficient number of consecutive samples correctly, the process terminates (currently this is 64 times the class count).

We operate under a similar assumption as Skalak: that \$-family recognizers are typically employed in problem domains where good prototypes appear in dense regions of the sample space. We also assume that most, if not all, gestures reside in a *sloppiness space* [5], so that rushed and sloppy instances are still distinguishable. Using these assumptions, instead of evaluating a candidate solution over the entire training dataset, we can randomly sample from the dataset. That is, samples are drawn with replacement and evaluated against the fittest solution and candidate solution, until either one solution clearly out performs the other, or a predetermine number of iterations pass (we use 256 times the class count in our evaluation). Also, to ensure good test coverage, in each iteration we test one sample from each class. Since each result is a Bernoulli trial (either a sample is classified correctly or not), the sequence of all results is a Binomial distribution. Therefore we can use an exact Binomial test to compare the solutions. The minimum variance unbiased estimator of the success rate is given by:

$$\hat{p} = \frac{x}{n}, \quad (1)$$

where x is the number of successes in a set of n Bernoulli trails. Let $\hat{p}_0$ be the success rate estimate for the fittest solution and $\hat{p}_c$ the estimate for a new candidate solution. As solutions are iteratively evaluated, we conduct a one-tailed hypothesis test to eliminate any candidate solutions that are unlikely to improve accuracy:

$$H_0 : \hat{p}_c = \hat{p}_0 \\ H_1 : \hat{p}_c < \hat{p}_0, \quad (2)$$

```
RANDOM-MUTATION-HILL-CLIMB (Samples, k)
for i ← 0 to k do
    Fittest[i] ← RANDOM-SAMPLE(Samples)
FittestRecognizer ← GENERATE-RECOGNIZER(Fittest)
count ← 0
max ← 32 * k
TestMutations ← 256
while count < max do
    Alternate ← Fittest
    MUTATE-ONE(Samples,Alternate)
    AlternateRecognizer ← GENERATE-RECOGNIZER(Alternate)
    c1, c2, n ← 0, 0, 0
    for i ← 0 to TestMutations do
        for j ← 0 to Gesture-Type-Count(Samples) do
            S ← RANDOM-SAMPLE-OF-TYPE(Samples,j)
            c1 ← c1+IS-RECOGNIZED(FittestRecognizer, S)
            c2 ← c2+IS-RECOGNIZED(AlternateRecognizer, S)
        k ← FIND-CRITICAL-VALUE(c1, c2, n)
        if c2 < k then
            break
    if c2 > c1 then
        Fittest ← Alternate
        FittestRecognizer ← AlternateRecognizer
return Fittest
```

```
FIND-CRITICAL-VALUE (correct1, correct2, n)
α, pf, comb ← 0.8, 1.0, 1.0
psuccess ← correct1/n
pfail ← 1.0 − psuccess
ps ← psuccess^n
for k ← n to 0 and α > 0 do
    α ← α − comb * ps * pf
    comb ← (comb * k)/(n − k + 1)
    ps ← ps/psuccess
    pf ← pf * pfail
return k
```

where the null hypothesis is that candidate solution is approximately as good as fittest solution. Note, however, that the usual normal approximation to the binomial distribution is inappropriate because the success rate is often too high. For this reason we must conduct an exact test and manually find the critical value of the rejection region.

The cumulative distribution function (CDF) of the binomial distribution is as follows:

$$P(X \leq k) = \sum_{i=0}^{k} \binom{n}{i} p^i (1-p)^{n-i}, \tag{3}$$

where random variable X is the number of successes and p, again, is the probability of success. Given a level of significance, such as $\alpha = .05$, it is actually more efficient to solve the inverse problem: to find the critical value for the upper tail, $1 - \alpha$, and calculate the summation backward from n down to k for $P(X > k)$. Why? First note that Equation 3 contains a binomial coefficient, which can be solved incrementally as the CDF is being calculated by using the following relation:

$$\binom{n}{k-1} = \binom{n}{k} \frac{k}{n-k+1}, \tag{4}$$

where k represents the number of successes in n trials, and the initial condition is $\binom{n}{k=n} = 1$. Second, note that because the success rate is high, the k containing $\alpha = .05$ of the lower tail (or equivalently the k containing $\alpha = .95$ of the upper tail) is close to n. For example, with $n = 1500$ and $p = .95$, then 5% of the distribution falls under $k = 1439$.

EVALUATION

We ran a large scale evaluation of the proposed selection techniques and their effect on error rates. We compared to the baseline, using all available prototypes, and the current trend of random selection for reduction. In this way, we could determine if there was an improvement over random selection and how close the results came to the best possible result. We chose to evaluate the proposed selection methods on three different datasets, with details shown in Table 3.

Recognizers

We used a number of $-family recognizers to insure that the results were consistent regardless of which recognizers were used:

Protractor. Protractor [8] is a speed-optimized version of the traditional $1 recognizer. Protractor aligns the candidate gesture and dataset prototype to minimize the distance between the two unistroke and uses the inverse minimum cosine distance between the samples.

$N-Protractor. $N-Protractor [3] is a speed-optimized version of the $N recognizer which leverages the optimizations proposed in Protractor to decrease the overall computation time of $N while maintaining similar error rates.

Penny Pincher. The Penny Pincher recognizer [14] is a reduced complexity recognizer that emphasizes speed and simplicity while maintaining high recognition rates. Penny Pincher reduces the matching process to addition and multiplication, allowing for significantly shorter matching times.

	Penny Pincher								
	$1-GDS			SIGN			MMG		
k	GA	RM	Rand	GA	RM	Rand	GA	RM	Rand
1	2.0	1.5	8.8	4.8	4.1	14.1	23.4	22.6	37.8
2	0.9	0.6	4.8	2.4	1.5	8.8	11.3	8.7	25.5
3	0.5	0.5	3.4	2.0	1.1	6.0	8.6	4.5	20.2
4	0.4	0.5	2.5	1.8	0.9	4.5	6.3	3.2	16.2
5	0.2	0.5	2.3	1.3	0.9	4.2	5.2	2.4	14.0
n	<0.1	<0.1	<0.1	0.4	0.4	0.4	0.8	0.8	0.8
	Protractor								
	$1-GDS			SIGN			MMG		
k	GA	RM	Rand	GA	RM	Rand	GA	RM	Rand
1	2.3	1.6	12.0	16.0	16.0	32.7	23.4	23.7	35.6
2	1.0	0.8	6.7	14.5	13.2	27.8	9.6	6.9	23.3
3	0.8	0.7	4.8	13.8	13.1	24.8	7.0	4.3	18.5
4	0.6	0.5	3.6	13.9	12.2	23.4	5.8	3.6	15.5
5	0.6	0.5	3.1	13.9	12.7	23.1	5.1	3.2	13.4
n	0.2	0.2	0.2	13.5	13.5	13.5	3.0	3.0	3.0
	$N-Protractor								
	$1-GDS			SIGN			MMG		
k	GA	RM	Rand	GA	RM	Rand	GA	RM	Rand
1	5.0	4.2	14.7	15.9	16.2	31.1	12.0	12.0	20.4
2	1.3	0.9	7.6	12.6	11.1	24.3	5.6	4.1	12.0
3	0.9	0.5	5.5	11.7	10.7	20.8	3.9	2.1	9.3
4	0.7	0.8	4.1	10.7	10.1	19.0	3.5	1.7	7.4
5	0.6	0.7	3.7	11.1	10.6	18.4	2.7	1.7	6.1
n	0.1	0.1	0.1	9.4	9.4	9.4	0.5	0.5	0.5

Table 1: Absolute error rates (in %) for all datasets, selection modes, and recognizers for template counts $k = [1, 5]$ and baseline ($k = n$) using remaining samples as templates after removing the candidates.

	$1-GDS		SIGN		MMG	
Recognizer	Mem	Speed	Mem	Speed	Mem	Speed
Penny Pincher	98.3	95.7	99.7	99.5	97.5	95.2
Protractor	98.3	97.7	99.7	99.7	97.5	96.8
$N-Protractor	98.3	97.4	99.7	99.6	97.5	97.7

Table 2: Percent reduction in memory consumption and runtime for $k = 5$ compared to baseline. Note that metadata overhead is excluded from the memory consumption calculation.

Procedure

In order to determine the effect of the reduced datasets on the error rates of the $-family recognizers, we randomly generated a number of tests for each combination of recognizer, dataset, and selection mode. The evaluations were user independent, so samples for each gesture type from each user were combined together. A prototype was selected from each gesture class within the selected dataset and was designated a candidate to be matched. The candidate was matched against the best reduced dataset generated using one of the selection methods. The candidate was not included in the gesture selection process for that particular test. Error rates for this cross-validation were recorded for $k = [1, 5]$, where $k * T$ is the number of prototypes to which the dataset should be reduced, and T is the number of distinct classes in the complete dataset. The variance of the resulting error rates were minimized by running tests with each configuration 500 times.

Name	Ref	Multistroke	Gestures	Participants	Total Samples
$1-GDS	[17]	No	16	10	4800
SIGN	[1]	No	17	20	33154
MMG	[3]	Yes	16	20	3200

Table 3: Datasets used to evaluate selection methods. Additional details can be found in the associated references.

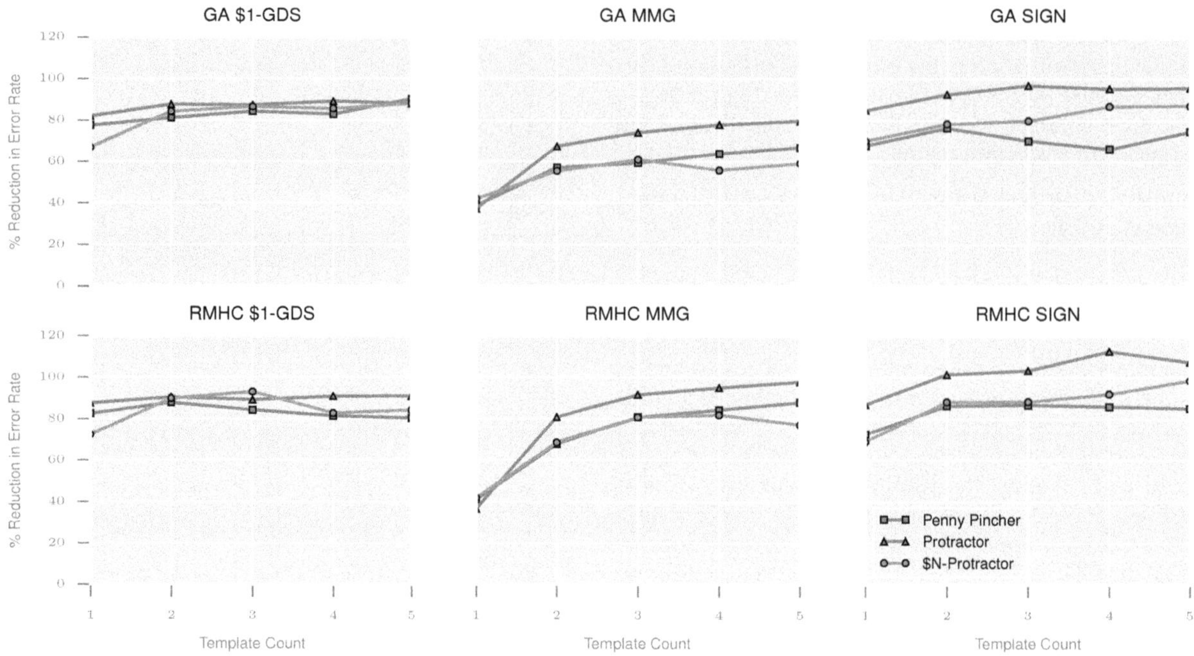

Figure 1: Percent reduction in error rates relative to random selection error rates and baseline for different sample counts per gesture class for each dataset. The baseline is represented by 100% reduction in error rate and random selection is represented by 0%; that is, charts were generated using the equation $100 * (random - method)/(random - baseline)$. In all cases, RMHC and GA were significantly closer to baseline accuracy than random selection with substantial reductions in error rate.

Results

Results for the evaluation are shown in Table 1. For visualization purposes, we elected to report the percentage decrease in error rate in lieu of the absolute error rate because we are not comparing recognizers. We wanted to see how close to baseline error rates the selection algorithms were able to reach. These results are presented in Figure 1. Each of the recognizers improved dramatically over random selection in all configurations. We compared the RMHC and GA error distributions to random selection for each dataset, recognizer and level of k, which resulted in 90 pairwise comparisons. Using Welch's unequal variances t-test with a Bonferroni correction, all results were significant ($p < .05/90$). Error rates were reduced by over 70% in all cases for $1-GDS, 35% for SIGN, and 25% for MMG. Table 2 also shows the reduction in time and space efficiency for $k = 5$. It is clear that reducing the size of the dataset reduces the computational load of the recognition process while still reaching similar recognition rates to baseline, according to Table 1.

DISCUSSION AND CONCLUSIONS

The results of the experiment point toward a clear benefit in using a supervised selection algorithm to reduce the number of prototypes while still maintaining only slightly worse error rates than when using the entire dataset. This idea is compounded in situations when there is a temporal constraint on recognition. Each configuration rapidly approached the baseline accuracy of the dataset for that particular recognizer.

Also notable is the fact that RMHC and GA performed similarly. Both methods are heavily influenced by the mutation genetic operator. Mutation is the primary method of exploration in GA with crossover being used to consolidate good candidates into potentially higher fitness individuals. RMHC is able to reach similarly optimal prototype subsets without the use of crossover or multiple candidates in each iteration. For this reason, we recommend practitioners use RMHC in lieu of GA. We have provided pseudocode for RMHC.

There are almost no downsides to carrying out this calculation, save the brief additional implementation time and time to carry out the preprocessing and selection, which is negligible for RMHC. However, we found that $N-Protractor was slow to carry out selection, particularly when working with a large, multistroke dataset (MMG). One possible way to solve this is to use a faster, more efficient recognizer like Penny Pincher during the selection process and then use the resultant subset of strokes to build a different $-family recognizer.

We proposed two alternative techniques for prototype selection that intelligently select prototypes that will best maintain the low error rates of the recognizer. Previous research [10] has found that there are methods to improve the performance of GA relative to RMHC. However, both techniques perform better than random selection in all cases tested here, and RMHC is simpler to code with similar execution time.

ACKNOWLEDGEMENTS

This work is supported in part by NSF CAREER award IIS-0845921.

REFERENCES

1. Almaksour, A., Anquetil, E., Quiniou, S., and Cheriet, M. Personalizable pen-based interface using lifelong learning. In *2010 International Conference on Frontiers in Handwriting Recognition (ICFHR)* (Nov 2010), 188–193.
2. Anthony, L., and Wobbrock, J. O. A lightweight multistroke recognizer for user interface prototypes. In *Proceedings of Graphics Interface 2010*, GI '10, Canadian Information Processing Society (Toronto, Ont., Canada, Canada, 2010), 245–252.
3. Anthony, L., and Wobbrock, J. O. $n-protractor: A fast and accurate multistroke recognizer. In *Proceedings of Graphics Interface 2012*, GI '12, Canadian Information Processing Society (Toronto, Ont., Canada, Canada, 2012), 117–120.
4. García, S., Luengo, J., and Herrera, F. *Data preprocessing in data mining*. Springer, 2015.
5. Goldberg, D., and Richardson, C. Touch-typing with a stylus. In *Proceedings of the INTERACT '93 and CHI '93 Conference on Human Factors in Computing Systems*, CHI '93, ACM (New York, NY, USA, 1993), 80–87.
6. Herold, J., and Stahovich, T. F. The 1-cent: Recognizer: A fast, accurate, and easy-to-implement handwritten gesture recognition technique. In *Proceedings of the International Symposium on Sketch-Based Interfaces and Modeling*, SBIM '12, Eurographics Association (Aire-la-Ville, Switzerland, Switzerland, 2012), 39–46.
7. Leiva, L. A., Martín-Albo, D., and Plamondon, R. Gestures À go go: Authoring synthetic human-like stroke gestures using the kinematic theory of rapid movements. *ACM Trans. Intell. Syst. Technol. 7*, 2 (Nov. 2015), 15:1–15:29.
8. Li, Y. Protractor: A fast and accurate gesture recognizer. In *Proceedings of the SIGCHI Conference on Human Factors in Computing Systems*, CHI '10, ACM (New York, NY, USA, 2010), 2169–2172.
9. Llorens, D., Prat, F., Marzal, A., Vilar, J. M., Castro, M. J., Amengual, J.-C., Barrachina, S., Castellanos, A., Boquera, S. E., Gómez, J., et al. The ujipenchars database: a pen-based database of isolated handwritten characters. In *Proceedings of the Sixth International Conference on Language Resources and Evaluation (LREC'08)*, N. Calzolari, K. Choukri, B. Maegaard, J. Mariani, J. Odijk, S. Piperidis, and D. Tapias, Eds., European Language Resources Association (ELRA) (Marrakech, Morocco, may 2008). http://www.lrec-conf.org/proceedings/lrec2008/.
10. Mitchell, M., and Holland, J. H. When will a genetic algorithm outperform hill-climbing?
11. Park, H.-S., and Jun, C.-H. A simple and fast algorithm for k-medoids clustering. *Expert Systems with Applications 36*, 2 (2009), 3336–3341.
12. Rubine, D. Specifying gestures by example. *SIGGRAPH Computer Graphics 25*, 4 (July 1991), 329–337.
13. Skalak, D. B. Prototype and feature selection by sampling and random mutation hill climbing algorithms. In *Machine Learning: Proceedings of the Eleventh International Conference*, Morgan Kaufmann (1994), 293–301.
14. Taranta, II, E. M., and LaViola, Jr., J. J. Penny pincher: A blazing fast, highly accurate $-family recognizer. In *Proceedings of the 41st Graphics Interface Conference*, GI '15, Canadian Information Processing Society (Toronto, Ont., Canada, Canada, 2015), 195–202.
15. Vatavu, R.-D., Anthony, L., and Wobbrock, J. O. Gestures as point clouds: A $p recognizer for user interface prototypes. In *Proceedings of the 14th ACM International Conference on Multimodal Interaction*, ICMI '12, ACM (New York, NY, USA, 2012), 273–280.
16. Vatavu, R.-D., Vogel, D., Casiez, G., and Grisoni, L. Estimating the perceived difficulty of pen gestures. In *Proceedings of the 13th IFIP TC 13 International Conference on Human-computer Interaction - Volume Part II*, INTERACT'11, Springer-Verlag (Berlin, Heidelberg, 2011), 89–106.
17. Wobbrock, J. O., Wilson, A. D., and Li, Y. Gestures without libraries, toolkits or training: A $1 recognizer for user interface prototypes. In *Proceedings of the 20th Annual ACM Symposium on User Interface Software and Technology*, UIST '07, ACM (New York, NY, USA, 2007), 159–168.

Maximizing Correctness with Minimal User Effort to Learn Data Transformations

Bo Wu
Computer Science Department
University of Southern California
4676 Admiralty Way
Marina del Rey,CA
bowu365@gmail.com

Craig A. Knoblock
Information Sciences Institute
University of Southern California
4676 Admiralty Way
Marina del Rey, CA
knoblock@isi.edu

ABSTRACT
Data transformation often requires users to write many trivial and task-dependent programs to transform thousands of records. Recently, programming-by-example (PBE) approaches enable users to transform data without coding. A key challenge of these PBE approaches is to deliver correctly transformed results on large datasets, since these transformation programs are likely to be generated by non-expert users. To address this challenge, existing approaches aim to identify a small set of potentially incorrect records and ask users to examine these records instead of the entire dataset. However, because the transformation scenarios are highly task-dependent, existing approaches cannot capture the incorrect records for various scenarios. We present a approach that learns from past transformation scenarios to generate a meta-classifier to identify the incorrect records. Our approach color-codes these transformed records and then presents them for users to examine. The method allows users to either enter an example for a record transformed incorrectly or confirm the correctness of a transformed record. Our approach also can learn from the users' labels to refine the meta-classifier to accurately identify the incorrect records. Simulation results and a user study show that our method can identify the incorrectly transformed records and reduce the user efforts in examining the results.

ACM Classification Keywords
H.5.2. Information Interfaces and Presentation: User Interfaces; D.2.4. Software Engineering: Program Verification; K.8.1. Personal Computing: Database processing

Author Keywords
Programming by Example; Data Transformation; Program Synthesis

INTRODUCTION

IUI 2016, March 7–10, 2016, Sonoma, CA, USA.
ACM 978-1-4503-4137-0/16/03.
http://dx.doi.org/10.1145/2856767.2856791

There are over 500 million users that are using spreadsheets to manage their data. These users come from various backgrounds and lack the necessary programming skills to automate their tasks. Programming-by-example (PBE) approaches [12] enable these users to generate programs without coding. Recently, these approaches have been successfully applied to data transformation problems [6] to save users from writing many task-dependent transformation programs.

To use a PBE system for data transformation, users are only required to provide input-output pairs (also referred to as examples). The PBE system generates the programs that are consistent with given examples. For example, Figure 1(b) shows the dimensions for a set of artworks. To extract the first degree from the dimension, the user enters "10" as the output for the first entry. The PBE approach generates programs that can transform the inputs into corresponding outputs specified in the examples. It applies the program to the rest of records. If the user finds any incorrect output, she can provide a new example. The approach refines the program to make it consistent with all given examples. The user often interacts with the system for several iterations and stops when she determines that all records are transformed correctly.

Despite the success of generating programs using PBE approaches, the correctness of the results is still an issue. Real-world data transformation often involves thousands of records with various formats. Each record consists of *raw data (input)* and *transformed data (output)*. The users are often not aware of all the variations of the data that they should transform. They know whether the records are transformed correctly when they see them. But they lack the insight of the unseen formats of the records buried in the middle of datasets.

To help users verify whether the records are transformed correctly, existing PBE approaches [6, 13, 19] provide recommendations or highlight certain records for the users. The user checks these records and provides new examples for those incorrect records. Here, we consider a record as *a correct record* when it is transformed into the expected format. Otherwise, the record is considered incorrect (referred to as *an incorrect record*).

To generate such recommendations, there are several challenges. First, the dataset is usually huge. The users need to see the results and provide additional examples if necessary on the fly. Fully transforming the entire dataset and analyzing all

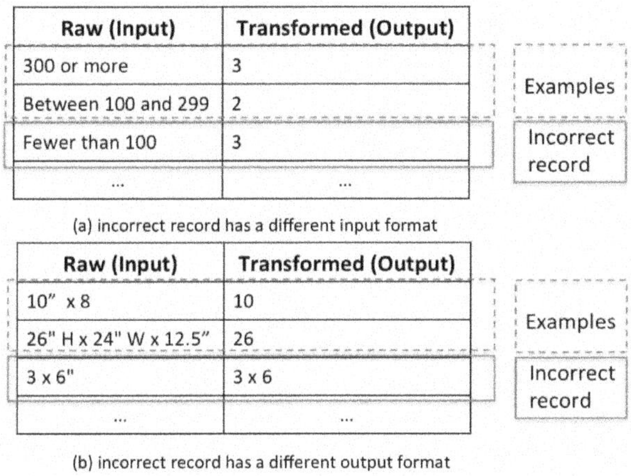

Figure 1. Different rules for recognizing incorrect records

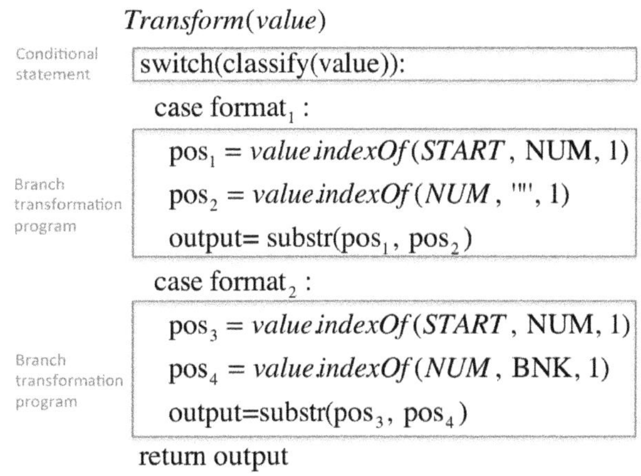

Figure 2. An example transformation program

the transformed records to generate recommendations takes too long to be practical.

Second, the users' intentions are highly task-dependent and there is no universal rule for determining whether the results are correct. Meanwhile, the approach should be able to hypothesize users' intentions accurately to provide useful recommendations. For example, the scenario in Figure 1(a) is to encode different texts into numbers. The users want to transform the three records into "3", "2" and "1" respectively. After giving the two examples in the dashed rectangle, the learned program does not transform the 'Fewer than 100' into the expected value '1', as it has not seen an example of that type before. The problem is that 'Fewer than 100' has different words from the inputs of the two examples when they are represented using the bag-of-words model [4]. To capture this incorrect record, we can use a rule to identify the records that have different words in the *input* from the examples. However, in Figure 1(b), the counts of numbers, blank spaces, quotes and "x" in the inputs are the same for the third and the first record. We need to use a different rule that identifies the records with different *output* formats to locate the incorrect records since the output of the third record contains an "x" and blank spaces, which the first two records do not have.

Third, the recommendation should place the incorrect records at the beginning so that users can easily notice these records. Otherwise, users have to examine many correct records before identifying the incorrect one, which is a burden.

Fourth, users are often too confident with their results to examine the recommended records, which they regard as an extra burden [14, 10]. Even when there are incorrect records in the recommendation, the users may ignore them and stop providing more examples.

To address the challenges above, our approach samples records to allow users to focus on a small portion of the entire dataset. It statistically guarantees that a user-specified percentage of records of the entire dataset are transformed correctly with certain confidence when all records in the small sample are transformed correctly. Our approach also maintains a library of different classifiers representing different rules for checking whether a record is transformed correctly. It uses an ensemble method to combine these different classifiers to automatically identify incorrect records in various scenarios. To save users' time in checking the recommendations, we provide users two ways to label the recommended records: (1) users can confirm a recommended record is correct or (2) they can provide the expected outputs for the incorrect records. Our approach then learns from these labels and provides users with refined recommendations. Finally, in addition to providing the recommendation that exposes incorrect records to users, we have also developed a method that identifies a minimal set of records that the user should examine before finishing the transformation.

Our contributions are summarized below:

- minimizes the user effort in obtaining a user-specified correctness,
- allows users to focus on a small sample of a large dataset,
- combines multiple classifiers based on different perspectives for verifying the correctness of records,
- refines recommendations when users confirm certain recommendations are correct or incorrect,
- manages user overconfidence by requiring users to examine certain records before finishing the transformation.

PROGRAMMING BY EXAMPLE

Our approach is built on the IPBE approach [21, 20, 22], which extends the previous PBE approach [6]. The approach is based on a domain specific transformation language (DSL), which supports a restricted, but expressive form of regular expressions, which also includes conditionals and loops. The approach synthesizes transformation programs from this language using examples.

For example, after the users provide examples for the first three records shown in Figure 1(b), the transformation program is shown in Figure 2. The program has a function ($classify(value)$) to recognize the format of the input ($value$). Based on the input format, it uses the conditional statement *switch* to invoke the corresponding branch transformation program to transform the input. Here, $format_1$ refers to the format

$$branch = segment_1 + segment_2 + ...$$
$$segment = const \mid substr(p_s, p_e, offset = 0) \mid loop(w, branch)$$
$$p = indexOf(leftcxt, rightcxt, c + offset)$$
$$loop(w, branch) = branch_1 + branch_2 + ... + branch_w$$

Figure 3. The DSL for branch transformation programs

of the first and second records where a double quotation separates the first degree information from the rest of the string. The $format_2$ corresponds to the format of the third record where a blank space separates the first degree from the rest.

The syntax of the branch transformation program is a concatenation of several segment programs as shown in Figure 3, where it returns a string concatenating the outputs of all its segment programs ($segment_i$). This language allows the users to perform simple string deletion, insertion and reordering. For simplicity, the branch program in Figure 2 only contains one segment program. A segment program can be specified in three ways: (1) a constant string (*const*), (2) extracting substring from the input between two positions ($substr_i$) or (3) a loop statement ($loop(w, branch)$). The *substr* program also has an offset with a default value 0, which is omitted by default. This parameter is described later with the loop statement. The two position programs (p_s and p_e) in the *substr* program specify the start and end positions in the input to extract the substring. A position program identifies a location in the input. The position programs can be specified using (1) an absolute position, or (2) restricted regular expressions that identify the context of the given position, which can be represented using a triple as (leftcxt, rightcxt, occ). The "leftcxt" describes the left context of the position and "rightcxt" describes the right context. The "occ" refers the occ-th appearance of the position with the specified context. The "occ" is computed by c + offset. Here, c is a number. The "offset" is 0 except it is in a loop statement. The contexts are all specified using token sequences. Our approach tokenizes texts into token sequences. The different types of token are defined as follows. START represents the beginning of the input string. END is for the end of the input string. UWRD represents an uppercase letter, LWRD means a sequence of lower letters, the BNK means a blank space, NUM refers to a sequence of digits and WORD refers to a sequence of alphabetical letters, etc. Each punctuation is a token, such as Dquot, which refers to a double quotation. Therefore, (NUM, Dquot, 1) means the first occurrence of a position whose left is a number and whose right is a double quotation mark.

Our language also supports loop statements, which is a concatenation of w non-nested branch programs. The ith non-nested branch program in the loop statement ($branch_i$) has an offset value of i-1. By having the offset values from 0 to $w-1$, the loop statement can repeatedly extract substrings of the same pattern and concatenate these substrings.

In order to generate the transformation program, IPBE [21, 20, 22] first creates traces [9] for the given examples. A trace essentially specifies the input-output pairs for all transformation steps of each particular example when transforming the raw data into the target data. For example, one trace for the first example in Figure 1(b) is $[substring = \text{“10”}(pos_1 = 1, pos_2 = 3)]$. The trace specifies a way to transform the raw data into the target output. It dictates that the program should contain one segment program and its output should be a string "10". It also specifies that the substring should be extracted between position 1 and 3. Thus, the first position program (pos_1) should output 1 and the second (pos_2) should return 3. With the traces of examples, the IPBE generalizes over these specific traces to derive programs.

When the user provides a new example, IPBE tries to refine the previous program to generate a new program that is consistent with all given examples. If such a program does not exist, the approach partitions the examples into multiple clusters using constrained agglomerative clustering [20]. Each cluster contains the examples of the same format. IPBE learns a multi-class SVM classifier [2] to recognize these different formats.

To learn the classifier, the approach first converts the records into features vectors. The features can be categorized into two types: (1) counts of tokens and (2) the average indices of tokens in the sequence. As shown in Figure 4, the string "6 x 8" is converted into a sequence of tokens. Each token has its type and content. The feature vector contains the counts for different tokens, such as the 2 under NUM, which means there are two NUM tokens. It also contains the average positions of these tokens. For example, first NUM has an index of 1 in the token sequence and the second NUM has an index of 5. Thus, the average position (NUM_pos) is 3.

<table>
<tr><td>Text</td><td colspan="5">6 x 8"</td></tr>
<tr><td>Token sequence</td><td colspan="5">NUM(6) BNK LWRD(x) BNK NUM(8) Dquot(")</td></tr>
<tr><td rowspan="2">Feature vector</td><td>NUM</td><td>BNK</td><td>NUM_pos</td><td>BNK_pos</td><td>...</td></tr>
<tr><td>2</td><td>2</td><td>3</td><td>3</td><td>...</td></tr>
</table>

Figure 4. The token sequence and feature vector for a string

After learning the SVM classifier, IPBE uses this classifier as the *classify* function in the *switch* statement, shown in Figure 2, to choose the branch program that should be invoked to transform the raw data. IPBE learns a branch transformation program for each cluster of examples. Finally, it combines the conditional statement with the branch programs to create the final transformation program.

VERIFYING THE TRANSFORMED DATA

To verify the correctness of the transformed data, our approach samples records from the entire dataset. The approach then identifies the potentially incorrect records and recommends these identified records for the users to examine. When the recommendations are shown to users, they can provide the target values for the incorrect records or they can confirm a record is transformed correctly. Our approach uses the records that the users have edited or confirmed as new examples to refine the recommendations.

The user interface of our system is shown in Figure 5. The interface consists of three areas:

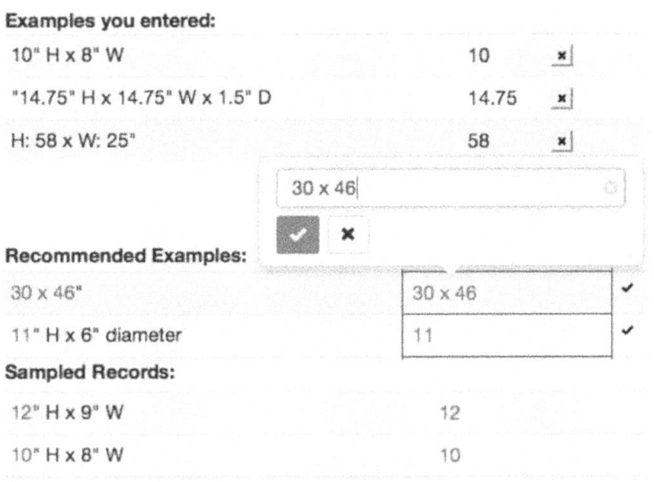

Figure 5. User interface

- Examples a user entered: this area shows all the examples provided by the user. There are also buttons with cross icons used for deleting previous examples,
- Recommended examples: this area shows all the potentially incorrect records for users to examine. If the user finds an incorrect record, she can click the record and enter the target output in the popup window as in Figure 5. She can also click the button with a check icon to confirm that the record is correct,
- Sampled records: this area shows all the records in the sample, which the user can also correct.

The records in the GUI are color-coded. The substrings that are extracted from inputs are colored in the same color in both the input and the transformed result. As shown in Figure 5, the "10" is colored blue in both the input and output of the last record to indicate the correspondences between the input and output. By providing the color-coding, the users gain some insight into the learned programs. Users are more likely to notice when there is a irregular color pattern, which is likely a sign of incorrect records.

SAMPLING RECORDS

Our approach uses hypothesis testing to decide whether the number of incorrect records in the entire dataset is below a certain percentage. The hypothesis is *the percentage of incorrect records is smaller than p_{lower}*. The alternative hypothesis is *the percentage of incorrect records is not less than p_{upper}*. The p_{lower} represents that the percentage of incorrect records that we want to achieve in the dataset. The p_{upper} refers to a percentage of incorrect records that we want to avoid ($p_{upper} \geqslant p_{lower}$).

We use the binomial distribution $B(n,p)$ to model the distribution of incorrect records since each record is either transformed correctly or incorrectly. The parameter n is the number of sampled records. The parameter p is the probability that a record is incorrect, which can also be interpreted as a p fraction of records that are transformed incorrectly. To find the sample size for testing the hypothesis, we use the binomial cumulative distribution function as shown in Formula 1 [3]. $Pr(x < Z_a; n, p)$ represents the probability that the number of incorrect records (x) is less than Z_a in the binomial distribution $B(n, p)$. We use $1-\alpha$ and $1-\beta$ to adjust our confidence level and power for the hypothesis test: (1) α controls the probability of rejecting our hypothesis when the hypothesis is true and (2) $1-\beta$ controls the probability of rejecting the alternative hypothesis when it is false. The confidence level $1-\alpha$ is set to 0.95 and the power $1-\beta$ is set to 0.80 in practice [3]. The z_α is the allowable number of incorrect records. If the incorrect number of records x is smaller than z_α, our hypothesis passes the test with confidence $1-\alpha$ and power $1-\beta$ over the alternative hypothesis. Given α, β, n, p_{upper} and p_{lower}, we can calculate z_α based on Formula 1.

Since the user ideally stops when there are no incorrect records in the sample, x is zero and it is strictly smaller than z_α.

$$\begin{aligned} &Pr(x < z_\alpha; n, p_{upper}) > 1-\beta, \\ &where\ Pr(x < z_\alpha; n, p_{lower}) < \alpha \end{aligned} \quad (1)$$

Demanding a lower error percentage, a higher confidence and power of the hypothesis requires a larger sample. For example, when $p_{lower} = 0.01$, $\alpha < 0.05$, the alternative hypothesis is $p_{upper} \geqslant 0.02$ and $1-\beta > 0.8$, we need a sample of 910 records. If we change the $p_{lower} = 0.001$ and $p_{upper} \geqslant 0.002$, the sample size is 9635. However, we can configure the parameters to achieve the balance between sample size and level of confidence to meet different user requirements.

RECOMMENDING RECORDS

Our approach automatically examines the records in the sample to identify potentially incorrect records (line 2 to line 9 in Algorithm 1). It sorts these records and recommends them for the users to examine. Our approach has two phases. First, it identifies the *records* ($R_{runtime}$) with runtime errors. Runtime errors are the errors that occur during the execution of transformation programs and cause the programs to exit abnormally. Second, our approach identifies the *questionable records* ($R_{questionable}$) with potential incorrect results when there is no record with runtime errors.

Finding the records with runtime errors

Our approach finds the records with runtime errors. These records cause the learned program to exit abnormally in execution. There are two types of runtime errors: (1) the position program cannot locate a position and (2) the segment program has a start position larger than the end position.

For example, the approach applies the learned program shown in Figure 2 to a new input "H: 24 x W: 7 " to extract the first degree information. The program uses the first branch program to transform this record. The start position program cannot locate a position in the input and outputs "-1", as "24" does not appear at the beginning of the input. The end position program cannot locate a position either, because there is no """ after "24". The corresponding segment program also has a runtime error, as both its start position and end position are smaller than 0 (-1). The other case of a runtime error is

Algorithm 1: Algorithm for recommending records

Input: Set of all the records R, transformation program P and MetaClassifier F
Output: Recommended set of Records R^*
$R_{runtime}$ = [], $R_{questionable}$ = [], R^* = []
R_s= sample(R)
for *record r in* R_s **do**
  r_t = applyTransformation(r, P)
  if r_t *contains runtime error* **then**
    r_t.score = number of failed position programs
    $R_{runtime}.add(r_t)$
  else
    score = F.getScore(r_t)
    if *score* < 0 **then**
      r_t.score = score
      $R_{questionable}$.add(r_t)
    end
  end
end
if $R_{runtime}.isEmpty()$ **then**
  sort $R_{questionable}$ acscendingly based on record score
  $R^* = R_{questionable}$
else
  sort $R_{runtime}$ acscendingly based on record score
  $R^* = R_{runtime}$
end
return R^*

that the segment program has a start position bigger than the end position. In this case, the two position programs of the segment program both successfully locate two indexes in the input. However, the end position is before the start position, which only causes a runtime error of the segment program. To identify the records with runtime errors, our approach applies the learned program to the sampled records, collects all the records with runtime errors and puts them into the set $R_{runtime}$.

Building a meta-classifier for detecting questionable records

The set of binary classifiers used for building the meta-classifier can be categorized into 3 types: (1) classifiers based on the distance (f_{dist}), (2) classifiers based on the agreement of different programs ($f_{program}$), and (3) classifiers based on the format ambiguity ($f_{ambiguity}$).

Classifiers based on distance

This type of classifier calculates the distances from records to a set of records. Based on the distribution of the distances, this type of classifier identifies the records with distances that are larger than certain standard deviations from the chosen references. To calculate the distance between two records, the approach first converts the records to feature vectors and then calculates the Euclidean distance between the two vectors. The features used here are the same as introduced in the previous section.

This type of classifier ($f_{dist}(e_i|\,r,t,c)$) is shown in Function 2. It classifies each record e_i as either a correct record (1) or an incorrect record (-1) based on its distance ($d_{e_i,r}$) from the reference (r). N is the number of records. Each classifier of this type can be characterized using a triple (r,t,c). The r represents the *reference*. It has two values: "all records" or "examples". The string "all records" specifies that the approach calculates the distance between the feature vector of the record (e_i) with the mean vector of all records except e_i. The string "examples" means that the approach computes the distance from the record (e_i) to the mean vector of the examples. The t has three values: "input", "output" or "combined". "input" and "output" here mean that only inputs or outputs of the records are used to create feature vectors. The "combined" means the input and output are concatenated into one string to create the feature vector. The σ is the distance standard deviation. The $c\sigma$ indicates the number (c) of standard deviations. For example, a classifier $f_{dist}(e_i|``examples", ``input", 1.8)$ identifies the records whose inputs are more than 1.8 standard deviations (σ) away from the mean vector of the inputs of examples .

$$f_{dist}(e_i|\,r,t,c) = \begin{cases} -1 & d_{e_i,r} > c\sigma \\ 1 & d_{e_i,r} \leqslant c\sigma \end{cases} \quad (2)$$
$$where\,\sigma = \sqrt{\tfrac{1}{N}\textstyle\sum_i (d_{e_i,r}-\mu)^2},\ \mu = \tfrac{1}{N}\textstyle\sum_i d_{e_i,r}$$

Since parameter triple (r,t,c) has many configurations, our approach generates all configurations. Here, the value for c is selected from a set of predefined decimal numbers. The approach uses each configuration to create a binary classifier and adds the classifier into the library of classifiers.

Classifiers based on the agreement of programs

This type of classifier identifies the records in which consistent programs disagree about the transformation results. Typically, our approach can generate multiple programs that are consistent with a given set of examples. Each program can be considered as an interpretation of the examples. The classifiers of this type maintain a set of programs that are consistent with the examples. The binary classifier identifies the records (output -1) that the programs produce different results for the same input. Providing examples for these records can help to clarify a user's intention and guide the system to converge to the correct programs. However, to build such classifiers, directly generating all the consistent programs and evaluating all these programs on records is expensive because there are usually a large number of consistent programs for a few examples.

To reduce the computational cost in building this type of classifier, we exploit the fact that the approach can independently generate the position programs. Our approach generates all the consistent position programs instead of the entire set of branch programs and then evaluates these position programs on the records. This modification greatly reduces the number of programs that our approach is required to generate and evaluate, as the set of complete programs can be considered as a Cartesian product of sets of position programs. For example, in Figure 6, the start and end position of the substring "10" can both be represented using a set of programs. Every start position program can combine with any end position program to form a segment program. There would be 16 segment programs if there are 4 start position programs and 4 end position programs. But the total number of start and end position pro-

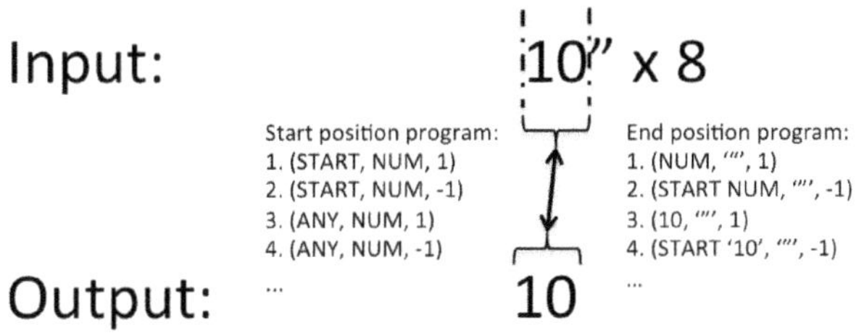

Figure 6. Candidate position programs for one segment

grams is only 8. Our approach only needs to generate and evaluate 8 position programs instead of 16 segment programs.

Classifiers based on the format ambiguity

This type of classifier aims to capture those records that are labeled with the wrong format. The transformation program has a conditional statement, which is used to recognize the format for a record before applying any transformation. We use a SVM multi-class classifier as the conditional statement as described in the Programming-by-Example section. The SVM classifier not only classifies the records into their formats but also outputs the probability of a record belonging to that format. To identify the records that are potentially labeled incorrectly by the SVM classifier, our approach selects the records with a probability below a threshold θ. To select the right θ, our approach first creates a classifier using each θ in a predefined set and adds the classifier into the classifier library. Later, our approach selects the classifier with the θ having the best performance described in the next section.

Combining classifiers using ADABOOST

We use ADABOOST [5] to combine classifiers above to create a meta-classifier ($F(e)$) for classifying whether a record (e) is transformed correctly as shown in Function 3. The meta-classifier outputs -1 for incorrect records and 1 for correct records. The output is 1 if the weighted sum of the output of a set of binary classifiers (f_i) is no less than 0; and it is -1 if the sum is negative. During training ADABOOST iteratively selects the binary classifier (f_i) from a pool of classifiers described above to minimize the error on the misclassified training instances. It also assigns weights (w_i) to these classifiers indicating their importance in the final meta-classifier.

$$F(e) = sign(\sum_i w_i f_i(e)) \tag{3}$$

Our approach only uses ADABOOST to select the binary classifiers and learn their weights **once** to create the meta-classifier. Our approach uses this meta-classifier for all future transformations. Notably, the meta-classifier only defines the binary classifiers to be used and the weights for them. The approach still learns the binary classifiers constituting the meta-classifier for each specific transformation. Our approach learns the parameters for the binary classifiers (f_i) from the examples, records, and consistent programs that are unique to each iteration. It combines these learned binary classifiers with the assigned weights to create the meta-classifier.

Sorting the recommended records

Since the approach recommends multiple records, it places the records that are more likely to be incorrect and contain more valuable information on the top of the recommendation area shown in Figure 5. This saves users' time in examining the recommended records and the system can also obtain more informative examples from the users. Our approach calculates a score (*getScore* line 6 in Algorithm 1) for each record (r) to measure how likely a record is incorrect and how much information the record can provide in synthesizing the program as shown in Equation 4.

$$getScore(r) = \begin{cases} failed\ subprogram\ count & Runtime\ error \\ -\sum_i w_i * f_i(r) & No\ runtime\ error \end{cases} \tag{4}$$

The records with runtime errors are all incorrect. The score for these records is the number of failed subprograms including segment and position programs. A higher score means the approach can learn more information from this record, if the user provides an example for this record. The approach sorts these records in descending order.

As to the records without runtime errors, we assume that the records that are more likely to be incorrect can provide more information for the system. The approach uses $-\sum_i w_i * f_i(r)$ in Function 3 as the score for each record. The w_i is the weight for all the binary classifier used in the meta-classifier. The $f_i(r)$ outputs the label (-1 or 1) for a record (r). A higher score indicates more classifiers or the classifiers with heavier weights consider the record as an incorrect record. The approach sorts these records in descending order.

Minimal test set

We want to ensure that the user has examined a minimum number of records. Users are recommended to validate at least one record in a minimal set of records by either confirming the correctness of the record or entering a new example for that record. Since there are multiple consistent programs given a set of examples, these programs conflict with each other as they generate different results on same records. The minimal test set contains the records in which these consistent programs disagree on the outputs. Ideally, we should ask users to review the outputs and select the correct ones so that they can identify the corresponding correct programs. However, fully generating all the programs and executing them on records is too computationally expensive. Therefore, our approach only generates all the consistent position programs and evaluates them on the records to approximate all the programs that should be tested. To identify the minimal test set, our approach uses the same set of records that are labeled as incorrect by the classifier based on the agreement of programs. Our approach highlights these records with blue borders as seen in Figure 5. When the minimal test set is empty, there are no conflicting position programs.

EVALUATION

To evaluate the performance of our approach, we performed experiments on simulated data and a user study to compare our system with alternative approaches. Transforming a dataset usually requires several iterations in the evaluation. An *iteration* starts when the user provides a new example and ends when the system has learned the transformation program and applied the program to the rest of the data records.

Experiment on Simulated Data

The experiment has two goals: (1) test whether our recommendation can capture the incorrect records, and (2) test whether our approach can place at least one incorrect record on top so that users can easily notice the incorrect records.

Dataset

We used the 30 scenarios published in our previous work [21]. Each scenario contains about 350 records. The data was gathered from student mashup projects in a graduate-level course, which required the students to integrate data from multiple sources to create various applications. They were required to perform a variety of transformations to convert the data into the target formats. Each scenario contains two columns of data. The first column shows the raw data and the second column shows the transformed data.

Experiment setup

To collect the training data for learning the meta-classifier, we need to have both the transformation results and the labels to indicate whether these records are correct or not. Our approach first selects a record, provides the expected output and uses this record as an example. The system learns the transformation program and applies the program to the rest of records. The system compares the transformed data with the expected output and labels each record as correct or incorrect. It also calculates the confidence of the conditional statement on each record. After collecting the data for the iteration, the system starts a new iteration by identifying the first incorrect record and providing an example for that record. The process ends when all the records are transformed correctly. Our approach collects training data from all iterations of the 30 scenarios. We divided all the scenarios into 5 groups and ran 5-fold cross-validation. Our approach trained the meta-classifiers using 4 groups of training data and tested the meta-classifier on the remaining group.

We used two metrics below to evaluate our approach and alternative approaches in each scenario:

- iteration accuracy: the percentage of iterations in which our recommendations contain at least one incorrect record out of all the iterations having incorrect records.

- mean reciprocal rank (MRR): the average of the reciprocal rank of the first identified incorrect record. Q is the total number of iterations and $Rank_i$ is the index of the first incorrect record in the recommended list in the i-th iteration. If the recommendation fails to include the incorrect record and there exists one, the $\frac{1}{Rank_i}$ is set to 0.

$$MRR = \frac{1}{Q}\sum_{i=1}^{Q}\frac{1}{Rank_i}$$

We compared our current approach[1] with the state-of-the-art approach (Approach-β) [20] and a baseline approach. The *Approach-β* also provides recommendations for users to examine. There are two main differences between our approach and approach-β. First, our approach learns a meta-classifier from a pool of classifiers, while Approach-β only uses one classifier that is just one of the classifiers in our pool. Second, our approach recommends multiple records for users to review, while Approach-β only recommends one record. The *baseline* approach like many existing approaches does not provide recommendations. The baseline only randomly shuffles the transformed records for users to examine and users directly examine these shuffled records.

Results

As shown in Figure 7, our approach accurately captured the incorrect records in the recommendation. The average iteration accuracy of our approach in all scenarios is 0.98 compared to 0.83 for Approach-β. The iteration accuracy is left blank for baseline as the baseline approach does not provide any recommendations. The improvement is mainly due to two reasons. First, our approach recommended multiple records compared to Approach-β, which only recommended one record in each iteration. Second, our meta-classifier is an ensemble of a library of classifiers. The classifier used in Approach-β is just one in the library. This ensemble of classifiers enables our approach to capture a boarder range of incorrect records. Only scenario 9 and 18 have iterations in which our approach failed to detect the incorrect records. These iterations require examples for unseen input formats that are similar to previous examples, which means the system fails to detect the difference. One example from scenario 9 is shown in Table 1. The user intended to extract the full prices for student tuition (1st and 2nd record). Since the third record only has the credit price, this record should be transformed to "NULL". However, given only the first and second record as examples, our approach did not know the user required a different transformation for the third record since the record shared a very similar format with two previous records. Thus, our approach did not recommend the 3rd record as a potentially incorrect record for users to examine.

Our approach can place the incorrect records on top of the recommendation, as the average MRR of our approach in all scenarios is 0.75. It saved users' time from fully exploring a long list of records. The average MRR of Approach-β in all scenarios is 0.68. Approach-β did not place the incorrect record on top for most of iterations that did not have runtime errors. The MRR of the baseline approach was calculated based on the index of the first incorrect record in the transformed records. We can see both our approach and Approach-β are well above the baseline, as the randomized shuffling can place the incorrect records in the middle of the list.

User study

The goal of this experiment is to test whether the users using our approach can achieve better correctnesses than the users of Approach-β with no more user effort.

[1]The documentation and code of our system are available on Github (https://github.com/areshand/Web-Karma)

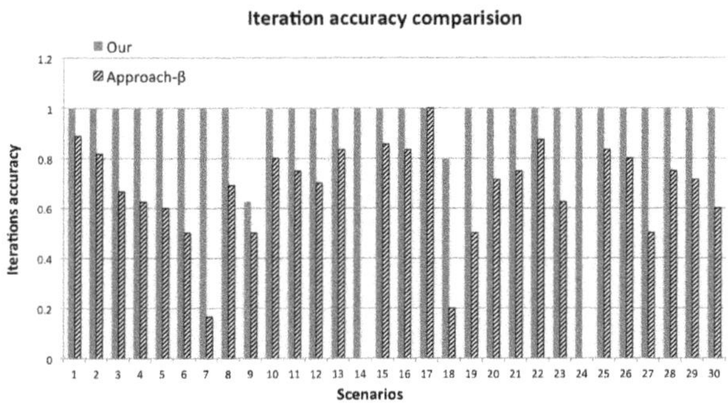

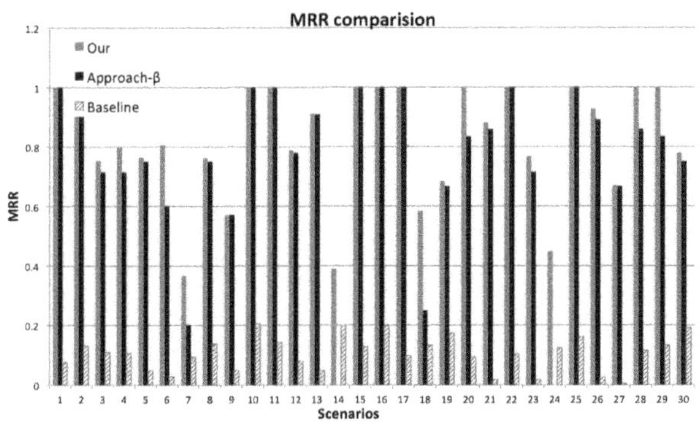

Figure 7. Comparison results

Raw	Transformed
$33,926 per year (full-time)	$33,926
$42,296 per program (full-time)	$42,296
$1,286 per credit (full-time)	**$1,286**

Table 1. One typical example of a failed iteration

Dataset

We collected 5 scenarios with about 4000 records for each scenario on average to evaluate the approaches. The first 2 records and the description of the scenarios are shown in Table 2 to demonstrate the transformation. These transformations involve transforming text into URIs by adding prefixes, replacing blank spaces with underscores or reordering substrings such as s1, s2 and s5. The rest of the scenarios focus on extracting substrings from the inputs such as s3 and s4.

Experiment setup

We used three metrics to measure the user performance (1) correctness, which is the percentage of correct records when the users stopped transforming, (2) iteration time, which is the average time (in seconds) used by users in one *iteration* and (3) total time, which is the averaged total time (in seconds) used by users to transform a scenario.

We recruited 10 graduate students and divided them into two groups ($group_A$ and $group_B$). We asked $group_A$ to use our system and asked $group_B$ to use the Approach-β. We asked them to work on one sample scenario to learn how to use the two systems. We then described the goal on the other 5 scenarios and asked them to transform the scenarios into the target formats. We used the training data gathered in the simulated experiment to train our meta-classifier for recommending records. The p_{lower} and p_{upper} were set to 0.01 and 0.04. Our approach sampled 300 records in every iteration.

Results

The results of the user study are shown in Table 3. Our approach achieved a correctness higher than 0.99 in all scenarios. These scores were within the expected correctness range. Compared with Approach-β, we can see our approach also achieved a higher score for correctness in all 5 scenarios. Users in $group_A$ not only had higher correctness rates, but also used less time per iteration for 4 out of 5 scenarios and used the same amount of time on the remaining scenario. We performed a paired one-tail t test for the hypothesis that *our approach uses less time per iteration and has a higher correctness than Approach-*β. The result shows that the improvements are statistically significant ($p < 0.05$).

In the user study, we found that users using our approach used less total time in 3 out of 5 scenarios. This was due to the fact that users using our approach were willing to perform more iterations. We found that the users in $group_A$ provided more examples than users in $group_B$, as users in $group_A$ can simply click a button to confirm a correct record as a new example. The users confirmed several examples (2 - 5 examples) before stopping the transformation process. Thus, the number of examples (Example#) provided by the users in $group_A$ is higher than the numbers in $group_B$ as shown in Table 3. The $group_A$ users provided 11.1 examples and users in $group_B$ only provided 8.4 examples on average. Providing more examples gives users more opportunities to refine the recommendation and examine more records, which in turn leads to a higher correctness rate. We found when the recommendation contained incorrect records on top, it largely reduced the time users used to examine the results compared to the time spent by users to directly examine the results when the recommendation failed to capture the incorrect records.

In the user evaluation, we observed that our approach recommended a large number of records for users to examine for certain iterations. For most of the iterations, the recommendations had the incorrect records on top of the recommended list and the users identified these incorrect records. For the remaining iterations, users missed certain incorrect records in the recommendation. But the users still obtained correctness scores that satisfied the requirement (p_{lower}=0.01 and $p_{upper} = 0.04$), as the numbers of unidentified incorrect records were smaller than the allowable number Z_α (7).

We also asked users for their feedback on the color-coding of the results. All users said the color-coding helped them to identify incorrect records by highlighting irregular color patterns. Some users also mentioned that it would be more helpful if different formats could also be colored differently

RELATED WORK

Programming-by-example (PBE) approaches [11, 8, 6] are effective in generating transformation programs for simple scenarios without coding. FlashFill [6], which is an example PBE system, is already integrated into Excel 2013 to help users transform the data. Here, we review the closely related work focusing on verifying the correctness of user-generated programs [10]. The techniques used to verify the correctness of programs can generally be categorized into three types: (1) testing the generated programs following formal software

Scenario	description	Input	Output
s1	change into URI	WidthIN	http://qudt.org/vocab/unit#Inch
		HeightCM	http://qudt.org/vocab/unit#Centimeter
s2	change into URI	Dawson, William	William_Dawson
		Lauren Kalman	Lauren_Kalman
s3	extract issue date	Thor I#172 (January, 1970)	January, 1970
		Machine Man II#2	NULL
s4	extract first degree	7 x 9 in.	7
		6 13/16 x 8 7/8 in.	6 13/16
s5	change into URI	American	thesauri/nationality/American
		South African	thesauri/nationality/South_African

Table 2. Scenarios used in user study

Scenario	Our approach				Approach-β			
	Correctness	Iteration Time	Total Time	Example#	Correctness	Iteration Time	Total Time	Example#
s1	1	16	182.4	11.4	0.828	16	144	9
s2	0.998	17	227.8	13.4	0.994	26	234	9
s3	0.992	16	185.6	11.6	0.873	36	313.2	8.7
s4	0.997	14	196	14	0.983	17	187	11
s5	0.999	12	64.8	5.4	0.872	22	94.6	4.3
Average	0.997	15	171.32	11.1	0.91	23	194.56	8.4

Table 3. User study results

testing strategies, (2) detecting potentially incorrect results and asking users to verify them, and (3) visualizing the results to reveal irregularities and outliers. Existing approaches usually combine techniques from multiple categories to maximize the chance of detecting errors in the generated programs.

As the users are often overconfident about the correctness of their results, a program testing plan can be designed and users are provided with feedback on the completeness of the tests. The testing feedback may motivate the users to review the results more thoroughly. The WYSWYT ("What You See is What You Test") [18, 16, 17] describes an approach to test spreadsheet programs. The approach asks users to provide test cases by validating the correctness of certain values. To ensure it has obtained enough test cases, the approach provides a criterion called definition-use coverage to find the values that users should validate. The criterion is developed based on the data-flow adequacy [15] to test the correctness of cell references in spreadsheets. Our approach is inspired by this approach of recommending that users examine a minimal set of records to address the overconfidence problem. However, our approach only focuses on transforming a column of data into another other column. There are no cell dependences that we can leverage to decide which records to examine. Moreover, recommended records can also help users to explore the dataset and increase the chances that they will notice unexpected inputs to refine their programs. This helps users understand and refine the task requirements rather than merely testing the programs. Earlier work [1] introduced assertions into the spreadsheet program testing. It allows users to specify their expectation and converts them into assertions. The assertions specify allowed cell values in the form of Boolean expressions. Whenever a conflict between an assertion and a cell value happens, the cell value is shown to the users. Our approach is different from this earlier work in that our approach only asks user to provide examples.

Many approaches have been developed to identify the potentially incorrect records. The work by Galwani [6] highlights the entries that have two or more alternative transformed results. This method generates multiple programs and evaluates these programs on all the records to identify these records with different results. This method is equivalent to one of the classifiers used in our approach to identify incorrect records. Our approach supports more methods for detecting potentially incorrect records and combines these different methods using a meta-classifier. Moreover, our approach places all identified records together in one area so that users do need to go through all the records to find them. LAPIS [13] highlights the texts that have potentially incorrect matches. Their approach identifies the matches that are different from the majority of matches. Wolfman et al. [19] extends Lau et al.'s approach [11] by reducing the user effort using a mixed initiative approach that combines several interaction modes. The approach by Wu et al. [22] recommends only one example for users to examine and the recommendation is only based on the distance from the records to the examples. Compared to the approaches above, our approach learns more powerful rules that can identify incorrect records in various scenarios. Our approach recommends and sorts multiple records so that the users are more likely to catch the incorrect records without examining a large number of records.

Different visualization methods have been proposed to help users gain insight into both the data and learned programs. OpenRefine [7] supports a large number of ways to visualize data and it also allows users to customize the visualizations, such as using histograms, facet graphs, etc. Users may notice an irregular pattern when watching these visualizations to uncover potentially incorrect results. Data Wrangler [8] translates transformation programs into natural language so that users can read these programs. They can then verify whether the programs are as expected. Our approach is orthogonal to the approaches above. Our approach color-codes the substrings in the records so that users can understand how the raw inputs are transformed into the outputs.

CONCLUSION AND FUTURE WORK

We presented an approach that is designed to help users of PBE systems to obtain correct results with minimal effort. The approach samples a set of records for automatic inspection. It then uses an ensemble of classifiers to identify potentially incorrect records from the sampled records and presents these records for the users to examine. A user can provide labels for these records by either entering examples for incorrect records or confirming a record is correct. The approach learns from these labels to update the recommendation. We performed a simulated experiment on collected scenarios. The results shows that our approach can identify incorrect records in nearly all iterations and can also place the incorrect records on top so that users can easily notice them. We also performed a user study. The results show that our approach can save users time and significantly improve correctnesses compared to alternative approaches.

In the future, we plan to introduce existing orthogonal methods for verifying the correctness of results and programs. For example, we can provide histograms to visualize both the raw data and transformed data to provide users a better overview of the data. Translating the transformation programs to readable natural language text can also help users gain insight into the generated programs.

ACKNOWLEDGEMENTS

This material is based on research sponsored in part by the National Science Foundation under Grant No. 1117913.

REFERENCES

1. Margaret M. Burnett, Curtis R. Cook, Omkar Pendse, Gregg Rothermel, Jay Summet, and Chris S. Wallace. 2003. End-User Software Engineering with Assertions in the Spreadsheet Paradigm. In *ICSE*.
2. Chih-Chung Chang and Chih-Jen Lin. 2011. LIBSVM: A library for support vector machines. *ACM Transactions on Intelligent Systems and Technology* (2011).
3. M.M. Desu and D. Raghavarao (Eds.). 1990. *Sample size methodology*. Academic press Inc.
4. Ronen Feldman and James Sanger. 2006. *Text Mining Handbook: Advanced Approaches in Analyzing Unstructured Data*. Cambridge University Press.
5. Yoav Freund, Robert E Schapire, and others. 1996. Experiments with a new boosting algorithm. In *ICML*.
6. Sumit Gulwani. 2011. Automating String Processing in Spreadsheets Using Input-output Examples. In *POPL*.
7. David F Huynh and Mazzocchi Stefano. *OpenRefine http://openrefine.org*. `http://openrefine.org`
8. Sean Kandel, Andreas Paepcke, Joseph Hellerstein, and Jeffrey Heer. 2011. Wrangler: interactive visual specification of data transformation scripts. In *CHI*.
9. Emanuel Kitzelmann and Ute Schmid. 2006. Inductive Synthesis of Functional Programs: An Explanation Based Generalization Approach. *Journal of Machine Learning Research* (2006).
10. Andrew J. Ko, Robin Abraham, Laura Beckwith, Alan Blackwell, Margaret Burnett, Martin Erwig, Chris Scaffidi, Joseph Lawrance, Henry Lieberman, Brad Myers, Mary Beth Rosson, Gregg Rothermel, Mary Shaw, and Susan Wiedenbeck. 2011. The State of the Art in End-user Software Engineering. *ACM Comput. Surv.* (2011).
11. Tessa Lau, Steven A. Wolfman, Pedro Domingos, and Daniel S. Weld. 2003. Programming by Demonstration Using Version Space Algebra. *Mach. Learn.* (2003).
12. Henry Lieberman (Ed.). 2001. *Your Wish is My Command: Programming by Example*. Morgan Kaufmann Publishers Inc.
13. Robert C. Miller and Brad A. Myers. 2001. Outlier Finding: Focusing User Attention on Possible Errors. In *UIST*.
14. Raymond R. Panko. 1998. What We Know About Spreadsheet Errors. *J. End User Comput.* (1998).
15. Sandra Rapps and Elaine J. Weyuker. 1985. Selecting Software Test Data Using Data Flow Information. *IEEE Trans. Software Eng.* (1985).
16. Gregg Rothermel, Margaret Burnett, Lixin Li, Christopher Dupuis, and Andrei Sheretov. 2001. A Methodology for Testing Spreadsheets. *ACM Trans. Softw. Eng. Methodol.* (2001).
17. Gregg Rothermel, Lixin Li, Christopher DuPuis, and Margaret Burnett. 1997. *What You See is What You Test: A Methodology for Testing Form-based Visual Programs*. Technical Report.
18. Karen J. Rothermel, Curtis R. Cook, Margaret M. Burnett, Justin Schonfeld, T. R. G. Green, and Gregg Rothermel. 2000. WYSIWYT Testing in the Spreadsheet Paradigm: An Empirical Evaluation. In *ICSE*.
19. Steven A. Wolfman, Tessa A. Lau, Pedro Domingos, and Daniel S. Weld. 2001. Mixed initiative interfaces for learning tasks: SMARTedit talks back. In *IUI*.
20. Bo Wu and Craig A. Knoblock. 2014. Iteratively Learning Conditional Statements in Transforming Data by Example. In *Proceedings of the First Workshop on Data Integration and Application at the ICDM*.
21. Bo Wu and Craig A. Knoblock. 2015. An Iterative Approach to Synthesize Data Transformation Programs. In *IJCAI*.
22. Bo Wu, Pedro Szekely, and Craig A. Knoblock. 2014. Minimizing User Effort in Transforming Data by Example. In *IUI*.

AutoManner: An Automated Interface for Making Public Speakers Aware of Their Mannerisms

M. Iftekhar Tanveer[1], Ru Zhao[2], Kezhen Chen[3], Zoe Tiet[4], Mohammed (Ehsan) Hoque[5]
Rochester Human-Computer Interaction (ROC-HCI), University of Rochester
{[1]itanveer, [5]mehoque}@cs.rochester.edu
{[2]rzhao2, [3]kchen33, [4]ztiet}@u.rochester.edu

ABSTRACT
Many individuals exhibit unconscious body movements called mannerisms while speaking. These repeated changes often distract the audience when not relevant to the verbal context. We present an intelligent interface that can automatically extract human gestures using Microsoft Kinect to make speakers aware of their mannerisms. We use a sparsity-based algorithm, *Shift Invariant Sparse Coding*, to automatically extract the patterns of body movements. These patterns are displayed in an interface with subtle question and answer-based feedback scheme that draws attention to the speaker's body language. Our formal evaluation with 27 participants shows that the users became aware of their body language after using the system. In addition, when independent observers annotated the accuracy of the algorithm for every extracted pattern, we find that the patterns extracted by our algorithm is significantly ($p < 0.001$) more accurate than just random selection. This represents a strong evidence that the algorithm is able to extract human-interpretable body movement patterns. An interactive demo of AutoManner is available at `http://tinyurl.com/AutoManner`.

Author Keywords
Public Speaking; Body Language; Interface Design

ACM Classification Keywords
I.5.0 Pattern Recognition: General; H.5.m. Information Interfaces and Presentation (e.g. HCI): Miscellaneous

INTRODUCTION
Have you ever felt unaware of your body language while giving a public speech? What did you do with your hands? Did you move around while speaking or stand still? How did you use your gestures to emphasize a point that you wanted to make?

Our conscious mind can process only 40 bits of information per second [22, 38]. As a result, we become easily overwhelmed in public speaking while thinking about what to say next. In this situation, many of our innate functions are delegated to the subconscious mind, which can process up to 4 million bits per second. This often results in unconscious and possibly repetitive patterns of movements. These movements include gripping or leaning, tapping fingers, whole body movements (such as rocking, swaying, pacing), jingling pocket change, adjusting hair or clothing, etc. The Toastmasters group [36] refers to these as *mannerisms*. These can significantly distract the audience.

In this paper, we present—AutoManner—an interface to automatically extract and visualize the repetitive patterns of the speaker's movements during public speaking. AutoManner captures and analyzes body language using a Microsoft Kinect [39] depth sensor to make speakers aware of their mannerisms. We implement a subtle feedback technique that involves pinpointing frequent movements and asking questions about their meanings. In our experiment with 27 participants, the users reported that the use of AutoManner made them aware of their mannerisms.

Most of the existing systems [27, 24, 6, 33] that assess the quality of public speech utilize a supervised classification approach. In supervised methods, the system either assigns the speakers to a predefined category or a number indicative of the quality of the speech. Although this *supervised approach* is beneficial for ontological categorization, it may not provide any insights about the strengths and weaknesses of an individual. For example, it usually does not offer any insight as to why particular body language is rated poorly, or which patterns in their body movement were not effective. In addition, a supervised approach is unable to detect idiosyncratic or unexpected body movements, as it is difficult to define all possible patterns that a person may show in a given context.

One possible way to solve this problem is to share the videos with public speaking experts and get subjective feedback. Challenges include identifying those experts and paying for their time. Another possibility is to obtain cheap micro-level annotations in the cloud using crowdsourcing [26]. However, crowdsourcing poses an inherent threat to the speaker's privacy. Speakers may not feel comfortable about real people viewing their videos and judging their speaking performance and body language. In this paper, we address this challenge by developing a fully automated framework that allows users to obtain feedback while being in complete control of their data.

In one of our previous projects [35], we proposed a sparsity-based algorithm to extract repetitive body movements (behavioral cues). In the AutoManner interface, we use this

IUI 2016, March 7–10, 2016, Sonoma, CA, USA.

DOI: http://dx.doi.org/10.1145/2856767.2856785

algorithm to automatically extract and show these repetitive movements to the speaker.

However, not every repetitive movement is bad. Specific gestures can be distracting (mannerism) or meaningful depending on how cohesive it is with the verbal content [13]. Currently, the proposed interface cannot determine the context of the verbal content. Nevertheless, it makes the speakers aware of their body language by highlighting the repeated body movements and asking questions about them. Reflection through answering questions about body language is a subtle way to show the speaker's idiosyncrasies and mannerisms. In our experiments, we found evidence supporting this design, as the participants reported becoming self-aware of their body language. A similar effect of awareness might also be achieved if one carefully watches and annotates the entire video. AutoManner automatically highlights the regions of repetitive body movements, thus eliminating the tedious manual observation and annotation process.

We claim the following contributions in this paper:

- We develop an intelligent interface that can automatically extract repetitive patterns of body language and visualize them to make public speakers aware of their body language.
- We formally evaluate the interface with 27 public speakers. They self-reported to become aware of their mannerisms after using our interface.
- Our experiment provides strong evidence ($p < 0.001$) that the algorithm we used is able to extract more accurate and human-interpretable body movement patterns than just random sampling.
- To the best of our knowledge, this is the first attempt to automatically analyze mannerisms in public speaking.

LITERATURE REVIEW

Nonverbal behavior (e.g. body language, vocal prosody, facial expressions, etc.) is an important modality for interpersonal communication. It is shown to be predictive of human communication skills in many different domains—for instance, patient satisfaction [11], analysis of persuasiveness [30], dating [28], job interviews [2, 23], etc. Body language is an important component of nonverbal behavior [16]. Cognitive neuroscientist Beatrice de Gelder [10], after an extensive literature review, concluded that body language is as reliable a metric as facial expressions.

Constituents of a Good Public Speech

Both verbal and nonverbal behaviors are important factors in good public speaking [32]. Strong speakers communicate ideas through a delicate interplay between verbal content and body language (body postures, head and hand movements, etc.). Schreiber et al. [29] analyzed the characteristics of good public speeches in order to develop a rubric for judging public speaking competency. Their work substantiates the importance of congruence between verbal and nonverbal factors during public speaking.

Experts on public speaking [13, 9, 18, 36] usually stress the importance of coherence in verbal content and body language. Hoogterp mentioned in his book [13] that body language should be synchronized with a speech for effective nonverbal communication. In addition, hand gestures should convey the same meaning as the verbal content. The Toastmasters group [36] pointed out that eliminating distracting mannerisms was necessary for conveying spontaneous and genuine feelings through body language.

Automated Assessment of Public Speaking Competence

A considerable amount of work has been done to model and automatically predict the performances of public speaking. Pfister and Robinson [27] proposed a real-time system to classify affective states and to assess public speaking skills. They extracted prosodic features such as pitch, intensity, and *MFCC* to classify a speaker's affective states into one of nine discrete categories (absorbed, excited, interested, joyful, opposed, stressed, sure, thinking, unsure) using a Support Vector Machine (SVM). Similarly, they classified public speaking skills into one of six discrete classes (clear, competent, credible, dynamic, persuasive, and pleasant).

Nguyen et al. [24] proposed an online feedback system that provides feedback about a speaker's body language on a scale of five degrees, from bad to excellent. They used a Kinect skeleton tracker to track the postures and gestures of the speaker. They then used a nearest-neighbor classifier to compare those movements to a set of predefined templates of postures and gestures in order to determine the quality of the speaker's speech. This method cannot account for completely novel body language. In addition, this method is not suitable for assessing cases where a gesture is meaningful in one context but not meaningful in another. Chen et al. [6] described a multimodal sensing platform for scoring presentation skills. They used syntactic, speech, and visual features (e.g. hand movements, head orientations, etc.) with supervised regression techniques (Support Vector Regression and Random Forest) to predict a continuous score indicating public speaking performance. They claimed a correlation coefficient of 0.38 to 0.48 with the manually annotated ground truth.

All the systems discussed so far utilize supervised classification/regression approaches. This may be an artifact of similar trends in human action/activity recognition literature [1, 7, 19, 37]. Recently, some work has been done on unsupervised analysis of human action detection. Niebles et al. [25] proposed a method of unsupervised learning of human action categories using a Latent Dirichlet Allocation model. Zhou et al. [40] proposed Aligned Cluster Analysis (ACA), which detects patterns in signals using k-means clustering and dynamic time warping. Tanveer et al. [35] proposed a sparse coding based approach for detecting common behavioral cues for body language. In this paper, we use the method mentioned in Tanveer et al. for capturing the fidgeting patterns and the mannerisms of public speakers.

Design of Effective Feedback

Feedback is an important component for any nonverbal skills assessment and training system. The predicted skill levels

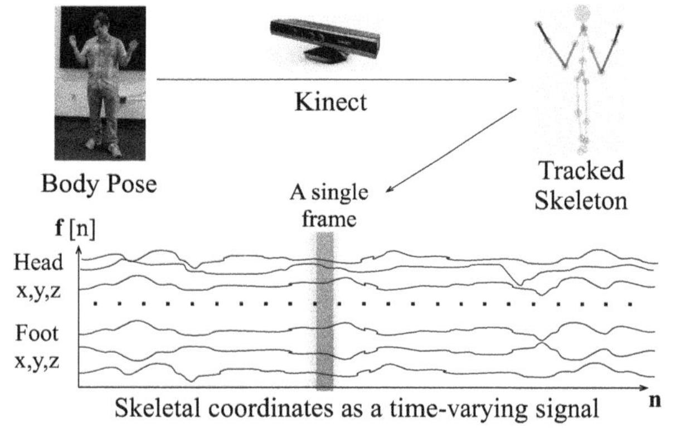

Figure 1: Steps for capturing the Motion Capture (MoCap) signal.

and useful recommendations should be effectively and intuitively conveyed to the users. A significant amount of work has already been done on designing useful feedback systems. For instance, Hoque et al. [14] showed that it is possible to improve job interview performances by reviewing one's own videos augmented with raw features such as smile, head movements, speech, and prosody. They used a virtual avatar to practice the job interviews. Tanaka et al. [33] also employed virtual characters for practicing social skills for people with Autism Spectrum Disorder (ASD). Tanveer et al. [34] designed a system to provide live feedback on prosodic behavior using Google Glass. They utilized *secondary display* phenomenon for minimizing distractions during the speech.

Chollet et al. [8] performed extensive analysis on learning strategies and usefulness of a virtual audience in public speaking training. They analyzed the efficacy of an interactive learning framework (Cicero [3]) where speakers can practice speaking in a safe and engaging environment with a virtual audience. The virtual audience can provide nonverbal feedback to signal elevated attention, rapport, lack of interest, or disagreement. They show that the interactive virtual audience results in significant progress in perceived attention and combined improvement compared to the traditional ways of providing feedback.

TECHNICAL DETAILS

Many public speakers display their own idiosyncratic body language, which makes it difficult to compile an exhaustive list of all movement patterns. Without an exhaustive list, we cannot train a supervised classification system to detect patterns of body movements. To address this challenge, we have developed an algorithm to extract common body movements automatically—without any human supervision on segmenting or labeling of a training dataset. In this section, we describe this method.

Data Capture

In order to sense the movements of the speakers, we record the speaker's activity using a Kinect [39] depth sensor. Kinect uses an infrared projector and sensor arrangement to record depth images of the region in front of the device. We use a

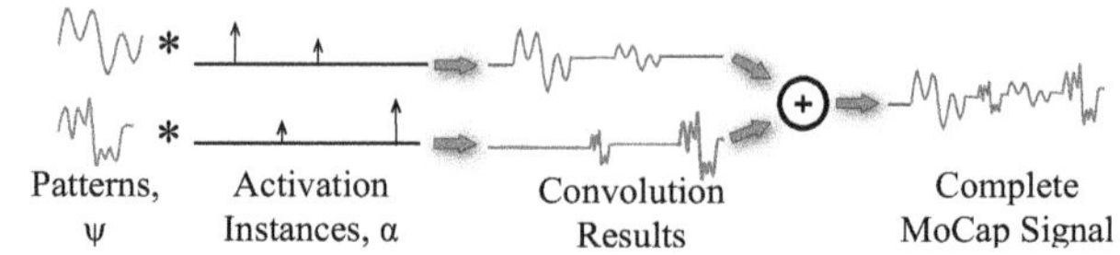

Figure 2: A simplified illustration of MoCap signal model. Only one component is shown ($k = 1$).

skeleton tracker [31] to extract the 3D coordinates of a person's body from the depth images. The skeleton tracker can track twenty joint locations of the person's body, as shown in Figure 1. We refer to the time-sequence of all the joint locations as a Motion Capture (MoCap) signal.

Preprocessing

The motion capture signal is a high dimensional vector-valued signal. At each time-instance, the signal consists of 60 (20 joints × 3 components—x, y, z) components. Due to the logistics of the experimental setup (i.e. to limit the total study time) we needed to reduce the dimensionality of the input signal. We did it by applying Principal Component Analysis (PCA) [15] at the frame level. The number of basis vectors for PCA was determined through a heuristic evaluation over a sample dataset. We kept the basis vectors corresponding to the k largest eigenvalues that account for 99% of the total variance of the signal. The value of k usually varies from five to 16, depending on the contents of the signal. PCA helps to reduce the noise in the MoCap signal by eliminating low energy principal components.

Extracting the Behavioral Cues

Behavioral cues are defined as small meaningful repetitive patterns in a person's gestures, posture, touching behavior, facial expressions, eye behavior, vocal behavior, etc. [16, 37] In this paper, we disregard the aspect of "meaning" for behavioral cues and use it interchangeably as "body movement patterns." In our prior research [35], we proposed an unsupervised algorithm to extract human-interpretable patterns of body movements from MoCap signals. Our algorithm was inspired by the *Shift Invariant Sparse Coding (SISC)* algorithm, proposed by Morup et al. [21]. In this project, we have developed an interface to display these patterns to the speakers as potential mannerism candidates. We briefly describe the technique in this section. Please refer to Tanveer et al. [35] for an elaborate discussion of this algorithm.

Mathematical Model

Let us assume that the MoCap signal, $\mathbf{f}[n]$, has k components, and the length of the signal is N. The behavioral cues are manifested in the signal as a specific pattern of variations. The patterns can appear at any location in the signal. Let us assume that there are D unique patterns and we denote any d^{th} pattern as $\psi_d[m]$. We also denote the signal representing the activation instances of the dth pattern as $\alpha_d[n]$, which is just a collection of impulse functions, as shown in Figure 2. We model the MoCap signal through a superposition of all the patterns repeated at the corresponding activation instances. It can be described mathematically as in Equation (1).

$$\begin{aligned}\mathbf{f}_m[\mathrm{n}] &= \sum_{d=0}^{D-1} \alpha_d[n] * \psi_d[m] \\ &= \sum_{d=0}^{D-1}\sum_{u=0}^{N-1} \alpha_d[u]\psi_d[n-u].\end{aligned} \tag{1}$$

Here, the asterisk ($*$) symbol denotes the convolution operation. Convolution of any signal with an impulse function results in a time-shift of the signal into the time-location of the impulse function.

Problem Formulation

We extract the behavioral cues by estimating ψ and α that minimize the total squared error between our MoCap model and the actual MoCap signal. However, without any suitable constraint, this minimization problem has many solutions. In order to get a unique solution, we enforce a sparsity penalty over the activation instances, α. In other words, we assume that any particular pattern occurs only sporadically over the signal. This assumption is reasonable because, in reality, it is not possible for a particular pattern to occur densely without distorting itself. The mathematical form for the optimization problem is shown in Equation (2).

$$\begin{aligned}\hat{\psi}[m], \hat{\alpha}[n] &= \underset{\psi,\alpha}{\operatorname{argmin}} \underbrace{\frac{1}{2}\left\|\mathbf{f}[n] - \mathbf{f}_m[n]\right\|^2}_{P(\psi,\alpha)} + \lambda \left\|\alpha\right\|_1 \\ \text{s.t.} \quad & \|\psi\|_F^2 \le 1 \quad \text{and,} \quad \forall_n \alpha[n] \ge 0.\end{aligned} \tag{2}$$

Here, the $P(\psi, \alpha)$ term represents the squared error. The ℓ-1 norm of α is the term for enforcing sparsity and λ is a multiplier controlling the relative proportion for the error term and the ℓ-1 norm. The constraint $\|\psi\|_F^2 \le 1$ makes sure that ψ cannot grow arbitrarily large. Finally, the constraint $\alpha[n] \ge 0$ ensures that the activation instances are non-negative. This is important to make sure that the extracted patterns are not upside down.

Algorithm

The objective function in this optimization problem is non-convex, in general. However, it is convex over one of the parameters (α or ψ) when another parameter is fixed. Therefore, we can solve it using an *Alternating Proximal Gradient Descent* approach. The complete procedure is shown in Algorithm 1. We alternatively keep one parameter fixed and update another, and vice versa. As the error reduces at each iteration of the gradient descent process, the algorithm is guaranteed to converge.

However, we cannot calculate the gradient of the objective function at all the points. The ℓ-1 norm of α is non-smooth, and thus non-differentiable. We use an *Iterative Shrinkage Threshold Algorithm (ISTA)* [5] to solve this problem. We use the gradients of the smooth part (i.e. $P(\psi, \alpha)$) to update the parameters. Then, at each iteration, we apply a *shrink* operation over α to enforce sparsity. We also project α to the set of non-negative numbers to enforce the non-negativity constraint. The gradients of $P(\psi, \alpha)$ with respect to ψ and α are shown in equations (3) and (4) respectively.

Algorithm 1: Learning the Behavioral Cues

Input: $\mathbf{f}[n]$, M, D and λ
Output: ψ, α
Initialize;
$i \leftarrow 0$;
$\alpha \leftarrow 0$, $\psi \leftarrow$ random;
while *not Converge* **do**
  Update ψ;
  reconstruct $\mathbf{f}_{model} \leftarrow \sum_{d=1}^{D-1} \alpha_d * \psi_d$;
  calculate $\nabla_\psi P$ using $\mathbf{f}, \mathbf{f}_{model}$ and α [Eq. (3)];
  $\psi^{(i+1)} \leftarrow \mathbf{project}(\psi^{(i)} - \gamma_\psi \nabla_\psi P)$;
  Update α;
  reconstruct $\mathbf{f}_{model} \leftarrow \sum_{d=1}^{D-1} \alpha_d * \psi_d$;
  calculate $\nabla_\alpha P$ using $\mathbf{f}, \mathbf{f}_{model}$ and ψ [Eq. (4)];
  $\alpha^{(i+1)} \leftarrow \mathbf{shrinkandproject}(\alpha^{(i)} - \gamma_\alpha \nabla_\alpha P)$;
  $i \leftarrow i+1$

$$\frac{\partial P}{\partial \psi_{d',k'}[m']} = \sum_{n=0}^{N-1}\{f_{\text{model},k'}[n] - f'_k[n]\}\alpha_{d'}[n-m'] \tag{3}$$

$$\frac{\partial P}{\partial \alpha_{d'}[n']} = \sum_{k=0}^{K-1}\sum_{n=0}^{N-1}\{f_{\text{model},k}[n] - f_k[n]\}\psi_{d',k}[n-m'] \tag{4}$$

The **shrinkandproject** method is shown in equation (5).

$$\begin{aligned}\alpha[n] &\leftarrow \text{sgn}(\alpha[n])\text{max}(0, |\alpha[n]| - \gamma\lambda) \quad \forall_{0 \le n < N} \\ \alpha[n] &\leftarrow max(0, \alpha[n]) \quad \forall_{0 \le n < N}\end{aligned} \tag{5}$$

Please note that, although the algorithm simultaneously solves two convex problems, the whole objective function is not convex, in general. Therefore, it is not guaranteed that the algorithm will reach the global optima when it converges—it may settle upon a local optima. We randomly initialize the algorithm, run it multiple times, and choose the lowest value to make it more likely to reach the global optima. The length of each pattern is heuristically set to two seconds in this application.

Speedup Techniques

While designing the user studies for the system, we needed to extract the behavioral cues between two consecutive speeches by a speaker. This situation imposed additional constraints on the convergence time for the algorithm. We wanted to ensure that it does not take more than five minutes to converge for a three-minute MoCap sequence. To achieve this, we reduced the dimensionality of the signal using PCA, as described before. We also set the number of patterns to be extracted at five, as makes the program linearly slower. However, even with these settings, the algorithm took about twenty minutes to converge, which is unacceptable, according to the study design.

We choose the step-sizes (γ_ψ and γ_α) using a *bold driver* [4] method to further speed up the algorithm. Choice of step size

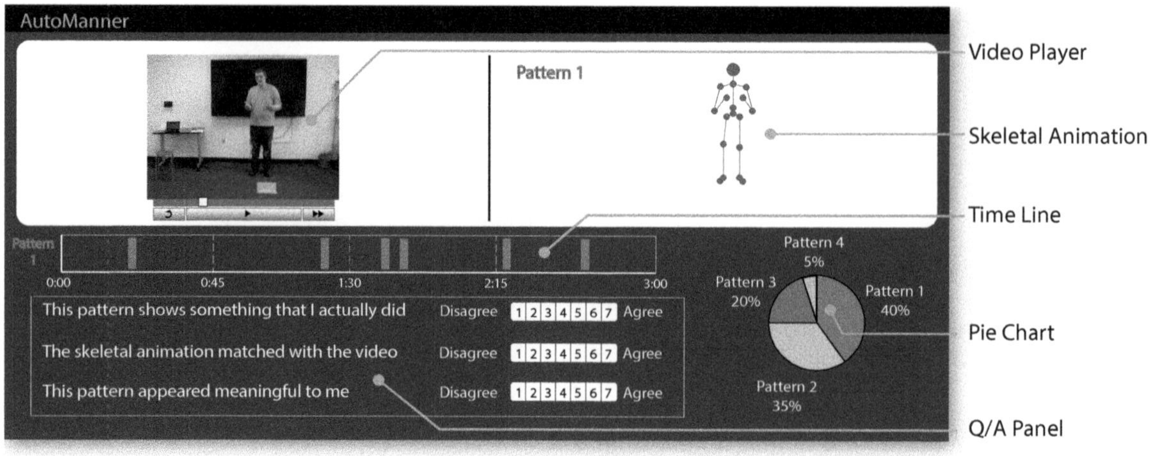

Figure 3: A screenshot of the user interface designed to analyze body language. A live sample is available at: `http://tinyurl.com/AutoManner`

is important, as too small a value will make the algorithm slow to converge. On the other hand, large step sizes will make it diverge from the optimum. In the bold driver method, the step-sizes are slowly increased (by five percent) at each iteration that reduces the value of the objective function. If the value of the objective function increases at any iteration, the step size is largely penalized (by 50 percent decrease) because it indicates the step size is too large. We find in empirical tests that bold driver is faster to perform than a typical *Line Search* approach, described by Tanveer et al. [35]. In addition, it takes a lower number of iterations than a constant step size. We reduced the convergence time to below five minutes by using the bold driver approach. Finally, we use simultaneous parallel jobs to rerun the algorithm and choose the results from the best performing job. We use a cluster computing environment for the parallel execution of the jobs.

DESIGN OF THE INTERFACE

The SISC algorithm described above extracts the common behavioral cues related to the speaker's body language. However, the appropriateness of the body language is largely dependent on the context of the speech—which is difficult to automatically assess. Therefore we design a user interface to make the speakers think about their own body language using a question-answer technique. We automatically extract the body movement patterns and ask questions to induce thoughts about the meaning of the cue in context of verbal content. We hypothesize that the process of thinking about a specific pattern of body movement will make them aware of their body language.

There are two main components in the interface. The first component shows the video of the speech and asks some questions about the overall quality of the speech. The video could be played normally, or fast-forwarded to quickly review the body movements in the entire speech. The second component of the interface is designed to make the speaker review and think about the extracted behavioral cues (i.e. patterns of body movements) one at a time. The speaker reviews the extracted behavioral cues and answers three questions related to each of them. This is shown in Figure 3. The interface also incorporates a video player for watching the whole speech. In addition, it contains a panel for a skeletal animation, a timeline, a pie chart, and a Q/A section. The *skeletal animation* in the upper right side of the interface represents a specific pattern of body movement (i.e. behavioral cue). This is the ψ parameter as denoted in Algorithm 1. The *timeline* shows the corresponding activation instances (α) for that specific pattern. The users can click on the time instances to play the region of the video where the pattern is activated. This allows the user to judge the verbal context for that specific behavioral cue. The *pie chart* gives a general overview to the relative proportion of the extracted patterns. The algorithm extracts the top five patterns of body movements. However, there might be less than five patterns depending on how diverse the speaker's body language is. In case the number of extracted pattern become less than three, the interface will display the following warning: "You did not move enough. For good body language you should move more and move purposefully".

A question-answer panel asks the users to rate three statements related to each pattern shown in the interface. These are listed in the "Pattern Specific Ratings" row of Table 1. The first statement makes the speaker observe the skeleton movements. The second statement makes them analyze the occurrences of the patterns in the timeline. The third statement makes them judge how coherent of the patterns are with the context of the speech. As we discussed before, the primary objective of these questions are to make the users think about the body language. Observing the skeletal movements will make them aware of a specific movement in their body. Besides, analyzing the time-instances of the pattern occurrence will provide a good idea on the context of the speech. We prepared a video tutorial[1] that explains the use of the interface. The participants of the user study watched it before their first interaction with the interface.

[1] `http://tinyurl.com/AutoMannertutorial`

Figure 4: Lab settings for the public speaking study

RESEARCH QUESTIONS

We wanted to answer the following research questions related to AutoManner in this paper.

- How useful is the interface? Do the users report becoming more self-aware of their body language?
- How well does the developed algorithm accurately identify the relevant behavioral patterns? If independent observers (e.g. workers of Mechanical Turk) annotate the accuracies of each time instance, is there any significant difference of accuracy between the treatment and the placebo patterns?
- Does the AutoManner interface help speakers improve their body language?

These questions are of different levels of difficulty which we attempted to answer from various perspectives using both quantitative and qualitative metrics. We decided to answer the first question from the user's point of view. We asked the users to evaluate the usefulness by annotating their opinions about a few statements. We also asked their subjective opinions in a free form question-answer session to gain more insight about AutoManner's efficacy. In the second question, we wanted to know the algorithm's accuracy. This could have been objectively answered by calculating error between the original signal and the extracted patterns. However, we are more interested on human-perception of the algorithmic efficiency, rather than just an error rate. Therefore we recruited Mechanical Turk^{TM} workers to observe and annotate the correctness of time instances that the algorithm detected. The turkers annotated the meaningfulness of the patterns as well. In the third question, we attempted to seek any improvement in the participants body language.

STUDY DESIGN

The design of the formal user study is focused on answering the research questions described above. Figure 5 illustrates an outline of the study. We asked the participants to deliver three speeches, each of which is three minutes in duration. After each speech, the participants rated their own speeches. Once they finished self-rating, they started interacting with the interface. The interaction involved observing each pattern of body movements and answering a few questions. Once finished the interaction, the participants rated the whole interface for its the usefulness. The same process continues for the second speech. No interface was shown after the third speech—the participants only rated themselves. The measures are shown in Table 1. All these statements were rated in a 7-point Likert scale [17].

Self-Ratings (for each speech)	Overall, I'm happy with the quality of my speech. I was purposely moving about. I was using a variety of gestures. My gestures were appropriate with the speech.
Pattern Specific Ratings (for each pattern)	This pattern shows something I actually did. The skeleton animation matched with the video. This pattern appeared meaningful to me.
Interface Ratings (Asked after reviewing all the patterns)	The feedback was very helpful. The feedback made me aware of my body language. This feedback made me aware of at-least one gesture that I make too frequently. I will use the system if it is available

Table 1: List of measures rated by the participants. All of these statements were rated in a 7-point Likert scale where higher values indicate better.

Baseline, Treatment, and Placebo

Among the three speeches, the first one was delivered without any interaction with our interface. Performance in this speech is considered as a baseline in the study. In order to evaluate the correctness of the algorithm, we prepared two different versions of the feedback interface. In one version, the interface showed the real patterns and time-instances extracted by the algorithm. We refer to this as the *treatment* interface. In another version, we faked the patterns by randomly sampling 2-second windows from the MoCap signal. The time-instances of these patterns were also randomly selected in the time-line. This version of the interface is referred as the *placebo*. In order to collect sufficient data, we made each participants to interact with both the placebo and the treatment—however, their order was counter-balanced. Participants with odd ID-number saw the placebo interface first, whereas even ID holders saw the treatment interface first. The participants did not know their ID number and the fact that there were two different versions of the interface.

Demographics, and Lab Settings

Twenty-seven people participated in the user study. Among them, 14 were female and 13 male. All of participants were undergraduate students at the University of Rochester. They declared themselves as native speakers of English. We recruited the participants by putting flyers around the campus and also by posting invitations in the student's Facebook pages. The participants received ten dollars in the form of Amazon gift cards for participating in the study. The study took approximately forty minutes to finish.

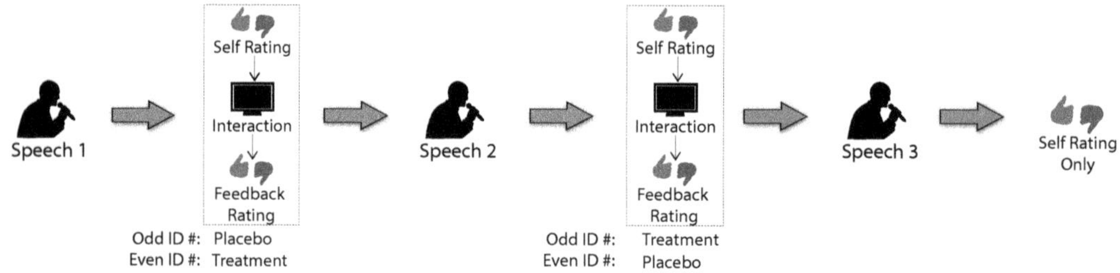

Figure 5: Design of the user-study to answer the research questions

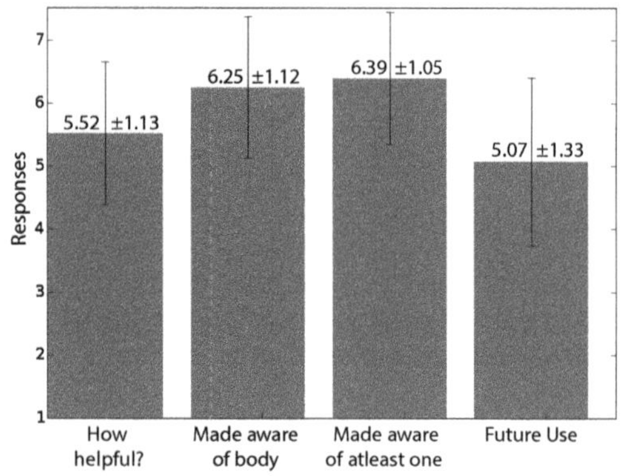

Figure 6: Interface related responses by the participants. The error-bars show one standard deviation from the mean. The dotted line shows the maximum value of Likert Scale.

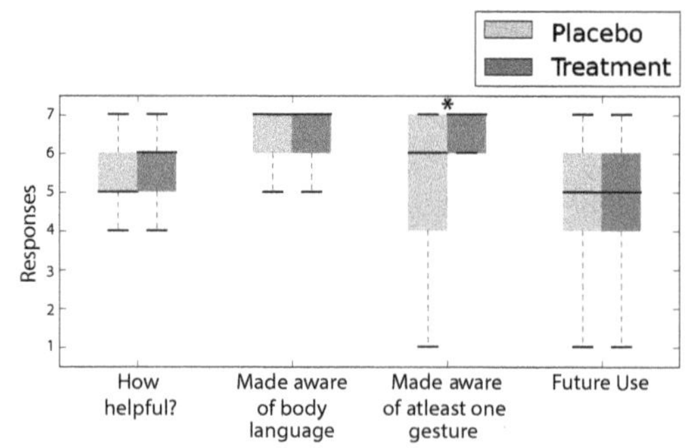

Figure 7: Box-Whisker plot for interface related responses. The ratings are grouped in placebo and treatment interfaces.

During the study, we video-recorded the speeches using a Canon Rebel T3 DSLR camera. We captured the full body motion capture (MoCap) as well, using a Kinect depth sensor and Microsoft SDK. We used a custom arrangement for time-synchronized records of the video and the MoCap signal. A picture of the recording arrangement is shown in Figure 4. The speakers chose three topics from a list of sample topics (e.g. favorite pastime, favorite book/movie/superhero, etc.) that we supplied for convenience. However, they were free to choose any other topic of their interest. The topics were decided at least one day ahead to allow the participants to prepare for the speech.

Finally, we randomly selected 7 participants to conduct short one-to-one interviews at the end of study. In this interview, we asked for their subjective opinions about the interface and audio-recorded their responses. This interview was done only after we finished the study. We asked if the participants liked the interface or not and the reasons for liking or disliking it. We also asked if they could realize that there were two different versions of the interface—one real (treatment) and another fake (placebo). In addition, we asked them to guess which one was real and which one was fake. Finally, we asked if the interface helped them become aware of their body languages or not.

RESULTS

In order to evaluate the usefulness of the interface, we analyze the participants' responses to the interface related measures (i.e. the third row in Table 1) in our study. These responses are recorded in a 7-point Likert scale. We compute the average of the aggregated responses from the real feedback only. In other words, the average is calculated by considering the responses after the first speech for the participants with even ID number, and responses after the second speech for participants with odd ID number. The average responses are shown in Figure 6. The error bars represent one standard deviations from the average. It is evident from the figure that most of the responses are more than 5 in the 7-point Likert scale. The participants provided higher ratings in the measures related to the awareness of body language. This represents the fact that AutoManner can successfully make the users aware of their body language.

We perform a group-wise analysis in order to observe the differences in the participants' responses in placebo and treatment interface. We group all the responses after interaction with the placebo interface as "*placebo*"; and that after the treatment interface as "*treatment*". A Box-Whisker plot for these two groups is shown in Figure 7. In this plot, the box represents the lower and upper quartile of the data. The horizontal bar inside the box represents the median. The whiskers represent the range of the data. We also conducted a Wilcoxon-Mann-Whitney Rank Sum test [12] to measure the statistical significance of differences between the groups. Throughout the paper, we use single, two, and three asterisk symbols to represent a rejection of the null hypothesis with 0.05, 0.01, and 0.001 significance levels respectively. Notice that there is a statistically significant difference ($p < 0.05$) in the responses for the third statement. It is clear from the figure that the responses for the placebo group varies widely in comparison to the treatment group. Responses for other

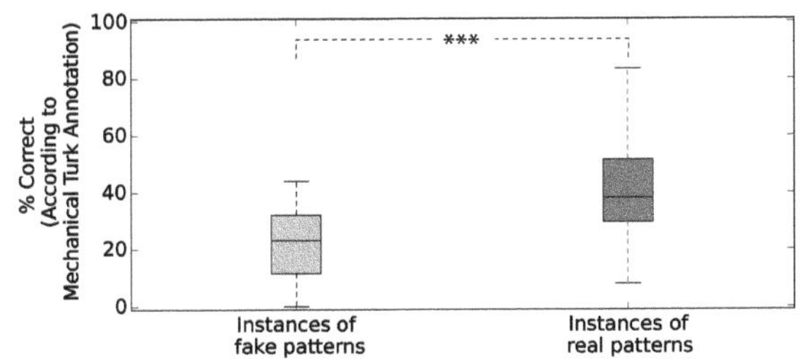

Figure 8: Box-Whisker plot for the percentages of instances for real and fake patterns. The three asterisk symbol represents a statistical significance with $p < 0.001$

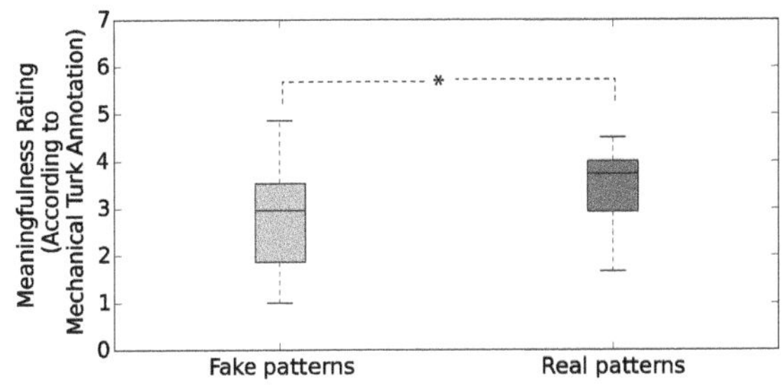

Figure 9: Ratings for "meaningfulness" of the patterns as annotated by the turkers. $p < 0.05$

measures are not statistically significant. This result makes sense considering the fact that the third statement is directly related to the parameter that we manipulated in the placebo and treatment interface.

In the second research question, we want to evaluate the efficacy of the algorithm from human perspective. On this regard, we require annotations on the accuracy of each time-instances. However, this is a huge task as there are as many as 50 time-instances for each pattern and 5 patterns per video. It was impractical to ask the participants to annotate the accuracy for each instance in the video. We solve this problem by recruiting thirty workers in the Mechanical Turk[2] website. In order to ensure high quality in the answers, we accept the turkers who completed at-least 1000 tasks with 99% acceptance rate. In addition, we perform a qualifying round; where we manually selected 30 turkers based on their performance on annotating a ground truth. These filtering and qualification round techniques were performed in light to the work of Mitra et al. [20].

We use an interface similar to AutoManner for the turkers to view the videos, patterns, and time-instances. The only difference between the mechanical turk interface and the original AutoManner is in the questions asked through the interface. This interface requires the turkers to annotate the answer to the following question for each time-instance: "*Does the skeletal animation match with the video at this time-instance?*". The turkers respond either yes or no. In addition, while evaluating the patterns, they annotate if they agree to the following statement: "*This body movement pattern conveys a meaning*". The response is recorded in a 7-point Likert scale. Three different turkers annotate the same data-point. We consider the mode (i.e. majority vote) of the responses as the turker response for a particular data point.

For the placebo videos, we extract the corresponding real patterns using the SISC algorithm. These real patterns were also shown to the turkers and received annotations. In our experiment, the turkers did not have any knowledge about the treatment or placebo groups of the patterns. For each pattern, we calculate the percentages of the time-instances that the turkers marked as correct. We represent the data in two groups—one for the fake patterns (placebo), another for the corresponding real patterns from the same videos. Figure 8 represents a box-and-whisker plot of these accuracies. It is evident in the figure that there is a clear difference in the perceived accuracy between the instances of the fake patterns and the real patterns. The mechanical turk workers were not aware of the differences in the patterns at all. In addition, different workers annotated different instances of the patterns. Despite this, we observe a statistically significant difference between the time-instances of real patterns and fake patterns. This is a strong evidence that the SISC algorithm performs significantly well in detecting and localizing the patterns. As the correctness of the time instances were marked by human annotators, this result also represents that the algorithm is able to extract human-interpretable body movement patterns.

We illustrate the turker's responses over the statement—"This body movement pattern conveys a meaning" in Figure 9. It is evident from this figure that the difference of responses between the fake and the real patterns is not as significant as the differences in their time instances (i.e. Figure 8). This drop in significance may appear surprising, but it is actually expected as the real patterns may or may not be meaningful depending on the context. On the other hand, we expect the fake patterns to be less likely to be meaningful. Therefore it is expected that there will be differences between the groups but less significant than Figure 8. This result might also be an indication to the fact that the question of "meaningfulness" is comparatively more subjective and vague than the previous scenario. Nevertheless, the statistical significance implies that the algorithm is more accurate than just random samples from the MoCap signal.

In the third research question, we ask if there is any improvement in the speaker's body language due to the use of our interface. In general, this is a difficult question to answer with strong affirmation. Typically, change of behavior is a gradual process and requires motivation and effort from within the person. Moreover, it may be hard to immediately notice any change in a person's behavior given a short exposure to a stimuli. Our interface could possibly make the speakers aware of their body language. However, how well they are able to internalize and reflect on the given insights is out of the current scope of the paper.

Nonetheless, to measure improvement in body language, we analyze how the speakers' self-ratings differ from the first speech to the last speech. The result is shown in Figure 10. The top plot of Figure 10 shows the average of self ratings in

[2]https://www.mturk.com/mturk/welcome

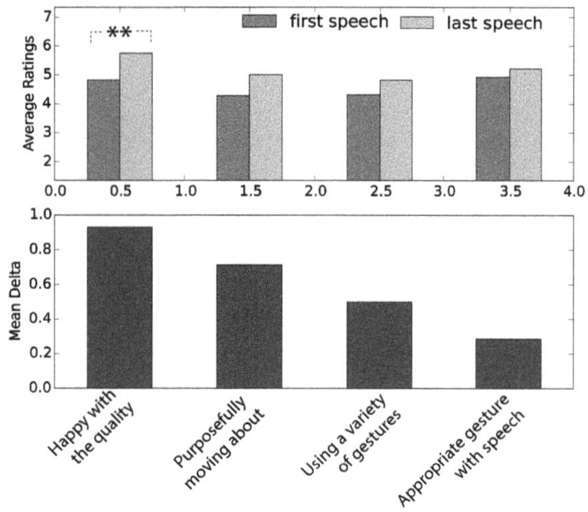

Figure 10: Participants' self ratings about their speech

the first video and the third video. Although there is an improvement in the average, only the first measure ("Overall, I am happy with the quality of my speech") is statistically significant ($p < 0.01$). We also computed the average *delta* as shown in the bottom plot of Figure 10. Mean delta is computed by taking away the ratings of first video from the rating of the third video for each participant, and then computing the average. The plot shows the mean delta is positive for all the self measures. These are evidence to the fact that there is an improvement over the participants' speaking. However, we cannot immediately claim that this improvement is a direct impact of using AutoManner. There are other considerations should be taken into account. Firstly, these are self-reports and the participants knew which one is their first speech and which one is last. That knowledge may lead to a bias for this result. Secondly, even if there are true improvements in their speaking, we never know if that is due to the usage of AutoManner or just due to practicing public speaking three times in the study.

Besides the measures as required for answering the research questions, we collect a few additional measures, as well. For example, we collect the participants' ratings on the accuracies of the patterns. We make some interesting observations while analyzing the responses of these measures as illustrated in Figure 11.

It is evident from this data that the participants could not actually differentiate between the fake patterns (placebo) and the real patterns (treatment). In addition, they sometimes rated patterns from the placebo interface higher than those from the treatment interface. This result is surprising especially given the fact that there is strong statistical significance for the difference in the mechanical turkers' annotations. As we shall discuss in the next subsection, this effect became more evident when we analyzed the participants' opinions in one-to-one interviews. In the Discussion section, we elaborate the reasons of this effect. We shall also describe how these two experiments focus on two different levels of the same question and thus one is inherently difficult to answer than another.

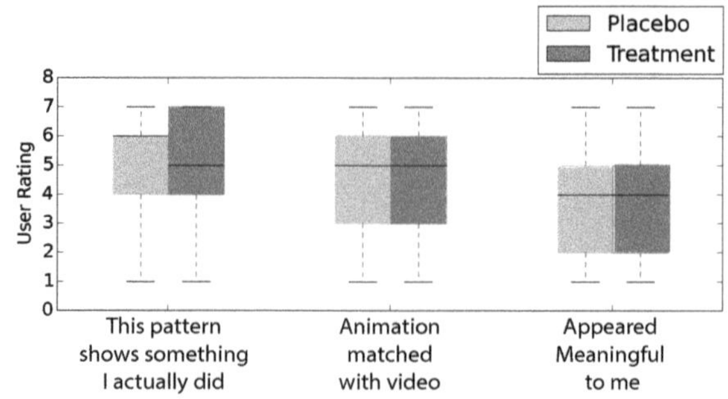

Figure 11: Participants' response to pattern-specific statements in the interface

SUBJECTIVE EVALUATION

We notice an overall trend of positive responses in the subjective interviews. When asked if the participants think they became aware of their body language, all of them replied in affirmation. One participant responded,

> *"It definitely made me more aware. It showed that I make the gestures sporadically. I was consistently showing the same gesture repeatedly throughout the three minutes of my talk."*

While the participants highly praised the fact that they became aware of their body languages, they also raised questions about the accuracy of the interface. For example, one participant mentioned,

> *"Sometimes the skeleton and what I was doing didn't match ... and sometimes I wasn't sure whether or not, cuz there was part which did match and part which didn't match at all. So I'm not sure to say yes or not to it."*

Some of the participants complained that the algorithm is actually picking the same patterns,

> *"It was a good idea here, but I'm not sure it picks up all of my gestures that well ... It seems like it's picking up all the same gestures. For example, I swayed a lot. It picked up the swaying but put it as five different gestures"*

However, another participant said, "*I would say, more than half are accurate.*". We thought these discrepancies were just due to the fact that the participants watched not only a treatment interface but a placebo interface as well. So perhaps they were referring to the errors in the placebo interface.

When we asked if the participants realized that there were two different styles in the interface—one real and another fake—none of them answered in affirmation. They appeared perplexed. One of the participant even argued that it was not possible because,

> *"I [the participant] remember both of them [the placebo and treatment interfaces] had the same thing [i.e. same pattern]!"*.

Their answers to guess which interface showed the real pattern also appeared random. This provides strong evidence

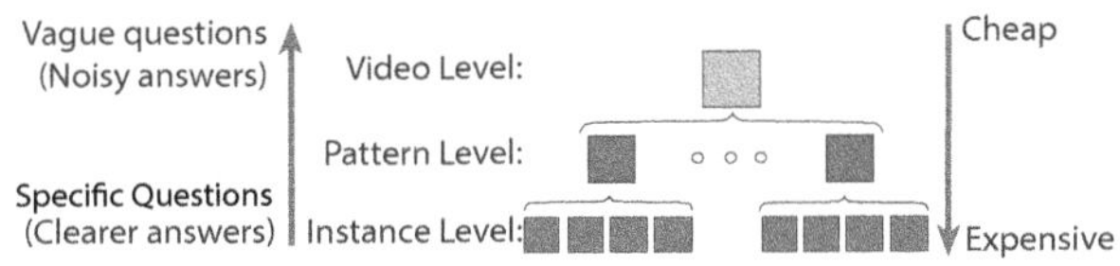

Figure 12: An illustration of our experience in mechanical turk data collection process

that the participants believed, in some cases, the placebo interface was as good as or even better than the treatment interface. We discuss more on this in the next section.

DISCUSSIONS

We became interested in knowing why the participants were unable to differentiate between the placebo and the treatment interfaces. In order to find the answer, we manually went through the interfaces. In this process, we found several patterns similar in both the placebo and the treatment interface. We found that the method that we used to generate the fake patterns was responsible for this problem. We generated the fake patterns by (uniformly) randomly picking a two-second window from the MoCap sequence and randomly assigning the time-instances for each pattern. We assumed, as the time-instances were completely random, it was a good strategy for designing the placebo interface. However, this argument is not valid when a single movement is repeated many times throughout the video. In that case, even a randomly selected window may pick up accurate gestures as the same pattern is repeated in the original sequence. In addition, the time instances may match in some cases due of the existence of high number of same patterns. Therefore, perhaps, our randomly sampled fake patterns, in some instances, might have overlapped with the real patterns. In retrospect, this outcome was not obvious during the initial stage of our exploration. We consider this as an important knowledge acquired in the process of experimentation to inform our future work.

A question still remains unanswered in the explanation above. Why the mechanical turk annotations were not as affected as the participants' annotations? The answer to this question resides in the way we collected data in these two experiments. Turkers annotated one time-instance at a time. When they looked at a certain time-instance, they only decided if the current movement in the video is matching with the skeletal movements or not. On the other hand, when the participants decide if a pattern matched with the video, they were presented with all the time-instances at once. In order to decide this match, they needed to watch several time-instances and summarize what they can *recall*. We hypothesize, these two processes are fundamentally different and thus it is unfair to make a direct comparison between the two results.

From this experience we gained interesting insights on designing behavior related questions in general as shown with an illustration in Figure 12. It is easier to answer specific questions that require less memory. On the other hand, it is difficult to answer questions where a person needs to decide an answer by remembering answers to a large quantity of smaller questions. For example, in our study, the task that asked the participant to match a particular time-instance of a video with the skeletal animation is simple; whereas, answering if a pattern is meaningful or not is context dependent and thus, hard. Unfortunately, it is more expensive to collect responses for more specific questions because they need a lot of questions to be answered. A well designed study needs to find a balance in this trade-off.

Finally, we sought answer to one last question: why did the participants like the interface and claim that they became aware of their body language if they were confused about differentiating the real and fake patterns? We argue that, although becoming self-aware is dependent on algorithmic accuracy, this dependence is not linearly related. The users only need a few correct samples to become aware of their body language.

FUTURE WORK

This work can help future experiments that follow a similar design. We think this experience has enough potential to generate numerous interesting questions related to study design and careful choice of questions in behavioral experiments. In the future, we shall continue our endeavor to design better interfaces with more appropriate choices of artificial intelligence components. We can possibly try other interesting unsupervised approaches for extracting body movement patterns. Unsupervised analysis of nonverbal behaviors is a lightly-explored and open field of research with numerous possibilities.

In this paper, we could not decisively determine whether the speakers actually improved their body language as a result of using this interface, or they just felt that they did better due to the interaction with a new technology. In the future, we shall try to evaluate this aspect using the opinions of public speaking experts. We shall also try to run a longitudinal study in order to tease out the novelty effect.

CONCLUSION

We presented an automated interface to make public speakers aware of their mannerisms. We used an unsupervised, *Shift Invariant Sparce Coding* (SISC) algorithm to automatically extract the common body movement patterns of the speaker. We showed these patterns as potential mannerism candidates. We designed a subtle question and answer-based scheme to provide non-judgmental feedback on mannerisms. Our experiments show that the speakers liked the interface, as they became aware of their body language. In addition, mechanical turk worker's annotations reveal that the algorithm we used in this system can extract human-interpretable patterns of body language.

ACKNOWLEDGMENTS

We would like to thank the anonymous reviewers for their detailed and encouraging feedback. Thanks to Tergel Purevdorj for helpful comments on the interface. This work was supported in part by Grant W911NF-15-1-0542 with the US Defense Advanced Research Projects Agency (DARPA) and the Army Research Office (ARO). Special Acknowledgment to Microsoft Azure for providing the computational platform.

REFERENCES

1. Aggarwal, J. K., et al. Human activity analysis: A review. *ACM Computing Surveys (CSUR)* (2011).
2. Anderson, K., André, E., Baur, T., Bernardini, S., Chollet, M., Chryssafidou, E., Damian, I., Ennis, C., Egges, A., Gebhard, P., et al. The tardis framework: intelligent virtual agents for social coaching in job interviews. In *Advances in Computer Entertainment*. Springer, 2013, 476–491.
3. Batrinca, L., Stratou, G., Shapiro, A., Morency, L.-P., and Scherer, S. Cicero-towards a multimodal virtual audience platform for public speaking training. In *Intelligent Virtual Agents*, Springer (2013), 116–128.
4. Battiti, R. Accelerated backpropagation learning: Two optimization methods. *Complex systems 3*, 4 (1989), 331–342.
5. Beck, A., and Teboulle, M. A fast iterative shrinkage-thresholding algorithm for linear inverse problems. *SIAM journal on imaging sciences 2*, 1 (2009), 183–202.
6. Chen, L., Feng, G., Joe, J., Leong, C. W., Kitchen, C., and Lee, C. M. Towards automated assessment of public speaking skills using multimodal cues. In *Proceedings of the 16th International Conference on Multimodal Interaction*, ACM (2014), 200–203.
7. Cheng, G., et al. Advances in human action recognition: A survey. *arXiv preprint arXiv:1501.05964* (2015).
8. Chollet, M., Wörtwein, T., Morency, L.-P., Shapiro, A., and Scherer, S. Exploring feedback strategies to improve public speaking: an interactive virtual audience framework. In *Proceedings of the 2015 ACM International Joint Conference on Pervasive and Ubiquitous Computing*, ACM (2015), 1143–1154.
9. D'Arcy, J. *Technically speaking: A guide for communicating complex information*. Battelle Press Columbus, OH, 1998.
10. de Gelder, B. Why bodies? twelve reasons for including bodily expressions in affective neuroscience. *Philosophical Transactions of the Royal Society B: Biological Sciences 364*, 1535 (2009), 3475–3484.
11. DiMatteo, M. R., Hays, R. D., and Prince, L. M. Relationship of physicians' nonverbal communication skill to patient satisfaction, appointment noncompliance, and physician workload. *Health Psychology 5*, 6 (1986), 581.
12. Fay, M. P., and Proschan, M. A. Wilcoxon-mann-whitney or t-test? on assumptions for hypothesis tests and multiple interpretations of decision rules. *Statistics surveys 4* (2010), 1.
13. Hoogterp, B. *Your Perfect Presentation: Speak in Front of Any Audience Anytime Anywhere and Never Be Nervous Again*. McGraw-Hill Education, 2014.
14. Hoque, M. E., Courgeon, M., Martin, J.-C., Mutlu, B., and Picard, R. W. Mach: My automated conversation coach. In *Proceedings of the 2013 ACM international joint conference on Pervasive and ubiquitous computing*, ACM (2013), 697–706.
15. Hotelling, H. Analysis of a complex of statistical variables into principal components. *Journal of educational psychology 24*, 6 (1933), 417.
16. Knapp, M., Hall, J., and Horgan, T. *Nonverbal communication in human interaction*. Cengage Learning, 2013.
17. Likert, R. A technique for the measurement of attitudes. *Archives of psychology* (1932).
18. Lucas, S. E. *The art of public speaking*. International Book Publishing Company, 2008.
19. Metaxas, D., and Zhang, S. A review of motion analysis methods for human nonverbal communication computing. *Image and Vision Computing* (2013).
20. Mitra, T., Hutto, C., and Gilbert, E. Comparing person-and process-centric strategies for obtaining quality data on amazon mechanical turk. In *Proceedings of the 33rd Annual ACM Conference on Human Factors in Computing Systems*, ACM (2015), 1345–1354.
21. Mørup, M., et al. Shift invariant sparse coding of image and music data. Tech. Rep. IMM2008-04659, Technical University of Denmark, 2008.
22. Murphy, J. *The power of your subconscious mind*. Courier Corporation, 2012.
23. Naim, I., Tanveer, M. I., Gildea, D., and Hoque, M. E. Automated prediction and analysis of job interview performance: The role of what you say and how you say it. *Automatic Face and Gesture Recognition (FG)* (2015).
24. Nguyen, A.-T., Chen, W., and Rauterberg, M. Online feedback system for public speakers. In *E-Learning, E-Management and E-Services (IS3e), 2012 IEEE Symposium on*, IEEE (2012), 1–5.
25. Niebles, J. C., Wang, H., and Fei-Fei, L. Unsupervised learning of human action categories using spatial-temporal words. *International journal of computer vision 79*, 3 (2008), 299–318.
26. Park, S., Shoemark, P., and Morency, L.-P. Toward crowdsourcing micro-level behavior annotations: the challenges of interface, training, and generalization. In *Proceedings of the 19th international conference on Intelligent User Interfaces*, ACM (2014), 37–46.
27. Pfister, T., and Robinson, P. Real-time recognition of affective states from nonverbal features of speech and its application for public speaking skill analysis. *Affective Computing, IEEE Transactions on 2*, 2 (2011), 66–78.
28. Ranganath, R., Jurafsky, D., and McFarland, D. It's not you, it's me: detecting flirting and its misperception in speed-dates. In *Proceedings of the 2009 Conference on Empirical Methods in Natural Language Processing: Volume 1-Volume 1*, Association for Computational Linguistics (2009), 334–342.

29. Schreiber, L. M., Paul, G. D., and Shibley, L. R. The development and test of the public speaking competence rubric. *Communication Education 61*, 3 (2012), 205–233.

30. Shim, H. S., Park, S., Chatterjee, M., Scherer, S., Sagae, K., and Morency, L.-P. Acoustic and para-verbal indicators of persuasiveness in social multimedia. In *Acoustics, Speech and Signal Processing (ICASSP), 2015 IEEE International Conference on*, IEEE (2015), 2239–2243.

31. Shotton, J., Sharp, T., Kipman, A., Fitzgibbon, A., Finocchio, M., Blake, A., Cook, M., and Moore, R. Real-time human pose recognition in parts from single depth images. *Communications of the ACM 56*, 1 (2013), 116–124.

32. Strangert, E., and Gustafson, J. What makes a good speaker? subject ratings, acoustic measurements and perceptual evaluations. In *INTERSPEECH*, vol. 8 (2008), 1688–1691.

33. Tanaka, H., Sakti, S., Neubig, G., Toda, T., Negoro, H., Iwasaka, H., and Nakamura, S. Automated social skills trainer. In *Proceedings of the 20th International Conference on Intelligent User Interfaces*, ACM (2015), 17–27.

34. Tanveer, M. I., Lin, E., and Hoque, M. E. Rhema: A real-time in-situ intelligent interface to help people with public speaking. In *Proceedings of the 20th International Conference on Intelligent User Interfaces*, ACM (2015), 286–295.

35. Tanveer, M. I., Liu, J., and Hoque, M. E. Unsupervised extraction of human-interpretable nonverbal behavioral cues in a public speaking scenario. In *ACM Multimedia (ACMMM'15)* (2015).

36. Toastmasters International. Gestures: Your body speaks. Online Document. Available at `http://web.mst.edu/~toast/docs/Gestures.pdf`, 2011.

37. Vinciarelli, A., Pantic, M., and Bourlard, H. Social signal processing: Survey of an emerging domain. *Image and Vision Computing 27*, 12 (2009), 1743–1759.

38. Wilson, T. D. *Strangers to ourselves*. Harvard University Press, 2004.

39. Zhang, Z. Microsoft kinect sensor and its effect. *MultiMedia, IEEE 19*, 2 (2012), 4–10.

40. Zhou, F., et al. Aligned cluster analysis for temporal segmentation of human motion. In *FG'08* (2008).

Desitra: A Simulator for Teaching Situated Decision Making in Dental Surgery

Narumol Vannaprathip
Faculty of ICT,
Mahidol University,
Nakhonpathom, Thailand
narumol.van@student.mahidol.ac.th

Peter Haddawy
Faculty of ICT,
Mahidol University,
Nakhonpathom, Thailand
peter.had@mahidol.ac.th

Siriwan Suebnukarn
Faculty of Dentistry
Thammasat University,
Pathumthani, Thailand
ssiriwan@tu.ac.th

Patcharapon Sangsartra, Nunnapin Sasikhant, Sornram Sangutai
Faculty of ICT,
Mahidol University,
Nakhonpathom, Thailand
{patcharapon.san, nunnapin.sas, sornram.san}@student.mahidol.ac.th

ABSTRACT
Use of simulation to teach decision making in surgery is challenging partly due to the situated nature of the decisions, with situation awareness playing a critical role in making high quality decisions. Thus simulation systems need to be able to provide the key cues needed in making decisions with high fidelity. In this paper we present the first version of Desitra, a simulation environment for teaching decision making in dental surgery. System design was driven by an observational study of teaching sessions for endodontic surgery in the operating room which identified perceptual cues used in decision making as well as tutorial intervention strategies used by surgeons. Desitra provides an open environment for learning decision making – students carry out dental procedures and are free to make mistakes. The pedagogical module monitors the student actions and intervenes when students make mistakes, providing as little guidance as necessary to keep students on a productive learning path. The system is implemented to run on Android tablets to be maximally accessible. Preliminary evaluation of the system shows that Desitra effectively captures key perceptual cues.

Author Keywords
surgical decision making; surgical simulation; serious games; intelligent tutoring systems

ACM 978-1-4503-4137-0/16/03...$15.00
DOI: http://dx.doi.org/10.1145/2856767.2856807

ACM Classification Keywords
H.5.2 Information interfaces and presentation (e.g., HCI): User Interfaces (D.2.2, H.1.2, I.3.6); I.6.3 Simulation and modeling (G.3): Applications; K.3.1 Computers and education: Computer Uses in Education;

INTRODUCTION
Surgical skill training has been traditionally based on the Halstedian apprenticeship model [10] whereby the surgical trainee attempts to perform a task with guidance and close supervision from an expert surgeon [20]. But shortened training programs, reduced working hours for residents and limitations on available operating room time [9] have strained this model and interest has concomitantly increased in use of simulation for training. Surgical simulation has the potential to provide students with increased training time outside the operating room, objective assessment of procedures, and formative feedback without the need for close direct supervision of experts in limited supply [17]. But despite the fact that 75% of the important events in the operating room are related to decision making and only 25% to technical (psychomotor) skills [15], a statistic that holds in the more specific context of dental surgery as well [3], work on surgical simulation has focused mainly on technical skills and has not fulfilled its potential in supporting teaching of decision making skills [1]. In this paper we focus on surgical decision making, which is the ability to consider available options, choose the option appropriate to the situation, implement the selected option, and review its outcome [4]. Decision making in surgery has a number of distinct characteristics which make it particularly challenging, including high stakes, uncertainty of outcomes at the level of individual patient, and potential irreversibility [13]. While decision making is involved in all three phases of surgery: pre-operative, intra-operative, and post-operative, our focus is on intra-operative decision making. Intra-operative decision making has the important

aspect of being situated – situation awareness is a key component of decision making and decisions are made in the context of carrying out psychomotor tasks, which provide important context and information for the decisions.

While some computer-based systems for teaching decision making skills have been developed [5,7,11,12,16,18], insufficient attention has been given to directly supporting perceptual cues as well as teaching strategies that instruct students in how to use them. The importance of understanding cues in surgical decision making has been emphasized by Sevdalis et al [13]. In this paper we present the first version of Desitra, a simulation environment for teaching decision making in dental surgery. System design makes use of an observational study of teaching sessions for endodontic surgery in the operating room which identified perceptual cues used in decision making as well as tutorial intervention strategies used by surgeons. Desitra provides an open environment for learning decision making – students carry out dental procedures and are free to make mistakes. The pedagogical module monitors the student actions and intervenes when students make mistakes, providing as little guidance as necessary to keep students on a productive learning path. Pedagogical emphasis is placed on how to reach good decisions rather than on simply memorizing the details of a given surgical procedure. The system is implemented to run on Android tablets in order to be maximally accessible. Evaluation of the system shows that Desitra effectively captures key perceptual cues.

DECISION MAKING IN SURGERY

Surgical procedures are organized into three basic phases: pre-operative, intra-operative, and post-operative. In the pre-operative phase, the patient's condition is diagnosed, the objective of the procedure is defined, the surgical plan is developed, and the needed tools, equipment, and materials are selected and prepared. Surgical planning is a hierarchical process. The plan created in the pre-operative phase is a high-level plan, with the specific way in which each action is executed determined in the intra-operative phase when the relevant perceptual and other information is available. This form of abstract action instantiation is the primary type of decision made in the intra-operative phase. The other two types of decisions, which are closely related, are how to recover from errors and how to respond to unexpected events. The focus of the current paper is on teaching the first type of decision, with the other two types left for a subsequent version of the system.

In this paper we illustrate key concepts using the procedure of root canal. Root canal was selected because it is a complex procedure involving a variety of qualitatively different steps and requiring perceptual judgement dependent on patient anatomy information that is not fully available preoperatively. The root canal procedure includes six main stages: rubber dam application, access opening, length determination, mechanical intervention, trying master cone, and root canal obturation; each with several steps. While the plan is created in the pre-operative phase, low-level details are determined in the intraoperative phase. For example, the first step of access opening consists of initial drilling. For this step the endodontist must evaluate the patient's radiography, select the correct type of bur with the appropriate size head corresponding to the pulp chamber width, determine the appropriate depth of drilling, and determine the side of the tooth from which to drill. The drilling must follow the correct outline shape to open access to the root canals in the pulp chamber without unnecessarily removing tooth mass.

RELATED WORK

Servais [12] provides an approach to teaching intraoperative decision making by asking students to answer questions concerning actions to be taken. After any error in judgement the student is informed of the consequence and asked to reevaluate. LapSkill [11] provides video clips of stages of laparoscopic surgery and asks students to answer multiple choice questions related to the situation shown in the clip. Flowers presents a 3D simulation using SECOND LIFE™ [5] which portrays a real life clinical scenario. It focuses on social interaction in patient management.

SICKO [7,18] is a non-immersive game for teaching patient management and clinical decision making. Players select a patient to manage, order tests, diagnose the patient's condition, and determine whether to prescribe medication or to send for surgery. If surgery is chosen, the player answers multiple choice questions to select the appropriate actions. When a player chooses a correct action, score points are given with positive feedback for positive outcomes. If an incorrect action is chosen, score points are deducted. The effect is shown to the player and the player is not given the chance to correct the action. The patient's status dynamically responds to the interventions chosen by the player. The dynamic intraoperative environment in SICKO allows players to deal with unexpected events over time.

SimPraxis [16] provides a simulated environment for teaching pre- and intra-operative decision making in laparoscopic surgery. In the intra-operative setting, students select instruments and instrument placement. When the chosen action (instrument and location) is correct, positive feedback is provided and a video clip plays showing the portion of the procedure using that instrument. When an incorrect action is chosen the effect of the action is explained and students must try the step again. Video clips are produced from actual surgical procedures and thus provide a high level of realism. However, the fact that video clips need to be obtained from real surgical procedures in the operating room limits the ability to support variations on procedures, to show outcomes of errors, and to provide practice for unexpected events.

OBSERVATIONAL STUDY

An observational study of five teaching sessions of root canal treatment was conducted at the student clinic in the Faculty of Dentistry, Thammasat University. Each surgical trainee carried out root canal treatment on a patient under the supervision and guidance of an endodontic instructor. Actions and discussions in the intraoperative sessions were recorded via video camera and transcribed. The transcript and video were analyzed to identify key information cues for decisions, types of errors and teaching strategies.

Surgeons use various information in making intraoperative decisions, including patient information, medical knowledge (anatomy, physiology, and pathology), surgical procedure knowledge, and visual and tactile perceptual information. From the observational study and interviews with endodontists we identified the information used at each decision step in the procedure. This information was used to inform the design of the simulation and the content of the feedback messages. For example, after selecting the outline shape to locate the canal orifice before beginning drilling, there should not be any fracture on the patient tooth (visual and experience). The surgeon selects the drill type (surgical procedure), the drill size by evaluating the patient's radiography (visual, patient information), the drilling depth (surgical procedure), the entry point to drill (visual, medical knowledge, and surgical procedure), and the direction to drill (visual, medical knowledge, and surgical procedure).

Three types of procedural errors were observed: errors in selecting an action, errors in dealing with unexpected events, and mistakes in recovering from errors. In this paper, we focus on the first type.

In a study of a large variety of surgical procedures Hauge [6] identified 27 teaching behaviors in the operating room, covering the spectrum of operating room activities. Our thematic analysis of the teaching sessions for root canal treatment [19] showed seven of these to be used: give guidance, give order, provide demonstration, give assistance, give hint, give explanation, and give feedback. These were often used in combination. Instructors responded to student errors with a variety of strategies. The factors that most influenced feedback for errors were the number of sequential errors committed in that stage, the criticality of the step, and the remaining time to carry out the procedure. Time and criticality (which tend to trigger giving an order or assistance) are important factors primarily due to the use of real patients, so we focus on the number of errors. For the first error instructors gave feedback and typically provided guidance by simply informing the student of the error and the possible consequences. For the second error in a stage, the instructor additionally provided more specific information about such aspects as surgical technique. For the third error, instructors would typically intervene by demonstrating how the action should be carried out while providing verbal explanation.

SYSTEM DESIGN

Simulation design

The simulator provides an intraoperative environment in which the student can see the patient from a facial view and a close up view of the working tooth. The upper right corner of the screen provides radiography and patient case information. The student can view the enlarged radiography to assess the anatomy of working tooth, as in Figure 1. The student performs a surgical task by selecting tools from the horizontal scrollable tray at the bottom of the screen, and placing them in the preparation tray or on the working tooth. Figure 2 shows the simulator immediately after the student places a drill on the working tooth. The system requests the student to specify the drilling depth (vertical slider or real value), drilling entry point, and drilling direction (drop down menus).

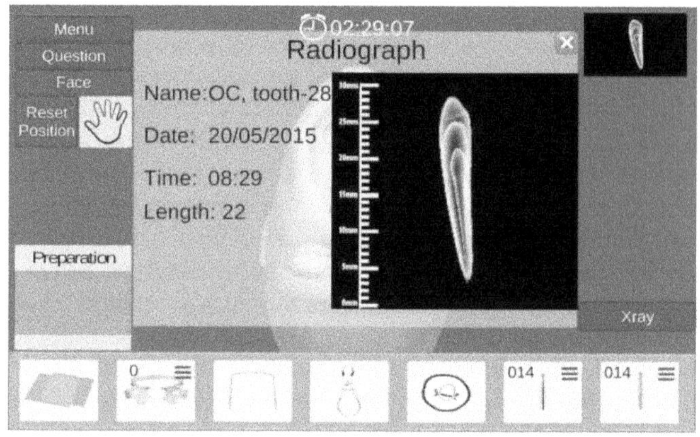

Figure 1. The enlarged radiograph panel allowing student to assess the anatomy of working tooth with patient's information.

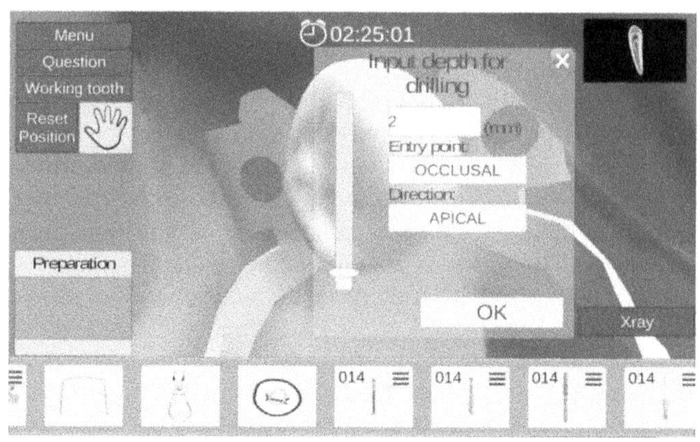

Figure 2. Close up of working tooth (with rubber dam applied) showing the information the user must specify as part of the drilling decision stage.

Teaching strategy and error handling

The first time an error occurs in a stage Desitra uses the giving guidance strategy by explaining the consequence of the error and displaying an image when relevant. The second time the student makes a mistake, the system again gives guidance but with additional specific information e.g.

the surgical technique. If a third mistake is made, the system demonstrates the correct action(s) accompanied by verbal explanation.

For example, suppose the student is at the initial drilling stage and has selected the safe-tipped taper bur (incorrect tool type) with tool number, drilling depth, entry point for drilling, and direction to drill. The system displays the error message: "You are using a safe tipped taper bur as the initial drill. The safe tipped taper bur can be damaged and the tooth is at risk of being fractured." If the student tries again by selecting the round diamond bur but the tool number is too large, a second error message is displayed explaining how to select the proper size along with an image of the consequence of the error as shown in Figure 3.

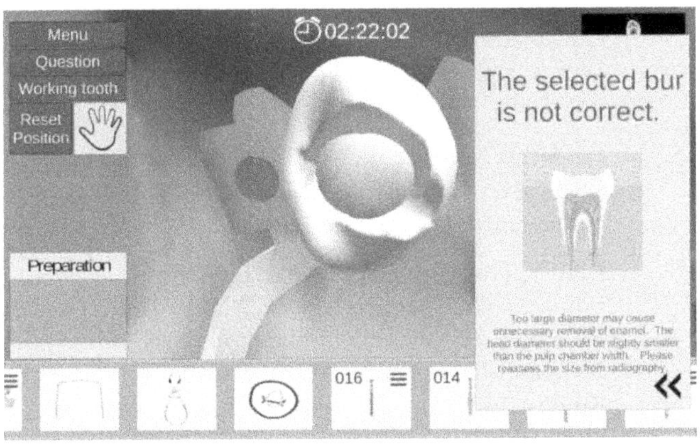

Figure 3. The second error message when too large drill was selected.

IMPLEMENTATION

We follow the basic ITS architecture of user interface, student model, pedagogical module, and the domain knowledge repository [2,8]. The simulator is the user interface component which sends a data stream of student actions to the student model. Currently the student model only keeps a record of the actions. The domain knowledge repository stores the sequence of all actions in the procedure. The pedagogical module checks the correctness of student actions against the domain knowledge and generates interventions according to the teaching strategy described above.

As shown in Figure 4, the system design follows the gaming ITS architecture of Sottilare [14]. The Unity game engine is used for simulation using 3D tool and patient models produced with MAYA. The tutoring modules reside in the android engine plugin. Desitra is designed to run on Android tablets in order to provide maximum accessibility to users. While a richer simulation including tactile feedback can be achieved using a virtual reality environment, the increase in usability and low cost were factors driving our choice of the tablet platform.

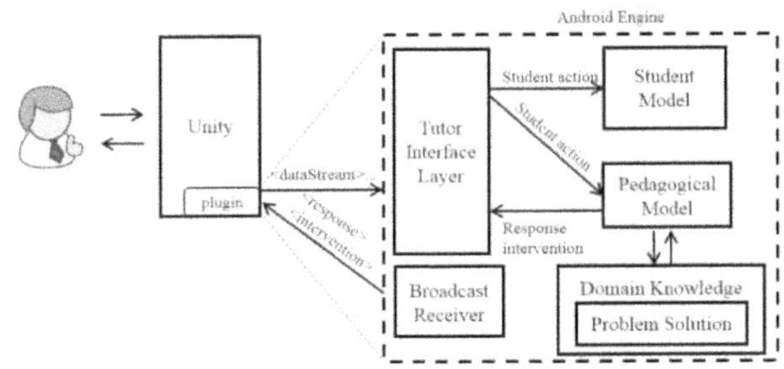

Figure 4. Desitra implementation architecture.

EVALUATION

We sought to determine the extent to which Desitra captures the key perceptual cues at the various decision stages. A stage of rubber dam application and two sub steps of access opening including outline drawing, and initial drilling were selected for evaluation since they represent a variety of decisions. Two expert endodontists were each asked to identify the important perceptual cues and other information needed for decision making for each of these three decisions. After doing so, they were asked to rate the simulation on a 5-point Likert scale as to how well it captures the cues they identified, with 5 designating excellent and 1 designating poor.

The two endodontists identified the same cues and information except that one identified tactile information as important for decision making in the initial drilling stage while the other did not. In terms of how well the system rendered the identified cues, both found the simulation did well (score 4-5) in providing information concerning the state of the working tooth, outline on the tooth, the radiograph, patient case information, and the tools. They disagreed on how well the system conveyed the stage of the procedure (scores 3 and 5). In the case of the initial drilling stage, one endodontist scored the drilling information 5 while the other gave a score of 3 because he wanted to see drilling motion which is not rendered in the simulation.

CONCLUSIONS AND FUTURE WORK

Our initial evaluation of Desitra suggests that it does a good job of capturing most of the key perceptual cues for the decisions in the three stages evaluated. The interventions in the pedagogical module of Desitra place emphasis on how to reach good decisions rather than on memorization of surgical steps. Although the current version is limited to the root canal procedure, the tutoring strategies used are fully general. Future work will focus on covering more procedures, adding a student model to personalize tutorial interaction, automatically generating content of interventions based on a causal domain model, and evaluation of effectiveness in teaching intraoperative decision making.

ACKNOWLEDGMENTS

We thank students and faculty of the Faculty of Dentistry, Thammasat University for support in the observational study and evaluation process. We also thank the anonymous reviewers for their valuable feedback.

REFERENCES

1. Dana K Andersen. 2012. How can educators use simulation applications to teach and assess surgical judgment? *Academic Medicine : Journal of the Association of American Medical Colleges* 87, 7: 934–41.
2. Joseph Beck, Mia Stern, and Erik Haugsjaa. 1996. Applications of AI in education. *Crossroads* 3, 1: 11–15.
3. A W Evans. 2001. Assessing competence in surgical dentistry. *British Dental Journal* 190, 7: 343–346.
4. R. Flin, S. Yule, S. Paterson-Brown, N. Maran, D. Rowley, and G. Youngson. 2007. Teaching surgeons about non-technical skills. *The Surgeon* 5, 2: 86–89.
5. Michael G Flowers and Rajesh Aggarwal. 2014. Second Life^{TM}: a novel simulation platform for the training of surgical residents. *Expert review of medical devices* 11, 2: 101–103.
6. Linnea S. Hauge, Jeanne A. Wanzek, and Constantine Godellas. 2001. The reliability of an instrument for identifying and quantifying surgeons' teaching in the operating room. *The American Journal of Surgery* 181: 333–337.
7. Dana T Lin, Julia Park, Cara a Liebert, and James N Lau. 2015. Validity evidence for Surgical Improvement of Clinical Knowledge Ops: a novel gaming platform to assess surgical decision making. *The American Journal of Surgery* 209, 1: 79–85.
8. Indira Padayachee. 2002. Intelligent tutoring systems: Architecture and characteristics. *Proceedings of the 32nd Annual SACLA Conference.(Cité p. 2)*, August: 1–8.
9. Vanessa N Palter and Teodor P Grantcharov. 2010. Simulation in surgical education. *Canadian Medical Association Journal* 182, 11: 1191–1196.
10. Vanash M. Patel, Oliver Warren, Kamran Ahmed, et al. 2011. How can we build mentorship in surgeons of the future? *ANZ Journal of Surgery* 81, 6: 418–424.
11. Sudip K. Sarker, Saif Rehman, Meera Ladwa, Avril Chang, and Charles Vincent. 2009. A decision-making learning and assessment tool in laparoscopic cholecystectomy. *Surgical Endoscopy* 23, 1: 197–203.
12. Elliot L Servais, Wayne W Lamorte, Suresh Agarwal, Wayne Moschetti, Sandeep K Mallipattu, and Steven L Moulton. 2006. Teaching surgical decision-making: an interactive, web-based approach. *The Journal of Surgical Research* 134, 1: 102–106.
13. Nick Sevdalis, Rosamond Jacklin, and Charles Vincent. 2012. Surgical Decision-Making: A Multimodal Approach. In *Safer Surgery: Analysing Behaviour in the Operating Theatre*, Rhona Flin and Lucy Mitchell (eds.). Ashgate, 353–340.
14. Robert A. Sottilare and Stephen Gilbert. 2011. Considerations for adaptive tutoring within serious games: authoring cognitive models and game interfaces.
15. Frederick Spencer. 1978. Teaching and measuring surgical techniques: the technical evaluation of competence. *Bull Am Coll Surg* 63, 3: 9–12.
16. Linh N Tran, Priyanka Gupta, Lauren H Poniatowski, Shaheen Alanee, Marc a Dall'era, and Robert M Sweet. 2013. Validation study of a computer-based open surgical trainer: SimPraxis(®) simulation platform. *Advances in medical education and practice* 4: 23–30.
17. Shawn Tsuda, Daniel Scott, Jennifer Doyle, and Daniel B Jones. 2009. Surgical skills training and simulation. *Current problems in surgery* 46, 4: 271–370.
18. Jamie Tsui and Stanford Edtech. 2014. Septris and SICKO: Implementing and Using Learning Analytics and Gamification in Medical Education. *Educause*, March: 1–7.
19. Narumol Vannaprathip, Peter Haddawy, and Siriwan Suebnukarn. 2015. A Preliminary Analysis of Tutorial Intervention Strategies for Teaching Decision Making in Dental Surgery. *Proceedings of the 2nd International Conference on Innovation in Education.*, 382–390.
20. Kyle R. Wanzel, Myléne Ward, and Richard K. Reznick. 2002. Teaching the surgical craft: From selection to certification. *Current Problems in Surgery* 39, 6: 583–659.

Toward Intelligent Tutorial Feedback in Surgical Simulation: Robust Outcome Scoring for Endodontic Surgery

Myat Su Yin, Peter Haddawy
Faculty of ICT,
Mahidol Unviersity
Nakhon Pathom, Thailand
myat.su@student.mahidol.ac.th,
peter.had@mahidol.ac.th

Siriwan Suebnukarn
Faculty of Dentistry,
Thammasat University
Pathum Thani,
Thailand
ssiriwan@tu.ac.th

Phattanapon Rhienmora
School of Science and
Technology,
Bangkok University
Klong Toey, Thailand
phattanapon.r@bu.ac.th

ABSTRACT
Numerous VR simulators have been developed as a means of addressing limitations of the traditional apprenticeship approach to dental surgical skill training. Most existing simulators support intra- and extra-coronal procedures such as carries removal. In this paper we address the problem of automated outcome assessment for endodontic surgery. Outcome assessment is an essential component of any system that provides formative feedback, which requires assessing the outcome, relating it to the procedure, and communicating in a language natural to dental students. This paper takes a first step toward automated generation of such comprehensive feedback. Our system automatically computes reference templates based on tooth anatomy, which provides flexibility to adjust parameters such as tolerance and to create new templates on demand. Detailed scores are transformed into the standard scoring language used by dental schools. Preliminary evaluation of our system on fifteen outcome samples with three expert endodontists shows a high degree of agreement with expert scores.

ACM Classification Keywords
H.5.2. **[Information Interfaces and Presentation (e.g. HCI)]**: User Interfaces (D.2.2, H.1.2, I.3.6); I.6.3 **[Simulation and Modeling (G.3)]**: Applications; K.3.1 **[Computers and Education]**: Computers Uses in Education.

Author Keywords
Surgical simulation; virtual reality; automated outcome assessment; formative assessment; intelligent tutorings.

INTRODUCTION
Acquisition of fine motor skill is essential for dental students. The mainstream approach to dental skill training combines didactic lectures with a surgical master apprenticeship model. Dental schools have increasingly been seeking ways to address a number of limitations of this approach to training, including subjectivity of evaluation, scarcity of available experts, and lack of standardization. Over the past decade, a variety of computer-based simulation systems have been developed as a way to address these limitations and dental schools have begun to incorporate simulators into their curricula. Among the various types of simulators, Virtual Reality (VR) simulators are becoming popular as they have the ability to record kinematic data on how a user performs each step of a task, with numerous dental VR systems developed academically and commercially [2, 3, 5, 6, 7, 8, 10, 11, 14, 15, 16, 17]. However, the full promise of such systems has yet to be realized due to the lack of sufficient support for formative feedback. Without such a mechanism, evaluation still demands dedicated time of experts in scarce supply.

Effective formative feedback requires assessment of outcome, procedure, and the relation of procedure to outcome, coupled with the ability to communicate the assessment in a language natural to dental students. In this paper we take a first step toward such a comprehensive approach to automated formative feedback by presenting the first algorithm for outcome scoring in the challenging area of endodontic surgery. The approach provides scores to the 3D voxel structure commonly used in VR dental simulators at a sufficient level of detail to allow correlation with procedure kinematic variables collected by such simulators. The fine-grained voxel level scores provide the precise error information that can be difficult to quantify in irregular 3D objects such as teeth with complex internal anatomy. To effectively communicate outcome score results, detailed level scores are translated into the language of the coarser level standard scoring system used by dental schools. The algorithm has been implemented for the procedure of access opening to the root canals. Agreement between system scores and those of expert endodontists is evaluated on fifteen outcome samples with a range error types and severity. Results show a high degree of agreement between system scores and those of experts, while at the same time highlighting the variability in the subjective expert judgements.

IUI 2016, March 7–10, 2016, Sonoma, CA, USA.
©2016 ACM. ISBN 978-1-4503-4137-0/16/03...$15.00
DOI: http://dx.doi.org/10.1145/2856767.2856810

DENTAL SIMULATOR AND DATA COLLECTION
In this study, we employed the VR dental simulator developed by Rhienmora et al. [9]. The simulator operates on a standard PC with nVidia GeForce 9600GT graphics card and two PHANToM Omni haptic devices in a dual configuration,

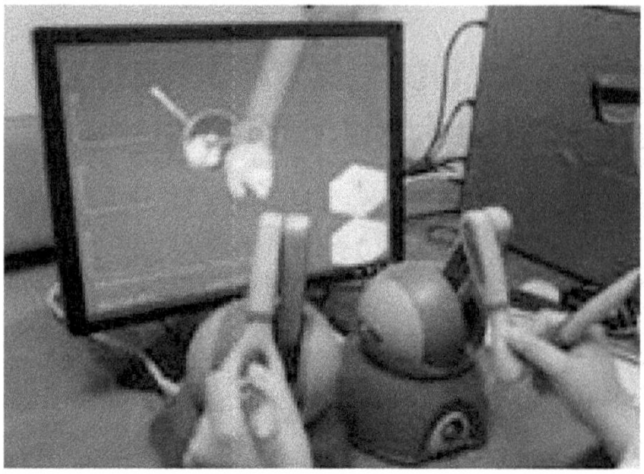

Figure 1. Simulator interface

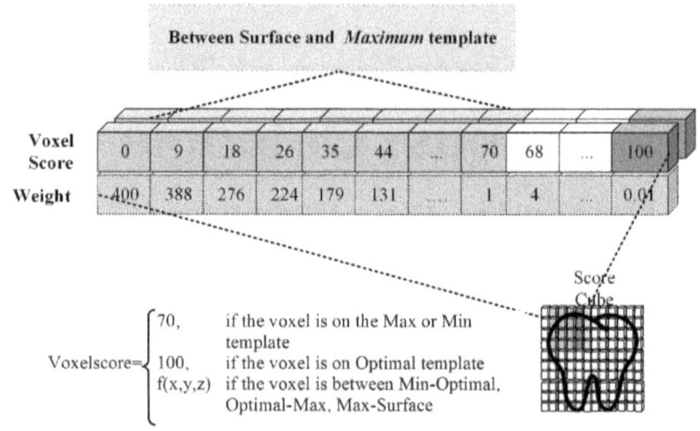

Figure 2. Portion of score cube between surface and Max

representing a hand-piece and a dental mouth mirror (Figure 1). The simulation software was developed in C++, OpenGL, and OpenHaptics SDK (HDAPI). The tooth model was acquired using three-dimensional micro-CT (RmCT, Rigaku Co., Tokyo, Japan) with a resolution of 50 x 50 x 50 μm, tube voltage of 90 KV, and tube current of 150 μA. Tomographic images were obtained using comprehensive dental imaging software (i-VIEW, Morita Co., Tokyo, Japan). Three-dimensional reconstruction was performed using 600 of these two-dimensional images processed by volume rendering. The tooth is stored in the form of a three dimensional grid of voxels representing the density of the structure at each point with a value between 0 and 255.

We have selected access cavity preparation of the root canal treatment procedure to demonstrate and evaluate our approach. This procedure was chosen because it exclusively involves drilling, which is supported by the simulator, and the desired outcome is challenging to score because it is a complex function of the internal tooth anatomy. In this preparation phase, the endodontist drills a small access hole through the surface of the tooth crown to gain access to the pulp chamber and root canals for treatment. The ideal result of access opening preparation is to create an unobstructed passageway to the pulp space and the apical portion of the root canals. The ideal shape of the opening is a function of the tooth shape, tooth size, and the number and location of the root canals. The number and location of the root canals can differ in the same tooth (e.g. mandibular left second molar) across different patients.

METHOD

To provide formative tutoring feedback automated outcome scoring (AOS) must have the ability to identify the type, location and severity of errors and be robust enough to account for a variety of possible outcomes. Since the optimal access opening route is an unobstructed passageway to the pulp space, we first locate the pulp chamber from the training tooth and project vertically from the base of the pulp chamber to capture the morphological information (shape, size and location) of the pulp. Using the projection, the areas on the training tooth are virtually removed to create the optimal outcome template. To permit a clinically acceptable amount of variation in outcome, Max (maximally acceptable) and Min (minimally acceptable) templates are defined by expanding and compressing the optimal template, respectively. Given a tooth and a procedure, a wide range of outcomes is possible. Our approach to outcome scoring is to evaluate the voxels in the tooth volume and label them with scores with respect to reference templates. In AOS, a new tooth volume is created and the voxels tagged with scores according to their locations. We call this a score cube.

As shown in Figure 2, the score cube is a 3D volume of the same size as the training tooth. To fill in the cells of the score cube, we first define a voxel scoring function. In practice, endodontists evaluate each access opening preparation on a scale between 0 and 100, with 0 representing perforation, 1-69 representing unacceptable, and 70-100 representing clinically acceptable. Following this scoring scheme, the score of 100 is assigned to the optimal template area and the score of 70 is assigned to Max and Min templates. The values of the voxels between Min-Optimal, Optimal-Max, Max-Surface are filled using linear interpolation.

Initially, we computed the overall outcome score as the average of the scores of voxels on the drilled area surface. But in a comparison with scoring by endodontists, we found that our scores computed in this way did not correspond well with the expert scores. In subsequent interviews we found that experts assign a significantly higher weight to more severe errors than to minor errors, such that a wall with a small area that is significantly over drilled (close to perforation) is given a much lower score than a wall with numerous small amounts of over drilling, even if the average amount of over drilling in the second case is greater than in the first case. Thus, the linear scheme was adjusted with a non-linear five-parameter logistic weight function [1] to apply higher weight to more severe errors at the voxel level. The parameters were estimated by curve fitting with least squares method prior to the experiments (Figure. 3).

To effectively communicate the assessment results, feedback should be made in a language easily comprehensible to students. Endodontic surgeons evaluate and communicate about errors in terms of scores for the four axial walls (Lingual,

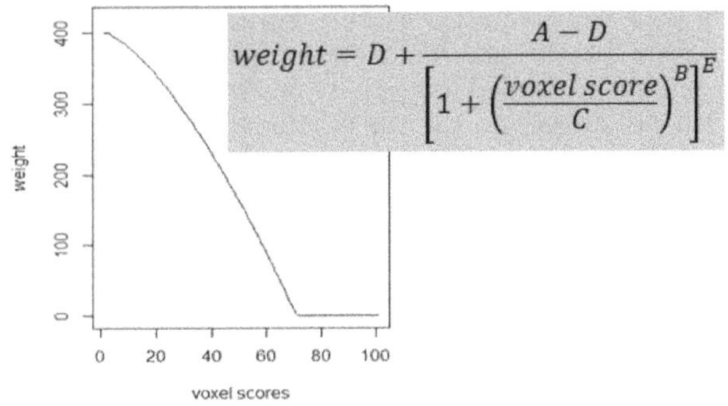

Figure 3. Nonlinear weight function

Buccal, Mesial, Distal), the pulpal floor, and an overall score. AOS thus translates the weighted voxel-level scores into these six scores. This is done by first extracting the surface contour from the drilled outcome area. The contour of the wall is then mapped onto the score cube and the voxels on the surface are assigned the weighted score points accordingly. The wall score is computed as the average weighted scores of the drilled area surface on the tooth slices in the wall region. The overall outcome score is determined in the same manner.

RELATED WORK

The Dentsim [6] and EPED [3] simulators provide training in intracoronal and extracoronal restoration by using plastic teeth and tracking kinematic data of the instruments using sensors. Training cases include cavity preparation in which the main task is to remove carries while preserving healthy tooth structure. The systems provide evaluation with respect to reference templates in terms of floor depth, outline shape, outline centralization, hand-piece positioning, wall angles, retention, floor smoothness, and wall smoothness. Because plastic teeth do not model internal tooth anatomy, the simulators do not cover endodontic surgery. A number of VR dental simulators have also been built for teaching intracoronal and extracoronal restoration. The common approach to outcome assessment is to analyze the amount tooth mass removed from the virtual tooth. The HapTel [16] and VOXEL-Man [17] simulators provide the percentage of caries removed, the percentage of healthy tissue removed, and injuries (e.g. pulp exposed). Both simulators support only cavity preparation. The MOOG Simodont [8] simulator supports cavity, crown, and bridge preparation but information on outcome assessment is not provided.

The Kobra VR simulator from Forsslund Systems [15] provides training in wisdom tooth extraction. Training cases cover bone removal, separation of crown and roots and positioning of elevator. The analysis report is provided on how much the operator has carved into risk areas by measuring the removed amount of bone, enamel, dentin and pulp on the virtual tooth. None of the above VR simulators supports outcome assessment for endodontic surgery.

Much work on automated outcome scoring has been done in the context of otology surgical skill training simulators. In evaluating mastoidectomy performance, Sewell et al. [12] used a Naïve Bayes classifier based on estimates of the probability that each voxel is removed by an expert and a novice to provide skill level classification of users. Their work was later extended by integrating various process-based features and incorporating metrics for exposure to critical anatomic structure into scoring [13]. Similarly, Kerwin et al. [4] present an approach to automated scoring of virtual mastoidectomy performance on a voxel level. They create a fully partitioned segmented dataset by defining surgically important regions on an iconic temporal bone. Then using earth mover distance, parts of an expert-drilled bone are compared with a student-drilled bone. A decision tree is created using the features derived from these comparisons to determine scores of surgical performance.

EXPERIMENTAL EVALUATION

We sought to evaluate the degree of agreement between AOS and human expert scores over a range of outcomes, including varying numbers of errors, types of errors, and severities. Fifteen outcome samples using the mandibular left second molar were prepared by an experienced endodontist who is familiar with the use of the VR system. During data collection, the expert deliberately committed a range of errors on the training tooth to reflect the types of errors committed by the students during the access opening procedure. The set of outcomes contained optimal results and those with errors including perforation of the walls, floor, and both, as well as various combinations of more minor over drilling and under drilling errors. Three endodontists (R1, R2, R3) who had professional training and experience in root canal treatment participated as raters in the experiment. The raters were selected on the basis of expertise levels which varies from one year to more than ten years of experience. The raters received verbal instructions to score the four axial walls (Lingual, Buccal, Mesial, Distal) and the pulp floor using the standard scoring scheme to which they were accustomed. Human raters normally score outcomes using the external view of the tooth, making it difficult to see some errors. Thus any differences in rating between AOS and the human raters could be due to limitations of perception or to differences in judgement. In order to separate these two factors and determine the extent of the influence of perception on scoring, we ran three sets of experiments. In experiment I the raters were provided with a 360 degree external view (Figure 4 (a)) of the drilled tooth

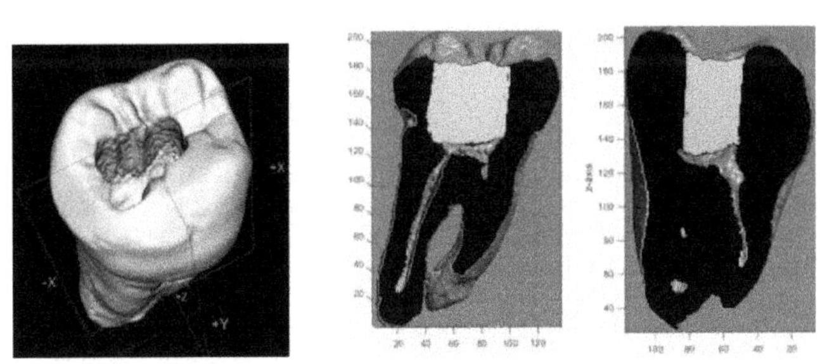

(a) Experiment I (b) Experiment II

Figure 4. Example views the experiments I and II

just as they would have in a clinical setting with a real patient. In experiment II the level of information provided to the raters was increased by additionally providing mid cross-sectional views of the drilling area (Figure 4 (b)). This provided raters with visual information on the depth, size and shape of the drilling at the center of the pulp. In experiment III the ideal drilling area based on the internal anatomy of the tooth along with the acceptable drilling areas were provided as visual guidelines for all axial walls and the pulp chamber floor from both lateral and top views (Figure 5) separately.

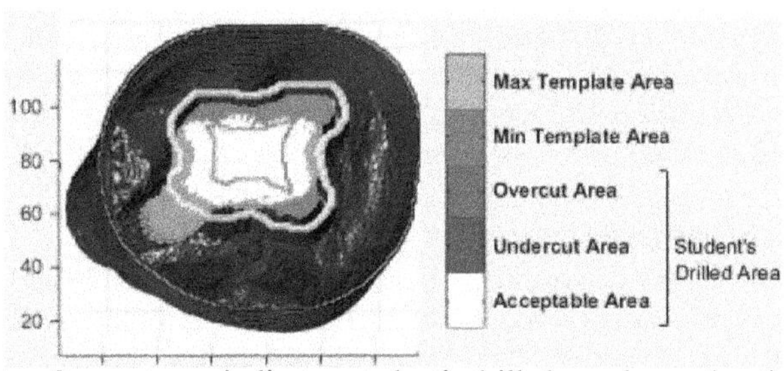

Note: *Overcut area* indicates student's drilled area beyond optimal template; *Undercut area* indicates student's drilling needs further extension to get the optimal result; *Acceptable area* represents student's drilling within the optimal drilling area.

Figure 5. Min, Max and Optimal templates overlaid on student's drilling area from the top view

In each experiment, raters gave a score on the four axial walls, the pulp floor, and the overall outcome score was computed as the average of the five component scores. Inter-rater agreement for each experiment was determined using the concordance correlation. Concordance correlation tests whether two raters assign the same scores.

RESULTS AND DISCUSSION

Table 1 shows the range of scores, the mean and the median for the three raters and AOS. While the minimum for all is zero, the maximum for R2, R3, and AOS are quite close, while that for R1 is significantly higher (94). The mean and median values for AOS, R2, and R3 are again quite close but those for R1 are lower. To examine the degree of subjectivity in scoring of outcomes, we evaluated the agreement among the three experts.

	AOS	R1	R2	R3
Minimum	0	0	0	0
Maximum	85	94	87	84
Mean	65.6	59.9	66.4	66.6
Median	73.5	64	74	77

Table 1. Overall outcome score ranges in experiment I

Table 2 (columns 1-3) shows the concordance correlation among the three pairings of the raters. Raters R2 and R3 are generally well correlated across the experiments, while rater R1 is mostly poorly correlated with the other two. Weaker correlation between raters R2 and R3 is observed for their pulp floor scores in experiment II. Post experiment interviews indicated that this was likely due to difficulties in perception. They may have relied too heavily on the cross sectional view which, because it was taken mid-volume, revealed only half of the drilling area, thus raters needed to estimate the depth the drilling in the rest of the pulp floor. Since rater R1 disagreed with the consensus score, he was excluded from the analysis of agreement with AOS.

Experiments		R1-R2	R1-R3	R2-R3	AOS-R2	AOS R3
Overall	I	0.7	0.68	0.99	0.99	0.99
Outcome	II	0.36	0.33	0.97	0.99	0.97
	III	0.74	0.62	0.95	0.98	0.95
Axial	I	0.55	0.52	0.8	0.69	0.67
Walls	II	0.6	0.46	0.74	0.75	0.81
	III	0.42	0.27	0.71	0.7	0.9
	I	**0.03**	**0.09**	0.69	0.82	0.86
Floor	II	0.28	0.44	0.43	0.86	**0.28**
	III	**0.13**	0.23	0.88	0.81	0.82

Note: Correlation values are significant for 95% confidence interval except when indicated with bold font face

Table 2. Concordance correlation coefficients between human raters and AOS

Table 2 (columns 4, 5) shows the concordance correlation between AOS scores and those of the two raters R2 and R3. Both types of correlation are very strong for the overall outcome across all three experiments. But we see differences among the experiments moving to the component scores. All AOS scores are substantially correlated (above 0.7) except for the axial walls in experiment I and the floor for AOS-R3 in experiment II. Examining the variation in correlation values between AOS and the two raters from experiment I through experiment III shows no clear pattern of increase in response to increasing amounts of information provided. This suggests that the disagreement in scores is likely due to disagreement in judgement between AOS and the human raters rather than perceptual effects. This is no surprise given the lack of agreement among the human experts.

CONCLUSIONS

Our experimental results show disagreement among human expert scores, reflecting the subjective nature of human outcome scoring. Even in cases where additional perceptual information was provided, the correlations did not uniformly increase, which indicates the disagreement in scores is likely due to disagreement in judgement. Almost all our experiments showed a high degree of correlation between AOS and the two human raters whose scores were themselves well correlated. Given the lack of perfect correlation among the human experts, we would not expect to be able to do much better than this.

Our next steps will include a more thorough evaluation of the algorithm with a larger group of experts, as well as extending the work by identifying the portions of the procedure responsible for each error and combining this with procedure analysis [10] to provide formative feedback.

REFERENCES

1. M Baud. 1993. Data analysis, Mathematical modeling. In *Methods of Immunological Analysis, Vol .1: Fundamentals*, Rene Masseyeff, Winfried Albert, and Norman A. Staines (Eds.). VCH Publishers, Inc., New Yourk, 656–671.
2. Gilad Ben Gal, Ervin I Weiss, Naomi Gafni, and Amitai Ziv. 2011. Preliminary assessment of faculty and student perception of a haptic virtual reality simulator for training dental manual dexterity. *Journal of dental education* 75, 4 (2011), 496–504.
3. CDS-100-EPED Inc. 2015. EPED. (2015). Retrieved October 2, 2015 from http://www.eped.com.tw.
4. Thomas Kerwin, Gregory Wiet, Don Stredney, and Han-Wei Shen. 2011. Automatic scoring of virtual mastoidectomies using expert examples. *International Journal of Computer Assisted Radiology and Surgery* 7, 1 (May 2011), 1–11. DOI: http://dx.doi.org/10.1007/s11548-011-0566-4
5. Min Li and Yun Hui Liu. 2007. Dynamic modeling and experimental validation for interactive endodontic simulation. *IEEE Transactions on Robotics* 23, 3 (2007), 443–458. DOI: http://dx.doi.org/10.1109/TRO.2007.895062
6. DentSim Ltd. 2014. DentSim Labs - For perfect dental preps. (2014). Retrieved September 4, 2014 from http://www.dentsimlab.com/.
7. Min Li and Yun-Hui Liu. 2004. A virtual endodontics testbed for training root canal skills. In *IEEE International Conference on Robotics and Automation, 2004. Proceedings. ICRA '04. 2004*. IEEE, 841–846 Vol.1. DOI: http://dx.doi.org/10.1109/ROBOT.2004.1307254
8. Moog Inc. 2015. MOOG Simodont Dental Trainer. (2015). Retrieved September 7, 2014 from http://www.moog.com.
9. Phattanapon Rhienmora, Kugamoorthy Gajananan, Peter Haddawy, Matthew N. Dailey, and Siriwan Suebnukarn. 2010. Augmented reality haptics system for dental surgical skills training. In *Proceedings of the 17th ACM Symposium on Virtual Reality Software and Technology - VRST '10*, Vol. 1. ACM Press, New York, NY, 97–98. DOI:http://dx.doi.org/10.1145/1889863.1889883
10. Phattanapon Rhienmora, Peter Haddawy, Siriwan Suebnukarn, and Matthew N. Dailey. 2011. Intelligent dental training simulator with objective skill assessment and feedback. *Artificial Intelligence in Medicine* 52, 2 (Jun 2011), 115–121. DOI: http://dx.doi.org/10.1016/j.artmed.2011.04.003
11. V. A. Sandoval, R. A. Dale, W. D. Hendricson, and J. B. Alexander. 1987. A comparison of four simulation and instructional methods for endodontic review. *Journal of dental education* 51, 9 (Sep 1987), 532–8. http://www.ncbi.nlm.nih.gov/pubmed/2442230
12. Christopher Sewell. 2007. *Automatic Performance Evaluation in Surgical Simulation*. Ph.D. Dissertation. Stanford University.
13. Christopher Sewell, Dan Morris, Nikolas Blevins, Sanjeev Dutta, Sumit Agrawal, Federico Barbagli, and Kenneth Salisbury. 2008. Providing metrics and performance feedback in a surgical simulator. *Computer Aided Surgery* 13, 2 (Mar 2008), 63–81. DOI: http://dx.doi.org/10.1080/10929080801957712
14. Siriwan Suebnukarn, R Hataidechadusadee, N Suwannasri, N Suprasert, P Rhienmora, and P Haddawy. 2011. Access cavity preparation training using haptic virtual reality and microcomputed tomography tooth models. *International endodontic journal* 44, 11 (Nov 2011), 983–9. DOI: http://dx.doi.org/10.1111/j.1365-2591.2011.01899.x
15. Forsslund Systems. 2014. Forsslund Systems. (2014). Retrieved September 9, 2014 from http://www.forsslundsystems.com/.
16. Brian Tse, William Harwin, Alastair Barrow, Barry Quinn, Jonathan San Diego, and Margaret Cox. 2010. Design and Development of a Haptic Dental Training System - hapTEL. In *Eurohaptics*, Vol. 1. 101–108. DOI: http://dx.doi.org/10.1007/978-3-642-14075-4
17. Voxel-Man. 2014. VOXEL-MAN Dental - Virtual Reality Dental Training Simulator. (2014). Retrieved September 7, 2014 from http://www.voxel-man.com/.

ViZig: Anchor Points based Navigation and Summarization in Educational Videos

Kuldeep Yadav, Ankit Gandhi, Arijit Biswas, Kundan Shrivastava, Saurabh Srivastava, Om Deshmukh
Xerox Research Centre, India
kuldeep.r@xerox.com, om.deshmukh@xerox.com

ABSTRACT

Instructional videos are one of the most popular ways of teaching and learning in an online setting. However, navigation in videos is linear as compared to other instructional resources such as textbooks, where a table of topics and a multi-faceted index of different anchor points i.e., list of figures, tables aid in efficiently navigating to a desired point of interest. There is a lack of appropriate techniques and interfaces which can support such textbook-style navigation in instructional videos.

This paper presents a novel approach to automatically localize and classify different anchor points in a video including figures, tables, equations, flowcharts, code snippets and charts. Our approach uses a deep convolution neural network in a semi-supervised fashion where the training data is obtained from the unconstrained Internet images. On an anchor point dataset of about $10K$ images, the proposed algorithm leads to a classification accuracy of 86%. Further, we designed a system $ViZig$ that uses these localized anchor points along with a automatically generated list of topics for non-linear video navigation and studied its effectiveness in real-world. Our user studies with 18 participants establish that the proposed video navigation mechanism provides statistically significant time savings as compared to the popularly used time-synched transcript along with youtube-style timeline scrubbing.

ACM Classification Keywords

H.5.1 Multimedia Information Systems: Video

Author Keywords

Video Navigation; MOOCs; Convolutional Neural Network; Deep Learning; Education;Video Indexing; Video Summarization

INTRODUCTION

Massive Open Online Courses (MOOCs) is a large-scale Internet revolution which offers free online courses delivered by qualified professors from world-known universities and attended by millions of students remotely. The growth of MOOCs has been remarkable and it is expected that global MOOCs market will grow at a compound annual growth rate (CAGR) of 56.61% between 2014 and 2018 [10]. Major MOOC providers like Coursera and Edx have a few million students registered on their platform [11] and thousands of new participants continue to enroll every day [21]. However, a very small fraction of participants (around 10%) actually finish a course on MOOCs [1]. Various studies concluded that MOOC participants spend a significant amount of time in navigating to the right content, which suits their learning goals [22, 23].

Instructional videos are one of the most popular ways of teaching and learning in an online setting. MOOCs have been producing a lot of quality educational content that is openly available for individual consumption. Due to this reason, they are also seen as game changers for students worldwide, who may not have easy access to quality instructors. However, there are many challenges associated with online viewing of these videos including limited non-linear navigation support, lack of efficient summarization, and limited meta-data to search for relevant videos. Multiple studies conducted on MOOC platforms indicated that participants often perform non-linear navigation in educational videos [22]. For example, certificate earning students were found to spend only about 4.4 minutes on an average on a 12 to 15 minute video. The same study states that certificate earners, on an average, skip 22% of the video content in MOOCs. Further, it has been found out that there is a point of interest every 2 minutes in a given education video and students often go back to specific points of interest to get help during assignments or while preparing for examination [23].

Traditionally, navigation in videos is linear as compared to other instructional resources such as books, where a multi-faceted index or table of content (list of figures/tables) aids in non-linear navigation. We point out the importance of book-like multi-faceted indices for educational videos using two different information-seeking scenarios. Consider a student Alice, who has been taking an online course on computer networks. Let us assume that she recently learned about various TCP protocols with the help of educational videos. While solving assignment problems, she wanted to refer back to the diagram which depicted the packet format of these protocols. Availability of an interface that lists the figures dis-

IUI 2016, March 07–10, 2016, Sonoma, CA, USA .

http://dx.doi.org/10.1145/2856767.2856788

cussed in the video along with their occurrence timestamp would enable Alice in navigating to her point of interest as quickly as possible. In a different scenario, Arun is an instructor teaching data structures and algorithms and he wants to find video content for his classroom to teach the heap sort algorithm. Specifically, he is looking for videos that contain flowcharts and code snippets both to complement his style of teaching. Presence of a video data library with such multi-faceted indexing can aid Arun in efficiently locating suitable videos for his class. Indeed, all the major word processing and document markup languages realize the utility of such multi-faceted index points in textual document navigation and provide techniques to generate a list of these anchor points as the document is being composed.

However, there has been little research work that localizes and classify different visual anchor points in an educational video. These anchor points include figures, tables, equations, flowcharts and code snippets. Localization of these anchor points is important because most of the discussion in an educational video is centered around them. Further, these anchor points could provide a multi-faceted indexing of the video and potentially help in non-linear navigation, searching, and efficient summarization of video content. Such automatic localization of anchor points and creation of multi-faceted index is non-trivial and requires intelligent processing of the video content.

To address this problem, we propose a novel approach for automatically localizing and indexing videos based on the anchor points[1]. The main contributions of this paper are as follows:

1. **Anchor point localization and Classification:** In this paper, a novel approach is proposed for automatic localization and classification of anchor points. We collect a large anchor point dataset of around $10K$ images from the web and train a deep convolutional neural network (CNN) for automatic classification of these anchor points. The trained deep model leads to a classification accuracy of 86%. The trained CNN is afterwards applied to a complex dataset of 25 educational videos and it was able to provide accuracy of nearly 80% in classifying different anchor points.

2. **ViZig System:** We design and implement an end-to-end system that aim to enable non-linear video navigation using automatically generated multi-faceted index i.e. combination of anchor point localization and classification framework along with list of topics generated from the audio-visual content. The proposed system also introduces jigsaw pages to summarize a video using the list of anchor points. Proposed non-linear navigation system is planned to be integrated with TutorSpace platform [12], which allows instructors to search and curate multimedia content from different MOOC providers.

3. **User Study & Evaluation:** We conduct a preliminary user study with 18 participants to evaluate the effectiveness of the *ViZig* system. Our results indicate statistically significant difference between the transcript-based navigation system and proposed approach; latter being less time consuming, a higher perceived utility of navigation components of proposed system and high acceptance of the proposed system by the users for their day-to-day video consumption.

[1]Now onwards anchor points are used to refer the set of figures, tables, equations, flowcharts, code snippets, and charts

RELATED WORK

We outline previous research in two broad categories: video event detection and non-linear video navigation for educational videos. In video event detection, we cover prior research work in analyzing video content which aims to localize objects or event in the video. For non-linear video navigation, we cover prior interfaces, techniques, and systems that aim to facilitate navigation to desired points of interest in a video.

Video Event Detection

A thorough survey of various technical strategies employed for video content analysis and their applications to various domains can be found in [30]. Several research work aim to classify different visual objects especially in surveillance videos[13, 14, 15]. However, semantics of educational videos are different and therefore, it created its own set of research challenges.

In the domain of educational videos, [31] presents novel middle-level visual features to extract the written text and figures from a video lecture. Authors in [32] present a video analysis technique to extract semantically meaningful structure in the lectures to support task based queries. The Talk-Miner system [33] analyzes instructional videos to identify unique slide images, uses OCR techniques to automatically identify the text on the slides and provides an index for easy search and retrieval of spoken as well as written words.

The proposed approach is a first of its kind where both list of topics and visual anchor points are automatically extracted from the educational video. Furthermore, these anchor points are automatically classified into six different categories, which makes the indexing and non-linear navigation easy and multi-faceted. For classification of anchor points, we use a deep learning based framework, which have recently shown high promise on object recognition tasks in complex images.

Non-linear Video Navigation

There have been research efforts to use visual and textual (transcript) information for providing non-linear video navigation in educational videos. NoteVideo [26] identifies different conceptual objects using rule-based techniques and creates a summarized image using them. This image can be used for quickly navigating to the part of the video where the given object has first appeared. Swifter [29] is a system for locating a scene in the given video. It improves the traditional timeline scrubbing technique by overlaying a grid of pre-cached thumbnails on the video timeline interface for quick navigation. Panopticon [28] works in a similar way and displays video thumbnails on the screen without excluding any frames. These thumbnails get enlarged and corresponding audio is played potentially helping in the navigation process. None of these systems automatically localize the anchor points or classify into different categories as performed by proposed system.

LectureScape system [27] uses previous user interaction data collected from logs to help in navigation. Along with interaction data, it uses data-enhanced transcript search and a visual summary representing points with high interaction activity. However, this system require interaction data for bootstrapping purpose and use limited multimedia content for enabling non-linear video navigation. In [7, 8], the authors analyzed the audio-visual content in educational videos and automatically creates a list of topic such that users can find a topic of their interest in educational videos as quickly as possible. The authors in [1] proposed an audio-visual content-centric method for video navigation. Although visual content is analyzed to identify frames with "maximum written content", anchor points are not localized in their approach.

In this paper, we proposed an automatic and scalable framework for localizing and classifying different anchor points in a video. These anchor points along with list of automatically extracted set of topics [7] creates a multi-faceted index for a given educational video. We demonstrate that such a multi-faceted index significantly aids in navigating through an educational video. To the best of our knowledge, this is one of the first effort to automatically create such a multi-faceted indexing of educational videos and use it for non-linear video navigation.

SYSTEM DESIGN

Humans are adept at navigating through a book or text document i.e., they use table of content to get an idea of the flow of the document or to infer the timeline of different concepts discussed. Table of content provides indexes for both textual and visual components in a document i.e., topics, figures, tables, etc. These indexes also help in non-linearly navigating to a desired point of interest in text documents (books). There are similar requirements observed for MOOC videos where users would like to have a multi-faceted index comprising of list of topics and various anchor points i.e., figures, tables, charts, etc. Proposed system design addresses these requirements and uses the automatically generated multi-faceted index to enable book-style skim-through of an instructional video. In this section, we present the different navigation components of the proposed system: list of topics, anchor points visualization, and a 2-D timeline, along with their respective interaction techniques.

List of Topics

This component provides a time-aligned view of different topics (concepts) discussed in a video and is generated automatically by analyzing the audio-visual content (i.e. spoken transcript and visual content extracted from slides) of the video. As shown in Figure 1a, list of topics is placed on the left-side of the video and the user has the flexibility to click on any of the topics to navigate to the beginning of the topic in the video. The list of topics can be used for non-linear video navigation as well as to get a quick textual summary of what is discussed in the video without even playing it. In the later subsections, we discuss how list of topics are tied to other navigation components such as the 2-D timeline.

Anchor Points Visualization

The anchor points consists of different visual cues commonly found in educational videos i.e., figures, tables, equations/proofs, charts, code snippet, flowcharts, etc. Most of the time, anchor points are the central part of the discussion in the video and the instructor uses them for providing graphical representation of concepts as well as for various other use-cases. For example, flowchart is a widely used graphical representation for explaining different algorithms. Unlike a textbook, where there is a table of content and two other graphical categories (list of figures and list of tables), the proposed system has six different categories of anchor points as mentioned earlier.

In the next section, we discuss our comprehensive framework to localize and classify different anchor points in a video. The framework discovers the presence of these anchor points with their respective positions on the video timeline, where as the classification framework assigns them into one of the six different categories outlined above. Furthermore, we have separate modules to infer caption of these anchors points with the help of video transcript as well as to estimate their importance based on the visual information flow.

We design a web-based interface where different anchor points are stacked like a "jigsaw puzzle" on the video to assist in the navigation process. A single snapshot of "jigsaw puzzle" is termed as "jigsaw page" as shown in Figure 1a. User can click on any of the anchor points as part of jigsaw page and the system navigates to the point where that particular anchor point is first appeared in the video. For example, in an instructional video discussing heap sort, flowchart of an algorithm could be an anchor point stacked in jigsaw page and user can click on it directly to navigate it to the portion of the video where flowchart is being discussed. We apply a size restriction on jigshaw pages, which is of the size of the video thumbnail in the player. Multiple jigsaw pages are created if there are many anchor points which can not fit into one. To assign different anchor points to jigsaw pages, we consider their importance and space constraints. The anchor points which are more important than others will found their position earlier than others. User have flexibility to navigate between all the jigsaw pages with the help of a "next" button. For implementation purpose, the jigsaw pages are created as video-based annotations and they can be shown or hidden based on the users' preferences. We believe that jigsaw-based interface is ideal for anchor point visualization and navigation for following reasons:

1. It places many anchor points in a single window and helps in quick non-linear video navigation requiring minimum number of clicks from the user. Also, it maintains the form-factor of different anchor points i.e., a figure is displayed in nearly the same dimensions as in the video.

2. Stacking and prioritizing anchor points in a jigsaw page provide a quick summary to the user and in some of the

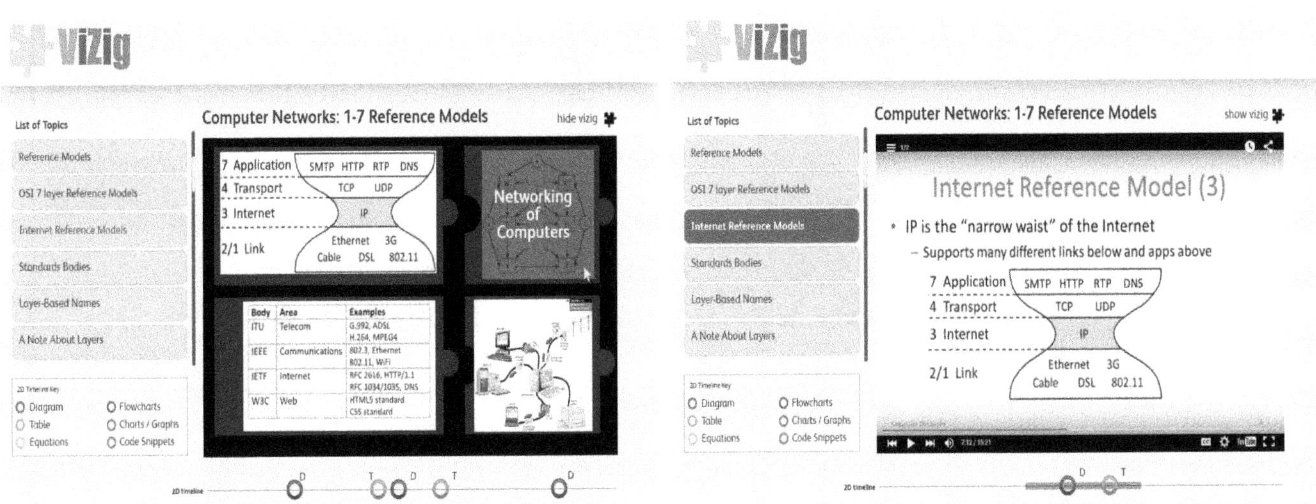

(a) Start view with a jigsaw page. 2-D timeline show location of different anchor points with their cateogories

(b) Topic-specific view. Thick part of 2-D timeline demonstrates the coverage of selected topic

Figure 1: Snapshots of the *ViZig* system prototype with different navigation components

cases, user can make a decision whether to play a video or not.

3. Jigsaw page based interface can be invisible or visible with a single click and hence, it minimizes the distraction to the user. User may choose to make it visible explicitly when needed.

2-D Timeline

Our system design incorporates a 2-D timeline which is used in conjunction with the concept list and jigsaw pages for navigation in the videos. The 2-D timeline is placed in parallel to the video player timeline and it is used to provide additional information which is difficult to incorporate in a traditional video player. Whenever, a user selects any topic to navigate using list of topics, locations of different anchor points are highlighted on the 2-D timeline with their respective icons as well as a topic-specific jigsaw page will be visible if user has enabled it. As shown in Figure 1b, User can click on any of the icons displayed on the 2-D timeline and quickly navigate to the part of the video where it has been discussed. This feature is helpful especially in large duration videos when a user is looking for topic-specific visual cues. Whenever, a user clicks on any of the anchor point in the jigsaw page, the portion of video is highlighted on the 2-D timeline, where the corresponding anchor point has been discussed. This feature helps in presenting coverage of an anchor point to the user. For example, a user can get to visualize how much time a teacher has spent discussing a particular figure or a table or a flowchart.

MULTI-FACETED INDEX CREATION

Figure 2 shows the main building blocks of the proposed system. We describe the details of each of these building blocks in this section.

Frame Extraction

First, we extract frames from the full video at the rate of 10 frames per second. After extraction of all these frames, the next step is to extract only the unique frames using the unique frame extraction approach proposed in [7]. It is important to extract the unique frames and process only those for anchor point classification to reduce the overall computational complexity of the classification process.

Topic List Creation

We use the method proposed in [7] to automatically create topic list i.e. table of content for educational videos. The method analyses the audio-visual content to automatically segments an educational video into relevant topics and label each segment with the corresponding topic. From the beginning times of different topic segments and their corresponding topic labels, the method generates the table of content. Such indexing of an educational video based upon topics will help users to quickly and efficiently navigate to the topic of interest in video.

First, the method defines and quantifies the saliency of visual words extracted from slides along with the spoken words obtained from the speech transcript. For quantifying visual saliency of words, the method uses different visual cues such as size, boldness, position, isolation, underlineness, etc. present in slides. The saliency of spoken words from speech transcript is computed in an unsupervised graph-based ranking model, TextRank. Second, the text from both the modalities is combined in a dynamic programming framework to estimate the time instants of topic changes in an educational video. The topic segmentation cost function in the dynamic program is defined in such a way that it simultaneously minimizes saliency-based metric of words common to two adjacent segments and maximizes the saliency-based metric of words unique to either of the two segments. Finally, the

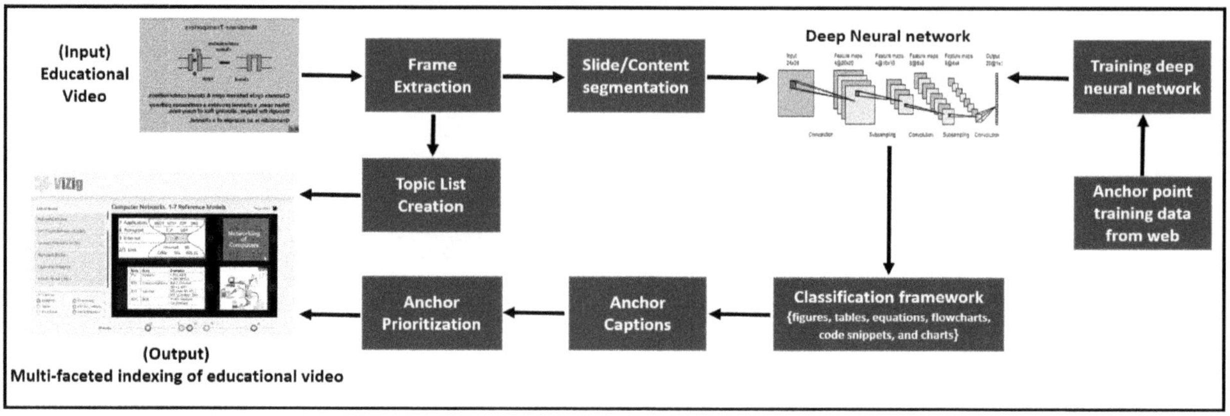

Figure 2: Pipeline of the proposed multi-faceted index creation approach.

method selects a representative 'title' for each topic and creates a table of content for an educational video.

Slide/Content Segmentation

In each frame along with the slide/board, other objects such as professor, chair, table, projector might also be present. It is important that we automatically extract only the slide/board region for further processing. First, we use normalized cut segmentation algorithm [9] to find out different segments in a frame. We also trained a classification model to identify the slide/board segments from other kinds of segments in the video. Once, we localize the segments that belong to the slide/board regions, we group them using several rule based heuristics. Eventually, we obtain one slide/board rectangular region in each frame. Once we extract these regions we remove the text from those. This step is necessary such that the text regions in a slide do not degrade the anchor point classification results. We use a state-of-the-art text localization method [16] method to perform this step. All pixels in the the detected text areas are set to the average RGB value of the whole slide/board region. These text-removed slide/board regions are fed into the deep neural network for classifying them into one of the anchor point categories.

Deep Learning for Anchor Point Classification

In this section we describe how different anchor points are automatically classified in an educational video. We use a state-of-the-art deep convolutional neural network (CNN) architecture [2] for this classification task. First we describe the details about how a CNN works and then how the CNN architecture is used in our anchor classification problem.

Convolution Neural Networks (CNN)

Convolutional neural networks or CNNs are a special kind of feed-forward neural networks for processing data that has a grid-like topology such as image data which are usually represented as two-dimensional grids of pixels. Any neural network which has at least one layer of convolution operation is called a CNN. CNNs have been extremely successful in many practical computer vision tasks such as image classification [2], object detection [3, 4], object tracking [5], semantic segmentation [6] etc.. CNNs usually have different kinds of layers such as convolution (CONV), rectified linear unit (RELU), pooling (POOL) and fully-connected (FC) layer. When a multi-channel color image is fed to a CNN, the image is transformed by these layers to a different feature representation or the corresponding class/category label of the image. We note that the CONV/FC layers perform transformations that are a function of not only the activations in the input volume, but also of the parameters (the weights and biases of the neurons). On the other hand, the RELU/POOL layers will implement a fixed function. The parameters in the CONV/FC layers will be trained with gradient descent (similar to traditional neural network training) so that the class scores that the ConvNet computes are consistent with the labels in the training set for each image. Now we describe the operations of each of these layers in further detail:

- CONV layer: The convolution layer is the core building block of a CNN and it's output volume can be interpreted as neurons arranged in a 3D volume. The CONV layer's parameters consist of a set of 3-dimensional filters whose parameters are learned through gradient descent. Every filter is small spatially (along width and height), but extends through the full depth of the input volume. During the forward pass, each filter is convolved across the width and height of the input volume, producing a 2-dimensional activation map of that filter. Intuitively, the network will learn filters that activate when they see some specific type of structure or pattern at some spatial position in the input. Stacking these activation maps for all filters along the depth dimension forms the full output volume. Every entry in the output volume can thus also be interpreted as an output of a neuron that looks at only a small region in the input and shares parameters with neurons in the same activation map (since all these numbers result from applying the same filter). The backpropagation for a convolution operation (for both the data and the weights) is also a convolution (but with spatially-flipped filters).

- POOL layer: It is common to insert Pooling layers in-between successive CONV layers in a ConvNet architecture. Its function is to progressively reduce the spatial size of the representation to reduce the amount of parameters and computation in the network, and hence to also control overfitting. Pooling helps to make the representation of image invariant to small translations of the input. This means that if we translate the input by a small amount, the values of most of the pooled outputs do not change. The Pooling Layer operates independently on every depth slice of the input and resizes it spatially, using the MAX operation. The most common form of pooling layer with filters of size 2 by 2 is applied with a stride of 2 downsamples every depth slice in the input by 2 along both width and height, discarding 75% of the activations. Every MAX operation would in this case be taking a max over 4 numbers (little 2x2 region in some depth slice). In addition to max pooling, the pooling layer can also perform other functions, such as average pooling or L2-norm pooling. Average pooling was often used historically but has recently lost preference compared to the max pooling operation, which has been shown to work better in practice. During backpropagation the backward pass for a max operation has a simple interpretation as only routing the gradient to the input that had the highest value in the forward pass. Hence, during the forward pass of a pooling layer it is common to keep track of the index of the max activation (sometimes also called the switches) so that gradient routing is efficient during backpropagation.

- RELU layer: RELU layer applies an elementwise activation function, such as the max(0,x) thresholding at zero to all outputs. However this step leaves the size of the volume unchanged.
- FC layer: Neurons in a fully connected layer have full connections to all activations in the previous layer, as seen in regular neural networks. Their activations can hence be computed with a matrix multiplication followed by a bias offset. In this stage every node in the output is connected to every node in the input.

Alexnet

In this subsection we describe a pre-trained CNN which was used for the imagenet [17] classification task. Imagenet is a large scale visual recognition challenge where more than million images from 1000 classes are required to be classified. The proposed approach in [2] developed a neural network model called Alexnet which improved the state-of-the-art imagenet classification results by a significant amount. Researchers in the computer vision community have often used the Alexnet architecture for other kinds of computer vision applications [18, 19]. If the training dataset for a classification problem is not significantly large, then training a deep neural network from scratch might lead to over fitting. That is why it is a common practise to use a pre-trained architecture and fine-tune only the top few layers of the network for a different classification task. We also use the Alexnet architecture along with fine-tuning in the proposed deep learning approach. We hope that the pre-trained network will extract low level features such as edges, corners etc. from images and then due to the fine-tuning step we will be able to extract the high-level features such as table/equation/code patches and learn a classification model to identify the anchor points.

Alexnet contains contains eight layers with weights; the first five are convolutional and the remaining three are fully-connected. The output of the last fully-connected layer is fed to a 1000-way softmax which produces a distribution over the 1000 class labels. This network maximizes the multinomial logistic regression objective, which is equivalent to maximizing the average across training cases of the log-probability of the correct label under the prediction distribution. The kernels of the second, fourth, and fifth convolutional layers are connected only to those kernel maps in the previous layer which reside on the same GPU. The kernels of the third convolutional layer are connected to all kernel maps in the second layer. The neurons in the fully-connected layers are connected to all neurons in the previous layer. Response-normalization layers follow the first and second convolutional layers. Max-pooling layers follow both response-normalization layers as well as the fifth convolutional layer. The ReLU non-linearity is applied to the output of every convolutional and fully-connected layer.

Dropout: Although combining the predictions of many different models is a very successful way to reduce test errors it appears to be too expensive for big neural networks that already take several days to train. So a recently-introduced technique, called dropout is used in Alexnet where the output of each hidden neuron is set to zero with probability 0.5. The neurons which are "dropped out" in this way do not contribute to the forward pass and do not participate in backpropagation. So every time an input is presented, the neural network samples a different architecture, but all these architectures share weights. At test time, all the neurons are used but their outputs are multiplied by 0.5, which is a reasonable approximation to taking the geometric mean of the predictive distributions produced by the exponentially-many dropout networks.

Proposed CNN for Anchor Point Classification

In the proposed CNN for anchor point classification we use the same architecture as used in Alexnet. However we fine-tune the final three layers for the network such that the network can be used for index classification. First, we remove the 1000 node final layer (used to classify 1000 classes form imagenet [2]) from the network and add a layer with only six nodes because we are trying to classify the anchors into six classes. Since the weights of this layer is learned from scratch we initialize the learning rate equal to 0.01 (same as Alexnet). While fine-tuning we also fine tune the previous two fully connected layers before this layer. However these layer weights are not learned from the scratch. We use a learning rate of 0.001 for these layers while performing the gradient descent with the anchor point classification training data. Once the CNN has been fine-tuned a new test anchor point image is forward propagated through this network to find the classification label.

Anchor Caption Generation

After the unique frames are classified into corresponding anchor points, the next step is to automatically generate a caption for each of the anchor points. The proposed method prefers spoken information over the visual information to generate these captions. Such a preference is motivated by

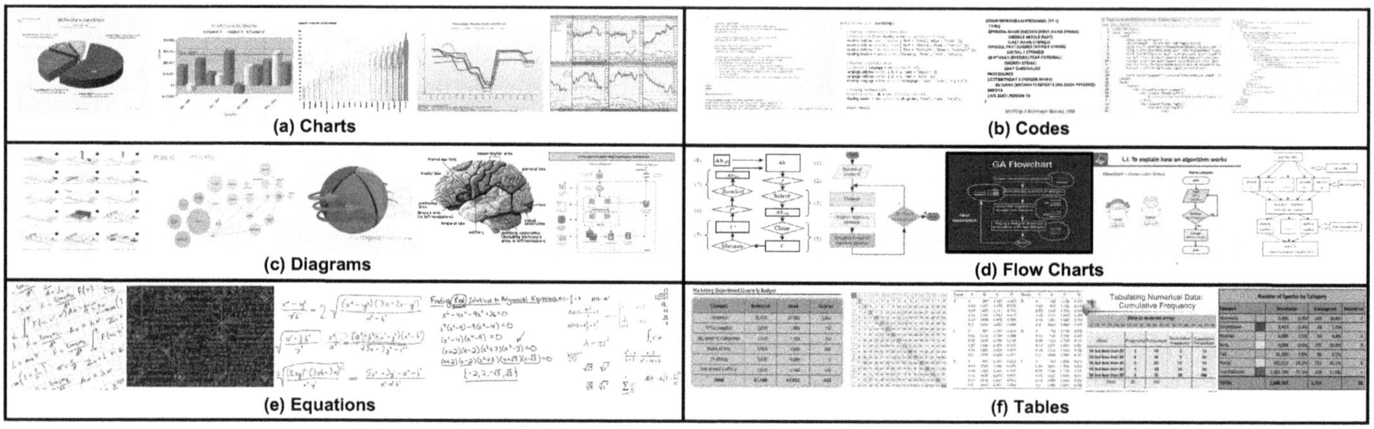

Figure 3: Few example images of the dataset comprising of classes - charts, codes, diagrams, flow charts, equations and tables.

Anchor Points Category	No of Images
Charts	3195
Codes	551
Diagrams	3097
Flow Charts	890
Equations	1238
Tables	1001

Table 1: Descriptive statistics about the dataset collected from web-based search engines

the system design where the entire visual frame corresponding to the anchor point is displayed to the user and thus the visual information is already present as part of this visual display. For every unique anchor point, a_i, the start time t_s^i and the end time t_e^i where the anchor point is displayed in the video are identified. It is assumed that the spoken description between times t_s^i and t_e^i corresponds to the anchor point a_i. The transcript of the spoken description between times t_s^i and t_e^i is passed through the unsupervised graph-based text ranking model, TextRank [35] and the top 2 most highly ranked phrases are chosen as the caption for the a_i anchor point. In the TextRank algorithm, the ranking of a phrase is determined by the number of other phrases that link to it and the strength of these links. The strength of the link between two phrases is defined by the normalized co-occurrence count over the entire video transcript: the number of times the two phrases co-occur within a window of $N(= 10)$ words.

Anchor Prioritization

The relevance quotient of an anchor point a_i is defined as a linear combination of (a) the duration that the anchor point is displayed in the video ($D_i = t_e^i - t_s^i$), and (b) the average TextRank of the two highly ranked phrases that constitute the anchor caption ($TR_i = (TR_1 + TR_2)/2$). The linear combination is given by: $RQ_i = 0.5D_i + 0.5TR_i$. Anchor points with higher relevance quotient are prioritized higher.

Dataset Collection

In this section, we describe the dataset, which we have collected for the evaluation of our framework. For training purpose, we needed to collect labeled data for different anchor points. To avoid large-scale labeling of data, we downloaded 9972 images from multiple image search engines (Google, Flickr, Bing, Yahoo and Ask Geeves) comprising of 6 different classes - charts, code snippets, diagrams, flow charts, equations and tables. The images are downloaded by providing multiple text queries followed by manual filtering. Manual filtering involves the removal of completely irrelevant images, for example, removing the images of wooden tables from table class. The per class statistics of the dataset is mentioned in Table 1. Figure 3 shows the example images from each of these classes. 'Chart' class comprises of all types of graph or any graphical representation of data including histograms, pie-charts, line, bar graph, scatter plot, etc. 'Code snippets' have images containing source codes, pseudo codes, or algorithms. 'Diagrams' class represent images having visual or symbolic representation of information. 'Flow charts' class represents images that define workflow or process. 'Equations' class have images comprising mostly of mathematical equations. 'Tables' class have images in which information or facts are arranged in rows or columns. Classifying an image into one of these classes is a very challenging task because of huge intra-class variations and interclass similarities.

Experimental Results

In this section, we report the anchor point classification results obtained using the proposed framework. We perform experiments in two different setups. In the first one, we perform training and testing both on the web images to examine the robustness and scalability of our approach on diverse set of images available for anchor points. However, in the second setup, we train our framework on the web images and tested on frames extracted from educational videos.

In the first setup, we perform a 10-fold cross validation experiment using the web images. All the web images are randomly partitioned into 10 different splits. Afterwards, we

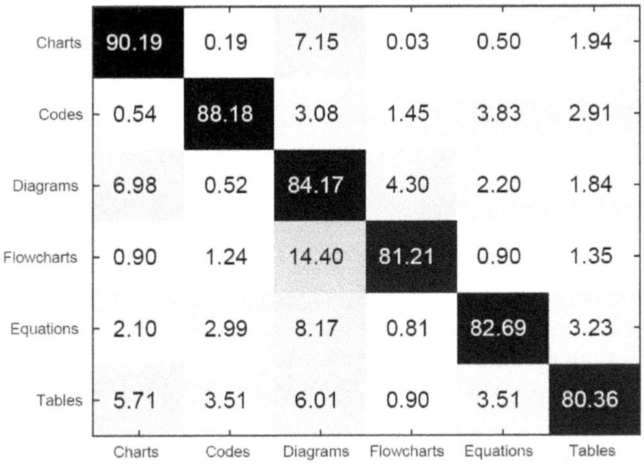

Figure 4: The confusion matrix for classification of different anchor points.

perform the classification task 10 times where each time testing is done on one of the splits and the CNN-based training is performed using the remaining nine splits. We obtain an average accuracy of 85.5% with a standard deviation of 1.22% (chance accuracy is only 32.04%). We also look at the confusion matrix in Figure 4 to understand which set of classes are confused most during classification. We find that flowcharts are classified as Diagrams 14.4% of the times. Overall, we find that almost all of the classes are confused with the Diagram class. Although, the categories were clearly defined such that intersection among the categories is minimized, there were some images which can belong to multiple categories, e.g.: some flowcharts or charts could have been included in the diagram class too. These images contributed to the increased confusion between the diagram category and others. However, we did not manually remove these images from our experimental setup and still achieve an accuracy of around 86%. That clearly demonstrates the robustness of the proposed approach.

In the second setup, we evaluate our approach on slide/content frames automatically extracted from educational videos. For this experiment, we choose a dataset of 25 educational videos taken from different MOOC providers i..e. $NPTEL$, $Coursera$ and EdX. The duration of these video ranged from 8 minutes to one hour. Proposed method identified a total of 122 anchor points on these set of videos and achieved an accuracy of 80.34% for anchor point classification. There was a slight degradation in classification accuracy because videos are recorded under varied situations including variations in camera angle, ambience light, lecturer positioning in the video, slides style, and use of handwritten text in videos. Even after all of these challenges, proposed approach show strong robustness in classifying different anchor points. We believe that our approach of training the deep neural network on web-based images is promising because it can scale very fast where new training images or categories can be added without much efforts. In the next section, we conduct a user study to evaluate the effectiveness of different anchor points for non-linear video navigation.

USER STUDY

We designed and developed our proposed system *ViZig* that provides capabilities for non-linear video navigation in educational videos. To understand and quantify the effectiveness of the proposed system in real-world, we conduct a user study with a selected group of participants. For comparison purpose, we developed a web-based prototype of a baseline system, where the transcript of the video is displayed alongside the video and youtube-style timeline scrubbing is used for navigation. Our baseline system was inspired by the video navigation system used by major MOOC providers (e.g., EdX) and e-learning organizations (e.g., Khan Academy). Our study was informed by the following research questions.

1. R1: How does the navigation time compare across the two interfaces (baseline & proposed) when different categories of tasks are presented to the user?
2. R2: What is the users' perceived utility of the different navigation components of the proposed *ViZig* interface?
3. R3: What is the user's perceived usability of the different features of the proposed *ViZig* system and how inclined would the users be in using these as part of their day-to-day educational video content consumption?

Participants

We recruited 18 participants for the study. All participants were tech savvy with basic exposure to video navigation systems such as YouTube. All of them were fresh computer science and electronics graduates from different engineering colleges in India. Out of the 18 participants, eight were female (mean age=25.2, stdev=1.3, max=27, min=24) and ten participants were male (mean age=26.3, stdev=2.4, max=31, min=23). Seventeen participants had prior exposure of watching MOOC videos and they were enrolled in Coursera and EdX courses.

Study Methodology

We selected two videos from a popular introductory "computer networking" course. The videos were of 14 and 16 minute duration and were created by the same instructor. The videos were selected considering the participants demographics so that all of them could follow the instructional content. All participants studied some form of computer networking course during their formal education. Previous studies [23, 22] have shown that often users return to a given point of interest in educational videos due to variety of reasons such as solving an assignment, preparing for an exam, or while revising a concept. To emulate a similar setting, the researchers shared the link of the selected videos to the participants and asked them to see the video thoroughly, just after their recruitment in the study.

After two days, each user was met individually, was explained the context of the study, the design of the two prototypes and the tasks. The study was designed in such a way that each participant got to use the baseline and the proposed *ViZig* interfaces on two separate videos to minimize the learning from repetitive tasks. While nine out of eighteen participants saw the first video with baseline system ($BV1$ followed by $PV2$) the other half used the proposed system with the second video ($PV1$ followed by $BV2$). The user had to answer six questions of three different task categories after viewing the video. They were allowed unlimited number of attempts, until they believed they had successfully completed all the tasks.

Three different task categories were designed to emulate a typical navigation experience when a user is likely to return to a point of interest of an already watched video. The task categories are as following:

1. **Visual Search:** In this task, a textual clue was given related to an anchor point and the user was required to navigate to the point where it has been discussed in the video. For example, users were asked to navigate to the point where "the relation between networking layers and protocols is discussed".
2. **Multi-modal Search:** For this category, both textual and visual clues were given to the participants and they were required to navigate to the point where both of these clues co-occurred. For example, users were asked to navigate where "session information is maintained in OSI reference models".
3. **Problem Solving Tasks:** For this category of tasks, we gave a set of questions inspired from in-video short quizzes, which are given in MOOCs to maintain student engagement. The participants were asked to find the portion of a video where the answer of a given question lies and write the answer on a paper for verification.

As mentioned earlier, participants were given a total of six tasks, two from each of three different task categories. We recorded the task completion time for each category for every participant as well as their responses to different tasks. The user study was followed by taking participants' feedback on a quantitative questionnaire (based on Likert scale), and one on one semi-structured interviews. We will now discuss our study results in the next section.

Results

All users completed all the tasks successfully with both the prototypes. To answer our first research question, we compared the task completion time for both the videos across both baseline and proposed interfaces. As shown in figure 5, the mean time for task completion was observed to be higher for baseline interface as compared to the proposed interface. Observe that, task completion time for different categories included the time taken to perform two tasks. We observed a statistically significant difference between the mean time for all three tasks categories – Task Category (TC)-1 ($t(17)=2.5223$, $p=0.0168$), TC-2 ($t(17)=2.7824$, $p=0.0090$) and TC-3($t(17)=2.0682$, $p=0.0468$). The results indicate that participants were able to navigate faster using proposed interface as compared to baseline for all the different task categories i.e. visual search, multimodal search and problem solving. Hence, we conclude that proposed interface is much more effective than baseline for variety of different navigation queries.

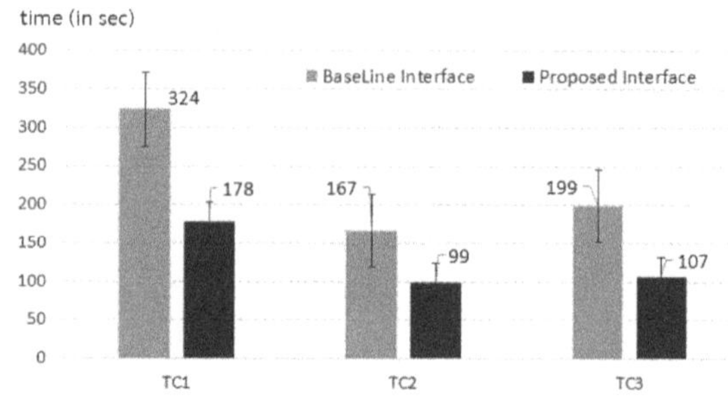

Figure 5: Comparison of mean navigation time (in sec) for different task categories across both the interfaces

To answer our second research question [R2], we collected responses from the qualitative questionnaire. This questionnaire was based on the Likert Scale (0-highly unsatisfactory; 7-highly satisfactory). Our results indicated that the proposed system was liked by the participants. All participants showed positive interest of using the system for their day to day video viewing experience (weighted average 5.11 out of 7). The concept of timelines and creative used of jigsaw pages to summarize the content was overall satisfactory (weighted average 5.28 out of 7). Participants ranked visual search (weighted average 6.22 out of 7) as a most suitable task to perform with the proposed system prototype. This was followed by multimodal search (weighted average 6 out of 7), searching for concepts (weighted average 5.94 out of 7) and navigation during solving problems (weighted average 5.56 out of 7).

Participants showed their likeliness towards the jigsaw based video summarization (weighted average 6.39 out of 7) as well as identified it as most helpful navigational feature in the proposed system. Overall, the participants found the system satisfactory and easy to use (weighted average 5.94 out of 7) and believed that it had all the capabilities required for video navigation (weighted average 5.11 out of 7). During one on one interaction, all participants commented positively about the system. Many believed ($n = 16$) that proposed system will be highly effective for them for non-linear video navigation as well as searching through video content. This summarizes answer to our third research question [R3].

In qualitative feedback, an enthusiastic participant commented - "Jigsaw is very good to review the key concepts described in the video. If one forgets the concept, he can directly navigate to a specific portion without searching for it." Another commented, "I like the way visuals are exploited and linked to the concept timeline." Many others ($n = 11$) reported that the proposed system is extremely suited for revision purpose and if someone has watched the video before and already know the content. While, most of the users shared positive responses, few of them (n=4) showed some concerns about the placement of the jigsaw summarization in the video pane itself. A participant commented, "I wish the jigsaw did not overlap with the video. It could have been more like the thumbnail concept that typically YouTube videos provides." Many participants (n=16) appreciated the concept of proposed system for low internet bandwidth settings. A participant commented, "In my office, the internet just dont' work. This navigation is very helpful in such conditions. Instead of manually sliding the timeline and waiting for video to buffer, I can directly go to the desired section of the video by a single click." Adding to our surprise, a user summarized, "You know what, I realized that I will surf the table of content only if I am not confident about the topic of the video. If I am fully confident, I will directly check the Jigsaw to find if it has what I need."

The quantitative & qualitative results with the verbal feedback from the preliminary user study demonstrate that proposed interface not only leads to more efficient navigation but is also preferred by the users as compared to baseline transcript based navigation technique.

SYSTEM LIMITATIONS

Proposed system have few known limitations. Automatic extraction of list of topics only work with slide-based videos and provide poor accuracy on blackboard or handwritten videos. Similarly, accuracy of anchor point classification also slightly decreases when blackboard based images are considered. These limitation can restrict the coverage of our non-linear video navigation system on certain type of videos. There is a need of investigating new techniques to overcome these limitations and making multi-faceted indexing ubiquitous for educational videos.

DISCUSSION & CONCLUSION

This paper introduces techniques to create a multi-faceted index by analyzing the multimodal content of educational videos. We successfully demonstrate the utility of such a multi-faceted index for efficient video navigation and found that it is much more effective as compared to the transcript-based interface that is provided by many MOOC providers. Such a multi-faceted index has broader applicability beyond enabling non-linear video navigation. We highlight some of these application scenarios in this section.

Enabling Multi-faceted Video Search & Selection

With the proliferation of new education paradigms such as blended or flipped learning, instructors are using lot of video content as part of their classroom teaching [20]. However, they spend a significant amount of time in searching for appropriate videos for their classroom. The proposed multi-faceted index will have information about the list of topics as well as the location and identity of the various anchor points. Such an index will allow the instructor to perform fine-grained video search such as "heap sort algorithm with a flowchart" or "dynamic programming with a coding snippet". The fine-grained video search functionality will help her in retrieving the most relevant videos w.r.t. her search term. Furthermore, the combination of the topic list and the anchor points provide a quick summary of the educational video without even the need to play the video, thus making the selection of appropriate videos time efficient.

Navigation Capabilities for Video Curation

Consider the above example, an instructor select an appropriate video for her class. However, she wanted to make some minor changes in the visual or audio content i.e. overlaying few of the images or equations with her own or adding voice-overs for some of the examples in the video. There are education-specific tools such as VidWiki [34] that provides an online tool to add advanced video annotations, which may correct existing errors, introduce new (or replace) content (i.e. figures), or translation of the video content in different languages. However, these tools only provide curation capabilities without any efficient video navigation techniques. Further, the annotations performed by VidWiki could be made more effective using capabilities of proposed system, which provides multimedia navigation capabilities, which aids in efficient content exploration as well as using anchor point localization to identify portions of the video that need intervention.

Optimize for Bandwidth-constrained Settings

In many parts of the world, Internet bandwidth conditions are not good enough for smooth video streaming. There is a high dropout rate as well as a poor engagement with video content/interactions in such conditions. Recent studies found that 40% of users stop watching a video, if it takes more than 10 seconds to load [25]. The multi-faceted index proposed in this paper has a very low bandwidth overhead compared to that of complete video streaming, and thus could be helpful in designing systems for low-bandwidth conditions. For example, a user can get a summary of the video using the index information and subsequently, she can make a decision to stream a video for further viewing or not. Also, she has the flexibility to stream only a part of the video in which she is interested in, as compared to streaming the entire video. For example, after looking at the list of the topics, she may choose to watch only one or two specific topics in a video.

As part of future work, we will be integrating *ViZig* system with TutorSpace platform [12] and plan to conduct user studies with large number of participants in a more realistic settings. Also, we intend to improve the accuracy of table of content generation as well as extending anchor point classification to more complex videos such as blackboard or handwritten videos.

ACKNOWLEDGEMENTS

Authors would like to thank all the user study participants for their time and valuable feedback in improving the system. We would like to thank Deepali Jain for her help in collecting part of the dataset as well as initial analysis.

REFERENCES

1. Yadav, K., Shrivastava, K., Mohana Prasad, S., Arsikere, H., Patil, S., Kumar, R., & Deshmukh, O. (2015, March). Content-driven Multi-modal Techniques for Non-linear Video Navigation. In Proceedings of the 20th International Conference on Intelligent User Interfaces (pp. 333-344). ACM.
2. Krizhevsky, A., Sutskever, I., & Hinton, G. E. (2012). Imagenet classification with deep convolutional neural

networks. In Advances in neural information processing systems (pp. 1097-1105).

3. Girshick, R., Donahue, J., Darrell, T., & Malik, J. (2014, June). Rich feature hierarchies for accurate object detection and semantic segmentation. In Computer Vision and Pattern Recognition (CVPR), 2014 IEEE Conference on (pp. 580-587). IEEE.
4. He, K., Zhang, X., Ren, S., & Sun, J. (2014). Spatial pyramid pooling in deep convolutional networks for visual recognition. In Computer VisionECCV 2014 (pp. 346-361). Springer International Publishing.
5. Hong, S., You, T., Kwak, S., & Han, B. (2015). Online Tracking by Learning Discriminative Saliency Map with Convolutional Neural Network. arXiv preprint arXiv:1502.06796.
6. Long, J., Shelhamer, E., & Darrell, T. (2014). Fully convolutional networks for semantic segmentation. arXiv preprint arXiv:1411.4038.
7. Biswas, A., Gandhi, A., & Deshmukh, O. (2015). MMToC: A Multimodal Method for Table of Content Creation in Educational Videos. ACM Multimedia conference 2015.
8. Gandhi, A., Biswas, A., & Deshmukh, O. Topic Transition in Educational Videos Using Visually Salient Words. Educational Data Mining 2015.
9. Shi, J., & Malik, J. (2000). Normalized cuts and image segmentation. Pattern Analysis and Machine Intelligence, IEEE Transactions on, 22(8), 888-905.
10. MOOC Growth Rate, `http://www.prweb.com/releases/massive-open-online/courses-market-2014-2018/prweb12018014.htm`
11. MOOCs 2014 Report, `https://www.edsurge.com/news/2014-12-26-moocs-in-2014-breaking-down-the-numbers`
12. TutorSpace Platform, `http://www.xrci.xerox.com/tutorSpace-at-scale-personalized-learning`
13. Chen, L., Feris, R., Zhai, Y., Brown, L., & Hampapur, A. (2008, September). An integrated system for moving object classification in surveillance videos. In Advanced Video and Signal Based Surveillance, 2008. AVSS'08. IEEE Fifth International Conference on (pp. 52-59). IEEE.
14. Javed, O., & Shah, M. (2002). Tracking and object classification for automated surveillance. In Computer VisionECCV 2002 (pp. 343-357). Springer Berlin Heidelberg.
15. Zhang, Z., Cai, Y., Huang, K., & Tan, T. (2007, September). Real-time moving object classification with automatic scene division. In Image Processing, 2007. ICIP 2007. IEEE International Conference on (Vol. 5, pp. V-149). IEEE.
16. Neumann, L., & Matas, J. (2013, December). Scene text localization and recognition with oriented stroke detection. In Computer Vision (ICCV), 2013 IEEE International Conference on (pp. 97-104). IEEE.
17. http://www.image-net.org/challenges/LSVRC/2014/.
18. Donahue, J., Hendricks, L. A., Guadarrama, S., Rohrbach, M., Venugopalan, S., Saenko, K., & Darrell, T. (2014). Long-term recurrent convolutional networks for visual recognition and description. arXiv preprint arXiv:1411.4389.
19. Long, J., Shelhamer, E., & Darrell, T. (2014). Fully convolutional networks for semantic segmentation. arXiv preprint arXiv:1411.4038.
20. Chetlur, Malolan et al. "EduPaL: Enabling Blended Learning in Resource Constrained Environments." ACM DEV 2014.
21. Lindsay Ryan, MOOCs are on the Move: A Snapshot of the Rapid Growth of MOOCs, `https://www.efmd.org/index.php/blog/view/250-white-paper-moocs-massive-open-online-courses`
22. Guo, P. J., & Reinecke, K. (2014, March). Demographic differences in how students navigate through MOOCs. In Proceedings of the first ACM conference on Learning@ scale conference (pp. 21-30). ACM. Chicago
23. Kim, J., Guo, P. J., Seaton, D. T., Mitros, P., Gajos, K. Z., & Miller, R. C. (2014, March). Understanding in-video dropouts and interaction peaks inonline lecture videos. In Proceedings of the first ACM conference on Learning@ scale conference (pp. 31-40). ACM.
24. Cutrell, E., Bala, S., Bansal, C., Cross, A., Datha, N., John, A., ... & Thies, W. (2013). Massively Empowered Classroom: Enhancing Technical Education in India, MSR Technical Report.
25. Krishnan, S. S., & Sitaraman, R. K. (2013). Video stream quality impacts viewer behavior: inferring causality using quasi-experimental designs. IEEE/ACM Transactions on Networking (TON), 21(6), 2001-2014.
26. Monserrat, T. J. K. P., Zhao, S., McGee, K., & Pandey, A. V. (2013, April). NoteVideo: facilitating navigation of blackboard-style lecture videos. In Proceedings of the SIGCHI Conference on Human Factors in Computing Systems (pp. 1139-1148). ACM.
27. Kim, J., Guo, P. J., Cai, C. J., Li, S. W. D., Gajos, K. Z., & Miller, R. C. (2014, October). Data-driven interaction techniques for improving navigation of educational videos. In Proceedings of the 27th annual ACM symposium on User interface software and technology (pp. 563-572). ACM.
28. Nicholson, J., Huber, M., Jackson, D., & Olivier, P. (2014, April). Panopticon as an eLearning support search tool. In Proceedings of the 32nd annual ACM conference on Human factors in computing systems (pp. 1221-1224). ACM.

29. Matejka, J., Grossman, T., & Fitzmaurice, G. (2013, April). Swifter: improved online video scrubbing. In Proceedings of the SIGCHI Conference on Human Factors in Computing Systems (pp. 1159-1168). ACM.

30. Hu, Weiming, et al. "A survey on visual content-based video indexing and retrieval." Systems, Man, and Cybernetics, Part C: Applications and Reviews, IEEE Transactions on 41.6 (2011): 797-819.

31. Choudary, Chekuri, and Tiecheng Liu. "Summarization of visual content in instructional videos." Multimedia, IEEE Transactions on 9.7 (2007): 1443-1455.

32. Altman, Edward, Yu Chen, and Wai Chong Low. "Semantic exploration of lecture videos." Proceedings of the tenth ACM international conference on Multimedia. ACM, 2002.

33. Adcock, John, et al. "Talkminer: a lecture webcast search engine."Proceedings of the international conference on Multimedia. ACM, 2010.

34. Cross, A., Bayyapunedi, M., Ravindran, D., Cutrell, E., & Thies, W. (2014, February). VidWiki: Enabling the crowd to improve the legibility of online educational videos. In Proceedings of the 17th ACM conference on Computer supported cooperative work & social computing (pp. 1167-1175). ACM.

35. Mihalcea, Rada, and Paul Tarau. "TextRank: Bringing order into texts." Association for Computational Linguistics, 2004.

AnalyticalInk: An Interactive Learning Environment for Math Word Problem Solving

Bo Kang
University of Central Florida
Orlando, FL 32816 USA
bkang@cs.ucf.edu

Arun Kulshreshth
University of Central Florida
Orlando, FL 32816 USA
arunkul@knights.ucf.edu

Joseph J. LaViola Jr
University of Central Florida
Orlando, FL 32816 USA
jjl@eecs.ucf.edu

ABSTRACT
We present *AnalyticalInk*, a novel math learning environment prototype that uses a semantic graph as the knowledge representation of algebraic and geometric word problems. The system solves math problems by reasoning upon the semantic graph and automatically generates conceptual and procedural scaffoldings in sequence. We further introduces a step-wise tutoring framework, which can check students' input steps and provide the adaptive scaffolding feedback. Based on the knowledge representation, *AnalyticalInk* highlights keywords that allow users to further drag them onto the workspace to gather insight into the problem's initial conditions. The system simulates a pen-and-paper environment to let users input both in algebraic and geometric workspaces. We conducted an usability evaluation to measure the effectiveness of *AnalyticalInk*. We found that keyword highlighting and dragging is useful and effective toward math problem solving. Answer checking in the tutoring component is useful. In general, our prototype shows the promise in helping users to understand geometrical concepts and master algebraic procedures under the problem solving.

Author Keywords
Semantic Representation; Inference and Reasoning; Scaffolding Generation; User Modeling; Intelligent Tutoring System; Learning Techniques.

ACM Classification Keywords
H.5.2. User Interfaces: Graphical user interfaces (GUI).; I.2.4. Knowledge Representation Formalisms and Methods: Representations.; I.2.1. Applications and Expert Systems: Natural language interfaces.

INTRODUCTION
Mathematical word problem solving is a complex task which requires users to abstract the symbolic knowledge representation to formulate the math concept, manipulate and transform symbolic knowledge, and infer unknown knowledge [30]. As the quantitative representation of such problems changes, the solving task becomes more difficult, which affects users' reasoning process [16, 21].

DOI: http://dx.doi.org/10.1145/2856767.2856789

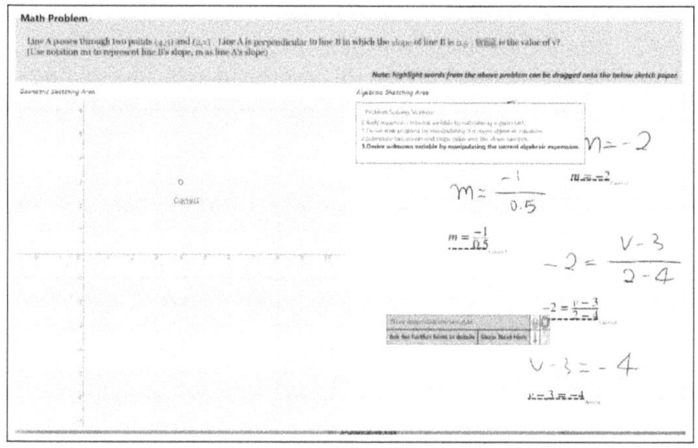

Figure 1: An example scenario where a user wants to solve the given math word problem on the dual geometric-algebraic workspace. In *AnalyticalInk*, the user drags the highlight words from the problem statement onto the below workspace to gain insight of problem's initial condition. Further, the user can sketch solving steps and query the system to check their correctness. As the current step is recognized a wrong, the system provides scaffoldings in visual widgets to guide the user's problem solving.

In this paper, we present *AnalyticalInk*, a novel math interactive learning environment prototype, which helps users to understand geometric concepts and solve geometry-and-algebra math problems. We illustrate a semantic graph knowledge representation to capture the key information of natural language based math word problems. The system relies on this representation to automatically solve the math problem and generates a scaffolding trace, which derives from known facts toward the unknown problem question as a sequence of scaffolding steps. We further demonstrates a step-wise tutoring framework upon the auto-generated scaffolding trace of a math problem. Such tutoring framework can check users' input steps and further provide adaptive scaffolding to help guiding a user through solving the problem.

The user interface of *AnalyticalInk* simulates the semantic word highlighting and dragging learning technique [8]. It lets users have a sense of the key information of a given problem and further allows them to drag information onto workspaces to either acquire the initial condition of a problem or reinforce geometric concept understanding. Interactive words directly map to annotated semantic words, which are defined by using the problem representation semantic. In addition, *AnalyticalInk* applies the theory of iterative development between the conceptual understanding and the procedural skill pruning from the math cognitive research [28].

The user interface provides both an algebraic canvas and a geometric canvas to let users determine the connection between geometric concepts and related algebraic procedures when solving geometry-and-algebra related problems. Lastly, *AnalyticalInk* supports sketch based user interactions, which have been shown to improve conceptual understanding, problem understanding and inferential reasoning during problem-solving [10, 25]. Figure 1 shows *AnalyticalInk*'s user interface. There are four contributions in this paper:

- A novel semantic graph based representation of geometry-and-algebra math problems is presented. We propose an automated reasoning process upon this knowledge representation to solve math word problems and generate scaffolding traces.
- A step-wise tutoring framework, which verifies users' input steps and further provides step-based adaptive scaffolding to guide user solving a problem.
- The novel learning environment *AnalyticalInk*, which embeds learning techniques to promote the math learning. The user interface of *AnalyticalInk* uses the sketch based natural input to let users reason during math problem-solving.
- The usability evaluation of *AnalyticalInk* is shown. The tutoring framework is evaluated and discussed. A comparative evaluation of the keyword highlighting and dragging learning technique is described.

RELATED WORK

Our work is closely related to three research areas: Computational Semantics of Natural Language, Intelligent Tutoring System (ITS), Learning based Interactive User Interface.

Computational Semantics and Reasoning

Our work considers the formal language representation of natural language descriptions. Specifically, both frame semantics and abstract meaning representation (AMR) are related to this work and have been explored in the natural language processing community. Frame semantics is a linguistic theory that interprets the meaning of words based on their semantic frames [9]. Abstract meaning representation converts a sentence to a directed, acyclic graph (DAG) containing a set of nodes and edges [6]. The nodes correspond to concepts and edges as semantic relations. Our intermediate knowledge presentation of geometry-and-algebra math problem is directly inspired by the AMR problem semantic.

Previous works have been developing statistical methods to parse math word problems as template based equations and further employing a solver to obtain the solution [23, 31, 35]. Instead of template-based methods, our work presents an intermediate semantic to capture relations of math concepts. However, this work does not consider the semantic parsing or the word alignment problem. Instead, we directly annotate given geometry-and-algebra math problems with our defined problem semantic. Using the annotated problem semantic, we focus on simulating how students plan to solve a problem as a constraint searching process upon the semantic graph. Due to the human learning purpose, we also consider the sequential scaffoldings generation instead of retrieving a single problem answer during the above search process. Gulwani et.al. used the program synthesis to automatically solving the ruler/compass based geometry construction problem [13]. Our automatic solving and scaffolding generation is based on the search upon the semantic graph, which is similar to the program synthesis methodology. However, as geometric math problems are different, our goal is to generate scaffolding traces, which covers both geometrical concepts and algebraic procedures.

Intelligent Tutoring System

Intelligent Tutoring System (ITS) research attempts to design and integrate instructional scaffolding methodologies into the system to promote a deeper level of learning [19]. The core of ITS is a cognitive tutor, which applies production rules to build up the domain dependent expert system [3]. Model-tracing tutor is built upon the cognitive tutor, which provides the flag feedback, the buggy feedback and a chain of scaffoldings [15, 26]. The state-of-the-art algebra cognitive tutor includes procedural scaffolding to derive algebraic expression or equations [18]. In *AnalyticalInk*, besides procedural scaffoldings that derive math expressions and equations, the auto-generated scaffolding trace also includes conceptual scaffoldings to guide geometric concept matching, geometric relation detection and concept reification processes. *AnalyticalInk* can be categorized as a step-based tutoring system [32], which requires users to enter multiple steps to accomplish the problem solving process.

In addition, student modeling is another component of ITS to evaluate students' knowledge master level. Knowledge tracing is the state-of-the-art probabilistic graphical model to predict learning mastery per skill [7]. In this work, we do not consider how well users comprehend the certain knowledge component. Instead, we only check the correctness of user input steps and give the adaptive scaffolding feedback based on the matching result.

Learning based Math User Interface

Educational psychology research showed the evidence that highlighting keyword is one effective learning technique toward the natural language understanding [8]. Hefferman and Koedinger considered the problem acquisition from natural language narratives toward math expressions as a symbolization process [14]. They built a cognitive model in order to provide scaffoldings to guide this process. Instead of building a cognitive model, *AnalyticalInk* implements the keyword highlighting learning technique and further provides the dragging operation upon colored semantic keywords. Mathematical cognitive science research revealed that developing the conceptual understanding and the procedural skill follows an iterative process. They proved it by conducting the experiment using the decimal fraction domain knowledge. We applied this finding to guide the design of *AnalyticalInk*, which emphasizes the iterative view of geometric concepts and algebraic procedural skills development.

Sketch is a powerful means of interpersonal communication. Forbus et.al. illustrated the importance of sketching to support the conceptual knowledge, visual understanding, and language [10]. In addition, Oviatt et.al. described the term *inferential reasoning* from the interaction perspective to design effective computational cognitive tools [25]. *AnalyticalInk* follows the sketch-based cognitive models to simulate pen-and-paper environment upon the user interface of interactive learning system. Previously, several pen-based math prototypes systems have been described, such as *MathPad*^{2} [24] ,*Hands-On Math* [33] and geometry theorem proving [17], Anthony et.al. demonstrated the effectiveness by integrating pen-based natural input with an intelligent tutoring system for algebra equation solving [5].

PROBLEM REPRESENTATION

When learning geometry concepts, students often encounter following types of math problems:

Problem1: Find the midpoint of the line segment joining $A(-2,2)$ and $B(4,6)$?

Problem2: There exists two points $A(2,4)$ and $B(5,v)$, the distance between A and B is 5. What is the value of v?

Problem3: There are two points $A(2,y)$ and $B(-1,4)$. The y-coordinate of point A is -1. What is the distance between these two points?

Problem4: Given an equation $2y+2x-y+2x+4=0$, graph this equation's corresponding shape? If it is a line, what is the slope of this line?

Problem5: A line passes through points $(2,3)$ and $(4,v)$, the slope of this line is 5. What is the value of v? What is the y-intercept of the line?

Problem6: Line A passes through $(-1,2)$ and $(5,8)$. Line B is parallel to line A, and also crosses point $(1,0)$, what is the general form of line B?

Problem7: Line A passes through two points $(4,3)$ and $(2,v)$. The line is perpendicular to line B in which the slope of line B is $1/2$. what is the value of v?

These natural language narrative math problems all cover geometric concepts. When reasoning such concepts, algebraic procedural derivations are required to infer the same concept, or from one toward the other. The geometric concept understanding and the algebraic procedural derivation are performed in an iterative manner so as to solve such problems [28]. The geometric concept can be subdivided into three types of knowledge: *knowledge entity* (such as a point or a line), *knowledge attribute* (such as the y-coordinate of a point, or the slope of a line) and *knowledge relation* (such as two lines are parallel, one point is on the line).

The pattern of question and answer, in the above math problems, is deriving from several given concept instances toward unknown concept instances. This attributes to the planning of math problem solving [30]. For instance, Problem1 introduces two points and a line, and lets users derive the midpoint entity through the internal relation between these points. Problem6 shows two lines and three points; the point-and-line relation and the line-and-line relation are implicitly specified in the problem narrative. Users need to derive one line's general form from the given entities. In addition, Problem1, 3, 4 and 6 require users to build and reason knowledge relations both in the forward manner. However, Problem2, 5 and 7 let users to build relations in the forward manner, but reason for unknown geometric concepts in the backward manner.

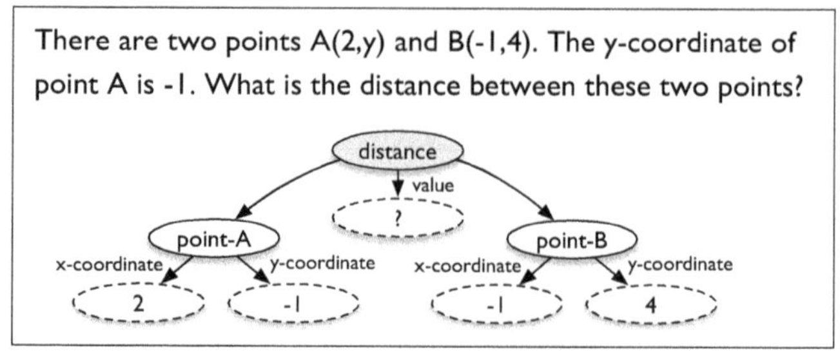

(a) Problem 3's semantic DAG representation.

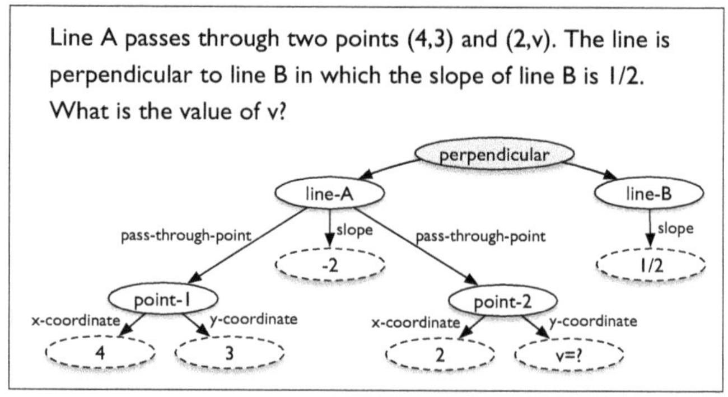

(b) Problem 7's semantic DAG representation.

Figure 2: Two math problems' semantic graph representations.

Syntax: We formulate the syntax of geometric concept knowledge as follows. All concept knowledge can be illustrated as the combination of a label, following by a colon and knowledge instance in the end. The label and colon is optional which depends on the problem description. For the *knowledge entity*, we currently model three entities: the point, the line and the circle. A point concept is represented in 2-dimensional Cartesian coordinates. The *knowledge attribute* is represented as the equation where the left side of it is a literal and the right side of the equation is a numeric value or an expression. The *knowledge relation* is represented as a function where the name of it is the relation and its arguments are knowledge entities. For the problem question, its syntax is an equation where the left side of it is a label or identity and the right side is a question mark. For instance, Problem3 contains two point knowledge entities as $A(2,y), B(-1,4)$, a knowledge attribute $y=-1$, its question can be represented as $d=?$. Similarly, Problem7 contains two point entities $(4,3),(2,v)$, two line entities $A: line, B: line$, a knowledge attribute $B: m=1/2$, three knowledge relations $pass-through(A,(4,3)), pass-through(A,(2,v)), perpendicular(A,B)$, its question can be represented as $v=?$.

Semantic Representation of Math Problems

In the semantic level, each math problem can be represented as a directed acyclic graph (DAG) using the syntax of geometric concepts. Figure 2 demonstrates two math word problems' corresponding DAG semantic representations. The graph contains a set of nodes and edges. The nodes are divided into three categories, including concepts, attributes, and semantic relations. A concept (represented using an ellipse) corresponds to a semantic entity, such as a point or line. Multiple attributes (dashed ellipse) can be associated with a concept. For example, a point may have two attributes: x-coordinate and y-coordinate. A line may have multiple attributes including slope, y-intercept, pass-through-point, and corresponding equation. A semantic relation (shaded ellipse) captures relationship between two concepts. For example, Problem7 shows that line B is perpendicular to line A ('perpendicular'); Problem3 displays distance between point A and B ('distance'). A semantic relation may be associated with one or multiple attributes. A query term corresponds to an attribute with unknown value.

SYSTEM OVERVIEW

We illustrate the process to generate the semantic DAG per math problem, and describe the scaffolding trace synthesis during the semantic DAG generation. Based on the generated scaffolding trace, we present our model-tracing tutor. We show a hybrid match-and-verify framework upon the tutor, which can solve multiple solution paths' verification and further provide the adaptive scaffolding. Last, we show the sketch-based user interface of *AnalyticalInk*, which incorporates learning techniques: semantic word highlight/dragging and dual geometry-and-algebra problem solving.

Automatic Reasoning and Scaffolding Generation

Instead of semantic parsing geometry-and-algebra math problems, we annotate math word problems according to the syntax of geometric concepts. Each natural language math problem is expressed as a sequence of the annotated geometric concept. This annotation process simulates how students prime initial conditions of a math problem. Based on annotated syntax geometric concepts, we present our problem-solving plan approach to derive from known concepts toward unknown concepts. Figure 3 shows the higher level description to use the semantic DAG to simulate the problem solving plan process.

Input: Let **S** be a sequence of annotated syntax concepts.

Output: Let **G** be the semantic DAG representation.

Initiate G.

For every input s in S:

Step 1: geometric concept m = **Syntax Pattern Match**(s)

where m can be geometric entities, attributes or relations.

Step 2: semantic relations R = **Constraint-Checking** (G, m)

For every relation r in R:

Step 3: **Update-Graph**(G, r)

Step 4: **Graph Bottom-up Reification**(G)

Figure 3: A semantic DAG based constraint search method to simulate the human problem-solving plan process.

The scaffolding generation is executed in all four steps of problem-solving plan method. In detail, a scaffolding step or a trace step is synthesized by performing a pre-defined rule to derive a geometric concept from one state to another. After executing a sequence of rules, a scaffolding trace will be generated. In the scaffolding trace, there are two different types of generated scaffolding steps: the geometric concept scaffolding and the algebraic procedural scaffolding. We give further explanations of these two types and their relations in the following subsections.

Syntax Pattern Match

The goal of step 1 is to parse annotated geometric concepts as knowledge instances. Based on the geometry concept syntax, we use the parsing expression grammar (PEG) to parse geometric entities, attributes and relations [11]. In the syntax level, variations of geometric concept format exist. For example, the syntax level of a line concept contains the *line general form*, the *line point-slope form* or the *line slope-intercept form*. In addition, algebraic manipulations should be performed to transform an algebraic expression as a geometric concept. For example, the annotation $2y + 2x - y + 2x + 4 = 0$ in Problem4 needs to be simplified using algebraic rule-derivations toward a recognizable line concept format $4x + y + 4 = 0$. To uniform the syntax of geometric concept, we build an algebraic rule-based expert system behind the PEG. Such expert system incorporates production rules with the arithmetic expression calculation and the algebraic expression manipulation.

In step 1, if the annotation matches the grammar without any rule-derivation, no scaffolding will be generated. However, if rules have been triggered to uniform the annotation as the geometric concept syntax format, both the geometric concept scaffolding and a sequence of algebraic procedural scaffoldings will be synthesized. The geometric scaffolding guides users to manipulate the algebraic expression so as to transform syntax annotations. Algebraic procedural scaffoldings are production rule derivations to explain this geometric scaffolding. Each procedural scaffolding or trace step records both geometric concept's formats before and after the rule derivation with the production rule itself. For example, transforming $2y + 2x - y + 2x + 4 = 0$ as a line concept format $4x + y + 4 = 0$ generates a sequence of procedural scaffoldings. These algebraic procedural scaffoldings apply rules such as the algebraic associative rule, the identity rule and arithmetic calculations in a recursive manner. The geometric conceptual scaffolding internally contains the procedural scaffolding trace. This geometric conceptual scaffolding is attached onto the recognized geometric concept knowledge.

In certain circumstances, the annotation contains the ambiguity to transform as a semantic knowledge. For instance, the input $x = 1$ can be either recognized as a line entity or an attribute. To discriminate it, the context information is required to further check if the literal x already exists. As such conflict happens case by case and depends on the context of existing input, we currently apply the case-based reasoning approach to perform the conflict resolving process [22].

Relation Constraint Checking and Graph Update

The goal of step 2 is to determine if any relation exists between any concepts of DAG and the current semantic concept m. Such relation searching process can be attributed to a constraint-solving problem (CSP) [29]. Algorithm 1 shows the search procedure upon the semantic DAG.

Data: Current geometric concept m.
Data: Current semantic DAG G.
Result: Detected semantic relations
Part1: unary-relation constraint Search:
for *node* g_i *in* G **do**
  if *Relation_Check(*g_i, m*)* **then**
    Generate unary-relation.
  end
end
Part2: binary-relation constraint Search:
for *node* g_i *in* G **do**
  for *node* g_j *in* G **do**
    if *Relation_Check(*g_i, g_j, m*)* **then**
      Generate binary-relation.
    end
  end
end

Algorithm 1: Constraint Checking on DAG.

Relation_Check function determines the existence of relation. We use the case-base reasoning approach to detect relations [22]. Semantic concept types, concept label information all guide the relation detection. When relations are found between current semantic concept m and any concepts on the semantic graph, certain geometric relation procedures will be executed either in a forward or backward reasoning manner. This leads to two types of geometric concept generation: the geometric concept instance generation upon existing DAG nodes or the new geometric concept node generation. The generated instance in the first type will be cached in the existing geometric concept DAG node. Step 3 of the method updates the graph by adding the current geometric concept m and its relation with others geometric concepts on the semantic DAG. If step 2 generates a new geometric concept node, the method in Figure 3 will be recursively called so as to add this geometric concept onto the semantic DAG.

For instance, in the Problem3, after the annotated inputs $A(2, y)$ and $B(-1, 4)$ have been added onto the semantic DAG, we recognize the annotated input $y = -1$ as a geometric attribute in the step 1 of the method. In the step 2, as the label constraint between $y = -1$ and $A(2, y)$ is satisfied, the unary relation between these two geometric concepts is found. The relation procedure to substitute a geometric attribute into a geometric concept is executed. This will generate a geometric concept instance $A(2, -1)$, which is cached onto the existing geometric concept node $A(2, y)$. Step 3 adds the current concept $y = -1$ onto the DAG and build the relation with $A(2, y)$. Similarly, for the next annotated input $d =?$, after recognizing it as a query of geometric distance attribute, we find the binary relation between $d =?$ and $A(2, y)$, $B(-1, 4)$. The binary distance relation procedure is applied, which brings all instances of A and B into the distance function to calculate distance attribute instances. Since there is only one instance A and B respectively, the single distance attribute instance $d = 5$ is generated by substituting the point's X and Y variables into the distance function and further compute the result. The generated $d = 5$ distance instance is attached onto the geometric query node $d =?$.

In addition to the above forward reasoning scenario, the backward reasoning scenario exists, such as Problem7. After parsing annotated inputs $(4, 3), (2, v)$, $A : line, B : line, pass - through(A, (4, 3)), pass - through(A, (2, v))$ and $B : m = 1/2$ onto the semantic DAG, recognizing the annotation $perpendicular(A, B)$ as the geometric relation, Step 2 of the method detects the binary relation between it and other two geometric concepts: line A and line B. When the geometric perpendicular relation procedure is executed, we translate the $perpendicular(A, B)$ as the perpendicular utility function $m * m1 = -1$, where $m = 1/2$ has been specified as the line B's slope in another DAG node. The backward reasoning is performed by substituting m's value into the perpendicular utility function, and the new geometric attribute $m1 = -2$ is synthesized. Step 3 further adds this new geometric attribute onto the graph, and triggers the recursive call to the method to detect its relation with other existing nodes on the semantic DAG. As $m1 = -2$ represents the line A's slope, its binary relation with (4,3) and (2,v) is detected recursively and a new geometric attribute $v = 7$ is generated.

In step 2, when a geometric relation procedure is executed, the geometric relation scaffolding will be generated according to the pre-defined instruction templates. For instance, when the distance relation is detected and the distance relation procedure is triggered in the Problem3, a sequence of geometric relation scaffoldings or a scaffolding trace can be generated, such as "substitute a given point into the distance function.", "derive the distance attribute value by manipulating the distance function.". Similar as step 1, the geometric scaffolding may contain algebraic procedural scaffoldings to achieve the goal of geometric scaffolding. In the above distance derivation scaffolding, the algebraic expression manipulation and simplification procedures is required as a linear sequence of algebraic rule derivations.

DAG bottom-up Reification
Step 4 attemps to perform the variable substitution (or reification) using existing relations, and further to propagate this substitution to other concepts through relations. Algorithm 2 shows this bottom-up reification procedure. For instance, in Problem3, reifying the attribute $y = -1$ into the geometric point $A(2, y)$ generates a new cached point instance $A(2, -1)$, which depends on $A(2, y)$. Under some circumstances, the existing DAG can become a cyclic graph. For instance, in Problem7, after the geometrical attribute $v = 7$ is generated in the step 2, a unary relation is detected between it and the geometric concept $(2, v)$. The reification procedure is executed by substituting the value of v into the geometric concept $(2, v)$. The cyclic graph is formed after this relation is added onto this semantic DAG. In order to prevent the infinite constraint propagation, the halt checking process should be conducted so that the propagation can be terminated when the geometric concept node has been visited. Executing the reification procedure will produce the geometric reification scaffolding. For instance, the scaffolding trace of Problem7 contains one geometric scaffolding "Reify the equations internal variable by substituting a given fact.".

Scaffolding Trace Propogation on DAG

Data: Current graph node g_i.
foreach *Graph edge* e_i *in* g_i*'s out edges* **do**
  Graph node $g_j \leftarrow e_i$.target
  if *HaltChecking*(g_j) **then**
    break;
  end
  if *Reify*(g_j, g_i) **then**
    Propagate the reification recursively.
  end
end

Algorithm 2: Reification propogation on the directed graph.

In the automated reasoning (shown in method 3), four steps can generate different types of geometrical scaffoldings, in which each one might contain an algebraic scaffolding trace or a sequence of algebraic scaffolding step. Geometrical scaffolding is attached onto the instance of geometric concept node. When a geometric concept instance is generated, geometrical scaffoldings from other related geometric concepts should be propagated onto this concept instance first. Then the current geometric scaffolding is added onto it. For instance, in Problem7, the scaffolding trace from $m1 = -2$ will be added onto the new generated node $v = 7$. Further geometric relation scaffoldings to derive from $m1 = -2$ to $v = 7$ will be appended after previous scaffoldings onto the $v = 7$. After the reasoning method is completely executed, each geometric concept node may contain a geometric scaffolding trace.

A Step-Wise Tutoring Framework

The generated scaffolding trace is used to construct our model-tracing tutor behind the *AnalyticalInk*. As the scaffolding trace is a linear sequence of geometric scaffoldings, where each of them could contain a linear sequence of algebraic scaffoldings, the scaffolding trace can be seen as a two dimension linear structure. Figure 4 shows this two dimension scaffolding trace structure in a directed graph manner. The outer graph node maps to the geometric concept state and the outer graph edge encodes each geometric scaffolding step to transform one geometric concept from one state to another. A graph node can link to a sequence of inner graph nodes, where each inner node represents the geometric concept's state after applying the algebraic procedural scaffolding. The inner graph edge encodes the algebraic procedural scaffolding. After executing inner algebraic procedures, the inner node directs back to the same outer node. Each directed graph of scaffolding trace maps to a math problem's solving plan. The model-tracing tutor in the *AnalyticalInk* is composed by directed graphs of math problems.

Match-and-Verify User Input Step

Figure 5 shows the method to verify a user's input steps. After parsing the raw user input as a geometric concept m, step 2 attempts to match m with a graph node among the directed graph of scaffolding trace. If the user input does not match any nodes on the scaffolding trace graph, we further evaluate it by adding it on the problems semantic DAG (step 3). This will trigger the automated reasoning method to check its relations with other geometric concepts on the semantic DAG. After processing it, if the auto-reasoning procedure deduces

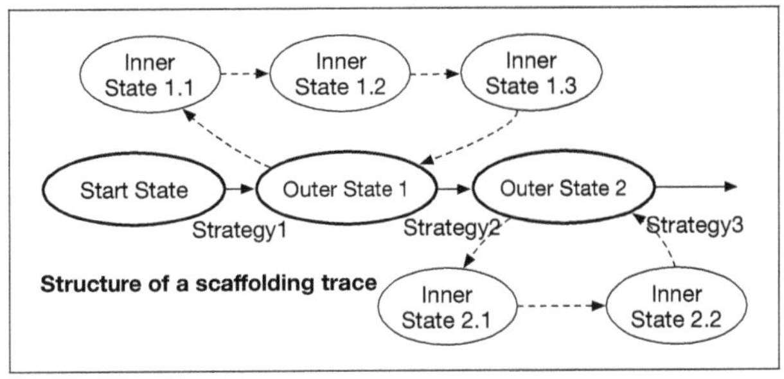

Figure 4: The direct graph structure of a scaffolding trace.

Input: Let s be the user's current input step.
Input: Let G be the semantic DAG representation of a math problem.
Input: Let G' be the scaffolding trace graph of the current problem.
Output: Let v as the boolean value to determine the correctness of s.
Initial: v := false
Step 1: geometric concept m = **Syntax Pattern Match**(s)
  where m can be geometric entities, attributes or relations.
Step 2: v = **Match State on Scaffolding Trace Graph**(G', m)
If v : = true return v
Step 3: <v,t> = **Match Concepts on Semantic DAG**(G, m)
  where t is a scaffolding trace to transform m to another state
If v := false return v
Step 4: **Update Trace**(G', t)
return true

Figure 5: The hybrid match-and-verify approach to check the user answer.

the user input as a geometric concept with the auxiliary scaffolding trace, we can compare geometric concept states with every state from our automated scaffolding trace. If any two states matched from these two scaffolding traces, it implies that the current user input can direct to the same goal as the automated scaffolding traces derivation, but with a different tracing path. Under this circumstance, the system will update the directed graph of scaffolding trace to insert this new scaffolding trace as different branches (step 4).

Adaptive Scaffolding Selection

According to user inputs, selecting adaptive scaffolding is critical in ITSs [20]. Using scaffolding trace directed graph, we keep a user flag to record the user's current solving status. If the user input is verified as a correct step, the user flag will be directed to the corresponding matched graph node. If the current input is verified as a wrong step, it implies that the system did not match any graph node state. Under this circumstance, the system will utilize the user flag to trace back as the latest correct status of a graph node that the user has been explored. The scaffolding selection is achieved by looking ahead onto the outer edge of current graph node.

AnalyticalInk: Interactive Math Learning Environment

Based on the model-tracing tutor, *AnalyticalInk* learning system keeps track and guide students problem solving by analyzing their interactive inputs. The user interface of system

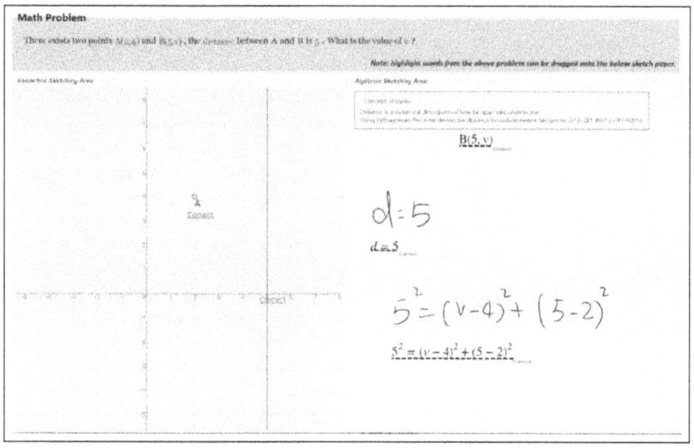

Figure 6: An user scenario where the participant was solving Problem2 using *AnalyticalInk*. The participant dragged $A(2,4)$ onto the geometric side and $B(5,v)$ onto the algebraic side. The participant draw a line onto the geometric side and sketched $d = 5$ onto the algebraic side. She queried the system and was given the flag feedback. The participant further dragged the distance concept word and the system showed her the "distance" concept explanation. The participant continued to solve the problem.

mainly contains three regions (shown both in Figure 1 and Figure 6). The top region presents the math problem. Below it, there are two working regions: algebraic and geometric work spaces. Scaffoldings are shown as visual widgets onto the system.

Keyword Highlighting and Dragging Interaction

Highlighting keywords of a math problem has been shown to be an effective learning technique in the knowledge acquisition phase [8]. Based on our semantic problem representation, we implement this learning technique and further extend it to allow users drag certain semantic words from the top problem region onto the bottom workspace to get the initial condition or the concept definition from the given problem.

From syntax annotations of a math problem, we further annotate each syntax word to align it to the corresponding phrase in the problem. For instance, in the Figure 6, syntax annotations of the problem can be: $A(2,4)$, $B(5,v)$, $d = 5$, $v = ?$. $A(2,4)$ and $B(5,v)$ syntax words directly map to the corresponding phrase in the problem. As $d = 5$ is extracted from several problem phrases relations, we annotate it onto the phrase "5" of the problem. We mark the $v = ?$ to align with the phrase "v" in the end of problem narratives. Aligned phrases will be color highlighted in the math problem. In addition, these highlight words can be dragged from problem region to either algebraic or geometric region, which depends on the type of geometric concept. In the Figure 6, $A(2,4)$ is dragged onto the geometric side. As $B(5,v)$ is not a concrete point from the initial condition, so it can be dragged only onto the algebraic side. As the type of the syntax word $d = 5$ is a geometric attribute, this phrase can be dragged onto the algebraic workspace only. Dragging the query phrase from the math problem will visualize geometric conceptual scaffoldings to give students guidance toward the current math problem solving. In Figure 1, dragging the phrase "What" triggers the system to show up all geometric conceptual scaffoldings in the problem solving strategy visualization box. In addition, during the problem acquisition phase, concept glossary explanation is another learning technique to support help seeking [1]. In *AnalyticalInk*, besides syntax word highlighting and dragging, we also annotate certain geometric concept words to be highlighted and draggable. In Figures 6, when dragging the phrase "distance", the system shows the extra explanation of concept distance in the visual widget. These concept explanations are manually annotated into the system.

Geometric Concept and Algebraic Procedural Understanding

AnalyticalInk lets users input the geometric shape concepts, such as a point, a line or a line segment in the geometric workspace, and input algebraic expressions in the algebraic workspace. The system can deduce from a geometric shape to its corresponding algebraic format or vice versa. As quantities in the math problem can have different natural narratives, geometric concept understanding and algebraic procedural derivation need to be iteratively proceeded in order to solve such math problems [28]. For instance, in Figure 6, students need to acquire the geometric point concept, and the distance concept's formula. By deriving the distance formula algebraically, students can finally get the distance geometric concept understanding in the geometric side. Conversely, in Figure 1, students need to acquire the geometric concepts, such as the point, the line slope, lines' perpendicular. Students need to use the slope and the perpendicular's algebraic formula to derive the geometric concept procedurally.

Sketch Input and Gesture Query

Sketch-based cognitive model has been proved to foster the perceptual and conceptual knowledge understanding [10]. Sketching has also shown its effectiveness to facilitate reasoning during math problem solving [25]. *AnalyticalInk* embodies the sketch as its input mode to simulate how students use the pen-and-paper to conduct math problem solving. The system lets users write math expressions, equations on the algebraic canvas, draw geometric shapes and labels on the geometric canvas. The system provides the real-time handwriting recognition feedback as the recognized math typeset offset, which is shown below the hand-drawn strokes. The handwritten math equation recognition is based on StarPad [34]. The geometric shape detection is built by recognizing low-level sketch primitives [27]. Students can further manipulate beautified shapes by touch.

In addition to the sketch input, the system supports the inferential reasoning by letting the user write a question mark as the reasoning tool. *AnalyticalInk* uses the template-matching approach to recognize the handwritten question mark [4]. When the handwritten question mark is recognized, if the written region is near any geometric shapes or algebraic expressions, the system will trigger the match-and-verify procedure. Otherwise, the system will directly show a next-step scaffolding toward the user. By verifying users' input, *AnalyticalInk* provides the flag feedback to indicate the current step's correctness (shown in Figure 1). If the current step is wrong, two scaffolding visualization widgets will be shown on the user interface. The problem solving strategy visual widget on the top of the algebraic canvas presents the linear sequence of geometric concept scaffoldings. One step is highlighted among this sequence to represent the current student problem solving status. The other scaffolding widget shows

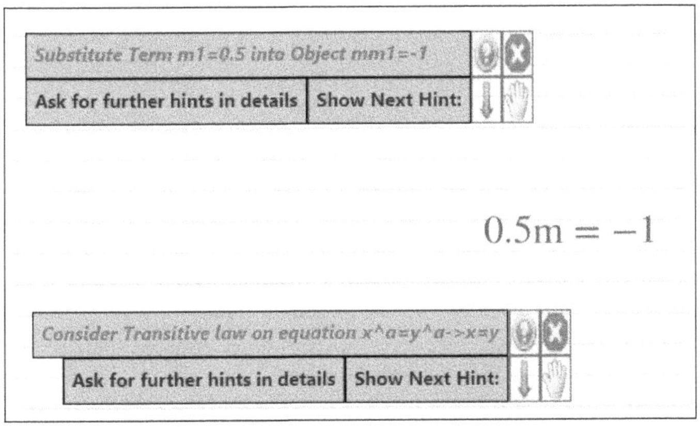

Figure 7: An example shows the algebraic procedural scaffolding derivations. The top didactic scaffolding in the visual widget and the middle math typeset forms one step algebraic procedural scaffolding. Clicking the down arrow on top of the scaffolding visual widget generates another visual widget below to give the next step meta-cognition scaffolding before showing the step's didactic scaffolding, which is similar to the one in the top widget.

the algebraic procedural scaffolding within the current geometric concept scaffolding. Before showing a didactic scaffolding step, the system first shows the corresponding meta-scaffolding or meta-cognition hint to inspire students' self-motived reasoning. Figure 7 displays a meta-cognition hint: *"Consider Transitive law on equation"*. Students can retrieve additional procedural scaffoldings by clicking the down arrow image on the widget.

EVALUATION

AnalyticalInk currently models 15 geometric concepts, which are commonly described in the coordinate geometry section of the geometry course, such as point, line, x-axis, origin, midpoint, line slope, circle, circle radius, length, perpendicular, intersection. Our geometric concept syntax can annotate geometrical mathematical problems. We have used it to annotate 30 problems (Problem1-7 are samples of them). Our current work did not formally evaluate the correctness of reasoning and the scaffolding generation. Instead, two human tutors were recruited to proofread the generated scaffolding trace per problem manually. Both tutors separately showed that the generated scaffolding traces of 30 annotated problems are the correct solutions.

To evaluate the effectiveness of the tutoring framework, learning techniques of *AnalyticalInk*, we performed a human-centered usability evaluation of the current interactive learning prototype system. We performed a with-in subjects study with the keyword highlighting and dragging (with or without) as the independent variable. Both conditions provides the tutoring scaffolding, the dual-canvas problem solving and the natural sketch input. The dependent variables were several aspects of the user events we recorded (see Table 1). This evaluation did not consider the learning effect of the system. R1 considers total user inputs, where R2 and R3 track users' inputs onto the geometric and algebraic canvas. R4 is calculated as the number of times the user makes a question-mark gesture to asks for a hint without input steps. R5 is calculated as the number of times the system writes the same gesture near to user input so as to evaluate it. R6 is calculated as

R1:	The number of steps the user inputs.
R2:	The number of steps the user inputs on the algebraic side.
R3:	The number of steps the user inputs on the geometric side.
R4:	The number of times the user makes a query.
R5:	The number of times the system evaluates user inputs.
R6:	The number of times the system shows the meta scaffolding.
R7:	The number of times the system shows the scaffolding.
R8:	The number of times the user rectifies an input step.

Table 1: The log file of user event record per problem.

the number of times the system evaluates the user input as wrong. Thus, R5 contains the count of R6. R7 is calculated by counting the number of times the user clicks the down arrow image to retrieve the scaffolding from visual widget. R8 is a counter that records two consecutive queries where the previous query check the user's step as a wrong step, and the current query verifies the user input as a correct step.

We hypothesize that the tutoring framework can help students to check their steps and give appropriate scaffolding feedback in demand. The keyword highlighting and dragging learning technique facilitate their problem understanding. We assume *AnalyticalInk* have the potential to guide students' geometry concept understanding and algebraic procedural skills.

Tasks and Experiment Procedure

We recruited 10 participants (with 9 of age 18 and one of age 17) who were currently taking a college algebra class. The experiment was conducted on a Microsoft Surface 3 Pro. Participants were asked to use the stylus and touch during the experiment. The study asked participants to use *AnalyticalInk* to solve two sets of 10 math word problems (one set with keyword highlighting-dragging and one without). The difficulty level of the problems in the two sets was same. We achieved this by changing numerical values but keeping the problem statement same. The order of conditions was balanced across participants based on the latin-square design.

Since each participant had to solve two sets of similar problems, we asked participants to complete the study in two sessions on consecutive days where each session takes about 70 to 80 minutes to finish. Because of the similarity of problems between two sets, participants might apply the lessons learned in the first session toward the second session, which should be minimized. Though putting one-day delay cannot completely reduce such side effect, it is acceptable for our usability evaluation goal. The problem-solving sessions were video-recorded.

In the first session, participants filled a pre-questionnaire, which collected information about their age, if they have taken the algebra course and their comfort level to solve math problem. They were then introduced to *AnalyticalInk* by letting them use it to solve a sample problem under the guidance of a moderator. The moderator gave instructions on how to use the system, answered participants' queries. Participants then began solving a set of ten problems (with or without keyword highlighting and dragging depending upon the balanced order). The second session was the same as the first session with no pre-questionnaire. During problem-solving sessions, we asked participants talk-aloud to express what they are cur-

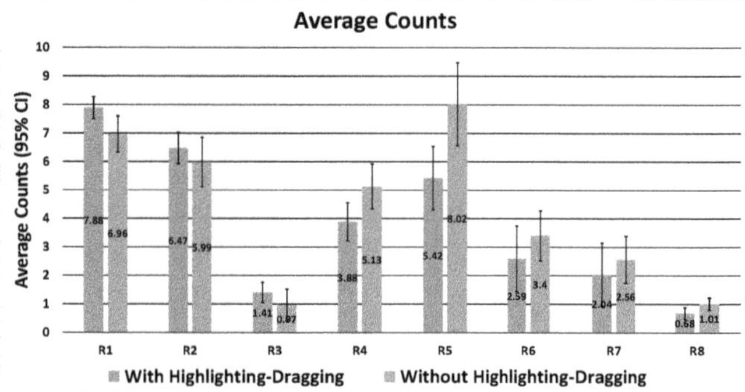

Figure 8: The average mean of each record in the user event log file.

rently doing and what they plan to do for the next action. This allowed the moderator to help participants in case they forget how to use the system to perform certain actions. During the problem solving, participants can explore the learning system to solve each problem. They can perform the keyword dragging, sketch out knowledge input either in the algebraic or the geometric canvas, query the system, and explore the scaffolding trace. When participants tried to verify a written solving step, as the system analyzed recognized expressions instead of participants' written form, participants were instructed to make sure that the recognized typeset expression matches their written form. After completing the two sessions, participants were asked to fill out a questionnaire that required them to rate *AnalyticalInk* on a variety of metrics (shown in Table 2).

Result

From user log files and their questionnaire feedback, we found the evidence that the answer checking of the tutoring framework is useful to guide students' math problem solving. Students prefer to use the keyword highlighting and dragging learning technique. In general, the system is useful to help students to learn geometric concepts and to improve algebraic procedural derivations.

Figure 8 shows the quantitative result from log files under two conditions (with or without the keyword highlighting and dragging learning technique). In both conditions, students either checked their input steps (R5) or asked for a next-step hint based on the last correct step (R4). Students made the error-rectification once in average for each problem solving (R8). In other words, the answer checking in the tutoring framework is effective to help students to correct their own wrong inputs. The users asked for next-step hints (R4) significantly more times without the keyword highlighting and dragging compared to when the technique was present ($t_9 = -2.727, p < 0.05$). The number of times the user input evaluation (R5) took place was significantly higher when the keyword highlighting and dragging was absent ($t_9 = -2.933, p < 0.05$). The number of times the user rectified their input (R8) was significantly less with this learning technique ($t_9 = -2.4, p < 0.05$).

Figure 9 shows the user's qualitative feedback on metrics. Students believed that step verification is useful (Q5). However, students reported that the current geometric concept scaffolding (Q6) and algebraic procedural scaffolding (Q7) is not that useful as verifying input steps. The user feedback indicated that the keyword highlighting and dragging had a low cognitive load to perform it (Q3-Q4). This learning technique helped them to improve geometric concept understanding and accelerated their math problem solving (Q1-Q2). Nine out of ten participants preferred to use this learning technique during their problem solving (Q16). The participant, who preferred to show original math problem without this learning technique, remembered most of geometric concepts and did not face issues during problem solving. Students agreed that providing both algebraic-and-geometric workspaces is effective for their problem solving (Q8). The log file summary also indicated that students used both algebraic and geometric workspaces to solve math problems (average count of R1, R2 and R3). Students believed that the sketch-based input was effective for math problem solving (Q9). Overall, students gave the positive feedback (Q11-Q12) on the effectiveness and usefulness of *AnalyticalInk*. In general, they were satisfied with the current prototype system (Q15).

Keyword Highlighting and Dragging	
Q1	To what extent did the keyword highlighting and dragging consolidate your math concept understanding?
Q2	To what extent did the keyword highlighting and dragging accelerate your math problem-solving?
Q3	How hard did you have to work (mentally and physically) to accomplish your level of performance?
Q4	To what extent did you feel frustrated using this learning technique?
Tutoring Answer Check and Scaffolding	
Q5	How useful was it to verify your solving step?
Q6	How useful and effective was the current geometry concept scaffolding to help your problem solving?
Q7	How useful and effective was the current algebraic procedural scaffolding to help your problem solving?
Overall User Experience	
Q8	How useful and effective was it to let you interact with both the geometric and the algebraic sides?
Q9	How useful and effective was the pen-and-gesture input-and-query flow for the math problem-solving?
Q10	To what extent did you think the current system should let you freely input, edit and query the knowledge?
Q11	How engaged did you feel to use *AnalyticalInk*?
Q12	How useful and effective was it to use *AnalyticalInk*?
Q13	How easy was it to use *AnalyticalInk* for the first time?
Q14	How easy was it to use *AnalyticalInk* after you get familiar with it?
Q15	How satisfied did you feel with this math tutoring system?
Q16	Regarding the keyword highlighting and dragging learning technique, which interaction method would you prefer?

Table 2: Post-Questionnaire. Except for Q16, participants responded to questions on a 7 point likert scale. (1 equals strongly disagree and 7 equals strongly agree).

DISCUSSION AND FUTURE WORK

The current *AnalyticalInk* can handle a limited set of annotated geometry math problems. As part of this paper, we did not systematically evaluate the annotation syntax of geometric concepts and corresponding semantic. Future work should

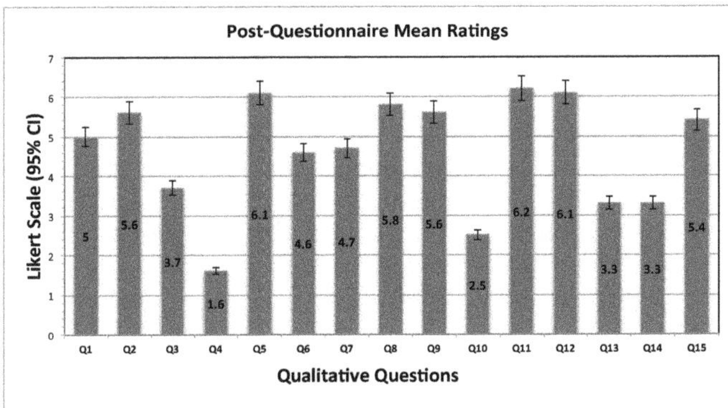

Figure 9: Mean participant ratings of individual aspects of *AnalyticalInk*'s user interface. Except for Q16, in Q3, Q4, 1 was the most positive answer and 7 was the most negative answer; in other questions, 1 was the most negative answer and 7 was the most positive answer.

evaluate its variability to handle large-scale math geometry word problems.

Step-wise Tutoring Framework: For the answer checking of the tutoring framework, though participants gave the positive feedback, we observed that the system sometimes did make the false positive matching-and-verification errors. Variations of written formats are attribute to such error. For instance, one participant sketches "x+2+4+1=x+2+5=x+7", which was recognized as a wrong step. However it was correct if the expression can be divided as two algebraic equations. Future work should handle more written formats. Participants informed they were unsatisfied with the current geometric concept and algebraic procedural scaffoldings. We summarized three reasons based on our observation and user feedback. First, current scaffolding narratives follow the rigorous rule-based description to derive geometric concepts. But participants commented out that verbalized example-based narratives should also be present so as to explain applied rules intuitively. Second, current geometric concept scaffoldings are insufficient for students who do not master the concept. The current geometric concept scaffolding covers the simple description to describe the process to transform to the corresponding algebraic procedurals. Rich geometric concept level pedagogical scaffoldings are required before showing the algebraic procedural scaffolding. Third, the adaptive scaffolding selection is not accurate. When the system recognizes the current user step as a wrong step, the system shows the scaffolding based on the last correct step. However, the current user step might slip several rule-based steps, in which the user might only made one rule deduction error. Under such circumstance, the current system cannot skip these correctly applied rule steps and show the error deduction scaffolding accurately. Future work should refine the scaffolding narrative and augment pedagogical concept-based scaffoldings. Annotated error-based scaffolding should be built into our model-tracing tutor. Based on such improvements, the adaptive scaffolding evaluation should be conducted to measure efforts and outcomes of the system toward learning [12].

Keyword highlighting and dragging: The log file quantitative data implied that students asked for less hints and checked less input steps with this learning technique (R4 and R5). R8 showed that students rectified wrong steps few times with this technique. Our observation indicated that with this learning technique, students spent more time to understand the initial condition of a math problem. By highlighting keywords of a problem, students increased their engagement and substantially built the solving scheme or a plan. Dragging such semantic words onto the workspace reinforced their planning. By dragging geometric concept words, they can retrieve and memorize explanations to facilitate the later problem solving. We believed this learning technique increased students' certainty to input correct steps, which indirectly reduced the times to query the system(R4), verify steps (R5).

User experience of the system: Though participants rated sketch-and-gesture flow to be effective to facilitate their problem solving. However, they reported that the system still has constraints to let them freely input, edit and query the knowledge (Q10). From our observation, participants faced sketch recognition errors during problem solving and recognition errors hindered the solving process. We gave participants pre-instructions to minimize making the recognition errors before the study. For a written step, if the participant did not want to query it, she can ignore the recognition error if it exists, and further derived the next step. However, if the participant wanted to query a step, the recognition result for the current step must be matched with her written intention. When learning to use the system, participants reported that it was not easy to use the system for the first time (Q13). Such perception existed even they got familiar with the system (Q14). By observing their actions during the study, though the cognitive load of sketching are low, sketch recognition errors affected their reasoning. It makes participants feel that the system is not easy to use even when they get familiar with it. Further sketch recognition improvement should be investigated.

CONCLUSION

In this paper, we present *AnalyticalInk*, an interactive math learning environment to facilitate geometry math problem solving. The graph representation of geometry math problems was illustrated. Based on it, we showed the automated reasoning method to solve these problems and generate instructional scaffoldings. When tutoring students to solve such problems, we described a hybrid match-and-verification framework to verify users' solving steps. The user interface of *AnalyticalInk* highlights keywords of a problem, and further supports the keyword dragging to the geometry-and-algebra workspaces. The system lets students use both geometry-and-algebra workspaces to understand geometrical concepts and derive algebraic procedures in an iterative manner. We conducted a usability evaluation of the system. Our results showed that the user step verification was useful. The keyword highlighting and dragging learning technique helped users to understand a problem and plan to solve it. The sketch input and gesture query supported the natural input and reasoning during the math problem solving. Overall, users were satisfied with the current *AnalyticalInk*.

ACKNOWLEDGMENTS

This work is supported in part by NSF CAREER award IIS-0845921. We would like to thank Fei Liu to revise the math problem semantic representation. We would like to thank the members of ISUE lab for their support and the anonymous reviewers for their useful comments and feedback.

REFERENCES

1. Aleven, V., McLaren, B., Roll, I., and Koedinger, K. Toward tutoring help seeking. In *Intelligent Tutoring Systems*, J. Lester, R. Vicari, and F. Paraguau, Eds., vol. 3220 of *Lecture Notes in Computer Science*. Springer Berlin Heidelberg, 2004, 227–239.
2. Aleven, V., Mclaren, B. M., Sewall, J., and Koedinger, K. R. A new paradigm for intelligent tutoring systems: Example-tracing tutors. *International Journal of Artificial Intelligence in Education 19*, 2 (2009), 105–154.
3. Anderson, J. R., Corbett, A. T., Koedinger, K. R., and Pelletier, R. Cognitive tutors: Lessons learned. *The journal of the learning sciences 4*, 2 (1995), 167–207.
4. Anthony, L., and Wobbrock, J. O. A lightweight multistroke recognizer for user interface prototypes. In *Proceedings of Graphics Interface 2010*, GI '10, Canadian Information Processing Society (Toronto, Ont., Canada, Canada, 2010), 245–252.
5. Anthony, L., Yang, J., and Koedinger, K. R. A paradigm for handwriting-based intelligent tutors. *Int. J. Hum.-Comput. Stud. 70*, 11 (Nov. 2012), 866–887.
6. Banarescu, L., Bonial, C., Cai, S., Georgescu, M., Griffitt, K., Hermjakob, U., Knight, K., Koehn, P., Palmer, M., and Schneider, N. Abstract meaning representation for sembanking. In *Proceedings of the 7th Linguistic Annotation Workshop and Interoperability with Discourse* (August 2013).
7. Corbett, A. T., and Anderson, J. R. Knowledge tracing: Modeling the acquisition of procedural knowledge. *User modeling and user-adapted interaction 4*, 4 (1994), 253–278.
8. Dunlosky, J., Rawson, K. A., Marsh, E. J., Nathan, M. J., and Willingham, D. T. Improving students learning with effective learning techniques promising directions from cognitive and educational psychology. *Psychological Science in the Public Interest 14*, 1 (2013), 4–58.
9. Fillmore, C. J. *The need for a frame semantics in linguistics*. Scriptor, 1977.
10. Forbus, K. D., Ferguson, R. W., and Usher, J. M. Towards a computational model of sketching. In *Proceedings of the 6th international conference on Intelligent user interfaces*, ACM (2001), 77–83.
11. Ford, B. Parsing expression grammars: a recognition-based syntactic foundation. In *ACM SIGPLAN Notices*, vol. 39, ACM (2004), 111–122.
12. González-Brenes, J. P., and Huang, Y. Your model is predictivebut is it useful? theoretical and empirical considerations of a new paradigm for adaptive tutoring evaluation. In *Proceedings of the 8th Intl. Conf. on Educational Data Mining* (2015).
13. Gulwani, S., Korthikanti, V. A., and Tiwari, A. Synthesizing geometry constructions. In *ACM SIGPLAN Notices*, vol. 46, ACM (2011), 50–61.
14. Heffernan, N. T., and Koedinger, K. R. The composition effect in symbolizing: The role of symbol production vs. text comprehension. In *Proceedings of the Nineteenth Annual Conference of the Cognitive Science Society*, Lawrence Erlbaum Associates Hillsdale, NJ (1997), 307–312.
15. Heffernan, N. T., Koedinger, K. R., and Razzaq, L. Expanding the model-tracing architecture: A 3rd generation intelligent tutor for algebra symbolization. *International Journal of Artificial Intelligence in Education 18*, 2 (2008), 153.
16. Ilany, B.-S., Margolin, B., et al. Language and mathematics: Bridging between natural language and mathematical language in solving problems in mathematics. *Creative Education 1*, 03 (2010), 138.
17. Jiang, Y., Tian, F., Wang, H., Zhang, X., Wang, X., and Dai, G. Intelligent understanding of handwritten geometry theorem proving. In *Proceedings of the 15th international conference on Intelligent user interfaces*, ACM (2010), 119–128.
18. Koedinger, K. R., Anderson, J. R., Hadley, W. H., and Mark, M. A. Intelligent tutoring goes to school in the big city.
19. Koedinger, K. R., Booth, J. L., and Klahr, D. Instructional complexity and the science to constrain it. *Science 342*, 6161 (2013), 935–937.
20. Koedinger, K. R., Brunskill, E., Baker, R. S., McLaughlin, E. A., and Stamper, J. New potentials for data-driven intelligent tutoring system development and optimization. *AI Magazine 34*, 3 (2013), 27–41.
21. Koedinger, K. R., and Nathan, M. J. The real story behind story problems: Effects of representations on quantitative reasoning. *The Journal of the Learning Sciences 13*, 2 (2004), 129–164.
22. Kolodner, J. *Case-based reasoning*. Morgan Kaufmann, 2014.
23. Kushman, N., Artzi, Y., Zettlemoyer, L., and Barzilay, R. Learning to automatically solve algebra word problems. In *Proceedings of the 52nd Annual Meeting of the Association for Computational Linguistics (Volume 1: Long Papers)*, Association for Computational Linguistics (Baltimore, Maryland, June 2014), 271–281.
24. LaViola, Jr., J. J., and Zeleznik, R. C. Mathpad2: A system for the creation and exploration of mathematical sketches. In *ACM SIGGRAPH 2004 Papers*, SIGGRAPH '04, ACM (New York, NY, USA, 2004), 432–440.
25. Oviatt, S. Interfaces for thinkers: Computer input capabilities that support inferential reasoning. In *Proceedings of the 15th ACM on International Conference on Multimodal Interaction*, ICMI '13, ACM (New York, NY, USA, 2013), 221–228.
26. Paquette, L., Lebeau, J.-F., Beaulieu, G., and Mayers, A. Designing a knowledge representation approach for the generation of pedagogical interventions by mtts. *International Journal of Artificial Intelligence in Education 25*, 1 (2015), 118–156.

27. Paulson, B., and Hammond, T. Paleosketch: accurate primitive sketch recognition and beautification. In *Proceedings of the 13th international conference on Intelligent user interfaces*, ACM (2008), 1–10.

28. Rittle-Johnson, B., Siegler, R. S., and Alibali, M. W. Developing conceptual understanding and procedural skill in mathematics: An iterative process. *Journal of educational psychology 93*, 2 (2001), 346.

29. Russell, S., and Norvig, P. Artificial intelligence: a modern approach.

30. Schoenfeld, A. H. Learning to think mathematically: Problem solving, metacognition, and sense making in mathematics. *Handbook of research on mathematics teaching and learning* (1992), 334–370.

31. Seo, M. J., Hajishirzi, H., Farhadi, A., Etzioni, O., and Malcolm, C. Solving geometry problems: Combining text and diagram interpretation. In *Proceedings of the 2015 Conference on Empirical Methods in Natural Language Processing, EMNLP 2015, Lisbon, Portugal, September 17-21, 2015* (2015), 1466–1476.

32. Vanlehn, K., Lynch, C., Schulze, K., Shapiro, J. A., Shelby, R., Taylor, L., Treacy, D., Weinstein, A., and Wintersgill, M. The andes physics tutoring system: Lessons learned. *Int. J. Artif. Intell. Ed. 15*, 3 (Aug. 2005), 147–204.

33. Zeleznik, R., Bragdon, A., Adeputra, F., and Ko, H.-S. Hands-on math: A page-based multi-touch and pen desktop for technical work and problem solving. In *Proceedings of the 23Nd Annual ACM Symposium on User Interface Software and Technology*, UIST '10, ACM (New York, NY, USA, 2010), 17–26.

34. Zeleznik, R., Miller, T., Li, C., and Laviola Jr, J. J. Mathpaper: Mathematical sketching with fluid support for interactive computation. In *Smart Graphics*, Springer (2008), 20–32.

35. Zhou, L., Dai, S., and Chen, L. Learn to solve algebra word problems using quadratic programming. In *Proceedings of the 2015 Conference on Empirical Methods in Natural Language Processing*, Association for Computational Linguistics (Lisbon, Portugal, September 2015), 817–822.

Author Index

www.ingramcontent.com/pod-product-compliance
Ingram Content Group UK Ltd.
Pitfield, Milton Keynes, MK11 3LW, UK
UKHW051412290926
15471UKWH00009B/1571

9 781450 344692